OREGON
GEOGRAPHIC
NAMES

OREGON GEOGRAPHIC NAMES

LEWIS A. McARTHUR

SIXTH EDITION
REVISED & ENLARGED
BY

LEWIS L. McARTHUR

OREGON HISTORICAL SOCIETY
PRESS

The production of this edition of *Oregon Geographic Names* was supported through significant funds provided by The Thomas Vaughan Fund for Publication in Oregon Country History, and by funds from Mr. C.M. Bishop, Jr., the Honorable Robert C. Belloni, the Honorable Malcolm F. Marsh, the Honorable Owen W. Panner, the Honorable John F. Kilkenny and by Lewis L. McArthur. Additional funding was provided by an anonymous gift in memory of Borden F. Beck, Jr. (1923–89), in recognition of his service as a member of the Oregon Geographic Names Board (1983–89), and his profound knowledge of, and passion for, the history and lore of his native state.

Library of Congress Cataloging-in-Publication data

McArthur, Lewis A. (Lewis Ankeny), 1883–1951.
    Oregon Geographic Names / Lewis A. McArthur.—6th ed., rev. & enl. / by Lewis
L. McArthur.
      p.   cm.
    Includes index.
    ISBN 0-87595-236-4 (cloth): $29.95.
    ISBN 0-87595-237-2 (paper): $19.95.
    1. Names, Geographical—Oregon. 2. Oregon—History, Local. I. McArthur, Lewis
L. II. Title.
F874.M16   1992
979.5°003—dc20   92-17234
                                                     CIP

First edition   1928
Second edition, revised and enlarged   1944
Third edition, revised and enlarged   1952
Fourth edition, revised and enlarged   1974
Fifth edition, revised and enlarged   1982
Copyright, 1928 and 1944:   by Lewis A. McArthur
Copyright, 1952, 1974 and 1982:   by Lewis L. McArthur

Designed and produced by the Oregon Historical Society Press.

The paper used in this publication meets the minimum requirements of American National Standard for Information Sciences—Permanence of Paper for Printed Library Materials, ANSI Z39.48–1984.

Printed in the United States of America.

CONTENTS

PREFACE

The original compiler of *Oregon Geographic Names*, Lewis A. McArthur was born in The Dalles on April 27, 1883. The son of Lewis Linn and Harriet Nesmith McArthur, he had an early association with Oregon history through both grandfathers. William P. McArthur made the earliest government survey of the northern Pacific Coast including the mouth of the Columbia River. James W. Nesmith, father of Harriet Nesmith, came to Oregon in the emigration of 1843 and was long active on the political scene of territorial government and early statehood.

McArthur was educated at the Portland Academy and graduated from the University of California in 1908. During his college years he worked for the *Oregonian* when Harvey Scott was editor and after graduation he spent two years with the then young Oregon Electric Railway under Guy W. Talbot. In 1910 Talbot left to found the Pacific Power & Light Co. and McArthur came along as one of the first employees. He was appointed vice-president and general manager in 1923 and continued with the company until his retirement in 1946.

Governor Oswald West appointed him to the Oregon Geographic Board in 1914 and he became its secretary in 1916, a position he occupied until illness forced him to resign in 1949. During the period between the two world wars the thoughts about a volume on Oregon place names jelled and resulted in the first edition in 1928. The research for this work was a wonderful combination: reading the journals of Northwest explorers, traders, trappers, naturalists and military men, and conversing with many pioneers who had been on the ground when some of Oregon's early history was made. Lewis A. McArthur never passed up an opportunity to question anyone who might add to his knowledge of local history.

McArthur was active in many fields besides the electric utility business. He was an advisor to government agencies engaged in topographic mapping and primary surveying. He was an avid stamp and book collector and served as president and for many years as director of the Oregon Historical Society. After he relinquished the position of general manager of the Pacific Power & Light Co. in 1936, he still traveled extensively throughout the state. In due course he brought out a second edition of *Oregon Geographic Names* in 1944 and finally a third in 1952. His first wife, Mary Lawrence Hewett, died in 1943 and in 1946 he married Nellie Pipes, the long-time librarian of the Oregon Historical Society. In 1950 McArthur's health began to fail rapidly and he died in Portland on November 8, 1951. However, he had completed all the text for the third edition which was put in final form by Nellie P. McArthur. The present compiler is his son, Lewis L. McArthur.

Through the three editions produced under the guidance of Lewis L. McArthur, the original text has been changed only as necessary corrections and revisions required. Every effort has been made to maintain the original style and there is intentionally no distinction between new and original material. The preface to the 1944 edition was reprinted for 1952 and then modified slightly for the 1974 edition. The major change in the 1982 preface was the complete revision of the tables of language of origin and type of name. These 1982 categories have now been superseded by new standards described in the present introduction.

This edition of *Oregon Geographic Names* is published by the Oregon Historical Society through its publishing arm, the Oregon Historical Society Press. Adair Law, the late George T. Resch and Susan Applegate of the Press have capably handled the editing, design and production while Press Director Bruce Taylor Hamilton has amicably resolved the inevitable problems. The Oregon Historical Society Board of Directors Publications Committee has been unflagging in its support.

A volume such as this is beyond the capabilities of one person. It is not possible to list all the persons who have provided or checked information but credit in the text is given in many instances while the Regional Research Library staff of the Oregon Historical Society has been a constant and obliging resource.

The 1974 edition was computer composed by Gordon Nelson of San Bruno, California and the 1982 edition was updated by him on the same program. This system was not available in 1990 so the electronic file was transferred to Word Perfect by the Poorman Douglas Co. of Portland. The compiler then revised all the composition codes in accordance with the *Chicago Guide to Preparing Electronic Manuscripts*. The internal biographical and geographical indexing was converted with the valuable help of Bruce Craig. The book is now in the compiler's desktop computer where additions and corrections are already accumulating.

INTRODUCTION

The format of this edition of *Oregon Geographic Names* has been changed slightly and additional abbreviations have been used to conserve space. The headings continue in **bold** type but the county name is shown in small capitals with the word "county" omitted. Land survey descriptions such as "section 4, township 2 north, range 4 east" have been condensed to "s 4, T 2N, R 4E." A few abbreviations have been used to save space. Some of these are for agencies that have had name variations other than those shown; the current abbreviation is used regardless of the actual initials at the time referred to in the text. The abbreviations are listed below along with pertinent comments. Other abbreviations are self-explanatory.

BLM	Bureau of Land Management
CPO	Community post office
GNIS	Geographic Names Information System (described later in this introduction)
ODOT	Oregon Department of Transportation
OGNB	Oregon Geographic Names Board (formerly the Oregon Geographic Board)
OHQ	*Oregon Historical Quarterly*
OHS	Oregon Historical Society
OPA	Oregon Pioneer Association
OR&N	Oregon Railroad and Navigation Company
OSHD	Oregon State Highway Division (formerly Oregon State Highway Department)
USBGN	United States Board of Geographic Names (formerly United States Geographic Board)
USBR	United States Bureau of Reclamation
USC & GS	United States Coast and Geodetic Survey (formerly the United States Coast Survey)
USCE	United States Army Corps of Engineers
USFS	United States Forest Service
USGS	United States Geological Survey

Where there is historical significance to a distinction, the present abbreviation has not been used and the name is presented in full, such as the U.S. Topographical Engineers in connection with Fremont. There have also been many changes in the corporate organization and names of railroads. The most prominent example is the new Burlington Northern, Inc., that includes the Great Northern Railway, Northern Pacific Railroad, Oregon Electric Railway and several others. An effort has been made to use the modern name for present stations and current text but in most historic references the original name is retained.

The origins of geographic names in Oregon may be traced roughly to six periods in the history of the state, and in most instances the names themselves indicate approximately the epoch in which they were applied. The six periods may be described as follows:

First: The period of aboriginal Indian life, which is reflected in Oregon by the existence of a considerable number of Indian place names, some of which were applied by the Indians themselves, and some later by the whites. These names are characterized by Willamette and Tualatin, approximations of the Indian name of the feature or the area including it.

Second: The period of exploration. By sea this resulted in names strongly Spanish with an English admixture such as Heceta Head, Cape Blanco, Cape Meares and Mount Hood. Overland exploration, influenced by the fur trade, brought English and French names such as Astoria, John Day and The Dalles.

Third: The pioneer period resulted in the application of a large number of eastern place names to Oregon communities, generally for sentimental reasons, and also resulting in the use of many pioneer family names for Oregon features such as streams and mountains. During this period a number of political subdivisions were named for well-known national figures who may or may not have played a part in Oregon's development. Examples of this period include the eastern names Portland and Salem, Eugene and Roseburg for pioneer settlers, and Linn and Washington counties for national figures. "Pioneer" settlements in many parts of eastern and central Oregon, of course, occurred in later decades than those in the western part of the state.

Fourth: The Indian wars and the mining periods caused the application of the names of soldiers and also the picturesque nomenclature that always follows the early pursuit of gold. Howluk Butte and Steens Mountain and Althouse Creek, Steamboat Creek and Luckyboy are typical.

Fifth: The homestead era. During the fifty years between 1875 and 1925, nine million acres qualified for final entry and thousands of family names were applied to creeks and buttes. There was also a multiple application of names generic to the land laws and the farming and grazing occupations such as School Section Creek, Homestead, Freezeout Ridge and Dipping Vat Creek.

Sixth: The modern period of made-up names, real estate phraseology and the current efforts to apply a suitable historic or Indian name to something that bears an unsatisfactory title. Vanport, Wood Village and Lincoln City represent the first two groups while Kelley Point, Salishan and many other examples demonstrate a laudable trend on the part of most public and private bodies currently applying new names.

In 1981, the U.S. Geological Survey completed phase I of the Geographic Names Information System, or GNIS, for Oregon. This has been augmented by a phase II project and now consists of about 45,000 names currently shown on their Oregon quadrangles and other basic maps. Each name is given a distinctive number, defined by a generic and located by civil division (county), latitude and longitude and the quadrangle or quadrangles on which it appears. After eliminating the innumerable Beaver, Bear, Sheep, Rock, Sand, Squaw, Fish, Huckleberry and the like, there are probably 15,000 features worthy of serious study. The writer has information under headings covering 5,473 names with some 1,979 more mentioned in the text. This is over a third of the more important ones in the state. From a historical point of view, it is apparent that practically all the best-known names of the state are mentioned.

As mentioned in the preface, the complete text is on-line in WordPerfect 5.0. The names of each heading have been shifted to Dbase IV. Oregon has a tape of its complete GNIS II and the compiler has a modified GNIS database in Dbase IV. All of the heading names in the sixth edition have been matched with the GNIS where they are identified by the distinctive number or IDNO. Names that are not now in the Oregon GNIS do not have an IDNO and thus are readily identified for subsequent entry. The compiler has categorized the 5,473 heading names according to American Name Society preliminary standards. The Dbase program allows analysis in a multiplicity of combinations and the following table shows the breakdown of the basic types.

Biographic	56%
Physical	13
Biological	5
Activity	11
Coinage & Mistakes	3
Miscellaneous	3
Unknown	2
Superimposed Indian	4
Transfers	3
	100%

"Biographic" names are a given name or surname of an individual or the name of a group. These names are further divided into "Associated" (names of persons associated with a feature such as a postmaster or homesteader) and "Commemorative" (the names of persons whom the namer intended to honor or commemorate). "Physical" names describe or denote a physical characteristic. "Biological" names refer to any flora or fauna or subdivision thereof. "Activity" names refer to or describe an activity, human or natural. "Coinage" names combine phonemes or letters without standard lexical meaning or reflect errors in transmission. "Miscellaneous" names do not readily fit into any other category. This last type contains many of our most interesting names. It is the subject of much study and will certainly be further divided. "Unknown" is obvious. "Superimposed Indian" are Native American names of various dialects and jargons. They derive from all parts of North America and were applied to features by settlers either arbitrarily or because they resembled names used by local Indians. There are some two hundred more Indian names that originated with local Native Americans but fall into the Biographic, Physical or Biological categories. Lastly, "Transfers" are those names brought in from other parts of the country as mentioned in the "Third" naming period. In a few more cases, the original origins are known and these names are included in their appropriate classes in the same manner as the just mentioned Indian names.

The majority of Oregon place names are Biographic or Physical. It may be said in explanation that it has not always been easy to draw the line between the Biographic divisions of Associated and Commemorative. It is the belief of the compiler that if a stream flows through the donation land claim of Balthasar Jones, a pioneer of 1850, and that the stream was named Jones Creek about the time Mr. Jones settled on the land, then the name is Associated. The matter of honoring Balthasar Jones was not considered when the stream began to be called Jones Creek. The whole business was a matter of descriptive convenience. On the other hand, the name Lake Abert is classified as being Commemorative because Colonel Abert was a well-known army officer who did not live in the vicinity of the lake; Captain Fremont named the lake in honor of his superior. It seems to the compiler that there should be a clear distinction between these two classes of names, although there are some cases where the segregation has been difficult. It is apparent that as more names are studied, the percentage of Biographic and Physical applications will increase, as most of the unimportant names are in these categories.

Earlier editions of this book contained a breakdown of names by language of origin devised by the late Lewis A. McArthur. This breakdown has not been satisfactory and the American Name Society is doing preliminary studies of linguistic classification. The compiler hopes some broad categories may be established prior to a future edition. However, one initial survey has been made. Of the 5,473 headings, 403 or 7.36% are of Native American origin. These include both the English approximations of names actually used by local Native Americans and the "Superimposed" names previously described. These 403 names are now all classed "Indian" but will be classified linguistically in the future.

Errors of fact have an irritating way of creeping into a work of this sort. Every effort has been made to check all the data published, but—notwithstanding this—mistakes frequently occur, and there are probably a number herein that have not been detected. Even government archives are not infallible. Donation land claim records in the branch land office show many inconsistencies, and affidavits of a claimant made but a few months apart bear gross disagreements in dates of birth and marriage and other data. The pioneers did not worry much about such matters and did not foresee the difficulties that would befall an investigator a century and a half later. Other fruitful sources of error are the printed reminiscences of popular "oldest living residents," who do not realize that they cannot remember so well as they did fifty years earlier.

Records of the Oregon provisional and territorial governments are not always consistent in the spellings of geographic names. Sometimes the forms used in the manuscript bills as passed are not the same as the styles used in the printed session laws and journals. Official records give both Tuality and Twality as the name of one of Oregon's original four districts and when the name was changed to Washington County, the printed law used the spelling Tualitz, possibly a printer's error. The compiler has found it impossible to reconcile all these discrepancies.

Similar difficulties are found in the records of Oregon post offices. Some of the records must be used with caution. *Caveat lector.* These records, kept at Washington, D.C., run back for over a century, and some of the entries are almost indecipherable. Then there are cases where post office records are continued from one book to another, and in the transfer minor changes have been made in the spellings of the names of the post offices and sometimes in the names of the postmasters. There are other places where it is almost impossible to follow the history of eastern Oregon post offices that have been in different counties at different times. Some post offices and postmasters jumped about like fleas. The late Lewis A. McArthur relied upon records laboriously copied from post office records. In recent years the study of post offices has been stimulated by philatelists and postmark collectors. Richard W. Helbock has produced an excellent compendium in *Oregon Post Offices*. The compiler not only uses it for verification but recommends it for dates and locations of offices not covered by this volume.

Currently post offices are being continually discontinued and established. The writer has endeavored to show the post office information current as of January 1, 1991, but statements in the text to the effect that names are used by Oregon post offices must be accepted in a general sense and not as of any particular date unless specified.

A good deal of nonsense has been written about the meaning of Indian names. The late Lewis A. McArthur knew many Indians. They eked out a living amidst hard circumstances and it seems improbable that Oregon Indians ever made up geographic names because of "moonlight filtering through trees," "sunshine dancing on the water," "rose petals floating on water" and "water rippling over pebbles." Competent researchers have found that most Indian names were based on much more practical and everyday matters.

Place names are integral to our knowledge and understanding of our history. Human activities, excepting those relying solely on intellect, involve spatial relationships and these are, in turn, defined by place names. History, onomastics, geography and linguistics ideally should form a multi-disciplinary team to study these relationships. It is a curious fact that academic historians have, with a few exceptions, ignored this important facet of history. Most place name research in the United States has been done by academics in the fields of modern language and geography or by non-academics as a hobby or an avocation. It is regrettable the details of local history that exerted so great an influence on our past have so little interest to today's history scholars in our universities.

The compiler hopes that a seventh edition of this book may be forthcoming at some future date, and with that in mind corrections and suggestions are earnestly requested. Correspondence addressed to Lewis L. McArthur, Oregon Historical Society Press, 1200 sw Park Avenue, Portland, Oregon 97205, will be welcomed.

Oregon Counties
and County Seats

Aaron Mercer Reservoir, POLK. This impoundment on Rickreall Creek a mile north of Socialist Valley is storage for the City of Dallas water supply. It is named for Aaron Mercer, a member of the Dallas Water Commission from 1949 to 1955, and a member of the Dallas City Council for many years thereafter. The USGS Socialist Valley quadrangle uses the full name but Resolution 1579 of the City of Dallas, dated Apr. 21, 1969, calls for Mercer Reservoir.

Abberdeen, LINN. Efforts to learn the reason for this odd name for a Linn County post office have not been fruitful. No real Aberdonian would waste the extra letter in the spelling, and the style must have been selected by someone other than a Scot. Abberdeen post office was established June 13, 1892, with Mary Flauger postmaster. The office was closed Apr. 24, 1894, and the business turned over to Lacomb post office. About 1890 one John Flaugher started a store at his home about eight miles east of Lebanon and applied for a post office which was supposed to have been named in compliment to a former home, Aberdeen, Michigan. The compiler has been unable to find a place called Aberdeen, Michigan, in available records, but there may have been one about 1890.

Abbey Creek, LINCOLN. Abbey Creek empties into Yaquina River in S 14, T 11S, R 10W. Edwin A. Abbey bought government land along the creek in the 1880s. The family were early residents of Newport.

Abbot Creek, JEFFERSON. Abbot Creek flows into Metolius River from the west about twelve miles southeast of Mount Jefferson. It was formerly called Eagle Creek, one of many of that name in Oregon. In 1930 Robert W. Sawyer of Bend recommended that the name of the stream be changed to Abbot Creek to commemorate Henry Larcom Abbot, who as a young lieutenant in the U.S. Army attached to the Pacific Railroad Surveys, passed along its banks on Sept. 28, 1855. The change was made by decision of USBGN. Abbot had a long and distinguished career. He was born in Massachusetts in 1831 and was graduated from West Point in 1854. He served with distinction in the Civil War and reached the brevet rank of major-general of volunteers, awarded "for gallant and meritorious conduct during the Rebellion." After the war his activities covered a wide range of military engineering, and he retired in 1895 only to serve for another three decades as a consultant to the government and to private enterprises. He died in 1927. The USFS has applied the name Abbot Butte to a point, elevation 4318 feet, in the northwest corner of T 12S, R 9E. It is just west of Abbot Creek and was named on that account. *See also* Camp Abbot.

Abbot Pass, CLACKAMAS, WASCO. In 1935 the USFS renamed the old High Rock road for Henry Larcom Abbot who crossed the Cascade Range westbound near Clear Lake on Oct. 8, 1855. For further information regarding Abbot *see* Abbot Creek. Abbot's route ran from Clear Lake to Dry Meadow to Fryingpan Lake while Abbot Road crosscs at Abbot Pass some five miles to the south. Between Fryingpan Lake and High Rock both the road and Abbot's 1855 route pass through Abbott Burn which, as noted under that heading, was named during the 1890s for James Abbott. One faction claims that Abbot Pass takes its name from the road and is thus spelled correctly while another says it was really the sheep crossing and should be spelled Abbott for the Wapinitia sheep man. The mass confusion resulting from the proximity of Abbot and Abbott was further compounded by the frequent misspelling of both names so the USBGN in *Decision List 7102* settled on the form Abbot. The road to Hell must be paved with the same good intentions had by people who bestow honorary names.

Abbott Burn, CLACKAMAS. Abbott Burn was named for James Abbott, a well-known stockman of Wapinitia. It is near the headwaters of Salmon River.

Abbott Butte, DOUGLAS, JACKSON. The following quotation from a letter by Captain O. C. Applegate, of Klamath Falls, indicates the origin of this name: "In very early times Hiram Abbott, usually known as Hi. Abbott, was, I believe, a resident of Big Butte Creek, or of that vicinity, and had some employment, as a sub-agent, perhaps, with the Rogue River Indians. He never was in any way connected with the Indian service on the Klamath reservation. I am of the impression that Abbott Butte on the Umpqua divide was named for him." The spelling Abbot is wrong.

Abernethy Creek, CLACKAMAS. This stream rises at an elevation of about 1100 feet ten miles southeast of Oregon City, and flows into the Willamette River at Oregon City. It was named for George Abernethy, first governor of Oregon under the provisional government. He was elected to this position on June 3, 1845. He died on May 2, 1877. He was long engaged in the mercantile business in Oregon City. His biography appears in OPA *Transactions* for 1886. *See also* Scott's *History of the Oregon Country*. George Abernethy once owned the island in the Willamette River at the edge of Willamette Falls at Oregon City. It was formerly known as Governors Island but is now known as Abernethy Island. In 1924 Professor Edwin T. Hodge of the University of Oregon applied the name Abernethy Island to a geographic feature in the lava fields near McKenzie Pass. This was also in commemoration of Governor Abernethy. The Southern Pacific Company selected the name Abernethy for a station in Lane County on the Cascade line in honor of Governor George Abernethy.

Abert Rim, LAKE. Abert Rim is one of the impressive fault scarps of Oregon, and is said to have a height of 2000 feet above Lake Abert. The upper 600 feet is practically vertical cliff. This rim is named for Lake Abert, which lies at its western foot. For the origin of the name, *see* Lake Abert. Captain John C. Fremont visited the lake and rim on Dec. 20, 1843, and wrote quite accurately of this rim, as well as of others in south central Oregon. Abert Rim and surrounding country are well described in USGS *WSP 220*. The highest part of the rim is just east of the south end of Lake Abert.

Abes Mountain, DOUGLAS. According to Fred Asam, this mountain five miles southeast of Red Butte was named for Abraham Wilson, an early resident of the area and a packer for the USFS during the 1920s.

Abiqua Creek, MARION. Abiqua Creek rises on the west slope of the Cascade Range, and joins Pudding River about three miles northwest of Silverton. It was on the Abiqua Creek that a skirmish or battle was fought in Mar. 1848, and several Indians were killed. Thirty years later there was lively disagreement between various old timers who either minimized, maximized or equivocated the extent of the engagement and the casulties. For a discussion of this battle by John Minto, *see* the *Oregonian*, Mar. 12, 1877; by James W. Nesmith, Mar. 15, 1877; by John Minto, Mar. 20, 1877; by A. F. Johnson, Mar. 22, 1877; by John Warnock, Apr. 3, 1877. The most extensive research on the subject is contained in Down's *A History of the Silverton Country*, p. 47. The compiler of these notes has been unable to learn the meaning of the Indian name Abiqua. It may have referred to a small tribe or to a camping place along the stream. The USBGN has decided on the spelling of Abiqua. The accent is on the first syllable.

Ace Williams Mountain, DOUGLAS. This prominent nose above the north bank of Little River three miles southeast of Glide was named for Asa Williams who settled near its base about 1854. The spelling of the first name has been corrupted for many years.

Acker Rock, DOUGLAS. This point south of South Umpqua River near the headwaters was named for Hiram L. Acker, originally from Texas, who settled at nearby Tallow Butte in 1913. It has an elevation of 4112 feet and in 1989 was still the site of a USFS fire lookout.

Ackerley Lake, LANE. Ackerley Lake is a small body of water between Munsel and Clear lakes north of Florence. It takes its name from an early family in the area. Lafayette C. Ackerley came to Florence in the 1880s and took a homestead on North Fork Siuslaw River some seven or eight miles upstream. Soon after, a brother, Clarence Ackerley, and his wife Carrie settled nearby. Ackerley Lake is some distance from the homesteads but it was named for the family. *See The Siuslaw Pioneer*, 1982.

Acton, MORROW. Acton was a post office on Butter Creek in the east part of the county and about 16 miles north-northeast of Heppner. This post office was established July 11, 1879, with John Barker first postmaster. With one exception it remained in service until June 19, 1888. It was not far from the place called Pine City and was probably in the east or northeast part of T 1N, R 27E. It may have been named for a family but the compiler has not been able to get further information about it. However, it should be noted that there are a good many places elsewhere named Acton and the locality in Morrow County may have received its name by transfer.

Acton Gulch, MALHEUR. Acton Gulch empties into Lake Owyhee from the west. It was named for Roy and Orin Acton who built and operated a wild horse trap in this canyon.

Ada, LANE. The post office of Ada was named for Miss Ada Wilkes, a daughter of an old-time resident. Ada Wilkes was subsequently Mrs. Ada Cleveland. Ada post office was established in 1892 on the Douglas County list.

Adair Point, CLATSOP. There are three small promontories between Hug Point and the community of Arch Cape. The northernmost of the three is Adair Point, named in the 1890s by the Samuel Adair family who owned the property that is now the Hug Point State Park parking lot. Adair, the son of General John Adair, first collector of customs at Astoria, was also prominent in Clatsop County affairs and the father of Lieutenant Henry Rodney Adair for whom Camp Adair was named. The Samuel Adair family had a summer home on the high ground above the small waterfall in Fall Creek. Adair Point is misnamed on some maps as Austin Point but this was corrected by the USBGN in *Decision List 8903*.

Adair Slough, CLATSOP. Adair Slough empties into Youngs Bay. It takes its name from John Adair and his wife, Dr. Bethenia Owens-Adair, the first woman doctor in Oregon. Dr. Owens-Adair came to Oregon in 1843 with her parents and settled on Clatsop Plains. After living in Douglas County, she married John Adair. About 1887 they moved to Clatsop County and established a farm along the upper reaches of the slough. The form Adams Slough is a typograhical error. For further information *see Dr. Owens-Adair: Some of Her Life Experiences*. Bruce Berney of the Astoria Public Library uncovered this connection in 1983.

Adair Village, BENTON. Adair Village succeeded to and was named for Camp Adair. After World War II, the military camp was closed and most buildings removed. The large hospital facility remained and in 1946 was leased to Oregon State University for student and faculty housing. The university converted the wards into 30 faculty and 320 married student apartments. A local government was organized and Adair Village post office was established Sept. 1, 1947. When the postwar student boom slackened, the university gave up the lease and the post office was closed in 1951. From 1957 to 1969, the U.S. Air Force maintained the base as a radar station. When they ceased operations, the property was sold and the individual houses were placed on the market. In 1976 Adair Village was incorporated. The City Hall is still one of the original wartime buildings. Kenneth Mumford has articles about Adair Village in the Corvallis *Gazette-Times*, Mar. 11, and Apr. 22, 1984 and Aug. 21, 1989. For origin of the name, *see* Camp Adair.

Adams, UMATILLA. This town is about 13 miles northeast of Pendleton on Wildhorse Creek. It was named for John F. Adams, part of whose homestead is now included in the town. The post office was established July 9, 1883, with William H. McCoy, postmaster.

Adams Creek, COOS. Adams Creek empties into Shutter Arm of Tenmile Lake. It is named for early settler William Adams who in 1884 filed on government land near the end of Templeton Arm.

Adams Creek, DOUGLAS. This creek runs north into Elk Creek in Scotts Valley. BLM records show Thomas J. Adams patenting a homestead along the creek in 1871.

Adams Creek, WALLOWA. This stream drains Ice Lake and flows into West Fork Wallowa River about four miles south of Wallowa Lake. It was formerly known as Fall Creek, but USFS officials changed the name to Adams Creek to avoid confusion with other Fall creeks. J. H. Horner of Enterprise informed the writer in 1931 that the present name commemorates one Tom Adams who had some mining claims on the stream.

Adams Mountain, LANE. Adams Mountain, elevation 4955 feet, is in the southwest part of T 22S, R 1E. It was named for Oscar P. Adams, an early resident of Lane County. For a short article about Adams by Jack Howard, *see* Cottage Grove *Sentinel*, Mar. 28, 1929. For biography, *see* Hines' *Illustrated History of the State of Oregon*, p. 485. Adams was born in Pennsylvania in 1828 and came to Oregon in 1854. After mining and other activities, he settled on a farm at what is now Cottage Grove in 1858. He spent much time prospecting and mining in the Calapooya Mountains and Adams Mountain was named on that account.

Adams Point, KLAMATH. Adams Point is the prominent high ground north of Lost River halfway between Merrill and Malin. It is named for J. Frank Adams, a prominent early settler, whose home ranch was nearby. Adams was born in California in 1855 and came to Klamath County in 1879 where he accumulated large land holdings and was active in irrigation affairs. He helped found the Bohemian community of Malin and in 1972 the Klamath County Historical Society erected in Malin Community Park a brass memorial plaque in his memory. There is a station on the Burlington Northern, Inc., called Adams Point. Adams died in 1929. For further information *see* Gaston's *Centennial History of Oregon*, v. 4, p. 707.

Adamsville, MORROW. Adamsville post office was established Apr. 15, 1884, with Silas W. Miles first postmaster. It was discontinued June 30, 1885. Old maps show the place in the vicinity of the present site of Hardman.

Adel, LAKE. Adel is a post office on Deep Creek where it debouches into Warner Valley. C. A. Moore, in a communication in the *Oregonian* on Sept. 18, 1926, says the office was named by Bert Sessions, who owned the land where it was first established in 1896. He named it for a former sweetheart. A more intriguing source is suggested by Judge Virgil Langtry of Portland who states that Mrs. Jacob Messner, an early settler in the Warner Valley, had recalled to her grandchildren that the name was a compliment to Leda, a cow of many virtues belonging to a local resident. Since the spelling was reversed, one can only assume the compliment was back-handed.

Adkisson Creek, WASCO. Joshua Adkisson came from Virginia and settled near Boyd in 1894. Adkisson Creek empties into Butler Canyon north of Tygh Valley.

Adobe Camp, HARNEY. Adobe Camp was a very small military installation established on Silvies River in Harney Valley on Sept. 18, 1865, by Captain L. L. Williams of H Company, First Oregon Volunteer Infantry. *See* Oregon Adjutant General's *Report*, 1865–66, p. 82. A plat of level ground was laid off about 25 yards square, protected by a sod wall 30 inches high, with an inside ditch 30 inches deep. The compiler does not know the exact location of the camp, but it seems to have been near what was later called Camp Wright when that post was established Oct. 3, 1865. It may be assumed that Captain Williams abandoned Adobe Camp at that time. *See also* Camp Wright.

Adrian, MALHEUR. When a branch of the Oregon Short Line Railroad was built into this part of the county, there was a post office called Riverview on the east side of Snake River, and railroad officials did not desire to have a station of the same name on the west side. Reuben McCreary, who platted the townsite of Riverview on the west side, suggested that if that name was unsatisfactory, the name Adrian be used, which was adopted by the railroad on Feb. 13, 1913. This was to commemorate his birthplace, Adrian, Hancock County, Illinois. Riverview post office with its descriptive name was established on the east side of the river on Aug. 22, 1911, with John E. Holley postmaster. About 1915 the office was moved west across the river to the vicinity of Adrian station, and the name of the office was changed to Adrian on Nov. 10, 1919. Earlier editions of this book ascribe the name to James Adrian, a local sheepman, but Adrian did not arrive in the area until 1916.

Agate Beach, LINCOLN. This is a descriptive name. The sea beach between Newport and Yaquina Head has long been noted for the very fine agates found there. Dealers in Newport make a specialty of cutting and polishing these stones.

Agate Desert, JACKSON. Agate Desert is northeast of Central Point and just south of Rogue River. It was named for the minerals found there in some abundance. It is not a desert in the exact sense of the word. Some of Agate Desert was used for the development of Camp White in World War II. On Feb. 13, 1901, a post office with the name Agate was established in the area, with Jefferson S. Grigsby first and only postmaster. The office was closed Apr. 30, 1907, and the area was then served from Central Point.

Agency Creek, POLK, YAMHILL. Agency Creek rises on the east slope of the Coast Range, and flows for the greater part of its length in Yamhill County, joining Yamhill River near Grand Ronde. It was named because of the United States Indian Agency at Grand Ronde, which was established in pioneer days.

Agency Hill, KLAMATH. This is a prominent landmark just north of Klamath

Indian Agency. The Klamath Indian name is *Yanaldi*, which describes the ridge extending from Klamath Agency to a point north of Fort Klamath.

Agency Lake, KLAMATH. This name is generally used in referring to the north arm of Upper Klamath Lake, so called because of the Klamath Indian Agency nearby.

Agency Plains, JEFFERSON. These plains lie at an elevation of from 2300 to 2400 feet, and are bordered on the west by the Deschutes River and on the east by Mud Springs Creek. They were so named because they were near the agency of the Warm Springs Indian Reservation.

Agness, CURRY. Agness post office was established Oct. 16, 1897, and was named for the daughter of Amaziah Aubery, the first postmaster. Agness is situated on Rogue River. Amaziah Aubery was born in northern California Dec. 24, 1865, and came to Curry County in 1883. He married Rachel Fry on Feb. 22, 1887. It is said that the name was improperly reported to the postal authorities, hence the unusual spelling.

Ahalapam Cinder Field, DESCHUTES, LANE. This cinder field lies on the summit of the Cascade Range just north of the Three Sisters. It was named in 1924 by Professor Edwin T. Hodge of the University of Oregon. Ahalapam is one of the forms of the Indian name *Santiam*, and was used because the Santiam River probably at one time headed in the region.

Aims, CLACKAMAS. Aims is the name of a locality about five miles airline northeast of Sandy, north of Bull Run River and just within Clackamas County. Aims post office was established Jan. 11, 1886, with Eleazor S. Bramhall first postmaster. The office was closed Aug. 31, 1907. In Aug. 1946, Harry E. Bramhall of Troutdale wrote the compiler that it was first planned to call this post office Bramhall, but it was concluded that the name was too long. Since it was the hope or aim of the local residents to develop a substantial community, it was concluded to adopt the name Aims, which was done. The spelling Aims is that used in postal records, and by USGS, but in recent years road signs have been installed with the spelling Ames. Mr. Bramhall, who did not approve the style Ames, said that the name Aims was proposed by Lloyd C. Lowe.

Ainsworth, SHERMAN. Ainsworth is a locality just east of the mouth of Deschutes River. It has had several names. In 1909 the Harriman railroad system began the construction of a line south from the Columbia River up the Deschutes Canyon into central Oregon, and the construction was carried on by the Des Chutes Railroad Company. The point of departure from the main line of the Oregon Railroad & Navigation Company was called Deschutes Junction. The junction was about a mile and a half east of the station called Deschutes, now Miller. When the railroads reached central Oregon, a station Deschutes was established a few miles north of Bend. This called for new names for the older stations, so Deschutes was changed to Miller and Deschutes Junction was changed to Sherman, because it was in Sherman County. The change to Sherman was made in 1912. This name later caused confusion with other stations named Sherman in Oregon and elsewhere, so in Oct. 1930, the station was renamed Ainsworth. This was in honor of Captain J. C. Ainsworth. Captain Ainsworth was one of the most prominent of Oregon's pioneer citizens. He was born in Ohio on June 6, 1822, and came to Oregon in 1850. As a youth he became acquainted with steamboat activity on the Mississippi River. After reaching Oregon he became interested in transportation. He was the leading spirit in the founding of the Oregon Steam Navigation Company. He moved to Oakland, California, in 1880, and died near that city on Dec. 30, 1893. His son, John C. Ainsworth, became a prominent Oregon businessman and gave freely of his time to public affairs. In 1936 much of the branch line up Deschutes River was scrapped, and the junction at Ainsworth was abandoned. However, the locality is still known as Ainsworth. For editorial comment about Captain Ainsworth, *see* the *Oregonian*, Dec. 31, 1893.

Ainsworth State Park, MULTNOMAH. The original tract of this park was donated to the state by John C. and Alice H. Ainsworth. Ainsworth was the son of Captain J. C. Ainsworth, mentioned above.

Airlie, POLK. This was the southern terminus of the narrow gauge line of the Oregonian Railway Company, Limited. The tracks were subsequently widened to standard gauge, and the property acquired by the Southern Pacific Company. The station was named for the Earl of Airlie in Scotland. He was president of the Oregonian Railway Company, Limited, and visited Oregon during the course of construction. Most of the track on the Airlie branch was taken out in 1929.

Ajax, GILLIAM. Ajax is a locality about 16 miles airline northwest of Condon, between Ferry and Devils canyons. It supported a post office at one time, but now there is not much in the place. The office operated intermittently from 1888 to 1921. There is a story to the effect that a cowboy named Gardner volunteered to carry the mail for the new office, without pay, and that he suggested it be named after the steamer *Ajax*. Gardner had come to Oregon from California on that ship and had a sentimental interest in the name.

Alamo, GRANT. *Alamo*, a Spanish word meaning poplar or cottonwood tree, was made famous in American history in 1836 when a small band of Texans was annihilated by Mexican troops. The Texans were defending their positions in the Alamo Chapel in San Antonio. As a result of this encounter the name Alamo has been used in many places throughout the country. Alamo post office was about six or seven miles by road southwest of Granite and is said to have been named for the Alamo Mine nearby. The compiler cannot determine if the mine was named for the local tree growth or by someone interested in Texas history. In any event the post office was established May 19, 1900, with Fred McCoy first postmaster. Available records are incomplete and the compiler cannot tell when the office was discontinued, though it did not have a long life, perhaps not much after 1905.

Albany, LINN. "Albany was founded in 1848 by Walter and Thomas Monteith, named after Albany, New York" (Bancroft's *History of Oregon*, v. 2, p. 716). The first settler arrived in 1846, (*Oregonian*, Nov. 18, 1888). In 1848, the Monteiths bought the squatter's claim to the townsite from Hiram Smeed for $400 and a horse. The first house in Albany, then the finest residence in Oregon, was built in 1849 by Monteith brothers, at Washington and Second streets. The first store was established in 1849. The town of Takenah was started in 1849, near Albany, and by act of Jan. 12, 1854 (*Oregon Session Laws*, p. 27), the legislature gave that name to both towns, but in 1855, the name Albany was restored by the legislature. The first school was operated in 1851, the first flour mill in 1852. The first steamboat arrived in 1852. For additional information about the Monteiths and early history of Albany, *see Oregon Journal*, Dec. 5, 1925, editorial page. C. H. Stewart of Albany calls attention to the fact that Bancroft's statement that Albany was named at the request of James P. Millar cannot be true because Millar did not arrive in Albany until 1851. Postal records indicate that Albany post office was established on Jan. 8, 1850, with John Burkhart first postmaster. The name of the office was changed to New Albany on Nov. 4, 1850. At this point the record becomes confused. It shows that James P. Millar became postmaster on Jan. 3, 1852, on which date the name was changed back to Albany. However another entry shows that Millar became postmaster on Jan. 3, 1853, and the name was changed on that date. It is probable that the second entry is correct and that the clerk forgot about the new year when he wrote the entry dated Jan. 3, 1852. James H. Foster became postmaster at Albany on July 16, 1853. In 1925 George H. Himes wrote that Takenah, the name applied in 1849 to the locality of Albany, was an Indian word which referred to a hole in the ground, apparently near the mouth of Calapooia River where the current had cut away the bank.

Albee, UMATILLA. A post office with the name Snipe was established at this locality on June 17, 1881, undoubtedly taking its name from nearby Snipe Creek. John H. Clifford was postmaster. On Apr. 17, 1882, the name was changed to Alba and in 1887 a plat for the community was filed using the same form. *Alba* is the Latin word for white. Sometime near the turn of the century the place became known as Albee for the Albee brothers, well-known local stockmen, and on July 30, 1907 the name of the post office was changed to conform. The compiler does not know the reason for this discrepancy in names. Possibly the land was platted with an old family name, at a time when Albee was spelled Alba. Possibly the similarity of names is merely a coincidence. Albee, like many other small communities in eastern Oregon, has suffered the ravages of time beginning with the depression of the 1930s and accelerating during World War II. The post office was closed on Oct. 31, 1943 and now all that remains are a few weatherbeaten buildings entirely on private property. Barbara Curtin gives a more recent picture in an article in the *Oregonian*, Sept. 20, 1976, p. BI.

Alberson, HARNEY. For more than a score of years Alberson was a post office on the extreme east edge of Harney County, in the locality of T 30S, R 36E. As with similar offices, it was moved around a little. The office was established Sept. 20,

1907 with William E. Alberson first of nine postmasters. The office was named in honor of the official, who was an early settler in the vicinity of Juniper Lake. The office was discontinued Sept. 29, 1930.

Albert, CLATSOP. Albert was a small community and post office on the upper reaches of Blind Slough a little to the south of Aldrich Point. The office was established Sept. 11, 1901, with Nels Haglund first postmaster. The place was named for Albert Berglund, who was the second postmaster. The office was closed out on Sept. 15, 1913, with all papers to Blind Slough.

Albina, MULTNOMAH. Albina is now a part of Portland, but it was originally a separate municipality. It was laid out in 1872 and incorporated in 1887. Portland, East Portland and Albina were consolidated in 1891. It was named for Albina V. Page, the wife of William W. Page, by Edwin Russell, one-time manager of the Bank of British Columbia in Portland. Page, a native of Virginia, came to Oregon in 1857 and died in Portland in 1897. Albina was settled upon (donation land claim) by James L. Loring and Joseph Delay. Litigation between them was won by Delay, who sold to W. W. Page, Edwin Russell and George H. Williams, who laid out the town. It was later purchased by William Reid and J. B. Montgomery, and settlement began in 1874. Albina post office was in service from 1876 to 1892.

Albion, WASHINGTON. Albion post office was in service on the extreme north border of the county from Mar. 17, 1902, to Dec. 31, 1908. It was about due south of Vernonia. George M. Holt was the only postmaster. In Apr. 1949, Mrs. Lura E. Christenson wrote that Holt came from Albion, Illinois, and he named the office for his old home in the Midwest.

Alco Creek, JACKSON. Alco Creek flows into Elk Creek about eight miles airline northeast of Trail, and Alco Rock, elevation 4479 feet, is a little to the north of the headwaters of the stream. According to D. W. Pence of Eagle Point, these features were named for an early settler, about whom little seems to be known. He had a place near the mouth of Alco Creek. On May 1, 1896, a post office was established for the locality, with the name Alcoe and with Richard P. Winsly postmaster, but the office was never actually put in operation, and Winsly's appointment was rescinded June 24, 1896.

Alder Slope, WALLOWA. Alder Slope is a well known part of the Wallowa Valley, lying southwest of Enterprise and at the base of Wallowa Mountains. Alder was one of the first communities in the valley. It was named for the alder trees that grew around the Beecher cabin. The first Quaker Meeting House in the Wallowa Valley was built at Alder about 1888. The townsite was platted in 1886, but the newer community of Enterprise drew the trade and now Alder is mostly a memory, with Alder Slope as its legacy. The name alder has been used in many places in Oregon, and in the western part of the state generally refers to the presence of the red alder, *Alnus rubra*. In the eastern part of the state the name alder is more likely to refer to mountain alder, *Alnus tenuifolia*, or white alder, *Alnus rhombifolia*. Alder post office, the third in what is now Wallowa County, was established Apr. 5, 1878, with Henry Beecher first postmaster. The office was discontinued Oct. 9, 1890.

Alder Springs, LANE. Alder Springs is a place on McKenzie Highway about 15 miles east of McKenzie Bridge and for a very long time it has been a popular spot. In early days it was sometimes called Isom Corral. In the summer of 1898 Claude Branton and Courtland Green were helping a man named John Linn drive some stock from the Cobb place near Sisters, west over McKenzie Pass into the Willamette Valley. It turned out that the word "helping" was euphemistic, to say the least. On the evening of June 15, 1898, while the party was camped at Alder Springs, Branton shot and killed Linn with a revolver. Branton was later tried and convicted for his part in the affair. He was hanged at Eugene, May 12, 1899. Green turned state's evidence and pleaded guilty to a charge of murder in the second degree. He was sentenced to life imprisonment, but was pardoned after a time. A remarkable fact about the murder transpired at the trial. After Linn was killed, he was buried and a fire built over his grave. As they sat by the fire, one of the assassins performed on the Jew's harp while the other furnished vocal music. They did not have the aid of the radio in those days.

Aldrich Mountain, GRANT. Aldrich Mountain was named for Henry Aldrich, an early rancher. Aldrich, along with his son, Elmer O. Aldrich, was one of a party of ranchers who encountered a band of marauding Paiute Indians in 1878. Young Aldrich was killed and his mutilated body was later found in Aldrich Gulch which was then named for him. The family name later transferred to Aldrich Mountain and the Aldrich Mountains to the east. Aldrich Creek does not flow in the gulch but runs north to John Day River.

Aldrich Point, CLATSOP. This point was named for R. E. Aldrich who at one time lived there and had a small mercantile establishment. In pioneer days it was known as Cathlamet Point for the Cathlamet Indians. For information about that name, *see* Cathlamet Bay.

Aldrich Spring, CROOK. This spring in S 2, T 12S, R 17E, was named by USFS ranger Douglas C. Ingram for John Aldrich. Aldrich for many years was a foreman for the Baldwin Sheep and Land Company who founded the famous Hay Creek Ranch. This information came from the 1948 notes of J. O. F. Anderson on file at the Ochoco National Forest.

Alecs Butte, YAMHILL. Alexander Carson, generally known as Alec Carson and sometimes called Essen, was a well-known western hunter and trapper in very early days. Mrs. Alice B. Maloney has put together some bits of his biography which are printed in *OHQ*, v. 39, p. 16. Carson was on the upper Missouri River as early as 1807. He was for a time a member of Wilson Price Hunt's party traveling west in 1810. In 1814 he appears to have been trapping in the Willamette Valley and was classed as a "freeman" or free American trapper not connected with the British fur companies. He was in Peter Skene Ogden's brigade that trapped the Snake country in 1824–25. Indians killed him at the small hill now known as Alecs Butte in 1836. This butte is about a mile and a half south of Yamhill, west of the Tualatin Valley Highway and east of North Yamhill River. In 1944 it was part of the William Fryer farm. The compiler has an original letter from T. J. Hubbard of Fairfield to James W. Nesmith, dated Sept. 24, 1858, telling about the murder of Carson. The substance of the letter is that in Apr. or May 1836, Carson, then sick, spent two or three weeks at Hubbard's home. He had with him his Nefalitin (Tualatin) Indian trapper Boney, Boney's wife and Boney's son, 12 or 14 years old. Carson had confidence in the Indian. When he was well enough to travel, the party of four set out and camped the first night at Ellicks Butte (now Alecs Butte). In the night Boney compelled his son to murder the sleeping Carson with a shotgun. Other Indians were at the camp and they plundered Carson's property. Click-kowin, a part Tillamook Indian, had a hand in the murder and shared in the plunder. He was later shot by Waaninkapah, chief of the Nefalitins. Hubbard said he never knew why Boney committed the crime, which was the first to mar the friendly feeling between Indians and whites in the Willamette Valley.

Alexander Butte, DOUGLAS. Alexander Butte is northwest of Dillard, and has an elevation of about 1600 feet. It was named for David Alexander, an early settler, who lived near its foot.

Alfalfa, DESCHUTES. Alfalfa is a well-known district in Deschutes County about 15 miles east of Bend, named for the forage crop grown there under irrigation. Alfalfa post office was established Jan. 29, 1912, with Sibyl C. Walker first of several postmasters. The office was closed Dec. 26, 1922, and the business was turned over to Bend. The compiler does not know who named the place, but the name is appropriate.

Alford, LINN. Alford is a station on the Southern Pacific line between Halsey and Harrisburg. It bears the name of Thomas Alford, a pioneer of 1850, upon whose donation land claim it is situated. The station was originally known as Muddy, on account of Muddy Creek, which flows nearby. This name appears in the *Oregonian* as early as Nov. 7, 1857. A post office was established in this locality in Feb. 1874, with the name Muddy Station. It was in service about a year. Liverpool was the name of a post office that served the area in 1877–79. The name of the railroad station was changed from Muddy to Alford some time after 1900.

Algoma, KLAMATH. This town was named for the Algoma Lumber Company. The name is said to be an Indian word formed from *Algonquin* and *goma*, meaning Algonquin waters. Various forms of the name have been used in several states.

Alice Lake, LINN. In the years following World War II the Oregon Fish and Game Commission had an extensive fish planting program in the high Cascade lakes. One of the important planting crews was headed by Reino Koski and included Charlie Campbell and Tom McAllister, later outdoor writer for the *Oregonian*. Most of the smaller lakes were unnamed and had to be designated for the records so between 1947 and 1950 they named many of the Cascade lakes. Alice Lake in the Eight Lakes Basin was named for Alice Koski, Reino's wife.

Alicel, UNION. Alicel is a station on the Joseph branch of the Union Pacific Railroad. It is reported that when this branch line was built about 1890 Charles Ladd, a local resident, had the station named for his wife, Alice Ladd. After the death of Mr. Ladd his widow married a Mr. Tucker and subsequently lived in Seattle. Alicel is in the Grande Ronde Valley.

Alkali Lake, LAKE. This playa occupies the south part of a broad shallow basin northeast of Lake Abert. The water is highly concentrated, the dissolved salts averaging 10 percent of the weight of the total brine. This lake, together with many other lakes, playas and streams, received its name on account of the alkaline salts dissolved in the water.

Allegany, COOS. Allegheny is the modern spelling of a Delaware Indian word for the Allegheny and Ohio rivers. The word is used for many features in the United States, including the Allegheny Mountains in the eastern United States, and for a county, city and river in Pennsylvania. There are several variations of the spelling. This post office was established Mar. 25, 1893, with Wiiliam Vincamp first postmaster. The compiler has been unable to learn why the spelling of the place in Oregon, Allegany, differs from the form generally used, Allegheny.

Allen Canyon, WALLOWA. Allen Canyon opens into Lostine Valley three miles west of Lostine. The canyon and Allen Canyon Ditch, diverting water from Little Bear Creek into the canyon, were both named for rancher Neil Allen, who constructed the diversion ditch.

Allen Canyon, WASCO. The old Free Bridge Road in eastern Wasco County descended the upper part of this canyon which was named for John W. Allen. Allen bought government land nearby in 1884.

Allen Creek, CROOK. Allen Creek is a major tributary of McKay Creek. It is named for Benjamin F. Allen who was born in Illinois in 1833. He came to Oregon with his wife, Matilda, and four children in 1868 via the Isthmus of Panama. The family took a homestead at the mouth of Allen Creek in 1871. Allen became a prominent cattleman of Crook County and served a term as county commissioner before moving to Portland in 1898.

Allen Creek, JOSEPHINE. Allen Creek is southwest of Grants Pass. It was named for Lafayette Allen who took up a homestead land claim on its banks in 1867.

Allen Creek, TILLAMOOK. Allen Creek is the main watercourse through Camp Meriwether. It was named by the Boy Scouts to honor E. E. Allen, Sr. Allen came to Sandlake in 1905 and for years the Boy Scouts maintained a supply point on his property at the end of the automobile road.

Allingham Guard Station, JEFFERSON. This forest guard station and USFS forest camp of the same name are on the site of the oldest known homestead in the upper Metolius River area, filed by David W. Allingham prior to the establishment of Camp Sherman.

Allison Creek, HARNEY. This creek flows into Silver Creek in Howard Valley.

It is named for Jesse Allison who was homesteading along it in 1911 when the USFS built a ranger station near its mouth. They named the installation for Allison. The original log cabin is still standing in 1990 and listed on the National Register of Historic Places. The present name is Allison Guard Station. Allison Spring near the cabin and Jessie Spring, a mile to the northeast, are also named for Allison. *See also* Howard Valley.

Alma, LANE. Alma is in the southwest part of Lane County on the Siuslaw River. On Mar. 13, 1919, Mrs. W. H. Weatherson of Portland wrote the editor of the Eugene *Register* that Alma was named for Alma Johnson, daughter of Arthur and Alice Johnson, early settlers in the community. Before 1928, A. H. Hinkson of Eugene, who was familiar with the history of the place, informed the compiler that the name was selected by A. P. Condray. Condray was the first postmaster and the post office was established in 1888. *Alma* is a Latin word meaning kind or bountiful.

Almasie Creek, LANE. Michael Almasie was a native of Austro-Hungary. After emigrating to the United States, he took a homestead north of Lake Creek below Greenleaf on the creek which now bears his name. The name Chappell Creek for this stream is wrong.

Almeda, JOSEPHINE. Almeda post office, serving a place on Rogue River about 15 miles northwest of Merlin, was named for the Almeda Mine nearby. On Feb. 27, 1947, A. E. Voorhies, publisher of the Grants Pass *Courier*, wrote the compiler that the mine was named about 1904 or 1905 by J. F. Wickham, who promoted and owned the copper property. The name was given in compliment to Miss Almeda Hand, niece of Mr. Wickham. Almeda Hand was then a little girl living in Spokane. Almeda post office was established Feb. 15, 1912, and was discontinued July 15, 1920. Josephine Donoghue was the first of three postmasters.

Aloha, WASHINGTON. Aloha post office was established on Jan. 8, 1912. It was supposedly named by Robert Caples, a railroad man, but the reason for the name was unknown. In 1983, Joseph H. Buck of King City informed the compiler that his uncle, Julius Buck, was the first postmaster and that he named the office Aloah after a small resort on Lake Winnebago in Wisconsin. During the application process the last two letters were transposed by the Post Office Department resulting in the shift from a midwest Indian name to an Hawaiian word. The Buck family had come to Oregon from Wisconsin in 1907 and settled west of Beaverton. An 1894 atlas shows a small community named Alloa in Wisconsin about thirty miles north of Madison but Joseph Buck said that this name had no connection.

Aloysius, JOSEPHINE. Aloysius post office apparently operated at the Leonard ranch in the Althouse district. Mary E. Leonard was the postmaster. Aloysius post office was established July 12, 1888, and was discontinued Nov. 30, 1889. The available business was turned over to Althouse. James T. Chinnock, long a student of southern Oregon history, wrote from Grants Pass in Apr. 1948, substantially as follows: "Lawrence Leonard and Mary Ellen Leonard, his wife, were pioneer settlers in the Illinois Valley in Josephine County. Lawrence Leonard was a native of Ireland, his wife of Ohio. They owned several farms and also mining property. Among the children was William Aloysius Leonard, born in 1875, died in 1915. Aloysius post office was established in 1888 with Mrs. Leonard postmaster, and I am sure the establishment was given the middle name of this son." Aloysius is the patron saint of the young, and his name is frequently given to Catholic children.

Alpha, LANE. The post office at Alpha was established in 1890, and was named for Alpha Lundy, the daughter of the first postmaster, Mrs. Flora B. Lundy. Alpha is the first letter of the Greek alphabet.

Alpine, BENTON. This little settlement was named because of its location near the top of one of the foothills of the Coast Range. The situation is not particularly alpine in character but is attractive nevertheless. The community took its name from the Alpine School. This school had been operated with the name for several years prior to the time the community was started. The post office was established in 1912, according to information furnished by the postmaster in 1926.

Alpine, MORROW. Just what there was to suggest the name Alpine for a post office in eastern Morrow County about 20 miles north of Heppner the compiler cannot imagine, but that is the record. This office was established Oct. 3, 1884, with G. H. Parsell first postmaster. It continued in service until July 27, 1894, when it was closed out to Galloway, a nearby office. A directory for 1886 says Alpine was a special supply post office, but there is no explanation of the term. The compiler's recollection of the locality is that it is not alpine in character, and the name may have been brought in from elsewhere. As of 1940 a diagram of Morrow County showed a precinct called Alpine in the northeast part of the county.

Alsea, BENTON. The name Alseya Settlement appears on the Surveyor General's map of 1855. The legend stretches along the river, and the center of the settlement is a little to the west of the present community Alsea. This is the earliest appearance of the name for the place that the compiler has been able to locate. It was not until July 1871, that Alsea post office was established, with Thomas Russell postmaster. The early history of the locality is largely concerned with the difficulties of communication and transportation. Some of these problems are set out in an article in *OHQ*, v. 44, p. 56, by J. F. Santee and F. B. Warfield, with the title "Account of Early Pioneering in the Alsea Valley." Paul V. Wustrow became postmaster on Mar. 30, 1876, and held the position until May 28, 1898, nearly a quarter of a century. Colonel Wustrow was a well-known character in the Alsea Valley and was of European birth and up-bringing, but whether Russian or German, the compiler cannot learn. He is said to have coined the name Waldport at the request of David Ruble, who founded that community. For information about the origin of the name Alsea, *see* Alsea River.

Alsea River, BENTON, LINCOLN. *Alsea* is said to be a corruption of *Alsi*, the name of a Yakonan tribe that lived at the mouth of Alsea River. Lewis and Clark give *Ulseah*. Duflot de Mofras gives *Alsiias* in his *Exploration*, 1844, v. II, p. 335. Wm. P. McArthur gives *Alseya* on his chart accompanying the report of the U.S. Coast Survey for 1851. The name has many variations, but there is no doubt that it was originally pronounced with three syllables, and not with two as at present. Alsea River rises in the Coast Range and flows into Alsea Bay at Waldport. The town of Alsea is in the southwest part of Benton County.

Altamont, JOSEPHINE. Altamont is a corruption of Spanish for high mountain. Altamont post office was established Apr. 16, 1884, with Benjamin M. Parker first and only postmaster. The office was closed June 21, 1886. The available geographic information about this place is meagre, but perhaps sufficient for its importance. Early gazetteers show a place called Alta and also Altamont at a point on the railroad about 21 miles north of Grants Pass and that was doubtless the location of the post office mentioned above. There had been an earlier post office named Leland near the highway crossing on Grave Creek about four miles east of the railroad. After Altamont post office was closed in 1886, Leland office was moved west to the railroad, but the exact date of this move cannot be determined from the records. The compiler thinks it was in the early 1890s. It seems probable that the location of the old Altamont office and the present Leland railroad station were in approximately the same place.

Altamont, KLAMATH. This community is just southeast of Klamath Falls, and is said to have been named for Altamont, the famous racehorse. It was applied to the locality by Jay Beach, a prominent horseman. Altamont post office was in service from Jan. 1895, to Feb. 1902, with George W. Smith postmaster.

Althouse Creek, JOSEPHINE. Althouse Creek and Althouse Mountain near the Oregon-California line were named for the Althouse brothers of Albany. They were pioneer prospectors and miners in southern Oregon. Althouse post office was established near the lower reaches of Althouse Creek in Oct. 1877, with Charles H. Beach first postmaster. This office was in service for about thirty years.

Alvadore, LANE. Alvadore is a town about 10 miles northwest of Eugene and about a mile northeast of Fern Ridge dam. It was formerly on a branch line of the Southern Pacific. It was named for Alvadore Welch of Portland, a public utility promoter and manager, who built the Portland, Eugene and Eastern Railway through the community. The railway was later acquired by the Southern Pacific Company, and in 1936 the track in this vicinity was torn up. Welch died in 1931.

Alville, GILLIAM. Alville is a place about eight miles airline northwest of Condon that has from time to time had a post office. An office called Igo was established early in 1891 with J. J. Fix postmaster. It was in operation either at or near the present site of Alville until the end of 1892. Alville post office was opened early in 1901 and was named for the first postmaster Allen McConnell. Alville is near the head of Ferry Canyon.

Alvord Lake, HARNEY. This is an alkali lake of varying size near the south end of Steens Mountain, from which it receives its main water supply through Wildhorse Creek. In wet weather the lake overflows Alvord Desert, a playa to the north which occupies a large part of Alvord Valley. These geographic features were named by then Captain George B. Currey of the First Oregon Cavalry, during the Snake War of 1864 for Brigadier-General Benjamin Alvord of the U.S. Army. He was paymaster of the Department of Oregon, 1854–62. In 1861–65 he was in command of the Department of Oregon. He was born at Rutland, Vermont, Aug. 8, 1813; died Oct. 16, 1884. He was held in high esteem in the Pacific Northwest, and Indian depredations in eastern Oregon, after his departure, made his absence all the more regrettable. For a biographical sketch, *see* the *Oregonian*, Mar. 3, 1865. *See also* Camp Alvord. A post office named Alvord was in service in this area from Aug. 1874, to Apr. 1881. J. G. Abbott was the first postmaster.

Amazon Creek, LANE. This is a small stream with a big name. Amazon Creek flows through the southwest part of Eugene and its waters eventually reach the Long Tom River. The compiler has been unable to get the facts about the original application of the name, but it was suggested by R. V. Mills of the University of Oregon that it was because the creek widened out over such a large area of flat lands during flood stages. After Fern Ridge Dam was completed a diversion canal with a dam and weir was constructed to connect Amazon Creek to Fern Ridge Reservoir. This was designed to help control flood waters in the flat plain including west Eugene.

Amelia City, MALHEUR. The U.S. Engineer map of the Department of the Columbia, 1885, shows Amelia City at the north end of Malheur County, a little east of the town of Malheur. It was a mining town that mushroomed in the locality of Mormon Basin. J. Tracy Barton, in *OHQ*, v. 43, p. 228, gives a little of the history of Amelia City and says that the place was named for Amelia Koontz, a preacher's daughter, who eloped with a miner. The new diggings had not yet been named, and local enthusiasts could not resist the chance to honor the young bride. However, it must be recorded that another origin of the name has been suggested. Amelia Young is said to have been Brigham Young's favorite wife, and her name has been perpetuated in several places on that account. Many years ago the compiler was told that Amelia City was named for Mrs. Young because it was in the vicinity of Mormon Basin. The matter is of little consequence today as Amelia City is hardly a ghost town, less than that, if possible.

Ames Creek, LINN. Ames Creek, near Sweet Home, is named for a family of early settlers. Lowell Ames, Sr., came to the Sweet Home area in 1852 and sired a family of six sons. According to *History of Linn County*, p. 66, the family as a whole is entitled to credit for the name.

Amine Peak, WHEELER. Amine Peak, elevation 3486 feet, is in the west part of the county, about 11 miles airline southeast of Clarno. Amine Canyon drains northwest toward John Day River. These two features were named for Harriet Amine Saltzman, member of a well-known pioneer family at Burnt Ranch in early days. This information was furnished in 1931 by Jay Saltzman, a brother of Miss Saltzman. The spelling Aymine is wrong.

Amity, YAMHILL. This name was the result of an amicable settlement of a local school dispute. Amity was the name of a school, first applied in 1849 by Ahio S. Watt, pioneer of 1848, who was the first teacher in a log building that was built by two rival communities which were seeking school advantages. The post office was established July 6, 1852, with Jerome B. Walling postmaster.

Amity Hills, YAMHILL. Amity Hills are a northern spur or extension from the Eola Hills. They are separated from Eola Hills by a pass between Amity and Hopewell. This pass has an elevation of 451 feet. Amity Hills have an elevation of 880 feet in their northwestern part. They were named for the town of Amity, nearby. These hills are also known as Yamhill Mountains, but that name does not reflect the best use. *See* Eola Hills.

Amos, LANE. Amos is a locality on one of the tributaries of Coast Fork Willamette River at a point 14 miles south of Cottage Grove. The post office was in service from Apr. 23, 1898, to Nov. 1, 1902, with John Sutherland postmaster. The end of the post office was brought about by moving it two miles and changing the name to London. Sutherland continued as postmaster at London. In Feb. 1947, Mrs. George A. Powell of Eugene, a daughter of John Sutherland, wrote the compiler that Amos post office was named for one of her brothers, John Amos Sutherland. In 1902 Sutherland moved north two miles to the place previously called London. Levi Geer had developed a mineral spring at London and apparently Geer selected the name London, though the compiler does not know why. When the Amos post office was moved to London, the name was changed to fit the new location. Sutherland and Geer operated a general store at London, and for a time at least the office was in one corner of the store with Emma Sutherland, now Mrs. Powell, assistant postmaster in charge. London post office continued in service until Jan. 15, 1919, when it was closed out to Cottage Grove.

Amota Butte, LAKE. This butte is south of the Paulina Mountains, in the extreme northwest corner of the county, near Indian Butte. It is named with the Chinook jargon word for strawberry, presumably because the plant grows on the butte.

Ana River, LAKE. Ana River is a short, spring-fed stream that flows into the north end of Summer Lake. W. H. Byars, who surveyed the lands bordering the lake, named the river for his small daughter, later Mrs. S. W. Thompson of Salem. Byars was a well-known pioneer resident of Oregon, and was surveyor general from 1890 to 1894.

Anchor, DOUGLAS. Anchor post office was established Feb. 3, 1906, at the Thomas ranch on upper Cow Creek with James W. Thomas postmaster. The ranch was at the mouth of Meadow Creek and was known as Meadows Ranch.

The name Anchor was given by Miss Charity Thomas, and was suggested by the fact the Thomas family used an anchor for its stock brand. Miss Thomas later married Paul Ludwig and in 1926 was living in Yoncalla. In 1936 Anchor post office was some five miles west near the mouth of McGinnis Creek while in later years Anchor School was located two and a half miles east near the site of the previous Binger office. The post office may also have had other locations. Anchor office was closed Feb. 15, 1940.

Anderson, JOSEPHINE. Anderson or Anderson Station was one of the famous old stopping places on the stage road about two miles north of Selma. This was on the route of travel between Grants Pass and Crescent City and is now on the Redwood Highway. The Anderson family was well known. Anderson post office was established June 6, 1889, with Mary Anderson postmaster. The name of the office was changed to Selma on July 10, 1897. The office may have been moved to the new location at that time.

Anderson Creek, LANE. Anderson Creek flows into the upper reaches of Dorena Reservoir. Alfred J. Anderson homesteaded near its mouth in 1889.

Anderson Creek, LINCOLN. In Sept. 1945, Andrew L. Porter of Newport told the compiler that Anderson Creek was named for Carl Anderson who had a homestead in the northwest quarter of S 4, T 11S, R 11W. Anderson lived near the stream for many years and was well known. Anderson Creek flows into Big Creek just northeast of Newport.

Anderson Lake, LAKE. This lake is one of the Warner Lakes. It is said to have been named for Thomas A. Anderson, a nearby resident.

Anderson Spring, JEFFERSON. Anderson Spring southwest of Ashwood was named for Christian G. Anderson who settled there prior to World War I.

Anderson Spring, KLAMATH. This spring is about a mile east of Kerr Notch in the southeast rim of Crater Lake and is one of the sources of Sand Creek. It has an elevation of approximately 6800 feet. It was named for Frank M. Anderson by Captain O. C. Applegate in 1888.

Anderson Valley, HARNEY. Anderson Valley is so called because one G. W. "Doc" Anderson lived therein. It is about 25 miles southeast of Malheur Lake. Anderson post office was established in 1908.

Andrews, HARNEY. This community was named for Peter Andrews, who settled in the Wildhorse Valley about 1880. The post office was established Oct. 6, 1890 on Andrew's property, later the Kueny Ranch, with Andrews first postmaster. In 1900, the office was moved a short distance north to the locality called Wild Horse on property owned by George A. Smyth, Jr., and Smyth became postmaster. Some local citizens referred to Wild Horse disparagingly as "Wild Hog" so Smyth changed the name to Andrews in compliment to his friend.

Andy Creek, LANE. Andy Creek runs into Fall Creek from the south about ten miles east of Winberry. The creek and Chichester Falls near its mouth are both named for Andrew Chichester, a homesteader along Fall Creek in the 1890s.

Aneroid Lake, WALLOWA. Aneroid Lake and Aneroid Point, one of the high peaks of the Wallowa Mountains, are among the show places of northern Oregon. The lake was named in the fall of 1897 by Hoffman Philip, at that time a member of a party making an investigation for the United States Fish Commission. He made a barometric determination of the elevation of the lake, using an aneroid barometer, and applied the name on that account. These facts are related in a letter by Philip, printed in the Enterprise *Chieftain* for Nov. 16, 1933. At that time Philip was American minister to Norway and the letter was written from the American legation at Oslo. It is an interesting coincidence that prior to 1897 the lake appears to have been called Anna Royal Lake, but the reasons given for the name Anna Royal are not as conclusive as they might be. J. H. Horner, long a student of Wallowa history, told the compiler that the name was applied in 1893 in honor of Miss Anna Royal of Walla Walla, who was the first white woman to climb up to the lake. The compiler has also been furnished with the spelling Anna Royl. However, in the story printed in the *Chieftain*, mentioned above, it is said that the name was applied by a Professor M. G. Royal, who attended a teachers' institute at Joseph in 1893 and was the guest of J. D. McCully. His mother's name was Mary Ann (Stanley) Royal, and it is said he named the lake for her. The compiler has been unable to reconcile all these discrepancies. The name Aneroid is now so well established that it seems improbable that it will be supplanted by the older style.

Angell Peak, BAKER, GRANT. Angell Peak, elevation approximately 8675 feet, is situated at the summit of the Blue Mountains, a little to the south of the junction of Union, Grant and Baker counties. Angell Peak was named by the USFS to honor Albert G. Angell, a member of the service in Oregon for nearly 30 years. More than half of that time he spent on the Whitman National Forest. He also served on the Deschutes National Forest and at the regional office in Portland up to the time of his death in 1941.

Anglersvale, TILLAMOOK. The post office Anglersvale was first called Firglen. It was established with that name on Sept. 8, 1916, with L. S. Miller postmaster. The name was changed to Anglersvale in Nov. 1916, and the office was closed in Feb. 1919. According to J. H. Scott of Nehalem, Miller was a civil engineer connected with the Pacific Railway and Navigation Company. A fishing camp was established on Nehalem River about opposite the mouth of Cook Creek. The place was first called Firglen, though the records show that some tracts were platted with the name Minnehaha. There were accommodations for fishermen who traveled to the place by rail and thus furnished traffic for the railroad. The change of name to Anglersvale was because it was thought to be a name that would be better advertising. As the automobile came into greater use, fishermen were diverted to other streams. Anglersvale was at or close to the place now known as Batterson.

Angora, LINCOLN. Angora post office which was a few miles west of Alsea was named for the goats raised in the vicinity. It was in the southeast part of T 13S, R

9W, on or near Fall Creek at a point not far above the mouth of that stream. The office was established Mar. 11, 1899, with Otto Dieckhoff first postmaster, and was discontinued June 29, 1907.

Anidem, LINN. Anidem is one of those names which was formed by spelling another word backward. Oregon has had a number of post offices with this type of name but most of them have faded from the picture. Anidem was established Jan. 10, 1896, with William B. Lawler first postmaster when mining activity was resumed near the old location of Quartzville. Lawler was apparently the principal in Lawler's Gold Mines, Ltd., the company which undertook the revival. Albert Burch was the manager and he gives further details in *OHQ*, v. 43, p. 108. The post office was discontinued June 16, 1902. Lawler had previously lived at a community or locality called Medina, possibly in Colorado. Why he chose to burden his mining development with such an odd name as Anidem is a mystery to the compiler. In 1906 there were approximately a dozen post offices in the United States with the name Medina but none in Colorado. However, there may have been a Medina mine in Colorado. These post offices were probably all named for Medina in Arabia, although it is of course possible that in some cases the name Medina was of Spanish origin. The compiler does not know why the name Medina turned out to be so popular in the United States.

Ankeny Bottom, MARION. This bottom has a general elevation of about 200 feet and is situated on the east bank of the Willamette River just north of the mouth of the Santiam River. It was named for Henry E. Ankeny, son of Captain A. P. Ankeny, who developed a farm there in the 1870s. Henry E. Ankeny was born in West Virginia in 1844, came to Oregon in 1850 with his father, and died Dec. 21, 1906. *See* Carey's *History of Oregon*, v. 2, p. 538. The Buena Vista Road passes over Ankeny Hill about three miles north of the bottom. Ankeny post office was at or near the Ankeny home on the northeast edge of Ankeny Bottom. It was established in Feb. 1889. The name of the office was changed to Sidney in May 1894, and moved about a mile west to a new location.

Anlauf, DOUGLAS. This is a station north of Drain, on the Siskiyou line of the Southern Pacific Company. It was named for a pioneer family of the vicinity. The post office was established May 1, 1901, with James A. Sterling first postmaster.

Annie Creek, KLAMATH. This stream, together with Annie Spring, which is its principal source, was named for Miss Annie Gaines in 1865. She and Mrs. O. T. Brown were the first white women to descend to the waters of Crater Lake. She always spelled her name Annie. Miss Gaines was later Mrs. Augustus C. Schwatka of Salem, hence a sister-in-law of Frederick Schwatka, the arctic explorer. Authorities at one time used the spelling Anna, but the USBGN has officially adopted the style Annie.

Annie Creek, LANE. Annie Creek rises southeast of Fairview Peak in the Bohemia district. It was named for Annie Oglesby, who was an early resident. Loren Hunt told the writer in 1968 that the nearby Noonday Mine was originally named

Annie Mine but he was not able to explain the change, which occurred many years ago.

Anns Butte, DESCHUTES. This butte is just west of the confluence of Deschutes River and Little Deschutes River south of Bend. It was named for Ann Markel who taught at Bend High School just after the turn of the century. Miss Markel tried homesteading near the butte and later married Vernon Forbes, one of the first legislators from Deschutes County.

Anoka, COLUMBIA. This post office was situated on the Ralph Rogers homestead on Pebble Creek two or three miles above an earlier office called Pebble. The only postmaster at Anoka was Mrs. Ralph Rogers, the same person as Mrs. Lou A. Rogers, mother of Nelson Rogers, Oregon's late state forester. The office was in service from Aug. 9, 1902, until Apr. 30, 1907. Omar C. Spencer reported that the office was named at the request of one Randolph, who had had post office experience at Anoka, the well-known place in Minnesota on the Mississippi River, a little upstream from Minneapolis. There are several places of this name in the United States. *Anoka* is an Indian word and it is said to mean "on both sides of."

Antelope, WASCO. Antelope Valley was probably named in 1862 by members of the party of Joseph Shearer, while packing supplies into the John Day mines. *See* Bancroft's *History of Oregon*, v. 1, p. 787. There were many antelope in central Oregon in pioneer days, hence the name. Antelope post office was established Aug. 7, 1871, and Howard Maupin was first postmaster, the office taking its name from the valley. The 1862 Shearer party also named Muddy Creek, Cherry Creek, Burnt Ranch and laid the foundation for Bakeoven. After World War II, the community languished until the 1980s when followers of Bhagwan Shree Rajneesh, who had started the city of Rajneeshpuram on the site of the old Muddy Ranch, came to dominate the town. On Sept. 18, 1984, by a vote of 57 to 22, the charter was amended to change the name from Antelope to Rajneesh. This received considerable publicity throughout the state for feelings about the Bhagwan and his followers were sharply divided. The Bhagwan's problems came to a head in the fall of 1985 when Anand Sheela, his personal secretary and spokeswoman, decamped to Europe, reportedly with a substantial sum of the sect's money. A short time later the Bhagwan was indicted on federal immigration charges. After an abortive attempt at flight, he pleaded guilty and returned to India. Meanwhile, on Nov. 6, 1985, the remaining residents, both original and Rajneeshee, voted 34 to 0 to restore the original name. The Post Office Department, relying on the efficiency of Zip Code, 97001, never changed the name from Antelope.

Anthony, BAKER. Anthony was a post office at the confluence of Eagle Creek and Little Eagle Creek. It operated intermittently from Aug. 3, 1903, until May 15, 1907, when it was closed to Sparta. Charles W. Hallford was the first and, probably, only postmaster. The office served a mining community that operated during the summer. It was named for Alfred W. Anthony, best known as an ornithologist but also a mining engineer, who developed the nearby Anthony Mine.

Anthony Lakes, BAKER, UNION. These lakes form a source of Anthony Creek, a tributary of North Powder River. The lakes were at one time known as North Powder Lakes, but the USBGN has officially decided on Anthony Lakes. The lakes take their name from the creek which is named for William 'Doc' Anthony who came to Baker county in 1864 and settled along its banks. Anthony, who was listed in the 1880 census as both a farmer and M.D., ranched on this property and for a time collected toll for the Dealy Wagon Road. His farm was about a mile north of the mouth of the creek. Anthony died in Oct. 1914 at age 85. In the 1930s skiers began to utilize the slopes above Anthony Lakes and after World War II, a major ski area was developed.

Antler, LAKE. Antler was a pioneer post office in Lake County that went out of service many years ago. In Oct. 1945, J. O. Jewett of the *Lake County Examiner-Tribune* was kind enough to look into the history of this office and as a result, was able to report as follows: "The first Antler post office was established in Dec. 1875, with B. S. Chandler postmaster. Chandler was a native of Ohio and an early settler in Wisconsin and served in the Civil War. Chandler State Park bears his name. The post office was in the Crooked Creek district about a half mile north of the present ranchhouse of Dr. W. Hayden Fisk of Lakeview, and in 1945 the remains of the old log cabin still stand there, about 15 miles north of Lakeview. This office was operated until Apr. 1879. Later, citizens living in that community wanted to re-route the stage line to include a stop there, so it was necessary to reestablish the office. This was done in Nov. 1891, with R. A. Paxton postmaster. This office was a few miles further north on Loveless Creek about the site of the present Fred Reynolds ranch. This office was closed in Oct. 1892." While there is no direct evidence as to the origin of the name, it is probable that Mr. Chandler had some deer horns on the premises, possibly nailed above the front door of the cabin.

Antoken Creek, WASCO. This stream is on the Warm Springs Indian Reservation in the east part of the Mutton Mountains. It flows into Deschutes River. In May 1943, the compiler was informed by J. E. Elliott of the Warm Springs Agency that the creek bears the name of an Indian who lived near its mouth many years ago and who died in 1905. Indians report that the word has no special meaning.

Antone, WHEELER. This place was named in the early 1890s for Antone Francisco, a pioneer settler. He was of Portuguese descent. The post office was established on Sept. 17, 1894 with Sylvester S. Wolever first postmaster. Except for one three-year period, it operated until Nov. 30, 1948.

Apiary, COLUMBIA. One of the most remarkable names in Oregon geographic history is Apiary, for a place about eight miles southwest of Rainier. Apiary post office was established Aug. 28, 1889, with David M. Dorsey first postmaster. The office was closed on Mar. 24, 1924. The office was so named because Dorsey had a bee ranch.

Apple Creek, DOUGLAS. Apple Creek flows into North Umpqua River four miles east of Steamboat and is the site of the USFS Forest Camp of the same name.

Jessie Wright of Cap's Illahee stated in 1967 that many years ago a USFS construction crew was camped nearby and George Collins, the cook, began to prepare dried apples for supper. Collins' experience as a cook must have been largely theoretical as he made no provision for the increase in volume. The creek was named for the surfeit which it carried away.

Applegate Butte, KLAMATH. Applegate Butte and Little Applegate Butte nearby are on what was the Klamath Indian Reservation, east of Fort Klamath. They bear the name of Philip Applegate, a grandson of General E. L. Applegate, a member of one of Oregon's prominent pioneer families. Philip Applegate was long a forester in the Klamath country.

Applegate Peak, KLAMATH. This peak is on the south rim of Crater Lake and is just above Vidae Cliff. It has an elevation of 8126 feet and was named for Captain O. C. Applegate of Klamath Falls. Oliver Cromwell Applegate was born in what is now Polk County, June 11, 1845, son of Lindsay Applegate. He performed important service during the Modoc War and was Indian agent at Fort Klamath for a number of years. He had great influence over the Indians and did much to promote their welfare. He was a much respected citizen of Klamath Falls, where he lived for many years, and where he died Oct. 11, 1938.

Applegate River, JACKSON, JOSEPHINE. Applegate River and its tributaries rise in the Siskiyou Mountains. It flows into Rogue River west of Grants Pass. The valley through which it flows is known as the Applegate district, and there is a post office called Applegate in Jackson County. Applegate is an honored name in Oregon history. Jesse, Lindsay and Charles Applegate came to Oregon from Missouri in 1843, and for many years were prominent in pioneer affairs. Lindsay and Jesse Applegate went into southern Oregon on an exploring expedition in 1846, particulars of which may be found in Lindsay Applegate's account in *OHQ*, v. 22, p. 12 *et. seq.* and also in Carey's *History of Oregon*, p. 444. In 1848, Lindsay Applegate was a member of a party of Willamette Valley settlers who visited the Rogue River Valley in southern Oregon on the way to the mines in California. This party prospected on the stream now known as Applegate River, which was named in compliment to Lindsay Applegate. *See OHQ*, v. 22, p. 3.

Appleton, WALLOWA. This post office was established in Sept. 1902, and operated until July 1913, with Miranda Rebecca Applegate postmaster. She homesteaded the land where the post office was situated about two miles east of Flora. It was planned to have the office named for Miranda Applegate but that was not possible because there was already an Applegate post office in Oregon. Accordingly a suitable name was coined by using part of the name Applegate.

Arago, COOS. Arago post office is about six miles south of Coquille. In May 1927, Mrs. T. P. Hanly of Bandon informed the compiler that Arago was named by her father, the late Henry Schroder, for Cape Arago. The office was not named for a racehorse, as is sometimes asserted. The community was formerly called Halls Prairie, but postal authorities rejected a name of two words.

Arant Point, KLAMATH. This point, with an elevation of 6815 feet, is about one mile south of Annie Spring. It was named for William F. Arant of Klamath Falls, formerly superintendent of the park. Arant died on Nov. 23, 1927. For his obituary, *see* the *Oregonian*, Dec. 4, 1927, sect. I, p. 8.

Arata, MULTNOMAH. Arata was the name of a station about a mile east of Fairview on the electric interurban line. The station was named for a local resident, S. A. Arata, who operated a farm nearby. The railway was torn up some years ago and the station was abandoned. The location is shown on the USGS map of the Troutdale quadrangle, 1918 edition. S. A. Arata was born in Genoa in 1864 and came to the United States in 1871. He came to Oregon about 1883, and for many years was in the grocery business in Portland. He retired in 1910 and moved to his farm. He died May 3, 1948, in Portland.

Arcadia, MALHEUR. Arcadia post office was established on the Malheur County list on Nov. 11, 1896, with Theodore T. Danielson first of six postmasters. The office remained in service with short interruptions until May 26, 1908, when it was closed out to Nyssa. The office, named for the pastoral area of Greece, was a few miles north of Nyssa, and served the K.S. & D. orchard area. The K.S. & D. Fruit and Land Company was promoted by Messrs Kiesel, Shilling and Danielson, who projected the development about 1890 and incorporated the company about 1897. There were some 1320 acres of land in the project, under the Owyhee ditch, and it was planned to develop an extensive fruit growing and processing community. The promoters selected the name Arcadia in the expectation that life on the project would be ideal. For more information, *see History of Baker, Malheur and Harney Counties*, p. 553. The compiler has been informed that the plan for a fruit growing community was abandoned many years ago and the land was later devoted to the general crops grown in the area.

Arcadia, WALLOWA. Thomas Gwillim was an early settler in Wallowa County, and like several others, he was so impressed by the character of his surroundings that he expressed his appreciation by applying a romantic name to a post office. Arcadia office was established Jan. 8, 1887, with Gwillim postmaster. It operated until Jan. 1897, at a point a little to the northwest of the present site of Zumwalt. Arcadia, a region in Greece, was noted for its pastoral, peaceful simplicity.

Arch Cape, CLATSOP. This cape is in the extreme southwest part of the county, at the south end of Cannon Beach. It was named because of the natural arch in the rocks. Arch Cape post office was established June 27, 1912, with William C. Adams first postmaster. It was discontinued Aug. 31, 1913, but has been reestablished.

Ardenwald, CLACKAMAS. Ardenwald was named about 1888 for Arden M. Rockwood, whose father owned the site of the community and platted it. *Wald* is German for a wood, and the combination name was used because of the woods in the neighborhood, and because of the name Rock-*wood*. Arden was a family name.

Argenti, MARION. Argenti townsite was near Silver Creek about a dozen miles southeast and upstream from Silverton, very close to Silver Creek Falls. Argenti post office was established in Apr. 1889, with George A. Lehman first of six postmasters. The office was closed in Sept. 1904, with all papers to Sublimity. There is a local story in Silverton and in Salem to the effect that Herbert Hoover, then a resident of Salem, worked as a chainman on the survey party that laid out the original townsite. *See* Dean Collins' story in the *Oregon Journal*, Apr. 19, 1940. It is said that there was a post office, store, blacksmith shop, hotel and two sawmills in the place, but these establishments have completely disappeared. *Argenti* is a Latin word meaning "of silver," a name obviously suggested by Silver Creek nearby.

Arkansas Hollow, WALLOWA. This small valley empties into Swamp Creek about eight miles north of Enterprise. James T. Baker, formerly of Madison County, Arkansas, homesteaded there in the early 1890s and the place was named for his former home.

Arko, WALLOWA. Arko post office was established in 1895 but discontinued in 1902. The place was in the north end of the county, a few miles northwest of Troy. It was named by Mary C. Loy, wife of the first postmaster, for Arkoe, Nodaway County, Missouri, but somehow the spelling was changed.

Arleta, MULTNOMAH. Arleta is part of Portland. It was named for Arleta Potter, daughter of T. B. Potter of the Potter-Chapin Realty Company, which put the addition on the market.

Arlington, GILLIAM. This town is on the south bank of the Columbia River at the mouth of Alkali Canyon. In pioneer days the place was known as Alkali. The post office at Alkali, which was then in Wasco County, was established on Nov. 7, 1881. Local residents did not consider the name Alkali suitable for a growing community, and at a town meeting N. A. Cornish suggested that the town be named Arlington, supposedly because there were a number of southerners living in the community at the time and it was the home of General Robert E. Lee. However, an ulterior motive lay hidden, for many years later his daughter, Nellie C. Cornish, in *Miss Aunt Nellie*, p. 28, says the name was selected to honor her father whose full name was Nathan Arlington Cornish. Cornish apparently neglected to mention this connection and the honor went unknown, at least during his lifetime. The name of the community Alkali was changed to Arlington by an act passed at a special session of the legislature and approved Nov. 20, 1885 and the Post Office Department conformed on Dec. 31, 1885.

Armet, LANE. Armet was a station on the original Southern Pacific Cascade line between Lowell and Oakridge. The place was formerly called Blakelyville, which was the name of the post office, but the railroad adopted the name Eula for the station. *See* Eula for the history of these names. The post office was later changed to Eula, but by that time the railroad found there was confusion between Eula and Eola, so about 1925 the station name was changed to Armet, the name of a head armor used in the Middle Ages. This name was selected arbitrarily by railroad officials. Properly the word is accented on the first syllable, but the name of the station was accented on the last syllable. Eula post office was taken out of service in the fall of 1943. The railroad was relocated when Lookout Point Dam was completed after World War II but the name survives on Armet Creek.

Armin, WALLOWA. Armin is said to have been named for one Armin Bodmer, of the Wallowa Valley, at a time when he was courting a young widow, Affie B. Hanna, who lived in the place.

Armitage, LANE. Armitage was named for George H. Armitage, an early settler nearby. He was born in New York in 1824, and came to Oregon in 1848, by way of California. For his biography, *see* Walling's *History of Lane County*, p. 490. He operated the first ferry across the McKenzie River. For an editorial about his public services, *see* the *Oregonian*, Aug. 4, 1928. McKenzie post office was established on Jan. 21, 1854, with George H. Armitage postmaster. It was apparently near the present site of Armitage station. The office was discontinued in Oct. 1859.

Armstrong Creek, GRANT. This stream is near Galena. It was named for W. W. Armstrong, a pioneer resident of the neighborhood. He was a veteran of the Civil War, and came to Oregon with government troops in 1866, and was for a time stationed at Camp Logan, near what is now Strawberry Mountain. He was a resident of Grant County for many years.

Army Hill, DOUGLAS. Army Hill is an elevation of sand on the west bank of Umpqua River, two miles north of its mouth. It was named because of the soldiers at Fort Umpqua. Fort Umpqua was a post at Umpqua City from 1856 to 1862. Umpqua City was a pioneer trading post near the mouth of Umpqua River.

Arnold Ice Cave, DESCHUTES. Arnold Ice Cave has been so known for a number of years, and the name is apparently established. However, the late Robert B. Gould of Bend told the writer that the name of Arnold came to be applied to this cave as a result of the misreading of a county road sign, which bore directions for Arnold (ranch) and the ice cave. Visitors combined the two names on the signboard, with the result that "Arnold Ice Cave" is now well known by that name. For additional information about the naming of this cave *see* editorial in Bend *Bulletin*, Apr. 18, 1927.

Arock, MALHEUR. This name was first applied in May 1922, and the post office was established in 1926. The name was suggested by T. Townley Garlick, due to the proximity of a large rock with picture writing, supposedly of Indian origin.

Arrastra Creek, JACKSON. An arrastra is a crude mill for grinding ore. The operation generally consists of dragging heavy stones over the ore, which has been placed in the bottom of a pit. The grinding stones are moved around by beams operated by mules or horses. There were a good many arrastras in southern Oregon in the days of the quartz mining, and Arrastra Creek was named for such a mill. The stream is tributary to Wagner Creek south of Talent.

Arrow, LAKE. Arrow post office was another office that was in operation during the days of the homesteaders in northern Lake County. It was situated a few miles northeast of Silver Lake, and is said to have been named for the Indian arrowheads found in the vicinity. The office was established May 21, 1910, with Edith Reigel postmaster. It was discontinued Feb. 28, 1918.

Arrowwood Point, CROOK. Arrowwood Point is the highest peak at the east end of the Maury Mountains southeast of Prineville. At one time this point was called Maury Mountain, which was confusing because the east-west range is called Maury Mountains. Accordingly about 1932, when it was planned to make a lookout development on the peak, the name was changed to Arrowwood Point, because of the presence of arrowwood shrubs on the summit. This shrub is the *Philadelphus lewisii* or syringa, also called Lewis mock orange. The new name was suggested by W. O. Harriman, USFS forest supervisor.

Arstell Creek, TILLAMOOK. Arstell Creek is tributary to Nestucca River near Cloverdale. It apparently is named for Ambrose Arstill who patented government land along it in 1890. The compiler cannot account for the difference in spelling.

Arthur, BAKER. Arthur was the name selected for a post office in the north part of the county to the northeast of Keating. The office was established as a result of mining activity in the Balm Creek area. It was in service from Feb. 25, 1929, to June 30, 1930, when it was closed to Keating. The writer does not know the activities of the mining industry mentioned. The name Arthur was derived from W. J. Arthur, more generally known as Johnny Arthur.

Arthur, MULTNOMAH. In earlier days a well-known Multnomah County post office was Arthur on the west shore of Sauvie Island a little north of Holbrook. This office was established July 26, 1880, with Mary Taylor postmaster. The office was closed Nov. 30, 1904, apparently as the result of the extension of rural free delivery. Mary Taylor was the only postmaster the place ever had. A good deal of effort has been made trying to learn the origin of this name, but with no result. The place was not named for President Chester A. Arthur because he was not president when the office was established, in fact he had not even been elected vice-president. The office was established about the time the Republicans nominated the Garfield-Arthur ticket in Chicago in the summer of 1880, and it may have been named because Arthur's name was in the news, but this is just a guess.

Asbestos, JACKSON. Asbestos locality and post office were named for the fireproofing material, deposits of which are to be found in the north part of Jackson County. The post office was established Aug. 15, 1893, with May Sackett first postmaster. It was closed Aug. 31, 1918, with papers to Beagle. It was situated in T 33S, R 2W, near Evans Creek. F. W. Libbey of the State Department of Geology and Mineral Industries calls the attention of the compiler to the fact that the word asbestos is a commercial term rather than a definite mineral name. There are a number of minerals which are called asbestos, the most important of which is

chrysotile, a fibrous variety of serpentine. Fibrous tremolite, another type of asbestos, is known to occur in Jackson County. Prolonged breathing of air contaminated with asbestos fibers can have serious or fatal consequences and during the
mid 1960s most uses of asbestos were discontinued.

Aschoff Buttes, CLACKAMAS. These buttes lie about five miles east of Marmot
and are north of Little Sandy River. They were named for Adolf Aschoff, who was
born in Germany on May 21, 1849, emigrated to the United States in 1869 and
came to Oregon in 1882. He settled at what is now Marmot on Mar. 16, 1883 and
was for many years a prominent guide and forester in that part of the state. He was
an enthusiastic advocate of all things tending to preserve and popularize the scenic features of Oregon. He died in Portland on May 16, 1930. For obituary, *see*
Oregon Journal, May 17, 1930. *See also* Marmot.

Ash, DOUGLAS. This post office was established July 24, 1894, and the first
postmaster was Charles L. Parker. The post office department asked for a short
name and he suggested Ash as there were many of those trees in the vicinity.

Ashland, JACKSON. Ashland was named by Abel D. Hellman, whose birthplace
was Ashland County, Ohio. Matthew P. Deady is the authority for the statement
that the town was named in honor of Henry Clay's birthplace, which was near
Ashland, Virginia (Deady letter in the *Oregonian*, May 13, 1884). Both explanations are possibly correct. Hellman was born in 1824. The town in Oregon was
named in 1852 (Walling's *History of Southern Oregon*). The flour mill was built by
Abel D. Hellman, John Hellman, Eber Emery, Jacob Emery and James Cardwell.
Ashland Mills in 1855 is described by T. J. Dryer, *Oregonian*, June 23, 1855; *see also*
Apr. 4, 1903. For notes on Ashland in 1855, Feb. 2, 1855. Ashland Mills post office
was established on May 17, 1855, with Abel D. Hellman first postmaster. The name
of the post office was changed to Ashland on June 14, 1871. Hellman and associates
built a sawmill before they built the flour mill and supplied lumber to the Jacksonville mines. For further information, *see* article by Fred Lockley in the *Oregon
Journal* for May 2, 1928, editorial page and Kay Atwood's book on early Ashland
and Abel Hellman, *Mill Creek Journal*.

Ashwood, JEFFERSON. Near Ashwood is a butte known as Ash Butte because
of the volcanic ash deposits on its sides. When the post office was established
about 1898, the word Ash was combined with Wood to form the name. This was
done to honor Whitfield T. Wood, who settled in the vicinity in the 1870s. His
son, James Wood, was the first postmaster.

Aspen Lake, KLAMATH. Aspen Lake is west of Upper Klamath Lake, and is fed
by streams from the east side of Aspen Butte. These features and others so named
in the state are distinguished by the presence of that beautiful tree, the quaking
aspen, or *Populus tremuloides*. In *The American Fur Trade of the Far West*, General
H. M. Chittenden says: "Another species of the genus populus was the *Populus
tremuloides*, the quaking asp, or the *tremble* of the French. The superstitious voy-

ageurs thought this was the wood of which the Cross was made and that ever since the crucifixion its leaves have exhibited that constant tremulous appearance which has given rise to the name. The wood of the quaking asp was preferred by the trappers as a fuel for cooking, because it had little odor and did not taint the meat."

Astoria, CLATSOP. The name Astoria is full of historic significance, for about it is woven the story of the discovery, exploration and development of the great Oregon country. It was near here that Captain Robert Gray discovered the mouth of the Columbia River and gave to the United States its claim to the title of the territory. It was near here that Lewis and Clark passed the winter of 1805–6 and it was here that the first commercial settlement of Americans was made on the Pacific Coast in 1811. This settlement was the direct result of the organization of the Pacific Fur Company in 1810 by John Jacob Astor of New York, and it was fitting that his name should be given to the company's initial enterprise. John Jacob Astor was born in Germany in 1763, and after four years in London, came to New York when he was 20. By his energy and industry he grew to be a leading figure in the commercial life of the city, where he died on Mar. 29, 1848, leaving a large fortune. The bibliography of John Jacob Astor's relations with Oregon is unusually large. Washington Irving's *Astoria*, published in 1836, is picturesque in style, but gives a good general account of Astor's enterprise. The first chapters of Scott's *History of the Oregon Country* treat the founding of Astoria quite fully, and include many references invaluable to those interested in the matter. The Astor party on the ship *Tonquin* arrived off the mouth of the Columbia River on Mar. 22, 1811, and after two disastrous days of strenuous effort, succeeded in landing in the estuary. Three weeks later, Apr. 12, the party began to build a post and bestowed upon it the name of the originator and chief owner of the enterprise. The place was called Astoria until the fall of 1813, when it was taken over by the British, and rechristened Fort George. *See* Carey's *History of Oregon*, p. 246. Fort George it remained until it was nominally returned to the United States in 1818. The name Astoria was gradually restored with pioneer settlement. Attention is called to the fact that the first trading post at Astoria is sometimes called Fort Astor rather than Astoria. The compiler has never found any authority for the name Fort Astor. Lewis and Clark hibernated on what is now known as Lewis and Clark River, a few miles southwest of the present city of Astoria. Their camp was called Fort Clatsop. The city of Astoria is situated on a peninsula between the Columbia River on the north and Youngs Bay on the south, and the high ridge in between is known as Coxcomb Hill. It has an extreme elevation of 595 feet at the bench mark in the base of the Astoria Column. Astoria post office was established on Mar. 9, 1847, with John M. Shively first postmaster. This was the first American post office on the Pacific Coast. Statements to the effect that the first post office at Astoria was in the John Adair house do not seem to be correct. General Adair got to Astoria in Apr. 1849, more than two years after the post office was established. On

Apr. 10, 1852, General Adair wrote to Joseph Lane as follows: "When I came to the country, or shortly after, you know Shively, who was postmaster and resided on the hill at Fort George, left for the mines, leaving no one to take care of the office ... McClure, who was one of Shively's bondsmen, would not allow a mail bag to go into his house and demanded of the P.M. Genl an immediate release as surety. I consented to take the poor bantling." John Adair became postmaster on Nov. 8, 1849; Butler Anderson on Nov. 11, 1850, and Sam'l A. Seymore on May 27, 1852. These data are from postal records at Washington, D.C.

Athena, UMATILLA. This town is about half way between Walla Walla and Pendleton. For many years it was known as Centerville. The name caused confusion with Centerville in Washington County, and also with Centerville in Klickitat County, Washington. In 1889 the town authorities decided on a change and asked D. W. Jarvis, local school principal, to suggest a new name. Jarvis, being of a romantic and classical turn of mind, suggested Athena, which was adopted. Athena was one of the most important goddesses of Greek mythology, and with Zeus and Apollo represented the embodiment of all divine power. She was the goddess of counsel, war, arts and industries. To the Romans she was known as Minerva. The post office of Centerville was established Oct. 11, 1878, with Wm. T. Cook as first postmaster. The name was changed to Athena May 16, 1889.

Athey Canyon, POLK. This canyon is on the west slope of Eola Hills about two miles northeast of McCoy. It was named for a pioneer family of the north Willamette Valley.

Attwell Creek, HOOD RIVER. This stream near Cascade Locks was named for Roger G. Attwell and his wife Mary Attwell, pioneer settlers. Attwell was born in New York City and arrived in Oregon in Aug. 1852. He settled near the present site of Cascade Locks on Apr. 12, 1853. *See* land office certificate 5041.

Atwood, MORROW. When Atwood post office was established on Oct. 22, 1883, it was on the Umatilla County list. Morrow County had not yet been organized. Henry C. Thompson was the first postmaster and with a short intermission this office ran along until Nov. 20, 1888. Whether it was always in what is now Morrow County the compiler cannot tell. It was on Butter Creek which, in that locality, is very close to the Morrow-Umatilla county line. The office may have been in the two counties at different times but when it was discontinued it certainly was in Morrow County.

Auburn, BAKER. Gold was found on Griffin Creek in Oct. 1861, and within a few weeks the eastern Oregon gold rush was in full fever. Thousands of miners and prospectors poured into the Blue Mountains and also into parts of Idaho where there were similar discoveries. A camp sprang up in the Blue Canyon district a little south of Griffin Creek. This camp was about eight miles airline southwest of Baker City and it rapidly became one of the largest settlements in eastern Oregon. A paragraph from Isaac Hiatt's *Thirty-one Years in Baker County*, p. 30, gives the following account of the founding of the place: "On the 13th of

June 1862, a meeting was called by Wm. H. Packwood, Ed Cranston, Geo. Hall and others at which time it was resolved to lay out a town to be called Auburn, and the next day a street was located from Freezeout gulch to Blue canon, and building lots taken on each side, and in a short time a number of buildings were put up and Auburn assumed the usual appearance of a new mining town. The diggings in that vicinity were thereafter called the Auburn mines." Many interesting stories have been written about the rise and fall of this camp, which is now not even a ghost town, but the compiler has never seen any information about the reason for the application of the name. Upward of 25 places in the United States have been named with the word made famous by Oliver Goldsmith in the first line of his *Deserted Village*, a name that turned out to be truly prophetic as far as the Oregon camp was concerned. According to Irving L. Rand of Portland there were no buildings left in Auburn, Oregon, in 1945. Many miners came to eastern Oregon from the Sierra Nevada region of California and the compiler is of the opinion that Auburn, Oregon, was named for the well-known California mining town, which was in turn named by miners who came from Auburn, New York. The compiler admits he has no evidence to support this theory but it is pleasing to contemplate. It is a matter of interest that there is a place called Blue Canyon in the Sierra Nevada not very many miles northeast of Auburn, California. There is nothing on modern maps to recall the mining camp of Auburn except the Auburn Ditch now used for irrigation. The post office at Auburn, Oregon, was established Nov. 1, 1862, with William F. McCrary first postmaster. This was the first post office in northeastern Oregon. It was in operation continuously until Oct. 31, 1903. *See also* Baker City.

Audison Creek, WALLOWA. This stream empties into Saddle Gulch in T 2S, R 49E. It bears the name of George Audison, hunter and trapper, who had a dugout there in the early 1880s.

Audrey, BAKER. Audrey post office was established in Mar. 1902 and was discontinued in Apr. 1918. The first postmaster was Lemuel D. King. The writer has been told that the office was named for Audrey King, daughter of the first postmaster. This office was in the extreme southwest corner of T 11S, R 37E, on North Fork Burnt River about nine miles southeast of Whitney, at the old King ranch and stage stop. Miss Audrey King married Charles Davidson. She was appointed postmaster at Audrey in Aug. 1912, after her marriage, and served until the office was discontinued as of Apr. 15, 1918. In 1949 it was reported that the Davidsons were then living in Salem.

Augur Creek, LAKE. There are two streams of this name in Lake County. One is immediately northwest of Lakeview and flows into Thomas Creek. The other is 20 miles further northwest and empties into Chewaucan River via Dairy Creek. The compiler is certain both were named for Captain C. C. Augur, U.S. Army, (born in 1821 and graduated from West Point) who was a participant in early Indian wars in Oregon. The names were doubtless applied during the Snake

War in 1864. During the Civil War he became major-general of volunteers, and was a brigadier-general in the regular establishment. He died in 1898.

Augusta, BAKER. Augusta post office operated from Aug. 10, 1871, to Oct. 11, 1872, with William T. Atkeson postmaster. The office was on Eagle Creek not far from the place later called Sanger, and is said to have been named for a Miss Augusta Parkwood, the first unmarried woman resident. *See* Sanger.

Augusta Creek, LANE. Augusta Creek is an important tributary of South Fork McKenzie River, flowing in from the south. It was named for Miss Augusta Young, daughter of Carl Young, an early day forest ranger in the McKenzie River country. Augusta Young was later Mrs. Starr.

Aumsville, MARION. This community is on the site of Henry L. Turner's pioneer farm. Turner and his sons and son-in-law, Amos M. Davis, built a flour mill there, and for a time the place was called Hoggum, because there were so many pigs about. Before the mill was completed, Amos Davis died, on Dec. 26, 1863. Turner was very fond of his son-in-law, who was generally called Aumus, and after Amos' death, he named the place Aumsville. Post Office authorities state that the first post office was called Condit, and was established July 10, 1862, with Cyrenius Condit postmaster. The name of the office was changed to Aumsville Mar. 11, 1868, with John W. Cusick postmaster. The Condit post office was first on the Condit property about three miles southwest of the present site of Aumsville. About 1865 it was moved about a mile and a half west to the William Morris place. It was moved to Aumsville when the name was changed in 1868.

Aurora, MARION. Aurora was the center of a German colony, and is now on the main line of the Southern Pacific Company and also on the Pacific Highway East about 28 miles from Portland. The town was founded by Dr. William Keil on Mar. 20, 1857, and was named for his daughter. Keil was born in Prussia in 1811 and died in 1877. The colony was founded in 1855, coming from Bethel, Missouri, where Dr. Keil founded a colony in 1845. After his death, private property succeeded his communal system. *See* Scott's *History of the Oregon Country*, v. 2, p. 324, which refers to several articles on the subject. Aurora Mills post office was established Dec. 30, 1857, with William Keil first postmaster. The name was changed to Aurora on Dec. 10, 1894.

Austin, GRANT. This community was named for Mr. and Mrs. Minot Austin, early settlers, who operated a small store and hotel not far from the present site of the town. The post office was established in 1888.

Austin Creek, TILLAMOOK. Austin Creek flows into Little Nestucca River about three miles above Meda. It was named for Henry Austin who homesteaded nearby in 1903.

Austin Hot Springs, CLACKAMAS. In 1903 Seth Austen patented 151 acres on Clackamas River three miles above the mouth of Collawash River. The hot springs on this plot as well as nearby Austin Point and Austin Meadow were all named for him, but the incorrect spelling Austin now prevails.

Austin Point, CLATSOP. Austin Point is the southernmost of the three small promontories south of Hug Point and north of Arch Cape community. It bears the name of James P. Austin who owned the property. Austin was the first postmaster at Cannon Beach when that office was established in 1891 near the north end of what is now the community of Arch Cape. It is near where the cannon from the *Shark* washed up on the beach. On some maps Adair Point was misnamed Austin point but this was corrected by the USBGN in *Decision List 8903*. Some years ago Austin Point was called Asbury Point for Robert C. F. Astbury but this name did not prevail. Astbury is remembered by Asbury Creek which runs by what was his property. The compiler cannot account for the change in spelling. Austin Creek south of Austin Point is also named for James Austin.

Averill Lake, MARION. This lake is some two miles west of Olallie Lake. It is named for Ed Averill who was a State Fish Protector for many years in the 1920s.

Avery, BENTON. This was a station on the Southern Pacific Company line about two miles south of Corvallis. It was named for Joseph C. Avery, a pioneer of 1845. He was the first owner of the site of Corvallis, which was then known as Marysville, and he sold the first town lots in 1849. Avery was a prominent and progressive citizen engaged in farming and mercantile business and was appointed postal agent for Oregon and Washington in 1853. He was several times a member of the Oregon legislature. He was born in Pennsylvania in 1817 and died at Corvallis June 16, 1876. *See* Corvallis.

Awbrey Mountain, JEFFERSON. This butte, at one time known as Sheep Rock, is in the extreme southeast part of the county, northeast of Grizzly. It bears the name of a pioneer stockman, Marshall Clay Awbrey, who was born at Camden, Ray County, Missouri, on Jan. 16, 1829, and died at Soldiers' Home, Roseburg, on Jan. 16, 1921. He served in the Mexican War, came to Oregon in 1850 and also served in the Rogue River Indian War. He began operations in central Oregon in the late 1860s. Awbrey Heights are just west of Bend and form a butte with an elevation of 4234 feet, covered with scattered timber. These heights together with Awbrey Falls on the Deschutes River several miles north of Tumalo were also named for Marshall C. Awbrey.

Axehandle Spring, JEFFERSON. Axehandle Spring and Axehandle Ridge are eastward of Ashwood, and the general locality was once known as Axehandle. Later on the name Donnybrook was used as the result of a little social affair in Calf Gulch, but the post office was called Kilts. The reader will find entertaining information under those headings. The following quotation from an editorial by Phil Brogan in the Bend *Bulletin*, Apr. 20, 1943, tells of the origin of the name Axehandle: "Shortly before the turn of the century, the community, then in Crook County, was known as Axehandle, named by wood haulers from Antelope community who secured fuel in the western spur of the Blue Mountains. One of their stopping places was a big spring. Old timers say some of the first wood haulers past the place found a broken axe handle and named the water hole Axehandle spring. The name gradually extended to the entire community, to take in the Bannon, Morgan, McLennan, Brogan, Eades, Crowley and Creegan ranches."

Axtell, LINCOLN. Axtell was the name of a post office on Yachats River in the extreme southern part of the county, about six or seven miles east of Yachats, applied in compliment to a local family. The office was established in May 1891, with John D. Axtell first postmaster. The office was closed in Aug. 1903, with papers to Waldport. The compiler visited the area in 1968 and noted that while nothing is left to mark the locality, the USFS has constructed a small fish ladder near the mouth of Axtell Creek. This, one of the marked exhibits on the Cape Perpetua Auto Tour, is a typical example of a minor stream improvement to better spawning access.

Ayers Canyon, MORROW. Thomas W. Ayers settled where this canyon empties into Butter Creek south of Service Buttes. Ayers was born in Iowa in 1840 and came to Oregon in 1862. He moved to the Butter Creek area with several brothers and sisters in the 1860s.

Azalea, DOUGLAS. Douglas County is noted for its azaleas and this post office was named on account of their abundance in that locality. There are two well-known members of the *Ericaceae* of this type in Oregon, the *Azalea occidentalis* or western azalea, and *Azaleastrum albiflorum*, or small white. The name Azalea has been used for post offices in Douglas County at two separate times and places, and the post offices Starvout, Booth and Azalea have at different times all served more or less the same territory in upper Cow Creek Valley. Starvout post office was established Feb. 18, 1888, with H. L. Miser postmaster. The name of the place was changed to Booth on Aug. 24, 1907, probably because the name Starvout was suggestive of an unsatisfactory locality. The name of Booth post office was changed to Azalea on May 6, 1914. In the meantime there had been another Azalea post office which was established Oct. 17, 1899, with Joseph A. Wharton first postmaster. This post office was discontinued Sept. 30, 1909. The postmaster at Azalea in 1925 told the writer that Mrs. Maggie Picket suggested the present name of Azalea for the former Booth post office. The writer does not know who suggested the name of the original Azalea post office, which is shown on the 1900 postal map at a point on Cow Creek about ten miles southwest of Riddle.

Baby Rock, LANE. This rock is on the southwest shoulder of Heckletooth Mountain, and above the track of the Southern Pacific Company just southeast of Oakridge. It was named by the Indians. Mrs. Lina A. Flock gave the compiler an unusual legend about the name. Indians who slept near the rock were believed to have been bitten by some animals that left the footprints of a baby. The wounds were fatal. Finally two Indians determined to exterminate these peculiar animals, and hiding in the rocks above, they surprised the visitors, jumping down on them and covering them with blankets in such a way that they could not escape. The animals were twisted in the blankets and burned up. Indian Charlie Tufti would never go near this rock. Mrs. Flock's grandfather, Fred Warner, was of the opinion that the peculiar animals were porcupines, which make tracks not unlike a small baby. Indians asserted that the baby tracks remained about the rock for many years, hence the name.

Baca Lake, HARNEY. This is a small overflow lake near Donner und Blitzen River south of Malheur Lake. It has an elevation of about 4160 feet. *Baca*, or *vaca*, is the Spanish word for cow, and the lake was supposedly named by Mrs. Dolly Kiger because so many cattle watered there. However, John Scharff, for many years with the Malheur National Wildlife Refuge, related a different origin. He stated that Primo Tero "Tebo" Ortega, one of Pete French's vaqueros, told him the correct form was *Boca*, a Spanish word for mouth or in this case outlet. The form Baca is now firmly fixed in local usage.

Bachelor Flat, COLUMBIA. According to a news story in the St. Helens *Mist*, June 28, 1929, Bachelor Flat was named because of the presence of so many unmarried men in the locality, which is about three miles southwest of St. Helens. The news story contains an interview with Charles Gable, who in 1880, settled near the present Bachelor Flat School. Gable related that there were five or six young bachelors in the neighborhood, who were cronies, and that at a gathering one night he suggested the name Bachelor Flat, which has prevailed through many years.

Bacona, WASHINGTON. This was a community in the extreme north part of the county. When the post office was established in May 1897, it was named for the first postmaster, Cyrus Bacon. The place went into a decline in the 1930s, probably as a consequence of the Tillamook Burn, and the office was closed in Jan. 1934. Bacona was over 1600 feet in elevation and in the early days, snow and bad weather frequently isolated the inhabitants. By the 1970s only a sign marked the location. *See* article by Ralph Friedman in the *Oregon Journal*, Aug. 29, 1974, p. A3.

Bade, UMATILLA. Bade is a station on the Union Pacific Railroad between Milton and Weston. It was named for William G. Bade, a nearby resident. For many years this station was called Bates, and it is said this was because a German section foreman misinterpreted Bade's name in transmitting it to the railroad company headquarters.

Badger, SHERMAN. Badger, a post office in what is now Sherman County, was not named for the animal that burrows in the ground, but for Thomas R. Badger, the postmaster. Badger post office was established on the Wasco County list on Dec. 19, 1882. The name of the office was changed to DeMoss Springs on Aug. 5, 1887, with Thomas J. Cocking as the new postmaster. Early in Dec. 1945, Giles L. French of Moro undertook to get together some of the history of the Badger office. According to Mr. French, Thomas Badger and a brother Ephraim Badger came to what is now Sherman County from Illinois. They left after a few years but their later history is not available to Mr. French. In any event, Thomas Badger had his post office down Barnum Canyon a few miles from Moro. This would make the Badger place about a half mile south and west of DeMoss Springs. Doubtless the office was moved at the time the name was changed.

Badger Creek, HOOD RIVER, WASCO. The badger, *Taxidea americana*, is so plentiful throughout Oregon, especially in that part east of the Cascade Range, that it is not surprising that many geographic features were named for it. Badger holes are in evidence in many localities, and Badger creeks are particularly plentiful. The creek mentioned at the head of this paragraph has its source in Badger Lake, in Hood River County, with an elevation of 4472 feet. A mile southeast is Badger Butte, with an elevation of 5981 feet, a well-known landmark.

Bagby Hot Springs, CLACKAMAS. These springs are in T 7S, R 5E. They were named for Robert W. Bagby, a prospector and miner who frequented the area. He lived between Molalla and Wilhoit. He died on Oct. 8, 1927. For his obituary, *see* the *Oregonian*, Oct. 9, 1927, sect. I, p. 17. The spelling Bagsby is wrong.

Bagnell, CURRY. In pioneer days a man named William Bagnell operated a ferry on Rogue River about five miles northeast of Gold Beach, then known as Ellensburg. The compiler has been unable to get much of Bagnell's history. On June 7, 1894, Bagnell post office was established at the ferry, with John R. Miller first and only postmaster. The office was closed to Gold Beach, Apr. 4, 1895.

Bailey Butte, WHEELER. This butte just west of Mitchell was named for Ezekiel Bailey who settled there in the 1880s.

Bailey Butte, WHEELER. Bailey Butte in the West Branch country was named before the turn of the century for early settler Lee Bailey.

Bailey Hill, LANE. This hill southwest of Eugene was named for John Bailey who settled there in 1857. The land was originally the donation land claim of Jackson Wright, Bailey's brother-in-law.

Bailey Mountain, CURRY. Bailey Mountain, elevation 3920 feet, is about 12 miles airline west of Kerby. The following quotation is from a statement made by the USFS to the USBGN, which adopted the name Dec. 4, 1941: "The name suggested is in honor of one of the first miners to settle in this area. He had a claim and built a cabin nearby that is still known as Bailey Cabin. The date of his death is unknown."

Baird, GILLIAM. Baird post office was established Dec. 8, 1884, and was named for J. C. Baird, the first and only postmaster. The office was discontinued Feb. 8, 1886. In Mar. 1948, J. D. Weed of Condon wrote the compiler that he came to Gilliam County on Jan. 17, 1899, and lived that winter at Shutler. Mr. Weed says that the Junction House was situated at Shutler Station and he was told in early days there was a post office there called Baird. The Junction House was the point where emigrants from the east traveling the Oregon Trail reached Alkali Canyon. From this point the Oregon Trail went westward up Alkali Canyon and along Rock Creek to John Day River.

Baiseley Creek, BAKER. Baiseley Creek near Pleasant Valley was named for

James Baiseley who discovered gold in the area in 1893. The Baiseley family were well-known Baker County prospectors in the early days.

Bakeoven, WASCO. During pioneer gold excitement in Canyon City, an enterprising trader started from The Dalles with a pack train of flour. After crossing the Deschutes River, Indians drove off his horses in the night and left him with his supplies. He constructed a rough clay and stone bakeoven and made bread which he sold to miners and prospectors going to the mines. The old oven was in existence for many years after the owner abandoned it. H. H. Bancroft, in his *History of Oregon*, v. 1, p. 787, says that the baker was a German and that the event occurred when Joseph H. Sherar took a party to the mines in 1862. Bakeoven Creek takes its name from the same incident. The post office of Bake Oven was established Dec. 1, 1875, with Mrs. Ellen Burgess first postmaster. This office was discontinued Oct. 30, 1913 with mail to Flanagan. Flanagan in turn was discontinued July 13, 1914 and Bakeoven was re-established on the same date. The offices apparently moved about as the original office was near the location shown on the USGS Shaniko quadrangle while the Bakeoven office was near Flanagan (site) on the Dead Dog Canyon quadrangle.

Baker Bridge, CLACKAMAS. This bridge was named for Horace Baker, who took up a donation land claim nearby in pioneer days. His land office certificate was number 4967. The bridge is near Carver.

Baker Canyon, MORROW. Baker Canyon empties into Eightmile Canyon. It was named for Lorin D. Baker who settled there at the turn of the century.

Baker City, BAKER. Baker City was, of course, named for Baker County. The post office was first established on Mar. 27, 1866, with William F. McCrary as postmaster. In 1911 the name of the post office was changed to Baker to conform to the new style adopted by the incorporated community. The one word form continued for 78 years but in an election on Nov. 7, 1989, the city voted to return to the original name. For additional information about the origin of the name, *see* Baker County and also editorial in the *Oregonian*, Nov. 13, 1925, p. 14. McCrary was the first postmaster at Auburn post office, which was established Nov. 1, 1862. It is reported that McCrary moved the office to the present site of Baker City in the fall of 1865 and opened a variety store. Whatever the facts are about this unauthorized move, the Baker City office was established Mar. 27, 1866, with McCrary postmaster. Despite McCrary's move, Auburn continued to have a post office until Oct. 1903.

Baker County. Baker County was created Sept. 22, 1862, by the state legislature (*General Laws* of 1862, p. 112). It was made from the eastern part of Wasco County. It was named for Edward Dickinson Baker (1808–61) who was elected United States senator from Oregon in 1860. He was killed at the battle at Balls Bluff just after he had been appointed a major-general. His biography appears in the *Oregonian* Jan. 15, 1875, by Tom Merry; May 31, 1908, by Clark E. Carr; Jan. 19, 1896. He first came to Oregon in Dec. 1859, and, in the following Feb. moved his family to

Oregon. For the narrative of his death, *see* the *Oregonian* July 16, 1893, p. 4; Oct. 21, 1906, p. 49; tribute to his strong oratorical power, Apr. 5, 1899, p. 3, by P. B. Johnson; reminiscences of Baker, by George H. Williams, July 29, 1906, p. 41; Baker's speech in Union Square, New York, in Apr. 1861, May 30, 1906, p. 8; his oration over the body of Senator Broderick, Oct. 14, 1883; his reply to Breckenridge, July 30, 1905, p. 43; description of the grave of E. D. Baker at San Francisco, Mar. 13, 1892; June 4, 1872, p. 3. For biographical narrative, by William D. Fenton, *see OHQ,* v. 9, pp. 1–23. A more recent work is *Lincoln's Constant Ally: Life of Col. Edward D. Baker* by Dr. Harry C. Blair and Rebecca Tarshis. For a description of Baker County in 1880, *see* the *Oregonian* for Dec. 28, 1880; in 1885, Oct. 19, 1885, by Alfred Holman; in 1881, Dec. 6, 1881, by George H. Atkinson. Details concerning the origin of Oregon counties may be obtained from *OHQ,* v. 11, No. 1, for Mar. 1910, which contains an address on the subject by Frederick V. Holman. Baker County had an area of 3093 square miles in 1989.

Baker Creek, YAMHILL. Baker Creek rises in the Coast Range and flows east to Panther Creek just west of North Yamhill River. It was named for John G. Baker who was born in Kentucky in 1818 and came to Oregon in 1843. He settled just north of the present site of McMinnville and for six years was sheriff of Yamhill County under the provisional and territorial governments.

Baker Gulch, WALLOWA. Baker Gulch drains into Joseph Creek in T 4N, R 45E. It was named for James, Sam and John Baker who had a hunting camp there in the 1890s. They were the sons of James T. Baker of Arkansas Hollow.

Bakersfield, WASHINGTON. Bakersfield post office was about five miles northwest of Thatcher. It was named in compliment to the family of the only postmaster, Sylvia S. Baker. The office was established Dec. 2, 1899, and was ordered closed to Thatcher, Dec. 16, 1901.

Balch Creek, MULTNOMAH. Danford Balch settled near what is now Willamette Heights in Portland in 1850. Balch was hanged on Oct. 17, 1859, for killing his son-in-law, Mortimer Stump, on the Stark Street ferry. For history of the tragedy of the Balch family, *see* Scott's *History of the Oregon Country,* v. 3, p. 352, and also story in *Oregonian* Aug. 14, 1938, magazine section. Balch creek was named for this family. At one time the creek furnished the city water supply.

Bald Butte, LANE. Earl Walker of Oakridge told the compiler this high ground on the west end of Kitson Ridge was originally called Hills Mountain for John Hill, the early settler. The change of name is hardly an improvement.

Bald Mountain, CURRY. Bald Mountain, elevation 2967 feet, is a prominent point about ten miles airline southeast of Port Orford, and has been so called since the days of the mining excitement in the 1850s. Glisan in *Journal of Army Life* uses the name on Mar. 15, 1856, and it is apparent that the name was in vogue before that date. On modern maps, Bald Mountain is the northwest end of a prominent ridge and Rocky Peak, elevation 3023 feet, is at the southeast end and about a mile away. It is possible that in early days the name Bald Mountain was applied to the ridge rather than to either of the two points. Davidson, in *Coast Pilot*, 1889, describes these features, though the wording is not entirely clear. He seems to call the northwest peak Pilot Knob and the southeast point Bald Peak, with an elevation of 3056 feet. He describes the ridge as a double peak above all the immediate mountains, and says the Indian name was *Chus-suggel*. In early days the expression Pilot Knob was used by mariners to describe all of the ridge referred to at the beginning of this paragraph. Preston's *Map of Oregon*, 1856, has the name Pilot Knob applied to the entire ridge, but that does not agree with Glisan.

Bald Peter, JEFFERSON. Bald Peter, elevation 6540 feet, is a conspicuous landmark on the Warm Springs Indian Reservation about six miles east of Mount Jefferson. This mountain bears a descriptive name sometimes applied by surveyors to points, rocky at the top and bare of timber. While this name may be derived directly from the Latin word *petrus*, meaning rock, it is more probably an allusion to Saint Peter, the rock on which the church was founded. There is another point called Bald Peter Butte, elevation 3725 feet, on the north boundary of the reservation in Wasco County, doubtless named for the same reason.

Bald Peter, LINN. J. L. Gilbert, an early postmaster at Berlin, stated that this Bald Peter with its barren top was not given the generic name described above, but rather was specifically for Peter Powell who took a donation land claim on McDowell Creek. The compiler has never seen a picture of Mr. Powell but assumes he suffered from a common affliction of the American male. Bald Peter Creek, a tributary of Crabtree Creek, rises on its north slopes.

Baldock Slough, BAKER. Baldock Slough is one of the channels of Powder River north of Baker. Hiatt, in *Thirty-one Years in Baker County*, p. 36, has an account of William Baldock, who came into the Baker Valley from Colorado in the fall of 1862. He was attracted by the fine stand of wild hay growing in the valley, and worked up a market for it in Auburn. He got a scythe from some source and made pitchforks from forked willow sticks. He harvested the hay and found ready buyers in the mining camps. Baldock Slough was named for this man or some member of his family.

Baldwin Creek, HOOD RIVER. Baldwin Creek drains the northeast part of upper Hood River Valley, and flows into East Fork Hood River. It was named for S. M. Baldwin, who, in 1878, homesteaded a tract through which the stream flows.

Baldwin Hills, JEFFERSON. The hills west of Hay Creek were named for Dr. David Baldwin who established the Baldwin Sheep and Land Company in 1873. This was the beginning of the famous Hay Creek Ranch. For further information *see East of the Cascades* by Phil Brogan and *OHQ*, v. 39, p. 384.

Baldy Lake, GRANT. This is a small lake on the north slope of Ireland Mountain, so named because at one time Ireland Mountain was known as Bald Mountain.

Ballard Landing, BAKER. Ballard Landing is a place on Snake River in the extreme northeast corner of Baker County, named for a local resident. A post office with the name Landing was in operation in this locality from Dec. 22, 1900, until May 10, 1904, with Eli F. Ballard postmaster.

Ballston, POLK. Ballston was named for Isaac Ball who took up a donation land claim where the town now stands. The post office was originally established as Ballsville on Sept. 19, 1878, with Andrew N. Martin postmaster. The name was changed to Ballston on July 19, 1880. Isaac Ball was one of the early champions of the west side narrow gauge railroad project. *See OHQ*, v. 20, p. 144.

Balm, TILLAMOOK. Several varieties of cottonwood trees are called balm or balm-of-Gilead, and in consequence the name Balm has been applied geographically to places inhabited by these trees. A post office named Balm was in operation in Tillamook County from May 1897, until Dec. 1911. Everett R. Bales was the first postmaster. The office was on Foley Creek, not far above the mouth and about two miles southeast of Mohler. The office moved about, depending on the postmaster. The office is supposed to have been named for some balm trees, which are not common in that part of Oregon, but the compiler does not know which variety. Mohler post office was established the day the Balm office was closed and it may be assumed that the Balm office was moved to Mohler and the name changed.

Balm Mountain, DOUGLAS. Balm Mountain is in the northeastern part of the county in the Calapooya Mountains and has an elevation of 6088 feet. It was named for a brushy plant known as mountain balm, or mountain lilac, *Ceanothus velutinus*. This plant is also called snow bush and sticky laurel.

Baltimore Rock, COOS. Baltimore Rock is south of the entrance to Coos Bay and north of Cape Arago, not far from the lighthouse. George Davidson, in *Coast Pilot*, 1889, says it was named because the schooner *Baltimore* struck on it and was wrecked.

Ban, MULTNOMAH. Ban was a station north of Linnton. It was named for Shinzaburo Ban, a prominent Japanese merchant of Portland who also operated a shingle mill near the station. Ban was born in Tokyo and came to the United States in 1891 when he was 37 years old and had already enjoyed a successful career in Japan. For further information about Ban and other early Japanese settlers in Oregon *see* Barbara Yasui's article, "The Nikkei in Oregon, 1834–1940," *OHQ*, v. 76, p. 229 *et seq.*

Bancroft, COOS. It is reported that the Post Office Department named this office, but the reason is not known. The post office was established July 28, 1891, with Burrel R. Banning first postmaster.

Bandon, COOS. Bandon is a community on the south side of the mouth of the Coquille River. It was named by George Bennett who settled not far from the present town in 1873. Bennett was a native of Ireland and named the new city for Bandon, on Bandon River, County Cork, Ireland. He married Katherine Ann Scott Harrison, and three children were born to them, two of whom were prominent citizens of Coos County. Bandon was almost completely destroyed by fire on

Sept. 26, 1936, but was rebuilt. For historical sketch of Bandon, *see* the *Oregonian*, Sept. 28, 1936. For history of Bandon and Coquille River by George Bennett, *see* *OHQ*, v. 28, p. 311, and v. 29, p. 20. An Englishman, William Davidson, known locally as Billy Buckhorn, is said to have been the first resident. Bandon post office was established Sept. 12, 1877, with John Lewis first of a long line of postmasters.

Bangor, COOS. Bangor was a townsite laid out on the west side of Pony Slough, now within the city of North Bend. "Major" L. D. Kinney, who came to Coos Bay about May 1902, from Maine, promoted the townsite and also expected to build a belt line railroad at Coos Bay and a railroad from Coos Bay to the Willamette Valley. The promotions did not mature. Bangor was named for Kinney's former home in Maine. A post office with the name Bangor was established Nov. 8, 1902, with Edwin H. Wall postmaster. The office was never in active operation and the order was rescinded Mar. 10, 1903.

Banks, WASHINGTON. Banks was named in compliment to Robert Banks, a pioneer resident, and his father, John Banks. The name is said to have been selected by Joe Schulmerich and Joed Hartley. Banks post office was established Jan. 21, 1902, with Ewell S. Turner first postmaster. It was at first planned to name the office Turner, probably for the first postmaster, but this could not be done because of duplication with Turner in Marion County. Banks post office was discontinued in Dec. 1904, and the business was turned over to Greenville. Early in 1907 the Greenville office was moved north a few miles to the location of the old Banks office. A local petition restored the old name Banks Apr. 1907.

Bannister Creek, LANE. This creek flows into Lookout Point Lake. A. J. Briem, in his notes on file at the OHS, says that the stream was named in the old days because an iron bar was installed near its mouth as a bannister to help travellers across an awkward spot.

Bannock Ridge, MALHEUR. Bannock Ridge is west of the site of Rockville. In 1978 Alfred McConnell of Ontario, who was raised in the area, provided the following information about the name. In the early days some Indians stole a particularly fine stallion from the Ruby Ranch. The ranch hands chased them north to Cow Lakes where the Indians, allegedly Bannocks, turned the horse loose. However, their pursuers followed them up onto what is now Bannock Ridge and killed them. The Bannocks or Bannacks were a subdivision of the Shoshone Nation centered in eastern Idaho. After an abortive uprising in the winter of 1862–63, they were placed on Fort Hall Reservation but numbers of them continued to summer on Camas Prairie in southwest Idaho. In 1878 there was a second uprising under Chief Buffalo Horn. During a protracted summer campaign, troops under the command of Major-General O. O. Howard pursued them through southeast Oregon and north through Grant County into the Blue Mountains. Defeated in several battles, the Indians dispersed in the fall and eventually returned to Fort Hall. Mark V. Weatherford gives many details in *Bannack-Piute War, The Campaign and Battles*.

Bar Creek, DOUGLAS. William J. and Hugh A. Barr settled on this creek in Camas Valley shortly after the Civil War. The Barr brothers found the fertile, isolated valley a fine spot to make money, literally, but they made a hasty departure after they were discovered minting their own coins from lead.

Barber, LINCOLN. Barber post office was established Mar. 30, 1911, and was discontinued Jan. 31, 1912. Clarinda Barber was the only postmaster in the history of the establishment. The compiler is informed that the office was at or near the mouth of Wolf Creek, on Elk Creek about three miles downstream from Harlan. It was named in compliment to the family of the postmaster.

Barbra, CLATSOP. Barbra is an unusual name for a place but that is the way it is written in postal records. Barbra was in the extreme south part of Clatsop County, on North Fork Nehalem River, near the middle of s 28, T 4N, R 9W. In later years the Markham and Callow logging camp was in operation a little to the northeast on the Necanicum Highway. Barbra post office was established May 24, 1892, with Thomas Mitchell the first and only postmaster. The office was closed May 26, 1900, with papers to Nehalem. Mrs. Rose West Johnson, RFD Warrenton, Oregon, wrote a letter explaining that Barbra post office was named for the wife of the postmaster, Thomas Mitchell. The Johnsons were old timers on Clatsop Plains and could recall the days when carriers took the mail through from Seaside to Nehalem.

Bare Creek, WALLOWA. This stream flows into Imnaha River from the west in T 2N, R 48E. It was named for Ike N. Bare who settled on its banks about 1887. He came into the Wallowa Valley in the late 1870s, according to J. H. Horner of Enterprise, and formerly lived in Iowa and Colorado. Bare was a typical frontiersman and also a rustic fiddler and minstrel. Bare Creek was once known as Fall Creek, but that name has sunk into disuse.

Bare Island, KLAMATH. This island is in Upper Klamath Lake not far from Modoc Point. It was so named because it was bare of any considerable stand of timber. The Klamath Indian name of this island was *Aushme*. Those Indians had a legend that it was created by one of their deities who threw a game-stick into the lake.

Barite, WHEELER. Barite was a name once used for a post office in the extreme southeast corner of the county, probably on or near Birch Creek southeast of Antone. Barite post office was established Mar. 22, 1901, with Reuben Fields postmaster. The office was closed Aug. 20, 1906. Barite, also called barytes and heavy spar, is sulphate of barium, frequently used in paint making. In Dec. 1945, F. W. Libbey, director of the State Department of Geology and Mineral Industries, wrote the compiler that he had no knowledge of barite in the locality mentioned, but as it is not an uncommon mineral, it is quite possible that it could have been found there.

Bark Cabin Creek, GRANT. Bark Cabin Creek is a tributary of South Fork Murderers Creek about 25 miles southwest of John Day. So called because an old trapper's cabin by the creek was covered with bark from nearby trees, the name Dark Cabin is incorrect.

Bark Creek, BENTON. Bark Creek flows northward from the foothills of Marys Peak. In 1937 Mark Phinney of Philomath interviewed Jerry E. Henkle, a well-known Benton County pioneer, who said the stream was named in the spring of 1856 by a party of neighbors looking for grazing land. They tried to cross this stream at a place so miry that they had to lay large pieces of fir bark to keep their horses from sinking. They called the stream Bark Creek.

Barkley Spring, KLAMATH. Barkley Spring is on the east shore of Upper Klamath Lake between Algoma and Modoc Point. It is a well-known locality, and bears the name of James Barkley, native of Ireland, who served at Fort Klamath as sergeant in C Company, 1st Oregon Cavalry, and was discharged there about 1866. He lived in a small cabin near the spring for some years, then moved to a home in Yonna Valley. Still later he was thrown from a cart near the spring and killed.

Barklow Mountain, COOS, CURRY. This mountain with an elevation of 3559 feet was named for a well-known pioneer family of Coos County.

Barlow, CLACKAMAS. Barlow is on the main line of the Southern Pacific Company in Clackamas County, and also on the Pacific Highway East. It was named for William Barlow. He was a son of Samuel K. Barlow, who opened the Barlow Road. William Barlow's reminiscences are in *OHQ*, v. 13, p. 240, where it is stated that he was born Oct. 26, 1822, in Marion County, Indiana, and it was in that state that his father had married Susannah Lee. The Barlows came to Oregon in 1845, traveling over the Cascade Range by what was later known as the Barlow Road, and arrived in Oregon City Christmas night. William Barlow engaged in various enterprises, and among other things, in 1859 started the first black walnut trees grown in Oregon. Samuel K. Barlow bought the donation land claim of Thomas McKay on Sept. 17, 1850, and afterwards sold this place to his son William. The railroad was built through the place in 1870, and the station was named for William Barlow. For additional information about the Barlow family, *see* article by Fred Lockley, editorial page of the *Oregon Journal*, Dec. 24, 1937.

Barlow Creek, HOOD RIVER, WASCO. This stream rises on Barlow Butte and both bear the name of Samuel K. Barlow, the builder of Barlow Road. *See* Barlow Road heading for additional information. The Barlow Road followed along Barlow Creek between White River and Barlow Pass. For discussion of the use of the name Zigzag, describing this creek, *see OHQ*, v. 19, p. 75. The early use of the name Zigzag instead of Barlow for this stream seems to the compiler improbable.

Barlow Road, CLACKAMAS, WASCO. The Barlow Road was named for Samuel Kimbrough Barlow, a pioneer of 1845, who developed the first made road in the state of Oregon. For a description of the difficulties the Barlows had getting over the Cascade Range on what was later the Barlow Road, *see OHQ*, v. 13, p. 240. In the fall of 1845, Joel Palmer was with the Barlow party after they left The Dalles. Palmer was instrumental in locating Barlow Pass and the way around Mount

Hood. *See* Palmer's *Journal of Travels Over The Rocky Mountains*, pp. 62 through 83. For a history of the road itself, *see OHQ*, v. 13, p. 287. For story about the road and a map, *see Sunday Oregonian*, magazine section, May 29, 1938. Barlow started the work when he came over with the emigration, and finished it the following year. From the summit of the Cascade Range westward to Sandy the Mount Hood Loop Highway is in substantially the same location as the Barlow Road, though modern engineering has solved some of Samuel K. Barlow's greatest difficulties. East of the summit the Barlow Road has been in disuse for many years for a considerable distance down the eastern slope, especially where it traversed the canyon of White River. The Oak Grove Road from Salmon River Meadows to Wapinitia was not a part of the original Barlow Road, though frequently spoken of as such. On July 27, 1925, a memorial tablet was dedicated to Samuel Kimbrough Barlow at a point on the Mount Hood Loop Highway just east of Government Camp. This tablet, which is on a large boulder, was unveiled in 1923 but could not be put in place then owing to difficulties over the title to the site. On the same boulder is another tablet dedicated to Susannah Lee Barlow, wife of S. K. Barlow. Samuel K. Barlow was born in Nicholas County, Kentucky, on Jan. 24, 1792. He died at Canemah, Oregon, July 14, 1867, and is buried beside his wife at Barlow.

Barnegat, TILLAMOOK. Barnegat is one of Oregon's ghost post offices, although the name is still used occasionally to refer to a locality on the narrow neck of land south of Bayocean. In Sept. 1943, O. K. Tittle of Tillamook wrote the compiler that Barnegat post office was first situated about two miles south of the place where the Bayocean Hotel was built later. The office was established at the instigation of A. B. Hallock, who was the first postmaster. When Hallock died Oct. 30, 1892, the office was moved a mile south to the Bert Biggs place and was operated by Mrs. Biggs, who was a daughter of Webley Hauxhurst. It is said that Hallock named Barnegat for his former home on the Atlantic Coast. The only Barnegat on the Atlantic Coast is of course Barnegat Bay, a well-known inlet on the shore of New Jersey north of Atlantic City. However, the biography of Hallock in the files of the Oregon Historical Society fails to show that he ever lived close to the Atlantic Ocean. In 1929 H. C. Sutherland of Portland told the compiler that his father, Thomas A. Sutherland, went shooting on Tillamook Bay in the 1870s and named Barnegat Bay, Tillamook County, because of similar activity on Barnegat Bay in New Jersey. It was the impression of the Sutherland family that Thomas A. Sutherland applied the name to the southwest part of Tillamook Bay and not to a place on land. Barnegat Bay in New Jersey is said to have been named by Henry Hudson with the Dutch word "breaker's inlet." Barnegat post office in Tillamook County was not established until 1891, and it is possible that the post office was named for the Barnegat Bay designated by Sutherland. The name of this office was changed from Barnegat to Bayocean in Feb. 1909.

Barnes, CROOK. For some years, Barnes was a post office in the south part of

Crook County. The office was discontinued July 31, 1925, and mail was then handled through Roberts post office. Barnes office was named for Harry Barnes as it was established at his ranch in May 1909, and he was the first postmaster.

Barnes Butte, CROOK. Barnes Butte is a spur or ridge extending from the foothills just northeast of Prineville. It was named for Elisha Barnes, a pioneer resident of Prineville.

Barnes Road, MULTNOMAH. This road leads westward from the head of West Burnside Street, in Portland. It was named for William Barnes, who came to Oregon in 1861, and took up land west of Portland in Washington County. He died Apr. 4, 1909. An electric railway was opened up Barnes Road in 1893, but service was abandoned in the fall of that year. Traces of the old line were visible in the 1930s. Barnes Heights in Portland got its name from the same source.

Barnes Valley, KLAMATH. Barnes Valley is in the extreme southeast part of the county, very close to the Lake County line. In fact it is probable that part of the valley is in Lake County. Early in 1948 Miss Frances L. Barnes, of Portland, wrote that the valley was named for her uncle, Captain James Thornton Barnes, and that she lived thereabouts as a small child over 60 years ago. Captain James Thornton Barnes was born near Little Orleans, Indiana, in 1819, and later moved with his family to Missouri. He served in the Mexican War, went to California in 1850 and came to Oregon in 1851 to join his brother, Daniel P. Barnes, a pioneer of 1847. James T. Barnes served in the Rogue River War and reached the rank of captain. For many years he was actively engaged in stock business in the Goose Lake and the Sprague River valleys. He died May 18, 1889, at Jacksonville.

Barnesdale, TILLAMOOK. Miss Lucy E. Doughty, Bay City, told the compiler that this place, which does not now have a post office, was named for Frank Barnes, who settled in the valley of Foley Creek about 1910. Barnesdale post office was established Apr. 18, 1912, with Frank Barnes first postmaster. The office was discontinued June 15, 1925.

Barnett, GILLIAM. This was a railroad station south of Arlington. The correct spelling is Barnett and not Burnett, as is shown on some maps.

Barney, CROOK. Barney post office was in operation from Sept. 6, 1913, to Jan. 15, 1918, with William A. Barney postmaster, and the office was named in his honor. The place was on the upper reaches of Mill Creek, about where the stream crosses the line between T 13S, ranges 17 and 18E. The Barney homestead was in S 25, T 13S, R 17E. The office served a small sawmill community about a mile north up Mill Creek. It is reported that most of the improvements were later destroyed by fire.

Barnhart, UMATILLA. The following information is paraphrased from a letter written the compiler by George A. Hartman of Pendleton, in 1947: Jeremiah Barnhart probably lived on the land ten miles west of Pendleton when the railroad established a siding, and his name was applied to the station. He did not homestead the place. He and Bob Thompson were partners in the sheep business for a number of years prior to the death of Thompson, who was killed by a sheepherder about 1894. The siding is on the Union Pacific Railroad and close to Umatilla River. A post office named Barnhart was established May 20, 1897, with Stella Jackson postmaster. This office was never in service and the order for its establishment was rescinded.

Barnhouse Spring, WHEELER. This spring in S 2, T 13S, R 23E, bears the name of Jacob L. Barnhouse who homesteaded on the upper reaches of Mac Creek in 1905.

Barnum Canyon, SHERMAN. Henry Barnum was one of the first settlers in the vicinity of Moro. He moved to this part of what then was Wasco County about 1867 and became a prominent early citizen.

Barr Creek, JACKSON. Mrs. Frances Aiken Pearson, who was born in Prospect in 1885, told the compiler that this creek was named because of a cattle bar to prevent livestock straying from the adjacent Red Blanket Ranch.

Barren Valley, MALHEUR. Barren Valley lies between South Fork Malheur River and Owyhee River southwest of Crowley. Louis Scholl, a draftsman and cartographer, accompanied Wallen in 1859 and was with Steen's expedition in 1860 when it passed through this area. It is not named in any known account, but when Scholl returned to The Dalles in the fall of 1863, he prepared from memory for Brigadier-General Benjamin Alvord a "Map of Major Steen's Field Notes of 1860" to be used in the following spring's campaign. This shows Barren Valley north of Alvord Valley but there is nothing to indicate the name was used prior to 1863. Lieutenant John Bowen accompanied Captains Currey and Drake during the 1864 expeditions and Barren Valley does appear on his map. This was enough to fix the name although Williamson's map of the late 1860s shows Banner Valley, probably a typographical error. The descriptive name will appear appropriate to anyone familiar with the local geography.

Barrett, HOOD RIVER. Dr. P. G. Barrett settled in the Hood River Valley in 1871, and for many years was the only physician in the valley and popular throughout the entire territory. He lived about three quarters of a mile south of the site of Barrett School, and at one time all the west side of the Hood River Valley was known as the Barrett District. He died in 1900. Barrett Spur on the north side of Mount Hood was also named for Dr. Barrett. Mrs. Barrett was interested in botany. She died in New York in 1924, aged 92 years.

Barrett, UMATILLA. This is a station on the Union Pacific Railroad just west of Milton. C. A. Barrett, a pioneer stock raiser of the county, owned land at this point and the station was named for him. For Barrett's reminiscences of pioneer and farming conditions in this section of Oregon, *see OHQ*, v. 16, p. 343.

Barron, JACKSON. Barron was a post office about ten miles southeast of Ashland, near to, but possibly not actually on the Southern Pacific railroad. It was named for a local family. The office was established June 18, 1875, with James Tyler first postmaster. That was of course before the railroad was built. The office was closed Oct. 15, 1910.

Barstow, MULTNOMAH. This station on the Oregon Electric Railway, just east of Garden Home, was named for W. S. Barstow, of New York City, a prominent engineer and public utility operator, who was interested in the construction of the railroad. He died on Dec. 26, 1942, at Great Neck, Long Island.

Bartlett, WALLOWA. Bartlett was named for Theron A. Bartlett, who owned the land on which the post office was situated. The office was established on May 14, 1904, and Bartlett was the first postmaster.

Barton, CLACKAMAS. This place was named for Barton, Wisconsin, by an old resident, E. H. Burghardt, who had formerly lived there. He settled near the mouth of Deep Creek and started a small flour mill and store, and later had the post office established with the name of his old home in the East. His daughter, Mrs. Anna Burghardt Davis, was living at Tangent, Oregon, in 1925. Her father was born in 1851 and died in 1912. He came to Oregon about 1876. Barton post office was established May 16, 1896, with Burghardt first postmaster.

Barton Lake, HARNEY. Barton Lake was named for an early settler, William Barton. It is about ten miles south of Malheur Lake.

Bartrum Rocks, DOUGLAS. These two prominent rocks form a double summit about eight miles east of Steamboat. They were named for Smith C. Bartrum an early USFS employee and first supervisor of the Umpqua National Forest when it was formed in 1905.

Barview, TILLAMOOK. This community was named in 1884 by L. C. Smith. It is just north of the bar at the entrance to Tillamook Bay and affords a fine view of the bay, bar and ocean. The style Barview has been adopted by the USBGN and not Bar View.

Basche Ditch, BAKER. Basche Ditch near Keating was named for the Peter Basche family. Basche was an early settler whose family is still well known in Baker County.

Basey Canyon, MORROW. Basey Canyon south of Heppner was named for Isaac Basey who settled there in the 1880s.

Bashaw Creek, MARION. Bashaw Creek drains Ankeny Bottom in the extreme southwest part of the county and flows into the Willamette River. It was named for Joseph Bashaw who was born in France in 1820 and settled on the land Oct. 1, 1851. The Land Office plat of this section indicates the spelling Bashan, but this is an error as the original application for the donation land claim is made out Bashaw.

Basin, GRANT. Butler Basin is a prominent expansion of the John Day Canyon just north of Picture Gorge and is notable for being the site of some of the most remarkable of the John Day fossil beds. A post office with the name Basin was established in this area on July 10, 1907, with William B. Bales postmaster. The office was closed out to Dayville in Apr. 1916. It was about seven miles south of Kimberly.

Baskett Slough, POLK. This slough originates in the intermittent lakes west and south of Mount Baldy about four miles northeast of Dallas. It flows eastward several miles and joins Mud Slough. It was named for George J. Baskett who was born in Kentucky in 1817 and who settled on a donation land claim near this slough in Oct. 1850. Baskett spelled his name with two "t's" as indicated and this style of name for this geographic feature has been officially adopted by the USBGN.

Bastendorff Beach, COOS. Bastendorff Beach is on the west part of Coos Head, south of the entrance to Coos Bay. It bears the name of a local family. The spelling Bastendorff appears in signatures to deeds in the files of the Oregon State Highway Commission.

Bates, GRANT. This post office is in the east part of the county near Austin. It was named for Paul C. Bates, an insurance man of Portland. Bates was instrumental in negotiating the purchase of timber lands by the Oregon Lumber Company, and when that company began operations, it suggested the name of Bates for the post office. Paul C. Bates was born in Massachusetts in 1874 and came to Portland in 1896. He died in Portland on Feb. 4, 1943. For obituary, *see* the *Oregonian*, Feb. 6, 1943. For biography, *see* Carey's *History of Oregon*, v. 3, p. 20.

Bates Butte, DESCHUTES. Bates Butte is west of Deschutes River and north of Fall River. It received its name from George Bates, a homesteader who settled nearby.

Batterson, TILLAMOOK. The railroad station Batterson on Nehalem River about six miles east of Mohler bears the name of S. M. Batterson, a local landowner. *See* Anglersvale.

Battle Ax, MARION. This mountain is in the eastern end of the county on the western slopes of the Cascade Range, and has an elevation of 5547 feet. There are two stories as to how it received its name. One is to the effect that it is sharp and has the appearance of a battle ax, while the other is that it was named by an old woodsman of the North Santiam Valley for a brand of chewing tobacco which was popular in the 1890s, and which he used liberally while exploring in the neighborhood of the mountain.

Battle Bar, CURRY. On Apr. 27, 1856, there took place one of those indecisive skirmishes that characterized the Rogue River Indian War of 1855–56. This fight lasted all day. The Oregon volunteers were on the north side of Rogue River about a mile west of what is now the east boundary of Curry County. The Indians —men, women and children—were on a bar on the south bank of the river, now called Battle Bar, in S 17, T 33S, R 9W. Neither side was able to cross the river so the combatants spent the time taking pot shots. *See* Walling's *History of Southern Oregon*, pp. 266–68.

Battle Creek, CLATSOP. This stream is situated about six miles southeast of Astoria on the Tucker Creek road. J. B. Kilmore of Astoria informed the compiler that it was named because of a boundary dispute between two farmers.

Battle Creek, DOUGLAS. This tributary of Twelvemile Creek south of Camas

Valley was named for one of the many skirmishes between settlers and Indians in the early days. The trouble was precipitated when local braves stole a horse belonging to Nancy Martindale, the daughter of a Camas Valley founder. The renegades were overtaken at this creek as they fled south towards Rogue River.

Battle Creek, GRANT. This stream flows into John Day River west of Dayville. J. E. Snow told the compiler that about 1870 two bands of Indians had a fight about two miles up this creek, near the canyon, hence the name.

Battle Creek, JACKSON. Battle Creek and Battle Mountain are in the northwest part of the county near the headwaters of Evans Creek. These features are named for the battle of Evans Creek, fought against Rogue River Indians in this locality Aug. 24, 1853.

Battle Creek, MARION. This stream heads on the east slopes of Prospect Hill about eight miles south of Salem and flows eastward to Mill Creek near Turner. Its name commemorates one of the few conflicts between settlers and Indians in the Willamette Valley. It was at a point near this stream that a party of Oregon Rangers engaged in a minor encounter with a band of eastern Oregon Indians in June 1846, as a result of cattle depredations. One Indian was killed in the excitement, and peace was finally restored by gifts.

Battle Creek, WALLOWA. This small stream flows into Snake River in T 3S, R 49E, east of Lookout Mountain. It was named because of a squabble and fight between two old prospectors who were living near its mouth in the early 1880s. Each went up and down the river to tell his version of the row, and other prospectors soon had a name for the creek.

Battle Mountain, UMATILLA. Battle Mountain, about 25 miles south of Pilot Rock on the Pendleton-John Day Highway, was named for a fight of whites against Indians in 1878, said to have been the last of such battles in Oregon. In 1930 the state aquired some 420 acres along the highway adjacent to the mountain and in 1934, established Battle Mountain State Park.

Battle Ridge, CROOK, WHEELER. Battle Ridge projects south from Wolf Mountain near the intersection of Crook, Grant and Wheeler counties. It was the scene of a major "sheep shooting" incident when a large flock of William R. Mascall's sheep were slaughtered about 1900. This serious affair did have a humorous twist. The sheep herder was warned and instructed to move by a written note posted on a tree by his camp. He did not know how to read and remained with his flock where he was captured and held prisoner while the helpless animals were killed. He was "allowed" to "escape" and fled to Dayville in what is even today reported to be record time. Some time later after the National Forest was created, the same herder again had sheep a few miles to the north. A USFS ranger came to his camp while he was gone and posted a Fire Notice on a nearby tree. The herder's education had not progressed so when he returned, he didn't wait but again fled for home. J. O. F. Anderson has a full account of these matters in his 1948 notes on file at the Ochoco National Forest.

Battle Rock, CURRY. This historic landmark is at the shore line of Port Orford and is a massive block of rock standing well above the water. In June 1851, Captain William Tichenor, who was at that time in command of the steamer *Sea Gull* operating between the Columbia River and San Francisco, endeavored to establish a commercial enterprise at Port Orford. He engaged J. M. Kirkpatrick and a number of others to go to Port Orford where the party was landed and provisioned on what is now known as Battle Rock. The party was besieged by Indians and an actual battle was fought on June 10, 1851, at which time 17 Indians were killed, mostly by fire from a small cannon. Kirkpatrick and his party finally succeeded in stealing away from the rock after several days' siege and made their way north along the coast until they reached settlements of the whites. When Captain Tichenor's representative returned by sea he found the contingent gone and assumed it had been murdered by the Indians. For an account of this battle *see Pioneer History of Coos and Curry Counties*, chapter 3, which consists of a statement by Captain Kirkpatrick.

Batts Meadow, HOOD RIVER. This meadow near Blue Ridge on West Fork Hood River was named for Batt Senecal, an old time USFS ranger at Dufur. Senecal ran horses in the area.

Baty Butte, CLACKAMAS. Baty Butte is near the headwaters of a branch of Molalla River. It was named for Andrew Jackson Baty. He was a farmer who lived on Dickey Prairie, about five miles southeast of Molalla. He was a pioneer settler in this locality, and spent much of his time hunting in the Cascade Range. This mountain was named for him, probably by the USGS party which prepared the maps accompanying Professional Paper Number 9, *Forest Conditions in the Cascade Range Forest Reserve*, Washington, 1903. The mountain was at one time known as Whitespot.

Baxter Creek, MALHEUR. Baxter Creek empties into Jordan Creek at Jordan Valley. It is named for John Baxter, one of the first settlers, who started the community in 1864. At that time the town was known as Baxterville.

Baxter Creek, TILLAMOOK. This stream was named for William T. Baxter, a pioneer of Oregon, who settled in Tillamook County about 1871. The stream is a tributary to Kilchis River.

Bay City, TILLAMOOK. For many years that part of Tillamook County around Bay City has been known as "down the bay," and when the county was first organized, the voting precinct for that section was called Bay Precinct. The town was established in 1888 and named by Winfield S. Cone. It is said that Cone came from Bay City, Michigan, and that he thus had a double reason for naming Bay City, Oregon, as he did. The post office at Bay City was established June 17, 1889, with Onslow Young first postmaster.

Bayocean, TILLAMOOK. This place was on the long neck of land lying between Tillamook Bay and Pacific Ocean. It was named in 1907 by the Potter-Chapin Realty Company of Portland, which established it as a summer resort, and named it because of its proximity to the two features mentioned. In the 1920s, much of the sand spit on which the resort was situated was washed away by the ocean and the facilites were subsequently completely destroyed. Bayocean post office was established in Feb. 1909, by change of name from Barnegat. *See* Barnegat.

Bays. The important bays and harbors of the Pacific Ocean in Oregon from north to south, are: Columbia River, Nehalem River, Tillamook Bay, Netarts Bay, Nestucca Bay, Siletz Bay, Yaquina Bay, Alsea Bay, Siuslaw River, Umpqua River, Coos Bay, Coquille River, Port Orford and Chetco Cove. It is an interesting fact that while most of the capes and headlands of Oregon were discovered and named before Lewis and Clark arrived, few of the harbors had been seen by white men up to that time. On Aug. 17, 1775, Captain Bruno Heceta anchored off the mouth of the Columbia River, the entrance to which he gave the name of *La Asuncion*, apparently because of the celebration of the *Asuncion de Nuestra Senora*, or the Assumption, on Aug. 15. Although the currents led him to believe he was near a river, he did not make the entrance, and thus lost the honor of discovering the Columbia. He named the north cape of the entrance *Cabo San Roque* and the south *Cabo Frondoso*, now Point Adams. John Meares was the next explorer to make any important mention of Oregon bays and harbors. For details of Meares' voyage off the Oregon coast, *see* Cape Meares. Meares passed the mouth of the Columbia on July 6, 1788, and while he recognized the fact that he was off a bay, he failed to identify the place as the mouth of a river. By nightfall of the same day he discovered and named Quicksand Bay, and while he says that the bay had a sand bar closing its mouth, his other observations indicate without much doubt that he had found Tillamook Bay. During the same year Captain John Kendrick and Captain Robert Gray brought the first American fur trading enterprise to the north Pacific Coast in the *Columbia Rediviva* and the *Lady Washington*. Robert Haswell, second mate of the *Lady Washington*, kept a diary, but notwithstanding the latitudes and landmarks mentioned along the Oregon coast, it is impossible to trace the course of the vessel with accuracy. Bancroft, in his *History of the Northwest Coast*, v. 1, p. 188, indicates some of the difficulties in interpreting the writing. It is possible that Alsea Bay or Yaquina Bay was seen by the ship. On Aug. 12, 1788, the *Lady Washington* anchored off Tillamook Bay. On Aug. 14, the ship crossed the bar, and at first the Americans had no trouble with the natives but on Aug. 16, the Indians made a murderous assault and killed a member of the crew. Two days later the ship got away, and in his diary Haswell makes the following observation: "Murderers Harbour, for so it was named, is I suppose the entrance of the river of the West it is by no means a safe place for aney but a very small vessel to enter the shoal at its entrance being so aucwardly situated the passage so narrow and the tide so strong it is scarce possible to avoid the dangers." Data on other bays in Oregon will be found under their respective headings.

Bayview, LINCOLN. Bayview is on the northeast part of Alsea Bay. The post office was established about 1901, and the name was chosen by Daniel M. Oakland, the first postmaster, because of the view of Alsea Bay that could be had from where the office then stood.

B. C. Creek, WALLOWA. This stream is near the south end of Wallowa Lake and drains B. C. Basin. It bears the initials of Breedan and Camp, who located some silver claims in the basin about 1905.

Beach Mountain, LANE. Beach Mountain lies south of the Southern Pacific Railroad between Fields and Frazier. According to Earl Walker of Oakridge, it was named for Charles T. Beach, an early settler, who ranched on Hills Creek about a mile and a half downstream from Kitson Hot Springs. Beach was USFS district ranger at Oakridge in 1909–1911.

Beagle, JACKSON. Beagle was named for William Beagle, an early settler and one-time postmaster. The community is a few miles north of Upper Table Rock and west of Rogue River.

Beagle Creek, GRANT. This Beagle Creek is a small tributary of Bull Run Creek about two miles west of the summit. William and Lucinda Beagle came to Oregon in pioneer days, probably originally from Kentucky with a stopover in Missouri. They had several children including Oliver H. P. Beagle of the Beagle Creek near Medical Springs. There were at least four other boys named James, John, William and F. M. The Beagle brothers were the discoverers of the Buffalo Mine north of Granite, one of the more productive mines in that area, but whether all or only some of them were involved is unknown. F. M. Beagle was the first postmaster when Sumter post office was established in 1874.

Beagle Creek, UNION. Beagle Creek near Medical Springs, bears the name of one Beagle who kept a little inn on the stream in 1864, on the pack trail between Columbia River and the Boise mines. Oliver H. P. Beagle came to Oregon in 1843 when he was eleven years old and had many stirring adventures, some of which are described in an article by Fred Lockley in the *Oregon Journal* for July 13, 1927. He operated a pack train in northeast Oregon in the 1860s and he and his wife lived there for a time. Beagle Creek was probably named for him.

Beal, KLAMATH. This station on the Burlington Northern Inc., seven miles south of La Pine, was named for Pearley Beal whose homestead was next to the station.

Beale Canyon, UMATILLA. Beale Canyon is about eight miles southeast of Nye in West Birch Creek drainage. Charles W. Beale settled there in 1886.

Beale Lake, COOS. Beale Lake lies against the dunes four miles south of Tenmile Creek. It is named for George Beale who took up land just east of the lake in 1882. The USGS Reedsport quadrangle of 1956 uses the form Beale but the Lakeside quadrangle of 1985 shortens it to Beal Lake. BLM original entry records show the longer spelling.

Beals Creek, DOUGLAS. This creek rises north of Beals Mountain and flows into South Umpqua River. Both features were named for Oliver N. Beals who was born in Crawford County, Indiana in 1839 and took up a land claim along the creek in 1868. Numerous maps use Beal but the form Beals is correct. The USBGN affirms this in *Decision List 6801*.

Beamer Ranch, LANE. This was the ranch of Jessie Brock, a longtime resident of the Oakridge region. It was on South Fork Salt Creek on the flats just above where the Southern Pacific Cascade Line crosses Salt Creek on a large steel trestle. Lawrence D. Hills in *Tales From The Hills*, p. 14 *et seq.*, gives an account of this remarkable woman.

Bear Creek, JACKSON. This is an important tributary of Rogue River, draining the valley in which Medford and Ashland are situated. It was for some years known as Stuart Creek, but is now called by a name of little significance. Stuart Creek, and Camp Stuart, a pioneer military establishment, were named by then Captain George B. McClellan, for his brother officer Captain James Stuart, who died June 18, 1851, not far from the stream. Stuart was wounded the day before near Rogue River while leading a charge against a band of hostile Indians. For additional data, *see* Camp Stuart. For story about the origin of the name Bear for this creek, *see* the *Oregonian*, Nov. 9, 1913. Bear Creek flows through Medford, and that city was named for the middle ford of the stream.

Bear Creek, WALLOWA. This important tributary of Wallowa River heads in the Wallowa Mountains in T 3S, R 43E, and flows into the Wallowa just west of the town of Wallowa. The name, Bear Creek, for this stream has been adopted by the USBGN. The principal tributary of Bear Creek is Little Bear Creek, flowing in from the east. Pioneer settlers in the Wallowa Valley found many bears along this stream. The wild animals were very destructive of cattle.

Bear Creek, WALLOWA. This stream heads near the Oregon-Washington state line and flows southeast into Grande Ronde River in T 6N, R 43E. In 1931 J. H. Horner told the compiler that the stream was named by a sheepherder employed by Judge Chester F. Miller of Dayton, Washington, who ran into nine bears all at one time frolicking on its banks. This sounds like a record.

Bear Flat, WALLOWA. Bear Flat is about on the line between T 1N, ranges 48 and 49E, on the ridge between Horse and Pumpkin creeks. It was named because Ben Johnson and Waldo Chase killed several bears there, among them two grizzlies. Charles and Guy Horner built the first cabin and corrals on this flat, according to information from J. H. Horner in 1931.

Bear Gulch, WALLOWA. Bear Gulch is an important canyon in the east part of T 1S, R 47E, and empties into Little Sheep Creek. It was named by George A. Wilson who had a remarkable experience with a bear in this gulch. Wilson's dogs chased a bear, and the excited animal jumped on a pack horse. This was too much for the patient nag, who bucked the bear off and then scattered the pack down the canyon. Wilson was a stock man with a place at the mouth of the gulch.

Bear Island, BENTON. This island in the Willamette River, and Bear Chute just to the east, were named for Owen Bear, a nearby pioneer settler. The record of his donation land claim is in land office certificate 327.

Bear Paw Forest Camp, WASCO. Tom Carter of the USFS told the compiler in 1969 that this forest camp on US-26 is so named because a skinned out bear paw was found nearby when the site was selected in the 1920s.

Beardsley Bar, MARION. Beardsley Bar is on the east bank of Willamette River, about three miles northwest of Salem. It was named for W. W. Beardsley, who owned a farm near the bar.

Bearway Meadow, WHEELER. In 1969 George W. Nelson, who was raised in Mitchell, told the compiler the curious origin of this name west of Waterman. During the 1860s a man called Berry Way robbed and killed a packer named Gallagher. Way escaped with a large quantity of gold and while he was later caught and hanged, the loot was never recovered. He said before his execution that it was hidden in a meadow marked by blazed trees west of where Waterman now stands. Nelson said that he was well acquainted with this meadow and the two trees and when he was a boy, it was still called Berry Way Meadow. The treasure has proven as elusive as the gold at Neahkahnie or the Bluebucket Mine. For more information on outlaws, *see* Judith K. Kenny's article in Pendleton *East Oregonian*, Sept. 3, 1959.

Beatty, KLAMATH. Annie E. Taylor, postmaster at Beatty, reported in 1925 that this place was named for the Rev. J. L. Beatty, a missionary who lived in that section of the Klamath Indian Reservation. Beatty is on Sprague River, on the highway between Klamath Falls and Lakeview.

Beatys Butte, HARNEY. This prominent butte is in the southwest part of the county, and Beatys Springs are nearby. These features were named during Colonel C. S. Drew's Owyhee Reconnaissance with the 1st Oregon Cavalry in 1864, and serve to perpetuate the memory of Sergeant A. M. Beaty, who is especially mentioned in Drew's report for the zealous performance of his duties. The USC&GS gives the elevation of this butte as 7916 feet.

Beaver, TILLAMOOK. It is not surprising that the name of the animal that exercised such influence in the history of the West should be attached to so many geographic features. There are three post offices in Oregon with Beaver as the dominant part of the name, and several score of creeks, mountains and buttes. The American beaver (*Castor canadensis* and its sub-species) occupied a wide field on this continent and existed in great numbers. Beavers are heavily built, and are covered with long, coarse hairs overlying the short, dense and silky underfur to which beaver skins owe their value. The abundance and high value of this fur had a great influence in the early exploration and development of North America. Beaver skins were the one ready product of the western world which the merchants elsewhere were eager to purchase, and as a consequence the competition in trapping was keen to the point where it caused international complications. Beaver skins passed as a standard of barter. Beavers belong to the rodent family, a group notable for low mental powers. Beavers are an exception to this rule, however. They have extraordinary intelligence, though probably not as great as sometimes stated. They apparently understand something about hydraulic operations and save themselves much labor by digging canals for floating and transporting sticks and branches needed for food. They live entirely on twigs and bark, and have a gnawing capacity that is startling. There appears to be no truth in the reports that they use their flat tails as trowels, and they do not transport mud thereon. This is done by means of their front paws. The beaver is considered to be a symbol of industry, and pioneers of Oregon were quick to associate this idea with the new commonwealth. The first money was known as "Beaver Money."

Beaver Creek, CLACKAMAS. The name of Beaver Creek community was first used for a school district in the early 1850s, and came from the name of the stream that flows into the Willamette River near New Era. Beaver Creek community is south of Oregon City and is a rather loosely defined area or district adjacent to the stream. In 1945 its commercial activity was centered at the Beaver Creek cross-roads, elevation 528 feet, where the Beavercreek post office was in operation. The postal history of this area is complex. A post office named Beaver was established in Dec. 1868, with James K. Graham postmaster. The office was closed in Sept. 1871. Beaver post office was reestablished in Mar. 1882, with C. F. Vonderahe first postmaster, and operated until Feb. 1883. In 1945 the writer was told that this office was near the present locality of the Carus School. A post office called Mink was in service from Feb. 1886, until May 1894. This office was about three miles southeast of the present Beaver Creek store, possibly on the Highland road. It was named by using an adaptation of the name of a local family, Moehnke, for Charles Moehnke was at one time postmaster of the office. The locality around the Mink post office was later served by an office called Shubel, which was operated from Dec. 1897, until Sept. 1904, with Gustav A. Shubel postmaster. In the early 1890s a post office named Beaver Creek was established, although the writer does not know its exact location. The name was changed to Beavercreek, probably in 1896. This office was in operation well after the turn of the century, and during its later life it may have been at the Beaver Creek store. Joseph R. Hoff took over this store and petitioned for a post office. An office with the name Hoff was established in Apr. 1916, with Hoff postmaster. Later Hoff disposed of the store and the name of the office was changed to Beavercreek Dec. 15, 1922, and that was the style used in 1945. There are streams called Beaver Creek in almost every county in the state. The beaver were very numerous through early days in Oregon, a fact that is attested by examination of the journals of the various fur hunters. For instance, on Sunday, Apr. 22, 1827, Peter Skene Ogden mentioned in his diary that McKay had taken 735 beaver and otter skins on two small streams discharging into Clammitte (Klamath) River in about three weeks. No wonder we have so many Beaver creeks, and so few beaver.

Beaver Hill, COOS. For well over half a century Beaver Hill has been a well-known name in western Oregon because of its application to the Beaver Hill coal mine about 12 miles airline south of the city of Coos Bay. The mining community

Beaver Hill had a railroad, but never had a post office with its own name. The place is shown with fidelity on the USGS atlas sheet of the Coos Bay area mapped in 1895–96, but there is nothing on the map to indicate that the name was used for a hill or other topographic feature. The USGS Riverton quadrangle of 1971 shows "Beaver Hill (site)" in S 17, T 27S, R 13W, the location of the mine, but also shows a topographic feature, Beaver Hill, some two and a half miles southwest. This hill once had a lookout and now supports a radio facility and towers. The name of the hill probably derives from the name of a nearby survey monument. The name of the mine was obviously applied because it was on one of the upper tributaries of Beaver Slough which drains south into Coquille River. There is a good deal of interesting information about the mine in the Nineteenth Annual Report of the USGS, from the pen of Dr. J. S. Diller. If the mine is ever reopened doubtless it will be in the news. Mrs. Mary M. Randleman of Coquille, authority on the history of that part of Oregon, called attention to the fact that Preuss post office was established at the mining community of Beaver Hill, Apr. 17, 1917, with Cora E. Holmes first of two postmasters. The office was discontinued Feb. 15, 1924. Preuss post office was named for Rosa Preuss, a school teacher of the neighborhood. It is probable that the post office department would not accept the name Beaver Hill because of possible confusion with other post offices such as Beaverton, Beavercreek, *et al.*

Beaver Landing, COLUMBIA. Beaver Landing was the name of a short-lived post office established Mar. 21, 1879, and discontinued on May 1 of the same year. Jacob S. Rinearson was the only postmaster and it may be assumed that the post office was somewhere near the Rinearson place northwest of Rainier. There has been a railway station in this locality called Rinearson and of course Rinearson Slough is well known. Beaver Landing was doubtless named because it provided an easy way of getting from the Columbia River up to the headwaters of Beaver Creek in the hills above the river.

Beaver Marsh, KLAMATH. Beaver Marsh is a place on US-97 about six miles south of Chemult, prominent since the days of stagecoaches and freight wagons in central Oregon. The topographic feature bears a descriptive name. The community has never had a robust growth, as may be seen from its postal history. Beaver Marsh post office was established June 30, 1927, and was discontinued Aug. 22, 1928. William Zumbrunn was the only postmaster. Miller Creek flows through the place.

Beaverton, WASHINGTON. Beaverton received its name because of the existence nearby of a large body of beaverdam land. Soil of this character was sought by pioneer settlers because of its productivity. The town was laid out in 1869 by George Betts, Joshua Welch, Charles Angel, W. P. Watson and others. Beaverton post office was established in Mar. 1872, with George W. Betts, first postmaster. Prior to World War II, Beaverton was a city of modest size serving a residential and farming community. After the war it became the center of the high technology electronics industry and because of its continued growth is now one of the larger cities in Oregon.

Beckley, HARNEY. Beckley was in Catlow Valley. In 1911 Charles D. Beckley started a general store where the post office was established in Apr. 1912, and the place was named for him. The post office was closed in 1926 and little evidence of the community remains

Bedfield, KLAMATH. Bedfield, a locality in the Poe Valley a few miles southeast of Olene, was named for Bedfield, near Framlingham, Suffolk, England. Edward Freuer came to Klamath County from the Bedfield in Suffolk in 1882 and engaged in the stock business. He named his new home in compliment to his former English home, and when a post office was established in Mar. 1892, Freuer was the postmaster and named the office, which, at first, was in his house. The post office was in operation until Aug. 1909. The Freuer place was also called the Seven-springs Ranch.

Bedrock Creek, CLACKAMAS. Ralph Lewis told the writer that he named this creek west of Bull Run Lake about 1906 because of the smooth, exposed bedrock on its flat bottom. He added that the creek he named was nearer Thunder Rock but later mapmakers affixed the name permanently to the stream north of Blazed Alder Butte.

Beech Creek, GRANT. This post office is about ten miles north of Mount Vernon. B. C. Trobridge of John Day, who settled in the John Day Valley July 19, 1862, wrote the compiler that Beech Creek was named for a pioneer settler who lived near the mouth of the stream. The post office was established Jan. 26, 1900, by James T. Berry, and it seemed appropriate to name it after Beech Creek because it was near the headwaters of that stream.

Beeler Ridge, WALLOWA. This ridge is just west of Imnaha River. It was named for Jake Beeler, of Joseph, a freighter.

Beerman Creek, CLATSOP. Beerman Creek flows into Necanicum River south of Seaside. It was named for Fred Beerman, who took up a donation land claim in the vicinity.

Beetle Spring, CROOK. A story in the Prineville *Central Oregonian*, Sept. 11, 1969, attributed to Fred Houston, says that the USFS established a beetle control camp at this spring in the early 1930s.

Beetles Rest Spring, KLAMATH. This is the well-known spring at Klamath Agency. The stream formed by this spring is quite short. The Klamath Indian name for the stream was *Tgulutcham Kshuteleh*. The first part of the name is descriptive of a small beetle with a green or purple shell. The second part of the name indicates to "live underneath or live below," indicating that the beetles lived in this particular locality. The stream flows into Crooked Creek.

Beggars Tick Marsh, MULTNOMAH. This wetland northwest of SE 111th and Foster Road on the outskirts of Portland is Multnomah County's first designated wildlife refuge. Its name comes from the Beggars Tick or *Bidens frondosa*, a native plant species commonly known as Tickseed or Sticktight. The refuge was dedicated in Apr. 1990. *See* the *Oregonian*, Apr. 19, 1990, p. C2.

Belknap Crater, DESCHUTES, LINN. This is one of the important features of the Cascade Range, and lies just north of McKenzie Pass. The crater and its enormous lava fields are easily seen from the McKenzie Highway and produce a spectacle that is awe inspiring to say the least. The crater has an elevation of 6877 feet. It was named for J. H. Belknap, an early resident along the McKenzie River, and a son of R. S. Belknap who developed Belknap Springs. J. H. Belknap was interested in the toll road that was built over McKenzie Pass in the early 1870s.

Belknap Creek, BENTON. Belknap Creek flows into Muddy Creek three miles west of Monroe at the location of what was once known as the Belknap Settlement. The Orem and Ransome Belknap families came to Oregon in 1847 and George Belknap and Jessey Belknap followed in 1848. Their adjoining claims in the broad valley of Muddy Creek gave rise to the name. Nearby Belknap Spring is named for the same people. For more information, *see* "Chronicle of the Bellfountain Settlement" by Robert M. Gatke, *OHQ*, v. 38, p. 265 *et seq*.

Belknap Springs, LANE. R. S. Belknap located these springs in Nov. 1869, and conceived a plan for developing them. Salt Springs post office was established Oct. 26, 1874, with Belknap postmaster. The name of the office was changed to Belknaps Springs June 15, 1875. About 1891 it was changed to Belknap Springs.

Bell Canyon, MORROW. This canyon north of Willow Creek and east of Lexington was named for Frank E. Bell who took up land near its head in 1889.

Bellamy, LINCOLN. Information about Bellamy post office is unsatisfactory, but the following data are the best that the compiler can lay hands on. Bellamy office was established May 24, 1898, with Ola A. Tveitmoe first postmaster. The office was four or five miles north of Toledo on the road to Siletz and the postal facilities were intended for a small colony of Scandinavians living in the vicinity. It was closed to Toledo on June 15, 1899. The compiler has had no success in getting the reason for the selection of the name for this office. It may have been intended to compliment a local resident or even someone living at a distance.

Belle, LANE. Belle post office was established at the main forks of Indian Creek in western Lane County on Aug. 25, 1906, with Daisy Belle Wilkinson first and only postmaster. The office was closed Aug. 31, 1908. Belle post office of 1906 was in the same locality as Hermann post office when that office was first established in 1889. In Jan. 1947, Smith L. Taylor of McKenzie Bridge, formerly a resident of western Lane County, informed the compiler that Belle post office was named with the postmaster's middle name.

Belle Passi, MARION. This is one of Oregon's ghost towns, situated about a mile south of Woodburn. The name came before the public in Feb. 1942, as the result of the erection of an historical marker by members of Belle Passi chapter of the Daughters of the American Revolution of Woodburn. The marker is on the Pacific Highway East, and commemorates the establishment of a pioneer community that eventually succumbed probably because of the development of Woodburn, which had the advantage of railroad service. The Rev. Neill Johnson located at the place about 1851. He was a member of the Cumberland Presbyterian denomination, and he soon built a church and later a school. In 1857 a contract was let to carry mail by stage from Portland to Sacramento, and this furnished an opportunity for a post office. Johnson suggested the name Groveland for a place in Illinois, but authorities objected because the name was too common. The Oregon Historical Society has a letter written by John L. Johnson, son of Neill Johnson, in which it is said that Johnson then recommended a name he had found, possibly in Humboldt's *Cosmos*, describing a place in Italy. J. L. Johnson gives this as Bell Passi, meaning good pass or beautiful place. Now the place in Italy, which is on the island of Sicily, is Belpasso. The post office in Marion County was officially Belpassi. The younger Johnson calls it Bell Passi and the marker uses the spelling Belle Passi. This selection of styles seems reasonably ample. Postal authorities inform the compiler that the post office at Belpassi was established on June 15, 1860. The name was changed to Gervais on Nov. 6, 1871.

Belle Vue Point, MULTNOMAH. This point is on the east shore of Sauvie Island and the west bank of Columbia River, just north of the mouth of Willamette River. The name Belle Vue Point was adopted for this feature by USBGN on Feb. 7, 1934. Belle Vue Point was named by Lt. W. R. Broughton, R.N., of the Vancouver expedition, on Oct. 29, 1792. It seems certain that at that time the arrangement of islands and channels at the mouth of Willamette River differed from the condition that now exists. About 1930 Mr. J. Neilson Barry of Portland made an extensive study of the problem and it was his conclusion that the locality that now bears the name Belle Vue Point was the proper place. Federal agencies accepted his recommendations.

Bellevue, YAMHILL. This community is on the Salmon River Highway about nine miles southwest of McMinnville. The name is descriptive but the compiler does not know who applied it. The place is on the Hathaway Yocum donation land claim. Yocum came to Oregon in 1851 from Illinois. Records at the Oregon Historical Society indicate that Bellevue was settled about 1860. Muddy post office was established in this locality in May 1855, with George Davis postmaster. It may have been on Muddy Creek a little northeast of Bellevue. The name was changed to Bellevue in Apr. 1869. The records do not indicate exactly where pioneer post offices were situated and frequently they were moved around to fit the convenience of the postmasters.

Bellfountain, BENTON. H. L. Mack, county clerk of Benton County, informed the compiler in Dec. 1926, that he lived in Bellfountain for 13 years and there was no question in his mind but that it was named for a town of the same name in Ohio by local residents who had previously lived in the Ohio town. In Ohio the name is spelled Bellefontaine. A post office called Dusty was established in this locality Dec. 6, 1895, with Helen Elgin first postmaster. The name of the office was not satisfactory, for obvious reasons. Postal records are not entirely clear, but it seems apparent that the name of the office was changed to Bellfountain July 31, 1902. The office was closed in Jan. 1905. The general area of Bellfountain was known in early days as Belknaps Settlement. *See OHQ*, v. 38, p. 266 *et seq*.

Belmont, DOUGLAS. Belmont post office was named with the middle name of Durward Belmont Hunt, the first and only postmaster. The office was established July 5, 1913, and was discontinued Aug. 15, 1914. Durward B. Hunt, then living at Redmond, wrote on Feb. 28, 1947, substantially as follows: "Belmont post office was situated in s 31, T 24S, R 3W, on the Nathaniel H. Rone homestead, thirteen miles east of Oakland. As far as I know the name Durward Belmont originated in the novel *Lena Rivers*, written by Mary J. Holmes."

Belshaw Creek, GRANT. This creek is tributary to John Day River from the north, nine miles west of Mount Vernon. The farm and orchard of Charles Belshaw were near its mouth. Belshaw was born in England in 1833 and came to Eugene in 1853 and on to Canyon City in 1862. He was one of the earliest orchardists in the John Day Valley and developed the Belshaw prune. For a short biography, *see History of Baker, Grant, Malheur and Harney Counties*, p. 505.

Beltz Dike, TILLAMOOK. F. A. Beltz, a lumberman and former county judge, built this dike in the 1930s to drain his ranch bordering Sand Lake.

Ben Jones Bridge, LINCOLN. This concrete structure carries the Otter Crest Loop of the old Oregon Coast Highway over Rocky Creek north of Newport. It is named for the late Ben F. Jones, who is considered to be the father of the plan to build the coast highway. The span was dedicated to Jones' memory on Sept. 17, 1927. For account of dedication and picture, *see* the *Oregonian*, Sept. 18, 1927, sect. I, p. 1. The Coast Highway, US-101, has been re-routed over Cape Foulweather so this bridge is no longer on the main highway.

Ben More Mountain, DOUGLAS. Ben More Mountain is south of Elkhead. The name is apparently of Scottish origin for *Ben* is Gaelic for "mountain" or "peak" and *More* means "big" or "dark." The compiler has no information as to who first applied the name or why.

Bend, DESCHUTES. This city derived its name from Farewell Bend, a point on the Deschutes River, which received its descriptive name because it was at this place travelers over the pioneer roads had their last view of the river. For a considerable distance in central Oregon Deschutes River occupies a canyon, and there are comparatively few places where it would have been easy in pioneer days to get a wagon down to the water's edge and ford the stream. The most accessible of these places, and the point where a canyon was not in evidence was at a pronounced double bend in the river where the city of Bend is now situated. It afforded a good place to camp in pleasant surroundings. It is certain that it was thus used in the days of the emigrations, but just how early cannot now be determined. It was also used when the road was opened over McKenzie Pass. The place began to be known as Farewell Bend, and the name was appropriate irrespective of the destination of the traveler, north, south, east or west. This origin of the name has been objected to on the ground that emigrant travelers would not say farewell when they meant goodbye, for farewell meant a place where the fare was good. Nevertheless the compiler is of the opinion that farewell in the sense of goodbye was not an uncommon use of the word, and meant that the emigrants were sorry to leave the pleasant spot. Bend was platted by Pilot Butte Development Company, and the plat was filed for record on June 7, 1904. The history of Bend post office is a little complex, and is given under the heading Deschutes in this volume. *See also* Pilot Butte. In Nov. 1927, Captain O. C. Applegate of Klamath Falls informed the compiler that the Warm Springs Indian name for the ford where the city of Bend is now situated was *Wychick*. Captain Applegate was unable to secure a translation of the word.

Bend Glacier, DESCHUTES. This glacier lies on the north slope of Broken Top. It was named in 1924 by Professor Edwin T. Hodge of the University of Oregon in honor of the city of Bend.

Bendire Creek, MALHEUR. Bendire Creek and Bendire Mountain are in the north end of the county and were named for Captain and Brevet Major Charles Bendire, U.S. Army. Major Bendire was a noted ornithologist and pursued the study of bird life in many parts of the Pacific Northwest. After retirement from the army he was honorary curator of the department of Oology of the National Museum in Washington. He was the author of *Life Histories of North American Birds*, published in special bulletins of the Smithsonian Institution in 1892 and 1895.

Beneke Creek, CLATSOP. Beneke Creek flows into Fishhawk Creek from the north at Jewell. The name has been spelled in various styles, but recent government maps use the form Beneke. The name is that of a family of early settlers and the spelling Beneke is furnished by county authorities.

Benham Falls, DESCHUTES. These falls were named for J. R. Benham, who filed on land nearby about 1885. The government rejected his filing. Benham was born in Oregon, and settled in Prineville in 1876. He moved to what is now Deschutes County in 1879. The falls were named for Benham by a Mr. Hutchinson, who was at the time promoting central Oregon irrigation enterprises.

Benjamin Spring, WALLOWA. This is a spring on the Summit Trail about a half mile north of Lookout Mountain in T 3S, R 49E. The spring was named for Benjamin Marks, a pioneer settler, who died in 1913. The name has been approved by decision of the USBGN.

Bennett Butte, COOS. This butte, elevation 2185 feet, is in Coos County near the northeast corner of Curry County. It is a well-known point about 10 miles east of the Pacific Ocean. In Nov. 1943, Mrs. Mary M. Randleman of Coquille wrote the compiler that the mountain was probably named during the Coos County gold rush. Two prospectors, Hudson and Bennett, operated in the locality and the butte was apparently named for Bennett. The butte was a meeting place for

Indians, as it was on the dividing line between tribal hunting grounds. Mrs. Randleman was also authority for the statement that Bennett Prairie, near the mouth of Johnson Creek, was named for the same miner.

Bennett Creek, DOUGLAS. Bennett Creek flows into Elk Creek in Scotts Valley. Joseph and Elijah Bennett both claimed land along it in the 1860s. The compiler does not know how the two were related.

Bennett Creek, LANE. This creek is tributary from the west to Coast Fork Willamette River. It originates in the hills north of Cottage Grove and flows into the Coast Fork just north of McFarland Butte. It was named for Scott Bennett, a landowner near its banks.

Bennett Pass, HOOD RIVER. This pass is the highest point on the Mount Hood Loop Highway, and has an elevation of 4673 feet. It lies about six miles southeast of Mount Hood on the ridge dividing the drainage of Hood River from White River. It is not on the main summit of the Cascade Range. The pass was named for one Samuel Bennett, a Wasco County stockman.

Bennett Rock, DOUGLAS. Combs in *God Made A Valley*, p. 59, says this peak north of Camas Valley was named for J. W. Bennett, a solitary resident with an unexplained and unending supply of gold dust.

Benson Creek, COOS. This creek flowing into Coleman Arm of Tenmile Lake is named for Ole Bentson or Benson who homesteaded near its mouth in the 1880s. BLM records use the form Bentson but Peterson and Powers in *A Century of Coos and Curry* use the form Benson.

Benson Glacier, UNION, WALLOWA. Benson Glacier is an ice field on the northeast and east sides of Eagle Cap in the Wallowa Mountains. It is impossible to determine from existing knowledge just what county it is in. It was named about 1914 by a party of climbers and the name was suggested by Clyde B. Aitchison in compliment to Governor Benson. Frank W. Benson was born at San Jose, California, Mar. 20, 1858. He came to Oregon with his parents in 1864 and except for a short time lived most of his life in Douglas County. He taught school, and was county clerk from 1892 to 1896. He served as secretary of state for Oregon from Jan. 15, 1907, until his death on Apr. 14, 1911. During that time he was governor from Mar. 2, 1909, to June 17, 1910. He was a citizen of high character, and was greatly esteemed.

Benson Plateau, HOOD RIVER. Benson Plateau southeast of Eagle Creek is a relatively level area with an elevation over 4000 feet. It appears to have been named for Thomas C. Benson who was born in Missouri in 1853 and came to eastern Oregon in 1864 as a boy. He worked as a drover and stockman in Umatilla County and around 1900 lived for a period in Cascade Locks. The compiler was told many years ago that Benson ran stock on Benson Plateau but this could not have been possible. Benson was active in the Portland Union Stockyards in the 1920s. He died in Portland on Mar. 17, 1930.

Benson State Park, MULTNOMAH. This park near Multnomah Falls honors

Simon Benson, pioneer lumberman and philanthropist. Benson was born in Norway on Oct. 8, 1852, and came to Oregon in 1878 after an interlude in Wisconsin. For the ensuing 30 years he pursued the lumber business with diligence and perseverance and amassed a considerable fortune. In 1910 he sold his timber interests and devoted his time to business and philanthropic affairs. He was an early member of the State Highway Commission and a strong advocate of good roads. He purchased the property that includes Benson State Park and donated it to the city of Portland who later conveyed it to the OSHD and the USFS. His other benefactions included the well-known bronze drinking fountains that adorn the streets of downtown Portland and $100,000 to School District #1 which was used to start Benson Polytechnic School. Benson died in Beverly Hills, California, on Aug. 5, 1942. For further information and comment, *see* the *Oregon Journal* of the same date.

Benton County. Benton County, which is in the west part of the Willamette Valley, was created Dec. 23, 1847, by the provisional legislature (*General and Special Laws of 1843–9*, p. 50). It was named in honor of Thomas Hart Benton, who was born in North Carolina on Mar. 14, 1782, and died in Washington, D.C. on Apr. 10, 1858. For 30 years he was a member of the United States Senate from Missouri, and one of the great events of his active life was his espousal, with his colleague, Senator Lewis F. Linn, of the extension of the control of the United States into the Oregon country. For an excellent short biography of Senator Benton, *see* the *Encyclopedia Britannica*. *See also* Scott's *History of the Oregon Country*. Benton County has an area according to ODOT of 676 square miles, and an excellent map of the county is published in the Benton County Soil Survey by the U.S. Bureau of Soils of the Department of Agriculture.

Berdugo, HARNEY. Berdugo post office was situated in the Catlow Valley near the Roaring Springs Ranch and was named for Joaquin "Chino" Berdugo, one of Peter French's early vaqueros. The post office was established Aug. 17, 1915, with Rita M. Kiphart first and only postmaster. The office was closed Sept. 29, 1927, with papers to Blitzen.

Berkley, LANE. Berkley post office was established Mar. 1, 1907, with David B. Allison first and only postmaster. The office was closed Dec. 31, 1908, but the record fails to show what other office fell heir to the business. Berkley post office was situated a little north-northeast of the present location of Noti. The place was named with the second name of the postmaster, David Berkley Allison.

Berkley, UMATILLA. Berkley post office was named for a small community in Boone County, Iowa. The Umatilla County office was in the farm home of Thomas Coleman Gettings, who, with his family, came from Iowa to Umatilla County in 1902. Berkley post office was established July 1903, and operated until Feb. 28, 1905. It was in S 20, T 4N, R 37E, about ten miles east of Weston.

Berkshire Creek, LANE. Berkshire Creek is about two miles north of Mapleton. Dale Steinhauer in the *Siuslaw Pioneer*, 1980, p. 11, states this creek is named for Elbert Levi Berkshire who came to Goshen in 1868 and settled on this tributary of the Siuslaw in 1886.

Berlin, LINN. Berlin is a community near Hamilton Creek, about seven miles southeast of Lebanon. In the early days of the county the Bellingers, Burrells and other pioneer families living in the vicinity were admirers of fine racing stock. The annual fair at Albany did not seem to satisfy their sporting spirit, so they began to hold their own races near the residence of Mr. Burrell. Burrell entertained all comers with true western hospitality. Finally the attendance was so large that he was forced to make a charge for meals and his home was referred to as Burrell's Inn. When the post office was established it was decided to name the place Burl Inn. This was cumbersome and the consolidation, Berlin, was adopted. Early in Oct. 1944, residents of Berlin were astonished to learn that arrangements had been made to change the name of their community to Distomo for the place in Greece so horribly treated by the Germans. This change in name, to be accompanied by a blast of nationwide radio and other publicity, was said to be in the interest of democracy, but the promoters of the plan were not sufficiently interested in practical democracy to ask the local residents for their views about the business. These local citizens organized a democratic revolt and the scheme was abandoned. A project to change all the names in this country so as to eliminate those commemorating places and people of nations with which the United States had at one time or another been at war would have surprising results.

Bernhardt Creek, LANE. This creek empties into Siuslaw River from the south near Wendson. It was named for Robert and Mary Bernhardt who came to the Siuslaw area in 1885. According to an article in the *Siuslaw Pioneer*, 1959, by Jennie Bernhardt Simpkins, the Bernhardts settled on Lawson Creek next to the Lawson family. The Lawsons soon moved to the Gardner area and while the stream has shown on some maps as Lawson Creek, she states it has been known as Bernhardt Creek for many years.

Berry, MARION. Berry was a railroad station on North Santiam River a few miles southwest of Detroit. It was named for a family of early settlers on the river. Berry post office was established June 8, 1893, with Ira S. Hatfield first of four postmasters. The office was closed Jan. 13, 1906. Nearby Berry Creek was named for Press Berry, a member of the family.

Berry Creek, BENTON, POLK. This creek flows through the donation land claim of Thomas W. Berry, and it was named for him. The record of his claim is in land office certificate 2323. Berry Creek is southeast of Airlie.

Bertha, MULTNOMAH. This was the name of a railroad station on the Southern Pacific West Side branch southwest of Portland where the line entered the Tualatin Valley. It was named for Mrs. Bertha Koehler of Portland, wife of Richard Koehler, for many years manager of the Southern Pacific Lines in Oregon and their predecessors. The early name of the community and later the post office was Hillsdale, but the railroad was unwilling to adopt that name for the station on account of possible confusion with Hillsboro on the same line. *See* editorial page of Portland *Telegram*, Jan. 18, 1926. Bertha station is a thing of the past and the long abandoned right of way is now occupied by Bertha Boulevard. However, Hillsdale remains as the name of a substantial district adjacent to Wilson High School. Mrs. Koehler died in Portland Nov. 20, 1943. For many years after the West Side railroad was built, the station on the watershed between the Willamette and Tualatin drainage was called Summit, but there were several other places in Oregon known as Summit, and this fact led railroad authorities to change the name. The change from Summit to Bertha took place about 1890.

Bessey Creek, COOS. Bessey Creek flows into South Fork Coos River about a mile west of Dellwood. H. E. and Elmer Bessey, brothers, came to Coos County in the 1880s and started an early day creamery near the mouth of the creek that now bears their family name. In 1894, H. E. Bessey married Josephine McIntosh whose mother and father were both Coos County pioneers. The *Oregonian*, Apr. 7, 1973, has a story with picture of Mrs. Bessey preparing to celebrate her 100th birthday the following day.

Bessie Butte, DESCHUTES. Bessie Butte, 4768 feet high, is ten miles south of Bend east of Lava Butte. It was named for Bessie Wilkinson, the second telephone operator in Bend, who in common with numerous other local residents applied for a homestead near the city.

Besters Ford, TILLAMOOK. About 1880 Stephen D. Bester took up land on the Wilson River about five miles east of Tillamook and for many years the Bester family made the place its home. A ford was developed for the use of settlers further up the stream and later when a wagon road was built the Besters kept the toll gate. An interesting account of these matters is contained in a letter by Frank D. Bester printed on the editorial page of the *Oregonian*, Apr. 8, 1945. As a youth, Frank Bester, son of Stephen, operated a boat at the ford and accommodated the travel. This ford was a mile downstream from the Wilson River Highway bridge over Wilson River.

Bethany, MARION. Bethany is a community about two miles west of Silverton on the road west to Chemawa. The locality was named in pioneer days, possibly as early as Apr. 1851, when Bethany Christian Church was organized. However, Silverton outgrew Bethany. Bethany School serves to keep the name alive. For a history of the locality and of a proposed college, *see* Salem *Statesman*, Oct. 30, 1931. *See also* Down's *History of the Silverton Country*. Efforts made by members of the Christian Church to establish a college or institution at Bethany failed for lack of funds. The churches continued their interest in the project and it is possible that the development of Bethel Institute at Bethel in Polk County was a result of the earlier effort. *Bethany* is a Hebrew word meaning "House of Poverty" and the name was applied to a place in Palestine not far from Jerusalem. The word has been used as a place-name in many parts of the United States, frequently as part of some church activity.

Bethany, WASHINGTON. The name Bethany is applied to a crossroads trading center about four miles northwest of Cedar Mill, but in earlier days Bethany was at the crossroads about two miles northeast of the present community of that name. Ulrich Gerber came to Oregon from Switzerland in the middle 1870s and settled on North Plains in the south part of s 17, T 1N, R 1W. He was instrumental in getting Bethany post office established in July 1878, at a point about a mile east of the present Bethany School. He suggested the name and was the first postmaster. The office was later moved to the crossroads on the west line of section 19. Bethany post office was discontinued in 1904 but the name for the community is still in use. A Presbyterian church stands at the northwest corner of the original Bethany crossroads of Ulrich Gerber. The Bethany Baptist Church is about a mile south of these crossroads.

Bethel, POLK. All that remains of this community is a school, situated at the base of the Eola Hills about a mile east of McCoy. Bethel is in a little vale called Plum Valley, and the locality was named in 1846 by the Rev. Glen O. Burnett for Bethel Church in Missouri where he had served as pastor. John E. Smith's booklet *Bethel*, published by the author in 1941, gives an account of this and subsequent events. Dr. Nathaniel Hudson settled nearby in 1851 and in 1852 opened Bethel Academy, a private undertaking. Bethel Academy was short lived. In 1854 Dr. Hudson moved to a new claim west of Dallas. In 1855 G. O. Burnett and Amos Harvey organized a new school called Bethel Institute. A building was erected and the institute opened in Oct. of that year. In Jan. 1856, the legislature officially chartered the school with the name Bethel Institute and it operated with that name until Oct. 1860, when the legislature granted a new charter with the name Bethel College. The college failed financially in 1861, and efforts to turn it over to the Christian Church were unsuccessful. *See* Monmouth. Bethel Institute and Bethel College seem to have been community affairs and while the Christian Church gave moral support, it does not appear that the church actually furnished funds. *Bethel* is a Hebrew word meaning "House of God." The name was applied to a holy city of Palestine originally known as Luz.

Bethel School, MARION. Bethel School is on the south side of the penitentiary road about six miles east of the business section of Salem. In early days Dan Early operated a sawmill in this locality, cutting some of the fine timber that grew there. Soon after the mill was torn down a group of Dunkards (members of the Church of the Brethren) settled in the place and built a church on the site of the mill. This they called the Bethel Church. The Dunkards lived a quiet life there for some years but the group gradually dwindled to the point where the church could no longer be maintained. The building was sold to the newly formed Bethel school district, made up from parts of other districts. The old building was used until about 1925, when a new school was built. There is more information about the name and place in a short neighborhood story by Mrs. J. R. Carruthers in the Salem *Statesman*, Oct. 1, 1931.

Betzen, LANE. Betzen was a station on the Southern Pacific between Mapleton and Cushman named for Betty Zentner, daughter of one of the engineers on the construction of the railroad.

Beulah, MALHEUR. Beulah was named for Beulah Arnold, daughter of the first postmaster. She was later Mrs. Roy S. Rutherford. Beulah post office was established Dec. 16, 1884, with Thomas L. Arnold first postmaster. The use of Miss Arnold's name is said to have been suggested by a family friend, J. C. Roberts, an early stockman of the Harney Valley.

Beverly Beach, LINCOLN. Beverly Beach is a small community north of Yaquina Head and Beverly Beach State Park adjoins it on the north. In 1981 Florence May Christy sent the compiler the following statement giving the origin of the name: "During the early nineteen thirties my husband, Curtis F. Christy, and I owned the property which is now known as Beverly Beach, Lincoln County, Oregon. Our goal was to establish a small seaside community on this property. In choosing a name for this site my daughter, Florence Daneene Christy Pearson, who at that time was a small child, was asked what she would like to call the community. Her favorite doll at that time was named Beverly, and her choice of that name established the location as Beverly Beach, which it has remained to this day."

Bewley Creek, TILLAMOOK. This branch of Tillamook River carries the name of J. C. Bewley, an early settler and one time deputy U.S. Marshal.

Bible Creek, TILLAMOOK, YAMHILL. A. S. Bible was born in Tennessee Mar. 16, 1834. He established a store in Sheridan in 1879 and was also a merchant in Willamina. He retired from these activities in 1898. *See Portrait and Biographical Record of the Willamette Valley*, p. 570. He operated a ranch near the Tillamook-Yamhill line north of Willamina and the names Bible Ranch and Bible Creek resulted from this activity. The stream flows into Nestucca River.

Biddle Pass, JEFFERSON. Biddle Pass, elevation about 5450 feet, is due east of Mount Jefferson. East of the pass the ground rises sharply to the southeast to form Bald Peter, a well-known landmark on the Warm Springs Indian Reservation. In 1920, Henry J. Biddle of Portland and Vancouver, who was an enthusiastic sportsman and naturalist, decided to investigate the feasibility of building a trail around the east base of Mount Jefferson. He made up a small party, including himself, Charles C. Giebeler of Detroit, the compiler of these notes and three amiable packhorses. As the result of two weeks in the field, enlivened by minor misadventures, excessively rough lava fields, fallen timber, boulders and yellow-jackets, Mr. Biddle concluded that the territory was not suitable for the type of construction he had in mind. The party camped at the south end of the pass on the night of Aug. 14, 1920, and went through the pass next day. At that time there was no evidence that a white man had been there before. Mr. Biddle died Sept. 27, 1928, and the compiler suggested to the USBGN that the pass should be named in his honor, which was done on Mar. 6, 1929.

Bieberstedt Butte, JACKSON. Bieberstedt Butte is in S 28, T 36S, R 3E. It is named for Carl Bieberstedt who took up government land east of Lakecreek in the 1880s. Bieberstedt Creek flows north into Willow Creek reservoir.

Big Butte, JACKSON. Big Butte post office took its name from Big Butte Creek. The post office was established May 9, 1878 with George W. King first postmaster. Henry H. Pope was appointed postmaster July 11, 1882, and John A. Obenchain on Oct. 6, 1888. The office was closed to Brownsboro on Mar. 31, 1908. It is reported to the compiler that Big Butte post office was moved several times, though it was generally in the neighborhood of T 35S, R 2E.

Big Butte Creek, JACKSON. Mount McLoughlin was known by the early settlers in the Rogue River Valley as Snowy Butte. Big Butte Creek had its rise near Snowy Butte and was so named on that account. It flows into Rogue River. A smaller stream rising in the same vicinity was christened Little Butte Creek. The name Butte Creek when applied to Big Butte Creek is incorrect.

Big Canyon, WALLOWA. This canyon carries Deer Creek which flows into Wallowa River just east of Minam. It has been shown with various names on older maps, including Bear Creek, Deep Canyon Creek, Little Minam Creek and Sheep Creek. The USBGN once named this Big Canyon Creek but changed to Big Canyon and Deer Creek in *Decision List 6601*.

Big Cliff Dam, LINN, MARION. This is a regulating structure for Detroit Dam a short distance upstream. Big Cliff Dam was completed in 1953 and named for a nearby prominent rock face.

Big Creek, CLATSOP. Big Creek has been known by that name for many years, and yet at one time it must have had another name. Old maps show it as Tillasana Creek, changed later to Tilly Ann Creek and even Tilly Jane Creek. The writer has been unable to determine where these older names originated. H. S. Lyman in *OHQ*, v. I, p. 321, says that the Indian name for the locality near Knappa was *Tle-las-qua*, which may have been the same as *Tillasana*.

Big Eddy, WASCO. Big Eddy was at the western end of the obstructions in the Columbia River at The Dalles. It was at this point that eastbound travelers and freight began the portage around these obstructions. As far as the writer can determine the name was not used in the days of exploration but probably came into use at the time of gold discoveries in eastern Oregon just after 1860.

Big Hole, LAKE. Big Hole is a sunken spot in the northwest part of the county, with an area of about a quarter of a square mile. It is roughly circular, and its bottom is about 300 feet below the surrounding land level. The name well describes it. Big Hole Butte lies just to the northeast.

Big Lake, LINN. Big Lake is just south of Santiam Pass and US-20. It is one of the higher lakes in the Cascade Range with an elevation of 4644 feet and has become a popular spot for camping and boating. The old Santiam Wagon Road passes near the north shore and the lake was probably named by the Andrew Wiley party in 1858. The name is, of course, descriptive.

Big Log Creek, CROOK, JEFFERSON. USFS ranger J. O. F. Anderson, in his notes on file at the Ochoco National Forest says: "Named for a large log on the creek said to be seven feet in diameter, which measurement I must doubt. The largest pine tree I ever saw on the Ochoco was 71" DBH, on the south bank of Auger Creek." Big Log Creek empties into Trout Creek in s 23, T 11S, R 17E, near the headwaters of Trout Creek.

Big Meadows, CURRY. This descriptive name for an area in the northeast part of Curry County has been in use since the days of the Rogue River Indian War of 1855–56. Big Meadows are near the southeast corner of T 32S, R 10W, about two miles airline north of Rogue River. Fort Lamerick was established in this locality May 1, 1865. According to L. J. Cooper, USFS ranger at Galice, this stockade was near the quartercorner between sections 1 and 2, T 33S, R 10W. The Big Meadows referred to above are not the same as Big Meadows at the Big Bend of Rogue River near Illahe, where there was a sharp engagement with the Indians at the end of May 1856.

Big Noise Creek, CLATSOP. This stream is about 20 miles east of Astoria. It was named in early days because of the fact that there was a sluice gate near its mouth used to control the water for floating logs. This sluice gate made an excessive noise and the stream was named on that account.

Big Prairie, LANE. Big Prairie post office was probably the first post office in the upper valley of Middle Fork Willamette River. This office was established July 14, 1873, with Addison Black first postmaster. The office operated until Dec. 10, 1879, with one intermission. The name was descriptive of the locality. Old maps show Big Prairie at or near the present locality of Westfir. The modern name for the plateau northeast of Westfir is High Prairie, and that was probably the reason for the name of the post office. The compiler does not know if the post office Big Prairie was near the Middle Fork or up on the plateau.

Big Rayborn Canyon, UMATILLA. Big and Little Rayborn canyons were both named for William Rayborn who in 1903 bought land on the north slope of Weston Mountain.

Big Spring, CROOK. This spring in s 29, T 14S, R 23E, was known in the old days as Dead Dog Spring. It was a locating point on the "Deadline" established in 1898 by the cattlemen of the Paulina Sheep Shooters. The original name came after a flock of Ed Shown's sheep and one of his herder's dogs were killed nearby.

Biggs, SHERMAN. Biggs is a station on the Union Pacific Railroad main line at what was the junction with the now abandoned branch south into Sherman County. It was named for a nearby landowner, W. H. Biggs, who was born in Belmont County, Ohio, May 12, 1831 and who came to Sherman County in 1880. The small local community is known as Biggs Junction because this is where US-97, running north and south, makes an important intersection with I-84.

Biggs Cove, TILLAMOOK. Biggs Cove was in Tillamook Bay just northeast of the town of Cape Meares. It was named for John A. Biggs who came from Kansas and settled in Tillamook County about 1885. When the Tillamook Bay spit was repaired after World War II, the cove was replaced by Cape Meares Lake. *See* Cape Meares Lake.

Biglow Canyon, SHERMAN. This canyon opens into the John Day River about six miles up from the Columbia. It was obviously named for a person but the compiler can find no trace of anyone by this name. Biglow post office in S 20, T 2N, R 18E, operated from 1894 to 1902 with Anne F. Lyman first postmaster.

Billy Creek, LANE. This tributary of Christy Creek is named for William J. "Billy" Pengra who was interested in the mining activity near Sinker Mountain.

Billy Meadows, WALLOWA. These meadows are about 25 miles northeast of Enterprise. They were named in the 1880s for William Smith, better known as Billy. He was a pioneer sheepherder employed by R. Frank Stubblefield and is said to have been a native of England.

Bilyeu Creek, LINN. This stream rises on the northwest slope of Snow Peak and flows northwestward into Thomas Creek. It bears the name of the Bilyeu family, members of which have lived on its banks since 1852. The stream is sometimes called Neal Creek, but that is not the name originally applied.

Binder Slough, CLATSOP. Binder Slough runs west off Youngs River south of Astoria. Charles Binder was the first husband of the maternal grandmother of Dorothy O. Johansen, long time professor of History at Reed College in Portland. Dr. Johansen reported that Binder was a rather mysterious individual who came to Oregon from Germany in the 1850s. He moved to Astoria where he ran a ship chandlery business and took up a claim along Binder Slough. Binder died in 1875 and in due course Sophie Schmeer Binder married Louis Kirchhoff.

Bingen Gap, HOOD RIVER. This is the geologic name for the cut four miles long and 2000 feet deep that the Columbia River has made through the Bingen anticline. Both the gap and the anticline were named for Bingen, Washington, situated in the gap on the north bank. The town in turn was named for the famous German city, Bingen on the Rhine.

Binger, DOUGLAS. The place called Binger was in the upper Cow Creek Valley at the mouth of French Creek, later the site of Anchor School. Binger post office was established July 16, 1894, with Isaac N. French postmaster. The office was closed Sept. 20, 1902, and mail was sent to Galesville. Binger Hermann was representative in Congress from the first Oregon district when the office was established and it may be assumed it was named in compliment to him.

Bingham Creek, DOUGLAS. Bingham Creek is tributary to Middle Fork Coquille River south of Camas Valley. It was named for Samuel Bingham who homesteaded nearby in 1876.

Bingham Lake, KLAMATH. Bingham Lake is south of Crescent Lake. It was named for Cy J. Bingham, for many years connected with the USFS and later sheriff of Grant County.

Bingham Lake, LINN. Bingham Lake is in Bingham Basin and Bingham Ridge is just to the south. Judge John B. Waldo named Bingham Basin for his old friend and companion, Edward W. Bingham, who died in Portland Jan. 1, 1904. Bingham was born in Pennsylvania in 1851. He came to Oregon in 1869 and two years later, when he was 21 years old, passed the bar examinations. In the middle 1880s, he was involved in the construction of the Northern Pacific Railway from Kalama to Puget Sound but after that he practiced law in Portland until his death. He was active in civic affairs and was known as the father of the Australian ballot and the direct primary in Oregon. He was an avid hunter and outdoorsman and accompanied Judge Waldo on several early expeditions to the Cascade Range. The old Mount Jefferson summit record shows that he and Judge Waldo climbed to the base of the pinnacle on Aug. 13, 1879. This was before the first complete ascent of the mountain when the pinnacle was still considered unclimbable.

Bingham Mountain, COOS. This mountain which has an elevation of 2287 feet, is in the valley of South Fork Coquille River. It was named for Isaac Bingham, a pioneer settler, and a conspicuous figure in the Indian fighting near Port Orford.

Bingham Prairie, CROOK. Bingham Prairie is in the Ochoco Mountains four miles south of Opal Mountain. It, and adjoining Bingham Spring, were named for Cy J. Bingham, one of the first USFS rangers on the Ochoco National Forest. Bingham was later for many years supervisor of the Malheur National Forest.

Bingham Springs, UMATILLA. Bingham Springs are in the east part of the county, on Umatilla River, eight miles east of Gibbon, and well up in the Blue Mountains. The springs have had a number of names. In earlier days the style Warm Springs was generally used. The place was for a time a station on the Thomas and Ruckel stage line through the Blue Mountains, and there was a toll gate at the stage house. The 30 by 50 foot main building was built of square, hewn tamarack logs about 1864. From the La Grande *Mountain Sentinel* notice of 1867, quoted under the heading Meacham, A. A. Meacham appears to have operated the station during 1867–68. Later, a man named Tip Parrent is said to have owned or operated them. Early in the 1880s Parrent sold the establishment to John B. Purdy who added the kitchen and dining wing, and secured a post office called Purdy on June 9, 1881, with William Parrent postmaster. This sounds as if Tip Parrent and William Parrent were the same man. Purdy became postmaster Aug. 7, 1882, and ran the office until Sept. 17, 1891, when it was closed. During Purdy's ownership, the place was known as Purdy Springs. About 1892 Dr. John E. Bingham of Walla Walla bought the springs and changed the name to Bingham Springs. A number of improvements were made and the place served as a popular resort for Portland, Pendleton and Walla Walla people. The writer of these lines spent many happy days there swimming in the pool, fishing in the Umatilla River and setting up pins in the bowling alley for guests who were willing to spend small sums for the service. The Union Pacific Railroad changed the name of Gibbon station to Bingham Springs, but the post office at Gibbon, which served the springs, continued with the name Gibbon. After the turn of the century the springs were called Wenaha Springs, probably for the Wenaha River in the Blue Mountains, but the name Bingham Springs has been restored and is in use at this writing. Many years ago the railroad changed the name of its station from Bingham Springs back to Gibbon.

Birch Gulch, WALLOWA. Birch Gulch drains into Snake River in T 4N, R 49E. The place is named for the birch trees that grow there. These trees are probably the red birch, sometimes called the water birch, *Betula fontinalis*.

Bird Butte, CLACKAMAS, WASCO. This butte is in the Cascade Range, north of Frog Lake. It was named for George Bird, a forest ranger, who bled to death nearby as the result of an accident.

Birdseye Creek, JACKSON. This stream flows into Rogue River two miles south of the town of Rogue River. It was named for David Birdseye, who took a donation land claim that included the mouth of the creek. In 1855, Birdseye completed a hewn log house that lasted well over 100 years and in 1974, was listed on the National Register of Historic Places. In the 1980s it was restored, including some original furnishings, by descendants of the original family, only to be destroyed by fire in November 1990.

Birkenfeld, COLUMBIA. Anton Birkenfeld, a native of Germany, settled in the Nehalem Valley in 1886 and founded the community of Birkenfeld about 1910. The place was named for him.

Bishop Creek, COLUMBIA. This stream, tributary to Tide Creek from the southwest, is sometimes shown on maps as Bashop Creek. In 1943, Wales Wood of Saint Helens wrote that the correct spelling was Bishop for Frank B. Bishop. Wood got his information from James Anlicker of Goble, member of a pioneer family of Columbia County, who was conversant with the matter.

Bishop Meadows, WALLOWA. These meadows are in T 3N, R 42E, and were named for Oliver N. Bishop who settled in the middle Wallowa Valley in the 1880s. He wintered stock on the meadows, as there was a good crop of wild hay there.

Bissell, CLACKAMAS. In 1927 it was reported by old residents that this town was named for W. S. Bissell who was postmaster general of the United States from 1893 to 1895. Wilson Shannon Bissell was born in New London, New York, in 1847, and when appointed to the cabinet was a practicing lawyer at Buffalo where he was a partner of Grover Cleveland. During his incumbency as postmaster general many improvements were made in the postal service, including a cut in transcontinental mail time, and the Bureau of Engraving and Printing taking over the work of printing postage stamps, previously done by private agencies. In 1902 he was made chancellor of the University of Buffalo, and died in 1903.

Bitter Lick, JACKSON. Bitter Lick is in the north part of the county about four miles northwest of Persist. The name is descriptive, and was given because of the strong taste of a fairly large spring. Bitterlick Creek, which took its name from the lick, flows southward into Elk Creek at a point close to Bitter Lick.

Blachly, LANE. Blachly is three miles from Triangle Lake, a well-known place in the Coast Range. Residents of the neighborhood formerly received their mail at Franklin post office, now discontinued. The office at Blachly was established June 27, 1892, and named for William Blachly, a local resident. William Blachly was born in Illinois in 1844 and came to Oregon in 1854. He died at Blachly on Feb. 16, 1934. See the *Oregonian*, Feb. 19, 1934, p. 8.

Black Butte, DESCHUTES, JEFFERSON. This imposing butte is one of the most important landmarks in the Deschutes Valley, not only on account of its characteristic dark color, but also on account of its symmetry. It stands well apart from the peaks of the Cascade Range, and has an elevation of 6415 feet, with a USFS lookout at the summit, which is in Jefferson County. From its north base flows the Metolius River, full bodied from a giant spring. It is not known who named Black Butte, but the title is fitting. It had this name as early as 1855, and an interesting picture of it is shown in Pacific Railroad Surveys *Reports*, v. VI, p. 90. In the diary of Lt. Henry L. Abbot in *OHQ*, v. 33, p. 19, Black Butte is called Pivot Mountain, also an appropriate name. Abbot was one of the engineers connected with the Pacific Railroad Surveys. He did not use the name Pivot Mountain in the printed report, but Black Butte.

Black Butte, DESCHUTES. In 1970 a subsidiary of Brooks Scanlon Lumber Company began development of a resort community on the site of the old Black Butte Ranch directly south of Black Butte. The first inhabitants took up residence in 1971 and Black Butte post office was established Sept. 16, 1971 with Wendell Clore first postmaster.

Black Butte, LANE. The geographic feature Black Butte is at the headwaters of Coast Fork Willamette River, about 20 miles south of Cottage Grove. The mountain was named for its characteristic dark color. A post office named Harris was established near the butte on Dec. 28, 1898, with William Harris postmaster, and it was named in compliment to this postal official. On Aug. 10, 1901, the name of the office was changed to Blackbutte and it operated with that name until Aug. 31, 1957.

Black Creek, LANE. Black Creek, a tributary of Salmon Creek, rises just west of Waldo Lake. It is named for Amos R. Black who in 1905 initiated an irrigation and power project using water from Waldo Lake. After final approval of Black's water application in 1908, he conveyed a portion to Frederick and Nellie Ray of Helena, Montana. They in turn organized the Waldo Lake Irrigation and Power Company and hired Simon Klovdahl to design and construct a tunnel and headgate to draw water from the lake. The works were completed in 1914 but little water was drawn for the permit was rescinded in 1915 and all land restored to the National Forest. In 1916 and again in 1960 the tunnel gates were capped to control leaking. Before this venture, the stream was known as South Fork Salmon Creek but the 1912 Cascade National Forest map uses the current Black Creek. The outlet of the tunnel is actually into Klovdahl Creek and then to Nettie Creek, a small tributary of Black Creek. Nettie Creek is probably a typographical error for Nellie honoring Mrs. Ray. Klovdahl is remembered by Klovdahl Bay in Waldo Lake. For further information *see* Eugene *Register-Guard*, Oct. 2, 1960, sect. 6.

Black Hills, KLAMATH. These hills occupy a number of square miles in the southeastern part of what was Klamath Indian Reservation. They were named on account of their color. The hills have a maximum elevation of about 6300 feet.

Black Place, JEFFERSON. This ranch northeast of Sampson Mountain was the homestead of Addison Black about the turn of the century.

Black Rock, POLK. Black Rock was the western terminus of the Southern Pacific Company branch line west from Dallas. It was on the Little Luckiamute River. It is generally believed the town was named because of an exposed ledge of black shale rock. The railroad was taken up after World War II and when the compiler visited the area in 1984, there was little evidence of civilization.

Blackhorse Canyon, MORROW. Legend has it that in the early days this canyon east of Lexington was the range of a horse rancher named Wade. Wade had one trait in common with Henry Ford, he didn't care what color a horse was as long as it was black.

Blackhorse Creek, WALLOWA. Blackhorse Creek flows into Imnaha River in the extreme southwest corner of T 4S, R 48E. It was named in the late 1890s by Horace J. Butler for a horse that strayed into the canyon and wintered there.

Blacklock Point, CURRY. M. S. Brainard wrote the author in 1967 that this point north of Cape Blanco was named for John Blacklock who was born in Scotland and lived near the point for many years. He died in Bandon on June 8, 1905. A post office named Sandstone operated nearby from Oct. 1890 to May 1891 with Annie J. Blacklock postmaster.

Blackmore Creek, WALLOWA. Blackmore Creek is a small stream flowing into Imnaha River in T 1S, R 48E. It was named for Fred Blackmore, a homesteader.

Blacks Island, DOUGLAS. Blacks Island is a small, marshy tract of land in the mouth of Smith River northeast of Reedsport. The Southern Pacific Company railroad trestle crosses the west end of the island. The name is said to be in commemoration of Arthur Black of the Jedediah S. Smith party which was massacred by the Indians in this vicinity on July 14, 1828. Black was one of the four who escaped. Fifteen members of the Smith party were killed. Black escaped alone and made his way to the Tillamook country, thence to Vancouver. For details, *see* Smith River. The compiler does not know who applied the name Blacks Island or when it was done, but it is in general use.

Blacksmith Shop Well, MORROW. This well in Sand Hollow just east of Finley Buttes supplied water for the field blacksmith shop and corral maintained by John S. Kilkenny. Completed in 1904, it was the first drilled well in Morrow County and was 290 feet to water. For a full account of Kilkenny and his many Irish Morrow County contemporaries *see* "Shamrocks and Shepherds" by John F. Kilkenny, *OHQ*, v. 69, p. 101 *et seq.*

Blaine, CURRY. Blaine post office is listed in Curry County for a few months in 1891. It was closed to Ophir. Eliza Woodruff was the only postmaster. The compiler has not been able to turn up much information about this office although it seems probable that it was named for James G. Blaine, candidate for the presidency of the United States in 1884. The Woodruff family lived not far from Ophir but early residents of the locality are of the opinion that Blaine post office was never in actual operation. That, of course, may be true.

Blaine, TILLAMOOK. Blaine is on the Nestucca River. It was named by the first postmaster, William Smith, for James G. Blaine (1830–1893), at one time Republican candidate for the presidency of the United States. Smith was appointed postmaster of Blaine in 1892 by John Wanamaker.

Blair Lake, LANE. Blair Lake northeast of Oakridge was named for Frank Blair of Lowell, who at one time ran some cattle near the lake. He is said to have discovered it.

Blake Flat, WHEELER. Grover C. Blake was born in West Virginia in Feb. 1884. He came west with his family via Kansas and Colorado and then emigrated to Oregon in 1904. He settled near West Branch and took up a homestead on the flat that bears his name. In May 1909, Blake went to work for the USFS and served in various locations until his retirement in 1944. His reminiscences, *Blazing Oregon Trails*, contain a wealth of information about early days in Wheeler County.

Blakeley, UMATILLA. This station was originally called Eastland for Robert E. Eastland, who received a patent to land nearby on Mar. 30, 1880. The name was later changed to Blakeley for William M. Blakeley, a wheat grower in the vicinity.

Blakes, BAKER. This station east of Huntington was named for Thomas J. Blake of the Iron Dyke mine at Homestead, who was instrumental in securing the construction of the Homestead branch of the Union Pacific Railroad.

Blalock, GILLIAM. Blalock is a station on the Union Pacific Railroad west of Arlington. It was here that Dr. Nelson G. Blalock, a pioneer citizen of Walla Walla and a veteran of the Civil War, hoped to develop an extensive horticultural establishment along the south bank of the Columbia River. Blalock died in Walla Walla, Mar. 14, 1913, aged 77 years. The flat land along the river suitable for agriculture was inundated in 1968 by the pool behind John Day Dam and there is now little to recall Dr. Blalock's hopes.

Blalock Mountain, UMATILLA. Blalock Mountain lies in the northeast part of Umatilla County, between North and South forks of Walla Walla River. It has an elevation of over 4500 feet. It was named for Dr. Nelson G. Blalock whose name is attached to the community of Blalock, Gilliam County. For information about Dr. Blalock, *see* Blalock. At one time Dr. Blalock cut timber and wood on top of Blalock Mountain and flumed it down into the two forks of the Walla Walla River. It is on that account that Blalock Mountain bears its name.

Blanchet, WASHINGTON. Blanchet post office was named for Francis N. Blanchet, first Catholic archbishop of Oregon. The office was at the place now known as Verboort. Blanchet post office was established Feb. 11, 1898, with Bertha Vandehey first and only postmaster. The office was discontinued Apr. 26, 1898, and the compiler has been told it was never in regular service. As early as 1893, an effort had been made to establish Verboort post office but the appointment of Sarah Mark as postmaster was rescinded in May 1894. However, it seems probable that Blanchet post office was planned to be on or near the grounds of the Church of the Visitation at Verboort.

Bland Mountain, DOUGLAS. This peak is near the confluence of Days Creek and South Umpqua River and Bland Creek rises on its south slopes. The 1860 census lists Henry and Mary Beckworth Bland and children including John, age 8 months. Records of the BLM also show that Henry M. Bland homesteaded along the creek in 1863. These items are mentioned in detail because Reinhart in *The Golden Frontier*, p. 149, mentions staying near Days Creek in 1858 with John Bland and his wife, the eldest Beckworth girl. The father may possibly have been called John by his wife or friends but this ceased after the birth of their son.

Blann Meadow, WHEELER. Blann Meadow southwest of Waterman was the location of the homestead taken by Isaac Blann in 1890. For a brief biography, *see Illustrated History of Central Oregon*, p. 692.

Blanton, GRANT. Blanton was a post office in Bear Valley named for David Blanton, the first postmaster. The office was established June 9, 1888, and was closed Sept. 14, 1891. It was reestablished Mar. 15, 1892, with Madison Waddell postmaster and was closed again June 12, 1895. In Sept. 1946, Edward I. Southworth of Seneca wrote the compiler that the Blanton post office was on the old Burns-Canyon City stage road about four miles north of the present town of Seneca.

Blattner Creek, LINCOLN. This is a tributary of Big Creek north of Newport. George Blattner took up a homestead nearby in the early 1890s.

Blazed Alder Creek, CLACKAMAS, MULTNOMAH. This creek received its name from a 24″ blazed alder tree near its confluence with Bull Run River. The tree was a bench mark established during the early City of Portland watershed surveys. Blazed Alder Creek rises on the slopes of Blazed Alder Butte but Ralph Lewis of Parkdale said that the butte took its name from the creek. He was in the area during the 1906 fire and stated that the butte was then already so named.

Blevins Creek, CROOK. Blevins Creek empties into Duncan Creek in S 17, T 14 S, R 19 E. Presumably it was named for I. M. Blevins, an early settler on Ochoco Creek and the father of Lee Blevins, for many years a USFS district ranger on the Ochoco National Forest.

Blevins Spring, WHEELER. This spring north of Derr Meadows was named for Jim Blevins, an early employee of the Fopiano Ranch.

Blind Slough, CLATSOP. Blind Slough opens off the Prairie Channel of the

Columbia River about halfway between Knappa and Brownsmead. The slough wanders about a good deal and gets nowhere in particular. One fair-sized branch pinches out suddenly and that was probably the reason for the name. Blind Slough post office was established near this water on May 2, 1910, with John W. Crow first of four postmasters. The office was closed out to Brownsmead Dec. 15, 1924.

Blitzen, HARNEY. This post office was about ten miles south of Narrows. It was named for the Donner und Blitzen River which flows into Malheur Lake. The river was named during the Snake War of 1864, when troops under the command of Col. George B. Currey crossed it during a thunder storm, and gave to it the German name for thunder and lightning. A second office named Blitzen was established Apr. 10, 1916, but it was some 35 miles south of the original location. This office, south of Frenchglen, was closed in 1943.

Blitzen Butte, DOUGLAS. USFS ranger Fred Asam named this summit a mile east of Thunder Mountain. Asam was born in Austria and came to this country as a young man so he applied the German word for lightning to match the nearby Thunder.

Blizzard Ridge, JEFFERSON. This ridge was named on a winter day about 1900 by John O'Kelly of the OK Ranch. O'Kelly was headed south towards home when he encountered such a severe snowstorm that he had to return to Ashwood.

Blodgett, BENTON. Blodgett is said to have been named for a pioneer settler, William Blodgett. The post office was established with the name of Emrick early in Apr. 1888, with James A. Wood first postmaster. The name was changed to Blodgett on May 8 of the same year. Emrick was the name of a local family.

Blodgett Creek, LANE. Blodgett Creek is a tributary of Brice Creek three miles southeast of Disston. It was named for John Blodgett, an early settler.

Blood Creek, LANE. Blood Creek is west of Black Butte. Herbert W. Blood homesteaded there in 1896.

Bloody Run, JOSEPHINE. This stream is three miles east of Grants Pass. It was so called because of an incident in the Rogue River Indian War in the 1850s. In 1944 W. A. Moxley of Lebanon wrote that there was a sharp skirmish at this point and one of the white men, separated from his companions, was shot while he was stooping to get a drink from the stream. His blood ran into the water and this gave rise to the name of the run.

Blooming, WASHINGTON. Blooming is a locality about two miles south of Cornelius but not a commercial community. Many years ago it was known as the German Settlement. In Dec. 1945, Ed Demmin of Hillsboro wrote the compiler that the Rev. Mr. Paul of the Lutheran Church wanted a better name for the community and selected the title Blooming, which he thought descriptive of the floral conditions and pleasant prospects generally. Blooming post office was established Feb. 27, 1895, with Heinrich Paul first postmaster. The office was closed Nov. 28, 1904, because of the extension of rural delivery. The writer has been told that it was a residence post office, not in a store. It seems probable that the man who named the place was the same person as the first postmaster, but the compiler has no proof of it.

Bloomington, POLK. Postal authorities have informed the compiler that this post office was established May 25, 1852 with Eli W. Foster first postmaster. Preston's *Map of Oregon* of 1856 shows Bloomington in the site of the community now known as Parker. Bloomington post office was closed in June 1863. The descriptive name seems to have been tinctured with too much optimism.

Bloucher, HOOD RIVER. This was a station on the Mount Hood Railroad west of Odell. It was named for H. E. Bloucher, a local resident.

Blowout Creek, LINN. This creek flows into Detroit Reservoir. It was named because of a great landslide resembling a blowout of the mountainside. The Blowout Creek drainage is geologically unstable and there are numerous other smaller land slips along the creek.

Blowout Creek, WALLOWA. Blowout Creek empties into Bear Creek in the southeast part of T 2S, R 42E. It was named by Leander McCubbin and others who camped near the stream in pioneer days and had trouble getting a fire started because the wind blew so hard.

Blue Box Pass, WASCO. This pass is on US-26 about one mile south of Frog Lake and one and one half miles south of Wapinitia Pass through the Cascade Range. Blue Box Pass has an elevation of 4024 feet and is some 70 feet higher than the main pass. The word pass is a misnomer since here the highway merely crosses the ridge separating Frog Lake and Clear Lake drainages as it follows this ridge to the south. Ivan M. Woolley in "Mt Hood or Bust: The Old Road," *OHQ*, v. 60, p. 54, says that the Clackamas Lake road turned off at this point and the location was marked by and named for a blue box containing a USFS telephone.

Blue Heron Bay, COOS. Blue Heron Bay is on the south side of Tenmile Lake between Rocky and Willow points. Its name was approved by the OGNB in 1988 at the request of local residents. The name was chosen because the bay is a nesting and feeding area for several Great Blue Herons or *Ardea herodias*.

Blue Lake, MULTNOMAH. This Blue Lake in the extreme southeast corner of the county was named by Pete and Jim Odell and Jake Lenz. They were on a hunting expedition when they looked down from above and said that the lake looked exactly like a blue huckleberry.

Blue Mountain, UMATILLA. This is a station on the Union Pacific Railroad southwest of Milton. It is on Dry Creek just north of the horseshoe curve made by the railroad in getting from Weston down into the Walla Walla Valley. When the railroad was being extended south from Walla Walla it was for some time dead-ended at Blue Mountain, and as the station was the last one on the way into the Blue Mountains, it was named for those features, although no one seems to know just why the singular form was used.

Blue Mountains. The Blue Mountains constitute one of the largest uplifts in the state and the main range together with its spurs and offshoots extends into several counties. The backbone of the Blue Mountains begins in Grant County and runs northward through Baker, Union, Umatilla and Wallowa counties in Oregon and into Walla Walla, Columbia, Garfield and Asotin counties in Washington. They consist largely of sedimentary and metamorphic rocks and are divided into five general sections. From west to east these are: Ochoco, Aldrich, Strawberry, Greenhorn and Elkhorn mountains. The Blue Mountains are separated from the Wallowa Mountains in northeastern Oregon by Powder River and Grande Ronde River. The highest point in the Blue Mountains is Rock Creek Butte, a peak on Elkhorn Ridge a few miles west of Baker. Rock Creek Butte has an elevation of 9097 feet. Strawberry Mountain near Prairie City is the highest peak in the southwest part of the Blue Mountains. It has an elevation of 9052 feet. One of the first references to these mountains is by Gabriel Franchere, one of the Astorians. On arriving at the Walla Walla River, he wrote: "A range of mountains was visible to the s.e., about fifty or sixty miles off." He does not give the mountains a name. On July 9, 1811, David Thompson of the North West Company of Montreal, refered to them as Shawpatin Mountains, but in his entry for Aug. 8, 1811, he said: "Beginning of course to see the Blue Mountains between the Shawpatin and the Snake Indians." In a footnote, T. C. Elliott, editor of the Thompson Journal, said: "Apparently the first record of this name Blue as applied to these mountains." (*OHQ*, v. 15, pp. 57 and 121.) Alexander Ross, J. K. Townsend, David Douglas, Peter Skene Ogden, John Work and other early travelers continued to use the name Blue Mountains. One of the early references is by the Rev. Gustavus Hines (*Oregon: Its History, Condition and Prospects*, 1851, p. 323): "As you approach the Blue Mountains on the south, particularly on the Umatilla and Walla Walla rivers, the hills disappear, and you find yourself passing over a beautiful and level country, about twenty-five or thirty miles broad, on the farther borders of which rise with indescribable beauty and grandeur, that range which, from its azure-like appearance, has been called the 'Blue Mountains.'"

Blue River, LANE. Blue River is remarkable in color, and is well named. The color apparently comes from the rocky bed and is not inherent in the water itself. The Blue River mines were discovered in 1863, and the stream was doubtless named about that time. Large stamp-mills were installed, but the ore was low grade, and the mills have not been operated for many years. *See* the *Oregonian*, Dec. 8, 1863; Nov. 2 and Dec. 17, 1889 and July 3, 1897. Blue River post office is near the mouth of Blue River where that stream flows into the McKenzie. It was established Jan. 18, 1886, with J. M. Davis first postmaster.

Bluebucket Creek, GRANT, HARNEY. This stream rises just west of Antelope Mountain in the southeastern part of Grant County, and after flowing through Antelope Swale in Harney County, joins a tributary of Malheur River. The name has been applied in recent years to preserve an interesting Oregon romance. The mystery of the location of the real Bluebucket Creek will probably never be solved. Members of the Meek party of 1845 picked up yellow pebbles and hung them under a wagon in a blue wooden bucket. The bucket was either lost or abandoned later, and it was not until some time had elapsed that the emigrants realized that they had possibly found gold. An interesting discussion of the episode and possible locations of Bluebucket Creek may be found in Scott's *History of the Oregon Country*, v. 3, p. 336. It is generally thought that the discovery must have been on a tributary of either the John Day or Malheur River, though suggestions that the locality was near Steens Mountain and also Tygh Valley have also been advanced. Columns have been written on the subject. As far as the writer knows there is nothing to connect the name of the stream in Harney County with the gold discovery, but it is used to preserve the tradition, and may not be far from the true locality.

Bluejoint Lake, LAKE. This is one of the lakes of the Warner Valley. It was named for the bluejoint grass that grows nearby in great profusion.

Bly, KLAMATH. *Bly* was a word of the Klamath Indians meaning up or high. According to Captain O. C. Applegate of Klamath Falls, it meant the old village *up* Sprague River from Yainax. White people appropriated the name and applied it to a town east of the Klamath Indian Reservation. A. S. Gatschet in his *Dictionary of the Klamath Language* (U.S. Geographical and Geological Survey, Washington, D.C., 1890) gives the word as *p'lai*, and says that it meant among other things the Sprague River Valley and sometimes simply the Sprague River as distinguished from the lower country along the Williamson River. *P'laikni* were people living high up, or along the upper reaches of Sprague River. *P'laikni* was also used to mean heavenly, or the Christian God. A post office called Sprague River was established in this vicinity on Nov. 12, 1873, with John W. Gearhart first postmaster. The name of the office was changed to Bly on Jan. 31, 1883.

On May 5, 1945, the community was the scene of the only World War II deaths in the contiguous 48 states. A Japanese balloon carrying incendiary bombs, designed to start forest fires, malfunctioned and landed without detonating. It was disturbed by a picnic group and exploded killing one woman and five children. The authorities did not wish to inform the Japanese of their success and the news was suppressed for several months. Bert Webber in *Silent Siege; Japanese Attacks Against North America in World War II*, gives a detailed account, with pictures, of the Japanese balloon operation and this tragedy. The *Sunday Oregonian*, May 5, 1985, p. F4, has a short article commemorating the 40th anniversary.

Blybach, TILLAMOOK. Blybach post office was on Nehalem River, about four or five miles east of what is now Mohler, about a half a mile east of the place later called Foss and just east of the E. H. Lindsey ranch. It was established Sept. 5, 1892, and was named for the postmaster, Hattie Blybach. The office was closed Mar. 5, 1896.

Boardman, MORROW. Boardman is a station on the Union Pacific Railroad not far from the Columbia River. It was named for Sam Boardman, a well-known resident of Oregon. Boardman has an elevation of 281 feet. Samuel H. Boardman was born in Lowell, Massachusetts, and for some years followed the construction and engineering business. In 1903, while stationed at Leadville, Colorado, he became interested in the Pacific Northwest and came to Oregon. He got a job with A. M. Drake at Bend, but on the way to central Oregon, he ran into smallpox at Shaniko, and lost interest in the Deschutes country. He returned to Portland. In the same year he filed on a homestead where the town of Boardman is now situated. For 13 years Sam and Mrs. Boardman snuffed sand and worked to develop irrigated land. At odd times he was engaged in railroad and highway construction and Mrs. Boardman taught school to help with the expenses. The town was platted in 1916. S. H. Boardman was continually interested in the phenomena of nature, and as a result of employment by the Oregon State Highway Department about 1916, he put his attention to roadside improvement and state park development. He was engaged in this activity for many years and the splendid results of his work are too well known to require comment. For a 1988 appraisal, *see The Park Builders, A History of State Parks in the Pacific Northwest*, chapter 6 by Thomas R. Cox. Boardman died on Jan. 26, 1953. *See Oregon Journal*, Jan. 27, 1953. In the 1960s the town of Boardman was relocated to the south during the construction of the John Day Dam and much of the original townsite is now covered by Lake Umatilla.

Boaz Mountain, JACKSON. Boaz Mountain, elevation about 3500 feet, is in the south part of T 39S, R 3W. It was named for Kinder Boaz who homesteaded nearby in 1876. The name is sometimes spelled Boaze in official records.

Bob Creek, WALLOWA. Bob Creek flows into Snake River in S 10, T 3N, R 50E. J. H. Horner of Enterprise told the compiler in 1928 that the stream was named because Lu Knapper and some companions had an experience with several wildcats in this canyon in the late 1880s.

Boeckman Creek, CLACKAMAS, WASHINGTON. Boeckman Creek flows into Willamette River just east of Wilsonville. It was named for Ernest A. Boeckmann who settled there in 1875.

Bohemia, LANE. Bohemia Mountain in the Bohemia mining district is a well-known geographic feature in eastern Lane County. It was named for a wandering prospector and miner called "Bohemia" Johnson. For nearly 30 years there was a Bohemia post office serving this neighborhood. The office was established on the Douglas County list on Apr. 26, 1893, with John B. McGee acting as the first of seven postmasters. The office oscillated back and forth between Douglas County and Lane County and for the last 15 years of its life it was in Lane County. It was discontinued Dec. 7, 1922, with mail to Disston. It is possible that some of the change in county lists was due to the moving of the Douglas-Lane boundary in this area.

Bohemia Mountain, LANE. This mountain is one of the summits of the Calapooya Mountains, a spur of the Cascade Range, and is in what is generally referred to as the Bohemia mining district. It was named for a wandering mountaineer and prospector, James Johnson, who was supposed to have been born in Bohemia. He was popularly known as "Bohemia" Johnson. He discovered the Bohemia mines in 1863. *See* the *Oregonian*, Jan. 20, 1900, and Scott's *History of the Oregon Country*, v. 1, p. 343.

Bohna, MALHEUR. Railroad company records indicate that this station near Malheur River was named for Ernest Bohna, who formerly owned land nearby. The siding is between Juntura and Harper.

Boiler Bay, LINCOLN. From time to time the *Oregonian* prints an editorial about an Oregon geographic name. These editorials, which are of nice reading length, are frequently erudite and accurate, but beyond all that, they are always sprightly. Such an editorial appeared on Nov. 10, 1942, and the secondary subject was Boiler Bay, though the title was otherwise. Boiler Bay, as many people know, is a little more than a mile north of Depoe Bay and is bounded on the west by a long, low promontory known as Government Point. The bay takes its name from a marine boiler "fast on a rocky shoal that is prolific of butter clams at low tide." The boiler and a shaft are the remains of a small freighter, the *J. Marhoffer*, built at Aberdeen, Washington, in 1907, and engaged in the coastwise trade. The ship was lost on May 18, 1910, enroute from San Francisco to the Columbia River, as the result of the explosion of a gasoline torch. The skipper was able to bring the flaming ship to shore, and the crew, with one exception, was saved. The cook died of exposure. The captain had brought his wife along, and there are stories to the effect that she greatly inspired the shipwrecked sailors by her courage. A letter in the *Oregonian* for Jan. 10, 1943, says that the early name for Boiler Bay was Briggs Landing for a pioneer family. However, a bay and a landing are not exactly the same thing.

Boiling Point, UMATILLA. Boiling Point, elevation about 3250 feet, was a place on old US-30 on Emigrant Hill southeast of Pendleton. It got its name because it was the locality where the old teapot automobiles began to boil over on a hot day. Boiling Point post office was in service from Nov. 1932, to Dec. 1935. Arthur G. Greer was the only postmaster. The fire under this community was extinguished when it was bypassed by the new highway, I-84.

Bolan Creek, JOSEPHINE. For many years this creek and other nearby features have been known variously as Bolan, Bollon or Bolland. After an early investigation of this supposed Indian name, the USBGN adopted the present spelling. However, the publication of the Reinhart recollections, *The Golden Frontier*, provides a different source. Reinhart describes how he and several others crossed the divide from Althouse Creek in 1853 and built a small community at the forks of Sucker Creek. Their buildings, including a bowling alley, were all burned in 1855 by the Indians. Reinhart returned in 1857 to what he says was then known as Bowling Creek where he staked a claim and constructed another alley. His description of how three men carried 30 balls and 20 pins over the divide from

Althouse Creek convinces the compiler that in those days men were strong of purpose as well as back.

Bolon Island, DOUGLAS. Bolon Island is in the Umpqua River north of Reedsport. This island has apparently had several names including Bone, Bowline and Dewars, but Warren P. Reed of Reedsport says that there is no doubt but that it was originally called after a settler by the name of Bolon. The USBGN has adopted the form Bolon.

Bolt, JACKSON. Bolt is on the south side of Rogue River about six miles east of the west boundary of Jackson County, at the point where the old Pacific Highway crosses Foots Creek. This place and Bolt Mountain on the Applegate River about seven miles southwest of Grants Pass, was named for John Bolt, a member of the firm of Kubli and Bolt, pioneer packers and merchants of southern Oregon.

Bonanza, KLAMATH. *Bonanza* is a Spanish word meaning prosperity. This place is said to have been named because of a number of fine springs in the vicinity. Good water is always a source of prosperity in a country that needs irrigation.

Boner Flat, WALLOWA. Boner Flat is in the Wallowa Mountains, in the east part of T 5S, R 45E. It bears the name of George W. Boner who ranged sheep in the vicinity about 1889. Boner Spring in T 3N, R 45E, is named for the same man. The spelling Bonner is wrong.

Boneyard Creek, WALLOWA. This stream flows into Sheep Creek in S 16, T IS, R 48E. One Charles Holmes lost most of his cattle in the canyon during a hard winter in the 1890s and the bleached bones became a landmark.

Bonifer, UMATILLA. Bonifer is a railroad station about two and a half miles southeast of Gibbon. It bears the name of a well-known rancher of the vicinity. The station was named in 1928.

Bonita, LANE. *Bonita* is a Spanish word meaning pretty. The compiler does not know why it was applied to a Lane County post office on Brice Creek. It may have been in compliment to a girl or possibly because of a pleasing outlook. Bonita post office was established Mar. 2, 1904, and operated until Feb. 20, 1908. Fred W. Lee was the first postmaster. Bonita was a little to the southeast of the center of T 22S, R IE.

Bonita, WASHINGTON. This was a station on the Oregon Electric Railway a short distance south of Tigard. It was named by a local resident, Geo. W. Cassaday, who was of a romantic turn of mind and selected the Spanish word for pretty or graceful.

Bonneville, MULTNOMAH. This is an historic spot in Oregon, and for many decades it was a popular picnic grounds for people living along the Columbia River between Portland and The Dalles. The railroad company maintained an "eating house" at Bonneville, where tired travelers paid a modest sum for all they could eat. The station was named for Captain (later Brigadier General) Benjamin L. E. Bonneville, the hero of Washington Irving's *The Adventures of Captain Bon-*

neville. He was born in France in 1795, graduated from West Point and fought with gallantry through the Mexican War. He explored the west from 1832–5, and visited many parts of Oregon and may have been the first white man to go into the Wallowa country. He died in 1878. For details of his life and travels *see* Scott's *History of the Oregon Country*, v. 1, pp. 170 and 297. The locality of Bonneville became nationally known as the site of the Bonneville Dam, construction of which was started in Sept. 1933, by the USCE and completed in July 1938 at a cost of $83 million. The impounded water forms Lake Bonneville. The main features are a dam, two powerhouses, a ship lock and fishways. The dam is across the main or north channel of the Columbia River and is 1090 feet long. The original powerhouse stands across the channel south of Bradford Island and contains generators with a total rated capacity of 518,400 kilowatts. The second powerhouse was constructed on the north side of the river starting Apr. 1978 and finishing Sept. 1986. It is 985 feet long and involved a tremendous excavation along with the relocation of the Washington town of North Bonneville. This addition cost $662 million and has a rated maximum capacity of 558,000 kilowatts. The original ship lock is south of the powerhouse, 76 feet wide by 500 feet long. This is being replaced with a new lock 86 feet wide by 675 feet long, the same dimensions as the locks at the other dams on the Columbia. At normal river stage the lift is 59 feet. This project is scheduled for completion in 1993 at an estimated cost of $330 million. For details of construction and equipment of Bonneville Dam, *see* article by Col. C. R. Moore, *Oregon Blue Book, 1941–1942*, p. 191 and *Water Power in the "Wilderness" The History of Bonneville Dam* by William F Willingham. In 1925 the USBGN, at the suggestion of J. Neilson Barry of Portland, applied the name of Mount Bonneville to a conspicuous peak about three miles south of Wallowa Lake, previously known as Middle Mountain.

Bonney Butte, HOOD RIVER. This butte is in the extreme southwest part of the county, and has an elevation of 5593 feet. Just east of it is Bonney Meadow. These two features were named for a Wasco County stockman, Augustus A. Bonney. He was born in Marion County, Oregon, Apr. 14, 1849, graduated from Willamette University in 1871, and settled in Tygh Valley in 1875.

Boomer Hill, DOUGLAS. Boomer Hill is the high ground at the head of Van Dine Creek a few miles west of Myrtle Creek. George Abdill of Roseburg told the compiler it was named because of the many mountain beaver, *Aplodontia rufa*. These are often called "boomers" for their distinctive sound.

Boone Creek, LANE. Ray Engels, retired USFS ranger at McKenzie Bridge, told the compiler in 1971 that this creek in South Fork McKenzie River drainage was named for one Boone, an early Forest Service cook.

Boone Slough, LINCOLN. This slough and nearby Boone Island bear the name of J. Morris Boone who filed on a homestead there in 1876.

Boones Ferry, CLACKAMAS. Alphonso Boone brought his family to Oregon in 1846 by the Applegate route. He was a grandson of Daniel Boone. About 1847, his son Jesse V. Boone, began to operate a ferry across the Willamette River just west of the present site of the 1-5 highway bridge at Wilsonville. A road leading south from Portland to this ferry was, and still is, known as Boones Ferry road. Another son, Alphonso D. Boone, became associated with his brother Jesse in the ferry. Jesse was killed in 1872. Chloe Donnelly Boone, daughter of Alphonso Boone, married George L. Curry, one time governor of Oregon, for whom Curry County was named. For post office history, *see* Wilsonville.

Booneville Channel, BENTON. This is a branch of the Willamette River flowing on the west side of John Smith Island and Kiger Island, a few miles south of Corvallis. Early maps of the Willamette Valley show the community of Booneville near this point and it is presumed that the channel was named for this community. The name should not be spelled Boonesville.

Booker Creek, LANE. Booker Creek is about five miles northeast of Walton. Andrew W. Booker was an early settler who filed on a homestead along the creek in the 1880s.

Boot Creek, WASCO. Boot Creek is tributary to Ward Creek west of Antelope. J. A. Rooper of Antelope told the author it was named for one Booten who ranched near its mouth in the early days. He was unable to explain the elision.

Booth, DOUGLAS. Booth is a station on the Southern Pacific Company line from Eugene to Coos Bay. It is near the extreme south end of Siltcoos Lake. In June 1948, Mrs. F. K. Davis of Eugene, daughter of the late Robert A. Booth, wrote the compiler that this station was named for her father. He was one of the most prominent western Oregon lumber men and was a founder of the Booth-Kelly Lumber Company of Eugene and elsewhere. Mrs. Davis wrote that R. A. Booth and A. C. Dixon of Eugene bought an island in Siltcoos Lake and that was the reason the railroad station was named Booth. The railroad station was named prior to 1918 but the compiler does not know just when. Booth post office was established near the railroad station in Sept. 1934, with Mrs. Clara P. Law first postmaster. It is reported that there has been some lumbering activity at this place. The post office was discontinued in 1944. The place called Booth in western Douglas County should not be confused with Booth post office in the upper Cow Creek valley, which was named for Winfield S. Booth. That post office was in service from 1907 to 1914. It had previously been called Starvout and in 1914 the name of the office was changed to Azalea.

Booth, JOSEPHINE. Booth was named for its postmaster, Henry E. Booth. The office was established Jan. 22, 1897, and was closed Dec. 31, 1898. An old map shows the place on Rogue River a few miles northwest of Grants Pass and about the same distance southwest of Merlin. The writer does not know the reason for the establishment.

Booth Hill, HOOD RIVER. Named for George Booth, an early settler in the Hood River Valley, who is said to have set out the first commercial orchard in the valley. He sent 20 boxes of Newtowns to the Buffalo fair in 1901 and received a gold medal and sold the apples for $7 a box. It is reported that Booth settled near the foot of the hill in 1885. For many years travelers hesitated to attempt the muddy road up Booth Hill in the winter, but the Mount Hood Loop Highway has solved the difficulty with some change in location from the old road.

Booth Lake, JEFFERSON. Booth Lake is just east of the Cascade Range divide two miles south of Three Fingered Jack. There is no positive information but Pete Cecil of the USFS Remount Station at Fish Lake informed the compiler in 1990 that Booth Lake was probably named for Robert Booth who was a gate keeper for the Santiam Wagon Road at Cache Creek in the old days.

Borax Lake, HARNEY. Borax Lake lies just south of Alvord Lake and is the only habitat of the Borax Lake chub or *Gila boraxobius*. It takes its name from the borax refining that was conducted there from 1898 to 1907. It is interesting to note that the company began as the Twenty Mule Team Borax Company but they failed to register the name. The next year an unconnected concern did register the name and started the now well-known business in California. The Oregon venture then changed to the Rose Valley Borax Company. Shaffer and Baxter have an excellent history of the operation in *OHQ*, v. 73, pp. 228–44. At one time the lake was called Hot Lake for its temperature ranges from 60 to 90 degrees Fahrenheit.

Boren Creek, LANE. Boren Creek flows into Martin Creek about a mile east of Divide. It was named for Charles Boren who took a donation land claim in the vicinity. Boren came to Oregon in 1853 from Illinois.

Boring, CLACKAMAS. The town of Boring was named for W. H. Boring, an old resident of the neighborhood. The district was known to old settlers as the Boring neighborhood, and in 1903 a townsite was platted and called Boring Junction. The Post Office Department and the builders of the interurban railway adopted Boring as the name of the community.

Bosley Butte, CURRY. Bosley Butte is in the southwest part of the county. F. S. Moore of Gold Beach informed the compiler that this peak was named for Julia Bosley, a young woman, who in early days was a member of a party that made a trip to the large prairies lying south of and extending across to the east side of the peak. Miss Bosley was one of the few of the party to ascend to the top of the mountain and it was named in her honor.

Boston Mills, LINN. About 1858 R. C. Finley and associates established a community and grist mill on Calapooia River about a mile and a half east of the present town of Shedd. They called the place Boston Mills, presumably because one or more of the proprietors came from the Massachusetts city. A small butte nearby was named Bunker Hill. The community became a stage stop and made a little growth. Boston Mills post office was established on Sept. 22, 1869, with William Simmons postmaster. Efforts to get the railroad through the place were unsuccessful and Boston Mills began to decline. The railroad was built through Shedd and the post office was moved to that place and the name changed to Shedds on Aug. 28, 1871. Shedds post office was changed to Shedd in 1915.

Boswell Springs, DOUGLAS. Boswell Springs are situated just west of the old Pacific Highway at a point about three miles south of Drain. They were discovered about 1853 by Conrad Snowden who later, along with Dr. Daniel Payton, built a resort hotel. At this time the place was variously known as Snowden Springs and Payton Springs. Captain Benjamin D. Boswell bought the establishment in the 1890s and renamed it for himself. The hotel burned about 1901 and while some of the facilities were rebuilt, the operation slowly declined. The springs were completely abandoned in 1950. Boswell post office was established Apr. 9, 1895, with B. F. Sanders postmaster. The office was closed sometime between 1906 and 1909, but the writer cannot tell the exact date. Stephen Dow Beckham gives more information and a picture in *Land of the Umpqua*, p. 253.

Boulder Creek, MARION. Boulder Creek flows into the North Santiam River east of Detroit. Boulder Creek was named in 1874 by T. W. Davenport of the Marion County road surveying party. *See OHQ*, v. 4, p. 248.

Boundary Creek, DOUGLAS. This tributary of Little River was named by USFS ranger Fred Asam because of its location near the National Forest boundary. The boundary was subsequently moved east near Wolf Creek.

Boundary Creek, LANE. Boundary Creek is so named because it flows into Fall Creek near the west boundary of the Willamette National Forest.

Bour, JOSEPHINE. The mining locality called Bour was given the family name of George, David and John Bour who were engaged in placer operations shortly after the turn of the century. Bour post office was established in May 1906, with Geneva M. Bour first postmaster. The office was discontinued in Feb. 1907. The Bour placer was situated on Illinois River about midway between the mouths of Deer Creek and Josephine Creek, a little downstream from Kerby. Nobody seems to know whether the post office was ever in actual operation or merely authorized. George Bour, living near Kerby in 1948, was of the opinion that the post office never was in service.

Bourbon, SHERMAN. Bourbon was a station on the Union Pacific Railroad, originally the Columbia Southern, about seven or eight miles southeast of Grass Valley. The station was established for a wheat shipping point. Giles French of Moro wrote the compiler about this name on June 1, 1946, as follows: "The name originated directly from that of the famous early-day tipple, which has been preserved to this time and is, in normal times, in conflict with Scotch and Rye. Bourbon you will recognize as the drink of the frontier, the product of good American corn, the elixir of the common man. Some say that when the first construction crew went to Bourbon to stake out the site of the first warehouse they found a bottle that once contained Bourbon and named the place for that reason. Another story is that the crew built the warehouse a little askew of the railroad and the reason for such lack of constructive ability was laid to a superabundance of Bourbon. Bourbon attained some local fame during World War I because Charles (Puss) Schwartz, an elderly bachelor, retired from farming, always gave his occupation as an employee of the 'shipyards at Bourbon.' Even yet Grass Valley residents use it as an occasional excuse for their vagrancy." The compiler thinks that Mr. French is well acquainted with the subject and that this account should be given great weight. It is pleasing to know that these historic names are being preserved in Sherman County.

Bourne, BAKER. Bourne was named for Jonathan Bourne, Jr., of Portland, who was at one time interested in eastern Oregon mines. He was United States senator from Oregon from 1907 to 1913. He was born in New Bedford, Mass., Feb. 23, 1855, and graduated from Harvard in 1877. He came to Portland in the following year and in 1880 was admitted to the Oregon bar. After his term in the Senate, he lived in Washington, D.C., and died there Sept. 1, 1940. Bourne post office was established in Mar. 1895, and discontinued May 31, 1927.

Bowden Crater, MALHEUR. Bowden Crater is a characteristic volcanic vent in the south-central part of the county about six miles northeast of the old Bowden ranch on Rattlesnake Creek. The crater got its name from the ranch, and the title was applied by Dr. Israel C. Russell of the USGS about 1902. *See* USGS Bulletin 217, *Geology of Southwestern Idaho and Southeastern Oregon*, p. 57. Dr. Russell gives an interesting description of this crater, which is unusual in that there seems to be a complete absence of the products of explosive eruptions such as lapilli and volcanic bombs. Bowden Crater is an isolated example of volcanism and Dr. Russell says that the adjacent lava flow, covering about a hundred square miles, apparently all came from the single crater. In 1902 the remains of the raised rim of the central elevation of Bowden Crater was about 600 feet in diameter enclosing a basin about 40 feet deep. The Bowden ranch was on Rattlesnake Creek a little to the south of the center of T 34S, R 41E. A post office named Bowdens was in operation here from Oct. 1890, until Apr. 1898. John B. Bowden was the first postmaster.

Bowen Valley, BAKER. Powder River passes through Bowen Valley just south of Baker. The valley was named for Ira B. Bowen who had a ranch there and a sawmill near Auburn. Ira B. Bowen and his brother, John P. Bowen, were among the earliest settlers in Baker County.

Bowers Slough, BENTON. This slough joins Willamette River from the north about four miles west of Albany. Two brothers of the name of Bowers lived in this vicinity in pioneer days and the slough was named for them.

Bowlus Hill, UMATILLA. This hill is just north of the forks of Walla Walla River. It was named for Louis Bowlus, a nearby landowner of the 1860s.

Bowman Creek, CURRY. Bowman Creek flows into Pacific Ocean north of Cape Ferrelo. It was named for Jonas W. Bowman, an early day blacksmith in Langlois, who homesteaded on the creek in 1879.

Bowman Creek, UMATILLA. Bowman Creek flows into Camas Creek near the Union County line. Henry Bowman took up land near its mouth in 1883.

Bowman Creek, WALLOWA. Bowman Creek is in T 3S, R 43E, and flows into Lostine River. It was named for Robert B. Bowman, who traveled over the trail along the stream to get to his mining claim. This was an old elk trail, and in early days the stream was sometimes called Elk Trail Creek.

Bowman Dam, CROOK. In 1961 Crooked River was dammed southeast of Prineville creating Prineville Reservoir. In 1973 at the instigation of a number of Crook County residents, the dam was named to honor Arthur R. Bowman who was born in Kansas in 1882 and moved to Prineville before World War I. He was active in many local affairs including reclamation work and was a member of both the Oregon and National Reclamation Associations where he was a strong supporter of the Crooked River Project. He died in Bend in 1970.

Box, BENTON, LINCOLN. A post office with the terse name Box was established on the Lincoln County list Jan. 28, 1897, with Mary J. Grier first postmaster. It was on or near Lobster Creek in the extreme southeast corner of Lincoln County. This office seems to have oscillated back and forth across the Benton-Lincoln county line, for it was first in one county, then the other. It was on the Benton County list as of July 21, 1906, but the writer cannot learn what happened to it after that except that it was not a post office in 1913. Polk's *Oregon and Washington Gazetteer* for 1907–08 says that the locality served by Box post office was frequently called Lobster Valley. John E. Davis of the Oregon Department of Agriculture at Salem was kind enough to send in the following story: "Before the post office was established a big box was placed beside the road and when any of the neighbors went to or from Alsea, the nearest post office, they carried the mail for all in Lobster Valley. Mail for those in the valley was placed in this box, from which it found its way into the various homes. None of the names first submitted for the post office was acceptable to the department and it occurred to someone to call it Box. This information came from Thomas Taylor who was postmaster at two different times."

Box Canyon, LANE. Box Canyon opens into the North Fork of Middle Fork Willamette River north of Moolack Mountain. Its descriptive name was given about 1880 by Charles McClane and Major Sears.

Boyd, WASCO. This name is reported as being derived from T. P. Boyd who settled in the vicinity about 1883 and with his sons operated a flour mill. When the post office was established, Mar. 6, 1884, G. H. Barnett, a local merchant, suggested the name of Boyd as being both short and appropriate. John E. Barnett was the first postmaster.

Boyer, LINCOLN, TILLAMOOK. John and Julia Boyer were among the early settlers on Salmon River and they operated the Salmon River toll road 1908–1920. The predecessor of this toll road was called the Elk Trail and it was used at a much earlier date. A post office called Boyer was established Aug. 18, 1910, with Mervin O. Boyer first of three postmasters. The compiler is informed that M. O. Boyer was a son of John Boyer and that the post office was in John Boyer's house. It was in the extreme north end of Lincoln County, probably not more than a mile from the county line. This office was discontinued Mar. 31, 1915. At a much later date the name Boyer was applied to a community on the Salmon River Highway in the extreme southeast corner of Tillamook County and about four miles northeast of the former Boyer post office. This little community now called Boyer is about a half mile northeast of the stone monument erected on the highway in 1926 to John and Julia Boyer. It is where the highway crosses Little Nestucca River. Boyer community does not have a post office as this paragraph is written in May 1948. For information about Salmon River Highway and John Boyer, *see* Leslie M. Scott's article "Military Beginnings of the Salmon River Highway," *OHQ*, v. 35, pp. 228–34.

Boyle Lakes, POLK. These are intermittent ponds about two miles northwest of Rickreall, and they are generally dry in summer. They were named for Dr. James W. Boyle, a pioneer of Oregon, who was born in Virginia in 1815, and came to this state in 1845. Dr. Boyle settled on the land near these lakes in 1850. He married Josephine P. Ford. For additional information about Dr. Boyle, *see* article by Fred Lockley on editorial page of *Oregon Journal*, July 27, 1927.

Bracket Mountain, CLACKAMAS. This mountain, elevation 5018 feet, is in T 6S, R 5E. It was named by W. B. Osborn, Jr., of the USFS, because it resembled a printer's bracket, or brace, placed horizontally with the point up, as follows:

Bradbury, COLUMBIA. This station and a slough in the Columbia River nearby were named for C. A. Bradbury, an early settler. Wilkes shows this slough as Kinak Passage, in an atlas accompanying *U.S. Exploring Expedition*, v. 23, Hydrography, but does not explain the name. The name of the railroad station was later changed to Locoda. For information about C. A. Bradbury, *see* Fred Lockley's story in the *Oregon Journal*, Apr. 15, 1945.

Braden, UMATILLA. Braden post office was in operation on the northern border of the county from Mar. 1891, to Sept. 1891. Jennie Braden was the postmaster. The post office was a room in the Braden home, which was on the lower Walla Walla road about four miles north of Milton. The house disappeared many years ago. It was near what was later called the Engel Chapel. It was in S 15, T 6N, R 45E.

Bradetich Well, DESCHUTES. Bradetich Well in Millican Valley was named for George and John Bradetich who established the Pine Mountain spread of Black Angus cattle. The two brothers came from southern Europe and started a small dairy farm in Bend. After this had grown to be one of the best known in the state, the brothers began their beef cattle operation. In 1969 George Bradetich was still active and running the ranch with his son Phil.

Bradford Island, MULTNOMAH. This island in the Columbia River has become very well known as a result of the Bonneville Dam. The south end of the dam itself is on the island, and much of the fish ladder structure. The north end of the original powerhouse is also on the island. The island was named for Daniel F. and

Putnam Bradford, brothers, who were pioneer steamboat operators on the Co-lumbia River. Among other things they rebuilt the portage road at the Cascades in 1856. Later another portage road was built on the south side of the river, and eventually both were absorbed by the Oregon Steam Navigation Company. For details of the fight with Indians on this island *see* OPA *Transactions* for 1896. Asser-tions that Bradford Island is the Strawberry Island of Lewis and Clark are not substantiated by the maps of the explorers. It is apparent from both text and maps that Lewis and Clark used the name Brant Island for what is now known as Bradford Island. Their Strawberry Island is now Hamilton Island, close to the north bank. However, on the return journey, Patrick Gass used the name Straw-berry Island in error for what was then Brant Island, now Bradford. This was on the evening of Apr. 9, 1806. The Astorians had the Gass journals but not those of Lewis and Clark, and as a result applied the name Strawberry Island to the wrong landmark. This error has been perpetuated by several subsequent editors and writers.

Bradley Creek, DOUGLAS. John V. Bradley was born in Missouri in 1828. He came to Oregon and served under Nesmith in the Indian Wars. In the 1850s he settled near Glide where he took a donation land claim. Bradley was married to Cynthia Tipton.

Bradley Trail, DOUGLAS. This trail is a well-known route of travel along the North Umpqua River in the eastern part of the county. It was named for William Bradley, a pioneer trapper and mountain stockman, who is said to have been born near Oakland, and to have worked his way into the headwaters of the North Umpqua River as early as 1875, when he was a young man. He traded deer meat and hides with the Indians, taking ponies in return, which he sold in Eugene and other points. This trade opened up a trail across the Cascade Range, which has ever since been known as the Bradley Trail, and much of it has been put on modern standards by the USFS. Bradley Creek, a tributary of the North Umpqua rising west of Windigo Butte, also bears the name of the same man. Bradley was killed by a horse in 1909, dying near his lonely cabin at Illahe.

Bradwood, CLATSOP. The Bradley-Woodward Lumber Company was incor-porated July 15, 1930, and one of its activities was the development of a mill and community on the south bank of the Columbia River about two miles upstream from Clifton. The name of the new town, Bradwood, was made synthetically from the name of the company. After the supply of large, old growth timber was exhausted, the mill closed permanently in June 1962. A major fire in 1965 destroyed most of the facilities and by 1984 only five residents remained. Bradwood post office was established Apr. 17, 1931 and closed along with the mill. The *Sunday Oregonian*, Jan. 8, 1984, section E, devotes a full page with pictures to the then current situation.

Brandenburg Butte, DESCHUTES, LINN. In 1986 the USFS needed names for two small features south of Santiam Pass because the area between US-20 and Big

Lake was being heavily used by cross country skiers and other winter sports enthusiasts. Brandenburg Butte is the 4888 foot high protuberance on the north ridge of Mount Washington just east of Big Lake. The name was selected to commemorate John W. Brandenburg, Sr., who came to Linn County about 1850. He was with Andrew Wiley in the 1859 road viewing party. Brandenburg died of typhoid fever in 1864 at age 60 but his son John, Jr., was also a well-known citizen of Linn County and one time deputy sheriff. The second feature, Claypool Butte, immediately to the north and 4851 feet high, was named for Joseph Claypool, a member of a family prominent in Linn and Crook counties. He was born in 1850 and as a young man tended the affairs of the Fish Lake station west of Lost Lake.

Brandt, DOUGLAS. This station on the Southern Pacific Company line in Cow Creek canyon was probably named for one of the Brandt family whose three members working in various capacities for the early Oregon & California Rail Road included Superintendent John Brandt, Jr.

Brandy Bar, DOUGLAS. Brandy Bar is in Umpqua River about fifteen miles east of Reedsport. On Aug. 6, 1850, the schooner *Samuel Roberts* of the Klamath Exploring Expedition grounded on this bar and the party was forced to spend the night there. There was some brandy aboard the ship which was used too freely during the night to the exasperation of the owner. The place was called Brandy Bar because of this incident. *See OHQ*, v. 17, p. 355.

Braton Hollow, JACKSON. Braton Hollow runs into Evans Creek from the south above Wimer. Darlin Brayton took up government land in the area in 1885.

Braunsport, COLUMBIA. Braunsport post office was established in Nov. 1891, with Johann B. Braun postmaster. The office operated under Braun's guidance until Nov. 9, 1901, when it was discontinued. In Dec. 1945, Omar C. Spencer of the Portland bar wrote the compiler that Braunsport was on Beaver Creek approximately five miles southwest of Vernonia, and that it was named for the first postmaster, who was a native of Germany. Mr. Spencer added the historical fact that there was a school at this place called Braunsport School, where he, Mr. Spencer, taught four months during the summer of 1897. The place on the USGS Vernonia quadrangle of 1979 shown as Braun is a little to the north of Braunsport.

Bravo Creek, CURRY. This tributary of North Fork Chetco River was named for cattleman John C. Bravo who came to this area in 1892 from Switzerland.

Bray Mountain, COOS. Bray Mountain is near the headwaters of Johnson Creek ten miles southwest of Powers. Dodge in *Pioneer History of Coos and Curry Counties* has several references to Iredel Bray. He says that Bray was a member of the "Coarse Gold" Johnson party that discovered gold on Johnson Creek in 1854 and that he subsequently had a cabin nearby during the Indian troubles of 1855. The diary of John Evans, the discoverer of the Port Orford meteorite, under date of Sunday, July 19, 1856, tells of meeting Bray near what is now the Powers Ranch and that Bray invited the party to partake of two freshly killed bear hanging in his cabin. Bray later patented a homestead near the present community of Powers.

Bray Point, LANE. Bray Point was named for a local family. The promontory is about a third of a mile south of Bob Creek and just north of Agate Creek. While not large, Bray Point presents a bold front to the sea and affords a fine view to travelers on US-101, the Oregon Coast Highway.

Braymill, KLAMATH. This post office had a comparatively short life. The name of the office was coined by taking the last name of W. M. Bray, principal owner of the Sprague River Company, which operated a sawmill at that point, and combining it with the word "mill." Surely ingenuity could go no further. Braymill station was formerly called Meva.

Breeds Flat, WASCO. In 1902 Walter L. Breed filed for a homestead on this flat between the forks of Mill Creek.

Breitenbush, MARION. Breitenbush post office and Breitenbush Hot Springs, on Breitenbush River about ten miles northeast and upstream from Detroit, got their names from the river. Breitenbush post office was established Mar. 21, 1928 with Merle D. Bruckman postmaster and closed Sept. 30, 1953 with mail to Detroit.

Breitenbush River, MARION. John Minto's account of the 1873 exploring party in *OHQ*, v. 4, p. 248, says that this river was named for John Breitenbush, a pioneer hunter who preceded them in the North Santiam River region. He gives no other information about the man but *Reminiscences of Southern Oregon Pioneers* contains a 1938 interview with Frederick R. Breitenbusher who was born at Buena Vista in 1862. Breitenbusher says that the pioneer hunter was his father, Lewis Breitenbusher, who crossed the plains in 1849 and after living in Buena Vista, moved to Linn County where he stayed for 12 years. The form Breitenbush has been firmly established since Minto's time.

Brennan Palisades, CROOK. The Brennan Palisades are a group of eroded volcanic pillars on Evans Creek, a tributary of Mill Creek, about 15 miles east of Prineville. They are named for Claude C. Brennan, a member of an early Crook County family, who operated an adjoining ranch for many years prior to his death in 1983. Phil Brogan has an article with picture in the Bend *Bulletin*, Feb. 14, 1970.

Brenner Canyon, MORROW. This canyon which empties into Rhea Creek was probably named for John E. Brenner who filed for a homestead there about the time of World War I. Brenner was the son or grandson of Peter Brenner, an early Morrow County settler, who came to the Eightmile area in the 1880s.

Brewer Ranch, LAKE. Ellsbury Brewer took up the land where this ranch stands on Bridge Creek prior to World War I.

Brewer Reservoir, JEFFERSON. In 1874 William Brewer took a homestead where Awbrey Creek joins Hay Creek. Hay Creek was later dammed and the reservoir is named for this early settler.

Brewster, LINN. This station north of Lebanon was named for Alexander Brewster, on whose land it was situated.

Brice Creek, LANE. This stream rises on the western slopes of the Cascade

Range and flows into Row River. It was named for Frank Brass, a prospector of early days. Brass fell into the stream on a prospecting trip and a companion named the creek for him. Time has brought about the change in spelling. The stream was formerly called Frank Brice Creek, but in 1943, the USBGN, in the interest of simplicity adopted the style Brice Creek. Brice Creek seems to be the form used locally.

Bridal Veil Falls, MULTNOMAH. The romantically inclined never fail to name at least one important waterfall in a state Bridal Veil. The falls in Oregon bearing this name are quite attractive during the higher stages of water, even though they are to a certain extent obscured by the bridge of the Historic Columbia River Highway. They have borne this name since pioneer days. There is a community nearby named Bridal Veil. The creek forming the falls is also known as Bridal Veil Creek. It heads on Larch Mountain.

Bridge, COOS. Bridge was a post office and community on Middle Fork Coquille River about eleven miles east of Myrtle Point, named for a nearby bridge over the stream. A post office named Angora served this locality, in part, in earlier days. It was established in Aug. 1883, and was closed in May 1894. Bridge post office was established July 6, 1894, with Thomas E. Manly postmaster. An effort was made to call the reestablished office Angora but for some reason the Post Office Department did not approve of the suggestion. It seems probable that the office at Bridge was not in the same place as the former office of Angora, but the records are not clear.

Bridge Creek, GRANT. Bridge Creek lay along the first route of travel from northeastern Oregon into the John Day mines. This route was at first nothing more than a trail. During the mining excitement of the early 1860s, the packers made some improvements so their work could be carried on more expeditiously, and among other things they built some pole bridges over what is now Bridge Creek. This fact gave rise to the name. The stream is southwest of Austin.

Bridge Creek, MARION. Bridge Creek is a stream southwest of Silverton, the waters of which find their way into Abiqua Creek, but the compiler does not know just how. He has been told that the stream was named in pioneer days because of a convenient bridge, but he does not know its location. Bridge Creek post office was established near this stream in Nov. 1919, and operated until Nov. 1923, when it was closed to Hullt. Edward Trenter was the only postmaster. This office was a little to the east of Hullt, near the north quartercorner of S 9, T 8S, R 2E. It was very close to the old Bridge Creek school and the two establishments were both named for the stream. In 1932–33 a new post office called Cedar Camp was in service in the same location with Mrs. Edith M. Filer, postmaster. Cedar Camp was apparently named because of the cedar lumber and shingle making in the vicinity.

Bridge Creek, WHEELER. This stream heads in the mountains in the south part of the county, and flows into John Day River. One branch flows through Mitchell. H. H. Bancroft in his *History of Oregon,* v. 1, p. 787, says that it was named because Shoeman and Wadley, California prospectors, built a small bridge over it of juniper logs, while enroute to the John Day mines. This was about 1862. On July 2, 1868, a post office named Bridge Creek was established in what is now Wheeler County with Alfred Sutton postmaster. Sutton was a prominent Wasco and Wheeler county pioneer. Sutton Mountain north of Mitchell bears his name. Bridge Creek post office, which was finally closed in 1882, was on the Sutton place, which was very close to the mouth of the stream, where it joined John Day River.

Bridgeport, BAKER. C.A. Moore, of Baker, in a letter in the *Oregonian,* Aug. 7, 1926, p. 8, gives the early history of this community. In 1861–63 considerable placer gold was discovered at Clark Creek, several miles southeast of Bridgeport. Supplies were packed from Baker over the old Creighton road, crossing Burnt River near where Hereford now is, and then down the river on the south side to these mines, where there were some stores and a post office. Bridgeport is on the south bank of the river, which could not then be forded. The need for a wagon road and a shorter route to Clark Creek led Dr. Jacob M. Boyd and James W. Virtue and associates, in 1868, to begin the construction of a toll road from Baker to what is now Bridgeport, and in 1869 this road was made passable for the entire distance. At the south end of the road, where it crossed the river, there was a bridge some 200 feet long, and since this was the terminus of the toll road, it was decided to call the place Bridgeport.

Bridgeport, POLK. Bridgeport is an unorganized locality on Little Luckiamute River about three miles east or downstream from Falls City. It is said to have been named for a pioneer bridge over the stream, but the compiler does not know the exact location of the structure. Bridge Port post office was established June 1, 1854, with Samuel T. Scott first postmaster. The name of the office was very soon changed to Bridgeport. It continued in operation until Jan. 13, 1874.

Briedwell, YAMHILL. Briedwell was a station on the Oregonian Railway narrow gauge line, later the Southern Pacific, at a point about two miles west of Amity, in the south part of the county. It was named for John W. Briedwell, a local resident, who was the first postmaster. Briedwell post office was established Aug. 16, 1887, and discontinued Oct. 31, 1888. Recent maps show a Briedwell School at this place, but the rest of the community is a thing of the past.

Briem Creek, LANE. Briem Creek on the south slopes of Hehe Mountain about ten miles south of Blue River was named for Alfred J. Briem, USFS district ranger in the area for 17 years.

Briggs Landing, LINCOLN. Briggs Landing, in Boiler Bay, was named for Joe Briggs, who lived nearby.

Briggson, UMATILLA. Briggson post office served an area about eight miles east-southeast and up in the Blue Mountains from Weston in what is known as the Wildhorse Mountain district. One Dan Briggs fostered the idea of an office in this locality, but it was decided to put it at the McCorkell place rather than at the

Briggs ranch, as Briggs lived too far back in the mountains. However, when the office was established, it was named in his honor. Briggson post office was established June 2, 1896, with William McCorkell first and only postmaster. The office was closed Apr. 30, 1909, with papers to Weston.

Brigham Creek, WALLOWA. Brigham Creek flows into Bear Gulch from the west in S 26, T 1S, R 47E. It was named in pioneer days because of an event that suggested Mormonism, hence the use of Brigham Young's first name.

Brighton, TILLAMOOK. This post office and railroad station were near the mouth of Nehalem River, in the northwest part of the county. The town was platted about 1910 with the name of Brighton Beach although it is not directly on the ocean. This place, together with many others in the United States, was named for Brighton, the fashionable seashore resort on the south coast of England. The post office was established May 21, 1912 with James R. Minich first postmaster and closed Mar. 15, 1954.

Brightwood, CLACKAMAS. Brightwood is said to have been named by a Mr. Alcorn, a property owner, because of the pleasing effect of the sun shining on the cottonwood trees in the spring. The first local post office was called Salmon, because it was very close to Salmon River, a stream named in pioneer days. Salmon post office was established in Apr. 1891, with Winnie McIntyre first postmaster. The name of this office was changed to Brightwood on May 6, 1910. Brightwood is about a quarter of a mile east of Salmon River on the old Mount Hood Loop Highway. The compiler does not know if the post office was moved this distance when the name was changed in 1910, or at some other time.

Bristow Prairie, LANE. This prairie on the summit of the Calapooya Mountains was named for Elijah Bristow, the founder of Pleasant Hill, near Goshen. *See* Pleasant Hill. Bristow hunted on the prairie. He was born in Virginia in 1788, and came to Oregon in 1846. *See* Walling's *History of Lane County*, p. 475.

Britt Creek, DOUGLAS. This creek one mile west of Idleyld Park bears the name of William Britt who was born in Ireland and came to the United States in 1877. He homesteaded near the mouth of the creek where he built a hotel and kept the travel. Britt died in 1900, age 81 years.

Britten, BAKER. Britten was a post office in the mining district in the Blue Mountains between Baker City and Sumpter, named for a local family. The office was established Sept. 25, 1884, with Elizabeth E. Britten postmaster. Britten post office was discontinued May 9, 1893.

Broadacres, MARION. About the time the Oregon Electric was opened for service between Portland and Salem in 1908, a station with the descriptive name Broadacres was established at a point about three miles west of Hubbard. There was not a great deal of business there at first, but in a few years it was necessary to have a post office. This office called Broadacres was opened in June 1914, and was discontinued in Dec. 1928, with the business turned over to Hubbard. John R. Foulds was the first postmaster.

Broadbent, COOS. Broadbent was named for C. E. Broadbent, who built a cheese factory in the community some time prior to the date the post office was established, which was in 1916.

Broadmead, POLK. Mead is the Anglo-Saxon word for meadow, and Broadmead means Broadmeadow. The post office was established Jan. 8, 1915, with Wm. H. Morris postmaster. The office was closed in 1942 and Broadmead no longer exists as a community.

Broady Creek, WALLOWA. This stream is in the northeast part of the county. It was named for a broad-horned cow that belonged to Tom Green. She ranged along this stream.

Brock Creek, LANE. This creek is 15 miles northeast of Oakridge. It was named for Stewart Brock who had a cabin and a small ranch nearby before the turn of the century. Earl Walker, a long time resident of Oakridge, added that Brock owned a farm near Shedd to which he later returned.

Brockway, DOUGLAS. Brockway, a little to the southwest of Roseburg, was once known as Civil Bend, a name said to refer to the boisterous activity of visitors to the horseraces. Civil Bend post office was in service from Sept. 1881, to Oct. 1888. When the office was reestablished in 1889, postal authorities objected to a name with two words, so a new name was selected in honor of B. B. Brockway, a pioneer resident. *See* Civil Bend.

Brogan, MALHEUR. This town was started by D. M. Brogan and was given his name in 1909. It is in the north part of the county at what was the north end of the now abandoned Union Pacific Railroad Company's branch from Vale.

Brogan Creek, CROOK. Phil Brogan of Bend informed the compiler in 1970 that this tributary of East Fork Mill Creek was named for his great uncle, Tom Brogan of Antelope, who used the area for summer graze. The tenor of those times is cogently described by Mr. Brogan's comment: "He was a stern old guy, and I certainly earned my $1 a day, plus board and bunk."

Broken Hand, DESCHUTES. This prominent gendarme or rock outcrop is on the east ridge of Broken Top about one and one half miles east of the summit. It has an elevation of 8376 feet. In 1966 Judge John F. Kilkenny proposed the name to honor Thomas "Broken Hand" Fitzpatrick who passed through central Oregon as a scout with Fremont in the fall of 1843. Fitzpatrick, though a man of many accomplishments, is less remembered than his friends and contemporaries who included Smith, Meek, Carson and Bridger. He was with the party that discovered South Pass in 1824 and he served as scout and guide for Father DeSmet, Fremont, Kearney and numerous others. Later he was Indian Agent for the Upper Platte and arranged the council of 1851 at Fort Laramie. Fitzpatrick was born in Ireland in 1799 and died in Washington, D.C., Feb. 7, 1854. He acquired his nickname early in his career when a rifle exploded and crippled his left hand. Hafen and Ghent have an excellent biography in *Broken Hand, The Story of Thomas Fitzpatrick, Chief of the Mountain Men.*

Broken Top, DESCHUTES. Although badly shattered, this mountain is one of the important peaks in the Cascade Range. It is southeast of South Sister and has an elevation of 9165 feet. From the aspect of its jagged summit it is not difficult to see why it was named. On its northern slope is Bend Glacier, on its south slope is Crook Glacier.

Brokencot Creek, CURRY. This stream is in the southeast part of the county in the Siskiyou Mountains. It rises east of Chetco Peak, and flows northward into Chetco River. It was named for Brokencot Camp, an old stopping place near its headwaters, distinguished by some worn out and now memorialized specimens of camp equipment.

Brookings, CURRY. Brookings was founded about 1908 as a company town for the Brookings Lumber & Box Company. John E. Brookings was president and as chief executive officer lived on the Pacific Coast, while his cousin, Robert S. Brookings, provided the major financial support. Robert Brookings lived in the east and devoted much of his time to semi-diplomatic missions and support of the arts. It was he who hired Bernard Maybeck, a San Francisco architect later involved in the Panama-Pacific Exposition, to lay out the townsite, certainly the only early plat in Oregon to receive the attention of such a qualified professional. Brookings post office was established Jan. 4, 1913.

Brooks, MARION. This is a station on the main line of the Southern Pacific Company nine miles north of Salem. It was named for Linus Brooks, who was born in Ohio in 1805, and came to Oregon from Illinois in 1850 and settled near the present site of the community. For additional information about the Brooks family, *see* editorial page of the *Oregon Journal*, June 25, 1927.

Brooks Meadows, HOOD RIVER. Brooks Meadows are drained by one of the branches of Dog River. These meadows were named for Caleb G. Brooks, who began to run cattle there about 1877. Brooks was a native of Iowa, and came to The Dalles with his family about 1870. He died in 1899, but his sons continued to use Brooks Meadows for cattle until about 1920.

Brooten Mountain, TILLAMOOK. Brooten Mountain has an elevation of 533 feet and forms the high ground east of Pacific City and south of Nestucca River. Shortly after World War I, H. H. Brooten uncovered a deposit of fossil kelp at the base of this mountain. He capitalized upon it through an advertising campaign worthy of the television claims of modern headache remedies and customers came from far and near to soak in the odoriferous baths. The name is all that remains to show for Mr. Brooten's enterprise.

Brophy Hill, JACKSON. Brophy Hill is two miles east of Lakecreek. Vern Brophy Whome was a prominent rancher near Lakecreek in the 1930s and the hill is called by his middle name.

Brothers, DESCHUTES. Brothers is on the Central Oregon Highway, US-20, between Bend and Burns, in the southeast part of the county. Brothers post office was established in Sept. 1913, with Patrick H. Coffey first postmaster. Phil Brogan of Bend told the compiler there were several fraternal family groups that settled in the area of whom the various Stenkamp brothers comprised one of the more notable. He thought the community was named for the many homesteading brothers and not in contradistinction to Sisters, the community northwest of Bend. However, an article by Charles Hutchinson in the Prineville *Central Oregonian*, Feb. 26, 1970, p. 6, gives a different origin. Sumner Houston, born in the Bear Creek area and the son of early homesteader Charley Houston, was working at the Frank Percival ranch east of Pine Mountain. A name was needed for a sheep camp and Houston noted three nearby similar hills with the Three Sisters looming in the background. He suggested the name Three Brothers Sheep Camp. The hills became known as the Three Brothers and the name, in abbreviated form, was attached to the post office when it was founded some years later.

Broughton, LANE. Broughton post office was named for the family of Thomas Broughton, the first and only postmaster. He was appointed May 8, 1891, and served until May 1, 1893. The compiler has been unable to get information about the exact location of this post office but it probably was slightly west of Elmira.

Broughton Bluff, MULTNOMAH. Lieutenant William Robert Broughton, commander of the armed tender *Chatham* of the Vancouver expedition, explored the Columbia River in the fall of 1792, and as far as known, was the first white man to visit the vicinity of the mouth of Willamette River. Broughton reached a point east of Troutdale on Oct. 30, 1792. He wrote quite accurately of the geography of the mouth of Sandy River, and his maps, though on a small scale, were carefully made. The bluff east of Troutdale has always been a prominent landmark, but bore no name until 1926, when at the request of the Girl Scouts of Portland, the USBGN officially adopted for it the name of Broughton Bluff. William Robert Broughton was born in England in 1762. He entered the Royal Navy at an early age and in 1776 after the battle of Bunker Hill he and his commanding officer, while engaging in a salvage operation, were captured by American troops. After the war he served in various capacities and in 1791 in command of the *Chatham*, discovered and named the Chatham Islands off New Zealand. His subsequent activities with Vancouver are well known. In later years he continued exploration and in 1797 was wrecked off the coast of Formosa with his ship *Providence*. Broughton then served in the Java Sea, retired as captain and died in Italy in 1821. For further details of his life, *see* Meany's *Vancouver's Discovery of Puget Sound*, p. 264. In the summer of 1974, Sir Charles Madden visited Portland to open the Oregon Historical Society's memorable Cook Exhibition. To commemorate the exploration by the British Navy, he participated in naming Chatham Island and Broughton Reach in the Columbia River. Broughton Reach is the stretch of the river running east from Flag Island where Broughton looked upstream for 15 miles and saw that the Columbia did not rise on Mount Hood but extended farther inland.

Brower, MULTNOMAH. Brower was the name of a post office in the hills about two miles south-southeast of Bridal Veil at the north base of Pepper Mountain. It was named for George W. Brower who, with Eldridge H. Thompson, had a logging and lumber business thereabouts in the 1890s. Brower post office was established Dec. 20, 1889, with Robert C. Bell first postmaster. The compiler does not know the closing date, but it was probably about 1895.

Brown, BENTON. Brown post office was established July 5, 1902, with Clara Huggins first and only postmaster. The office was closed Mar. 10, 1903. Robert Johnson informed the compiler that the office was situated at the home of William and Clara Huggins on the Brown place some eight or ten miles southwest of Corvallis.

Brown Creek, GILLIAM. Brown and Buckhorn creeks join to form Lone Rock Creek a mile south of Lonerock. Brown Creek is named for William C. Brown who ranched and ran sheep along the creek in the 1880s. In 1971, Scott Brown, William Brown's son then age 92 years, provided this information to Judge John F. Kilkenny.

Brown Meadows, WALLOWA. These meadows are in s 16, T 4N, R 41E. They bear the name of John Brown, a homesteader.

Brown Mountain, WALLOWA. This is a high peak in the Wallowa Mountains northwest of Eagle Cap. It was named because of its characteristic color near the top.

Brownlee, BAKER. Two men named Brown and Lee, uncle and nephew, settled on the Idaho side of Snake River in the 1860s. Later on, the men established a ferry across the river and when the railroad was built down the Oregon side, the company named the station Brownlee. Brownlee post office was established Dec. 17, 1910, and operated intermittently until July 1943. In 1959 the Idaho Power Company completed Brownlee Dam. This 395 foot high dam forms a slackwater pool extending to within ten miles of Weiser and has a maximum generating capacity of 450,000 kilowatts.

Browns Mountain, DESCHUTES. Browns Mountain, elevation 5330 feet, is south of Crane Prairie, and Browns Creek is nearby. These features were named for John A. Brown, a black homesteader who settled in the neighborhood. Brown was a trapper and hunter and also ran some stock. C. J. Keefer is authority for the statement that he always paid his bills in gold which led to the notion that gold was buried near the homestead. Brown died in Prineville in 1903 but rumors of buried treasure near Crane Prairie have been more durable.

Brownsboro, JACKSON. This place was named in 1853 for Henry R. Brown, on whose land the community was established. Brownsboro is on Little Butte Creek. A post office was established in the locality in Feb. 1873, with the name Brownsborough and with John Bilger first of a long list of postmasters. The name of the office was changed to Brownsboro on June 25, 1892.

Brownsmead, CLATSOP. This community developed on the bank of the Columbia River as the result of diking and reclamation, carried on by W. G. Brown, a well-known engineer of Portland. His name coupled with the Anglo-Saxon word for meadow formed the name of the community. It was formerly known as Brody.

Brownsville, LINN. Brownsville is on the Calapooia River near the foothills of the Cascade Range, and has an elevation of 356 feet. It was laid out in 1853, and named by James Blakely in honor of Hugh L. Brown, who started the first store there. Both these men were pioneers of 1846. Blakely built the first house in the fall of 1846. For biography and portrait of Blakely, *see* the *Oregonian*, Apr. 17, 1901, p. 10. For description of Brownsville in 1889, the *Oregonian*, Jan. 18, 1890. For description in 1894, Jan. 1, 1895, p. 11. Postal records show that Brownsville post office was established on Jan. 8, 1850, with the name Calapooya with H. H. Spalding first postmaster. This was changed to Brownsville on May 18, 1859.

Browntown, JOSEPHINE. This place is a relic of the past. It was a mining town on Althouse Creek, about three miles south of Holland. Walling, in his *History of Southern Oregon*, p. 455 says that it was named for one Webfoot Brown, the pioneer Brown of the vicinity, and that at one time the place had 500 inhabitants.

Bruce, BENTON. Bruce is the name of a small community on the Pacific Highway West about ten miles south of Corvallis. It is on the Major James Bruce land claim and was named on that account. A post office named Bruce was established in July 1900, with Lucinda Norwood first postmaster. The office was closed in May 1905.

Bruces Bones Creek, CURRY. John Quiner of the OSHD told of the naming of this creek north of Cape Ferrelo. In the 1950s Bruce Schilling was a chainman with the crew completing the survey for the new alignment of US-101. At the end of the day when the crew started to leave, Schilling headed in the wrong direction and because of the heavy brush had considerable difficulty finding his way out of the deep gully. The rest of the party saw him but could not make themselves heard over the sound of the surf. Ron Brazeau, the transitman, then commented that they would find Bruce's parched bones next spring when they returned. No doubt the story bore considerable repeating and the name was soon firmly fixed.

Brush College, POLK. Brush College is situated in the southeast part of the Eola Hills. It was named because of the character of the nearby ground cover. For a story about Brush College school and community by Mrs. W. N. Crawford, *see* Salem *Statesman*, Oct. 8, 1931.

Brush Creek, CURRY. Brush Creek drains an area southeast of Port Orford and flows into Pacific Ocean just north of Humbug Mountain. It seems to be the consensus in Curry County that this stream was named for Gilbert Brush, a young Texan, who was a member of the T'Vault exploring party in those parts in 1851. To say that he had hair-raising adventures is apposite, since Coquille Indians "lifted" part of his scalp. *See* Bancroft's *History of Oregon*, v. 2, pp. 196–200, and Dodge's *Pioneer History of Coos and Curry Counties*, p. 26. Preston's *Map of Oregon*, 1856, shows this stream as Savage Creek, but Preston possibly confused it with Euchre Creek, a little further south, which George Davidson, in *Coast Pilot*, 1889 says was called Savage Creek. *See* Euchre Creek. Preston's knowledge of Curry County geography was necessarily sketchy.

Brushy Creek, WALLOWA. Brushy Creek flows into Little Sheep Creek approximately 12 miles east of Enterprise. It was named because of the unusually dense brush growing along its banks. The first homesteader on this stream was William Waln.

Bryan Creek, YAMHILL. Bryan Creek in the Chehalem Valley was probably named for Tom Bryan who farmed the lower reaches in the early days. Bryan was one of nine sons of Francis and Sarah Bryan who lived north of Newberg. All the sons as well as two daughters married into local pioneer families so the name was well known.

Bryant Lake, LINN. This is a small slough lake about a mile west of Albany. It was named for Hub Bryant, a pioneer resident. Bryant Park, in Albany, was given to the city by the same man. He owned considerable land in the vicinity of the lake.

Buchanan, HARNEY. Buchanan is a locality about 20 miles east of Burns on the Central Oregon Highway where the highway begins to climb up out of Harney Valley. The place bears the name of a local family. Buchanan post office was established on May 1, 1911, with Hattie E. Buchanan first postmaster. The office was closed June 30, 1919, but the place is still referred to as Buchanan. For biography of Joseph W. Buchanan and his wife, Hattie, *see History of Baker, Grant, Malheur and Harney Counties*, p. 715.

Buck Creek, MULTNOMAH. This stream flows into Sandy River just north of Gordon Creek. It has also been known as Trapper Creek, but the USGS has adopted the name Buck Creek, which seems to represent the best local use.

Buck Fork, DOUGLAS. Buck Fork was the name of a post office on Buck Fork, a tributary of North Myrtle Creek. Fred Asam, an early USFS ranger, homesteaded nearby before the creek was named and was one of the settlers instrumental in establishing the office. During a discussion regarding a name, Asam remarked: "I have just killed a forked horn buck. Why not call it Buck Fork?" The office was in operation from Sept. 1910 until Aug. 1927. Nearby Buck Peak was apparently named for the stream.

Buck Island, KLAMATH. Buck Island is near the lower end of Upper Klamath Lake. It is one of many features in Oregon named for some event connected with a deer. In pioneer days it was called Rattlesnake Island.

Buck Peak, HOOD RIVER, MULTNOMAH. This peak west of Lost Lake was named in July 1906 by R. S. Shelley of the USFS. Shelley and Ralph Lewis were locating trail and came across a large buck sunning himself near the summit.

Buck Point, JACKSON. Buck point is south of Willow Creek Reservoir near Mount McLoughlin and Buck Point Creek rises on its north slope. They apparently are named for Norman L. Buck who took up land along the creek in 1902.

Buck Rock, JACKSON. Buck Rock is a well-known landmark northeast of Trail.

It was named in 1860 by Albert Winkel, a pioneer hunter and trapper. Its top was frequented by deer.

Bucket Lake, BAKER. Bucket Lake is west of Elkhorn Peak. Herbert Ensminger of Haines stated in 1968 that in 1920 he, Raymond Ward and Omar Maxwell stocked Bucket Lake and nearby Rock Creek Lake with trout. The fish were trucked to Eilertson Meadow and taken the rest of the way by pack train. Bucket Lake was already so called because of the bucketlike basin it is in.

Buckhorn Springs, WALLOWA. Buckhorn Springs are well known. They are in T 3N, R 48E. The place was frequented by deer and many horns were shed there. Campers found the horns and made piles of them.

Buckneck Mountain, DOUGLAS. This mountain is on the divide between Rogue River and North Umpqua River, northwest of Crater Lake, and has an elevation of 6173 feet. The origin of the name is not known, but it was applied by a sheepherder some time prior to 1906.

Buckskin Peak, CURRY, JOSEPHINE. This peak, elevation 3925 feet, is in the Siskiyou Mountains slightly more than six miles north of the Oregon-California state line. The summit of the peak is covered with the so-called "buckskin boulders." They are of many sizes but all of peculiar buckskin color.

Budd Creek, COOS. Budd Creek bears the name of an early settler. It flows into Cunningham Creek northwest of Coquille.

Buell, POLK. Buell is in the northern part of the county, and was named for Elias Buell, who started a mill there and a small store in pioneer days. Elias Buell's land office certificate was numbered 4165. Buell post office was established in Mar. 1900.

Buena Vista, POLK. The compiler was informed by E. M. Croisan, of Salem, that Buena Vista was named by his grandfather, Reason B. Hall, whose donation land claim formed the site of the community. Hall was born in Georgia in 1791, and settled on his land claim in 1847. He named Buena Vista about 1850, because some of his relatives participated in the battle of Buena Vista in Mexico. About the time he named the community, he started Halls Ferry across the Willamette River. James A. O'Neal built a warehouse in Buena Vista, the first mercantile establishment, about 1850. Later one of Reason Hall's sons started another Halls Ferry north of Independence. *Buena Vista* is Spanish for beautiful view or good view.

Buffalo, LAKE. Buffalo was a post office in the northeast part of the county, just northwest of the center of T 27S, R 21E, about a dozen miles east of Christmas Lake. It was established Apr. 11, 1913, with Samuel W. Stanton first of four postmasters. The office was discontinued June 29, 1918. A news item in the *Lake County Examiner*, Lakeview, Feb. 13, 1947, says that the office was named because a nearby juniper tree was so shaped that it looked like a buffalo. The story is credited to S. V. Carroll, well-known resident of the county.

Buford Creek, WALLOWA. This stream rises in Oregon a little north of Flora, and flows northward into Washington, where it drains into Grande Ronde River. It was named for Park Buford, a pioneer settler nearby. The locality became important because Buford Canyon was used for the highway from Enterprise to Lewiston. Park Buford is reported to have died as a result of a rattlesnake bite, which he received while reaching under his cabin trying to find a pup.

Bug Butte, KLAMATH. On Mar. 1, 1926, L. D. Arnold of the Indian Field Service wrote the USBGN from Klamath Agency as follows: "Bug Butte, not Big Butte, is a newly coined name for the butte two miles southeast of Council Butte in sections 24 and 25. It has been so named because bark beetles have in the past five years killed nearly all the pine trees." This insect is the western pine beetle, *Dendroctonus brevicomis. See* Essig's *Insects of Western North America*, p. 514, and news article in Bend *Bulletin*, July 14, 1927.

Bug Creek, WHEELER. This small creek in the Ochoco National Forest just north of the Crook County line was named by USFS ranger Grover Blake before World War I. He had an insect control camp on the creek with about 60 men cutting and peeling lodge pole pines infected with the pine bark bug.

Bugby Hole, CLATSOP. Bugby Hole is the name of a very deep place in the Columbia River about midway between Wauna and Bradwood, close under the precipitous cliffs to the west of the stream. There was a railway flag stop nearby known as Bugby Hole. In Sept. 1943, Seth F. Michael of the USCE office in Portland wrote the compiler that Bugby Hole was named for an earlyday settler who carried on some logging operations in the vicinity. Bugby Hole has a depth of over 100 feet at low water and is remarkable on that account.

Bull Mountain, WASHINGTON. This mountain is situated about three miles southwest of Tigard and has an elevation of 711 feet. G. W. Tefft of Beaverton told the writer in 1927 that it was named for a band of wild cattle that ranged on the hill in pioneer days. These cattle were gradually killed off with the exception of one bull and thus the descriptive name was attached to the hill in question.

Bull of the Woods, MARION. This peak, elevation 5510 feet, is in the northeast part of the county but a short distance from the Clackamas County line. One account asserts it was named for a nearby mining claim or prospect but Ron Burnett in an article in *Mazama*, Apr. 1979, p. 3, relates that William R. Bagby of the hot springs family once shot a large bull elk and told his friends: "I got the Bull of the woods." Regardless of the application, "Bull of the woods" is an old logger's term. Walter F. McCulloch in *Woods Words*, p. 21, gives three definitions all relating to big or important men in the logging industry.

Bull Run Lake, CLACKAMAS, MULTNOMAH. Will G. Steel is authority for the statement that the Klickitat Indian name for Bull Run Lake was *Gohabedikt*, meaning Loon Lake. It is not surprising that such a name was not used by white men. The lake undoubtedly received its present name from Bull Run River, not *vice versa*. The compiler has no evidence that the lake was called Chitwood for an old settler, as it seems improbable that anyone could have settled in such a locality.

Bull Run Lake has an area of about .6 of a square mile, and an elevation of 3161 feet. The outlet is through underground springs forming Bull Run River, but a dam now regulates part of the leakage. Contrary to general belief, no drainage from melting snow or ice on Mount Hood enters Bull Run drainage basin. A chemical description of the water may be secured from USGS *WSP 363*. The intake point for the Portland water supply is about 20 miles down stream from the lake. Economically, Bull Run Lake is the most important lake in Oregon, for it is the source of the water supply for much of the population of the Portland metropolitan area.

Bull Run River, CLACKAMAS, MULTNOMAH. George H. Himes, late curator of the Oregon Historical Society, said the name of Portland's water supply, Bull Run, may have started from the presence of wild cattle on that river in the pioneer period (1849-55). According to Charles B. Talbot, who arrived in Oregon in 1849, cattle escaped from immigrants in that vicinity and ran wild a number of years. The place was called by the settlers Bull Run. For further history of the name Bull Run, *see* the *Oregonian*, Mar. 29, Apr. 5, 1897, p. 8; July 30, 1901, p. 12. The locality called Bull Run is about three miles northeast of Sandy, in Clackamas County, and near Bull Run River. The first post office was Unavilla, established in May 1893. The compiler does not know the reason for selecting this odd word. The name was changed to Bullrun in Nov. 1895, and to Camp Namanu in Jan. 1939. *See* Camp Namanu.

Bullard Creek, LAKE. M. W. Bullard moved into the Goose Lake Valley in 1869 and settled at the present site of Lakeview. Bullard Creek and Bullard Canyon, just east of the town, bear his name. For a description of his activities, *see Illustrated History of Central Oregon*, p. 844. Bullard Creek and the Bullard ranch played a prominent part in the county seat squabble of 1876. The legislature created Lake County in Oct. 1874, and named Linkville, now Klamath Falls, temporary county seat until an election to be held June 5, 1876, at which time a permanent county seat was to be selected by majority vote. At the appointed election Bullard Creek rolled up a count of 120 against 88 for Linkville, but 120 was not a majority of the 384 votes cast. About 75 votes were cast for Goose Lake, Goose Lake Valley, Bullard's Ranch and Bullard's Creek in Goose Lake, which were not counted for Bullard Creek. On Aug. 10, 1876, the county commissioners ordered the scattered votes to be included in the Bullard Creek total and directed that the county seat be set up at the Bullard house. However, the county clerk would not comply. In accordance with the legislative act, the election was held again on Nov. 7, 1876. By that time the town of Lakeview had been organized, and it carried the election. Six years later the people of Linkville and the Klamath Valley succeeded in getting a county of their own cut off from Lake, and called it Klamath.

Bullards, COOS. This town is near the mouth of Coquille River and was named for Robert W. Bullard, who was born in Iowa Nov. 26, 1857, and died July 11, 1925. In 1882 he established a general merchandise store at what is now Bullards, and also a ferry across the river. The post office was named for him. He came to Coos County in 1877. He married Malinda A. Hamblock.

Bulldog Rock, DOUGLAS. This rock is near the summit of the Calapooya Mountains in the northeastern part of the county and has an elevation of 5801 feet. It was named by USFS supervisor E. H. McDaniels on account of the prominence with which the bluff stood out from its immediate surroundings, in defiance of the elements.

Bullock Creek, DOUGLAS. This creek flows into Jackson Creek above South Umpqua River. It was named for William A. Bullock who homesteaded there in the 1890s.

Bully Creek, MALHEUR. There are several stories concerning the origin of the name of this stream, all apparently revolving around the fact that when a man fell into its waters many years ago, his friends stood about and cried out "Bully! Bully!" T. T. Geer, in the *Oregonian*, Feb. 9, 1921, says that during a debate in the legislature in 1889 on a bill to change the name of the stream, David P. Thompson told the story and said that the incident happened while he, Thompson, was engaged in surveying townships for the government. In a letter in the *Oregonian*, Apr. 21, 1927, Glen Livingston relates the story, saying that it came from D. P. Thompson and that it applied to Bull Run River. On Apr. 27, 1927, Henry E. Reed, in the *Oregonian*, replied to Livingston, saying that the incident did not happen on Bull Run River. He says that Thompson told him it happened to some soldiers in the 1850s. The legislature of 1889 changed the name of this stream from Bully Creek to Alder Creek and Thompson was a member of the house of representatives at the time. It seems probable to the compiler that the story told by Governor Geer is the correct one, and that the incident happened while Thompson was surveying. It does not seem probable that there were soldiers on Bully Creek in the 1850s. Despite the act of the legislature, the name of the stream has remained Bully Creek, and it is universally so known. The act is printed on p. 158 of the *Laws of Oregon*, fifteenth legislative assembly, 1889. A post office called Bully was established near this stream Apr. 3, 1882, with Nancy Kime first postmaster. This office did not operate continuously. The name was changed to Westfall in Feb. 1889. The office was doubtless moved from time to time.

Bunchgrass Creek, WASCO. This stream is in the extreme northwest part of the Warm Springs Indian Reservation, and flows into Warm Springs River. There are a number of geographic features in Oregon named for bunchgrass, a valuable natural forage of the eastern part of Oregon. Hitchcock and Chase in *Manual of Grasses of the United States* list *Festuca idahoensis*, sometimes called *F. ovina ingrata*, the blue bunchgrass of the prairies, which is densely tufted. The bluebunch wheatgrass, *Agropyron spicatum*, is taller and grows generally on dry hills.

Buncom, JACKSON. Buncom was a community at the confluence of Sterling Creek and Little Applegate River. The post office was established Dec. 5, 1896 with J. Parks first postmaster, and closed Dec. 15, 1917. There was little left of the town in 1980. Dean Saltmarsh of Jackson County, in an interview with Kay Atwood in 1975, said that the name was a mispronunciation by Chinese miners of the name of a local settler. The settler's actual name has long been forgotten.

Bunker Hill, COOS. Bunker Hill is a neighborhood in the south part of the city of Coos Bay, and is remarkable for the fact that it was not named for the historic spot in Boston. Prior to 1900 it was just another timbered hill rising above tidewater near the mouth of Coalbank Slough. It was called Bunker Hill because of the coal bunkers nearby and the application of the name came without formality. About 1906 the area was platted for homes by the Flanagan estate and the title Bunker Hill seemed natural. The coal bunkers were principally on Isthmus Slough to the east of Bunker Hill, but there were also some on Coalbank Slough to the west. It was here that the ocean vessels took on their cargoes of coal from the Newport mines.

Bunker Hill, LINN. About 1858 R. C. Finley and associates established a community and grist mill on Calapooia River about a mile and a half east of the present town of Shedd. The locality was called Boston Mills. Just southeast of the site of the Finley enterprises was a small butte, which took the name Bunker Hill because it was so close to the Boston Mills. This little butte is about a half mile west of Saddle Butte and south of the east-west road.

Bunker Hill, MARION. Bunker Hill is one of the highest points in the group of hills south of Salem. It has an elevation of 956 feet, and lies about two miles west of the Pacific Highway East and a mile north of Ankeny Bottom. In a letter written to Ladd & Bush, Bankers, dated Feb. 1, 1915, John W. Jory gives information about the origin of this name. The letter was published in the *Ladd & Bush Quarterly*, Apr. 1915. Jory wrote that in pioneer days Bunker Hill was known as Bald Hill to distinguish it from other hills in the vicinity. He was of the opinion that the name was changed to Bunker Hill either by Perry Watson or by Henry E. Ankeny. The name Bunker Hill has been in general use since about 1870. Stories to the effect that the hill may have been named for a local resident seem to be erroneous, and Bunker Hill near Boston, famous in the American Revolution, is no doubt the origin of the name.

Bunyard Creek, LAKE. Bunyard Creek flows into Silver Creek near the town of Silver Lake. It was named for Jesse Bunyard, one of the very early homesteaders in the area, who was born in Missouri on Oct. 2, 1843. He came west with his mother in 1854 and settled in Umatilla County in 1866. In 1876 he moved to Silver Lake where he took up his homestead along this creek. He is reported to have sowed the first crop of grain in the Silver Lake area.

Burch Creek, BENTON. Burch Creek empties into Alsea River four miles west of Alsea. It is not named for the tree but for A. A. Burch who filed for water rights in 1924.

Burghardts Mill, CLACKAMAS. This little settlement is about a mile west of Barton and is near Clackamas River. It was named for Ernest H. Burghardt, one of the early settlers in that community. It was he who secured the establishment of the Barton post office. The mill is occasionally referred to as Burkhards Mill but that form is incorrect. For additional information, *see* Barton.

Burkemont, BAKER. Burkemont is a locality in the extreme northern part of the county, about 20 miles northeast of Baker City. It was named for Judge Thomas Carrick Burke, who was at one time interested in mining development at that place and was later a resident of Portland and collector of customs.

Burleson, LAKE. Burleson post office was established May 25, 1914, with Mima E. Petit postmaster and was in operation until Jan. 31, 1915. It was named in compliment to Albert S. Burleson, postmaster general from 1913 until 1921. The office was about 16 miles east-northeast of the town of Silver Lake.

Burlington, LINN. In Mar. 1947, Leslie L. Haskin of Newport, a student of Linn County history, wrote the compiler in substance as follows: "It is commonly said the town of Burlington was renamed and called Peoria. This is not correct. The town of Burlington was started in 1851 with a ferry run by John Smith and a store by John Donald. The townsite was mapped by James Freeman in 1853. The place had at that time two dwellings, two stores, one smithy and a ferry. However, the river silted up and spoiled the boat landings. Because boats found no suitable landing places, they passed the town and it died. The site of Burlington was the better part of a mile down the river from Peoria, and they were two different towns. Some buildings were moved from Burlington to Peoria." Burlington post office was established Nov. 17, 1855, with William M. McCorkle postmaster. The name of the office was changed to Peoria on Nov. 7, 1857, and it was doubtless moved to the new location about that time. There had been some settlement at Peoria as early as 1851, but active growth did not follow until later. Mr. J. C. Irvine wrote from Lebanon that Burlington, Oregon, was on the donation land claim of his grandfather, James Martin, who came to Oregon in 1852. It was in sections 5,6,7 and 8, T 13S, R 4W. Mr. Irvine said that before coming to Oregon his grandfather farmed for some 20 years near Little York, Illinois. The nearest market town was Burlington, Iowa. It is a matter of family tradition that Burlington, Oregon, was named for Burlington, Iowa.

Burlington, MULTNOMAH. Burlington is the name of a community north of Portland. The plat was filed for record on Mar. 24, 1909, by Ruth Trust Company. Herman Wittenberg was president of the company and named the place Burlington, but it is not known why he selected that name.

Burma, LANE. Burma was an operating station on the Southern Pacific line north of Eugene, and was established to help clear trains at the north end of Eugene Yard. Traffic became congested at this point in 1941, and when the station was put in service, the name was selected because of the traffic bottleneck then existing on the great Burma Road between India and China. Burma station was officially established by the railroad on Nov. 27, 1942, but it was actually put in service about the beginning of 1942. The station is now Eugene Yard.

Burns, HARNEY. This community was named for Robert Burns by George McGowan, a pioneer resident who was a great admirer of the Scottish poet. Elevation 4148 feet. In Feb. 1943, Archie McGowan of Burns furnished the compiler with some data about his father, George McGowan, who moved into the Harney Valley from the Willamette Valley in May 1882. George McGowan first stopped at the little settlement of Egan, about two and a half miles southwest of the present site of Burns, and engaged in the mercantile business. He soon decided to enlarge his business and move to a new location. He took Peter Stenger into partnership in the fall of 1883, and the two established themselves at the present locality of Burns, one reason being that it was nearer the Stenger ranch. Stenger wanted to name the new place Stenger, but McGowan thought otherwise, calling attention to the fact that Stenger was frequently pronounced Stinger, and the name Stingertown would be bad advertising. McGowan suggested Burns, and early in 1884 the community was established with that name. George McGowan died in Portland Jan. 31, 1930, aged 85 years. For story on the hanging of a portrait of George McGowan in the new Burns post office, *see* Burns *Times-Herald*, June 13, 1941. Egan post office was established July 31, 1882, with George McGowan postmaster. The name was changed to Burns Jan. 22, 1884. The name Egan is said to have been that of a local Indian celebrity. Chief Egan was a prominent leader of the Paiutes during the Bannock War of 1878 and he was active in Harney County. *See* Fred Lockley's column in the *Oregon Journal*, May 1, 1934.

Burnside, CLATSOP. David Burnside, for whom this place was named, was a native of Ireland. He came to the United States about 1825, and was naturalized in Apr. 1832. He arrived in Oregon in 1847. He married Mary Ann (last name not given) in Philadelphia, in Aug. 1853. He settled on his donation land claim in 1855, and the nearby station was subsequently named on this account. His land office certificate was numbered 3606. Marys Creek in Clatsop County was named for his wife.

Burnt Bridge Creek, LANE. Burnt Bridge Creek flows into Middle Fork Willamette River a few miles below Westfir. According to C. B. McFarland of Oakridge, the name came into use as a result of the Dead Mountain fire of 1910, which destroyed the wagon bridge over the stream. The name Burnt Ridge Creek is wrong.

Burnt Ranch, WHEELER. Burnt Ranch is a place on the south bank of the John Day River at the extreme western edge of Wheeler County. The name was applied in 1866. The ranch was on the old military road from The Dalles to Canyon City. The buildings were burned during an Indian uprising and from that time the place was known by its present name. The original Burnt Ranch was near the mouth of Bridge Creek, but the post office moved about, depending upon the home of the postmaster. At one time the office was far enough west to be in Jefferson County. Burnt Ranch post office was established Jan. 15, 1883, by change of name from Grade. Addie S. Masterson was the first postmaster.

Burnt River, BAKER. Burnt River is an important stream rising in the Blue Mountains and draining the southern part of the county. It joins Snake River east of Huntington. Exact information about its name is not available, and there are two theories about the matter, one being that Burnt River was so called because of the burned timber along its banks and the other because of the burned looking rocks, especially along the lower reaches. As far as the writer knows, the first mention of Burnt River is in the Peter Skene Ogden journals for Friday, Oct. 28, 1825. T. C. Elliott was of the opinion that the name came from the burned woods, because fur-traders reached the upper parts of the stream first where the burned looking rocks are not so much in evidence. During the times in question the stream was frequently mentioned as the *Riviere Brule*, by the French-Canadians. It is, of course, evident that the trappers named the stream, and that pioneers proceeding along the lower part of the river 25 years later had nothing to do with it, though they doubtless thought the name was appropriate because of the dry character of the country they traversed. Mr. Elliott thought that the name was probably first applied to the river by Donald McKenzie possibly as early as 1818. *See OHQ*, v. 13, p. 71. For many references about the name Burnt River, *see Discovery of the Oregon Trail* (Stuart's Narrative edited by Rollins), pp. 79 and 95. In the first edition of *Astoria*, v. 2, p. 122, Burnt River is appropriately called Woodpile Creek apparently on account of driftwood accumulations. The compiler has seen later editions of *Astoria* with this name spelled Woodvile, a meaningless error.

Burnt Woods, LINCOLN. This post office is in the eastern part of Lincoln County, near Tumtum River, where the remains of forest fires are still much in evidence. The office was established in 1919, and a list of suggested names was sent to the Post Office Department. On the list was Burnt Woods, proposed by H. G. Downing, and this was the name chosen by the authorities.

Burnt Woods, WASHINGTON. Washington County has had more than its share of forest fires and it is not surprising that there was once a post office in the county called Burnt Woods. This office was a mile or so north of the place called Glenwood, as Glenwood was situated in 1945. Burnt Woods post office was established Sept. 12, 1879, with Mrs. Mary J. Evans postmaster. The office was closed Sept. 17, 1883. Later a post office named Glenwood was organized to serve the same general locality, but it may not have been in exactly the same place. Glenwood post office was subsequently moved a couple of miles south to a site on Gales Creek.

Burroughs, UMATILLA. The compiler has been unable to get much information about Burroughs post office, except that it was in service from May 10, 1893, to July 12, 1895, with Barney F. Hogue the only postmaster. Hogue is said to have lived in Coombs Canyon four miles west of Sparks Station, southwest of Pendleton, in a locality sometimes referred to as Burroughs. There was a smithy and some other buildings in the locality. Postal records show that a post office called Bissell was established with Benjamin L. Burroughs postmaster on Apr. 27, 1893, but Bissell post office was never in operation. Judging from available information

Burroughs post office was in the same neighborhood as the Bissell office and was named for the Bissell postmaster.

Bus Point, WASCO. Eric Gordon of the USFS named this point in S 19, T 4S, R 11E, for Lewis D. "Bus" Reavis who worked for Gordon in the 1920s. Dr. Reavis told the writer in 1969 that he had just topped a 120-foot tree to prepare a fire lookout platform and his boss named the spot in his honor.

Bush, MARION. Bush is the name of a station on the Burlington Northern in north Salem. It commemorates Asahel Bush, the prominent editor and publisher of the Salem *Statesman* during the second half of the nineteenth century. Bush was born in Massachusetts in 1824 and came to Oregon in 1850. He was associated with W. S. Ladd in the Salem Ladd & Bush Bank and was influential in the Democratic Party. He died in Salem on Dec. 23, 1913. The Bush house in Salem is listed in the National Register of Historic Places and is the central feature of Bush Pasture Park.

Bushnell Creek, DOUGLAS. This creek above Tenmile was named for Linus Bushnell who took up a donation land claim there in 1854. Bushnell Rock, northwest of Tenmile, was apparently named for Archie L. Bushnell, a more recent member of the family.

Buster Butte, LANE. This butte and other features of the same name are on Steamboat Creek near the summit of the Calapooya Mountains. They were named in 1921 by USFS ranger Fred Asam for his faithful old packhorse, Buster.

Butcher Bill Creek, MORROW. This creek and Butcher Bill Meadow north of Lake Penland are named for "Butcher Bill" Floren, an early settler who ran stock in the area. BLM records show Sylvester W. Floren took up land in the meadow in 1896. *See* USBGN *Decision List 7202*.

Butcher Knife Ridge, HOOD RIVER. Ralph Lewis of Parkdale told the writer that this ridge east of Lost Lake was named about 1900 because Pete Lenz remarked to hunting companions that the brush on this ridge was so thick you couldn't stick a butcherknife into it.

Butcherknife Creek, WALLOWA. One day in the early 1890s Jack Shields and Dick and Alex Warnock found an old butcherknife on this stream, and named the creek on that account. Butcherknife Creek is a tributary of Lightning Creek.

Butler, POLK. On Feb. 16, 1861, a post office with the name Grand Ronde was established in the north part of Polk County, at the site of Fort Yamhill. Benjamin Simpson, an Indian agent, was the first postmaster, and the area served was about a half mile north of the present locality of Valley Junction. On Oct. 3, 1894, this office was moved about three miles northwest to Grand Ronde Agency in Yamhill County, but without change of name. This move left the Fort Yamhill area without a post office. A new office was established in the locality, with the name Butler, on Mar. 16, 1895, and with J. C. Ellis first of two postmasters. The office was named in compliment to Judge N. L. Butler of Dallas, who owned a large farm nearby. According to Mr. Ellis the farm was then being operated by James

Shepherd, and Shepherd suggested the use of the name. Butler post office was discontinued June 30, 1911.

Butler Basin, GRANT, WHEELER. This is a large basin in the John Day Valley north of Picture Gorge. It was named for an early settler, Frank Butler, a one-armed rancher who lived in a little cabin near the present site of Cants Ranch. Butler was the only resident of the basin in 1877. The name Upper Basin is occasionally used for this geographic feature, but Butler Basin seems to be the generally accepted form. There was once a post office in this locality called Basin.

Butler Canyon, WASCO. US-197 follows Butler Canyon from Tygh Valley north to Tygh Ridge summit. Jonathan Butler was born in Illinois in 1833 and came to Oregon and Wasco County with his family. Butler settled near Kingsley and helped develop the road in the canyon that bears his name.

Butler Mountain, WHEELER. Butler Mountain lies just north of Richmond. It was named for two brothers, John D. and George O. Butler who raised stock in the Richmond area before the turn of the century. The two had adjoining homesteads on the north slopes of the mountain.

Butte, LAKE. Butte post office was on the east border of the county line a little south of Wagontire Mountain. The office was established Dec. 21, 1911, with Josiah E. Pope first postmaster. This was at the time that many dry farmers and homesteaders were coming into central Oregon. The office was closed Oct. 31, 1922, and the mail was then handled through Wagontire office. Butte post office was named for a well-known point, Elk Butte, near the east border of T 27S, R 22E.

Butte Creek, CLACKAMAS, MARION. Down, in *A History of the Silverton Country*, says that Butte Creek was probably named for Graves Butte, or Lone Tree Butte, so called because at its summit was a gigantic fir. The butte is now known as Mount Angel. Butte Creek was so known in the days of pioneer settlement. A post office with the name Bute Creek was operated from Jan. to Nov. 1851, with Jeremiah Jack postmaster. This office was reestablished with the name Butte Creek in 1867, and the name was changed to Marquam in Nov. 1889.

Butte Creek, WALLOWA. J. H. Horner of Enterprise told the compiler in 1931 that the Indians called the locality of this stream *Tusco-wall-a me*, meaning a place where the owls lived. In early days the stream was called Owl Creek, but the name was gradually changed to Butte Creek because it rises near Oregon Butte in Columbia County, Washington. Butte Creek flows south into Oregon and drains into Wenaha River in T 6N, R 41E.

Butte Creek, WHEELER. This stream rises near Fossil and flows into John Day River. It was so named because of Black Butte, a prominent point near its source, which serves as a landmark. Black Butte has an elevation of about 4000 feet and is about two miles northeast of Fossil.

Butte Disappointment, LANE. Butte Disappointment is on the north side of Middle Fork Willamette River, east and northeast of Lowell. It has a maximum elevation of 2409 feet and is a very prominent landmark. Walling in his *Illustrated*

History of Lane County gives an account of the naming of this feature. In 1848 a party of settlers led by Elijah Bristow of Pleasant Hill undertook a foray against marauding Indians. The posse tried to ascend the river on the northeast bank, but was blocked by Fall Creek, which was in flood. The settlers mistook Fall Creek for the main stream, and returned to the Hills place, crossed the river and followed up the southwest bank. When they reached a point about opposite the present site of Lowell, they found to their disappointment that they were on the wrong side of the Middle Fork. They could not proceed on that side and had to give up the expedition. Because of this episode the name Butte Disappointment was applied to the prominent hill on the north side. A post office named Butte Disappointment was established May 8, 1872, with Samuel Handsaker, postmaster. It was at or near the present site of Dexter and was named for the prominent point a few miles eastward. The name of the office was changed to Dexter on July 19, 1875.

Butte Falls, JACKSON. Settlers in the Rogue River Valley refered to Mount McLoughlin as Snowy Butte, and the two main streams draining to the northwest from that mountain were known as Big and Little Butte creeks. At the falls on Big Butte Creek a settlement sprang up that took its name from the natural feature.

Butter Creek, UMATILLA. Butter Creek is a tributary of Umatilla River, and the old pioneer road crossed it west of Echo. *See* Scott's *History of the Oregon Country*, v. 3, p. 316. The writer has heard of two theories about the origin of the name. The diary of John T. Kerns, published in OPA *Transactions* for 1914, says under date of Sept. 9, 1852, that Butter Creek was named because some volunteers took butter from the stores during the Cayuse War. Miss L. C. McKay, for many years a resident of eastern Oregon, confirmed this statement, and informed the writer that the butter was taken from the officers' mess so the enlisted men could have hot cakes. The other story is to the effect that a party of pioneers found some stale butter on the banks of the stream. The writer has no confirmation of this story.

Butterfield, CLATSOP. Butterfield was a station just north of Gearhart. It was named for Charles Butterfield, who married Margaret Gearhart, daughter of a Clatsop Plains pioneer.

Butterfield Lake, COOS. This lake five miles southwest of Tenmile Lake is on the 1887 homestead of Lysander Butterfield.

Buttermilk Creek, BENTON. This very small stream flows southward through Philomath into Marys River. A letter printed in the Philomath *Review* for Jan. 15, 1942, signed by F. S. Minshall, gives the origin of the name. Many years ago a creamery did a thriving business on the banks of this brook, and ran its surplus buttermilk into the drain. This activity was of no great consequence in the cold months of the year, but in summer, the resulting stench aroused local residents to indignation. A septic tank was installed, but it overflowed. Farmers carried away the surplus milk for hog feed, but they could not carry away the odor. A "Smelling Committee" was appointed by the council, but as is frequently the case with committees, little was done. Finally the creamery got into financial trouble and closed, thus bringing an end to the business. The name Buttermilk Creek remains, however.

Butteville, MARION. Butteville is on the east bank of the Willamette River in the extreme north part of the county and has an elevation of 103 feet. It was named for a well-known hill about a mile to the southwest, called by the early settlers on French Prairie *La Butte*, a form of name still used by the USGS on its map of the Sherwood quadrangle, which shows the geography of this region. *La Butte* has an elevation of 427 feet. Butteville was laid out prior to 1850 by Abernethy and Beers. The Oregon Electric Railway has a station called Butteville about two miles east of the town. This station was formerly called Chopunnish, a northwest Indian name, but was changed to Butteville to avoid confusion. Postal officials inform the compiler that Butteville post office was established with the name Champoeg on Apr. 9, 1850, with F. X. Matthieu first postmaster. The name was changed to Buteville Sept. 9, 1850, and to Butteville probably in the 1860s, although the date of this change is not clear in the records. The office was discontinued in the summer of 1905.

Button Springs, LAKE. Lee Button was a pioneer homesteader northeast of Fort Rock. He is mentioned in Charles H. Sternberg's *Life of a Fossil Hunter*. Sternberg was in the locality in 1877. Button Springs are in T 23S, R 16E, and they have given their name to the Button Springs Ranch, which is well known in Lake County. The springs were not named because of their size or shape.

Buxton, WASHINGTON. Henry T. Buxton settled in this place in 1884, and was appointed its first postmaster in 1886. He was a son of Henry Buxton, a pioneer of 1841, and the town was named for his family.

Byars Creek, MARION. This creek flows into Breitenbush River northeast of Detroit. Byars Creek and Byars Peak nearby were named for W. H. Byars, surveyor general for Oregon from 1890 to 1894.

Bybee Bridge, JACKSON. This bridge crosses Rogue River not far from Upper Table Rock. It was named for William Bybee who operated a ferry at this point for many years in the early days. Bybee also ran sheep in the upper Rogue River valley and Bybee Creek in the northeast corner of the county bears his name.

Bybee Lake, MULTNOMAH. This is a small overflow lake on the south bank of Columbia River north of St. Johns. It was named for James Bybee. According to land office certificate 2234, Bybee was born in Kentucky on Dec. 1, 1827, and arrived in Oregon in the fall of 1850. He settled on his claim near Columbia River in the fall of 1853, and made final proof in Nov. 1859, and was then unmarried. The lake was largely on his property, and not on that of James F. Bybee, a pioneer of 1845, who was a nearby settler.

Byrds Point, WHEELER. This prominent bluff above Burnt Ranch was named for William Byrd who homesteaded nearby in 1882.

Byron Creek, DOUGLAS. In 1853 John Byron took up a donation land claim along this creek south of Olalla.

Cabbage Hill, UMATILLA. The notion that the Oregon Trail, US-30, comes down Cabbage Hill into Umatilla Valley east of Pendleton does not seem to be borne out by facts. The highway traverses and descends Emigrant Hill and is not on Cabbage Hill at all. Cabbage Hill is a long spur extending southwest from Emigrant Hill, ending at Table Rock above McKay Creek. Cabbage Hill School is about a mile south of the Oregon Trail. The geography of this locality is shown on the USGS topographic map of the Cabbage Hill quadrangle. In Mar. 1946, the compiler received a letter from Mrs. J. E. Jones of Elgin containing a statement by her uncle, G. L. Dunn of Gibbon, about Cabbage Hill. Dunn says that in the fall of 1897 he was herding sheep on the hill above North Fork McKay Creek and he named the area Cabbage Hill because of a prominent cabbage patch near the top of the slope. This name was adopted by the local residents and has been in use ever since. Dunn says the cabbages were on land farmed by one Huderman.

Cabell City, GRANT. Cabell City was on Onion Creek about eight miles north of Granite in s 1, T 8s, R 35-1/2E. Fred E. and John B. Cabell located the nearby La Bellevue Mine about 1879 but it was not as productive as the Buffalo Mine some three miles to the southeast. The Cabell brothers were listed in Granite precinct in the 1900 census, presumably at Cabell City. Only Cabell Cemetery has survived. In 1980 the USFS described it as a 14 by 20 foot plot surrounded by an iron fence and containing the graves of Fred Cabell, his wife Johanna, and their eight year old daughter. The wife's headstone is inscribed "Johanna Cabell, Oct 17, 1844, Apr 12, 1923." The other two graves are located by single, unmarked headstones. Fred Cabell died in May 1914, age 70. A newspaper clipping in the OHS *Scrapbook* file states he was buried on the slopes of Cabell Mountain. This must refer to the high ground that rises north of Cabell City site and runs eastward to the presently unnamed 7317 foot summit above the La Bellevue Mine.

Cabin Creek, DOUGLAS. This stream flows into Calapooya Creek near Oakland. Both the Southern Pacific Company line and I-5 follow Cabin Creek between Oakland and Rice Hill. It is said that the Rev. J. A. Cornwall built a cabin on this stream in the fall of 1846, in which he and his family spent the following winter. This is believed to have been the first cabin built in Douglas County by citizens of the United States, and the stream was named for it.

Cable Cove, BAKER. Cable Cove was at the headwaters of Silver Creek northwest of Bourne. It was named for Henry Cable who with Erwin Cable patented the Columbia Quartz Mine in 1892. It was on the North Pole-Columbia lode and produced over $3,500,000 in gold and silver before closing in 1916. Henry Cable was one of the early prospectors in the area having first located the Columbia in 1888. He also patented at least two other nearby claims, the Consolidated Fractional and the California. N. S. Wagner, retired Department of Geology and Mineral Resources veteran, provided this information in 1986 and added that he understood Cable started as a pack string freighter from Umatilla Landing to Fort

Boise before he became interested in mining. For a time there was a post office in the vicinty of Cable Cove which operated with the name Cableville. Cableville post office was established Oct. 24, 1901, with Thomas Costello the first of five postmasters. The office was discontinued in May 1909. The Cables must not be confused with Fred Cabell of Cabell City although they may have been cousins for the claim filed for the California Mine shows Johanna and Bessie Cabell as part owners along with Henry Cable.

Cache Creek, WALLOWA. This creek flows into Snake River in T 6N, R 47E, in the extreme northeast of Oregon. It was named by A. C. Smith, a pioneer of the Wallowa Valley. He and some companions were scouting in the neighborhood in the 1870s and found Indian caches on a bar at the mouth of the stream.

Cadle Butte, CROOK. Cadle Butte south of Veazie Creek has an elevation of 5106 feet. It was named for John F. Cadle who homesteaded on Ochoco Creek at the turn of the century.

Cahill Creek, CLACKAMAS. This is a short stream that flows northward into Beaver Creek about two miles east of New Era. It bears the name of Enos Cahill, who was born in Ohio in 1844, a Union soldier in the Civil War and later a homesteader on the banks of this stream. He held a number of public offices in Clackamas County and died in 1913. He was favorably remembered in the neighborhood, and in 1941 a group of former students of Leland School asked to have his name applied to this stream which has its source in a number of springs on the Cahill homestead. The name has been adopted by USBGN.

Cain Creek, LANE. Cain Creek flows into Lookout Point Lake. John and Henry Cain both homesteaded along Middle Fork Willamette River in the 1890s but A. J. Briem, in his notes on file at the Oregon Historical Society, says the stream was probably named for John Cain.

Cairn Basin, HOOD RIVER. Cairn Basin is a secluded alpine meadow just east of Cathedral Ridge on Mount Hood and the site of one of the stone shelters on the Timberline Trail. It takes its name from the large cairn constructed in 1922 by C. Edward Graves and the Hood River exploring party. At various times the cairn fell into disrepair but in the late 1960s a group of Crag Rats undertook periodic maintenance.

Cake, MALHEUR. Cake post office was in the extreme northern part of the county, almost on the watershed between Burnt River and Malheur River, and at the head of Mormon Basin. The office was established to serve the headquarters of the Rainbow Mine, and the mine itself was just over the line in Baker County. Cake was the name of a Portland business man who was interested in the development of the property. Cake post office was established Feb. 3, 1917, with Isaac Blumauer first postmaster. Carl H. Connet was the second postmaster, and he wrote from Albany in Aug. 1946, giving some information about the place. The office was closed in Mar. 1920. It was reestablished June 21, 1922, with the name

Rainbow Mine, but closed on May 31 of the following year. The mine was named because of association with the place where the pot of gold was supposed to be. There has been a change of the county boundary in this locality, but it is not clear just how it affects the information recorded above.

Calamut Lake, DOUGLAS. Calamut Lake is in the extreme northeast part of the county. The writer has been unable to secure definite information as to how it got its name, but it seems probable that it may have been an early form of Klamath, and may have been so called by emigrants. The form of spelling here used is that adopted by the USBGN.

Calapooia River, LINN. Calapooia River rises in the western slopes of the Cascade Range and joins the Willamette River at Albany. The name has the same origin as Calapooya in Douglas County. However, the territorial Linn County Court established the spelling Calapooia at its first session, July 1, 1850, and this form has since been used locally. The OGNB confirmed this spelling on Dec. 7, 1962 and the USBGN in *Decision List 6401*.

Calapooya Mountains, DOUGLAS, LANE. These mountains are a westward spur of the Cascade Range and constitute the watershed between the Willamette and Umpqua rivers. Calapooya Mountains join the Cascade Range at Cowhorn Mountain with an elevation of 7666 feet in the northeast corner of Douglas County. The Indians of the Willamette Valley were of the *Kalapooian* family. Calapooya Mountains bear the name. *See* Lewis' *Tribes of the Columbia Valley*, p. 178. The Calapooya Indians were indolent and peaceful, and not disposed to trade *ibid*. The name is given as *Calapoosie* by David Douglas in his journals, *OHQ*, v. 6, p. 85; *Col-lap-poh-yea-ass*, by Alexander Ross, in *Adventures of the First Settlers on the Oregon*, pp. 235, 236; *Call-law-poh-yea-as*, in his *Fur Hunters of the Far West*, v. 1, p. 108; *Kala-pooyhas*, in Townsend's *Narrative*, p. 175; *Callapuya*, by Wilkes. Lewis and Clark give *Collapoewah*; Parker's journal gives *Calapooa*; Lee and Frost *Calapooyas*. *Calapooya* is properly the name of a division of the *Kalapooian* family formerly living between Willamette and Umpqua rivers. The USBGN has adopted the spelling Calapooya. Calapooya Creek rises on the south slopes of Calapooya Mountains in Douglas County and flows through Oakland and joins the Umpqua River at Umpqua. The origin of the name of the stream is the same as that of the Calapooya Mountains.

Caldwell Creek, CLACKAMAS. Caldwell Creek is a small tributary of Henry Creek from the north just east of Rhododendron. In Jan. 1980, John C. Caldwell of Oregon City wrote the compiler and told how this creek got its name. His father, J. B. "Boots" Caldwell, was an Oregon City business man who would often spend weekends at his father-in-law's cottage in Rhododendron. A regular diversion was to spend a few solitary hours fishing some small stream in the neighborhood and the one now called Caldwell Creek was a favorite. One day in the 1930s Caldwell was visiting a friend, Ralph S. Milln, deputy surveyor of Clackamas County. Milln was busy putting the finishing touches on a new map and said: "Boots, how would you like to have a creek named for you? I have a lot of them that need names." The fishing stream came at once to mind and the name was applied forthwith. Naming regulations were less involved in those days and the few federal rules were often bent.

Calf Gulch, JEFFERSON. Calf Gulch is east of Ashwood, in the Donnybrook country, and is the veritable spot where an event took place that gave Donnybrook its name. The general locality was once called Axehandle, and additional information will be found under that heading. The Bend *Bulletin*, Apr. 20, 1943, says editorially: "one of the community's names, Donnybrook, was derived from a little social affair in Calf gulch, where guns, as well as axe handles, were used, and one man, Tom Kinney, received a bullet wound." *See also* Donnybrook and Kilts. Calf Gulch was named during the days of pioneer stockmen, but the compiler does not know the exact reason.

Calico Creek, LANE. Calico Creek flows north into Silk Creek near Royal. It was named by Amanda Babcock for its proximity to Silk Creek. Amanda and Morton Babcock came to the Cottage Grove area in the late 1880s and settled near Royal. Mrs. Babcock also named nearby Muslin Creek which flows into Silk Creek from the north. Earlier maps had these two names reversed but they were in error. This information came from Amanda Babcock's niece, Edith Hayden.

California Gulch, BAKER. California Gulch, which is about ten miles airline southwest of Baker, drains south into Powder River. It is just a little west of the famous pioneer mining camp of Auburn. It was named in the eastern Oregon gold rush of the early 1860s because of the presence of many California miners in that part of the diggings. Hiatt in his *Thirty-one Years in Baker County* has a good deal to say about the rivalry between the visitors from California, called Tarheads, and the Oregonians, dubbed Webfeet.

Calimus, KLAMATH. The Southern Pacific Company formerly had a station named Sprague in Klamath County, but in 1926 changed the name to Calimus to avoid duplication. The name Calimus was taken from Calimus Butte.

Calimus Butte, KLAMATH. This is an important landmark near the center of the Klamath Indian Reservation and is used as a lookout station. Captain O. C. Applegate, authority on the Klamath country, said the origin of the name was obscure. One Klamath Indian told him it meant Flat Butte.

Calkins Creek, TILLAMOOK. Charles W. Calkins homesteaded in southern Tillamook County in 1902 and his son, David Calkins, ranched along Calkins Creek near the new alignment of US-101 over Cascade Head. Another son, Elmer Calkins, told the author in 1968 that this creek was called Shinglebolt in the early days because a small shingle and shake mill was located nearby. Early maps showed this stream as Caulkins Creek but this was corrected on the USGS Neskowin quadrangle of 1985. There is a second, small Calkins Creek emptying directly into Salmon River about a mile west of the US-101 bridge.

Calor, KLAMATH. Calor is a station on the Southern Pacific Company Cascade

Line just north of the Oregon-California state line. The name is synthetic and was made up from parts of the names of the two states. There are many of these combination names in the United States.

Calvert, DOUGLAS. Calvert post office was established May 3, 1892, with Mrs. John (Laura V.) Applegate first and only postmaster. The office was closed Sept. 5, 1894, and the business turned over to Louis post office. Calvert was about four miles east of Yoncalla in Scotts Valley on what had been the R. M. Kelly donation land claim. Mrs. Applegate planned to name the office Scott Valley, but postal authorities objected to a name with two words and also because it was so nearly the same as Scottsburg in the same county. It was then planned to name the office Kelly, but this was unacceptable to the authorities because of duplication. At length Calvert was selected. It is reported that Calvert was a family name in the Applegate clan.

Camas Valley, DOUGLAS. The word Camas is used to describe geographic features in many parts of Oregon, including Camas Valley in Douglas County, Camas Swale in Lane County, Camas Swale in Douglas County, Camas Creek in Umatilla County, and others. The name is taken from that of a favorite food of the western Indians, the *Camassia* bulb, a plant related to the scilla. The word was derived from the Nootka Indian word *Chamass*, meaning "fruit" or "sweet." It was adopted into the Chinook jargon as camas, kamass, lacmass, and lakamass. The locality of Camas Valley was a place where the Indians gathered supplies of the sweetish bulbs of the blue-flowered "Lakamass."

Cambrai, WASCO. Cambrai is a station on the Burlington Northern Inc. just south of Maupin. The 1961 Oregon Trunk Gold Spike issue of the Spokane Portland and Seattle Railway *Dope Bucket* states that Cambrai was a coined word with no local significance that originated in 1917 when the station was named. The compiler does not know why the name came to be applied but it was much in the news in the late fall of 1917. The battle of Cambrai was a major engagement between the English and Germans during World War I. It commenced on Nov. 20, 1917 and was centered about the French town of that name.

Camelot Lake, DESCHUTES. Ray Engels, former USFS ranger at McKenzie Bridge, thought that the lake basin southwest of Wickiup Plain must resemble the jousting fields of King Arthur's time. He thus named two of the lakes Camelot and Lancelot.

Camp Abbot, DESCHUTES. On Dec. 4, 1942, the War Department announced that an army engineer replacement and training center would be named Camp Abbot, in honor of Brigadier-General Henry Larcom Abbot. Abbot's distinguished career is described in this volume under the heading Abbot Creek. On Sept. 2, 1855, in command of a detached party engaged on one of the projects of the Pacific Railroad Surveys, he camped on the site of the engineer center. Camp Abbot was dedicated on Sept. 2, 1943, and was in active service for about a year.

Camp Adair, BENTON, POLK. Henry Rodney Adair was a scion of a prominent

Oregon pioneer family and was a native of Astoria. He was graduated from West Point and became a lieutenant of cavalry in the regular army. He was killed at Carrizal, Mexico, about 90 miles south of El Paso, June 21, 1916, when Mexican soldiers made a surprise attack on a small detachment of American troops. Lieutenant Adair conducted a spirited defense but the few troopers in his immediate vicinity were greatly outnumbered and many were killed. Camp Adair, on the west side of the Willamette Valley north of Corvallis, contained about 50,000 acres and was built in 1942–43 as a training center for World War II. It was formally dedicated Sept. 4, 1943, although occupied by troops for some time prior to that date. *See* news articles, *Oregonian*, Aug. 27, 1943, and *Oregon Journal*, Sept. 4, 1943. The camp was named in honor of Lieutenant Adair. Camp Adair post office was established June 1, 1942. It was discontinued May 23, 1946.

Camp Alden, JACKSON. After the battle of Evans Creek, Aug. 24, 1853, which was an important event in the Rogue River Indian outbreak, General Lane put the white soldiers into a camp at Hailey Ferry near Upper Table Rock. This camp was called Camp Alden in compliment to Captain Bradford Ripley Alden of the Fourth U.S. Infantry, who had been severely wounded on Evans Creek. After a few weeks, Fort Lane supplanted Camp Alden. The exact location of Camp Alden is not known. Hailey Ferry later became Bybee Ferry. Walling's statement in *History of Southern Oregon*, p. 220, to the effect that Alden died two years later from the effect of his wound is not borne out by Heitman's *Historical Register*, which gives the date as Sept. 10, 1870.

Camp Alvord, MALHEUR. Camp Alvord was established in June 1864, in what is now known as Alvord Valley at the east base of Steens Mountain just south of Little Alvord Creek. Lieutenant J. A. Waymire and troops of the First Oregon Volunteer Cavalry had camped in the locality early in the year and had dug some rifle-pits during an engagement with the Indians. In June, Captain George B. Currey of the same regiment, in command of cavalry and infantry, found these pits and used the site until September for an establishment which he called Camp Alvord in compliment to Brigadier-General Benjamin Alvord. For a history of Alvord, *see* Alvord Lake. Currey caused some additional earthworks to be thrown up in the form of a star, but the compiler has been unable to learn of any permanent structures. The Oregon Adjutant General's *Report*, 1865–66, says this camp was broken up late in Sept. 1864. On Aug. 31, 1865, Major W. V. Rinehart, commanding the First Oregon Volunteer Infantry at Fort Klamath, issued a letter order to Captain F. B. Sprague directing him to take a detachment of the regiment to the Alvord Valley and establish Camp Alvord on Horse Creek in a position with "natural advantages, such as security against attack, and the severities of winter, its healthfulness, and convenience to wood, water, and grass." The Horse Creek mentioned is now called Wildhorse Creek. Sprague found Captain Borland of the same regiment already encamped on Horse Creek at a site probably near the northeast corner of S 26, T 35S, R 33E, by the mouth of the canyon about one and one half miles northeast of Andrews. Camp Alvord was used until June 1866, when on the recommendation of Major-General F. Steele, commanding the Department of the Columbia, it was evacuated and the troops moved about 25 miles southeast to a spot on Whitehorse Creek along the Chico Road. The new post was called Camp C. F. Smith. *See* Camp C. F. Smith.

Camp Baker, JACKSON. Alice A. Sargent wrote a short account of Camp Baker in the Medford *Mail-Tribune*, Sept. 13, 1931. The camp was established in 1862 and was garrisoned by part of the First Oregon Volunteer Cavalry. It was named in honor of Major-General E. D. Baker who was killed at the battle of Balls Bluff in 1861. *See* Baker County. The site of Camp Baker was about a half a mile west of Phoenix. The various buildings were built of hewn pine logs. Coleman Creek flowed between the mess hall and the stables. In 1931 there were a few mouldering logs to mark the spot. The compiler does not know when the camp was evacuated but it was used as late as 1865. In Jan. 1944, T. V. Williams of Medford wrote the compiler that the D.A.R. marker for Camp Baker stands about 75 feet west of Coleman Creek on the south side of the east-west road through the middle of s 16, T 38S, R 1W.

Camp Barlow, CLACKAMAS. Camp Barlow is mentioned in official military records, but it does not seem to have been a formal establishment and was perhaps not more than a campground. It was used in the 1860s as a place of enlistment or rendezvous for Oregon volunteers. Tradition at Oregon City says that the camp was on the property of William Barlow adjacent to Molalla River, or just northeast of the present community of Barlow. In Mar. 1944, William Tull of Canby reported that his grandfather, William S. Tull, was one of the first to enlist at Camp Barlow, and that Mrs. William Barlow served dinner to the recruiting staff the first day. The record shows that William Tull, aged 18, enlisted in E Company of the First Oregon Volunteer Cavalry on Feb. 5, 1862. Camp Barlow does not seem to have been long in use.

Camp Blossom, CLACKAMAS. Camp Blossom is about one-half mile west of Timberline Lodge at timberline on Mount Hood. Before the lodge and all weather access road were built in 1937, Camp Blossom was the usual staging point for climbs of the south side. Fred McNeil in *Wy'east "The Mountain"*, p. 114, states that Lige Coalman insisted that the original Camp Blossom was some distance east at the head of the old timberline road and that Judge M. C. George selected a new site in 1907 when the original campsite was taken over by a USGS survey party making the first contour map of Mount Hood. The Camp Blossom cabin was built by Coalman in 1916 as a supply base for the summit lookout. It has since been torn down but the hearth and chimney base are still visible. Regardless of whether or not the cabin site was the original Camp Blossom, the location was used very early by climbers for tree carvings still readable in 1974 show names and dates back to 1890. While no definite proof is available, the writer believes that Camp Blossom, wherever it may have first been located, was named for James M. Blossom, a pioneer hardware merchant of Portland. Blossom was born in Maine in 1817 and came to Oregon in 1852. The *Oregonian* for Aug. 6, 1859, has an account of the climb of Mount Hood on July 26, 1859 by T. J. Dryer and six others including J. M. Blossom. The account describes Blossom as the nimrod of the party and comments on the campsite at timberline. The description could apply to innumerable places but their route came within a mile of Timberline Lodge.

Camp Carson, UNION. For many years the origin of the name Camp Carson for a place near the headwaters of the Grande Ronde River was a mystery. An 1887 War Department map shows an abandoned Camp Carson site ten miles southeast of the spot now called Camp Carson Mine. The mine is in Tanner Gulch, sections 15 and 22, T 6S, R 36E. There is no record of any military establishment with the name Camp Carson but a letter, on file at the Union County Museum, dated July 29, 1927, signed by Mrs. Turner Oliver, summarizes an interview with Samuel Williamson whose father and brother were two of the original developers of the mine in 1863. He states that Tanner Gulch was named for Mr. Tanner, one of the developers along with his father, but he gives no name for the mine. Mr. Ben Francy of the USFS informed the writer in 1982 that the name was undoubtedly applied about 1872 after James Carson of Michigan became a part owner. The heyday of the area was between 1895 and 1900 when a group of French capitalists purchased the property and installed an extensive hydraulic mining operation. As of the 1980s, little remains to show of their efforts.

Camp Castaway, COOS. This appropriate descriptive name was applied to a military camp used by soldiers and sailors who got ashore from the wreck of the transport *Captain Lincoln* a couple of miles north of the entrance to Coos Bay. The *Captain Lincoln* sailed from San Francisco Dec. 28, 1851, with C Troop of the First Dragoons under command of Lieutenant H. W. Stanton. A medical officer, Dr. Francis Sorrel, was also on board. Instead of making Port Orford, the ship got into difficulties and in very bad weather was wrecked on the morning of Jan. 3, 1852. A report, dated at Benicia, Mar. 24, 1852, is in the annual report of the Secretary of War, dated Dec. 4, 1852, p. 109, and gives many details. There are other reports and letters about Camp Castaway in the same volume. Stories of the wreck are in Dodge's *History of Coos and Curry Counties*, p. 144, *et seq. See also* Victor's *Early Indian Wars of Oregon*, p. 290. Camp Castaway was apparently used about four months, and was a tent town. The troopers finally reached Port Orford after some remarkable adventures.

Camp C. F. Smith, HARNEY. This camp was established in June 1866 by troops relocated from Camp Alvord which was abandoned at the same time. *See* Camp Alvord. The new camp was on a low point of land just above Whitehorse Creek about a mile northeast of the Whitehorse Ranch. Lt.Col. M. A. Reno's *Inspection Report* dated Oct. 14, 1867 gives details of several permanent buildings. Presumably it was named for Major-General Charles Ferguson Smith, a distinguished officer of the regular army. This camp was abandoned Nov. 9, 1869.

Camp Colfax, MALHEUR. This camp was used for a few months during the Indian wars of the 1860s and is mentioned in the Oregon Adjutant General's *Report*, 1865–66. It is described as being where the Canyon City-Boise road crossed Willow Creek. *A Webfoot Volunteer, The Diary of William M. Hilleary 1864 –1866* has some amusing references to the post as well as some specific information. Hilleary's unit, F Company of the First Oregon Volunteer Infantry, established Camp Colfax about Aug. 24, 1865, on South Willow Creek about six miles east of Ironside Mountain. It was apparent that temporary protection would not stand against the weather, so in late October logs were snaked and hauled in from Ironside Mountain and at least two and maybe three cabins were built, with common walls so as to save logs. The roofs were poles and willows, covered with earth and there were good fireplaces of stone. The camp seems to have been used as a way-station by outfits other than F Company. The detachment proceeded to Fort Boise at the end of the year and Hilleary says with satisfaction that the cabins were set fire on Dec. 27, 1865, and the soldiers marched away. He does not say for whom the camp was named, but it was probably intended to honor Schuyler Colfax, popular member of Congress from Indiana and in 1865 speaker of the House of Representatives. Colfax visited Oregon in the summer of that year.

Camp Creek, CLACKAMAS. This stream rises near Government Camp, and flows westward into Zigzag River. Laurel Hill, the terror of the emigrant trains, lies between these two streams like a wedge, and over its brow travellers on the Barlow Road let their wagons down by ropes snubbed around trees. It seems probable that this stream was named for its connection with Government Camp. *See* Government Camp. Joel Palmer of the Barlow party mentions Camp Creek under date of Oct. 13, 1845, but the description in his journal shows this to be a tributary of White River some 15 or 20 miles southeast of Government Camp. The name has not prevailed in the original location and the exact stream can no longer be identified.

Camp Creek, DOUGLAS. This stream flows into Mill Creek, north of Loon Lake. Camp Creek was named in 1853 by a party from Scottsburg headed by L. L. Williams which camped on the stream on the way to Loon Lake. *See* Walling's *History of Southern Oregon*, p. 439.

Camp Creek, LANE. Camp Creek is a prominent stream that flows into McKenzie River from the north between Thurston and Walterville. It was called Camp Creek in very early pioneer days. There are two stories about the origin of the name, both of which may be true. One is that pioneer settlers found an Indian camp near the stream, called *Chaston* by the Indians themselves. On the other hand Walling, in *Illustrated History of Lane County*, p. 468, says that the stream was named because a party of pioneers chasing Indian stock thieves camped there. Walling gives several paragraphs of history of the little valley of Camp Creek. Camp Creek post office was established July 12, 1871, with William Pattison, Jr., first of seven postmasters. This office was closed to Springfield, Sept. 15, 1922. It is apparent from an inspection of maps of various dates that Camp Creek office moved a good deal depending on the availability of postmasters.

Camp Creek, LANE. The stream referred to in this heading rises south of Stony Point and flows south into Siuslaw River near Alma in the west part of the county. Writing of this stream, P. M. Morse, Lane County Engineer, under date of Aug. 4, 1943, says "has usually been called Camp Creek, as it has been a favorite camping spot during the summer and for hunters during the deer season."

Camp Creek, WALLOWA. This stream drains a considerable area in the vicinity of Zumwalt and flows into Sheep Creek a little above Imnaha. In early days stockmen going from Wallowa Valley into the Imnaha country found a good campground near the mouth of the stream, and as a result the name Camp Creek was applied. Also the Indians had a campsite on the stream which they used traveling from Chesnimnus south to other localities. The first homesteader on the stream was Waldo Chase. Trail Creek flows into Camp Creek.

Camp Currey, HARNEY. According to the Oregon Adjutant General's *Report*, 1865–66, Camp Currey was established in the fall of 1865 at Indian Springs on what is now known as Silver Creek. In Jan. 1944, J. C. Cecil of Burns wrote the compiler that Camp Currey was at what at that time was known as the Cecil 71 Ranch, a pioneer landmark. "Pat" Cecil sent the following extract from a statement made by the Adjutant General's Office at Washington, Apr. 23, 1930: "The camp was established in August, 1865, and was abandoned in May, 1866. No formally declared reservation existed at this point. It was occupied on September 30, 1865, by Companies D and I, 4th California Infantry, detachment of Company E, 1st Washington Territorial Infantry and a detachment of Company K, 1st Oregon Infantry. In November, 1865, the 2nd Battalion, 14th U.S. Infantry, was stationed at this post. Company K, 1st Oregon Infantry, was also at the post. It was commanded on September 30, 1865, by Captain L. S. Scott, Company D, 4th California Infantry, and on November 30, 1865, 1st Lieut. Frank W. Perry, Brevet Major, Company E, 2nd Battalion, 14th U.S. Infantry, assumed command of the post and remained until the post was abandoned in May, 1866." In addition "Pat" Cecil wrote the compiler: "Many years ago we removed the foundation stones of about forty cabins, measuring about 10 by 12 feet, and judging by the charred remains, I think they were built of hewed logs. There is an excavation on the hillside that may have been used as a cellar or storehouse. There were three graves back of the camp, apparently of soldiers." The camp was named for Colonel George B. Currey, who had been an officer in the First Oregon Volunteer Cavalry but who had succeeded to the command of the Columbia District when Brigadier-General George Wright was drowned. The spelling, Curry, is wrong.

Camp Dahlgren, CROOK. Camp Dahlgren was established Aug. 22, 1864, by Captain John M. Drake of the First Oregon Volunteer Cavalry, and was named for Colonel Ulric Dahlgren who was killed Mar. 2, 1864, in a cavalry engagement near Richmond, Virginia. Drake had already occupied Camps Maury and Gibbs, but had to move because of poor forage. Camp Gibbs was apparently on what is now known as Drake Creek near the north base of the Maury Mountains, and Camp Dahlgren is described as being 20 miles to the northeast on Beaver Creek. Drake's report says that Camp Dahlgren was abandoned Sept. 20, 1864, but he gives no details about its location. It was probably not far from the present town of Paulina.

Camp Day, KLAMATH. In the files of the Oregon Historical Society are family letters from Lieut. Lorenzo Lorain of the Third Artillery which give a few details of a march made by a detachment of two officers and 66 enlisted men of Company L, 3rd Artillery, under the command of 1st Lieutenant Alexander Piper, from Fort Umpqua to a point near Klamath River, where a post called Camp Day was established. Piper and his party left Fort Umpqua June 26, 1860, and proceeded by way of Scottsburg and Canyonville to the Rogue River Valley. The soldiers passed through Jacksonville, and from that point followed the Yreka road to the junction with the emigrant trail from the Klamath country. This trail was followed to the vicinity of Klamath River, where a camp was made July 16, 1860, apparently on Spencer Creek about half a mile from the river, although the identification is by no means certain. This establishment was called Camp Day, in honor of Lieutenant Edward Henry Day, also of the Third Artillery. Day was a native of Virginia and a classmate of Piper's at the Military Academy. He died Jan. 2, 1860, and this circumstance undoubtedly impelled Piper to select his name for the camp. Piper left Camp Day with his troops Oct. 6 and arrived at Fort Umpqua Oct. 18, 1860. Lorain was interested in photography, which was a novelty in 1860. He took pictures of Camp Day and these along with Piper's journal are reproduced in an article in *OHQ*, v. 69, pp. 223 *et seq*.

Camp Elliff, DOUGLAS. Preston's *Map of Oregon*, 1856, shows the Elliff place in S 11, T 32S, R 5W. This is near where I-5 first reaches Cow Creek Valley after going south from Canyonville. A post called Camp Elliff was established in this locality in the Rogue River War of 1855–56, which was occupied by Captain Laban Buoy and a detachment of B Company, Second Oregon Mounted Volunteers, mostly from Lane County. It was Buoy's duty to keep the road open along Cow Creek. The compiler has found no record of any permanent structures at this camp. *See* Victor's *Early Indian Wars of Oregon*, p. 368.

Camp Gibbs, CROOK. This camp at the north base of Maury Mountains was in use for a short time in the summer of 1864 during the Snake War and was probably named for Governor Addison C. Gibbs. Camp Maury was established on what is now Maury Creek on May 18, 1864, but because of poor forage, the post was moved west about five miles on July 21, 1864, and named Camp Gibbs. The compiler does not know the exact location, but it seems apparent that it was on or near what is now known as Drake Creek. Captain John M. Drake of the First Oregon Volunteer Cavalry was in command of the camp. The post was moved again Aug. 22, on account of poor forage. The new post was called Camp Dahlgren.

Camp Gordon, DOUGLAS. Camp Gordon is one of the elusive military camps used in the Rogue River War of 1855–56. It is described by Mrs. F. F. Victor in *Early Indian Wars of Oregon*, p. 368, as being eight miles above the mouth of Cow Creek. The compiler is of the opinion this means up the main route of travel, for there was no road up Cow Creek itself. Eight miles south along the route of travel would put Camp Gordon somewhere on Canyon Creek south of Canyonville. The camp was in command of Captain Samuel Gordon and was doubtless named for him.

Camp Grant, DOUGLAS. This trail shelter just southeast of Red Butte was named arbitrarily by USFS ranger Fred Asam.

Camp Ground, MULTNOMAH. Camp Ground post office was established on May 19, 1884, with Edward F. Wright postmaster, and remained in service only until June 9, 1884. In fact the office may never have been in actual operation. It was just at this time that Gresham post office was established. That event took place on May 15, 1884, and James F. Roberts was the first postmaster at Gresham. There was a good deal of rivalry between the proponents of the two offices, Camp Ground and Gresham, and not a little bad feeling developed among the partisans. William H. Stanley wrote from Gresham in July 1947, that the proposed offices were within rock throwing distance of each other, at or near the intersection of Main Street and Powell Valley Road. Gresham beat Camp Ground to the draw. Mr. Stanley says that a campground was situated near Main Street and Powell Valley Road, with some small cabins used during camp meetings. Edward F. Wright had some connection with this campground, probably managed it at camp meetings.

Camp Hancock, WHEELER. Camp Hancock is a memorial to Lon W. Hancock, an amateur paleontologist and geologist. Hancock was born in Harrison, Arkansas in 1884. He left school at an early age and spent most of his adult life as a Post Office employee in Portland. He had an abiding interest in fossil hunting and during the 1940s he began taking young boys on outings in the Clarno area. These became more complex and in 1951 Lon and his wife took 14 boys and ten volunteer staff members for the first formal 12-day summer camp at Camp Hancock under the sponsorship of the Oregon Museum of Science and Industry. Interest grew apace and the early tent camp has grown to a modern, well-equipped facility. Hancock died in 1961 and left his collection of more than 10,000 fossils and artifacts to OMSI.

Camp Henderson, MALHEUR. Camp Henderson was one of the establishments of the Indian wars of the 1860s. On May 26, 1864, Captain George B. Currey of the First Oregon Volunteer Cavalry camped on Crooked Creek about eight miles southwest of the mouth of Jordan Creek and called the place Camp Henderson in compliment to J. H. D. Henderson, representative in Congress from Oregon, 1865–67. The stream was called Gibbs Creek in honor of Governor A. C. Gibbs, but that name did not persist. Camp Henderson was not long in use and was a very simple establishment. *See* Bancroft's *History of Oregon*, v. 2, p. 499

and Oregon Adjutant General's *Report*, 1865–66, p. 36. Preston E. Onstad in *OHQ*, v. 65, pp. 297 *et seq.*, has further details and pictures. He states that the location was on Crooked Creek just south of the present US-95 highway bridge.

Camp Kuratli, CLACKAMAS. This is the Salvation Army youth camp on the Clackamas River at the mouth of Deep Creek. It was formerly known as Camp Trestle Glen because of the two railroad trestles on the abandoned Portland Traction Company line. Reuben Kuratli gave generously of his time and labor to renovate the old facilities and the Salvation Army commemorated him with the name.

Camp Lincoln, GRANT. Camp Lincoln, named for Abraham Lincoln, was established by Lieutenant J. A. Waymire of the First Oregon Volunteer Cavalry Mar. 15, 1864, and abandoned May 1, 1864. It was used during the Indian outbreaks, but was a temporary post. *See* Oregon Adjutant General's *Report*, 1865–66, pp. 67, *et seq.* It was on South Fork John Day River, but the compiler has been unable to get the exact location. Probably it was near the present community of Dayville.

Camp Logan, GRANT. Camp Logan was established Sept. 2, 1865 by Captain A. B. Ingram, Company K, First Oregon Volunteer Infantry, during the Indian troubles. It was not a large camp and not long in use although according to Lt.Col. M. A. Reno's inspection report of Oct. 1867, it was then still occupied by regular army troops. William M. Hilleary, in *Recollections of a Linn County Volunteer* in the Oregon Historical Society Library says quarters were built for 40 men. This was in Aug. or Sept. 1865. The place is mentioned in the Oregon Adjutant General's *Report*, 1865–66, but no details are given. In Jan. 1944, R. H. Sullens of Prairie City wrote the compiler that Camp Logan was on Strawberry Creek about six miles south of Prairie City near what at that time was the Roger Kent ranch. This information agrees with War Department maps, although the stream was apparently known in 1865 as Indian Creek and later as Logan Creek. In fact Strawberry Mountain was once called Logan Butte on account of the camp. The post was named for William Logan, Indian Agent at Warm Springs Reservation during the early 1860s. C. W. Brown of Canyon City has written the compiler confirming the location at the Kent ranch and says there were several log houses, the remains of some of them still in evidence in Jan. 1944. Formerly this was the J. J. Cozart ranch. An old box stove from Camp Logan is still in use at the Prairie City Grange Hall.

Camp Maury, CROOK. Camp Maury was about 30 miles airline southeast of Prineville, on the south side of Crooked River Valley near the base of Maury Mountains. It was named for Colonel R. F. Maury, who took a prominent part in the Snake War of 1864, and was at the time in command of the First Oregon Volunteer Cavalry. The camp was in the southeast quarter of S 20, T 17S, R 21E, on the southeast side of Maury Creek and just west of Rimrock Creek. It had been occupied previously by a command under Major Enoch Steen, and the site had been selected for a supply depot. A company of the Oregon Cavalry under command of Captain John M. Drake made camp at the place in the evening of May 18, 1864, and Drake, in his journal, says he named it for Colonel Maury. It was on May 18 that Lieutenant Stephen Watson and two men were killed by Indians. They were buried by the side of a small knoll south of the camp and at the edge of the timber. The bodies were later moved to Camp Watson, a more important establishment to the northeast. The account given by Bancroft in *History of Oregon*, v. 2, p. 498, is wrong in some particulars. Camp Maury was occupied until July 21, 1864, when the depot was moved five miles west to a place called Camp Gibbs. This was done to get better forage. In Jan. 1943, Mrs. Florence Knox of Post wrote about Camp Maury and said that a number of stone walls were still standing, three or four feet high, apparently built to protect sleeping soldiers. The site of the camp is on the J. T. Stewart homestead.

Camp McDowell, UMATILLA. Camp McDowell was established on Camas Prairie on May 31, 1865, by Captain Abner W. Waters and a detachment of Company F, First Oregon Volunteer Infantry. According to *A Webfoot Volunteer, The Diary of William M. Hilleary, 1864–66*, it was on what they called Humbug Fork John Day River and was called Camp Humbug. The stream is now known as Camas Creek. On June 11, 1865, the camp was moved a short distance and renamed Camp McDowell for Major-General Irvin McDowell, then commanding The Military Department of the Pacific. It was abandoned on July 11, 1865, when the troops returned to Fort Walla Walla. For information about McDowell, *see* McDowell Peak.

Camp McKinley, MULTNOMAH. The Spanish-American War broke out Apr. 20–22, 1898, and no time was lost in mobilizing the Oregon National Guard. A camp was officially established Apr. 29, 1898, on the racetrack grounds at Irvington Park, named Camp McKinley in honor of President William McKinley and it was at this camp that the Second Oregon Infantry was mustered into the service of the United States. Camp McKinley was just east of what is now Northeast Seventh Avenue, between Northeast Brazee and Northeast Fremont streets in Portland. The locality no longer shows any traces of camp or racetrack. Between May 11 and May 16, 1898, the Second Oregon was moved to the Presidio of San Francisco, from which post it embarked for Manila on May 25, to be away from the United States for more than a year. Brigadier-General Raymond F. Olson of the Oregon Military Department, on Oct. 8, 1947, sent the compiler a copy of part of General Orders No. 2, dated Apr. 29, 1898, establishing Camp McKinley, but added that no orders of disestablishment could be found and it was assumed that the camp officially ceased its life on May 19, 1898, when the last of the state and federal property was removed. The compiler recalls visiting the camp several times, and has no recollection of anything more than the most temporary sort of facilities.

Camp Meriwether, TILLAMOOK. Camp Meriwether is the summer camp of the Boy Scouts, Portland area. It is on the ocean front about two miles south of Cape Lookout and not far from Sand Lake. It was named for Meriwether Lewis in 1925 by G. H. Oberteuffer, scout executive of the Boy Scouts of America, Portland area.

Camp Millard, CLACKAMAS. The ground for this camp was given to the Boy Scouts of America in 1925 by Mrs. Alvira Millard in memory of her son, Samuel Brown Millard. The facilities were expanded and cabins were built in 1937. The camp was used by the army during World War II and after the war was again a popular spot for the Boy Scouts. By the 1980s it did not fit into the plans of the Columbia Pacific Council and in 1990 they disposed of the property to concentrate in other locations.

Camp Namanu, CLACKAMAS. The Camp Fire Girls of Portland and vicinity have a summer camp a little northwest of Bull Run, on Sandy River just below the mouth of Bull Run River. The name of this place and its summer post office is Camp Namanu. *Namanu* is said to be an Indian word meaning beaver, and that animal was once plentiful in the locality. The compiler does not know from what Indian language *namanu* is taken. The Chinook jargon word for beaver is *ee-na*. Namanu may be a variation of the Chinook jargon word *ne-nam-ooks*, meaning land otter. A Camp Namanu post office was established Jan. 7, 1939, by change of name from Bullrun. Elaine S. Gorman was the first postmaster.

Camp Polk, DESCHUTES. Camp Polk is about three miles northeast of Sisters on the west bank of Squaw Creek, and there is now little to show that it was once a military post. The camp was established in 1865 at the time of Indian uprisings in eastern Oregon. Captain Charles LaFollette was commanding officer of Company A of the First Oregon Volunteer Infantry and a resident of Polk County. His company was stationed at this camp and he named the place in honor of his home county. Some cabins were built and the troops spent the winter of 1865–66. About 1870 Samuel M. W. Hindman settled near the camp and for a time ran the post office. Mrs. Nellie M. Miller, long a resident of Sisters, died in July 1941, and left a substantial sum to be used in improving and maintaining the Camp Polk cemetery, also known as the Hindman cemetery. The locality of Camp Polk is shown on the USGS map of the Sisters quadrangle. A post office with the name Camp Polk was established in Mar. 1875, with Samuel M. W. Hindman postmaster. In July 1888, the office was moved about three miles southwest to the community of Sisters and the name was changed to agree with the new locality.

Camp Rilea, CLATSOP. Camp Rilea was founded in 1927 as Camp Clatsop, a summer training area for the Oregon National Guard. Prior to this, places in southern Oregon had been used but the termination of land grant railroad military rates in 1926 made it desireable to have a location nearer the central Willamette Valley. Additional land was added during the 1930s and at the start of World War II the camp was operated as a federal post for troop training and staging. It is now wholly owned by the state of Oregon and in 1959 was renamed Camp Rilea in honor of Major-General Thomas E. Rilea, long time Adjutant General of Oregon. Rilea was born in Chicago, Illinois on May 5, 1895 and died in Portland on Feb. 4, 1959. For obituary, *see* the *Oregonian*, Feb. 4, 1959, p. 1.

Camp Russell, MARION. When the First Oregon Volunteer Infantry was organized in 1864–65, at least four companies appear to have been mustered in at a place called Camp Russell, but the *Report* of the Adjutant General, 1865–66, fails to locate the camp. However, *Recollections of a Linn County Volunteer* by William M. Hilleary of F Company, on file at the Oregon Historical Society, say that the camp was on the Fair Grounds at Salem. Among other things, Hilleary says: "One wing of the old pavilion was fitted up for squad room, in which were our bunks. It was our sitting room, parlor, bedroom, hall, all in one. Another wing of the pavilion was occupied by the kitchen and culinary department, which was dubbed 'Hotel de Russle' for it was here that we, with an eye on the main chance, 'rustled' for our grub." This camp was named in honor of Major-General David Allen Russell, who was killed at the battle of Opequan, Virginia, Sept. 19, 1864. Russell had served in Oregon and was a popular soldier and his death occurred about the time the camp was established. The order naming the camp is in the *Official Records of the Union and Confederate Armies*, v. 50, part 2, p. 1086.

Camp Russell, POLK. This was a logging camp three miles southwest of Valsetz, the site of a logging operation owned by George Russell.

Camp Sherman, JEFFERSON. This post office is on the Metolius River about two miles north of its source. It was named because of the fact that a number of families from Sherman County spent their summer vacations at this camp.

Camp Spencer, JOSEPHINE. Camp Spencer was a place used in the Rogue River War of 1855–56, and is mentioned in Victor's *Early Indian Wars of Oregon*, p. 366. It is described as being on the lower Applegate River. Mrs. Victor gives neither the exact location of the camp nor the reason for the name.

Camp Stuart, JACKSON. A list of military establishments in Oregon should include the name of Camp Stuart, although it is not mentioned in Heitman's *Historical Register*. In 1917, Princeton University Press published *Mexican War Diary of George B. McClellan*, edited by William Starr Myers. On p. 14 is a note of an entry by McClellan on a page otherwise blank, of an event several years after the Mexican War. The note as printed is: "On the 18th June, 1851, at five in the afternoon died Jimmie Stuart, my best and oldest friend. He was mortally wounded the day before by an arrow, whilst gallantly leading a charge against a party of hostile Indians. He is buried at Camp Stuart—about twenty five miles south of Rogue's River [Oregon?], near the main road, and not far from the base of Cishion (?) Mountains. His grave is between two oaks, on the left side of the road, going south, with J. S. cut in the bark of the largest of the oaks." Captain James Stuart was graduated from West Point in 1846 and served with distinction in the Mexican War, gaining two brevets. Stuart was wounded in an engagement probably near Rogue River a little upstream from Upper Table Rock. Walling in *History* *of Southern Oregon*, p. 197, gives an account of the incident and says that Stuart was buried near the present town of Phoenix, close to the site of the Colver house, but mentions no military establishment. There is additional information in Bancroft's *History of Oregon*, v. 2, p. 227. The camp was used intermittently at least as late as 1853. The stream flowing northward through the valley at this point was named Stuart Creek in honor of James Stuart, but settlers later changed the name to Bear Creek, which cannot be considered an improvement. The compiler is of the opinion that McClellan wrote *Ciskiou*(?) in his note and not "Cishion (?).

Camp Warner, LAKE. Camp Warner occupied two places in the Warner Valley, some distance apart. In 1866 troops from Vancouver made a reconnaissance into southeast Oregon, and, among other things, selected a site for Camp Warner on the west side of the Warner Valley. Soldiers were sent from Boise, Idaho, with orders to build the camp, but the command reached the east side of the Warner Valley and concluded that it would be impractical to cross the string of lakes and swamps. Accordingly, the camp was built a little east of the valley on the north part of Hart Mountain and named for Brevet Captain William Horace Warner, who was killed by Indians in Sept. 1849, probably in Surprise Valley, just over the line in California. For information about the event, *see* Warner Valley. The Camp Warner mentioned in this paragraph is now generally known as Old Camp Warner. The winter of 1866–67 was very severe and the troops at Old Camp Warner suffered great hardships. Major-General George Crook, then a lieutenant-colonel, took command at Boise in 1866, and in 1867 made an inspection of the Warner Valley. He disapproved of the camp and the locality and was provoked by the story that the troops could not cross the lakes. He caused a rock causeway to be built in a few days and relocated Camp Warner in the west part of the valley, at about the place originally selected by the troops from Vancouver. For additional information about Camp Warner, *see History of Central Oregon*, p. 811, *et seq.* Therein it is stated that the troops were moved from the camp in October and Nov. 1873. Heitman's *Historical Register* lists Camp Warner but gives no details. There is also some information in Bancroft's *History of Oregon*, v. 2, p. 536. *See also* Stone Bridge. In Oct. 1943, C. H. Langslet, county assessor at Lakeview, informed the compiler that the second location of Camp Warner was on Honey Creek in the southwest part of T 36S, R 22E, at what is now known as Fort Warner Ranch. The USGS Little Honey Creek quadrangle dated 1968 shows the site in S 33 on Dent Creek, a small tributary of Honey Creek.

Camp Watson, WHEELER. All that is left of Camp Watson is on a little stream called Fort Creek about five miles west of Antone. The place is clearly shown on the USGS Derr Meadows quadrangle. Camp Watson was named in honor of Second Lieutenant Stephen Watson of the First Oregon Volunteer Cavalry who was killed in action with Snake Indians on the upper reaches of Crooked River May 18, 1864. According to the report of Captain H. C. Small of Company G of the Oregon Cavalry, he selected the site of Camp Watson Oct. 1, 1864, and his command

133

built huts for the winter. The name was applied by order of Brigadier-General Benjamin Alvord. It is apparent that there was a temporary Camp Watson a little earlier in the campaign four miles to the east. Late in 1866 the Oregon volunteers were recalled to Fort Vancouver and mustered out of service, but the camp was occupied by federal cavalry and infantry detachments for several more years. Local tradition says that a log stockade about 15 feet high was the main defense, and there were several groups of log cabins and a blacksmith shop. In addition there was a building used for a stage station. A large meadow was used for a parade ground. In 1935 there were reported to be seven graves at Camp Watson, but it could not be determined if Watson's body was in any of them. A post office with the name Camp Watson was established to serve the locality on Nov. 11, 1867, with Charles L. West first of four postmasters. This office was discontinued Nov. 3, 1886, with papers to Caleb.

Camp White, JACKSON. George Ared White was born in Illinois July 18, 1881. When but a youth he became interested in military life and served in the Spanish-American War. He came to Oregon from the Rocky Mountain states in 1904 and joined the staff of the *Oregonian*. The compiler recalls many pleasant weeks spent with George White and Gene Howe in 1905 reporting the Lewis and Clark Fair for the *Oregonian*. In 1915 George White became adjutant general for Oregon and from that time on his rise in military rank was remarkable. He served with distinction in World War I. Successively he held more important positions and was major-general in command of the 41st Division when that organization was called into the federal service Sept. 16, 1940. He served with that rank until his death Nov. 23, 1941. He received many honors from both government and private agencies. Under the name Ared White he gained wide popularity as an author. Camp White, near Rogue River in southern Oregon, was north of Medford, and was named in honor of George A. White. It was a large installation of over 900 buildings for use in World War II. The camp was authorized in Jan. 1942, and the first concrete was poured Mar. 11. The camp was officially dedicated Sept. 15, 1942, with Mrs. White the guest of honor although the first troops had arrived in July. Camp White was deactivated in Apr. 1946. Most of the buildings were removed and much of the land sold off. The hospital complex was retained and, in 1948, turned over to the Veterans Adminstration for a domiciliary facility. *See also* White City.

Camp Withycombe, CLACKAMAS. Camp Withycombe, which is just east of Clackamas station, is named for James Withycombe, governor of Oregon from 1915 to 1919. In Feb. 1944, Colonel Elmer V. Wooton, acting adjutant general of Oregon, wrote the compiler: "Camp Withycombe was established in 1909, under a lease arrangement with option to purchase. The United States Government was the lessee and the purchase option was exercised in 1910. Originally known as the Clackamas Rifle Range, it was redesignated Camp Withycombe during World War I and in 1934 was officially designated as Camp Withycombe. The original tract was added to several times, so that now the area embraced in the camp site totals 257 acres."

Camp Wright, HARNEY. Camp Wright was used during the Indian troubles of the 1860s. According to the Oregon Adjutant General's *Report*, 1865–66, it was established Oct. 3, 1865. It was occupied by Captain L. L. Williams and H Company of the First Oregon Volunteer Infantry, and it was situated on Silvies River close to the east end of Wright Point near what was later Island Ranch. It was named for Brigadier-General George Wright who was drowned in the wreck of the *Brother Jonathan. See* Wright Point. The camp was not many months in use and was not substantially fortified. *See* Bancroft's *History of Oregon*, v. 2, p. 514 and p. 490, footnote. *Recollections of a Linn County Volunteer* by William M. Hilleary on file at the Oregon Historical Society say that the soldiers protected themselves by building up sod walls with roofs of poles covered with earth.

Campbell Canyon, MORROW. This canyon empties into Willow Creek five miles below Heppner. It was named for a well-known family that included Morrow County pioneer, Eugene F. Campbell, and County Judge William T. Campbell.

Campbell Falls, DOUGLAS. The USFS has adopted the name Campbell Falls for a drop in South Umpqua River, in S 13, T 29S, R 1W, just above the mouth of Boulder Creek. These falls were named to commemorate Robert G. Campbell, a former employee of the USFS who was killed in action in World War II, Nov. 12, 1944.

Campers Flat, LANE. Campers Flat, on Middle Fork Willamette River, supposedly was named because emigrants and other travellers on the Oregon Central Military Wagon Road would stop to rest and graze their stock at nearby Big Pine Opening.

Canaan, COLUMBIA. In Dec. 1985, Robert M. Hamill of Corvallis wrote the compiler and gave the following information about this small community west of Deer Island. Perry Usher settled on a claim and gave an acre for a school and grounds. He was so impressed with the good soil and lush growth, he told his friends he was in the Land of Canaan. The school was called Canaan until 1955 when the district was consolidated with Saint Helens. B.L.M. records show that Aaron P. Usher filed on a homestead at Canaan in Oct. 1886. Of course he may have lived on the ground prior to the actual filing date.

Canary, LANE. This place received its unusual name because local residents could find none other that would satisfy both postal authorities and railroad officials. Many names were suggested but to no avail. The writer is informed that Canary has no local significance and it is not known who suggested it.

Canby, CLACKAMAS. Canby was named for Major-General Edward R. S. Canby, commander of the Department of the Columbia, who was killed by Modoc Indians on Apr. 11, 1873, at a peace parley not far from the California-Oregon line south of what is now Klamath Falls. For a short account of the Modoc War, *see*

Scott's *History of the Oregon Country*, V. 2, p. 334. *See also* Jeff C. Riddle's *The Indian History of the Modoc War*, which gives detailed accounts of the war and subsequent happenings. Edward Richard Sprigg Canby was a veteran of the Seminole, Mexican and Civil wars. In 1874 Fort Canby, Washington, at the mouth of the Columbia River, was named for him. Stories to the effect that the community of Canby was once called Knighttown for Adam Knight, an early resident, could not be confirmed in June 1943. Adam Knight, then still living, denied all knowledge of the matter. The general locality from Canby north to the Willamette River was called Baker Prairie.

Canemah, CLACKAMAS. Canemah was founded in 1845 by A. F. Hedges. During many years it was the loading and unloading point for the portage around Willamette Falls. Leslie M. Scott says that *Canemah* is supposed to have been the name of an Indian chief.

Canfield Hill, CURRY. Canfield Hill is north of Rogue River five miles above Wedderburn. It was named for Jason W. Canfield who was born in Ohio in 1843 and homesteaded here on Rogue River before the turn of the century.

Cannery Hill, TILLAMOOK. Cannery Hill is the high ground projecting northward into Nestucca Bay. Before the bay was closed to commercial fishing, a cannery was located on the west side of the hill. When local roads were developed after World War I, fish were taken elsewhere for processing and now all that remains is the name.

Cannery Mountain, LINCOLN. Cannery Mountain, elevation 1065 feet, is on the south side of Siletz River about two miles southeast of the present site of Kernville. This mountain is about south of and across the river from the site of the former Kern fish cannery and it was named on that account. For information about the cannery, *see* Kernville.

Cannibal Mountain, LINCOLN. Cannibal Mountain, elevation 1946 feet, in the Coast Range about five miles south of Tidewater, has one of those names that seems to defy efforts to find a reason for the application. The region is not noted for its cannibals, unless they be deer flies and mosquitos, and it seems hardly likely that anyone ever named the peak for such pests. The compiler has an old map with the name Cannonball Mountain for this peak, but in 1946, H. G. Hopkins, district ranger for the USFS at Waldport, tried to learn the history of the name of the mountain and could find no one in the locality that ever heard of Cannonball. The point was sometimes called Canniber Mountain, supposed to be an Indian name meaning saddle, but search so far has disclosed no such Indian word. Canniber was also said to be derived from the fact that old timers went to the place for canning berries, but this seems fanciful. Hopkins reports that stories that two well-known hunters went there to get venison to eat raw were denied as ridiculous by one of the hunters still surviving. Stories that a pioneer trapper, during a snowstorm ate his Indian wife rather than starve are of the guidebook type rather than for jury trial.

Cannon Beach, CLATSOP. Lieutenant Neil M. Howison, U.S. Navy, arrived in the Columbia River July 1, 1846, in the schooner *Shark* for the purpose of making an investigation of part of the Oregon country for the government. For details of his visit, *see* Carey's *History of Oregon*, p. 451. For details of his report, *see OHQ*, v. 14, p. 59. The *Shark* was wrecked on attempting to leave the Columbia River on Sept. 10, 1846, and part of her deck and a small iron cannon drifted ashore south of Tillamook Head, thus giving the name to Cannon Beach. For information about this disaster *see OHQ*, v. 14, p. 355. In 1930, the cannon and the capstan of the *Shark* were mounted on a concrete base in a turnout on the east side of US-101 near the north end of the community of Arch Cape and just south of Hug Point State Park. The capstan may not have belonged to the *Shark*. The City of Cannon Beach has marked both north and south US-101 exits with replicas of the cannon, but the original was located near where it washed ashore. In 1989, the cannon and capstan were removed to Astoria by the Clatsop County Historical Society.

Cannon Beach is a well-known seashore resort, and is of historic interest. In Jan. 1806, William Clark climbed over Tillamook Head and visited the locality. At the south end of Cannon Beach is Arch Cape, which blocks automobile travel on the beach itself. Hug Point, about two miles north of Arch Cape, originally blocked beach traffic, but a narrow road was cut around its face in the solid rock. This route for automobile travel was abandoned long ago after the completion of the original Oregon Coast Highway. Other important points are Humbug Point, Silver Point, and Chapman Point, which is at the north end and is a southern spur of Tillamook Head. Haystack Rock, 235 feet high, is one of the prominent sights on the beach itself. Ecola Creek flows into the ocean at the north end of Cannon Beach. The community has been known by various names including Elk Creek and Ecola, but the Post Office Department in 1922 changed the office name from Ecola to Cannon Beach to agree with the natural feature and to avoid confusion with Eola, where mail was frequently missent. Cannon Beach is about eight miles long. Cannon Beach post office was established May 29, 1891, with James P. Austin postmaster. This office was near Austin Point south of Hug Point, not far from the spot where the old cannon stood and several miles south of the present Cannon Beach community. The office was closed Nov. 2, 1901. The office called Ecola was established Nov. 25, 1910, with Lester E. Bill postmaster. This office was at the place called Elk Creek, now called Cannon Beach community. The name of the office was changed to Cannon Beach on May 25, 1922, when Eugene Lamphere was the postmaster.

Canoe Encampment Rapids, MORROW. These rapids were flooded out when John Day Dam was built. They were in the Columbia River between Castle Rock and Blalock Island. The encampment at the foot of the rapids was a popular one with the fur traders and trappers. The name appears in early journals, but when first so used cannot be determined. It has been suggested that possibly the name was originally applied by traders because of an encampment of Indians with canoes at that point, as it seems strange that the traders themselves would single out those rapids as being particularly associated with their canoes, which they had with them at all rapids.

Cantor Creek, MALHEUR. Cantor Creek empties into Antelope Reservoir southwest of Jordan Valley. It is apparently named for Alex Canter, one of the early settlers in Jordan Valley, who had a homestead nearby.

Canyon City, GRANT. This historic community is the county seat of Grant County, and derives its name because of the fact that it is situated in a canyon about two miles south of the John Day River. This part of the state was the scene of gold discoveries in the fall of 1861 and for some time there was a great influx of miners. Canyon City post office was established in what was then Wasco County on Apr. 23, 1864. Grant County was formed from part of Wasco County on Oct. 14, 1864. Canyon City suffered from a disastrous fire on Apr. 18, 1937, a large part of the community being destroyed.

Canyon Road, MULTNOMAH, WASHINGTON. Canyon Road, at the head of Southwest Jefferson Street, Portland, was a highly important factor in the development of the city. Rival communities such as Linnton, Milton and Saint Helens were at a disadvantage because they did not have as good access to the rich farm lands of the Tualatin Valley. The road was named because it traversed the canyon of Tanner Creek. *See* Tanner Creek. Canyon Road was first opened in the fall of 1849 (letter of Joseph Smith in the *Oregonian*, July 13, 1884). Citizens of Portland formed, for the improvement of the road in 1850, the Portland and Valley Plank Road Company, which was chartered by the legislature and organized at Lafayette July 30, 1851. Subscription for funds opened Mar. 10, 1851, at Portland, Hillsboro, Lafayette, Nesmiths Mills, Marysville (Corvallis), Albany and Salem. Grading began in 1851. Stephen Coffin took the contract for laying the planks. The first plank was laid Sept. 27, 1851, amid ceremonies. In Sept. 1851, Thomas Stephens became superintendent. For further work, *see* advertisements in the *Oregonian* in 1851. The work soon lapsed for lack of funds (article by George H. Himes, *ibid.*, Aug. 14, 1902). The first plank was laid near the present Art Museum. The route was surveyed by Daniel H. Lownsdale. The road was badly damaged by rains in the winter of 1851–52, *Oregonian*, Jan. 10, 1852. A statement of the work on the road appears Apr. 3, 1852. The sum of $14,593.83 was expended up to that time. On May 10, 1852, the third and fourth installments to stock subscriptions were called for. In the summer of 1852 a scandal, or rupture, occured in the company, and new directors were elected, *Oregonian*, Aug. 7, 1852. An earlier road, built by F. W. Pettygrove, passed through what is now Washington Park. The Sunset Highway, US-26, has long replaced the old Canyon Road for the route is a primary access to Portland from the Tualatin Valley.

Canyonville, DOUGLAS. Canyonville is an historic community of Oregon, and is situated at the north end of Canyon Creek Canyon, where this defile opens into the valley of the South Umpqua River. It was in this canyon that the immigrants of 1846 had such great hardships on their way into the Willamette Valley. The canyon was known in pioneer days as Umpqua Canyon. For a graphic description of the difficulties experienced here by the pioneers of 1846, *see* Bancroft's *History of Oregon*, v. 1, p. 563. For information concerning the proposed location of a railroad in the canyon, *see* Scott's *History of the Oregon Country*, v. 4, p. 5. The railroad route finally selected ascended Cow Creek from Riddle and joined the old stage road not far from Glendale. The stage route for many years continued up Canyon Creek and today travelers over I-5 may see where there have been earlier routes through the canyon. The total descent from the pass at the head of Canyon Creek to Canyonville is nearly 1300 feet, most of which occurs in the south part of the canyon. Difficulties have continued here in modern times, for on Jan. 16, 1974 nine men working in a Pacific Northwest Bell Company relay station about a mile south of Canyonville were killed when a massive earthslide swept away the building. For details, *see* the *Oregonian*, Jan. 18, 1974. Canyonville was for many years known as North Canyonville, the post office having been established with that name July 6, 1852, with John T. Boyle, postmaster. There was a locality farther south known as South Canyonville, but this was not a post office. The post office name was changed to Canyonville June 1, 1892. Canyon Creek is erroneously supposed by many to be Cow Creek. The freeway does not follow the canyon of Cow Creek although it does traverse that stream through a wide valley east of Glendale. The pass at the head of Canyon Creek is 2015 feet in elevation. Canyonville has an elevation of 747 feet. Those who have visited this part of the state will realize that Canyon Creek and Canyonville are appropriate names.

Cape Arago, COOS. Cape Arago is the western point of a large headland just south of the mouth of Coos Bay. The northern point of this headland is Coos Head. Captain James Cook sighted it on Mar. 12, 1778, and named it Cape Gregory for the saint of that day. Since 1850 this cape has been called Cape Arago, and is officially so known by the USBGN. Dominique François Jean Arago (1786–1853) was a great French physicist and geographer. He was the intimate of Alexander von Humboldt, and his friendship with Humboldt "lasted over forty years without a single cloud ever having troubled it." The name Cape Arago first appeared on the USC&GS chart prepared by William P. McArthur in 1850, and issued the following year. It seems apparent that McArthur applied the name Arago as the result of the naming of Humboldt Bay, California, which took place about the same time. Humboldt Bay was named in 1850 during the visit of a company of miners styled the Laura Virginia company or association. A. J. Bledsoe, in *Indian Wars of the Northwest*, 1885, p. 118, gives an account of the exploration of the Laura Virginia expedition in the ship *Laura Virginia*, and he says that Humboldt Bay was named at the solicitation of a member of the party who was an admirer of the great scientist. Elsewhere it is reported that the name was selected by Lieutenant Douglass Ottinger, captain of the *Laura Virginia*, but this does not agree with Bledsoe. McArthur visited Humboldt Bay and mapped it in 1850 and a few weeks later charted Port Orford which he named Ewing Harbor for his Coast Survey schooner *Ewing*. He charted the vicinity of Cape Arago shortly after leaving Ewing Harbor. It seems obvious that the well-known friendship between Arago and Humboldt suggested the name for the cape. Family tradition says that McArthur was greatly interested in mathematics and physics and it seems certain that he was familiar with the association of Arago and Humboldt. The compiler is of the opinion that Cape Arago was named on account of this friendship. H. R. Wagner, in *Cartography of the Northwest Coast of America*, v. 2, p. 373, says that Cape Arago is the same as Cabo Toledo of Bodega's and Heceta's larger map of 1775.

Cape Blanco, CURRY. Cape Blanco is in north latitude 42° 50′ 14″ and is the most westward point in Oregon, but not, as some suppose, of continental United States. *Blanco* is a Spanish word meaning white. In 1602 Sebastian Vizcaino sailed from Acapulco at the head of an exploring expedition, and after one of his ships had turned back at Monterey, Vizcaino in his ship and Martin de Aguilar in a *fragata*, left Monterey on Jan. 3, 1603, sailing northward. During a storm the two ships separated and Vizcaino sailed up the coast alone, reaching a point which he named Cape San Sebastian on Jan. 20. He returned to Acapulco without meeting the *fragata*. In the meantime de Aguilar also sailed northward, and he records that on Jan. 19 he reached the 43rd parallel, and found a point which he named Cape Blanco. North of the cape he reported a large river. Here he turned back. Most of the crew of the *fragata*, including de Aguilar, died on the way to Acapulco. H. R. Wagner in *Cartography of the Northwest Coast of America*, v. 1, p. 111, describes this voyage and calls attention to the fact that Cape Blanco was mentioned in the instructions, so that name was already in use before 1602. The recorded latitudes of this expedition are too great and there is nothing to show that the members ever reached the coast of Oregon or saw what is now Cape Blanco. The large Heceta-Bodega map prepared as a result of the 1775 expedition refers to this point as *Cabo Diligensias*. Bodega was off the cape Sept. 27, 1775. *See* Wagner's *Cartography*, v. 2, p. 376. On Mar. 12, 1778, Captain James Cook writes of his discovery of Cape Arago, which he called Cape Gregory, and stated that he thought he observed the Cape Blanco of de Aguilar in proximity. He was too far away to see the mouth of Coos Bay. On Apr. 24, 1792, Captain George Vancouver sighted what we now know as Cape Blanco, and named it Cape Orford in honor of George, earl of Orford, his "much respected friend." Vancouver determined its latitude as 42° 52′, very nearly its true position. There was some speculation on Vancouver's ship as to whether or not it was the Cape Blanco of de Auguilar, but the position and its dark color "did not seem to intitle it to the appellation of cape Blanco." Vancouver brings up the matter again in his *Voyage of Discovery* in the latter part of the entry for Apr. 25. He passed and identified Cape Gregory (now Cape Arago) of Captain Cook, and made a reasonably accurate determination of its latitude, though he noted the difference between his figures and Cook's. There was no other important point and he said: "This induced me to consider the above point as the cape Gregory of Captain Cook, with a probability of its being also the cape Blanco of D'Aguilar, if land hereabouts the latter ever saw." Vancouver finished his observations for the day by expressing a doubt that Cook saw Cape Blanco or any other cape south of Cape Gregory on Mar. 12, 1778, and stated that it was fair to presume that what Cook saw was an inland mountain. Notwithstanding all these facts the name Cape Blanco has persisted for the most western cape of Oregon, even though it may not have originally been applied to it, and Vancouver's name Cape Orford has fallen into disuse and has been decided against by the USBGN. Part of the name is still in use in Port Orford, which is just south of the cape. Cape Alava, Clallam County, Washington, is the most westward point in the 48 contiguous states, with a longitude of 124° 44'. It is in approximate latitude 48° 10'. It is more than 10' of longitude further west than Cape Blanco. Authorities are not unanimous as to the color of Cape Blanco, but George Davidson, whose opinion carries great weight, says in the *Coast Pilot* for 1869 that the rocks were of a dull white appearance but bright when the sun shone on them. However, this is probably more or less true of other capes in the neighborhood. For illustrated story about Cape Blanco and the lighthouse, by Alfred Powers, *see* the *Oregonian*, Sunday, Sept. 15, 1915.

Cape Falcon, TILLAMOOK. Cape Falcon is the next cape south of Arch Cape, and has been known in the past as False Tillamook Head, which lies further north. On Aug. 18, 1775, Captain Bruno Heceta, while cruising along the north Pacific Coast discovered a cape in latitude 45° 43' north and named it Cape Falcon. While this is not far from the correct latitude of what we now know as Cape Falcon, 45° 46', the records of Heceta are so meager as to make it impossible exactly to identify his discovery. Cape Falcon as we now know it derived its name from Heceta, irrespective of what point he originally discovered. The present application of the name was made by George Davidson of the USC&GS in 1853, as being preferable to a name with the "false" in it. Heceta speaks of Cape Falcon, but Fray Benito de la Sierra, one of his chaplains, uses the expression "a range of high hills, to which we gave the name *Sierra de Montefalcon*." *See California Historical Society Quarterly*, v. 9, p. 235. The day of Santa Clara de Montefalco is Aug. 18, and this name was obviously given in her honor. Cape Falcon has been the cause of considerable misunderstanding among students of Oregon history. Greenhow, in his *History of Oregon and California*, appears to have started the trouble by confusing Cape Falcon, or as it was sometimes known, False Tillamook Head, with Clarks Point of View. This he does in two places, one in chapter IV and another time in appendix E. This error has been perpetuated by both great authorities on the Lewis and Clark expedition, Coues and Thwaites. As a matter of fact Clarks Point of View was on Tillamook Head, as is clearly shown by Clark's description of the view he had from the point and also by two maps in *Original Journals of the Lewis and Clark Expedition*, atlas volume. Davidson perceived this error. *See Coast Pilot* for 1869. However, Davidson was of the opinion that the Cape Grenville of

Meares was the same as Cape Falcon, but this seems improbable to the writer. At the time of his discovery of Cape Falcon, Heceta also named *La Mesa* or The Table, putting it some 15 minutes of latitude further south than the cape, with no indication as to whether it was an inland mountain or not. It seems to the compiler that *La Mesa* must have been what is now Cape Meares, or some flat-topped mountain inland. It is improbable that the name *La Mesa* had anything to do with Neahkahnie Mountain. The latitude given for *La Mesa* is much too far south, and the summit of Neahkahnie Mountain is not prominent and flat as seen from the sea. There are several more imposing and higher points in the immediate vicinity.

Cape Ferrelo, CURRY. Bartolome Ferrelo (Ferrer) was a pilot in the expedition of Juan Rodriguez Cabrillo, a Portuguese, who sailed from Mexico in June 1542, for the purpose of exploring the coast of California. When near the 34th parallel of north latitude Cabrillo sank under the fatigue of the voyage and turned the command over to Ferrelo. The latter discovered a cape on the 41st parallel which he called *Cabo de Fortunas*, and on Mar. 1, 1543, found himself to be as far north as the 44th parallel, but on the following day bad weather drove him south. It is now not easy to determine how far north Ferrelo came, nor what he actually discovered. H. R. Wagner in *Cartography of the Northwest Coast of America*, v. 2, p. 373, says that *Cabo de Fortunas* was probably the modern Point Arena, and apparently Ferrelo saw no more land north of that. His latitudes were considerably in error. There is nothing to connect the Cape Ferrelo with Bartolome Ferrelo the pilot, though it was named in his honor by George Davidson of the USC&GS, probably in 1869. Cape Ferrelo is but a short distance from the Oregon-California boundary line. It is the first prominent headland north of St. George Reef, and while not projecting seaward to any considerable extent, it is nevertheless noticeable on account of its bold rugged face.

Cape Foulweather, LINCOLN. Cape Foulweather was discovered and named by Captain James Cook, the English explorer, on Mar. 7, 1778. This was the first geographic feature that Captain Cook named in his voyage to the north Pacific Ocean. On the day of his discovery the weather was particularly inclement. The *Coast Pilot* for 1869 gives a detailed account of this cape and incidents surrounding its discovery, compiled by George Davidson.

Cape Kiwanda, TILLAMOOK. This cape was once known as Sand Cape, but Kiwanda is the name in general use and the one adopted by the USBGN. Cape Kiwanda is a low, yellow, rocky point, much broken and eroded, projecting about one half mile from the general trend of the coast. Behind the cape are bright sand dunes, and it is probable that these rather than sand on the cape itself suggested the name Sand Cape. There is some uncertainty about the origin of the name Kiwanda, and it is said to mean "wind mountain." However, John W. Meldrum of Oregon City, former surveyor general of Oregon, said that Kiwanda was the name of a Nestucca Indian chief and local celebrity. This origin of the name seems much more probable, as the name Wind Mountain is not applicable to the cape.

Cape Lookout, TILLAMOOK. Cape Lookout is one of the most prominent on the Oregon coast. It projects into the ocean one and one-half miles and has a narrow promontory over 400 feet high on its seaward end. East of the cape the mountains rise to an elevation of over 2000 feet. Cape Lookout bears its present name in error which will doubtless never be corrected. The name was originally applied by John Meares to what is now known as Cape Meares, which he described fully and accurately, and his description was subsequently corroborated by Vancouver. The name was probably changed to the new position on the USC&GS charts of 1850 and 1853. Cape Lookout is about ten miles south of Cape Meares and is much more prominent, which is doubtless the reason for the change. Having once become attached to the new cape it was deemed inadvisable to attempt to restore the name to the old location and as a result George Davidson applied Meares' name to the feature that Meares called Cape Lookout. For further information on this point, *see* Cape Meares and also refer to United States *Coast Pilot* for 1869.

Cape Meares, TILLAMOOK. Cape Meares is just south of Tillamook Bay, and bears the name of the most interesting of all the early explorers of the north Pacific Coast. Meares is well described in the following words by Professor Edmond S. Meany in his *History of the State of Washington*, p. 25: "John Meares, a retired lieutenant of the British Navy, was the most unconventional and interesting personality of all those figuring in these early marine annals. He sailed under double colors, he succeeded as fur hunter and geographer, he was the pioneer of two great industries, he sought to plant a colony of Chinese men with Kanaka wives, he wrote a book, he precipitated a quarrel between England and Spain which came near embroiling also the new republic of the United States in a serious war. There was nothing dull about John Meares. In 1786, he sailed from Bengal with two vessels, the *Nootka* and *Sea-otter*, names redolent of furs and adventure. Little is known of this voyage except that it was confined to the shores of Alaska. In 1787 English merchants in India fitted out two ships, the *Felice Adventurer* and the *Iphigenia Nubiana*, and placed them in command of John Meares and William Douglas. To avoid excessive port charges in China and to evade licenses from the South Sea and East Indian monopolies, a Portuguese partner was taken in, who procured from the governor at Macao, Portuguese flags, papers and captains. In case of need the real masters would appear as clerks or super-cargoes. While little use was made of this scheme, the trick of double colors is condemned as a cheat, closely akin to piracy. In May 1788, Meares in the *Felice* arrived at Nootka, and for two pistols bought some land from Chief Maquina. He at once erected a little fort, and began an important enterprise. He had brought the framework of a schooner. His ship's company included fifty men, crew and artisans, part of each group being Chinamen. This little schooner, the *North West America*, was the first vessel built in this part of the world and this also was the first introduction of Chinese labor on the Pacific Coast." While Meares' organization was engaged in these activities, he himself set sail on an exploring expedition along the coast. He passed the mouth of the Columbia River on July 6, 1788, but he failed to identify it as a river. By nightfall of that same day he had discovered and named three important features, the first of which he referred to as Cape Grenville, and the next Quicksand Bay, the third feature he christened Cape Lookout, and the volume containing the story of his travels has a very fine plate showing this cape together with the remarkable rocks a little to the southwest. Having failed to discover the new river he was seeking, he returned to Nootka. For further information about the history of Nootka and the controversy between England and Spain over Meares' enterprise, *see* Meany's *History*. It is not easy at this time to identify Cape Grenville. George Davidson supposes it to be Cape Falcon. Quicksand Bay seems to be what is now known as Tillamook Bay. Meares' description and pictures of Cape Lookout, beyond all doubt, refer to what we now call Cape Meares, and the rocks that Meares christened Three Brothers are now known as Three Arch Rocks and form a bird sanctuary that is frequently written about. George Davidson applied the name of Cape Meares to the feature herein described in 1857. Davidson was for many years connected with the USC&GS and is considered the authority on the early explorations of the Pacific Coast. It appears that through some misunderstanding the USC&GS adopted the name Cape Lookout on its charts of 1850 and 1853 for a point about ten miles south of Meares' original location. The name of Cape Lookout having become so well established in its new position and attaching to a point quite striking in appearance, it was apparently thought by Davidson best to leave the name where it was and honor Meares by applying his own name to the feature that he discovered. Professor Meany's remarks about Meares being the pioneer of two great industries refer to shipbuilding and timber exporting. When the *Felice* started for China she carried with her a deck load of spars, the first to be shipped from the Pacific Northwest. The spars were lost in rough weather, but this does not rob Meares of the glory of starting our lumber industry.

Cape Meares Lake, TILLAMOOK. After World War II, the Pacific Ocean cut through the Bayocean peninsula which formed the west side of Tillamook Bay. The breakthrough was at Biggs Cove just north of the high ground forming Cape Meares and the narrowest spot on the peninsula. The second ocean entry posed serious problems for Tillamook Bay and the USCE constructed a substantial dike from Pitcher Point northwest to the southern extremity of what was then Bayocean Island. The dike altered the current and sand reestablished the old shoreline, changing what had been Biggs Cove into a lake. Nearby residents, capitalizing on this natural accretion, renamed the impoundment Cape Meares Lake. Biggs Cove was named for John A. Biggs who came to Tillamook County about 1885. He was a son-in-law of Webley Hauxhurst, a companion of Ewing Young in 1835. This is another example of commercial interests eliminating a good, historic name.

Cape Perpetua, LINCOLN. Cape Perpetua, which is in the extreme southwest corner of the county, is one of the historic geographic features of Oregon. It was discovered on Mar. 7, 1778, by Captain James Cook, the famous English explorer, and it has been frequently asserted that he named the cape because the bad weather seemed to hold him perpetually in sight of it. It is apparent from a careful reading of his journals that this was not the case, but that he named the headland for St. Perpetua, who was murdered in Carthage on Mar. 7, 203, for it was on St. Perpetua's Day that he made his discovery. A pious gentleman informs the writer that Perpetua the Martyr was a noble lady of Carthage, and in the face of her father's pleading and tears, professed the faith and was thrown to the beasts and beheaded.

Cape Ridge, LANE, LINCOLN. Cape Ridge gets its name because its western end forms Cape Perpetua. It lies between Yachats River on the north and Cummins Creek on the south, and Cape Creek, a short stream in between the two, bisects it unequally, with the larger part to the north, this terminating in the Cape. Cape Ridge rises rapidly from the cape and about a mile and a half from the ocean, it has an elevation of 1400 feet, and about three miles from the ocean there is a well defined summit 1947 feet high. This ridge together with others extending from the ocean finally blends itself into the Coast Range at higher elevations. For geography of this feature, *see* USGS Waldport quadrangle.

Cape Sebastian, CURRY. Cape Sebastian gets its name from the fact that on Jan. 20, 1603, Sebastian Vizcaino on an exploring expedition north from Mexico sighted a high white bluff near what he determined to be the 42nd parallel. He named it in honor of the saint of that day, San Sebastian. This point marked the northern limit of his voyage, but his recorded latitudes are much too high. What cape he saw and named it is not now possible to determine with accuracy, but the name Cape Sebastian is fixed on a cape in north latitude 42° 19' 40". The name was first applied to this feature by George Davidson in the USC&GS *Coast Pilot* for 1869, p. 112. For more information about Vizcaino's voyage, *see* Cape Blanco. Cape Sebastian is prominent from north or south, and rises abruptly from the sea to a height of about 700 feet. The style Cape San Sebastian is wrong for this feature and is not in accord with the name given by Davidson.

Capes. The first exploration of the Oregon country by white people was by the sea, and on account of presumed ease of identification, capes and promontories were sought after and named by the early navigators. Cape Blanco was the first geographical feature of the state to be named by a white man, although it is not at all certain what feature was originally so identified. For a period of nearly 200 years explorers carried on the work of naming the headlands of Oregon before the interior was touched upon. The history of the naming of the Oregon capes is therefore worthy of study, particularly in view of the fact that much uncertainty exists as to what some of the early navigators saw and named on their charts. In order that the matter may be understood, it is necessary to have a table of latitudes, shown below. This table gives the positions north of the equator of the important capes of the state, such positions being taken from the publications of the usc&gs except for that marked (a) which is scaled from reliable maps, and is approximate. The positions marked (lt) are for the lighthouses on the capes, and all others are for some important triangulation point on the cape, though not necessarily in the exact center, or on its most westward point.

NAME	NORTH LATITUDE
Point Adams	46° 12′ 38″
Tillamook Head	45° 57′ 54″
Arch Cape	45° 48′ 10″
Cape Falcon (a)	45° 46′ 04″
Neahkahnie Mountain	45° 44′ 38″
Cape Meares (lt)	45° 29′ 12″
Cape Lookout	45° 20′ 16″
Cape Kiwanda	45° 13′ 03″
Cascade Head	45° 03′ 41″
Cape Foulweather	44° 46′ 21″
Yaquina Head (lt)	44° 40′ 37″
Cape Perpetua	44° 17′ 15″
Heceta Head (lt)	44° 08′ 15″
Cape Arago (lt)	43° 20′ 29″
Cape Arago	43° 18′ 10″
Coquille Point (usgs)	43° 06′ 52″
Cape Blanco (lt)	42° 50′ 14″
Cape Sebastian	42° 19′ 40″
Crook Point	42° 15′ 07″
Cape Ferrelo	42° 06′ 08″

Cape Blanco is the most westward point in Oregon and its lighthouse is in west longitude 124° 33′ 45″. The most westward triangulation station on the cape is in longitude 124° 33′ 50.712″ and is close to the edge of the cliff of the middle point. For detailed information on the above points *see* usc&gs *Special Publication 175* and supplemental data. The table of latitudes given above will be of use in considering the discoveries on the Oregon coast, and will also indicate why it is impossible now to determine exactly what features each explorer recorded since, in some instances, the headlands are not unlike and are near together. The matter of fog and low lying clouds must also be taken into account. For instance it seems incredible that Heceta could so accurately describe the mouth of the Columbia River, then miss Tillamook Head completely and hit upon Cape Falcon.

Captain Cook Point, LANE, LINCOLN. Captain Cook Point is the first prominent point south of Cape Perpetua, and Captain Cook Chasm is a well-known landmark at the end of the point. The Oregon Coast Highway, US-101, crosses this chasm on a concrete viaduct. These features bear the name of Captain James Cook, R.N., one of the greatest explorers of all time. He sailed along this part of the Oregon coast in 1778, and on Mar. 7 of that year discovered and named Cape Perpetua, just north of Captain Cook Point. James Cook was born in 1728 in Yorkshire, and joining the Royal Navy in 1755, he soon began to demonstrate his talents as a navigator. Before 1776 he had made two very important voyages and, above all, had made remarkable advances in the prevention of scurvy. He sailed from England in 1776 on his third and last voyage, during which he sighted the Oregon coast. After important discoveries in Alaska, he visited the Hawaiian Islands, where he met death at the hands of natives on Feb. 14, 1779. Distinguished honors were paid to him by many countries. The compiler was unable to find that any geographic features had been named for him in the 48 contiguous states and in 1931 recommended to the USBGN that the name Captain Cook Point be applied to the Oregon promontory. The board adopted the name in October of that year.

Captain Gray Mountain, TILLAMOOK. This high ground just northeast of Garibaldi is prominent from the sea as you enter Tillamook Bay. It was named in 1988 to commemorate Captain Robert Gray's entry into Tillamook Bay on Aug. 13, 1788 in the *Lady Washington*. This was, so far as is now known, the first landing by white men on the coast of the State of Oregon and the first landing from an American ship on the Pacific Coast of North America. Gray was also the first American to circumnavigate the globe which he did on this same voyage. The OGNB met at Garibaldi on Aug. 13, 1988 to participate in the local celebration which included a floral airdrop on the 1420 foot summit. The name was approved by the USBGN in *Decision List 8801*. One of Gray's crew was killed by hostile natives. In consequence, the bay was given the name Murderers Harbor. *See* Bays.

Captain Keeney Pass, MALHEUR. Jonathan Keeney was born in Indiana on Apr. 27, 1813. As a young man he was with Sublette in 1834 and then worked for the American Fur Company under Jim Bridger. He later spent several years in Missouri raising a family and made an uneventful trip to the Willamette Valley with the emigration of 1846. He arrived in Oregon in the early fall and is reported to have been a member of the first party to bring wagons over the newly completed Barlow Road. Keeney settled in Linn County and in 1855 was elected Captain, Company C, Oregon Mounted Volunteers when that unit was mustered in for the Rogue River Indian War. About 1860 he moved to Walla Walla and thence to the Boise basin where he maintained a ferry and kept the travel near the mouth of Malheur River, dying near there on Aug. 15, 1878. The emigrant road ran from south of Nyssa northwest to Vale and in 1975 the low divide between these two points was named Captain Keeney Pass to honor this Oregon pioneer.

Carberry Creek, JACKSON. This stream is formed by Steve and Sturgis forks, and flows into Applegate River. It was for a time also known as Steamboat Creek, but it is now universally known as Carberry Creek, in memory of Jim Carberry, an early placer miner. It was called Carberry Creek in pioneer mining days, and that name seems to have antedated the form Steamboat Creek. *See OHQ,* v. 23, p. 154.

Carcus Creek, COLUMBIA. Carcus Creek, west of Apiary, flows north into Clatskanie River. In 1941 Sinclair Wilson of Portland, who knew much of the early history of the county, told the compiler that many years ago this stream was called Carcass Creek because a local resident found a dead horse on its banks. However, the formal style of spelling soon gave way to the form now universally used throughout the county. Efforts to adopt the original spelling have been unavailing, and the name Carcus Creek seems to be here to stay.

Cardwell Creek, JACKSON. Cardwell Creek flows into Sams Creek north of Gold Hill. It bears the name of John A. Cardwell who was born in England and came to southern Oregon in 1860. He filed on government land along the creek in 1865.

Carey Bend, MARION. This bend in Willamette River near Dayton is named for John and Ruth Carey whose donation land claim included the area. John Carey was born in Philadelphia in 1802 and came to Oregon in 1847.

Carey Creek, CURRY. Government land records show that in 1897 Robert A. Carey applied for a homestead along this creek which flows into Chetco River east of Brookings.

Carey Stearns Ranch, DESCHUTES. This ranch in the La Pine area was owned by one of the sons of Sidney Stearns, the early Deschutes and Crook county cattleman.

Carico, COLUMBIA. Carico was a post office in the woods about six miles west of Deer Island, but the place did not develop into a community. The office was established Dec. 4, 1889, with Mrs. Lydia Pinckney first postmaster. Her husband, Nelson Pinckney, became postmaster on Mar. 25, 1904, and the office was closed to Deer Island on May 15, 1913. In June 1947, Mrs. Nellie C. Buss of Saint Helens, daughter of Mr. and Mrs. Pinckney, told the compiler that the office was named for one John Carico who had squatted on a claim in the locality prior to the arrival of the Pinckneys. John Carico moved away many years ago and the compiler knows nothing of his history.

Carle Creek, LANE. William T. Carle took a homestead on this tributary of Maple Creek just above Siltcoos Lake. Carle settled at Siltcoos Lake in 1886 and filed his claim in 1891. He was later postmaster at Alene.

Carll, DOUGLAS. Carll was a post office on the upper reaches of Cow Creek named for a local family. This office served the area later served by Binger and by Anchor. The office was established Oct. 22, 1883 with George McCormick first of five postmasters. Carll office was closed July 16, 1894, and it seems probable on that date the name was changed to Binger, although the official record is not exactly precise on this point. As with many other offices of this type, it was doubtless moved from time to time.

Carlson Creek, LANE. Carlson Creek flows into Garoute Creek from the west.

It apparently is named for Otto E. Carlson who homesteaded nearby at the turn of the century.

Carlton, YAMHILL. A. E. Bones, postmaster at Carlton, wrote in Oct. 1925, that the place was named for John Carl, Sr., and that it was done at the request of R. R. Thompson of Portland at the time the west side railroad established a station there about 1874. Carl was an early settler in the neighborhood and Thompson owned a farm there. It has been stated elsewhere that the town was named for Wilson Carl, an ex-county commissioner. Possibly the two were members of the same family. Carlton post office was established July 21, 1874, with F. J. Fryer first postmaster.

Carmichael Canyon, MORROW. Carmichael Canyon empties into Skinners Fork in the upper Willow Creek drainage. It was named for John A. Carmichael who was born in Pennsylvania in 1853 and came to Oregon in 1877.

Carnahan, CLATSOP. This community is on Clatsop Plains and was named for Hiram Carnahan, a pioneer of 1846. He was born in Tennessee in 1820. After arriving in Oregon he visited the California mines, but returned and settled in Clatsop County about 1849. He married Mary E. Morrison. For information about the Carnahan family, *see* editorial page of the *Oregon Journal*, June 30, 1928. Hiram Carnahan died in Jan. 1896.

Carnation, WASHINGTON. This post office just south of Forest Grove was established May 20, 1905, with Clarence L. Bump first postmaster. It was so named because the Carnation Milk Products Company formerly had a condensery nearby, and Bump's store where the post office was situated was the Carnation store. This post office was operated with the name South Forest Grove from Apr. 1906, until Nov. 1914, when the old name Carnation was restored.

Carney Butte, UMATILLA. Carney Butte has an elevation of 4813 feet and is about a mile east of Battle Mountain summit. It was named for an early family. One member, Leonard S. Carney, took up government land as early as 1876.

Carney Canyon, UMATILLA. This canyon five miles south of Vinson was named for Samuel J. Carney who settled near its mouth in the 1890s.

Carnine Canyon, GILLIAM. This canyon running to Sixmile Canyon east of Condon was named for J. M. Carnine, a veteran of the Civil War, who settled nearby in 1901. *See Illustrated History of Central Oregon*, p. 586.

Carpenterville, CURRY. Carpenterville is on the old Oregon Coast Highway about 16 miles north of Brookings. In 1921 D. W. Carpenter and his family settled at this locality and among other things operated a small mill for fence lumber. Carpenter later moved to California and then to Bandon, but his sons continued to run the mill. He returned to the place about the time the highway was built and started a store and tourist cabins. In Apr. 1932, a post office was established and named for the family.

Carpet Hill Creek, LANE. A few miles below Westfir, Carpet Hill Creek flows into Middle Fork Willamette River from the north. Jess McAbee, a pioneer resident of Lowell, is authority for the story of this name. The old Middle Fork road crossed the toe of a hill near the creek, and a large, smooth, sloping rock caused the oxen to slip and lose their footing. One outfit overcame the difficulty by laying a large carpet over the rock, and as a result the creek soon had its present name.

Carroll Rim, WHEELER. In 1971, at the suggestion of Phil Brogan, this high ground facing Painted Hills State Park was named for Samuel Carroll. Unfortunately, due to a typographical error in the proposal, the USBGN in *Decision List 7201* applied the name to a similar feature six miles to the east on the southeast end of Sutton Mountain. In 1986, James Morris of the National Park Service questioned the location and the mistake was rectified. Carroll was born in Illinois in 1820 and came to Linn County in 1847 where he took a donation land claim. About 1870 he moved to the Painted Hills area and raised a substantial family. Carroll Creek near West Branch was named for a son, Samuel Carroll, Jr., and Carroll Butte on the headwaters of Marks Creek was named for another son, Charles.

Carson, BAKER. The postmaster of Carson in 1925 wrote that this community was apparently named for Tom Corson who settled about 1870 on a small stream flowing into Pine Creek. Neighbors pronounced his name Carson and applied it to the stream in question and subsequently to a small sawmill which was called the Carson Mill because it was situated on the creek. When the post office was established July 26, 1893, the name was applied to it as well. The office was discontinued in Apr. 1952. The area is served by a rural route out of Halfway.

Carter, LANE. This was a station on the Cascade line of the Southern Pacific Company east of Lowell. It was named for Joe Carter, an old settler of the neighborhood.

Carter, MALHEUR. Carter post office was one of those establishments that did not last long. It appears on the Malheur County list as of July 15, 1898, and was discontinued Nov. 2, 1901, with papers to Rockville. William C. Carlton was the only postmaster. The post office was named for an early settler, one Carter, whose initials are not available to the compiler. Carter post office was on Carter Creek, 18 or 20 miles eastward of the place known as Watson and something over 20 miles north of Sheaville. Carter Creek was also named for the pioneer settler. His home was near the junction of Carter Creek and Succor Creek.

Carter Branch, LINN. This stream flows into Beaver Creek about seven miles northeast of Lebanon. It was named for a family of early settlers nearby.

Carter Creek, LANE. Carter Creek flows into Maple Creek about four miles up from Siltcoos Lake. Leonard B. Carter homesteaded there in the 1890s.

Carter Lake, DOUGLAS. This is a long, narrow lake in the extreme northwest corner of Douglas County about one-half mile from the Pacific Ocean. It was named for an early settler, Ira Carter, who lived on its shore.

Carter Spring, JEFFERSON. In 1888 Richard H. McCarter took up a homestead including this spring near Pony Butte. The Scottish prefix has vanished along with most of the small ranchers.

Cartney, LINN. This is a station on the Oregon Electric Railway north of Harrisburg. It apparently was named for J. M. McCartney, an early settler in the neighborhood, as the station is on part of what was his land. The compiler does not know why his full name was not used.

Cartwright, LANE. D. B. Cartwright was born in Syracuse, New York, in 1814 and came to Oregon in 1853. He settled in the upper reaches of Siuslaw River and established a hotel and stage station which he called Mountain House. After World War II the building was still standing about eight miles west of Cottage Grove and a picture of it was published in the *Sunday Journal*, Dec. 9, 1945. It was torn down in the summer of 1973. Cartwright died in 1875. William Russell, a native of Ohio, came to Oregon in 1848, and in 1866 married Miss N. C. Cartwright. He took over the activities of the Mountain House and was instrumental in having a post office established with the name of his father-in-law. This occurred on Aug. 7, 1871, and the office continued under Russell's direction until Sept. 18, 1890. For biographies of Cartwright and Russell *see Illustrated History of Lane County*, p. 482; for picture of the Mountain House, p. 232. In May 1946, P. M. Morse, Lane County Engineer, informed the compiler that the Mountain House was situated on the east side of the Territorial road in the extreme west part of s 30, T 20S, R 4W.

Cartwright Creek, CROOK, JEFFERSON. Cartwright Creek flows into Trout Creek in s 26, T 11S, R 17E. Records of the Ochoco National Forest say it was named for an early settler. In 1884 Charles M. Cartwright bought government land two miles downstream on Trout Creek. Theodore Cartwright also took property nearby in the 1870s. *See Illustrated History of Central Oregon*, p. 734.

Carus, CLACKAMAS. Carus is a locality on SH-213 about seven miles south of Oregon City and a little to the southwest of Beaver Creek. Carus post office was established June 7, 1887, with David Hunter first postmaster, and was discontinued July 27, 1907. The origin of this name has long been a mystery, and some information dug up early in 1946 merely adds to the confusion. The compiler has been informed by two reliable persons that it was planned to name the place Carns, and that is the way the name was sent to the postal authorities at Washington. It was not unusual to misread an "n" for a "u" and the name was innocently converted into Carus when the office was established. It may have been intended to name the office for a Carns in another state, or what is more probable, for a family named Carns.

Carver, CLACKAMAS. Carver was a post office near Baker Bridge on Clackamas River. It was at the site of the former office of Stone, which was established a number of years before, and was later discontinued. The old office was called Stone because of the number of large boulders in the locality. About 1915 Stephen S. Carver promoted an interurban line from Portland into this part of Clackamas County, and a townsite at Stone was surveyed and platted with his name, Carver.

The post office of Carver was established June 3, 1924, and closed Feb. 28, 1939. S. S. Carver was born in Iowa in 1866 and died at Carver on Nov. 25, 1933. For obituary, *see* the *Oregon Journal*, Nov. 27, 1933.

Carver Glacier, DESCHUTES. Jonathan Carver was the first person known to have used the name Oregon, which he did in his book published in 1778. The only place in Oregon where his name has been perpetuated is in Carver Glacier, which is on the north slope of the South Sister and is one of the sources of Squaw Creek. It was named in 1924 by Professor Edwin T. Hodge of the University of Oregon. Carver was born at Weymouth, Massachusetts, Apr. 3, 1710. He served in the French and Indian wars, and later became an adventurous traveler. He had difficulties in getting the story of his travels published, and soured and discontented, he went to England where he was in a measure successful. He died in want in London in 1780. For his travels Carver outfitted at Mackinac and went to Green Bay, on Lake Michigan, and from there, by portage and river, to the Mississippi at Prairie du Chien, and then up the Mississippi to the Saint Peter, to spend the winter of 1766–67. He returned by way of Lake Superior, in 1767. Carver's *Travels* have been criticized as to their originality, and questions of plagiarism have been discussed by historical and literary authorities for many years. He is alleged to have plagiarized the writings of Charlevoix, Lahontan and James Adair, and the parallels have been freely quoted. For narrative of Carver's travels and discussion of this "plagiarism," *see The American Historical Review*, v. 11, pp. 287–302, by Edward Gaylord Bourne. *See also Bibliography of Carver's Travels*, 1910, and *Additional Data*, 1913, by John Thomas Lee, published by the Wisconsin Historical Society. For details of Carver's family and of his birth, *see The Wisconsin Magazine of History*, v. 3, No. 3, p. 229, by William Browning. While Jonathan Carver originated the form of the name Oregon, it now seems probable that he did not originate the name itself. That was apparently done by Major Robert Rogers, an English army officer who was commandant at the frontier military post at Mackinac, Michigan, during the time of Carver's journey into the upper valley of the Mississippi. For particulars of this matter *see OHQ*, v. 22, No. 2, for June 1921, containing an article by T. C. Elliott. *See* Oregon. Rogers used the form Ourigan.

Cascade Head, TILLAMOOK. Cascade Head is a jagged, wooded cape with a cliff on the seaward side about three miles long and in places over 100 feet high. It was named because of the fact its face is cut deep by gorges through which the waters of three creeks are discharged from cascades 60 to 80 feet high. The name was applied to it by George Davidson of the USC&GS in the *Coast Pilot* for 1869.

Cascade Locks, HOOD RIVER. The federal government adopted a plan for permanent improvements at the Cascades of the Columbia in 1875, and began work in 1878. For the history of the construction of the Cascade locks *see* the *Oregonian*, Jan. 1, 1895, p. 8. The locks were completed Nov. 5, 1896. The community was named for the locks. Scott's *History of the Oregon Country*, v. 3, p. 190, gives a detailed history of the various aids to transportation developed at this point. The locks were submerged early in 1938 as a result of the construction of Bonneville Dam, but the town was not disturbed. The steel cantilever "Bridge of the Gods" was raised about 40 feet to facilitate navigation.

Cascade Range. The Cascade Range is the great mountain backbone of Oregon and Washington, and divides both states into separate climatic and geographic provinces. Probably the first attempt at a name for the range was by the Spaniard, Manuel Quimper, 1790, who roughly mapped it as *Sierras Nevadas de S. Antonio*. In 1792 George Vancouver, the English explorer, gave names to a number of the most prominent peaks, but referred to the range as "snowy range," "ridge of snowy mountains," or "range of rugged mountains." Lewis and Clark, 1805–1806, mention the named peaks and frequently refer in general terms to the range of mountains. Lewis wrote: "The range of western mountains are covered with snow," while Clark wrote: "Western mountains covered with snow." (Thwaites' *Original Journals of the Lewis and Clark Expedition*, v. 4, pp. 313 and 305–306.) "Western Mountains" is the nearest to a name for the range adopted by Lewis and Clark. John Work, of the Hudson's Bay Company, wrote in Dec. 1824: "A ridge of high mountains covered with snow." (*Washington Historical Quarterly*, v. 3, pp. 213, 215.) David Douglas, the botanist, in writing his journal had great need of a name for these mountains and he seems to have been the first one to use the name "Cascade." He refers again and again to the "Cascade Mountains" or "Cascade Range of Mountains." (*Journal Kept by David Douglas*, 1823–1827, pp. 221–222, 252, 257, 342.) Douglas does not claim to have originated the name for the range, and earlier use of it may yet come to light. William A. Slacum's report, 1836–1837, says the mountains called "Klannet Range, from the Indians of that name." (*OHQ*, v. 13, p. 201.) Hall J. Kelley, early enthusiast of the Oregon country, who is sometimes referred to as "The Boston Schoolmaster," sought in a memoir (1839), to change the names of the great peaks by calling them after former presidents of the United States and to christen the range "Presidents' Range." The Wilkes Expedition, 1841, charted the mountains as Cascade Range. Kelley's memoir is in 25th Congress, 3rd Session, *House Report 101, Supplemental Report*, dated Feb. 16, 1839, p. 47. The original report, dated Jan. 4, 1839, is generally referred to as the Cushing report and the supplement of Feb. 16, 1839, is an addition. Kelley's memoir is listed as Appendix O, and is dated Boston, Jan. 31, 1839. It was addressed to the Committee on Foreign Affairs of which Caleb Cushing of Massachusetts was chairman. On pp. 53–54 Kelley says: "The eastern section of the district referred to is bordered by a mountain range running nearly parallel to the spine of the Rocky Mountains and to the coast, and which, from the number of its elevated peaks, I am inclined to call the Presidents' Range." In a footnote Kelley adds: "These isolated and remarkable cones, which are now called among the hunters of the Hudson's Bay Company by other names, I have christened after our ex-Presidents, viz:

1. Washington, latitude 46 degrees, 15 minutes [Saint Helens or Adams]
2. Adams, latitude 45 degrees, 10 minutes [Hood]
3. Jefferson, latitude 44 degrees, 30 minutes [Jefferson]
4. Madison, latitude 43 degrees, 50 minutes [Three Sisters]
5. Monroe, latitude 43 degrees, 20 minutes [Diamond]
6. John Quincy Adams, latitude 42 degrees, 10 minutes [McLoughlin]
7. Jackson, latitude 41 degrees, 20 minutes [Shasta]

Farnham's *Travels in the Great Western Prairies* was published in 1843. Page 96 (New York edition) describes the Presidents Range and its several peaks. Farnham mentions ten peaks south of the 49th parallel (Canadian boundary). "Five of these latter have received names from British navigators and traders. The other five have received from an American traveler, Mr. Kelley, the names of deceased Presidents of the Republic. Mr. Kelley, I believe, was the first individual who suggested a name for the whole range. For convenience in description I have adopted it. And although it is a matter in which no one can find reasons for being very much interested, yet if there is any propriety in adopting Mr. Kelley's name for the whole chain, there might seem to be as much in following his suggestion that all the principal peaks should bear the names of those distinguished men . . . I have adopted this course." Farnham's names and positions, together with modern names are:

1. Mount Tyler, 49 degrees [Baker]
2. Mount Harrison [Rainier]
3. Mount Van Buren [Olympus]
4. Mount Adams, 45 degrees [Adams]
5. Mount Washington [Hood]
6. Mount Jefferson, 41-1/2 degrees [Jefferson]
7. Mount Madison [Three Sisters]
8. Mount Monroe, 43 degrees, 20 minutes [Diamond]
9. Mount Quincy Adams, 42 degrees, 10 minutes [McLoughlin]
10. Mount Jackson, 41 degrees, 10 minutes [Shasta]

Some of Farnham's positions, as well as those of Kelley, are widely erroneous, yet it is surprising that they are as good as they are. Farnham's position for Mount Jefferson is obviously a typographical error for 44 degrees, otherwise it does not fit the sequence. The latitudes of both authors are generally too low. These presidential names were started by Kelley, and were confused by later writers who adopted his names but not his locations. In this way, difference of names appears as to Mount Adams, Mount Saint Helens, Mount Hood and other peaks. The original names remain with Mounts Hood, Saint Helens, Rainier, Baker and Jefferson; otherwise with Adams, Three Sisters, McLoughlin and Shasta. John

Work, in his journal (*OHQ*, v. 10, pp. 308–09, by T. C. Elliott), calls Mount Adams Mount Saint Helen, Mount Saint Helens Mount Rainier, and Mount Rainier Mount Baker.

The name Cascades was first that of the narrows of the Columbia River, which yet bears the title. This name for the Columbia River narrows is used commonly by writers as far back as the Astor expedition. In the Cushing supplemental report, referred to above as containing the Kelley memoir, there is also a memoir of Nathaniel J. Wyeth, dated Feb. 4, 1839, which uses the name Cascade mountains. In Greenhow's *History of Oregon and California*, the name Far-West mountains is suggested. *See also* Bancroft's *History of Oregon*, v. 1, p. 164, note. As far as the writer knows, but one tribe of Indians had a name for the Cascade Range as such. The Klamath Indians called it the *Yamakiasham Yaina*, literally "mountains of the northern people." Cascade Range is the official form of name adopted by the USBGN and the feature to which it applies extends from Canada to the gap south of Lassen Peak in California. The Cascade Range is primarily volcanic in character and particularly in Oregon and in northern California its crest is made up of the remains of a series of giant volcanoes. The Cascade Range differs essentially in construction and in origin from the Sierra Nevada of California and there is no connection between the two. The highest point in the Cascade Range in Oregon is Mount Hood, 11,237 feet, and the lowest pass is the gorge of the Columbia River. The important routes of travel through the Cascade Range in Oregon include I-84 along the Columbia River at water level, and the Mount Hood Loop Highway, SH-35, which in certain sections follows closely the Barlow Road, and which has a maximum elevation of 4647 feet where it goes through Bennett Pass on a spur east from the main range. The elevation of the roadway at Barlow Pass is 4161 feet. The Warm Springs Highway, US-26, goes through Wapinitia Pass at an elevation of 3952 feet, but this highway also crosses a higher spur east of the main divide, at Blue Box Pass, elevation 4025 feet. Santiam Highway, US-20, goes through the north part of Santiam Pass, in the vicinity of what was once called Hogg Pass, at an elevation of 4817 feet. The old Santiam toll road goes through Santiam Pass about three miles south of Santiam Highway at an elevation of 4773 feet, but here again the road reaches higher ground two miles east of the main divide at an elevation of 4774 feet. The McKenzie Highway, SH-242, takes the place of the McKenzie toll road. Its maximum elevation is 5325 feet. The next highway to the south is the Willamette, SH-58, which goes through Willamette Pass at 5128 feet just west of Odell Lake. The old Oregon Central Military Road goes through Emigrant Pass west of Summit Lake at an elevation of about 5600 feet. The Diamond Lake Highway, SH-138, crosses through a pass north of Crater Lake at an elevation of 5925 feet. Crater Lake Highway, SH-62, has a summit elevation of 6016 feet, west of Annie Spring. The Lake of the Woods Highway, SH-140, crosses south of Mount McLoughlin at an elevation of 5105 feet. The highest point on the Green Springs Highway, SH-66, between Ashland and Klamath Falls is 4695 feet at Hayden Pass.

The backbone of the Cascade Range and the foothills have been accurately mapped by the USGS from the Columbia River to the California border. This work was started about 1900 and finally completed after World War II at 1/62,500 scale or one inch to the mile. By 1990 it was further refined at 1/24,000 and accurate elevations determined. These heights are shown in the following table of elevations. They probably are not subject to much change.

NAME	ALTITUDE	NAME	ALTITUDE
Mount Hood	11,239 feet	Maiden Peak	7,818 feet
Olallie Butte	7,215 feet	Mount Yoran	7,100 feet
Mount Jefferson	10,497 feet	Diamond Peak	8,744 feet
Three Fingered Jack	7,841 feet	Cowhorn Mountain	7,664 feet
Mount Washington	7,794 feet	Howlock Mountain	8,324 feet
Belknap Crater	6,872 feet	Mount Thielsen	9,182 feet
Black Crater	7,251 feet	Mount Bailey	8,368 feet
North Sister	10,085 feet	Mount Scott	8,929 feet
Middle Sister	10,047 feet	Hillman Peak	8,151 feet
South Sister	10,358 feet	Garfield Peak	8,054 feet
Broken Top	9,175 feet	Applegate Peak	8,126 feet
Bachelor Butte	9,065 feet	Union Peak	7,709 feet
Irish Mountain	6,893 feet	Mount McLoughlin	9,495 feet

In the 1980s the USGS remapped the area surrounding Crater Lake National Park and determined new elevations for Mount Bailey and Mount Thielsen, which are shown above. The 1920 elevation for Mount McLoughlin is not used because it refers to the top of the lookout house and not the groundline. It should be noted that the Cascade Range extends well into California and includes both Mount Shasta and Lassen Peak.

Cascade Summit, KLAMATH. Cascade Summit railroad station in the extreme northwest corner of the county, came into being with completion of the Southern Pacific Cascade Line in 1925–26. The station is just east of the summit tunnel through the Cascade Range and got its name on that account. The elevation is 4841 feet. Cascade Summit post office was established Sept. 8, 1927, with Oliver M. Shannon first postmaster and discontinued June 28, 1980.

Cascades, HOOD RIVER. The Cascades of the Columbia River were caused by natural obstructions. According to carbon dating, there was a massive earth slippage north of the river about 1260 AD. This was certainly one of the largest in the United States in the last millennium and it is now referred to as the Cascade Landslide. The remains are largely in Washington and extend roughly from

Bonneville Dam to Cascade Locks. It is estimated that more than four billion cubic yards of earth moved south off the Table Mountain massif and for a short period of time, perhaps only hours, completely blocked the Columbia River. Re-slumped slide material can be seen one hundred feet or more above the river on the south bank near Ruckel Creek. Lewis and Clark, 1805–1806, the first white men to see this geographical feature, used the word "cascades," but not as a name. The Upper Cascades they called "Great Shute." Alexander Ross, in his *Adventures of the First Settlers on the Oregon*, writing as of 1810–1813, mentions the cascades a number of times, indicating the obstruction in the river. David Thompson, of the North West Company of Montreal, on July 13, 1811, referred to "Rapids and Falls" and on July 27 to "Grand Rapid." John Work, of the Hudson's Bay Company, on June 22, 1825, wrote: "Embarked at 3 o'clock and reached the Cascades at 1." (*Washington Historical Quarterly*, v. 5, p. 85.) David Douglas, the botanist, in his journal for 1826 uses the word often, but not always for the same locality. Rev. Henry Harmon Spalding, writing from Fort Walla Walla on Oct. 2, 1836, uses the words: "The Cascades or Rapids." For an account of the fight with the Indians at the Cascades *see* OPA *Transactions* for 1896. The Cascades were submerged early in 1938 as a result of the construction of Bonneville Dam.

Cascadia, LINN. This post office was so named because it was situated in the Cascade Range. It was established in 1898.

Case Creek, MARION. Case Creek flows into Champoeg Creek near Champoeg. It is named for William M. Case, a pioneer of Oregon, who was born in Indiana in 1820 and came to Oregon in 1844. In the following year he took a donation land claim on this creek about three miles south of Champoeg. Case built a large home on the property in 1858 which was still standing in 1990. He died on his own farm on Feb. 11, 1903, and the building eventually fell into disrepair. In the 1970s it was purchased by Wallace K. Huntington of Portland and completely restored under the supervision of architect Gilman Davis. The building is on the National Register of Historic Places.

Casey, CLATSOP. Casey post office was on Youngs River about ten miles south of Astoria. It was named for a local family. The office was established in Aug. 1903, with Catherine Quinn postmaster. Casey office operated until Aug. 1911, when it was closed out to Astoria.

Cason Canyon, GILLIAM. Cason Canyon is southwest of Condon. It was named for Pemberton F. Cason, a nearby resident. The next canyon to the east, Pemberton Canyon, bears Cason's first name. *See* Pemberton Canyon. For biography, *see Illustrated History of Central Oregon*, p. 618.

Cason Canyon, MORROW. Cason Canyon empties into Rhea Creek at Ruggs. It was named for James P. Cason and his wife Mary who settled there in the early days. Cason was a son of Fendel Cason of Clackamas County and came to Oregon with his family in 1843. Mary Ellen Marsh Cason came west in 1847. Her mother died en route and Mary Ellen stopped at the Whitman Mission. She was there at the time of the massacre and was one of the women held captive by the Indians and rescued by Peter Skene Ogden in Dec. 1847.

Cassiday Butte, CURRY. This butte, 1818 feet high, southeast of Carpenterville was named for William F. Cassiday, an early settler.

Cassiday Creek, DOUGLAS. Cassiday Creek empties into Smith River six miles above Reedsport. Hugh Cassiday came to the Smith River country in the 1870s and settled near the mouth of Cassiday Creek. His daughter married Peter Cowan, the son of John Cowan, postmaster at nearby Sulphur Springs. Descendants of this pair were still living in southwest Oregon in the 1980s.

Casteel Spring, UMATILLA. The Casteel family is well known in the Pilot Rock area but Lloyd Waid of the USFS in Ukiah believes this spring was named specifically for Mick Casteel.

Castle Creek, JACKSON, KLAMATH. The various branches of Castle Creek rise on the west slope of the rim of Crater Lake, and Castle Creek itself flows into Rogue River. It was named Castle Creek because of the many spires and pinnacles in the canyon. Castle Crest is the high ground just east of Rim Village in Crater Lake National Park. Early maps show Castle Creek heading just south of Rim Village but because of a signing mixup, this branch is now known as Dutton Creek. This leaves the head of Castle Creek separated from Castle Crest by Munson Ridge and Munson Valley.

Castle Rock, CLATSOP. Castle Rock stands in the Pacific Ocean about a mile northwest of Arch Cape and has an elevation of 157 feet. It has upward projections that simulate battlements with some degree of fidelity and as a whole looks not unlike a castle. The name is apposite.

Castle Rock, MORROW. It does not seem to have taken much imagination on the part of early settlers to build rock castles in the air, for there are Castle rocks in most of the counties of the state. The one in Morrow County about a mile northwest of the present railroad station Castle was probably the best known. It was a low bluff said to actually resemble a castle from the river. This formation as well as the old railroad and highway grades were inundated by Lake Umatilla behind John Day Dam.

Castro Spring, MALHEUR. This spring about 15 miles south of Jordan Valley is on property that belonged to Fred Castro. Nearby Castro Ridge is named for the same man. He was buckaroo boss for Pick Anderson in the early days. Hanley and Lucia in *Owyhee Trails* describe the activities of both these men.

Catalpa Lake, WASCO. This lake 1.3 miles east of Frog Lake Butte was named by a fish planting crew of the Oregon State Game Commission about 1950. The catalpa, *Bignoniaceae catalpa*, is not native to the Pacific Northwest and the compiler is unable to explain the application.

Catched Two Lake, WALLOWA. This is a small lake in T 4S, R 43E, on the divide between Lostine and North Minam rivers. J. H. Horner, an old-time resident, reported that many years ago Lyle Shumway was herding sheep in the area. His camptender neglected to set up the tent and after a row he departed and Shumway spent the night under the stars. The camptender and a friend returned the next day and Shumway recounted that "he catched two damn fools today." He publicized his opinion by carving "Catched Two" on a board and posting it nearby.

Catching Creek, COOS. Catching Creek is an important stream tributary to South Fork Coquille River. It was named for Ephraim C. Catching, an early settler in the vicinity of Myrtle Point. Other geographic features in Coos County are also named for E. C. Catching or for his family.

Catching Creek, DOUGLAS. James Catching was born in Tennessee in 1827 and came to Oregon in 1847 with his brother, Ephraim. He took part in the Cayuse War and then moved to California. In the 1850s he returned to Oregon and spent some time in the Coos Bay area where one brother, Ephraim Catching, was an early well-known settler. James Catching then moved to the lower Cow Creek Valley where he and another brother, John, took donation land claims southwest of the present town of Riddle. Gaston has a biography of James Catching in *Centennial History of Oregon*, v. 3, p. 309.

Cathedral Ridge, HOOD RIVER. This ridge is one of the northwest spurs from Mount Hood and it is notable for the impressive cathedral-like spires along its summit. It was named in 1922 by a party of explorers from Hood River, led by C. Edward Graves, who was living in Arcata, California, in 1943. This party also named Eden Park, Wy'east Basin and Vista Ridge.

Catherine Creek, UNION. Catherine Creek is an important tributary of Grande Ronde River southeast of La Grande. It was named for Catherine Godley, the daughter of Thomas and M. E. Godley, early settlers near Union. Information about the Godley family is sparse and the compiler is indebted to John W. Evans of Eastern Oregon State College for unearthing the above facts. The Godleys were among the earliest Union County settlers. Captain Seth Weldy, 23rd Infantry, in his report dated Aug. 15, 1867, describing his march from Fort Dalles to establish an outpost on Willow Creek in Malheur County, says that the detachment camped by Catherine Creek on July 27, 1867. Little Creek near Union was originally named Julianna Creek for the Godley's other daughter.

Cathlamet Bay, CLATSOP. Cathlamet Bay is on the south side of the Columbia River east of Tongue Point. Like many other Indian names, its meaning is hard to trace. Myron Eells identified the term with the Indian word *Kalama*, which is a town in Washington. On Nov. 11, 1805, Lewis and Clark passed near the Indian village of Cathlamet and referred to *Calt-har-mar* nation of Indians. Thwaites refers to this nation as an extinct Chinookan tribe. It was obviously a small unimportant group of natives, and there is a possibility that the name of the tribe was associated with the word *calamet*, meaning stone, indicating that the Indians lived in a stony place. The Indian village of *Caltharmar* was on the south bank of the

Columbia River, possibly not far from the present site of Knappa. Thomas N. Strong of Portland is authority for the statement that after the visit of Lewis and Clark, the Caltharmar nation, much reduced by disease, crossed the Columbia River and settled near the present town of Cathlamet, Washington. Wilkes, in *U. S. Exploring Expedition*, v. 23, p. 335, and in accompanying atlas refers to Cathlamet Bay as Swan Bay.

Catlow, HARNEY. This place and several other geographic features nearby were named for John Catlow, who was born in Yorkshire in 1824, and who, after emigrating to the United States, engaged in mining and stock raising in several parts of the west. He had extensive holdings in Harney County. He died in 1901. For biography, *see History of Baker, Grant, Malheur and Harney Counties*, 1902, p. 701.

Cave Junction, JOSEPHINE. This is the name of a community and post office on the Redwood Highway about 30 miles southwest of Grants Pass where the branch highway goes east to the Oregon Caves. In 1935 traffic into the caves had resulted in a community developing at the junction and a post office was applied for, with the name Caves City. The name was not satisfactory to the authorities, partly because the use of the word City implied that the place was incorporated, which was not a fact. Other suggestions were made, but on May 29, 1936, the USBGN adopted the name Cave Junction, which seemed to be satisfactory to those concerned. The post office was established in 1936.

Cave Mountain, KLAMATH. This mountain east of Chiloquin between Williamson and Sprague rivers is named for the prominent cave in its lower slopes.

Caverhill, GRANT. The post office of Caverhill was established through the efforts of W. S. Caverhill, a local resident, and it was accordingly named for him. The post office was established Feb. 7, 1916, and Nellie Caverhill was first postmaster.

Caviness, MALHEUR. Caviness is a locality about 15 miles west of Brogan and about ten miles southeast of Ironside, both airline measurements, named for a prominent local family. It is in the stock country. Caviness post office was established Jan. 24, 1908, and was closed Dec. 15, 1910. William P. Caviness was the place's only postmaster.

Cavitt Creek, DOUGLAS. Cavitt Creek is a tributary of Little River about 20 miles east of Roseburg. It was named for Robert L. Cavitt, a bachelor, who settled along its banks. Cavitt came west before the Civil War but returned to fight. After the war he again came west and later went to the Klondike where he found only frozen feet. He then settled for good on his claim along Cavitt Creek only to be burned to death by a fire in his cabin.

Cayuse, UMATILLA. Cayuse is a railroad station and post office about 11 miles east of Pendleton and is one of the few geographical features in the state named for the Cayuse Indians. In 1924 Professor Edwin T. Hodge of the University of

Oregon applied the name Cayuse Crater to a vent in the south part of Broken Top Mountain in Deschutes County. The Cayuse Indians were a Waiilatpuan tribe, formerly living at the headwaters of Walla Walla, Umatilla and Grande Ronde rivers, and between the Blue Mountains and Deschutes River. The tribe was closely associated with the neighboring Walla Wallas and Nez Perces, but was linguistically independent. After 1855 the tribe was moved to the Umatilla Reservation. Their language is practically extinct, and their members have been absorbed by other tribes. Alexander Ross gives the name *Cajouse* in *Adventures of the First Settlers on the Oregon*, p. 127; Townsend's *Narrative* gives *Kayouse*; Palmer gives *Caaguas* and *Kioose* in his *Journal*, 1847, p. 53; Hale gives *Cailloux* in his *Ethnography and Philology*, p. 214; Scouler gives *Cayoose*; Wyeth, *Cayouse* and *Skiuse*; George Wilkes, *Kiuse*; Farnham, *Skyuse*; John Work, *Kyauses*; Washington Irving gives *Sciatogas*. The Cayuses had linguistic affinities with the Molallas of western Oregon. Indian horses have come to be called "cayuses" because the Indians of that name were large breeders of the animals. The name formerly had only local use, but later spread over the Pacific Northwest. Cayuse in Umatilla County was formerly a stage station, and was at the foot of what was known as Meacham Hill. Cayuse post office was established Oct. 29, 1867, with John S. White first postmaster. There is a Cayuse Canyon opening onto Rock Creek northeast of Condon in Gilliam County. It was doubtless so named because cayuse ponies pastured there.

Cazadero, CLACKAMAS. This was a station on the Estacada line of the Portland Electric Power Company near which the Cazadero power plant of the company is located on the Clackamas River. For many years previous to the time the company made its additional development further up the river, Cazadero was the end of the interurban line. It was named by the original promoters of the line, and the word is Spanish, meaning a place for the pursuit of game. The name was doubtless suggested by Cazadero, California.

Cecil, MORROW. This is a railroad station on the Union Pacific Heppner branch in the western part of Morrow County, at an elevation of 619 feet. A post office named Cecils was established a mile to the south in 1867 and operated until 1870. Cecil post office was established on July 1, 1902 and operated as both an office and rural branch until 1974. It derived its name from the Cecil family, large landowners in the neighborhood who gave land for the post office.

Cedar Camp, MARION. Cedar Camp post office was established Nov. 26, 1932, and operated until July 22, 1933. Mrs. Edith M. Filer was the only postmaster. This office was a little to the northeast of Hullt and in the same locality as the older Bridge Creek post office. Cedar Camp was so known because there were several cedar shingle camps in the vicinity. Cedar Camp appears to be a name synonymous with the Bridge Creek locality. The compiler has been told that Cedar Creek is another name for Bridge Creek, but he cannot find any official sanction for the name Cedar Creek as applied to the stream.

Cedar Mill, WASHINGTON. This suburban community north of Beaverton at the intersections of Barnes and Cornell roads is located on the site of the sawmill established in 1855 by Justus Jones and his son, John Halsey Jones. Justus Jones and his family came to Oregon in 1853 and took a claim near Clatskanie. In 1855 he moved to Washington County and bought a squatters claim along Cedar Mill Creek from one Joe Walters. Here he erected a small sawmill with a "muley" or sash saw powered by an overshot waterwheel. In 1869 Jones sold the mill to John Q. A. Young and W. R. Everson. He then moved into Portland where he and his son established the Jones Lumber Company on Macadam Road. This well-known enterprise continued until shortly after World War II in what is now the John's Landing area. John Quincy Adams Young was the son of Dr. Elam Young, a well-known Oregon pioneer, who, with his family, came to Oregon in 1847. Young, who was working in the Whitman sawmill at the time of the massacre on Nov. 29, 1847, escaped, but his son James was killed. The Young family arrived in Oregon City in 1848 and soon thereafter settled near the present site of Hillsboro. In 1856, Young married Elizabeth Constable of Hillsboro, moved to the Cedar Mill area and, with Everson, participated in the operation of the Jones sawmill. The post office at Cedar Mill was established Jan. 27, 1874, with Young the first postmaster. He named the place because he specialised in cutting cedar siding, shingles, shakes and other products, most of which were used in buildings in the town of Portland, which was then growing rapidly. For more information, *see* the *Oregon Journal*, Sept. 15, 1981, p. 4MW. The style Cedar Mills is wrong, although often seen in print.

Cedar Mountain, MALHEUR. Cedar Mountain consists of several rounded summits the highest of which is 5564 feet. It is in T 26S, R 41E, approximately 12 miles southwest of the south end of Lake Owyhee. It has been called both Cedar Mountain and Juniper Mountain in the past but in 1975 the USBGN in *Decision List 7502* settled on the former name. There are no cedars in this part of Oregon but the common juniper, *Juniperus occidentalis*, was often miscalled cedar by early settlers.

Celilo, WASCO. On Mar. 9, 1957 the final closure was made at The Dalles Dam and Lake Celilo, the impounded pool, began to form. This pool with a normal elevation of 160 feet contains 330,000 acre feet of water and powers the 1,806,800 kilowatt rated capacity of the 26 turbines. It also inundated The Dalles of the Columbia from Big Eddy to Celilo Falls. In addition to the lake, the name Celilo is perpetuated in Celilo Village built by the USCE to replace Indian facilities at their traditional fishing grounds. In bygone days the name was used for a railroad station, for the navigation canal along the south bank of the Columbia River, and for "the rather low but romantic horseshoe shaped falls at the rock reef composing the upper end of this obstruction (Dalles) below which the Indian was accustomed to stand with his spear to pierce the jumping salmon. Like all other river falls these were known to the fur traders as The Chutes, and where the name 'Celilo' was first used or whence it came is not known." T. C. Elliott, *OHQ*, v. 16, p. 133 *et seq*. Gustavus Hines, in *Oregon: Its History, Conditions and Prospects*, Buffalo, 1851, p. 14, says: "A boy whose Indian name was Ken-o-teesh, belonging to the Si-le-lah tribe, was received into the mission in April and died on the 19th of the following August." Whether Si-le-lah is the same as Celilo is a matter of conjecture, although a study of Oregon tribal names gives no other solution. Early journals of fur traders and travelers do not mention Celilo. Celilo was used in 1859, according to Mr. Elliott, who said there are several suggested meanings, including "tumbling waters," "shifting sands," and the name of an Indian chief, etc. Dr. Leo Frachtenberg of the Smithsonian Institution, in the *Oregon Journal*, Dec. 31, 1917, said Celilo is a Yakima word meaning "cleft in the bank." Mr. Elliott's article referred to above gives more theories about the name and much information about the Celilo Canal. Stories to the effect that Celilo is a name based on a remark of a steamboat captain, "I see, lie low," may be dismissed as fiction.

Cemetery Hill, WALLOWA. Cemetery Hill is in s 20, T 1N, R 48E, near Imnaha. In 1931 J. H. Horner told the compiler that it was named because more than a dozen Indian graves were found there in pioneer days by Jack Johnson and others. A. C. Smith talked to the Indians about the origin of these graves but could learn nothing. They told him the graves were very old.

Cemetery Ridge, WALLOWA. This ridge is in the northeast part of the county and extends from Buckhorn Springs northeast. It is in townships 3 and 4N, R 48E. According to J. H. Horner of Enterprise, it was named because in the vicinity were the remains of some Indians killed in a battle between Nez Perces Indians and a band of renegade Snakes. The circumstances of this fight were within the memories of the older Indians in the Wallowa Valley.

Centerville, WASHINGTON. Centerville was the name of a small community on Dairy Creek at the road crossing about two miles north of Cornelius. The principal activity of the place revolved around the Trullinger mills, but today there is little to show for it. The locality was probably named because it was about the center of the Tualatin Plains, although it may have been named because it was supposed to be near the center of the county. Centreville post office was established Oct. 11, 1866, with Edward Jackson first postmaster. This office was closed Mar. 30, 1874. Ingles post office was established at the same place or nearby on Sept. 28, 1881, with William S. Ingles, postmaster. The name of this office was changed to Centerville on Sept. 2, 1889, and the office was closed Sept. 30, 1904. These three offices may not all have been in exactly the same place, but they were in the same general locality.

Central, LINN. Central was one of the earliest post offices established in what is now Linn County. The office was established June 13, 1852, with Joel Ketchum postmaster, and it was discontinued Apr. 19, 1861. Early maps show the place about nine miles east of Albany and a little south. The office bore a descriptive name, probably because it was in a central location between Albany and the early settlements to the east.

Central, MULTNOMAH. On June 13, 1900, a post office named Central was established on the Multnomah County list. The office was discontinued Dec. 14, 1903. James Channing was the first and only postmaster. According to the Portland city directory of 1902 the post office was at the southeast corner of Claremont Avenue and the East Ankeny street carline. Because of the change in Portland street names the location of this post office should now be described as the southeast corner of NE Glisan Street and NE 53rd Avenue. This falls within the limits of Center Addition, a tract that was platted in 1890. A question arises as to why the name of the post office Central differed from the name of the addition Center. This discrepancy was doubtless caused by the fact that there was then a post office in Washington County called Centerville and postal authorities undoubtedly did not wish to run the risk of fostering further confusion. Also there was a community in Clackamas County called Center. This old Central post office had of course no connection with a later Portland office called Central station.

Central Point, JACKSON. This community received its name because two important pioneer wagon roads of the Rogue River Valley crossed at this point which was near the center of the valley, thereby suggesting the name. One of these roads was the north and south road from the Willamette Valley and the other was the road leading from Jacksonville, which was then the center of settlement, northeast to Table Rock, Sams Valley and other localities. Central Point was named by Isaac Constant who was a pioneer of 1852 and who also lived near the crossroads. Magruder Brothers established a store at this point about 1870 and a post office was soon given the name of Central Point. The town is on the Siskiyou line of the Southern Pacific Company and on I-5 and has an elevation of 1272 feet.

Cerro Gordo, LANE. Cerro Gordo is a point on the north side of Row River about five miles east of Cottage Grove. The words are Spanish and mean a rich hill in a mining district, otherwise a fat or round hill. *Gordo* also means obese. In 1945 John C. Veatch of the Portland bar told the writer that a number of veterans of the Mexican War settled in the vicinity of this butte and presumably displayed their knowledge of Spanish by naming the mountain. There is a notion that this hill resembles the one in Mexico where the battle of Cerro Gordo was fought but Mr. Veatch thinks this improbable and that the real reason for the name was that the slopes are of a golden brown in late summer, giving the appearance of a gold or rich mountain. Mr. Veatch was well acquainted with the locality because he was born there.

Chadwell, CLATSOP. Chadwell is a locality on Lewis and Clark River about four miles south of Miles Crossing and south of Astoria. It bears the name of a place in England. Mr. and Mrs. William True were early settlers in the Lewis and

Clark Valley. They came from Chadwell, England, and when the local post office was established Feb. 20, 1882, True was the first postmaster and he named the place for his former home. The Clatsop County office was closed July 27, 1898, with papers to Melville. *See* information in the "Astoria Column" in the *Astorian-Budget*, June 7, 14, 20, and 26, 1946.

Chadwick Canyon, DOUGLAS. This canyon running into South Umpqua River at Missouri Bottom was named for Jacob J. Chadwick who settled near its mouth in 1868.

Chain Canyon, WASCO. J. A. Rooper, who was born on the old Rooper Ranch, told the compiler in 1969 that this canyon that empties into Ward Creek was named because in the early days someone found a piece of abandoned chain presumably left by emigrants who strayed into the rough defile.

Chamberlain Hill, MULTNOMAH. Chamberlain Hill is east of Sandy River and north of Springdale. It bears the name of Elijah D. and Sarah Ellen Chamberlain who came to Oregon from Kansas in 1881 and settled in the Springdale area.

Chamberlain Lake, TILLAMOOK. This lake on the Camp Meriwether property of the Boy Scouts of America was named for the former owner, E. A. Chamberlain. It is a pleasant fresh water swimming spot within a few hundred yards of the Pacific Ocean. Chamberlain's father, Ezra B. Chamberlain, took up a homestead north of the lake in 1886.

Chambers Lakes, DESCHUTES, LANE. These are a small group of moraine lakes on the crest of the Cascade Range between the Middle and South Sisters. They were named in 1924 by Professor Edwin T. Hodge for James Blair Chambers, an early merchant of Eugene. Chambers was born in Quincy, Ohio in 1833 and came to Oregon in 1884. He moved to Eugene in 1887 and founded Chambers & Son Hardware Company. His son, Frank L. Chambers, succeeded to the business in 1890 and lived to be an extremely prominent Eugene business man. James B. Chambers died in Eugene in 1902.

Chambers Spring, WHEELER. Chambers Spring near the headwaters of Fry Creek south of Mountain Creek was named for Calvin Chambers who homesteaded nearby at the turn of the century.

Champagne Creek, DOUGLAS. This stream flows into Umpqua River from the south a few miles northwest of Roseburg. It is in a locality known as the French Settlement because it was here that a number of French-Canadians established a sort of colony in the 1850s. One of these settlers was Joseph Champaign and the creek bears his name. Dean Byrd of Salem reported in 1990 that the family used the form Champaign and this was the style on Joseph's tombstone. It is unlikely the current spelling of the creek's name will be revised. For data about the French Settlement, *see* Walling's *History of Southern Oregon*, p. 428.

Champion Creek, LANE. Champion Creek, in the Bohemia mining district, was named for the Champion mine, which is situated near its headwaters. Champion post office was in operation in this locality from Sept. 1909, until Oct. 1918.

Champlain, MULTNOMAH. A post office with the name Champlain was in service at Holbrook from Jan. 27, 1892, to May 21, 1892, with Fred Gaskell postmaster. Information about the origin of the name is unsatisfactory. Holbrook post office had been in operation at or near this place from Sept. 1887, to Oct. 1888, when it was closed to Arthur. Millard C. Holbrook of Portland wrote the compiler in Sept. 1946, that Fred Gaskell was associated with his (Holbrook's) grandfather, Samuel Wilson, in a general merchandise store on the Holbrook farm. Gaskell applied for a post office to replace the discontinued office, and the name Champlain was suggested as being that of a nearby stream. The name Champlain was changed to Holbrook by postal authorities on May 21, 1892, and thus the old title was put back in service. Mr. Holbrook adds that the name Champlain is not known in the area and there does not seem to have been any stream called Champlain Creek. Just what Gaskell had in mind is a mystery.

Champoeg, MARION. The name Champoeg (Champooick, in early official records of the provisional government) is variously explained. According to F. X. Matthieu, the name was derived from the French words *Campment du Sable*, "camp of sand" (*OHQ*, v. I, p. 88). According to other testimony, the origin is from French *champ* ("field"), and an Indian word, probably *pooich* ("root"); or the word may be purely Indian, designating a root or weed. According to H. S. Lyman, the name is not of French, but of Indian origin; *Cham* (hard *ch*), as in *Chehalem, Chenamus, Chemeketa, Calapooya, OHQ*, v. I, p. 176. Frederick V. Holman says *Champoeg* is an Indian word, *Champoo*, a weed, (*OHQ*, v. II, pp. 22–23). Henry B. Zenk in a 1976 Master's thesis at Portland State University entitled "Contributions to Tualatin Ethnography: Subsistence and Ethnobiology," mentions the yampah or false caraway plant, called by the Kalapuyans *apu i jik*. He then notes on p. 87: "This term is given as the source of the name Champoeg (for which Gatschet has *ca mpuik*." Wilkes map of 1841 shows Champooing.

Champoeg was the site of the first warehouse of the Hudson's Bay Company on the Willamette River, south of Oregon City, and the shipping place for wheat from the Willamette Valley. The accessibility of Champoeg by land and water caused it to be chosen as the meeting place to consider a provisional government. The site of the Champoeg meeting place and monument is on the south bank of the Willamette River midway between Newberg and Butteville. The settlement of Champoeg is about a half mile to the south on Mission Creek. Events leading up to the Champoeg meeting of May 2, 1843, are set forth in Scott's *History of the Oregon Country*, v. 2, p. 3, where begins Harvey W. Scott's address on the occasion of the unveiling of the Champoeg Monument on May 2, 1901. On Feb. 15, 1841, Ewing Young died at a point not far from the present site of Newberg and as he left considerable property and no heirs, the necessity of a civil government was manifest. Some little headway toward securing a government was made, but it was not until two years later that the movement acquired enough momentum to amount to anything. Two preliminary meetings were held in the spring of 1843, at the second of which a committee was appointed, and this committee was to report at a meeting to be held at Champoeg on May 2, 1843. At the appointed time about an equal number of American and British citizens met, and by a narrow margin, the Americans gained control of the situation and started the organization that developed into the provisional government of Oregon, the first government by Americans on the Pacific Coast.

The site of the Champoeg meeting is now owned by the State of Oregon, and is a State Park. The State built a memorial building which was dedicated May 2, 1918. For further details of Champoeg Memorial Building, *see* Scott's *History of the Oregon Country*, v. 2, p. 221. In the 1970s the State Parks Department found in private storage Theodore Gegoux's huge 1923 history painting of the Champoeg meeting entitled "Inception of the Birth of Oregon." This was painted long after the Champoeg meeting but Gegoux used photographs, portraits and recorded descriptions for the likenesses of over 20 of the actual participants. The picture, fully restored in its original frame, is now hanging in the park Visitor Center. Champoeg post office was established Apr. 9, 1850, with F. X. Matthieu first postmaster. The name was changed to Buteville on Sept. 9, 1850. A post office named Champoag was then established on July 10, 1851, with Robert Newell postmaster. The name was changed to Newellsville on Aug. 2, 1864, and to Champoeg on May 24, 1880. This office was discontinued in the summer of 1905.

Chandler, POLK. Chandler post office was about five miles south-southwest of the site of Valsetz, and a little north of the southwest corner of the county. It was in operation from Apr. 1895, until July 1900, and bore the name of the first postmaster, Thomas C. Chandler. It was closed to Rocca. The office was on North Fork Rock Creek. Chandler Mountain nearby got its name from the same source as the post office.

Chanticleer Point, MULTNOMAH. Chanticleer Point is about one mile west of Crown Point on the Historic Columbia River Highway. It was named by Mr. and Mrs. A. R. Morgan who purchased the property in 1912 and erected a popular resort called Chanticleer Inn after the cock in *Reynard the Fox*. The spot has a fine overlook of the lower Columbia River Gorge and the name of the inn was soon attached to the viewpoint. In 1931 the building was destroyed by fire and the property subsequently passed to Julius L. Meier and was included in his country estate. In 1956 the Portland Women's Forum resolved to purchase 3.7 acres including the main overlook to be donated to the State Park system. A large stone marker was dedicated in May 1960 but title was not passed to the state until Oct. 1962. The name Portland Women's Forum State Park was specified by the grantor but fortunately Chanticleer Point is preserved in the inscription on the marker.

Chaparral Creek, WALLOWA. This is a tributary of Minam River. Chaparral is a word that is often supposed to refer to a specific bush or shrub, but such is not the case in the western United States. Chaparral means any dense thicket of low shrubs, especially those that bear thorns. There is no such thing as a chaparral plant in this part of the world. In Spain and in other places *chaparral* refers frequently to dense growths of low evergreen oak trees, and it is from *chaparro*, an evergreen oak, that the word is derived.

Chapin Creek, MORROW. Chapin Creek is in the south part of the county and flows into Rock Creek about six miles southeast of Hardman. It bears the name of George Chapin who homesteaded in the neighborhood in early days. The spellings Chopen and Chapen are wrong.

Chapman, COLUMBIA. Chapman took its name from Simcoe Chapman, who operated a logging enterprise in the eastern part of Columbia County. Simcoe Chapman was born in Ontario, Canada, in 1840. As a young man he engaged in lumbering and logging activities, a business which he followed all his life. He operated in Michigan and Minnesota, and came to Oregon in 1901. He founded both the Chapman Timber Company and the Chapman Lumber Company. He died in 1923.

Chapman Creek, DOUGLAS. This creek flows into North Fork Smith River in s 17, T 20S, R 10W. It is named for Robert Chapman who filed for a homestead along the creek in 1879. This creek has been shown on some maps as Sulphur Creek but this is wrong. The USBGN has confirmed the name Chapman.

Chapman Creek, JOSEPHINE. This stream is about four miles southeast of Kerby. It bears the family name of William Chapman, a pioneer settler on its banks.

Chapman Hill, POLK. Chapman Hill is in the southeast part of Eola Hills, about two miles northwest of Salem. It has an elevation of a little over 400 feet. It was named for a Captain Chapman, who lived near the hill. Chapman Corners just to the north is named for the same man. In other days Chapman Hill was known as Schindler Hill but that name seems to have fallen into disuse.

Chapman Point, CLATSOP. Chapman Point is the first important projection into the sea north of Ecola Creek and the first outlying southern point of Tillamook Head. It received its name from W. S. Chapman, a civil engineer of Portland who owned the point and considerable property nearby.

Chapman Slough, HARNEY. This slough is part of Silvies River south of Burns. It was named for a pioneer settler along its banks, John Chapman.

Chapman Spring, WHEELER. This spring on the north end of Sutton Mountain was named for Archie Chapman who homesteaded there in 1900. Chapman was the son of George W. Chapman who settled near Richmond in 1869.

Charbonneau, CLACKAMAS. Charbonneau is a planned residential community south of Willamette River and east of I-5 near Wilsonville. Work was started in the early 1970s and largely completed by 1980. The place is named for Jean Baptiste Charbonneau, son of Lewis and Clark's guide, Sacajawea.

Charcoal Cave, DESCHUTES. This cave just southwest of Arnold Ice Cave was named by Dr. L. S. Cressman, University of Oregon anthropologist, because of the large, inexplicable deposit of prehistoric charcoal found on its floor. Phil Brogan gives more details in an article in the *Oregonian*, Mar. 25, 1973.

Charcoal Point, DOUGLAS. Charcoal Point on North Umpqua River about nine miles east of Steamboat was named by USFS ranger Fred Asam for a natural charcoal outcrop.

Charleston, COOS. Charleston was named for Charles Haskell, who is said to have taken up a claim at the mouth of South Slough in 1853.

Charlotte, LANE. Charlotte post office was in service so long ago that the compiler knows little about it except its location, and that information is none too reliable. Charlotte post office was established in June 1880, and was discontinued in Apr. 1881. Edgar P. Hayfield was the only postmaster. The office was named for his younger sister Charlotte Hayfield. A map dated 1889 shows Charlotte near the southwest corner of T 16S, R 1W. This puts it about two miles south of Mohawk.

Charlton, COLUMBIA. This station on the west bank of the Columbia River south of Goble was named for A. D. Charlton of Portland, for many years general passenger agent for the Northern Pacific Railway.

Chase, YAMHILL. William O. Chase was the first of five postmasters at Chase, and the office was named in compliment to him. Chase was about seven or eight miles west of McMinnville, in the west part of T 4S, R 5W. The office was established Mar. 24, 1896, and operated until Aug. 30, 1905.

Chase Mountain, KLAMATH. Francis Landrum of Klamath Falls informed the writer that this mountain southwest of Keno was named for George Chase who in the 1890s built the stage station at the junction of the Agar and Applegate roads. This was near Klamath River in S 32, T 39S, R 7E.

Chaski Bay, KLAMATH. This bay is on the south side of Crater Lake, and lies between Phantom Ship and Eagle Point. It was named by Will G. Steel for a minor deity of the Klamath Indians. A. S. Gatschet in his *Dictionary of the Klamath Language* gives the word as *Tchashkai*, meaning weasel. The "Weaslet" was a mythical being often alluded to by western Indians, and conjurers frequently mentioned weasels because of their curious pranks and tricks.

Chatfield, WASCO. This was a siding on the Union Pacific Railroad near Mosier. The station was named in 1920 for Roy D. Chatfield, a fruit grower in the neighborhood, who was at one time manager of the Mosier Fruit Growers Association. He was the donor of Memaloose Park, now owned by the state. It was east of Mosier.

Chatham Island, MULTNOMAH. In the last week of June 1975, Admiral Sir Charles Madden, BT. GCB, Chairman of the Board of Trustees of the National Maritime Museum and former Commander-in-Chief of the British Home Fleet and NATO came to Portland to attend the opening of the memorable Cook Exhibition put on by the Oregon Historical Society. To commemorate the part played by the Royal Navy in the exploration of Oregon, the OGNB, at the suggestion of the compiler, voted to call the unnamed island south of Flag Island, Chatham Island for the ship commanded by Lieutenant William R. Broughton of Vancouver's expedition, and Sir Charles participated in an appropriate ceremony. There have been a number of British ships of this name. Broughton's command was launched in 1758 and continued in service until 1814. She was a vessel of 135 tons and carried a crew of 55 officers and men. It is interesting to note that Broughton, who was in the Columbia River in Oct. 1792, had discovered the Chatham Islands near New Zealand the previous year and named them for his ship. For information about Broughton, *see* Broughton Bluff. For information about Cook, *see* Captain Cook Point.

Chautauqua Lake, CLACKAMAS. A partly filled lake between Gladstone and I-205 is all that is left to remind Oregonians of one of the social phonenema of the first quarter of the twentieth century. The Chautauqua Movement was started in the summer of 1874 by John H. Vincent and Lewis Miller as a training operation for Sunday School instructors, and took its name from its location on the shore of Chautauqua Lake, New York. During the balance of the nineteenth century it grew and gradually shifted emphasis to the general field of adult education utilizing both professional educators and popular luminaries such as William Jennings Bryan. Melvil Dewey taught library management while developing his Dewey Decimal classification system between 1900 and 1910. About 1900 the system was tremendously expanded by the establishment of travelling groups or Chautauquas which visited innumerable cities in the United States. A favorite operating spot would be a wooded area near a lake, similar to the founding location in New York. The subject has been well covered in *We Called it Culture*, by Victoria and Robert Ormand Case and *The Chautauqua Movement*, by John H. Vincent. Chautauqua Lake in Oregon was in Gladstone Park, part of the Fendel Cason claim and now a summer camp for the Seventh Day Adventist Church. The park featured a giant assembly hall with wood roof trusses carrying a clear span remarkably long for its day. The Oregon City *Enterprise-Courier*, July 23, 1954, has an excellent account of the Oregon Chautauqua. Gannett says *Chautauqua* is an Indian word that has been the subject of much controversy. Meanings are varied and range from "foggy place" through "where the fish was taken out" to "place of easy death."

Cheatem Holler Camp, GRANT. This spot at the head of Myrtle Park Meadows was named by USFS employee Leo Gunther for one Cheatum or Cheatham. An incident involving Mr. Cheatum, a bottle of whiskey and an irate Mrs. Cheatum was responsible for Gunther's terminology.

Cheeney Creek, CLACKAMAS. Cheeney Creek is a tributary of Salmon River south of Welches. This stream was formerly called Sheeny Creek, a name applied by a survey party in the early 1870s because of an episode connected with the Jewish camp cook, who was unfamiliar with the woods. Many years later the USFS changed the name to Cheeney.

Chehalem, YAMHILL. Joseph B. Rogers owned property where Newberg stands today. In 1848 he had the town of Chehalem platted but he died in 1853 and his original settlement passed into obscurity. Chehalem was one of the earliest post offices in Yamhill County. It was established Mar. 14, 1851, the same day as Lafayette and North Yam Hill offices. The only earlier office in the county was Yam Hill Falls, established Jan. 8, 1850. Chehalem post office was discontinued Jan. 6, 1852. Daniel Dodge Bayley was the first postmaster at Chehalem. Bayley was born in Vermont in 1801. He and his family were among those who came to Oregon in 1845 by the Meek Cutoff. They arrived in the Chehalem Valley in Sept. 1845, and settled on a place near what is now Newberg. The Chehalem office was at the Bayley home. *See* West Chehalem. Daniel Dodge Bayley later went to Tillamook Bay, where he named the town of Garibaldi, and served as first postmaster.

Chehalem Mountains, WASHINGTON, YAMHILL. These are the highest mountains in the Willamette Valley, and that section of the valley north of them is generally known as the Tualatin Valley, drained by Tualatin River. The Chehalem Mountains and some independent spurs extend from the Willamette River east of Newberg northwest to the foothills of the Coast Range south of Forest Grove. The highest known point at the southern end is due north of Newberg, and has an elevation of 1447 feet. At a point on the northern end east of Wapato is a summit of 1633 feet, called Bald Peak. It may be assumed that the modern word Chehalem comes from the Indian name *Chahelim*, listed under the heading Atfalati (Tualatin), *Handbook of American Indians*, v. 1, p. 108. This name is given by Gatschet in 1877 to one of the bands of Atfalati, a division of the Kalapooian family of Indians. Gatschet lists more than 20 of these bands, all living in the general vicinity of the Chehalem Mountains. H. S. Lyman in *OHQ*, v. 1, p. 323, refers to a point near the mouth of what is now known as Chehalem Creek and calls it *Cham-ho-kuc*, but gives no meaning or explanation.

Chehulpum Creek, MARION. This stream rises in the hills northeast of Jefferson and flows westward into a branch of the Santiam River. It has also been known as Doty Creek, but in 1934 a number of local residents petitioned to have the Indian name adopted. The petition was approved by the Marion County Court and the OGNB. In Feb. 1935 the USBGN adopted the name Chehulpum Creek for the stream, which flows under old Pacific Highway East just south of Looney Butte. George H. Himes is authority for the statement that *Chehulpum* was an Indian word meaning Beaver Illahe, or land where beaver were plentiful. Jacobs in *Kalapuya Texts*, p. 163, says the meaning is a place "up above, upstream, up-country."

Chemawa, MARION. Chemawa is one of the Indian names in the state that has several fanciful meanings attributed to it, including "our old home," "true talk" and "gravelly soil." There is little on record to substantiate any of the meanings.

Silas B. Smith, Clatsop County pioneer, is authority for the statement that *Che-may-way* was the Indian name for a point on the Willamette River about two and a half miles south of Fairfield where Joseph Gervais settled in 1827–28. The same name was applied to Wapato Lake. Indian names were bestowed generally on account of physical peculiarity, and not for sentimental reasons, and the name may mean "gravelly soil," but gravel is neither peculiar nor abundant at either one of the places mentioned. Many Indian names began with *Che* and *Cham*, particularly those applied to places in the Willamette Valley, such as *Chemawa, Chehalem, Chemeketa* and *Champoeg*. For information on this matter, *see* article by H. S. Lyman, *OHQ*, v. 1, p. 316. Chemawa has an elevation of 165 feet.

Chemult, KLAMATH. This community, elevation 4758 feet, is toward the north end of the county, on US-97. It is also a station on the Southern Pacific Cascade line and the junction with that line and the Burlington Northern, Inc. The name is that of a Klamath Indian chief who was one of the 26 who signed the treaty of Oct. 14, 1864. The geography of the locality is shown on the USGS map of the Chemult quadrangle.

Chenoweth Creek, WASCO. Chenoweth Creek rises in the hills west of The Dalles, and after flowing across Chenoweth Flat reaches the Columbia River southeast of Crates Point. This stream was named for Justin Chenoweth who was a prominent pioneer of Oregon. He was born in Clark County, Illinois, Nov. 17, 1825, and was educated as a surveyor. He started to California in 1849 by way of New Orleans and Panama, but on reaching New Orleans he changed his plans and proceeded up the Mississippi to Saint Louis and thence to Fort Leavenworth. At Fort Leavenworth he joined, as a civilian, the party of the First U.S. Mounted Rifles which reached The Dalles in the fall of 1849. Chenoweth lived for a short time in the Willamette Valley, taught school, was a clerk for the territorial legislature and was employed in the territorial library. He married Mary H. Vickers, at Butteville, Dec. 9, 1852. He settled on a claim west of The Dalles, and carried the mail between The Dalles and the Cascades in a small boat. He was actively engaged in surveying public lands, both as a private surveyor and as United States surveyor at the Vancouver land office. His cousin, Francis A. Chenoweth, was one of the promoters of the tramway at the Cascades and it is a family tradition that Justin surveyed the line. He left The Dalles about 1866. He died in Portland Mar. 16, 1898, and his obituary appears in the *Oregonian*, Mar. 20, 1898. Nathan Olney owned a store near Crates Point before Chenoweth settled there, and Chenoweth Creek was then known as Olney Creek, but that name did not persist. The name of the geographic feature near The Dalles is frequently spelled Chenowith, but the USBGN has officially adopted the form Chenoweth. Dr. William C. McKay was authority for the statement that the Wasco Indian name for the locality of Chenoweth Creek was *Thlemit*, which means a caving or washing away of the banks.

Cherry Creek, JEFFERSON. This creek was named on account of the wild cherries growing along its banks. It flows into John Day River near Burnt Ranch, and was one of several geographic features in central Oregon named by the pack train party of Joseph H. Sherar on the way to the John Day mines in 1862. *See also* Antelope, Bakeoven and Muddy Creek. Cherry Creek post office was named for the nearby stream. The office was established on the Crook County list on June 23, 1884, with Mrs. Harriet P. Tucker first postmaster. The office was closed June 21, 1886. All the evidence available to the compiler shows that this office was in what is now Jefferson County, but that may not have been the fact.

Cherry Creek, WALLOWA. William Duncan, a pioneer stockman, named this stream because of the many wild cherry trees that grew along its banks. Cherry Creek flows into Snake River in T 5N, R 48E.

Cherry Grove, WASHINGTON. Cherry Grove was founded in 1911 by August Lovegren. Lovegren came to this country from Sweden in 1883 and for many years operated a lumber mill at Preston, Washington. Mr. Lovegren wanted a name connected with fruit for the new community and thought of Appleton but there was already a place by that name in Oregon. His cousin, Anna Ryberg, then suggested Cherry Grove after her home in Goodhue County, Minnesota. Cherry Grove post office was established May 8, 1912 and operated until June 30, 1959.

Cherryville, CLACKAMAS. Cherryville is near the Mount Hood Loop Highway east of Sandy. The name is said to come from the wild cherries growing in the neighborhood.

Chesher, LANE. The pioneer post office Chesher was named for James P. Chesher, its first postmaster. The office was established Apr. 1, 1875, and was closed Aug. 21, 1890. It was reestablished Dec. 27, 1892, the name was changed to Varien and it went with that name until June 7, 1895, when it was closed again. For a short biography of J. P. Chesher, *see Illustrated History of Lane County*, p. 500. The post office was a few miles west of what is now Veneta, not far from the present community of Noti, in the Coast Range on the upper drainage of Long Tom River. The name should not be confused with Cheshire, later applied to a place west of Junction City. The name Varien came from Paul Varien Bollman, son of John W. Bollman, the postmaster at the time the name was changed.

Cheshire, LANE. Cheshire was a station on the line of the Southern Pacific Company south of Corvallis. It was near the Long Tom River. It was platted in 1913 as Hubert, but this caused confusion with another station on the same line, Huber, so the railroad company changed the name to Cheshire. The name Hubert was selected to compliment Hubert Cheshire, a favorite small boy of the neighborhood. Hubert post office was established Mar. 20, 1914, with Henry C. Ball postmaster. The name of the office was changed to Cheshire on May 12, 1914. The Cheshire family had been prominent in the locality.

Chesnimnus Creek, WALLOWA. This stream flows into Joseph Creek, and for many years was shown on maps as Chesninimus Creek. Investigations by the

USFS indicated that this spelling was in error, and the USBGN adopted the shorter form. The word is Indian in its origin and according to J. H. Horner of Enterprise means Thorn Butte, referring to a locality near the head of the stream where there were several thorn thickets. The Indians camped there and called the place *Sis-nim-mux*, accent on the second syllable. The suffix *mux* meant butte or mount.

Chester, MULTNOMAH. Chester post office was in operation from May 6, 1893, to May 31, 1894, with Rudolph Baumann postmaster. This suburban office appears to have been an independent establishment. An old Portland directory lists the address of R. Baumann and Sons at the southeast corner of N. Willamette Boulevard and Gay Street. The compiler must assume that Chester was the name of some member of Baumann's family.

Chestnut Spring, WALLOWA. Chestnut Spring is about ten miles southeast of Minam. It bears the name of Ed Chestnut, who had a homestead in the vicinity. He was an early settler on Cricket Flat.

Chetco River, CURRY. The name is applied to various features in southwest Oregon, and is derived from the name of a small Indian tribe that lived along the lower reaches of the river. Early day spelling was Chetko and Chitko. For information about the Chetco Indians, *see Pioneer History of Coos and Curry Counties*, edited by Orvil Dodge. Mount Emily in the southwest part of Curry County is sometimes known as Chetco Peak, but the real Chetco Peak is in the east part of the county and has an elevation of 4660 feet. *See* USGS topographic map of the Chetco Peak quadrangle. The spelling Chetco has been adopted by the USBGN. For editorial about an Indian woman, Lucky Dick, the last of the Chetcos, *see* the *Oregonian*, Jan. 23, 1940. A post office named Chetco was among the earliest in southwest Oregon. This office was established Mar. 3, 1863, with Augustus Miller first postmaster. It was discontinued Nov. 15, 1910. Old maps show this office at various places on the coast between the mouth of Chetco River and the Oregon-California state line. It probably moved with the availability of a postmaster.

Chewaucan Marsh, LAKE. This is a large marsh, fed principally by Chewaucan River and draining into Lake Abert. The elevation of the upper end of the marsh is 4311 feet and that of the lower end 4291, according to the Strahorn railroad survey. The name is derived from the Klamath Indian words *tchua*, meaning wild potato, and *keni*, a general suffix meaning locality or place. The wild potato is generally known in Oregon and Washington as the wapato, arrowhead or sagittaria. It was an article of food with many tribes. *See* USGS *WSP 220* and *363* for information about the marsh. *See also* the *Oregonian*, Sept. 14, 1925, p. 11, for information about the wapato.

Chickahominy Creek, HARNEY. Chickahominy Creek flows into Silver Creek north of Riley. The name is old and while there is no definite information, it must have been named by units of the 1st United States Cavalry Regiment about June 23, 1878, at the time of the battle of Silver Creek in the Bannock War. Colonel Reuben F. Bernard, commanding the 1st Cavalry, had been a second lieutenant in the same regiment during the Peninsular Campaign in the late spring of 1862. He fought at the battles of Mechanicsville and Gaines Mill, both along the Chickahominy River in Virginia, on June 26 and 27, 1862, so either the near anniversary or the arrangement of the battle suggested the name.

Chicken Hill, GRANT, UNION. Chicken Hill is in the Blue Mountains on the watershed between the Grande Ronde and North Fork John Day rivers. The local tradition about the origin of the name is to the effect that in the days of the mining fever a freighter was hauling in supplies from Columbia River points and on top of an otherwise bulky load were several crates of chickens for the mining camps. The load capsized before reaching the top of the hill and the chicken coops were so badly smashed that the fowls escaped into the brush, crowing and cackling. The locality has been called Chicken Hill ever since.

Chicken Whistle Creek, LANE. This is a small tributary of Battle Creek heading on the Chicken Whistle Art Farm near Crow. The farm is owned by Bel and Chuck Ivey. Bel Ivey, in a whimsical vein, described the stream as: "nearly as big as a chicken whistle." The writer has little knowledge of obscure musical instruments so the reader must look elsewhere for information about this device, if such a device ever was.

Chickenhouse Gulch, GRANT. This gulch was named for a sheepherder's cabin built there in the early days. The cabin was very rough and so were the herders when they referred to their abode.

Chico, WALLOWA. The town of Chico was named by George Harris, who had formerly lived in Chico, California. When he took up a homestead in Wallowa County, he named it for his former home. *Chico* is a Spanish word meaning little. Chico, California, is laid out on the old Spanish land grant, *Rancho del Arroyo Chico*. This *rancho* was in 1854 certified to General John Bidwell, an early California pioneer, who laid out the town of Chico. Stories to the effect that Chico, California, was named for a governor, Chico, seem to have no foundation and the compiler can find no record of any such person.

Chief Joseph Mountain, WALLOWA. This mountain has been known at various times as Tunnel Mountain and Point Joseph, but in 1925 the USBGN officially named it Chief Joseph Mountain in honor of the famous Nez Perce Indian chief. Joseph, or Young Joseph as he was sometimes known, was born near the mouth of Imnaha River in June 1837, and died at Nespelem, Colville Indian Reservation, Sept. 21, 1904. He was the son of Old Joseph, who died about 1871, and the grandson of Ollicut, a Cayuse Chief. Old Joseph took his wife from a band living near the mouth of Asotin Creek. In May 1877, Young Joseph and his band began to threaten the white settlers in the Wallowa Valley, claiming the valley as his ancestral home. After some skirmishing and encounters, the Indians finally began their famous journey to Montana, pursued by troops. Chief Joseph made his last stand at the Battle of the Big Hole, Aug. 9, 1877, and on Oct. 4, 1877, he surrendered to Colonel Nelson A. Miles at Bear Paw, Montana. For references to this matter, *see* Scott's *History of the Oregon Country*, V. 2, pp. 104 and 332. For additional information on Joseph, *see The Nez Perce Indians and the Opening of the Northwest*, by Alvin M. Josephy, Jr. For news story about launching of Liberty ship named for Chief Joseph, *see* the *Oregon Journal*, Mar. 28, 1943, main sect. p. 15.

Chilcoot Mountain, DOUGLAS. This mountain is in S 6, T 25S, R 1E, just south of the Lane County line. USFS rangers Fred Asam and Ed Lough named this while locating a trail. They had considerable difficulty crossing this peak and felt it must be similar to Chilkoot Pass in the Klondike. Chilcoot Creek and the ridge of the same name nearby were named sometime later. There is no explanation for the different spelling.

Chiloquin, KLAMATH. Chiloquin is the whiteman's form of a Klamath Indian family name *Chaloquin*. Chaloquin was the village chief of the old Indian town of *Bosuck Siwas*, or Painted Rock, and his name was given as *Chaloquenas* in the treaty of 1864. Two sons, George and Mose Chaloquin, served with the state troops in the Modoc War.

Chilson Creek, UMATILLA. In the early part of the twentieth century, a Sanford W. Chilson decided to make his home along this creek running through Bridge Creek Flats.

China Cap, UNION. This peak is in the southwest part of Wallowa Mountains and has an elevation of 8638 feet as shown on the USGS map of the China Cap quadrangle. While the compiler has no written record of when it received its name, it is obvious from its picture that it bears a close similarity to the hats worn by Chinese laborers throughout the Pacific Northwest in the early days of development, and it must have been named on that account.

China Creek, WALLOWA. This is a small stream flowing into Snake River from China Gulch in T 4N, R 49E. In the days of placer mining in the Pacific Northwest and particularly near Lewiston there were a great many Chinese panning for gold, and there are China bars, China creeks and China flats in many parts of Oregon, Washington and Idaho. It was at these points that large colonies of Chinese carried on their mining operations.

China Ditch, GILLIAM. The City of Arlington lies at the mouth of a long draw named Alkali Canyon. Most of the year this canyon is dry but when the Condon branch of the Union Pacific was built in 1904, a drainage ditch was dug alongside the railroad grade. Much of the work was done by Chinese laborers. When the job was finished, one family stayed and built a laundry west of the ditch which soon became known as China Ditch. This drainage was later called China Creek but at the request of Marion Weatherford, a long-time resident, the anachronism was eliminated and the dry watercourse was given back its original name. *See* USBGN *Decision List 8801*.

China Hat, DESCHUTES. China Hat is a butte east of Paulina Mountains. It received its name because, when viewed from Fort Rock, it resembled the style of hat worn by Chinese during early days of the Pacific Northwest.

Chinchalo, KLAMATH. This was a station on the Cascade line of the Southern Pacific Company. It bore the name of a Klamath Indian chief and *shaman*. According to Will G. Steel his domain was in the Klamath Marsh country. He was a signer of the treaty of 1864 as Makosas.

Chinidere Mountain, HOOD RIVER. This mountain is just west of Wahtum Lake and has an elevation of 4674 feet. H. D. Langille, pioneer resident of Hood River Valley and an authority on the Mount Hood region, said that Chinidere was the last reigning chief of the Wasco Indians, and that this mountain was named for him.

Chinook Bend, LINCOLN. Chinook Bend is about three miles upstream from Kernville, at a point where the Siletz River makes a pronounced bend first south, then north. The geography of the locality is shown on the USGS map of the Devils Lake quadrangle. In Nov. 1945, Andrew L. Porter of Newport wrote the compiler as follows: "Chinook Bend was so named because the early run of Chinook salmon would lie there and wait for the rain to make fresh water before going up to the spawning ground. It was a good place to troll for salmon."

Chinquapin Mountain, JACKSON. There are a number of geographic features in Oregon named for the western chinquapin, *Castanopsis chrysophylla*; of these Chinquapin Mountain, in the southeast part of Jackson County, is probably the best known. The western chinquapin is sometimes called the golden leaved chestnut. In the lower mountain altitudes it grows into a handsome tree, 75 feet high in some places. On the high mountains it is generally a shrub. It is found generally on the slopes of the southern Cascade Range and the Sierra Nevada.

Chisholm Canyon, SHERMAN. Duncan P. Chisholm was born in Glen Elg, Scotland in 1860. Along with many other Scots caught by the agrarian decline of the Highlands, he emigrated to the United States and in 1888 homesteaded above this canyon six miles east of Kent. Wool was a common cash crop of the small rancher in this area and Chisholm's fleece won a gold medal at the Lewis and Clark Fair in 1905. He was a man of remarkable physical strength and many stories are told of his ability to lift or move incredible weights.

Chitwood, LINCOLN. This was a station on the line of the Southern Pacific Company between Corvallis and Toledo. George T. Smith, postmaster at Chitwood, wrote in 1925 that the station and post office were named for Joshua Chitwood, who lived near the present site of the community when the railroad was built down the Yaquina River. This railroad was built between 1881 and 1885. For details of this construction *see* Scott's *History of the Oregon Country*, v. 4, p. 334.

Chitwood Creek, TILLAMOOK. This creek rises on Cascade Head and spills into the Pacific Ocean. It was named for John D. Chitwood, the first postmaster at Emma.

Chloride, BAKER. Chloride post office was established in the Blue Mountains on June 18, 1901, with George B. Rogers first postmaster. The office was closed on May 28, 1904. It was installed to serve a mining development in the east part of T

8s, R 37E. In Dec. 1945, LeRoy A. Grettum of Baker wrote the compiler as follows: "This post office was at the Chloride Mine in the Blue Mountains near the headwaters of Rock Creek, west of Haines. According to people in Haines who were working there at the time, both the post office and the mine shut down in the spring of 1904 because a very bad snow slide carried away a lot of surface improvements and the resulting debris blocked the tunnel." According to F. W. Libbey of the State Department of Geology and Mineral Industries the name Chloride was doubtless applied because of the presence of silver chloride in the local outcrops. Mr. Libbey wrote: "Chloride is not an uncommon name in western mining camps. In the early days in the West a lessee or prospector who followed a thin vein or small high-grade ore deposit was called a chlorider. According to Albert H. Fay in his *Glossary of the Mining and Mineral Industry* the term is said to have originated at Silver Reef in southwestern Utah when the rich silver chloride ores were being worked. The name was later extended to apply to similar workers in other fields and to other types of high-grade deposits."

Chocktoot Creek, LAKE. This creek flows into Sycan Marsh from the east, and was named for a well-known Indian chief of the Paiute or Snake tribe.

Choptie Prairie, KLAMATH. Choptie Prairie is between Saddle Mountain and Chiloquin Ridge. The name is derived from a Klamath Indian word meaning secluded, or hidden, which well describes the place.

Christensen Slough, BAKER. John C. Christensen came to Baker County in 1869 and settled near Haines. This slough bears his family name.

Christman, LANE. Christman post office was established Jan. 6, 1888, and discontinued Sept. 6, 1893, with Mattie Kirk the only postmaster. It was on Row River southeast of Cottage Grove, probably in the northeast part of T 21S, R 2W. In 1947 John C. Veatch of Portland, reared in the Cottage Grove area, wrote the compiler as follows: "I think this office was on the ranch of Wes Christman who lived on Row River a few miles from the Star office. As I remember, Wes moved into Cottage Grove about 1893 and this was probably the reason for closing the office."

Christmas Creek, WALLOWA. This small stream flows into Snake River in s 32, T 4N, R 50E. It was named by James Tryon and Lu Knapper. They took their sheep to the canyon for winter range on Christmas Day, 1888, and built a cabin on the creek.

Christmas Lake, LAKE. Christmas Lake is a small body of water in T 26S, R 18E, about 25 miles east of Fort Rock. The name is one of the puzzles in Oregon nomenclature. It is frequently asserted that John C. Fremont discovered and named the lake in question, which is not a fact. A map of the Oregon territory accompanying Senator Lewis F. Linn's report, prepared under the direction of Col. J. J. Abert in 1838, shows a river flowing from a lake near what is now known as Drew Valley, the river being labeled Christmas River. It is not clear where this name was obtained, but it is possible that such a stream may have been named by

Hudson's Bay Company men. Fur brigades visited central Oregon as early as 1825, and may have had something to do with the name of Christmas River. During the second exploring expedition of Captain Fremont, which left Kansas in May 1843, its leader conducted the party through the Deschutes Valley, and after naming a number of geographic features, he arrived in the Warner Valley and on Dec. 24, 1843, he reached and named Christmas Lake. This lake is much further southeast than the lake now known by that name, and there is but little doubt that it was what is now known as Hart Lake that Fremont christened. It is an important member of the Warner Lakes group, and near the central part of the valley. There is at present no information as to how the other Christmas Lake got its name, but it is some distance from Fremont's route, and there is no evidence that he ever knew of its existence. The surveyor general of Oregon issued a map of the state in 1863 which shows Christmas Lake in the Warner Valley in the place where Fremont discovered and named it. It has been called Hart Lake for many years.

Christy Creek, LANE. This is the largest tributary of North Fork Willamette River. It was named for one "Doc" Christy, a veterinarian of Eugene, who located a mining claim near its mouth in the early days.

Chrome Ridge, GRANT. Chrome Ridge is south of John Day River and just west of Fields Creek. It is one of several geographic features in Oregon named for the mineral chromite. In July 1945, Dr. F. W. Libbey, director of the State Department of Geology and Mineral Industries, wrote the compiler as follows: "The word chrome is used rather loosely to mean chrome ore or chromite. Chromite is found in lenticular deposits at various places in southwest Oregon and central Oregon, especially in Grant, Josephine and Curry counties. Thus there is the connection between chromite deposits and the word chrome which has been applied to some geographic features in Oregon. Chromite or chrome ore is usually considered to be a chemical mixture of ferrous oxide and chromic oxide. However, it never occurs in nature as this theoretical compound because it always contains impurities such as silica, alumina and magnesia. The chromite ore in Grant County is, generally speaking, lower grade than the chromite ore of southwest Oregon. The Grant County ore averages a lower percentage of chromic oxide." Chromite was not searched for in pioneer days and the use of the name for Oregon geographic features is relatively modern.

Chucksney Mountain, LANE. This mountain, elevation 5756 feet, is about 12 miles north of Waldo Lake. It bears the name of a local Indian celebrity who made his home in the valley of Middle Fork Willamette River.

Cinnamon Butte, DOUGLAS. This butte is about five miles north of Diamond Lake, and has an elevation of 6400 feet. It was named by O. C. Houser of the USFS in 1908 because of the characteristic color of the brush and rock formation near its summit. The USBGN has adopted this name.

Cipole, WASHINGTON. The name of this station on the Southern Pacific line west of Tualatin is pronounced *si-pole*. Cipole is near the large onion-raising lands of the county and the name represents an imperfect representation of the Italian word for onions, *cipolle*, pronounced *chi-po-le*.

Circle Bar, HARNEY. This railroad station was named for the Circle Bar Ranch which used that brand. It is about nine miles southeast of Crane.

Circle Creek, CLATSOP. Circle Creek and its tributaries drain a considerable part of Tillamook Head. The stream got its name because of its circular course, though it far from describes a complete circle. The Circle Creek bridge was a well-known structure on the Oregon Coast Highway southwest of Cannon Beach Junction. The relocation of US-101 eliminated the horseshoe curve crossing.

City Creek, LANE. City Creek rises on the east side of Bohemia Mountain and flows southeasterly to Steamboat Creek. It is so named because Bohemia City, the mining town of the early 1900s, was located near its headwaters.

Civil Bend, DOUGLAS. Civil Bend is one of the amusing place names of Douglas County. It was applied in derision because the locality was so uncivil. The Bend is a prominent reverse kink in South Umpqua River a little to the southwest of Roseburg. The name is said to refer to the boisterous activities of visitors who came to see the horse races in early days. According to Israel B. Nichols, an old timer in the locality, in the Roseburg *News-Review*, May 7, 1948: "there was always lots of drinking and lots of fights, so they called it Civil Bend." Civil Bend post office was in service from Sept. 1881, to Oct. 1888, with James M. Dillard first postmaster. When the office was reestablished in 1889, postal authorities objected to a name with two words. A new name, Brockway, was selected in honor of B. B. Brockway, a pioneer settler.

Clackamas, CLACKAMAS. The Indian word *Clackamas* has been used as the name for two post offices in Clackamas County, at different times and places. The first of these offices, established Sept. 29, 1852, with the name Clackemas and John Foster postmaster, was put on the Marion County list, but was changed to the Clackamas County list with the revised spelling Clackamas on Mar. 22, 1853. It was discontinued Oct. 18, 1853. Preston's map of 1856 shows the site of the office about two miles northwest of what was later Logan. When the Oregon & California began railroad service from Portland south on Sept. 5, 1870, to the place then called Waconda, a station between Milwaukie and Oregon City was called Marshville and it is shown that way on the first time card. *See* Scott's *History of the Oregon Country*, v. 4, p. 30, for a facsimile of this time table. It is not clear just why the name Marshville was applied, as there is very good land drainage in the locality, though topographic maps show a small swampy area about a mile to the south. The name Marshville may have been named for a person, Marsh. There are references to the place by the name Marshfield, but that was not the railroad name. On Dec. 8, 1873, a post office was duly established at the locality with the name Clackamas, and with Noah N. Matlock first postmaster. The railroad was not long in changing the station name from Marshville to Clackamas. All was then brought into harmony.

Clackamas County. This county, together with Clackamas River and other features in Oregon, received its name from the Clackamas Indians, a Chinookan tribe, living along the river. The remnants of the tribe were moved to the Grand Ronde Reservation. It was formerly a large tribe. Lewis and Clark use the form *Clackamus*, and other forms are *Klackamus*, in George Wilkes' *History of Oregon* and on Charles Wilkes' map of 1841; *Clackamus; Nekamus*, in *OHQ*, v. 1, p. 320; *Kluckamas*, in Townsend's *Narrative: Akimmash, Clackamis, Clackamos, Clackemus, Clackemurs, Klackamat, Thlakeimas, Tlakimish*, and many others. Clackamas County was one of the original four districts of early Oregon, the other three being Twality, Yamhill and Champooick. It was created July 5, 1843, and at present has an area of 1890 square miles. An excellent map of Clackamas County is published by the Bureau of Soils of the Department of Agriculture. For full information concerning this county, *see OHQ*, v. 11, No. 1, which contains an article by Frederick V. Holman on the origin of Oregon counties.

Clagett Lake, MARION. Clagett Lake is one of the Firecamp Lakes above South Fork Breitenbush River. It was named many years ago for Ben Clagett, a State Fish Protector who was in the area in the 1920s with William L. Finley.

Clark Branch, DOUGLAS. Walling, in his *History of Southern Oregon*, p. 441, says this stream north of Myrtle Creek was named for James A. Clark, whose land claim was near its mouth. William Hudson later owned the property.

Clark Butte, LANE. A. J. Briem, in his notes on file at the OHS, says that both this butte and Clark Creek on the upper reaches of Fall Creek were named for early settler Austin Clark.

Clark Creek, HOOD RIVER. This creek drains one of the lobes of Newton Clark Glacier, and is named Clark Creek on that account. The next large stream to the north is called Newton Creek for the same reason. Both are tributaries of East Fork Hood River.

Clark Creek, UNION. Clark Creek is the correct name of this stream, not Clarks. The creek was never owned by anyone named Clark, and the possessive of this and many other geographic names should be discarded.

Clark Glacier, LANE. This is the westward of the two small glaciers on the south side of the South Sister, and was named for William Clark in 1924 by Professor Edwin T. Hodge of the University of Oregon. So far as known it is the only geographic feature in the state named for the great explorer except the Lewis and Clark River in Clatsop County. Thwaites' *Original Journals of the Lewis and Clark Expedition* gives a detailed account of the exploration, and on p. xxvii of the first volume is a short biography of William Clark. He was born in Virginia on Aug. 1, 1770, and was the younger brother of George Rogers Clark (1752–1818). At the age of 23 he was a first lieutenant in General Anthony Wayne's western army. He retired from the army in 1796 with brevet rank of captain, and lived quietly with his family, occupied chiefly in adjusting the affairs of his older brother until 1803 when he was invited by Meriwether Lewis to join Jefferson's proposed exploring expedition to the Pacific Ocean. After the expedition Jefferson appointed Clark brigadier-general of the militia of Louisiana, and also Indian agent for Louisiana. Subsequently Clark was surveyor general for Illinois, Missouri and Arkansas. He died on Sept. 1, 1838. For details of Clark's life, *see* Coues' *History of the Expedition of Lewis and Clark*, v. 1. William Clark spelled his name without the final "e," though that form has been used in many places, especially in Clarke County, Washington, until 1926, when the state legislature cut off the "e." For editorial comment on this error, *see* the *Oregonian*, Dec. 3, 1925.

Clark Spring, UMATILLA. This spring located three miles above the mouth of Bridge Creek was named for Ralph G. Clark, an early homesteader.

Clarke, CLACKAMAS. Clarke is a crossroads community in the Highland district about fifteen miles southeast of Oregon City. In pioneer days this was known as the Ringo Settlement. About 1870 one "Friday" Jones bought some property there for "1 yoke of oxen, a shotgun and $200." This he sold in 1876 to Irving L. Clarke, the latter transaction covering 320 acres. Clarke started a store and a little later got a post office. This office, called Clarkes, was established May 13, 1889, with Clarke first postmaster. The office was closed Dec. 13, 1904. Raymond Caufield of Oregon City was good enough to gather these facts from George A. Clarke, a son of Irving L. Clarke, in Sept. 1945.

Clarke Springs, JEFFERSON. These springs and the nearby orchard on the old Madras-Ashwood road were on the homestead of James G. Clarke who settled in eastern Jefferson County about 1900.

Clarks Canyon, MORROW. This canyon runs northwest into Willow Creek just west of Lexington. It was named for Oscar Clark who settled near its mouth in 1864.

Clarks Creek, BAKER. This stream is a tributary of Burnt River. It is said to have been named for a miner who accidentally shot himself there in the early 1860s. There was at one time a post office known as Clarksville near this stream. This office was organized to serve a territory near placer diggings developed along Burnt River in 1861–63.

Clarnie, MULTNOMAH. The origin of the name Clarnie is obscure, but the following explanation is derived from trustworthy sources. Two locators of the Oregon Railroad & Navigation Company decided to name the railroad station after their daughters, the name of one being Clara, and that of the other being Jennie. They combined syllables of the two names to make Clarnie. This station is five miles west of Fairview.

Clarno, WHEELER. This post office was on John Day River near Clarno Bridge, and when it was closed in 1949 happened to be in Wheeler County. Clarno was named for one of the earliest white settlers on John Day River, Andrew Clarno. The Clarno post office was generally situated not far from the bridge, depending upon who could be prevailed upon to take the postmastership. Sometimes it was in Wasco County, sometimes in Wheeler. Clarno has an elevation of

1304 feet. Clarno post office was established Sept. 15, 1894, with Nannie Chichester postmaster. It was then in Gilliam County, as Wheeler County had not yet been formed. When Andrew Clarno settled on John Day River, he had no neighbors. Stockmen in those days did not feel the need of any. When he heard that a friend had settled on a homestead about 20 miles to the east, near the present site of Fossil, he rode over on horseback, and said: "Bill, don't you think you're crowding me a little?" Maps and postal records of the 1880s show a post office named Crown Rock in the present locality of Clarno, but the compiler has been unable to get information about it, except that it was named for a prominent rock formation nearby.

Classic Ridge, TILLAMOOK. Classic Ridge is between Nehalem and Neahkahnie Mountain. Classic Lake is east of the ridge. These features were named by J. H. Edwards of Portland, who was interested in music, and had hopes of developing a community of persons devoted to the arts.

Clatskanie, COLUMBIA. Silas B. Smith, Clatsop County pioneer, is quoted in the *OHQ*, v. 1, p. 322, to the effect that *Tlatskani* was a point in the Nehalem Valley reached by the Indians from the Columbia River either by way of what we now know as Youngs River, or by way of Clatskanie River. The Indians used the word *Tlats-kani* by applying it to certain streams indicating the route they took to get to *Tlats-kani*, and not as the name of the streams for Indians were not in the habit of naming streams. White men carelessly applied the name to the stream. Clatskanie River in Columbia County, and Klaskanine River in Clatsop County were thus named, and Clatskanie, a town, developed near the point where the former joined the Columbia River. Clatskanie is the spelling adopted by the USBGN for the features in Columbia County. The locality *Tlats-kani* in the hills south of Clatskanie River was named for the Tlatskanai Indians, who lived along the river and in the Nehalem Valley to the south. *See Handbook of American Indians*, v. 2, p. 763. There are many variations in the spelling of the name. A news story in the Rainier *Review*, Oct. 2, 1931, says that the town of Clatskanie was first known as Bryantville, which was platted early in 1884. A similar story is carried in an Historical Records Survey release printed in the *Review*, Mar. 27, 1936. The compiler is unable to reconcile these statements with the fact that Clatskanie is shown on the official post office list as early as Dec. 1871.

Clatsop, CLATSOP. Clatsop post office was established near the south end of Clatsop Plains in July 1894, with Alexander Tagg first postmaster. This office operated with one intermission until July 25, 1919, when the business was turned over to Warrenton. The office was of course named for the county and for the Clatsop Indians. It was doubtless moved from time to time. The Tagg place was about a half a mile east of Clatsop school.

Clatsop County. Clatsop District was created by the provisional legislature by an act passed June 22, 1844, and comprised parts of the northern and western parts of Twality District. F. V. Holman's article on the history of Oregon counties in

OHQ, v. II, p. 24, gives detailed information about the formation and boundaries of the county. *Clatsop* is the name of an Indian tribe; mentioned in Lewis and Clark *Journals* and Gass' *Journal*. For description of Clatsop County in 1855, *see* the *Oregonian*, June 16, 1855. For history of Clatsop County, by Preston W. Gillette, *ibid.*, Nov. 20, Dec. 12, 1895; Jan. 18, 1896. For narrative of the Clatsop Indians, by Preston W. Gillette, Oct. 23, 1899, p. 6; his narrative of Mrs. Michel, last of the Clatsops, Mar. 10, 1903, p. 3; his narrative of pioneers of Clatsop County, Nov. 20, 1895, p. 6; Jan. 18, 1896; description of Clatsop County in 1881, by Alfred Holman, Sept. 9, 1887; biography and portrait of Mrs. Michel, Feb. 26, 1905, p. 22. *Clatsop* is given as *Tlahsops* by Silas B. Smith, in the *OHQ*, v. I, p. 320. Townsend's *Narrative* gives *Klatsop*. Hale, in *U. S. Exploring Expedition, Ethnography and Philology*, 1846, p. 215, gives *Tlatsap*. In OPA *Transactions* for 1887, p. 85, the name is *Tschlahtsoptchs*. Dart, in *Indian Affairs Report* for 1851, gives *Clatsops*. Lewis and Clark give *Clat Sops, Clatsops*, etc. Farnham, in *Travels*, New York, 1843, p. III, gives *Clatstops*. There are many other variations. The Clatsops were of the Chinookan family, formerly at the mouth of the Columbia River, on the south side, between Tongue Point and the ocean, and south to Tillamook Head. Lewis and Clark spent the winter of 1805–06 among them at Fort Clatsop. Clatsop County has an area of 934 square miles, according to ODOT. The name Clatsop has been applied to many geographic features in Oregon, including Clatsop Plains and Clatsop Spit.

Claxtar, MARION. Claxtar is one form of the name of the Tlatskanai Indian tribe, generally known as Clatskanie. For information about this tribe *see Handbook of American Indians*, v. 2, p. 763. Lewis and Clark passed the Indian village of Claxtar or Clack-star on the Columbia near Deer Island on Sunday, Mar. 30, 1806. It is more probable the tribe was part of the Upper-Chinook group. When the Oregon Electric Railway was built officials used this name for a station north of Salem, adopting the spelling employed by Lewis and Clark.

Claypool Bridge, LINN. This bridge was about four miles north of Lebanon. C. H. Stewart of Albany wrote the compiler in 1927: "In early days the old Indian trail south through the Willamette Valley crossed the South Santiam near this point. The bridge is on the donation land claim of Samuel R. Claypool, a prominent pioneer citizen of that locality."

Clayton Creek, CLATSOP. Clayton Creek is a small stream emptying into the Pacific Ocean just north of Humbug Point. It was apparently named for S. F. Clayton who in 1883, with his wife Sarah Clayton, patented land along the creek.

Clayton Creek, JACKSON. This creek south of Ashland is named for Henry W. Clayton, an early Jackson County settler, whose donation land claim was near where I-5 crosses the stream. For a short biography *see History of Jackson County*, p. 351.

Clear Creek, COLUMBIA. Clear Creek flows into Nehalem River from the west in the extreme southwest corner of the county. Its name is of course descriptive. Many years ago there was a post office called Clear Creek, but it did not last long.

Old maps show the place close to the mouth of the stream. Clear Creek post office was established Jan. 11, 1878, with Henry D. Sluter (Sleeter?) postmaster. The office was discontinued Jan. 22, 1879.

Cleawox Lake, LANE. This lake is about a mile south of Siuslaw River and a mile east of the Pacific Ocean. It has an elevation of 82 feet. The name is obviously an Indian one but the writer has been unable to get its meaning. The USBGN has officially adopted the name Cleawox Lake instead of Cleawok Lake or Buck Lake.

Cleek, JEFFERSON. Cleek post office was established on the Wasco County list May 19, 1881, with Harley A. Belknap first and only postmaster. The office was discontinued Feb. 21, 1883, and the business turned over to Hay Creek. The best available information is to the effect that the office was at the Henry A. Cleek ranch two or three miles west of what was later Grizzly post office. Belknap rented the Cleek place while the Cleeks were at The Dalles for a time. The ranch was one of the points where stage coach horses were changed. The compiler has not been successful in getting the exact location of the place, but it seems to have been on or near Willow Creek.

Cleetwood Cove, KLAMATH. This cove was named for the boat from which Will G. Steel sounded Crater Lake for the government in 1886. In a dream Steel fancied he heard the word applied to a golden arrow. The dream was so vivid that he christened his boat *Cleetwood*.

Clem, GILLIAM. Clem was named for a well-known Gilliam County character, Clemens Augustus Danneman, who owned a ranch where travelers could get accommodations. He was a native of Germany and a veteran of the Civil War. He was born Oct. 13, 1835. He came to America about 1856, to Oregon 1879, and settled in Gilliam County. Clem is a station on the Condon branch of the Union Pacific Railroad.

Cleo, COOS. Cleo is a station on the Southern Pacific Company line south of Coos Bay. This station was named by using, backward, the initials of the name of a lumbering concern, Oregon Export Lumber Company, which was then operating nearby.

Cleveland, DOUGLAS. F. M. Good came to Oregon from Kentucky in 1853 and was one of the early settlers near the present community of Cleveland, west of Winchester. He started a sawmill and flour mill, and named his brand of flour for the Cleveland flour mill in Ohio. Thus the place in Oregon received its name indirectly for the city in Ohio. Cleveland post office was established Dec. 16, 1874, with Francis M. Good first postmaster, who was the F. M. Good just mentioned. The office was discontinued Feb. 15, 1923.

Cleveland Cave, DESCHUTES. Cleveland Cave is one of the numerous volcanic tube ice caves in the Bend area. It was named for George Cleveland who discovered it while working as a forester near Wanoga Butte. Phil Brogan reports on this in the *Oregonian*, June 15, 1958.

Cliff, LAKE. Mrs. Helen Parks of the Fort Rock Valley Historical Society wrote in 1989 to say Cliff post office was named for J. L. Cliff, a land locator who settled in the area. The office was in operation from Jan. 1906, until June 1920, in the north part of the Christmas Lake Valley.

Cliff Spring, LAKE. R. A. Long of Fort Rock told the compiler in 1972 that this spring near Bridge Creek was named for Cliff Buick and not for nearby precipitous slopes.

Clifford, BAKER. Clifford was a stage station near the upper reaches of North Fork Burnt River on the stage road from Baker to Canyon City. It was a popular stopping place operated by Mr. and Mrs. Marsh Young. The Youngs were warm personal and political friends of Judge Morton D. Clifford and they named the place in his honor. Clifford post office was established Mar. 10, 1894, with Nellie Clark first postmaster. The office was discontinued effective Sept. 15, 1901. Morton D. Clifford was born in Iowa in 1859 and with his widowed mother came to Grant County in 1871. He attended school at Canyon City and read law under W. Lair Hill at The Dalles. He was a lifelong Democrat. He served as district attorney and also as circuit judge until 1904 when he moved with his family to Baker. He had an extensive law practice from which he retired a few years before his death, which occurred in Portland on his 82nd birthday, May 22, 1941. Judge Clifford married Edith Haseltine in 1885.

Clifton, CLATSOP. Clifton was a settlement on the south bank of the Columbia River long before the railroad was built and at one time J. W. and V. Cook, pioneer salmon packers, had a cannery there. The name is descriptive of the cliffs above the river. Clifton post office was established Jan. 6, 1874, with Vincent Cook first postmaster. J. H. Middleton, who was living near Waldport in 1927, and who went to Clifton in the fall of 1873, told the compiler that Clifton was the name of the farm of Stephen G. Spear, and that he was of the opinion that Spear named the place Clifton before the property came into the possession of V. and J. W. Cook. Members of the Cook family are also of the belief that Spear named the place before the Cooks became established there.

Clifton, HOOD RIVER. This name has been applied to the locality about three miles west of Hood River, where I-84 begins to drop down from the top of the well-defined cliffs that characterize the place. The highway has an elevation at this point of about 250 feet above the river.

Climax, JACKSON. Appeals for information about the name of this place brought an interesting letter from Mrs. Walter F. (Bertha B.) Charley of Central Point, who was postmaster at Climax from 1920 to 1933. In July 1946, Mrs. Charley wrote in substance as follows: "The proposed post office at Climax was a popular project among the people of upper Antelope Creek valley, and the petition, circulated by John Wyland, was signed by every adult then living there. It seems that that word 'climax' was a favorite of this man, who stated that 'the climax of his efforts was a tee-total landslide.' He suggested that the post office, when established, be named Climax. The post office was first in the home of Jacob Worlow,

Mrs. Worlow being the first postmistress. The office traveled about the community as new postmasters were appointed, and was in at least six different homes. Finally I was appointed in 1920, and was the last postmistress, serving until 1933, when the patrons dwindled to so few that the office was closed. The few people remaining in the settlement drive twenty-five miles to Medford for mail." According to postal records Climax office was established Nov. 10, 1891, with Mary E. Worlow first postmaster. The office was closed Aug. 11, 1933, with all papers to Eagle Point. The place is east of Medford.

Cline Falls, DESCHUTES. Cline Falls are on the Deschutes River about four miles west of Redmond. The McKenzie Highway crosses the river just south of the falls. They were named for Dr. C. A. Cline (1850–1926), a well-known dentist of Redmond, who owned the falls. Cline Buttes just southwest of the falls received their name from the same source. Dr. Cline died July 19, 1926. For obituary, *see* the *Oregonian* for July 22, 1926, p. 20.

Cline Hill, BENTON, LINCOLN. Cline Hill is the summit where US-20 crosses the Coast Range between Newport and Corvallis. The name commemorates Walker F. Cline, a pioneer homesteader.

Cloud Cap, KLAMATH. Cloud Cap is the highest point on the east rim of Crater Lake and has an elevation of 8070 feet above sea level and 1893 feet above the water of the lake. It received this somewhat fanciful name from J. S. Diller of the USGS, because of its high dome.

Cloud Cap Inn, HOOD RIVER. Cloud Cap Inn is an historic building at the 6000 foot timberline level on the northeast side of Mount Hood. There is a fine year-round spring in the vicinity and in 1885, Mr. and Mrs. David R. Cooper started a tent camp nearby to accomodate summer tourists. In 1889, William M. Ladd and C. E. S. Wood erected the hewn log structure to provide first class facilities. The building was designed by William Whidden, well-known Portland architect, and was located to provide an outstanding view of the north side of the mountain. The summer season was only some three months long and winter sports had not yet become fashionable so the venture was never a financial success. The inn operated sporadically under various ownerships until World War II when it was abandoned and turned over to the USFS. About 1956 the Crag Rats, a mountain rescue and climbing organization in the Hood River Valley, were given custody in return for certain necessary maintenance. The building was listed on the National Register of Historic Places in 1974 and later incorporated in a 1400 acre Historic District. By 1988 the exterior had been largely restored and in 1989 the USFS sponsored a 100th anniversary party including descendants of many of the people originally involved. Erskine Wood, the son of C. E. S. Wood, told the compiler that the name Cloud Cap was suggested by his mother, Nan Wood.

Clover, MALHEUR. Clover post office was established as of Apr. 3, 1882, and was closed Jan. 9, 1883. Josephine M. Reeves was the first postmaster. The compiler has been told that this post office was named for Clover Creek, but no one has come up with a definite locality for the establishment. Clover Creek was named in pioneer days because of the growth of wild clover along its banks.

Clover Flat, LAKE. Clover Flat is a descriptive name for a locality about seven or eight miles airline west of Valley Falls. Clover Flat post office was established Dec. 31, 1914, with Janie N. Bryan first and only postmaster. The office was closed out to Paisley on Mar. 15, 1918.

Cloverdale, DESCHUTES. Cloverdale is a small community a few miles east of Sisters on the highway to Redmond. It was named by R. A. Ford, a teacher and later county school superintendent. Ford farmed nearby and surveyed the Cloverdale Ditch which parallels Squaw Creek. An article in *Ruralite*, v. 24, no. 9, Sept. 1977, gives the history of the place and tells of Alvin Cyrus, the son and grandson of early residents. *Ruralite* was published by Ruralite Services Inc., Forest Grove, Oregon.

Cloverdale, TILLAMOOK. Cloverdale was founded and named by Charles Ray (1851–1925), who settled in Tillamook County about 1884 on the farm that subsequently became the site of the community. He later established a store, hotel, bank and cheese factory at Cloverdale, and was a charter member of Cloverdale Grange. It is apparent that the name is descriptive of the surroundings, which constitute fine dairy country. The name was suggested by Cloverdale, California, where Ray occasionally visited.

Clymer, MARION. Clymer post office, which operated with one break from May 1883, to May 1901, served an area a little to the southeast of Macleay in the vicinity of McAlpin school. The office was named for the first postmaster, Mary Clymer.

Coal Creek, COLUMBIA. Coal Creek flows into Pebble Creek from the east at a point about three miles south of Vernonia. The stream got its name from small coal outcrops along its banks. In fact there have been mining operations in some of these outcrops but so far not on a large scale.

Coal Creek, DOUGLAS, LANE. Coal Creek empties into Middle Fork Willamette River near Campers Flat. Earl Walker, longtime resident of Oakridge, stated that six or seven men built a large log cabin a couple of miles above the mouth of the creek and tried to develop a coal mine. About a half mile above the cabin they had several tunnels but the deposit was not extensive enough to pay. He said the only one whose name he remembered was Jim Sears who used to walk out to what was then Hazeldell to pick up the mail.

Coal Creek, LINCOLN. Coal Creek, which flows into Pacific Ocean a couple of miles north of Yaquina Head, was named in pioneer days because of supposed coal deposits along its course. In Oct. 1945, Andrew L. Porter of Newport told the writer that this coal-like mineral was just large pieces of shale. He tried to burn some without success. In earlier days this stream was on the Siletz Indian Reservation and could not be prospected. Some people thought they were being deprived of a good fuel supply until the true nature of the rock was determined.

Coal Point, CURRY. This point is about three miles south of Port Orford and just north of Humbug Mountain. It is immediately north of Brush Creek. It is believed that Coal Point is the one mentioned by George Davidson in the USC&GS *Coast Pilot* for 1869, which he says was named because of the reported existence of coal in the vicinity, but he could find none after careful examination.

Coalbank Slough, COOS. This slough is a branch of Coos Bay. It received its name in pioneer days. Upon its waters a great deal of coal was taken out of the coal mines in light craft and in sea-going boats.

Coalca, CLACKAMAS. Coalca is a station on the Southern Pacific Company railroad about a mile north of New Era. It was named for an Oregon Indian. To the east, and up on the side hill above the highway, is a natural rock formation called Coalcas Pillar. This pillar is a rock spire with a peculiar knob or capstone at the top. In earlier days the station near this point was called Rock Island for the natural feature in the Willamette River, but due to confusion with other places of the same name, the railroad company changed its station list.

Coaledo, COOS. Coaledo was named because of a coal lead or vein. The place is on Beaver Slough a few miles northwest of Coquille. George Bennett, in *OHQ*, v. 28, p. 346, says a man named Vandenburg was the first settler in the locality. Postal records for 1875 show Coaledo post office, established in that year.

Coalman Glacier, CLACKAMAS, HOOD RIVER. In the 1930s it became evident that the ice mass on the south face of Mount Hood above Crater Rock was not directly connected with Zigzag and White River glaciers. Thousands of people have toiled up this final pitch called either "The Chute" or "The Hogsback" depending upon the location of the route up the ever changing ice. In 1970 Elijah Coalman, the most famous of the Mount Hood guides, died and the OGNB promptly recommended that this be called Coalman Glacier. Lige Coalman was born near Sandy, Oregon on Nov. 26, 1881. He first climbed Mount Hood at the age of fifteen and in the ensuing 31 years made a total of 586 ascents, a record not likely to be surpassed. He was instrumental in the design and construction of the USFS summit lookout on Mount Hood and spent three summers on top prior to World War I. Coalman was later very active in youth work with the YMCA and spent several years at Spirit Lake on Mount Saint Helens. In 1938 he moved to California where he spent his remaining years. For further information *see Mazama*, 1970 and editorial comment in the *Oregon Journal*, July 1, 1970.

Coalmine Creek, DOUGLAS, JACKSON. Coalmine Creek flows south across the county boundary in T 31S, R 1E, and drains into Sugarpine Creek. It got its name because of the discovery on its banks of some black rock that appeared to be coal. However, subsequent investigation showed that the substance was not coal. *See also* Kettle Creek. A deer lick at the junction of Sugarpine and Coalmine creeks is called Coalmine Lick.

Coast Fork, LANE. Coast Fork post office, named for Coast Fork Willamette River, was established Dec. 28, 1867, with George W. Rinehart postmaster. The office was closed Oct. 1, 1872. Gill's map of Oregon of 1874 shows the place on the railroad about four miles south of Creswell, but the railroad was not built when the office was established, so the legend on the map may be for a later railroad station and not for the post office as originally established. Local tradition is to the effect that the post office was a little east of the present site of Creswell.

Coast Fork Willamette River, LANE. This is the smallest of the three streams that combine in the neighborhood of Eugene to form Willamette River. The other two are McKenzie River (formerly McKenzie Fork) and Middle Fork. Coast Fork was so named because it headed more nearly toward the coast than did the other two. It has been so called since pioneer days.

Coast Range. Mountains close to the sea are characteristic of almost the entire eastern shores of the Pacific Ocean. From Bering Sea to Cape Horn ranges of varying heights are constantly visible from the ocean, and Oregon is no exception to the rule. The entry made by Meriwether Lewis in his diary for Apr. 1, 1806, shows that he perceived quite clearly that the mountains along the coast were separated from the Cascade Range by a valley drained by a large river. However, the term Coast Range does not seem to have been used by early explorers in the Oregon country, and the name was doubtless developed by the pioneer settlers. Between the Columbia River and the Siuslaw River the Coast Range is rather well defined, particularly west of the Willamette Valley, but from the Siuslaw south, the Coast Range gradually merges with spurs from the Cascade Range until finally both are consolidated with the Klamath Mountains, whose name is used by geologists in referring to the group near the Oregon-California line, part of which is popularly referred to as the Siskiyou Mountains. The Coast Range of Oregon is, however, geologically, quite independent both of the Cascade Range and of the Klamath Mountains and its dividing line with the latter is considered by geologists to be at or near Rogue River. However, government map makers use the name Coast Range continuously from Oregon into California, and do not employ the term Klamath Mountains. Interesting information about these mountain groups will be found in USGS *Bulletins 196* and *546* by Dr. J. S. Diller. The style Coast Range has been officially adopted by the USBGN. The Coast Range is an irregular group of maturely dissected hills and peaks, and while the main divide is generally parallel to and about 30 miles from the coast, this divide is frequently not in line with the highest summits. From the Columbia River south to Rogue River there are several important peaks. The best available elevations for these peaks are shown in the following table, in most instances to an established survey marker. However, the reader must remember survey markers are not always at the actual summit but differences are rarely more than a few feet.

NAME	ALTITUDE
Saddle Mountain (USCE)	3283 feet
Onion Peak (USCE)	3057 feet

NAME	ALTITUDE
Neahkahnie Mountain (USC&GS)	1621 feet
Mount Hebo (USC&GS)	3154 feet
Euchre Mountain (USGS)	2452 feet
Marys Peak (USC&GS)	4097 feet
Table Mountain (USGS)	2820 feet
Grass Mountain (USC&GS)	3603 feet
Prairie Peak (USCE)	3422 feet
Roman Nose Mountain (USGS)	2859 feet
Kenyon Mountain (USC&GS)	3254 feet
Mount Bolivar (USC&GS)	4319 feet

Mount Bolivar is the highest peak in the Oregon Coast Range north of Rogue River. There are higher peaks in the Oregon Coast Range south of Rogue River. The Columbia River cuts the Coast Range to water level. The next stream to find its way through the Coast Range is the Nehalem, which pursues a winding course, first east, then north, and finally west and southwest until it reaches the ocean. In the north part of the range the highest summits lie in a well-defined line beginning at Clatsop Crest on the Columbia River, passing through Saddle Mountain and Neahkahnie Mountain. South of the Nehalem and north of the Siuslaw there is a succession of peaks and mountains most of which are west of the drainage divide. The South Yamhill River cuts deeply into the Coast Range from the Willamette Valley with a resultant pass to the ocean of but little over 700 feet. Yaquina River does the same, except from the west. The Siuslaw River has cut a pass below 500 feet, and the Umpqua River cuts through the range at water level.

Coburg, LANE. Coburg was originally called Diamond as it was located on John Diamond's donation land claim. A blacksmith named Charles Payne or Paine operated a smithy where Coburg is now situated and named the place about 1865 for a very fine imported stallion named Coburg, apparently imported from and named after Coburg, Germany.

Coburg Hills, LANE. These hills are a spur of the Cascade Range. They lie between the Willamette Valley and the Mohawk River. McKenzie River swings around their southern end. They have an extreme elevation of over 3000 feet. Coburg Hills take their name from the town of Coburg just to the west.

Cochran, WASHINGTON. Cochran post office and railroad station were named for Judge Joseph W. Cochran and J. Henry Cochran, brothers, of Ashland, Wisconsin, who owned a large tract of timber in the locality.

Cochran Creek, LINN. Cochran Creek is a stream northwest of Brownsville. It flows into Butte Creek north of Saddle Butte. William Cochran was a pioneer landowner on the upper part of this stream, and it was named for him.

Coe Glacier, HOOD RIVER. This is one of the important glaciers on the north slope of Mount Hood and has its source near the top of the mountain. It lies east of Pulpit Rock, and Coe Branch flows northeast from its base. It was named for Captain Henry Coe, a pioneer resident of the Hood River Valley, who with several others, operated a stage line to the mountain.

Coffee Creek, DOUGLAS. This stream flows into South Umpqua River from the north about 15 miles east of Myrtle Creek. Reinhart in *The Golden Frontier*, p. 152, says a party of soldiers chasing hostile Indians camped by this creek about 1858. They were out of coffee and made fun of one of their companions who complained bitterly of this lack. The name Coffee Creek continued even after the discovery of gold.

Coffee Island, MARION. Coffee Island is in the Willamette River southwest of Saint Paul. It was named for the Coffee family, early settlers on the east bank of the river.

Coffeepot Creek, LANE. This stream flows into Middle Fork Willamette River south of Oakridge. According to C. B. McFarland of the USFS, the creek was named in pioneer days. A coffeepot fell out of an immigrant's wagon and was run over by a wheel and ruined. John H. Hill, an early resident of the vicinity, vouched for the story.

Coffin Butte, BENTON. Coffin Butte lies about three miles southwest of Suver, and just west of US-99W. It has an elevation of 732 feet. Viewed from the southwest, this hill has a remarkable resemblance to a coffin, hence the name applied.

Coffin Canyon, GILLIAM. Coffin Canyon emptying into Thirtymile Creek southwest of Condon is named for one of Gilliam County's earliest settlers. George Coffin settled near its mouth in 1877.

Coffin Mountain, LINN. Coffin Mountain is a name that well describes this 5771 foot peak south of Idanha. When viewed up Blowout Creek from Detroit Lake it appears as a flat top box of awesome proportions. The name is very old.

Coffin Rock, COLUMBIA. Coffin Rock is in the Columbia River a little more than a mile north of Goble. It is so called because it was an Indian burial place. Broughton mentions it in his report on Oct. 28, 1792. "Mr. Broughton continued to proceed against the stream, and soon passed a small rocky islet, about 20 feet above the surface of the water. Several canoes covered the top of the islet, in which dead bodies were deposited." The first use of the name Coffin Rock that the compiler has seen is in Coues' *Henry-Thompson Journals*, v. 2, p. 796, under date of Jan. 11, 1814. This islet should not be confused with Mount Coffin, a point on the Washington shore west of Longview.

Cogswell Creek, LAKE. This stream flows westward into Goose Lake at a point about ten miles south of Lakeview. Members of the Cogswell family were pioneer settlers in Goose Lake Valley as early as 1869, and the stream was named for M. Cogswell or one of his relatives.

Colby Spring, CROOK. Charles Colby bought 40 acres of school section lieu land that included this spring southwest of Conant Basin. He also at one time owned the old Way Ranch on Crooked River west of Combs Flat Road. For further information on the sale of "school sections" by the state after withdrawal, *see* School Section Cabin.

Cold Camp Creek, WASCO. In 1862 Joseph H. Sherar named Cold Camp near the headwaters of this creek on The Dalles-Canyon City road. The creek flows westerly to Antelope Creek.

Cold Springs, UMATILLA. Cold Springs railroad station, Cold Springs Wash, Cold Springs Reservoir and Cold Springs Canyon are all well-known geographic names in northwest Umatilla County. The station is on the Union Pacific Railroad on the south bank of Columbia River about ten miles east of Umatilla. The names are all descriptive. A post office named Arroyo was established in these parts on July 15, 1878, with Clinton V. B. Reeder postmaster. The name of the office was changed to Cold Springs on Apr. 2, 1880, with Andrew C. Bryan postmaster. This office was short lived and was closed probably in 1883. *Arroyo* is a Spanish word meaning rivulet or small stream, and in the western United States the term is frequently used for intermittent creeks or dry watercourses. The name Arroyo was doubtless suggested by Cold Springs Wash. Cold Springs Reservoir was formed when the wash was dammed in the early 1900s to provide storage for irrigation water diverted from the Umatilla River.

Colebrook Butte, CURRY. This butte has an elevation of 2046 feet and is about ten miles south of Port Orford and two miles east of the Pacific Ocean. Euchre Creek flows around its eastern and southern slopes. It was named for a pioneer settler, F. W. Colebrook, who located a homestead nearby about 1860. Colebrook was born in Scotland, Oct. 13, 1816, and came to Oregon about 1858. He died May 21, 1889.

Colegrove Butte, CURRY. This butte southeast of Carpenterville was named for Delmar Colegrove who took over the Raleigh Scott holdings in this area in 1902.

Coleman Arm, COOS. This arm of Tenmile Lake is named for William and C. P. Coleman. Peterson and Powers in *A Century of Coos and Curry* say that the Colemans bought out the Ole Benson farm for their dairy operation. Apparently at one time the post office at Templeton was on their property for Miss Albina Coleman was the first postmaster.

Coleman Canyon, JEFFERSON. Coleman Canyon is west of Hay Creek and north of Hay Creek Ranch. It was named for Henry Coleman, a partner in Teal & Coleman, the famous ranchers of Trout Creek in the 1870s. Phil Brogan tells of their history in *East of the Cascades*.

Coleman Creek, JACKSON. Coleman Creek drains an area south of Medford. It bears the name of M. H. Coleman, a pioneer of 1853, who was the first settler on the stream.

Coleman Creek, LANE. Coleman Creek is a small tributary of Maple Creek in s

12, T 19S, R 11W. It is named for Mattie Coleman who homesteaded at its mouth before World War I. The name Tenmile Creek is incorrect.

Coleman Mountain, HARNEY. This mountain and a nearby creek were named for a stockman who lived in that vicinity. These features are about 35 miles east of Burns.

Coles Valley, DOUGLAS. This valley was named for Dr. James Cole, the first settler therein. It is along the Umpqua River northwest of Roseburg. Dr. Cole established his home in the valley in 1851. *See* University of Oregon *Extension Monitor* for Sept. 1924. For information about the Cole family, *see* story by Fred Lockley in the *Oregon Journal*, Aug. 17, 1937. Coles Valley post office was established in Dec. 1860 with F. M. Good first postmaster. The office operated intermittently until 1916.

Colestin, JACKSON. Colestin was a post office and a station on the Southern Pacific Shasta line three miles south of the Siskiyou summit tunnel. It was named for Byron Cole who came to Oregon in 1851 and with his brother, Rufus, took a donation land claim straddling the Oregon-California border where they established a stage station called Cole's and kept the travel. Byron Cole sold his interest in the station in 1859 and shortly thereafter acquired several hundred acres to the north including a mineral spring. In 1883, when the railroad was expected to be completed through to California, he built a hotel. A post office with the name White Point was established Aug. 8, 1883 with Ed J. Farlow first postmaster. Cole became postmaster in October of the same year. When the railroad was finally built through in 1887, a station was installed named Colestin. The post office name was changed to Colestin Apr. 3, 1892, and the office was closed Sept. 30, 1943. The railroad station was closed many years ago but in 1983 there were still two or three buildings standing. In recent years the forms Colestein and Colestine have both been used but these are incorrect. *See also* White Point.

Collard Lake, LANE. This lake is about three miles north of Florence. It was named for Roy L. Collard who took up a homestead near the lake.

Collawash River, CLACKAMAS, MARION. This important tributary of the Clackamas River was first named Miners Fork because of the mining activity near its headwaters in northern Marion County. There is a Colowesh Basin in Washington just north of The Dalles and a local chief named Colwash lived nearby in the early days. Jacobs in *A Sketch of Northern Sahaptian Grammar*, says "tcalu-, kalu-, possibly means in origin basket work" and "wac or wass site" as in Wascopam. *Kalu-wass* seems to mean a place where awl baskets were made. This is appropriate for the site in Washington but does not indicate direct Indian application to the extensive, wooded watershed of the Oregon river. The compiler has been unable to learn when or under what circumstances the present name was first applied.

College Creek, WALLOWA. College Creek is a short tributary of Imnaha River in the eastern part of the county. A. N. Adams, a local rancher better known as

Sam, named this stream. He was a Civil War veteran, and pioneer of Wallowa Valley. He applied the name after a school had been established nearby.

College Crest, LANE. In the 1850s there was an educational institution in Lane County called Columbia College. It was situated in the south part of Eugene and the name of the institution has been perpetuated in a geographic name College Crest. This term is applied to an upland, most of which is in s 6, T 18S, R 3W. College Crest is not near the University of Oregon and was not named for that institution. In 1909 J. O. Story and Wesley Whitbeck filed a plat for College Crest but whether they originated the name the compiler does not know. About that time, Fred S. Williams, Jr., settled in the area and in 1913 applied for a post office to be called College Crest. This office was duly established June 13, 1913, and Williams was appointed postmaster, but he asserted that he had never received any notice from the Post Office Department and did not know that the office had been established. Williams operated a neighborhood store and he planned to run the post office in connection with this store. The little store which was to have been the post office was situated at the northwest corner of what is now Friendly Avenue and Lorane Highway in Eugene. At one time there was a street car waiting station at this point.

Collier Creek, CURRY, JOSEPHINE. This stream, now part of the boundary line between the two counties, was named for an early resident, and old maps and records show it as Cole Collier Creek. The first part of the name is now omitted. Collier Butte and Collier Bar were named for the same man

Collier Glacier, LANE. Collier Glacier heads on the west side of North Sister and drains into White Branch. It is the largest glacier in the Three Sisters region and was named for Professor George H. Collier of the University of Oregon, who made an ascent of the Three Sisters in 1880. Professor Collier was a prominent early-day instructor, and came to Oregon from Ohio in 1868. His son, Dr. Arthur J. Collier, was also an instructor at the University of Oregon and a well-known geologist.

Collings Mountain, JACKSON. This mountain is in the southwest part of the county, and has been shown at times as Collins Mountain. The USFS informs the compiler that it was named for a local resident named Collings, and that Collins is wrong.

Colorado Lake, LINN. This lake which has an elevation of 195 feet, lies on the south bank of the Willamette River a few miles east of Corvallis. The compiler has been unable to obtain information as to why this lake is called Colorado Lake.

Colson, KLAMATH. Colson post office was given the family name of the first and only postmaster, Mary E. Colson. The office operated from Mar. to Dec. 1895. It was in the northwest corner, probably in s 7, of T 40S, R 10E. An old map shows this post office very close to the banks of Lost River, at a point seven or eight miles northwest of Merrill.

Colton, CLACKAMAS. Colton is situated on Milk Creek at an elevation of 706

feet. It was named about 1892. Two local residents, Joshua Gorbett and a man named Cole each wished to name it for the other, but the Post Office Department objected to Gorbett because it was too much like Corbett, in Multnomah County. As a result, Colton was selected.

Columbia City, COLUMBIA. This city, just north of St. Helens, was founded in 1867 by Jacob and Joseph Caples. Columbia City was ambitious to become the terminus of Ben Holladay's Willamette Valley railroad in 1870, at the time Portland became the terminus of the west side line with a bonus of $100,000. The prospective community was named for the Columbia River, but the expected growth has not materialized. Columbia City post office was established Aug. 16, 1871.

Columbia County. This county was created Jan. 16, 1854, by the territorial legislature. It comprised the northeast part of Washington (Twality) County as it was after Clatsop County had been created. It was named for the Columbia River, its northern and eastern boundary, and St. Helens is its county seat. The area of Columbia County is 693 square miles (ODOT).

Columbia River, northern boundary of Oregon. Columbia is one of the most abundantly used geographic names in America. Aside from the beauty of the word, its history reflects efforts to honor the achievements of Christopher Columbus. Its greatest use in the Pacific Northwest is as the name of the great river. Captain Robert Gray, in the American vessel *Columbia Rediviva*, on May 11, 1792, at 8 A.M. sailed through the breakers and at 1 P.M. anchored in the river ten miles from its mouth. On May 19, Gray gave his ship's name to the river. (*United States Public Documents*, Serial No. 351, House of Representatives Documents 101.) This was the American discovery and naming of the river. Prior to this, the river's existence had been suspected and other names had been suggested. In 1766–1767, Jonathan Carver, while exploring among the Indians of Minnesota, wrote about a great river of the West and called it Oregon, a word which he may have stolen. On Aug. 17, 1775, Bruno Heceta, Spanish explorer, noted the indications of a river there. He called the entrance *Bahia de la Asuncion*, the northern point *Cabo San Roque* and the southern point *Cabo Frondoso*. Later Spanish charts showed the entrance as *Ensenada de Hecata* and the surmised river as *San Roque*. In 1788 John Meares, English explorer and fur trader, sought for and denied the existence of the Spanish river *Saint Roc*. He called the Spaniard's *Cabo San Roque* Cape Disappointment and the entrance he changed from *Bahia de la Asuncion* or *Ensenada de Heceta* to Deception Bay. That was the situation when Captain Gray made his discovery. In 1793, Alexander Mackenzie, of the North West Company of Montreal, made his memorable journey to the western coast. He came upon a large river which he said the Indians called *Tacootche-Tesse*. This afterwards turned out to be Fraser River, but for a time it was confused with the Columbia. Captain Meriwether Lewis mapped it as a northern branch of the Columbia, spelling it *Tacoutche*. Arrowsmith's 1798 map of the Columbia River was made from Broughton's survey. The name Columbia is not used but instead, the sheet is entitled *Plan of the River Oregan*. William Cullen Bryant in his great poem *Thanatopsis*, 1817, revived and gave wide circulation to Oregon as the name of the river. Another literary name was Great River of the West, which, of course, did not disturb Columbia as a geographic term. *OHQ*, v. 22, Dec. 1921, contains the "Log of the Columbia" by John Boit. This furnishes many interesting details of the discovery of the mouth of the Columbia River by one who was there at the time. The first examination of the Columbia River for the USC&GS was made in 1850 by Lieut.-Commanding Wm. P. McArthur, U.S. Navy. For account of this survey and McArthur's comments on the Columbia River, *see OHQ*, v. 16, No. 3, Sept. 1915, which contains an article by Lewis A. McArthur. This article, among other things, contains the first hydrographic notice ever published by the Coast Survey for the Pacific Coast. It is entitled *No. 3 Columbia River, Oregon*, and gives sailing directions for entering the Columbia River as far as the harbor at Astoria by Lieut.-Commanding Wm. P. McArthur, U.S. Navy, assistant in the Coast Survey. For a more recent overview, *see* article by Don Holm in *Sunday Oregonian*, Northwest Sect. July 20, 1975.

Colvin Creek, MORROW, WHEELER. This stream heads in the extreme northeast of Wheeler County and flows northeast into Morrow County, where it joins Porter Creek. Its waters eventually find their way into North Fork John Day River. Colvin Creek bears the name of John Colvin, who had a homestead on the stream about a half mile east of what is now the Heppner-Spray Highway and about 18 miles south of Hardman. The spelling Colivin is wrong.

Combs Creek, LANE. Combs Creek is tributary to Coast Fork Willamette River about two and a half miles south of London Springs. Henry Combs bought government land there in 1889.

Combs Flat, CROOK. On Oct. 18, 1947, Remey Cox of Prineville wrote as follows: "Combs Flat is a benchland area embracing most of sections 13 and 36, T 15S, R 17E. It was named because it was the home ranch of James Combs, whose lands extended north to the area now in the Ochoco Irrigation district reservoir. Norval Powell, scion of another pioneer Crook County family, now occupies the shrunken remnant of the Combs ranch, and there is a county road debouching from our well-known Ochoco Highway a few miles east of Prineville and connecting with the Crooked River Highway below Post." James Parker Combs was born in Indiana and was married to Jane Dyer of that state. The Combs came to Oregon in 1852 and settled near Lebanon, moving in 1870 to what was later Crook County. For biographical information about members of the family, *see* Crook County *News* of Prineville, Aug. 4, 1930, and Prineville *Central Oregonian*, Mar. 20, 1947. The flat is sometimes incorrectly spelled Coombs.

Comegys Lake, HARNEY. Comegys Lake, off the north end of Steens Mountain, is named for Lloyd and Elmer Comegys who both homesteaded nearby. There appears to be no basis for the name Cummings Lake and the USBGN adopted Comegys in *Decision List 8201*.

Comer, GRANT. Comer post office was near the junction of Comer Gulch and Dixie Creek, about eight miles north of Prairie City. It was named for R. H. J. Comer, Grant County pioneer printer and mining man, who lived on Dixie Creek and in Prairie City for many years. According to a letter of Mrs. Louise King, printed in the Canyon City *Eagle*, Mar. 7, 1947, Comer came from Canada. He was an old-time printer and printed the seven scattered numbers of *The City Journal*, which appeared in Canyon City in 1868 and 1869. It is probable that he wrote most of the contents of the little sheets. Comer's main interest was in mining, and on Sept. 6, 1869, he published the last issue of the *Journal*, which included the following paragraph: "With this issue we (i. e. the typo) withdraw from public life to more remunerative occupation of again swinging the pick and shovel. To a majority a newspaper is a very easy thing to run, but we cannot see it, so the outside world will remain in ignorance of the advantages of this section of Oregon." Comer is said to have been blown to bits many years ago in Prairie City by mine caps. Comer post office was established Jan. 10, 1896, with Henry A. Hyde first postmaster. The office was discontinued May 15, 1907.

Committee Creek, CROOK. Committee Creek flows into North Fork Crooked River and Committee Spring is in S 4, T 16S, R 21E. Ralph Elder, a USFS ranger in the 1920s, reported that the "Sheep Shooters" used to meet under a huge pine tree near the spring. Both the spring and the creek owe their names to the war between the sheepmen and the cattlemen around the turn of the century. *See* Sheep Shooter Tree and Battle Ridge.

Company Hollow, WASCO. Company Hollow is a little vale in S 12, T 1N, R 14E, about three miles south of Fairbanks School. In Feb. 1949, Judge Fred W. Wilson of The Dalles wrote the compiler as follows: "Company Hollow got that name because prior to 1863 when J. C. Ainsworth and the Oregon Steam Navigation Company completed the portage railroad from The Dalles to Celilo, passengers, mail and freight had to be hauled by teams and the company used this hollow and surrounding country for pasturing its horses." Company Hollow was well known for its fine stand of bunchgrass. Wasco County has a road in this locality officially called Company Hollow road. English post office was near this hollow.

Compass Creek, HOOD RIVER. Compass Creek is the tributary of Coe Branch that flows from Langille Glacier on Mount Hood. Van Embree of Parkdale named it after he lost his compass while building the Timberline Trail crossing.

Comstock, DOUGLAS. This station on the Southern Pacific Company line in the north part of the county was named for James J. Comstock, an early day sawmill operator.

Conant Basin, CROOK. Conant Basin and Conant Creek are on the north slopes of Maury Mountains southeast of Prineville. They bear the name of Ed G. Conant, pioneer stockman of the locality. *See* the *Oregonian*, Sept. 18, 1927, sect. V. p. 1. Conant was born in Cuba, but not of Cuban blood. He settled in Crook County in Nov. 1869, and raised horses until his death in the 1890s.

Concomly, MARION. This station on the Oregon Electric Railway about three miles southwest of Gervais was named for Chief Comcomly, head of the Chinook tribe, who is described in Irving's *Astoria*, and also in Alexander Henry's journal. He died in 1830, and his grave was visited by Wilkes in 1841. For references to Chief Comcomly, *see* Scott's *History of the Oregon Country*, v. 2, p. 139. The spelling used by the railway company is a variation of the original name. Lewis and Clark met Comcomly on Nov. 20, 1805, and gave him medals and a flag. Irving describes him in a decidedly humorous vein. His daughter married Archibald MacDonald of the Hudson's Bay Company and their son Ranald MacDonald is an interesting figure in northwest history. Ranald MacDonald wrote *The Narrative of His Life*, edited by Lewis and Murakami, which the Oregon Historical Society issued in a new edition in 1990 (the original published version was brought into print in 1923 by the Eastern Washington State Historical Society). This "Narrative" contains much interesting information about Comcomly and his family, and also about MacDonald's visit to Japan in 1848–49, which is of great historic interest. An editorial in the *Oregonian* for Nov. 29, 1893, treats of MacDonald's pretensions to the Chinook throne.

Condon, GILLIAM. Condon is the county seat of Gilliam County, and has an elevation of 2844 feet. It is an important trading center on SH-19 and is also the southern terminus of the Condon branch of the Union Pacific Railroad. About 1883 a man named Potter owned a homestead just north of Thirtymile Creek, upon which there was a fine spring. He platted the land around the spring, but became involved in financial difficulties, and the land became the property of Condon and Cornish of Arlington. Condon and Cornish sold lots in the townsite, and in 1884 David B. Trimble took the necessary steps to secure a post office, and was appointed the first postmaster. Trimble suggested the name Condon, which was adopted by the department. The office was established July 10, 1884. Harvey C. Condon, for whom the place was named, was a practicing lawyer and located in Arlington, or as it was then known, Alkali, about 1882, and was a member of the firm of Condon and Cornish. He was the son of Judge J. B. Condon, a pioneer jurist of eastern Oregon, and the nephew of Dr. Thomas Condon, Oregon's great geologist. H. C. Condon lived in the state of Washington during the latter part of his life, and died at Vaughn, Washington, June 21, 1931. After World War II, it was the location of two U.S. Air Force stations.

Condon Butte, LANE. This butte is about five miles northwest of North Sister and one mile east of the McKenzie Highway. It was named in 1924 by Professor Edwin T. Hodge of the University of Oregon in honor of Dr. Thomas Condon (1822–1907), distinguished geologist, scientist, Congregational minister and for many years a member of the faculty of the University of Oregon. Dr. Condon's discoveries of the prehistoric horse had a large influence on the conclusions of scientists and went far to establish evolutionary theories. The richest field of his discoveries was in the John Day Valley. For details concerning his life and work, *see* Scott's *History of the Oregon Country*, V. 3, p. 169, McCornack's *Thomas Condon* and Clark's *The Odyssey of Thomas Condon*. Dr. John C. Merriam of the Carnegie Institution selected the John Day fossil bed as the scene of intensive investigations looking toward the development of Dr. Condon's discoveries.

Condon Creek, LANE. Condon Creek empties into North Fork Siuslaw River a few miles above its mouth at the oxbow bend known as The Portage. It is named for Frank Condon, an early settler. Condon filed on a homestead alongside the creek in 1884. Isaac Condon, perhaps a brother, took an adjoining homestead the following year.

Conley, UNION. Conley is a station on the Joseph line of the Union Pacific Railroad north of La Grande. The station and Conley Lake to the east are named for Frank Conley, an early wheat rancher. About 1900 he sold his property to the Mormon Church who established the community of Nibley near Conley Lake. Mount Harris, northeast of La Grande, was once known as Mount Conley.

Conley Creek, DOUGLAS. Conley Creek, in North Umpqua River drainage three miles northeast of Rock Creek Guard Station, was named for John A. Conley who homesteaded near its mouth in 1903.

Connell Spring, CROOK. This spring in S 17, T 14S, R 22E, is named for L. Connell who settled on Summit Prairie in 1880 and lived on Peterson Creek until World War I. This information is taken from a report made in 1936 by USFS ranger Ralph Elder to the Regional Office. The USGS Keys Creek quadrangle dated 1966 shows this as Cold Springs.

Connley, LAKE. Connley post office and Connley Hills between Fort Rock and Silver Lake were named for a local family. The compiler has seen the name spelled in other ways, but Connley was the style used by postal officials. Connley post office was established Apr. 18, 1912, with Warren B. Graham first of three postmasters. The office was closed out to Fort Rock on July 31, 1920.

Conser, LINN. Conser is a station on the Oregon Electric Railway about four miles north of Albany. This station was named for John A. Conser, who owned land nearby. He was the son of Jacob Conser, a pioneer of 1848.

Contorta Point, KLAMATH. This point is on the east shore of Crescent Lake. It was named in 1925 by F. W. Cleator of the USFS because of the abundance nearby of lodgepole pine, *Pinus contorta*.

Conyers Creek, COLUMBIA. Conyers Creek drains an area south of Clatskanie and flows into Clatskanie River at Clatskanie. It bears the name of the Conyers family, several members of which have been prominent residents of the area and have occupied important posts both in public affairs and in business.

Cook Creek, LINCOLN. Willmon Cook took up government land on this tributary of Simpson Creek northwest of Chitwood. Cook came to the area in the early 1900s.

Cook Creek, TILLAMOOK. S. M. Batterson, for many years a resident of the lower Nehalem Valley, informed George B. McLeod of Portland in Aug. 1927, that this stream was named for a local character, Indian Cook, who settled near the mouth of the creek in 1877 or 1878. Cook is said to have been a Cherokee, and there was some feeling against him on the part of the Tillamooks, although he married a Tillamook woman. Cook was a man of fine character, and was murdered by his enemies, not far from the present site of Nehalem.

Cook Slough, CLATSOP. This is a small tidal slough that joins Youngs Bay. It is situated a short distance east of Miles Crossing. Cook Slough takes its name from Geo. W. Cook, who was an early settler on land nearby. He was born in Vermont in 1818 and came to Oregon in 1850.

Cooks Meadow, HOOD RIVER. Cooks Meadow is a half mile south of Brooks Meadow. It is named for Osmer White Cook who was born in Iowa in 1847 and came to the Threemile country southwest of The Dalles in 1874. Cook ran cattle on the meadow in the early days.

Coombs Canyon, UMATILLA. This canyon drains into Umatilla River from the south, just west of Rieth. According to James H. Raley of Pendleton, it bears the name of Calvin Coombs, who settled in the vicinity in the late 1870s. The name Comas Canyon as applied to this canyon is wrong.

Coon Town, HARNEY. Coon Town is now nothing more than a flavorful place name in Oregon history. Even in full vigor before the turn of the century, it was only a tiny community in s 23, T 28S, R 33E, on the homestead of a well-known rancher, Sylvester "Coon" Smith. The name came from the nickname of its principal citizen and was without racial connotation.

Cooper Creek, CLACKAMAS. This creek runs from the vicinity of Fryingpan Lake south to the north end of Timothy Lake. When Oak Grove Fork was dammed to create Timothy Lake it flooded out Cooper Lake in the same basin and Cooper Creek was so called to perpetuate the name. T. H. Sherrard of the USFS informed the compiler that the lake was named for Warren Cooper, now deceased. Cooper, the son of David R. Cooper for whom Cooper Spur was named, was for several years district ranger for the USFS at Parkdale.

Cooper Mountain, WASHINGTON. This is a prominent hill about four miles southwest of Beaverton and has an elevation of 794 feet. It was named for Perry Cooper who was born in Ohio in 1825 and was a pioneer of Oregon. He settled on the slopes of this mountain in Mar. 1853.

Cooper Spur, HOOD RIVER. David Rose Cooper was an early settler in Hood River Valley, and lived not far from the present community of Mount Hood. He had a camping place on the east slope of Mount Hood and the spur was named for him. This was about 1886. Cooper Spur separates Eliot Glacier from Newton Clark Glacier.

Coopers Ridge, LINN. Coopers Ridge is the high ground south of Idanha. Earl Stahlman of Detroit told the writer that it was named for Jack Cooper who ran a regular pack train to Breitenbush Hot Springs in the early days.

Coopey Falls, MULTNOMAH. Coopey Falls were named for Charles Coopey, for many years a well-known tailor in Portland. Coopey was a native of England. He owned land adjacent to the falls that bear his name.

Coos Bay, COOS. As the result of votes at two city elections held Nov. 7 and Dec. 28, 1944, the name of the community Marshfield was changed to Coos Bay, thus doing away with a geographic title that had been in use for 90 years. On Jan. 8, 1965, the city of Empire also voted to consolidate under the new name and in 1983 the community of Eastside followed suit. For the history of these names, *see* Marshfield, Empire and Eastside. The new name was of course taken from the natural feature, Coos Bay. For comments on the origin of the name Coos, *see* Coos County.

Coos City, COOS. Coos City was one of the early post offices of Coos County and it was named for the county or the bay. It was established June 25, 1873, with Henry A. Coston first postmaster. The office continued in service until Mar. 18, 1884. It was situated on Isthmus Slough about five miles south of Marshfield as it was then known. There is little left of the community, but the name is retained by the Coos City bridge. An important road turned eastward at this point headed to Roseburg.

Coos County. Coos County was created Dec. 22, 1853, by the territorial legislature. It was originally formed from the west parts of Umpqua and Jackson counties. *Coos* is an Indian name of a native tribe who lived in the vicinity of Coos Bay. The name is first mentioned by Lewis and Clark, who spell it *Cook-koo-oose* (Thwaites' *Original Journals*, v. 6, p. 117). The explorers heard the name among the Clatsop Indians. Alexander R. McLeod in his journal of 1828 gives the name *Cahoose*; Slacum, in his report of 1837, gives the name of Coos River *Cowis*; Wilkes, in *Western America*, spells it *Cowes*. The spelling has been variously *Koo'as, Kowes, Koos, Coose*, and finally *Coos*. For description of Coos Bay, *see* the *Oregonian*, June 11, 1873, article signed "Northwest." For description of the Oregon coast south of Coos Bay, by the same writer, July 9, 1873. One Indian meaning of Coos is "lake," another, "place of pines," Aug. 26, 1902, p. 12. Perry B. Marple, who began exploiting Coos Bay in 1853, spelled the word *Coose*, and said it was an Indian perversion of the English word coast, meaning a place where ships can land. *See* his advertisement, the *Oregonian*, Jan. 7, 1854. Another version is that the Indian word was made to resemble the name of a county in New Hampshire, (*Oregonian*, Dec. 9, 1890, p. 6). The Coos Indians were of the *Kusan* family, formerly living at Coos Bay. Lewis and Clark estimated their population at 1500 in 1805. The name is often used as synonymous with the family name. Hale, in *U. S. Exploring Expedition, Ethnography and Philology*, 1846, p. 221, gives the name as *Kwokwoos* and *Kaus*; Parrish, in Indian Affairs *Report* for 1854, p. 495, gives *Co-ose*. Interesting details of the early history of southwest Oregon may be found in Orvil Dodge's *Pioneer History of Coos and Curry Counties*, published in Salem in 1898. Coos County has an area of 1586 square miles. In 1844 Duflot de Mofras got off the prize pun in the history of Oregon geographic names when he published his work

Exploration du Territoire de l'Oregon. He called Coos River *la riviere aux Vaches*, or Cows River, apparently after talking to some of the Scots employed by the Hudson's Bay Company.

Coos Head, COOS. Coos Head is the point on the south side of the entrance to Coos Bay. It extends northward from Cape Arago, but is much lower than the main part of the cape. Between Coos Head and the west point of Cape Arago is the Cape Arago Lighthouse, a well-known landmark. The locality of this lighthouse is sometimes called Gregory Point, perpetuating after a fashion the name Cape Gregory, which was originally applied by Captain James Cook in 1778. *See* Cape Arago.

Coos River, COOS. Coos River, named for the stream nearby, was the third post office in Coos County. It was established Mar. 7, 1863, with Amos C. Rogers first postmaster. This office was closed Sept. 20, 1864. The office was opened again Feb. 10, 1873, with Frank W. Bridges postmaster and was closed Sept. 24, 1875. Available maps show the location of this office on Coos River near the mouth of the Millicoma. It may have been in a different locality the first time, but probably not far away. Rogers and Bridges were well-known pioneer settlers in the locality.

Cooston, COOS. Cooston is on the east shore of Coos Bay and the origin of the name is the same as that of Coos County. Cooston post office was established May 13, 1908, and the first postmaster was William E. Homme, who named the place. The office was discontinued in July 1939.

Copeland Creek, DOUGLAS. Copeland Creek rises in T 27S, R 2E, and flows into North Umpqua River near Eagle Rock. It was named for Thomas Bent Copeland who prospected along its banks. Copeland was born in St. Joseph, Missouri in 1850, and came to Oregon in 1864. He and his brother Matt homesteaded on Scott Mountain north of Glide. Copeland Butte, four miles north of Glide, is also named for T. B. Copeland.

Copeland Creek, JACKSON, KLAMATH. Copeland Creek was named for Hiram Copeland of Fort Klamath. The stream rises west of Crater Lake and flows into Rogue River.

Copeland Spring, KLAMATH. Copeland Spring is near Williamson River east of Klamath Marsh. In 1986, the USFS proposed the name to remember John Henry Copeland. Copeland was born in 1910 at Klamath Agency. In his early years he worked at various jobs on the reservation and discovered this spring in 1937 while logging for Weyerhaeuser Lumber Company. After service in World War II, he graduated from Oregon State University and spent much time working with young people and coaching boxing at the Oregon penitentiary. He died in Eureka, California in Apr. 1984.

Copper, JACKSON. Copper is the name of a locality on Applegate River, near the mouth of Carberry Creek and about a mile north of the Oregon-California line. It got its name from the copper mining activity in the vicinity, especially at the Blue Ledge mine just over the line in California. The post office was estab-

lished in Nov. 1924, with Mrs. Mamie Winningham first postmaster. The office
was discontinued in May 1932.

Copper, WALLOWA. A post office with the name Copper was established Jan. 5,
1904, with Anna Bigham postmaster. It was in operation until May 3, 1907, at
which time the office was closed and all papers sent to White Bird, Idaho, the
most convenient nearby office. Copper post office was in S 14, T 3N, R 50E, and was
established to serve some copper mine claims in the vicinity. There is a pinnacle
called Copper Mountain in the locality and also a Copper Creek flowing into
Snake River. The post office was about a half mile west of Snake River.

Copperfield, BAKER. Copperfield was on the west bank of Snake River. The
place had a meteoric career. About 1900 there were many prospectors in the place
and it was called Copper Camp, because of the character of the nearby ore. Soon
after this the community was definitely named Copperfield, and by 1910 there
were about 1000 inhabitants, the increase in population being due to the digging
of two tunnels by the railroad company and by the predecessor of the Idaho
Power Company, near the Oxbow. In 1914 Copperfield became really famous
when Governor Oswald West sent his secretary, Miss Fern Hobbs, double armed
with determination and a signed declaration of martial law, to clean up the morals
of the place. The community was trying to recover from the struggle between
Miss Hobbs and the Power of Darkness, when fire swept away most of the buildings, so it was impossible to determine if Righteousness had prevailed. Two more
fires made Copperfield a thing of the past but the community was rejuvenated in
1965 with the name Oxbow. *See* Oxbow.

Copperfield Draw, KLAMATH. This spot east of Chiloquin was named for early
settlers David and Anna Copperfield.

Coquille, COOS. This name is applied to a city, a point and a river in Coos
County, south of Coos Bay. Coquille is a word of unknown origin, probably
Indian, but with French spelling. The French word means a shell. *Scoquel* appears
in the *Oregonian*, Jan. 7, 1854, in an advertisement of the Coose Bay Company.
The name is there said to be Indian for "eel." *Coquette* appears on a map of John B.
Preston, surveyor-general of Oregon, 1851, probably intended for *Coquelle*. It ap-
pears *Coquille* in Preston's map of 1856. Canadian-French fur traders may have left
the form of name among the Indians. *See OHQ*, v. 19, pp. 73–74, by Leslie M.
Scott, and also the *Oregonian*, for Sept. 3, 1907, where Harvey W. Scott makes
some comments on the pronunciation of the name. Captain William Tichenor in
Pioneer History of Coos and Curry Counties, p. 29, says the Indian name of this
stream was *Nes-sa-til-cut*, but gives no further information. In an article in the
Coos Bay Times, Nov. 29, 1943, Mary M. Randleman, Coos County pioneer, says
the word is of Indian origin and cites a number of early uses of the style Coquelle
and Coquel. The *Handbook of American Indians*, v. 1, p. 871, lists the Mishikhwut-
metunne Indians, who lived along the Coquille, and says that the Chetco names
for some of these Indians was *Ku-kwil-tunne*, and *Kiguel* is a form listed as being

used as early as 1846. This seems to indicate an Indian origin of the name. On Oct. 25, 1938, the *Oregonian* printed on its editorial page an interesting letter from Sam Van Pelt, an aged Indian living at Brookings, who recounted the difficulties of spelling Indian names with "English" letters. "Coquilth" was the result of his efforts to produce the correct sound, but no interpretation of the word was furnished. The letter and accompanying editorial are well worth reading. Interesting information about the founding of the town of Coquille is given in an article in the *Coquille Valley Sentinel* for Nov. 20, 1941. In Coos County there have for many years been spirited differences of opinion about the pronunciation of the name Coquille. *See* editorial in the *Oregonian*, Oct. 17, 1938, as well as editorial mentioned above.

Coquille Point, LINCOLN. Coquille Point is on the east shore of Yaquina Bay about a half mile north of Yaquina community. The place is said to have been named for some Indian families who lived there many years ago and were supposed to have been members of the Coquille tribe of Coos County. The writer does not know how they became settled at Yaquina Bay.

Corbell Butte, KLAMATH. Corbell Butte, the 5389 foot high point on the north end of Chiloquin Ridge, was named for an early day family. Corbell served in the army at Fort Klamath during the Modoc troubles.

Corbett, MULTNOMAH. This community on the Historic Columbia River Highway between Sandy River and Crown Point was named for Senator Henry Winslow Corbett, one of Oregon's prominent pioneer citizens, for many years a resident of Portland. Mr. Corbett owned a farm nearby. For a concise biography of Mr. Corbett, *see* Carey's *History of Oregon*, v. 2, p. 305. Scott's *History of the Oregon Country* has biographical information about Senator Corbett in v. 1, pp. 108 and 280, and Harvey W. Scott's tribute, v. 5, p. 183. For many years there was a station named Corbett on the Union Pacific Railroad at the base of the bluff below the community. The station is gone but there is a small commercial cluster where a road leaves I-84 and climbs the hill to connect to the historic highway. Corbett post office was established Dec. 20, 1895 with William H. H. Reed first postmaster.

Corbin, CURRY. Walter F. Riley wrote the compiler from San Jose, California, in Mar. 1947, that Corbin was named for a man interested in the operations of a sawmill in the locality. Corbin was on Mussel Creek, about 15 miles south of Port Orford, and when the USGS map of the Port Orford quadrangle was made in 1897–98, the place was about a mile east of the old coast road between Port Orford and Gold Beach. Corbin post office was established May 8, 1901, with Richard D. Jones postmaster. The office was discontinued in Jan. 1910, and had four different postmasters, so it may have been moved from time to time.

Cord, MALHEUR. Cord was a rural office on Duck Creek on the west edge of the county about 25 miles southeast of Venator in Harney County. Cord post office was established Apr. 13, 1897, with Thomas M. Seaward first postmaster.

The office, which was named in compliment to Mrs. Cordelia Seaweard, wife of the postmaster, was closed Dec. 31, 1917, with papers to Mooreville.

Cordes, COOS. For a number of years the Southern Pacific Company maintained a railroad station with the name Coos near the north shore of Coos Bay and about two and a half miles north of North Bend. In the latter part of 1944 the name of the city of Marshfield, also on the railroad, was changed to Coos Bay. The similarity of names of two stations so near together was unsatisfactory and as a result the company changed the name of Coos siding to Cordes. R. C. Cordes deeded part of the right of way at this point when the railroad was built.

Cornelius, WASHINGTON. Cornelius was named for Colonel T. R. Cornelius, a pioneer of 1845. He was the son of Benjamin Cornelius, who with his family emigrated to Oregon during that year as a member of the Meek party. The family settled on Tualatin Plains. Colonel Cornelius served in the Cayuse War of 1847–48, and the Yakima War of 1855–56. He served 20 years in the Oregon legislature, and in 1861 raised a regiment of volunteer cavalry. He was a merchant and also for a time ran a sawmill. Colonel Cornelius was born in Nov. 1827, and died June 24, 1899. The town of Cornelius is between Hillsboro and Forest Grove and has an elevation of 175 feet. Cornelius post office was established Dec. 18, 1871.

Cornett Lake, KLAMATH. This small lake in S 23, T 24S, R 5E, was named in 1949 by a fish planting crew of the Oregon State Game Commission for Marshall Cornett, president of the Oregon Senate, who was killed in a plane crash on Oct. 28, 1947.

Cornucopia, BAKER. This name is derived from Latin words meaning "horn of plenty" and the word is frequently applied to mines and other enterprises where there are large hopes of success. In 1885 mines were discovered on the southern slopes of the Wallowa Mountains in Baker County, and among the prospectors were several who came from Cornucopia, Nevada, who suggested that name for the new camp. Some mining activity in the area continued until World War II. Cornucopia post office was established Dec. 7, 1885 and ran until June 1942.

Cornutt, DOUGLAS. George B. Abdill of Roseburg provided the following information about this station on the Southern Pacific Railroad five miles southwest of Riddle. In the early days the stop was called Glenbrook for the Glenbrook Farm of William H. Riddle but from time to time it was confused with the more important Glendale station to the south. In 1906 the name was changed to Cornutt to honor pioneer settler Noah Cornutt. The place was of minor importance until it became the shipping point for the Hanna Mining Company when they opened their nickel operation in 1954. In more recent years the nickel mine has only operated sporadically.

Corral Basin, WALLOWA. Corral Basin is in the northwest corner of T 3S, R 43E. It was named because Standley and Sturgill built some sheep corrals there, made of heavy poles and logs. This was in the late 1880s. Sturgill was undoubtedly Jacob "Jake" Sturgill, for whom Sturgill Peak, some seven miles to the south was named. Corral Basin is on the north slope of Bald Mountain. Sturgill Creek rises on the south slope and flows south to North Minam River.

Corral Creek, CLACKAMAS. Corral Creek drains the east slope of Parrett Mountain and flows into the Willamette River one mile west of Wilsonville. There are many other Corral creeks in Oregon, especially east of the Cascade Range. The word was originally Spanish and meant an enclosure or pen for stock. It was possibly from the same source as the South African Dutch word *kraal*. There were two reasons for describing creeks with this word. The first was that stockmen built their corrals with streams running through them as a matter of convenience. In the second place there were many valleys, especially in eastern Oregon, where rock formations produced natural corrals, with water running through them.

Corral Creek, JACKSON. George F. Wright of Jackson County was the authority for the following facts concerning the naming of this Corral Creek near Pinehurst. His uncle, William A. Wright, said that in the middle 1860s a gang of rustlers built a set of corrals along the creek. They would round up cattle in the Rogue River valley, bring them to the corrals and obliterate the brands, then drive them to the Klamath basin for sale. Vigilantes apprehended three of the thieves and hanged them in thick brush where Lincoln Creek empties into Keene Creek. George Wright's father, Thomas J. Wright, told of seeing the bones and fragments of clothing still hanging in 1866, and many years later he showed George the rotting log remnants of the corrals.

Corral Creek, WALLOWA. Corral Creek flows into Imnaha River in T 3N, R 48E. J. H. Horner of Enterprise told the compiler that the stream was named for a corral built nearby in 1884. A trail follows down this creek from the locality called Indian Village. It was in this general locality that a fight took place between Nez Perces and a band of renegade Snake Indians. This fight is well remembered. *See* Cemetery Ridge.

Corset Creek, LINN. Corset Creek is tributary to Rainbow Creek two miles southeast of Idanha. George and Arly Dickie, who were raised in the area, told the writer in 1977 that they well remembered an old fashioned corset securely constraining a burgeoning tree trunk near this stream. The garment itself and the cause of its curious location are now both lost in antiquity.

Corvallis, BENTON. In the winter of 1847–48 Joseph C. Avery began to lay out the community now known as Corvallis. In 1846 Avery settled on property on the north side of Marys River where it flows into the Willamette, and in the same year William F. Dixon settled on land just to the north. Avery's building sites were known as the Little Fields. The first lots are said to have been sold in 1849. The place was first called Marysville, and while Avery probably selected this name, the evidence is not positive. He was using his own name for the post office in 1850. It is generally believed that the place was named because it was on Marys River, but there may have been additional reasons. The origin of the name Marys River is uncertain. *See* Marys River, where it will be seen that the river name was in use at least as early as 1846. In 1853 the legislature changed the name of the locality from Marysville to Corvallis. Information about the early history of Corvallis may be found in *History of Benton County*, p. 422. E. A. Blake, in a letter printed in the Corvallis *Gazette-Times*, June 7, 1935, says that Marysville was named for Mrs. John Stewart, also known as Aunt Mary Stewart, one of the first settlers in Corvallis. On the same page is a reprint of an interview with Mrs. Stewart, giving incidents of the early history of the place. Mrs. Stewart is authority for the statement that J. C. Avery told her he would name the community Marysville for her because she was the first white woman to live there. Joseph C. Avery was the first owner of the site of Corvallis, and he was a pioneer of 1845. He died in 1876. Avery made up the name Corvallis by compounding Latin words meaning heart of the valley. It is said that the name Marysville was changed to prevent confusion with Marysville, California. Corvallis has an elevation of 224 feet and the geography of its immediate surroundings may be seen on the USGS map of the Corvallis quadrangle. Avery's post office was established Jan. 8, 1850, with J. C. Avery postmaster. The name was then changed to Marysville Sept. 9, 1850, with Alfred Rinehart postmaster. Avery became postmaster again on Mar. 14, 1851; Wayman St. Clair on Nov. 5, 1851; Geo. H. Murch on Jan. 7, 1853, and Avery again on June 7, 1853. The name of the office was changed to Corvallis on Feb. 18, 1854. The name Marysville was applied to another post office, Forks of Mary's River, for a few weeks in the summer of 1850. This was probably an error, the authorities at Washington applying the change to the wrong office. *See OHQ*, v. 41, p. 55 for records of these offices.

Coryell Pass, LANE. This pass is on the narrow shelf of ground between the Willamette River and the hills about a mile south of Springfield Junction. It is occupied by the tracks of the Southern Pacific Company, with the old Pacific Highway just above. It was named for Abraham H. Coryell, a pioneer of 1847, who lived nearby, and the pioneer routes of travel led through this gap. Paul Bristow, grandson of Elijah Bristow, in notes on file at the Lane County Pioneer Museum, says that Coryell picked this odd site for a homestead because it was near the confluence of the Middle and Coast forks Willamette River, the head of navigation, and thus had great commercial possibilities. A memorial stands just east of the highway at this point bearing the following inscription: "Coryell Pass. Oregon Trail 1846. Erected by Oregon Lewis and Clark Chapter, D.A.R. 1917."

Cosper Creek, POLK, YAMHILL. This stream is near Grand Ronde, and was named for a pioneer family. Casper Creek is wrong.

Cottage Grove, LANE. Cottage Grove is an important community in the southern part of Lane County, on the line of the Southern Pacific Company and adjacent to I-5. Its elevation is 641 feet and the Coast Fork Willamette River flows through it. The post office was first established east of the present site of Creswell, Mar. 3, 1855, with G. C. Pearce as postmaster. Pearce had his home in an oak grove, and named the post office Cottage Grove. Andrew Hamilton became postmaster in Sept. 1861, and he moved the office to the present site of Saginaw. When Nathan Martin was postmaster in the latter 1860s the office was moved to a point on the west bank of Coast Fork Willamette River in the extreme southwest part of what is now the town of Cottage Grove. When the railroad was built through in the 1870s a station was established more than half a mile north and east of the post office. This was the start of a bitter neighborhood controversy that ran on for nearly two decades. The people living near the post office would not allow it to be moved to Cottage Grove railroad station, so a new post office was established at that point and named Lemati. *Lemati* is a Chinook jargon word meaning mountain, but why it was selected as a name for the new post office is not apparent. *Lemiti* is the generally accepted spelling of the word as used elsewhere in Oregon. Cottage Grove was incorporated in 1887, but in 1893 the eastsiders rebelled and secured a charter for East Cottage Grove. The name of this place was changed to Lemati by the legislature in 1895, and the railroad station sported two names on its signboard, although Lemati was in small letters. The differences were subsequently composed and an act was passed in 1899 to consolidate the places with the name Cottage Grove. Lemati post office, as a rival to Cottage Grove, was in operation from Nov. 21, 1893, to Sept. 5, 1894, with Laban F. Wooley postmaster. However, on Mar. 28, 1898, the name of the Cottage Grove office was changed to Lemati and it operated that way until May 10, 1898, when the name Cottage Grove was restored. Perry P. Sherwood was postmaster at that time.

Cotton, MULTNOMAH. Cotton was a station on the line of the Portland Electric Power Company about a mile west of Gresham. It was named for William Wick Cotton (1859–1918), a well-known attorney of Portland, who owned a large farm near the station. Cotton was a native of Iowa, and studied law at Columbia University, New York City. He came to Portland in Oct. 1889, and practiced law continuously until his death, at which time he was counsel of the Oregon-Washington Railroad & Navigation Company and other important corporations.

Cottonwood, LAKE. Cottonwood post office was named for Cottonwood Creek which flowed nearby the office. The place was about ten miles southwest of Lakeview, and Rial T. Striplin was the only postmaster the office ever had. Cottonwood office was established May 1, 1897, and was discontinued Nov. 1, 1897, with papers to Lakeview. The office was near the west quarter-corner of S 34, T 39S, R 19E. Cottonwood Creek flows very close to this land corner.

Cottonwood Creek, LAKE. This stream is northwest of Goose Lake and drains several townships. There are a score of Cottonwood creeks in Oregon, and all serve to testify to the popularity (no pun intended) of members of the *Populus* group, including *Populus angustifolia*, *Populus trichocarpa* and others. General H. M. Chittenden, in *The American Fur Trade of the Far West*, says that one of if not the most important tree in the fur trade business was the cottonwood. Not only were cottonwoods beautiful trees, but lines of them were welcome sights to the trappers and travelers, indicating water courses and fuel supplies. They provided shelter in winter and summer and rather surprisingly, fairly good horse feed. Ponies ate and throve on cottonwood bark quite successfully. Most of the Cottonwood creeks in Oregon have borne their names so long that it is impossible to say who named them.

Cottrell, CLACKAMAS. Cottrell is a crossroads locality in the extreme north part of the county on the Bluff Road about five miles north-northwest of Sandy. The post office was established Mar. 26, 1894, with Charles Andrews first of two postmasters. The office was closed June 29, 1904, probably because of the extension of rural free delivery. In addition to the locality Cottrell, there is a Cottrell School nearly a mile eastward, and at one time there was a station Cottrell on the Mount Hood electric railway about a mile north of the community. This station was in Multnomah County, but the electric railway and station have been abandoned. Cottrell was named for the family of Mrs. Charles Andrews, *nee* Cottrell.

Couch Lake, MULTNOMAH. It is not suprising that thousands of Portland residents have never heard of Couch Lake but in the Vanport flood of June 1948, this pond made an effort to reestablish itself. Its success was short-lived. Couch Lake was in the vicinity of Portland Union Station. It was named for Captain John Couch, one of the founders of Portland. An account of Captain Couch and his activities will be found in Oregon Pioneer Association *Transactions* for 1886. Captain Couch built a home on the west bank of this lake according to an article in the Oregon *Sunday Journal* for Oct. 20, 1946. The lake covered about 22 Portland city blocks and had a depth of about 15 feet. The compiler has a dim recollection of this body of water of about 1890 and as he recalls it the lake had been reduced in size by that time. In the 1880s this lake and surrounding land were bought by the Northern Pacific Terminal Company which had been organized in 1881. The first contract for filling the lake was let in 1888. The material used was ballast from incoming ships and sand from the river bed. The Union Station was formally opened Feb. 14, 1896, and the first train left it that evening. Due to financial problems there was a long delay between the property purchase and the station completion. The architects of the station were Van Brunt & Howe of Kansas City. If McKim, Mead and White of New York ever drew any plans for this station, as has been reported, they were not used. The building is listed on the National Register of Historic Places and, in the late 1980s, was taken over by the Portland Development Commission who directed a complete refurbishment. The extra passenger and freight trackage was removed but the station is still an important Amtrak facility. In 1990 during Mayor J. E. "Bud" Clark's administration, the Portland Development Commission planned to remove one of the two historic train sheds and two more tracks, leaving only five. This was strongly opposed by those believing in the probable resurgence of rail traffic, for it would be difficult to handle the 1990 scheduled trains and impossible to accommodate any future increase. When this edition went to press the matter was still unresolved.

Cougar Reservoir, LANE. This six mile long artificial lake was formed by damming South Fork McKenzie River about three miles south of Rainbow. It is a combination flood control and hydro-electric project and is an excellent example of how names proliferate. Originally Cougar Reservoir, it was changed to Cougar Lake by the USCE but at the request of the local residents the USBGN restored the earlier name. The name Cougar was given by Congress in 1950 in conjunction with the legislation for Cougar Dam. This was named because the preliminary surveys designated the site from its proximity to Cougar Creek, a minor nearby stream. In common with many other man-made objects, it is regrettable that a name of more distinction or historical significance was not selected. There are many features in Oregon named for the cougar or *Felis concolor*. Vernon Bailey in *Mammals and Life Zones of Oregon* has a good account of these animals.

Council Butte, KLAMATH. This butte is near Sprague River about two miles from Yainax. The USBGN adopted the name Council Butte in 1927, thus bringing to an end a controversy of many years standing. Gatschet, in *Dictionary of the Klamath Language*, uses the name *Yainaga* for this butte. *Yainaga* is the diminutive of *yaina*, meaning hill or mountain. For many years now the butte has been officially known as Council Butte, and the name Yainax Butte became transferred to a mountain with an elevation of 7226 feet, about 12 miles to the southeast. The name Council Butte had its origin in the council held at the little butte when a treaty was signed between the whites and certain Snake Indians on Aug. 12, 1865. Government surveyors used the name Council Butte in 1866 when they surveyed the township. In later years efforts were made by some of the older residents of the county to have the name Yainax returned to the little butte near Yainax community, but it was not considered practicable to do so because the name Council Butte had been so long in use by some of the government bureaus. *See* Yainax and Yainax Butte.

Council Creek, DOUGLAS. Council Creek runs north to Cow Creek about three miles southwest of Riddle. It takes its name from the council held near its mouth in 1853 when Joel Palmer, Superintendent of Indian Affairs, met with several bands of lower Cow Creek Indians. George Riddle tells of this meeting in *Early Days in Oregon*, p. 78.

Council Crest, MULTNOMAH. This is the highest point on a range of hills south of Portland. Its elevation is 1073 feet. It was a part of the John B. Talbot donation land claim and was subsequently owned successively by C. A. Beal, James Steel, and Graham Glass, Sr. The hill was for a time known as Glass Hill and was later called Fairmount, which name is still retained by the boulevard which encircles it. On July 11, 1898, delegates to the National Council of Congregational Churches met on top of this hill. Some discussion was had concerning a good name for it. A delegate from Portland, Maine, suggested Council Crest. This name was at once approved by Geo H. Himes, who was present, and a report of this meeting was sent to newspapers. Indians at one time may have used the crest as a meeting place and signal station because of its wide outlook, but there is no historic record of it. For additional information about the naming of this crest, *see* the *Oregonian*, editorial page July 29, Aug. 5, 1927. For denial that the crest was used by Indians as a signal point, *see* interview with Miss Ella Talbot, *Oregon Journal*, Mar. 15, 1914. Before World War II, there was an old fashioned Amusement Park on the summit. This had the traditional merry-go-round, minature train, Fun House, scenic railway and the usual row of concessions. The Council Crest streetcar line passed completely around the west end and the station at Council Crest Park was always busy on summer weekends. The wooden observation tower, long in use on top of Council Crest, was torn down late in 1941, and in 1942 a steel standpipe with a capacity of 500,000 gallons of water was built in its place. The city later added an open observation area encircled by a low wall with locating arrows pointing to the five prominent mountains visible from the crest, Jefferson, Hood, Saint Helens, Adams and Rainier.

Courthouse Rock, GRANT. This is a well-known landmark in the west part of the county. The name is quite descriptive. *See* Courtrock.

Courthouse Rock, WASCO. This prominent flat topped rock with vertical sides is two miles west of Antelope. Its descriptive name is very old.

Courtney Creek, LINN. Courtney Creek, south of Brownsville, was named for John B. Courtney, who operated a pioneer sawmill near the point where the stream leaves the foothills. He settled in the vicinity in 1846.

Courtney Creek, WALLOWA. Courtney Creek was named for pioneer stockmen, Lins, Alex and Bent Courtney. It is in the north part of the county.

Courtrock, GRANT. Courthouse Rock is the name of a peculiar formation in the hills in the west part of the county. This rock may be seen for many miles in all directions. When the post office was established nearby in Apr. 1926, postal authorities selected the name Courtrock from among several that were suggested. Mrs. Viola A. Lauder was the first postmaster. The office was closed on May 31, 1953, and little now remains.

Couse Creek, UMATILLA. Couse is derived from the Nez Perce word *kowish*, and is the name of an edible root used for making bread. Piper and Beattie in their *Flora of Southeastern Washington* give its botanical name as *Cogswellia cous*. It is a member of the natural order *Umbelliferae*. The stream in Umatilla County rises in the western slopes of the Blue Mountains and flows into Walla Walla River southeast of Milton-Freewater. There are probably other geographic features in the state with the same name, due to the fact that the root was found plentifully in such localities.

Cove, JEFFERSON. The place on Crooked River known as Cove is not inappropriately named. At this point, which is about two miles south of the old river mouth, the stream was in a canyon with an overall depth of some 900 feet. About half way down from the bluffs west of Culver, there is a bench or shelf, and this shelf is closed on the east by rock walls, forming a natural cove. Further down into the canyon there was another natural cove near the river. The county highway from Culver to Grandview crossed Crooked River at the Cove Bridge, and after passing over a rocky divide several hundred feet high, made a second descent this time to cross the Deschutes River. It then climbed a seven-mile grade to the bench west of the Deschutes. In 1940 the OSHD acquired several thousand acres including the early farmsite at the Cove bridge. This was developed into The Cove Palisades State Park, one of the most popular units in the State Parks System, but with the completion of Round Butte Dam the site was flooded by Lake Billy Chinook. Portland General Electric Company financed the relocation of the park facilities to the present location on the high ground between the Palisades and the Island where the old county highway crossed over from Crooked River to Deschutes drainage.

Cove, UNION. Cove lies in a natural pocket where Mill Creek flows from the Wallowa Mountains, and it has an elevation of 2893 feet. It is on the east edge of the Grande Ronde Valley and at the west foot of Mount Fanny. The first family settled there on Oct. 9, 1862, and on June 4, 1863, a post office was established which was given the name of Forest Cove, for descriptive reasons. Samuel G. French was the first postmaster and he probably suggested the name. On June 29, 1868, post office authorities eliminated the first part of the name because of the confusion with Forest Grove in Washington County. As a result of this simple action there arose in Union County a feud that lasted many years. In 1864 Union County was created, and as was frequent in pioneer days, there was contention over the location of the county seat. In 1872 a bill was passed putting the matter to a vote, and the two communities that received the highest vote in the preliminary balloting were to be eligible for the final election. Some votes were cast for Forest Cove by old timers to whom the new name did not mean much, and as a result an attempt was made to deprive Cove of its position in the contest. T. T. Geer's *Fifty Years in Oregon*, chapter XXXVI, gives an entertaining account of these matters.

Cove Orchard, YAMHILL. This is a descriptive name applied to a community in the northern part of the county. It was platted with this name by F. C. Graham of Portland.

Coverdale, WALLOWA. Coverdale is a locality in T 5S, R 47E, close to Imnaha River, but it is not a community. It is a campground and forest guard station. The place was named in 1909 by J. Fred McClain, a forest ranger, for Marion Coverdale, a hunter and trapper who lived on Prairie Creek in the early 1880s.

Cow Creek, DOUGLAS. This stream is one of the historic landmarks of southern Oregon. It is tributary to the South Umpqua River and for a large part of the way from Glendale to Riddle it occupies a narrow defile through rugged mountains. The Siskiyou line of the Southern Pacific Company shares Cow Creek Canyon with the creek. For many years very high water in the stream has been a menace to traffic. It is popularly supposed that I-5 passes through Cow Creek Canyon but this is not true. South of Canyonville I-5 follows Canyon Creek, which is also in a narrow defile. Some miles to the south the highway crosses Cow Creek, but at this point the creek occupies a wide valley. Walling's *History of Southern Oregon*, p. 424, says an immigrant recovered his cattle from thieving Indians in this valley, from which fact the creek derived its name.

Cow Gulch, GRANT. Cow Gulch drains into Murderers Creek from the north about a mile up from the mouth of the creek. It has been so called for a long time. The name was applied because the gulch was a natural collecting point for cattle.

Cow Valley, MALHEUR. Cow Valley is east of Ironside and Cow Valley Butte is on its north edge. It was named in the 1880s when cattle were gathered in this ten mile long basin for fattening on the lush grass prior to being driven to Wyoming. The coming of the railroad shortened the drive and the dry years after the turn of the century ended the grass. In 1937, the Circle Bar ranch rented the valley for summer graze. Rankin Crow was put in charge and he later bought a sizeable piece of property and installed the first private, deep well irrigation system. The water restored the valley and he raised fine stands of alfafa and other feed crops.

Cowhorn Mountain, DOUGLAS, KLAMATH. This mountain is at the summit of the Cascade Range, at the junction with the spur known as Calapooya Mountains. In pioneer days it was known as Little Cowhorn to distinguish it from Big Cowhorn, farther south, now Mount Thielsen. It had a peculiar spire or rock pinnacle on its summit, making it resemble Mount Thielsen, and the two peaks were named because of resemblance to a cow's horns. Many years ago the pinnacle on Little Cowhorn fell off.

Cox Creek, LINN. Cox Creek is a stream east of Albany that heads near Spicer and flows northwest to the Willamette River. West of the north Albany exit from I-5 it forms Waverly Lake. Cox Creek was named in pioneer days for Anderson Cox, a prominent Linn County citizen and member of the Oregon constitutional convention. Cox took up a donation land claim on this stream. Willard Marks of Albany told the compiler in 1942 that when he was much younger, youthful cronies spent Sundays and holidays in the vicinity of this stream, doubtless fishing and otherwise obtaining physical refreshment. In 1911–13 the USGS mapped the area and applied the name Second Periwinkle Creek to the stream, apparently overlooking Cox Creek as having the first title. Thus the matter rested for three decades until local residents bestirred themselves to get the old name restored. This was done on Feb. 26, 1942, by decision of the USBGN, and the official designation is now Cox Creek.

Cox Island, LANE. This island in Siuslaw River is about two miles upstream from Florence. It is named for Captain William Cox, a prominent early day resident. The island was apparently acquired by Cox from one John Lyle in the 1890s. About 1902 Cox built a fine two story house to which were later added several ancillary buildings. In 1903 the Siuslaw Boom Company acquired the island and for many years used it as a headquarters for their log rafting operations on the river. In 1953 it passed to Champion International Company and in 1977 they in turn donated it to The Nature Conservancy for preservation as a natural area. In Oct. 1979, the two story house, the only remaining building, was listed in the National Register of Historic Places while The Nature Conservancy proceeded with plans to restore the structure so that it could be used as a base for their Cox Island preserve. As of 1989, restoration funds were still lacking and the house was in poor repair. For conditions in 1983, *see* the *Oregonian*, June 26, 1983, p. C7.

Coxcomb Hill, CLATSOP. This is the summit of the ridge south of Astoria, between the Columbia River and Youngs Bay. The compiler has been unable to learn who first applied the name. The spelling used is the customary form applied to court fools and jesters who wore an imitation coxcomb, and were frequently called coxcombs. The Astoria Column, given by Vincent Astor as the result of efforts made by Ralph Budd, then president of the Great Northern Railway Company, stands at the top of Coxcomb Hill. It depicts important events in the history of the Pacific Northwest. It was dedicated July 22, 1926, before a notable gathering. The bench mark in the base of the Astoria Column has an elevation of 595 feet, and the top of the tower dome, at the base of the finial, has an elevation of 720 feet.

Coyote Creek, LANE. The word Coyote is used to describe a number of geographic features in Oregon, including a station in Morrow County, a butte in Baker County known as Coyote Point, and several streams. Coyote is derived from the Mexican or Aztec name *coyotl*, the word for the prairie wolf, or barking wolf of western North America, *Canis latrans*. The Chinook jargon word for the coyote was *talapus*, with which was associated an idea of deity, or god of the plains. According to Jarold Ramsey, author of *Coyote Was Going There: Indian Literature of the Oregon Country*, coyote, the trickster or transformer, appeared as a: "culture hero to tribes as separate as the desert Paiutes and the coast Coos." Early settlers looked upon the coyote as a nuisance because of his noisy habits and his tendency to pay a midnight visit to the chicken roost, on which occasion he could be perfectly quiet. Creeks and points where coyotes were seen or heard had the name of the animal attached, and possibly some were named because of the fact that a coyote had been killed nearby. According to Walling's *History of Lane County*, p. 456, The creek in Lane County that now empties into Fern Ridge Reservoir was named by the Applegate road party of 1848. They killed two coyotes near where the road crossed the creek. They hung the skins on a nearby tree and christened the stream.

Coyote Well, DESCHUTES. This Coyote Well is just north of US-20 four miles west of Millican. According to R. A. "Reub" Long a "coyote well" was a hidden water hole and this location along the course of Dry River must have originally met the specifications. *See The Oregon Desert*, p. 396. There are other Coyote wells in eastern Oregon.

Cozad Mountain, DOUGLAS. This prominent mountain northeast of Oakland was named for a pioneer of that neighborhood, Jonathan Cozad, who is said to have come to Oregon in the 1850s. The accent is on the second syllable.

Cozine Creek, YAMHILL. This stream rises in the eastern foothills of the Coast Range and flows through McMinnville where it joins South Yamhill River. It was named for Samuel Cozine, who was born in Kentucky in 1821 and was a pioneer of Oregon. He settled on land adjacent to the present site of McMinnville in 1849.

Crabtree Creek, LINN. This creek rises in Crabtree Lake on the west slope of the Cascade Range and flows into South Santiam River just east of the forks of the Santiam. The lake has been known both as Wolf Lake and Crabtree but the OGNB approved the latter in the summer of 1966. The stream and lake, were named for John J. Crabtree, a native of Virginia, who crossed the plains in 1845. After wintering on the Tualatin Plains, Mr. and Mrs. Crabtree bought the William Packwood claim east of the forks of the Santiam in the spring of 1846. *See* editorial page *Oregon Journal*, Dec. 3 and 4, 1924, and Carey's *History of Oregon*, v. 2, p. 203. The station on the Southern Pacific branch North of Lebanon was named for a cousin, Fletcher Crabtree.

Craggy Rock, WHEELER. Named by the pioneer Maurice Fitzmaurice family who homesteaded in the Rowe Creek area in the early 1880s, Craggy Rock is a conspicuous remnant of a basaltic flow, slightly tilted, on the range skyline about ten miles south of Fossil. From the top, some 400 feet high at one point, can be obtained a grand panoramic view of the mountainous, deeply eroded lands just north of John Day River. The compiler cannot improve upon the preceeding text furnished by central Oregon author and amateur geologist Phil Brogan.

Craig Lake, LANE. Craig Lake is near the summit of McKenzie Pass. It is a pond at the side of the McKenzie Highway. It was named for John T. Craig, one of the founders of the McKenzie toll road, who died of exposure in Dec. 1877, while in pursuance of his duties as a mail carrier across the pass. *See* article on editorial page of the Portland *Telegram*, Sept. 17, 1925. A masonry tomb has been built over the remains of John Templeton Craig, close beside the highway, and on July 13, 1930, a bronze plaque on the headstone was dedicated in his honor. This was done by the Oregon Rural Letter Carriers Association. Robert W. Sawyer of Bend made a short talk about Craig, which is printed in *OHQ*, v. 31, p. 261. Craig was born in Wooster, Ohio, in Mar. 1822, and came to Oregon in 1852. Much of his mature life was involved with the McKenzie road construction.

Craig Lake, LINN. This is a small lake on a bench southeast of Maxwell Butte. Tom McAllister informed the compiler in 1990 that he strongly suspected the lake was named for T. J. "Tom" Craig who was in charge of the railroad car *Rainbow* for the Oregon Fish and Game Department. The *Rainbow* was a special baggage car equipped in 1912 for transporting fingerling trout. They were moved to various spots throughout the state where local sportsmen would often assist in planting the lakes and streams. McAllister has an article about the *Rainbow*, with pictures, in *The Creel*, of The Flyfisher's Club of Oregon, v. 1, no. 1, Dec. 1961.

Craig Mountain, UNION. Dunham Wright of Medical Springs informed the compiler in 1927 that this mountain west of Union bears the name of "Pap" Craig, a pioneer resident of the county, former sheriff and also county judge.

Crale, LANE. Crale is a station on the Southern Pacific Cascade Line southeast of Lowell. It is at the mouth of Crale Creek which in turn is named for John Crail who homesteaded there in the 1870s. A. J. Briem, a long time USFS ranger in the area, mentions several members of the Crail family in his notes on file at the OHS. Both he and the BLM records use the form Crail but it is not likely that the spelling will be corrected at this late date. C. B. McFarland of Oakridge told the compiler in the 1950s that one member of the family had a mellifluous voice and was much in demand for funerals.

Crane, HARNEY. The community Crane was named because of its situation near Crane Creek and Crane Creek Gap, prominent geographic features in the Harney Valley. Crane post office was first established on June 10, 1895, with Henry C. Turner first postmaster. The office was discontinued June 30, 1903, but was reestablished Oct. 11, 1916, when the railroad was completed from Ontario. From then until 1924, when the railroad was finished to Burns, Crane was an important shipping point for livestock. The post office may have been moved a time or two.

Crane Creek, HARNEY. Crane Creek is prominent because the valley of the stream and Crane Creek Gap to the west form a natural pass between the drainage area of South Fork Malheur River and Harney Valley. Crane Creek is doubtless named for the sandhill crane, *Grus canadensis tabida*, formerly a common summer resident of eastern Oregon. For information about this bird, *see Birds of Oregon*, Gabrielson and Jewett, p. 229. A smaller bird, the little brown crane, has been known in Oregon. The California heron or blue crane is found generally in western Oregon.

Crane Creek, LAKE. Crane Creek flows into Goose Lake a few miles south of Lakeview. Crane Mountain, elevation 8447 feet, is a little to the southeast of the creek and about five miles south of the Oregon-California state line. These two features were named for an early settler. *History of Central Oregon*, p. 816, says this man's name was Samuel Crane and that he settled on the creek in 1869. The compiler has a statement from John Venator of Lakeview, made in 1943, to the effect that his father bought land from a man who was called "Bill" Crane and that the creek and peak were named for him. The two Cranes may have been brothers or otherwise related. In any event, the geographic features do not seem to have been named for the bird, despite the popular notion.

Crane Prairie, DESCHUTES. Crane Prairie, before the regulating dam for irrigation storage was built at its lower end, was a natural meadow, with several river channels cutting across it. The main stream flowing through the prairie is Deschutes River. When unregulated, the water stands on the prairie in the spring, but by midsummer the meadows are comparatively dry. The dam built at the south end of the prairie can be made to hold back sufficient water to flood the entire area several feet deep. This has been done to such an extent that the natural woods fringing the prairie have been water killed and present a desolate appearance. The prairie is so called because of the number of cranes that fish there. When full, the water surface of the reservoir has an elevation of about 4440 feet and covers an area of about seven square miles.

Cranston Ditch, BAKER. Cranston Ditch runs along Powder River near Keating. Edward P. Cranston came to Baker County in 1862 and was an early, prominent citizen. The ditch was probably named for his son, Herbert Cranston, who had a large ranch in the area and was at one time postmaster at Keating.

Crater Creek, CLACKAMAS. This creek runs south into Little Crater Meadows and eventually drains to Timothy Lake. It was named in the early days before the diminutive was added to Little Crater Lake.

Crater Lake, KLAMATH. This is a mountain lake between five and six miles in diameter, with an area of about 21 square miles, situated in the caldera of the extinct volcano, Mount Mazama, on the summit of the Cascade Range. It is fed by small streams from melting snowbanks on the inner slopes of the rim, and has no visible outlet. Elevation 6177 feet. This lake is one of the deepest in the world, and soundings have been made of 1996 feet. The highest point on the rim is Hillman Peak, 8156 feet above the sea. The water is an intense blue. Crater Lake was discovered on June 12, 1853, by John W. Hillman and a party of prospectors, and was christened Deep Blue Lake. It has been known at times as Mysterious Lake, Lake Majesty, Lake Mystery, and other similar names, but on Aug. 4, 1869, it was named Crater Lake by a party of visitors from Jacksonville, Oregon. For information about the discovery of the lake and the various names, *see Mazama*, v. 1, no. 2. *See* Mount Mazama for information about the mountain. For particulars about the unveiling of the tablet in memory of J. W. Hillman, *see* the *Oregonian*, Sept. 21, 1925, p. 1 and editorial. Crater Lake National Park was created by an act of Congress May 22, 1902, and embraces about 250 square miles of land and water. The lake may be reached by highway from Medford, Fort Klamath, or Bend. The USGS publishes a contoured map of Crater Lake National Park, and the National Park Service issues maps and other valuable information. For many years the most comprehensive story of the park and its geology was that in USGS Professional Paper 3, *Geology and Petrography of Crater Lake National Park*, by Diller and Patton, Washington, 1902. In more recent years there has been a demand for an appraisal of the older theories about the origin of the lake and for a popular account of the business. The latter need was met by the publication of *Crater Lake, the Story of its Origin*, by Howel Williams of the University of California, Berkeley, 1941. This volume, full of interest and well illustrated, was followed by *Geology of Crater Lake National Park, Oregon*, also by Williams, published by the Carnegie Institution at Washington, D.C., 1942. This is a more formal publication of great scientific importance. Crater Lake is one of nature's marvels. It is more in the nature of a scenic wonder than anything else the writer has ever seen. Oddly enough it is not a real crater lake at all, because it occupies a caldera far larger than the crater of the original mountain. Crater Lake has been the subject of so much writing and is so well known to the public that the writer does not feel it necessary to elaborate. There are, however, two illusions about the lake that should be dispelled. The lake does freeze over, contrary to popular belief. In 1949 the ice was thick enough for a park ranger to walk to Wizard Island. Also many people discuss the possibility of underground outlets from Crater Lake. It is doubtful if there are any. The lake receives almost its entire supply direct from precipitation, as the drainage area is but a little larger than the lake. It is fairly certain that evaporation accounts for all of the outgo from the lake, without allowance for underground flow. In 1988 and 1989 investigations were made using the deep water midget submarine *Alvin* to determine if there were hot springs in the floor of the lake. Results to 1990 have been inconclusive

Crater Peak, KLAMATH. This peak was named by engineers of the USGS because of the extinct crater in its summit. It has an elevation of 7265 feet.

Crater Rock, CLACKAMAS, HOOD RIVER. Crater Rock is a well-known point on the south slope of Mount Hood. It was so named because of the smouldering crater on its north side, between the rock and the slope of the mountain. Crater Rock was formed during a volcanic event about 1700 AD. It is near what once was the central axis of the mountain, but an earlier major volcanic event about 200 AD destroyed much of the south side in a fashion similar to Mount Saint Helens in Washington. The preponderance of precipitation on the southwest slope of Mount Hood has also resulted in the slope wearing away more rapidly than the other sides, causing the summit to shift gradually northeast.

Crates Point, WASCO. This is a conspicuous promontory west of The Dalles, around the toe of which flows the Columbia River, changing course from north to west. It is part of the east portal of the Columbia River Gorge. A nearby railroad station is known as Crates. These features were named for Edward Crate, a French-Canadian who came to Oregon as an employee of the Hudson's Bay Company in 1838. He was born in Canada about 1821. After Peter Skene Ogden rescued the survivors of the Whitman massacre, Crate is said to have been a member of the boat crew that brought them down the river. He served in Thomas McKay's company in the Cayuse War of 1848. Crate stayed in Oregon City until 1850 and in April of that year went to The Dalles to settle. The records of the land office indicate that he made settlement on his claim on Apr. 1, 1851, at the place now called Crates Point, which he selected because it was adapted to landing boats. The Crate claim was near the river under the slope of the bluff. The name on the original application at the land office is spelled Crete, but the family abandoned this form of spelling long ago. According to Dr. William McKay, the Indian name of the locality of Crates Point was *Thleyap Kanoon*, which referred to a variety of freshwater mussels. These were gathered and used for a great feast and general good time. Crate was married to Sophia Boucher, a native of New Caledonia, on June 24, 1844, at Vancouver. The marriage record is in St. James parish register. She was born about 1830. The couple had 14 children, some of whom became well-known citizens of Oregon. Edward Crate died in 1894. In a list of Indian names for localities near The Dalles, Dr. McKay gives *Kat-ka Talth* for the mountain at Crates Point. This means Flint Mountain. In 1990 The Columbia River Gorge Commission selected a site near Crates Point for the proposed Interpretive Center.

Crawford, YAMHILL. This was a station between Lafayette and Newberg, and was named for Medorem Crawford, who was born in Orange County, New York, June 24, 1819. He came to Oregon in 1842 with Dr. Elijah White, and took a prominent part in the affairs of the state. He died Dec. 27, 1891. For biographical information, *see* Scott's *History of the Oregon Country*. Medorem Crawford was esteemed by all who knew him and his narrative of the emigration of 1842 appeared in OPA *Transactions* for 1881.

Crawfordsville, LINN. Crawfordsville is on Calapooia River about eight miles above Brownsville. It was named for Philemon V. Crawford, upon whose land the town was built. He was born in Madison, Indiana, in 1814, and crossed the plains in 1851. The town was founded in 1870 by Crawford and Robert Glass. Crawford died in Eugene Feb. 1, 1901. His son, Jasper V. Crawford, was first postmaster at Crawfordsville. Information to the effect that the place was named for George F. Crawford is wrong.

Crazy Creek, CROOK. USFS ranger J. O. F. Anderson's 1948 notes on file at the Ochoco National Forest say this creek was named for a slightly unbalanced sheep herder who lived along side it. Crazy Creek is tributary to Deep Creek three miles above North Fork Crooked River. The next stream to the west is Stupid Creek, probably so named because it runs south between Crazy and Looney creeks. *See* Looney Creek.

Crazyman Creek, WALLOWA. Crazyman Creek follows a circuitous course through T 4S, R 48E, and drains into Imnaha River. In 1931 J. H. Horner of Enterprise told the compiler that the stream was named in the early 1880s because of an incident involving Jack Johnson, who was hunting. Johnson, looking down into the canyon, saw a man who acted as if demented, cavorting and jumping about. Johnson found the man to be Scotty McKinnel, who was camped nearby with John Williamson, William Ellis and Dock Fake. McKinnel's antics were caused by surprise at seeing another man in the neighborhood. The party named the stream Crazyman Creek because of this event.

Crescent, CROOK. Crescent post office was established on the Crook County list July 31, 1886, with Nettie M. Powell postmaster. The office was closed in Sept. 1888, re-opened in Dec. 1888, and closed again Oct. 1, 1890. It had another resurgence in May 1891 with Henry D. Jory postmaster and was finally closed in Apr.

1895 with papers to Mitchell. This office was always near the east end of Big Summit Prairie. Earlier statements that there had been an office of this name in Deschutes County were incorrect due to an error in record transcription.

Crescent, KLAMATH. This town, with an elevation of 4452 feet, is an important trading point on US-97, The Dalles-California Highway about 50 miles south of Bend. It was at this place that the proposed junction of the Harriman north-south and east-west railroads was to have been situated, with the name of Odell, for Odell Lake. Odell post office was established on August 19, 1901 with Eva Graves first postmaster. She and her husband, Charles Graves, were instrumental in establishing the community. There was another Odell in the state in the Hood River Valley, so in 1907, the Graveses changed the name to Crescent for Crescent Lake, one of the large lakes of the Cascade Range located 15 miles to the west.

Crescent Lake, KLAMATH. This is one of the impressive mountain lakes of Oregon, on the east slope of the Cascade Range just southeast of Diamond Peak. It is fed principally by Summit Creek, and its outlet is Crescent Creek, which flows into Little Deschutes River. Its south shore is skirted by the old Oregon Central Military Road, and the Southern Pacific Cascade line passes a little to the east of the lake. It is named because of its shape. The normal elevation is about 4837 feet, but there is some variation due to water storage. USGS *Professional Paper 9* describes this lake in detail. The geography of the lake and its immediate surroundings are shown on the USGS maps of the Crescent Lake, Odell Lake and Summit Lake quadrangles. Crescent Lake was named in July 1865, by B. J. Pengra and W. H. Odell, while making a reconnaissance for the Oregon Central Military Road. Pengra's report, dated Nov. 29, 1865 is in part on file at the Oregon Historical Society.

Crescent Lake, KLAMATH. When the Cascade line of the Southern Pacific Company was constructed, a station called Simax was established near the north end of Crescent Lake. *See* Simax Bay. The railroad company later changed the name of the station Simax to Crescent Lake for the lake a half a mile to the south.

Crescent Mountain, LINN. Crescent Mountain is about 20 miles east of Cascadia and four miles north of the South Santiam Highway. The name is descriptive and has been in use for a very long time. The mountain, as seen from the air, is a well-defined ridge, shaped like a horseshoe, open to the east. Crescent Creek, which flows eastward, drains the horseshoe. The highest point is on the southwest turn, elevation 5761 feet.

Creston, MALHEUR. Creston is a descriptive name and was given because the post office was on a divide or crest east of South Fork Malheur River. The name was proposed by T. R. Beers in 1910.

Creswell, LANE. Creswell was named by Ben Holladay for John A. Creswell, postmaster general from 1869–74. John A. Creswell was born in Maryland in 1828, and served as U.S. representative and as senator before joining the cabinet. In 1874 he was appointed counsel of the United States in the Alabama Claims matter and served until 1876. He died Dec. 23, 1891. Creswell station was named by Holladay before the post office was established. The post office was established on Mar. 4, 1872 with John L. Gilfry first postmaster. Creswell has an elevation of 543 feet and is on the Shasta line of the Southern Pacific Company and I-5. Creswell Butte, about a mile to the south, has an elevation of 982 feet.

Creswell Canyon, MARION. This is a canyon in the hills north of Jefferson and its lower end is crossed by the old Pacific Highway East just north of Steiwer Hill. It was named for Donald C. Creswell, a pioneer of Oregon. He was born in Tazewell County, Illinois, in 1830, and his land office certificate 4993 says that he arrived in Oregon on Oct. 10, 1852. He cultivated his donation land claim near this canyon beginning Oct. 31, 1853. He was married to Mary Ann Rush on Nov. 30, 1851, in Louise County, Iowa. He spelled his name without a "t."

Crews Creek, BAKER. Willis W. Crews came to Baker County in 1880 and settled at the mouth of this creek near Keating. Crews built the first lime kiln in the Baker area.

Cribbins Hill, COOS. This is a small hill south of Myrtle Point. It was named for William Cribbins, a pioneer settler nearby.

Cricket Flat, UNION. J. H. Horner of Enterprise told the compiler in 1927 that this flat was named for the very large crickets which infested this place in the early 1870s. William Knight, whose parents settled at what is now Cove, Oregon, in the 1860s, informed Horner that his father drove hogs from Cove to Cricket Flat to feed on these crickets. Cricket Flat was considered to be a fine hog pasture. General O. O. Howard crossed this flat in the late summer of 1878 and camped about three-quarters of a mile west of the present site of Elgin.

Crims Island, COLUMBIA. Broughton discovered Crims Island and nearby islets in the Columbia River on Oct. 26, 1792, and named them Bakers Islands for the second lieutenant of Vancouver's ship *Discovery*. This seems to be the same island that Lewis and Clark named Fannys Island, in honor of Frances, William Clark's youngest sister. Wilkes gives the name Gull Island in the atlas accompanying *U. S. Exploring Expedition*, v. 23, Hydrography. James F. Crim took up a homestead on the island and received his patent Feb. 10, 1871. The USBGN adopted the name Crims Island on Oct. 5, 1927, at the suggestion of the compiler of these notes. With the lapse of time Wilkes' name Gull Island has become transferred to a small isle north of the west end of Crims Island.

Cripple Creek, CLACKAMAS. This stream flows into the Clackamas River from the east in T 5S, R 6E. In 1927 W. C. Elliott, civil engineer of Portland, told the compiler that a surveyor in his employ cut his foot with an ax at this point in 1897.

Criterion, WASCO. An editorial in the Bend *Bulletin*, Nov. 10, 1959, gives information about this name for a point on The Dalles-California Highway south of Maupin. When the post office was established on Sept. 11, 1913, three names were proposed, Canfield, Three Notch Juniper and Criterion. The last was suggested by J. Elmer Lindsay who stated that he found the word by chance in a dictionary and thought that it would be most appropriate for what the founders thought would be a model community. The first preference was for Three Notches and the second was for Criterion. The Post Office Department objected to the first name because it was made of two words and adopted the second preference. The word criterion means a standard by which to judge of the character or excellence of an object or thing. Pioneer stockmen called the locality Three Notches because of three cuts in a prominent juniper tree, still standing in 1946, east of the highway. Criterion Summit is the highest point on The Dalles-California Highway between The Dalles and Redmond. The bench mark just west of the highway has an elevation of 3362 feet and the highway summit is a couple of feet lower. This was once known as Lakeview Summit, but why is a mystery. There are no lakes within miles of the place. Criterion post office was established in Sept. 1913, and closed in June 1926.

Croisan Ridge, MARION. Croisan Ridge and Croisan Gulch lie not far from the east bank of the Willamette River just southwest of Salem. These features were named for a prominent Marion County pioneer family. The first member of this family to live in Oregon was born in Bavaria in 1812 of Huguenot parents. He emigrated to the United States in 1839 and came to Oregon over the Applegate route in 1846. After various pioneer experiences, including a trip to California, he settled on a donation land claim southwest of Salem in Mar. 1850. *See* editorial page, *Oregon Journal*, Dec. 18 and 19, 1925. He died Sept. 14, 1875. The original application for the land claim shows the name spelled in various ways, including Croisant, Croisint and Crossint. The given names of this pioneer settler were John Henry. While the land office records seem to indicate that the spelling Croisint was the correct one, present members of the family state that the name was really Croisant. The second generation in Oregon found the name so frequently mispronounced that the final "t" was dropped and the name has become Croisan. The Croisan family tradition says the name originally meant growing, the French for which would be *croissant*. *Croissant* is also the French for crescent.

Cromwell, UNION. Old maps show Cromwell on the railroad at a point between Telocaset and North Powder. The post office was established July 24, 1882, and was closed Dec. 2, 1884. Julius T. Cromwell was the only postmaster and the office was named for him. Polk's *Gazetteer* for 1886–87 says that Cromwell was also called Antelope Valley. The post office was close to Antelope Creek wagon bridge on the original homestead of Robert Brannan.

Cronin Creek, CLATSOP, TILLAMOOK. Cronin Creek empties into Nehalem River about 12 miles south of Elsie. It is named for Patrick Cronin, a veteran of the Civil War, who in the 1880s homesteaded at its mouth. About 1900 Cronin moved his family to Forest Grove where he was engineer of the city light plant and town marshall. This information was supplied by James A. Cronin II, Patrick's great-grandson.

Crook, CROOK. Crook, a place on the headwaters of Bear Creek, was named for the county. Available maps show the office moved about a little, apparently depending on who would accept the postmastership. Crook post office was established June 16, 1886, with Nancy Hinton postmaster. The office was finally closed in Nov. 1908.

Crook County. Crook County was created Oct. 24, 1882, from a part of Wasco County after Lake County had been taken off on the south. (*Special Laws* of 1882, p. 178.) For many years it was one of the large counties of central Oregon, but is now diminished in size as the result of the creation of Deschutes and Jefferson counties. It has an area of 2986 square miles, according to ODOT. Prineville is its county seat. Crook County was named for George Crook, major-general in the U.S. Army, who was born near Dayton, Ohio, Sept. 8, 1829; died at Chicago, Mar. 21, 1890. He was graduated from West Point in 1852. Prior to the Civil War he served in the West and was wounded in 1857 in the Pit River country. He made a brilliant record in the Civil War, and afterwards in Indian wars of the west. *See* Scott's *History of the Oregon Country*, v. 2, p. 184, and v. 5, pp. 223–25.

Crook Peak, LAKE. Crook Peak was undoubtedly named for Major-General George Crook, who fought Indians throughout south central Oregon in several campaigns. *See* Crook County. Crook was in the territory west of Warner Valley near what is known as Crook Peak in 1867. *See* Bancroft's *History of Oregon*, v. 2, p. 535, *et seq*. The USC&GS gives the elevation of Crook Peak as 7834 feet.

Crook Point, CURRY. This point is in approximate latitude 42° 15′, and is within 20 miles of the Oregon-California boundary. It is also about five miles south of Cape Sebastian. The point is moderately low, but terminates seaward in a rock knoll 160 feet high, with lower ground immediately back of it. It was named for A. H. Crook, who for many years operated a large stock ranch nearby.

Crooked Creek, KLAMATH. This is a stream near Klamath Agency, tributary to Wood River. It bears a descriptive name. The Klamath Indian name is *Yanaldi Koke*, literally "Stream bordered by the Yanaldi Ridge." *Koke* is the Klamath word for stream. For additional information, *see* Agency Hill.

Crooked Creek, LAKE. This stream drains Antelope Valley north of Lakeview and flows north into Lake Abert. The correct name is Crooked Creek and not Crook Creek. There is a story to the effect that it was named for Major-General George Crook but such is not the case. It owes its name entirely to its physical characteristics.

Crooked Creek, MALHEUR. This stream has a descriptive name. It joins Owyhee River a few miles below the mouth of Jordan Creek near the place called Rome. Captain George B. Currey of the First Oregon Volunteer Cavalry calls the stream Gibbs Creek in the Oregon Adjutant General's *Report*, 1865–66, p. 35, in compliment to Gov. Addison C. Gibbs. Currey established Camp Henderson on Gibbs Creek May 26, 1864. The name Gibbs Creek has not prevailed.

Crooked Finger Prairie, MARION. This prairie is southeast of Silverton. According to Down's *A History of the Silverton Country*, p. 3, it bears the name of a

Molalla chief. He is supposed to have died at Grand Ronde Agency, although there is another story to the effect that he was shot near the Clackamas River. Stivers Vernon has a two part article in the *Sunday Oregonian*, Apr. 29 and May 6, 1934, Magazine Sect. in which he claims Loshuk or Crooked Finger was killed near the prairie in 1847.

Crooked River, CROOK, DESCHUTES, JEFFERSON. This stream was named during the fur trading period, and the name bestowed is unusually appropriate. Arrowsmith's map of North America, London, 1824, with pen corrections probably to 1832-33, shows Crooked River by name and in good detail. A map prepared under the direction of Col. J. J. Abert, dated 1838, shows the name Crooked River. This map is attached to the Cushing report, more properly described as 25th Congress, 3rd Session, House report 101, entitled *Territory of Oregon*, with supplemental report. USGS *Bulletin 252*, by Dr. I. C. Russell, is the standard handbook of the geology of central Oregon and contains much valuable information about Crooked River. In 1925 the USGS made an extended survey of the topography and geology of Crooked River between its mouth and Trail Crossing, with particular reference to the remarkable springs that feed the stream in this section. The state of Oregon and the U.S. Reclamation Service published a bulletin in 1915 entitled *Ochoco Project* which contains much other information about Crooked River. For information about the highway bridge over Crooked River near Terrebonne, *see* the *Oregonian*, Aug. 1, 1926, sect. 7, p. 1.

Crooks, UNION. Crooks is a station on the Union Pacific Railroad in the Blue Mountains. It was named for William Crooks, who was born in New York City in 1831, and died in Portland Dec. 17, 1907. He was for some years an official of the railroad. For his biography, *see* the *Oregonian*, Dec. 18, 1907. Colonel William Crooks was the son of Ramsay Crooks, of the Astor overland party. For adventures of Ramsay Crooks, *see* Irving's *Astoria*. He was born in Scotland in 1787, and died in New York City June 6, 1859. He was credited with being "the strongest man, next to Mr. Astor himself, who at any time stood at the helm in the home office at New York." (Chittenden.)

Crooks Creek, LINN. This stream is in the extreme north part of the county and is intermittent in character and its waters eventually find their way into the Willamette River about eight miles north of Albany. This stream was named for John T. Crooks, who took up a donation land claim nearby.

Cross Hollows, WASCO. Cross Hollows is just south of Shaniko and is named for the prominent right angle crossing of two canyons. It was the location of Sherar's station where John Ward kept the hotel. Cross Hollows post office was established May 23, 1879. For further information, *see* Shaniko.

Cross Keys, JEFFERSON. Much research has been expended on the origin of the name of Cross Keys post office, first established on the Wasco County list, but applicable to a locality now in the extreme north part of Jefferson County. The locality is just south or southwest of the mouth of Cow Canyon, and close to the banks of Trout Creek. The post office was doubtless moved from time to time. An office with the name Trout Creek was established July 3, 1878, with Jasper A. Friend postmaster. William Heisler became postmaster on Oct. 17, 1878, and on Feb. 13, 1879, Robert Ashby became postmaster. On this date the name of the office was changed to Cross Keys. Edward G. Bolter became postmaster on July 8, 1879, and ran the office until Sept. 24, 1898, when it was closed to Ridgeway. It was reopened a few weeks later and ran until July 31, 1902. There is a notion in central Oregon that Cross Keys was named for the place in Wales, but so far the compiler has found no confirmation of the statement. It has been asserted that either Heisler, Ashby or Bolter applied the name, but these assertions are also without confirmation. Statements that Cross Keys was several miles south in the valley of Hay Creek are not confirmed by any maps in the possession of the compiler. A later office called Willowdale was not far from the original site of the Trout Creek office.

Croston, MARION. Croston was the name of the post office on the east bank of Willamette River at the east landing of Halls Ferry. This landing was several miles down stream from Independence. The post office was established Dec. 22, 1884, with Benjamin F. Hall first of three postmasters and continued in service until Mar. 19, 1901. When it was established, Croston post office was put on the Polk County list, but this must have been in error, for there is nothing to indicate that it ever operated in Polk County. It is obvious that the name was intended to indicate a place where there was a crossing, in this case a ferry.

Crow, LANE. Crow was named for James Andrew Jackson Crow and his wife, Helen Fisk Crow, who came to Oregon by wagon train and were among the founders of the community. The post office at Crow was established Nov. 6, 1874, with Alexander Wood first postmaster. Will G. Steel told the compiler that the word Crow was a literal translation of an Indian word *Andaig*, applying to the locality, but search failed to bring any confirmation of the statement.

Crow Creek, WALLOWA. Crow Creek is northeast of Enterprise and flows northward to join Joseph Creek. According to J. H. Horner of Enterprise, the stream was named by A. C. Smith and Jasper Matheny in the late 1870s because they found the birds so thick in the aspen groves along its banks.

Crow Ridge, WALLOWA. This ridge lies between Joseph and Deer creeks in the northeast part of the county. It was named for Bert Crow, first settler on the ridge in the early 1880s. He was the first man to take a wagon from this ridge down to Grande Ronde River.

Crowcamp Creek, HARNEY. Crowcamp Creek rises on the west slope of Crowcamp Mountain, elevation 5887 feet. This high ground on the east side of Harney Valley has been known as the Crowcamp Hills. Second-Lieutenant John F. Noble, Company G, 1st Oregon Cavalry, a member of Captain John M. Drake's command, kept a diary of the expedition from Fort Dalles to the Harney Valley. They camped at "Smith's Camp" the nights of June 16 and 30, 1864. The spot is where Crowcamp Creek emerges from the hills into Harney Valley and Noble's diary, on file at the OHS Library, under the latter date calls the stream Crow Creek. *See OHQ*, v. 65, pp. 56 *et seq*. Old timers in the area say that the hills and creek were named for James Rankin Crow, a stock herder working for Todhunter & Devine, pioneer cattlemen. Crow discovered an excellent spring in the locality, and camped there. Later the Crowcamp Ranch was established nearby. However, Crow could not have predated 1864. In the early 1870s, Crow and his wife, Ann Elizabeth Crow, homesteaded in Stone House Canyon near Mann Lake.

Crowfoot, LINN. Crowfoot is a crossroads community on the South Santiam Highway about two miles south of Lebanon. It has not had a separate post office, but has been served through Lebanon. All the available evidence says that the locality got the name Crowfoot because the roads intersecting there came together in a pattern that suggested the track left by a crow's foot. This is shown clearly by the USGS map of the Lebanon quadrangle. Katherine Harris, in a column headed "Off the Record," in the Lebanon *Express* for Jan. 23, 1947, gives a good deal of history about the place called Crowfoot. It was named many years ago, apparently by Hester Sturdevant, an early resident of the locality. The Grange Hall, then one of the important buildings at Crowfoot, was formerly the old college hall at Sodaville. When the college was abandoned, the building was moved to Crowfoot.

Crowley, POLK. This station is on the Southern Pacific Company line between Holmes Gap and Rickreall, and was named for Solomon K. Crowley, an early resident of the neighborhood. He was born in Missouri in 1833 and came to Oregon in 1852. *See* Hines' *Illustrated History of the State of Oregon*, p. 1012.

Crowley Creek, MALHEUR. Crowley Creek was named for G. B. Crowley who with his son James Crowley settled along its banks in 1874. In May 1878, during the Bannock War, Indians burned their home but the family escaped injury. Crowley post office was established Mar. 2, 1911 and closed Jan. 29, 1935.

Crown Creek, MARION. Crown Creek rises on Elkhorn Mountain and flows north into Little North Santiam River. It takes its name from the Crown Mine, an operation of the Crown Mining and Milling Company, located along its bank.

Crown Point, MULTNOMAH. In 1884 Lorens Lund, a native of Schleswig Holstein, took up a homestead on the high ground above and including Crown Point. His family farmed the homestead for many years and when the Columbia River Highway was built, Lund donated the land on which the Vista House was constructed. His daughter, Thora Lund, told the writer in 1973 that her father always referred to the top of the bluff as "The Point" and he would often walk down from the farmhouse on a summer evening to watch the sunset. Gertrude G. Jensen, an authority on the Columbia River Gorge, said Marshall Dana of the *Oregon Journal* first used the present name when discussing plans for the Vista House. He said it would "put the crown on Crown Point." The compiler has been unable to find when this first use occured but Crown Point is used by Samuel Lancaster in *The*

Columbia, and in numerous newspaper accounts of the construction and dedication of the highway prior to World War I. Crown Point was designated a National Natural Landmark in Aug. 1971, and the Vista House, a remarkable example of Jugendstil architecture designed by Edgar M. Lazarus, was entered in the National Register of Historic Places on Nov. 5, 1974.

Crown Rock, WHEELER. Crown Rock was a post office not far from the present site of Clarno. Huntley post office was established Feb. 28, 1876, with Joseph Broughton first postmaster. The compiler has not been able to get the history of the name. The name of the office was changed to Pine Creek on June 23, 1876. This name was of course for Pine Creek, a prominent stream flowing into John Day River from the east. On Dec. 10, 1877, the name was changed again, this time to Crown Rock for a prominent geological formation in the vicinity, apparently a rimrock of basalt.

Crutcher, MALHEUR. Crutcher post office was established on the Malheur County list Mar. 20, 1900, with Elliott W. Crutcher first and only postmaster. The office bore his family name. It was in operation only until Aug. 13, 1901, when it was closed to Jordan Valley. The compiler has not been able to learn the exact location of this office but obviously it was in the east part of the county and south of Vale.

Crutcher Bench, CLACKAMAS. This side hill bench lies just north of the junction of Sandy and Zigzag rivers. It was named for H. P. Crutcher, who filed a claim on the bench about 1890.

Cruzatte, LANE. Cruzatte, a station on the Cascade line of the Southern Pacific Company, was named for a member of the Lewis and Clark party, Peter Cruzatte. Lewis and Clark spelled his name in several ways, and named a stream in Washington for him, now known as Wind River.

Cryder Butte, KLAMATH. Cryder Butte is south of Davis Lake in the extreme north part of the county. It was named for W. W. Cryder, the first and only supervisor of the short lived Paulina National Forest prior to World War I.

Crystal, KLAMATH. This name was originally applied to a fine stream flowing into Upper Klamath Lake near Pelican Bay. In 1925, Postmaster S. A. Brown reported that he thought the stream was named in 1891 by G. W. Malone and John Young. Crystal, as the name of the office, was proposed by the first postmaster, D. G. Brown, in 1894, when it was established through his efforts.

Cucamonga Creek, HARNEY. This stream rises on the northwest slopes of Steens Mountain, and enters Kiger Creek, a tributary of Donner und Blitzen River. The name is derived from Cucamonga Creek, San Bernardino County, California, and was applied to the Harney County stream by Mrs. Dolly Kiger. *Cucamonga* is an Indian name and according to Mrs. Nellie Van de Grift Sanchez, in *Spanish and Indian Place Names of California*, was originally applied to a native village about 42 miles east of Los Angeles, and later to a land grant. Mrs. Kiger wrote the compiler in 1927 that she lived in the Harney Valley from 1874 to 1878 and that one of her neighbors, Mace McCoy, had formerly lived in California and frequently spoke of Cucamonga wine, a variety made in the southern part of the state. Mrs. Kiger named Cucamonga Creek because she liked the sound of the word.

Cullaby Lake, CLATSOP. A lake on Clatsop Plains, about two miles long, fed by small streams. The present outlet is through a ditch into Skipanon River. Many years ago this lake drained through Neacoxie Creek, which first flowed northward and then turned south and emptied into the estuary of Necanicum River. Shifting sands have from time to time interfered with the flow of Neacoxie Creek and thus changed the drainage from Cullaby Lake. In later times, extensive cranberry culture developed along the shores of the lake. Its elevation is near sea level. Silas B. Smith is authority for the statement that the Indian name for this lake was *Ya-se-ya-ma-na-la-tslas-tie*. *See OHQ*, v. 1, p. 322. It was later named for Cullaby, a well-known Indian character on Clatsop Plains. Cullaby had a peculiar light complexion, and was a son of the Indian whom Lewis and Clark saw on the last day of the year 1805, and whom they described as "freckled with long dusky red hair, about 25 years of age, and must certainly be half white at least."

Culp Creek, LANE. Culp Creek is a post office as well as a stream tributary to Row River southeast of Cottage Grove. Culp Creek was named for John Culp, who settled in this neighborhood a few years prior to 1900. A logging company established a camp there and called it the Culp Creek camp, and when the post office was established Feb. 24, 1925, the name naturally attached itself to the new office. Geo. E. Potter, a local merchant, was the first postmaster. For additional information, *see* Cottage Grove *Sentinel*, Mar. 28, 1929.

Cultus Creek, DOUGLAS. Cultus Creek heads on the South Myrtle Creek divide and flows north into Cavitt Creek. Former USFS ranger Fred Asam informed the compiler in 1968 that the name was applied by a U.S. Land Office surveyor called Sturdevant who had considerable trouble finding his way about in the rough terrain and who considered the whole area very troublesome. For the Indian meaning, *see* Cultus Lake.

Cultus Lake, DESCHUTES. *Cultus* is a Chinook jargon word, quite expressive, meaning bad or wholly worthless. It is used in many places in the Pacific Northwest, generally because of the lack of one or more of the pioneer traveler's greatest needs, "wood, water and grass." Cultus Prairie meant that the horse feed was poor. The word found its way into the jargon from the Chinook Indian word *kaltas*. In addition to Cultus Lake in Deschutes County, there is also a Little Cultus Lake and Cultus Mountain. The latter was doubtless named for the lakes. Cultus has been spelled in many ways, including Kultus, Cultos and Cultis, but the USBGN has adopted the form Cultus.

Culver, JEFFERSON. In the latter part of 1900 at a dinner party of old settlers living in the Haystack country O. G. Collver was requested to make an application for a post office and to act as postmaster. A number of names of old settlers were submitted to the department, and Culver was adopted, this being the ancestral name of Mr. Collver. O. G. Collver was born in Roseburg on Feb. 10, 1854, and went into central Oregon in June 1877. He was appointed postmaster of Culver Oct. 31, 1900. The site of Culver post office as first established was about five miles east of the present town. O. G. Collver died in Portland Nov. 14, 1939. For a short biography, *see* Madras *Pioneer*, Nov. 23, 1939.

Cumley Creek, LINN. Cumley Creek was named for Jennings B. Comley who patented a homestead near its mouth, now inundated, just above Detroit Dam. Comley was an early, prominent citizen of Albany and a member of the first city council. During the later part of the 19th century it was common for individuals to file for homesteads on land with a good timber cover. After proving up, they would sell to a logging or lumber company. When Comley filed in 1893, the railroad had been completed to Idanha and the area was alive with great expectations. For a short biography of Comley, *see* Lang's *History of the Willamette Valley*, p. 833.

Cummings Creek, GRANT. Cummings Creek is a tributary, from the north, of John Day River, 13 miles east of Dayville. J. E. Snow, of Dayville, informed the compiler in Oct. 1927, that James Cummings settled on this stream in pioneer days. He came from Maine and was a bachelor. Members of his brother's family still lived in the neighborhood at that time. James Cummings' house was one of those burned by the Indians in 1878. The stream was named for him.

Cummins Creek, LANE. This creek and Cummins Ridge to the south are in the extreme northwest corner of the county. They were named for F. L. Cummins, an early homesteader. The form Cummings is wrong.

Cumtux, CURRY. Cumtux was a short lived post office near the present community of Agness. It was established on July 29, 1895 with Henry P. Moore postmaster and discontinued the following October. The office at Illahe, several miles upstream, had been established the previous January and, apparently, there was insufficient business for two offices. The office at Agness was not established until two years later. *Cumtux*, usually spelled *Kumtux*, is a Nootkan word whose most important meaning is "understand." The compiler is indebted to Forrest Dunn of Lebanon for the information about the location of the office.

Cunningham Canyon, MORROW. This canyon empties into Butter Creek at the Umatilla County line. It was named for Charles Cunningham, the founder of the Cunningham Sheep and Land Company, who was born in County Galway, Ireland in 1846. Cunningham came to the United States in 1864 and after service in the navy took a land claim at the mouth of the canyon in 1878. He was a prominent person in the livestock industry and at one time was president of the *Woolgrowers Stock Journal*.

Cunningham Creek, COOS. This stream is north of the town of Coquille. It was named for Evan C. Cunningham, a pioneer settler on its banks.

Cupids Knoll, POLK. In Nov. 1972, the voters of Colorado disapproved a measure to complete the financing for the 1976 Winter Olympics which had been awarded to Denver. This necessitated choosing a new location. Amid the well organized and advertised appeals from the world's great winter sports areas one tiny voice from the Willamette Valley was audible. The good burghers of Monmouth with pardonable pride and commendable financial acumen made one last, desperate effort to save these events for the western United States. However, the International Olympic Committee felt the proposal to hold all alpine events on 321 foot high Cupids Knoll with a total budget of $2.25 did not quite come up to their august standards. A full account of these proceedings can be found in the *Oregon Journal*, Dec. 18, 1972, sect. 2. Cupids Knoll was named in the days when automobiles were less plentiful and students at the then Oregon Normal School were wont to seek seclusion within walking distance. The compiler's unrelated namesake, Scott McArthur of Monmouth, was kind enough to pass on this information before the knoll lapsed back into obscurity. He added that the city had terminated the romantic activity by installing a chain link fence.

Cupit Mary Mountain, LANE. Cupit Mary Mountain, elevation 6175 feet, is a prominent point just west of Waldo Lake. In Mar. 1943, C. B. McFarland, for many years a ranger with the USFS at Oakridge, furnished the compiler with information about Cupit Mary. She was the youngest daughter of an Indian known as Old Moses, who lived at an Indian village near what is now Oakridge. She was not well thought of by other Indians. Her name, Cupit, is reported to be an Indian word meaning last, indicating her position among Old Moses' children. It is doubtless the same as the Chinook jargon word which Gibbs gives as *ko-pet*, meaning stop, the end or enough. Both Old Moses and Mary's mother probably had had enough. *Ko-pet* is accented on the second syllable.

Cupper Creek, GRANT. Cupper Creek is in the northwest corner of the county and flows south into North Fork John Day River a few miles west of Monument. The name of this stream perpetuates a type of story that is full of human interest, but perhaps not romantic enough to get the attention it deserves. The history of the immigration of the Cupper family illustrates what it took to develop that part of Oregon that produces livestock. Henry Adams Cupper and his wife, Cordelia Harriet Cupper, together with three small children, left England in Jan. 1877, and after a stormy voyage across the Atlantic, reached the end of rail travel at Redding, California. They took stage to Linkville, now Klamath Falls, and Cupper got a job of sorts in the Poe Valley. They spent the winter in Ashland and in the spring started with wagon and team looking for a location to settle. They journeyed near what is now La Pine, and got lost, but finally reached Farewell Bend where they "loaded up with water and crossed the desert to Prineville." From Prineville they continued northward, crossing John Day River at McDonald Ferry and then turned southeast through Lone Rock to Heppner. At Heppner they undertook to freight a load of provisions in to Bill Welch. Avoiding the Indians, they delivered the cargo, and were so impressed with the Welch Ranch, the natural meadows and the abundance of game that they arranged to buy the squatters' right. Welch is said to have assumed that they would not stay, and he would get the place back. In the meantime the Indians had attacked Long Creek, and so many settlers returned to Heppner that they swept the Cuppers along with them. The Cuppers remained at Heppner six weeks and then returned to the ranch and braved the rest of the Indian troubles. Cupper brought sheep into the cattle country, which did not endear him to his neighbors. They raised a large family and lived on the ranch until 1918. They moved to Salem and celebrated their golden wedding anniversary on Oct. 1, 1922. Mr. Cupper died in Jan. 1923, and Mrs. Cupper in 1938, when she was 90 years old. Cupper Creek is still 50 miles from a railroad and some seven miles from a post office.

Curiosity Creek, WALLOWA. Curiosity Creek flows into Imnaha River in S 32, T 2N, R 48E. It was named in 1883 by Hugh Conahar for a curious limb of an alder tree. The branch grew back into the tree like a jug handle.

Currant Creek, JEFFERSON, WASCO. The old road from The Dalles to Canyon City passed along Currant Creek before reaching John Day River. The creek was named in early days for the profusion of wild currants that grew along its banks and *The History of Central Oregon*, p. 637, describes a pack train ambush in 1862 when Indians secreted themselves behind these bushes.

Currin Creek, CLACKAMAS. Currin Creek is a tributary of Eagle Creek near Estacada. It was named for the Currin brothers mentioned under Currinsville.

Currinsville, CLACKAMAS. This was a station on the now abandoned line of the Portland Electric Power Company two miles north of Estacada. It was named for George and Hugh Currin, who were pioneer settlers in Clackamas County and took up donation land claims near this point. For editorial comment about the members of the Currin family, *see* the *Oregonian*, Nov. 19, 1943. *See also* editorial page, the *Oregon Journal*, Sept. 25, 1928. A post office named Zion was established in this general locality on June 24, 1874, with William H. H. Wade first postmaster. The name of the office was changed to Currinsville on Jan. 8, 1884, with George J. Currin postmaster. The office was closed Feb. 16, 1906. Zion post office was obviously named by a biblical enthusiast.

Curry County. Curry County was created Dec. 18, 1855, and was taken from the south part of Coos County. It was named for George Law Curry, who was born at Philadelphia July 2, 1820; died Portland July 28, 1878. On arrival at Oregon City he acted as editor of the *Oregon Spectator* from Oct. 1, 1846, until the end of 1847, and in Apr. 1848, published the *Oregon Free Press*. He represented Clackamas County in the provisional legislature of 1848–49, served as chief clerk of the territorial council of 1850–51, and represented Clackamas in the house of the territorial legislature in 1851. In 1853, President Pierce appointed Curry secretary of the territory of Oregon. A few days after taking that office, he became acting governor through the resignation of Governor Joseph Lane. In Dec. 1853, Governor John W. Davis arrived, but in Aug. 1854, Davis resigned, and Curry was acting governor until appointed governor a few months later. He served as governor until the territory became a state, in 1859. "He was of singularly amiable disposition, honorable, and gifted with a versatility of such degree that whatever he undertook was well performed." (OPA *Transactions* for 1878, p. 80.) He was editor of the Portland *Advertiser*, the third daily newspaper at Portland, first published Jan. 1, 1861, and the *Evening Journal*, Jan. 25 to Apr. 25, 1876. For biography of himself and his wife, Chloe Boone Curry, *see* the *Oregonian*, Feb. 12, 1899. For his narrative of early history of Oregon, Mar. 15, 1872, p. 3; Feb. 28, 1872, p. 3. Curry was territorial governor when Curry County was created. For early history of Curry County, *see* the *Oregonian* for Feb. 14, 1886, by O. W. Olney. *See also* Scott's *History of the Oregon Country*, v. 5, p. 222, for a tribute to Curry. *The Pioneer History of Coos and Curry Counties*, edited by Orvil Dodge, contains much interesting material about early days in Curry County. Bancroft, in *History of Oregon*, v. 2, p. 415, says it was first proposed to name this county Tichenor, for Captain William Tichenor of Port Orford, a member of the legislative council from Coos County. Tichenor declined this honor saying that his constituents wanted the new county named for Governor Curry. Curry County had an area of 1623 square miles in 1990.

Curtin, DOUGLAS. This place was named for Daniel Curtin, who operated a sawmill there in the early 1890s. Curtin is on I-5 and the Southern Pacific railroad about seven miles northeast of Drain.

Cushing Falls, WASCO. Cushing Falls are on Fifteenmile Creek a short distance above its mouth. They carry the name of Milo M. Cushing who came to The Dalles in 1852 with the Fourth United States Infantry Regiment. Cushing is credited with erecting the first hotel and commercial building in The Dalles and for many years he lived near the falls that now bear his name. He was born in Truxton, New York in Jan. 1820, and died in The Dalles in 1906. In 1854 he married Mary Piggott, the first marriage in Wasco County after its formation.

Cushman, LANE. Cushman is a station on the Coos Bay line of the Southern Pacific Company on the north bank of the Siuslaw River. It is about a mile east of Cushman community, which was formerly Acme. It was named by the railroad company for C. C. and I. B. Cushman, local residents. The company already had an Acme on its lines and did not wish to duplicate that name, and after the station was changed, the post office authorities followed suit. The name Acme was originally applied by Mrs. W. A. Cox, an early settler. It is said that Mrs. Cox dreamed she was to live in a place called Acme, so when her husband platted a townsite in Lane County, the place was called Acme. Cushman post office was established July 3, 1916 by change of name from Acme. The office was closed in 1961 with papers to Florence.

Cusick Mountain, WALLOWA. Cusick Mountain is some three miles southeast of Eagle Cap and forms the south buttress of Hawkins Pass. It is named for William C. Cusick, the pioneer botanist of eastern Oregon. Cusick came to Oregon in 1853 as a small boy and spent much of his adult life near Union where he amassed a substantial botanical collection. He died in 1922. For further information, *see* Corning's *Dictionary of Oregon History*, p. 68.

Custer, COOS. Custer post office in the south part of the county was named for Custer M. Hermann, son of Cass M. Hermann, a prominent Coos County pioneer. The office was at the Cass Hermann stock ranch on the mail road south from Myrtle Point to Eckley, Curry County, and was in the hills just north of the head of Rowland Creek. Custer Hermann did not live to maturity. Custer post office was established July 19, 1893, with Cass M. Hermann first and only postmaster. The office was closed May 17, 1901. A. H. Bender of Myrtle Point, a nephew of Cass M. Hermann, sent in the information about this name.

Cutler City, LINCOLN. Cutler City, just south of Taft and on the east shore of Siletz Bay, has had a remarkable development as a resort town. It was started by Mr. and Mrs. George Cutler, who are said to have acquired the property from "Uncle Charley" DePoe, a Siletz Indian. The Cutlers formerly lived near Dallas. Mr. Cutler died in 1913 and Mrs. Cutler in 1939. For obituary of Mrs. Cutler, *see* the *Oregon Journal* for June 19, 1939. On Dec. 8, 1964, Cutler City voted to become part of a new community to be called Lincoln City.

Cutsforth Corner, MORROW. This spot three miles north of Lexington was named for a well-known local resident, Orville Cutsforth.

D River, LINCOLN. D River connects Devils Lake with the Pacific Ocean at Lincoln City. It is the shortest river in the world, about 100 yards long, although it is difficult to define exactly where the lake ends and the river begins. US-101 crosses D River and the entire course of the stream may be seen from a viewpoint adjacent to the bridge.

Dad Spring, WALLOWA. Dad Spring is in S 19, T 2N, R 50E. It was named for Elbert B. Wilson, who was generally known as "Dad" or "Snake River" Wilson. He came to Wallowa County in July 1900, and ranged cattle near this spring in the summers. This spring was at one time known as Brigham Spring because it was on Mormon Flat.

Dads Creek, GRANT. Dads Creek flows into John Day River just east of Prairie City. It is named for Hokum "Dad" Rinehart, who built a mining or sluice ditch on it in the 1860s. This information, forwarded by Dorsey Griffin, came from Ernest Ricco who later owned most of the land along the creek.

Dahlin Creek, LANE. Dahlin Creek flows into Mercer Lake from the north. John L. Dahlin took a homestead along it in 1892.

Dairy, KLAMATH. This place was named by William Roberts, pioneer settler. He is said to have lived in the Rogue River country and also in the Klamath country as early as 1865. He selected the word Dairy because he had previously lived in a community by that name in an eastern state. The post office of Dairy was first established May 8, 1876, with Roberts postmaster. The valley in which Dairy is situated was at one time known as Alkali Valley, but now bears its Klamath Indian name, Yonna Valley. *See* Yonna Valley.

Dairy Creek, MULTNOMAH. Dairy Creek is on the east part of Sauvie Island. It drains Marquam Lake into Columbia River. It was named for a small dairy operated nearby by a French-Canadian employee of the Hudson's Bay Company. This was in pioneer days. For additional data *see* Marquam Lake.

Dairy Creek, WASHINGTON. Dairy Creek and its tributaries are an important part of the Tualatin River drainage. The main stream is formed by two long branches which join a few miles northeast of Forest Grove. West Fork Dairy Creek rises near Buxton and East Fork Dairy Creek rises in the extreme south part of Columbia County north of Mountaindale. Dairy Creek has been so called for a long time. While the evidence is not positive, it is probable that the stream was named by employees of the Hudson's Bay Company during the fur trading period. The company operated a dairy on what is now Dairy Creek, but the compiler does not know the exact location. On July 5, 1882, George B. Roberts, retired Hudson's Bay Company employee, wrote to Mrs. Frances Fuller Victor: "Wyeth's Fort William . . . was located with the view to easy communication with the Tualatin plains. Our people used that road over the hills and we had a dairy there on what is now called Dairy creek." Roberts is referring to the Logie Trail. The date the dairy was established is uncertain, but by inference it must have been prior to 1840.

Daley Creek, JACKSON. In Sept. 1947, Miss Venita Daley of Medford sent the compiler data about her grandfather, William Carter Daley, and the geographic features in the east part of Jackson County named for him. These features include Daley Creek and Daley Prairie. The creek, which is about four miles long, starts at a spring in the south part of the prairie, and flows west to join Deadwood Creek. Daley Creek is in T 37S, R 4E. The creek and the prairie were named many years ago in memory of an elk hunting expedition organized by Daley, an Ashland pioneer of 1864, and his brother-in-law, Samuel B. Hamilton, Jacksonville miner of 1856. These two built a hunting cabin near Daley Creek about 1873, and for several years packed in from Ashland. Daley shipped a considerable number of beaver and other pelts from Ashland to San Francisco, where there was a ready sale. Daley abandoned the campsite and cabin after game laws became effective and bought a ranch about a mile above Lakecreek post office, where he farmed for nearly 35 years. He died at his home in Eagle Point in 1930, aged 84. He was a well-known resident of the Little Butte Creek area.

Daley Lake, TILLAMOOK. This lake is near the ocean about two miles southwest of Oretown. It is known as Fletcher Lake and also Daley Lake. D. R. S. Daley was an Oregon pioneer. He came to Tillamook County in the 1870s and took up a homestead near the south end of the lake. Fletcher Lake is a modern name and in the opinion of the writer is not the correct one.

Dallas, POLK. Dallas is said to have been called Cynthia Ann originally. It was settled in the 1840s on the north side of Rickreall Creek, but was moved more than a mile south in 1856 because of inadequate water supply. It was named for George

Mifflin Dallas (1792–1864), vice-president of the United States from 1845 to 1849. Dallas was vice-president during Polk's administration, and when a name was needed for the county seat of Polk County, it was but natural that Dallas was chosen. A narrow gauge railroad was built into Dallas in 1878–80 as a result of a county seat fight with Independence. Independence was after the county seat honor, but citizens of Dallas raised $17,000 and secured the branch line, and this settled the contest for the seat of government. Dallas post office was established Oct. 22, 1852, with John E. Lyle postmaster. Attention is called to discrepancies in the available information about the early name Dallas. It appears both as Cynthian and Cynthia Ann. An article in the *Oregon Spectator*, Feb. 10, 1852, makes sarcastic reference to Cynthian. It is reported that this name was chosen by a Mrs. Lovelady in memory of a place in Kentucky, but the name in Kentucky is Cythiana. Mrs. Harriet McArthur and Judge C. H. Carey of Portland and Captain O. C. Applegate of Klamath Falls informed the compiler in 1927 that the place was named for Mrs. Jesse Applegate, whose given name was Cynthia Ann. The Applegates lived in Polk County at the time the place was named.

Dalreed Butte, MORROW. Dalreed Butte is in the extreme west part of the county about two miles north of Willow Creek. Roy Scott, postmaster at Cecil, Oregon, wrote the compiler in 1927 that this butte received its name about 50 years previously. It was named for Dallas Reed, who lived near the butte at that time.

Daly Creek, BAKER. Daly Creek is south of Richland. The stream was named for an early settler. Dunham Wright of Medical Springs told the compiler that Daly came to Oregon in 1862. *See also* letter from H. E. Daly on editorial page, the *Oregonian*, Oct. 7, 1927.

Daly Lake, LINN. Daly Lake is on the upper reaches of Pyramid Creek at the head of Middle Santiam River drainage. An article in the Salem *Capitol Journal*, Aug. 18, 1906, p. 6, tells of an expedition by Judge John B. Waldo and George Downing during which they took 275 trout from Daly Lake in one day. Daly Lake was named for D. R. S. Daley of Oretown in Tillamook County, who accompanied Judge Waldo on several trips to the Cascade Mountains. The form Daly was in use as early as 1906 although Waldo in all his letters uses the form Daley Lake.

Daly Spring, CROOK. This spring on Williamson Creek in the Bear Creek Buttes was named for the Dealy family who settled there about the time of World War I.

Damascus, CLACKAMAS. Mrs. John C. Elliott of Clackamas, Clackamas County, wrote the compiler in Sept. 1945, that Damascus was named by Henry Pedigo, who did so because of a verse in the Bible. The compiler has not been able to identify the verse. Damascus post office was established Aug. 26, 1867, with John S. Fisher first postmaster. It was closed in Aug. 1904.

Damewood Creek, LANE. This creek is a tributary of Sharps Creek three miles above Culp Creek. It is named for Joe Damewood, a member of a family of early settlers.

Damon Creek, GRANT. This stream flows into John Day River from the north, west of Mount Vernon. Patsy Daly of Prairie City told the compiler it was named for Robert Damon, who settled nearby in the 1860s. The *History of Baker, Grant, Malheur and Harney Counties*, p. 486, in a short biography, says Damon was born in Scituate, Massachusetts, in 1828 and came to Grant County in 1870.

DaMotta Branch, DOUGLAS. In the early days this tributary of Deer Creek just east of Roseburg was known as Goose Creek. Phil DaMotta came to Roseburg before the turn of the century where he was a barber by profession and a horse breeder by hobby. His farm was on this fork of Deer Creek and the name soon changed to DaMotta Branch. George B. Abdill of Roseburg furnished this information and added that the form DeMonty, shown on some maps, was incorrect.

Danebo, LANE. Edward F. Bailey of Eugene told the writer that this area west of Eugene was named in the early 1900s because of the large number of Danish settlers.

Danger Bay, KLAMATH. Will G. Steel, the authority on Crater Lake, told the compiler that this name was ill-chosen, as he never saw the time that danger befell anyone boating on Crater Lake. However, it is an old name, and will doubtless remain.

Daniels Creek, COOS. This stream flows into South Fork Coos River about seven miles east of Coos Bay. It bears the name of an early settler, William Daniels, who lived near the mouth of the creek. S. B. Cathcart wrote in 1929 that Daniels left the locality many years ago.

Danner, MALHEUR. It is reported that this town was originally known as Ruby, but the postal authorities would not accept the name for a post office. Several other names were submitted including Danner, which was suggested in honor of J. H. Danner, one of the pioneer settlers in the community. Robert E. Danner, his son, was the first postmaster. The office was established Apr. 3, 1920.

Dans Creek, CURRY. M. S. Brainard of Brookings told the writer that this creek near Illahe was named for a well-known character named Indian Dan who homesteaded nearby in the 1860s.

Dant, WASCO. In 1950 Dant & Russell, Inc., established a perlite mine near Frieda on the Oregon Trunk Railway in Deschutes Canyon. Frieda was renamed for Thomas Dant, president of Dant & Russell, Inc. The mine has since been abandoned and according to reliable reports from a visiting fisherman little commercial activity remains.

Dardanelles, JACKSON. Dardanelles was a place of importance in pioneer days in the Rogue River Valley, but the community passed into discard. Dardanelles post office was established Oct. 19, 1852, with William G. T'Vault postmaster. T'Vault was a prominent pioneer of southwest Oregon and started this settlement south of and across Rogue River from the present town of Gold Hill. At this point the river passes from a wider valley into a much more constricted section, with hills close on each hand. Apparently this natural setting suggested the Strait of the Dardanelles to T'Vault, although it could hardly be more than a suggestion. T'Vault was a newspaper editor of prominence and had a wide range of interests. The original Dardanelles gets its name from the city of Dardanus. It is said that the first quartz mill in southern Oregon was installed near Dardanelles in 1860. There are interesting references to this event in Walling's *History of Southern Oregon*, pp. 329 and 379.

Darling Canyon, GILLIAM. Darling Canyon empties into Thirtymile Creek halfway between Condon and Lonerock. Linus W. Darling built one of the first buildings in Condon in 1887 where he operated a drug store and later served as postmaster. Darling also patented a Timber Culture claim and owned land near the head of Darling Canyon.

Darrow Rocks, POLK. These rocks are in the Willamette River about five miles downstream from Salem, and Darrow Chute is just below the rocks. The name is spelled Darrough on some maps, but this does not seem to be correct. Hedda S. Swart of Salem kindly investigated the history of the name in 1943 and found that William and Marion Darrow conveyed some property at this locality to William McGee in 1874. This record is found in the deeds in v. 8, p. 481, at the Polk County courthouse, Dallas. Swart had this spelling confirmed by Mr. and Mrs. John Schindler, local residents of long standing. The USCE, in their work along the river, use the spelling Darrow and not Darrough.

David Hill, WASHINGTON. David Hill, about three miles north west of Forest Grove, was named for Frederick W. David who homesteaded there in 1876. His daughter, Mary David, married the son of Harmon Thatcher for whom nearby Thatcher is named.

Davidson, JOSEPHINE. Davidson post office was near Applegate River in the extreme east part of the county, about five miles southeast of Murphy. The office was named for J. E. Davidson, whose place was next door to the post office. Davidson, a younger brother of Elijah J. Davidson the discoverer of the Oregon Caves, was born in Independence, Polk County, Sept. 6, 1866, and in Mar. 1947, was living in Grants Pass. Davidson post office was established June 12, 1900, with Alice R. Bailey first and only postmaster. The office was closed to Murphy Oct. 11, 1907. Mr. Davidson informed the compiler that the office was kept in the country store of W. S. Bailey, and Mrs. Bailey was the official postmaster. The office was closed by the advent of rural free delivery.

Davidson, MORROW. On Apr. 26, 1893, Davidson post office was established on the Morrow County list with Gamaliel Davidson first and only postmaster. The office was named for the postmaster, and after a relatively short life, it was closed Aug. 27, 1897, with all papers to Eightmile. The post office was about ten miles west-northwest of Hardman and just north of Rock Creek.

Davidson Hill, HOOD RIVER. This is the hill on the west side of Hood River Valley north of Tucker Bridge. It was named for William Davidson, who settled at this point about 1880.

Davidson Hill, POLK. Davidson Hill is two miles west of Buena Vista. It was named for Carter T. Davidson, born in 1802, a pioneer of Oregon of 1852, who settled on a donation land claim nearby in the fall of the year he came to Oregon. It has an elevation of about 425 feet.

Davies Junction, WASHINGTON. Davies Junction is the junction of US-26 and SH-47 west of Forest Grove. It is named for William Davies and his brother, Harry Davies, who came to the area about 1905 and had a sawmill east of Garrigus Creek. This information came from William's son, Hubert E Davies, who farmed in the area for many years.

Davin Spring, CROOK. This spring is about six miles east of Paulina, and was named for John Davin, a Frenchman who came to Paulina from Nevada about 1890. The name is not connected in any way with that of John Devine, pioneer stockman of southeast Oregon.

Davis Canyon, MORROW. Davis Canyon empties into Eightmile Canyon. It takes its name from Charles N. Davis who ranched there in the first part of the century.

Davis Creek, DESCHUTES. Davis Creek is the official name given by USBGN to the outlet of Davis Lake. The stream flows nearly two miles underground beneath a superficial lava flow before coming to the surface. It is joined by the flow of other large springs, apparently not fed by the lake, and is tributary to Deschutes River. Davis Creek is below the water surface of Wickiup Reservoir at higher stages and resumes its flow only as the reservoir is drained.

Davis Creek, GRANT. This stream is just west of Austin. Patsy Daly of Prairie City wrote the compiler in 1927 that it was named for Jim Davis, an early day miner.

Davis Creek, WALLOWA. Davis Creek flows into Snake River in T 2N, R 51E. It was named for Ben Davis, who had a squatter's claim on its banks.

Davis Creek, WALLOWA. This stream, which is about ten miles long, flows northward and joins Swamp Creek in the extreme southwest corner of T 4N, R 45E. It was named in the 1870s for James Davis, hunter, trapper and Indian interpreter.

Davis Creek, WASCO. Davis Creek is a small tributary of Standard Hollow near Emerson on Fifteenmile Creek. It was named for D. O. Davis who took up land along it in the 1880s. Davis was a businessman in The Dalles who, in common with others, availed himself of the Homestead Act to increase his land holdings.

Davis Lake, DESCHUTES, KLAMATH. This is one of Oregon's important mountain lakes and has an area of a little over four square miles. It is fed principally by Odell and Moore creeks and the USGS gives its normal elevation as 4389 feet. The south shore of the lake is a grassy flat, but the north end is dammed by a rough flow of jagged lava. The outlet, Davis Creek, is subterranean for nearly two miles. After it comes to the surface, it is joined by streams from other large springs, apparently not fed from the lake, and makes its way to Deschutes River. Davis

Lake was named for one "Button" Davis, stockman of Prineville, who was formerly from Shedd in Linn County. He ran stock in the vicinity of the lake, according to information furnished in 1927 by W. P. Vandevert of Bend. Davis Mountain, just east of the lake, was named for the same man. The names were probably applied before 1880.

Davis Spring, WALLOWA. This spring is in S 29, T 3N, R 47E. It was named for Frank Davis, who ranged sheep there.

Dawson Creek, TILLAMOOK. Dawson Creek is a small tributary of Nestucca River just east of Cloverdale. It was apparently named for James J. Dawson, an early homesteader. Dawson is listed in the 1870 Tillamook County census, age 40 years.

Day, SHERMAN. Day was a station on the line of the Union Pacific Railroad near the mouth of John Day River. It was originally known as John Day, but this name was confused with the station John Day in Clatsop County, and also with the post office John Day in Grant County, so the railroad cut the words in half. For the origin of the name, *see* John Day River. The name of the station in Clatsop County was changed to Van Dusen.

Day Creek, DOUGLAS. William P. and George W. Day both took up donation land claims in Camas Valley in 1853. The brothers were prominent early settlers and William Day was the first man to plant and raise a garden in the valley. The creek was undoubtedly named for the family rather than either of the individuals.

Day Ridge, WALLOWA. Day Ridge is a well-known divide between Mud and Courtney creeks, southwest of Flora. It bears the name of Len and Foster Day, who homesteaded there in the early 1890s. William Fornier was the first white settler on the ridge.

Days Creek, DOUGLAS. Walling, in his *History of Southern Oregon*, p. 441, says this stream was named for Patrick and George Day who settled near the mouth of the creek in 1851. It is an important tributary of South Umpqua River northeast of Canyonville. The post office near the mouth of Days Creek was for some years called Day's Creek, but the name was changed to Days Creek about 1890.

Dayton, YAMHILL. Dayton was settled in the winter of 1848–49 by Joel Palmer and Andrew Smith, and was named for Dayton, Ohio, the former home of Smith. Dayton post office was established on June 5, 1851, with Christopher Taylor postmaster. Edward L. Bill became postmaster on May 25, 1852; Joel Palmer on Aug. 2, 1852; and Cyrus Jacobs on Aug. 16, 1853. The principal landmark at Dayton is the Grand Ronde Blockhouse in the northwest corner of the City Park. This structure was built by Willamette Valley settlers on Fort Hill in the Grand Ronde Valley in 1855 and 1856. In 1856 federal troops established Fort Yamhill adjacent to Fort Hill. Among the famous officers stationed at this military establishment were P. H. Sheridan, A. J. Smith, D. A. Russell, and W. B. Hazen. Fort Yamhill was abandoned as a military post in the 1860s and the blockhouse was moved to Grand Ronde Agency. After Grand Ronde Agency was abandoned by the government the blockhouse fell into disrepair. John G. Lewis, a patriotic citizen of Dayton, fearing that the building would disappear, secured permission from authorities to move the logs to Dayton, which was done in 1911. The structure was rebuilt and dedicated to Joel Palmer, a founder of Dayton and donor of the City Park. General Palmer was one of Oregon's outstanding pioneer citizens and was superintendent of Indian affairs, 1853-57. *See* Palmer Peak.

Dayville, GRANT. The original site of the Dayville post office was some three miles west of the present location. The first office was established Dec. 8, 1868, with James N. Brackett first postmaster. The place was named for John Day River, which was named for John Day, a member of the Astor expedition. It is of interest to note that during a period of 50 years there were but three postmasters at Dayville, the second being John W. Lewis and the third J. E. Snow. The present site of the community is at the mouth of South Fork John Day River.

Dead Indian Creek, JACKSON. This creek and Dead Indian Mountain are in Jackson County, and the Dead Indian Road extends from near Ashland past these two geographic features to Upper Klamath Lake in Klamath County. It is said that about 1854 some settlers from Rogue River Valley found two dead Rogue River Indians in some deserted wigwams near the creek, and supposed that Klamath Indians had killed them in a fight. They named the stream for their discovery. For many years the road did not extend over the Cascade Range, but in 1870 Captain O. C. Applegate and a band of Klamath Indians opened the road all the way to Pelican Bay on Upper Klamath Lake.

Dead Mountain, LANE. Dead Mountain is the high ground north of Salmon Creek east of Oakridge. C. B. McFarland of the USFS said that this was formerly known as Green Mountain but took its present name after the forest fires of 1883, 1898 and 1910.

Dead Point Creek, HOOD RIVER. This stream is a tributary of West Fork Hood River, not far from Dee. Various maps have shown it as Dry Point Creek and Burnt Creek. Ross Winans, an early resident of the vicinity, informed the compiler that the pioneer name of this stream was Dead Point Creek, and in his opinion that was the correct name. Winans never heard it called Burnt Creek. The stream was named in contradistinction to Green Point Creek nearby, as one creek rises on a point covered with green timber and the other on a point covered with dead timber.

Deadhorse Canyon, CLACKAMAS. This canyon drains into North Fork Molalla River. Dee Wright, native of Molalla, told the compiler that in pioneer days several stray horses were lost in this canyon and perished, hence the name. Deadhorse Butte nearby took its name from the canyon.

Deadhorse Ridge, WALLOWA. Deadhorse Ridge is a prominent divide between Bear Gulch and Sheep Creek, and the northeast end is in T 1S, R 48E. Deadhorse Lake is on the ridge. According to J. H. Horner of Enterprise this lake was named by George A. Wilson and James Simmons in the late 1880s. They turned out a blooded stallion to range and the horse ran himself until too warm and was found dead in the lake.

Deadman Canyon, WASCO. Deadman Canyon was named because when the area was first settled in the 1880s a body was found in a cave near the mouth of the canyon where it empties into Ward Creek north of Willowdale.

Deadman Creek, WALLOWA. This creek in T 5S, R 46E, does not seem to have been named for a corpse. The stream drains into Imnaha River, and according to J. H. Horner of Enterprise, it was named by James Dale in the early 1890s, because he said he might just as well be dead as to be in such a lonesome place. He was a sheepherder for Aaron Wade.

Deadman Pass, UMATILLA. Deadman Pass is a gap on Emigrant Hill southeast of Pendleton and its formation is shown at the east edge of the USGS map of the Cabbage Hill quadrangle. This is not a pass for east-west travel on the Oregon Trail but is a transverse pass across the ridge, hence a dip on the highway. It gets its name as the result of an incident of the Bannock War, in July 1878, recounted by Fred Lockley on the editorial page of the *Oregon Journal*, Aug. 8, 1931. George Coggans, traveler en route from La Grande to Pendleton and four teamsters, James Myres, Olney P. McCoy, Charles McLoughlin and Thomas Smith, were killed by Indians in the vicinity of what is now known as Deadman Pass.

Deadman Spring, WASCO. This spring, in the northwest part of Warm Springs Indian Reservation, was named because an outlaw Indian was killed there many years ago by a posse.

Deadwood Creek, LANE. Deadwood Creek, which drains a considerable area in the western part of the county, flows into Lake Creek which in turn flows into Siuslaw River. Deadwood Creek got its name in early days because of the dead timber snags adjacent to its banks, the result of extensive forest fires in the Coast Range. Deadwood post office, named for the stream, was established Apr. 15, 1884, with Thomas Pope first postmaster. The office was near the mouth of Deadwood Creek, It was discontinued to Greenleaf June 15, 1914, but reopened Feb. 15, 1950.

Deady, DOUGLAS. Until World War II a flag station on the Southern Pacific line north of Roseburg and located on his donation land claim was the only geographic feature in Oregon to bear the name of one of the state's most distinguished citizens, Judge Matthew P. Deady, 1824–93. This station is now long abandoned leaving nothing to honor Deady, a pioneer of 1849, and for more than a half century a member of the bench and bar of his adopted state. He was president of the constitutional convention in 1857, and later prepared codes of civil and criminal procedures. He was for more than 30 years United States district judge for Oregon. For an estimate of his life by Harvey W. Scott, *see* Scott's *History of the Oregon Country*, v. 5, p. 188. Deady Hall at the University of Oregon, now a National Historic Landmark, bears his name. He was president of the board of regents of the university for many years.

Deal Creek, UNION. Deal Creek flows down Deal Canyon on the west edge of La Grande. It bears the name of Robert Deal who was born in Ohio in 1840 and came to La Grande by ox-team in 1864. He was in the freighting business until the arrival of the railroad in 1884. He continued in the community, farming and raising stock, until his death on Jan. 30, 1936, age 95. Robert Deal was a substantial and well-known citizen.

Dean Creek, CURRY. This creek flowing through Gold Beach was named for George Dean, an early settler and county clerk in the 1860s.

Dean Creek, GRANT. Dean Creek, east of Canyon City, was named for a man who operated a small sawmill there during the mining excitement of the 1860s.

Dean Point, TILLAMOOK. Dean Point projects southward along the west side of Nehalem River just south of the town of Nehalem. It bears the name of George Dean, well-known settler in the Nehalem area, who at one time owned land on the point.

Deardorff Mountain, BAKER, GRANT. Fleming Byars Deardorff settled in this part of eastern Oregon about 1870 and this mountain was named for him. It is 7207 feet high. There is a Deardorff Creek just southwest of the mountain, flowing into John Day River. The creek is in Grant County. Deardorff was a son of Joseph M. Deardorff, pioneer of 1853, who settled near Oakland, Douglas County, where members of the family still reside.

Deathball Rock, LANE. This rock is southeast of Blue River. It received its name because of an attempt made by a surveying party cook to bake some biscuits. It appears that he was not entirely successful. Deathball Mountain is a little southwest of Deathball Rock and seems to have been named after the rock was named. The name is found on early surveys going back to the 1880s but the exact feature named has been a subject of some controversy.

Dedman Ranch, WHEELER. Robert H. Dedman owned this ranch at the head of Dedman Canyon southeast of Fossil. The style Deadman is wrong.

Dee, HOOD RIVER. Dee was named for Thomas D. Dee, business associate of the late David C. Eccles and a stockholder in the Oregon Lumber Company. The name was used when the lumber company mill was built at Dee in 1906.

Dee Wright Observatory, DESCHUTES. This USFS structure adjacent to SH-242 just east of McKenzie Pass was built of native lava to provide shelter for the many travellers who stop to view the comparatively recent lava flows and the several major Oregon summits visible from this spot. A peak finder is located inside the building and the summits can be observed through suitably located openings in the walls. The structure is named to honor Dee Wright, a long time guide, trail builder and packer for the USFS. Wright was born near Molalla in 1872 and grew up among the Molalla Indians. He was well versed in their habits and folklore and was fluent in the Chinook Jargon. Among other projects, Wright used mules to pack the material for the Mount Hood Lookout up to Crater Rock where Lige Coalman and others back packed it to the summit. Wright was a well-known character and raconteur in western Oregon. He died in Eugene in Apr. 1934 and when the observatory was completed shortly thereafter, the USFS named it to honor his memory.

Deer Creek, DOUGLAS. This stream rises in the hills east of Roseburg and joins South Umpqua River at Roseburg. Its name dates back to pioneer days and the community of Roseburg was known as Deer Creek as late as 1854. The name of the place was subsequently changed to Roseburg because of the settlement of Aaron Rose, who settled at the site of the present city of Roseburg on Sept. 23, 1851. He crossed the plains to Oregon from Michigan in that year. *See* Roseburg.

Deer Island, COLUMBIA. Deer Island, in the Columbia River, was named by Lewis and Clark. They first visited the island on Nov. 5, 1805, on their way down the Columbia, and again on Mar. 28, 1806, on their return. It was on the second visit that the party had good luck getting venison. Captain Lewis noted in his diary that the Indian name for the island was *E-lal-lar*, or Deer Island. The compiler is unable to identify this Indian word. The town of Deer Island, which is on the mainland, was named for the island.

Deer Meadows, CLACKAMAS. R. S. Shelley and Ralph Lewis of the USFS named this meadow about 1906 when they watched a doe and fawn feed and play one Sunday morning.

Deering, JOSEPHINE. In June 1948, Fred Ahlberg was kind enough to write the compiler that Deering post office was situated in the southeast quarter of S 11, T 41S, R 9W, in the extreme southwest part of Josephine County and about a mile and a half north of the California state line. This location is about a quarter-mile east of the Redwood Highway. The post office was established in Nov. 1902, and was discontinued in Dec. 1908. David S. Webb was the only postmaster. The compiler is of the opinion that Deering post office was named for the Deering school nearby and the school was named for a family of early settlers. In July 1948, L. C. Moffitt, Josephine County school superintendent, wrote that he got this information from Lincoln Savage, who was superintendent about 1900.

Degner Canyon, JEFFERSON. Trout Creek flows through this canyon near its headwaters. Ernest and Jonathan Degner both homesteaded nearby about the time of World War I.

Del Norte, HARNEY. *Del Norte* is a Spanish expression meaning of or from the north. On July 12, 1888, a post office named Del Norte was established in Harney County, with Francis M. Jordan first and only postmaster. The office was discontinued July 20, 1889, with papers to Burns. In Sept. 1946, Archie McGowan of Burns told the compiler that Del Norte post office was in the vicinity of Saddle Butte a few miles northwest of Crane. The Jordan family lived at a place generally called the Crossing, on Malheur Slough, and moved away many years ago. No one in the locality appears to know just why the post office name was selected.

Delaine, LAKE. Delaine post office was established Aug. 5, 1912, with Walter S. Lyon first and only postmaster. The office was closed to Plush on Aug. 15, 1913.

The place was in s 9, t 35s, r 26e, and east of the Warner Valley. It is now in the Hart Mountain Antelope Refuge. This post office was named for the Delaine sheep, as Lyon ran sheep of that breed in the area. Dr. John Leonard Lyon of Lakeview was a partner in the enterprise and a brother of the postmaster. Delaine is a word that has been used to describe a number of things. It refers to a fine dress goods, and also to a superior type of soft wool. Delaine Merino sheep were developed in southwest Pennsylvania and in areas in the neighboring states of West Virginia and Ohio.

Delake, LINCOLN. A. C. Deuel, postmaster at Delake in 1925, told the writer that Delake was the name agreed upon by himself and Judge Frank L. Mann, Lincoln County resident, because it was the way many local Finnish people pronounced Devils Lake. Delake post office was near Devils Lake. It was established in Jan. 1924. On Dec. 8, 1964, Delake voted to become part of a new community to be called Lincoln City.

Delco Creek, WASCO. This stream heads on the ridge west of Cow Canyon and runs westward towards Deschutes River. It is named for Johnny Delco who herded sheep for Hinton and Ward in the late 1800s. The family is one of Oregon's oldest and descends from Jean Baptiste Delcour who came from Montreal as a fur hunter for the Hudson's Bay Company and later took a donation land claim on French Prairie.

Delena, COLUMBIA. Delena is on the Columbia River Highway east of Clatskanie. Postal records show that Delena post office was established Apr. 22, 1892, with Lincoln J. Meserve first of nine postmasters. The office was discontinued Mar. 15, 1922, although its operation was not continuous for the three decades indicated. In Nov. 1947, W. N. Meserve of Grays River, Washington, wrote the compiler that Lincoln J. Meserve, his brother, named the post office. W. N. Meserve says that his brother found the name in a classical dictionary or in a book on mythology. Stories that the place was named for a town in Nebraska are wrong, says Mr. Meserve. Also it has been reported that Delena was the name of a girl in the Meserve family, but Mr. Meserve says that this is not a fact. The compiler has been unable to find any trace of a place called Delena in Nebraska.

Dell, MALHEUR. An army map of 1887 shows a place called Dell about 10 miles northwest up Willow Creek from Vale. Dell post office was established in June 1881, with George W. Perkins first postmaster. The office continued in operation until Feb. 1911. The compiler does not know why it was named unless the title was descriptive of some locality on Willow Creek. The difficulty in getting localized information about a place like Dell is shown in the following quotation from the *Illustrated History of Baker, Grant, Malheur and Harney Counties*, p. 553, written as of about 1902: "Dell is located at Cole's ranch . . . on Willow Creek. It is simply a post office, which shifts from one ranch to another as the postmasters die or resign, or the national administration changes. In this portion of Willow Creek Valley are located some of the best hay and grain ranches in the county." To add to the difficulty about the history of the post office Dell is the fact that old postal records indicate the existence of an office called Snake that may have been a predecessor of Dell. Snake office was established Apr. 5, 1881, with James S. Stark first postmaster. The records seem to show that the name was changed to Dell within a couple of months, but the date and nature of the change are not clear. The name Snake seems to indicate that the office was on or near Snake River. The office may have been moved from Snake River not far away to Willow Creek when the name was changed.

Dellmoor, CLATSOP. Dellmoor was a station and locality about three miles north of Gearhart and just east of US-101, the Oregon Coast Highway. It was named for the late J. S. Dellinger of Astoria, editor of the *Astorian*. Dellinger, among other things, was interested in cranberry culture on Clatsop Plains, and it is probable that he devised the name Dellmoor himself. The style Delmoor is wrong and not in accord with the original spelling.

Dellwood, COOS. Dellwood is a place on South Fork Coos River about 12 miles airline east of Coos Bay. The locality was formerly called Idlewood, but when the post office was established Nov. 2, 1940, postal officials would not approve of that name because of possible confusion with Idleyld in Douglas County. Several new names were suggested, but the form Dellwood was chosen because it was not unlike the old name. Leo A. Lindros was the first postmaster and kindly sent the compiler the above information.

Delmar, COOS. Delmar is a well-known name for a place on Isthmus Slough a few miles south of Coos Bay and a little to the north of Coaledo. It is on US-101, the Oregon Coast Highway, and is near the mouth of a drain coming in from the west that is sometimes called Delmar Creek or Delmar Gulch. The best available information is to the effect that Delmar was named for Delmar Hennessey. The Hennessey family was interested in a coal mine project near the head of the gulch. Delmar post office was established Mar. 16, 1914, with Lemuel V. Cole first of five postmasters. The office was discontinued July 15, 1918, but there was still a store at Delmar in 1947 and a little commercial activity in the vicinity.

Delp Creek, LANE. This is a tributary of Fall Creek. It was named for a mining prospector, George Delp.

Dement Creek, COOS. This stream is a tributary from the west of South Fork Coquille River. It was named for Samuel M. Dement, who was said to have been the first white man who actually settled with his family in South Fork Valley. He was born in Ohio, Oct. 5, 1822. He came to California in 1852, and settled in Oregon in 1853. He died in Dec. 1885.

Democrat Gulch, JOSEPHINE. This is an historic place southeast of Kerby. It was named during the pioneer gold mining days of the Illinois Valley because of the political views of some of the prospectors.

De Moss, SHERMAN. De Moss was a station on the Union Pacific Railroad. There was at one time a post office there by the name of De Moss Springs. The station was named for a celebrated pioneer family of the county, members of which styled themselves the "Lyric Bards." They were musical entertainers, and made extended tours when wheat growing did not require their labors at home. They also operated a recreation park in connection with the springs. Professor James M. De Moss was the leader of the "Lyric Bards." He was born in Indiana May 15, 1837. He was reared in Iowa and in 1862 moved to Powder Valley, Oregon. He located in Sherman County in 1883. He is said to have been the founder of the town of North Powder, Union County, where he kept the stage station.

Dencer, MARION. Dencer post office was in operation for a few years in the Jacob Dencer home at a point about a mile or so southwest of the community called Liberty, and was named for the first postmaster. The office was established Feb. 12, 1889, with Dencer postmaster and was continued until Apr. 20, 1892, when the name was changed to Rosedale. When the name was changed the office was moved two miles southeast to the Rosedale community on Battle Creek.

Denio, HARNEY. Aaron Denio settled in this locality in 1885 and the place was named for him. The post office was established in Sept. 1888. The community was located within a few yards of the Nevada border and after World War II, a number of business establishments relocated to the south in Nevada to avail themselves of more liberal liquor and gambling laws. The post office was also moved and opened on the Nevada list on Dec. 31, 1950. Aaron Denio was born in Illinois in 1824 and after various rovings, emigrated to California in 1860. For 25 years he engaged in milling, mining and farming in California and Nevada, then settled in the extreme south edge of Oregon. He died at Denio in 1907. For additional information about his ancestry and life *see OHQ*, v. 47, pp. 200–201. For more recent information on Denio, *see* a story by Mark Kirchmeier in the *Oregonian*, June 16, 1979, p. D3.

Denmark, CURRY. The writer was informed by the postmaster of this community in 1925 that the first settlers were natives of Denmark, hence the name adopted. He must refer to Captain N. C. Lorentzen, who settled there in 1878, according to Dodge's *Pioneer History of Coos and Curry Counties*. Lorentzen and his daughter, Lena Lorentzen, were drowned near Humboldt Bay in Dec. 1892, at the time of the wreck of the barge *Majestic*.

Denning Spring, UMATILLA. This spring on the upper reaches of Pearson Creek was named for Dick Denning, a contract logger who built the road up the creek.

Dennis Creek, LANE. Dennis Creek is named for W. B. Dennis who opened the nearby Black Butte Mine in 1898. The mine produced mercury from what was once described as the largest low grade cinnabar deposit in the world but operations were sporadic and ceased many years ago.

Denson Canyon, UMATILLA. Forest H. Denson settled along this canyon near McKay Creek before World War I.

Dent, COLUMBIA. Dent was the name used for a post office from June 1892, to

Oct. 1898. Frances M. Fuller was the only postmaster. This office was a few miles west of Rainier and close to Beaver Creek. It was closed out to Delena. W. N. Meserve wrote in Nov. 1947, that the place was apparently given the family name of Mrs. U. S. Grant, but Mr. Meserve could give no reason except that the name Dent was terse. Members of the Meserve family were reared at Delena on Beaver Creek and their opinions about the history of the area are doubtless reliable.

Dent Creek, LAKE. Dent Creek is a small tributary of Honey Creek on the west side of the Warner Valley. New Camp Warner was actually on this stream, less than a mile from Honey Creek. Dent Creek was named for John H. Dent who homesteaded the land when it was opened for entry after the military departed. Dent's Final Certificate was dated Sept. 3, 1889.

Denver, CLATSOP. Denver, a locality in the Nehalem Valley, was not named for the Colorado city of the Plains, but for William J. Denver, the postmaster. The post office was established May 26, 1884, and discontinued Oct. 31, 1888. The business was turned over to the Jewell office, and little remains in the place.

Denzer, LINCOLN. This post office was named for its first postmaster, Frederick C. Denzer. It was established Apr. 10, 1909.

Depoe Bay, LINCOLN. Depoe Bay is a popular place on the Oregon Coast Highway. The exact origin of the name has been obscured by time, although there is a general knowledge of the matter. The bay and other geographic features in Lincoln County, including a creek flowing into Yaquina River near Toledo, appear to have been named for an Indian who was associated in some way with an early-day army or Indian supply depot in the Siletz territory. He assumed or was given the name Depot, but it appears to have been entered on the records as Depoe, and that is the form now generally used. The spelling Depoe has been adopted by the USBGN for the community, bay and two streams, while Depot is correct for the stream near Toledo. The name is generally pronounced without stress on either syllable. For editorial comment about the name Depoe Bay, *see* the *Oregonian*, Sept. 9, 1936, where it is said that the bay was named for Willie DePoe, a Siletz Indian. He was also known as "Old Charley" and his wife's name was Matilda. An interesting item about the bay appears under a Pendleton dateline in the *Oregon Journal* for Nov. 8, 1935, and recounts the fact that Dr. F. W. Vincent of Pendleton and his grandfather cruised up the Oregon coast north from Newport in 1878 and observed a break in the shoreline. Lowering the sails of their 40-foot boat, they finally rowed it into the little harbor. "We found there the anchor chains of a sea-going craft, two headlights and the letters 'U.S.,' so we named the little spot 'Wreckers Cove'," said Dr. Vincent. That name has not prevailed.

Depot Slough, LINCOLN. This slough forms the tidal end of Depot Creek and empties into Yaquina River near Toledo. At one time the slough was spelled Depoe and the creek Depot but the OGNB decision of June 1961, and USBGN *Decision List 6203* eliminated this inconsistency. Both features were named for William DePoe who is discussed under Depoe Bay. The spelling Depot may have been selected originally to avoid confusion with North and South Depoe Bay creeks that empty into Depoe Bay.

Derby, JACKSON. Derby, a locality northeast of Eagle Point, was named for William H. Derby, well-known local settler. The post office was established Jan. 23, 1892, with Derby first of a series of five postmasters. The office was closed May 15, 1919, with papers to Eagle Point. The locality name continues in use, even though the post office has been closed.

Derby Creek, TILLAMOOK. Derby Creek rises on Giveout Mountain and flows southeast to Nehalem River east of Cochran. In 1977 the OGNB voted to name this stream for Captain George Horatio Derby, U.S. Topographical Engineers. Derby was stationed in Oregon as a lieutenant in 1855 when he reconnoitred the military road from Astoria to the vicinity of Forest Grove. Part of the alignment followed or came near to this creek. Derby graduated from West Point in 1846. He was wounded in the Mexican War but his military career was undistinguished and he died prematurely in 1861 at age 38. However, his memory is preserved through his alternate career as a humorist. His writings under the pen name John Phoenix, Esq., appeared in the *Knickerbocker* magazine and the *Atlantic*, often accompanied by his own illustrations. For further information, *see* article by Robert Frazier in the Eugene *Register-Guard*, June 26, 1977, p. 17A, and *The Veritable Squibob* by George R. Stewart.

Derr Meadows, WHEELER. Derr Meadows west of Antone and Derr Creek running through them were named for Martin Derr, rancher from Caleb, who had summer range in the area. In the 1880s Derr built a cabin and corrals. Later when the land was taken into the national forest, the USFS established a guard station and summer ranger headquarters.

Derrick Lake, LINCOLN. This lake in S 18, T 10S, R 9W, is named for homesteader Rufus Derrick. He came to the area prior to World War I. At one time it was called Demick Lake but this was corrected in USBGN *Decision List 5401*.

Derry, POLK. This station on the line of the Southern Pacific Company just east of Rickreall was named by James W. Nesmith for Derry, New Hampshire, where his family had resided. In 1912 an effort was made to change the name of Derry to Loganberry. For editorial on the subject, *see* the *Oregonian*, Aug. 12, 1912. *See also* news items and letters, Aug. 13, 14, 1912.

Deschutes, DESCHUTES, SHERMAN, WASCO. There have been several post offices and localities in Oregon named Deschutes, in compliment to Deschutes River. In 1943 the name was used for a place between Redmond and Bend, no longer a post office but a station on the Burlington Northern, Inc. A post office named Deschutes Bridge was in operation from Mar. 3, 1860, to Dec. 6, 1860, with John Moran postmaster. It was on the Wasco County list, but Fred W. Wilson of The Dalles informed the writer that the office was doubtless at the east end of the old toll bridge over Deschutes River, near the mouth, and therefore in what is now Sherman County. A post office named Deschutes was established in July

1868, with Ezra L. Hemingway postmaster. Hemingway owned land at what is now known as Sherars Bridge and at one time owned the bridge itself. This post office was in that place. Joseph H. Sherar became postmaster on Jan. 11, 1872, and the name was changed to Sherars Bridge Jan. 4, 1883. An office called Deschutes was established Feb. 20, 1888, with Rosa Burrell postmaster. This office operated until Oct. 14, 1893, and according to Judge Wilson was probably at the east end of the bridge at the mouth of the river, in the same location as the Deschutes Bridge office first mentioned above. In later years a railroad station named Deschutes was established at the mouth of Deschutes River and when the railroad was built up the Deschutes Canyon a station called Deschutes Junction was established about a mile and a half east of Deschutes. When the railroad reached central Oregon, Fred S. Stanley asked that the name Deschutes be given a station between Redmond and Bend. Stanley was accommodated and the two older stations at the mouth of the river were changed. Deschutes was named Miller and Deschutes Junction was named Sherman, which was changed to Ainsworth in Oct. 1930. In the meantime Bend post office was established Jan. 18, 1886 with John Sisemore postmaster. This office was probably in the Sisemore cabin in the south part of what is now Bend. Sisemore asked for the name Farewell Bend, but the postal authorities objected to two words. After some other incumbents, William H. Staats became postmaster of the Bend office on Apr. 18, 1899. The records are not quite clear from this point. Staats apparently tried to change the name of the office to Pilot Butte, and this was ordered May 13, 1901, but for some reason the new name was not actually used. Staats' next move was to get the name of the Bend office changed to Deschutes on Dec. 30, 1902. It is reported that Staats took the office away from the Sisemore place to his own locality further downstream, but the date of this move cannot be determined from the records. On Mar. 7, 1904, a new Bend office was established near the former Pilot Butte Inn and began to compete with Staats' Deschutes office. The Deschutes office operated until June 1906, when it was discontinued. The name Deschutes was given to the office between Redmond and Bend in July 1911.

Deschutes County. This county was created Dec. 13, 1916, out of a part of Crook County. Bend is the county seat. Deschutes County was named for Deschutes River which was known during the period of fur trading as *Riviere des Chutes* or River of the Falls. For derivation of the name, *see* Deschutes River. The County has an area of 3040 square miles.

Deschutes River, DESCHUTES, JEFFERSON, KLAMATH, SHERMAN, WASCO. Lewis and Clark discovered the Deschutes River on Tuesday, Oct. 22, 1805, and referred to it by an Indian name *Towornehiooks*. *See* Thwaites' *Original Journals of the Lewis and Clark Expedition*, v. 3, p. 147. However, on their return journey the explorers called the stream Clarks River, presumably for William Clark. (v. 4, p. 292, and also atlas volume, map 32, part 1, and map 40.) Neither of these names prevailed. The Klamath Indians apparently referred to the Deschutes as *Ko-*

lamkeni Koke. Koke was a general name for stream, while *kolam* referred to a wild root used for food, possibly a species of *Aralia*. *Keni* was a suffix meaning place. A literal translation would be stream of the place where the kolam grew. In the fur trading period the stream was known as *Riviere des Chutes* or *Riviere aux Chutes*, meaning River of the Falls. As a result of the modern tendency to simplify geographic names, the expression is now universally written Deschutes. The trappers applied their name because the river flowed into the Columbia near the falls of that river and not because of any falls in the Deschutes itself. The following two quotations show this very clearly: ". . . I lost no time in joining Mr. Finan McDonalds party who I found encamped on the River of the Falls of the Columbia, about four days march from the Main stream." Peter Skene Ogden under date of Oct. 10, 1826, in *Fur Trade and Empire*, p. 281: "3. Mr. Ogden Hunted last winter in the Space of country Bounded on the north by the Head waters of the River of the Columbia falls, on the west by the Umqua, from thence East to the River Malheur in the Snake Country." John McLoughlin, Aug. 11, 1827, in *The Letters of John McLoughlin, First Series*, p. 49. F. N. Blanchet, in *Historic Notes*, 1883, p. 14, has a paragraph about the name *La Riviere des Chutes* and says that it was for the *Chutes* in the Columbia River and not for the falls in the stream itself. The Rev. A. F. Waller, in his diary under date of May 8, 1845, refers to the Deschutes River by an Indian name, *Wanawont*. The diary gives no explanation of the name.

Desert, JEFFERSON. Desert post office was established June 21, 1890, with William G. Rogers first postmaster. It was named for the surroundings. The office was closed in Apr. 1892. The record shows that an effort was made to revive the office in May 1904, with James O. Colb postmaster, but apparently the revival was not completed. It is possible that the 1904 office was in a different location from the earlier office. According to information sent by Devere Helfrich of Klamath Falls, Desert post office was in the northwest part of T 13S, R 14E, near Gray Butte School. According to Mr. Helfrich it is probable that Desert post office was at different times in sections 5 and 6 of the township mentioned above, and very close to the first location of Lamonta post office. Mr. Helfrich was born in the immediate neighborhood. Desert and Lamonta post offices were between ten and twelve miles airline southward of Madras.

Desert Cone, KLAMATH. Desert Cone is north of Crater Lake, and has an elevation of 6651 feet. It is at the west edge of Pumice Desert, and is named on that account.

Desert Ridge, DOUGLAS, KLAMATH. This ridge is north of Crater Lake, and has an elevation of 6941 feet at its highest point. It is about a mile long. It gets its name because it is just west of Pumice Desert.

Despain Gulch, UMATILLA. Despain Gulch is east of Hermiston, and the intermittent stream therein flows into Cold Springs Reservoir. This gulch was named for Jerry DeSpain, prominent Umatilla County pioneer.

Deter, JACKSON. Deter post office was named for the David M. Deter family.

This family owned a cattle ranch near the site of the post office. Deter was a flag station on the Southern Pacific Company line in the Siskiyou Mountains a couple of miles south of the summit tunnel, probably at what was once known as Gravel Pit Spur, one mile north of Colestin. The post office was established July 15, 1920, with Grace Deter postmaster and finally closed in 1931.

Detroit, MARION. Charles C. Giebeler, the well-known postmaster and packer of Detroit, wrote the compiler in 1925 that the first name suggested for this community was Coe, but the post office authorities disapproved of the name because it was too much like Cove in eastern Oregon. Detroit was the name then selected because of the presence in the community of a number of Michigan people. Detroit post office was established Oct. 16, 1891, with Vanness G. Danforth first postmaster. The original townsite was inundated in the summer of 1952 when the USCE finished Detroit Dam, a 463 foot high concrete gravity structure that impounds 340,000 acre feet of water and has an installed generating capacity of 100,000 kilowatts. Detroit community was relocated about half a mile northwest of the original site on slightly higher ground. It is now a popular headquarters for water sports.

Devils Backbone, CLACKAMAS. This is a narrow divide between Sandy and Bull Run rivers. It was named in pioneer days because of the great difficulty emigrants experienced in getting their wagons past the place.

Devils Backbone, KLAMATH. Well named. This is a gigantic series of serrated rocks forming a vertical backbone on the inside rim of Crater Lake. Its name is imaginative.

Devils Canyon, GILLIAM. There are a number of canyons of this name in the state, at least two of which are in Gilliam County, opening into the canyon of John Day River. They are so called on account of the unusual rock formations suggestive of satanic influences, and also because they are so difficult to get through.

Devils Garden, LAKE. Devils Garden is northeast of Fort Rock. It is an irregular area of several square miles, with a growth of juniper trees. It is surrounded by extensive lava flows, which form a striking contrast to the enclosed tract which is mostly of ordinary soil. The surrounding lava has given the place its name.

Devils Horn, DESCHUTES. This butte of peculiar color is in the south part of Paulina Mountains. It is composed of lava of a reddish hue, and its shape is suggestive of the name that has been given it. It is several hundred feet high.

Devils Lake, LINCOLN. Devils Lake is near the Pacific Ocean in the northwest part of the county. It was named because of an Indian legend which is to the effect that a giant fish or marine monster lived in the lake and occasionally came to the surface to attack some hapless native. There are several versions of the story but this one is sufficient to indicate the origin of the name. The post office was called Delake, a corruption of Devils Lake. *See also* Neotsu.

Devils Lake Fork, TILLAMOOK, WASHINGTON. Devils Lake Fork, one of the larger tributaries of Wilson River, heads in the extreme west edge of Washington County and flows northwest to join the main stream near Wilson River Highway. The fork has become well known in recent years because of the conspicuous steel viaduct that carries the highway over the stream. Devils Lake Fork takes its name from the fact that it drains a small body of water called Devils Lake, so called as a result of Indian nomenclature. The Indians, particularly of the Coast Range region, were fearful of a number of lakes and localities that were supposed to be inhabited by skookums, or evil wood-spirits. Some of the lakes are still called Skookum lakes, others are called Devils lakes. Many Indians avoided these places, and considered them haunted.

Devils Pulpit, HOOD RIVER. This is a prominent shelf or bench on the east slope of Preachers Peak, at the summit of the Cascade Range, south of Lost Lake. It was named when R. S. Shelley of the USFS named Preachers Peak for his father. The remark was made that if the preacher were there, the Devil wouldn't be far away. *See also* Preachers Peak.

Devils Run, WALLOWA. Devils Run is a stream flowing into Chesnimnus Creek in the southwest corner of T 4N, R 47E. It was named because of the roughness and swiftness of the water.

Devils Stairway, DOUGLAS. This series of rocky ridges is in S 26, T 25S, R 2E. Before the USFS trail was developed, it was difficult to traverse and Perry Wright, an early settler, named it Devils Ladder. This was later changed to the present form.

Devine Canyon, HARNEY. Devine Canyon is north of Burns, and is traversed by the Canyon City-Burns Highway, US-395. Devine Ridge is nearby. They bear the name of John Devine, noted Harney County pioneer. John S. Devine was born in Richmond, Virginia, in Nov. 1839, and settled in Harney County in 1868, where he made his home until his death in Burns, Sept. 1901. The firm of Todhunter & Devine established the famous Whitehorse Ranch in the south end of the county, and the partners were among the so-called cattle barons, around whom gathered so much controversy. There is a Devine Rock near Wildhorse Lake and Devine Flat near Crowcamp Creek, both named for John Devine. The John Devine monument in Devine Canyon was dedicated on July 22, 1928. For description of exercises and address by John W. Biggs of Burns, *see OHQ*, v. 29, p. 236. The selection of the name Devine Canyon is curious because its location is far from Devine's area of operation and there is nothing to connect him to this feature. In 1990 it was reported that the monument was in disrepair and the drinking fountain had been turned off due to a contaminated water supply.

Devitt, BENTON. This community got its name from the two Devitt brothers who operated a sawmill nearby for a number of years.

Dewey, YAMHILL. Dewey is a crossroads locality about five miles northeast of Yamhill and near the north end of Ribbon Ridge. The Lakeview School is in the same general locality. Dewey post office was established on June 21, 1898, with

P. W. Watkins postmaster. The country was ringing with praise for Admiral George Dewey at the time because of his victory at the battle of Manila Bay, and the office was named in his honor. The office was discontinued on Sept. 30, 1904. Lakeview School was so named because it overlooks Wapato Lake to the north.

Dewies Canyon, JEFFERSON. This canyon rises in the Baldwin Hills and empties into Mud Springs Creek. It was named for Frank L. Dewies who applied for a homestead near its head in 1914.

Dexter, LANE. Dexter post office was established in May 1872, and was first called Butte Disappointment. This name was derived from a local landmark which was so named by pioneers in 1848. On July 19, 1875, the post office name was changed to Dexter. Samuel Handsaker, was then postmaster. His son, John Handsaker, in an interview with Myron Tinker, Eugene *Register-Guard*, June 3, 1951, stated that the family had a "Dexter" brand cook stove with the name emblazoned on the front. He always understood that the name of the cook stove was the source of the place-name.

Deyoe Creek, TILLAMOOK. Deyoe Creek is a tributary of Devils Lake Fork, Wilson River, near its headwaters. It is named for Daniel and Jacob Deyoe who took up adjacent government land about 1900. The form Deo Creek is incorrect.

Diablo Mountain, LAKE. *Diablo* is the Spanish word for devil. Diablo Mountain is east of the north end of Summer Lake, and has an elevation of 6145 feet, according to the USC&GS. Diablo Canyon is nearby. It is said that the canyon was named first, because it was rough and difficult to travel, and the name, Diablo Mountain, came later. The name, Mount Diablo, appears to be wrong.

Diamond Craters, HARNEY. Diamond Craters and the old Diamond post office both got their names from the Diamond Ranch, which was established in pioneer days by Mace McCoy. This ranch used a diamond-shaped brand. Mrs. Dolly Kiger applied the name of the ranch to the community about 1874, according to information given the writer by C. H. Smyth, postmaster at Diamond in 1925. In 1927 Mrs. Minerva J. Kiger, of Corvallis, wrote the compiler that she was the Dolly Kiger referred to above. She confirmed the history of the name Diamond as given herein. Diamond Craters are about six miles northwest of Diamond post office site. There are about 20 of them occupying an area of some five square miles, described in USGS *Bulletin 217*. In the 1970s the craters were in the news because stone dealers were removing the *pahoehoe* or sheet lava to sell for veneer stone. The variety of craters and other examples of volcanism within such a small space makes the area unique and the BLM has made various plans to protect it. There is an excellent illustrated article by Connie Hofferber in the *Oregonian*, Aug. 3, 1979, p. E1, and a follow up by Pauline Braymen, Apr. 2, 1982, p. D2, when Interior Secretary James Watt designated it an Outstanding Natural Area.

Diamond Hill, LINN. Diamond Hill is on the east edge of the Willamette Valley about six miles north of the south line of Linn County, and about ten miles north of Coburg, Lane County. The compiler is of the opinion that Diamond Hill was named for John Diamond, prominent Lane County pioneer, whose home was near Coburg. Diamond Peak and Diamond Lake in the Cascade Range were named for the same man. John Diamond was born in Londonderry, Ireland, in 1815, and emigrated to New York in 1833. He lived at times in the states of New York, Michigan, Illinois, and emigrated to Oregon in 1847. He took up a claim where the town of Coburg now stands. He sold the property in 1858, and after three years of traveling, settled just east of Coburg. For additional biographical information, *see* Walling's *History of Lane County*, p. 488. Along with other pioneers, he made explorations into the Cascade Range, which accounts for the application of his name to geographical features in that area. The compiler does not know the circumstances of the naming of Diamond Hill. It seems certain that Diamond did not live in the locality, which was about ten miles north of his homestead. He may have had some business interests there, or possibly pastured stock there. John Diamond was a sturdy citizen and neighbors may have complimented him on that account. Diamond Hill post office was established on the Linn County list on Sept. 16, 1858, with James H. Pierce first postmaster. This office was closed Sept. 28, 1869. An office with the name Diamond was in service from Apr. 23, 1887, to Oct. 4, 1887, with David H. Pierce postmaster. It was doubtless in the same community.

Diamond Lake, DOUGLAS. This is one of the important mountain lakes of Oregon, and lies in the southeast part of the county between Mt. Thielsen and Mt. Bailey. It has an elevation of 5182 feet. About 1927 George H. Kelly of Portland and Wm. P. Vandevert of Bend, both of whom were familiar with the history of the middle Cascade Range, informed the compiler that Diamond Lake was named for John Diamond. This was the same man for whom Diamond Peak was named. Diamond discovered the lake from the summit of Diamond Peak in 1852. The name has nothing to do with the shape of the lake. *See* Diamond Hill.

Diamond Lake, KLAMATH. Diamond Lake is a station on the Cascade line of the Southern Pacific just northeast of Beaver Marsh. It was named for the large lake about 20 miles westward. In 1911, when the Oregon Trunk was surveying a railroad from Bend to Klamath Falls, Joseph Ringo platted a community named Lonroth in S17, T28S, R8E. In the 1920s when the Southern Pacific Cascade line was built, they named their station at this location Lonroth. They also had a station five miles south named Diamond Lake. Shortly after the line was opened, the railroad changed the name from Lonroth to Diamond Lake and renamed the other Diamond Lake station Yamsay. This was about 1926. Edward Gray in *History of Early Northern Klamath County*, p. 270, says Ringo named the townsite for an associate of the Hunter Land Company. Earlier editions of this book say the name came from Elias Lonnrot, 1802–1884, Finnish philologist and discoverer of the *Kalevala*, the great epic of Finland. The reader may choose either source.

Diamond Lake, UNION. Diamond Lake is in T 5S, R 43E, and drains into Elk Creek, a tributary of Minam River. Diamond Lake was not named because of its shape. The lake is inaccessible and a sheep herder named Diamond agreed to stock it with fish, which was a difficult task, owing to the rugged character of the surrounding country. The lake was named for him.

Diamond Peak, KLAMATH, LANE. This is a fine peak of the Cascade Range, and has an elevation of 8750 feet according to the USGS. For the geography of the region surrounding the mountain, *see* the USGS map of the Diamond Peak quadrangle. The writer has been told that there is a small living glacier on Diamond Peak, but he has no direct knowledge of it. Diamond Peak was named in 1852 for John Diamond, pioneer settler near Coburg, Oregon, who was a member of a party of road viewers opening a road between Middle Fork Willamette River and Idaho for an immigration route. The report is contained in the *Journal* of the Oregon territorial council, 1852–53. *Appendix*, pp. 13–15. Other viewers were: William M. Macy, W. T. Walker, William Tandy, Alexander King, Joseph Meadows and J. Clarke. For additional references, *see* Scott's *History of the Oregon Country*, v. 4, p. 8. For information about John Diamond, *see* editorial page of the *Oregon Journal*, June 4, 1931.

Diamond Prairie, WALLOWA. This little prairie is west of the town of Wallowa. It is said to be named because of its shape.

Diamond Rockpile, LANE. This point is in the southeast corner of the county south of Diamond Peak and has an elevation of 6437 feet. It received its name because of its peculiar formation and its nearness to Diamond Peak.

Dibblee Point, COLUMBIA. Dibblee Point is on the old Dibblee farm four miles west of Rainier where the Columbia River bends west. John Dibblee was born in New Brunswick, Canada. In 1862 he married Sarah Weston and two years later they came to California. In 1869 they moved to Oregon and Dibblee bought Charles North's donation land claim where he ran a substantial dairy farm for many years. John Dibblee died in 1910 but his son, H. R. Dibblee, continued the operation and was a prominent citizen of the area. In later years a sand island formed in the river north of Dibblee Point. This was sometimes known as Dibblee Island but the correct name is Lord Island.

Dick Bluff, CROOK. Dick Bluff is south of Opal Mountain in S 10, T 12S, R 18E. It and nearby Dick Creek, a tributary of Trout Creek, were both named for Dick Hinton of Antelope who grazed sheep in the area prior to the creation of the National Forest. The early form was Dicks Bluff but the possessive has been dropped for many years.

Dick Point, TILLAMOOK. John A. Biggs, who was born nearby, told the writer in 1971 that when he was a very small boy, an Indian called Indian Dick lived at this spot near the mouth of the Tillamook River.

Dickey Prairie, CLACKAMAS. Dickey Prairie is about four miles east-southeast of Molalla. The prairie was an old Molalla Indian campground. The property was homesteaded by one of the Dickey family and it was given his name by general usage.

Diffin, GRANT. Jimmy Diffin is said to have been the last surviving resident of the old mining town of Robisonville in the Blue Mountains south of Granite, and Diffin post office was probably named for him. Former County Judge R. R. McHaley of Prairie City has an interesting paragraph about Jimmy Diffin in a letter published in the Canyon City *Eagle* for Mar. 7, 1947. Diffin preserved his independence till the very end and refused to be sent to the county farm as a public charge. He was frequently called "49 Jimmy." Diffin post office was established Mar. 19, 1890, with John H. Mitchell the first and only postmaster. The office was discontinued Apr. 10, 1891.

Dillard, DOUGLAS. John Dillard, for whom the town of Dillard was named, was born in Missouri in 1813 and came to Oregon by ox team in 1850. In 1852 he settled on a donation land claim about 11 miles south of Roseburg and when the railroad was built through that part of the state about 1882 a station was established and named for Dillard. He continued to live on his claim until his death in 1892. *See* Down's *A History of the Silverton Country*, p. 132, note 19.

Diller Glacier, DESCHUTES. This is a large important glacier on the east slope of Middle Sister. It was named for Dr. Joseph Silas Diller, for many years connected with the USGS and the authority on the geology of western Oregon. He was the author of a number of important bulletins of the USGS and several geologic folios. His most popular work was the Geological Survey's *Guidebook of the Western United States*, Part D., *The Shasta Route*. The name Diller Glacier seems to have been applied by Dr. I. C. Russell of the USGS in Aug. 1903. *See* USGS *Bulletin 252*, p. 125. Dr. Diller was born in Pennsylvania in 1850 and graduated from Harvard (Lawrence) in 1879. He joined the USGS in 1883 and was a valued member of the organization until his retirement in 1923. Most of his field-work was in southwest Oregon and northern California. His knowledge of the geology of those areas was profound. He died at Washington, D.C. Nov. 13, 1928.

Dilley, WASHINGTON. Dilley was named for Milton E. Dilley, pioneer resident. Dilley post office was established Dec. 31, 1873 and continued until May 1, 1961. For a description in the 1970s, *see* the *Oregonian*, Feb. 22, 1977, p. B3W.

Dillon, WASCO. This was a station on the railroad near the Celilo Canal. It was named for an army officer, Captain Theo. H. Dillon, who was a member of the engineer corps and assisted in the construction of the canal. One of the construction camps was known as Dillon's Camp, which the railroad company called Dillon.

Dillon Falls, DESCHUTES. This white water cataract on Deschutes River some nine miles southwest of Bend is well known to anglers. The name is derived from Leander Dillon who homesteaded nearby about 1890 and later figured in the timber claim contests of 1906. Dillon moved to Prineville and died there in a fire on Jan. 25, 1907.

Dinah-mo Peak, MARION. This is a 6441 foot high peak about three miles north of Jefferson Park. It was named in 1985 to commemorate Dinah Beth Ross who was born in Wisconsin in 1956 and came to Oregon in 1977 after extensive travel in Europe and Asia. Dinah Ross had a great love and respect for nature and wilderness. She was a resource specialist and taught for the Multnomah County Outdoor Education Program. She moved to Breitenbush Hot Springs where she became assistant business manager and led many wilderness hiking and cross country ski tours. She was killed in an automobile accident Sept. 9, 1983, and there was an immediate movement by the community and a number of outdoor organizations to honor her memory. The selection of this prominent, unnamed peak met with unanimous approval and the USBGN concurred in *Decision List 8503*.

Dinger Lake, CLACKAMAS. Forest ranger Joe Graham of Clackamas Lake is authority for the statement that this lake was named because Mack Holloman caught fine trout therein, calling them "humdingers." Only the last part of the word was applied to the lake.

Dinner Creek, CLACKAMAS. Dinner Creek is a small stream tributary to Clackamas River about two miles above Roaring River. W. C. Elliott, well-known civil engineer of Portland, told the writer that he named the stream in 1897 because his surveying party stopped there for dinner.

Dinwiddie Valley, LINN. C. H. Stewart of Albany wrote the compiler in 1927 as follows: "This valley, in the hills southwest of Brownsville, I am told was named for a little old bowlegged Scotchman named Hugh Dinwiddie, who for many years was secretary of the Brownsville Woolen Mills."

Dipping Vat Creek, WHEELER. This creek rises south of Little Summit Prairie and flows to Paulina Basin. There are Dipping Vat creeks and springs also in Grant, Harney and Malheur counties and numerous similar names elsewhere in eastern Oregon. They originated with an act of the 1907 Legislature "To suppress and avoid contagious and infectious diseases among sheep." Prior to that time, scab and other afflictions had wiped out the native rimrock sheep. Serious infection of domestic sheep prompted the legislation which included provision for a State Sheep Inspector and an annual dip to U.S. Department of Agriculture specifications. The animals were totally immersed and where flocks ran into the thousands, a large water supply was needed. Consequently many streams and springs bear the name of this early, odoriferous adjunct of the large bands of range sheep.

Discovery Point, KLAMATH. Crater Lake was discovered on June 12, 1853, by John W. Hillman and a party of prospectors. The party first came on the lake at a point on the southwest rim. This place has since been called Discovery Point to commemorate the event.

Disston, LANE. Disston post office was established Oct. 25, 1906, with Crampton Jones first postmaster. The early records show his name as Cranston Jones, but Mrs. R. L. Gawley informed the compiler in 1967 that she knew Jones well and was present when he received notice of the appointment. Her husband was one of the organizers of the first saw mill at Disston and she stated that the name of the mill and town both came from the well-known Disston saws.

Divers Creek, HOOD RIVER. L. M. Baldwin of Hood River gave the compiler the following interesting facts about this name. Davis Divers came to Oregon City in 1852 and moved to Hood River Valley in 1862 where he took up a homestead not far from Odell. While raising a large family, he would frequently travel afoot over the mountains to Oregon City by way of what came to be known as the Divers Trail. Baldwin's uncle told him that he had been over the trail many years ago and thought it had originally been a route used by Indians in the area. It is not clear whether the creek was named to honor Divers or because the Divers Trail crossed it.

Divide, DOUGLAS, LANE. Divide is a natural name for a station on the Southern Pacific a few miles southwest of Cottage Grove on the watershed between the Willamette and the Umpqua rivers. Eastward the drainage is toward Coast Fork Willamette River and to the west is Pass Creek, a tributary to Elk Creek. Divide station is in Lane County close to or on the summit. The actual divide has an elevation of about 740 feet while the benchmark in the overpass over both the railroad and I-5 is 766 feet. Divide post office was established to serve this neighborhood on May 31, 1900, with Edna Hedrick first postmaster. This office was on the Douglas County post office list. The office is shown on the Lane County list as of May 10, 1909, and it was discontinued Jan. 15, 1921. The office may have actually been moved from one county to the other, the writer thinks it probable that a relocation of the county boundary brought about the change.

Divide, WALLOWA. Divide was the name of a post office that operated in Wallowa County from Jan. 1891, until Nov. 1893, with Annie E. Shaw first postmaster. This office was situated in what is called the Divide country between Sheep Creek on the east and Little Sheep Creek on the west. When Annie E. Shaw had the office it was in S 11, T 3S, R 46E, and during the rest of its existence it was not far away. When the office was first asked for, it was suggested by Joe Wasson that it be named Threebuck because it was near the headwaters of that stream, but it was decided that the name was too cumbersome.

Dixie, BAKER. Dixie, a locality on Burnt River about five miles north of Lime, was named because it was near the confluence of Burnt River and Dixie Creek, which flows in from the west. Dixie Creek was named in the mining days because of the prevalence of southerners on its upper reaches. Dixie post office was established Mar. 21, 1913, and was discontinued Apr. 30, 1924. The post office was not in the mining area, but close to the railroad along Burnt River. In the 1980s little remained but the sign to mark the location of the community.

Dixie, WASHINGTON. Dixie post office was established in the extreme northeast corner of Washington County on Nov. 21, 1887, with John Dix first of four postmasters. It seems obvious that the office was named for the family of the postmaster and not for Dixie, the land of the magnolia and the mockingbird. The office was five or six miles southwest of Scappoose, and when it was closed May 4, 1905, it was closed to that office. The name Dixie Mountain is still used for a prominent ridge in that part of the state. The fact that the office was named for the family was confirmed by a letter dated Feb. 2, 1948, signed by W. D. Moreland of the Skyland Land Company, which operated in Multnomah and Washington counties. Mr. Moreland said that when real estate in this area was put on the market in 1933 it became desirable to adopt a name for the locality. The property was near Wallace school, but that name was considered rather unsatisfactory. A community picnic was held about 1936–37 at the John Tannock picnic grounds. There was a good deal of discussion about a place name. When a formal vote was taken nearly 80 percent of those present were in favor of Dixie to commemorate the old Dixie post office and John Dix, its postmaster.

Dixie Creek, GRANT. This stream flows into John Day River near Prairie City. Patsy Daly of Prairie City told the compiler in 1927 that the stream was named during the mining excitement of the early 1860s because there were so many southerners mining along its banks.

Dixie Jett Gulch, WALLOWA. Dixie Jett Gulch drains into Sheep Creek in T 2S, R 47E. The name is an odd one, and was applied to commemorate a settler who built a cabin in the canyon. The compiler has been furnished with several spellings of this man's name, all purporting to be the veritable form. These include: Dick Se Jett, Dixie Jett and Dick Surjett. The man himself, a prospector and hunter, went his way many years ago. The USFS uses the spelling Dixie Jett because it is the simplest and is in general use.

Dixon, WASCO. Dixon is a station on the Burlington Northern, Inc. line in Deschutes Canyon. It was named for T. F. Dixon, former vice president and general manager of the Spokane Portland and Seattle Railway.

Dixon Creek, BENTON. Dixon Creek, north of Corvallis, was named for William F. Dixon, pioneer of Oregon, who took up a donation land claim nearby. For information about him, *see* land office certificate 903.

Dixonville, DOUGLAS. Dixonville is about five miles east of Roseburg. The post office was established Sept. 16, 1901, and named for R. B. Dixon who owned the land where the post office and other buildings were situated.

Do Little Flat, WHEELER. Grover C. Blake told the compiler that this flat south of Lawson Mountain was named because the local homesteaders had little or nothing to do. In the peak of the homestead activity after the turn of the century, many settlers would eke out a minimum existence until they were able to patent their land and then would immediately sell to one of the large and well organized local ranchers.

Doane Creek, POLK. Doane empties into South Yamhill River two miles southwest of Willamina. It takes its name from Nehemiah Doane whose donation land claim included the mouth of the stream. Some maps show Doane Creek as the smaller stream three quarters of a mile to the west but that is incorrect.

Doane Lake, MULTNOMAH. Doane Lake is an overflow lake on the west bank of the Willamette River near the Burlington Northern, Inc. bridge. Doane Point is in the same neighborhood. These features were named for Milton Doane who took up a donation land claim there. Doane's name has been spelled several ways, and it appears as Done on land office plats, but he could not read and write, hence the variety of styles. Doane is the form in general use, and adopted by the USBGN. The lake has been filled with material dredged from the river.

Dobry Point, WASCO. This point above Lost Creek north of the Barlow Road was named for Jack Dobry, an employee of the USFS before World War II.

Doc Canyon, WALLOWA. This canyon drains into Bear Creek, south of Wallowa. It was named for one "Doc" Cussins who herded sheep nearby.

Dodge, CLACKAMAS. Dodge, a place about four miles southeast of Springwater, was named for a local family. The post office was established Mar. 25, 1896, with Almon T. Dodge first of five postmasters. The office was closed May 31, 1914.

Dodge Canyon, DOUGLAS. Dodge Canyon, west of Oakland, was named for J. R. Dodge, who took up a donation land claim near its mouth.

Dodge Island, MULTNOMAH. Dodge Island is in Bull Run Lake. It was named in honor of Frank T. Dodge, superintendent of Portland Water Works, 1889–1913. A metal tablet was installed on a rock on this small islet in Sept. 1918. For a photograph of the tablet, *see* the *Oregonian*, May 12, 1918. For an article about the dedication of the tablet, Sept. 15, 1918.

Dodson, MULTNOMAH. Dodson is a railroad station just west of Warrendale. The name of the station comes from Ira Dodson, an early settler in that part of the county. Dodson station has been moved several times and was once near the present location of Warrendale.

Dodson Mountain, DOUGLAS. Dodson Mountain is an important peak east of Dillard, with an elevation of about 3200 feet. It was named for Samuel Dodson, pioneer stockman who settled nearby. His land was still owned in 1926 intact by his son, Samuel Dodson, Jr.

Doerner Creek, DOUGLAS. George Abdill of Roseburg informed the writer in 1969 that Doerner Creek north of Flournoy Valley was named for John Doerner who came to Douglas County in the 1880s and farmed along the stream. His son, Charles Doerner, was county clerk of Douglas County for a number of years.

Dog Creek, DOUGLAS. This creek rises south of Dog Mountain and flows into North Umpqua River just west of Horseshoe Bend. It was named in 1916 by Perry Wright, an early settler. Wright, with two dogs, was crossing the creek on a partly submerged log over very turbulent water. The dogs both slipped off and were only rescued with considerable difficulty. This again goes to show that man is a dog's best friend.

Dog Lake, LAKE. Dog Lake is west of Goose Lake and was formerly called Dogleg Lake because its outline on a map is strongly suggestive of a dog's hind leg. The name has become contracted as a matter of convenience. Dog Mountain to the north takes its name from the lake.

Dog River, HOOD RIVER. In pioneer days Hood River was known as Dog River because a party of travelers ate dog meat there in preference to starving. Mrs. Nathaniel Coe of Hood River Valley objected to the name, and secured a change to Hood River, on account of Mount Hood. The name Dog River is now applied to a stream heading in Brooks Meadows southeast of Parkdale, and flowing into East Fork Hood River. It is the source of The Dalles water supply. *See* Hood River.

Dog Thief Point, CLATSOP. Dog Thief Point overlooks the Sunset Highway about seven miles east of Elsie. It is near the old Astoria-Tualatin Plains Military Road of 1855, and there has been a supposition that the name is a corruption of "Dog Robber," the military slang for an officer's orderly. In early 1980 after some lengthy investigation by a number of people, J. W. Forrester, Jr., of Astoria forwarded the following facts provided by Henry Rierson, lifelong resident of the area. Rierson stated that about 1900, two men from Astoria were walking east over the military road. They stopped for the night at Joe Lynch's place near Elsie and after they left the following morning, Lynch found that his shepherd dog was missing. He gave chase and later found the men with his dog camped in a lean-to on the mountain. The animal returned to Elsie with his master, Lynch proclaimed that the hill should be called Dog Thief Mountain and another strange place name entered the Oregon rolls.

Doghouse Gulch, GRANT. Doghouse Gulch, which drains into South Fork John Day River about 15 miles south of Dayville, got its name as a result of a sarcastic reference to a shanty occupied by a sheepherder. The structure apparently was short of some of the modern conveniences.

Dogwood Creek, CLATSOP. This stream is about 18 miles east of Astoria. It was at one time known as Hall Creek, after an early settler, but the name did not persist. There are few trees of the forest that are held in such affectionate esteem as the dogwood, and yet the name of the tree is almost never used for a geographic feature. At least that is the situation in Oregon, where hundreds of place-names have been applied for firs, cedars, pines, oaks, willows and cottonwoods. The Pacific dogwood, *Cornus nuttallii*, is a lovely tree and should not be neglected.

Dole, DOUGLAS. Dole is a station on the Southern Pacific Railroad four and a half miles north of Myrtle Creek near the site of the old Ruckles station. It apparently was named for Edward Dole who married the daughter of early settler Samuel L. Stevenson.

Dollar Lake, HOOD RIVER. This lake is near the north end of Barrett Spur, north of Mount Hood. The name is descriptive. Richard J. Grace of Portland wrote the compiler: "Dollar Lake is apt, as the lake is very small for a permanent one and is almost perfectly round."

Dollar Lake, WALLOWA. Dollar Lake is in the Wallowa Mountains in T 4S, R 45E, and was named by J. Fred McClain because it was so nearly circular.

Dollarhide, JACKSON. In 1875, H. C. Dollarhide filed on land along the old stage road from Ashland to Siskiyou summit where he farmed and kept the travel. When the railroad was built through in 1887, the alignment at this point made a wide turn to gain elevation. This was known as Dollarhide Curve and at one time was the location of a station.

Dolph, TILLAMOOK. This community was named for Joseph N. Dolph, who came to Portland in 1862. He served as city attorney and as United States attorney and also in the state legislature. He served as United States senator from Oregon in 1883–95, and had large influence in the Senate and was a close friend of President Harrison. He was born in New York in 1835 and died in Portland in 1897. *See* the *Oregonian* for Mar. 11 and Mar. 19, 1897. Dolph was named for him while he was in the Senate. It was for a time a post office.

Dominic, MARION. This was a station northeast of Mount Angel. It was named for Father P. Dominic, O.S.B., for many years a moving spirit in the activities of Mount Angel College.

Dompier Creek, DOUGLAS. Dompier Creek flows into South Umpqua River two and one half miles northeast of Tiller. It was named for a family of early settlers.

Don Lake, LINN. This small lake in T 12S, R 6E, was named for Don Carlos Stahlman, son of Fred Stahlman the early USFS district ranger at Detroit.

Donaca Lake, LINN. Donaca Lake is south of Detroit, and drains through Donaca Creek into Middle Santiam River. W. B. Donaca came to Oregon in 1852 and settled in Linn County in 1861. For a good many years he was a merchant in Lebanon. This lake and the creek were named for him or for some member of his family.

Donahue Creek, MULTNOMAH. This small tributary of Bridal Veil Creek is the only feature on the map today that remains to commemorate the Bridal Veil Lumber Company operation on the slopes of Larch Mountain. Part of their logging was contracted to Donahue & Kelley with M. C. Donahue supervising. The lumber company operated a railroad from their mill at Palmer south along the slopes of Larch Mountain and there was a station named Donahue where the railroad crossed this creek not far from the present Larch Mountain Road.

Donald, MARION. Donald is a station on the Oregon Electric Railway, on French Prairie, northwest of Woodburn, and was named for the late R. L. Donald, of Portland, who was an official of the construction company that built the railway.

Donaldson Canyon, MORROW. This canyon south of Heppner was named for Samuel C. Donaldson who was born in Pennsylvania and came to Morrow County in 1871. He was a large landowner and sheepman before the turn of the century. The proper name for the stream in the lower end of the canyon is Shobe Creek.

Donnelly Butte, HARNEY. Donnelly Butte is about 30 miles northwest of Burns and has an elevation of 6033 feet. At one time it was called Black Butte but was renamed to honor Edgar W. Donnelly, USFS district ranger in the area for many years.

Donnelly Creek, CROOK. This creek flows into North Fork Crooked River in T 15S, R 22E. The stream and nearby Donnelly Spring were named for R. N. Donnelly, prominent sheepman. Donnelly was born in Tennessee and came to Oregon in the early days. He was the father of long time USFS employees W. A. and E. W. Donnelly, and at one time a member of the Oregon Legislature. He died near Richmond in 1936.

Donner und Blitzen River, HARNEY. This stream was named during the Snake War of 1864, when troops under the command of Colonel George B. Currey crossed it during a thunder storm, and gave it the German name for thunder and lightning. The river is frequently called simply Blitzen.

Donnybrook, JEFFERSON. This name is now applied to a school in the east end of the county, but some years ago Donnybrook referred to the whole community. Phil Brogan, in the Bend *Bulletin*, Apr. 20, 1943, discusses the name with sympathetic understanding as follows: "It was in the community's range epoch that a group of Celts, celebrating some undetermined occasion at a sheep cabin in Calf gulch, just over the ridge from Axehandle, did the thing in true Donnybrook style. There was no fair, but one fine fight. Joe Brannon heard of the party and with typical Irish wit, called the locality Donnybrook. And gradually that name spread to the community, and the county school, below Axehandle spring, was named the Donnybrook school. For many years the community was known as Donnybrook far and wide. Then came the homesteading era. Across Currant Creek and near the shadow of Coyote mountain, Jesse Kilts homesteaded. Eventually, as homesteaders moved in, a post office was obtained, and postal officials named the community after the postmaster. Since then the community, Axehandle of pioneer days and Donnybrook of the ranch era, has been known, at least to Uncle Sam, as Kilts." The original Donnybrook is a suburb in the southeast part of Dublin, famous for a fair held under license from King John in 1204. The entertainment furnished at the fair reached such specialized disorder that the institution was abolished in 1855. Phil Brogan reported that he had seen the name of the Oregon school called Donnybrooke. If this is true, and it probably is, the compiler thinks the authorities in Jefferson County better put a stop to such nonsense.

Dooley Mountain, BAKER. This is a prominent point south of Baker, near the Baker-Unity Highway. It bears the name of a well-known eastern Oregon pioneer, John J. Dooley, who came to the vicinity of Baker in 1862. For many years he was connected with various mining and construction enterprises in Oregon and Idaho, and built a toll road near the mountain which bears his name. A letter by J. C. Bowen is printed on the editorial page of the *Oregon Journal*, June 7, 1929, and it recounts some of the history of John J. Dooley and his kindly wife. At that time the Dooleys were 92 and 89 years of age, respectively, and lived in Baker.

Dora, COOS. Dora post office was established Aug. 10, 1874, with John H. Roach postmaster. It has been reported that the place was named for Dora Roach, apparently the small daughter of the first postmaster.

Dorena, LANE. This post office was established in 1899 with Alfred H. Bigelow first postmaster. The place was named for Dora Burnette and Rena Martin by consolidating parts of their first names. In 1949 the USCE completed Dorena Dam on Row River and the impoundment, Dorena Lake, flooded the townsite. The community was relocated near the head of the lake five miles up river. The dam is an earth fill flood control project with about 70,000 acre feet of usable water storage. The recreation facilities are operated by Lane County.

Doris Creek, LANE. Mrs. R. L. Gawley, who lived in Disston many years ago, told the compiler in 1967 that this tributary of Layng Creek was named for the daughter of Elza Holderman, an early USFS ranger.

Dorman, UMATILLA. Dorman post office was in the south part of the county, probably not far from Ukiah. It was established Oct. 3, 1887, and named for James W. Dorman, the first postmaster. The subsequent history of this post office is not clear. The name was changed to Dale on Nov. 11, 1891, but whether the office was moved at that time is not certain. In any event, the office was shown on the Grant County list in 1903 with the name Dale. The compiler has been to Dale several times and finds it hard to fit the name to the geography, although the man who selected the word may not have had the same difficulty. This part of Oregon is deeply cut by canyons. It does not seem that the name Dale describes them very accurately. The name Dale as applied to this locality may have had a significance other than topographic.

Dorrance Meadow, DESCHUTES. This meadow five miles west of La Pine was named for early day homesteader Samuel H. Dorrance. Dorrance was later killed by J. L. Melvin of Melvin Butte.

Dosch Road, MULTNOMAH. Few Oregon pioneers have been so greatly respected as Colonel Henry E. Dosch. His contributions to the development of the state were substantial, and his character such as to win him a host of friends. He was born in Germany June 17, 1841. He emigrated to St. Louis, Missouri, in Jan. 1860, and had been in the United States but little more than a year when he enlisted in the northern army, and finally reached the rank of acting colonel of volunteers. In 1863 he crossed the plains, and after visiting California arrived in The Dalles in 1864. After various mercantile experiences in eastern Oregon and elsewhere, he retired in 1890, and devoted the remainder of his life to horticulture. His knowledge of the state and its products was profound. He represented Oregon at every important exposition beginning at the World's Columbian Exposition held at Chicago in 1893. For many years he resided near Hillsdale, and the county road between Green Hills and Hillsdale was named for him. There was also a station on the Southern Pacific west of Bertha called Dosch. Colonel Dosch died at Portland in 1925.

Dothan, DOUGLAS. Dothan post office was established in Mar. 1896, to serve the locality of West Fork station on the Southern Pacific Company railroad in Cow Creek Canyon. It is said that the station agent, one Hudson, thought that the name of the post office should be different from the station name in order to avoid confusion in accounts. He suggested the name Dothan which he found in biblical history. Dothan was a place near Samaria in Palestine. Dothan post office in Oregon was closed in 1942. The post office list for Douglas County shows an office named Herman, established Apr. 15, 1886, with James W. Gilmore postmaster. The office was discontinued Dec. 13, 1887. The compiler has been told that this office served the locality of West Fork railroad station. It is possible that the office was named in compliment to Binger Hermann, then Oregon's representative in Congress, who may have assisted in getting it established. It will be noted that there is a discrepancy in the spelling.

Dotyville, LINN. The early-day post office called Dotyville in Linn County was named in compliment to the Doty family, local residents. Dotyville was near the south line of T 10S, R 1W, and just a little to the southeast of Scio. The office was established Oct. 3, 1884, with J. A. Richardson first postmaster. The office continued in operation until Oct. 6, 1890. The place is not shown on modern maps.

Double Corral Creek, WHEELER. This creek is in the south part of the county west of Derr Meadows. Early sheepmen Martin Derr and Z. T. Keys brought the first sheep to this area in 1884. Later counting and separating corrals were built at the headwaters of the creek near Blevins Spring. These have been rebuilt several times and relocated slightly but are still in use.

Dougherty Slough, TILLAMOOK. This slough flows westward under the Oregon Coast Highway a half mile north of Tillamook and empties into Hoquarten Slough. It bears the name of Nathaniel Dougherty, an early settler near Tillamook Bay and an esteemed and prominent pioneer of the county.

Dougherty Spring, WALLOWA. This spring, in the northeast part of T 4N, R 46E, was named for William Dougherty, who herded sheep there and established a camp for Hayes and Kernan about 1902.

Doughty Creek, TILLAMOOK. This stream was named for William Thomas Doughty, who settled in Tillamook County in 1870. It rises about two miles east of Bay City and flows south, thence west into Tillamook Bay. Its mouth is just north of Kilchis Point.

Douglas County. On Jan. 24, 1851, the territorial legislature created Umpqua County and named it for the Umpqua River. It is said that the short life of Umpqua County was due to political troubles. In any event, on Jan. 7, 1852, the territorial legislature created Douglas County out of the eastern part of Umpqua County. Another part of Umpqua County was added to Coos County in Dec. 1853, and the remainder was given to Douglas County in 1862. Douglas County was named for Stephen Arnold Douglas (1813–1861), distinguished American politician and Democratic candidate for the presidency in 1860. He was a strong supporter of Oregon in the Congress, and at the time Douglas County was named for him, he was in the United States Senate from Illinois. According to ODOT, Douglas County has an area of 5015 square miles.

Douglas Hollow, WASCO. Douglas Hollow drains into Fifteenmile Creek about a mile north of Emerson. It was named for John Douglas, very early Wasco County settler, who brought land near its mouth in 1864.

Dougren, LANE. Dougren is a station on the Southern Pacific Cascade Line west of Dexter. When the railroad was relocated around Lookout Point Dam, land for this station was purchased from a man named Green who stipulated that his name be used. The railroad already had a station named Green just south of Roseburg so Dougren was coined from the names Douglas Green.

Douthit Springs, CROOK. These springs and Douthit Creek in S 10, T 14S, R 19E, near Ochoco Creek were named for one Douthit, an early homesteader. The spelling Drouthit is incorrect.

Douty, TILLAMOOK. Douty post office was in the extreme northeast part of the county, established to serve the Douty Lumber Company. This enterprise was situated just a little northeast and over the county line from Cochran, Washington County. The Douty Lumber Company was named for one of its owners, F. A. Douty. There was a Southern Pacific Company railroad station called Douty but it did not have an agent. Douty post office was established Jan. 19, 1921, and was ordered discontinued Aug. 7, 1924. James M. White was the only postmaster.

Dover, CLACKAMAS. Dover post office was established June 16, 1890, with Frederick R. French first of a series of nine postmasters. The office was closed Aug. 31, 1911, so that the number of postmasters was large for a total service of 21 years, apparently a record for Oregon. Dover was a few miles southeast of Sandy. The first location is said to have been in S 32, T 2S, R 5E, but the USGS 15' map of the Cherryville quadrangle shows it a mile or so further south, toward the end of its service. In July 1947, William H. Stanley of Gresham, sent in some of the early history of Dover, secured from Mrs. Joel Jarl, daughter of Mrs. Ethel Roberts, third postmaster at Dover. According to Mrs. Jarl the first postmaster, Frederick French, was either a native of England, or of English descent and named the office for the locality in England where he himself or his forebears came from. In 1917 the old Dover area in Clackamas County was served by a rural carrier from Eagle Creek.

Doves Bar, MARION. This bar is near the east bank of Willamette River southwest of Salem. It was named for Bethuel Dove, who owned a nearby donation land claim on the west bank of the river in Polk County. Dove lived on what is known as Hayden Island.

Dovre Peak, TILLAMOOK. This point is in the northeast part of T 3S, R 7W, in the east part of the county. It bears the name of geographic features in the province of Christiansand, Norway. It was named by USBGN about 1930 at the suggestion of F. E. Berg, homesteader who lived in the vicinity of the peak.

Downey Gulch, WALLOWA. This gulch is in T 5N, R 47E, and is in the extreme northeast corner of the county. It was named for R. M. Downey, pioneer resident and at one time county assessor. Downey Gulch is tributary to Cook Creek. Downey Saddle in the same township was also named for R. M. Downey. There is a much smaller Downey Gulch in the north part of T 2S, R 47E, named for the same man.

Downing, UMATILLA. Downing is a station on the Union Pacific Railroad north of Weston. It was named for J. A. Downing who farmed the land through which the railroad was built.

Downing Creek, LINN. Downing Creek enters North Santiam River from the east about four miles south of Marion Forks. While there is no specific evidence, the writer feels confident that this stream was named by John Minto for George S. Downing, member of both Minto's 1874 survey party and the 1881 party which located the route to the present Santiam Pass.

Downing Point, LANE. Downing Point is an old name confirmed by the USBGN in *Decision List 8503*. It is the high ground south of the mouth of Weaver Creek and commemorates a miner named Downing, who along with a companion named Weaver, was lost nearby in a winter storm. *See also* Weaver Creek.

Downs, MARION. This was a station about two miles north of Silverton. It was named for James Down, native of Saltash, Devonshire, England. He was born in 1835, came to the United States during the Civil War, and settled in Oregon in 1864. He engaged in the hop and grain business. He died May 28, 1898. *See* Down's *A History of the Silverton Country*, chapter XXII.

Drain, DOUGLAS. This place was named for Charles Drain, pioneer settler in the locality. The donation land claim on which the town of Drain is situated was taken up by Warren Goodell. He sold it to Jesse Applegate who in turn sold the property to Charles Drain in 1861. In 1872 the Oregon & California Railroad (the actual name adopted on Mar. 16, 1870 was Oregon & California Rail Road Company) reached northern Douglas County. Drain and his son, John, had sold 60 acres of their land to the railroad for one dollar "in consideration of establishing a station ... and laying out a town to be called 'Drain.'" Drain post office was established on Apr. 25, 1872. Charles Drain, Sr. was once a member of the legislature, and his son, J. C. Drain, was also in the legislature and was speaker of the house. The town's most imposing residence, a Queen Anne style house built in 1893 for Charles Drain, Jr. The structure is still standing in 1990 and in 1978 was entered on the National Register of Historic Places. For additional information about the Drain family, *see* article by Fred Lockley on editorial page of the *Oregon Journal*, Aug. 8, 1927.

Drake Peak, LAKE. Drake Peak, with an elevation of 8407 feet, is a prominent point in the mountains northeast of Lakeview. It was named for John M. Drake, well-known officer in several campaigns against the Snake Indians in south central Oregon. He reached the rank of colonel toward the conclusion of the Snake War.

268   OREGON GEOGRAPHIC NAMES

For information about his activities in this territory, *see* Bancroft's *History of Oregon*, v. 2, p. 488, *et seq*. Drake Butte and Drake Peak, in the Maury Mountains in Crook County, are also named for Colonel Drake.

Draper, JACKSON. This place, southwest of Gold Hill, was named for Silas Draper, miner. Draper post office was established Feb. 9, 1882, with Draper first postmaster. The office was closed in Oct. 1912.

Draper Canyon, SHERMAN. In the 1870s, Norman Draper took up government land along this canyon. It opens into John Day River ten miles above the Columbia.

Dread and Terror Ridge, DOUGLAS. This ridge is on the south side of North Umpqua River in the northeast part of the county. It is about four miles long and has an elevation of 4896 feet. The name was applied by district ranger C. V. Oden of the USFS in 1908 because of the dense thickets of thorns and other brush which made the prospects of fire fighting in that section extremely disagreeable.

Dreadnought Island, KLAMATH. This island, in the west end of Crescent Lake, was named by F. W. Cleator of the USFS in 1925 because it resembled a dreadnought battleship.

Drew, DOUGLAS. This place is said to have been named for a local resident, Robert Drew.

Drew Creek, LAKE. This stream drains into Goose Lake. It was named for Lt.-Col. C. S. Drew, in command of the Owyhee Reconnaissance of the First Oregon Cavalry in 1864. The stream has been dammed for irrigation storage.

Drew Creek, LANE. Drew Creek is tributary to North Fork Siuslaw River in s 13, T 17S, R 11W. The *Siuslaw Pioneer*, 1982, p. 103, says it was named for an Indian named Frank Drew who came to the Siuslaw country as a boy in 1876. BLM records show that Frederick Drew took up an Indian Allotment in s 12, in 1897, but the compiler suspects the given name is in error as there are a number of other entries for Frank Drew in other locations.

Drewsey, HARNEY. Abner Robbins started a store at this place in the summer of 1883 and called it Gouge Eye, apparently to commemorate the frontier method of settling disputes. Norma Miller in *A Lively Little History of Harney County—A Centennial Souvenir Album*, gives a reported account of the confrontation and the dispute that caused it. About a year later Robbins applied for a post office but postal authorities were reluctant to accept the original name, so he substituted a new name, Drusy. Eventually the office was named Drewsey. *Oregon, End of the Trail (Oregon Guide)*, p. 468, says the new name was in compliment to Drewsey Miller, the daughter of a rancher. In 1926 the compiler was told that the name submitted to Washington was Drusy, which authorities changed to Drewsey. Drusy seems more like a girl's name. The *Oregon Guide* calls the name Gouge Eye unpleasant, but the compiler thinks it a stout, picturesque bit of nomenclature, much better than some of the gutless expressions of today.

Drift Creek, LINCOLN. Drift Creek post office was one of the very first in the southwest part of what is now Lincoln County, then Benton. It was established Aug. 6, 1874, with Matthew Brand postmaster, and was named for the stream flowing into Alsea Bay. The creek was named for the accumulations of driftwood on its banks. There is also a Drift Creek in Lincoln County flowing into Siletz Bay. The name of the office was changed to Collins in Jan. 1876, in honor of a local family. The name of this office was changed to Waldport in June 1881, and back to Collins in Feb. 1882. This post office called Waldport may have been on the north side of Alsea Bay, not on the south side. Collins was changed to Lutgens in May 1890, and Lutgens was changed to Stanford in July 1893. Stanford it remained until June 1897, when it became Lutgens again. The name of the office was changed to Nice in Apr. 1917, and was closed in Nov. 1919. This post office had eight names during its 45 years of service, a record in the opinion of the complier. No other Oregon office appears to have approached this mark. It is obvious that the office was moved a number of times. However, the offices mentioned above were all in the general vicinity of Alsea Bay. Lutgens was named for Albert H. Lutgens, also spelled Lutjens, and Nice was named for Harry Nice. Both of these men were local residents. The compiler has been unable to learn why Stanford post office was so named.

Drift Creek, MARION. This stream was named Drift Creek in early days because of the accumulation of driftwood along its banks. Its upper reaches were in heavily wooded country.

Drift Fence Campground, UMATILLA. This USFS campground northeast of Dale was named because of its proximity to a drift fence used to control open range livestock.

Drinkwater Pass, HARNEY. Drinkwater Pass is on US-20 east of Drewsey where the highway leaves the Malheur River valley. Clarence Drinkwater was a merchant in Drewsey before World War I and his wife, Castolia Drinkwater, was still living in Drewsey in the 1970s. The compiler does not know why their name was applied to this pass some distance to the east.

Driver Valley, DOUGLAS. Isaac and Samuel Driver both took donation land claims in this valley north of Calapooya Creek. Isaac Driver's claim was at the mouth of the valley near the old post office of Fair Oaks while Samuel's was in the upper part.

Drury Creek, LANE. Drury Creek, west of McKenzie Bridge, was named for Forrest Drury who homesteaded along it prior to World War I.

Drury Creek, LANE. This stream, a tributary to Mohawk River from the northwest, and Drury Butte south of Marcola were named for a family of early settlers. The post office and community Mabel, situated a little to the south of the mouth of the stream were named for Miss Mabel Drury.

Dry River, CROOK, DESCHUTES. This is the bed of an ancient river that once drained the High Desert. The course of the channel is well marked from the west end of the desert to Crooked River, a distance of more than 50 miles. In some places the dry bed is in a canyon, and in other places in a narrow defile between abrupt basalt walls. The Ochoco highway between Redmond and Prineville crosses this defile at a point where an excellent view may be had of it. In many places water may be uncovered by digging in the gravel bed.

Dryden, JOSEPHINE. Dryden, in the Deer Creek Valley east of Selma, was named for John Dryden, famous English poet, playwright and critic, who lived from 1631 to 1700. Mrs. Alma Harmon Kiphart of Eugene, a native of the Deer Creek country, sent this information, which has been confirmed by other sources. A paragraph from Mrs. Kiphart's letter of Mar. 20, 1947, is as follows: "Dryden post office was named by J. P. (Perry) Mills, Deer Creek Valley pioneer, for John Dryden the poet. Mr. Mills was a great reader and had in his possession many good books. It was through his influence that the post office was established. Early in 1900 he went to the Soldiers' Home at Roseburg, where he spent his last days. The establishment of this office is one of my fondest recollections." Dryden post office was established Feb. 8, 1892, with Mary E. Tolin first of a long line of postmasters. In the summer of 1946 the compiler drove up Deer Creek to satisfy his curiosity about this isolated office and found it still in service and in good order, but in 1979 it was no longer in operation.

Drylake, CROOK. This post office was in the south part of Crook County. There is a small lake nearby which fills with water in the early spring, but is generally dry during the late summer. For many years the stockmen have referred to this as Dry Lake or Dry Lake Flat. When the post office was established in Sept. 1913, the name Dry Lake was selected by local residents, but the post office authorities telescoped this name into one word and it has been so known ever since. The office was closed in Jan. 1937.

Duckworth, LANE. Duckworth was apparently named for a local family, but the compiler does not know for which one. Isaac W. Duckworth was postmaster at Long Tom office as early as 1859, and there may have been others of the name. Duckworth post office was established Mar. 4, 1884, with Gilbert D. Chamberlain first postmaster. Byron Ellmaker was appointed Nov. 25, 1884, and lost no time in getting the name changed to Elmira on Dec. 22, 1884. *See also* Elmira.

Dudley, JACKSON. Dudley was a post office in the mountains about six miles north of Butte Falls. It was established Apr. 2, 1909, with Theresa E. Spencer first and only postmaster. The office was closed Oct. 31, 1912, with papers to Butte Falls. In Feb. 1947, Judge J. B. Coleman of Medford wrote the compiler that Dudley post office was named for a Mr. Dudley who at one time owned or controlled what was known as the Dudley timber tract north of Butte Falls. Dudley post office was in the home of Mr. and Mrs. Spencer in S 12, T 34S, R 2E. A few years ago the old Spencer cabin was still standing with the mail boxes still in place therein, according to Judge Coleman.

Dufur, WASCO. According to the *History of Central Oregon*, the first settler in the neighborhood of Dufur was Lewis P. Henderson, who in 1852 established a home about four miles from the present site of the community. During the next three years Messrs. Reynolds, Marsh and Brown, stockmen, established ranches nearby. In 1863 David Imbler built a farmhouse where the town of Dufur now stands. In 1872 Andrew J. and E. Burnham Dufur bought a farm where Dufur is now situated. These two men were members of a well-known Wasco County pioneer family which came from New England by way of Panama to Oregon in 1859. On Jan. 11, 1878, the post office was established and named for the Dufur family. Chauncey A. Williams was first postmaster, and is said to have selected the name of the office.

Dukes Valley, HOOD RIVER. This is a sort of natural cove on the north slope of Booth Hill between the Mount Hood Loop Highway and Hood River. There seem to be plenty of legends as to how the valley got its name. The compiler is of the belief that it was named for a man named Duke who lived in the valley in the 1860s. There is a story, however, to the effect that it was named for a well-known ox, used by Peter Neal in logging operations, which much preferred wandering off into the secluded pastures of Dukes Valley to hauling logs. In 1886 Captain J. H. Dukes, veteran of the Civil War, came to the Hood River Valley, and the compiler has been told that Dukes Valley was named for him, although there is nothing to indicate that he actually lived in Dukes Valley, but in the town of Hood River, except for a short time when he lived near Oak Grove.

Duley Creek, CURRY. Duley Creek flows into Lone Ranch Creek east of Cape Ferrelo. It was named for Winfield S. Duley who lived on its banks before the turn of the century.

Dumbbell Lake, LANE. Dumbbell Lake is in the Cascade Range about two miles south of Horse Mountain. According to USFS records it was named by Dee Wright because of its shape.

Dumont Creek, DOUGLAS. This tributary of South Umpqua River northeast of Tiller was named for James and Frank Dumont who maintained a hunting camp nearby many years ago. This information was provided by Ira Poole of Canyonville.

Duncan, UMATILLA. Ida M. Wilbur, postmaster at Duncan in 1925, told the writer that the community was named for Isaac Duncan, veteran of the Civil War. He lived in the neighborhood for many years, and the name of Duncan was proposed for the place in 1899. The post office was established Oct. 28, 1899.

Duncan Creek, LAKE. Duncan Creek is near Silver Lake. It was named for George C. Duncan who first settled on the land where the stream emptied into Silver Lake. The Duncan family arrived in the Silver Lake Valley about 1873.

Duncan Ditch, BAKER. This ditch was named for the family of Charles H. Duncan who settled near Keating in the 1890s.

Duncanville, GRANT. Duncanville was a post office in the west or upper end of

Bear Valley, southwest of Canyon City. Postal records show that the office was established Sept. 27, 1897, with Wesley P. Duncan postmaster. The office was discontinued May 15, 1902, with all mail to Canyon City. It was named for the postmaster.

Dundee, YAMHILL. William Reid came to Oregon in 1874 from Dundee, Scotland. Among other things he became interested in Willamette Valley railroad construction, and he assisted in organizing the Oregonian Railway Company, Limited, a corporation of Dundee, Scotland, which succeeded to the interest of The Oregon Railway Company in 1880. The Oregon Company had previously taken over property of the Willamette Valley Railroad Company, which had gotten into financial difficulties. The Oregonian Railway Company made several narrow gauge extensions on the west side of the Willamette Valley, and an east side extension from Dundee. The town of Dundee was established and named for Reid's home in Scotland. For details of Reid's history and of the construction of the railroad mentioned above, *see* Scott's *History of the Oregon Country*. The post office history of Dundee is a little more complicated than ordinary. An office named Ekins was established there in 1881 which ran until the summer of 1882 when the name was changed to Dundee in commemoration of Reid's birthplace. The name Dundee was used for the post office name from July 25, 1882, until June 30, 1885, when the postal business was turned over to Lafayette. On Apr. 16, 1887, a new post office with the name Dundee Junction was established with Frank D. McCain first postmaster. The name Dundee Junction was used because there had been a good deal of talk about building a railroad bridge over Willamette River from Fulquartz Landing on the Yamhill County side to Rays Landing on the Marion County side. The east side narrow gauge line would thus be brought to Dundee where a junction would be made with the west side line and also a connection to Portland. The writer is of the opinion that the name Dundee Junction was in use by the railroad company prior to the time that Dundee Junction post office was established. In any event, the name Dundee Junction for the post office prevailed until Feb. 13, 1897, when it was changed to Dundee, the present style. The bridge has not been built.

Dundon Bridge, LINCOLN. Dundon Bridge is just west of Toledo, and the name is frequently misspelled. Alonzo T. M. Dundon was born in Peoria, Illinois, in 1852, and came to Oregon with his parents in 1864 in the train of Captain Frank Shedd. In 1866 the Dundon family settled near what is now Toledo. Alonzo Dundon ran a brickyard and also a freight line from Corvallis to the coast. He died Dec. 27, 1940. For obituary, *see* Toledo *Leader*, Jan. 2, 1941.

Dunes City, LANE. In the early 1960s there was a movement to establish a Dunes National Park in the Siltcoos Lake area. The local residents including Westlake and North Beach wished to avoid being included in the proposed park so in 1962 they voted to incorporate as Dunes City. Westlake post office, established in 1915, continues to serve the area and North Beach is retained as the name of the neighborhood near the mouth of Woahink Creek.

Dunlap Lake, MARION. This lake, northeast of Detroit, was named for Harry Dunlap who prospected nearby. The name was first applied about 1906, according to information furnished by Charles C. Giebeler of Detroit.

Dunning Creek, YAMHILL. Dunning Creek west of Carlton Lake was named for Alexander Dunning whose donation land claim was along its banks. He settled there in 1853 but left Yamhill County in 1858.

Dupee Creek, YAMHILL. Edward Dupuis and his wife took a donation land claim where this creek empties into Deer Creek in Gopher Valley. The stream bears their name but the compiler cannot account for the change in spelling.

Durbin, MARION. Durbin was a railroad station east of Salem. It was named for F. W. Durbin of Salem, who had a spur for loading cordwood. For information about the Durbin family, *see* the *Oregonian*, Aug. 1, 1926, sect. 1, p. 12.

Durham, WASHINGTON. Albert Alonzo Durham came to Oregon in 1847. He built a sawmill below Oregon City, which he sold. Then he built a sawmill at Oswego, where he did a large business until 1869. *See* advertisement of his sawmill at Oswego in the *Oregonian* in 1850–1851. He named Oswego for Oswego, New York. After operating at Oswego, he moved into Washington County and built a sawmill and a flour mill on Fanno Creek. These mills were operated by water power, and for a number of years the place was known as Durhams Mills. When the Oregon Electric Railway was built the station at this point was called Durham. A. A. Durham was born in Genesee County, New York, Mar. 15, 1814; he died in Washington County, Oregon, Apr. 4, 1898.

Durkee, BAKER. The community Durkee was named for a family of early settlers. The first post office in the locality was called Express Ranch, with C. W. Durkee first postmaster. It was established Apr. 21, 1865, but was later moved to Weatherby. *See* Express Ranch for the history of this office. The existing post office Durkee was established Feb. 26, 1902, probably by change of name from another office called Express.

Dusty, BENTON. In Feb. 1946, Robert Johnson of Corvallis wrote the compiler as follows: "Frank Elgin opened a country store five miles northwest of Monroe, and a post office was established therein with Helen Elgin, his daughter, postmaster. The storekeeper suggested the name Elgin for the new office but as many residents of the community came from Bellefontaine, Ohio, they wanted it named for their native heath. No agreement could be reached and as the store was located on dusty crossroads, the name Dusty was adopted. But the people of the community were not satisfied until the name was changed to Bellfountain and Bellfountain today is surrounded by a prosperous community." The post office at Dusty was established Dec. 6, 1895, with Helen Elgin first postmaster. Whatever the local argument may have been about the name of the office, the real reason why Elgin was not selected was because there was already an Elgin in Oregon and duplications were not allowed. Postal records are not entirely clear, but it seems probable that the name of the office Dusty was changed to Bellfountain on July 31, 1902.

Dutch Flat, WASCO. In the early 1870s a German settled on the plateau east of and above Mill Creek. His home was known as Dutchman's Cabin and the flat has been called Dutch Flat ever since.

Dutch Oven Camp, LANE. Dutch Oven Camp is on South Fork McKenzie River. S. L. Taylor of McKenzie Bridge is authority for the story of origin of the name. A burro, packed for a fishing party, fell over a cliff at this point and was killed. About the only part of the pack that was undamaged was a demijohn of whisky, but an iron Dutch oven was badly broken and the rest of the pack ruined. The remains of the oven lay in the vicinity for several years and caused the application of the name.

Dutcher Creek, JOSEPHINE. Dutcher Creek flows into Rogue River from the southwest nine miles downstream from Grants Pass. It takes its name from John Dutcher whose donation land claim was near its mouth.

Dutchman Butte, DOUGLAS. Before the turn of the century a German named Adolph "Chris" Swagerman lived in Elk Valley just west of this 3907 foot summit. Swagerman was a solitary individual who disliked visitors. The butte was given the vernacular name so often applied to his compatriots.

Dutchman Flat, DESCHUTES. The late Judge H. C. Ellis of Bend was responsible for the story that a German sheepherder and party discovered the flat years ago when they were blocked by snow near Sparks Lake and forced to winter nearby. An editorial in the Bend *Bulletin*, Nov. 21, 1958, gives a more reasonable origin. After noting that snows on 6200 foot Dutchman Flat or even 5500 foot Sparks Lake are often 15 feet deep, they properly conclude that neither man nor sheep could have survived an ordinary winter. This comment is followed by the opinion of the Vandevert brothers that the flat was named for "Dutch John" Felderwerd who ranched near the present location of Bend in the 1880s. Felderwerd ranged sheep and cattle as far west as Sparks Lake and built and maintained cabins for his herders in many locations.

Dutchman Peak, JACKSON. Dutchman Peak is on the summit of the Siskiyou Mountains about nine miles west of Mount Ashland. It commemorates a German miner named Hensley who was caught in a sudden snowstorm and frozen to death in the 1870s. Nearby Deadmans Point owes its name to the same occurence.

Dutton Canyon, MORROW. This canyon just west of Heppner was named for William P. Dutton, an early homesteader. He was born in Vermont in 1852 and came to Rhea Creek about 1875.

Dutton Cliff, KLAMATH. This cliff is at the southeast corner of Crater Lake at an elevation of 8150 feet. It was named by Will G. Steel in 1886 for Captain Clarence E. Dutton, U.S. Army. There is also Dutton Creek in the park. It rises near Rim Village and flows southwest to Castle Creek.

Duwee Canyon, KLAMATH. This canyon lies to the south of Crater Lake, and is remarkable for its unusual spires and pinnacles. The name is from the Klamath Indian word *ti-wi*, indicating the rushing noise made by a cascade. A waterfall in the canyon has the same name. The spelling Duwee has been adopted by USBGN, and the style Dewie is obsolete.

Dwyer Creek, CURRY. This stream flows into South Fork Floras Creek near Edson Butte. It was named for P. F. Dwyer, an early settler.

Dyar Rock, KLAMATH. This rock is on the south rim of Crater Lake, and has an elevation of 7880 feet. It was named in 1872 by Captain O. C. Applegate for Leroy S. Dyar, of Ontario, California, then Indian agent on the Klamath Indian Reservation, and later a member of the Modoc Peace Commission. Dyar was the only member of the commission who escaped uninjured when attacked by Captain Jack and his band of Indians in the Lava Beds Apr. 11, 1873, at which time General E.R.S. Canby and Dr. E. Thomas were killed and chairman A. B. Meacham was wounded and left for dead.

Dyer Well, DESCHUTES. This well was on the property of Howard F. Dyer who homesteaded near Horse Ridge in 1912.

Eagle Butte, HOOD RIVER, MULTNOMAH. This butte was formerly called Eagle Creek Butte, because it was near the headwaters of the creek, but the name was cumbersome and the USFS has adopted the shorter form.

Eagle Cap, WALLOWA. This peak was for many years thought to be the highest mountain in eastern Oregon. In early days the Wallowa Mountains had a variety of names, including Eagle Mountains, and Eagle Cap was supposed to be the top of them all, hence the name. According to the USGS it has an elevation of 9595 feet so there are other peaks in the Wallowa Mountains that are higher.

Eagle Creek, BAKER, UNION. There are a good many geographic features in Oregon named for the eagle including mountains, streams and places. One of the most important is Eagle Creek which rises on the south slopes of the Wallowa mountains and flows southeastward into Powder River. This stream has played a prominent part both in the mining and in the irrigation history of northeast Oregon. An account of the naming of this stream is given by Isaac Hiatt in his book *Thirty-one Years in Baker County*, p. 30. Knight and Abbott were herding cattle in the Powder River Valley in 1861, and coming to a considerable tributary, they shot an eagle. That circumstance gave the name Eagle Creek to the stream.

Eagle Creek, CLACKAMAS. Eagle Creek is the name of a post office as well as of a stream. There are many streams of the same name in the state. A. C. Cogswell, postmaster at Eagle Creek in 1925, wrote the compiler that the place was called Eagle Creek as early as 1844, and that the name originated with Indians because there were so many eagles along the stream.

Eagle Point, JACKSON. Just east of the town of Eagle Point is a prominent rocky cliff, surmounted by pine trees, and in pioneer days this was a favorite nesting place for eagles. It was called Eagle Point. It is said that John Mathews suggested the name of this point for the post office, which was established about 1872, with Andrew McNeil first postmaster. By 1981 there was only one water-powered, stone ground gristmill still operating in Oregon. The mill, built in 1872, was placed on the National Register of Historic Places in 1976. For a story about the Butte Creek Mill in Eagle Point, *see* the *Oregonian*, Jan. 8, 1982, p. E1.

Eagleton, BAKER. Eagleton post office was in the extreme north part of the county a little to the northeast of Sanger. It was on one of the forks of Eagle Creek and took its name on that account. When established, the office was in Union County, but a change of boundaries brought it into Baker County. Eagleton post office was established Apr. 22, 1896, with Frank McGee first postmaster. It was closed in Feb. 1902. The compiler was told that the place was established in connection with mining activity.

Earl, LANE. Earl post office was established Apr. 26, 1898, with Arthur J. Johnson first postmaster, and was named for Earl R. Johnson, the small son of the postmaster. It is reported that several names were sent in and postal authorities selected Earl from the lot. The office was then in Douglas County, on the headwaters of Sweet Creek southeast of Point Terrace. About 1913 the Douglas-Lane county boundary line was changed and the office was then in Lane County. It was discontinued June 15, 1925. In Mar. 1947, Earl R. Johnson, then living on Crow Stage Route, wrote the compiler in part as follows: "At that time all the mail was carried on horseback over steep mountain trails, and though the mail came only once a week, mail day was really an event to the people in that out of the way station. The route led from Point Terrace at the mouth of Sweet Creek on the Siuslaw River up the creek to Earl, a distance of nine miles. I helped circulate the petition which led to the change of the county boundary. About the time Earl post office was established, an office was also established at Ord, which was about seven miles east over the mountains on the headwaters of Smith River. Horace Fisk was the first postmaster at Ord."

Early, SHERMAN. Early post office was established in the northeast part of Sherman County on Jan. 9, 1902, with Herbert K. Porter first of three postmasters. Members of the Wall family later ran the office, which was discontinued Aug. 30, 1919. On Sept. 10, 1946, Giles French wrote the compiler as follows: "Early was a post office on the north line of township two north just west of John Day River. At Early there was a flour mill where early-day farmers obtained their bread-stuff, and I am told the name was given the place because garden sass became edible early when grown there. The elevation is low and the sun shines brightly in the John Day Valley when it is cold and windy on the hills above. The Walls built a dam a short way above the mill and James Fox now grows alfalfa there. It would be a quiet and peaceful spot in which to retire from the cares of the world, the telephones, the Russians, bureaucracy, radio, UNRRA, the whips and scorns of time, the unworthy spurns that patient merit takes."

East Lake, DESCHUTES. This is a landlocked lake about two miles in diameter, occupying what was probably once part of the crater of a volcanic peak known to geologists as Mount Newberry. It is in the Paulina Mountains southeast of Bend. It is in the eastern part of the crater, opposite Paulina Lake, and is called East Lake on that account.

East Morrison Street, MULTNOMAH. In the summer of 1909 the Southern Pacific Company opened a new station to serve the east part of Portland and the official name was East Morrison Street. In the days of more frequent local train service, this station did a good business and the regular patrons were augmented by travelers who found they could not make the time to the Union Station but could catch their trains at East Morrison Street by judicious use of taxicabs or family automobiles. Station attendants and train crews saw the finish of many a close race. The East Morrison Street station was demolished in the winter of 1945 –46. For news story and pictures of the event, *see* the *Oregonian*, Jan. 13, 1946. The reference to the East Side station is incorrect. The railroad name-board read East Morrison Street, and at one time the lettering was gilt on a black background. The station served little or no passenger business in later years. The original Oregon & California Rail Road station established about 1879 was on what was known as L Street in East Portland, later East Washington Street. The building was generally called the L-Street station but the official name was East Portland. Later there was another station near the mouth of Sullivan Gulch which was called the East Side station, but still later East Portland, serving two railroads. *See* East Portland. After the station name East Portland was moved from East Washington Street to the new East Portland station near the mouth of Sullivan Gulch, it was necessary to adopt a new name for the old station. The railroad company decided on the style East Washington Street and that name was used up to the time that the new East Morrison Street establishment was put in service.

East Portland, MULTNOMAH. East Portland existed as a separate community from pioneer days until June 1, 1891, when an election was held on the proposal to consolidate the three communities Portland, East Portland and Albina. The proposal carried and the program became effective July 5, 1891. James B. Stephens was the founder of East Portland. In 1845 Stephens bought for $200 property previously owned by a French-Canadian, one Porier. Stephens laid out a town in 1850– 51 and filed the East Portland plat in 1865. The selection of the name seemed to have been natural, but not imaginative, and in this respect followed the pattern of much other Oregon nomenclature. For the early history of Stephens and East Portland by Leslie M. Scott, *see OHQ*, v. 31, p. 351. East Portland post office was established May 15, 1866, with Milton Hosford first postmaster. The office continued in service until Mar. 4, 1892, when it was consolidated with Portland. John M. Lewis was then postmaster of East Portland. When the Oregon & Califoria Rail Road began to operate about 1870, it had a station called East Portland. This station was near the foot of what was then L Street, now known as Southeast Washington Street. This station was popularly known as the L-Street station, although East Portland was its official name. This was not the same station as East Morrison Street, a later structure that served many years and was demolished in the winter of 1945–46. The railroad had a terminus farther north near the mouth of Sullivan Gulch, which was called the East Side Station. Later the Southern Pacific and the Union Pacific had a station near this point called East Portland, but it was a separate operating point from either the original East Portland or East Morrison Street.

Eastside, COOS. This is a descriptive name, because the community is on the east side of Coos Bay. This place was at one time the terminal of the old Coos Bay Military Wagon Road. It was originally called East Marshfield, but about 1908 the name was changed to the present style. In 1983 Eastside merged with and is now part of the city of Coos Bay.

Eaton Butte, DESCHUTES. This 5169 foot-high butte on the east shore of Wickiup Reservoir is apparently named for Robert E. Eaton, who patented land at its base in 1918.

Ebell Creek, BAKER. This creek where the Union Pacific Railroad leaves Sutton Creek was named for August Ebell who homesteaded along its banks. Ebell was a brother of George Ebell who came to Baker County in 1865.

Ebell Picnic Area, BAKER. This park in the narrow neck between Mill and Marble creeks was named for George Ebell, an early settler. He was the brother of August Ebell who settled near Encina.

Eber Creek, LANE. Eber Creek is five miles southwest of Monroe. It is named for Eber Taylor on whose donation land claim it is located. Taylor was born in Pennsylvania in 1811 and came to Oregon in 1852.

Echo, UMATILLA. This place was named for Echo Koontz, daughter of Mr. and Mrs. J. H. Koontz. The community was started about 1880, and the Koontz family was among the first to settle there. Echo is near the site of Fort Henrietta, so called for Mrs. Henrietta Haller, wife of Major Granville O. Haller, U.S. Army, who commanded troops in early Indian campaigns. When the post office at Echo was established, Major Lee Moorehouse, of Pendleton, tried to have the name Henrietta adopted, but as Koontz was interested in the town, his daughter's name was selected. James H. Koontz was born in Ohio in 1830 and came to Oregon in 1862, settling at Umatilla in 1863. Echo Koontz was born at Umatilla Landing and later was Mrs. Charles H. Miller. Koontz died in 1912. For additional information about the locality of Echo, once known as Brasfield Ferry, *see* story by Fred Lockley in the *Oregon Journal*, Aug. 30, 1931. In 1861–62 Thomas A. Brasfield ran a stage station called The Crossing along with the ferry and kept the travel.

Eckley, CURRY. Eckley is a place at the east edge of the county near North Fork Sixes River on the old mountain road from Myrtle Point southwest to Port Orford. The post office has had three different names. A post office called New Castle was established in this locality on Dec. 19, 1879, with Mrs. Charlotte Guerin first postmaster. The name was changed to Tell Tale on May 21, 1883 and to Eckley on June 29, 1883. This office was in operation until Dec. 15, 1916, when it was closed out to Myrtle Point. A study of the Guerin family history as printed in Dodge's *Pioneer History of Coos and Curry Counties*, indicated that Mrs. Guerin's daughter-in-law, Mrs. George H. Guerin, was a native of Wingate, a place near Newcastle-on-Tyne in the north of England. It seems more than probable to the compiler that the name New Castle for the Curry County post office was suggested by Mrs. George Guerin, or by somebody in the family in her compliment. That there was a difference in the spelling is not a great objection to this theory. So much for New Castle. The name Eckley for this post office came from Mrs. Guerin's grandson, Eckley Guerin, son of Mr. and Mrs. George H. Guerin. Eckley Guerin was born in Aug. 1882, and the name Eckley was applied to the post office June 29, 1883.

Eckman Slough, LINCOLN. Eckman Slough and Eckman Creek are south of Alsea Bay. The postmaster at Waldport wrote the compiler in 1927 that these two streams were named many years ago for a Scandinavian settler who lived nearby.

Ecola Creek, CLATSOP. Captain William Clark was the first white man of record to visit the vicinity of this stream, which he did on Wednesday, Jan. 8, 1806. On Jan. 3, Indians reported to Fort Clatsop that a whale had beached south of what is now known as Tillamook Head. On Monday, Jan. 6, Clark started south with a small party. On Tuesday, after visiting the site near Seaside where they had boiled salt, they ascended Tillamook Head. The next day they traversed the head and named Clarks Point of View. When they descended to the south, they came to the beached whale south of a wide creek. Clark called the stream *Ecola* or Whale Creek. From pioneer days until 1974 the stream was called Elk Creek but then at the instigation of the Oregon Lewis and Clark Trail Committee the original name was restored. The village near its mouth at the north end of Cannon Beach was first called Elk Creek, then Ecola, but for many years its postal name has been Cannon Beach. *See* Ecola Point and Cannon Beach for additional information. Thwaites on p. 324 of v. 3 of his *Original Journals of the Lewis and Clark Expedition*, is confused about Whale Creek and mistakes it for Nehalem River, the more important stream to the south. He has done the same with other features visited by Captain Clark during the first days in Jan. and identifies them with points too far south. *See* Tillamook Head.

Ecola Point, CLATSOP. Some time prior to 1900 J. Couch Flanders of Portland was attracted by the name Ecola and he applied it to a group of cottages owned by the Couch family on the south flank of Tillamook Head about two miles north of what was then known as Elk Creek. The name was attractive, and people living near the mouth of Elk Creek asked for a post office to be named Ecola, which was established Nov. 25, 1910. To avoid confusion R. L. Glisan and L. Allen Lewis then changed the name of the Couch family cottages to Ecola Point, because of the prominent projection nearby. Ecola Point is between Chapman Point and the main promontory of Tillamook Head. The name Ecola is no longer used for the post office, which is now Cannon Beach. George Gibbs, in his *Dictionary of the*

Chinook Jargon gives the word *ehkoli*, a whale, and indicates that it came from the Chinook Indian word *ekoli*, with the accent on the first letter. The modern spelling with the accent on the middle syllable is, however, firmly established.

Eddeeleo Lakes, LANE. These three lakes north of Waldo Lake were first stocked and fished by three early USFS employees. The name is a combination of the first names of Ed Clark, Dee Wright and Leo McMahon.

Eddyville, LINCOLN. This post office seems to have had more than the usual number of moves. It was first called Little Elk, because it was near the mouth of Little Elk Creek. About 1888 Israel F. Eddy, the postmaster, moved the office about a mile west and had the name changed to Eddyville. Some four years later the office was brought back to its original location and the name changed to Little Elk. About 1893 it was moved again to Eddy's place and was continued under the name of Eddyville until 1900 when it was moved back to the mouth of Little Elk Creek, but this time the name was not changed and the office still goes by the name Eddyville. Israel Eddy was a man of generous size and remarkable strength who on more than one occasion seized brawlers by the neck and dunked them in the horse trough. In 1908 at the wedding of a local young lady, he appeared with a coonskin cap and ear trumpet and regaled the assembly with the story of how he recovered from the flu by drinking a swig of piano polish mistaken for his medicine. Eddy died in 1911 at age 87 years.

Eden, COOS. Eden was the name used for a post office in the extreme southeast part of Coos County, in the very rough, mountainous country on West Fork Cow Creek. Eden post office was established July 21, 1914, with Edward A. Zimmerman first of three postmasters. The office was discontinued Jan. 14, 1922, with mail to Dothan on Cow Creek. The compiler has been told that transportation to this post office was very primitive and he puts great faith in the report. The name for the post office was doubtless suggested by that of Eden Ridge to the southwest. Eden Ridge has been so called for many years. The ridge and the post office apparently were named by people fond of isolation and pioneer living. About the time of World War I, John Eden filed a coal mining claim in the area. This may be just a curious coincidence.

Eden, WALLOWA. Wallowa County has had more than its share of post offices with names showing that its settlers seemed to be pleased with the prospects. Among these names have been: Paradise, Promise, Joy, Arcadia, Utopia, Eureka and Enterprise. There was also a post office called Lovely but that was the family name of the postmaster. A post office with the name Eden was established Oct. 2, 1907, with B. E. Puller, postmaster. Apparently the office never operated because the appointment was rescinded on Apr. 29, 1908. It was planned to put the office at the Puller ranch on the breaks of the Grande Ronde River a few miles southwest of Troy. The locality is generally known as Eden Ridge.

Eden Park, HOOD RIVER. Eden Park, on the northwest slope of Mount Hood, was named in the summer of 1922 by a camping party led by C. Edward Graves, then of Hood River, but living in Arcata, California, in 1943. At the same time the party applied the names Cathedral Ridge, Vista Ridge and Wy'east Basin. These names were all adopted by the USBGN.

Edenbower, DOUGLAS. Edenbower is a locality about two miles north of Roseburg. It was named as long ago as 1888 by a family that moved from the rigorous climate of Winnipeg, Manitoba, to the Umpqua Valley. This family was impressed by the warm sunshine of that part of Douglas County and coined the name Edenbower. In Apr. 1948, Mrs. John Ferguson wrote from Days Creek, Oregon, that Mr. and Mrs. Donald Ferguson and three children came to Roseburg from Winnipeg in 1888 and after living in town a short while bought a ten-acre tract, and proceeded to make it their home. Mrs. Ferguson was so much impressed by the climate and the surroundings that she wrote a poem in Nov. 1888, extolling the locality and referring to it as Edenbower. It was not long after this, perhaps in 1890, that a school was organized and Mr. Ferguson suggested that it be called Edenbower. The name was adopted. Edenbower community did not have a post office until Aug. 1, 1908. John Botcher was the first postmaster. This office was discontinued Jan. 31, 1919. The area is served now by a rural route. Mrs. Ferguson's poem, "Winter—A Contrast," will be found in the Roseburg *News-Review* for May 21, 1948. It appears in the column by Charles V. Stanton and along with it are some other items about Edenbower.

Edison Ice Cave, DESCHUTES. On June 6, 1910, a large fire blazed some 30 miles southwest of Bend. One of the firefighters was Jack Edison, who, when returning to camp with George Vandevert, discovered a cool opening in the earth, entered and found an ice cave. Not only was Edison's name given the cave but also the fire. Edison Butte nearby is named for the same man, apparently a member of a transient crew. Edison Ice Cave is about four miles west of Wanoga Butte.

Edson Butte, CURRY. Edson Butte is a prominent landmark about seven miles east of Langlois. Both it and Edson Creek that flows into Sixes River were named for Avery J. Edson who came from New York with the Applegate train of 1846. Edson operated the Pacific Hotel at Port Orford in 1854 and later took as his second wife Christina Geisel, survivor of the massacre north of Gold Beach.

Edwards Creek, TILLAMOOK. Edwards Creek rises on 3168 foot Edwards Butte and is tributary to South Fork Trask River. Both were named for John D. Edwards, an early day timber cruiser, who took up a timber claim near the creek in 1889.

Egg Creek, LINN. Roy Elliott, who was district ranger for the USFS at Detroit for many years, told the writer in 1978 that around 1915 a trail crew camped on this creek near the headwaters of Middle Santiam River. Roy Talbert was insulted by one Anderson, another member of the party, and Talbert retaliated by hitting Anderson with a hard-boiled egg.

Egli Ridge, HARNEY. Egli Ridge is just east of the north end of Wagontire

Mountain. Amel Egli was an early settler in s 28, T 25S, R 24E. Egli, his wife, Lucy, and son, Amel, age 2 years are listed in the 1880 census. The early post office of Wagontire was first know as Egli. *See* Wagontire.

Eight Dollar Mountain, JOSEPHINE. Eight Dollar Mountain, elevation 3992 feet, is one of the prominent features in the Illinois Valley. There are several stories as to how it got its name, the most probable being that it came about as a result of the discovery nearby of a gold nugget worth $8.00. Another version is that a man wore out a pair of shoes worth $8.00 walking around its base. Its sides are excessively rough and inasmuch as the distance is about 12 miles it is quite possible that the latter story may be true. The battle of Eight Dollar Mountain, a skirmish in the Rogue River Indian War, was fought in this locality Mar. 25, 1856. *See* Victor's *Early Indian Wars of Oregon*, pp. 391–92.

Eightmile, MORROW. The post office at Eightmile took its name from Eightmile Canyon, which was so named because its mouth was about eight miles up Willow Creek from the Columbia River. The name was first used by pioneer stockmen.

Eightmile Creek, WASCO. This stream was so called because the pioneer wagon road from The Dalles into central Oregon crossed it about eight miles from town. Eightmile Creek and Fivemile Creek join, and the combined stream, called Eightmile Creek, flows into Fifteenmile Creek. For information about the names of this group of streams, *see* Fifteenmile Creek.

Eilertson Meadow, BAKER. Herbert Ensminger of Haines was authority for the information that this meadow west of Hunt Mountain was named for Eilert Eilertson who had a cabin and fish pond near its lower end. Eilertson lived there in the summer and in Haines the rest of the year. He died in 1919.

Ekins, YAMHILL. The first post office to serve the locality now known as Dundee was named Ekins for the postmaster, Claudius Ekins, who was appointed June 7, 1881. The name of this office was changed to Dundee on July 25, 1882. For the further history of this office, *see* Dundee. Ekins post office was established about the time the narrow gauge railroad was being extended from Dayton northeast through what is now Dundee to Fulquartz Landing on the Willamette River. *See* Scott's *History of the Oregon Country*, v.4, p. 305, *et seq.*

Ekoms, CURRY. The order establishing Ekoms post office was dated June 20, 1899. George W. Billings was to be the first postmaster. However, for some reason, the office never went into service and the order was rescinded Sept. 15, 1902. In Apr. 1948, Mr. Billings wrote that the name Ekoms was made by spelling Smoke backward. The office was to be in the Rogue River area, and the method of getting a name may have been suggested by the method used to make the name Ragic for a post office further down stream. Ragic, or Cigar spelled backward, was the name of a post office on Rogue River near the mouth of Lobster Creek.

Elam, BENTON. Elam was the post office name for a small community known as Harris, near Philomath. The office was established Apr. 20, 1918 and discontinued Dec. 31, 1928. Postal authorities would not accept the name Harris for the post office because of similarity to Harrisburg in Linn County. Accordingly the office was named for Mrs. Gladys Elam, the first postmaster. *See* Harris.

Elbow Lake, DOUGLAS. This little lake is about a mile east of the Pacific Ocean, just west of Tahkenitch Lake. It is known as Elbow Lake on account of its shape. *See* the USGS map of the Siltcoos Lake quadrangle.

Elder Creek, JOSEPHINE. Elder Creek is about two miles east of Waldo. It was named for John Elder, pioneer rancher.

Eldorado, MALHEUR. Eldorado, as a geographic name, is taken from the Spanish expression *el dorado*, meaning the gilded, and by analogy a golden or otherwise valuable object. It also means a legendary land abounding in gold. Its principal use in the West is in the Sierra Nevada of California, where it is applied to the county in which gold was discovered in 1848. The name has been used in many localities and may be found spelled El Dorado and also ElDorado. Modern usage tends toward Eldorado. The place called Eldorado in Shasta Gulch in what is now the extreme north part of Malheur County was a few miles northwest of the community of Malheur. It was named in the days of the eastern Oregon gold rush of the 1860s, doubtless by some of the many Californians who took part in the excitement. Miners began to work the placers of Eldorado as early as 1865, and about 1868 a town was started. A writer in the *Oregonian* of about that time says that the embryo town rejoiced in the name El Dorado City and was indifferently supplied with everything but whisky. The place thrived for a few years, but when Eldorado ditch began to bring in the waters from upper Burnt River many miles away, it missed the town of Eldorado, which was abandoned in consequence. Early in the 1870s many of the movable structures were taken to a new locality called Malheur City. El Dorado post office was established Sept. 1, 1869, with Samuel B. Reeves first postmaster. The office was finally closed in Nov. 1879. Building Eldorado ditch was one of Oregon's remarkable construction enterprises. William H. Packwood was a moving spirit in the business. The ditch gathered the waters of a number of tributaries on the south side of Burnt River and conveyed them eastward to a pass in the ridge south of Burnt River called Shasta Gap. It went through this pass toward Shasta Gulch and the Willow Creek drainage, where it was extensively used in mining. The ditch was originally about 135 miles long. In recent years it has been used for irrigation.

Eldriedge Bar, MARION. Eldriedge Bar is on the Willamette River about three miles downstream from Wheatland. It got its name from Freeman E. Eldriedge, pioneer settler on French Prairie. Eldriedge School, north of Waconda, was named for the same man. He was born in Pennsylvania in 1826 and came to Oregon by way of California in 1846–47. For a time during the 1850s Eldriedge rented his farm near the Willamette River and operated a grist mill at Parkersville about ten miles eastward. He was instrumental in having the Parkersville post office established and was the first postmaster.

Elephant Mountain, DOUGLAS. This is in the northeast part of the county northwest of Diamond Lake, and has an elevation of 5950 feet. The name was applied by V. V. Harpham and O. C. Houser, of the USFS in 1908, because the mountain when viewed from the west is suggestive both in shape and size, of the animal whose name it bears.

Elephant Mountain, LANE. Mrs. R. L. Gawley, who lived for many years in Disston, told the compiler in 1968 that this mountain in the Bohemia district bore a singularly appropriate descriptive name.

Elgarose, DOUGLAS. Elgarose, a post office in the southeast part of T 26S, R 7W, a couple of miles northwest of Melrose was named by the first postmaster, John E. Carlson, for Algaros in Sweden. The Reverend Mr. Carlson was born in the place in Sweden, and thought to perpetuate its name in Douglas County when the opportunity presented itself. Elgarose post office was established Jan. 28, 1916, with Carlson postmaster. The office was closed Nov. 27, 1924, and the business turned over to Melrose.

Elgin, UNION. In early days the locality of Elgin was called both Indian Valley and Fishtrap, because of the presence of Indian fishing gear. Elgin post office was established on Sept. 28, 1885, with W. B. Hamilton postmaster. A news story in the Elgin *Recorder* for Feb. 18, 1932, is authority for the statement that when the application for a post office was being prepared, Hamilton heard his nephew and niece, Charlie and Lottie Hamilton, singing about the wreck of the steamer *Lady Elgin*, and he was so impressed by the name that he suggested the title Elgin for the post office. The news item in the *Recorder* is based on a statement from C. W. Hamilton, then 88 years old and living on Lower Cove market road. Presumably he was the nephew, Charlie Hamilton. The compiler has been unable to learn that the community was named for Elgin, Illinois. The wreck of the *Lady Elgin* was one of the worst lacustrine disasters in the history of the United States. This steamer was loaded with a group called the Union Guard, composed of Third Ward boys from Milwaukee, who formed an excursion to attend a mass meeting in the presidential campaign of 1860. The Union Guard went to Chicago to hear their favorite, Stephen A. Douglas, on Sept. 7. The excursion and the political rally were highly successful, and the happy crowd started back for Milwaukee, Irish lads and lassies dancing as the boat ploughed through a Lake Michigan fog. About midnight the *Lady Elgin* was hit by a lumber schooner, the *Augusta*, which proceeded on her way after being assured that the *Lady Elgin* was not seriously damaged. This was a mistake, because the steamer sank in a short time, with a loss of nearly 300 lives. This disaster was the subject of a lugubrious ballad that was popular for a couple of decades, and the community of Elgin, Oregon, appears to have been named for the melancholy song, "Lost on the *Lady Elgin*."

Eliot Glacier, HOOD RIVER. Eliot Glacier is one of the larger glaciers on Mount Hood and occupies the northeast part of the mountain north of Cooper Spur. It is the source of Eliot Branch, and its lower end is not far from Cloud Cap

Inn. It was named for Dr. Thomas Lamb Eliot, for many years one of Portland's most revered citizens. Dr. Eliot was born in St. Louis, Missouri, on Oct. 13, 1841, and graduated with the first class from Washington University in St. Louis, of which his father was chancellor. He came to Portland Dec. 24, 1867, and took over the pastorate of the Unitarian Church. For a short biography of Dr. Eliot, *see* the *Oregonian*, Oct. 13, 1925, p. 5. Dr. Eliot was at one time greatly interested in mountaineering and the glacier on Mount Hood was named for him on that account. He died in Portland Apr. 26, 1936. In 1925 the Mazamas research committee made a number of investigations as to the rate of flow of Eliot Glacier. These observations were carried on at an elevation of approximately 7800 feet, and notes were taken for 14 weeks. The investigations indicated that the stakes which were set in the glacier traveled about four feet a week. The maximum movement was near the center of the glacier and the movement near the side walls was somewhat less, and during part of the season the sides of the glacier moved eight inches a week. Additional observations at an elevation of 7200 feet indicated a movement of about two feet a week for the central part of the glacier. *See Mazama* for Dec. 1925. *Mazama*, monthly edition, for Aug. 1926, gives additional information about the flow of this glacier. The greatest record for a year of any of the marks was made by one on the upper line, which moved 183.7 feet.

Elk Butte, LAKE. Elk Butte is near the southwest corner of S 12, T 27S, R 22E, a little to the southwest of Wagontire Mountain. This is in an area where elk have not frequently been found because of the lack of water. In May 1947, Archie McGowan of Burns informed the writer that Elk Butte was named in the early 1890s by members of the Hutton, Egli and other local families who discovered the track of a lone elk which took them to what they called Elk Butte. They were positive they were on the trail of a stray elk, which was very unusual for the desert country of Lake County.

Elk City, LINCOLN. Elk City is at the junction of Elk Creek and Yaquina River, and was named for the creek. It is said to have been the first settlement in what is now Lincoln County. Postal records show that Newton post office was established in July 1868, with E. A. Abbey first postmaster. Marshall Simpson became postmaster in Nov. 1869. He was out of the office for a few years, but held the position again on Nov. 23, 1888, when the name was changed from Newton to Elk City. It is said that he instigated the change. Statements to the effect that Elk City was named by pioneer settlers about 1865 do not agree with the records unless the locality and the post office went by different names. This has happened at a number of places in Oregon.

Elk Creek, BENTON, LINCOLN. Jerry E. Henkle, Benton County pioneer, is authority for the statement that Elk Creek was named in 1856 by a party of explorers who went into the Coast Range looking for grazing land. The name was given because a fine bull elk was shot near one of the camps on the stream. Elk Creek rises on the west slope of Marys Peak and flows westward into Yaquina River.

Elk Creek, DOUGLAS. Elk Creek joins Umpqua River near the town of Elkton. The stream has borne the name of Elk Creek since the period of the fur traders. The writer does not know when the stream was first named, but John Work mentions it as Elk River in his diary on June 7, 1834. *See OHQ*, v. 24, p. 253. Elk appear to have been plentiful in the Willamette Valley and in the Umpqua country, and there are many features named for them in those parts of the state.

Elk Creek, DOUGLAS. Judging by the number of geographic names in Oregon commemorating elk, that animal must have been both plentiful and popular in the days of the fur traders and the pioneers. Elk furnished more than their share of early-day provisions. The 1988 Geographic Names Information System lists 39 Elk creeks in the state as well as numerous Elk flats, mountains, meadows and springs. An important stream named Elk Creek flows into South Umpqua River at Tiller, in the southeast part of the county. It was named in pioneer times. There was an Elk Creek post office near the mouth of the stream, established Dec. 18, 1877, with S. C. Cramer first postmaster. This office operated with the name Elk Creek until Aug. 22, 1884, when the name was changed to Perdue, in compliment to John Perdue, Sr., then postmaster. Perdue took office June 11, 1884 and the office was moved west and down South Umpqua River about six miles below the mouth of Elk Creek. The new locality became known as Perdue. It is not clear from available records just when this move was made. Tiller post office was established near the mouth of Elk Creek Oct. 15, 1902, with Alfred B. Marquam first postmaster, and was still in operation in 1989. Tiller was named for Aaron Tiller, local settler. The locality has become known because of its place on the Tiller-Trail highway.

Elk Flat, UNION. Elk Flat is east of Elgin. It is an extension, to the south, from Cricket Flat. In Jan. 1947, Geo. T. Cochran of La Grande wrote the compiler: "Elk Flat joins Cricket Flat on the south. There is probably no dividing line between the two areas. In pioneer days there were many elk that grazed along the south part of Cricket Flat, and from that fact the locality became known as Elk Flat. I can remember going there many times with my father to get our winter's meat in the form of Elk." Elk Flat post office was established Apr. 17, 1878, with Joseph M. Tucker first postmaster. The office was discontinued Nov. 11, 1886. Tucker took up a homestead and built a house and blacksmith shop in s 17, T 1S, R 40E. According to Mr. Cochran he later found that his improvements had been installed on the wrong land. This was such an irritation that he gave up the post office and returned to his old home in Iowa. However, he came back to Oregon later. The Elk Flat post office was continued at various locations, and during the time James S. Brayton had it (1881–1886), it was at the Brayton place on Owenby Hill in s 10 of the township mentioned above, about five or six miles northeast of Elgin.

Elk Horn, POLK. Elk Horn was one of the pioneer post offices of the county and as with many others it was not always in the same place. Without a doubt it was named for some incident connected with an elk's horns. Probably a pair was nailed over the door of the Buell home. Elk Horn post office was established Nov. 16, 1869, with Cyrus Buell postmaster. Buell was a prominent settler on Mill Creek and was interested in the grist mill that gave the stream its name. For about five years the post office was at the Buell place about two miles south or upstream from the highway bridge and present location of the community called Buell. On May 18, 1874, Thomas R. Blair was appointed postmaster of Elk Horn and during his incumbency the office was about two miles north or down Mill Creek from what is now Buell. The office was closed Oct. 4, 1882, but the locality, which is a little over four miles southwest of Sheridan by road, is still called Elk Horn.

Elk Lake, DESCHUTES. Elk Lake is a fine body of water southwest of Bend, and Elk Lake post office was nearby. The lake was named in 1906 by USFS ranger Roy Harvey of Eugene. The post office was established because the lake was and is extensively used for recreation purposes.

Elk Mountain, DESCHUTES, LANE. This prominent peak of the Cascade Range is south of South Sister and west of Elk Lake. The mountain and Elk Lake were named about 1906 by Roy Harvey. A band of elk came across the summit of the range every year from the west and spent most of the summer on the side of a butte, which Harvey called Elk Mountain. This is said to be the only place where elk range on the east slopes of the Cascade Range.

Elk Point, WASHINGTON. This is a prominent hill about 960 feet high, just west of the community of Sylvan. The Pointer family settled near this hill in pioneer days, and called it Elk Point because the animals browsed on the sides of the point in question. In later years this feature has been called Pointers Point, but this was not its original name and on June 3, 1925, the USBGN officially adopted the name Elk Point.

Elk River, CURRY. This is a well-known stream that flows into the Pacific Ocean between Cape Blanco and Port Orford. It has been known as Elk River since territorial days and was probably named during the gold rush to the beach placers in southwest Oregon. There were many elk in those parts. The style Elk River is used in an article by William V. Wells in *Harper's Magazine*, Oct. 1856, p. 591, describing experiences in southwest Oregon in Oct. 1855.

Elkhead, DOUGLAS. The community and post office were named because they were near the head or source of Elk Creek in the western slopes of the Calapooya Mountains. A post office with the name Elk Head was established here on May 28, 1877, with R. J. Hendricks postmaster. On Feb. 27, 1895, the name was changed to Elkhead, and the office was discontinued Mar. 31, 1926. The best available maps show the name in one word. Elkhead was sometimes called Shoestring.

Elkhorn, MARION. This is a community on Little North Santiam River a few miles northeast of Mill City. While the origin of the name is obvious, the writer does not know the circumstances in which it was applied. The USGS map of the Elkhorn quadrangle shows Elkhorn and Elkhorn Woods to be several miles apart in the valley. Elkhorn post office was established in Mar. 1892, with William D. Morehouse postmaster. The office was finally closed in June 1917. Its principal business doubtless had to do with mining activity along the upper reaches of Little North Santiam River. There was an earlier post office in this neighborhood called Ivie, established in June 1890, with Martha J. Heath postmaster. The name of this office was changed to Elkhorn in Mar. 1892, but the writer does not know if the offices were at the same place.

Elkhorn Spring, WALLOWA. This spring is in T 5S, R 42E. It was named by William Adams and Hector McDonald because of a pair of elk horns that lay nearby for a number of years.

Elkton, DOUGLAS. Elkton was laid out and named in Aug. 1850. *See OHQ*, v. 17, p. 356. However, it did not have a post office until Sept. 26, 1851. David B. Wells was first postmaster. Elkton received its name because it was at the junction of Elk Creek and the Umpqua River. At one time the Hudson's Bay Company maintained an establishment known as Fort Umpqua very close to the present site of Elkton. For further information, *see* Leslie M. Scott's article on John Work in *OHQ*, v. 24, p. 238 *et seq*. John Work visited the Umpqua River in 1834 and Fort Umpqua, which was on the south side of the Umpqua River at the mouth of Elk Creek, apparently did not exist at the time of Work's visit. He mentions "umpqua old fort" which appears to have been established in 1832 near Calapooya Creek. There was of course, later on, Fort Umpqua, near the mouth of the river, which had nothing to do with the Hudson's Bay Company forts.

Ella, MORROW. Ella post office was established Apr. 24, 1882, with Frank Oviatt first postmaster. The office was discontinued on Sept. 30, 1910. The place is about seven miles east of Cecil. Four miles south of Ella is Ella Butte. Roy Scott of Cecil wrote the compiler in 1927 that at the time the matter of establishing a post office was considered, a meeting was held in a blacksmith shop owned by Oviatt. It was decided that the office should be established in Oviatt's house, as that seemed to be the best location, but a name could not be agreed upon. Oviatt's little daughter, Ella, was playing around the blacksmith shop and having hurt herself, began to cry. One of the men told her that they would name the office for her if she would stop crying, which she did. Ella Butte was formerly known as Well Spring Butte. Well Spring was a prominent point on the immigrant road about five miles east of the location of Ella post office. The spring is mentioned in many emigrant journals.

Ellendale, POLK. This pioneer community was about two miles west of Dallas, on Rickreall Creek. In 1845 James A. O'Neal built the first grist mill in Polk County, a few hundred feet west of what was later Ellendale. About 1849 O'Neal sold the mill to James W. Nesmith and Henry Owen, who operated it until 1854, and then sold it to Hudson & Company. The post office O'Neals Mills was established Jan. 8, 1850, with O'Neal postmaster. The name was changed to Nesmiths on Aug. 21, 1850, with J. W. Nesmith postmaster. The office was discontinued

Oct. 22, 1852. Due to the length of time necessary to communicate with Washington, D.C., O'Neal's appointment may have been made after he had sold the mill. Reuben P. Boise came to Oregon in 1850, and took up a donation land claim at Nesmiths Mills in 1852. He named the place Ellendale for his wife, Ellen Lyon, native of Massachusetts, who sailed from New York to San Francisco in the record time of 89 days on the *Flying Cloud*. The mill flume took water from the creek on the south side and crossed to the north side near the present county bridge. One of Oregon's pioneer woolen mills was started in Ellendale in 1860. *See* Lomax, *Pioneer Woolen Mills in Oregon*.

Elliott, COOS. Elliott post office was on the property of James K. Polk Elliott near Catching Creek a few miles southwest of Myrtle Point. Elliott post office was established Sept. 24, 1883, and was discontinued Sept. 11, 1897. J. K. P. Elliott was the only postmaster. He was a prominent pioneer of the county.

Elliott Creek, COOS. Elliott Creek flows into South Slough from the east. It bears the family name of Hiram Elliott, pioneer of 1849, who was born in Ohio in 1812 and settled in Coos County in 1865. He was a farmer and logger who raised a large family in the South Slough area. Elliott died in 1888.

Elliott Prairie, CLACKAMAS. This prairie lies east of Pudding River and Butte Creek. It was named for William Elliott, who came to Oregon in 1846. He was born in Indiana in 1815 and served in the Florida War in 1836. He married Nancy Sconce in 1838. He died at Park Place Feb. 27, 1905. His wife died in 1888. Elliott served in the Cayuse and Yakima wars.

Elliott State Forest, COOS, DOUGLAS. Elliott State Forest, consisting of 71,105 acres, was established through an exchange of state school grant lands which were widely scattered throughout the national forests for a solid block of federal forest lands, formerly known as the Millicoma Tract. The first move to establish a state forest by this means was made in 1913 by Governor Oswald West and State Forester F. A. Elliott. The exchange was not completed until 1929. Elliott died in 1930 and the forest was named to commemorate his work. This forest lay in the path of the historic Coos Bay fire of 1868, which left the land denuded for years. A study made in 1923 showed that only about half the area was stocked. Twelve years later a survey showed that more than 90 percent was stocked with western conifers, while most of the rest of the tract was producing maple, alder, myrtle, madrona, and cascara.

Elma Creek, LANE. Elma Creek empties into North Fork Siuslaw River in S 29, T 16S, R 10W. It was probably named for Elma or Alma Poole, a wife or sister of Monroe Poole, first postmaster at Pawn.

Elmira, LANE. Amos F. Ellmaker, in 1925, informed the writer that Elmira was named by his brother, Byron Ellmaker, for Elmira, California, a place that he greatly admired. About 1884 Byron Ellmaker bought a location for a wood and iron smithy near the present site of Elmira, then called Duckworth. Ellmaker did not like this name and persuaded postal authorities to change it to Elmira.

Elmonica, WASHINGTON. So named for Eleanor and Monica Stoy, daughters of Sam B. Stoy, who lived there in 1909. Stoy was an insurance man of Portland at the time and coined the name from the names of his two daughters.

Elowah Falls, MULTNOMAH. These falls on McCord Creek were named by a committee representing the Mazamas and other outdoor organizations in 1915. The name is obviously Indian, but the writer has not been able to determine its meaning.

Elrus, LANE. This station, on the Coos Bay branch of the Southern Pacific Company, was named for Elmer Russell, owner of a lumber mill nearby.

Elsie, CLATSOP. Elsie was named for Elsie Foster, relative of the first postmaster, George Gragg, about 1892. The compiler is informed that an effort was made to name the office Clover, but the name was not accepted.

Elwood, CLACKAMAS. Elwood is a locality between Colton and Springwater southeast of Highland Butte, probably named for Elwood Sylvanus, son of a Presbyterian minister of the neighborhood. The Rev. Mr. Sylvanus bestirred himself about getting a post office in the early 1890s, and the office was established with the name Ellwood on Apr. 28, 1892, with Eunice T. Sylvanus postmaster. There seems to have been an error in the procedure, because the name of the office was changed to Elwood on Sept. 12, 1892. The office was closed June 30, 1914.

Ely, CLACKAMAS. Ely, also called Elyville, was a suburb on Molalla Avenue near Holmes Lane in the extreme south part of Oregon City. The locality is sometimes called Mountain View, probably because it is near the cemetery of that name. The place was named in honor of George and Fred Ely, who settled there in early days. They were well-known public spirited citizens. George Ely later went to Inglewood, California. Ely post office was in operation from early 1891 until late 1894, with George C. Ely postmaster. The office was in operation again from July 1895, to Dec. 1904. In 1984, the compiler had a note from Roberta Schuebel Caldwell, the granddaughter of Robert Beattie, the last postmaster. She said in part: "I have a visual memory and remember the little post office at the top of the hill on what is now Molalla Avenue. Grandpa had a little candy counter in the post office and there was always a little glass cupfull of 'penny candies' for us little girls when we went to see him there."

Ely Canyon, MORROW. John and George Ely homesteaded in this canyon in the 1880s. It empties into Willow Creek near Morgan.

Embody, LAKE. In Mar. 1947, Mrs. Delbert Cloud, New Pine Creek, Oregon, wrote the compiler that Embody was named for Charles Embody, who at one time operated a sawmill there. Embody was about 16 miles northwest of the town of Silver Lake, on the old Military Road. Mrs. Cloud's father, S. L. Porter, took up a homestead in the locality in 1903 and proved up on it in 1908. He operated a small mill, which he sold to Charles Embody of Portland. Embody post office was established Aug. 3, 1908, with Stephen S. Lowing first and only postmaster. The office was discontinued Feb. 15, 1910, with mail to Silver Lake.

Embree Slough, HARNEY. Earl H. Conser of Burns, who knew the facts of such matters, wrote the compiler as follows: "Embree Slough, near Burns, was named for one "Doc" Embree, through whose land the slough followed an irregular course. He had several initials, but I am unable to find anyone who knows them exactly. He was a doctor of sorts." This was Thomas Van Buren Embree, son of Cary Embree. Cary Embree was a pioneer of 1844 and a resident of Polk County.

Emele Ditch, BAKER. This ditch was named for the family of William D. Emele who settled near Keating in the 1880s.

Emerson, WASCO. Emerson was a community and station on the Great Southern Railroad on Fifteenmile Creek about 18 miles southeast of The Dalles. It was named for Chester W. Emerson who settled there in 1884. The railroad was torn up in the 1930s and little now remains except a local crossroads.

Emerson Creek, DOUGLAS. This tributary of South Umpqua River was named for Lemuel N. Emerson who homesteaded the nearby ranch in 1915.

Emery, JEFFERSON. The Post Route map of 1900 shows Emery at a point 17 miles by road northeast of Sisters and a little to the west of Squaw Creek. In July 1946, Sterling J. May, acting postmaster at Sisters, informed the compiler that the office was at the Trahan homestead, and that it was named for Emery Trahan. The office operated from Sept. 1899, to July 1901, with Antoine G. Trahan postmaster. The Trahan place was about three miles southwest of Geneva, in sections 8 and 17 of T 13S, R 11E.

Emigrant Butte, KLAMATH, LANE. Emigrant Butte lies west of Summit Lake, in the southeast corner of Lane County, at the summit of the Cascade Range. It has an elevation of 6535 feet. It was named because of the emigrants that traveled over the emigrant route nearby.

Emigrant Buttes, UMATILLA. These buttes are west of Stanfield, and have an elevation of 759 feet. They are close to the route of the Oregon Trail, and were named for the emigrants.

Emigrant Creek, JACKSON. Emigrant Creek is southeast of Ashland and is supposed to be so named because emigrants who crossed the Cascade Range over the southern route came down this stream into Rogue River Valley. Emigrant Lake was formed in 1926 when the creek was dammed for irrigation. The dam was raised and the lake enlarged with work completed in 1960. When full, the lake has an area of 790 acres and is a popular recreation spot as well as important for flood control.

Emigrant Hill, UMATILLA. Emigrant Hill is a very prominent ridge of the Blue Mountains, southeast of Pendleton. The Oregon Trail traverses this hill as it proceeds westward, then descends to the northwest to Umatilla River. Emigrant Hill is sometimes referred to as Cabbage Hill, but Cabbage Hill is a spur south from the main hill and the Oregon Trail does not touch Cabbage Hill. Geography of this locality may be found on the USGS map of the Cabbage Hill quadrangle.

Emigrant Hill was of course named in pioneer days because the emigrant trains traveled over it.

Emigrant Pass, KLAMATH, LANE. This pass is about one half mile west of Summit Lake in T 24S, R 5E. It was originally called Willamette Pass as the emigrant road through it followed Middle Fork Willamette River to within a few miles of the summit. In 1960 the crossing of SH-58 just north of Odell Lake was named Willamette Pass and this redesignated Emigrant Pass. The primitive road is rarely travelled and care must be taken to avoid confusing this early Willamette Road with the present highway.

Emigrant Springs, SHERMAN. Giles L. French of Moro was good enough to dig up some facts about this place in Dec. 1945. Emigrant Springs are of good size and situated in S 27, T 2S, R 18E, in the northeast corner of Sherman County. The Oregon Trail passed through the area about a half mile south of these springs, but many wagons pulled down the canyon and camped at the springs where the water was good. Some emigrants camped there several days to refresh their stock. A post office called Emigrant was established in this vicinity on Jan. 20, 1887, with William J. Peddicord first postmaster. The name was changed to Emigrant Springs on June 29, 1889, and the office was closed June 12, 1895. The record indicates that the office was at or near the springs after the name was changed, but before that it may have been at the springs or in fact on the Oregon Trail. It should be added that the office was on the Wasco County list when first established.

Emile Creek, DOUGLAS. Emile Creek rises north of Taft Mountain and flows westward into Little River about ten miles southeast of Glide. It was named for Emile Shivigny, native of France, who settled nearby about 1875.

Emma, TILLAMOOK. Emma post office was in service for about six years at a point on Neskowin Creek about five miles southeast of the present community of Neskowin. The office was named for Emma Chitwood, local resident, and the name Emma Trail was applied to a route of travel from what is now Otis over the mountain to Emma, where settlers on lower Salmon River got their mail until they had their own post office at Otis, in Apr. 1900. Emma post office was established Dec. 16, 1896, with John D. Chitwood first postmaster. The office was closed Feb. 26, 1903, and the business was turned over to Neskowin.

Empire, COOS. Empire City, as it was first known, was founded in 1853 by men from Jacksonville, called the Coos Bay Company, headed by Perry B. Marple. For a list of members of this company, *see* Scott's *History of the Oregon Country*, v. 3, p. 161. The name Empire City was suggested by the expectation that the town would be the center of a large region. Discovery of gold in northern California and southwestern Oregon led to the formation of the project, and stock in the company was offered for sale in the *Oregonian*, Jan. 7, 1854. Empire City was formerly county seat of Coos County. A custom house was established at Empire City in 1853 for the southern collection district of Oregon, with David Bushing collector. Empire City post office was established in Apr. 1858. It operated with that name until Oct. 1894, when the title was changed to Empire. On Jan. 8, 1965, the city voted to consolidate with Coos Bay and the name Empire, in use for over a century, like Marshfield, became a thing of the past.

Enchanted Prairie, COOS. This little prairie of about a hundred acres is an open spot alongside the Coos Bay-Roseburg Highway approximately four miles east of Bridge and about 25 miles east of Myrtle Point. In the summer of 1943 Mrs. Alice B. Maloney of Berkeley, California, wrote the compiler that the place had a special significance for the Indians, who buried their dead there in a sort of cavern. John Yoakam investigated it as a boy and local Indians threatened him with violence. Enchanted Prairie post office was established Jan. 9, 1871, with Rufus P. King first postmaster. The name of the office was changed to Angora Aug. 3, 1883. Angora post office, which was apparently named by a goat fancier, was closed May 5, 1894.

Encina, BAKER. *Encina* is Spanish for evergreen oak. J. C. Mayo, of Stayton, wrote that he named this station. During the time of railroad construction the siding was called Oak Cut, but this name was cumbersome, and Mayo, who had lived in Mexico, changed it to the form now used.

Endersby, WASCO. This place was named for W. E. Endersby, local settler. Endersby School is about three miles north-northwest of Dufur and the spelling is that used in 1946 by the county school authorities. It is also reported to be correct by members of the family. A post office called Endersly was in operation in this vicinity from Apr. 1892, to Oct. 1906, with George W. Fligg postmaster. All postal records available to the writer spell the name Endersly. No explanation has been found for the discrepancy in spelling.

Endicott Creek, COLUMBIA. The USBGN has adopted the name Endicott Creek for a short stream flowing generally northeastward to Tide Creek in S 29, T 6N, R 2W. This was in compliment to Lawson Edward Endicott who was born in Wisconsin in 1866 and died in Portland July 27, 1938. He was long a member of the Portland police force. He was for a number of years detailed to assist travellers at the Union Station where he was a familiar and able officer. He came to Oregon about 1883 and to Portland in the early 1920s. He was awarded a medal for bravery about 1914. The compiler of these notes remembers Endicott well and thinks he deserves the honor of having a stream named after him.

Endicott Creek, COOS. Endicott Creek is a tributary of Middle Fork Coquille River. This stream was named for J. J. Endicott, pioneer settler near its mouth.

Engels Creek, DOUGLAS. This creek which flows into Little River at Peel was named for Abraham A. Engels who crossed the plains in 1852 and settled in the Glide-Peel area sometime in the 1860s. He later filed several land claims but although the various entries in BLM records all use the form Engles, members of the family still living in the area state this is incorrect. The OGNB adopted the above form in June 1968.

English, WASCO. English post office got its name from the fact that it was situated on the English farm near Company Hollow about eight miles southeast of The Dalles. The office was established July 2, 1896, with Christopher C. English postmaster and was in operation until Aug. 12, 1898. Judge Fred W. Wilson wrote the compiler in Feb. 1946, as follows: "The roads were bad then, and the farmers in that vicinity did not want to travel through the mud for their mail. When the roads were made better the need no longer existed. There were a very few farmers served by the office."

English Mountain, LANE. This mountain lies southeast of McKenzie Bridge. It was named during World War I to honor the English people. French Mountain lies just to the west and was named at the same time.

Enola Hill, CLACKAMAS. Enola Hill lies just north of Zigzag River and west of Devil Canyon. The name Enola was made by spelling Alone backward. It was applied by a homesteader who had a home that was quite isolated.

Enright, TILLAMOOK. Enright is a station on the Southern Pacific Company branch line to Tillamook. It is in the east part of the county near Salmonberry River and is about midway between Timber and Wheeler. Enright post office was established May 27, 1932 and closed Feb. 28, 1943. Enright is said to have been named for Mrs. E. E. Lytle. Before her marriage she was Miss May Enright and was well known in Oregon railroad circles. E. E. Lytle was a prominent railroad builder and was instrumental in extending railroad service to Shaniko, in north central Oregon, and from Hillsboro west to Tillamook. Lake Lytle, on one of the Tillamook beaches, bears his name.

Enterprise, WALLOWA. Ben Weathers, postmaster of Enterprise in 1925, informed the writer that the community was named in 1887. A meeting was held in a tent owned by a mercantile company and several names were suggested, including Bennett Flat, Wallowa City, Franklin and Fairfield. Finally R. F. Stubblefield suggested Enterprise, and that name was selected by a majority vote. The post office was established Nov. 9, 1887, with Catherine Akin first postmaster.

Eola, POLK. The village of Eola was formerly known as Cincinnati, and so appears when the post office was established on June 5, 1851. It is said to have been named by A. C. R. Shaw because of the fancied resemblance of the site to that of Cincinnati, Ohio. The place was incorporated with the name of Eola by the territorial legislature on Jan. 17, 1856. Miss Abigail J. Scott, later Mrs. A. S. Duniway, taught school in Cincinnati in 1853, and during pioneer days an effort was made to establish the state capital there. The name Eola comes from *Aeolus*, god of the winds in Greek mythology. There seems to be good authority for the belief that the name Eola was suggested by a local musical enthusiast named Lindsay Robbins, who disliked the name Cincinnati, and offered the new name because he was fond of the Aeolian harp. However, Geo. H. Himes thought that Shaw suggested Eola as well as the original name, so there you are.

Eola Hills, POLK, YAMHILL. These hills, which have an extreme altitude of 1170 feet, extend from Eola on the south to a point near Amity on the north, a distance of about 15 miles. They constitute one of the important groups of isolated hills in the Willamette Valley. They have had various names, including Bethel Hills and Yamhill Mountains, but Eola Hills seems firmly established, except for the northern extension, which is separated from the main ridge by the pass east of Amity. This northern extension is known as Amity Hills. Eola Hills got their name from the village at their southern end. Bethel Academy, Bethel Institute and Bethel College were prominent pioneer establishments situated in Eola Hills. *See* Bethel.

Erhart Cove, LANE. In 1889 Peter Erhart and in 1890 George Erhart filed on government land alongside this cove in Siltcoos Lake. There is also an Erhart Lake along US-101 just north of the Douglas County line. Kate Erhart filed on government land along the lake in 1902 but the filing was later cancelled. The compiler does not know the relationship of these three people.

Erickson Ranch, WHEELER. Erickson Ranch south of Antone is near the site of the 1889 homestead of John C. Erickson.

Erk Hill, HOOD RIVER. This high ground north of Odell was named for William Ehrck, native of Germany and a stonemason by trade, who settled on the hill in early days. Ehrck did the stone work on Cloud Cap Inn in 1889. This information was provided by L. M. Baldwin of Hood River.

Erma Bell Lakes, LANE. These three mountain lakes are just west of the summit of the Cascade Range and about five miles north of Waldo Lake. They are shown on the USGS map of the Waldo Mountain quadrangle. They were named for Miss Erma Bell, for a number of years employed as a computer in the Portland office of the USFS. She died Apr. 27, 1918, as a result of an automobile accident near Troutdale, and it was thought proper to perpetuate her memory by naming these lakes for her.

Errol, CLACKAMAS. Errol station received its name from Joseph A. Strowbridge, Jr. His father came to this country from England many years ago on a four-masted vessel named *Errol*. The post office at Errol station was installed about Jan. 1, 1922.

Erskine, SHERMAN. This place is between Moro and Grass Valley, and has also been known as Millra, Erskineville and Erskine Springs. About 1882 C. A. Williams opened a store there and Erskineville post office was established Dec. 19, 1882, with Abiel Erskine postmaster. When the railroad was built through, the shorter name Erskine was used for the station. Erskineville post office was closed Apr. 20, 1907, but the locality still goes by the name Erskine.

Erwin, BAKER. The place called Erwin was named for a well-known stockman, John Erwin, who was born in New York state in 1839 and settled in Oregon in 1868. He served in the Civil War and was wounded. He developed a stock ranch in Lower Powder Valley northeast of Baker. His biography is in the *History of Baker, Malheur, and Harney Counties*, p. 304. Erwin post office was established July 13, 1892, with Mrs. Elizabeth A. Pierce first postmaster. The office was closed as of Nov. 15, 1910. Gill's map of Oregon, 1911, shows Erwin in S 17, T 8S, R 42E, a little northwest of Keating. The name of Erwin post office was not changed to Keating as is sometimes reported.

Esmond Mountain, JACKSON. Edwin Esmond took a homestead just north of Lakecreek in 1871. Esmond Mountain, six miles due east, presumably bears his name.

Estacada, CLACKAMAS. *Estacada* is a Spanish word and means staked out, or marked with stakes, and the principal use of the name in the United States is in northwestern Texas where the form *Llano Estacado* is employed to describe a tract of land that in English would be called a "staked plain." The Spanish name refers to the trunks of an upright desert plant that remain standing like stakes or poles over an area of many hundred square miles. The name was used in Oregon because it had a pleasing sound, with no thought of its original significance. In the summer of 1927 a number of letters were written to the *Oregonian* asserting that Estacada was named for a girl whose name was first given as Esther Keady or Esther Cady, and by later correspondents as Esther Williams. These letters were printed on the editorial page of the *Oregonian* for July 16, 25 and 27. Other letters denying this version and supporting the *Llano Estacado* version were printed on July 18, 23 and 29. W. P. Keady was a right of way agent for the railroad company that built into that section of Clackamas County, and on Apr. 7, 1909, he wrote from Spokane, Washington, to L. E. Belfils, Estacada, and gave his story of the application of the name. The letter is too long to quote in full, but the substance is that on Dec. 27, 1903, a meeting was held at the office of the Oregon Water Power Townsite Company, First and Alder streets, Portland. Townsite and railroad company officials suggested various names, as follows: G. W. Morrow suggested Rochester; W. H. Hurlburt suggested Lowell; W. P. Keady suggested Lynn and George J. Kelly suggested Estacado. Kelly's suggested name, Estacado, was drawn from a hat, and adopted for the townsite, but through an error in drafting was filed as Estacada. One of Keady's sons was named Lynn, which was probably the reason for the suggestion of the name Lynn mentioned above. George J. Kelly, in a letter on the editorial page of the *Oregonian*, July 23, 1927, gives his version of the matter, which is substantially the same as Keady's, except that he says he was responsible for the change from Estacado to Estacada. He was chief clerk in the office, and selected the name at random from a map of the United States which showed *Llano Estacado*, in Texas. The compiler of these notes spent several weeks in Estacada shortly after the town was established and was informed by a number of persons at the time that the *Llano Estacado* of Texas was the origin of the name.

Estes, BAKER. This small suburb on the northwest edge of Baker carries the name of Hardin W. Estes who was born in Mississippi in 1828 and came to Baker County with the White Horse company in 1862.

Estes Creek, DOUGLAS. This creek is near the headwaters of Middle Fork Coquille River above Camas Valley. It was named for Jesse Estes who homesteaded there in 1888. His family first went from Missouri to Colorado in 1859 where they settled in the Rocky Mountain valley that is now Estes Park.

Estrup, LANE. Estrup post office was established on the Lane County list as of Mar. 31, 1898, with Peter E. Peterson postmaster. This office was west of Junction City, probably not far from the place that was later called Horton. According to information which is believed to be reliable Peterson named the post office with a Danish name, but the compiler has been unable to learn the exact significance of the word Estrup. According to J. J. Winn, an old timer in Lane County, the name Estrup may have been derived from the name of a Danish queen, but reference books do not mention such a sovereign. Estrup is or was a family name in Denmark but the compiler can find no record of its being a given name. Jacob B. S. Estrup was a prominent member of the Danish government at various times in the latter half of the nineteenth century. It is reported that there is a village called Estrup in Schleswig-Holstein and in 1905 there was an Estruplund parish in Denmark. It seems obvious that the name of the Lane County post office had its origin in Denmark. According to post office records Samuel M. Horton was appointed postmaster of Estrup post office on Sept. 27, 1901. The office was discontinued Apr. 4, 1902. Mr. Winn says that Horton never actually served as postmaster.

Etelka, COOS. Etelka post office, which was established Sept. 23, 1891, was named for a famous Hungarian opera singer, Etelka Gerster, 1855–1920. Mlle. Gerster, whose married name was Etelka Gardini, had a distinguished career both on the continent and in the British Isles. She also sang in America. For additional information, *see* Grove's *Dictionary of Music and Musicians*, v. 2. Etelka post office remained in service until Mar. 30, 1909, with Julia A. Carman the only postmaster. It was about ten miles south of Myrtle Point, near South Fork Coquille River. In July 1948, Mrs. Mary E. Coke of San Diego wrote the compiler that she was a daughter of Mrs. Carman and that she selected the name Etelka from a magazine or catalogue. She was then a young girl. The compiler has been told that in recent years Etelka has been referred to as Etalka but that certainly was not the name of the post office.

Etna, JACKSON. Etna was an early-day post office located on upper Rogue River, and for a time at least the office was about four miles below the present site of Trail. Doubtless it moved around, but it was always close to Rogue River. The post office was established July 5, 1882, with William P. Knighten first of five postmasters, and was discontinued June 26, 1896, when Louis J. Marck was postmaster. In the summer of 1946 the compiler had some correspondence about this office with D. W. Pence of Eagle Point. It was Mr. Pence's recollection that Etna post office was named for the niece of one of the postmasters, possibly of Mr. Marck. Mr. Pence was of the opinion that Marck was the first postmaster, but this is not in accord with government records. The compiler thinks that the girl was probably the niece of one of the earlier postmasters, probably of the first, William P. Knighten.

Etna, POLK. Etna was a post office at the Riggs place a few miles north of Rickreall, but the reason for the name seems to have eluded historical records. The office was established Sept. 4, 1856, with Thomas J. Riggs first and only postmaster. It was discontinued May 8, 1868. Rickreall post office was out of service from 1857 to 1866, so there was need of another office in the locality. Despite help from various Polk County people, including Cecil L. Riggs of Dallas, the compiler has been unable to get the reason for the name Etna. There does not seem to have been any member of the Riggs family named Etna. Cecil Riggs wrote in Jan. 1947, that he had always thought the office was named for the mountain on the east coast of Sicily, but perhaps without any definite reason. Mount Etna had a violent eruption in 1852, which may have been news in the Willamette Valley soon enough to produce a post office name in 1856. This is no more than a theory.

Euchre Butte, LAKE. This is a prominent mountain north of Lake Abert. It is said to have been so named because of an historic card game played nearby by cowboys in pioneer days.

Euchre Creek, CURRY. This stream apparently takes its name from the Tututni Indian band *Yukichetunne*. The name indicates "people at the mouth of the river." The *Handbook of American Indians*, among others, gives the following forms of the name: *Euchees, Eucher, Euchre, Eu-qua-chee, Uchres* and *Yoquichacs*. George Davidson, in the *Coast Pilot*, 1889, p. 373, refers to the stream as Ukah Creek for the *U-kahtan-nae* Indians. Miners applied the style Euchre Creek in the early 1850s, apparently influenced by the name of the popular card game. Davidson says that the stream was also called Savage Creek, but that name is not explained and has not persisted.

Euchre Mountain, LINCOLN. Accurate information about the name of Euchre Mountain seems hard to obtain, but it is generally believed that the word Euchre was used by pioneer surveyors as an approximation of the Indian name of the mountain. The correct pronunciation and meaning of the Indian name are not now available. The USGS gives the height of Euchre Mountain as 2452 feet. The late Robert L. Benson suggested to the compiler in 1977 that the name might be another of the transplanted names that accompanied the southern Oregon Indians exiled to the Grand Ronde and Siletz reservations. *See* Rogue River, Polk County.

Euclid, LINCOLN. This office was established May 25, 1904, with Martin G. Lyon postmaster and closed Apr. 30, 1909. In 1949, F. W. Furst, supervisor of the Siuslaw National Forest, wrote that Euclid post office was at or near the site of an earlier office called Axtell, which had been discontinued in the summer of 1903. The Euclid office was just to the east of the mouth of North Fork Yachats River in T 14S, R 11W. It is reported that the name was given by Allen Beamer, a nearby resident who had a reputation for being a scholarly individual. Just why the name of the Greek geometrician was selected has not been explained. In the spring of

1908, Lyon gave up the office and the establishment was moved some distance upstream on the north side of Grass Creek.

Eugene, LANE. Eugene F. Skinner took his land claim at Eugene at the foot of Skinner Butte in 1846, and built his cabin, and in 1847 moved his family into it. His wife, Mary Cook Skinner, was the first white woman to dwell in Lane County. Skinner came to Oregon in 1846, and first settled at Dallas. He was born Sept. 13, 1809, in Essex County, New York, and died at Eugene Dec. 15, 1864. His wife was born Feb. 7, 1816, and died June 4, 1881. Eugene City in 1855 is described by Thomas J. Dryer in the *Oregonian*, June 23, 1855. The first steamboat to ascend the Willamette River to Eugene was the *James Clinton*, Mar. 3, 1857, *Oregonian*, Mar. 21, 1857. The Indian name of Skinner Butte was *Ya-po-ah, Oregonian*, Apr. 23, 1897, p. 3, or *Ya-po-oh*, Nov. 17, 1890. For notes on Eugene in 1885, Jan. 31, 1885. This post office was established with the name Skinner's on Jan. 8, 1850, with Eugene F. Skinner postmaster. The name was changed to Eugene City on Sept. 3, 1853, and to Eugene on May 29, 1889.

Eugene Glacier, LANE. Eugene Glacier is on the north slope of South Sister, between Skinner and Lost Creek glaciers. It was named for the city of Eugene in 1924 by Professor Edwin T. Hodge of the University of Oregon.

Eula, LANE. Eula post office was named for Eula Blakely, daughter of Joe Blakely, an early resident. The post office was established about the time the railroad was built, with the name Blakelyville, but the railroad company adopted a shorter name, Eula. To avoid confusion, postal officials changed the name of the office to Eula, and both station and office operated with this name until about 1925 when the railroad changed the station name to Armet because Eula was too much like Eola, Polk County. Armet was selected arbitrarily by the company. It is the name of a form of head armor used in the middle ages. Properly the word is accented on the first syllable, but not so at Armet.

Eureka, WALLOWA. Eureka post office was established in Aug. 1903, and operated until July 1906. Thos. E. Alyea was the first postmaster. The office was near the southwest bank of Snake River in T 4S, R 48E, and was established to serve the Eureka mines which were being developed in the vicinity. There was mining activity at various points between the Imnaha River and the stream called Eureka Creek which flows into Snake River about three quarters of a mile farther downstream. The office and presumably the creek were named for the Eureka mines. The writer does not know the exact location of the office, possibly it was on the river between the two tributaries. *Eureka* is a Greek expression meaning "I have found it," and the word is frequently applied to mines and other enterprises where there are high hopes of success. There is a bar in Snake River just below the mouth of the Imnaha, and this is known as Eureka Bar. In 1945 it was reported that mining activity in the locality appeared to have ceased many years before.

Eustis, WALLOWA. This post office was named for Harry R. Eustis, nearby homesteader. It was situated in S 15, T 3S, R 41E. The office was established Feb. 29,

1904, with Charles H. Campbell first postmaster and it was in operation until May 1907, at a point about ten miles north of Minam.

Evans, WALLOWA. R. L. Forsythe of Enterprise wrote the compiler in 1927 as follows: "When the branch line railroad was built from Elgin to Joseph in about the year 1909, the railroad people agreed to run the railroad through Lostine if that city would pay a bonus of $1500, the cost of the additional construction by reason of a cut that would have to be made through a small hill east of Lostine. One man, Mr. James Haun, prominent citizen of Lostine, was strongly in favor of paying the sum but a majority was against him and the proposition was lost. As a result the railroad missed Lostine by about one mile and a depot was established a mile away and named Lostine by the railroad company. Mr. Haun had said that he would leave the town if it failed to land the railroad. This he did by moving two good residence buildings out of Lostine and onto land that he owned near the depot. He, together with John McDonald and S. W. Miles, laid out a new townsite at this point, and the name of Evans was selected (in honor of Mrs. Sam Wade). The settlement soon grew to include ten or twelve houses, a couple of store buildings, three wheat warehouses, a church and school house, as well as a few smaller buildings. Later a post office was established at the new townsite with the name of Evans. The last few years has shown a decline in the place, one store building having recently been torn down and hauled away and a number of the residences and buildings stand vacant. Locally the place has always been known as Jim Town, Jim being Mr. Haun's first name. There is, of course, a post office at the original town of Lostine and also one at Evans. The railroad has never recognized the name of Evans and it is still called Lostine on its map even though the station is actually at Evans." Post office records show Evans post office was established June 3, 1913 and closed Jan. 31, 1940. In 1980 Lostine and Lostine Station were still a mile apart and Evans remained in decline.

Evans Creek, CROOK. Evans Creek is tributary to Mill Creek two miles below Steins Pillar. It is named for Henry Evans who in 1889 filed on a homestead nearby. His son, David Evans, in 1914 also filed on property near the mouth of the creek.

Evans Creek, HOOD RIVER. This prominent tributary of East Fork Hood River rises on the slopes of Mount Hood below Cloud Cap Inn. Captain H. C. Coe in an article in the Hood River *News*, Mar. 6, 1918, says that it was named for R. O. Evans, an early resident of Hood River who homesteaded along the creek.

Evans Creek, JACKSON. Evans Creek was named for a pioneer settler on Rogue River, who operated a ferry about three miles west of Evans Creek, and was also first postmaster for the office of Gold River. This office was near the site of the ferry. Davis Evans was generally known as Coyote Evans, but why, the compiler does not know. Gold River post office was established Apr. 18, 1855. The territorial legislature changed the name of Rogue River to Gold River in 1854, and reversed itself in 1855. The post office name Gold River was doubtless the result of this action. The battle of Evans Creek, an important encounter in the Rogue River Indian War, was fought on the headwaters of this stream Aug. 24, 1853.

Evans Well, DESCHUTES. This well south of Millican Valley was on the 1911 homestead of Clifton L. Evans.

Evarts, UMATILLA. Evarts post office in the south part of the county was named for one Squire Evarts, at one time a lawyer in Pendleton, later a storekeeper at Evarts and probably also justice of the peace. The compiler has been unable to learn if the name Squire was Evart's given name, or an honorary title. The post office at Evarts was established Nov. 11, 1885, with William Roberts first postmaster. The office was closed to Ridge Nov. 11, 1886. It is reported that Evarts had probably moved away from the locality before the post office was established. Sam E. Darr of Adams has written the compiler that Evarts' establishment consisted of a store, hotel and feed stable all under one roof on the old mail route from Nye to Alba. It was on the west side of the road, on a ridge, and about four miles north of the old post office Ridge on the same mail route. Mr. Darr says that Evarts also owned the store at Ridge. The site of Evarts post office is now on the Pendleton-John Day Highway about five miles south of the junction with the highway to Heppner.

Evarts Creek, DOUGLAS. This creek flows into Cavitt Creek two miles south of Little River. It was named for J. H. Evarts who was born in Michigan and came to the Pacific Coast in 1888. He was a long time resident of Peel.

Evergreen, HARNEY. Evergreen post office was established on June 30, 1882, with Miss Mary E. Bedell first postmaster. The office was finally closed Jan. 21, 1887, and the business turned over to the Riley office. The history of the office is contained in the Grant County records, because Harney County had not yet been organized, but the office was in what is now Harney County. Old maps show Evergreen on Silver Creek a little below Camp Currey. Evergreen was about 300 yards down Silver Creek from the Military road crossing, on the A. O. Bedell land, later the Cecil ranch. There was a small green meadow at this point, and the Bedell children named the office on that account.

Ewe Creek, JOSEPHINE. Edith A. Keyte in *Josephine County Historic Highlights*, p. 63, says that Ewe Creek is only correct phonetically. She was born and raised in nearby Merlin and says that the correct form should be Yew Creek for the many trees of that species that line its banks.

Ewing Young Historical Marker, YAMHILL. Ewing Young came to Oregon in 1834 and at the time of his death in 1841 lived in his cabin in Chehalem Valley near this marker. His nearby grave is beneath an oak tree that was planted as an acorn in 1846. Young's death and the necessity of probating his estate, created the need for a provisional government, which was organized in 1843. It is curious that the name of one of the most industrious and prosperous early settlers who posthumously gave the impetus to organized government lies overlooked amid a welter of names of little distinction.

Express Ranch, BAKER. The post office called Express Ranch was very promi-nent in Baker County during the days of the mining excitement. The office was established Apr. 21, 1865, with C. W. Durkee first postmaster. It was situated at or near the place later called Durkee and was named because it was a stopping place for stage coaches or expresses as they were frequently called. The name of this office was changed to Weatherby on July 2, 1879, and it was apparently moved at that time to the Weatherby place about ten miles to the southeast, down Burnt River. Andrew J. Weatherby was postmaster at the time the name was changed. The Weatherby office continued in operation until Feb. 1920. The removal of the post office to Weatherby left the Express Ranch without a post office, and a new office named Express was established Nov. 26, 1884, with Joseph McKay postmas-ter. The name of this office was changed, probably on Feb. 26, 1902, to Durkee, in compliment to the early settler of the locality. This change was doubtless made because the name Express was unsuited to an office situated on a railroad. Such a name would cause confusion in express shipments.

Face Rock, COOS. Face Rock is in the ocean, just a little off shore and about a mile south of the mouth of Coquille River at Bandon. The rock bears a striking resemblance to a human head, with a lifelike face peering up from the ocean and gazing toward the North Star. There are a number of Indian legends about Face Rock. The rock is sometimes called Graystone, but Face Rock is the name in general use.

Fair Grounds, MARION. The first of the long series of Oregon State Fairs was held in the first week of Oct. 1861, at grounds a little to the north of Oregon City. While the facilities were good, they were not entirely satisfactory, and it was decided to move the fair to the Marion County Fair Grounds in the northeast part of Salem. The fair was held there on four days beginning Sept. 30, 1862, and the place has since continued as the State Fair Grounds. For historical notes, *see OHQ*, v. 8, p. 317, *et seq.* A post office with the name Fair Grounds was established in Dec. 1871, and was discontinued in Mar. 1874. The office was reestablished with the name Fair Grounds in Apr. 1892, and was continued until Sept. 1914, when the business was turned over to Salem. It should be noted that the post office estab-lished in Apr. 1892, was officially called Fair Grounds. The name was reduced to one word, Fairgrounds, sometime about 1895 and it remained that way until the office was discontinued in 1914. However, the railroad station was two words, Fair Grounds, for many years.

Fair Oaks, DOUGLAS. Fair Oaks was an early-day office near Calapooya Creek a few miles eastward of Oakland, which received its name because of the surround-ing tree growth. The post office was established Apr. 5, 1878, with William R. Smith first of three postmasters. It was discontinued May 25, 1882, with mail to Oakland. Available maps are not in agreement as to its exact location, and it probably moved around a little to suit the postmasters.

Fairbanks, WASCO. Fairbanks is a locality on Fifteenmile Creek near the mouth of Company Hollow. When the Great Southern Railroad was built along the creek in 1905, a station named Fairbanks was established. W. H. McNeal in *History of Wasco County*, p. 276, says that it was named for Charles W. Fairbanks who had just taken office as vice president under Theodore Roosevelt. There is another story that it was named by Daniel Farrington for his old home in Maine. In 1891 Farrington had filed on a homestead some distance to the south near Wrentham so the latter explanation appears improbable. Fairbanks post office was established Oct. 31, 1905 with Cyrus Cooper postmaster. It was discontinued July 31, 1909 with papers to Freebridge.

Fairchild Spring, WALLOWA. Fairchild Spring, in T 4N, R 47E, was named by George Mitchell, Dr. C. T. Hockett, S. L. Burnaugh and F. I. Vergere for Henry Fairchild, who directed them to the spring for a hunting camp. It is in the northeast corner of the county.

Fairfield, MARION. Postal authorities have informed the compiler that this post office was established Mar. 24, 1852, with John C. Peebles first postmaster. Fairfield is not now a post office. The name is apparently descriptive and belongs to a locality about six miles south of St. Paul, on the east bank of the Willamette River. For short history of Fairfield, *see* Salem *Statesman*, Oct. 28, 1931. John C. Davidson is reported to have built the first store in 1856. Before the days of the railroads, Fairfield was an important shipping point for river freight.

Fairmount, LANE. Fairmount post office was established June 10, 1891, with Lavinna E. Yeager first postmaster. John Lyndon Marsh became postmaster Feb. 15, 1902, and the office was closed to Eugene Feb. 20, 1904. Fairmount is one of those pleasant and popular descriptive names that can be and have been used without overworking the imagination. It has been applied to almost any sort of rise in ground, sometimes but a few feet higher than the surrounding land. The popularity of the name is attested by the fact that in 1945 there were well over a dozen post offices in the United States with the word Fairmount in some form. The Fairmount in Lane County was just east of Eugene, and during the time that John L. Marsh had the office it was at what was in 1947, 1873 Franklin Boulevard, at the intersection of Villard (extended), within the present city limits of Eugene and a short distance east of the University of Oregon. By 1980 the building had gone in favor of a parking lot sandwiched between two of the currently ubiquitous fast food stores.

Fairview, COOS. Fairview is a locality or community on North Fork Coquille River about six miles northeast of Coquille. It does not now have a post office. The name is said to be descriptive. Fairview post office was established for the first time on May 7, 1873, with Francis Braden first postmaster. It was closed Aug. 15, 1913. It was because of the Fairview post office in Coos County that an office of the same name could not be established in Multnomah County to handle the mail at Fairview railroad station just west of Troutdale. A distinct name was necessary for the Multnomah County situation, and Cleone was chosen, though the railroad continued to use the name Fairview for its station. After Fairview office in Coos County was closed, the name of Cleone office in Multnomah County was changed to Fairview in 1914.

Fairview, MULTNOMAH. The locality, Fairview, west of Troutdale, on the Columbia River, has also been known as Cleone. Fairview was adopted, in 1855, as the name of a Methodist Sunday school, organized in 1853. The late Stephen Roberts proposed the name, and it was adopted in preference to Mount Pisgah and Mount Pleasant. After the Oregon Railroad & Navigation Company's line was built, about 1882, and a station was established, named Fairview, a confusion in mail matters ensued because an older Fairview existed in Coos County, Oregon. Milton Hosford proposed Cleone, which was accepted as the name of the post office, but the railroad adhered to the old station name Fairview. Cleone post office was established Mar. 27, 1883, with Hosford postmaster. Differences over the name of the place were composed, probably due to the abandonment of the Coos County office of Fairview, and on Jan. 14, 1914, the name of the office of Cleone was changed to Fairview. In 1927 Milton W. Smith of Portland told the compiler that it was his opinion that the community of Fairview was named in the early 1880s by Mrs. Hannah M. Smith, who platted the townsite. Mrs. Smith was the widow of Hiram "Redshirt" Smith. This does not agree with the data given above, which is from Scott's *History of the Oregon Country*, v. 2, p. 313. A news item in the *Oregonian*, Sept. 10, 1901, p. 9, says the name Fairview had been in use about 45 years, and this seems to substantiate the Scott version. It is probable that Mrs. Smith merely adopted the old name for her town.

Fairview Peak, LANE. Fairview Peak is the highest point in the Bohemia district with an elevation of 5933 feet. According to Fred Asam, an early USFS ranger, it was originally South Lookout Mountain but this was changed to Fairview to eliminate duplication.

Falcon Rock, TILLAMOOK. Falcon Rock, elevation 15 feet, is in the Pacific Ocean a little less than a mile westward of Cape Falcon. The rock got its name from Cape Falcon. For the origin of the name of the cape, *see* Cape Falcon. The rock is sometimes called Cape Falcon Rock, but that form does not reflect the best usage, and is not the style used on the charts of the USC&GS.

Fall Creek, DESCHUTES. Fall Creek heads in Green Lakes east of the South Sister, and flows south about four miles into Sparks Lake. It has a succession of falls and rapids, culminating in a fine drop of about 30 feet at a point about a half a mile north of Century drive. It gets its name from this fall, which is most attractive. Professor E. T. Hodge, in *Mount Multnomah*, pp. 61 and 62, gives a good description of this stream and adjacent points of interest.

Fall Creek, LANE. Fall Creek was a post office on the stream of the same name, which is tributary to Middle Fork Willamette River. Fall Creek post office was near the junction of Little Fall Creek and the main stream. The writer is told that many years ago the community was called Tay for the River Tay in Scotland, apparently by the Stuarts and other Scottish settlers in the neighborhood. James Stuart located there as early as 1853. Postal authorities inform the compiler that Tay post office was established Aug. 9, 1880, with A. R. Randall first postmaster. The name of the office was changed to Fall Creek on Aug. 3, 1885, apparently at the request of T. C. Randall, then postmaster. The stream has been known in the past as Big Fall Creek in contradistinction to Little Fall Creek, a tributary, but federal mapping agencies nearly always drop the word "Big" from pairs of names of this sort, and consider the larger stream the main stem, with "Little" applied to the tributary. In 1965 Fall Creek Reservoir was completed by the USCE. It is a 1820 acre pool retained by a 195 foot high rockfill dam operated for flood control and water conservation. The pool stores approximately 115,000 acre feet of water at a normal elevation of 830 feet and provides a popular lake for water sports.

Fall River, DESCHUTES. Fall River heads in giant springs, and after flowing through pine woods for some eight or ten miles joins Deschutes River from the west, north of Pringle Falls. About half way between the source of the river and its mouth, it descends a series of small falls and cascades with a total drop of about a hundred feet. It was from these falls that it received its name.

Falls City, POLK. This town was named for the falls in Little Luckiamute River, which are near the west edge of the community. The name was proposed at the meeting which was held to initiate proceedings for incorporation. This place was originally served from a post office called Syracuse, situated between Dallas and the present site of Falls City. Syracuse post office was established in Feb. 1885, with Frank K. Hubbard first postmaster. The name of the office was changed to Falls City in Oct. 1889, and the office was doubtless moved at that time. It is said that the name Falls City was suggested by a family that had previously lived in Falls City, Nebraska.

Faloma, MULTNOMAH. This post office was north of Portland and served a community which was at one time known as Bridgeton. About 1921 the post office authorities were requested to establish an office there, but they objected to the name Bridgeton because of the duplication of other similar names in the United States. A meeting of local citizens was held and it was decided to ask to have the place named Faloma. This name was made up by using the initials of three original landowners in the neighborhood, to-wit: Messrs. Force, Love and Moore.

Fandango Canyon, LAKE. This canyon east of Silver Lake is named with the word for a lively Spanish dance. The compiler has been unable to learn why.

Fangollano, MALHEUR. Charles J. Bush, postmaster of the nearby office of Harper, wrote the compiler in Dec. 1925, as follows: "Fangollano is the Spanish translation (*fango llano*) of Mud Flat, the name the locality bore before the post office was established. Those responsible for the later christening no doubt got their inspiration from hearing Spanish spoken by the Spanish and Basque sheepmen who are wont to graze their flocks nearby; and wishing to retain, I presume, something of the significance of the old name without advertising what they considered a certain obloquy that attached to it, they compromised on Fango-llano. The post office at Fangollano is now discontinued." It should be noted that the Fangollano post office was at Little Mud Flat, which is six miles west of Mud Flat.

Fanno Creek, POLK. This creek empties into Valsetz Lake and Fanno Peak and Fanno Ridge form the high ground to the northeast. They are named for O. A. Fanno who settled on the South Fork Siletz River in the 1890s. Andrew L. Porter, who made the first land survey of the area in July 1894, notes the location of the Fanno cabin at the mouth of the creek. Of course, this was long before the river was dammed to form Valsetz Lake.

Fanno Creek, WASHINGTON. Fanno Creek takes its rise north of Garden Home, and after flowing westward turns sharply to the south and enters Tualatin River just north of Tualatin. It was named for Augustus Fanno, who settled on its bank in pioneer days. Augustus Fanno was born in Maine in 1804. He came to Oregon in 1846, with his wife and little son. Mrs. Fanno died on the arrival of the family at Oregon City, and after casting around for a home, Fanno selected a spot in Tualatin Valley on the trail from Oregon City to Tillamook Bay. This claim was about 12 miles from Oregon City, on what is now called Fanno Creek. He was married a second time to Rebecca J. Denny, and died on his farm June 30, 1884. For information about the Fanno homestead, *see* the *Sunday Oregonian*, Nov. 13, 1983, p. C12.

Faraday, CLACKAMAS. This was the station for the Cazadero power plant of the Portland General Electric Company, on Clackamas River. It was named by O. B. Coldwell, vice president of the company, for Michael Faraday, the great British scientist, who discovered the induction of electric currents.

Farewell Bend, BAKER, MALHEUR. Farewell Bend on Snake River is where westbound immigrants turned northwestward from the river and took a pass through the hills to the present site of Huntington on Burnt River. Farewell Bend was named in the days of the pioneers. Today I-84 leaves Snake River at the same point and passes through the gap in the hills to Huntington. The geographic situation is the same as it was a century ago. Farewell Bend post office was in service from Mar. 19, 1867, until Nov. 19, 1867, with William H. Packwood post-master. This post office shows in the Baker County list, but it was in operation before Malheur County was formed, and in fact its location may have been in what is now Malheur County, very close to the Baker County line. The location of Farewell Bend, was also known as Olds Ferry, although the modern place of that name is on the Idaho side of Snake River. R. P. Olds began to operate a ferry at Farewell Bend as early as 1862, having obtained a license from authorities in what is now Idaho. His license to operate in Oregon was granted in Mar. 1865, although he had actually been in business for three years prior. *See* Hiatt's *Thirty-one Years in Baker County*, p. 94. Packwood was also interested in the ferry at Farewell Bend and in the Burnt River toll road.

Fargher, SHERMAN. Fargher was a station not far from the east end of Sherars Bridge. It was named for Arthur W. Fargher, nearby landowner. He was born on the Isle of Man in 1855. He came to the United States in 1870 and to Oregon in 1878. He was at one time employed by the predecessors of the Oregon-Washington Railroad & Navigation Company.

Farley, HOOD RIVER. This station, east of Cascade Locks, was formerly known as Herman for the nearby creek. *See* Hermann Creek. The name caused confusion with Sherman, a station east of The Dalles, and Farley was substituted in honor of a local resident.

Farm Creek, CLACKAMAS. Farm Creek lies in T 7S, R 6E. It was named by Joe Davis, Jim Russell, Andy Wyland and Joe Dickey, who prospected and mined in that part of the county in the 1880s. They found good horse feed at the head of Farm Creek and left their stock there to pasture, calling the place The Farm.

Farmer Creek, CURRY. M. S. Brainard of Brookings told the compiler in 1967 that this creek two miles east of Carpenterville was named for Henry Farmer, homesteader. Farmer was well known locally for his beautiful handmade rugs and enormous feet. He died at Gold Beach Mar. 7, 1945.

Farmer Creek, TILLAMOOK. This creek flows into Nestucca River two miles above Hebo. It was named for A. D. Farmer who homesteaded along it in 1879.

Farmington, WASHINGTON. Farmington, a place near Tualatin River eight or nine miles southwest of Beaverton probably was named for Farmington, Connecticutt. The post office was established Nov. 24, 1884, with Isaac B. Everson first of five postmasters. The office was closed Dec. 23, 1904, with papers to Hillsboro. The locality is still a well-known point on a secondary highway extending from Beaverton.

Farrell Lake, KLAMATH. This small lake just east of Snell Lake was named in 1948 by a fish planting crew of the Oregon State Game Commission for Robert S. Farrell Jr., Oregon secretary of state, who was killed in a plane crash Oct. 28, 1947.

Fashion Reef, MULTNOMAH. Fashion Reef is in the Columbia River a little downstream from Multnomah Falls. It was probably named for the river steamer *Fashion*. This boat, the first on the middle river, was built with the name *James P. Flint* in 1851 by the Bradfords and Van Bergen at the Cascades. She was sunk in Sept. 1852, apparently on what is now known as Fashion Reef. She was raised in 1853 and taken to Vancouver, where she was renamed the *Fashion* and put back in service. *See* Wright's *Marine History of the Pacific Northwest*, pp. 35 and 45. Whether the reef was named as the result of the grounding in 1852, or some later trouble, the compiler does not know, but thinks the first alternative the more probable.

Fate Creek, DOUGLAS. David and Mary Ann Fate came to Oregon in 1852 and the following year settled east of Roseburg. They later moved to the Days Creek area and bought land including Fate Creek. David Fate was the chairman of the first Republican Convention in Roseburg.

Faubion, CLACKAMAS. This post office was established late in 1925 and was named for a local family. W. J. Faubion was the first postmaster and the office was half a mile southeast of Zigzag ranger station, on the old Mount Hood Loop Highway. The post office was closed on Sept. 30, 1937 with mail to Zigzag and W. J. Faubion died the following year.

Faught Creek, CROOK. Faught Creek heads south of Drake Butte in the Maury Mountains. In 1877 James M. Faught came to Crook County, first ranching along Trout Creek and then moving to the Bear Creek country where he had a sheep operation. In later years two sons, Elam and Elmer Faught, ran the sheep ranch. Faught Creek was named either for James Faught or for his family. For a short biography, *see Illustrated History of Central Oregon*, p. 759.

Fawcett Creek, TILLAMOOK. This stream southeast of Tillamook was named for W. H. Fawcett, who took up a homestead nearby. His land office number was 997.

Feasters Rocks, MARION. This spot on Willamette River near Lambert Bend bears the name of Daniel Fiester who with his wife, Rachel Anne, took up a donation land claim nearby. Fiester arrived in Oregon in 1847 and worked as a miller for John McLoughlin in Oregon City. His large family became well known in Marion County and several members used the form Feaster at one time or another.

Fellers, MARION. This station south of Donald was named for the family of a pioneer settler on French Prairie, Francis Feller.

Fence Creek, WALLOWA. Fence Creek flows from the west into Imnaha River about six miles north of Imnaha. The stream takes its name from some stone fences built in the vicinity in very early days by A. C. Smith, one of the first white settlers in the Wallowa Valley. A news story about the activities of A. C. Smith appears in the Enterprise *Chieftain* for Oct. 3, 1940. For biography of A. C. Smith *see History of Union and Wallowa Counties*, p. 577.

Fennell Lake, LINN. This small intermittent pond southeast of Jefferson was named for J. Fennell, an early settler. The spelling Fennel is wrong.

Ferguson Creek, CROOK. Ferguson Creek rises in the Maury Mountains and flows south to Bear Creek. Thomas J. Ferguson took up land along its banks in 1911. According to an article by Charles Hutchinson in the Prineville *Central Oregonian*, Jan. 22, 1970, this creek was once known as Belknap Creek, possibly for Doctor Horace Belknap, the pioneer central Oregon doctor. However, in the early 1930s the USFS renamed the creek for Ferguson.

Ferguson Creek, LANE. This stream flows into Long Tom River south of Monroe. It was named for a pioneer family. *See OHQ*, v. 5, p. 136.

Fern, BENTON. Fern post office was in operation from Oct. 1899, until Sept. 1903, with Edward L. Davis postmaster. The office was on the Davis farm on the road between Philomath and Bellfountain, and got its name because of the fern-covered hill nearby. The Davis place was about four miles west of Greenberry.

Fern Hill, CLATSOP. Fern Hill has been used as a locality name in Clatsop

County for many decades. The place is about eight miles east of Astoria, close both to railroad and highway. Fern Hill post office was established Oct. 24, 1879, with Mrs. Mary A. Dennis postmaster. This office was closed Apr. 1, 1881. An office called Fernhill was established Nov. 16, 1901, with Margaret Lewis first postmaster. This office was closed May 12, 1922, with papers to Svensen. The fern growth is heavy in that part of the state, especially on cleared land, and the name of the plant has been used frequently in geographic nomenclature. The most prolific fern in the locality of Fern Hill is the eagle brake or bracken.

Fernvale, DOUGLAS. Fernvale post office was about four miles northeast of Glendale on Windy Creek. The office was established Oct. 9, 1906, with Helma Nelson first postmaster, and operated until May 31, 1924. The locality has a descriptive name with a mildly sentimental touch.

Ferry, CURRY. The post office Ferry took its name from the early-day means of getting across Chetco River at a point about a mile up from the stream's mouth. The ferry was not far from the present Oregon Coast Highway bridge but the writer does not know the exact location. Ferry post office was established Mar. 5, 1888, with Sarah E. Cooley first postmaster. The office was discontinued Sept. 22, 1898, and the business turned over to Harbor post office.

Ferry, WASCO. Ferry post office was named for the postmaster, William T. Ferry. The office was established Oct. 26, 1912, and was at or near a place called Dillon, close to the Celilo Canal. The name of the office was changed to Dillon on Apr. 8, 1914, and to Celilo on May 20, 1915. For information about the name Dillon, *see* Dillon. According to Judge Fred W. Wilson of The Dalles, Ferry at one time worked for the railroad and may have been employed on the construction of Celilo Canal. He was a man of considerable clerical ability.

Ferry Creek, COOS. Ferry Creek is south of the town of Coos Bay and east of Delmar. In Aug. 1943, Mrs. Mary M. Randleman of Coquille wrote the compiler that the stream was named for the Ferry family, pioneer settlers, and not for a ferryboat.

Ferry Creek, COOS. This stream flows into Coquille River near Bandon. According to information from Mrs. Emma Drane, pioneer resident of the locality, John Lewis operated a ferry on Coquille River near the mouth of this stream in 1870, and the creek took its name from the ferry. The style Fairy Creek is wrong according to Mrs. Drane. There was, however, an earlier ferry at this locality, mentioned by William V. Wells in a story of experiences in southwest Oregon in *Harper's Magazine*, Oct. 1856, p. 595, describing conditions in Oct. 1855. Wells says the scow ferry was operated by a Yankee and an Englishman and was "for man and beast." There is nothing to indicate that Ferry Creek was named for the first ferry.

Fiddle Creek, DOUGLAS, LANE. Fiddle Creek heads in the Coast Range and flows westward into Siltcoos Lake. The origin of the name is unusual, but certainly not improbable. In Dec. 1942, Millard Martin, postmaster at Ada, wrote the compiler that about 1894 two men passed through the neighborhood on the way from North Fork Smith River to the Siuslaw country with the intention of buying cattle. One of the men had the misfortune to break his leg, and the two were forced to retire to a cabin about a half mile from the present site of Ada post office and wait for the injury to heal. This made a long and tiresome wait and the injured man wished repeatedly for his fiddle to help him pass the time. This expressed desire caused the nearby stream to be called Fiddle Creek.

Fiddler Mountain, JOSEPHINE. Fiddler Mountain and Fiddler Gulch are about six miles northwest of Kerby. They are named for Dr. George Fiddler and his son William Fidler (it is not clear which form the family used). Dr. Fiddler came to California in 1849. He returned east and in 1853 brought his family to Oregon where he settled near Coburg. Both the Fiddlers prospected in southern Oregon but the features were probably named for the father. William Fiddler lived in southern Oregon for many years and was a member of the first party to make a serious exploration of the Oregon Caves. See *OHQ*, v. 23, pp. 270–273.

Fielder Creek, JACKSON. This creek and Fielder Mountain west of Evans Creek, were named for Thomas Fielder, pioneer settler.

Fields, LANE. Fields, a station on the Cascade line of the Southern Pacific Company, was named for two members of the Lewis and Clark party, Joseph and Reuben Fields. It is sometimes said that Fields station was named for L. R. Fields, for many years an operating official of the railroad company in Oregon, but such is not the case, as is shown by the company records.

Fields, HARNEY. Charles Fields took up a homestead where Fields post office is now situated. He established a "station and kept the travel and freight haulers." He sold out to John Smyth in 1911, and when the post office was established in 1913, Smyth had it named for Fields.

Fields Peak, GRANT. This peak, elevation 7360 feet, and Fields Creek nearby were named for Harvey Fields, pioneer stockman. Fields Peak is about eight miles southwest of Mount Vernon.

Fife, CROOK. Fife is in the southeast part of the county. The compiler is informed that the place was named for the county of Fife, Scotland, former home of the first postmaster. This postmaster was Thomas Balfour. The office was established May 17, 1890 and finally discontinued Nov. 15, 1937. It moved around somewhat and for a time was actually in Deschutes County.

Fifteenmile Creek, LAKE. Fifteenmile Creek was so named because the old road crossed it about that distance northeast of Fort Bidwell, California. The stream heads east of Goose Lake and flows southeast nearly to the California state line, where it empties into Twelvemile Creek. It in turn flows east and north and into Twentymile Creek. The flow from these streams eventually reaches the Warner Valley.

Fifteenmile Creek, WASCO. This is the stream that flows through Dufur, and it received its name in pioneer days because the road from The Dalles crossed it about 15 miles from The Dalles. The road also crossed Fivemile Creek and Eightmile Creek before it reached Fifteenmile Creek. The Dalles-California Highway extends along all of these streams between The Dalles and Dufur. The three streams combine before they flow into the Columbia, and the name Fifteenmile Creek follows through to the Columbia, even though at its mouth it is only about four miles from The Dalles. The mouth of Fifteenmile Creek is at Seufert, and there was a substantial concrete bridge carrying the old Columbia River Highway over the creek at that point, known as Seufert Viaduct. All highway traffic now moves over I-84 immediately to the north although the old viaduct was still standing in 1989. Old maps show Fifteenmile Creek as Nansene Creek, and there was once a community of that name in Wasco County, but the compiler has been unable to secure information about the word Nansene. This is probably the same stream mentioned by Fremont on Nov. 25, 1843, as Tinanens Creek. Nansene post office was established May 17, 1880, with William C. Adams first postmaster. The office has been discontinued.

Fin Roberts Creek, LANE. This is a tributary of Salt Creek east of Oakridge. It was named for one Fin Roberts, who it is said, resembled the creek in that he was always dry.

Final Falls, CLACKAMAS. This 45-foot high falls on the Salmon River is about seven and three quarters miles downstream from the mouth of Linney Creek. It is the final of six falls between Linney Creek and Welches. For details of this group, *see* Stein Falls.

Findley Buttes, WALLOWA. The Findley Buttes are in the Wallowa Valley between Enterprise and Imnaha. They are named for Florence Findley who took up a homestead there in the 1880s. These buttes are sometimes known as Brumback Buttes for N. W. Brumback, nearby settler, but Findley Buttes is the older name and in the opinion of the writer, the correct one. Florence Findley married J. J. Johnson, an old settler. There was an early day post office near the Findley Buttes called Joy, because nearby settlers were so happy to get mail service.

Findley Creek, WALLOWA. Findley Creek flows west into Imnaha River near Imnaha. It was named for the Findley family. *See* Findley Buttes.

Fingerboard Gulch, WALLOWA. This gulch and Fingerboard Saddle where it heads are in the southeast part of T 3N, R 49E. The gulch drains into Cow Creek, and it is named for a wooden fingerboard that was nailed to a tree at the beginning of the trail up the stream. This trail was used to go eastward to the James Tryon place in the early 1880s, according to J. H. Horner of Enterprise.

Fingerboard Prairie, LANE. This prairie owes its name to the fact that for many years there was a signboard nearby cut in the shape of a pointing finger. Fingerboard Prairie is about six miles northeast of Belknap Springs.

Finley, WALLOWA. Finley post office was established Sept. 11, 1913, with Virgil T. Floch postmaster, but the office was short lived and was closed Nov. 30, 1914, at which time John E. Jackson was postmaster. The office was in S 36, T 1N, R 46E, about 15 miles northeast of Enterprise. It was intended that the office should be named for the Findley Buttes nearby but somewhere along the line the letter "d" was dropped, presumably in error.

Finley Butte, DESCHUTES. Finley Butte just east of La Pine is a source of ballast cinders for the Burlington Northern Inc. It was named for David Alex Findley, an early settler and first postmaster at Lava. The form Finley has been in universal use for many years.

Finley Buttes, MORROW. These buttes are in T 3N, R 26E, about 15 miles south of Irrigon. They are named for William B. and Hannah Finley who homesteaded in the area about 1880.

Finley Lake, MARION. Finley Lake is about a third of a mile northwest of Olallie Lake. It apparently was named for William L. Finley, well-known Oregon naturalist.

Finn Rock, LANE. Finn Rock is a peculiar formation on McKenzie River not far from the mouth of Finn Creek. The rock resembles a shark's fin but was not named on that account but instead for Benjamin F. Finn, an early settler. Finn Creek was named for the same reason. Finn Rock post office, established Jan. 6, 1947, is no longer an independent station but operates as a community post office of Eugene.

Finney and Egan Lake, MARION. Old plats show James Finney and W. H. Egan as nearby landowners, and the lake was apparently named for them. It is southwest of Waconda.

Finzer, MARION. Finzer was a station on the Oregon Electric Railway about five miles southwest of Salem. It was named for William E. Finzer, at one time adjutant general of the Oregon National Guard. The state had a rifle range at this station, which was named Finzer on that account.

Fir, HOOD RIVER. Information about Fir post office is not contained in the available records of Hood River County, yet the office is known to have been in service about 1915. It was in S 6, T 1N, R 11E, approximately four miles southeast of Odell near Neal Creek, and was named for the fir forests in the locality.

Fir, WASHINGTON. Fir was the name of a post office in the valley of Gales Creek not far south from the 1945 location of the Glenwood office. In other words it was about four miles northwest of the town of Gales Creek. The office of Fir was established with the name Bateman on June 30, 1890, with Clara J. Collins postmaster. It was named in compliment to an early settler of the locality, whose name has been perpetuated in the Bateman store which is also about four miles northwest of Gales Creek office. On Apr. 27, 1891, the name of the office Bateman was changed to Fir and it operated with that name until Oct. 9, 1900. Clara J. Collins continued as postmaster through the life of Fir post office. The compiler does not know the exact origin of the name of Fir post office. It may have been named for the trees which grow vigorously in the locality, or it may have been suggested by the name of Fir Creek, a small stream flowing east from the Coast Range to join Gales Creek just southeast of the Bateman store. Fir Creek School is situated on the creek at the toe of the foothills on a side road about two miles northwest of the town of Gales Creek. For information about the varieties of firs growing in Oregon, *see* Firwood.

Fire Spring, KLAMATH. On July 29, 1938, the men fighting a forest fire in the Cascade Range west of Chemult found this spring in the southwest quarter of S 26, T 27S, R 6E. This was the only available water supply except that carried in by airplane, and in the circumstances, it was called Fire Spring. The name has been approved by the USBGN.

Firemans Leap, DOUGLAS. This is a steep bluff at the south end of Homestead Ridge on the upper reaches of Steamboat Creek. During World War II, the army provided paratroopers as smokejumpers for the USFS to counteract fires that might result from Japanese fire bombs. The jumpers were employed to fight a lightning-caused fire on Lemon Butte, some five miles to the northwest. One was killed and several injured when they jumped into extremely difficult terrain. While there is nothing to connect the feature Firemans Leap with the Lemon Butte accident, it appears to be named for the incident. This information was provided by Rex Wakefield who was district ranger for the USFS at Layng Creek during the 1940s.

Firholm, POLK. Firholm post office was very close to the place called Elk Horn. Elk Horn office, with Thomas R. Blair postmaster, was closed Oct. 4, 1882. Nathan Blair, son of Thomas, decided to petition for the reestablishment of postal facilities in the locality. It was planned to use a small shop near the Blair home, and as there were some prominent fir trees close by, the name Firholm was suggested for the new office. Firholm was established Apr. 8, 1883, with Nathan Blair postmaster. This office was closed July 9, 1883.

First Creek, LINN. This stream is the first tributary of South Santiam River from the north, east of Lebanon, and is named on that account. It has also been known as Calloway Creek, but federal mapping agencies use the style First Creek.

First Lake, LINN. First Lake is one of a series of four on the east bank of the Willamette River north of Albany. These lakes are named in order from Albany north. First Lake is the one nearest the city.

Firwood, CLACKAMAS. Firwood is a community near US-26 southeast of Sandy. It has been so called for many years. It is a nice descriptive name and, considering the enormous quantity of firs in Oregon, some people have thought it remarkable that there are not more geographic names with "fir" in them. There are many Pine creeks and Cedar creeks but few Fir creeks. George R. Stewart in *Names on the Globe*, p. 75, states: "the namer is more likely to use the uncommon term than the common one." but in Oregon's case "fir" was the uncommon term. The great firs of the Pacific Northwest were far better timber than the eastern firs that were held in low esteem by people familiar with eastern hardwoods and Michigan white pine. Mills and dealers avoided this opprobrium by using various pseudonyms, the most popular of which was "Oregon Pine," a term used by the

Hudson's Bay Company in the manifest of the first shipment of lumber from the Columbia River. By 1900 "Douglas Fir" was well established in the northwest but "Oregon Pine" was still a familiar designation in other parts of the United States until after World War I. The fir is Oregon's most important forest growth. These trees may be divided into two classes, the Douglas fir, and the balsam firs. The Douglas fir is also known as the Douglas spruce, and its botanical name is *Pseudotsuga menziesii*. It is not of the fir family, but is a false hemlock. It was first classified in 1792 at Nootka Sound as *Pinus taxifolia* by Archibald Menzies of Vancouver's command. Menzies' notes were mislaid and not published until many years after a second discovery in 1827 by David Douglas, the great botanist, who gave the name *Pseudotsuga taxifolia*. It is fitting that these two naturalists are both commemorated, Menzies by the botanical and Douglas by the common name. There are but two species of this *genera*, the Douglas fir and a near relative, the bigcone fir or *Pseudotsuga macrocarpa*. The Douglas fir is of great commercial importance in Oregon. The balsam firs are the true firs, and there are six that are of interest to Oregonians. They are much alike, and are frequently confused even by people familiar with the woods. Their names are often mixed, and colloquial expressions such as red fir, yellow fir and Oregon fir are employed in attempts to describe them to the uninitiated. Probably the most important of the six Oregon species are the noble fir, *Abies procera* and silver fir, *Abies amabilis*. These two trees are very important commercially and are often called larch by lumbermen although true larch, *Larix occidentalis*, only grows east of the Cascade Range. *Abies lasiocarpa*, or alpine fir, is small and not so important. The lowland white fir, *Abies grandis*, and the white fir, *Abies concolor*, are important lumber producers, and are generally known as white fir. The red fir of California, *Abies magnifica*, also grows in Oregon, together with its variety *shastensis*. With the exception of the California sequoias, the firs of Oregon are the most magnificent of our forest trees, and attain heights of over 300 feet. Diameters of ten feet are not uncommon. For detailed descriptions of the species mentioned above, together with their ranges, *see* Sudworth's *Forest Trees of the Pacific Slope*, and Mathews' *Field Book of American Trees*.

Firwood, COLUMBIA. Firwood was named for its natural, rustic surroundings. The post office was on or near Clatskanie River southeast and upstream from Clatskanie. A 1930s map shows the office in the extreme south part of T 7N, R 4W, but a later army map shows Fir Wood school in the next township to the east. There is no mention of the name on the 1957 USGS Clatskanie quadrangle but an abandoned school shows in S 32, T 7N, R 3W, just east of Swedetown. This may be the same as Firwood school on the army map. The post office may have been moved from time to time, and in fact been in both locations in its career. The post office with the name Firwood was established Feb. 14, 1917, with Percy A. Frazer first of three postmasters. The office was discontinued May 31, 1918, with mail to Clatskanie.

Fischer Island, BENTON. Fischer Island is the lower part of a land-area in Willamette River upstream from Corvallis. The upper part is Stahlbusch Island. Fischer is the correct spelling and not Fisher. The Fischer Flouring Mill Company owned the land.

Fish Lake, LINN. The Oregon GNIS lists II Fish lakes and innumerable Fish creeks but this Fish Lake and associated Fish Lake Creek are of special interest. They are adjacent to US-20 just west of Santiam Junction. Fish Lake was the site of the most popular stopping place, operated by Henry Burmister and Joe Claypool, along the old Santiam Road in the 1870s. The lake dries up in the summer and provides excellent forage. This made it a desirable stopping point for west bound parties and, later, the site for the USFS pack string headquarters and remount station. It is also known for its Hackleman Trout and a rare breed of sedge known as Fish Lake Sedge. This information was provided in 1990 by Pete Cecil of the USFS in Bend who added it was still the site of one of the few remaining USFS pack strings in Region 6.

Fisher, LINCOLN. Fisher post office was named for the fisher, *Mustela pennanti*. The compiler is indebted to Tom McAllister, the well-known outdoor writer, for the following information about this now rare animal: "This cat sized hunter of squirrels and other small animals is a member of the family *Mustellidae* which includes minks, martens, weasels, badgers, otters and skunks. Before its near disappearance in Oregon, it lived in undisturbed virgin forest at low to intermediate elevations and often followed stream courses on its solitary rounds. The fisher vanished in the Coast Range with loss of habitat, trapping and the use of poison baits to control coyotes and wolves, but in the 1980s it was reported again in the Cascade Range. Old time trappers prized the fisher for the beauty and high value of the pelts." Fisher post office was established Mar. 19, 1892, but was not always in one location. It is reported that Bennett Olsen suggested the name. Martin Johanson was the first postmaster, and J. W. Mink later held the office. Remarkable nomenclature.

Fisher Creek, LANE. Fisher Creek is a tributary of North Fork Willamette River and was named for a pioneer cattleman who grazed stock nearby.

Fishhawk Creek, CLATSOP, COLUMBIA. There are two streams called Fishhawk Creek tributary to Nehalem River from the north. One of these streams flows into the river in the extreme west part of Columbia County. The other flows into Beneke Creek at Jewell. These streams were named because of incidents connected with the many fishhawks in Oregon and it is surprising that more streams have not been named for them. Ernest E. Hogberg was appointed postmaster at Fishhawk, Columbia County, on Jan. 17, 1890, and he held the office until it was discontinued Aug. 15, 1910. It was at, or very close to, the mouth of this stream near the extreme west edge of Columbia County. The area is now served by Birkenfeld post office. On Feb. 14, 1917, another post office, this time called Fish Hawk in two words, was established in the east part of Clatsop County.

Florence M. Bennett was the postmaster but her tenure was short. The office was ordered discontinued Sept. 22, 1917. This office was doubtless on a short section of Fishhawk Creek that loops into eastern Clatsop County.

Fishtrap Creek, COOS. This is a tributary of Coquille River between Coquille and Myrtle Point. It was named because Indians in pioneer days had many traps for catching salmon there.

Fisks, GRANT. According to R. R. McHaley in a letter published in the Canyon City *Eagle*, Mar. 7, 1947, Fisks was about a half mile north of the present site of Austin. The place was named for D. Walter Fisk, who owned a station there. Fisks post office was established Nov. 29, 1905, with Sarah P. Cecil first and only postmaster. The office was closed July 14, 1906, with mail to Austin.

Fitzgerald Ranch, WHEELER. Thomas Fitzgerald started this ranch on Bear Creek in the 1890s. He was a well-known sheep man who, in 1904, had 1000 head slaughtered by the "Sheepshooters." Phil Brogan in *East of the Cascades*, chapter 13, describes the range wars between cattle and sheep ranchers including the activities of the self styled Crook County Sheepshooters Association. He estimates that more than 10,000 sheep were destroyed between 1902 and 1906.

Five Hundred Flat, GRANT. Five Hundred Flat is at the headwaters of Myrtle Creek. In 1974, A. G. Oard, supervisor of the Malheur National Forest, wrote giving the following information about the name: "This was a place where buckaroos from Silvies and Izee came to play mumbly-peg and trade horses. It is rumored that the horses they traded were not always their own. The name comes from the fact that they always played mumbly-peg to a limit of 500 points."

Fivemile Creek, COOS. Fivemile Creek is a little south of Cape Arago and flows into Pacific Ocean. The stream was named during the Coos County gold rush of 1853–55 because it was thought to be about five miles north of the mining town of Randolph on Whisky Run. The distance is in fact about four miles, but it doubtless seemed more to the tired gold seekers.

Fivemile Creek, DOUGLAS. This creek flows into Tahkenitch Lake. It was so named because it is about five miles long.

Fivemile Creek, WASCO. This stream was so named because the pioneer road from The Dalles into central Oregon crossed it about five miles from town. Fivemile Creek and Eightmile Creek join, and about a mile and a half from the junction the combined stream, Eightmile Creek, flows into Fifteenmile Creek. For information about the names of this group of streams, *see* Fifteenmile Creek.

Fivemile Point, COOS. This point was named by George Davidson of the USC&GS because it was thought to be about five miles south of Cape Arago. It was suggested to navigators as a range point from Cape Arago. *See Coast Pilot* for 1889.

Fivemile Rapids, WASCO. These great rapids of the Columbia River were named by USCE because of their distance east from the boat landing at The Dalles. They formed a part of The Dalles of the Columbia, and were formerly known as the Long Narrows, The Dalles and The Great Dalles. *See* The Dalles in this book and article in *OHQ*, v. 27, p. 115. Fivemile Rapids were inundated by Lake Celilo when The Dalles Dam was completed in 1957.

Flag Island, MULTNOMAH. This little island is on the south side of the Columbia River about midway between Troutdale and Corbett station, just upstream from Gary Island. It has been named Flag Island by USBGN because it was in this vicinity that Lieutenant W. R. Broughton of the Royal Navy raised the British flag on Oct. 30, 1792. The name was suggested by J. Neilson Barry of Portland, in 1929.

Flagg, LANE. Flagg was a station west of Eugene on the Southern Pacific Company line to Coos Bay. It was named for L. Randolph Flagg, who was a member of the contracting firm that built the railroad.

Flagstone Rock, DOUGLAS. In 1939 field officers of the USFS recommended that a prominent unnamed rocky, barren point in S 23, T 28S, R 1E, be named Flagstone Rock because of its appearance. The name was approved by the USBGN. Flagstone Creek is named because it heads near the rock.

Flagtail Mountain, GRANT. This mountain was named because of the large number of flagtail deer that formerly grazed in the vicinity. It is about 20 miles southwest of Canyon City.

Flanagan, WASCO. Flanagan was a community and post office on the east side of Deschutes River six or seven miles east of Maupin, named for a local family. Flanagan post office was established in Oct. 1905, with John Flanagan first postmaster, and operated until Mar. 1912. There is some question about the postmaster's first name which may have been Thomas.

Flatiron Point, DOUGLAS. Flatiron Point is a descriptive name used by the USFS to describe a very prominent pointed plateau that lies just south of the junction of North Umpqua River and Fish Creek. The point is about 20 miles northwest of Diamond Lake and is remarkable for its flat top and steep sides. The point is toward the north.

Flavel, CLATSOP. Named for Captain George Flavel, who once owned the land on which the community is situated. In 1892 ambitious schemes were put on foot to build a railroad from Salem to Flavel, and the townsite concern, the Flavel Land and Development Company, laid plans for a big terminal to rival Astoria. In 1897, a fine hotel was built, which enjoyed a short season of social gaiety, but Astoria was too strongly entrenched for the rival community, which so far has not made the expected development. Silas B. Smith said that the name of the Clatsop Indian village at what is now Flavel was *Konapee*.

Fleetwood, LAKE. Fleetwood, a post office in the north part of Fort Rock Valley, came as a result of the homesteading movement into that part of Oregon. The office was established Sept. 25, 1913 with Helen A. Fleet postmaster. The name was coined from the family name. The office was closed in June 1928.

Fleming Spring, BAKER. Boyd Fleming filed on land at this spring southeast of Pleasant Valley in 1919.

Fletts, GILLIAM. George W. Flett was an early settler on Rock Creek on the east edge of what is now Gilliam County at a point a few miles northeast of Gwendolen. He had a post office established with the name Flettville on Nov. 4, 1881, which operated until Feb. 25, 1884, with Flett postmaster. Another office called Fletts was established May 5, 1884, with Orlando Rowland postmaster. D. F. Stricklin and Henry M. Pitman were later postmasters. The office was closed on Apr. 12, 1888. Charles E. Stricklin, Oregon State Engineer, was reared in these parts and on Dec. 24, 1945, he wrote the compiler as follows: "Apparently the post office was moved around. When my father was postmaster, a bedroom in the residence was used. During Mr. Flett's tenure as postmaster, he erected a small building in front of his residence which was used as a post office. When Mr. Flett was postmaster, the post office was located in the vicinity of the Flett School, but at that time there was no school there and the post office was across Rock Creek from where the school is now situated."

Flickbar, BAKER. Flickbar post office was established on the Baker County list on May 3, 1897, with James Grant first postmaster. The office was discontinued in Apr. 1899. Flickbar sounds like the name of a five-cent slab of candy, but an investigation made by LeRoy A. Grettum of Baker in Dec. 1945, indicates that was not the source of the title. According to Mr. Grettum, Flickbar was about ten miles up Snake River from Robinette, just north of Quicksand Creek and between the old stations Titus and Park. A man named Flick owned a ranch there and did some placer mining on a bar in Snake River. When the post office was established, it was named in compliment to Flick and his gravel bar. Irving L. Rand of Portland informed the compiler that it was his understanding that the geographic feature called Flicks Bar was on the Idaho side of Snake River and not in Oregon.

Flock Mountain, WHEELER. John and Charles Flock settled in Mitchell near the turn of the century. John Flock served a term as city recorder but Charles' wife, Sally, took up government land on the west side of Flock Mountain so the name probably comes from this side of the family.

Flora, WALLOWA. Flora was a post office in the extreme north part of Wallowa County. It was named for the daughter of the first postmaster in that district, A. D. Buzzard. This information was given the compiler by N. J. Hansen, postmaster at Flora in 1925. The office was opened Oct. 6, 1890 and closed Dec. 27, 1966. The little of Flora that remains is described by Phil Adamsak in the *Oregon Journal*, July 31, 1981, p. 19.

Floras Creek, CURRY. Floras Creek is a well-known stream in the north end of the county, flowing into the Pacific Ocean north of Cape Blanco. About 1910 William H. Packwood told the compiler that in the summer of 1852 he was a member of Lieutenant H. W. Stanton's command which was ordered to cut a trail from Fort Orford up Rogue River to the Rogue River Valley. They had with them a civilian named Fred Flora, who had been engaged in mining near the coast and Floras Creek was named for him. An editorial in the *Curry County Reporter*, printed in 1939, mentions this man, but spells his name Fred Florey. It says that Florey had opened up a trail along Floras Creek before 1855. It seems possible that miners from California, who were familiar with Spanish, changed the spelling from Floreys Creek to Floras Creek. The compiler has never seen any evidence that Floras Creek was named for the pilot of a Spanish expedition along the coast. Martin de Aguilar is said to have had a pilot named Flores, but there is nothing to show that his expedition ever saw Oregon.

Florence, LANE. Florence is on the north bank of Siuslaw River near the mouth. The town is said to have been named for A. B. Florence, who was a member of the state senate at the sessions of 1858, 1859 and 1860, representing Lane County. According to another story, (*Oregonian*, Oct. 7, 1903, by Lionel Johnson), the town was named for a French vessel, wrecked about 1873, at the mouth of Siuslaw River. Alfred L. Lomax discusses the wreck of the Florence in *OHQ*, v. 36, p. 222. The actual date was Feb. 17, 1875. Lewis & Dryden have further information in *Marine History of the Pacific Northwest* including the comment that the ship was "a veritable floating coffin."

Flounce Rock, JACKSON. Flounce Rock is a peculiar geological formation north of Rogue River between Trail and Prospect. It bears a fancied resemblance to the flounces on a woman's dress. It was so named at a time when flounces were worn, by Hiram Abbott, pioneer resident of the neighborhood.

Flournoy Valley, DOUGLAS. Flournoy Valley, a couple of miles west of Lookingglass, was named for H. B. Flournoy, who settled there in 1850. Fort Flournoy blockhouse was built in the valley in 1855. *See* Walling's *History of Southern Oregon*, p. 419.

Fogarty Creek, LINCOLN. Fogarty Creek flows into the Pacific Ocean at Fogarty State Park. Both the creek and the park are named for John Fogarty, a former Lincoln County judge. Fogarty took a homestead along the creek in 1906. His father, Jack Fogarty, came to Lincoln County in the early 1880s.

Foland Creek, TILLAMOOK. Foland Creek flows into Nestucca River near Beaver. It was named for Merriman Foland who settled nearby in the 1880s.

Foley, TILLAMOOK. A post office with the name Folley was established near Foley Creek on June 7, 1888, with Frank Worthington first postmaster. This office was out of service for a short time in the latter part of 1893. The name of the office was changed to Foley on Dec. 27, 1894, and that is the way it remained until it was closed by an order dated July 13, 1906, and effective July 31, 1906.

Foley Creek, CROOK, JEFFERSON. In 1878 Elijah T. Foley homesteaded along this creek in T 11S, R 17E. Foley Butte to the southwest takes its name from the creek.

Foley Creek, TILLAMOOK. This stream is east of Nehalem Bay. Miss Lucy E. Doughty of Bay City wrote the compiler in 1927 that the search for the origin of this name had led to a story to the effect that when the first white people settled in that part of the country they found a cabin that had evidently been built by a white man. When the Indians were asked about it, the whites were informed that it had been constructed by a man named Foley. Who Foley was, whence he came, whither he went, is apparently unknown.

Foley Slough, HARNEY. This is a part of Silvies River east of Burns. It was named for an early settler, J. C. Foley.

Foley Spring, BAKER. E. W. Coles, who was born in Haines in 1878, told the compiler in 1973 that this spring northeast of Haines was named for an early settler.

Foley Springs, LANE. Walling, in *History of Lane County*, p. 466, says that Foley Springs were first discovered by William Hanley and William Vick. In 1865 a man named Alexander settled on the premises and in 1870 a Dr. Foley purchased the springs and opened them to the public under the name Bethesda Hot Springs. Lane County records seem to show that what Dr. Foley bought from Alexander was not more than a squatter's rights, for Abram A. Foley received a patent from the government for the property. It was dated Mar. 30, 1882, and filed for record Nov. 30, 1889. Dr. Foley operated the springs for nine years, when they passed into the hands of Henry Hill, who sold out to Peter Runey in 1882. Runey made extensive improvements and got a post office, which was called Foleysprings in compliment to Dr. Foley. Postal authorities spelled the name as one word, but ordinary mortals used the style Foley Springs. The water is hot, about 188 degrees, rendering the baths very agreeable when adequately tempered. The building Runey constructed about 1916 was destroyed by fire in Mar. 1981. *See* article in Eugene *Register-Guard*, Mar. 6, 1981.

Follyfarm, MALHEUR. This post office was formerly on the extreme east edge of Harney County, and received its name because of the farming operations of J. H. Neal, who attempted to irrigate land in adverse conditions. Neal, unlike many persons in similar circumstances, possessed a sense of humor, and called his place Neal's Folly, which subsequently became Folly Farm. The post office was established about 1909, and Neal suggested the name of his farm for the name of the office, and the authorities promptly accepted it, as being distinctive and non-duplicating, but coupled it into one word. Dorcas N. Neal was first postmaster. The office was later moved a short distance eastward to a road junction on the west edge of Malheur County. John Scharf informed the compiler in 1981 that J. H. Neal was the first homesteader on Smyth Creek and that he surveyed the early meander line of Malheur Lake.

Foots Creek, JACKSON. Walling, in *History of Southern Oregon*, p. 379, says this stream was named for O. G. Foot, a miner who prospected along the creek in early days. Foots Creek flows into Rogue River from the south a few miles west of Gold Hill. The community at the mouth of Foots Creek has been known as Bolt since pioneer days. A post office called Foots Creek was in operation near this stream from Apr. 1878, until July 1879, with Silas Draper postmaster. The writer does not know the exact location of the office, but Draper was interested in mining on the upper reaches of the creek and the office may have been near what was later known as Draper. *See* Draper.

Fopiano Creek, WHEELER. Fopiano Creek rises west of Waterman and flows to Mountain Creek. John Fopiano located along this creek in 1875 after mining near Canyon City. After he died in 1891, his wife's brother, James Wilson, moved from California to manage the ranch.

Force Lake, MULTNOMAH. This overflow lake on the south bank of the Columbia River south of the east end of Hayden Island was named for George W. Force, pioneer settler.

Fordice Creek, DOUGLAS. Fordice Creek flows through Hughes Canyon to North Umpqua River west of Glide. James M. Fordice came to the Rogue River Valley in 1853 but in 1859 he filed on land along Fordice Creek. His name has also been spelled Fordyce. The name Hughes Canyon comes from Washington J. Hughes who came to Douglas County in 1862 and ran the ferry at Lone Rock. He later homesteaded in Hughes Canyon.

Foreman Point, WASCO. This prominent nose about six miles east of Bear Springs is the site of a state forest lookout. It was named for a well-known Wapinitia family. Benjamin L. Foreman settled on Juniper Flat in 1889 and married Eliza Abbott, sister of sheepmen James and Joe Abbott.

Forest, KLAMATH. This post office is said to have been named for the fine stand of timber adjacent. The compiler is quite prepared to believe the statement. In 1902 the pine forests of the vicinity must have been magnificent. Forest post office was about seven miles west of Keno on the old Ashland road. It was just east of Spencer Creek. Forest post office was established May 20, 1902, with Nathan S. High first postmaster. The office was discontinued to Keno, Mar. 4, 1908. Forest post office was about three miles northeast of a later office called Wampus. Both places were on the old Pokegama-Klamath Falls freight and stage road as well as on the road to Ashland. Both probably owed a good share of their existence to the business between Klamath Falls and Pokegama.

Forest Crossing, CROOK. Forest Crossing of Crooked River is at the south end of Lone Pine Flat just north of O'Neil, in the extreme northwest corner of the county. The locality was named for Francis Forest, who was born in Polk County, Oregon, in 1857, and settled in Crook County in 1876. For biography, *see Illustrated History of Central Oregon*, p. 784.

Forest Grove, WASHINGTON. At a meeting of the trustees of Tualatin Academy (Pacific University), Jan. 10, 1851, the name Forest Grove was adopted for the community. The name Vernon was first proposed and rejected. J. Quinn Thornton moved to adopt the name Forest Grove and the motion was passed. Previously that part of the county was known as West Tualatin Plain. It seems probable that the name Forest Grove was the idea of Thornton himself. Thornton arrived at his homestead in the Willamette Valley in Nov. 1846, and he named his claim

Forest Grove. *See* Thornton's *Oregon and California in 1848*, v. 1, p. 239. The words Forest Grove seem to have stuck in his mind. Postal authorities inform the compiler that Tualatin post office was established Feb. 1, 1850, with David Hill first postmaster. The name was changed to Forest Grove on Dec. 31, 1858. David Hill was the founder of Hillsboro, and information about him will be found under that heading. The compiler has been unable to learn why Hill was postmaster of a community apparently situated several miles away. However, post offices were frequently moved considerable distances in pioneer days. Tualatin post office was just south of the present site of Forest Grove. For early history of Forest Grove by Fred Lockley, *see* the *Oregon Sunday Journal*, Mar. 22, 1931.

Forman Canyon, JEFFERSON. Roy and Frank Forman operated a wheat ranch immediately north of this canyon near Trout Creek before World War I.

Fort Bailey, JOSEPHINE. This was one of the camps or so-called forts used in the campaign against the Rogue River Indians in 1855–56. Data about its location are conflicting, but the statement by Victor, in *Early Indian Wars of Oregon*, p. 368, is probably correct. It is to the effect that the fort was five miles south of Cow Creek. That means that it was on Wolf Creek, at or close to the present community of Wolf Creek. It was apparently named for Captain Joseph Bailey of the Oregon Mounted Volunteers. Bailey was from Eugene. Fort Bailey is sometimes described as at Grave Creek, but Fort Leland is known to have been the post at that place.

Fort Birdseye, JACKSON. Fort Birdseye was one of the stockades used by the settlers during the Rogue River Indian uprising of 1855–56. It was on the south bank of Rogue River near the mouth of Birdseye Creek, at the David Birdseye place. In 1856 some of the logs from the stockade were used to build the Birdseye cabin. A D.A.R. marker has been placed on the south side of the old Pacific Highway at the site of the stockade. When Rogue River Valley settlers gathered in one of these stockades, they called it "forting up." For more information, *see* Birdseye Creek.

Fort Briggs, JOSEPHINE. In Jan. 1944, James T. Chinnock of Grants Pass wrote the compiler as follows: "Fort Briggs was on the George E. Briggs donation land claim in s 35, T 39S, R 8W, near Sucker Creek. This was a log house in the Illinois Valley at which settlers gathered during the Rogue River War of 1855–56. Briggs was a pioneer settler."

Fort Clatsop, CLATSOP. This was the first military establishment to be built in Oregon, and it served as the Lewis and Clark winter-quarters for 1805–06. The various factors which influenced the selection of a locality for winter-quarters are mentioned in Thwaites' *Original Journal of the Lewis and Clark Expedition*, v. 3, p. 246, *et seq*. The men were allowed to vote on the location. Lewis made a reconnaissance and on Dec. 5, 1805, rejoined Clark, reporting that he had found a good situation. Construction of a stockade about 50 feet square was started at once. This was built around seven cabins. On Jan. 1, 1806, Captain Lewis recorded in his orderly book that the fort was completed, and the first orders for its operation and security were officially issued on that date. The name Fort Clatsop is not given in the orders, but appears later in the journals. The party left the fort on the return trip at 1 P.M., Sunday, Mar. 23, 1806. On Mar. 20, Lewis wrote: "we have lived quite as comfortable as we had any reason to expect we should." The site of Fort Clatsop, three acres of land, is about three-quarters of a mile south of US-101, the Oregon Coast Highway, just west of Lewis and Clark River and is easily accessible by road. A restoration project was begun in 1958 under the National Park Service. The Fort Clatsop National Monument consists of a replica of the log stockade and cabins along with modern visitor facilities. *See* the *Oregon Journal*, Aug. 22, 1963. Postal records show that Fort Clatsop post office was established Nov. 10, 1852, with Thos. W. Shane first postmaster. Carlos W. Shane was a prominent pioneer of this locality and it is possible that the authorities misread his name and put it down Thos. Franklin Shane became postmaster on Feb. 18, 1854. The office was discontinued on Feb. 15, 1855. The office was in service again with other postmasters from Mar. 1876, to Sept. 1881. The name of the office established in 1852 is very indistinct in early postal records, and may in fact be Port Clatsop. In view of the fact that the Shanes lived at Fort Clatsop and also in view of the name used for the office in 1876, the compiler thinks that the style Fort Clatsop is correct. The locality could hardly be called a port.

Fort Dalles, WASCO. Fort Dalles was a regular military post used during various Indian disturbances from 1850 to 1866. It was situated on Mill Creek, in the west part of the community of The Dalles, and before it was abandoned, it had developed into a commodious post. Fort Lee was established at The Dalles in the fall of 1847 at the time of the Cayuse War, but it had nothing to do with Fort Dalles. In May of 1850 Colonel W. W. Loring, then stationed at Vancouver, sent two companies of the Mounted Rifles to The Dalles to establish a supply depot. Heitman, in the *Historical Register*, says the post was first called Camp Drum. This was apparently to commemorate Captain Simon Henry Drum, who was killed in the assault on the City of Mexico, Sept. 13, 1847. For information about Fort Dalles, *see Illustrated History of Central Oregon*, pp. 102–105. The first buildings were of logs, but some of them burned, and the post was reconstructed in 1856–57, rather elaborately. A Captain Thomas Jordan had charge of the new construction. There is no record of any fortifications or defenses, either before or after the reconstruction. The reservation at first very large, was finally reduced to 640 acres, with the northeast corner at the mouth of Mill Creek. In 1905 the Old Fort Dalles Historical Society secured possession of the only remaining building, the Surgeon's quarters. This building is now used by the society as a museum and is visited by a great many people each year. It was built in 1858 and its design gives a good idea of Fort Dalles after the development of 1856–57. Priscilla Knuth has an interesting and detailed account of the fort and its buildings in *Picturesque Frontier, The Army's Fort Dalles*.

Fort Flournoy, DOUGLAS. Fort Flournoy was a settlers defense blockhouse built in the Flournoy Valley in 1855. It was never actually used. Walling, in his *History of Southern Oregon*, p. 419, says the structure was built of hewn logs, about 18 feet square, with the superstructure about 28 feet square. This was a typical method of blockhouse construction. The building was still standing in 1883 a couple of miles west of Lookingglass.

Fort George, CLATSOP. The North West Company took over Astoria and the Astor enterprise in Oct. 1813, and the Astor post was named Fort George, presumably in compliment to King George III. Franchere says that the bargain for the transfer was signed on Oct. 23, 1813, but he does not say that the name was changed on that date. Captain William Black of the British sloop of war *Racoon* was in the Columbia River in December and pulled down the American flag on Dec. 12 or 13. In his report to the Admiralty, Black says that he named the post Fort George. Fort George was technically returned to the United States Oct. 6, 1818, but continued as a British post. Americans revived Astoria many years later. The compiler has been unable to find any contemporaneous record that the Astorians used the expression Fort Astor. They referred to the post as Astoria. Franchere says the Northwesters planned to move the factory to Tongue Point, but this was not done. A diagram of Fort George as of 1818 is on file at the Oregon Historical Society and shows it to be a substantial installation, more than 150 by 200 feet, with a stockade and other defenses. A note on the diagram shows that the original Astoria establishment was about 75 by 110 feet, apparently not fortified. In 1930 workmen excavating in Astoria found remains of the stockade, probably the north wall, running from Fifteenth to Sixteenth streets, between Duane and Exchange streets. A plan of the fort has been painted on the sidewalks and pavements in this vicinity.

Fort Harney, HARNEY. During the Indian outbreaks of the 1860s, there were a number of army camps in southeast Oregon, but most of them were temporary. It appears to have been the plan of the authorities to make Fort Harney something more permanent. However, the place was a fort in name only if evidence can be relied on. Fort Harney was established Aug. 16, 1867, and was first called Camp Steele. On Aug. 28, 1867, Major-General H. W. Halleck, commanding the Military Division of the Pacific wrote to Brevet Major-General George Crook at Camp Warner regarding the naming of military posts. His thoughts on name selection are concise: "As a general rule, I think military posts should not be named after civilians, but after military officers as a compliment for military services. In most cases, it would be most appropriate to adopt the names of those who have served in the country where the post is established. I, therefore, cannot approve the name of Camp Wood, but think the new post should be called Camp Warner, or if you prefer, New Camp Warner. There is already one Camp Steele in the Department of the Columbia, and it would, therefore, be improper to give the same name to another. The present name of Camp Wright would also be objectionable, as there is now a Camp Wright in California. As the new post is in Harney Lake Valley, I suggest the name of Camp Harney, after General Harney." On Sept. 14, 1867, the name was changed in compliment to Major-General W. S. Harney but the record is not clear whether it was first "camp" or if it proceeded directly to "fort." *See* Harney County. The post was near the mouth of Rattlesnake Creek and about two miles east or north of what was later the community of Harney. In 1864 troops had been in this vicinity at a place called Rattlesnake Camp. In Jan. 1944 Archie McGowan of Burns wrote the compiler: "A portable sawmill was established in the timber north of the fort and extra good pine lumber was cut and practically all of the buildings were built of this lumber. There never were many of them, probably two small houses for officers, a barracks, some sheds or barns with log corrals for the horses. I can remember as a boy seeing some of those logs still lying around the corral, but the houses were all torn down and moved away by the settlers just as soon as the fort was abandoned. I have been told there was really no stockade." The *Illustrated History of Baker, Grant, Malheur and Harney Counties*, p. 633, says Fort Harney was abandoned June 14, 1880. It was used in the Indian disturbances of 1878. By order of the president, the Fort Harney military reserve of 640 acres was created Jan. 28, 1876, but on Sept. 13, 1882, this was reduced to 320 acres. The compiler has a statement from the late J. J. Donegan of Burns to the effect that the rest of the reserve was restored to public entry Mar. 2, 1889, "and the fort was abandoned." War Department records say that the soldiers marched out June 13, 1880, and Donegan's statement means that the land was abandoned as military property in 1889. A post office with the name Camp Harney was established Aug. 10, 1874, with William T. Stevens first postmaster. The writer has been unable to learn why postal authorities did not use the official name as adopted by the War Department. The name of the office was changed to Harney Sept. 16, 1885, with Robert J. Ives postmaster. The office was doubtless moved to the new community at that time.

Fort Hayes, JOSEPHINE. Fort Hayes was a gathering place for settlers during the Rogue River War of 1855–56 and was close to what is now the Redwood Highway southwest of Grants Pass. Walling, in his *History of Southern Oregon*, p. 452, says that Fort Hayes was at the Thornton place, about nine miles north of Kerby. James T. Chinnock of Grants Pass was of the opinion that the fort was near the south end of Hayes Hill, probably at what is also known as Anderson Station. The compiler has not been able to get more definite information. Members of the Hayes family were early settlers in the Illinois Valley and the fort was named for them.

Fort Henrietta, UMATILLA. Fort Henrietta was built by a detachment of the First Oregon Mounted Rifles under the command of Major Mark A. Chinn in Nov. 1855, in the Yakima War. Chinn named the fortified post Fort Henrietta, in compliment to the wife of Major Granville O. Haller of the United States Army. The fort was a stockade one hundred feet square, built of large split timbers, with two bastions of round logs, and an outside stock corral enclosed with rails found on the ground. *See* Victor's *Early Indian Wars of Oregon*, p. 439. Fort Henrietta was near the west bank of Umatilla River not far from the present (1942) site of the Catholic Church in the town of Echo. Statements that the fort was near Well Spring do not seem to be substantiated by the records.

Fort Hill, POLK. Fort Hill, just northeast of Valley Junction, was named because Willamette Valley settlers built a blockhouse on its summit in 1855–56. The federal government sent troops to this place and established Fort Yamhill on Aug. 30, 1856. *See* Fort Yamhill for additional information. The blockhouse was later moved to Grand Ronde Agency and still later to Dayton and set up in a public park.

Fort Hoskins, BENTON. Data about most of the early military establishments in Oregon are neither plentiful nor accurate, but fortunately there is a good account of the history and physical facts of Fort Hoskins. This information is in an article by Colonel Oscar W. Hoop, U.S. Army, with the title "History of Fort Hoskins, 1856–65," in *OHQ*, v. 30, p. 346. Fort Hoskins was established as the result of the concentration of Indians at Siletz Agency and was named in honor of Lieutenant Charles Hoskins who was killed in the battle of Monterrey, Mexico, Sept. 21, 1846. Captain Christopher C. Augur, Fourth Infantry, and his command reached Kings Valley July 25, 1856, and according to army records printed in *OHQ*, v. 36, p. 59, Fort Hoskins was established the next day. It was on Luckiamute River near the mouth of what is now known as Bonner Creek, probably on land owned by Rowland Chambers, later by Franz. Later in the year Lieutenant P. H. Sheridan began to build a road or trail from the fort over the Coast Range to the Siletz country. Augur's selection of the site for the fort was not approved by Brigadier-General John E. Wool, his superior, and there was a good deal of controversy. Augur stuck to his guns and the fort stayed where it was until it was evacuated Apr. 13, 1865. A blockhouse was built in the Siletz country, but there was also a squabble about this, and it had to be moved. Colonel Hoop has written entertainingly of the establishment of Fort Hoskins and the life there. The present community and post office of Hoskins are close to the site of the fort, but there is nothing left of the establishment. Colonel Hoop says that Sheridan left Fort Hoskins for Fort Jones, California, May 19, 1857, and "this is the last we hear of Sheridan in the valley of the Willamette." The implication is wrong for Sheridan was at Fort Yamhill in 1861 and was not ordered east until September of that year. Heitman's *Historical Register* says Fort Hoskins was on Siletz River and Old Fort Hoskins was on the Willamette River six miles north of Corvallis. Neither of these statements, apparently based on official records, is correct. Fort Hoskins was actually about 15 miles airline northwest of Corvallis. Heitman's Fort Hoskins on Siletz River seems to have been the Siletz blockhouse. The official records of two forts may have been based on the notion that General Wool had the post moved, but as a matter of fact Captain Augur refused to budge.

Fort Kitchen, COOS. Fort Kitchen was a stockade where settlers "forted up" under command of an elected captain, William H. Packwood. It was about a mile south of the present town of Myrtle Point, on South Fork Coquille River near the mouth of Catching Creek. An account of the establishment of this fort in Nov. 1855, is contained in Dodge's *Pioneer History of Coos and Curry Counties*, p. 96, *et seq.*, where it is said the post was named for the creek. *See also* Victor's *Early Indian Wars of Oregon*, p. 373, *et seq*. It seems probable that the firm stand taken by Captain Packwood in dealing with local Indians was successful in avoiding bloodshed in the Coquille Valley. According to Dodge, *supra*, p. 211, the stream was named for E. C. Catching, pioneer settler. The Catching place became a rendezvous at an early date. It is the opinion of the compiler that the name Fort Kitchen came as the result of the mispronunciation of the family name.

Fort Klamath, KLAMATH. For the origin of the word Klamath, *see* Klamath County. The Klamath Indian name for the locality of Fort Klamath was *Iukak*, meaning within, or in the midst, and referred to the location close to or between mountains. The fort was established with two companies of soldiers in 1863. It was an important post during the Modoc, Snake and Paiute wars, and was at a point about a mile southeast of the present community. The troops were removed in 1889. For story about Fort Klamath, *see* the *Oregon Journal*, Oct. 24, 1937.

Fort Lamerick, CURRY. The locality of Big Meadows was important during the Rogue River War of 1855–56. It is in the extreme northeast part of Curry County, about two miles north of Rogue River and near the southeast corner of T 32S, R 10W. It is mentioned several times in Victor's *Early Indian Wars of Oregon* and also in Walling's *History of Southern Oregon*. On account of their strategic position, the Oregon Volunteers decided to establish a post at the Big Meadows, and a site was selected May 1, 1856. This post was called Fort Lamerick in compliment to Brigadier-General John K. Lamerick of the Oregon troops. Since hostilities were over in the summer of 1856, Fort Lamerick was short lived. In Feb. 1944, forest ranger L. J. Cooper of Galice kindly sent some information about Fort Lamerick. The post was very close to the quartercorner between sections 1 and 2, T 33S, R 10W, and was about 300 feet above the present (1944) site of the Frye barn. In 1896 there were remains of the fort, some rotting logs and what appeared to be a dugout. These remains were cleared off by C. J. Frye when he took up a homestead. Local tradition is to the effect that the fort was a crude affair, hardly more than low log breastworks enclosing a camping place. Despite that, Fort Lamerick was important as a rendezvous and merits recording.

Fort Lane, JACKSON. Fort Lane was built for service in the Rogue River War. It was established Sept. 28, 1853, and evacuated in Sept. 1856. *See OHQ*, v. 36, p. 59. In the files of the Oregon Historical Society is a letter from Captain A. J. Smith of the U.S. Dragoons, dated Dec. 18, 1853, and addressed to General Lane, saying that the fort had been completed and that the detachment of three companies of dragoons and one company of infantry was quite comfortable. The fort was named in compliment to General Joseph Lane, whose career is described under Lane County. Walling, in *History of Southern Oregon*, p. 231, says: "Appropriately named Fort Lane, it was commodiously and even handsomely built, and in a manner well adapted to the uses of such a post. A stockade enclosed quite a spacious area in which was a parade ground, together with barracks for private soldiers, houses for officers, an armory, hospital, and other necessary buildings, all built of logs." The D.A.R. marker for Fort Lane is about a quarter of a mile north of Tolo on the road to Gold Ray, near the Southern Pacific tracks. Stones for the marker were taken from the remains of the fort.

Fort Lee, WASCO. Fort Lee was the stockade or post established at The Dalles by the Oregon Volunteers during the Cayuse War in the fall of 1847. It was named for Major H. A. G. Lee of the expeditionary force. According to Bancroft's, *History of Oregon*, v. 1, p. 703, the only piece of ordinance at the governor's command was a ninepounder belonging to Oregon City. This was sent to The Dalles, which place was designated as army headquarters. The compiler does not know the exact location or the details of construction of Fort Lee.

Fort Leland, JOSEPHINE. Fort Leland was one of the posts used by the Oregon volunteers during the Rogue River Indian uprising of 1855–56. It was just north of where the old Pacific Highway crossed Grave Creek north of Grants Pass. For the history of the name Leland, *see* Grave Creek and Leland. Fort Leland was established in the fall of 1855 by the Oregon volunteers, and the name is mentioned several times by Victor in *Early Indian Wars of Oregon* and also in Walling's *History of Southern Oregon*. There are some ambiguities about the location, but the consensus is that it was at the Grave Creek House and that is the local tradition. Walling, p. 255, says that after the battle of Hungry Hill, Harkness and Twogood, proprietors of the Grave Creek House, built a stout stockade of timbers and prepared for a siege. This stockade appears to be what was called Fort Leland. Troops had their headquarters there for several months.

Fort Miner, CURRY. This fort was not a military establishment, but a log structure built by settlers and miners about a mile and a half north of the mouth of Rogue River, on an open prairie near the ocean. The fort was used during the Indian fighting in 1855–56 as a place of refuge. Rodney Glisan in *Journal of Army Life*, p. 290, uses the name Fort Miner under date of Mar. 8, 1856, and mentions the fort in several places. In one place, on Mar. 25, 1856, he refers to it as Citizen Fort, and it is apparent that the establishment was built some time in 1855. Dodge, in *Pioneer History of Coos and Curry Counties*, gives a good deal of information about the place and on p. 83 refers to it as "Miner's Fort." On p. 347 is the name "Fort Miners." Fort Miner seems to have been a semi-official name for the establishment. Glisan says it consisted of two log houses, surrounded by a high earth embankment. Dodge, on p. 361 of his history, gives some reminiscences of Judge Michael Riley, which include a statement that the Rogue River miners and settlers built their stockade at first on the south side of the river near the present site of Gold Beach. Riley was absent at San Francisco at the time and on his return in Jan. 1856, objected to the location because there was not enough open space around. Riley was responsible for building a new Fort Miner north of the river where there was no cover for attacking Indians.

Fort Orford, CURRY. Fort Orford was established Sept. 14, 1851, and evacuated in Oct. 1856. *See OHQ*, v. 36, p. 59. According to R. C. Clark, the first troops were sent from Astoria. On Oct. 18, 1851, 135 soldiers sailed from the Depot of the Military Division of the Pacific, Benicia, California, to garrison Fort Orford. The detachment was in command of Lt. Colonel Silas Casey, *see* annual report of the Secretary of War, dated Nov. 29, 1851. The soldiers built the fort with cedar logs and with lumber shipped from San Francisco. The buildings were at the community of Port Orford and the post was named on that account. Dr. Rodney Glisan was stationed at Fort Orford from June 21, 1855, to Aug. 21, 1856, and has written an interesting account of activities there in his *Journal of Army Life*. In addition to the military post, there was an earlier civilian stockade with blockhouses, also called Fort Orford. Captain William Tichenor's second expedition landed at Port Orford July 14, 1851, and immediately built the first Fort Orford. *See* Fort Point. For Tichenor's account of the establishment of the civilian fort, *see* Dodge's *Pioneer History of Coos and Curry Counties*, chapter 11. The army post was a few hundred feet northwest of the civilian Fort Orford. The civilian fort was destroyed by the Port Orford fire of Oct. 10, 1868.

Fort Point, CURRY. Fort Point is at the south edge of the town of Port Orford, overlooking the ocean. It is just northwest of the famous Battle Rock. On July 14, 1851, Captain William Tichenor's second expedition landed at Port Orford and built two blockhouses on Fort Point, with log defenses. This establishment was built as a place of refuge for local settlers. The government, on Sept. 14, 1851, established the military post of Fort Orford, but this was in addiiton to the original blockhouses. The blockhouse fort was destroyed in the fire that burned Port Orford Oct. 10, 1868.

Fort Rock, LAKE. This is a prominent rocky landmark. The rock is an isolated mass, imperfectly crescent shaped, nearly one third of a mile across, and its highest point is about 325 feet above the floor of the plain on which it stands. It has perpendicular cliffs 200 feet high in places. It is not surprising that it has been likened to a fort. An item in the Bend *Bulletin*, June 20, 1925, says that William Sullivan, an early resident, named Fort Rock. Sullivan settled in what is now Lake County in 1873. In 1938 prehistoric artifacts were discovered in a large cave in a then unnamed butte about a mile and a half to the northwest. This butte was subsequently named Reub Long Butte to honor the well-known Lake County rancher and writer but the artifact cave has always been and continues to be known as Fort Rock Cave. Dr. L. S. Cressman of the University of Oregon supervised extensive excavations that uncovered weapons, tools and even sandals, and subsequent carbon dating showed some items 9000 years old. Phil Brogan has a full description including pictures in *East of the Cascades*, chapter 4. The community of Fort Rock was founded and named by Ray Nash. The post office was established Mar. 9, 1908. There was considerable activity around Fort Rock during the homestead period before World War I but in recent years little remains.

Fort Rowland, COOS. William Rowland settled on South Fork Coquille River in 1853, on what is now known as Rowland Prairie, and his place was used as a settlers defense headquarters against the Indians in the fall of 1855. The stockade was called Fort Rowland. For information about Fort Rowland and William Rowland, *see* Dodge's *Pioneer History of Coos and Curry Counties*, pp. 97–100 and 187. *See also* Victor's *Early Indian Wars of Oregon*, p. 374. Mr. and Mrs. Albert Powers, well-known residents of Coos County, owned the Rowland property in 1945. According to Mrs. Powers the Rowland home was on the Rowland donation land claim in the southwest quarter of S 27, T 30S, R 12W, close to the line of the Robert Y. Phillips claim.

Fort Smith, DOUGLAS. Fort Smith was a post used by the Oregon Volunteers during the Rogue River War of 1855–56. *See* Victor's *Early Indian Wars of Oregon*, p. 368. It was at the place of William Henry Smith on Cow Creek. It was near the southwest corner of S 25, T 32S, R 6W, and about four miles up Cow Creek from the present town of Glendale, close to I-5. Available records do not describe any defenses, although there may have been a stockade.

Fort Stevens, CLATSOP. Isaac Ingalls Stevens was governor of Washington Territory, 1853–57, and delegate to Congress, 1857–61. He was killed while leading the Seventy-ninth Regiment New York Volunteers, at Chantilly, Virginia, against the Confederates, Sept. 1, 1862. He was major-general, and had seized the colors of the regiment after the color-sergeant had fallen. Governor Stevens was highly energetic and constantly active, and was very popular with the people of the territory. He was born at Andover, Massachusetts, Mar. 18, 1818. In 1839 he was graduated from West Point. He served with distinction in the war with Mexico. The route of his journey to the territory in 1853, laid out and surveyed, by him, as one for a railroad, was largely followed by the Northern Pacific. A biography, by his son, Hazard Stevens, is a meritorious book: *Life of Isaac Ingalls Stevens*, Houghton Mifflin & Company, 1900. For a prospectus of Stevens' railroad surveys, *see* the *Oregonian*, July 16, 1853; progress of the surveys, Oct. 1, 22, 1853. Stevens visited the eastern states in 1854. He left Portland Mar. 29, 1854. His report on his council with the Blackfeet, dated June 8, 1854, appears, *ibid.*, July 29, 1854. Fort Stevens, in Oregon, was named for him by Captain George H. Elliott, USCE, who built the fortifications there and at Cape Disappointment in 1864, *Oregonian*, Sept. 21, 1864. Fort Stevens post office operated from Feb. 20, 1899 to Jan. 31, 1949. Edward M. Philebaum was first postmaster.

In 1955 Clatsop County gave a large parcel of land immediately south of Fort Stevens to the state for inclusion in the State Parks system. In 1968 the parks system obtained control of the military reservation via long term lease from the

USCE and most of the area is now Fort Stevens State Park. It is not only one of the more popular camping areas but also attracts large numbers of visitors to Battery Russell and the other historic gun emplacements. In 1980, *Fort Stevens: Oregon's Defender at the River of the West*, a detailed history of the post by Marshall Hanft, was published by the State Parks and Recreation Division. *See also* Hanft's article "The Cape Forts: Guardians of the Columbia," *OHQ*, v. 65, pp. 325 through 361.

Fort Umpqua, DOUGLAS. This was a United States military establishment, not to be confused with Hudson's Bay Company forts of the same name. Fort Umpqua was established July 28, 1856. *See OHQ*, v. 36, p. 59. It was one of three forts set up to watch over the Indians at Grand Ronde and Siletz agencies. The other two were Fort Yamhill and Fort Hoskins. A letter in the Bancroft Library, University of California, dated Umpqua City, Mar. 20, 1862, with a signature that seems to be J. V. Cately, says that the post was built to accommodate two companies of soldiers, but on that date had but one lieutenant and 22 men. The post was at the same place as the community and post office of Umpqua City, about two miles north of the mouth of the river, on the west bank, not far from what is now known as Army Hill. Walling, in *History of Southern Oregon*, p. 438, says that in the summer of 1862 a paymaster visited the fort and found all the officers, commissioned and non-commissioned, away on a hunting trip. As the result of this episode, the post was abandoned.

Fort Vannoy, JOSEPHINE. Fort Vannoy was one of the more important posts used by Oregon volunteer troops during the Rogue River War of 1855–56. James T. Chinnock of Grants Pass furnished the compiler with the following information: "Fort Vannoy was on the north bank of Rogue River about four miles west of what is now Grants Pass, near the northwest corner of S 21, T 36S, R 6W, on the Margaret Vannoy donation land claim adjoining the James N. Vannoy claim. Vannoy was a pioneer of 1851 and established a ferry in that year. A man named Long operated a ferry a little below this point in 1850. Fort Vannoy was in no sense a fortification, but a headquarters camp for the volunteers of the 1855–56 Indian War. It was probably established in late October or Nov. 1855. The exact location cannot be determined, because there are no marks remaining. There was a group of log houses, and possibly some defense, such as log breastworks or a low stockade hastily constructed. The word fort seems to have been used for any place where the settlers gathered for mutual protection rather than for a place fortified. Fort Vannoy was important because it was used for headquarters as well as for settlers' refuge. The land is now owned by C. H. Eismann." A good article about Fort Vannoy, written by James T. Chinnock, is in Grants Pass *Courier*, Aug. 8, 1942.

Fort William, COLUMBIA, MULTNOMAH. Fort William was established on Sauvie Island by Nathaniel J. Wyeth, and occupied two sites. The first was near Warrior Point, where the fort was established temporarily in the autumn of 1834. Wyeth wrote on Oct. 6, 1834: "We are near the mouth of the Multnomah." About

May 1, 1835, the establishment was moved south opposite the Logie Trail, which was a route of travel into Tualatin Valley. This was to be the permanent location. It was on the west side of the island, in s 7, T 2N, R 1W. Owing to the commercial rivalry of the Hudson's Bay Company, Wyeth was forced to abandon Fort William. Carey, in *History of Oregon*, p. 302, says that Fort William was named for one of Wyeth's partners but does not say which one. The site is shown as Fort William Bend on the USGS Sauvie Island quadrangle.

Fort Yamhill, YAMHILL. In 1855–56 Willamette Valley settlers built a blockhouse on Fort Hill, near the present community of Valley Junction, as a protection against Indians who had been moved onto the reservation. The federal government sent troops to this place and established Fort Yamhill on Aug. 30, 1856. See *OHQ*, v. 36, p. 59. The fort was named for the Yamhill River. For the origin of the name Yamhill, *see* Yamhill County. There is a good general account of the activities at Fort Yamhill in Glisan's *Journal of Army Life*. Dr. Glisan arrived at Fort Yamhill early in Sept. 1856, and his journal runs through Feb. 10, 1859. It is well worth reading. The compiler does not know when Fort Yamhill was evacuated as a military establishment, but it was subsequent to June 30, 1865. Official records do not seem to warrant the use of the name Fort Sheridan for this establishment. The D.A.R. marker for Fort Yamhill is about a half a mile north of Valley Junction on the Three Rivers Highway and it says that the fort was about 300 yards east of the monument, which would place it close to Fort Hill east of Cosper Creek. In a general way this agrees with Glisan's description. After the army authorities abandoned Fort Yamhill as a military post, the Fort Yamhill blockhouse was moved from the top of Fort Hill to Grand Ronde Agency and used for a jail. It stood about where the Agency Community Hall stood in 1944. Later it was moved again, this time to Dayton and set up in a public park. After the blockhouse was moved to Dayton, dedication ceremonies were held Aug. 23, 1912, and an address was given by Judge M. C. George. It contains historical information about Fort Yamhill. See *OHQ*, v. 15, p. 64.

Foss, TILLAMOOK. Foss is a place on Nehalem River about four miles east of Mohler. The post office was in operation from 1928 to 1943. The office was named for Herbert Foss who had timber holdings in the locality. He was living in Mohler in 1943.

Fossback Marsh, LANE. This is a swampy area not far from the mouth of North Fork Siuslaw River. It was named for a pioneer family of the vicinity.

Fossil, WHEELER. The compiler is informed that this post office was established Feb. 28, 1876, at the ranch of Thomas B. Hoover, who was the first postmaster. He had discovered and was removing some fossil remains on his ranch at the time, and this suggested the name of the new office.

Foster, LINN. The post office was established Feb. 8, 1892, with Aaron H. Yost first postmaster. C. H. Stewart of Albany told the compiler in 1927 that the place was named for Parley J. Foster, who operated a grist mill in the neighborhood. In

1967, Mrs. William C. Foster added the fact that Parley's father, Alonson Foster, along with his son, also built a saw mill there in 1890

Foster Butte, DOUGLAS. This butte near the headwaters of Black Creek east of Red Butte was named for Roy Foster, nearby resident and part time USFS employee. This information was furnished by Fred Asam of Canyonville.

Foster Butte, LAKE. James Foster came to Oregon with the emigration of 1845 and settled in the Willamette Valley. In 1871 he moved to Lake County and settled where Foster Creek empties into Summer Lake, apparently near where Fremont camped in 1843. *See OHQ*, v. 46, p. 154. He was a well-known citizen of Lake County. Foster Lake and Foster Flat Meadow are also named for James Foster.

Foster Creek, CURRY. Foster Creek rises on Ophir Mountain and flows into Rogue River near Illahe. According to M. S. Brainard of Brookings it was named for Charles Foster who was born in New York about 1820. He came to Port Orford about 1851 and was a captain in the Gold Beach Guards during the Indian wars. He homesteaded near the mouth of Foster Creek where he died Apr. 21, 1883.

Foster Reservoir, CROOK. This reservoir in Rabbit Valley bears the name of William Foster who was born in Corvallis in 1848 and came to central Oregon in 1871. In 1872 he moved to the Bear Creek area and then rapidly expanded his holdings until at one time he was known as the "Central Oregon Cattle King." Foster was drowned in 1890 while trying to cross Crooked River on a horse in high water.

Foster Road, MULTNOMAH. Philip Foster came to Oregon in 1842, by sea. His wife was Mary Charlotte Pettygrove, sister of F. W. Pettygrove, one of the founders of Portland. Foster was born at Augusta, Maine, Jan. 29, 1805. During his first four years in Oregon, Foster engaged in the mercantile business at Oregon City. His farm, at Eagle Creek, was the first on the Barlow Road section of the Oregon Trail in the Willamette Valley. This made the Foster farm the most widely known in Oregon. The Foster place was, during many years, a depot of supplies for new settlers. He was preceded there by Samuel McSwain, pioneer probably of 1842. Foster died Mar. 17, 1884. Mrs. Foster died in 1879. For his biography, *see* the *Oregonian*, Mar. 28, 1884, p. 1. Foster Road bears his name. For detailed information about him and his early experiences in Oregon, *see* the *Oregonian*, Dec. 18, 1927, sect. 1, p. 10.

Fourbit Creek, JACKSON. Fourbit Creek is tributary to South Fork Big Butte Creek northwest of Mount McLoughlin. Anne Weatherford in *Real West*, Sept. 1967, has an interesting account of the naming of this stream. It appears that in the spring of 1859 Eli Ledford and four companions attempted to cross from Jacksonville to the Klamath country. Because of deep snow, they were unable to get through and they made camp at Rancheria Prairie. Here all the party were murdered but whether by Indians or renegade whites is unknown. Ledford's four companions were found first in a common grave but his body was finally located about a half mile away. Ledford habitually carried a money belt filled with 50 cent pieces, and while trying to escape the fate of his companions, he scattered the coins. For many years the fourbit pieces would occasionally be found in the prairie or along the banks of Fourbit Creek.

Fourmile Canyon, GILLIAM, MORROW. This canyon opens into Eightmile Canyon, and is so called on the assumption that its mouth is about four miles up Eightmile Canyon from the point where that canyon opens onto Willow Creek.

Fourmile Creek, COOS. A stream called Fourmile Creek flows into the Pacific Ocean a little more than seven miles south of Bandon, and the origin of the name of the stream is somewhat of a puzzle. It is said that it was so called because it was about four miles south of Coquille River, but it is nearly twice that far. Whoever did the original measuring greatly underestimated the distance. It is of interest to note that US-101, the Oregon Coast Highway, crosses the main branch of Twomile Creek at a point three miles north of Fourmile Creek, and something like five miles south of Bandon. Fourmile post office was established near Fourmile Creek on Mar. 3, 1906, with Harlan P. Dunning first and only postmaster. The office was closed to Langlois June 15, 1907. It was reestablished as Four Mile in 1947 and finally closed May 24, 1963.

Fourmile Lake, KLAMATH. So called because it was assumed that the lake was four miles long. This lake is just northeast of Mount McLoughlin in the heart of the Cascade Range.

Fourth Lake, LINN. This lake is the fourth of a series of four lakes, beginning at Albany and extending north along the east bank of the Willamette River. They are named in order from Albany.

Fox, GRANT. Fox takes its name from Fox Creek, an important tributary of North Fork John Day River. The name was applied to the stream in pioneer days on account of some incident that occurred on a hunting or prospecting trip that had to do with a fox. The post office was established about 1883.

Fox Butte, LAKE. Fox Butte is in the extreme north end of Lake County and southeast of the Paulina Mountains. In Dec. 1945, Avon D. Derrick of Fort Rock wrote the Bend *Bulletin* that the butte was named for a black fox seen there by his father, H. E. Derrick, in the summer of 1909. Stories to the effect that the feature was named for a nearby settler, one Fox, do not seem to be true.

Fox Canyon, SHERMAN. Fox Canyon opens into John Day River four miles from the Columbia. George Fox patented a homestead at its mouth in 1934.

Fox Creek, MARION. Charles C. Giebeler of Detroit, informed the compiler that this stream, which flows into Breitenbush River, was named for one Fox, camp cook for a party of trail builders. While camped near this stream Fox fell into a fire as the result of an epileptic fit, and was burned so badly that he died.

Fox Hill, UNION. Fox Hill is north of La Grande. It is named for Charles Fox who came to the Grande Ronde Valley in 1862 and started the first sawmill in the area. The mill was located along the river at the place once known as Orodell.

Fox Hollow, LANE. Fox Hollow drains a considerable area southwest of Spencer Butte and also southwest of Eugene and adds the water to Coyote Creek. It has been called Fox Hollow since pioneer days and while the natural assumption is that it was named for some incident connected with a fox, Cal M. Young, long a resident of Lane County, wrote the compiler in 1947 expressing his doubts. Mr. Young says that he was told many years ago that the hollow was named for the many fox squirrels that lived therein. These fox squirrels, also called Oregon gray squirrels, were so named because of their bushy tails. There was at one time a Fox Hollow post office near the road junction in s 5, T 19s, R 4w, with Mrs. Aslaug I. Knox postmaster. This office was in service from Nov. 27, 1922, to Sept. 1, 1924, in the Fred G. Knox farm home, and was closed by the extension of Rural Route 3 from Eugene.

Fox Valley, LINN. Fox Valley is a cove on the south side of North Santiam River about two miles east of Lyons. It has been so called since pioneer days and was named for John Fox, one of the first settlers. He had an Indian wife. Fox Valley post office was established July 21, 1874, with Abner D. Gardner first postmaster. The office operated on and off until May 6, 1907, when it was supplanted by rural free delivery.

Francis Creek, DOUGLAS. Francis Creek flows into South Umpqua River nine miles northeast of Tiller. It was named for Frances Rondeau, member of a pioneer Douglas County family and a sister of USFS employee John Rondeau.

Francisville, WHEELER. Information about this early-day post office is very meagre. It was established Jan. 4, 1883 and closed June 28, 1883. John F. Jordan was the first postmaster. Old maps show the office situated on Pine Creek a few miles east of what was later Clarno. The compiler has not been able to learn the origin of the name, or anything else about the place for that matter.

Franklin Butte, LINN. This butte is just southeast of Scio. Its greatest elevation is 911 feet. Riley Shelton, of Scio, informed the compiler in 1927 that the butte was named for Franklin M. Rice, who took up a donation land claim at the west and southwest part of the butte. It was at first called Paynes Butte, but the name was changed to the present form about 1860. Rice operated a blacksmith shop near the southeast corner of his claim, and some of the cinders remained there in the road for many years. Mrs. Rebecca Morris, pioneer of 1845 from Missouri, furnished these data to Shelton. Shelton was born near the butte in 1853, and was well acquainted with Rice.

Franklin Hill, MORROW. This hill near Matlock Canyon on the east edge of the county was named for early settler James C. Franklin.

Franklin-Smithfield, LANE. The Franklin-Smithfield controversy has been outstanding in Lane County for many years, and up to 1942 the difference of opinion had not been composed. The locality is on the Territorial road a few miles north of Elmira. There have been many news stories about the squabble. The most comprehensive that the compiler has seen are in Eugene *Register-Guard*,

Mar. 1, 1931, and by Professor John B. Horner in the *Oregonian*, May 14, 1933. It is not easy to follow all the arguments. About 1852–53 Daniel Smith made his homestead at what is now Franklin-Smithfield and in 1857 R. V. Howard established a store in the vicinity. In the meantime Franklin post office was established on Mar. 3, 1855, with Enos Elmaker postmaster. The compiler does not know if the office was at that time near the Smith home, or some distance away, as it seems to have been in several nearby localities. Howard attempted to have a post office called Smithfield, but this name ran afoul of Smithfield in Polk County, and the authorities would not allow duplication. It is not clear whether Howard wanted to change the name of the Franklin post office or establish a new one. In 1891 Daniel Smith laid out a townsite and filed the plat for Smithfield. In the meantime Franklin post office was in operation and it appears on the 1900 postal map. In 1909 the USGS mapped the locality as Smithfield. It was shortly after this that there began to be marked differences of opinion as to the name of the village. The controversy was acute in 1931 and in 1934 an effort was made to have the county commissioners adopt one of the names. The commission however passed a resolution calling for double-barrelled direction signs on roads and highways, reading both Smithfield and Franklin. This arrangement did not satisfy the partisans of the two names, but it represented the situation in 1943. By 1966 the Franklin contingent appeared to have triumphed for maps no longer included Smithfield. By 1990 dissension had ceased and the community is known only as Franklin.

Frankton, HOOD RIVER. This is a community on the west side of the Hood River Valley, and is said to have been named for one Frank Backus, who platted a tract of land with the hope of developing a town. E. L. Smith, well-known pioneer of Hood River, was interested in this enterprise.

Fraser Canyon, WASCO. Hugh Fraser homesteaded near the head of this canyon north of Antelope in 1883.

Frazer Creek, LINCOLN. This creek flows into Salmon River two miles from the Pacific Ocean. It was named for Alec F. Frazer, an early settler.

Frazier, LANE. Frazier, a station on the Cascade line of the Southern Pacific Company, was named for Robert Frazier, member of the Lewis and Clark party. *See also* Fields, Cruzatte and Pryor.

Frazier Mountain, CLACKAMAS. Frazier Mountain, elevation 5110 feet, was named for Donald Frazier, who died in 1918 in military service during World War I. He was a forest guard on the Mount Hood National Forest. The mountain was formerly called Shellrock Mountain, one of several in the state, and it was believed the new name would be more suitable than the duplication, as well as honor a man who died for his country. Frazier Mountain is in T 5S, R 7E.

Frazier Mountain, UNION. Dunham Wright of Medical Springs, wrote the compiler in 1927 that this mountain was named for an old hunter named Frazier, pioneer settler in Antelope Valley near Telocaset.

Fredenburg Butte, JACKSON. This butte is about three miles north of Butte

Falls and just north of the Fredenburg Ranch. Both bear the name of Francis M. Fredenburg who came to Jackson County in the 1870s. Older maps show both features as Frendenburg but this was corrected by the USBGN in *Decision List 8902*.

Freebridge, WASCO. Freebridge was a station on the Great Southern Railroad about four miles north of Emerson on Fifteenmile Creek. It was so called because here the old stage road to what is now Sherman County left Fifteenmile Creek to cross over the ridge to the Deschutes canyon where it in turn crossed the river at Free Bridge. The Free Bridge was the result of a plan by Wasco County to provide free going between The Dalles and Sherman County communities, so that the toll bridge at the mouth of Deschutes River could be avoided. The project was undertaken in Sept. 1885, and in October of that year a contract for the bridge was awarded to Hoffman and Bates of San Francisco and Portland. When railroad construction was started in the Deschutes canyon in 1909, advance camps of both lines were established in this area and supplied in part by wagon over the Free Bridge Road from the railroad along Fifteenmile Creek. The Deschutes Railroad, the Union Pacific line up Deschutes River, called their camp station Freebridge. It was located on the Sherman County side of the Deschutes River near the Free Bridge and about opposite the present Burlington Northern station called Kloan. Freebridge post office was established at the Fifteenmile Creek location on Jan. 29, 1908 with Frederick L. Petersen first postmaster. Ida Carlisle succeeded him on Nov. 24, 1908 and after the completion of the construction in the northern part of the Deschutes canyon, the post office was closed on July 30, 1910 with papers to Wrentham. W. H. McNeal, who devotes an entire page of *History of Wasco County* to this tangled toponomy, says the situation was clarified about 1920 when the Great Southern changed the name of their Freebridge station to Daneville. This name was apparently a compliment to Petersen who was a native of Denmark.

Freedom, COOS. Freedom post office was established May 21, 1878, with Yelverton M. Lowe first postmaster. This office was closed Jan. 8, 1883. In Sept. 1946, Mrs. Mary M. Randleman of Coquille wrote the compiler that the office, which was at the mouth of Beaver Slough, was named for patriotic reasons. When the post office was closed the mail was handled through Coquille.

Freedom, LANE. Post office records show that Freedom post office was established Feb. 17, 1858, with Thomas M. Awbrey first postmaster. The name of the office was changed to Lancaster on May 7, 1866, when Joseph S. Lyman was postmaster. It seems probable that this office was at or near the place called Lancaster, which is just southwest of Harrisburg. Walling in his *Illustrated History of Lane County*, p. 458, says that in the early 1850s a man named Woody started a house of entertainment in this locality and called it Woodyville. The term house of entertainment seems to have been a fancy name for a roadhouse. Walling also says that Johnson Mulkey bought the property, changed the name to Lancaster and built a sawmill. The writer has no information about the origins of the names Freedom or Lancaster. It is interesting to note that Lancaster, a city in Pennsylvania, is not far east of Harrisburg. The associations of names in Pennsylvania may have had something to do with naming a place Lancaster in Oregon because it was close to a town called Harrisburg. The author has no evidence to support this theory, but it is appealing. On Jan. 23, 1872, the name of Lancaster post office was changed to Junction City. It is probable that at that time the office was moved south so as to be on the recently constructed railroad. The first postmaster of the Junction City office was David McAlpine.

Freeman Dry Camp, LAKE. R. A. Long of Fort Rock said that this spot south of Oatman Flat was a camp site used by early day sheepman Roy Freeman. The form Feeman is incorrect.

Freewater, UMATILLA. In 1889, a townsite was platted just north of Milton and named New Walla Walla because of its proximity to the Washington city. J. B. Mahana was largely responsible for the initial filing which was refiled in 1890 as Freewater. The new community was established as a result of disatisfaction with the taxes and business restrictions of the city of Milton along with a major dispute over water-rights within the city. The rivalry between Freewater and Milton continued unabated until 1951 when the two cities finally merged. Milton-Freewater post office was established Sept. 1, 1951, and for further information, *see* Milton-Freewater. John B. Mahana was a controversial individual. In addition to being a promoter, he was an inventor of sorts and held patents to an ingenious single rail railroad system. For information on this subject, *see* the Union *Eastern Oregon Republican*, Oct. 30, 1890 and the Pendleton *East Oregonian*, Jan. 1, 1892. The compiler is indebted to John Evans of Eastern Oregon State College for dredging up this last interesting bit of early Umatilla County history.

Freezeout Creek, WALLOWA. This stream is in the eastern part of the county. It was named by one Jack Johnson because he nearly froze there one night. Johnson was a prominent pioneer character of the Wallowa country.

Freezeout Ridge, MORROW. This long north and south ridge about 13 miles east of Heppner divides the headwaters of Willow and Butter creeks. It was named in 1899 when John Kilkenny and James Carty lost 1000 head of sheep in a spring blizzard after shearing.

Fremont, LAKE. For some years, beginning about 1909, Fremont was a post office. It was about six miles west of Fort Rock. The name was probably suggested by the name Fremont National Forest, which was named for Captain John C. Fremont, who explored central Oregon in 1843. Regardless of the fact that Fremont made an accurate and valuable record of his trip through Oregon, he is frequently spoken of lightly, as a general who never commanded an army and an explorer who never made a discovery. He was born in Georgia in 1813. At the age of 25 he was appointed a second lieutenant in the topographical engineers of the army. He made several explorations in the west, and these, coupled with his experiences in California, led to his nomination by the Republicans in 1856 for the presidency. He served in the Civil War, and attained the rank of major-general.

He died in 1890. While his geographical work was of good character, too many claims were made in his behalf. *See* editorial in the *Oregonian*, Apr. 2, 1926.

Fremont Canyon, DESCHUTES, JEFFERSON. This canyon is northeast of Sisters. It is popularly supposed to be the canyon ascended by Captain John C. Fremont early in Dec. 1843, while he was on his way south through the Deschutes Valley.

Fremont Highway, DESCHUTES, KLAMATH, LAKE. SH-31 between La Pine and Lakeview was named in honor of Captain J. C. Fremont, who explored central Oregon in the fall of 1843. For data about Captain Fremont, *see* Fremont. The name Fremont Highway was suggested by Robert W. Sawyer of Bend, and it was adopted by the Oregon State Highway Commission Aug. 30, 1927. For article about Captain Fremont and Fremont Highway, by John W. Kelly, *see* magazine sect. *Oregonian*, Mar. 18, 1928.

Fremont Meadow, DESCHUTES. This little natural meadow is on Tumalo Creek in S 34, T 17S, R 11E, and lies within Shevlin Park, property of the city of Bend. Captain John C. Fremont and his exploring party camped in this vicinity on the night of Dec. 4, 1843, and mentioned following an Indian trail southward to a meadow, obviously on Tumalo Creek. In Sept. 1855, the officers of the Pacific Railroad Surveys, Williamson and Sheridan, followed a trail southward to the same locality and met Abbot who was traveling north. The position given is that of the meadow in question and the description is accurate enough for a check. This indicates that the Indian trail crossed Tumalo Creek at this meadow, sometimes called Upper Meadow, the same place used by Fremont in 1843. In Jan. 1943, the city of Bend and some interested residents asked to have the name Fremont Meadow adopted, which was done by the USBGN later in the year.

French Creek, DOUGLAS. This tributary of North Umpqua River near Glide was named for John H. French who was born in Missouri and came to Oregon with J. V. Bradley and Thorpe in 1851. French took a donation land claim along this creek just east of Bradley's claim.

French Creek, DOUGLAS. In the 1890s Isaac N. French, the first postmaster at Binger, settled where this stream empties into upper Cow Creek.

French Gulch, BAKER. French Gulch is in the vicinity of Auburn and it was an important place at the time of the eastern Oregon gold rush of the early 1860s. Some French miners operated in this gulch and it got its name on their account.

French Mountain, LANE. This mountain lies southeast of McKenzie Bridge. It was named during World War 1 to honor the French people. Just east is English Mountain, named at the same time.

French Pete Creek, LANE. This stream is an important tributary of South Fork McKenzie River. Smith Taylor told the compiler that it was named for French Pete, an early day sheepherder, who ranged his band along the stream. The compiler has been unable to get the rest of French Pete's name, but the omission may not matter. In the 1970s the creek became the point of a major confrontation between environmentalists and timber interests. The environmentalists were try-ing to preserve a substantial stand of young timber with a high potential value at maturity. Their efforts were eventually successful and the bulk of French Pete Valley was added to the Three Sisters Wilderness on Feb. 28, 1978. This section has one of the lowest elevations of any of the Oregon wilderness areas.

French Prairie, MARION. French Prairie lies in the Willamette Valley, between the Willamette River and Pudding River, north of Salem. Its general elevation is less than 200 feet and it is well shown on the USGS map of Saint Paul quadrangle. The prairie was named for the early French-Canadian settlers, most of whom were former employees of the Hudson's Bay Company. Early days on French Prairie are described by H. S. Lyman, in reminiscences of Louis Labonte in *OHQ*, v. 1, p. 169. For similar article by Lyman, reminiscences of F. X. Matthieu, includ-ing list of French-Canadian settlers, p. 73. For article about settlement of French Prairie, by Oswald West, *OHQ*, v. 43, p. 198.

French Settlement, DOUGLAS. This locality is mentioned under the heading Champagne Creek. It was a few miles northwest of Roseburg. A post office with the name French Settlement was in operation from Aug. 10, 1874, until Dec. 14, 1874, with John M. Wright postmaster. The place was named for a number of French-Canadians who established a colony there in the 1850s.

Frenchglen, HARNEY. Dr. Hugh James Glenn was born in Virginia in 1824 and spent his youth in Missouri, where he was married in Mar. 1849. In that year he emigrated to California, and after working in the mines, in 1853 he settled tem-porarily in what is now Glenn County, California. After several trips across the plains, he brought his family to California in 1868 and settled there permanently. In 1867 he began to buy land on a large scale and in 1874 he was reported to own 55,000 acres in the Sacramento Valley. He was known as the Wheat King. He was killed by Huram Miller on Feb. 17, 1883, on his Jacinto Ranch only 17 days after his oldest daughter Ella had become the bride of Peter French. French was born John William French in Missouri in 1849 and came to California as a child. During his teens he took the Christian name Peter and worked for Glenn on the Jacinto Ranch. In 1872 Dr. Glenn sent Peter French to southeastern Oregon as a scout and landbuyer. French bought large holdings for the Glenn account and became a partner in the French-Glenn business. He was impressed with the valley of the Donner und Blitzen River for cattle raising and among other properties, bought a small ranch from a local cattleman and prospector named Porter who was using a P branding iron. This place was a favorite of Pete French and became his head-quarters, with the name P Ranch. The P Ranch became one of the most famous properties of the West and was the center of very large holdings. Pete French was shot and killed near Sodhouse on Dec. 26, 1897, by Edward L. Oliver. This trage-dy was the result of an altercation over some land, and Oliver was acquitted by a jury. For many decades the P Ranch and the French-Glenn holdings were land-marks in Harney County. Frenchglen post office was near the P Ranch, and the name of the office perpetuates the name of the owners of the enterprise, with a single modification in spelling. A large part of the property is now in the Malheur Migratory Bird Refuge. For further details, *see* Malheur Lake and P Ranch. *See also* news stories in the *Oregonian*, Dec. 29, 30, 1897. Frenchglen post office was established by change of name from Somerange Dec. 1, 1926, with Robert Bradeen postmaster. After Bradeen's death, his brother, Jesse Bradeen, became postmaster on June 30, 1930. The office was closed in Dec. 1941, but reestablished on Mar. 20, 1947. *See also* Somerange.

Frickey Canyon, WHEELER. This tributary to Amine Canyon was named for William Frickey who homesteaded there in 1920.

Friday Creek, CROOK. Friday Creek rises on the Maury Mountains southwest of Drake Butte and flows south to Bear Creek. An article in the *Central Oregonian*, Oct. 23, 1969, quoted in part, gives the origin of the name: "Floyd Houston in the early days, spent a winter on Maury Mountain cutting rails on what is now Friday Creek. Floyd had been nicknamed by his old time friends 'Friday' due to the speed he worked, 'Slower than Friday,' although at his steady pace he cut nearly enough rails that winter to fence both a timber claim and a homestead."

Friend, WASCO. Friend was named for George J. Friend, as the post office established Feb. 28, 1903, was on his homestead. The name was proposed by Theo. H. Buskuhl, first postmaster.

Friendly Reach, MULTNOMAH. This is part of the Columbia River, about 8 miles long, from the mouth of the Willamette River eastward. It was named by Lieutenant W. R. Broughton on Oct. 31, 1792, in commemoration of the friendly behavior of an old Indian chief, who acted as a guide. The name was adopted by the government in 1926 at the request of the Camp Fire Girls.

Friends Peak, JEFFERSON. In 1881, Jasper Friend homesteaded on Trout Creek near the mouth of Cow Canyon and this peak to the south bears the name of his well-known family. Friend was first postmaster at Cross Keys near present Willowdale and was a brother of Columbus Friend who settled north of Antelope.

Frissell Point, LANE. This point, which is northeast of McKenzie Bridge, together with Frissell Creek to the north, and Frissell Crossing on South Fork McKenzie River, were named for "Uncle" George Frissell, pioneer settler on the upper McKenzie River.

Frizzell Ranch, WHEELER. Joseph Frizzell came to Wheeler County in the 1870s. He settled east of Fossil and then moved to a ranch on upper Girds Creek.

Frog Hollow, WHEELER. Frog Hollow is five miles southwest of Waterman on the road to Mitchell. George W. Nelson, who was raised in the area, told the writer in 1969 that the place couldn't have been better named. On a spring evening, the constant, blatant croaking compared favorably with the radio born rock and roll music of two generations later.

Froman, LINN. This was a railroad station southeast of Albany, named for Thomas Froman, pioneer resident of the neighborhood.

Fruita, WALLOWA. Fruita is situated in a park on Imnaha River near the mouth of Grouse Creek. When the post office was established, various names, including Imnaha Park and Grouse Creek were suggested, but postal authorities rejected them all, mostly because of duplication. Finally the department sent a *Postal Guide* and requested that a name of one word be selected that did not duplicate any other name in Oregon. A local resident by the name of T. F. Rich, had lived at Fruita, Colorado, and he suggested that name.

Fruitland, MARION. Fruitland is the name of a locality about five miles east of Salem and a mile north of the Penitentiary road, applied because of the excellence of the soil. Fruitland post office was established Sept. 5, 1892, with George H. Nichols postmaster. The office was closed Mar. 19, 1901, and the locality, which is thickly settled, is served from Salem.

Frustration Falls, CLACKAMAS. This 55-foot-high falls on Salmon River is about six and three quarters miles downstream from the mouth of Linney Creek. It is the fifth of six falls between Linney Creek and Welches and was named because it is so difficult to reach. For details about this group of waterfalls, *see* Stein Falls.

Fry, LINN. Fry is a railroad station between Albany and Lebanon, named for Olney Fry, Sr., a pioneer settler of the vicinity.

Fryingpan Lake, CLACKAMAS. This lake is south of Salmon River in the eastern part of the county. It is supposed to simulate the shape of a fryingpan, hence the name.

Fryrear Butte, DESCHUTES. This butte is east of Sisters, and was named for an early settler nearby, John B. Fryrear.

Fuego, KLAMATH. This station on the Cascade line of the Southern Pacific Company is named for Fuego Mountain to the east. *See* Fuego Mountain.

Fuego Mountain, KLAMATH. Fuego Mountain is in the east central part of what was the Klamath Indian Reservation. *Fuego* is Spanish for fire. Captain O. C. Applegate told the writer that in early days there were several bad forest fires on this butte, and owing to remoteness, they were hard to control. He thought this was the reason for the name.

Fuji Mountain, LANE. Fuji Mountain, a 7144 foot high, flat topped peak two miles south of Waldo Lake, is another of Oregon's mystery names. The name predates World War II and has no known connection to the famous Mount Fuji-yama in Japan. It certainly has no physical resemblance, either in size or prominence. The Eugene *Register-Guard*, Aug. 3, 1986, p. 1, has an article by Harry Esteve describing Fuji Mountain and a climb by an expedition of 25 Japanese exchange students.

Fuller Canyon, MORROW. James S. Fuller homesteaded in this canyon five miles west of Heppner about 1880.

Fuller Lake, DOUGLAS. This lake north of North Umpqua River in T 25S, R 3E, was named by USFS ranger Fred Asam for a boyhood friend, Joseph Faller. Asam was born in Austria and Faller was one of his early companions in his homeland. There is no record of when Faller Lake was changed to Fuller.

Fulton Canyon, SHERMAN. Fulton Canyon is in the northwest part of the county. It was named for the Fulton family, pioneer settlers in Wasco and Sherman counties. Colonel James Fulton was born in Missouri and came to Oregon in 1847. He served in the Indian wars and subsequently settled in Wasco County. Later he lived with other members of his family in Fulton Canyon. He was the postmaster at the post office of Fultonville, now discontinued. He died in 1896. In 1976 Giles French, the sage of Sherman County, was kind enough to provide the following details of Fulton's three sons and the geographic features connected with each of them. Fulton Canyon was named for John Fulton who took up a claim there in 1878 and later built an impressive home. He was for many years county judge of Sherman County. Frank Fulton Canyon, which comes into Fulton Canyon from the east about a mile south of the Columbia River, was named for another son. His home was near the center of S 20, T 2N, R 15E, about where the county road leaves the canyon to head north to Biggs Junction. Frank Fulton Canyon extends south only to the forks where the east branch becomes Locust Grove Canyon and the west branch Neece Canyon. Frank had a son named Charles who was occasionally inclined to the local tipple and some older residents referred to this feature as Whiskey Canyon. A third son of Colonel Fulton was Dave Fulton and he lived in Mud Hollow, the next canyon to the east. At one time this was called Dave Fulton Canyon but this name has not survived. In 1977 the USGS prepared new maps of the area and the nomenclature was adjusted to fit the above facts.

Fulton Ridge, WASCO. This is the high ground overlooking the south bank of the Columbia River and the west bank of the Deschutes. R. E. Newcomb of the USGS proposed the name in 1965 as descendants of the Fulton family still farm in the area. For information on the source, *see* Fulton Canyon.

Furnish Creek, LANE. This is a tributary of Salmon Creek east of Oakridge. It was named for James Furnish, forest ranger. Furnish was of the opinion that there was no such stream in the neighborhood and when it was finally discovered it was named for him as a reminder of his error.

Fuzztail Butte, DESCHUTES. Fuzztail Butte is ten miles north of East Lake. Phil Brogan of Bend informed the writer that a fuzztail was a wild or escaped horse whose unkempt tail was a sure sign of a lack of human attention.

Gaerky Creek, JACKSON. Gaerky Creek is tributary to Bear Creek from the north at Ashland. Kay Atwood of Ashland told the writer in 1983 that in the original 1854 Tax Assessment volume for Jackson County there is an entry for William Gerke's 160 acre claim. Gerke's name does not appear in subsequent records so it must be assumed he left southern Oregon during the Indian troubles.

Gage Creek, WHEELER. Gage Creek flows into West Branch Bridge Creek from the east. It was named for Isaac Gage who took up a homestead along its banks in 1876. He was not related to the Gage family who lived in West Branch about the turn of the century.

Gale, KLAMATH. On Apr. 10, 1890, the name of Tule Lake post office in the south part of Klamath County was changed to Gale. It seems probable that the office was moved, although the compiler does not have exact information. Williston D. Woodcock was the postmaster at the time the name was changed from Tule Lake. He continued to operate the Gale post office until Mar. 6, 1891, when the name was changed back to Tule Lake. In Sept. 1948, R. H. Anderson of Klamath Falls wrote that he had talked to a Mrs. Johnson, daughter of Woodcock, and in 1948 living at Lakeview. She said she remembered the circumstances of the post office very clearly. The family had difficulty in selecting a name for the new office and finally someone suggested that it be called Gale because of the severe winds and sand storms that then prevailed. This name was in use only about a year.

Gale Creek, DOUGLAS. Gale Creek flows into Fish Lake in S 6, T 29S, R 3E. It was named in 1983 for Leslie C. Gale, a USFS employee who worked on the trails and bridges in the area. Gale died in 1980. *See* USBGN *Decison List 8402.*

Galena, GRANT. Galena was a post office in the valley of Middle Fork John Day River, at a place once the site of Susanville post office. It is alleged that about 1901 a mine and its employees about two miles away up Elk Creek, secured the removal of the Susanville office to a point near the mine. This left the abandoned post office site without an office. A new office with a new name was petitioned for, and, due to the fact that there was a body of ore in the vicinity, Galena was suggested. Galena is a common ore of lead, chemically known as lead sulphite. A news story in the *Oregonian*, Sept. 7, 1943, announced the closing of Galena post office in Aug. 1943. Mrs. Genevieve Saling was the last postmaster. For editorial comment, *see* the *Oregonian*, Sept. 9, 1943.

Gales Creek, WASHINGTON. Gales Creek and Gales Peak nearby were named for Joseph Gale who came to Oregon in 1834, with Ewing Young, from California. He was born Apr. 27, 1801, near Washington, D.C. He settled on East Tualatin Plain and afterwards at the foot of Gales Peak, on a tributary of Tualatin River, and later in Eagle Valley, then in Union but now in Baker County. Gale, in his younger days, followed the sea; afterwards, he became a trapper in the Rocky Mountains. Gale was master of the *Star of Oregon*, the first ship to be built in Oregon, which was launched in the Willamette River in 1841 and finished in 1842. Lieutenant Charles Wilkes gave him papers for sailing the *Star of Oregon*. He sailed the schooner to San Francisco Bay. For story of this enterprise, *see* magazine section of the *Oregonian*, May 18, 1941, and OPA *Transactions* for 1891. Together with Alanson Beers and David Hill, Gale constituted the executive committee of the provisional government, elected July 5, 1843. He died in Eagle Valley, Union County, Oregon, Dec. 13, 1881. For his biography, *see* the *Oregonian*, Dec. 29, 1881, p. 4; Feb. 12, 1882, p. 4; Oct. 12, 1883, p. 1; May 9, 1877, p. 4. "Captain Gale has always been a man of great energy, brave, fearless and honest." (J. W. Nesmith, in an address before OPA on p. 12 of *Transactions* for 1880.) Gales Creek post office, named for the stream nearby, was established Sept. 10, 1874, with Lester Ray first postmaster. The place was sometimes called Gales City.

Galesville, DOUGLAS. Galesville was a pioneer post office in the Cow Creek Valley, established Oct. 14, 1854, with George F. Hall first postmaster. The office was closed Jan. 31, 1916, and the business turned over to Azalea. In Aug. 1946, Miss Bess A. Clough of Canyonville informed the compiler that two men, Gale and Goshen, first settled on the place later purchased by Daniel Levens, and when the post office was established, it was named for Gale, whose first name is not known to the compiler.

Galice, JOSEPHINE. The postmaster at Galice, in 1926, wrote the compiler that the place took its name from a French doctor, Louis Galice, who came as early as 1852, and discovered placer gold. It is said that this Frenchman is buried close to Galice Creek nearby. For additional details about the discovery of gold at Galice, and the history of the community, *see* Walling's *History of Southern Oregon*, p. 460.

Gallagher Canyon, WASCO. This canyon in the extreme southeast corner of the county is on the old The Dalles-Canyon City road. Grover C. Blake in *Blazing Oregon Trails*, p. 14, says that in 1863 one Gallagher, a packer, was camped along the trail at the mouth of this gulch. During the night his helper named Berry Way did him in, disposed of his body and departed with the pack train with a disputedly large amount of gold dust. Way was apprehended and later hanged in Canyon City but the gold was never recovered. The canyon has since carried the name of the ill fated Gallagher. *See also* Bearway Meadow.

Galloway, MORROW. Galloway is in the Butter Creek drainage northeast of Heppner. It is about two miles south of the locality called Pine City, and bears the name of an early settler. Galloway post office was first established July 31, 1886, with John J. Galloway postmaster. The office served intermittently until Sept. 30, 1915, when it was closed out to Echo.

Galls Creek, JACKSON. Named for Jacob Gall, who settled on this stream on Sept. 7, 1852. The spelling Galls is in general use. The form Gauls is wrong.

Garden Creek, WALLOWA. This stream is in T 6N, R 47E, and is in the very northeast corner of the state. It flows into Snake River, and according to J. H. Horner of Enterprise was named because an early settler had a fine garden on a bar at the mouth of the creek.

Garden Home, WASHINGTON. This name is mildly sentimental, and may be classified with Sweet Home, Pleasant Valley and others of that class. The community of Garden Home has existed for many years, and became prominent when the Oregon Electric Railway was built. The site of Garden Home station was somewhere east of the older settlement.

Garden Valley, DOUGLAS. This valley, at the junction of North and South Umpqua rivers gets its name from the character of the soil, which is well adapted to vegetable and garden products. *See* Walling's *History of Southern Oregon*, p. 432.

346   OREGON GEOGRAPHIC NAMES

Gardener Butte, JACKSON. This 2914-foot-high butte three miles northeast of Lakecreek was named for Raphael Gardener, Sr., who settled in the area in 1884. Early maps show Gardner Butte but this was corrected by the USBGN in *Decision List 8902*.

Gardiner, DOUGLAS. Gardiner is on the north bank of the Umpqua River near its mouth. It is an historic community of Oregon, and bears the name of a Boston merchant who sought to trade on the river. His vessel, *Bostonian*, was wrecked at the mouth of the Umpqua on Oct. 1, 1850. Most of the goods on the vessel were saved and moved to the location of what was subsequently the town of Gardiner. The place became the headquarters of the Umpqua customs district in 1851, with Colin Wilson as collector. *See* advertisement in the *Oregonian*, Dec. 6, 1851. The community is described in the *Oregonian* for June 23, 1855. The post office of Gardiner's City was established on June 30, 1851, with Geo. L. Snelling first postmaster. The form Gardiner City was used on Oct. 20, 1853, which was the date that Harrison Spicer became postmaster. The official name is now Gardiner.

Gardner Creek, TILLAMOOK. Gardner Creek flows into Deer Creek on the south slope of Cascade Head immediately adjacent to the headquarters of the Cascade Head Experimental Forest. Gayton Phelps wrote the compiler that it was named for Jesse N. Gardner who came to the Salmon River country before World War I. On Mar. 11, 1911, Gardner patented a land claim in S 21, T 6S, R 10W, and in 1935 the land was sold to the USFS.

Gardner Ridge, CURRY. Johnson Gardner came to Curry County in 1877 and settled on this ground near the mouth of North Fork Chetco River where he eventually raised a large family. This information was provided by M. S. Brainard of Brookings.

Garfield, CLACKAMAS. Garfield is about three miles east of Estacada. It is not now a post office. It was named for James A. Garfield, twentieth president of the United States. A post office with the name Leon was established in this locality May 1, 1893. The name was changed to Garfield May 26, 1897, and the office was closed Feb. 15, 1906.

Garfield Peak, KLAMATH. This peak is on the south rim of Crater Lake and has an elevation of 8054 feet. It was named by Will G. Steel for James R. Garfield, then Secretary of the Interior, on July 15, 1907. Garfield was the first cabinet officer to visit Crater Lake.

Garibaldi, TILLAMOOK. T. B. Handley, an attorney of Portland, wrote the compiler on Oct. 1, 1927, that his grandfather, Daniel Bayley, was one of the first white settlers in Tillamook County, and in the 1860s named the community of Garibaldi for the Italian patriot. D. D. Bayley was an ardent admirer of Garibaldi, and wanted his name perpetuated in Oregon. Giuseppe Garibaldi was born in Italy July 4, 1807. His life was at all times eventful, and he had been condemned to death before he was 27 years of age. He was a revolutionist in South America for several years, then returned to Italy in 1848 to join the revolution in that country.

Then for more than 15 years he was for the most part engaged in military activities connected with the establishment and early period of the kingdom of Italy. He died in 1882. The compiler has been unable to associate Joseph C. Champion with the naming of Garibaldi in 1848. In 1848 Garibaldi was just starting the most active part of his career, and it is doubtful if anyone in Oregon knew much about him at that time. Champion was the first white settler in what is now Tillamook County, having come from Astoria by boat in 1851. Champion lived in Garibaldi, but not, however, until he had lived at other places in the county. Garibaldi post office was established Aug. 9, 1870, with Daniel D. Bayley first postmaster. This was apparently the third post office in Tillamook County, although the office at Nehalem may have been established the same day. The Nehalem record is not clear. William Ralston became postmaster on Sept. 17, 1873, and the office is shown as closed on Feb. 29, 1876. Garibaldi office was opened again on Feb. 2, 1880. The name was changed to Hobsonville Feb. 6, 1883. It may be assumed that the office was moved to a new location at Hobsonville, although these early post office records do not contain information about moving of offices. The office at Hobsonville was closed Oct. 26, 1887, and the business was transferred back to Garibaldi, where an office had been reopened Sept. 1886. Except for a couple of interruptions, the Garibaldi office has been in operation ever since.

Garlinghouse Lake, BENTON. This is a small slough lake northeast of Monroe. Its elevation is 265 feet. It was named for William Garlinghouse, a pioneer settler nearby.

Garner, KLAMATH. Garner Lundy, a young man living on the east edge of Klamath County, had his first name perpetuated at Garner post office, which was established June 7, 1902. Lundy is said to have been the first student in the local school. This post office was across the creek from the George Boyd home ranch, in S 14, T 36S, R 14E, about four miles airline north of Bly. Jessie M. Boyd was the only postmaster. She ran the office until June 3, 1903.

Garoutte Creek, LANE. Garoutte Creek rises south of Black Butte and flows north to Little River. It was named for S. P. Garoutte who discovered the cinnabar deposits at Black Butte in the 1890s. The form Saroute Creek is incorrect. Bill Lynch has an interesting article in the Eugene *Register-Guard*, Mar. 10, 1980, giving a good deal of history of the Garoutte family and the creek name.

Garrigus Creek, WASHINGTON. Garrigus Creek empties into West Fork Dairy Creek near Manning. Jeptha Garrigus and his wife, America Garrigus, with their five children, lived along the creek in the 1880s. A son, Ora Garrigus, still owned some of the land in 1937.

Garrison, LINN. Garrison post office was in the locality later known as Upper Soda, and was established Aug. 9, 1892, with Charles H. Foster first of five postmasters. The office was closed Nov. 30, 1904. In Sept. 1946, William R. Mealey of Foster was kind enough to supply some history of various post offices in the vicinity of the South Santiam River, and said that Foster was the prime mover in getting the post route established as far as his home. He was given the privilege of naming his office, which he did with the family name of his mother-in-law, a Mrs. Garrison.

Garrison Butte, DESCHUTES. This small butte is about seven miles north of Sisters and just south of the Jefferson-Deschutes county line. While the evidence is not conclusive, it is probable that the butte was named because of its proximity to Camp Polk, an establishment built in the Indian wars, 1865–66. The site of the camp is about five miles south of the butte. The compiler has been unable to learn of any local resident named Garrison.

Garrison Lake, CURRY. This lake is shown on some maps as Garrison Lagoon, but the generally accepted name is Garrison Lake, and that style has been adopted by the USBGN. In 1931 Louis L. Knapp of Port Orford wrote the compiler that the lake was named for a pioneer settler, John B. Garrison, who was a member of the Tichenor party. Statements to the effect that the lake was named because U.S. troops were stationed nearby in 1851–56 do not appear to be correct.

Garwood Butte, DOUGLAS. Garwood Butte bears the name of Leroy E. Garwood, one-time administrative officer of the Umpqua National Forest, who died in Mar. 1944. The butte, which has an elevation of 7027 feet, is about seven miles west of Diamond Lake. It was formerly called Bear Butte, a name of no distinction. The name was changed in honor of Garwood by the USBGN early in 1946.

Gasco, MULTNOMAH. This was a station between Portland and Linnton. It was named for the Portland Gas & Coke Company, now the Northwest Natural Gas Company, whose plant was nearby.

Gaston, WASHINGTON. Joseph Gaston emigrated to Oregon from Ohio in 1862 and actively promoted the west side railroad southwest of Portland, which was built by Holladay and Villard. He built the narrow gauge line from Dayton to Sheridan in 1878. He wrote and published histories of Portland and of Oregon. He died July 20, 1913, aged 79 years. Gaston was named for him.

Gatch Falls, LINN. In 1874 the original Gatch Falls, some three miles northwest of Marion Lake, was named by John Minto and the Marion Road party to honor Professor Thomas M. Gatch. Gatch at that time was the popular president of Willamette University and a well-known educator who was later president of both the University of Washington and what was then known as Oregon Agricultural College. For a short biography, *see Willamette* [University] *Scene*, Winter, 1986. Trouble started almost at once as in the 1880s Nathan Gooch took a squatter's claim just above the falls and his name was firmly fixed by the local residents. In 1970 the OGNB recognized this fact and decided in favor of Gooch Falls while a sub-committee under Tom McAllister was instructed to locate a suitable substitute so that the name Gatch could be continued. Mr. and Mrs. McAllister, William Wessinger and the writer spent a delightful day inspecting the back reaches of Marion Creek and suggested that the lower of the double Marion Falls be renamed Gatch. Marion Falls are about one half mile downstream from Marion

Lake and were originally named Orla Falls by the Minto party for Orla Davenport, the daughter of their surveyor, T. W. Davenport. The name did not prevail and later Marion Falls was applied to the upper and the lower was known as Linn Falls. This latter name has also passed into disuse so the lower falls appeared a most acceptable substitute. The OGNB accepted the name Gatch Falls in Dec. 1972. For further information, *see* Gooch Falls.

Gate Creek, LANE. This creek is tributary to McKenzie River near Vida. An article in the Eugene *Guard*, July 12, 1893, says that Mr. Stormant applied the name because near its mouth there was a foot log crossing where the creek passed between two immense rocks. The arrangement had the appearance of a gate and gateposts. Gate Creek post office was established Dec. 30, 1874, with Thomas M. Martin postmaster. It was discontinued on Sept. 30, 1880, and reestablished May 29, 1891, with Benjamin F. Finn postmaster. The office was discontinued on July 22, 1895, and again reestablished Jan. 22, 1897. On Dec. 3 of that year the name of the office was changed to Elliston. Elliston post office was discontinued in Mar. 1900.

Gate Creek, WASCO. Gate Creek is a tributary of White River. It was named because one of the Barlow Road tollgates was built near the stream. *See OHQ*, v. 25, p. 167.

Gates, MARION. The post office which serves Gates was originally on the south side of North Santiam River and was therefore in Linn County. The office was established in Feb. 1882, with the name Henness and with Mrs. Jane Henness first postmaster. The name was changed to Rock Creek on Aug. 23, 1883. About 1892, W. R. Robertson, then postmaster, moved the post office across the river to a place called Gatesville and the name of the office was changed to Gates. This was in honor of Mrs. Mary Gates, one of the oldest settlers in the vicinity. The name Gatesville was first applied to the place about 1888. Mrs. J. P. McCurdy, postmaster at Gates in 1925, wrote the compiler as follows: "There was much opposition to the adoption of the new name of Gates by the older settlers who wished to retain the name of Rock Creek. A petition was signed to keep the old name. The party circulating the petition got drunk and lost it, and therefore the name of Gates remained." Page Mr. Volstead.

Gateway, JEFFERSON. Gateway is named for a natural depression in the terrain north of Madras, caused by erosion by Trout Creek and its tributaries. It is in effect a natural gate for the railroad and vehicular traffic north and south through central Oregon. The name was applied to the post office in 1913, possibly by George McFarland. The post office was originally known as Youngs, but it was not at the present site of Gateway. Youngs was named for Louis A. Young, a local resident, and was about three miles from where Gateway office was situated when it was closed in 1956.

Gatton Creek, MULTNOMAH. This small stream flows into Ramsey Lake just north of St. Johns. It was named for William Gatton, a pioneer of 1852, who settled near the present site of St. Johns. He was born in 1831, and died Mar. 24, 1924. For information about the Gatton property, *see* the Portland *Telegram*, Aug. 10, 1925, where the name is spelled Gratton, and letter from J. N. Pearcy, on editorial page Sept. 1, 1925. Drainage projects are changing and eliminating geographic features in the vicinity of Ramsey Lake.

Gawley Creek, CLACKAMAS. This stream is in the south part of the county and flows into Molalla River. A man by the name of Gawley prospected on the creek in early days, and it was named for him.

Gazley, DOUGLAS. Gazley is a locality just north of South Umpqua River a little to the north-northeast of Canyonville. It bears the name of James F. Gazley who came to Oregon in the early 1850s and took up land in the valley of the South Umpqua River. For further information, *see* OPA *Transactions*, 1919, p. 170. Gazley post office was established Sept. 16, 1915, with Belle Butcher first postmaster. The office was discontinued Jan. 29, 1935.

Gearhart, CLATSOP. Philip Gearhart was a pioneer settler on Clatsop Plains, and on part of his donation land claim is now located the beach resort of Gearhart. The record of Philip Gearhart is shown on land office certificate 3109. He was born in Pennyslvania in 1810, arrived in Oregon in 1848, and settled on his claim in 1850. He died in Sept. 1881.

Gearhart Mountain, LAKE. Gearhart Mountain is about ten miles northeast of Bly, very close to the Klamath-Lake county line. It has an elevation of 8364 feet, and according to the USFS was named for some incident connected with one Gearhart, a pioneer cattleman. James P. Gearhart and his brother, William H. Gearhart, were in the stock business in this part of Oregon from about 1873 to 1882 and traded into California. The mountain was probably named for one or both of the brothers. They were born in Howard County, Missouri, and came to Oregon in 1852, living in Benton County and later in Josephine County and also in California. The latter part of their lives was spent near Drewsey, Harney County. For biographies of the two brothers, *see Illustrated History of Baker, Grant, Malheur and Harney Counties*, pp. 687 and 703.

Geer, MARION. Geer is a railroad station east of Salem. It was named for the family of T. T. Geer. His parents were pioneers of Oregon and he himself was once governor of the state. His book, *Fifty Years in Oregon*, is one of the most interesting contributions to the intimate history of early days in Oregon.

Geisel Monument, CURRY. In a small state park just west of the Oregon Coast Highway about seven miles north of Gold Beach stands the Geisel Monument, marking the graves of John Geisel and his family. A granite shaft is inscribed: "Sacred to the memory of John Geisel, also his three sons, John, Henry, and Andrew, who were massacred by the Indians, Feb. 22, A.D. 1856, ages respectively 45, 9, 7, and 5 years. Also wife and mother died Sept. 20, 1899, age 75 years." There are individual grave stones and the plot is surrounded by an ornamental iron fence. The Geisel massacre was the outstanding tragedy in the early history of

Curry County. It is described in Dodge's *Pioneer History of Coos and Curry Counties*, pp. 346-48.

Geiser, BAKER. This mining camp was named for Albert Geiser, owner of the Bonanza mine. Geiser post office was established July 15, 1898, with Ed. Geiser first postmaster. The office was discontinued May 18, 1909.

Gekeler Slough, UNION. Gekeler Slough runs through the south part of La Grande. It is named for J. George Gekeler who settled along it in 1862.

Gellatly Creek, BENTON. Andrew Gellatly was born in Perth, Scotland in 1838. He emigrated to the United States in the 1860s and came to Philomath in 1870. He settled at the mouth of Gellatly Creek, a tributary of Greasy Creek two and a half miles west of Philomath, and farmed there until his death in 1898. There is another Gellatly Creek tributary to Marys River a few miles to the northwest. This is apparently named for Andrew's brother, Peter Gellatly, who settled nearby in 1875. Information on the Gellatly family was supplied by Portland attorney William A. Palmer, Andrew Gellatly's grandson.

Gem, BAKER. Gem was the name applied to the post office later called Sparta. Gem was named for a mine but the compiler does not know its exact location. William Lynn White served as postmaster from Aug. 7, 1871, to Oct. 29, 1872, when the name of the office was changed to Sparta. White did not continue as postmaster, which may mean that the office was moved at the time the name was changed. This is just assumption, however. When Gem post office was established it was in Union County in what was known as the Panhandle. The Panhandle was later attached to Baker County.

General Patch Bridge, DESCHUTES. This bridge over Deschutes River south of Sunriver was named for Lieutenant-General Alexander M. Patch U.S. Army. General Patch commanded the IV Army Corps during training manoeuvres near Camp Abbot in the fall of 1943 and later led the 7th Army in Europe.

Geneva, JEFFERSON. This post office was established about 1914 through the efforts of John T. Monical. His wife's name was Geneva Monical, and the office is said to have been named for her, as she was the first postmaster.

George, CLACKAMAS. This community was named for Melvin C. George, of Portland, former representative in Congress from Oregon. Judge George was born in Ohio in 1849. He came to Oregon when he was two years old. He was a practicing lawyer for many years and occupied various political positions, including that of circuit judge. He was representative in Congress from 1881 to 1885, and while he was in that position a petition was received at Washington for a post office in Clackamas County. Walter Q. Gresham was postmaster general at that time and suggested Judge George's name for the new office, which was accordingly adopted. The office was closed on Apr. 30, 1919. Judge George died Feb. 22, 1933.

George Creek, TILLAMOOK. F. E. Kellow of Cloverdale told the writer in 1971 that this creek north of Hebo was named in the early days for George Bodyfelt who homesteaded the surrounding land. Kellow said that his grandfather, George Kellow, specified the creek was not named for him but for Bodyfelt.

Gerber Reservoir, KLAMATH. Gerber Reservoir, in southeast Klamath County, stores water for irrigation. It was named for Louis C. Gerber, an early settler in the locality, who owned a considerable part of the reservoir site.

Gerdine Butte, DESCHUTES. Gerdine Butte, elevation 6600 feet, is in the extreme southwest corner of the county, about seven miles north of Maiden Peak and just east of the summit of the Cascade Range. It was named in compliment to Thomas Golding Gerdine, for many years a topographic engineer in the USGS. Major Gerdine was born at West Point, Mississippi, on June 2, 1872, and graduated from the University of Georgia in 1891. He joined the Geological Survey in 1893 and with the exception of short services for the General Land Office and for the War Department, he remained with the Survey until his death. He spent nearly ten years in difficult field work in Alaska, and in 1908 was appointed division geographer for the USGS in charge of operations in the Pacific Coast states and Hawaii. During the first World War he was in charge of War Department mapping in various strategic areas, but returned to the USGS early in 1919 and continued in charge of Pacific Coast work, with headquarters in Sacramento. He died in that city on Oct. 31, 1930. His knowledge of Oregon geography and topography was profound. The last piece of mapping carried on in Oregon under his supervision was that of the Maiden Peak quadrangle. The OGNB suggested that an unnamed butte in this area be called Gerdine Butte. Mount Gerdine in Alaska, elevation 12,000 feet, was also named in his honor.

Geren Island, MARION. Geren Island is in North Santiam River about a mile southeast of Stayton. It is named for John L. Geren, former City of Salem Director of Utilities who designed the water filtration facilities on the island. Geren died in 1982 and the name was approved by the USBGN in *Decision List 8702*.

Gerking Canyon, SHERMAN. The USGS Wasco quadrangle dated 1957 shows this canyon near Rufus as Girkling. This apparently was not satisfactory and the USBGN in *Decision List 5904* changed to Gherkin. The original homesteader and namesake was William Gerking who settled in S 20, T 2N, R 17E, in 1880. When the new USGS map of the Rufus quadrangle was published in 1971, the spelling was finally brought into accord.

Gerlinger, POLK. Louis Gerlinger, a well-known Oregon lumberman and railroad builder, promoted The Salem, Falls City and Western Railway, later purchased by the Southern Pacific Company. The crossing of this line and the original west side line a mile south of Derry was named in honor of Mr. Gerlinger.

Germantown Road, MULTNOMAH, WASHINGTON. Germantown Road was named when the thoroughfare was built westward from the Willamette River to serve settlements on the North Plains of the Tualatin Valley. Many of the settlers were Germans and Swiss and the road got its name on that account. This route of travel is very old, going back to the 1840s.

Gervais, MARION. Named for Joseph Gervais, a pioneer citizen of Oregon, and an early resident on French Prairie. Gervais came to Oregon with the Hunt party of the Astor enterprise in 1811, and for a number of years was engaged as a trapper for the various companies. He settled on French Prairie, but not at the present site of Gervais. Gervais is on the Peter Depot claim. Neill Johnson is said to have given the name to the town of Gervais. Gervais and Etienne Lucier may have named Pudding River in 1813. Both men voted at Champoeg in 1843 for a provisional government. Gervais died on French Prairie July 13, 1861, aged 84 years.

Gesner, MARION. Gesner was a railroad station east of Salem. It was named for the Gesner family, early settlers. Alonzo Gesner was at one time county surveyor, a fact which may have had to do with the selection of the name.

Getchel Meadows, WALLOWA. Getchel Meadows are in T 4N, R 46E, and were named for William Getchel who built a cabin in the locality and wintered there. He was for a time in the railroad service between La Grande and Enterprise.

Gettings Creek, LANE. This stream flows into Coast Fork Willamette River a few miles northeast of Cottage Grove. It was named for Samuel A. Gettings who lived in the vicinity in 1888. The spellings Gittings and Giddings are incorrect. The USBGN has adopted the spelling Gettings for this name and also for North Fork Gettings Creek, the name of a tributary.

Ghost Creek, CLACKAMAS. This small stream heads on the west side of Bird Butte and flows into Salmon River. The Wapinitia Highway, US-26, crosses it 1.5 miles north of Frog Lake. Ghost Creek was named because of ghost-like white tree trunks standing on the hillside nearby.

Ghost Ridge, HOOD RIVER. This ridge lies immediately east of Eliot Branch and runs from Cloud Cap down towards Inspiration Point. It takes its name from the whitened snags left after a series of early day fires. The first of these in 1886 was supposedly set by sheepman Johnny O'Leary who was trying to improve the grazing range. A series of natural fires came afterward but since World War II, new growth has gradually covered the ethereal remains.

Gibbon, UMATILLA. This is a station on the Union Pacific Railroad 20 miles east of Pendleton just west of the junction of Umatilla River and Meacham Creek. It bears the name of John Gibbon, 1827–96, a distinguished American army officer, who gained the rank of brevet major-general. In 1885–86 he was in command of the Department of the Columbia at Vancouver, Washington. For references to General Gibbon, *see* Scott's *History of the Oregon Country*, v. 2, pp. 104 and 283. During the railroad construction there was a station at or near the present site of Gibbon known as Mikecha. *See* Kamela. About the turn of the century the name of Gibbon railroad station was changed to Bingham Springs, because it served Bingham Springs resort about eight miles east up Umatilla River, but the name of the post office remained Gibbon. The name of the station was later changed back to Gibbon. Bingham Springs were named for Dr. John E. Bingham of Walla Walla, Washington.

Gibbs Creek, GRANT. Gibbs Creek flows into Middle Fork John Day River approximately a mile upstream from Galena. The creek and Gibbs Meadow in s 26, T 9S, R 32E, were named for George L. Gibbs who purchased land at the meadow during the 1920s. This information was provided by Orville Gibbs of John Day.

Gibraltar Mountain, LANE. USFS ranger A. J. Briem stated that this peak southeast of Vida was named Gibraltar Rock in the 1870s by Thomas Warner because of its resemblance to the original.

Gibson Creek, CROOK. This small tributary of Newsome Creek near its headwaters in the Maury Mountains was named for early settlers John and Molly Gibson who moved there in the 1880s.

Gibson Creek, LANE. This is a small tributary of Indian Creek two miles south of the old community of Reed. It was probably named for Andrew Gibson who in 1901 filed on government land near its mouth. Gibson never proved up his claim.

Gibson Gulch, POLK. Gibson Gulch is in the southeast part of the Eola Hills. Daviess Gibson was an early settler in the Eola Hills, and the gulch was named for him. He was an Oregon pioneer of 1849, and after returning to Illinois by Panama, came to Oregon again in 1852. He died prior to 1900, and was buried in Spring Valley.

Gibson Gulch, UMATILLA. Gibson Gulch empties into Stewart Creek about five miles east of Pilot Rock. It was named for Thomas S. Gibson who bought up numerous small homesteads to form a substantial ranch. One of these belonged to Milton E. Pomeroy who took up his claim in 1895. At that time the draw was called Pomeroy Gulch but the name did not prevail.

Giebeler Lake, MARION. This small lake a half mile southeast of Mount Beachie is named for Charles C. Giebeler of Detroit, Oregon. Giebeler was a long time resident of the North Santiam region and a well known packer and guide.

Gilbert, MULTNOMAH. Gilbert was a station on the Portland Traction Company line east of Lents Junction. The name is preserved in the Gilbert district of Portland including Gilbert School. The name comes from William M. Gilbert who in the late 1880s farmed near what is now SE 122nd Avenue and Foster Road. Gilbert died in Portland in 1950.

Gilbert Creek, YAMHILL. Gilbert Creek flows into Coast Creek in S 11, T 5S, R 7W. BLM records show Theodore H. Gilbert filed on a claim about a mile above its mouth in 1883.

Gilbert River, COLUMBIA, MULTNOMAH. Gilbert River pursues a meandering course on Sauvie Island, draining a number of lakes, and finally emptying into Multnomah Channel. W. H. H. Morgan, a pioneer resident of Sauvie Island, told the compiler in 1926 that the stream was named in fur trading days because a trapper, supposed to be in the employ of the Hudson's Bay Company, was drowned in it. He was a French-Canadian called Gilbert, and his name has been attached to the stream ever since.

Gilchrist, KLAMATH. Gilchrist is a mill town and post office on The Dalles-California Highway in the north end of the county. The community was developed in 1938 and the post office was established on Nov. 14, 1938. The town was named for Frank W. Gilchrist, vice president and general manager of the Gilchrist Timber Company.

Gilchrist Butte, WHEELER. This butte is north of the old community of West Branch. It was named for James C. Gilchrist, an early resident and one of the first USFS rangers.

Gilchrist Valley, CROOK, DESCHUTES. Gilchrist Valley is drained by one of the tributaries of Crooked River, and lies east of Hampton Butte. It is about 20 miles long, north and south, and ten miles wide, and its physical characteristics are well described by Dr. I. C. Russell in USGS *Bulletin 252*. Dr. Russell named the valley for Charles Adams Gilchrist, its first settler, as a tribute to his enterprise and hospitality. C. A. Gilchrist was born in Indiana Nov. 5, 1855. He lived in Missouri, California and New Mexico, and finally came to Oregon, and began ranching in what is now known as Gilchrist Valley. He married Miss Mabel F. Johnstone of Indiana in 1899. He died Mar. 3, 1926. *See* the Portland *Telegram* Mar. 5, 1926. During the latter part of his life he lived in Portland.

Gillespie Butte, LANE. Gillespie Butte is in the north part of Eugene and has an elevation of 605 feet. It was named for Jacob Gillespie who came to Oregon from Missouri in 1851 and took up a donation land claim near the butte in 1852. He was in charge of building the Cumberland Presbyterian church in Eugene and held a negro slave in this state. After the death of his wife, Amelia, in 1867, he married the widow of Alexander Goodpasture. *See* Goodpasture Island.

Gilliam County. Gilliam County was created Feb. 25, 1885, by the state legislature. It has a land area of 1237 square miles, according to the ODOT, and its county seat is Condon. The county was named for Colonel Cornelius Gilliam, who commanded the forces of the provisional government in 1847–48, after the Whitman Massacre, in the campaign against the Cayuses. He was killed toward the end of the campaign, Mar. 24, 1848, while drawing a rope from a wagon. The rope caught the hammer of a gun and discharged it. Gilliam was born in North Carolina in 1798. He came to Oregon in 1844. "He was brave, obstinate, impetuous and generous, with goodnatured abilities but little education. Thus died an honest and patriotic and popular man, whose chief fault as an officer was too much zeal and impetuosity in the performance of his duties." (Bancroft's *History of Oregon*, v. I, p. 725.) For a narrative of his death, *see* the *Oregonian*, June 29, 1888, p. 2, letter by William A. Jack, and Jan. 24, 1926, sect. 1, p. 20, article by Opal Clark of Heppner.

Gilman Canyon, MORROW. This canyon on the upper reaches of Balm Fork was named for David E. Gilman who settled along Balm Fork just after the turn of the century. The spelling Gillman is wrong.

Ginkgo Creek, JACKSON. This creek rises east of Rogue River and flows into

Mill Creek north of Prospect. Apparently in the early days a group of Chinese miners planted a ginkgo tree near one of their camps and when the tree was later discovered, the name was attached to the nearby creek. The ginkgo or *Salisburia adiantifolia* is native to China and Japan where it is a popular garden tree although there are now no known natural stands. The species is very old and at one time widespread as fossil ginkgo leaves have been found in the Eagle Creek gravels in the Columbia River Gorge.

Girds Creek, WHEELER. This stream was apparently named for William Gird of Corvallis. Gird was a well-known horse fancier and breeder in Benton County in the 1860s. He was also a close friend of T. B. Hoover and when this gentleman and his companions came to Butte Creek near Fossil in 1869 to raise horses in eastern Oregon, Gird probably accompanied or visited them. Old timers in Wheeler County say that the creek was named for a settler prior to 1872 and Oswald West in *OHQ*, v. 46, p. 148, says the creek in the John Day Valley was likely named for Gird. For further information on Gird, *see OHQ*, v. 48, p. 141.

Gist, DESCHUTES. A post office called Gist was established on the Crook County list on Feb. 14, 1907, and named for the first postmaster, Charles L. Gist. The office was a few miles southeast of Sisters on the old road, a little southwest of the highway from Sisters to Tumalo. When Deschutes County was formed in 1916, the office was put on the list for that county. It was closed on June 25, 1920, and the business was turned over to Tumalo.

Githens Mountain, CLACKAMAS. Githens Mountain is at the headwaters of Eagle Creek. It was named for George W. Githens and his son, Henry A. Githens, who were early homesteaders in the area. The Githens tended cattle and harvested the abundant native huckleberries for the Portland market. *See* USBGN *Decision List 8302*.

Glacier Creek, LANE. This creek rises east of Sunshine Shelter. Ray Engels of the USFS named it because of its proximity to Collier and Renfrew glaciers although it does not flow directly from either.

Glad Tidings, CLACKAMAS. Glad Tidings is a puzzle among Oregon geographic names. The place is about three miles northeast of Marquam on the Cascade Highway. The compiler has been quite unable to learn the character of the cheering news that produced the name. Glad Tidings post office was established Aug. 30, 1860, with George W. Jackson first postmaster. The office was closed to Butte Creek on Sept. 2, 1887. During this operation of 27 years no one seems to have made a record of the origin of the unusual name. It has been suggested that the good news had to do with the admission of Oregon as a state, but that event was about a year and a half earlier than the date of the post office, during which time the news must have become quite stale, and if the old stories can be believed, the news was none too well received when the event took place.

Gladstone, CLACKAMAS. The community of Gladstone was platted in 1893 and named for William Ewart Gladstone, the British statesman. However, The Gladstone Real Estate Association was incorporated in 1889, so that the name was really chosen at this earlier date. Harvey Cross of Oregon City was one of the incorporators of the association and was actively interested in developing the townsite, and is credited with selecting the name Gladstone. He was a great admirer of the prime minister. Gladstone post office was established June 30, 1890.

Glasgow, COOS. Glasgow is a small community on the north side of Coos Bay. It was started by speculators in the 1890s and, after an initial burst of enthusiasm, it languished for 30 years until the construction of US-101 when it became the northern terminus of the Coos Bay ferry. It is supposed to have been named by a Scot because it reminded him of Glasgow in Scotland, but the compiler has been unable to verify this. The promoters were the Pacific Coal & Transportation Company whose principals included Henry L. Pittock, Phil Metschan, Admiral Schley and several other well-known citizens.

Glass Buttes, LAKE. Glass Buttes are in the northeast corner of Lake County. They have an elevation of 6390 feet according to the USC&GS. There are two prominent rounded domes, and several lesser hills, and the whole group makes an important landmark. The buttes take their name from the obsidian or volcanic glass scattered over their slopes. They stand about 2000 feet above the surrounding plain, just south of US-20.

Glaze Lake, LANE. Prince Glaze was USFS guard at Frog Camp after World War I. This lake and nearby Prince Lake were both named for him.

Glaze Meadow, DESCHUTES. This meadow is just south of Black Butte. It bears the name of Tilman Glaze, an early settler in this part of what was then Crook County. Frances Juris has an account of Glaze Meadow with pictures in *Old Crook County*, pp. 8 and 9.

Glen, LINCOLN. Glen post office was in the west part of T 12S, R 9W, a few miles south of Salado. It was on upper Drift Creek or one of its tributaries. Glen post office was established Jan. 17, 1894, with Simeon J. Wilhoit first of three postmasters. The office was closed to Elk City on June 30, 1912. The name Glen is said to have been applied by Jerry Banks in honor of some town where he had lived previously, but the compiler has been unable to identify the place.

Glenada, LANE. Glenada townsite was platted by Geo. H. Colter about 1890. The writer is informed that since the place was in a circle of the Siuslaw River, it was called "Glen-Ada," the Ada being for Mrs. Colter. Why the circle of the river suggested Glen has not been explained. Postal authorities played havoc with Colter's name by condensing it into Glenada. The office was established about 1890 with Margaret I. Grant first postmaster. She was a sister of Mrs. Colter. Colter was born in Nova Scotia in 1846 and died on May 8, 1934.

Glenbrook, BENTON. The descriptive name Glenbrook was given a post office that operated in the foothills of the Coast Range a few miles west of Monroe. The office was established May 4, 1898, with Ella Atkins first postmaster. It was discontinued Jan. 17, 1905, about the time many other offices were closed because of the establishment of rural free delivery. The locality called Glenbrook is on Hammer Creek about three miles southwest of Alpine.

Glencoe, WASHINGTON. The community called Glencoe has been absorbed by the village of North Plains, of which it constitutes the northeast part. In Oct. 1945, the compiler was told by J. M. Brown of Hillsboro that Glencoe was named by Charles McKay for the place in Scotland with the melancholy history. McKay was a Scot, although available records indicate that he was born at sea in 1808. The naming of Glencoe, Oregon, must have been for sentimental reasons because physically the location does not resemble the place in Scotland by any stretch of the imagination. The post office at Glencoe was established Jan. 9, 1871, with William H. Silvers postmaster. The office was discontinued in Dec. 1904.

Glencullen, MULTNOMAH. Glencullen is a community in the extreme southwest part of Portland. It was named in compliment to Captain John Winchell Cullen, a prominent pioneer citizen of Oregon. Cullen was born at La Porte, Indiana, June 18, 1838, and came to Oregon in 1847. He fought in the Indian wars of 1855–56 and also in the Civil War. He took part in many affairs of importance in developing the state. He died in Portland Dec. 14, 1939, and is buried in Lone Fir Cemetery. For information about Captain Cullen, *see* editorial page of the *Oregon Journal* for Nov. 30, 1937.

Glendale, DOUGLAS. When the railroad was extended south from Roseburg in 1881–83, Solomon Abraham acted as right-of-way agent, and platted several communities, including the present site of Glendale. This site he named Julia, for Mrs. Abraham. The chief engineer of the railroad, Charles A. F. Morris, and Abraham got into a controversy about the townsites, and Morris changed the name of the station from Julia to Glendale, although the post office and townsite remained as before. This resulted in confusion, and the post office was subsequently changed from Julia to Glendale. There are several stories as to why the name Glendale was selected. Will G. Steel says it was suggested by G. Wingate, for the Scottish glens. Albert Abraham of Roseburg, son of Solomon Abraham, told the writer that Morris was a native of Glendale, Massachusetts, or Glendale, Scotland, and suggested the name himself. A large part of the Glendale business district was burned on July 11, 1928. Walling in his *History of Southern Oregon*, p. 426, says that it was first planned to name this place Montgomery because it was laid out on the L. D. Montgomery land claim, but that name did not prevail. L. D. Montgomery was the first postmaster at Julia office, which was established in Feb. 1883, and continued in office after the name was changed to Glendale in Aug. 1883.

Gleneden Beach, LINCOLN. Gleneden Beach is a type of descriptive name frequently found in seashore areas where there are high hopes of real estate sales. The place is about a mile south of the south end of Siletz Bay. Gleneden Beach post office was established Nov. 1, 1927, with William F. Cary first postmaster and was discontinued June 23, 1961. It is now a rural station out of Lincoln City.

Glenn, MALHEUR. Glenn post office was established on the Baker County list on Apr. 5, 1881, with William S. Glenn postmaster. The office was doubtless named for the postmaster. The office was moved to the Malheur County list when that county was organized in Feb. 1887, and it was discontinued in Dec. 1888. The office was situated near Willow Creek about nine miles northwest of Vale.

Glenn Creek, POLK. This stream flows through the south part of Eola Hills, just northwest of Salem. The writer is informed that it was named by C. A. Park, who lived nearby. Park is said to have named the stream because it ran through a glen or narrow valley, but in this event the name should be spelled Glen Creek. However, the style Glenn Creek has become well established through long use, and is the form used on government maps.

Glenora, TILLAMOOK. The name Glenora was applied about 1898 to a weather station near the old Wilson River wagon road. The name of this weather station has an interesting history. As far as the writer can determine the first use of this name in the Pacific Northwest was for a place on Stikine River in northern British Columbia. This area was called Cassiar district and there was a good deal of gold excitement there in 1873–75. A river landing was named Glenoraville but this was shortened to Glenora almost immediately. Glenora is said to mean vale or glen of gold. One of the first residents was Walter J. Smith, a former member of the Union army. After his discharge from the armed forces he engaged in mining and is said to have built the first house at Glenora, British Columbia. Mr. Smith later came to Oregon and in the spring of 1885 settled near the upper Wilson River. He liked the name Glenora and eventually tried to have it adopted for a post office, but the authorities objected because of the similarity to the name Glenwood used for an office in nearby Washington County. Mr. Smith had to be content with a post office named Wilson. Whether this office was named for the Wilson River or for William L. Wilson of West Virginia, the postmaster general, is a matter of argument. About 1898 a weather station was established at the James F. Reeher place with Mrs. Jennie A. Reeher in charge. The writer has been informed that Mrs. Reeher adopted the name Glenora for the weather station.

Glentena, LANE. In June 1947, Mrs. B. W. Inman of Noti wrote the compiler that Glentena post office was at or near the place later called Linslaw. Glentena office was established July 26, 1888, with Aaron C. Barbour first postmaster, and was discontinued Aug. 26, 1902. It was named for Mrs. Glentena Barbour, the wife of the first postmaster.

Glenwood, WASHINGTON. This name is said to have been originated about 1880, and was adopted because the natural surroundings suggested a glen in the woods. It is not inappropriate, differing in this respect from many similar names in the state. The post office was established in Aug. 1886, with Nira E. Catching postmaster. The office has not always been in the same location.

Glenwood Creek, LANE. This creek rises on Fairview Peak and flows west to Sharps Creek. About 1900, when there was considerable mining activity in the

Bohemia District, there was a stage stop called Glenwood near this creek on the way up the Hardscrabble Grade.

Glide, DOUGLAS. The post office at Glide was established in 1890, and Virginia C. Laird was the first postmaster. According to information furnished the compiler, Mrs. Laird had considerable difficulty thinking of a suitable name for the new office until one day she observed her small son playing about and singing "The River Goes Gliding Along." Without more ado Mrs. Laird christened the place "Glide," and it has been gliding along ever since.

Glisan Glacier, HOOD RIVER. In the summer of 1937, Kenneth N. Phillips, chairman, and other members of the Mazamas' Research Committee made a study of the ice fields on the northwest slope of Mount Hood, and among other things recommended that the name Glisan Glacier be applied to an ice stream lying between Sandy and Ladd glaciers and just east of Cathedral Ridge. The name was approved by USBGN in 1938. The name Glisan Glacier is in honor of Rodney Lawrence Glisan, well-known citizen of Portland, prominent because of his high character and his long devotion to the study of many phases of natural history and mountaineering and exploring and to outdoor photography. Rodney L. Glisan was born in Portland Apr. 3, 1869. He was educated at Bishop Scott Academy, and after studies in Paris, attended Yale, where he was graduated in 1890. He was admitted to the Oregon bar in 1892. He served in the Portland city council and also in the Oregon legislature and was on the Portland charter revision committee. He was much interested in sports and played on the first football team of the Multnomah Athletic Club and was a member of the Portland Rowing Club. He was president of the Mazamas in 1903 and later a vice-president of the American Alpine Club. He died in Portland May 6, 1934.

Goat Island, CURRY. Goat Island is in the Pacific Ocean west of Brookings. In 1935 it was declared a migratory bird refuge and is under special access restrictions to protect the great numbers and varieties of birds that nest there. For an interesting account of the island, *see* the Brookings *Pilot*, June 15, 1967. The name Goat Island is very old and the compiler has been unable to learn the circumstances connected with its application.

Goble, COLUMBIA. This place was first settled by Daniel B. Goble, in Apr. 1853. He took up a donation land claim, and later sold it to George S. Foster, who laid out the town and named it for the previous owner. Goble was born in Ohio in 1815 and arrived in Oregon in Aug. 1852. His land office certificate was numbered 4157. Before the railroad bridge was built across the Columbia River at Vancouver, Goble was the Oregon terminus for the train ferry to the Washington side at Kalama.

Gods Valley, CLATSOP, TILLAMOOK. Gods Valley lies east and south of North Fork Nehalem River, and drains into that stream by means of Gods Valley Creek, the mouth of which is in the extreme south part of Clatsop County. It was named many years ago. In Dec. 1945, J. H. Scott of Nehalem wrote the compiler in part as follows: "The valley was discovered by John Hunt and E. K. Scovell, who were hunting elk on the North Fork and followed a trail east over the ridge and down into an unknown valley where they found and shot several elk. It is reported that they were badly in need of meat, and when they shot the elk, one of them said, 'What shall we call this valley?' The other replied, 'We needed meat and God led us here, so let's call it Gods Valley.' Courtland Matthews has an interesting article in the *Sunday Oregonian*, Apr. 3, 1949, Sect. 4. giving an overview of the area as of that date and a slight variation in the origin of the name. He quotes Mrs. Charlie Alley, the sister-in-law of John Hunt, as saying that in 1876 Hunt returned from the excursion with Scovell and declared they had found a "Valley of the Gods." Both comments may be correct. The largest spruce tree in Oregon or Washington is said to be in the northern part of this valley, although the tree has been dead for many years.

Goen Creek, GRANT. This is a small tributary of John Day River just east of Fields Creek. In the 1880s, William Goen patented a homestead a couple of miles above its mouth and the creek was named for him.

Goff, SHERMAN. Goff is a station on the Union Pacific Railroad just east of John Day Dam. It was established in Jan. 1914, and named for H. W. Goff, the man from whom the railroad bought the original right of way about 1882. Earlier information that the station was named for Theodore H. Goffe, the engineer for the Oregon Pony at the Cascades in 1862, does not appear to be correct.

Gold Beach, CURRY. Gold was discovered in the sands of Curry County in the early 1850s and the beaches were named on that account. They were the scene of operations of hundreds of placer miners in pioneer days. This particular beach was at the mouth of Rogue River, and the settlement there was for some years known as Ellensburg, but it is said that there was confusion with Ellensburg, in Washington Territory, and the name was changed to Gold Beach. The name Ellensburg was derived from Sarah Ellen Tichenor, daughter of Captain William Tichenor. *See* Tichenor Rock. Bancroft and Mrs. Victor both refer to the fact that the settlement at the mouth of Rogue River was once known as Whaleshead, but Orvil Dodge says that is a mistake. What is now known as Whaleshead Island is some distance south of Gold Beach. For information about early history of Gold Beach, *see* Port Orford *News*, Dec. 14, 1926, where it is said that Sebastopol was one of the early names for the place. For additional history of Gold Beach, *see* editorial page *Oregon Journal*, July 20, 21, 1927, and under Fort Miner.

Gold Creek, CLACKAMAS, MARION. Gold Creek and a tributary, East Gold Creek, drain a large basin that is traversed by the Clackamas-Marion county line. Gold Creek flows into Little North Santiam River from the north just east of the west line of T 8S, R 5E. Gold Creek is in the very heart of the North Santiam mining area, and from time to time there has been a good deal of activity in that region. The stream was named for the gold ore that was uncovered. There were also silver, copper, iron, galena and other minerals. For an account of these discoveries, *see* Down's *History of the Silverton Country*, pp. 85 and 86. Down does not give the date of the discovery of minerals in the North Santiam area, but it seems probable that it was in the middle 1860s.

Gold Creek, POLK. Gold Creek flows into South Yamhill River from the south a little west of Willamina. It is sometimes shown on maps as Cold Creek but various county authorities have informed the compiler that Gold Creek is the correct name, not Cold Creek. The local school is officially known as Gold Creek School. The compiler has not been able to get the origin of the name; its history seems to be as closely guarded as the metal itself.

Gold Hill, JACKSON. Gold Hill was the scene of an early gold discovery in southern Oregon. There is now some controversy as to the exact location of the hill so known, but from what evidence the writer has seen it is quite certain that the original Gold Hill was on the south bank of Rogue River opposite the present community of Gold Hill. There seems to be no historic reason to believe that it was north of the town, even though so shown on some maps. The hill to the north is somewhat more imposing than the original Gold Hill to the south, and this may be the reason that some local residents tried to move the name. The town is of course named for the hill. In pioneer days the main settlement in this neighborhood was that of W. G. T'Vault at Dardanelles, on the south side of Rogue River.

Gold Lake, LANE. This lake lies between Odell and Waldo lakes near the headwaters of Salt Creek. C. B. McFarland, long time USFS district ranger at Oakridge, stated that it was named for one Gold, Amos R. Black's foreman on the Waldo Lake Irrigation and Power Company tunnel project.

Gold Ray, JACKSON. Colonel Frank Ray of New York was interested in the power development at the falls of Rogue River at Lower Table Rock, and named the place Gold Ray. This name caused confusion on the line of the Southern Pacific Company, because of the close proximity of Gold Hill, the next station to the west. The railroad name for Gold Ray is Ray Gold. The California Oregon Power Company used the original arrangement of the words.

Golden, JOSEPHINE. Golden post office was named for the mining activity of a locality a few miles southeast of Wolf Creek. The office was established Jan. 10, 1896, with Schuyler C. Ruble first postmaster, and continued in operation until Mar. 31, 1920. The place was on Coyote Creek and had quartz and stamp mills.

Golden Curry Creek, LANE. This creek on the east slopes of Elephant Mountain was not named for an exotic East Indian meal. It is a corruption of Gould & Curry, apparently named in the hope the area would emulate the famous Virginia City, Nevada, silver mine.

Golden Falls, COOS. These falls are in Glen Creek Valley northeast of Allegany. In Mar. 1929, S. B. Cathcart of Marshfield wrote the compiler that they were discovered by Frank Ross and soon thereafter they were visited by Dr. C. B. Golden, first Grand Chancellor of the Knights of Pythias of Oregon, E. A. Anderson and Thomas Hirst. At that time they were named Golden Falls in compliment to Dr. Golden. Some time later other falls were found on a stream nearby, and the names Silver Falls and Silver Creek were applied in contradistinction to Golden Falls in the belief that the first falls were named for the metal, which is not a fact, according to Cathcart.

Goldson, LANE. According to information received by the writer from Seth W. Harpole, postmaster at Goldson in Jan. 1926, the place was named for the first postmaster, J. M. Goldson. The post office was established about 1891.

Goltra, LINN. Goltra was a station between Albany and Lebanon named for W. H. Goltra, a pioneer settler of the vicinity.

Gone Creek, CLACKAMAS. Gone Creek is a curious example of *ex post facto* naming. When Portland General Electric Company cleared the reservoir site at Timothy Lake, they picked a location for a forest camp near a small unnamed stream. When the lake was filled, the creek was inundated leaving only the intermittent upper reaches. Ralph H. Millsap of the power company suggested this name for a creek that was of little importance until it was gone.

Gooch, LINN. This station, about two miles west of Mill City, was named for Fred Gooch, who once ran a sawmill there.

Gooch Falls, LINN. These falls on Marion Creek about three miles below Marion Lake have been the subject of more than usual controversy. They were originally named Gatch Falls by John Minto in 1874 to honor Thomas M. Gatch, a well-known pioneer educator. However, in the 1880s Nathan W. Gooch took a squatter's claim that included the falls and built a small cabin immediately above. His name was soon applied to the falls and as his family continued in the area, it has been so known locally for many years. The similiarity of the two names compounded the confusion as the map makers and purists used Gatch while the residents used Gooch. After some study, the OGNB in Dec. 1970 decided on Gooch Falls and this was confirmed by the USBGN in *Decision List 7102*. Concurrently steps were taken to apply the name Gatch to another falls on Marion Creek. *See* Gatch Falls.

Goodfellow Lakes, CLACKAMAS. These lakes are in T 2S, R 7E. They were named for one Goodfellow, a clothing manufacturer in Minneapolis, who owned land in this part of the county.

Goodman Creek, LANE. This creek empties into Lookout Point Lake. A. J. Briem, in his notes on file at the OHS, says that it was named for William Goodman, an early settler.

Goodpasture Island, LANE. This piece of land is off the east bank of Willamette River in the north part of Eugene. There has been considerable shifting of the main river channel to the west and the original island is now bounded on the east by intermittent and disconnected sloughs. It was not named for the succulent forage but for Alexander Goodpasture who took up a donation land claim in the area in 1853. After Goodpasture's death in 1862 his widow married Jacob Gillespie who lived near Gillespie Butte. To further cement the new family ties, Marcellus

M. Gillespie, the son of Jacob and his first wife Amelia, married Alexander and Elizabeth Goodpasture's daughter, Rachel. Two Goodpasture sons, William and Thomas, farmed the original land well into the twentieth century.

Goodrich Creek, BAKER. Goodrich Creek rises on the east slopes of Elkhorn Peak in the Blue Mountains west of Baker and flows eastward to join Pine Creek near the locality called Wingville. The stream was named in the mining days for A. C. Goodrich, who came into eastern Oregon from the mining regions of the Sierra Nevada with experience as a surveyor and in ditch construction. He made a survey for the Auburn Ditch and had much to do with the construction of the conduit. For details, *see* Hiatt's *Thirty-one Years in Baker County*, chapter 4. The Auburn Ditch reached the headwaters of Goodrich Creek.

Goose Creek, LANE. This little stream flows into McKenzie River from the north, just west of McKenzie Bridge. Scott Taylor of McKenzie Bridge has furnished the compiler with the history of the name. About 1870, Mr. and Mrs. John Sims were traveling eastward along the road on their way to have Thanksgiving dinner with Uncle George Frissell. Mrs. Sims had her baby in one arm and a dressed goose in the other. When her horse reached the creek, he jumped suddenly, and the goose fell into the water. Ever since that event, the brook has been known as Goose Creek.

Goose Lake, LAKE. The Klamath Indian name for Goose Lake was *Newapkshi*. Goose Lake seems to have been named during pioneer days rather than in exploratory times. The compiler has no record as to who named it, but there was good reason to call it Goose Lake. Wild geese frequented central Oregon in large numbers in early days. In his diary for Oct. 21, 1832, John Work of the Hudson's Bay Company fur brigade, mentions "pit lake." On the next day the party camped near the lake itself. *See California Historical Society Quarterly*, Sept. 1943, p. 205. This is clearly Goose Lake and the text of the diary implies that the trappers had been in those parts before. Pit River in this locality is shown on Arrowsmith's map of North America corrected to 1832–33. The map of the Territory of Oregon, prepared by direction of Colonel J. J. Abert of the U.S. Topographical Engineers, 1838, shows Pit Lake and the hot springs to the north. The name Pit Lake went out of use long ago.

Gooseberry, MORROW. Gooseberry is a locality west of Heppner near the west edge of the county. The place was known as Gooseberry Spring at least as early as 1872 and was well known to cattlemen. It was named for a large wild gooseberry bush just above the spring. Gooseberry post office is shown on the 1884 post office list, but it has been out of service for a good many years. There are many places in eastern Oregon named for wild gooseberry bushes.

Gooseberry Creek, WALLOWA. This stream flows into Chesnimnus Creek in T 3N, R 46E. In 1931 J. H. Horner of Enterprise told the compiler that it was named by Jack Johnson, George Vail and William Duncan because they found some very good wild gooseberries nearby, which they cooked and ate.

Gooseneck Creek, POLK. Gooseneck Creek flows into Mill Creek, southeast of Willamina. It is said to have received its name in early days because its course is curved like a goose neck.

Gopher Valley, YAMHILL. Vernon Bailey in *Mammals and Life Zones of Oregon* lists no fewer than 15 varieties of pocket gophers in the state, surely enough for all requirements. It is not surprising that a pleasant vale in the east foothills of the Coast Range was called Gopher Valley. This valley is north of Sheridan and drains south through Deer Creek into South Yamhill River. Gopher post office was established Apr. 6, 1899, with Edward H. Taylor postmaster. The office was discontinued Sept. 14, 1905. The office was on the east side of Gopher Valley about a mile south of Gopher School.

Gordan Peak, LINN. This peak at the headwaters of Quartzville Creek was named for Gordon Short. Short worked for the USFS from 1911 to 1957 and helped construct many of the fire lookouts. The compiler cannot reconcile the difference in spelling but it may come from confusion with Gordon Meadows and Gordon Lakes which have been spelled both ways. *See* Gordon Meadows. This information came from Gerald Williams' interview with Short in 1969. Williams was with the staff of the Willamette National Forest. The spelling Gordon was confirmed in USBGN *Decision List 8502*.

Gordon, SHERMAN. Gordon post office, Gordon Butte, and Gordon Ridge, all near Deschutes River in the west part of Sherman County, were named for Tom Gordon, an Irish homesteader who settled nearby in the middle 1860s. Giles French in the *Golden Land*, p. 61, relates how William Hand, editor of The Dalles *Mountaineer*, accompanied Governor George Woods' party of inspection over The Dalles Military Road in 1869. They stopped at Gordon's place and Hand mentions his well established orchard. In 1965 an effort was made, due to a cartographic error, to rename Gordon Butte McDermid Cone. This was thwarted by the timely intervention of Mr. French. Gordon Butte is in S 13, T 1N, R 15E, and is not the high ground four miles southeast at the end of Gordon Ridge. Gordon post office was established July 7, 1896, with Joseph P. Walker first and only postmaster. The office was closed Dec. 18, 1896.

Gordon Butte, WASCO. Gordon Butte is 4821 feet high and lies north of Badger Creek. It was named for Eric Gordon, USFS District Ranger at Dufur 1923-1945.

Gordon Creek, UNION. William Gordon, a rancher, had a place on this stream in the early 1870s and it bears his name. Gordon Creek flows into Grande Ronde River a little below Elgin.

Gordon Lake, KLAMATH. Gordon Lake is near Yamsay Mountain. It is named for William Gordon, for many years a field surveyor for Region 6, USFS. Gordon spent a great deal of his time in the field where, in his off hours, he was an ardent angler. He was supposed to have known most of the good fishing spots in the National Forests. After his death, his friends in the USFS and the OSHD named this favorite lake for him.

Gordon Meadows, LINN. Gordon Meadows and Gordon Lakes are in the Fall Creek drainage some three miles south of Upper Soda. The name comes from the Hyatt-Gordon Grazing Allottment. They were using the land at the turn of the century, probably for sheep. Efforts to learn more have been fruitless except that both names are spelled in a number of different ways. The most important variant is Gordan Meadows.

Gore Creek, JACKSON. Gore Creek is a tributary to Bear Creek at a point about three miles southeast of Medford. It flows in from the south and passes under the Pacific Highway. It was named in compliment to Elijah Emerson Gore and Mary Elizabeth Gore, who came to Oregon from Lee County, Iowa, in 1852. The Gores settled in the Rogue River Valley on Sept. 27 of that year. The first winter was spent at Jacksonville, and then the family moved to a donation land claim near what is now Voorhies station, and adjacent to the stream. The name has been approved by USBGN.

Gorman, SHERMAN. Gorman post office was established Aug. 25, 1892, and was discontinued on Oct. 5, 1900. John E. Morrow was the first of three postmasters. In June 1948, Giles L. French of Moro wrote the compiler that the Morrow family homesteaded in S 30, T IN, R 19E. It is believed that the name Gorman perhaps came from a local resident but that is not certain. There was a Gorman school district in this locality on what is known as Starvation Point. Mr. French says that name was given for obvious reasons.

Gorton Creek, HOOD RIVER. This creek near Wyeth received its name because Edwin Gorton had filed for a homestead along its banks during the 1890s.

Gosage Creek, LANE. Gosage Creek is south of Dexter. It is probably named for Thomas Gosage who came to the Dexter area in 1880, and in 1891 patented a homestead along the creek.

Goshen, LANE. In biblical geography, Goshen was a pastoral region in lower Egypt, occupied and colonized by the Israelites before the Exodus. The compiler does not know who applied the name to the Lane County community. Goshen post office was first established Sept. 6, 1874, with John Handsaker serving as first postmaster.

Gould Lake, COOS. Gould Lake is in S 36, T 23S, R 11W, on the upper reaches of Elk Creek. It is named for George A. Gould who homesteaded nearby in 1886. The lake was formed in 1894 when a massive landslide dammed Elk Creek just over the ridge from the Gould place. At times the lake has been called Elk Lake but the USBGN decided on Gould in *Decision List 8602*. The 1983 GNIS gazetteer for Oregon lists 138 place-names beginning with Elk, surely more than ample to honor the magnificent *Cervus alces*.

Gourlay Creek, COLUMBIA, WASHINGTON. This little stream is a tributary to South Scappoose Creek. It was named for Alexander Gourlay, a pioneer homesteader nearby.

Government Camp, CLACKAMAS. The First U.S. Mounted Rifles crossed the plains in 1849, and reached The Dalles in the fall of that year. Most of the soldiers were taken down the river to Vancouver by boat, but a small command was left behind with the wagons and animals. Before the horses and mules could recuperate from the overland journey, the command was ordered to Oregon City by way of the Barlow Road. Nearly two-thirds of the animals were lost on the trip, and 45 of the wagons were abandoned. There was much controversy both before and after the trip about the advisability of attempting it with the stock in such poor condition. The name Government Camp came from the fact that some of the wagons were abandoned nearby and remained as evidence of military activity. Government Camp is on US-26 and the Mount Hood Loop Highway and has an elevation of 3888 feet. Official reports about the First U.S. Mounted Rifles are to be found in 31st Congress, 2nd Session, Senate Executive Document 1, part II, p. 126, *et seq*. There are many interesting illustrations. The journals have been edited by Raymond W. Settle with the title *March of the Mounted Riflemen*, Clark Company, Glendale, 1940. *See also* Bancroft's *History of Oregon*, v. 2, p. 82, and Portland *Telegram*, editorial page, Mar. 1, 1926. Government Camp post office was established June 24, 1931, with Margaret Villegar first postmaster.

Government Cove, HOOD RIVER. Government Cove, formed when the pool was raised behind Bonneville Dam, is two and one half miles east of Cascade Locks. A substantial rocky hillock left above high water was quarried for jetty rock but this venture was abandoned. The slack water cove has also been used for the storage of log rafts. Either of these uses could have been the reason for the name which is now well established and shown on current maps.

Government Island, MULTNOMAH. Government Island is in the Columbia River. Broughton spent the night of Oct. 29, 1792, in the vicinity of this island. In fact, he may have camped on the island itself, or possibly on Lemon Island. Broughton spent the day of Oct. 30 exploring the Columbia River to a point above Sandy River, and returning in the evening, camping not far from his position of the previous night. The next white men to visit the island were Lewis and Clark, on Nov. 3, 1805. They called it Diamond Island, because of its shape. The Lewis and Clark maps indicate that what is now known as Government Island was then divided into two large islands, besides smaller ones, and it was the upper of the two larger islands that was named Diamond. The lower island is not named in the text, but the maps show it and another islet to the west as White Goose Island. This western islet is probably the Lemon Island of today. The two larger islands are now consolidated, though part of the dividing channel still exists. At the time of Lewis and Clark the western of the two larger islands was nearly consolidated with the islet to the west mentioned above. In Feb. 1850, the government reserved this island for military purposes, and raised hay on it. It was then called Miller's Island. The name, Government Island, came into use after government occupation. *See* Bancroft's *History of Oregon*, v. 2, p. 89, and the Secretary of War's annual report, dated Dec. 4, 1852, p. 123. The island can now only be approached by water. Glen Jackson Bridge on I-205 crosses the island but there is no vehicular or pedestrian access.

Gowdy Ranch, LAKE. This ranch on Silver Creek south of Silver Lake was started prior to World War I by James Gowdy.

Grabenhorst Corners, MARION. Grabenhorst Corners are about four miles south of Salem, on the Pacific Highway East. These corners were named for G. H. Grabenhorst, who owned land nearby.

Grade, WHEELER. Grade post office was established June 28, 1880, with George M. Wasson first postmaster. This office was named for a short section of the old stage road from Antelope to Mitchell. This section was known as "The Grade," and it had been cut out of the side hill on the southwest side of John Day River just south of the mouth of Cherry Creek, at the very west edge of what is now Wheeler County. The post office and toll house were in the southeast corner of T 9S, R 20E. In the summer of 1947 Mrs. Goldie Van Bibber (Mrs. Charles F.) Putnam of Inchelium, Washington, sent the compiler some very entertaining reminiscences of youthful experiences at The Grade. According to Mrs. Putnam the original stage and freight road in this locality was difficult and dangerous and it was improved by a man called "Monty," the improvements being made by hand labor over a period of several years. Monty did not live long to enjoy the fruits of his labor. Monty was another name for the postmaster, George Montgomery Wasson. Addie S. Masterson was appointed postmaster on Oct. 24, 1882, and the name of the office was changed to Burnt Ranch on Jan. 15, 1883. About this time the office was doubtless moved from its original location to the site of Burnt Ranch about four miles east, near the mouth of Bridge Creek. Grade office was reestablished in May 1896, by change from Burnt Ranch, and it was in the period of 1897–98 that Hattie Van Bibber, Mrs. Putnam's mother, was postmaster. The office was closed July 31, 1901. Grade post office and toll house was a natural stopping place for the freighters, and Mr. Van Bibber operated a smithy to take care of the trade. Among other matters Mrs. Putnam writes of the following: "Mother was postmistress; served meals to freighters at twenty-five cents and collected the toll for "Mac" Cornett, who was interested in the road. The toll was twenty-five cents for each horse, regardless of the number of wagons or their weight. We could not charge Indians and preachers, and naturally there was no charge to the neighbors. In good weather there were often ten, twelve or even twenty freighters camping along the road from the house far up past the blacksmith shop. It was a sight to remember to see the Grade at starting time, lined with freight teams pulling out toward The Dalles, loaded with huge sacks of wool. Not a few outfits had as many as three wagons and ten or twelve horses. Most drivers sat on a high seat and deftly manipulated a line for each horse. Many rode the left wheel horse and drove the leaders. At least one team in each outfit had warning bells on an arch fastened to the hames. Some horses were sleek and strong, well harnessed, others were pitiable creatures, victims of cruelty and ignorance. You could almost read a man's character by his team and wagon. One of the best outfits on the road belonged to Jack McCauley who had a family of ten children on a little homestead near the town of John Day. After I was grown I stayed one night with them when the stage broke down and was struck with the splendid discipline and high moral tone of the family."

Graeme, CLACKAMAS. The name of Graeme post office in the extreme west part of the county came from the Scottish family name Graham. There was a Graham's Ferry in this vicinity in early days and it was situated two or three miles upstream from Wilsonville. The compiler has been told that when an application was made for the establishment of Graham post office postal authorities objected to the name Graham because of possible confusion with Gresham post office in nearby Multnomah County. The name Graeme was used as a compromise. Graeme is an alternative form of the Scottish word Graham. The Graham family was well known in the locality and one member, Robert Graham, was living in Oregon City in 1948. Graeme post office was established Feb. 1, 1896, with T. Howard Baker first postmaster. It was discontinued Aug. 12, 1903. The compiler has been told that Baker bought the Graham house about the time Graeme post office was established.

Graham Butte, DESCHUTES. Graham Butte is about five miles southwest of Black Butte and Graham Corral is nearby. According to Phil Brogan of Bend, Mr. and Mrs. E. A. Graham arrived from California on Oct. 20, 1880 and soon settled on a homestead near Graham Corral. The location alongside the road to the Willamette Valley was a busy place in the summer and the Grahams kept the travel for the sheep and herders moving to the high pasture.

Graham Creek, JACKSON. This small creek north of Prospect was named for Edwin Graham who came from Texas prior to 1904 and endeavored to raise ginseng along this stretch of Rogue River. Mr. Graham's operation is not included in the inventory of Oregon's more successful agricultural ventures.

Graham Pass, CLACKAMAS. This pass is on the divide between Clackamas and Collawash rivers near the Marion County line. It was named for Joe Graham, a former USFS ranger.

Grand Island, YAMHILL. This is one of the largest islands in the Willamette River, and is so named on that account. It is separated from the rest of Yamhill County on the west by Lambert Slough, over which there is a bridge. In pioneer days it was known as Deer Island, which caused some confusion with Deer Island in Columbia County. Later it was called simply the Island. Island settlers organized a community club about 1913, and the name Grand Island was adopted by popular vote. For short history of Grand Island by Mrs. C. A. Ferguson, *see* Salem *Statesman*, Oct. 2, 1931. The island contains about 4000 acres of tillable land, mostly rich river soil. Statements that it is only 46 feet above sea level are not substantiated by government maps, which show that much of the area is about 100 feet above sea level, with one point 107 feet in elevation.

Grand Prairie, LANE. In pioneer days that part of the Willamette Valley floor northwest of Eugene and southwest of Harrisburg was generally referred to as Grand Prairie, but the name has sunk into disuse. Grand Prairie post office was established June 22, 1854, with Jonathan Butler first postmaster. E. Blachley became postmaster on Sept. 3, 1858, and Jonathan Butler, Jr., on Mar. 18, 1859. The office was closed Mar. 30, 1860. The office was of course named for the natural feature. In Feb. 1947, J. M. Nighswander of Eugene wrote the compiler that this office was probably near the "center, the school, or the thickest of the settlement." This center was near the northeast corner of the Andrew Jackson Simmons donation land claim, at the place later called Meadow View and also Grand Prairie School. Mr. Nighswander's mother was a daughter of Simmons, and his father, Francis Marion Nighswander taught school at Grand Prairie in 1873. Modern maps show Meadow View as a Burlington Northern siding about five miles south of Junction City, and also on the Pacific Highway.

Grand Rapids, CLATSOP. In Aug. 1892, articles of incorporation were filed in the Clatsop County records at Astoria for the Grand Rapids Improvement and Development Company. The compiler has been told that the enterprise was named for Grand Rapids, Michigan, and a program of lumbering and furniture manufacturing was planned. The community was to be at the bend of Nehalem River about four miles south of Jewell and Grand Rapids post office was established Dec. 28, 1892, with Horace M. Spencer first postmaster. The compiler has not found any record of a platted townsite with the name Grand Rapids and knows of no rapids in the river at that point that might warrant the name but a post World War II Metzger map shows an area marked Grand Rapids in the extreme southeast corner of S 23, T 5N, R 7W. The post office continued to operate until July 7, 1897, when it was closed out to Vinemaple. It seems apparent that Grand Rapids office was reestablished May 12, 1902, with Fred Springer postmaster, but available records give no postal history. At one time the Tideport Timber Company maintained an office, machine shop and roadhouse in the neighborhood and a place named Tideport shows on the Metzger map a little west of Grand Rapids.

Grand Ronde, POLK, YAMHILL. This name, as applied to a valley and two communities in western Oregon, is universally misspelled, but the style is so firmly fixed in the public mind that there seems little chance to change it. The USBGN tried to secure the use of Grande Ronde but without avail. The French word *ronde*, meaning circle or roundness, requires the adjective agreement *grande*, and the two words together may be taken as describing a fine large valley of excellent appearance, more or less hemmed in by hills. This valley and the one in Union County were named by French-Canadian trappers because of their aspect, but the valley in eastern Oregon is always called Grande Ronde. For many years there was a Grand Ronde Indian Reservation in Polk and Yamhill counties. There were 1064 Indians on this reservation in the census of 1867. The Grand Ronde Agency, which was in Yamhill County, was closed in the fall of 1925, but a community remains. *See* editorial in the *Oregonian*, Nov. 18, 1925. In the 1920s the railroad was extended from Willamina and the present Salmon River Highway was started along South Yamhill River. These both bypassed Grand Ronde Agency about a mile and a half south in Polk County and the present community of Grand Ronde grew up just west of the mouth of Rock Creek. Grand Ronde post office was established Feb. 16, 1861, with Benjamin Simpson first postmaster. The office was first at the site of Fort Yamhill, about a half mile north of what is now Valley Junction. About 1894 the office was moved to Grand Ronde Agency in Yamhill County, and in the early 1920s it was moved to the present site in Polk County. The post office has always been called Grand Ronde. In 1895 Butler post office was established at the locality of Fort Yamhill. The railroad was abandoned in the 1980s.

Granddad Butte, DOUGLAS. This butte in S 10, T 25S, R 2E, was named by USFS ranger Fred Asam for an aged prospector known only as "Grandad."

Grande Ronde Valley, UNION. This imposing valley has given its name to Grande Ronde River and also to La Grande. In this part of Oregon, the French name has retained both final "e"s. Grande Ronde, in eastern Oregon, is mentioned as early as 1827 by Peter Skene Ogden. In the copy of his journal at the Oregon Historical Society he says: "Saturday September 14th at 7 A.M. we started advanced one mile and reached Clay River or commonly Called Riviere deGrande Ronde. This river discharges in the South branch of the Columbia, about two days march across land from Fort Nez Percy." The name Clay River may have been applied because where the Grande Ronde River leaves the valley it is frequently very slightly yellow in appearance, or putty colored, doubtless due to valley drainage. Robert Stuart uses the name Glaise River several times in his journal early in Aug. 1812. *See Discovery of the Oregon Trail*, edited by P. A. Rollins, p. 76 *et seq. Glaise* is a French term for clay. Washington Irving quotes Bonneville as calling this stream *Fourche de glace*, or Ice River. Rollins suggests that *glace* is a misunderstanding of *glaise*, which seems likely, as the river where Bonneville saw it, hardly merits the name Ice. There are good descriptions of the Grande Ronde Valley in *Astoria* and in Stuart's narrative. It is obvious that Grande Ronde River was named after the valley.

Grandview, JEFFERSON. The name of Grandview suggests an hyperbole, but the compiler is of the opinion that the view justifies the name. Residents of the community enjoyed a view of the eastern slopes of the Cascade Range that was certainly inspiring. However, an inspiring view was not enough and by 1960 nothing remained except the remnants of abandoned homesteads.

Granger, BENTON. The Oregon Pacific railroad was put in service between Albany and Corvallis early in 1887. Granger was one of the early stations on this line about midway between the two cities mentioned. Granger post office was established Feb. 25, 1888, and it was in service until Sept. 30, 1903. Levi Joy was the only postmaster. The compiler has been informed that the place was named because of the well-known Granger movement which was prominent about that time. It is not known whether the station was established and named before the post office but the compiler thinks that was probably the case.

Granite, GRANT. Details of the early history of many Oregon mining communities are either nonexistent or hard to come by. Granite is no exception and the reader will just have to reconcile the following facts. Albert G. Tabor discovered gold along Granite Creek on July 4, 1862. He named his claim the Independence to commemorate the date and the area was promptly designated the Granite Creek Mines. By 1863 Granite City had been established and was so called on Alonzo Leland's *New Map of the Mining Regions of Oregon & Washington Territory* as well as the map prepared by Lieutenant John Bowen of Currey's command during the 1864 campaign against the Snake Indians. Some historians claim that the community was known as Independence and it was so shown on Foster's *Mining Map of Eastern Oregon* dated 1888 but the post office, established Mar. 26, 1878, was named Granite and this persisted until the final closure in 1957. The USGS Granite quadrangle dated 1972 shows Tabor Diggings about three miles down Granite Creek from Granite and the Independence Mine about the same distance upstream. The compiler does not know which of these two spots, if either, was the site of the original discovery nor if the community called Independence was the same settlement now called Granite. A paragraph in the *Oregonian*, Oct. 9, 1862 under a Granite Creek Mines dateline states that a town called Pleasant City had been laid out on Granite Creek but this name did not survive and the *Oregonian*, June 10, 1863 uses the name Granite City Mines. In a more recent vein, an article in the *Oregon Journal*, May 8, 1974 describes the revival of municipal government in Granite, a necessity caused by the resurgence of the population to eight from one in 1958. By 1990 it had surged another 25 percent to ten. Granite Creek was named for the granite rocks prevalent in the area.

Granite, JOSEPHINE. Granite, a Southern Pacific Company industrial station a couple of miles northwest of Grants Pass, was named for the immense quantities of decomposed granite in the locality, granite that the railroad used for ballasting hundreds of miles of tracks. This granite was of fine texture, packed well and was practically dustless, qualities of great value to a railroad. There was a good deal of railroad business at this point at the time when the Oregon lines were reballasted and a post office was found necessary. It could not be called Granite because of duplication with Granite in Grant County, then an operating post office. The office in Josephine County was therefore named Granite Hill. It was established June 12, 1905, and closed June 3, 1908. Lloyd B. Wickersham was the only postmaster. The railroad station was discontinued some years later.

Granny Creek, WALLOWA. Granny Creek is a short stream that flows into

Freezeout Creek in T 2S, R 48E. The creek was named for a favorite old mare owned by James Wilson and called Granny, which ranged along the stream in the late 1880s. She was killed by cougars and her body was found near the creek. At the head of the stream is a well-known natural lookout, Granny View Point. It commands a wide territory.

Grant, GRANT. Grant post office was established June 13, 1870, with William N. Bonham first postmaster. W. W. Stone became postmaster on Oct. 9, 1871, and the office was closed Apr. 14, 1873. This office appears to have been the third in what is now Grant County, preceded only by Canyon City and John Day City. The office was of course named for the county and for General U. S. Grant. In a letter printed in the *Blue Mountain Eagle*, Canyon City, Mar. 7, 1947, R. R. McHaley, former county judge, says: "William N. Bonham owned a ranch about a half mile northward from the present town of Mount Vernon, and W. W. Stone lived in the same neighborhood, so that this must have been the location of Grant post office. There was no town of Mount Vernon when Grant post office was created. I stayed all night at the Bonham residence in 1875, and there was no town of Mount Vernon then. The Bonhams kept a public stopping place at their ranch home." The compiler thinks that Mr. McHaley has solved the problem of the location of Grant post office. There was of course another Grant post office much later on in what is now Sherman County.

Grant, SHERMAN. Grant was a station on the railroad in the north part of Sherman County. It is not now a post office although it was at one time. The place came into being when the railroad was built in the early 1880s and it was known at that time as Villard in honor of Henry Villard, the great railroad man. The name was later changed to Grant for William Grant of The Dalles. In 1883 the community was burned. The townsite was platted in Nov. 1883, by William Murray and W. Lair Hill. The Columbia River flood in 1894 practically wiped out the town and citizens were forced to seek hillsides for safety.

Grant County. Grant County was created Oct. 14, 1864, and was named for General U. S. Grant, who at the time was at the height of his fame as a military leader for the northern armies. Grant County was carved out of parts of Wasco and Umatilla counties. Grant County has an area of 4497 square miles.

Grant Creek, CROOK. Grover Blake, one of the first USFS rangers in the area, told the writer in 1971 that the creek, spring, butte and meadows in the north part of the county were all named for one Grant, a very early sheep man from Antelope who used the area for summer graze.

Grant Creek, LANE. Grant Creek is tributary to Maple Creek three miles up from Siltcoos Lake. In 1891, James H. Grant filed on land along this creek.

Grant Hill, BENTON. Grant Hill is a 1005 foot high summit about a mile south of Pedee. It bears the name of R. J. Grant whose donation land claim included the hill.

Grant Island, CLATSOP. Grant Island in Youngs River bears the name of one of

Astoria's best known early citizens. Bridget Grant was born in Ireland in 1831, and came to Astoria in 1876 after some years in Massachusetts. Her husband drowned soon after coming to Oregon and Bridget opened a boarding house. She and her sons soon owned several hotels and boarding houses that catered to itinerant seamen and operated what was, in effect, an early hiring hall. *Calamity Jane and Other Wildcats*, has a chapter on Bridget Grant and among other nuggets relates: "She had, too, before many years her farm on Young's River. Here in slack seasons she would send seafaring guests for a season of wholesome country life which served a quadruple economic purpose. Isolation kept them sober and prevented their falling into the hands of rival agencies." Bridget Grant died in Portland in 1923, age 92 years.

Grants Pass, JOSEPHINE. Many stories have been circulated as to how this community got its name. Grants Pass citizens for the most part are inclined to the belief that the name was applied as a result of the capture of Vicksburg by General U. S. Grant. About the time the news arrived in southern Oregon, men were engaged in improving the road over the low hills north of the point where the city is now situated, and they celebrated General Grant's victory by naming the summit Grants Pass. This name was later applied to a nearby stage station and then to a post office, and on completion of the railroad the post office was moved from the stage station near the geographic feature called Grants Pass to a point near the railroad station and the present community took its name from the post office. On Oct. 12, 1921, Geo. H. Parker wrote Geo. H. Himes that the post office at Grants Pass was established in 1865 and the first postmaster was Thomas Croxton. Croxton desired to perpetuate the name of General Grant because of Grant's record in the Civil War, and asked the postal authorities to name the new office Grant. According to Parker the petition was refused because there was another Grant in Oregon. Government records indicate that the office was established Mar. 22, 1865, with the name Grants Pass, and with Croxton postmaster. This substantiates Parker's statement, although it does not prove that Croxton originated the idea of the name. The fact that he substituted Grants Pass for his original proposal indicates that the form Grants Pass was already in use. Wm. M. Colvig of Medford says E. B. Dimmick probably named the pass itself. Versions of the story ascribing the name to a visit of General Grant appear erroneous, because there is no evidence that General Grant was ever in that part of Oregon. He was stationed at Fort Vancouver from Sept. 1852, to Sept. 1853. The death of Colonel Bliss, of the adjutant-general's department, on Aug. 5, 1853, caused the promotion of Grant to the rank of captain of a company then stationed at Humboldt Bay, California. Grant made the journey from Fort Vancouver to Humboldt Bay by sea to San Francisco, and thence north to the place of his destination. He went to Fort Vancouver in 1852 by sea, from San Francisco. Stories to the effect that General Grant "passed" in a card game at Grants Pass may be dismissed as pure fiction. For additional information about the naming of Grants Pass, *see* editorial page *Oregon*

Journal, Aug. 30, 1927. For editorial about Grant's experiences in the Pacific Northwest, *see* the *Oregonian*, Mar. 7, 1943.

Grass Valley, SHERMAN. Pioneer settlers, without ever changing countenance, tell newcomers that in early days the rye-grass was so tall in this part of Oregon that it was well over a man's head. They even state that this was so when the man was on horseback. This accounts for the name. Grass Valley was incorporated as a result of a popular vote held Sept. 10, 1900.

Grass Valley Canyon, SHERMAN. Grass Valley Canyon heads in Grass Valley, hence the name. The canyon wanders northward through Sherman County, and finally joins the canyon of John Day River. This name is one of that class that is cumbersome, due to the fact that the name of one feature is used to describe another. Salmon River Glacier is another example. Grass Valley Canyon is an old name, however, and will probably persist.

Grater Butte, JEFFERSON. One of the earliest settlers on upper Trout Creek was James M. Grater who came to the Ashwood country in 1869. The 3643 foot butte was named for him although his two nephews, H. C. and L. G. Grater, were also well-known early settlers.

Grave Creek, JACKSON, JOSEPHINE. This stream rises in the northwest corner of Jackson County and flows into Josephine County. It receives Wolf Creek near Leland. In 1846 a girl named Martha Leland Crowley, died on what is now Grave Creek, and her burial there gave rise to the name. James W. Nesmith, in a letter published in the *Oregonian*, Nov. 23, 1883, wrote that in the late summer of 1848 he started for California with a party of gold seekers, and they found Miss Crowley's grave had been desecrated by Indians. They reinterred the remains, and called the stream Grave Creek. In Jan. 1854, the legislature passed an act changing the name of Grave Creek to Leland Creek, in honor of Miss Crowley, but the public did not accept the new name and it remains Grave Creek. Statements that Miss Crowley's name was Josephine and that the county may have been named for her cannot be substantiated by the compiler. *See also* Leland. Martha Leland Crowley was the daughter of Thomas and Catherine Linville Crowley, who came to Oregon from Missouri in 1846. Thomas Crowley and Martha Leland Crowley died in Oregon, but before the family reached the Willamette Valley. Thomas Crowley's daughter Matilda and a son Calvin also died on the trip out from Missouri, as well as Calvin's wife and child. In 1848 Mrs. Thomas Crowley was married to James M. Fulkerson in Polk County. *See* Grants Pass *Courier*, Jan. 23, 24, 26, 1934.

Gravelford, COOS. Gravelford is a place on North Fork Coquille River a few miles northeast of Myrtle Point. The name came from the natural ford in the stream. Gravel Ford post office was established in Apr. 1878, with Solomon J. McCloskey first postmaster. It was finally discontinued Apr. 30, 1934, with mail to Myrtle Point. The name in two words is the style used in post office records available to the writer, but the form Gravelford is used on the post route map of 1900 and on the USGS atlas sheet for the Bridge quadrangle.

Graveyard Point, CURRY. This point is a high headland southwest of the town of Port Orford extending southeastward into the harbor. In Feb. 1944, Louis L. Knapp of Port Orford wrote the compiler: "During the time the military garrison was maintained at Port Orford, two soldiers were buried on this point. Thereafter the oldtimers always spoke of the headland as Graveyard Point and it is generally known and referred to as such. No other burials have ever been made there."

Gray, CURRY. Gray post office was in service from Nov. 1884, to Nov. 1887, with Loftin Gray first and only postmaster. The office was obviously named for him. In May 1948, Douglas Cooley of Brookings wrote that this office was situated on Gray Flat, two miles north of Brookings.

Gray, LINN. This was a station on the Oregon Electric Railway southwest of Albany. It was named for Carl R. Gray, formerly president of the Oregon Electric and other roads, and later president of the Union Pacific Railroad Company at Omaha.

Gray Butte, JEFFERSON. There is a story, unconfirmed, that this butte was named for Dr. Asa Gray, the botanist, but residents nearby all say that the name is due to the characteristic color.

Gray Creek, CROOK. Gray Creek runs north to Big Summit Prairie. It and Gray Prairie are both named for John H. Gray. Gray was born in Linn County in 1855 and came to central Oregon in 1876. He was first county assessor and in 1896 sheriff of Crook County. He settled on Combs Flat but in 1899 he moved up Crooked River where he started the Bonnieview Ranch one and one half miles north of Post. About 1900 his son, Otto, filed a homestead on Gray Prairie and John Gray bought land there also.

Gray Creek, LANE. Gray Creek empties into Middle Fork Willamette River south of Oakridge. It is named for Israel J. Gray who came to the Oakridge area in the 1870s and homesteaded near the mouth of the creek.

Gray Eagle Bar, MARION. Gray Eagle Bar is on the east bank of Willamette River about three miles southwest of Salem. It received its name from the fact that the river steamer, *Gray Eagle*, was once stuck on this gravel bar for several days.

Green, DOUGLAS. This community three miles south of Roseburg was named for Jeptha Green who settled nearby in 1853. The station on the Southern Pacific Railroad was originally called Greens but the railroad has dropped the possessive.

Green Basin, MARION. The post office Green Basin, situated on North Santiam River about two miles east of Niagara, was named for a fine stand of green timber north of the office and in the vicinity of Rocky Top. A saw mill was operated near the post office. Green Basin post office was established Oct. 3, 1890, with John D. Montgomery first of four postmasters. The office was closed May 1, 1896, with papers to Niagara.

Green Hills, MULTNOMAH. Green Hills, the name of a residence district in the southwest part of Portland, was suggested by Henry Hewett when his own and neighboring property was platted in 1913. The style Greenhills is not that of the official plat and was not the form suggested by Mr. Hewett. The name Green Hills has extended its growth eastward until it now includes the Green Hills crossroads. The locality of the crossroads was known as Mount Zion in early days. According to Mrs. Hildegarde Plummer Wither, for many years a resident on Dosch Road, the name Mount Zion was applied by her grandfather, Albert Kelly, a son of Samuel Kelly of Kentucky, and brother of Oregon's well-known pioneer, Clinton Kelly. The Kelly family lived near the Mount Zion meeting house in Pulaski County, Kentucky, and had a sentimental attachment to the biblical name. In 1854 the Rev. Clinton Kelly suggested the name Mount Zion for what is now known as Mount Tabor in east Portland but his son Plympton Kelly was in favor of Mount Tabor and that name was adopted. It was about 1860–61 that Albert Kelly suggested the name Mount Zion for what is now called Green Hills. About the time mentioned Patton road was opened up to the pass in the hills and a small school was built at the southeast corner of what became the main intersection. This little school was just about the same location as the Green Hills service station in operation at this writing in 1990. The school house provided a meeting place for local residents and it was on this account that Kelly called the locality Mount Zion because of his sentimental interest in the Mount Zion meeting house in Kentucky. The selection was a little odd from a geographic point of view because Kelly gave the name Mount Zion to a pass in the hills and not to one of the summits. There was also a Mount Zion station on the Council Crest streetcar line just above the present intersection of Fairmount Boulevard and Talbot Road. The preceding stop on the Council Crest loop was Hewett Station. For many years the locality now called Sylvan was known as Zion Town. This name was originated by Nathan B. Jones. It is possible that the name Zion Town was applied because the place was so near Mount Zion School and crossroads. There was no town at Mount Zion.

Green Lakes, DESCHUTES. These are a group of one large and several small lakes directly between the South Sister and Broken Top. They are one of the sources of Fall Creek and the large lake has an elevation of 6505 feet. The name is descriptive, especially when viewed from above.

Green Mountain, LANE. This Green Mountain is three miles north of Disston and has an approximate elevation of 3450 feet. Loren W. Hunt of Cove, who lived nearby for many years, told the compiler that this peak was named for Claud Green, an early trapper.

Green Peter, LINN. For the meaning of the word peter when used to describe a rocky summit, *see* Bald Peter. Green Peter is situated northeast of Sweet Home and is the site of a forest lookout. Some maps and records refer to this point as Bald Peter, but the Linn County Fire Patrol has informed the writer that Bald Peter is about a mile north-northeast of Green Peter. In 1967 the USCE completed Green Peter Dam, a concrete gravity structure 380 feet high, on Middle Santiam River about one mile west of the mouth of Green Peter Creek.

Green Point, COLUMBIA. Broughton, of Vancouver's expedition, camped at Green Point on Oct. 26, 1792, and called it Point Sheriff, presumably after John Sheriff, master's mate of the *Chatham*.

Green Springs Mountain, JACKSON. Named because of the perennial verdure around the springs near the summit of this mountain on SH-66, the highway between Ashland and Klamath Falls. The highway was for many years known as the Green Springs Mountain Road. The form Green Spring is wrong.

Green Valley, DOUGLAS. This valley is northwest of Oakland. It seems to have been named because of its appearance. For the early history of the valley, *see* Walling's *History of Southern Oregon*, p. 439.

Greenback, JOSEPHINE. The locality called Greenback in the northeast part of the county was named for the Greenback mine, but the writer does not know the reason the mine was named unless it was expected that it would produce plenty of money. Generally miners were more interested in metallic money than that of the folding type. Greenback post office was established in Aug. 1902, with Carey W. Thompson first postmaster. The office operated until June 1908. The place was a couple of miles north of Grave Creek and about four miles airline east of the old Pacific Highway.

Greenberry, BENTON. Greenberry is a station south of Corvallis. It bears the given names of Green Berry Smith, a pioneer of 1845, who settled in Benton County in 1846, and who for a time lived on his farm near this station. Smith was generally called Greenberry, despite the fact that he had two given names. For further information, *see* Smith Hill in this book.

Greenburg, WASHINGTON. This was a station north of Tigard named by the officials of the Oregon Electric Railway Company for a local resident, and not because of any remarkable verdure. His family name was Greenburg. Greenburg Road serves a substantial suburban area that evolved in the 1980s.

Greenhorn, BAKER. Miles F. Potter in *Oregon's Golden Years*, p. 77, gives the following interesting account of this name. On the east slope of Vinegar Hill in s 7, T 10S, R 35E, there is a prominent rock or horn of green serpentine. The USGS Vinegar Hill quadrangle shows this point with an elevation of 7804 feet. It is highly visible and was known in the early days as the Green Horn. When the mining excitement developed during the 1860s, the name was corrupted to Greenhorn and applied to both the district and to Greenhorn Creek near the headwaters of North Fork Burnt River. An early community grew in the 1870s but Greenhorn post office was not established until May 24, 1902 with Burton Miller postmaster. The office was closed Dec. 15, 1919. Apparently the early postal needs of the area had been met by the Robisonville office, less than a mile to the northeast. Ellen Morris Bishop has an interesting article on the geology of the "green horn" and the surrounding area in the *Oregonian*, Jan. 14, 1987, p. E2.

Greenleaf, LANE. The name Greenleaf was first applied to this community about 1885, and when the post office was established about 1892, the same name was used for the office. It also was used for Greenleaf Creek, a stream flowing into Lake Creek where Greenleaf post office was first situated. The name is said to have been used because of the abundance of green maple trees in the vicinity. About 1908 the post office was moved some three miles down Lake Creek.

Greenman Creek, DOUGLAS. In 1908 John W. Greenman settled on Little River west of Wolf Creek along this creek which bears his name.

Greens Bridge, LINN, MARION. Greens Bridge is over North Santiam River about two miles east of Jefferson. It bears the name of Thomas Green, an early settler in the vicinity.

Greenville, WASHINGTON. Greenville, a crossroads community about two miles south of Banks, at one time had a post office, but commercially the place has dried up. The office was established Jan. 9, 1871, with E. W. Dixon first postmaster. The office operated under various postmasters until Apr. 1907, when it was moved north to the locality of the old Banks office and the name Banks restored. Greenville was apparently a descriptive name, bestowed because the locality was so verdant. The writer has not been able to find any evidence that the place was named for an individual.

Gregory Point, COOS. Gregory Point is the northwest promontory of Cape Arago. The Cape Arago Lighthouse is on this point. The name perpetuates the name Cape Gregory, originally applied by Captain James Cook on Mar. 12, 1778, to what is now called Cape Arago.

Greiner Canyon, GILLIAM. This canyon south of Condon was named for an early settler, Andrew Greiner, who homesteaded there in 1885. Members of the Greiner family still live in the Condon area after almost 100 years.

Gresham, MULTNOMAH. Gresham was named for Walter Quinton Gresham, (1832–1895), soldier and statesman. He made an enviable record in the Civil War, displaying gallantry in action, and in 1865 was brevetted major-general of volunteers. After the war he practiced law and became a member of the federal judiciary. He was postmaster general in Arthur's cabinet from Apr. 3, 1883, to Sept. 24, 1884, when he became secretary of the treasury, and served about a month in that position. He was a candidate for the Republican nomination for president in 1884 and 1888, but eventually drifted away from the Republican party, and was secretary of state in Cleveland's cabinet from Mar. 7, 1893, until his death on May 28, 1895. Gresham post office was established in May 1884, and the name was suggested by Benjamin F. Rollins because W. Q. Gresham was then postmaster general. Gresham named the post office of George, in Clackamas County, for Judge M. C. George of Portland. *See* George.

Gribble Prairie, CLACKAMAS. This prairie is a well-known locality about four miles southeast of Aurora. It was named for John G. Gribble, who was born on the line between North and South Carolina in 1799 and after migrating to Missouri, came to Oregon in 1846. He settled near Macksburg in 1847 on a donation land claim, and his name was applied to the prairie in consequence. Gribble Creek is also named for him. He died June 3, 1869. For additional information, *see Portrait and Biographical Record of Portland and Vicinity*, pp. 393 and 853.

Grice Hill, POLK. Grice Hill is in the Eola Hills about three miles northwest of Salem. It has an elevation of about 550 feet. It was named for L. Grice, a nearby landowner. There was a pioneer quarry on the east part of this hill from which a good deal of building stone was taken for construction in Salem. This was before the days of concrete.

Griffin Canyon, WHEELER. This gulch is tributary to Dry Hollow, south of Fossil. It has been shown as Griffith Canyon, but in 1931 the compiler was told Griffin was correct. This was confirmed by W. H. Steiwer of Fossil in Feb. 1944, stating the canyon was named for Tom Griffin.

Griffin Creek, BAKER. The locality of Griffin Creek just southwest of Baker City was one of the most prominent places in the early history of northeastern Oregon. It was close to this stream that Henry Griffin and others struck pay dirt on the evening of Oct. 23, 1861. This may be considered the beginning of placer mining in that section of the state and there was a good deal of subsequent activity, including the rise and fall of the town of Auburn. For the history of the discovery, *see History of Baker, Grant, Malheur and Harney Counties*, p. 142. The stream was of course named for the prospector. Griffin is buried with other members of his family in the Auburn cemetery. Sometime in the 1920s the Baker Chamber of Commerce erected an antique headstone with the name spelled Griffen. This is apparently in error since the many early records and references all use the form Griffin.

Griffin Creek, JACKSON. This stream rises in the mountains south of Medford and flows northward to join Bear Creek not far from Central Point. It was named for Captain B. B. Griffin, a pioneer of 1848, who settled in the Rogue River Valley in 1852. Griffin is the correct spelling.

Grindstone Ridge, WASHINGTON. Grindstone Ridge runs southward from South Saddle Mountain about four miles and terminates in Windy Point. It was named because an early settler with a timber claim on the ridge had a grindstone by his cabin. During the 1890s a surveying party sharpened their axes on the stone and its disappearance a short time later caused much local comment.

Grizzly, JEFFERSON. This post office was established about 1890, with Elsie Edmund first postmaster. It was named for Grizzly Mountain, a prominent butte about four miles to the southeast. The office was closed June 30, 1948.

Grizzly Mountain, CROOK. W. P. Vandevert of Bend in 1926 told the compiler that Grizzly Mountain received its name in the 1870s because of its grizzled color, and not because of any adventure with a grizzly bear.

Grizzly Mountain, CURRY. This mountain is three miles east of Gold Beach. There is a story to the effect that an early citizen nicknamed "Grizzly" lived on its slopes and hunted meat for the Gold Beach miners in the early days.

Grossman, WALLOWA. Grossman post office got its name from Grossman

Creek, situated about four miles southwest of Promise. The office was established in Dec. 1904, with Rhoda A. Pool, postmaster, and was closed in Mar. 1921.

Grossman Creek, WALLOWA. Grossman Creek was named for a pioneer trapper. He died many years ago near what is now Rondowa. Grossman Creek is about ten miles north of Minam.

Grouse, WALLOWA. This community is in the extreme north part of the county. It was at one time a post office. The place has also been known as Grouse Flat. In earlier days there were many grouse in the neighborhood. Grouse post office was established Jan. 28, 1896, with Samuel M. Silver first postmaster.

Grouse Butte, YAMHILL. Grouse Butte lies between Newberg and Parrett Mountain. Doris Jones Huffman of Newberg wrote in 1987 and said the butte was named in pioneer days for the abundance of grouse. It is on the donation land claim of Jesse Parrish and a descendant, Elery A. Parrish, operates the Grouse Butte Century Farm nearby.

Grouse Hill, KLAMATH. Grouse Hill is a prominent feature north of Crater Lake, and has an elevation of 7401 feet. It was so called because of the abundance of grouse found there.

Grouslous Mountain, CURRY. This mountain was named for John and Peter Groslouis who settled near Port Orford about 1853. Herman Reinhart, in *The Golden Frontier*, refers to them several times both when they lived in Curry County and later when they had moved back to their family home on French Prairie. Reinhart spells the name Grosluis and F. F. Victor, in *The Early Indian Wars of Oregon*, p. 324, speaks of John Grolouise. The correct spelling of this French family name is Groslouis and there were several of the family in Oregon in very early days.

Grove City, MALHEUR. On Apr. 3, 1888, a post office with the impressive name Grove City was established near Malheur River at a point about ten miles west of Vale. John F. Tilson was the first postmaster. This office was discontinued Sept. 19, 1899, with papers to Vale. The office was apparently named in consequence of Osborn Grove, a well-known place in the neighborhood.

Guano Lake, LAKE. This is a mud lake or playa about five miles long situated in T 39S, R 27E. It is fed by Guano Creek, an intermittent stream heading on Hart Mountain. Guano Lake has no outlet. The lake and creek were so named because of the guano deposits along their banks. The lake was named first, in the summer of 1864, during the Owyhee Reconnaissance of the First Oregon Cavalry under Lieutenant-Colonel C. S. Drew. *See* Drew's *Official Report*, p. 15. For a number of years the stream feeding the lake was called Warner Creek, but is now generally known as Guano Creek.

Guerin Creek, CURRY. Guerin Creek is a tributary of North Fork Floras Creek in the northeast corner of T 30S, R 14W. It is named for Alexander H. Guerin who homesteaded along it. Guerin, born in 1874, was the son of William S. Guerin, well-known early Curry County resident.

Guerin Prairie, CURRY. Guerin Prairie lies just north of the old site of Eckley on North Fork Sixes River. It is named for the Guerin family who were among the earliest settlers in the area. Charlotte Guerin was the sister of Captain William Tichenor. She came to southern Oregon in 1876 along with two of her sons, George H. and William S. Guerin. They all located in the Eckley area where Charlotte Guerin was postmaster at Eckley. George Guerin's wife, Priscilla, was born in England and was responsible for the early name, New Gate. Eckley post office was named for the their son. *See* Eckley.

Guild Lake, MULTNOMAH. This was a shallow lake within the city limits of Portland, on the west bank of Willamette River named for Peter Guild, a pioneer of 1847. After the Lewis and Clark Exposition of 1905, it was gradually filled with material sluiced down from the nearby hills and dredged from the river. After World War II the area was developed into an important industrial and distribution center commonly referred to as Guilds Lake.

Gull Island, COLUMBIA. This is a small island in the Columbia River north of Crims Island. Wilkes shows it as Weaqus Island in the Atlas accompanying *U.S. Exploring Expedition*, v. 23, Hydrography, but does not explain the name. Wilkes shows Crims Island as Gull Island, and it seems obvious that the name Gull later became attached to the smaller island to the north.

Gulliford Spring, UMATILLA. This spring on East Fork Butter Creek four miles south of Gurdane was named for the Gulliford family who in the early 1900s settled near Ukiah.

Gumbo, GILLIAM. A post office with the name Gumbo was established on the Gilliam County list on Oct. 18, 1892, with Zachariah J. Martin postmaster. The appointment was rescinded Nov. 15, 1892, and the office was never in service. The compiler has not been able to find the site for this proposed establishment, but supposes it to have been in a locality of gumbo, or sticky soil. Gumbo is the English form of the Louisiana-French *gombo*, meaning the okra plant, used to thicken soups. The word is derived from the African Congo expression *quingombo*, or okra. Not only is gumbo used to refer to thick soups, but also to the Negro-French patois of Louisiana and also to certain heavy, sticky soils. *See* Read's *Louisiana-French*, p. 122, published by the Louisiana State University Press.

Gumboot Creek, WALLOWA. This stream is in the southeast part of the county. It was named because Jack Johnson, a prominent pioneer stockman, once found an old gumboot in it. Gumboot Butte took its name from the stream. Johnson was one of the earliest settlers on Imnaha River.

Gumjuwac Saddle, HOOD RIVER. This pass is a mile southwest of Lookout Mountain, on the watershed between Hood River and Badger Creek. It is approximately 5200 feet in elevation. The name is not of Indian origin but a phonetic or illiterate rendition of Gum Shoe Jack, an early day sheepherder with an affinity for rubber boots, who resided nearby. Jack Springs is thought to be named for the same man.

Gunaldo Falls, YAMHILL. Gunaldo Falls are well known to those who traverse the Three Rivers Highway between Hebo and Grand Ronde. They are just northeast of the highway, on Sourgrass Creek, at a point about a mile east of Dolph. The compiler has been informed that these falls were given a synthetic name when a county road was built through in 1915–19. This name is said to have been made by taking the first letters of the last names of two county commissioners and a county judge. In May 1948, County Clerk A. R. McLaughlin wrote the compiler that William Gunning and W. S. Allan were county commissioners at that time and J. B. Dodson was county judge. Parts of their names have been handed to posterity in this scrambled form.

Gunter, DOUGLAS. Gunter post office was established in the fall of 1905, with J. O. Gunter first postmaster. Gunter petitioned for the office and suggested the name of his father-in-law, Craig. Other petitioners sent in Gunter's name, which was adopted by the authorities. Gunter was born in Indiana Aug. 7, 1852, and came to Oregon in Nov. 1885.

Gurdane, UMATILLA. The post office of Gurdane was named for John S. Gurdane, a pioneer settler of south Umatilla County. He was once a member of the state legislature. The post office was established in 1890.

Guy W. Talbot State Park, MULTNOMAH. For a description and history of this park, *see* Latourell Falls. Guy W. Talbot was born in Centerville, Michigan in 1873 and died in Portland on Dec. 1, 1961. He was employed by various railroad enterprises and became manager of the Oregon Electric Railroad in 1907. In 1910 he helped organize and became the first president of the Pacific Power & Light Company. For further information, *see* the *Oregonian* for Dec. 2, 1961.

Gwendolen, GILLIAM. Walter H. Guild, superintendent of the Oregon-Washington Railroad & Navigation Company at La Grande, informed the compiler in 1927 that Gwendolen was named for Miss Gwendolen Worthington, daughter of B. A. Worthington formerly vice-president and general manager of the railroad company. Information to the effect that the station was named for the daughter of a railroad conductor is wrong. The Condon branch line was built shortly before 1900 and the post office was established a few years later.

Gwinn, MALHEUR. This station about six miles east of Juntura, on the Union Pacific Railroad was named for Monte Gwinn, a stockman of Boise, Idaho. In 1943 it was reported that the station was no longer in service.

Gwynn Knoll, LANE. This is a knoll on the Pacific Coast in the northwest part of the county. It is south of Cape Perpetua. It was named for an early settler.

Gypsum, BAKER. According to information received by the writer from the postmaster at Gypsum in Jan. 1926, the place was named in the fall of 1907 on account of the gypsum deposit that is situated about a mile northwest of the station. General Charles F. Beebe of Portland was interested in the development of this deposit and probably suggested the name for the station. The post office was established about 1913, with J. C. McNaught as first postmaster. The post office was closed in the 1920s and the remnants of the community were inundated when Brownlee Dam was completed in 1959.

Haas Ridge, WALLOWA. Haas Ridge lies just west of Lightning Creek in the northeast part of the county. It was named for the Haas family, pioneer sheepherders.

Hackett Creek, CLACKAMAS. Hackett Creek flows west into Sandy River near Brightwood. It was named for John C. Hackett who settled near its mouth in the 1890s.

Hackleman Creek, LINN. This stream is near the South Santiam Highway. It rises in Tombstone Prairie just east of Tombstone Summit and flows eastward into Fish Lake. It bears the name of Abram Hackleman, one of the first settlers in Albany and one of the organizers of the Willamette Valley and Cascade Mountain Wagon-Road Company. Hackleman was born in 1831 and came to Oregon in 1847. He moved to Crook County about 1880. His name is often spelled Abraham, which is wrong, according to a letter from Willard L. Marks of Albany, dated Feb. 26, 1943.

Hadleyville, LANE. Hadleyville is the name of a locality on Coyote Creek about four miles southeast of Crow. Recent maps show a Hadleyville school in the area. Hadleyville was named for a local family. For biography of H. G. Hadley, an Oregon pioneer who settled in Lane County in the early 1850s, see *Illustrated History of Lane County*, p. 486. Hadleyville post office was established Oct. 3, 1890, with Frank Hadley the first of four postmasters. The office was closed to Crow on Oct. 31, 1903.

Hadsall Creek, LANE. In 1880 Mark Hadsall took a homestead near the mouth of this stream on the south edge of Mapleton. Amos Hadsall, who filed nearby in 1883, apparently arrived later as he is not listed in the 1880 census, so the stream was probably named for the former.

Haflenger Creek, LANE. Haflenger Creek empties into Horse Creek four miles above Foley Springs. It was named for Mrs. Ella Haflenger who operated the resort at the springs for many years. Mrs. Haflenger's first husband was Peter Runey who purchased the property at Foley Springs in the 1880s. The name on some maps is spelled Haflinger Creek but that is not correct. The compiler has a sample of the Foley Springs letterhead that has Mrs. Haflenger's name prominently displayed.

Hager Mountain, LAKE. Hager Mountain, about ten miles south of the town of Silver Lake, was at one time known as Hagerhorst Mountain for a pioneer settler in Silver Lake Valley. For many years it has been called by its modern name, which seems well established. The Klamath Indian name for Hager Mountain was *Chock-chock-lisk-se*. Some old maps call it Bald Butte.

Haig, MULTNOMAH. About 1889 a real estate addition was laid out in the southeast part of what is now Portland by Louis and Maria Feurer. This addition lies a little to the south southeast of Powell Boulevard. Most of the streets were given

German names, presumably by the Feurers. These German street names became subject to criticism in World War I and some of them were changed. As is natural with an activity of this sort there was a good deal of confusion. The name Karl Street was changed to Haig in honor of the great British field marshal. At the time of World War II so much traffic developed north of the Brooklyn yards that it was necessary for the Southern Pacific Company to extend its double track southward through east Portland. The railroad adopted the name Haig for the end of this section of double track and a station with this name was established for operating purposes.

Haines, BAKER. F. W. Castor, postmaster at Haines in 1926, informed the writer that the community was named for "Judge" I. D. Haines, of Baker City, who owned land on which the town was situated. The community was started in 1883, the year before the railroad was constructed through Baker Valley. The post office was established in Nov. 1884, with Florence A. Dorsett first postmaster. For story about the early history of Haines, *see* Baker City *Record Courier*, July 2, 1936.

Haines Creek, COOS, CURRY. This stream flows into Sixes River from the north at the site of Eckley. It is named for John Haines who was born in Illinois in 1828 and came to Curry County in 1859 where he settled near Eckley. His formal homestead filing was May 5, 1880.

Hale, LANE. Hale post office was near Elk City about five miles northwest of the place now called Noti, and was given the family name of the postmaster, George H. Hale. The office was established Aug. 4, 1886, and was closed out to Elmira on May 23, 1907. Lumbering was the chief industry.

Hale Butte, LINN. Hale Butte is about two miles west of Jefferson and has an elevation of 427 feet. It was named for Milton Hale, whose donation land claim took in part of the butte. Hale established Hale Ferry and the city of Syracuse on the Santiam River near the butte in pioneer days, but his town did not grow to maturity. Hale Butte has been shown on maps as Gale Butte, a typographical error. For information about Hale and Syracuse, *see OHQ*, v. 32, p. 195.

Haley, CLACKAMAS. Haley was a station about one mile northwest of Boring. It was named for P. W. Haley, a nearby resident.

Halfway, BAKER. An article printed in the Baker City *Democrat-Herald* on Aug. 29, 1935, which seems to be authoritative, says that the post office was established about 1887 on the Alexander Stalker ranch, now Canaday farm, and the office was named Halfway because it was about midway between Pine and Cornucopia. This appears to be correct. Later the office was moved and it is now much nearer Pine. The original significance of the name has been lost. The compiler has received several letters about this name, in which it is stated as a matter of historical fact that the place was named because it was halfway between the following points: Pine and Carson, Baker City and Cornucopia, Baker City and Brownlee and Brownlee and Cornucopia. Halfway is not midway between any of these places, as may be seen from an inspection of the map. C. A. Moore, in the

Oregonian, Dec. 13, 1926, editorial page, says Halfway is midway between Pine and Carson. This is not a fact. The compiler believes that the first paragraph printed above contains the most reliable information. In Jan. 1906, it was planned to change the name of Halfway post office to Bellevue, and an order was entered on Jan. 8, 1906, establishing the post office with the new name, and with George S. Gillett postmaster. For some reason the order was not put into effect and was rescinded Jan. 13, 1906. On Jan. 17 Gillett was appointed postmaster at Halfway and the business of that office appears to have been carried on without any ripples. Bellevue is a descriptive name that has been used in many places in the United States. The compiler has been unable to learn the reason for the proposal to change the name of Halfway post office to Bellevue.

Hall Creek, COOS. This stream joins Coquille River at Arago. It was named for David Hall, who took up a donation land claim near its mouth.

Hall Ridge, MARION. Earl Stahlman of Detroit told the writer that this high ground northeast of Detroit Dam was named for Bruce Hall who logged it many years ago.

Halls Ferry, MARION. Halls Ferry was a station on the Oregon Electric Railway not far from the site of Halls Ferry which crossed the Willamette River north of Independence. This ferry was first established about 1868 by Noah Leabo. He sold it to J. A. Colby about 1874 and B. F. Hall bought it about 1882 and after that it was known as Halls Ferry. B. F. Hall was the younger son of Reason B. Hall, who founded the town of Buena Vista. For information about the Hall family, *see* Buena Vista.

Halo Creek, LANE. *Halo* is the Chinook jargon word meaning none, and the name Halo Creek means that very little water flows in the stream, perhaps none at all at certain seasons. Halo Creek flows into Salmon Creek from the north about 12 miles east of Oakridge.

Halsey, LINN. This place was named for William L. Halsey, vice-president of the Willamette Valley Railway Company during the construction period. Halsey was one of the Holladay organization. The railroad was built through what is now Halsey in 1871, and the name was doubtless applied at that time. Halsey was not named for the man of that name connected with the Astor enterprise. For biography of William L. Halsey, *see* the *Oregonian*, Feb. 22, 1884, p. 3.

Hamaker Mountain, KLAMATH. Hamaker Mountain is a prominent point 6596 feet high southwest of Keno. It was named for John Wesley Hamaker who was a land law specialist and surveyor of Klamath County in the 1880s. He was later United States Land Commissioner in Klamath Falls. Both he and his brother, Joseph O. Hamaker, were involved in the land frauds at the turn of the century. One of the points of controversy was the use of assumed names and this may account for the numerous variant spellings.

Hambone Butte, CLACKAMAS. This butte is between Salmon and Roaring rivers. Its elevation is about 4900 feet. It was named by T. H. Sherrard of the USFS who said the name was arbitrary and had no peculiar significance.

Hamilton, GRANT. Hamilton was named for J. H. Hamilton, a pioneer stockman of the neighborhood and also the first settler where the town is now situated. Hamilton located there some time in 1874 and lived there until his death in 1909. The first store was built by Anson C. Frink who was the first postmaster. The Hamilton ranch was headquarters where settlers met to try the speed of their favorite horses, as Hamilton was a fancier of horseflesh.

Hamilton Canyon, UNION. Hamilton Canyon lies between Hilgard and Perry. It was named for Richard Hamilton who bought government land along the canyon in 1883.

Hamilton Creek, CURRY. Adam Hamilton homesteaded near this creek three miles east of Brookings in the 1880s.

Hamilton Creek, LINN. C. H. Stewart of Albany wrote the compiler in 1927 as follows: "Hamilton Creek is one of the foothill streams of Linn County east of Lebanon. I have been told it was named for a family that settled in that locality at an early date and only resided there a short time."

Hamlet, CLATSOP. Hamlet post office was established about 1905, with Albert Hill as first postmaster. The story of the name is printed in the Seaside *Signal* for Jan. 10, 1929. Herman Ahlers, an old settler on the Necanicum River, is authority for the statement that when he was postmaster at Necanicum, a petition was brought in by a man named Hutinen, living in the valley of North Fork Nehalem River, asking for a post office to be called Hamlet. Ahlers said he asked if the place was named for Shakespeare's play or because it was just a small community. Hutinen told him the latter. The same story contains a statement by A. W. Utzinger, also an old resident, that Hamlet was once called Push in honor of the Astoria Push Club and the name was changed to Hamlet in compliment to Harry Hamlet, member of the club, which was interested in the development of the locality. In a subsequent letter Ahlers denies all this and points to the fact that it was Necanicum post office that was called Push, not the Hamlet post office, and that the Astoria club had no interest in the locality. Government records confirm Ahlers' statement that Push was used at Necanicum and not at Hamlet.

Hamlin Prairie, DOUGLAS. Hamlin Prairie is on the divide between Elk Creek and Jackson Creek about seven miles southeast of Tiller. It was named for Edmund T. Hamlin who settled there in 1916.

Hammer Creek, BENTON. Hammer Creek bears the name of Jacob Hammer, a pioneer settler on its banks. The stream is west of Monroe. According to the article "Chronicle of the Bellfountain Settlement," *OHQ*, v. 38, p. 274, Hammer's family lived on the Caton homestead while the men of the settlement were away at the California mines. For biography of Jacob Hammer, *see History of Benton County*, Portland, 1885, p. 514.

Hammersley, JOSEPHINE. A post office with the name Hammersley was established June 7, 1894, with M. Hammersley postmaster. For some reason it was never placed in service and the appointment was rescinded Oct. 8, 1894. The compiler is informed that the office was intended to serve the locality of the

Hammersley mine on the extreme east edge of the county northeast of Grants Pass.

Hammond, CLATSOP. Named for Andrew B. Hammond, a pioneer of the Pacific Northwest. He was born in New Brunswick July 22, 1848, and in 1866–67 came to Washington and then settled in Montana, where he lived about 30 years, successfully engaged in mercantile and railroad affairs. From 1895 to 1898 he built the Astoria and Columbia River Railroad, later acquired by the Spokane, Portland and Seattle Railway Company. In later years he lived in San Francisco, where he died Jan. 15, 1934. He was one of the foremost business men of the Pacific Coast and was interested in timber, lumber, shipping, fishing and various mercantile enterprises. Silas B. Smith says that the Clatsop name of the Indian village near the present site of Hammond was *Ne-ahk-stow*. See *OHQ*, v. 1, p. 321.

Hamner Butte, KLAMATH. Hamner Butte is a prominent 7098-foot mountain southeast of Davis Lake. It was named for Thomas Frank Hamner, a homesteader near Black Rock south of the butte who patented government land just south of Black Rock in 1910. Hamner evidently went by both his given names. For much information about early residents in this area, see Edward Gray's *History of Early Northern Klamath County*.

Hampton, LANE. This station on the Southern Pacific Cascade Line was established when the railroad was relocated around Lookout Point Lake. It was named for Harry A. Hampton, railroad division engineer from 1922 to 1943.

Hampton Butte, DESCHUTES. Hampton Butte is really a group of dissected hills, part of which is in Crook County. The summit, with an elevation of 6333 feet, is apparently in Deschutes County. W. P. Vandevert of Bend told the compiler in 1926 that the butte was named for one Joe Hampton, who moved into Hampton Valley in the 1870s from near Eugene. There is a description of the butte in USGS *Bulletin 252*, which says that it was the result of explosive volcanic eruptions, which discharged acid lavas and probably furnished most of the material for the extended tuff sheets forming the surface of much of the adjacent country. The butte is of importance geologically and is well described in detail by Dr. I. C. Russell in the bulletin mentioned above. Hampton post office was established in 1911. Adna S. Fogg, the first postmaster, suggested naming the office for the butte. The office operated with one intermission until 1953. Currently Hampton, or as it is sometimes called Hampton Station, consists of a gas station and restaurant on US-20 east of Brothers between Bend and Burns. There is a short article with a picture in the *Oregonian*, Mar. 20, 1990, p. C4.

Hancock Creek, CLACKAMAS. Hancock Creek drains a small area east of Molalla. Its waters find their way into Molalla River. Isaac V. Trullinger is authority for the statement that a man named Hancock operated a small sawmill on the stream and the creek was named in compliment to him.

Handy, CLACKAMAS, MARION. The post office called Handy had an interesting history from two distinct aspects. It was given a descriptive name by its enthusiastic promoters who did not wish to travel miles for their mail. Also, it was moved bodily from one county to another though the distance was not great. There have been several Oregon post offices that have appeared on the lists for two different counties but these situations have generally been the result of moving the county boundaries. In the case of Handy the office was moved. Handy post office was established Apr. 18, 1896, on the Marion County list. Samuel Sweaney was the first postmaster. This office was moved to the Clackamas County list probably some time in Sept. 1898, and the new postmaster was Pearliette Killin. After this change the office went in service on the east side of Butte Creek near the Killin bridge. A little later Pearliette Killin became Mrs. Pearliette K. Pendleton. The office was discontinued in June 1903, apparently as a result of the extension of rural delivery. The following quotation is from the editorial of the Canby *Herald* for June 17, 1948: "The post office was established in 1896 by Samuel Sweaney on the Marion County side of Butte Creek serving Union community. The Sweaneys named it Handy for the simple and logical reason that it was handy to have a post office there instead of having to traipse all the way to Woodburn to get the mail."

Handy Creek, POLK. Handy Creek empties into what was Valsetz Lake at the old townsite. It bears the name of Arden R. Handy who homesteaded there at the turn of the century.

Haner Butte, DESCHUTES. Haner Butte, west of Wickiup Reservoir, was named for Joseph H. Haner. He came to central Oregon in 1901 from Minnesota and was active for many years as a timber cruiser and fire patrol supervisor. When Deschutes County was formed in 1916, Haner was the first county clerk. He died in 1953 at age 81.

Hanks Lake, LINN. Hanks Lake is in Hunts Cove on the south flank of Mount Jefferson. It is named for Henry C. "Hank" White who worked the area for the USFS about the time of World War 1.

Hanks Marsh, KLAMATH. Hanks Marsh is on the east side of Upper Klamath Lake between Klamath Falls and Algoma. It was named for James L. Hanks, a second cousin of Abraham Lincoln, who was born in Illinois in 1820 and came west in 1853. He settled alongside Upper Klamath Lake in 1873 where he became a successful rancher and stockman.

Hanover, BAKER. Some of the place names in the early mining areas present problems that so far have been unsolved by the compiler. Such a case is that of Hanover post office, established Nov. 3, 1888, with George L. Howard postmaster. The name of the office was changed to Cracker, Feb. 2, 1889, and it may have been moved at that time. Hanover has been widely used as a place name in the United States, and both the 1945 and 1988 *Postal Guides* contain lists of more than 20 post offices with the title Hanover or some adaptation of it. It is not surprising that a place in Baker County was named Hanover but it is more than likely that the name was brought from some other state rather than directly from Germany. Hanover in Baker County was near the mouth of Silver Creek, where that stream flows into Cracker Creek, nearly two miles southwest of Bourne. This office was operated with the name Cracker until it was discontinued Sept. 28, 1891. Cracker post office was obviously named for Cracker Creek, but the origin of that name is also a mystery to the writer.

Hanscombe Creek, GRANT. This creek rises on Hanscombe Mountain and flows north to Laycock Creek five miles south of Mount Vernon. BLM records show Charles S. Hanscom homesteaded a mile above the mouth of the creek in 1887 while the 1880 census lists C. S. Hanscomb. The compiler does not know which form of the name is correct.

Hansen Creek, MARION. Hansen Creek is east of Detroit. It was named for Elijah S. Hansen who took up government land near its mouth in 1900.

Happy, HARNEY. In the fall of 1916 plans were made to establish a post office called Happy, apparently in the hills just south of Happy Valley. Matilda McCrudden was appointed postmaster on Nov. 16, 1916, but the office was never operated and there is no further record.

Happy Camp Spring, WHEELER. Happy Camp Spring is in S 18, T 13S, R 23E, and Happy Camp Creek is just to the south running into Deep Creek. J. O. F. Anderson, in his notes on file at the Ochoco National Forest, says one of Ben Iremonger's herders always referred to this spring site as his "Happy Camp." Anderson first saw the spring in 1912 and there was evidence it had been used for many years.

Happy Valley, HARNEY. Mrs. Minerva J. Kiger, better known as Mrs. Dolly Kiger, of Corvallis, wrote in 1927: "George McCoy named Happy Valley. He said the settlers were so hospitable and happy." Mrs. Kiger lived near Steens Mountain from 1874 to 1878. Happy Valley was the site of George C. Smyth's ranch where he and his son, John Smyth, were killed by Indians in 1878. *See* Smyth Creek.

Harbor, CURRY. Harbor post office is where the old office of Chetco was once situated. The Chetco office was in operation from 1863 until 1910, in various places, and at one time was near the mouth of Chetco River at the present site of Harbor. Later it was moved southward several miles. When Harbor post office was established on Nov. 24, 1894, the name Chetco could not be used because the Chetco office was then serving the locality near the Winchuck River. It is reported that the new name was taken from the title of the Chetco Harbor Land and Townsite Company. For the history of the name Chetco, *see* Chetco River.

Hardesty Mountain, LANE. This peak, elevation 4270 feet, is in T 20S, R 1E. The notes of A. J. Briem, early USFS ranger, on file at the Oregon Historical Society, state that it was named for Charles Hardesty who was elected judge in 1854. Hardesty settled near Eugene in the early 1850s.

Hardin, CROOK. In June 1946, John W. Biggs of Burns told the writer that this post office was named for Colonel Hardin, a stockman who operated extensively in central Oregon in partnership with Amos Riley. Riley post office in Harney County was named for the other partner. These two did not live in Oregon, according to Judge Biggs, who said they had headquarters at Santa Rosa, California. However, they spent a great deal of time in Oregon and had many friends in the cattle country. The history of Hardin post office is slightly perplexing. All old maps available to the writer show the office in the extreme east part of Crook County near Grindstone Creek, in the locality later known as Angell Ranch. However, the office was first established on the Grant County list on May 23, 1882, with Seth Bixby first postmaster. It was transferred to the Crook County list without date. William McLagan became postmaster July 6, 1887, and the office was closed July 31, 1890. The significance of the original listing in Grant County is not clear. If it was an error, that is an end to the business. However, if the office was actually in what was then Grant County, the question arises as to whether it was in what is now Grant or what is now Harney. Grant, Harney and Crook counties come together in this locality. In early days the locality of Hardin was also called Twelvemile, probably because it was that distance from Paulina.

Harding, CLACKAMAS. George A. Harding, for more than half a century a much-respected resident of Oregon City, was born in Sydney, Australia, in 1843, and after a short visit in California, arrived in Oregon in 1857. He was a director of the Willamette Valley Southern Railway Company, and this station on that line was named for him on that account. He died Sept. 23, 1926.

Harding Butte, DOUGLAS. Harding Butte is north of North Umpqua River near Illahee Rock. It was named in 1920 by USFS ranger Fred Asam for President-elect Warren G. Harding.

Hardman, MORROW. Hardman is an old community north of Rock Creek that in recent years has languished. The first settlers were John F. Royse and his brother. Royse was a schoolteacher and started the first school in 1879 in a community called Dairyville. Locals often refered to the place as Rawdog. About the same time, David Hardman started a settlement about a mile away and on June 15, 1881, a post office was established with Hardman the first postmaster. Hardman came to Morrow County in 1878. For a brief biography, *see History of Umatilla and Morrow Counties*, p. 569. Locals were in the habit of refering to Hardman's town as Yallerdog. In 1882 The communities combined. The post office was moved to the site of Dairyville with the Hardman name retained. Hardman post office operated with intermissions until 1968. After the combination, the locals adopted the name Dogtown.

Hardscrabble Hill, LINN. Hardscrabble Hill is the northeast part of a butte about two miles southwest of Jefferson. Hardscrabble Hill itself has an elevation of 369 feet and is close to the west bank of Santiam River. This hill and other features in the state bearing the same name are so called because of the poor character of the soil and the difficulty of cultivating it. *See also* Hungry Hill and Needy.

Hardscrabble Ridge, LANE. This is the high ground that runs west from Fairview Peak terminating at the junction of Fairview and Sharps creeks. The name is so shown on the 1901 map of the Bohemia Mining District, not because of poor agricultural prospects but because it is a variant of "hardscramble." According to early travellers, it took from four to eight hours for a team to ascend this five mile stretch of steep wagon road.

Hardtack Island, MULTNOMAH. Hardtack Island is just southeast of Ross Island in Willamette River in the south part of Portland. It was once part of Ross Island, and probably still is at low water. It was known as Hardhack Island about 1905 on account of the *Spiraea douglasii* which grew there, but the influence of boating and yachting visitors overcame the botanical name and substituted one of nautical significance. Hardtack Island has been adopted as the official name by USBGN. *See also* Ross Island. Riverward from the south end of Ross Island is a gravel bar which was platted in 1868–69 as Toe Island, because of its shape. The three islands of the Ross Island group were charted as Oak Islands by Wilkes in 1841. Henry E. Reed, who had a wide knowledge of Portland history, was of the opinion that the name Hardtack Island was probably originally applied to Toe Island because of the well-known difficulty in tacking or bringing a sailboat about at that point on the river. Wind and currents were unobliging. There is not much of Toe Island left today. Whatever may have been the original application of the name Hardtack Island, it is now universally applied to the island southeast of Ross Island and east of what is left of Toe Island. The compiler remembers very well that about the beginning of the century the name Hardhack Island was used, but that name has not prevailed. The early plats show the name Ross Island covering both of the larger islands, Ross and Hardtack.

Hardy Creek, LANE. Hardy Creek is a tributary of South Fork McKenzie River. It was named for Charles A. Hardy, an attorney of Eugene, who built a hunting and fishing lodge near the mouth of the stream. Hardy Ridge nearby derives its name from the same source. Charles Albert Hardy was born in Michigan in 1874, graduated from the University of Wisconsin in 1896 and died at Portland on Nov. 29, 1937.

Hare, CLATSOP. In the early 1890s Levi Knapp, well-known pioneer settler of Clatsop County, operated a country store in the woods east of Astoria at or near the place later called Svensen. For convenience of local residents, James W. Hare, then postmaster at Astoria, arranged for a post office in the Knapp store and also for a supply route from Astoria. The new office was given the name Hare in compliment to the man who was so helpful to the little community. It was established Apr. 25, 1891, with Levi Knapp first postmaster. Victor H. Coffey carried the pouches from the river landing about a half mile to the store. Coffey became postmaster at Hare on May 8, 1893, about the time he took over the interest in the store. The office was either closed out to Svensen in 1895 or had its name changed to Svensen at that time, the compiler cannot tell which from the available records. The Svensen office records show that it was established Aug. 15, 1895, with A. B. Coe first postmaster, but Coffey became postmaster on Nov. 7, 1895, so to all intents the history of the two offices merged at that date. For additional information, *see* Astoria Column in the Astoria *Astorian-Budget*, June 14, 1946.

Hare, CURRY. Hare post office was established Apr. 21, 1898, in the extreme north part of the county about six miles east of Langlois on the road to Myrtle Point. The office was given the family name of the first postmaster, Joseph Hare. It was finally closed Aug. 15, 1913. For a short biography of Joseph Hare, *see* Dodge, *Pioneer History of Coos and Curry Counties*, appendix, p. 47.

Haring Creek, LANE. The *Siuslaw Pioneer*, 1982, p. 103, says this tributary of North Fork Siuslaw River a short distance above its mouth was named for Amos Haring whose family was the first to settle on the North Fork. BLM records show Haring's pre-emption claim was filed Sept. 9, 1880.

Harkens Lake, BENTON. This lake is about three miles northeast of Monroe. Its outlet is an intermittent stream flowing into Willamette River. Its elevation is 260 feet. It was named for a nearby settler.

Harl Butte, WALLOWA. Harl Butte is in the extreme northwest corner of T 3S, R 48E. It was named for John Harl who had a homestead near the foot of the butte.

Harlan, LINCOLN. James R. Harlan was one of the originators of the plan to secure a post office, and the office, when established about 1890, was named for him. He was first postmaster, according to information by the postmaster in 1926.

Harlow Crater, LANE. This is one of the small craters southwest of Black Crater and north of the North Sister. Professor E. T. Hodge of the University of Oregon named it for M. H. Harlow, one time president of the McKenzie toll road project. *See* Hodge's *Mount Multnomah*, p. 112.

Harms Creek, LANE. Harms Creek empties into Rat Creek north of Dorena Reservoir. John Harms had a donation land claim at the mouth of Rat Creek.

Harney, HARNEY. Harney is a community north of US-20 between Burns and Buchanan. It is at the site of Fort Harney and in the early part of the twentieth century had its own post office. *See* Fort Harney for its early history. *See also* Harney County.

Harney County. Harney County has a land area of 10,141 square miles, and is the largest county in Oregon. It was created Feb. 25, 1889, and was named for William Selby Harney who was appointed to the command of the Department of Oregon of the United States Army in 1858, and was recalled in 1859, for his summary seizure of San Juan Island, from the British, in July, 1859. He served in the Black Hawk War, and the Mexican War, and was in command of Union forces in Missouri in the early part of the Civil War. He was breveted major-general in 1865. He was a noted Indian fighter, and was popular in the Pacific Northwest. He died May 9, 1889. For obituary, *see* Scott's *History of the Oregon Country*, v. 5, p. 212. Harney County was not named until after Harney Lake and Harney Valley had been so called for a number of years, and the name of the county was undoubtedly suggested by the name of those features.

Harney Lake, HARNEY. The first written information about Harney Lake is in

Peter Skene Ogden's journal of his third Snake expedition, published in *OHQ*, v. II, p. 204, *et seq*. On Oct. 29, 1826, when the expedition was not far from what is now known as Harney Valley, Ogden wrote that Thomas McKay, who had been sent on in advance, rejoined the party and reported the discovery of "a country of rivers and lakes, one of the latter the water is salt." The entry for Tuesday, Nov. 1, is: "At sunset we reached the lakes. A small ridge of land an acre in width divides the fresh water from the salt lakes. The two lakes have no intercourse. The fresh water has an unpleasant taste 1 mile wide 9 long. In this Malheur lake discharges Sylvailles River and 2 small forks; but it has no discharge. Salt Lake at its south end is 3 miles wide. Its length at present unknown to us but appears to be a large body of saltish water. All hands give it a trial but none could drink it." Subsequent entries give more information about the lakes. There is no doubt in the mind of the writer that what Ogden called Salt Lake is the Harney Lake of today, and the fresh water lake is Malheur Lake. During certain stages Malheur Lake discharges into Harney Lake, with the result that Harney Lake gradually tends to get more alkaline. T. C. Elliott who edited the journals is slightly confused about the lakes, and in a footnote states that Harney is not salt, which is incorrect. J. J. Donegan of Burns told the writer that in the days of emigrations Harney and Malheur were known as Bitter lakes. The Indian name for Harney Lake is said to have been *Tonowama*. Harney Lake received its present name on July 7, 1859. Captain H. D. Wallen of the Fourth Infantry, in charge of a military expedition from The Dalles to Great Salt Lake, reached a body of water which he described as measuring about twenty by nine miles, unfit to drink. He applied the name Lake Harney in compliment to then Brigadier-General W. S. Harney in charge of the Department of Oregon. Details of this event are in 36th Congress, 1st Session, Senate Executive Document 34, which contains Wallen's report in full. Wallen mentions the sand ridge or dike east of Harney Lake and recounts the discovery of "Lake Stampede," now Malheur Lake or its arm, Mud Lake. This water was potable and he applied the name because his stock became unmanageable. Time has brought a change in the name of the alkali lake from Lake Harney to Harney Lake.

Harney Valley, HARNEY. Harney Valley was named for Major-General W. S. Harney. The valley is well defined, and has an average elevation of about 4100 feet. The south part of the valley is occupied by Harney and Malheur lakes and their marshes and meadows. The main and tributary valleys have an area of about 750 square miles, for the most part quite level. The name was applied as the result of the naming of Harney Lake or of the establishment of Fort Harney during the Snake War. *See* Bancroft's *History of Oregon*, v. 2, p. 488, *et seq*.

Harper, MALHEUR. Harper is on the Malheur River and it has been a post office since 1913. Harper was named for the Harper Ranch of the Pacific Livestock Company on which it is situated. The ranch, in turn, took its name from one of the early settlers near the Malheur River.

Harper Bridge, DESCHUTES. H. J. Overturf told the compiler in 1969 that this bridge over Deschutes River just below the mouth of Little Deschutes River was named for one Harper, an early homesteader.

Harper Creek, GRANT. Harper Creek flows north to John Day River at Mount Vernon. John Harper took a homestead at its mouth in 1902. Albert and Charlotte Harper also filed on land upstream prior to World War I.

Harper Creek, LANE. This creek flows into Lookout Point Lake. It is named for John Harper who took up land near its mouth in the 1880s.

Harriman, HARNEY. This place is just between Malheur Lake and Crane Creek Gap. Dr. Homer Denman owned the land where this community developed, and when the Oregon Short Line Railroad Company began to build from Ontario into the Harney Valley, Denman named his place for Edward H. Harriman, the railroad magnate. The post office was established in 1907 with Mrs. Bertha Denman first postmaster. After the railroad reached Crane in 1916, several buildings were moved to that town, the post office was closed and Harriman fell into a decline from which it never recovered.

Harriman, KLAMATH. Effective Oct. 1, 1947, the name of the post office Rocky Point on the west shore of Upper Klamath Lake was changed to Harriman in compliment to the memory of Edward H. Harriman, the railroad man. For several years Mr. Harriman maintained a summer camp near this place and he was very much interested in the development of that part of Oregon. The post office at Rocky Point had several names. It was called Lawrentz, Recreation, Pelican Bay and Rocky Point and later Harriman until finally closed on Feb. 15, 1954. The Harriman lodge was in this same locality but the compiler does not know if the various post offices and the lodge were in the same spot.

Harrington Creek, DOUGLAS. This creek in North Umpqua River drainage five miles northwest of Mace Mountain was named for Lee G. Herrington who took up timber claims in the vicinity just after the turn of the century.

Harris, BENTON. Harris was the name of the station served by Elam post office, not far from Philomath. The place has been a community since about 1890, and bears the name of a pioneer landowner. When the petition for the post office was circulated, residents asked that it be named Harris but postal authorities were afraid of confusion with Harrisburg, Linn County. For additional information, *see* Elam.

Harris Creek, CURRY. Harris Creek and Harris Beach State Park are both named for George S. Harris who was born in Perth, Scotland in 1836. After travelling to India and New Zealand, he came to the Pacific Coast in 1860 and settled in the Chetco country in 1871 where he bought several hundred acres along Harris Creek to run sheep. Harris died near Brookings on Jan. 4, 1925.

Harris Creek, JOSEPHINE. This is a small tributary of Jumpoff Joe Creek near Merlin. It bears the name of George W. Harris who took a donation land claim along its banks. Harris was killed by Indians on Oct. 9, 1855, at the beginning of the Rogue River uprising.

Harrisburg, LINN. Harrisburg was incorporated in 1866. Presumably it was named for Harrisburg, Pennsylvania. Some persons say the name was proposed by Hiram Smith, pioneer of 1853; others, by Asa A. McCully, pioneer of 1852. The locality was called Prairie Precinct in 1852. In that year D. and A. A. McCully started a store there. W. A. Forgey surveyed the site in 1853. At that time the place was named Thurston, and soon afterwards, Harrisburg. Thurston post office was established on Dec. 31, 1853, with Gamaliel Parrish postmaster. Harrisburgh post office was established in Nov. 1855, but records show that Thurston post office was not closed until Dec. 3, 1856. This inconsistency cannot be explained nor do the records show clearly when the name was changed to Harrisburg.

Hart Mountain, LAKE. Hart Mountain is a prominent landmark on the east side of Warner Valley. It has an elevation according to the USC&GS of 8020 feet. Its western face is abrupt and impressive and the bold escarpment stands over 3000 feet above the floor of Warner Valley. Near the foot of Hart Mountain is Hart Lake. Hart Mountain was at one time known as Warner Mountain. Wilson and Alexander established a ranch near the foot of the mountain and used a heart as a cattle brand. The vaqueros were not noted scholars and the ranch was immediately known as the Hart Ranch and has been so known ever since and Hart Mountain and Hart Lake derived their name from this source. It is not likely that the spelling will ever be changed, as the incorrect form is universally used.

Hartley Creek, TILLAMOOK. Hartley Creek empties into Nestucca River a mile above Cloverdale. It is named for the Hartley family who were early settlers. Metzger's 1930 map shows Louise Hartley owning a substantial holding just above the creek mouth. The form Hartney, used on some maps, is wrong.

Hartshorn Butte, WALLOWA. Hartshorn Butte is in sections 17 and 18, T 1N, R 48E. It was named for L. C. Hartshorn who ranged stock there in the 1890s. The butte was at one time called Masterson Butte for R. H. Masterson, but that name has fallen into disuse according to J. H. Horner of Enterprise.

Harvey Creek, LANE. Mrs. R. L. Gawley, who lived in Disston many years ago, told the compiler in 1967 that this tributary of Layng Creek was named for Harvey Holderman, the son of Elza Holderman, an early USFS ranger.

Harvey Creek, YAMHILL. Harvey Creek flows through the donation land claim of Andrew E. Hervey into Chehalem Creek at Newberg. Hervey was born in Pennsylvania and came to Oregon in 1852. He left Yamhill County prior to the Civil War and the present spelling came into general use.

Harvey Mountain, LANE. This mountain was named for J. Roy Harvey, who was a pioneer forest officer in the Pacific Northwest. He served in many positions with the USFS. Harvey Mountain is about six miles southeast of Blue River.

Hascall Spring, UMATILLA. This spring is on upper Birch Creek drainage north of Granite Meadows. Charles Hascall was a well-known early settler and cattleman on Birch Creek.

Hash Rock, CROOK. Allan Hasch was an early settler in central Oregon. *See* article by A. L. Veazie, *OHQ*, v. 39, p. 380. Ochoco National Forest records indicate that Hasch settled on Willow Creek in 1869 and may have had a mining claim near the rock. Abandoned tunnels and other signs of mining activity were visible until the 1930s. Hash Rock is about 20 miles airline northeast of Prineville and Hash Rock Creek rises on its east slopes.

Haskell Reservoir, BAKER. Haskell Reservoir is in Blue Canyon. It is named for Monroe Haskell who settled on the land before the turn of the century.

Haskin Butte, WALLOWA. Haskin Butte is in the south part of T 3N, R 46E. It bears the name of Robert J. Haskin, who took up a homestead in the neighborhood and ranged his stock there. The butte has also been called McKibbin and also Greenwood, but the style Haskin Butte has superseded the other forms. The name Haskins Butte is wrong.

Hastings Peak, WASCO. Hastings Peak is six miles east of Antelope. It was named for James A. Hastings who took up a homestead near its base in 1915.

Hat Creek, WALLOWA. Hat Creek is in the southeast part of the county and flows into Snake River. It was named many years ago when Alex Warnock was riding an unruly pony and had his hat bucked off near this stream. That hat hung on a bush for some time and the stream was named on that account. Hat Point, a prominent overlook near the headwaters of Hat Creek, was named for the stream.

Hat Rock, CROOK. Hat Rock is a descriptive name applied to a formation on the southeast slopes of Powell Buttes in the southwest corner of the county. This rock is near the middle of T 16S, R 15E. Hat Rock post office was named for this formation. The office was established Sept. 6, 1910, with Louisa E. Becker postmaster. The office was closed Nov. 18, 1911.

Hat Rock, UMATILLA. Hat Rock is a prominent monolith on the south shore of Lake Wallula nine miles east of Umatilla. Lewis and Clark mention a rock which resembled a hat in its shape under date of Oct. 19, 1805. This is the earliest description but it reappears in many subsequent journals. In 1951 the property was aquired by the state and incorporated into Hat Rock State Park.

Hatfield Spring, JEFFERSON. Hatfield Spring north of Teller Butte was named for the man who homesteaded the area in 1913, Ira J. Hatfield.

Hauser, COOS. Hauser is a station on the line of the Southern Pacific Company north of Coos Bay. It was named for Eric V. Hauser of Portland. About 1914 Eric Hauser and his sons had a construction contract on the railroad. The community now known as Hauser was then called North Slough, but the name was changed to Hauser because the old name suggested miasmatic surroundings.

Haven Island, CLATSOP. Haven Island in Youngs River is named for Captain Lewis G. Haaven who, in 1888, patented a homestead including the island. Apparently he continued his seafaring career until 1913 when he retired and devoted his time to improving his real estate. The *Astorian Daily Budget* has news items dated

Apr. 20, and Aug. 26, 1914 describing various dikes and other improvements. Haaven died in Portland Aug. 11, 1929. Bruce Berney of Astoria dug out this information in 1990.

Hawkins Pass, WALLOWA. Albert Hawkins was for many years on the staff of the *Oregonian* before he died on May 8, 1930. He was profoundly interested in Pacific Northwest history and geography and was a tireless pedestrian and climber in the most difficult circumstances. His enthusiasm for the Wallowa Mountains was immense, and on July 27, 1929, he was a member of a small party that climbed over a pass on the divide between Imnaha and the Wallowa drainage about three miles southeast of Eagle Cap. Shortly after his death a petition signed by various public officials and private citizens asked to have the pass named in his honor, which was done by USBGN. The compiler lists the pass in Wallowa County, but it is very close to the county line and in fact may be in Union County. For a biography of Albert Hawkins, *see* the *Oregonian*, May 9, 1930.

Hawley Canyon, JEFFERSON. Hawley Canyon was named for Henry Hawley who homesteaded east of Axehandle in 1912.

Hawley Creek, BENTON. This creek near Alpine bears the name of Chatman Hawley. Hawley was a son-in-law of Jessey Belknap. He came to the Belknap Settlement in 1848. The Belknap Settlement was west of Monroe near what was later called Bellfountain. *See OHQ*, v. 38, p. 265 *et seq.* for further information.

Hawley Creek, LANE. William W. Hawley homesteaded near the present town of Dorena in 1883. He was a freighter to the Bohemia mines and the creek and Hawley Butte near Dorena both bear his name.

Hawn Creek, YAMHILL. Hawn Creek flows into Yamhill River west of Lafayette. It was named for Jacob Hawn who settled near the present townsite in 1846. He operated a hotel and tavern and was first postmaster at Yam Hill Falls in 1850. The falls of Yamhill River are near the town of Lafayette and not downstream at Yamhill Locks.

Hawthorne, DOUGLAS. According to an article by Charles V. Stanton in the Roseburg *News-Review*, Feb. 14, 1947, Hawthorne post office was on Calapooya Creek about 15 miles east of Oakland, and was given the middle name of the postmaster, Erastus Hawthorne Cooper. The Hawthorne school was situated nearby. Hawthorne post office was established Feb. 10, 1905, with Cooper the first and only postmaster. It was closed July 20, 1911, with mail to Oakland. In Feb. 1947, Margaret Smith of Sutherlin wrote about the difficulties of mail service in the days before good roads. "The mail was delivered to Hawthorne each Tuesday and Saturday by Edgar L. Rone. He was assisted by the various youngsters of the neighborhood, who considered the trip to town and back a real privilege. Often the roads were impassable for wagons or hacks and the mail followed devious trails over hills and through fields on horseback. The boys were not afraid of fractious cayuses or roads of bottomless mud."

Hawthorne Spring, CROOK. This spring was named for Elmer Hawthorne, a

USFS forest guard who first camped there about 1915. It is just off West Fork Mill Creek near Hash Rock.

Hay Creek, JEFFERSON. There are a number of Hay creeks in Oregon but the most important historically is the stream that drains a considerable area east of Madras and flows northward to Trout Creek. This Hay Creek was named in pioneer days in central Oregon on account of the fine natural forage that grew in its valley. It had a natural attraction for stockmen, many of whom had come into the area from Linn County and from other parts of the Willamette Valley. There are many references to the early history of Hay Creek in the *Illustrated History of Central Oregon*, p. 699, *et seq*. Hay Creek post office was established on the Wasco County list in Dec. 1875, with Lafayette Tirrill postmaster. With one intermission this office continued in operation until July 1920. It was east of Madras, though it may have been moved from time to time. For many years the famous Baldwin Sheep and Land Company had its headquarters at Hay Creek.

Hayden Creek, WALLOWA. This stream is tributary to Little Sheep Creek in T 2S, R 46E. B. T. Hayden, who settled near the mouth of the stream in the early 1880s, ranged stock on its banks and as a result, the creek bears his name.

Hayden Glacier, DESCHUTES. This glacier is on the northeast slope of Middle Sister, and southeast of North Sister. It was named for Lieutenant E. E. Hayden, U.S. Navy, by Dr. I. C. Russell of the USGS. See USGS *Bulletin 252*, p. 125. Edward Everett Hayden, born in Massachusetts Apr. 14, 1858, was a member of the class of 1879 at the Naval Academy. He was ordered for special duty with the Smithsonian Institution and was attached to field parties of the Geological Survey in Nevada and Arizona in 1882, and visited the Cascade Range with J. S. Diller in 1883. The party fitted out for this trip at Red Bluff, California, and made a detailed inspection of many important localities, including Lassen Peak, Mount Shasta, Crater Lake and Mount Thielsen. While attempting to climb the Three Sisters, Ensign Hayden suffered a serious fall of some 200 feet. Diller got two men from camp and they started to carry the injured scientist to a place of safety. While this was being done a rock fell from the mountainside and struck Diller senseless. The packers took Diller to camp and Hayden had to lie out all night. After other adventures Hayden was finally landed at Prineville, where he was put on the stage and reached the hospital at Portland on Sept. 22, 1883, 14 days after the accident. On Nov. 11 his left leg was amputated at the thigh and he was able to proceed to his home in the East on Jan. 15, 1884. E. E. Hayden eventually became a rear admiral on the retired list and lived in Washington, D.C. He took part in much scientific work carried on by the Navy Department. He died in Baltimore on Nov. 17, 1932, and was buried at Arlington National Cemetery.

Hayden Island, MULTNOMAH. Hayden Island was discovered on Oct. 29, 1792, by W. R. Broughton, who reported the fact in the following language: "From Belle Vue point they proceeded . . ., passed a small wooded island, about three miles in extent, situated in the middle of the stream. Their route was between this island and the southern shore, which is low. . . . This obtained the name of 'Menzies Island'; near the east end of which is a small, sandy woody island that was covered with wild geese." Broughton named this Goose Island on Oct. 31. It is indeed unfortunate that the name of Archibald Menzies has not been perpetuated in Oregon geography. Memoir No. v of the Archives of British Columbia, entitled *Menzies' Journal of Vancouver's Voyage*, gives an excellent account of the great botanist and his work in the Pacific Northwest. Lewis and Clark reached Hayden Island on Nov. 4, 1805, and named it Image Canoe Island, because of the presence of a canoe with carved images at the bow. It is perhaps not surprising that Thwaites confused Image Canoe Island with Wapato, now Sauvie Island, when he edited the Lewis and Clark journals, for while Lewis and Clark maps are quite clear, the text is somewhat perplexing. Gay Hayden, a pioneer of 1850, owned all of or part of this island in pioneer days, and it has borne his name ever since. He was for many years a resident of Clark County, Washington. Some maps show the names of Shaw Island and Vancouver Island, but the USBGN has decided against these forms. Dr. John Scouler used the name Menzies Island on May 2, 1825, when he and David Douglas made a short excursion from Fort Vancouver and found a number of interesting plants. *See OHQ*, v. 6, p. 173. The 1980s saw increased commercial and residential development over most of the island. Larry Barber has an interesting article about the Hayden Island area of Portland in *Freshwater News*, Mar. 1989.

Hayden Lake, POLK. Hayden Lake is near the west bank of the Willamette River, two miles southwest of Eola. It was named for Benjamin Hayden, a picturesque pioneer lawyer of Oregon, who also achieved fame as a rustic raconteur. West of Hayden Lake is Hayden Slough and nearby in the Willamette River is Hayden Island, both of which were named for the same man.

Hayes Hill, JOSEPHINE. Hayes Hill was in pioneer days a place that travelers had to reckon with, between Rogue River and Kerby. The road was steep and hard to negotiate. Hayes Hill was named for Jarvis Hayes, a pioneer settler nearby. For additional information about this locality and Fort Hayes, *see* Walling's *History of Southern Oregon*, p. 452.

Hayesville, MARION. Homer Simmons of Tillamook wrote the compiler in 1970 to give the following information regarding this community on old Portland Road just north of Salem. He stated that his wife's great grandfather, Adam Stephens, bought the surrounding property in 1849 for a rifle, a pony and $30.00. During the Hayes-Tilden campaign of 1876 the local residents voted to name the area in honor of Rutherford B. Hayes.

Hayland, TILLAMOOK. The compiler is of the opinion that Hayland was a natural, descriptive name, selected by Mr. and Mrs. Mulligan, local landowners, because of the low grassy meadows of several acres. Hayland post office was established Apr. 16, 1888, with Mary J. Mulligan first and only postmaster. The office was discontinued Sept. 26, 1888, with papers to Dolph. This office was at the place now known as Boyer, very close to the John Boyer monument on the Salmon River Highway. It is possible that John Boyer purchased the property from the Mulligans, although that is not certain.

Haynes Creek, LANE. Haynes Creek flows into Chickahominy Creek north of Walton. At the turn of the century, William J. Haynes patented a homestead near its mouth. There were also several other members of the Haynes family located in the vicinity.

Haynes Inlet, COOS. Haynes Inlet is the large north arm of Coos Bay and is fed principally by Larson Slough and Palouse Creek on the east, and on the west it is joined but not exactly fed by North Slough. The mouth of the inlet is about a mile wide. The east shore of Haynes Inlet is traversed by US-101, the Oregon Coast Highway. Dodge, in his *Pioneer History of Coos and Curry Counties*, p. 134, says that the inlet was named for Henry Haines, an early day settler who discovered coal near the present site of Glasgow, just south of the inlet. However, on p. 16, Dodge spells the name Haynes. Whatever the facts are about the way that this pioneer spelled his name, the geographic feature has been called Haynes Inlet for many years and that is the style used on government maps.

Haypress Creek, WHEELER. This creek flows into Double Corral Creek west of Derr Meadows. *A History of the Ochoco National Forest*, says that the stream flows through Haypress Meadows where soldiers from Camp Watson cut hay in the 1860s. Remains of an old haypress were visible until the time of World War I.

Haystack, JEFFERSON. Haystack post office was established on the Crook County list June 21, 1890, with Elijah McClenahan first postmaster. The office was a little to the north of Haystack Butte and was named for that mountain. This happened before Jefferson County was formed. Haystack office was finally closed out to Culver Feb. 28, 1907. Culver post office had been established in 1900, only a little distance away, but apparently in a more strategic location. There was not enough business to support two offices.

Haystack Butte, JEFFERSON. Haystack Butte bears a descriptive name, due to its shape. It has been so known for many years, and the territory near its base is known as Haystack country. The butte lies east of Juniper Butte, and US-97, The Dalles-California Highway passes through a saddle between them.

Haystack Creek, WHEELER. Haystack Creek is not far from Spray. W. F. White, in a letter on the editorial page of the *Oregonian*, Nov. 8, 1927, says this stream was named for a mound in a field at the Fleming and Wagner ranch. This mound resembled a haystack, both in size and form. Stories to the effect that the stream was named because it washed away a haystack are not substantiated.

Haystack Rock, CLATSOP. Haystack Rock is a prominent monolith on Cannon Beach which has done far more than its share to advertise Oregon. It is 235 feet high and for many years it has been a popular and favorite landmark on the Oregon coast. It very much resembles a haystack, hence its name. The compiler has no idea when it was named or who named it.

Haystack Rock, TILLAMOOK. About a mile southwest of Cape Kiwanda is a very prominent pinnacle known as Haystack Rock. It has an elevation of 327 feet and is considerably higher than the Haystack Rock on Cannon Beach. It bears a descriptive name. Davidson, in the *Coast Pilot*, 1889, says that Cape Kiwanda was once called Haystack Point because of its proximity to Haystack Rock.

Haystack Rock, WALLOWA. Haystack Rock is a prominent point in T 4N, R 45E. It was named because of its resemblance to a haystack.

Hayward, WASHINGTON. The locality called Hayward is in sections 19 and 20 of T 2N, R 4W. It is northeast of Gales Creek and northwest of the Thatcher district. In the summer of 1948 Paul L. Patterson of Hillsboro was able to gather some interesting information about the name of this place. The story came from Nicklaus Bothman who homesteaded at what is now Hayward. There were several settlers and they got their mail at Greenville which was very inconvenient. An appeal was made to Binger Hermann, then representative in Congress from Oregon. Mr. Hermann was able to get the post office established and apparently suggested the name Hayward. It has been said that Mr. Hermann called attention to the fact that there was a place called Hayward in almost every state of the Union and Oregon should have one too. The difficulty about this story is that there do not seem to have been many places called Hayward but that difficulty is not an objection to the theory that Mr. Hermann named the place. Mr. Bothman was willing to accept Mr. Hermann's suggestion, after concluding that it would be better than to try to dig up a better name. A school district was formed and that was also named Hayward and later Mr. Bothman applied the name to the Hayward Cemetery where his little son was buried. As far as the compiler knows these names are still in use. Hayward post office was established Dec. 19, 1891. Katie Bothman was the first postmaster. It was discontinued Nov. 25, 1904, and the business turned over to Greenville. Another son, Robert Bothman, had a long career with the OSHD and in the 1980s was director of the Oregon Department of Transportation.

Hayward Peak, CURRY, JOSEPHINE. Hayward Peak bears the name of Stanton B. Hayward, a forester who served several years in the Siskiyou National Forest prior to his death on Nov. 29, 1939. The peak is about 20 miles northwest of Kerby on the high divide south of Illinois River. It has an elevation of about 4300 feet. The name was adopted by the USBGN on Dec. 4, 1941.

Hazel Mountain, WALLOWA. Hazel Mountain is in the northwest part of T 4S, R 43E. It was named for Hazel Taylor of Milton, Oregon, who at that time was camping nearby. The name was applied in Aug. 1913, by N. Jay Billings of the USFS.

Hazelau, MARION. Hazelau was a station on the Oregon Electric Railway about two miles southeast of Salem. It was named by R. G. Halberg, a landowner nearby. The compiler is informed that Halberg was born in Hazelau, Germany, and he wished to perpetuate the name of his native town. Atlases do not give a Hazelau in Germany, but do show a Haslau in Bohemia.

Heather, LANE. Heather is a station on the Cascade line of the Southern Pacific Company, named for the small plants that grow in the higher altitudes of Oregon. They are not true heather, although they are members of the *Ericaceae*, or heath family. These Oregon plants are *Phyllodoce*, and are low growing, with small, leathery evergreen leaves.

Hebo, TILLAMOOK. Hebo is a town at the junction of US-101 and SH-22 south of Tillamook. It was named for Mount Hebo, an important peak in the Coast Range nearby. *See* Mount Hebo. Hebo post office was established in 1882 with George M. Bodyfelt first postmaster.

Heceta Head, LANE. The following editorial by Harvey W. Scott, in the *Oregonian*, Aug. 20, 1895, effectively sums up Heceta's claim to fame: "The Columbia River was first seen by civilized man Aug. 17, 1775. Captain Bruno Heceta, commanding the Spanish corvette *Santiago*, in a voyage along the coast from Mexico, noticed an opening in the coast from which rushed a current so strong that he could not enter. His nautical observations, published with his report, show that the position of his ship was within one minute of the latitude of Cape Disappointment, which he called Cape San Roque. The smoke from forest fires then was not so thick as now, though it was the same time of year; for Heceta saw clearly the distant mountains. Heceta Head, further down the coast, perpetuates his name." There are several accounts of the voyage of Bruno de Hezeta (Anglicized spelling Heceta). The best summary is that of H. R. Wagner in *Cartography of the Northwest Coast of America*, v. I, p. 175. *California Historical Quarterly*, v. 9, p. 201, *et seq.*, contains Fr. Sierra's account. *See also* Cape Falcon and Columbia River. Heceta commented on shallow water some distance off-shore from what is now known as Heceta Head. Soundings by the USC&GS confirmed this discovery, and as a result, in 1862, George Davidson of the Coast Survey named Heceta Head and also suggested the name Heceta Bank. Both of these names were adopted by the government and have come into universal use, thus complimenting the Spanish navigator. The name Heceta is frightfully mispronounced on some parts of the Oregon coast, where it is called Heketa, with a strong accent on the first syllable. In Castillian the pronunciation would be *Ay-thay-tah*, with the accent on the second syllable. This sound is a little difficult for Oregonians, most of whom seem to have Anglicized the word into *Heseta*, with the accent on the second syllable. Doubtless that style will prevail. There was a post office called Heceta but it has been discontinued.

Heckletooth Mountain, LANE. Mrs. Lina A. Flock of Oakridge, member of a pioneer family of the neighborhood, wrote the compiler in 1927 that this mountain, four miles east of Oakridge, was named by her grandmother, Mrs. Elizabeth Stuart Warner, about 1872, because of the tall rocks with which it is surrounded near the summit. These resemble the teeth of a heckle, an instrument used in the handling of flax.

Heflin Creek, CROOK, WHEELER. This creek bears the name of Miles Heflin who homesteaded west of West Branch in 1900.

Hehe Butte, WASCO. There are a number of geographic features in Oregon named *Hehe*, the Chinook jargon for laughter or fun. The name is applied to a creek, trail and mountain in Lane County, and doubtless elsewhere. Indians used the name for places, not in the sense of funny, but because of the presence of good spirits, Hehes, in contrast to the Skookums, which were powerful and evil wood-gods. Hehe localities were considered good places to visit, and they were especially used for religious festivities, games and horseracing. The compiler has been informed by Indians that the locality of Hehe Butte on Warm Springs Indian Reservation was a place of good spirits and was used for contests of various sorts.

Heisler, JEFFERSON. William Heisler was one of the prominent pioneer operators in central Oregon and Heisler post office on Hay Creek northeast of Madras was named for him. This office was established in May 1905, with Alfred R. Lyle first postmaster. The office operated, but not continuously, until May 1910. William Heisler opened a store in Prineville in 1871, and was a contemporary of Barney Prine. He was appointed first postmaster at Prineville, then called Prine, in Apr. 1871. In Oct. 1878, he was appointed postmaster at Trout Creek, an office whose name was changed to Cross Keys in Feb. 1879. He was active in various enterprises in what are now Crook and Jefferson counties, and later in Wasco County. For a detailed biography, *see Illustrated History of Central Oregon*, p. 255.

Held, CROOK. Held post office was on the upper reaches of Bear Creek and south of Maury Mountains. It was named for Paul Held, the first postmaster, and had a relatively short life during the homesteaders' era. The office was established May 1, 1909, and was discontinued May 15, 1919.

Helena Mine, LANE. This claim was on the southeast side of Grizzly Mountain in the Bohemia District. Loren W. Hunt informed the compiler in 1967 that three brothers named J. J., R. J. and P. J. Jennings took out considerable free gold and operated a ten stamp mill. Nearby Helena Saddle took its name from the mine.

Helix, UMATILLA. Helix post office was established on May 6, 1880, with Mary Ann Simpson postmaster. The name first selected was Oxford, but postal authorities objected because of possible confusion with similar names elsewhere. In 1927 the writer was told that W. B. Henderson selected the name Helix, but the reason given was not plausible. Since then additional information came to light that indicated that the place was named because a local resident had a painful experience with an infection in the helix of his ear. The testimony is not as conclusive as it might be, but is probably true. In July 1942, W. H. Morrison of Pendleton, who lived in Helix when he was a boy, informed the compiler that in early days Dr. John Griswold was a prominent resident of Helix, and at a community meeting told the audience that about the time the post office was established, one of his patients developed a very sore ear and had to be taken to Pendleton for treatment. The patient was either Henderson or Peter Hjelseng. During a consultation with another doctor in Pendleton, the word helix was mentioned, and the sick man thought it would be a fine name for the proposed office. In Nov. 1927, H. V. Christensen of Helix, wrote the compiler and described the event. In Apr. 1942, Dr. F. W. Vincent of Pendleton visited Helix at the request of the compiler and made inquiries about the matter. He was told the story of the infected ear and was informed that Henderson was the patient. Dr. F. A. Kiehle of Portland told the compiler that he heard this story after he came to Oregon in 1908 from the secretary of one of the medical societies. Reports that Henderson's first name was Helix have not been substantiated.

Hellgate Canyon, JOSEPHINE. Because of inadequate communications, the physical characteristics of Hades are unknown. However, this appears to act as a stimulant to the use of "hell" as part of the name of many rough terrain features. Hellgate Canyon is a typical tortuous constriction of Rogue River five miles west of Merlin. The form Hellsgate is wrong.

Helloff Creek, TILLAMOOK. Helloff Creek flows into Nehalem River from the north near Rector, and got its odd name because the rough area along the banks of the stream presented such difficulties to cruisers and loggers. There is a little flat near the mouth of the creek, which was said to be just off hell. When a logging camp was established on the flat, it was called Helloff, and that name was used for the post office, which was established Jan. 17, 1920, with Francis E. Hays first of four postmasters. The office was closed Mar. 31, 1924, and little evidence remains of the place.

Hells Canyon, BAKER, WALLOWA. Prior to 1950 this name was applied to a rough, deep canyon that empties into Snake River in T 3S, R 49E. In the 1950s Wallowa County and the Snake River gorge were popular topics and the subject of several Sunday Supplement promotions. A touch of sensationalism was necessary and the publicists applied the name Hells Canyon to the valley of Snake River from about the present site of Oxbow Dam to the mouth of Grande Ronde River. Regardless of accuracy, the name is now in general use and the OGNB recognized this in Dec. 1970, when they voted to change the name of the original Hells Canyon to Hells Canyon Creek. The compiler of the sixth edition has a substantial file by the late Lewis A. McArthur protesting this name transfer, but feels that only a token objection can be taken to this *fait accompli*. It is doubtful that this will contribute much to the peace of mind of the departed.

Helmick Hill, POLK. Helmick Hill is just west of the point where the Pacific Highway West crosses Luckiamute River. It was named for Henry Helmick, a pioneer of 1845, who with his wife Sarah took up a donation land claim on the Luckiamute in 1846. Their home was at the base of the hill. Helmick died in 1877. In 1924 Mrs. Helmick presented to the state land adjacent to the highway for a park which was dedicated with appropriate honors, and named Sarah Helmick State Park. She celebrated her 100th birthday on July 4, 1923. For information about the Helmick family and the park *see OHQ*, v. 26, p. 444 *et seq*.

Helms Canyon, SHERMAN. Helms Canyon is three miles east of Rufus. It was named for C. I. Helms who had a horse ranch there in the early days. When the homesteaders began to arrive in the 1880s, Helms picked up and left for the Grand Coulee country. The compiler thinks he must have wanted his solitude in monumental doses if he left Sherman County in 1885 because of overpopulation.

Helvetia, WASHINGTON. Helvetia is a community on North Plains. Several Swiss families settled in the neighborhood and gave the place the Latin or Roman name of their mother country. For story of the early history of the community, *see* the Hillsboro *Argus*, Dec. 31, 1931. It is said that David Tschabold moved to adopt the name Helvetia at a meeting of the local school board in 1892.

Hembree, TILLAMOOK. The post office serving the Sand Lake section was first called Hembree, in compliment to a local resident. Hembree post office was established July 10, 1890, with Absalom J. Hembree first postmaster. The name of the office was changed to Sandlake on Jan. 18, 1898. The writer does not know to what extent it may have been moved around the neighborhood.

Hemlock, TILLAMOOK. There are a number of geographic features in Oregon named for the hemlock tree, which is an important part of our forests. The place in Tillamook County, which has been discontinued as a post office, was named for the western hemlock, *Tsuga heterophylla*, which grows in great abundance in the Coast Range. It is a fine large tree, growing 160 feet high, and even taller, and is characteristic of the middle, moist, forest zone, on western slopes, but is not common east of the Cascade Range. The other variety of hemlock in Oregon is known as mountain or black hemlock, *Tsuga mertensiana*, and is an alpine tree with little resemblance to the western hemlock. It has drooping slender branches, and its height is not often more than 60 feet. It grows near the timber line, and is not often found below 4000 feet in the Cascade Range, and in other mountains in eastern Oregon. It prefers a north exposure, and will endure dense shade. It grows in Oregon at elevations as high as 8000 feet. *See* Sudworth's *Forest Trees of the Pacific Slope*. The mountain hemlock has a rather larger cone than the western hemlock. Its leaves are rounded and plump looking, differing in this respect from other hemlocks. The leaves of the western hemlock are flat and grooved.

Hemstad, DESCHUTES. According to Robert W. Sawyer of Bend, Hemstad post office was named for a local homesteader, Olaf Hemstad. The office was near the middle of the northeast quarter of T 22S, R 16E, near the south boundary of Deschutes County, east of the Paulina Mountains and about 15 miles southeast of Millican. The post office was established Dec. 8, 1917, with Frank P. Drake first and only postmaster. It was discontinued Nov. 15, 1918.

Henderson Creek, LINCOLN. Henderson Creek flows into the Pacific Ocean about two miles south of Yaquina Bay. The Oregon Coast Highway, US-101, crosses the creek to the northeast of the old Lifesaving Station near the beach. In 1945 Mr. Andrew L. Porter of Newport told the writer that the stream was named for a nearby landowner who had moved away some years before.

Henderson Creek, LANE. This tributary of Maple Creek north of Mount Popocatepetl was apparently named for Laura Henderson who in 1903 patented a homestead along it.

Henkle Butte, DESCHUTES. Jeremiah E. Henkle was born in 1843 and came to Oregon when he was ten years old. He spent most of his life in Benton County, where he was well known. He enlisted in Company A of the First Volunteer Infantry in Dec. 1864, and served at Vancouver Barracks and at Fort Yamhill. The company left Fort Yamhill on Sept. 4, 1865, and arrived at Camp Polk near what is now the town of Sisters, on Sept. 23, 1865. Henkle spent the winter at the camp and was mustered out on June 30, 1866. *See* Oregon Adjutant General's *Report*, 1865–66, and also story by Fred Lockley, editorial page, *Oregon Journal*, June 25, 1935, which contains more data about Henkle. Henkle Butte, elevation 3390 feet, is on the north side of Squaw Creek about two miles northeast of the site of Camp Polk. In Feb. 1943, Billy Wilson of Sisters, then 86 years old and in good health, recalled the story of the naming of the butte. Wilson said the commanding officer at the camp put up a prize for the soldier who made the round trip from camp to the butte in the shortest time and Jerry Henkle won the race. The point has borne his name since that time. The spelling Hinkle is wrong.

Henline Mountain, MARION. Henline Mountain is about 12 miles northeast of Mill City, near Little North Santiam River. It was named for an early settler who was interested in a mining enterprise nearby.

Henry Creek, WALLOWA. Henry Creek drains into Imnaha River in T 4S, R 48E, opposite the mouth of Crazyman Creek. It was named for an Indian who camped near its mouth.

Henry Creek, YAMHILL. Henry Creek flows into Yamhill River just east of Lafayette. It was named for Anson B. Henry who owned a great deal of the land along its banks. Henry was born in New York about 1830 and made his way to Oregon in 1852 with Anson G. Henry who was thought to be his uncle.

Henry Hagg Lake, WASHINGTON. An impoundment created in 1974 by Scoggins Dam on Scoggins Creek. The 1150-acre reservoir is a multi-purpose lake for flood control, irrigation and recreation. It is named for Henry Hagg, a prominent Washington County dairyman and County official who died in 1971.

Henryville, COOS. In 1874 coal mining operations were undertaken on the east side of Isthmus Slough on or near the Charley Wheeler place about midway between what are now known as the Coos City bridge and Delmar. A Dr. Henry was one of the main promoters of this mining activity, and at first the mine held considerable promise of success. However, the success was not achieved. For a short history of the enterprise, *see* Dodge's *Pioneer History of Coos and Curry Counties*, p. 425. The mining activity called for a post office, and one was established with the name Henryville on Jan. 28, 1875, with Stephen D. Megeath first and only postmaster. The office was closed Apr. 7, 1876. The office was apparently named for the Dr. Henry mentioned above.

Hensley Butte, JEFFERSON. Hensley Butte is in the extreme southeast corner of the county at the headwaters of Allen Creek. It is named for Edward L. Hensley who filed a land claim nearby about 1905.

Heppner, MORROW. Named for Henry Heppner. He and Jackson L. Morrow opened the first merchandise store there, in 1873. The county was created and named in 1885. The town of Heppner was founded in 1873 (*Oregonian*, Sept. 15, 1877, p. 2). Morrow settled at Scott Prairie, near Shelton, Washington, in 1853, and was one of the founders of Tumwater. In 1855–56 he served in Captain Swindall's company in the Indian war. Heppner died at Heppner, Feb. 16, 1905, aged 76 years (biography and portrait, *Oregonian*, Feb. 18, 1905). Destruction of a large part of the town of Heppner June 14, 1903, by flood, was one of the great tragedies of Oregon. Heppner post office was established Feb. 3, 1873, with George H. Stansbury first postmaster. The post office has been in continuous operation. The earlier history of this office is confusing. It was first established on the Wasco County list with the name Butter Creek and with Stansbury postmaster. That was on June 3, 1872. It was later put on the Umatilla County list, and was on that list when the name was changed to Heppner. How the name Butter Creek happened to be applied to the office now called Heppner is hard to understand, as Heppner is a long way from Butter Creek. It is possible that Stansbury's office was actually on Butter Creek and he moved it bodily to a new location. Another office was established on Butter Creek on July 28, 1873, with John S. Vinson postmaster. That was at the place later known as Vinson, in Umatilla County. The new Butter Creek office may have followed the desertion by Stansbury.

Hereford, BAKER. At the time this community was being formed, it is said a Hereford bull was led through the settlement. Many residents were interested in stock, and someone suggested Hereford as the best name for the place.

Herlihy Canyon, KLAMATH. Herlihy Canyon is just east of Algoma. It was named for Stephen Herlihy who had a ranch and kept a hotel and stable on the old Fort Klamath road just after the turn of the century.

Herling, JACKSON. A post office with the name Herling was established on the Jackson County list on July 26, 1888, with Henry A. Bauten postmaster. It was discontinued on July 9, 1895, with papers to Jacksonville. Herling was the family name of people who lived about four miles southwest of Jacksonville on the road to Ruch, and the office was at the Herling place. The Ruch office had not yet been established. The Herling house was burned about the time the office was closed, and the Ruch office was established a couple of years later to take care of local postal needs.

Herman Creek, HOOD RIVER. Investigations by H. H. Riddle of Portland indicate that the spelling Herman is correct, Hermann is wrong. The stream was named for an early settler, James H. Herman.

Herman Creek, LANE. Herman Creek flows southward near the east line of T

16S, R 10W, into Indian Creek, a little to the northwest of Reed. It was named in compliment to Binger Hermann, prominent Oregon pioneer and for many years a representative in Congress from this state. The name was applied by Stephen Milledge, a local resident. There is a rather minor discrepancy in the spelling, but the form Herman has been so long in use that there is little likelihood that it will be changed.

Hermann, LANE. Hermann was a post office in western Lane county north of Mapleton and always at or near the main fork of Indian Creek. The office was named for Binger Hermann, Coos County pioneer, and for many years a representative in Congress from Oregon. He was in Congress at the time the office was established and doubtless was of some assistance in getting the installation. Hermann post office was established June 26, 1889, with Mrs. Laura J. Dickey first of four postmasters. The office was closed Mar. 16, 1900, with papers to Mapleton. There is still a Herman School at the forks of Indian Creek, but the spelling has been slightly changed. In 1906 a post office called Belle was established to serve the area, but it was closed in 1908.

Hermansville, COOS. Hermansville post office was situated about seven miles south of Myrtle Point on South Fork Coquille River and was named in compliment to Dr. Henry H. Hermann, one of the most prominent of the Coos County pioneers. Dr. Hermann was the prime mover in the Baltimore Company, an organization that came to Oregon by Panama in 1859. *See* Dodge's *Pioneer History of Coos and Curry Counties*, p. 390. For biography of Dr. Hermann, *ibid.*, Biographical Appendix, p. 41. It will be noticed that there is a slight discrepancy in the spelling of Dr. Hermann's name and the name of the post office, Hermansville. The compiler has been unable to get satisfactory early history of this post office. Levi Gant was the first postmaster, but the year of establishment is uncertain, apparently prior to 1872. With one intermission the office operated until Oct. 17, 1881. A. H. Bender of Myrtle Point, a grandson of Dr. Hermann, was been kind enough to furnish the compiler with information about several Coos County geographic names.

Hermiston, UMATILLA. Hermiston was named by Colonel J. F. McNaught, a pioneer settler in the community. The name was suggested by his wife, Jennie McNaught, who had recently read Robert Louis Stevenson's unfinished novel, *Weir of Hermiston*. Colonel McNaught liked the sound of the name, and found that it did not duplicate any other post office name in the United States. The railroad station at Hermiston was originally called Maxwell probably after A. L. Maxwell, who was at one time a passenger traffic official of the railroad company. Postal authorities would not accept the name Maxwell as a post office name because of duplication, and it was for this reason that Colonel McNaught picked out a new name.

Hershal, BAKER. A. C. Moore wrote in the *Oregonian*, Dec. 13, 1926, editorial page, that this place was named for Dr. Herschel E. Currey, a physician of Baker City. It was at one time known as Currey, but the post office was later called Hershal. The office was discontinued in 1928. For biography of Dr. Herschel Eugene Currey, *see* Gaston's *Centennial History of Oregon*, v. 2, p. 12. The compiler does not know why the post office name was spelled differently from the doctor's name.

Hess Creek, YAMHILL. This stream rises in the hills west of Dundee and flows east to Willamette River. It is named for Daniel Hess, an early settler. Hess was born in Kentucky about 1830. He came to Oregon with his father, John Hess, who took a donation land claim in what is now the north part of Newberg. This family was not related to Joseph Hess for whom the stream in Newberg is named.

Hess Creek, YAMHILL. This stream rises in the Chehalem Mountains and flows south through the eastern part of Newberg into Spring Brook and the Willamette River. It was named for Joseph Hess, a pioneer settler who operated a mill near where it is now crossed by US-99W. Hess came to Oregon with the Emigration of 1843 and took a donation land claim northwest of Newberg. The forms Hess Branch, Hess Mill Creek, Joseph Hess Mill Branch and Mill Creek are incorrect. *See* USBGN *Decision List 6003*. Alexander Henry visited the vicinity of Hess Creek on Jan. 24, 1814. *See OHQ*, v. 25, pp. 308–11. This Hess Creek should not be confused with the Hess creek which flows into Willamette River from the west two miles upstream.

Hewett Boulevard, MULTNOMAH. Hewett Boulevard is west of Council Crest, and connects Green Hills with Sylvan. It was named for Henry Hewett, a pioneer grain merchant and insurance man of Portland. Mr. Hewett was born at Hunters Hill, near Gateshead, County Durham, England, Jan. 15, 1847. He came to the Pacific Coast about 1864, and settled in Portland in 1870, and in the following year shipped the first cargo of wheat that ever went from Portland to the United Kingdom. He later extended his activities to include marine insurance, and was for many years Lloyd's Agent in Portland. He lived for a time at Twentieth and Glisan streets in Portland, where the Couch School now stands, and personally planted many of the shrubs now standing in the school yard. In 1888 he moved to the hills west of Council Crest and developed a country place, setting out many shrubs and trees brought from abroad. In the later years of his life he devoted himself entirely to the insurance business. He possessed a great fund of information about the marine history of the Pacific Coast. He died at his home on Green Hills Feb. 16, 1915.

Hibbard Gulch, BAKER. Hiatt in *Thirty One Years in Baker County*, p. 19, says that Mr. Hibbard arrived in 1863 and took up a claim near Morrison. This was southeast of Pocahontas and obviously near the gulch which bears his name.

Hickman Lake, CLACKAMAS. This lake and other geographic features in the northeast corner of the county were named for Orre Hickman, a forest guard in the early days of the USFS.

Hiddensprings, HARNEY. Hiddensprings post office was established June 21, 1916, with Mary E. O'Malley postmaster. The order was rescinded and the office apparently never operated. The name came from Hidden Spring near what is known as Clover Swale, a range district on the desert about 20 miles south of Harney Lake.

Hideaway Falls, CLACKAMAS. This 100-foot high falls on Tumbling Creek is about two thirds of a mile above Salmon River. It is one of a group of seven falls in the area and was named because it is so difficult to see even when one is directly in front. For details of this group, *see* Stein Falls.

High Camp, CLACKAMAS. This point is near North Fork Molalla River. Dee Wright, a native of Molalla, told the compiler that the camp was originally established by the Ogle family, pioneers of the Molalla Valley, and they gave the camp its descriptive name.

High Desert, DESCHUTES, LAKE. Early maps bear such names as Great Sandy Desert and Rolling Sage Plains, descriptive of that part of Oregon which is traversed by US-20 near the southeast corner of Deschutes County. Today the name High Desert is universally used, in contradiction to the Low Desert further south. The line of demarcation of the two deserts is not well defined, and the difference in elevation does not amount to a thousand feet.

Highland, CLACKAMAS. The Highland district is about eight or ten miles southeast of Oregon City, and Highland Butte, elevation 1728 feet, is within the area. Godfried Wallace, the first postmaster at Highland, is said to have originated the name, but whether first applied to the butte or the area, is unknown to the writer. Highland post office was established Feb. 21, 1870, with Wallace first postmaster. The office was in service until after the turn of the century, but the compiler has not been able to learn the exact date it was closed. The name Highland for the district is in general use.

Hildebrand, KLAMATH. This post office was first established with the name Edgewood in Aug. 1890, and with Newton F. Hildebrand first postmaster. The name of the office was changed to Hildebrand in December of the same year. From Oct. 1919, until May 1923, the name of the office was Hilderbrand, but the error was corrected. This office has not operated continuously and as with other early-day post offices, it may not always have been in the same place.

Hilgard, UNION. Hilgard was apparently named for Eugene W. Hilgard, Dean of the College of Agriculture at the University of California. He was a cousin of Henry Villard who built the railroad over the Blue Mountains and was engaged by Villard in the early eighties to make an agricultural survey of the area. A post office with the name Dan was established in this locality July 9, 1883, with George A. Steel postmaster. The name of the office was changed to Hilgard on Aug. 23, 1883, when Hilgard, a well-known individual, was in the Northwest. For information on Villard, *see* Villard Glacier.

Hill Creek, JACKSON. Hill Creek spills into Emigrant Reservoir south of Ashland. It is named for Isaac Hill whose donation land claim was along its lower reaches.

Hilliker Gulch, WALLOWA. This gulch in T 4N, R 48E, was probably named for some early day miner. J. W. McClaren stated in 1965 that he purchased the Hilliker claim from the Eureka Mining Co. and that Hilliker was gone prior to 1918.

Hillis Peak, JACKSON. Hillis Peak is two miles southeast of Wimer. It bears the name of William P. Hillis who owned several pieces of land along Evans Creek in the early 1860s. His son, William Hillis, succeeded to the property and farmed there until after the turn of the century.

Hillman Peak, KLAMATH. This peak is at the west edge of Crater Lake, and is the highest point on the rim above the lake, with an elevation of 8151 feet. It was at one time known as Maxwell Peak, for Sir William F. Maxwell, of Edinburgh, Scotland, who explored the Crater Lake region in 1871. It was later called Glacier Peak because on its slopes were found the first evidences of glacial scratchings, indicating the occurence of glacial action on Mount Mazama. Finally the USBGN adopted the name Hillman Peak, in honor of John W. Hillman, who was one of the party that discovered Crater Lake on June 12, 1853.

Hills Creek, LANE. This stream flows into Middle Fork Willamette River at Jasper. It bears the name of Cornelius J. Hills, who came to Oregon from Herkimer County, New York. He is reported as having crossed the plains three times. He was the father of Jasper Hills. *See* Walling's *History of Lane County*, p. 490.

Hills Creek, LANE. This stream is an important tributary of Middle Fork Willamette River, which it joins about four miles southeast of Oakridge. It drains a large area south of Salt Creek. It was named for John H. Hill, who settled near its mouth about 1870. At that time he was about 38 years old. His wife was generally known as Aunt Phoebe. The Hills had a ranch and kept the travel, and John Hill spent a substantial part of his time hunting and fishing. This stream should not be confused with Hills Creek near Jasper, which was named for Cornelius J. Hills. A post office called Hill was in operation from June 1882, to Dec. 1885, with John H. Hill postmaster. Hills Creek Dam and Reservoir on Middle Fork Willamette River were named because the damsite is just downstream from the former creek mouth. The earth fill dam is 304 feet high, stores 250,000 acre feet of water and has two 15,000 kilowatt generators.

Hillsboro, WASHINGTON. Hillsboro was named for David Hill who was born in Connecticut in 1809 and came to Oregon in 1842. He was at the Champoeg meeting on May 2, 1843, and was elected to the three-man executive committee of 1843–44. Hill was chairman of this committee and thus, in effect, Oregon's first elected governor. He settled at the site of Hillsboro at least as early as 1845 and represented Twality in the provisional legislature in 1847. He died May 9, 1850. Hillsboro was formerly spelled Hillsborough. Prior to 1849 the place was called Columbia and Columbus. The *Oregon Spectator* on Jan. 10, 1849, mentions Hillsborough, and Abraham Sulger as having a store there. On Jan. 10, 1850, the place was still referred to as Hillsborough. An early name of the locality was East Tualatin Plain; that of the Forest Grove locality, West Tualatin Plain. Postal authorities inform the compiler that Hillsborough post office was established Aug. 5, 1850, with Abraham Sulger first postmaster. The early abbreviation of the name of the place seems to have been Hillsboro', rather than Hillsboro. Hillsborough post office was discontinued Mar. 30, 1855, reestablished Oct. 3, 1855, and changed to Hillsboro on Apr. 20, 1892.

Hillsdale, MULTNOMAH. Hillsdale is a suburban community in southwest Portland. When the Southern Pacific Company West Side branch railroad was operated through Hillsdale, the company found it inadvisable to use the name Hillsdale for the station because of possible confusion with Hillsboro on the same line. The station was named Bertha for Mrs. Richard Koehler, wife of the railroad manager. The track has been torn up and Bertha station is no more. The name Hillsdale has been in use since pioneer days, and is quite suitable for the place. Hill is from the old Anglo-Saxon *hyl*, and Norse *holl*. Dale means a small valley. It comes from the same source as dell, and the German *thal* and Slavonic *dol*.

Hillside, DOUGLAS. Hillside post office was established Mar. 20, 1891, with George N. Elliot postmaster. The office was closed on Aug. 26 of the same year. An editorial in the Roseburg *News-Review* of Feb. 14, 1947, says that the office was situated on the Oakland-Elkton road in the Kellogg district. The editorial goes on to say that the Ross Hutchinson home was either on or near the site of the Hillside post office.

Hillside, WASHINGTON. Hillside is a community seven miles northwest of Forest Grove. The school district was organized in 1869 and the Congregational Church in 1884. The first pastor of the church was the Reverend Horace Lyman who was also first Superintendent of Schools in Washington County in 1850. The name comes, of course, from the local topography. This information was supplied by L. E. Bamford of Forest Grove.

Hilton Ridge, WALLOWA. Hilton Ridge is in the extreme northwest part of T 3N, R 47E. Hilton Creek is nearby. These two features were named for James Hilton, a little Englishman who ranged his horses in the vicinity. He had a homestead on Pine Creek.

Hines, HARNEY. Fred Herrick, a sawmill operator, founded the Fred Herrick Lumber Company and promoted the railroad north of Burns. The mill was just southwest of Burns, and a community was established with the name Herrick. In 1928 Edward Hines of Chicago bought the railroad and lumber business and operated it with the name Edward Hines Lumber Company. A post office named Hines was established Feb. 3, 1931, to serve the mill and the nearby community. In the 1980s, the mill was sold to the Snow Mountain Pine of Oregon, Ltd., who operated it until 1989 when they sold the company to an investment group headed by Donald A. Graves.

Hinkle, UMATILLA. Hinkle Freight Classification Yard is the principal northwest switching point for the Union Pacific Railroad. When the Oregon Railway & Navigation Company line was completed to Huntington in 1884 it branched off the Spokane line at Umatilla, Oregon and followed the Umatilla River to Pendleton. About 1915 a cutoff was built from Boardman that rejoined the main line at Hinkle. A station was needed and Joseph T. Hinkle, an early day Umatilla County attorney, sold the railroad .05 acres of land. He thus unknowingly assured himself a prominent place in local geography for while Hinkle languished in obscurity for a third of a century, it sprang into prominence when the completion of McNary Dam in 1951 required relocation of the tracks along the Columbia River. The Union Pacific then located a major yard at this junction and in 1976 began the expansion to its present importance. The Portland *Daily Journal of Commerce* for June 27, 1978, has a feature article including pictures. Joseph Hinkle died about 1933.

Hinkle Butte, JEFFERSON. This high ground east of Muddy Creek was apparently named for William S. Hinkle who filed on a homestead nearby in 1879.

Hinton Creek, LANE. Ray Engels of McKenzie Bridge told the writer in 1971 that this stream in the upper Separation Creek drainage was named for Jim Hinton, an early sheep man.

Hinton Creek, MORROW. Hinton Creek flows into Willow Creek at Heppner. It was named for John T. Hinton who settled five miles east of Heppner in 1864.

Hipower Creek, DOUGLAS. This creek rises south of Chilcoot Mountain and flows south into Canton Creek. In the early 1920s USFS rangers Fred Asam and Ed Lough were locating trail. They found themselves in this steep, rugged area and one remarked to the other: "It would take a high-powered man to get through this." At the end of their journey the name seemed even more appropriate so the stream was called Highpower Creek. It was subsequently shortened to the present form.

Hipp, BENTON. Hipp was the name of the post office that served the community of Alder. Postal authorities would not accept the name of Alder for a post office because of confusion with many other offices of that name. The name Hipp was suggested by L. M. Roser who was office manager of the Climax Lumber Company mill nearby. The compiler is informed that the name Hipp was made up from the initials of the given names of members of the families owning the mill. Hipp post office was established Apr. 18, 1922, with Efrann Anderson first postmaster. Roser was the second postmaster, and Rufus E. Wood held the position when the office was closed Jan. 15, 1930.

Hirsch Reservoir, DESCHUTES. This reservoir northeast of Millican near West Butte was apparently named for Max Hirsch who homesteaded nearby.

Hiyu Mountain, CLACKAMAS, HOOD RIVER. This mountain is just south of Bull Run Lake. Its name is the Chinook jargon word for much, or plenty, and is used to indicate that the mountain is large. There is a Hiyu Ridge in Lane County south of South Fork McKenzie River.

Hoaglin, DOUGLAS. The name Hoaglin is said to be of Indian origin. The writer was informed by the postmaster at Hoaglin in 1926 that the name had been used for the post office since about 1898. A nearby Indian told the postmaster that the word meant some sort of medicine. There is a community Hoaglin in Van Wert County, Ohio, and it is quite possible that the name of the place in Oregon came from that source. The name of the Oregon post office was changed to Idleyld Park on Dec. 1, 1932.

Hobo Lake, WALLOWA. Hobo Lake is in T 3S, R 43E. In early days Robert B. Bowman and others found a hobo camped at this lake, apparently living quite happily. They were not able to learn his identity. The lake has been known as Hobo Lake ever since.

Hobsonville, TILLAMOOK. In 1927 Miss Lucy Doughty of Bay City wrote the compiler as follows: "John Hobson and family were among the pioneers of Clatsop Plains. About the year 1885 Messrs. Hobson and Leinenweber of Astoria, erected a salmon cannery at the place since called Hobsonville. Frank Hobson, son of the Mr. Hobson mentioned above, came here about the time the cannery was built, and still lives at Garibaldi."

Hoevet, TILLAMOOK. Hoevet was a post office serving the extreme west part of Wheeler. This was the location of the original Wheeler post office but about 1931 the Wheeler office was moved eastward to the business district of the community at the request of local residents. This was done with the provision that an office would be provided to serve the Wheeler lumber mill and its employees, all in the west part of town. The new office was named Hoevet for C. R. Hoevet, at that time manager of the mill.

Hoffman Creek, LANE. This is a small tributary of Siuslaw River near Beck Station. It apparently is named for Ira Hoffman who took a homestead at its mouth in 1885.

Hoffman Dam, CROOK. According to Phil Brogan of Bend, this irrigation diversion dam on Crooked River four miles below Prineville Reservoir was built by Jim Hoffman, an early day rancher.

Hog Hollow, UMATILLA. Judge John F. Kilkenny told the author the early legend regarding the name of this canyon just south of Vinson. An emigrant train strayed from the Oregon Trail and during their wanderings a band of hogs escaped near this canyon. In time they turned wild and provided both food and sport for the chase.

Hogan, DOUGLAS. Hogan post office was established May 18, 1887, with James McKinney first postmaster. Hogan post office is reported to have been named for a local landowner who later moved to Roseburg and opened a store. Hogan post office was close to the banks of South Umpqua River, northwest of Roseburg. The name of the office was changed to Melrose on Oct. 10, 1890.

Hogan, MULTNOMAH. Hogan on the southeast outskirts of Gresham, once a station on the Portland Traction Company interurban line, is remembered by the brick factory and nearby Hogan Butte. The place was named for Eli Hogan who was born in Arkansas in 1865 and came to Portland, via Cascade Locks, in 1905. Hogan had a sawmill at the site. Sharon Nesbit has an interesting article in the *Gresham Outlook*, Nov. 14, 1987, p. 1. Hogan is now best known for the curious "Hogan Cedars," apparently a singular mutation of the western red cedar found only in a narrow strip of this valley of Johnson Creek near Gresham. This species was first classified in 1913 by dendrologist Camillo Karl Schneider as *Thuja plicata fastigata*.

Hogg Rock, LINN. Hogg Rock is a prominent point about a mile west of the summit of the Cascade Range. The Santiam Highway skirts its western and southern slopes. This rock was named for Colonel T. Egenton Hogg, promoter of the Yaquina railroad project. For a history of this project, *see* Scott's *History of the Oregon Country*, v. 4, p. 328. Among other things, Hogg proposed to extend his railroad through the Cascade Range into eastern Oregon. The style Hogg Butte is sometimes applied to this feature, but the compiler thinks it is wrong. For many years the name Hogg Pass was applied to the locality now used by the Santiam Highway in crossing the summit of the Cascade Range and the name Santiam Pass was used for the low point traversed by the Santiam toll road about three miles to the south. In 1929 there developed an agitation to apply the name Santiam Pass to both these localities on the theory that they constituted but one main geographic feature and also because the Santiam Highway would eventually draw the name Santiam Pass, to the elimination of Hogg Pass. The USBGN, in 1929, adopted the name Santiam Pass for the pass as a whole, rejecting the style Hogg Pass. John Minto, in *OHQ*, v. 4, p. 248, says that Hogg's name was probably applied by J. I. Blair of New York, who was connected with the Hogg enterprises. Minto also says that John B. Waldo first noted the apparent lowness of Santiam Pass. However, Andrew Wiley crossed the pass as early as 1859 and recognized its importance. *See* Wiley Creek.

Holbrook, MULTNOMAH. Philo Holbrook was a pioneer of Oregon, and owned a farm at the present site of Holbrook. When the post office was established, it was named for him.

Holcomb Creek, WASHINGTON. Holcomb Creek rises in the hills north of Helvetia and flows into Rock Creek about a mile north of the Sunset Highway. It was named for Stephen A. Holcomb, a pioneer settler, who took up a donation land claim nearby. Originally there was a small lake with the same name near where the two streams joined but this has been drained.

Holderman Mountain, LANE. This mountain on the headwaters of Mosby Creek near the Douglas County line was named for Elza Holderman, an early USFS ranger.

Holdman, UMATILLA. Holdman brothers were early settlers in this community, and when the post office was established in 1900, it was named for them.

Hole in the Ground, DOUGLAS. Perry Wright gave this descriptive name to a natural depression east of Calf Creek about two miles south of North Umpqua River. Wright homesteaded near Cap's Illahee in 1909 and made his living farming and hunting in the area until his death in 1966.

Hole in the Ground, DOUGLAS. Hole in the Ground is a geographic name that bids fair to equal Bear Creek in popularity. This one in T 29S, R 3E, was named by forest supervisor Smith C. Bartrum after he was benighted and had to camp in this peculiar depresssion filled with vine maple and rocks.

Hole-in-the-Ground, LAKE. This very remarkable place is well described by its name. It covers an area of about a quarter of a mile, and its floor is over 300 feet below the surrounding land level. It is about eight miles northwest of Fort Rock.

Holladay, CLATSOP. Holladay was the station a mile or so south of Seaside at the end of the railroad line from Portland. The line was abandonded and the rails taken up prior to 1980 and nothing exists in Oregon today of a geographic nature to call to mind one of Oregon's most important pioneer citizens. Ben Holladay came to Oregon in Aug. 1868, with what was considered immense wealth and plunged into the Willamette Valley railroad fight that was then raging. Holladay was a native of Kentucky and came west in 1856, and having made money in the overland stage business, he sold out to Wells Fargo & Company about 1866 and turned his attentions to Oregon. He allied himself with the east side, or Salem interests, and built in all about 240 miles of railroad. In 1873 his railroad defaulted, and today is part of the Southern Pacific system. Holladay's ventures and extravagances scattered his wealth. He died July 8, 1887, aged 68 years. For references to his activities and controversies *see* Scott's *History of the Oregon Country*, V. 3, p. 172. His name was applied to the station in Clatsop County because for some years he was interested in the Seaside House, a famous pioneer resort south of the present site of Seaside. A post office called Ben Holladay was established in Clatsop County on June 13, 1890, with C. C. Cooper postmaster. The office was closed Apr. 9, 1891.

Holland, JOSEPHINE. Holland post office was established in Apr. 1899, and the first postmaster was John M. Smock. The post office was named after a pioneer settler in the neighborhood, James E. Holland.

Holland Meadows, LANE. Lawrence D. Hills in his notes, *Places of Historical Interest in the Upper Willamette Valley*, says that Holland Meadows and adjacent Holland Point were named after Hugh Holland, an early settler, who built a cabin there for hunting and trapping. The meadows are on the divide between Layng and Larison creeks.

Holley, LINN. The post office at Holley was established about 1890 and George W. Pugh, an early settler and first postmaster, named the place after his home in Wisconsin. There is no record of a Wisconsin post office or major community of this name, but Lamar Newkirk, a grandson of Mr. Pugh, told the author in 1968 that this was the correct origin and that the name had nothing to do with holly trees or the shrub Oregon grape.

Hollo Creek, LANE. Hollo Creek comes into Lake Creek from the north about three miles below Greenleaf. It is named for Peter L. Hollo who was born in Norway and came to Oregon about 1845. He homesteaded along Lake Creek in the 1880s where he lived as a recluse. Hollo died near Springfield on Feb. 14, 1905. The form Hula, used on some maps, is incorrect.

Hollys Ridge, KLAMATH. Hollys Ridge is the east ridge of Mount Thielsen north of Cottonwood Creek. It was named in 1990 for Holway R. Jones who was born in New Orleans in 1922 and died in Eugene in 1986. Jones was a longtime member of the Sierra Club and was a driving force in the establishment of the Mount Thielsen Wilderness.

Holman Guard Station, LANE. This USFS installation west of Nimrod was named for L. G. Holman, a well-known state fire warden in the World War II era.

Holmes Creek, DOUGLAS. Holmes Creek on the west side of Camas Valley was named for Manasseh B. Holmes who came to Douglas County in 1854 and raised stock along this stream. Combs in *God Made A Valley* says that he was titled "General" by all who knew him.

Holmes Gap, POLK. Holmes Gap and Holmes Hill are five miles north of Rickreall, the former being a natural pass used by the Southern Pacific Company and by the Pacific Highway West. The gap has an elevation of 166 feet and the hill just to the east 567 feet. These features were named for Horatio Nelson Viscount Holmes, a pioneer of Oregon, who took a donation land claim at this point.

Holt Creek, BAKER. Holt Creek empties into Pine Creek in s 25, T 7S, R 47E. It apparently is named for Benjamin Franklin Holt who took up land near its mouth in 1917.

Holton Creek, JOSEPHINE. Holton Creek flows into the Illinois River just south of Kerby. It was named for Dr. D. S. Holton, a pioneer physician of the neighborhood. For biography of Dr. Holton, *see* Walling's *History of Southern Oregon*, p. 508. *See also* Kerby.

Home, BAKER. Home, a community on Snake River at the mouth of Conner Creek, was inundated in 1959 by the pool behind Brownlee Dam. Information about the origin of the name is unsatisfactory. The post office was established Aug. 1, 1918 and closed Feb. 28, 1946 with papers to Huntington. John W. Flick is said to have been the first postmaster. He asked for the name Marble but the department refused that name and called the place Home instead. This seems to have been satisfactory to the local residents. The writer has not been able to learn why the name of Home was selected. This office should not be confused with an earlier office called Home, established on the Baker County list in June 1878. This earlier office was in what is now Malheur County.

Home, MALHEUR. Home post office was established on the Baker County list in June 1878, with Alvin R. Roberts postmaster. The office was situated in what is now Malheur County near Willow Creek a few miles northwest of Vale. The history of the office is a little confusing. The office was discontinued in Nov. 1878, but was put in service again within a few weeks. There was another short interruption in 1879. At the time of these interruptions William S. Glenn was postmaster. The writer can find no record of this office after June 1880, and it may have stopped functioning in that month. It should be noted that Glenn was postmaster at the new office of Glenn, in the same general locality, in Apr. 1881. It is possible that when Glenn was postmaster at Home, he may have had the office at the place later called Glenn. There was not much formality about moving post offices in those days.

Home Creek, HARNEY. Home Creek flows westward from Steens Mountain into Catlow Valley, and the Home Creek Ranch near the stream is a prominent landmark. In his memoirs, *The Cattle Drives of David Shirk*, p. 115, Shirk says that he moved to the Catlow Valley on May 10, 1877 and built his house on a stream which he called Home Creek. This was immediately after his marriage to Frances Crow, the niece of Rankin Crow. Other members of the Shirk family settled nearby.

Homer, GRANT. Homer post office was established Sept. 20, 1889, with Wells W. Stone first postmaster. The office was in Bear Valley, in the same locality as the later offices Duncanville and Logdell. The second postmaster at Homer was B. S. Duncan, who was living at Mount Vernon in Mar. 1947. Mr. Duncan has recorded that he was postmaster at Homer for considerably more than a year, and that his salary amounted to 25 cents. He resigned, and the office was closed Nov. 4, 1895. Homer post office is said to have been named for Homer Stone, son of the first postmaster W. W. Stone. At least that is the opinion of Mr. Duncan. *See also* Logdell.

Homestead, BAKER. It is reported to the writer that Frank E. Pearce took up a homestead at this point in connection with his operations with the Iron Dyke Mine, and that the office was named on account of the homestead claim. This was about 1900. J. H. Pearson was the first postmaster, and he suggested the name. The community of Homestead was inundated by Hells Canyon Dam and the post office was closed May 1, 1965 with mail to the new office of Oxbow some six miles south.

Homestead Creek, LANE. This creek is part of Steamboat Creek drainage just north of the Douglas County line. It was named by USFS ranger Fred Asam because he thought it a very desirable homestead site. His opinion was not shared as no one ever filed upon this location.

Hominy Creek, WALLOWA. Hominy Creek flows into Snake River in T 1N, R 50E. It was named because Alex Warnock spilled a kettle of hominy when camping there.

Homly, UMATILLA. In 1928 the Union Pacific Railroad established an additional station east of Cayuse and named it Homly. The name was supposedly taken from a tombstone in the nearby Indian graveyard. If so, it was appropriate for Homly or Homily was a Walla Walla chief who remained friendly during the

Bannock War of 1878. The "Private Journal, 1878" of C. E. S. Wood, *OHQ*, v. 70, p. 34, states that Homily was present at the council at Umatilla on Aug. 26, 1878 and Wood in "Private Journal, 1879" tells of his visit to Homily's camp on Feb. 22, 1879, p. 167.

Hon Spring, CROOK. This spring in S 32, T 13S, R 19E, is named for early rancher Charles C. Hon who was born in Linn County in 1871 and ranched near the spring in the 1890s.

Honey Creek, LAKE. Honey Creek, one of the largest streams of the Warner Valley, was named in 1864, according to Judge William M. Colvig of Medford who wrote the compiler in Apr. 1927, as follows: "I was a cavalry soldier under Col. C. S. Drew in 1864, in what is known as the Colonel Drew Expedition, from Fort Klamath to Fort Boise, Idaho. I was one of sixty members of Company C, 1st Oregon Cavalry who went with Drew. In the fore part of August, 1864, we struck the Warner Lakes country, and scouted over the entire valley. I was with a small party that went up the west side to what is now known as Honey Creek. We camped on the creek bottom and noted that the leaves of the willows were heavily laden with a white substance that was as sweet as honey. It would scale off in flakes, often the size of a twenty-five cent coin. It only happens in hot, dry weather, and is the product of the drying up of honey dew, which falls during the night. We named it in our camp record Honey Creek. We gave Drew Valley, Crockett Springs, Beatys Butte, Sprague River and a great many other names now on the map. I know for I was company clerk and kept the records."

Honeyman, COLUMBIA. Honeyman was a station between Scappoose and St. Helens. It was established to serve a farm owned by William Honeyman, a prominent pioneer hardware dealer of Portland, and was named for him.

Hood Mountain, COOS. This mountain which has an elevation of about 1700 feet is in the valley of South Fork Coquille River. It was named for William L. Hood, a prominent stockman who owned land nearby.

Hood River, HOOD RIVER. This stream was discovered by Lewis and Clark on Tuesday, Oct. 29, 1805, and called Labeasche River, an improvised method of spelling the name of Francis Labiche, one of the French-Canadian watermen. *La biche* is French for female deer or doe, but in French-Canadian, it frequently was used to mean elk. There is nothing in the journals to indicate that game was seen at this point, and the river was named for the man. In pioneer days some travelers, being in a starving condition, ate dog meat near Hood River, and the unpopular name Dog River was the result, but not because of any suggestiveness of the French name. Later on, Mrs. Nathaniel Coe, a well-known pioneer resident of the valley, objected to the name Dog River and succeeded in changing local usage to Hood River on account of Mount Hood, its source. For narrative of settlement, in 1852, *see* the *Oregonian*, June 11, 1889, p. 3; May 9, 1881, p. 3; description, May 14, 1903; Oct. 4, 1914, p. 4. Hood River Valley is famed for apples and pears which producers there ship in large quantities. The name Dog River is now attached only to a small stream that heads in Brooks Meadows about eight miles southeast of Parkdale and flows into East Fork Hood River. In Oct. 1852, an advertisement in the *Oregonian* says that a road had been cleared from "Dog River to the ferry" which was one of the first on the Columbia. The name Hood River appears on a map as early as 1856.

Hood River, HOOD RIVER. The city of Hood River was named for the stream nearby. Hood River post office was established on the Clackamas County list on Sept. 30, 1858, with Nathan Benson first postmaster. Charles C. Coe became postmaster May 16, 1860.

Hood River County. This county was created June 23, 1908, and was taken from Wasco County. Since most of the new county was drained by Hood River, it was appropriate to name it Hood River County. According to the ODOT, it has an area of 538 square miles.

Hoodoo Butte, LINN. Hoodoo Butte, elevation 5721 feet, is a prominent point just south of Santiam Highway very near the summit of the Cascade Range. The place has become well known because it is a fine locality for skiing. The origin of the name is uncertain. Hoodoo may come from the word that indicates a run of bad luck or a Jonah. On the other hand, throughout the western part of the United States the word is used to refer to natural rockpiles or pinnacles of fantastic shape. The name Hoodoo Butte may have been applied during the days of the Santiam toll road because of difficulties in construction or travel, although the second reason given above is just as likely.

Hoodoo Spring, WALLOWA. This spring is in T 6N, R 42E. In earlier days, the place was hard to get to because of poor trails and in 1907 Roy Smith, a forest ranger, applied the name Hoodoo Spring.

Hoods Bar Light, MULTNOMAH. This navigation aid is on the north side of Government Island, in the Columbia River. It is sometimes suggested that Hoods Bar was named because of the excellent view of Mount Hood, but such is not the case. The Hood family were for many years landowners on Government Island, and the bar was named for the family. Frederick W. Hood and James Hood purchased a farm on Government Island in the early 1880s. The obituary of Frederick W. Hood was published in the *Oregonian*, Nov. 30, 1927, p. 8.

Hook, GILLIAM. Hook was the last name of the railroad station formerly called Squally Hook because it was at this point on the south bank of the Columbia River that rough weather was frequently experienced by steamboat men. In the interest of simplicity the railroad company eliminated the word Squally. A nearby post office was once known as Quinook, which was a name made up by taking parts of the station names of Quinton and Squally Hook. The present station name is Quinton.

Hooskanaden Creek, CURRY. This creek enters the Pacific Ocean northwest of Carpenterville. Dodge's *Pioneer History of Coos and Curry Counties*, p. 106, says that this name comes from the *Wish-to-na-tan* Indians who lived along the creek.

The early settlers had great difficulty with this Indian name and Hooskanaden was about as close as they could come. There have been numerous variants including Houstenader but the matter was resolved in *Decision List 8003*.

Hoover, MARION. Hoover post office, named for the first postmaster, was on North Santiam River two or three miles upstream from Detroit. The office was established in May 1907, with R. N. Hoover first postmaster. It was discontinued in Oct. 1916, and the business turned over to the Detroit office. The name has been retained in Hoover Ridge, the high ground between North Santiam and Breitenbush Rivers.

Hoover Creek, WHEELER. Hoover Creek is a tributary of Thirtymile Creek. It flows north of Black Butte about three miles from Fossil. T. B. Hoover settled nearby many years ago and the stream bears his name.

Hope, MALHEUR. Hope station near Malheur River was named for M. G. Hope, a landowner nearby. It is just west of Vale.

Hope Creek, WALLOWA. Hope Creek is tributary to Freezeout Creek just west of Freezeout Saddle in T 2S, R 48E. It was named in compliment to Harry Hope, who ranged stock there.

Hopewell, YAMHILL. Hopewell was named in optimism. It is at the east base of the Eola Hills at a point ten miles south of Dayton and a couple of miles west of Wheatland. Hopes of growth have not been fulfilled. Hopewell post office was established June 21, 1897, with John W. Spencer first postmaster in a series of four. The office was closed out to Amity on Jan. 9, 1903, doubtless as a result of the extension of rural free delivery. Hopewell does not appear in gazetteers of the middle 1880s.

Hopkins, CLATSOP. Hopkins post office was near Nehalem River at a point six or seven miles northeast of Jewell. It was named for the first postmaster, Thomas Hopkins. This post office was established Feb. 24, 1890, and was discontinued to Jewell Nov. 15, 1892. The office was reestablished Apr. 10, 1894, and continued in operation until July 14, 1902. There is little left of the community.

Hopmere, MARION. Officials of the Oregon Electric Railway named this station Chemeketa when the line was built, hoping to perpetuate the original Indian name of the locality of Salem. Local enthusiasts were not satisfied, and succeeded in changing the name to Hopmere. Adele Egan of Brooks said it truly depicted the scene in the early 1900s, a sea of hops in all directions. However, by the late 1900s, the hop fields were largely a thing of the past. Oregon lost not only a good Indian name but Hopmere is no longer apposite.

Hoquarten Slough, TILLAMOOK. This slough is at Tillamook. Miss Lucy E. Doughty, of Bay City, wrote the compiler in 1927, as follows: "I do not know the meaning of this name. It is thought to be of Indian origin. It has been in use since the first settlers came, as Mr. W. N. Vaughn used it in a memorial that he compiled. He always spelled the word 'Hoquarton.' Now the name is applied only to the slough and to a voting precinct in the city, but for a long time after we came here, Hoquarton Prairie was the name used for the neighborhood now known as Fairview. When a town was first laid out on the bank of this slough, it was named Lincoln, but as there was already a post office of that name in Polk County, the post office had to be Tillamook. The site had been called Hoquarton, the Landing, or Tillamook Landing. I think it was usually called Hoquarton by the settlers in the bay neighborhood and it was not until 1885 that I began to hear the town called Tillamook. Before that, when we said 'Tillamook' we meant the county." The government now uses the spelling Hoquarten for the slough. This style is well established.

Horn Creek, LINN. Horn Creek flows into North Santiam River just south of Marion Forks. William Horn was an early homesteader on the adjoining flats and Scott and Nan Young named this creek in his memory when they settled at Marion Forks in 1932.

Horning Gap, LAKE. Horning Gap is a pass in the hills north of Silver Lake, named for a homesteader.

Horse Canyon, UMATILLA. Lloyd Waid of Ukiah said that this canyon four miles east of Dale was named because its south facing slopes provided an excellent winter range for horses.

Horse Creek, LANE. This stream joins McKenzie River from the south, not far from McKenzie Bridge. George Frissell, an early settler on McKenzie River, is authority for the story that the stream was named because in pioneer days some emigrants succeeded in getting a wagon over the summit of the Cascade Range near the head of Horse Creek and got their wagon down on the west slope a considerable distance. They lost their horses, and the stream was named on that account. Many years ago the remains of the wagon were found near the bank of the stream which tends to substantiate the story.

Horse Creek, WALLOWA. Horse Creek is an important tributary to Imnaha River from the east. It was so named because Jack Johnson wintered his horses there in 1878–79.

Horse Heaven, JEFFERSON. In Aug. 1946, Frank E. Lewis, postmaster at Horse Heaven, wrote an interesting letter about the place, from which the following information has been condensed: "The name Horse Heaven for this area was given perhaps sixty odd years ago. At that time the springs were accessible to wandering herds and the grass was better. Then followed a period of overgrazing, fencing off the better springs and more line fences. The climate became drier. There is some open country in the area and at times one sees small bands of range horses. The grass seems to have come back. Here at Horse Heaven cinnabar was discovered about 1933. Active production of mercury began in 1934 and the Horse Heaven Mines, Inc., assumed control in 1936. The mine is now closed down after about ten years operation. The entire area was homesteaded in the 1920s I believe, but practically all the homesteaders have left. Horse Heaven is forty-six miles eastward of Madras and about eighteen miles east of Ashwood. The country is on the John Day side of the divide." Horse Heaven post office was established Apr. 23, 1938, with Mrs. Mary E. Finnell first postmaster. Mail went in twice a week from Ashwood. The office was closed in the summer of 1946.

Horse Heaven Creek, LANE. This stream rises in the Calapooya Mountains and flows southward into Steamboat Creek. Near the head of the creek, which is close to the Bohemia mining district, there was a natural pasture, where miners and prospectors fed their stock. The name Horse Heaven is used in a great many places in the west, indicating natural pastures along streams, where horses could be turned loose without fear that they would stray away, or good forage on ranges where large numbers of wild horses congregated.

Horsepasture Mountain, LANE. Ray Engels of McKenzie Bridge told the writer in 1971 that this 5660 foot summit south of Horse Creek was named because of the excellent pasture on the south slopes. This was important in the early days when the lookout was supplied by pack animals.

Horseshoe Lake, JEFFERSON. This lake is near the summit of the Cascade Range south of Olallie Butte. It drains to the north into Monon Lake. It was not named because of its shape, but because a horseshoe was found near its shore.

Horsetail Falls, MULTNOMAH. This name is supposed to be descriptive of the falls and has been in use since pioneer days. The lower falls, visible from the highway, are 176 feet high.

Horsfall Lake, COOS. Horsfall Lake is named for Doctor William Horsfall who took up government land nearby just after the turn of the century. Doctor Horsfall began his medical practice in Marshfield in 1892 and continued for more than 60 years in the same community. For an account of this early Coos County doctor, *see* Peterson and Powers, *A Century of Coos and Curry*, p. 167 *et seq*.

Horton, LANE. Three brothers by the name of Horton settled near the site of Horton post office in 1903. They were E. J. Horton, Sam M. Horton and J. C. Horton. They established a sawmill called Horton Mill. The post office was established the latter part of 1913 with the name of Horton. Sam M. Horton was the first postmaster and was still in office in Jan. 1926. Horton was a center of the dairying and lumbering community. The post office was discontinued Jan. 31, 1960.

Hoskins, BENTON. In 1856 the federal government established a fort in Benton County known as Fort Hoskins. It was named for Lieutenant Charles Hoskins, who was killed in the battle of Monterrey, Mexico, Sept. 21, 1846. He was appointed to the army from North Carolina. Fort Hoskins in Benton County was not a large military establishment. The post office of Hoskins was named in memory of the fort. Although Fort Hoskins is now nothing more than a memory, there was a time when it was an important post. Several officers who later achieved prominence in the military establishment were at one time in command at Fort Hoskins or were stationed there. Captain C. C. Augur was there in the late 1850s. He was later a major-general. Captain Frederick T. Dent, later a brigadier-general, was commandant at Fort Hoskins in 1861. He was a brother of Mrs. U. S.

Grant. General P. H. Sheridan in his *Personal Memoirs*, v. 1, p. 97, says "I spent many happy months at Fort Hoskins." For additional information, *see* Fort Hoskins.

Hosmer Lake, DESCHUTES. This lake is about one mile due east of Elk Lake on the Cascade Lakes Highway west of Bend. It was originally named Mud Lake, possibly because the large population of trash fish would rile the fine pumice silt bottom. In 1962 the OGNB approved the change to Hosmer Lake in memory of Paul Hosmer, a long time resident of Bend and a well-known amateur naturalist. For further information on Hosmer, *see* the Bend *Bulletin*, Jan. 19, 1962. By 1962 the trash fish had been eliminated and the lake restocked experimentally with Atlantic Salmon or *Salmo salar*.

Hospital Creek, LANE. Hospital Creek flows into Lookout Point Lake near Hampton. When the original railroad was built up the Middle Fork Willamette River in 1909, it was on the north side of the river. A construction camp hospital was established at the mouth of this creek.

Hot Lake, UNION. This is a steaming mineral lake at Hot Lake station near Union. The name is quite descriptive, although the compiler does not know when it was first used. On Aug. 7, 1812, Robert Stuart and companions traveling from Astoria to St. Louis, visited Hot Lake. As far as known this was the first time it was seen by white men. Washington Irving's *Astoria* describes the event in the following words: "In traversing this (Grande Ronde) plain, they passed, close to the skirts of the hills, a great pool of water, three hundred yards in circumference, fed by a sulphur spring, about ten feet in diameter, boiling up in one corner. The vapor from this pool was extremely noisome, and tainted the air for a considerable distance. The place was much frequented by elk, which were found in considerable numbers in the adjacent mountains, and their horns, shed in the springtime, were strewed in every direction around the pond." *See also Discovery of the Oregon Trail, Robert Stuart's Narrative*, edited by P. A. Rollins, p. 78. A station named Hot Lake was established when the railroad was built in 1883 and a post office followed. At the turn of the century there was a substantial health resort at the lake, segments of which are still being used in the 1990s. The post office was closed in 1943.

Hot Springs, LAKE. Hot Springs was one of the earliest post offices in what is now Lake County, and it was established in Dec. 1871, with William Greenman first postmaster. According to J. O. Jewett of the *Lake County Examiner-Tribune*, who gathered some data for the compiler in Oct. 1945, the office was at or near the Abram Tenbrook ranch about five or six miles south of Lakeview, approximately at the then site of the Ned Sherlock ranch. The office was named for the numerous hot springs on the east side of Goose Lake in the vicinity of the Tenbrook ranch. Abram Tenbrook became postmaster in Dec. 1872, and Robert H. Dunlap took the office in Apr. 1873. Charles Hagerhorst was postmaster at two different times. On Sept. 24, 1875, the name of the office was changed to Goose Lake, and the establishment was closed on Aug. 28, 1877. This was probably due to the fact that offices had been established at Lakeview and at New Pine Creek in Dec. 1876. Both of these places drew business from the older office. John Work in *Fur Brigade to the Bonaventura* mentions these springs under date of Oct. 22, 1832.

Houghton Creek, BAKER. This creek empties into Powder River at Keating. Philip Houghton took up government land just above its mouth in 1878.

Houlton, COLUMBIA. Houlton post office was situated at Saint Helens railroad station. The main town of Saint Helens is about a mile from the station. Houlton was originally called Milton. For information about this, *see* Milton Creek. The post office was established about 1890, and inasmuch as there was already a post office in Umatilla County by the name of Milton, it was necessary to find a new name for the Columbia County community. B. W. Plummer was the first postmaster, and he recommended the name Houlton for Houlton, Maine, his former home. The scheme of having post offices with different names serving the same community has never been satisfactory and it never worked well at Saint Helens. As a result the name of Houlton office was changed in the summer of 1946 to Saint Helens, Station A.

House Rock, DESCHUTES, LANE. This House Rock is on the summit of the Cascade Range, a few miles south of the Three Sisters, and has an elevation of 6737 feet. It is named because of its shape. It has also been called McArthur Hill in compliment to Judge Lewis L. McArthur, 1843–97, Oregon attorney and jurist, but that name has not prevailed.

Houston Butte, CROOK. This butte in the Bear Creek drainage north of Brothers was probably named for John W. Houston, a member of a well-known Crook County family, who homesteaded the area in 1910 although it may be attributed to his son, J. Floyd Houston.

Houston Lake, CROOK. Houston Lake is about seven miles west of Prineville and north of Powell Buttes. According to Fred Houston of Prineville, it was named because his father, Tom Houston, wintered his sheep there from 1908 to 1910. Tom Houston came to Crook County in 1895. He was a brother of J. Floyd Houston who settled in the Bear Creek Country.

Howard, CROOK. The community of Howard was in at least two different places in the Ochoco Valley, but the post office was abandoned about 1918 and now Howard is a ghost town. The original Howard was what is now known as the Ochoco Mines on Ochoco Creek near the mouth of Scissors Creek. It was named for a rancher and prospector who found gold there in 1872. Mining became active in the place for awhile, but the boom petered out in the early 1890s. It revived and with its resumption came a post office. It was about 28 miles northeast of Prineville. In 1909 the post office was moved to a point in the Ochoco Valley about 18 miles east of Prineville on the Ochoco Highway. The office was discontinued about 1918.

Howard Canyon, MORROW. This tributary of Little Butter Creek northeast of

Freezeout Ridge was named for James L. Howard who established a sheep ranch at its mouth in 1885.

Howard Canyon, MULTNOMAH. Howard Canyon is southeast of Corbett. It was named for James Howard who settled nearby in the 1880s.

Howard Meadows, WALLOWA. These meadows are in T 3N, R 41E. They drain through Howard Creek into Wallowa River. They bear the name of Abe Howard who took up a homestead in the vicinity about 1885. Howard was killed when a horse fell on him, and his sons buried him on the north edge of the meadows named for him.

Howard Spring, WALLOWA. This spring, in T 4N, R 47E, was named for General O. O. Howard, who camped in the vicinity in the summer of 1878 when he was leaving the Grande Ronde Valley. For information about General Howard, *see* Mount Howard.

Howard Valley, HARNEY. Howard Valley is south of the Grant County line and three miles east of the south extension of the line between Grant and Crook counties. In July 1878, General O. O. Howard was on the trail of the Bannock Indians and he camped for two days in Howard Valley before proceeding north. In 1911, the USFS built a ranger station at the mouth of the valley and named it for Jesse Allison, a nearby homesteader. In 1936 E. W. "Ci" Donnelly, USFS district ranger, stated that it should have been called Howard Valley Ranger Station but the name Howard has been retained for the valley, Howard Point at the mouth of Dodson Creek and Big and Little Howard springs. *See also* Allison Creek.

Howe, YAMHILL. Howe station near Carlton was named for William Addison Howe, a resident of Carlton and Portland for many years. He was born in Massachusetts, graduated from Harvard in 1881, and came to Oregon the following year. While a student at St. Mark's School in Massachusetts, Mr. Howe made and used the first baseball mask, by reinforcing a fencing mask with stronger wire. Mr. Howe died in Portland, Feb. 2, 1934.

Howell Prairie, MARION. Howell Prairie is west of Silverton, between the branches of Pudding River. It was named for a pioneer settler, John Howell, who came to Oregon in 1843. For information about Howell Prairie and the Howell family, *see* Down's *History of the Silverton Country*.

Howlock Mountain, DOUGLAS, KLAMATH. This is an important peak in the Cascade Range north of Mount Thielsen, and has an elevation of 8324 feet. It was at one time known as Walker Mountain, possibly for W. T. Walker of the road-viewing party that explored Middle Fork Willamette River in 1852. *See* Walker Mountain for additional information. About 1916, at the suggestion of the compiler hereof, the USBGN changed the name of the peak to Howlock Mountain, for a well-known Paiute Indian chief who ranged central Oregon. The reason for this change was that the name Walker Mountain was already applied to a prominent mountain southeast of Crescent, a comparatively short distance away, and it was thought advisable to avoid duplication.

Howluk Butte, HARNEY. Howluk Butte is 4780 feet high and is two miles east of Alvord Lake. It was named in 1860 by Enoch Steen during his campaign against the Snake Indians. Howluk or Howlock was a Paiute chief of some fame whose activities apparently reached as far west as Klamath Lake. The USBGN adopted the spelling Howluk in *Decision List 6601*. Howlock Mountain north of Mount Thielsen is named for the same man.

Hubbard, MARION. Hubbard was named for Charles Hubbard, who was born in Kentucky Feb. 14, 1800, and came to Oregon in 1847. A few months after his arrival in Oregon City with his family, he was visited by Thomas Hunt, a squatter not far from Pudding River, and induced to rent Hunt's land while Hunt went gold seeking in California. Hunt was never heard from again, and Hubbard bought the right in the claim from Hunt's widow, and settled there. He built a cabin in 1849 about where Hubbard High School stood in 1926. The railroad was built through that part of the Willamette Valley in 1870 and Charles Hubbard gave land for a station, and laid out a townsite, which was named for him. He died on Mission Bottom in 1884.

Hubbard Creek, CURRY. In Feb. 1944, Louis L. Knapp of Port Orford wrote the compiler as follows: "Hubbard Creek empties into the ocean one mile southeast of Port Orford. Captain William Tichenor, in founding the town of Port Orford in 1851, had as one of his partners Isaac M. Hubbard, who was also purser in the steamship *Sea Gull*. Mr. Hubbard was to have a land claim on the east side of the town through which runs this large stream. Thereafter people generally referred to it as Hubbard Creek." It is a coincidence that Dr. Alonzo Hubbard of Scituate, Massachusetts, made at least two trips to Curry County in very early days. An account of one of these trips is in a story with the title "Wild Life in Oregon," by William V. Wells, *Harper's Magazine*, Oct. 1856, but the compiler has found no evidence that connects Dr. Hubbard's name with the stream.

Hubbard Lake, MARION. Hubbard Lake, northwest of Waconda, was named for W. C. Hubbard, who owned land on its banks. He was an early settler.

Huber, WASHINGTON. Huber was a station west of Beaverton. It bore the name of Jacob Huber, an early resident. The community was established about 1910 and the post office in 1916. The post office was closed Dec. 31, 1953.

Huckleberry Mountain, WALLOWA. This point is a very prominent peak in the Wallowa Mountains and has an elevation of about 7550 feet. It is in the extreme northwest corner of T 2S, R 43E. It was named in early days by Sam Wade and William Masterson, who ran stock on the mountain. Their families camped on the mountain for many years.

Hudson, COLUMBIA. Hudson is a locality about five miles west of Rainier and close to Beaver Creek. It was named for a local family. Hudson post office was established June 20, 1892, and was discontinued Oct. 31, 1913. Susan A. Hudson was the first of five postmasters.

Hudson Bay, UMATILLA. This name is attached peculiarly to a tract of land, or a flat, and not to a body of water. Hudson Bay is west of Milton-Freewater and is so named because many years ago the Hudson's Bay Company operated a farm and grazed stock on the plain. The name is definitely established and is in universal use, notwithstanding its oddity. Isaac I. Stevens visited the Hudson's Bay Company farm on Nov. 4, 1853, and the visit is mentioned on p. 152 of the Pacific Railroad Surveys *Reports*, v. 12, book 1.

Hug Point, CLATSOP. Hug Point is on Cannon Beach. It is so called because it was necessary to hug the rocks to get around the point without getting wet. Before US-101 was built, a makeshift automobile road had been cut in the face of the point, but the writer felt that he would just as soon be drowned as scared to death.

Hughey Creek, TILLAMOOK. Mrs. Sylvester Siskey told the compiler in 1971 that this creek east of Tillamook was named for her grandfather, James Hughey. Mrs. Siskey at that date was still living on the family farm.

Hugo, JOSEPHINE. Hugo post office was established in 1896, and was named for Hugo Garber, an early settler who was instrumental in securing the office.

Hulbert Lake, LANE. This is a long, narrow lake fed by intermittent streams and surface drainage. It is four miles west of Harrisburg and has an elevation of 295 feet. It was named for Joseph Hulbert, a pioneer settler nearby.

Hullt, MARION. Hullt post office was first established about 1891 on the Hullt homestead and was named for that family, which settled there many years ago. C. J. Hullt was the first postmaster. The office was near the famous Silver Creek Falls, of which there are ten cascades in all, the highest of which is about 178 feet. The post office was discontinued in the summer of 1943.

Humboldt Basin, MALHEUR. A post office named Humboldt Basin was established June 29, 1869, with Marcus F. Colt postmaster, to serve a locality in what was then called Humboldt Basin and also Mormon Basin. The name Humboldt Basin for the geographic feature gradually gave way to the name Mormon Basin and that is the style now generally used. *See* Mormon Basin. Humboldt Basin post office was established on the Baker County list, but according to the best information available to the compiler it was actually in what is now Malheur County. This office was closed May 23, 1883. A new post office with the name Basin was established in the same general locality in Nov. 1894, with Andrew M. Johnson postmaster. This office was discontinued in Aug. 1895.

Humbug Creek, JACKSON. This stream, near Applegate, was named as the result of a quarrel over the value of a mining claim.

Humbug Creek, LINN. Humbug Creek flows into Breitenbush River at Humbug Forest Camp. Judge John B. Waldo, in his notes on his high Cascades trips states on Sept. 3, 1901: "Mr. Croner went deer hunting over on the head of Humbug Creek. (This is a name of ours given about twenty years ago and it has stuck)." Waldo does not say why the name was given in the first place.

Humbug Mountain, CURRY. This prominent landmark, elevation 1748 feet, is on the shore of the Pacific Ocean, about six miles southeast of Port Orford. It was once known as Sugarloaf Mountain, but its name was changed to Tichenors Humbug as the result of a mistake made by one of the exploring parties sent out by Captain William Tichenor. This party lost its way and went to the north of Port Orford instead of to the south. *See Pioneer History of Coos and Curry Counties*, p. 25. This was in 1851. Since that time Tichenors Humbug has become known as Humbug Mountain. George Davidson in the *Coast Pilot*, 1889, p. 373, says that in 1853 the mountain was called Mount Franklin and that the Indian name was *Metus*. Davidson does not explain these names, which have not prevailed.

Humbug Point, CLATSOP. This point is on Cannon Beach north of Hug Point. It has long been known as Humbug Point because travelers going along the beach flattered themselves that they had reached Hug Point only to find that they had been humbugged, and had a mile yet to go. The two points look much alike.

Hungry Hill, JOSEPHINE. Hungry Hill is a place in the mountains about seven miles west of Kerby in the Illinois Valley. Various points called Hungry Hill were generally named in the mining days because miners who worked at them went hungry because of poor diggings. There is another Hungry Hill in the north part of the county and also others in the state.

Hungry Hill, JOSEPHINE. This hill is an historic point in the south part of S 17, T 33S, R 7W, a few miles southwest of Glendale. Important engagements in the Rogue River Indian War were fought hereabouts on Oct. 31 and Nov. 1, 1855, called the battle of Hungry Hill and also the battle of Bloody Spring. *See* Victor's *Early Indian Wars of Oregon*, pp. 352-55. This Hungry Hill should not be confused with the point in the Illinois Valley west of Kerby.

Hungry Hill, LINN. This hill is southwest of the town of Scio, and has an elevation of 665 feet. Jefferson Myers was authority for the statement that it was named because the soil on its slopes was so poor and rocky that farmers who tried to till it were driven out by starvation.

Hunt Butte, JEFFERSON. Hunt Butte, on the headwaters of Muddy Creek, is 4115 feet high. It was named for Edgar O. Hunt who homesteaded the land in 1914.

Hunt Creek, CLATSOP. This stream is about 25 miles east of Astoria. It was named for Henry H. Hunt, a pioneer sawmill operator, whose mill began operations at Hunts Mill Point in 1844.

Hunt Creek, LANE. This stream flows into Row River east of Culp Creek. James T. Hunt settled near its mouth about 1883 and he and his family lived there many years. In 1967 his son, Loren W. Hunt, gave the compiler this information but added that when he was a boy the creek had no formal name.

Hunt Mountain, BAKER. Hunt Mountain bears an historic name, but the name was applied in modern times. It was at the request of J. Neilson Barry and other Oregonians that the USBGN attached the name of Wilson P. Hunt, leader of the Astor overland expedition, to the summit of the northeastern spur of Elkhorn Ridge, northwest of Baker City. For details concerning Hunt and the overland expedition, *see* Irving's *Astoria*. Hunt is mentioned as having seen the range northwest of Baker City, on Dec. 28, 1811. Wilson Price Hunt was chief partner in the Pacific Fur Company after Astor. He was born at Ashbury, New Jersey, about 1782. He went to Saint Louis in 1804, and engaged in the fur trade there. After the Astor enterprise at Astoria, he returned to Saint Louis, and was appointed postmaster there in 1822. He died in Apr. 1842. He was a man of remarkable energy, strong purpose and fidelity, and was highly respected.

Hunt Rock, CURRY. F. S. Moore, in *Curry County Reporter*, Dec. 16, 1926, says this is the correct name of the rock at Wedderburn, and not Hume Rock. Hunt Rock was named for James M. Hunt, a gold seeker of 1853, and a prominent pioneer settler at the mouth of Rogue River.

Hunter Spring, UMATILLA. Lloyd Waid of the USFS told the compiler that this spring south of Hidaway Creek in the east part of the county was named by the USFS in the 1960s as it was a favorite camping spot for the Nimrods.

Hunter Spring, WALLOWA. Hunter Spring is in the southeast part of T 3N, R 43E. It was named for Charles Hunter, who ran stock in the locality. Tom Willet, one of his men, found the spring, cleaned it out and carved Hunter's name on a nearby alder tree to commemorate the event.

Hunters, COLUMBIA. Hunters post office was established May 29, 1888, to serve a settlement a mile or so south of Goble. Stephen H. Walker was the first postmaster. Hunters was named for the Hunter family, local residents. The office was closed to Reuben in Oct. 1893. The name has survived in Hunter Bar, the southern projection of Sandy Island.

Hunters Cove, CURRY. Hunters Cove is just southeast of Cape Sebastian, and Hunters Island is south of the cove. F. S. Moore, of Gold Beach, wrote the compiler that in the early days sea otter hunting was an important industry, and those engaged in the business used small boats for cruising along the coast, and in heavy weather sought protection in the cove. This cove finally took its name from these sea otter hunters. Hunters Island took its name from the cove.

Hunters Hot Springs, LAKE. These springs are just north of Lakeview and are named for the late Harry A. Hunter who had large holdings in Lake County. The springs are mentioned by John Work in his journals under the date of Oct. 21, 1832. *See California Historical Society Quarterly*, Sept. 1943, pp. 205 and 215. Indians of northern California and Nevada used hot springs as places to deposit their dead.

Huntington, BAKER. This place was named for J. M. and J. B. Huntington, brothers, who settled there in 1882. The place was originally Miller stage station. J. B. Huntington bought out Miller. J. M. Huntington was the first postmaster.

Huntley Canyon, WHEELER. Joseph Huntley settled near the mouth of this canyon seven miles south of Fossil in 1866. He and Andrew Clarno were the first settlers in the Pine Creek area. *See Illustrated History of Central Oregon*, p. 640.

Huntley Creek, DOUGLAS. Carsena A. Huntley was born in Ohio in 1814. He came to Oregon in 1847 and in 1851 was one of the first settlers on North Umpqua

River where he took a donation land claim west of Glide. Huntley died in California in 1890.

Huntley Spring, CURRY. This spring west of Collier Butte was supposedly the favorite campsite of Nathaniel Huntley, a member of a well-known early Curry County family.

Hunts, JACKSON. Hunts was the name of a post office in the extreme east part of the county on the old mail route from Ashland northeast to Pelican Bay. The office operated from Apr. 1898, until June 1902, with Arthur F. Hunt postmaster, and it was named with his family name. The place was about 20 miles eastward of Ashland.

Hunts Cove, LINN. Hunts Cove and Hunts Lake are on the south flank of Mount Jefferson above Pamelia Lake. The name goes back to the 1880s but the exact origin is unknown. Judge John B. Waldo in his notes on his high Cascades trips mentions Hunts Cove on several occasions and he hiked to the cove while camped at Pamelia Lake in Aug. 1907, just before his death. The best opinion is that Hunts Cove is named for George Washington Hunt, a railroad developer interested in Hogg's Oregon Pacific Railroad. Hunt and Nelson Bennett were given contracts in 1887 to complete the line from the vicinity of Idanha to the summit. A good deal of clearing and grading was done but both contractors quit in Dec. 1887, after disagreements with the railroad. Hunt established a work camp near Circle Lake in Santiam Pass where he built three cabins for the crew. These were known as Hunts Railroad Cabins and Waldo stayed in them several times over the years. There was a George S. Hunt who managed the Curtis Lumber Company store in Detroit in 1905, but this was much later. The compiler feels certain that Hunts Cove was named for some connection with George Washington Hunt, a well known individual in Oregon.

Hunts Mill Point, CLATSOP. This point is between Clifton and Wauna. It was named for Hunts Mill, a pioneer sawmill owned by Henry H. Hunt and Ben Wood. This mill was built during the winter of 1843–44, and began operations in 1844. Edward Otey, a pioneer of 1843, was the millwright. Hunt Creek, nearby, was named for the same reason. Hunts Mill was the first sawmill in Clatsop County.

Hurlburt, MULTNOMAH. Mr. and Mrs. John Quincy Adams Hurlburt made settlement in the east part of Multnomah County about 1877 or 1878 at a point about three miles southeast of Springdale. The Hurlburt home was on a bench about a half mile northeast of Sandy River and about 800 feet west of what was later Hurlburt School. Hurlburt post office was established in the Hurlburt home on June 20, 1899, with John A. Hurlburt postmaster. By this time Mr. Hurlburt had discarded the Quincy part of his name. The office was closed Nov. 14, 1903, apparently because of the extension of rural free delivery.

Huron, UMATILLA. Huron is a station on the Union Pacific Railroad about eight miles northeast of Meacham. The station is also on Meacham Creek. Huron was apparently named for one Jake Huron, who in company with Eph Johnson, operated a pioneer sawmill in this locality. The mill was later purchased by Wilbur and Son. It produced much of the ties and timber used to build the railroad. It is said that Huron station was originally called Reardon for a track laying foreman. This name was later changed to Laka and still later to Huron, but the compiler does not know the dates. Huron post office was in operation from May 1905 to June 1913.

Hurricane Creek, WALLOWA. Named by C. A. Smith in the early 1880s. He explored the creek after a big storm and found a great many trees blown down. However, David Cole in the *Oregonian*, Aug. 29, 1986, says it was not blow down but avalanche debris. In 1931, J. H. Horner of Enterprise told the compiler that the first sawmill in the Wallowa Valley was built on this creek about 1878 by E. V. Cohorn.

Hurt Cabin, CURRY. This cabin on the upper reaches of Collier Creek in the east part of the county was named for E. G. Hurt who lived there in the early days.

Huston Canyon, MORROW. Huston Canyon northeast of Eightmile was named for Luther Huston who settled there in the 1890s.

Hutchcroft Creek, YAMHILL. Mrs. Harvey Stoller of Dayton supplied the following information regarding this tributary of North Yamhill River. The creek was named for John and Margaret Hutchcroft who came to Yamhill County in 1874 and bought part of the Elisha Bedwell donation land claim. They were well-known citizens of the area for many years. Hutchcroft was born in England and came to Oregon via Canada and Wisconsin.

Hutchinson, BAKER. Hutchinson was a station on the Union Pacific Railroad about five miles northwest of Haines. It was named for a local family. The post office was established Aug. 3, 1900, with James H. Hutchinson first postmaster. The office was discontinued Aug. 5, 1902.

Hyde Creek, BENTON. In 1901 John W. Hyde filed for a homestead in the northeast corner of s 6, T 13S, R 6W. This was duly patented. Hyde left the homestead and over the years, the creek that flowed through the property and emptied into Wells Creek became known as Cedar Creek. Hyde's name was transferred to the next west tributary of Wells Creek about a mile to the northeast. After World War II, maps used the form Hide and showed the creek in both locations. In 1985 the USBGN deferred to local usage and confirmed the relocation but corrected the spelling in *Decision List 8503*.

Hymes Creek, BENTON, LINCOLN. In 1969 this tributary of Tumtum River near Summit was named in honor of Alva D. Hymes. Hymes settled along its banks in 1906 and died there in 1942.

Ibex Butte, CROOK. Ibex Butte is in the south part of the county, in the northwest quarter of T 20S, R 23E. There is also a Little Ibex Butte nearby, and the two features are about 25 miles airline northwest of Suntex. These buttes bear the popular name of the rimrock or lava bed sheep. This wild sheep resembles the Rocky Mountain bighorn, but the two varieties are not identical. The lava bed bighorn ranged over a large part of eastern Oregon. There is a good deal about both varieties in *Mammals and Life Zones of Oregon*, by Vernon Bailey. There is a popular notion that there was at one time a post office called Ibex in the vicinity of the buttes, but the compiler has not been able to find any trace of it in post office records.

Ice House Creek, JACKSON. Dead Indian Road eight miles northeast of Ashland is located alongside Ice House Creek. In one spot the creek forms Ice House Lake and here Ashland residents harvested ice before the advent of mechanical refrigeration.

Idaho Point, LINCOLN. This is a prominent landmark on the south side of Yaquina Bay about two miles southeast of Newport. In times past it has been known both as Point Virtue and Hinton Point. Andrew L. Porter, a resident of the Yaquina Bay district since the 1860s, told the compiler in 1945 that the point was named for one Hinton who settled there in the early days. This was Rowland B. Hinton, a pioneer of 1846 who was a prominent resident near Monroe in Benton County. The name Idaho Point appears to have been the result of a real estate venture but after World War II it became well established. The USBGN made this offical in *Decision List 7602*.

Idanha, MARION. Idanha is a place on North Santiam River about four miles upstream from Detroit. John Minto in *OHQ*, v. 4, p. 248, says the original name was Muskrat Camp but that it was renamed by the proprietor of the resort hotel. T. Egenton Hogg's Oregon Pacific Railroad Company built east up the North Santiam River and reached the vicinity of Idanha in 1889. All construction ceased at the end of that year and there was little activity in the area until 1895 when, amid a rash of land entries, Idanha post office was established with Alma Kriesel postmaster. The origin of the name is apparent but the reason baffling. In 1887 Fred J. Kiesel of Ogden, Utah, was the principal incorporator of The Natural Mineral Water Company which bottled Idan-Ha water from the Ninety Percent Spring in Soda Springs, Idaho. The company went on to build the Idanha Hotel in Soda Springs and both the water and the hostelry became known throughout the northwest. Alma Kriesel had two brothers who were active in Idanha, Oregon, possibly in the resort hotel, and the compiler is certain that some member of the family was familiar with the Soda Springs operation. Extensive research has shown that both the Kiesel and Kriesel families came originally from Germany but no connection can be established. There is an Idaho legend to the effect that Idan-Ha, as the name was used on the bottle labels, was the Indian name for the legend or spot of the Spirit of the Healing Waters. More than this the reader must find or deduce for himself.

Idaville, TILLAMOOK. Idaville was platted about 1870 by Warren N. Vaughn, and the land was part of his donation land claim. He named the place for his oldest daughter, Ida Vaughn.

Idea, GILLIAM. Idea is obviously an odd name for a post office, but that is the record. This office was established Feb. 5, 1886, in S 10, T 4S, R 23E. This locality is on West Fork Dry Creek about 12 miles east of Condon. Earlier information placed the office much closer to Condon and confused the names of the people involved. In Jan. 1977, Mrs. Raymond Bennett of Bend wrote and clarified the matter giving the following facts. James Washington Hiatt was the first postmaster and he intended to name the office Ida for his sister-in-law, Ida Chance Keizur, the wife of Manly Keizur, a local rancher. Somewhere along the line the name was misspelled with this odd result. Hiatt was succeeded as postmaster by James Royse whose tenure was very short. The post office was closed July 26, 1889, and what little business there was, was turned over to Gooseberry.

Idiot Creek, TILLAMOOK. Idiot Creek flows into Devils Lake Fork Wilson River from the north about two miles west of the summit of the Coast Range on SH-6. The compiler pondered this name ever since it was officially applied in USBGN *Decision List 6503*. After some publicity in Nov. 1977 by Jim Jordan in the Portland *Daily Journal of Commerce*, Calvin Clayton who had worked the truck lines along Wilson River since World War II called to confirm the suspected origin. About one half mile up Idiot Creek was the site of Ryan's Camp, a logging operation in the Tillamook Burn. This was such an out of the way spot that supposedly only an idiot would go there to work, and the camp was popularly known as Idiotville. The name was applied to the stream in due course.

Idleyld Park, DOUGLAS. Idleyld Park is one of Oregon's mystery names. The place is on North Umpqua River near the mouth of Rock Creek, a locality formerly served by Tioga post office, later by the Hoaglin office. In Jan. 1946, K. D. Lytle of Roseburg, division engineer of the Oregon State Highway Division, wrote the writer that about 1918–19 an amusement hall was built in the place and the owner named it Idleyld Park for a similar place he had heard of in California. There is a post office in California named Idyllwild. If that name is the genesis of the Oregon name, there has been some fancy confusion along the line. As nearly as the writer can determine, the post office at Idleyld Park was established Dec. 1, 1932, by change of name from Hoaglin. Earl D. Vosburgh was postmaster at the time.

Idol, HARNEY. A post office with the name Idol was established on the Harney County list as of Mar. 25, 1892, with Joseph Morris first and only postmaster. The office was closed to Harney on Aug. 9, 1893. In 1947 Archie McGowan of Burns wrote the compiler that in the early 1890s gold was discovered on the head of Trout Creek north of Harney. There was a mild stampede to the diggings, but the gold petered out. Even to this day after the spring freshets small grubstakes of very fine gold are recovered. Joseph Morris, better known as Joe, moved his store from Harney to the new camp, which was called Idol City. No one seems to remember why this name was selected, unless it was because gold was the idol of miners the world over.

Igo, GILLIAM. In July 1946, J. D. Weed, then district attorney at Condon, sent the following information about Igo: "Igo was a post office in the Ferry Canyon country and it was named for John Igo, an early settler. There is a Grange hall there at the present time known as the Igo Grange." Igo post office was established in Feb. 1891, with James J. Fix postmaster. The office was closed in Dec. 1892, with papers to Condon. Old maps show Igo in the south part of T 3S, R 20E.

Ikenick Creek, LINN. This creek flows north into Clear Lake. It owes its unusual name to Isaac Nickerson who was commonly called Ike Nick. In the 1870s Nickerson and Henry Burmister kept the travel at Fish Lake Station. One winter he was caught in a blizzard and frozen to death. In the spring his body was found near the creek which now bears his nickname. Pat Cecil of the USFS in Bend provided this information which was found in *Sweet Home In the Oregon Cascades*, p. 19, by Carey and Hainline.

Ikt Butte, DESCHUTES. *Ikt* is the Chinook jargon word for one. The name was applied by the USFS to a butte northwest of Paulina Mountains, at a time when several buttes were named with the Indian series of numbers.

Illahe, CURRY. This is the Chinook jargon word meaning land or earth and is also used to connote country. George Gibbs states that it is derived from the Chinook Indian word *ilahekh*. There are of course, various spellings, but the government has adopted Illahe as a standard. Besides the post office in Curry County, there are other features bearing the name, including a place on North Umpqua River, Illahe Hill about four miles southwest of Salem, and Tenasillahe Island in the Columbia River.

Illingworth, TILLAMOOK. Illingworth post office was on Wilson River about 14 miles northeast of Tillamook, and was named in compliment to members of a local family. The office was established in June 1896, with James R. Harris first postmaster. The office was closed in Dec. 1899.

Illinois River, JOSEPHINE. C. H. Stewart, of Albany, wrote the compiler in 1927 that Illinois River was named as the result of the early discovery of gold thereon by the Althouse brothers of Albany. These brothers, Samuel, John and Phillip, were pioneers of 1847, emigrating from Peoria, Illinois, and settling in Albany, where they made their homes. They mined on Althouse Creek and Illinois River in southern Oregon in the early days of the placer diggings.

Illumination Rock, CLACKAMAS. On this rock occurred the first successful illumination of Mount Hood. This illumination was part of the Independence Day celebration in Portland on July 4, 1887. Will G. Steel organized a party that carried 100 pounds of red fire to this rock and the light was seen as far as the mountain was visible.

Image Creek, CLACKAMAS. Image Creek rises on Table Rock and flows northwest to Table Rock Creek in the south part of the county. Table Rock was a holy place of the Molalla Indians and a large, carved rock gave its name to the nearby creek. Gatschet gives the Molalla name for Table Rock as *Fautiha* or *Faudiha*.

Imbler, UNION. This community, north of La Grande, was named for the Imbler family, pioneer settlers. The post office was established Apr. 27, 1891, with Albert E. Imbler first postmaster.

Imnaha River, WALLOWA. Imnaha is a beautiful name for a stream that rises in the Wallowa Mountains, and flows to Snake River through one of the deepest river gorges on the continent. The word was used by William Clark, on a map issued with the original Lewis and Clark journals in 1814, in the form *Innahar*. As far as the writer knows, Captain Bonneville was the first white man to go into the Wallowa country. For information about this exploration, *see* Bonneville. He was in the vicinity of Imnaha River in January and February 1834. It is difficult to follow Bonneville's march as described by Irving, for the geography of the country is obviously confused, but the general character of the landscape is very well described, and Irving's somewhat extravagant style is quite suitable to the remarkable rock formations and almost bottomless canyons the traveler encountered. Besides the river, there is a post office named Imnaha. J. H. Horner of Enterprise, the authority on Wallowa County history, told the writer in 1927 that *Imna* was the name of a sub-chief and that it was the custom among the Indians to sound *ha* to indicate the territory ruled over by a chief. Thus Imnaha was the land ruled over by *Imna. See also* Wenaha River.

Imperial, DESCHUTES. This place is said to have been named by someone who had formerly lived in Imperial Valley, California.

Inavale, BENTON. Inavale post office was established July 2, 1896, with John Mitchell first postmaster and operated until May 4, 1905. The place was about eight miles southwest of Corvallis and about three miles west of Greenberry. The office was in a productive little valley and was given the descriptive name "In a vale" on that account.

Ince Camp, WASCO. Ince Camp is on the old road from Antelope to John Day River about two miles north of Currant Creek. It was named for the Ince brothers, Arthur and Elby, who homesteaded there in 1913.

Inch Creek, CLACKAMAS. This stream is in the east part of the county near Salmon River. It was named by W. B. Osborne of the USFS because it was about an inch long on a map on the scale of 1–62,500.

Independence, POLK. Independence was named by Elvin A. Thorp, who founded the community. The name was in compliment to Independence, Missouri. Thorp was born in Howard County, Missouri, in 1820. He came to Oregon in 1844, took up a donation land claim at the present site of Independence, Oregon, in June 1845. Independence post office was established Apr. 3, 1852, with Leonard Williams first postmaster.

Independence Prairie, LINN. This small prairie is at the junction of Marion Creek and North Santiam River. It was named by the Marion County road viewing party on Independence Day, July 4, 1874. John Minto was in charge of the party. Independence Rock, a little to the southeast, was named for the prairie.

Indian Beach, CLATSOP. This fine little beach, well hidden from general observation, is on the southwest front of Tillamook Head and about two miles airline northwest of the mouth of Ecola Creek. Indian Point is at the north end of the beach and Bald Point at the south end, and Canyon Creek flows over the beach just south of Indian Point. The compiler is of the opinion that this is the beach referred to by Captain William Clark on Jan. 8, 1806, in the following words: "... I proceeded on down a Steep decent to a Single house the remains of an old *Kil a mox* Town in a nitch immediately on the Sea Coast, at which place a great No. of eregular rocks are out and the waves comes in with great force." Clark adds that the Indians used the place to deposit their dead in canoes. His description is remarkably accurate and in addition, old Indians told Rodney L. Glisan about 1895 that Indian Beach had a village in ancient days and later was a *memaloose illahe*, or place of the dead. They also said that it was the place where Captain Clark first came down to the sea and brought the Indian woman. Clark's map of Tillamook Head (Point of Clark's View) is also remarkably accurate and shows Indian Beach with fidelity.

Indian Creek, HOOD RIVER. In pioneer days there was a permanent Indian town or camp in the flat where the main west side road crosses this creek, and the name was applied on that account.

Indian Creek, WASCO. This Indian Creek rises south of Shaniko and flows to Antelope Creek. In the early days the flats above Cross Hollows south of Shaniko were a gathering spot for Indians to trade and compete in tribal games. Dolph Kimsey who was raised in the area told the compiler that the Indian Creek valley was marked by innumerable Indian campsites.

Indian Mountain, HOOD RIVER. Before World War I, the springs on this mountain were a favorite camping spot for Indians on huckleberry and hunting trips. Ralph Lewis told the compiler that he had seen numbers of their camps and that they took many deer from the upper Eagle Creek valley.

Indian Ridge, LANE. In 1927 Smith Taylor of McKenzie Bridge told the compiler that Indian Ridge was named for an old Indian hunting trail that extended along its summit. The ridge is west of South Fork McKenzie River. The elevation of Indian Ridge Lookout is 5426 feet.

Indian Valley, UNION. Indian Valley is the flat land along Grande Ronde River just north of the mouth of Indian Creek, now largely occupied by the City of Elgin. It was named in the late 1860s because the first settlers found numerous Indian artifacts in the valley of Indian Creek. The Indians found the stretch of Grande Ronde River near Elgin excellent for fish traps and were frequent visitors. Prior to 1885 even the present community of Elgin was called Indian Valley. However, Indian Valley post office was about three miles up Indian Creek from its mouth near where the pioneer road from Summerville to Cricket Flat crossed the stream. It was established Apr. 10, 1873, with John W. White postmaster, and was discontinued Jan. 13, 1874. Indian Valley post office was reestablished June 11, 1877, with Joel Weaver postmaster. This office operated until Oct. 26, 1881. There were also three other postmasters.

Indianhead Rock, HOOD RIVER. This rock is about one half mile north of the intersection of Indian Creek with Lake Branch of West Fork Hood River. When the area was logged about 1960, this prominent rock became visible from the road and the USFS named it to help local area identification. The resemblance to an Indianhead is fanciful but the location near Indian Creek and Indian Mountain makes the name appropriate.

Ingle Creek, GRANT. Ingle Creek rises on Ingle Mountain and flows north to John Day River at Mount Vernon. Both features were named for William D. Ingle who was born in South Carolina and came west in 1859. Some years later he settled near Mount Vernon where he took up a land claim in 1871.

Inglis, COLUMBIA. Inglis post office, which was established Sept. 30, 1902, was given the family name of the first postmaster, John E. Inglis. Inglis post office and railroad station lay about midway between Clatskanie and Quincy. The office was out of service from 1910 to 1914, and was discontinued again in 1918.

Ingram Point, CROOK. This mountain is northeast of Prineville and bears the name of Douglas C. Ingram of the USFS. The name was applied on May 3, 1933, to honor Ingram, who lost his life in Aug. 1929, in a fire in Chelan National Forest. He was born in Scotland, Nov. 1882, and joined the USFS in 1909. He served in the field and in the Portland office, and was an authority on range management. He had an important collection of forest plants. He first used Ingram Point, then known as Tamarack Point, as a lookout and it is quite fitting that the place should bear his name. Ingram Butte, elevation 4333 feet, approximately 16 miles airline northeast of Oakridge and near the headwaters of Christy Creek, was named for the same man.

Inlow, LANE. In Jan. 1947, Elwin A. McCornack of Eugene wrote the compiler as follows: "The first wagon road from Eugene to Mapleton left the present route at Hale or Elk Prairie west of Noti and by following Chickahominy and Nelson creeks intersected the Lake Creek road near Greenleaf. For years this route was followed by Whisman Brothers four and six in hand stage coaches. On the Chickahominy end of this section there lived a pioneer settler by the name of Igo Inlow. His place was well known and it may be there was a post office established there at one time." Well, the post office actually was established on June 20, 1899, with Clemons E. Carlisle first postmaster. The office was closed to Hale on Jan. 16, 1901. In Apr. 1948, McCornack wrote that the office was named for "Doc" Inlow, father of Igo Inlow. The office was said to have been in "Doc's" house. His given name has not been recalled.

Ione, MORROW. The name of this small community in eastern Oregon furnished Harvey W. Scott with ammunition for a characteristic editorial which appeared in the *Oregonian* for June 22, 1903, after the Willow Creek flood of June 14 had brought into prominence various geographic names in that part of the state. He said: "Let us take advantage of the present occasion to correct the current pronunciation of 'Ione,' the town on Willow Creek, below Heppner. In current use they call it I-one, with accent on the last syllable, almost universally. But Ione is a name of three syllables, the accent properly on the second. So, many of our people say I-rene, two syllables, with accent on the last. But Irene is a name of three syllables, with accent on the second. We have a steamboat that most persons call Cal-li-ope, with accent on the final syllable. But Calliope is a name of four syllables with accent on the second. Again, in the name Arion, the accent is commonly placed on the first syllable. But the correct pronunciation places it on the second syllable making the 'i' long. Our schools and academies should insist on right pronunciation of these and other names. In Idaho, on the Oregon Short Line, they call a town Sho-shone two syllables, with accent on the ultimate. Now, Shoshone is not a classical Greek name, as the foregoing are, but an Indian one. Nevertheless, the Indians called it Sho-sho-ne, accenting the final syllable, as emigrants who came across the plains perfectly remember." The town of Ione was named by E. G. Sperry, who owned the land, in 1883, for Ione Arthur, a girl from Brownsville who was visiting the Sperry family. She was with her father, John Arthur, and others of her family. The post office was established in 1884, with Aaron Royse first postmaster. He ran the first store in the community.

Iowa Hill, WASHINGTON. Iowa Hill is a prominent point about three miles airline east of Gaston and just north of Laurelwood. It has an extreme elevation of about 1165 feet at its north end. This hill has been called Iowa Hill for many years because of the fact that several families of settlers came to the locality from Iowa.

Iowa Slough, COOS. Iowa Slough flows into Coquille River from the north just west of Riverton. Walling, in his *History of Southern Oregon*, p. 488, says the stream was once called Deadman Slough because of the murder of two white men, Venable and Barton, upon its banks in 1854. Five Indians were thought to be guilty of the crime and three were hanged. A post office named Iowa Slough was established in Mar. 1872, with Harrison E. Nosler postmaster. The office was discontinued in Nov. 1878.

Ipsoot Butte, KLAMATH. This butte, in the extreme northeast corner of the county, is named with the Chinook jargon word for hidden, or secluded. The word *ipsoot* should not be confused with *itswoot*, meaning bear.

Irish Bend, BENTON. Irish Bend is a land area with limits not exactly defined lying west of Willamette River and east of Long Tom River, a few miles northeast of Monroe. The name of the locality comes from a prominent eastward bend in Willamette River in T 14 south. Several Irish families settled in this vicinity about 1860, and gave the name to the river bend and to the bottom land west of the Willamette. The families of James Martin, James Herron and Robert Herron have been among the leading contributors to the development of the area.

Irma, CURRY. Irma was a post office on the old road about midway between Gold Beach and Harbor. It was very close to the north line of T 39S, R 14W. The office was established Feb. 11, 1895, with Clara A. Clarke first postmaster. This office was discontinued July 23, 1902. Dodge's *Pioneer History of Coos and Curry Counties* lists N. D. and Clara A. Clark as having settled in that part of Oregon in 1891. N. D. Clark appears to have been interested in a variety of things and was an inventor of sorts. Among the children of Mr. and Mrs. Clark was Irma, born in 1879, and it is reasonable to suppose that the post office was named for this 16-year-old girl. Post office records use the spelling Clarke but Dodge has simplified it. The compiler does not know which is correct but past experience has shown post office records in respect of the spelling of proper names are generally reliable. Emma Hardenbrook was appointed postmaster of Irma post office on June 20, 1898, and it is reported that the office was moved about five miles south at that time.

Iron Mountain, CLACKAMAS. Iron Mountain is the name applied to the area west of Oswego and north of Oswego Lake. In recent years the principal application of the title has been in the expression Iron Mountain Boulevard. An iron ore called limonite was mined extensively in this locality from 1867 to about 1894. F. W. Libbey of the Department of Geology and Mineral Industries has sent the compiler a short statement about this activity which was carried on at first by a company known as the Oregon Iron Company. A small blast furnace was built close to the town of Oswego in 1867, probably the first of such furnaces on the Pacific Coast. The furnace was used fairly continuously to 1886, when a new furnace of modern type was built and put into operation in 1888. Record of iron production ceased after 1894. The new furnace produced nearly 11,000 long tons in 1890 and the industry was of great importance to the Pacific Northwest. The chimney of the new furnace is still standing in George Rogers Park in Lake Oswego. It has been listed in the National Register of Historic Places.

Iron Mountain, COOS, CURRY. This mountain is a north-south ridge about 15 miles east of Port Orford and has a maximum elevation of about 4000 feet. The compiler does not know by whom the name was applied, but the style Iron Mountain was in use as early as Mar. 1856. *See* Glisan's *Journal of Army Life*, p. 295. In Dec. 1943, Earl K. Nixon, director of the State Department of Geology and Mineral Industries, wrote the compiler that the mountain was probably named because of the reddish-brown color of the rock mass and not because of the presence of iron ore as such. The rock outcrops are prominently stained with ferric oxide and there is a lot of manganese stain but no commercial ore deposits.

Iron Mountain, HARNEY. This is about ten miles west of Harney Lake and has an elevation of 5380 feet, according to the USGS. It is known as Iron Mountain because of the hard metallic appearance of the rock of which it is composed. During the Indian disturbances of the 1860s, this point was called Pleasanton Butte, apparently in compliment to a well-known officer in the regular army, Alfred Pleasanton, who had been stationed in the Pacific Northwest.

Iron Mountain, LINCOLN. Iron Mountain, elevation 654 feet, a conspicuous point near the Pacific Ocean about four miles north of Newport, is remarkable for its conical symmetry. The upper part is red brown and has a sort of burned, metallic appearance, hence the name. The mountain is just east of the Oregon Coast Highway.

Ironside, MALHEUR. The name Ironside was first applied in 1891. It is said that J. M. Young, who was the first postmaster, suggested the name of the post office. The name was chosen because of the proximity of Ironside Mountain, the most prominent geographical feature nearby.

Ironside Mountain, MALHEUR. This is the most important landmark in the north part of the county. The highest point is 7804 feet above the sea. It is so called because of its iron-like appearance.

Irrigon, MORROW. Irrigon is near the site of Grande Ronde Landing, a former rival of Umatilla. For information about these places, *see* Umatilla. Later the place was called Stokes, and it was a station on the railroad with that name even after Irrigon post office was established. Irrigon post office was established Nov. 16, 1903, with Frank B. Holbrook first postmaster. Addison Bennett made up the name of the place from the words Oregon and Irrigation. Irrigon was the scene of a promising irrigation enterprise, hence Bennett's style of name. He was editor of the first newspaper in the place, called the *Oregon Irrigator*, later the *Irrigon Irrigator*, its initial number appearing Jan. 27, 1904. After various ventures in the newspaper business, he served for many years as a staff writer on the *Oregonian* and died in Portland, Sept. 30, 1924. Stokes post office was in operation from May 26, 1897, until Apr. 25, 1899, with Douglas W. Bailey postmaster.

Irving Glacier, LANE. Dr. E. T. Hodge of the University of Oregon gave the name Irving Glacier to a small glacier between Middle Sister and South Sister. This was in commemoration of Washington Irving, the author of *Astoria* and *The Adventures of Captain Bonneville*.

Irwin Rocks, DOUGLAS. These rocks near Reston are named for William Irwin who settled nearby before the turn of the century.

Island City, UNION. Island City got its name because it is on an island formed by a slough which leaves Grande Ronde River west of the town and rejoins the river several miles to the east. The slough is south of the main stream.

Isolate, DOUGLAS. Isolate was named because of its isolation, and apparently well named at that. The office was near Days Creek (stream) about ten or twelve miles northeast of Canyonville, near the northwest corner of T 30S, R 3W. Isolate post office was established Apr. 17, 1917, with Thomas F. Epping first postmaster. The office was closed to Days Creek office on Apr. 30, 1919.

Israel Well, DESCHUTES. This well was on the 1912 homestead of John H. Israel five miles northwest of Brothers.

Isthmus Slough, COOS. Isthmus Slough was known as Wapello Slough in pioneer days, but the name was changed because the slough led to the isthmus over which there was a trail to Beaver Slough, a tributary of Coquille River. The isthmus lies east of Isthmus Slough. East of the isthmus are Ross Slough, Catching Slough and the mouth of Coos River. A post office named Isthmus was established in the vicinity of Isthmus Slough Dec. 11, 1871, with Gilbert Hall postmaster. The name of the office was changed to Utter City Feb. 11, 1875. The office was closed June 22, 1880. Utter City was named for the Utter brothers, who operated a coal mine.

Ivan, KLAMATH. Ivan, once a station on the Southern Pacific Company railroad between Klamath Falls and the California state line, is said to have been named shortly after the railroad was built. The compiler has been unable to get confirmed information, but several sources, generally reliable, are of the opinion that the station was named for Ivan Daniels. Daniels was a railroad employee, probably a pump expert, who is said to have been killed in a tunnel accident not far from the state line. Statements to the effect that the station may have been named for Ivan Kesterson, connected with a local sawmill enterprise, are wrong. In June 1948, Irving E. Kesterson wrote from Atherton, California, ruling out any connection between the station name and that of his brother Ivan. The two Kestersons were at one time associated in the operation of a sawmill near Ivan station. Irving Kesterson says that he bought the mill in 1917 and his brother Ivan joined the enterprise in 1918. The station had been named some years before. Ivan post office was established Nov. 18, 1926, with Andrew J. Hanan postmaster. The name of the office was changed to Worden in Mar. 1930. The office was doubtless moved several miles to Worden at that time. There had been a post office at Worden some years previously.

Ivison, LANE. Ivison was a post office on Wildcat Creek west of Eugene and a few miles east of Walton. The office was established Mar. 3, 1893, with Isaac S. Day first postmaster. Thomas T. McGlynn was appointed postmaster May 11, 1909. The office was discontinued Sept. 15, 1909, with mail to Elmira. In Feb. 1947, Mrs. C. A. Stephens of Eugene wrote the compiler that she was the daughter of Isaac Day, the first postmaster, and at the time the office was established, Day was asked to submit a name for the place. There was a schoolteacher boarding at the Day home, and the teacher was given the selection of the name, and she chose Ivison. She was with the impression that Day's given name was Ivison and not Isaac, and she selected Ivison in supposed compliment to Day. By the time the error became apparent, postal authorities had established the office with the name Ivison.

Ivy, CLATSOP. This railroad station east of Astoria was so named because of a heavy growth of ivy over the remains of a building south of the track.

Izee, GRANT. In 1927 J. E. Snow of Dayville told the compiler that this post office was so oddly named because a local stockman, M. N. Bonham, used the letters I Z for his cattle brand. Postal authorities inform the compiler that Izee post office was established Nov. 6, 1889, with Carlos W. Bonham first postmaster and was discontinued July 31, 1954.

Jack Creek, KLAMATH. Jack Creek is in the northeast part of the county. It heads east of Walker Mountain and flows generally southward to Klamath Marsh and Williamson River. It was originally Jackass Creek, but the passage of time has shortened the name. Dr. Thomas Condon on July 31, 1877, wrote while on a trip to Fossil Lake: "Finally we reached water (at Jackass Gulch), where we camped." *See Thomas Condon*, by Ellen Condon McCornack, p. 199. Despite the fact that there are more than 18 Jack Creeks in Oregon, it is improbable that the original name of Jackass Creek will be revived.

Jackass Butte, HARNEY. In 1987, Dorsey Griffin, who was familiar with the area, wrote to give information about this name. His father said the butte and adjoining Jackass Mountain, west of SH-206 north of Frenchglen, were named because of the feral donkeys or "jacks" that escaped or were left in the area by early prospectors. Jackass Creek flows west into Weed Lake.

Jackknife Canyon, SHERMAN. Mrs. Lulu D. Crandall of The Dalles told the compiler that her father, Z. Donnell, named Jackknife Canyon because of the circumstances connected with losing a jack knife near the canyon in the fall of a year in the late 1860s. He found the knife the following spring and named the canyon on that account.

Jackpot Meadow, CLACKAMAS. Jackpot Meadow is about ten miles south of Mount Hood and drains into Salmon River. It was named because after periods of wet weather it was easy to get into and hard to get out of.

Jacks Bridge, CLACKAMAS, MARION. Jacks Bridge is on Butte Creek about a mile southwest of Marquam. The name commemorates Jeremiah J. Jack, a native of Tennessee, a pioneer of 1847, and an early settler near Butte Creek. For biography, *see History of the Silverton Country*, p. 44. Bute Creek post office was established Jan. 24, 1851, with Jack postmaster. The office was discontinued Nov. 3, 1851. It was on the Marion County list. This office was reestablished in 1867 in Clackamas County with the name Butte Creek and in Nov. 1889, the name was changed to Marquam. For a time during the 1870s the office may have been in Marion County, although the records are conflicting.

Jackson County. The discovery of gold in southern Oregon in the early 1850s made it desirable to provide a county government for that part of the state and accordingly on Jan. 12, 1852, Jackson County was created and named for Andrew Jackson, seventh president of the United States. As then constituted the county comprised all that part of Oregon west of the Cascade Range and between the south boundary of Umpqua County and the north boundary of California. The county has been reduced in size considerably since its original establishment. Large areas have been taken to form most of Curry and Josephine counties to the west. According to ODOT in 1989, the area of the county is 2811 square miles. One of the earliest irrigation projects in Oregon was in Jackson County.

Jackson Creek, DOUGLAS. This stream was for many years called South Fork South Umpqua River, a name sufficiently cumbersome to call for a change. It was renamed by the USBGN for Clarence W. Jackson, who was killed by a truck in the state of Washington while in the employ of the USFS. He had formerly been a ranger on the Umpqua National Forest in Oregon.

Jackson Creek, MULTNOMAH, WASHINGTON. This stream is a tributary of McKay Creek and is about eight miles north of Hillsboro. The falls of this stream are known as Jackson Falls. These features were named for John B. Jackson, a pioneer settler who took up a donation land claim nearby.

Jackson Creek, TILLAMOOK. Jackson Creek flows through Cape Lookout State Park and empties into the south end of Netarts Bay. It was named for J. H. Jackson, an early settler at Netarts and road supervisor in the 1880s. The creek originally flowed into the Pacific Ocean but was diverted into Netarts Bay after World War II.

Jackson Hill, MARION. Jackson Hill is about eight miles south of Salem. For many years one of the main county highways went over this hill. When the Pacific Highway East was built south of Salem, a new route was followed which eliminated the bad grade over Jackson Hill. Jackson Hill is about one-half mile south of Sunnyside school. It was named for L. A. Jackson, a pioneer resident.

Jackson Lake, WALLOWA. Jackson Lake was named for J. H. Jackson, formerly a resident of Lostine, who first stocked it with trout. It is in the Wallowa Mountains about 20 miles south of Lostine, in the northwest quarter of S 2, T 4S, R 43E, and its waters drain into Lostine River.

Jacksonville, JACKSON. The development of Jacksonville began with the placer gold discoveries there in 1851–52. Leslie M. Scott told the compiler in 1927 that Jacksonville was named for Jackson Creek, upon which it is situated. Scott believed that Jackson Creek was named for one of the gold discoverers but a diligent search of census and other records fails to uncover anyone of this name. The current opinion is that the creek took its name from the county. For information about Jacksonville, *see* the *Oregonian*, Aug. 1, 1926, sect. 1, p. 12. After World War II great strides were made to preserve Jacksonville's historic buildings, culminating in its designation as a National Historic Landmark. Robertson Collins, a long time resident, preservationist, and in 1985 chairman of the Oregon State Advisory Committee on Historic Preservation, was instrumental in this movement. Jacksonville post office was established on Feb. 18, 1854, with R. Dugan first postmaster. Sylvester H. Taylor was appointed postmaster on Dec. 19, 1854.

Jacques Creek, DOUGLAS. This tributary of Elk Creek three miles southeast of Drew was named for Lott M. Jacques who homesteaded nearby in 1901.

Jakey Ridge, WALLOWA. This ridge is the high ground west of Sleepy Creek about eight miles north of Hat Point. It was named for Jakey Wilson whose family owned the Wilson ranch on the Idaho side of Snake River south of Pittsburg Landing. The form Jackey is incorrect.

Jalland Creek, HOOD RIVER. This creek is tributary to Badger Creek near Badger Lake. It was named by USFS ranger Eric Gordon for his mother whose maiden name was Jalland.

James, CLACKAMAS. James post office operated from Nov. 1904, to Mar. 1906, and was obviously named for Dudly (or Dudley) James its first postmaster. In May 1948, Isaac V. Trullinger, formerly a resident of Clackamas County, wrote that the James post office was situated near Milk Creek between Meadowbrook and Colton. Thomas W. Gerber wrote from Canby confirming Mr. Trullinger's statement and added that James post office was in the north part of S 5, T 5S, R 3E. The James family came into that part of Clackamas County about the turn of the century according to Mr. Gerber. There were nine sons and the old gentleman used to brag that he had sired a baseball team, although there is nothing to indicate that the sons ever played after they came to Oregon. Mr. Gerber contributes another morsel to the effect that about the time Dudly James, the oldest son, put up a little store building at the location mentioned above, it burned down and postal activities were transferred to the James house where they were continued until the post office was discontinued in 1906.

Jameson Creek, LANE. Jameson Creek enters McKenzie River from the north near Walterville. It is named for John C. and Eunice Jamison whose donation land claim included the stream. Their certificate number was 363. The compiler does not know when the map name was changed to the present form but early records all use the spelling Jamison.

Jamestown, BAKER. Jamestown post office was established on the Union County list on June 5, 1882, with James B. Sams first postmaster. The office was apparently named in compliment to the postmaster. It was finally closed on June 21, 1886. Jamestown was near Big Creek, in the extreme north part of Baker County, northeast of Baker City. The locality was once in Union County, but a subsequent boundary change brought it into Baker County. Jamestown was also called Big Creek, for the stream.

Jamieson, MALHEUR. Oregon Short Line Railroad Company officials named Jamieson for a Dr. William Jamieson, who was an early settler on Willow Creek. The post office was established in 1911, with J. L. Pope first postmaster.

Jamison Meadow, KLAMATH. This meadow west of Tea Table Mountain was part of the Jamison Ranch started by William J. Jamison at the turn of the century.

Japanese Hollow, WASCO. In 1908 three Japanese, S. Nishizasi, H. Okita and M. Yasui incorporated the Columbia Land and Produce Company. They purchased a sizeable tract of land in what soon became known as Jap Hollow where they raised produce for shipment to The Dalles. During the early days of World War II, all Japanese in western Oregon, Washington and California, including those who were citizens by right of birth in the United States, were evacuated to interior relocation camps. In 1989 Congress recognized this injustice and passed compensatory legislation. For further information about the Yasui family, *see* Lauren Kessler's article, "A Legacy of Success," in the *Sunday Oregonian*, Dec. 7, 1986, Northwest Magazine. In the early 1970s the form was changed to Japanese Hollow.

Jarboe Meadow, UNION. This meadow is about 15 miles north of Elgin, in the extreme north end of the county. It drains southward through Jarboe Creek into Lookingglass Creek and bears the name of William H. Jarboe, a local homesteader who was a well-known character of the vicinity. The compiler has seen Jarboe's original signature attached to a letter dated Dec. 29, 1898, written to Fay S. Le-Grow, then of Walla Walla, spelled as indicated. The styles Jarbeau and Jarbo are wrong.

Jasper, LANE. This is a siding on the Southern Pacific Company's Cascade line southeast of Springfield. It was named for Jasper B. Hills who was born in the locality in 1859. He was the son of Cornelius Joel Hills, who settled at the present site of Jasper in 1846. The place was named about 1880.

Jaynes Ridge, WALLOWA. This ridge is in the southeast part of the county. It was named for Barren Jaynes, a pioneer rancher.

Jean Lake, HOOD RIVER. This lake just northwest of Badger Lake was named by USFS ranger Eric Gordon for his eldest daughter, Jean.

Jeff Davis Creek, GRANT. This stream, which is just east of Prairie City, was named during the Civil War because there were southern sympathizers mining and prospecting on its banks.

Jeffers Slough, CLATSOP. Jeffers Slough drains an area west of Miles Crossing and flows into Lewis and Clark River. It was named for a landowner. The spelling Jeffries is wrong.

Jefferson, MARION. Apparently the earliest name for the locality of Jefferson was Conser's Ferry, named for Jacob Conser, the owner. Conser, a pioneer of 1848, was a prominent settler in the Santiam Valley who was mixed up with various business enterprises at several places, including Syracuse and Santiam City, about two miles downstream from Jefferson. He left Santiam City and took up a claim upstream and started his own community. He built his ferry in 1851, but it appears that he was still serving as postmaster at Santiam City in the summer of 1852. Jefferson Institute was established in the vicinity of the ferry, and the name of the institute was eventually adopted by the community, probably on account of the strength of the Democratic party in the neighborhood. The institute was of course named for Thomas Jefferson, third president of the United States. For early history of Conser and the community of Jefferson, *see* article by Jesse Steiwer Douglas in *OHQ*, v. 32, pp. 316–331. Milton Hale, a pioneer of 1845, was apparently first to sense the strategic importance of this general locality. He established Hale Ferry on the Santiam River, below the present site of Jefferson. He also established Syracuse on his claim on the south bank. Santiam City sprang up on Samuel S. Miller's claim on the north bank. Conser seems to have been ubiquitous. Moving from the vicinity of Scio, he became first postmaster at Syracuse when that office was established on Oct. 4, 1850. Jacob L. Miller became postmaster on Mar. 14, 1851. On July 27, 1852, the name was changed to Santiam City with Jacob Corson postmaster, an obvious misprint in the postal records for Jacob

Conser. Samuel S. Miller became postmaster on Oct. 16, 1852. Postal records of this office are confusing because Syracuse office is listed in Marion County, but the community was of course in Linn County. Santiam City office was listed in Linn County on Oct. 16, 1852, and the community is supposed to have been in Marion County. Douglas, in *OHQ*, v. 32, p. 195, *et seq*. mentions the complex history of these two places and Conser's activities. Conser's new community gradually drew business up river and Syracuse and Santiam City faded from the picture. The post office was changed to Jefferson on June 13, 1861.

Jefferson County. Jefferson County was created Dec. 12, 1914, and the territory comprising it was taken from Crook County. It was named for Mount Jefferson, which is one of the principal geographic features in the district, and stands at the west end of Jefferson County. For details concerning the name of the mountain, *see* Mount Jefferson. Jefferson County has an area of 1780 square miles.

Jefferson Park, JEFFERSON, MARION. Jefferson Park is a place of peculiar beauty across the Cascade Range wedged between Mount Jefferson on the south and the almost perpendicular walls of a great rock barrier to the north. The floor of the park is about a mile wide north and south, and probably three miles long from east to west. It was formerly known as the Hanging Valley, a name lacking in descriptive quality and appropriateness. The present name of Jefferson Park was given by Judge John B. Waldo who was there in the 1870s. It is much more suitable and, of course, was suggested by the mountain. The park is about 5900 feet above the sea, and the views to be had from it of the glaciers on the north slope of Mount Jefferson and of the great canyon of the Whitewater to the east must be seen to be appreciated. Jefferson Park Glacier dominates the north side of the mountain. For excellent pictures of the park and other information, *see Mineral Resources of Oregon*, v. 2, No. 1, and *Mazama* for Dec. 1925.

Jeffries Creek, LINCOLN. This stream, which flows into Big Creek just north of Newport, was named for a homesteader who settled in the northeast quarter of s 5, T 11S, R 11W.

Jennies Peak, WHEELER. This point, elevation about 4000 feet, is about 12 miles south of Fossil. It was named for Jennie Clarno in the early 1870s. The Clarno family were pioneer settlers in that part of John Day Valley.

Jennings Lodge, CLACKAMAS. Jennings Lodge was platted as a townsite about 1905 and became a post office in 1910. It was named by Judge B. F. Bonham for Berryman Jennings, an Oregon pioneer of 1847. He was receiver of the Oregon City land office under President Buchanan and helped build the *Lot Whitcomb*, the first steamer built on the Willamette River, at Milwaukie in 1850. Jennings post office was established Nov. 3, 1910, with Lenora D. Miller postmaster. The name of the office was changed to Jennings Lodge on Jan. 6, 1911.

Jenny Creek, JACKSON. Jenny Creek is formed about one and one half miles southeast of Howard Prairie Lake by the junction of Soda and Grizzly creeks. George F. Wright of Jackson County said the name was applied by U.S. soldiers in the 1850s. They were fording the creek in midwinter and a jenny, or female mule, slipped and drowned in the high water.

Jennyopolis, BENTON. This was an early day post office south of the present site of Corvallis. It was established Mar. 24, 1852, with Richard Irwin first postmaster. It was discontinued Apr. 18, 1857. Such a name would be a handicap to any community.

Jensen Spring, WALLOWA. Jensen Spring is on Summit Ridge at the headwaters of Freezeout Creek. It was named for Mart Jensen, an early settler, who died in 1901. This name has been incorrectly applied to Coyote Springs about three quarters of a mile northeast.

Jerome Prairie, JOSEPHINE. Jerome Prairie is about six miles southwest of Grants Pass. It was named for Jerome Dyer, one of the very early Josephine County settlers. Dyer along with Daniel McKew, was killed by Rogue River Indians on June 1, 1855.

Jessie Flat, WASCO. This flat in Sorefoot Creek drainage northwest of Clarno was named for Jessie McLennan who took a stock-raising homestead there in 1922. The Stock-Raising Homestead Act of 1916 increased the maximum homestead area to 640 acres when the lands were suitable only for grazing livestock, and required only certain range improvements before patenting. It was repealed in 1934 by the Taylor Grazing Act.

Jessie M. Honeyman Memorial State Park, LANE. This park which includes parts of Cleawox and Woahink lakes is one of the most popular overnight facilities in the Oregon State Parks system. It was named to honor Mrs. Walter J. Honeyman who was a long time resident of Portland and active in the early conservation movement. For many years she was president of the Oregon Roadside Council whose primary concerns were the beautification of highway roadsides and the preservation of existing natural environment. The park was dedicated July 12, 1941 with Mrs. Honeyman the honored guest. Jessie Honeyman was born in Glasgow, Scotland on June 2, 1852 and died in Portland on July 3, 1948. For obituary, *see* the *Oregonian*, July 5, 1948.

Jett, BAKER. Jett was a station on the Union Pacific Railroad about eight miles northwest up Burnt River from Huntington. It bore the name of a family of early settlers. A post office called Jett was at one time in operation in this locality. It was established July 13, 1895, with Mary F. Jett, postmaster and was closed Mar. 15, 1901.

Jewell, CLATSOP. This place was named after Marshall Jewell, postmaster general from 1874 to 1876. The name was given by W. H. Kirkpatrick, first postmaster at Jewell in 1874.

Jewett Lake, WALLOWA. Jewett Lake, elevation about 8300 feet, is on a high bench a mile south of Aneroid Lake. It is named for one of Oregon's most prominent biologists. Stanley G. Jewett was born in New Brunswick, Canada in 1885. He was a collector for the Field Museum in Chicago and for the U.S. Biological

Survey in the Pacific Northwest. In 1916 he was permanently employed by the agency which later became the U.S. Fish and Wildlife Service and he continued with them until his retirement in 1949. He made numerous collection trips in the Wallowa Mountains and hundreds of his specimens are in the National Museum of Natural History in Washington, D.C. and the U.S. Fish and Wildlife Service Collection. He was co-author of *Birds of Oregon* and collaborated on *Birds of Washington*. He died in Portland in 1955.

Jim Creek, JEFFERSON. Jim Creek is tributary to Awbrey Creek near Hay Creek Ranch. It was named because Jim Scates, Jim Connelly and Jim Howell all settled along its banks. The name Calivan Creek is wrong.

Jim Creek, WALLOWA. This stream enters Snake River in the northeast part of the county, about seven miles south of the Oregon-Washington state line. J. H. Horner informed the compiler that it bears the name of James Wright, who attempted to cross the creek on a small footlog, lost his balance and fell in. This was in the late 1870s. He squatted on a claim near the creek, ranged cattle there and started to build a log cabin on the place.

Jim Hunt Creek, CURRY. James M. Hunt was a gold seeker of 1853 and prominent pioneer settler near the mouth of Rogue River. He is mentioned in *Pioneer History of Coos and Curry Counties*. Jim Hunt Creek bears the name of this pioneer. It flows into Rogue River from the south about six miles northeast of Gold Beach. Hunt Rock at Wedderburn is named for the same man.

Jimtown, BAKER. Jimtown is a small community, once known as Langrell, located two miles northwest of Halfway. It is named for James H. Chandler who operated the local store from 1910 to 1916. The original town was started by Richard Langrell, an early Baker County resident and the man for whom Langrell Gulch was named. Langrell built the store building in 1904 and operated the facility until he sold to Chandler in 1910. The USGS Halfway quadrangle of 1956 used the name Langrell but that was corrected on the 1987 Jimtown quadrangle.

Jobs Garden, DOUGLAS. USFS ranger Fred Asam named this spot on the north bank of North Umpqua River west of Steamboat because the jumble of rocks and boulders was reminiscent of the Bible story.

Jockey Cap, CLATSOP. The name Jockey Cap has been applied to a prominent monolith standing close to the shore at a point a little south of Silver Point. The rock is plainly visible both from the beach and from the Oregon Coast Highway, and should be viewed from the southeast to get the characteristic appearance. The visor of the cap points to the southwest.

Joe Ney Slough, COOS. This slough is a tributary of South Slough of Coos Bay. S. B. Cathcart of Marshfield informed the compiler in 1929 that Joe Ney settled on the slough in pioneer days. He later went to Elk River in Curry County and bred horses. He died many years prior to 1929.

Joes Point, WASCO. This promontory three miles northeast of Fivemile Butte was named for Joe White, a very early USFS employee.

John Creek, DOUGLAS. Grover C. Blake of Roseburg told the compiler this story of place-name shuffling. John Creek is tributary to North Umpqua River in T 26S, R 1W. It was originally named Wright Creek for Perry Wright, an early settler who had a nearby timber claim. The next creek to the west was named Johnson Creek for another timber claimant but the names were switched in error by map makers. As there was already a Johnson Creek a few miles to the northeast near Johnson Butte, the newly switched name was abbreviated to John Creek.

John Day, GRANT. The town of John Day in Grant County took its name from John Day River. The post office, with the name John Day City, was established Jan. 20, 1865, with Abraham Himes first postmaster. This office was discontinued in Mar. 1871. The office was reestablished in July 1879, with the name John Day. For a good many years there was a station on the railroad just west of the mouth of John Day River in Sherman County called John Day, but due to confusion in shipments, the name was changed to Day. Similar difficulties with John Day station at the mouth of John Day River in Clatsop County resulted in a change to Van Dusen, for a well-known county family.

John Day River, CLATSOP. This stream, like the other of the same name, in eastern Oregon, was named for John Day of the Astor-Hunt overland party of 1811–12. For information about him, *see* John Day River, Gilliam County. John Day Point, just east of the river, takes its name from the stream. Lewis and Clark mention the river in their journals for Nov. 27, 1805, and give an Indian name *Kekemarke*. Wilkes, in *U.S. Exploring Expedition*, v. 23, Hydrography, atlas, shows this as Swan Creek. There was formerly a railroad station near this river, originally called John Day, but some years later changed to Van Dusen, in honor of the pioneer family of Astoria.

John Day River, GILLIAM, GRANT, JEFFERSON, SHERMAN, UMATILLA, WASCO, WHEELER. John Day River is one of the important rivers of Oregon, but due to the fact that it drains an area with little rainfall, the stream does not deliver much water. If it is remarkable in this respect, it is still more so for the great amount of suspended material it carries from its drainage basin. Measured in tons per square mile, the John Day carries off 198 a year, or practically double that of any other important stream in the state. (This calculation is at Dayville.) Its total delivery at the Columbia is more than 750,000 tons of suspended matter a year. It bears the name of John Day (1771–1819) of the Astor overland party. John Day was a Virginia backwoodsman. He was a member of the Astor-Hunt overland party, and he and Ramsay Crooks fell behind the main party in the Snake River country in the winter of 1811–12. They had several terrible experiences, but eventually got through the snow of the Blue Mountains and fell in with friendly Walla Walla Indians. These Indians aided the wanderers and sent them on their way down the Columbia River. In the vicinity of the mouth of John Day River Crooks and Day met hostile Indians who robbed them, even of their clothes. The two naked men started back to the Walla Walla country, but fortunately were rescued by Robert

Stuart's party which was descending the Columbia. John Day's name was applied to the Oregon river apparently because it was near the mouth of the stream that the two men were attacked. According to one account John Day went insane in Astoria in 1814 and was buried there, but T. C. Elliott cites McKenzie's statement that Day died in the Snake River country in 1820. *See OHQ*, v. 17, p. 373. Lewis and Clark named this stream Lepages River on Oct. 21, 1805, after one of their party. John Work uses the name Day's River in his journal for June 25, 1825. (*Washington Historical Quarterly*, v. 5, p. 86.) Peter Skene Ogden mentions John Day's river by that name Nov. 29, 1825. (*OHQ*, v. 10, p. 337.) For editorial by Harvey W. Scott showing impossibilities of Mrs. S. A. Weeks of Sherwood being daughter of John Day, *see* the *Oregonian*, Jan. 10, 1910. The fossil beds of the John Day country are among the most important in America. John Day Dam on the Columbia River just downstream from the mouth of John Day River was completed in 1968. It is a 105-foot-high concrete gravity structure impounding Lake Umatilla. The power-house generating capacity in 1979 was 2,160,000 kw.

John Henry Lake, WALLOWA. This lake was named for John Henry Wilson of Wallowa, who had mining interests nearby. It is in T 3S, R 43E.

John P. Amacher Park, DOUGLAS. This county park along North Umpqua River at Winchester is named for John P. Amacher who was born in Switzerland and came to America in 1920. He was a well-known citizen of Douglas County and one of the organizers of the Douglas County Parks Department. Amacher died in 1978, age 82 years. *See* Roseburg *News-Review*, June 19, 1978.

John Smith Island, BENTON. This is an island in the Willamette River south of Corvallis. It was named for a prominent citizen of Benton County, who lived in Corvallis for many years. He owned the island and other land in the vicinity.

Johnnie Spring, DOUGLAS. This spring near the headwaters of Cavitt Creek was named for John Rondeau, an early USFS employee. Rondeau Butte was named for the same man.

Johnny Cake Mountain, GRANT. In 1989, Ron Miller of Hillsboro told the compiler the origin of the name of this flat topped mountain seven miles north of Monument. His grandfather, John Westfall, a teenager, was herding sheep nearby about 1910. The mountain lies just north of the line between townships 7 and 8s, R 28E. When a survey crew asked the name, Westfall replied that it looked like a stack of cakes. The survey crew added his given name. In 1946, a USC&GS crew doing first order traverse established a triangulation station named Cake on the west edge of the summit.

Johnny Kirk Spring, GRANT. This spring is on John Day Highway, north of Dayville. It bears the name of an eccentric pioneer who settled in the John Day Valley, after taking part in the '49 gold rush to California. He came to Oregon about 1870. In the winter he lived in his bachelor's cabin near the spring that now bears his name; during the summer he mined and prospected in the Blue Mountains. He was popular because of his inveterate story-telling.

Johns Landing, MULTNOMAH. Johns Landing is a commercial and residential area built up along sw Macadam Street in southwest Portland. Prior to World War II this was a manufacturing and distributing area but these uses declined. The B. P. John Furniture Company was the largest operation and several of B. P. John's descendants bought up surrounding property and commenced the development of a 60-acre private urban-renewal project. John Storrs was the architect and John D. Gray the leading principal and the name, Johns Landing, was a logical consequence of the combination.

Johnson, LINCOLN. Johnson post office was at the Parmele place about half a mile up Drift Creek from the mouth of that stream on the east side of Siletz Bay. The office was established Mar. 11, 1899, with George S. Parmele first and only postmaster. The office was closed May 23, 1903, and what business there was was turned over to Kernville. Parmele operated a general store. The office was named in compliment to Jakie and Sissy Johnson, a local Indian couple, well and favorably known. Jakie is said to have been a Siletz Indian, but his wife was from California. The Johnsons held land by patent and part of the town of Taft is on property owned by the pair.

Johnson Canyon, MORROW. This canyon runs north into Little Butter Creek northwest of Lena. It was named for Felix Johnson, Sr., who settled near its mouth. Both he and his son, Felix, Jr., were well-known sheep men.

Johnson City, CLACKAMAS. Johnson City near Gladstone was incorporated by a 49 to 10 vote on June 16, 1970. At the time of the election it had the distinction of being owned entirely by one man, Delbert Johnson. Johnson started the development as a trailer court in 1959 and tried without success to have the 45-acre area annexed to Gladstone in 1968. The 1969 Oregon Legislature established a boundary review board to prevent a proliferation of small incorporated cities but the proponents had filed for an election before the effective date of the law. For further details, *see* the *Oregon Journal*, June 11, 1970, and the *Oregonian*, June 17, 1970.

Johnson Creek, CLACKAMAS, MULTNOMAH. U.S. land surveyors named this stream for William Johnson, a pioneer of 1846, who settled near what is now Lents, and there built a sawmill in the 1850s. Scott's *History of the Oregon Country* gives some additional facts and also has information about Johnson's sons Jacob and Jasper W. Johnson. *See also* the *Oregon Journal*, Aug. 20, 1934, editorial page.

Johnson Creek, COOS. Johnson Creek empties into Templeton Arm of Tenmile Lake. It is named for Stephen Johnson who homesteaded near the site of Templeton in the 1880s. Johnson operated an early grist mill and at one time Tenmile Lake was called Johnson Lake.

Johnson Creek, CROOK. Johnson Creek is west of Mill Creek and empties into Ochoco Creek east of Prineville. It is named for Ewen Johnson who came to Oregon in 1865. In 1867 he joined George Barnes in the Mill Creek area where they cut logs. Later both brought their families from the Willamette Valley.

Johnson Creek, GRANT, WHEELER. This stream flows into John Day River about 10 miles southeast of Spray. It was named for Henry Johnson, a pioneer stock man who settled near the mouth of the stream in the 1870s.

Johnson Creek, MORROW. This stream in the Butter Creek drainage south of Vinson was named for the well-known family of Felix Johnson, a native of Ireland. Johnson arrived in Morrow County in the 1870s with his two sons, Felix and James. They were well-known local stockmen and the creek was probably named for James Johnson whose own holdings were near its mouth.

Johnson Creek, MULTNOMAH. This stream, which formerly flowed from the neighborhood of Barnes Road across the northern part of Portland, has been partly confined to a drainage sewer and is no longer visible outside of the canyon west of Washington Park. It was named for Arthur Harrison Johnson, a leading meat dealer of Portland for many years. He arrived in Portland in 1852 and soon formed a partnership with Richard S. Perkins in the butcher business. In 1862 Perkins retired but Johnson continued and enlarged the business. His slaughterhouses were in the neighborhood of Twenty-third and Flanders streets, Portland. For information about Johnson, *see* Scott's *History of the Oregon Country*, v. 2, pp. 82 and 273, and for his obituary, *see* the *Oregonian*, Apr. 30, 1902.

Johnson Creek, UMATILLA. James Johnson took up property along this creek on upper McKay Creek drainage in 1917.

Johnson Creek, WALLOWA. This is a small tributary of Imnaha River from the east at a point about 25 miles east of Wallowa Lake. It was named for one Tom Johnson, who took up a homestead along the stream and ranged cattle there.

Johnson Heights, WHEELER. Hugh S. Johnson homesteaded in 1900 about eight miles north of Waterman at the north end of this prominent ridge.

Johnson Meadow, KLAMATH. BLM records show that in 1917, William E. Johnson filed on this land in sections 1 and 12, T 27S, R 9E. The filing was cancelled.

Johnson Meadows, LANE. These meadows in the Bohemia district were named for James Johnson, the discoverer of the Bohemia Mine. For further information, *see* Bohemia Mountain.

Johnson Mountain, COOS. Johnson Mountain is in the southwest part of the county and Johnson Creek flows around it on the south. These two geographic features were named for a pioneer miner, "Coarse Gold" Johnson, who discovered gold nearby in rich nuggets in 1854. The *Coos Bay News*, Aug. 31, 1887, contains an item to the effect that George Bailey had recently found the remains of a man in the woods south of Sixes River. The remains were identified as those of "Coarse Gold" Johnson, who discovered gold on what was later called Johnson Creek.

Johnson Prairie, JACKSON, KLAMATH. This prairie and the creek of the same name on the county line east of Howard Prairie Lake were named for Cal Johnson who settled there in early days.

Johnston Creek, LANE. Johnston Creek is tributary to Lake Creek below Greenleaf. It is named for James Johnston, a native of Ireland, who came to

Oregon in 1884. He homesteaded near this creek and lived there until his death in 1928. The spelling Johnson is wrong.

Jones Butte, UNION. Jones Butte is 3295 feet high and is about two miles north of Elgin. It is named for John E. Jones who was born in Wales in 1818 and emigrated first to the United States and then to the Pacific Northwest. In 1875 he brought his family across the Blue Mountains from Walla Walla and settled by the butte near Elgin or as it was then called, Indian Valley. Jones died in 1889. This information was provided in 1975 by his granddaughter, Ethel M. Chandler.

Jones Creek, JOSEPHINE. Jones Creek is a tributary of Rogue River, about two miles east of Grants Pass. John K. Jones was a pioneer settler near the banks of this stream and it was named in his honor. He and his wife were killed by Indians, and their heirs subsequently owned the claim.

Jones Creek, LANE. According to A. J. Briem, long time USFS ranger, this small tributary of upper Fall Creek was named for early settler Allison W. Jones.

Jones Hill, MORROW. Henry Jones who was born in England in 1834 settled southwest of Lena in the 1870s and this hill and nearby canyon both carry his name.

Jonesboro, MALHEUR. This station was named for William Jones, a local cattleman. The place is between Juntura and Harper, on the Union Pacific Railroad.

Jont Creek, POLK. Jont Creek is a small stream that rises in the extreme south border of the county and flows northeastward through Airlie. It was named for one Jont Williams, an early day homesteader in the vicinity.

Joppa, WASHINGTON. The *Pacific Monthly and Official Gazette*, date uncertain, but probably about 1880, contains the following: "Joppa is not the celebrated place where the timber was floated to build King Solomon's Temple, but a discontinued post office eight miles northwest of Forest Grove. A migratory peddler was the postmaster. The authorities in Washington City having learned that he carried the post office in his pocket, concluded it was rather an inaccessible place for the numerous population of Joppa to obtain their mail, and discontinued the office." The compiler has not been able to get much additional information about this post office except that it was established Mar. 13, 1874, with Alvin C. Brown the first of three postmasters. The office was closed July 5, 1876. It has been impossible to get the exact location of the office. It seems probable that the office was named by a biblical enthusiast. The original Joppa was one of the most ancient seaports of the world, on the coast of the Holy Land about 35 miles northwest of Jerusalem. The spelling of the more modern community on the coast of Israel is generally given as Jaffa.

Jordan Butte, MORROW. Jordan Butte just south of Ione was named for John Jordan who settled near the mouth of Rhea Creek in 1865. Jordan Canyon takes its name from the butte.

Jordan Craters, MALHEUR. Jordan Craters are a volcanic field located in a depression of the Owyhee Plateau about 30 miles west of Jordan Valley. Geologists estimate the most recent lava flow from the craters may have been between 4000 and 9000 years ago. For a detailed description, *see* Oregon Department of Geology and Mineral Industries *The Ore Bin*, v. 39, no. 8, Aug. 1977. The craters include a variety of volcanic features with Coffeepot Crater one of the more interesting.

Jordan Creek, CURRY. This creek east of Brookings was named for Robert Jordan who homesteaded nearby in the 1870s.

Jordan Creek, LANE. Jordan Creek flows into Coyote Creek about four miles upstream from Crow. Some maps show this stream with the name Jorden Creek, but in Dec. 1945, Merle Nighswander, an old timer of the vicinity, wrote the compiler that the correct spelling was Jordan. Mr. Nighswander added that the name was that of an early-day squatter on the banks of the creek.

Jordan Point, COOS. When USGS mapped the Coos Bay quadrangle in 1895–96, it applied the name Jordan Point to a feature on the east side of Coos Bay north of the mouth of Kentuck Slough. This name was supposed to be derived from James Jordan, an early settler who ranged Kentuck Slough as a hunter for the North Bend mill. *See* Dodge's *Pioneer History of Coos and Curry Counties*, p. 358. When the area was remapped nearly a half century later it was found that the name Jordan Point had wandered off to a low promontory on the north side of the bay just west of the Southern Pacific Company railroad. In 1866 Jordan took up government land at this point and what is now the adjacent Jordan Cove while four years later he bought property at the first mentioned location on the east side of the bay. It appears he may be entitled to have his name on both sides but in the 1970s the western position was firmly established and prominently identified by one of the largest wood chip loading facilities in Oregon. The eastern feature is now known as Glasgow Point. For further information, *see* Glasgow.

Jordan Valley, LINN. Jordan Valley is just south of North Santiam River, but it does not drain to that stream. Jordan Creek carries the waters of the valley southward into Thomas Creek, which flows into South Santiam River west of Scio. Local tradition says that Jordan Valley was named by Linn County's famous pioneer circuit rider, Joab Powell, in compliment to the Valley of the Jordan in the Holy Land. Many years ago there was a post office called Jordan on the lower reaches of Jordan Creek. This office was established Aug. 10, 1874, with Elias Forgey first of six postmasters. The office was closed out to Scio Oct. 21, 1905. This was due to the extension of rural free delivery. Most maps show this office close to the mouth of Jordan Creek, but it may have wandered around a little.

Jordan Valley, MALHEUR. Jordan Valley is the name of a post office in Jordan Valley on the banks of Jordan Creek, which is a tributary of Owyhee River. The stream was named for Michael M. Jordan who was the leader of a party that discovered gold on its banks in May 1863. Shortly thereafter, in 1864, he was killed in an Indian fight in the Owyhee country. *See* Bancroft's *History of Washington, Idaho, and Montana*.

Jory Basin, JEFFERSON. Jory Basin west of Ashwood was the location of the 1888 pre-emption claim of Lorinda P. Jory. Mrs. Jory was the daughter of A. H. Crooks and the wife of Stephen J. Jory. Crooks and Jory were murdered by Lucius Langdon near Grizzly in Mar. 1882 as the aftermath of a property dispute. Langdon was apprehended and a day or so later shot by a lynch mob in Prineville who also hanged a supposed accomplice named W. H. Harrison.

Jory Hill, MARION. Jory Hill, with an elevation of 737 feet, is southwest of Salem. Several members of the Jory family settled in this neighborhood in pioneer days on donation land claims, and the hill was named for them.

Joseph, WALLOWA. Joseph is a town in the Wallowa Valley and is named for Chief Joseph, (1837–1904), who claimed the valley as his ancestral home, which brought on a war with the whites, which resulted in Joseph's retreat to Montana. For details of his life, see Chief Joseph Mountain. Joseph Creek in Wallowa County also bears his name. In Jan. 1944, J. H. Horner of Enterprise told the compiler that the community of Joseph was first called Silver Lake and also Lake City. When the post office was established on Apr. 23, 1880 these two names were suggested but postal authorities would not accept them because of duplication with other Oregon places. Matt Johnson then suggested the name Joseph, which was accepted.

Josephine County. Josephine County was created Jan. 22, 1856, from a western part of Jackson County. It now has an area of 1631 square miles. It was probably named for Josephine Rollins, who was the daughter of the discoverer of gold in the Josephine Creek that bears her name, according to H. H. Bancroft, (*History of Oregon*, v. 2, pp. 415 and 713). This is confirmed by Walling, on p. 447 of his *History of Southern Oregon*, who says that Josephine County received its name from Josephine Creek, which was named for Josephine Rollins. Further confirmation is contained in a letter from the woman herself, dated Feb. 19, 1909, a copy of which is in possession of the Oregon Historical Society. She signs herself Virginia Josephine Rollins Ort, and says she was born in Morgan County, Illinois, in 1833. In 1850 the family started for California from Missouri, but finally landed in Oregon. The family again started for California in 1851, and several members, including Miss Rollins, went into the valley of the Illinois River near the stream that bears her name. Mrs. Ort says as far as she knew she was the first white woman in that part of Oregon, and that the county was named for her. She was married in 1854 to Julius Ort, in Colusa County, California, and in 1863 moved to Sonora County, where she was living at the time she wrote the letter. Walling's statement that Miss Rollins' married name was O'Kelly does not seem to be correct. According to Geo. H. Parker (letter to the *Oregonian*, Nov. 2, 1913), Josephine Rollins was then (1913) living at Sonoma, California; Parker wrote that he had received a photograph of her taken when she was 45 years of age; that she was the sister of the wife of Jacob Thompson, of Ashland; that she came with her father, in 1851, to the county now bearing her name. In 1846 a girl named Martha Leland Crowley died on what has since been called Grave Creek. The legislature, by act of Jan. 6, 1854, tried to change the name to Leland Creek, in honor of Miss Crowley (see *Special Laws* of legislature, p. 19). The general public never adopted the new name and the stream is still called Grave Creek. Assertions that Miss Crowley's first name was Josephine and that the county may have been named for her do not seem to be substantiated by the available records. Josephine Rollins was the first white woman who made her abode there, so that the name of the county is probably hers. For history of the grave of Martha Leland Crowley, by C. P. Fullerton, *see* the *Oregonian*, Nov. 23, 1883; by James W. Nesmith, Nov. 23, 1883: p. 2; by Matthew P. Deady, Dec. 5, 1883.

Josephine Creek, JOSEPHINE. This is a tributary of Illinois River west of Kerby. According to Bancroft's *History of Oregon*, v. 2, p. 713, it was named for Josephine Rollins, who was a daughter of the man who discovered gold in the creek. In another place, v. 2, p. 227, note 38, Bancroft makes the conflicting statement that Josephine Creek was named for Josephine Kirby whose father discovered gold nearby. The compiler has been unable to reconcile these statements, and in view of what is known about Josephine Rollins, suspects that the story of Josephine Kirby is wrong or possibly a typographical error. For further information, *see* Josephine County.

Joy, WALLOWA. Joy was a pioneer post office near the Findley Buttes, about 15 miles airline northeast of Enterprise. J. H. Horner told the compiler in 1931 that the office was named because of the joy settlers expressed at the possibility of mail service. These people did not then know about chain letters and junk mail. Newton W. Brumback was the first postmaster at Joy, in 1888.

Judd Creek, DOUGLAS. Judd Creek rises northwest of Nickel Mountain and flows to South Umpqua River north of Riddle. It is named for William W. Judd whose donation land claim straddled the stream. George Abdill of Roseburg told the compiler in 1979 that Judd came to Douglas County in 1852 and lived there until 1869 when he died as the result of being kicked by a horse. Abdill added that there is a reverse curve on the railroad where it crosses Judd Creek. About 1900 there was a bad collision between two light engines, the result of a train order mixup.

Judkins Point, LANE. Judkins Point, in the east part of Eugene, was named for Thomas H. Judkins, who settled on a farm just east of the promontory in 1853. Judkins was born in New York in 1803 and came to Oregon in 1851. He settled first near Monroe. He died in 1878.

Judson Rock Creek, LANE. This creek empties into Sharps Creek in S 16, T 23S, R 1E. Judson Rock is about a mile to the northeast in section 10. They both take their names from Frank Judson Hard, a miner from Colorado, who came to the Bohemia District in the 1890s. He purchased a number of claims and was active in the area until his death in 1920. For more information, *see Facts and Yarns of the Bohemia, Oregon Gold Mines* by Ray Nelson.

Judson Rocks, MARION. These rocks are in Willamette River about two miles northwest of Sidney. They were named for L. H. Judson, a nearby landowner of pioneer days.

Jump Off Joe Peak, GRANT. The Pacific Northwest has a near monopoly on features named Jump Off Joe. Oregon and Washington each have seven and the only other one in the 48 contiguous states is in California. Jump Off Joe Peak is a sharp ridge three miles south of Desolation Butte. In the early days an important sheep driveway ran along this ridge to the east end where there was a precipitous drop that required careful herding. The name was in common use among the sheep herders. This information was provided in 1974 by A. G. Oard, supervisor of the Malheur National Forest.

Jumpoff Joe Creek, JOSEPHINE. Jumpoff Joe Creek is in the extreme northeast corner of the county. I-5 crosses it south of Sexton Mountain. James W. Nesmith, in a letter printed in the *Oregonian* for Nov. 23, 1883, says the stream was named for an exploit of Joe McLoughlin, in 1837 or 1839, but does not state the nature of the exploit. McLoughlin died Dec. 14, 1848. Data in possession of Oregon Historical Society indicate the naming of the stream probably took place in 1828 rather than at the time mentioned by Colonel Nesmith. Joe McLoughlin, son of Dr. John McLoughlin, was in southern Oregon in a trapping party under the leadership of Alexander R. McLeod. The trappers camped one night on this stream and McLoughlin, who came in after dark, fell over the edge of the bluff and received very severe injuries, which, it is said, subsequently caused his death. Myron Eells gives this as the correct origin of the name, and practically the same facts are printed in *West Shore*, Oct. 1883, p. 26. Other stories about this name do not seem to be substantiated by historical records.

Junction City, LANE. About 1870 when the railroad construction war was being waged in the Willamette Valley, Ben Holladay had a scheme to build a west side railroad. It was to join his east side line at a point in the Willamette Valley, not further south than Eugene. Junction City was selected to be the place where the two roads were to come together. The west side railroad was not built according to plans and as a result the city never became a junction for railroad traffic, but 50 years later it did become a junction of the east and west branches of the Pacific Highway through the Willamette Valley. The name, therefore, is now quite appropriate.

June, LANE. June post office, which was situated on the upper reaches of Lost Creek south of Dexter, was established Jan. 3, 1899, with Malinda Mathews first postmaster. The office was discontinued Sept. 18, 1907, and the business was turned over to Zion, which was a few miles north down Lost Creek. June post office was named for Mount June, a prominent point to the southeast. Mount June was named because snow generally lies on its summit and slopes until that month of the year.

Juniper, UMATILLA. Juniper is a station on the Union Pacific Railroad, in the extreme north part of the county, close to the Columbia River. It is just north of the mouth of Juniper Canyon, which drains a considerable area north of Hold-man. These features were named for the scattering juniper trees of the locality. Juniper post office was established June 26, 1884, with John B. Davis first postmaster. Except for a period from June 1894, to Mar. 1898, this office was in service until Jan. 31, 1912, though it appears to have been in several different places, never very far from Juniper Canyon.

Juniper Butte, JEFFERSON. Juniper Butte is just south of Culver. It is a prominent feature on the landscape, and has a rather peculiar concavity on the north, like a natural amphitheater on a large scale. The compiler is unable to determine why it should have been called for the juniper tree any more than several other buttes in the neighborhood which have as many of these trees growing on their slopes. The juniper of Oregon is *Juniperus occidentalis*, or western juniper.

Juniper Mountain, LANE. Juniper Mountain is the high point on the west end of Juniper Ridge fifteen miles southeast of Oakridge. It is not named for the eastern Oregon *Juniperus occidentalis* but for an entirely different tree, the dwarf *Juniperus communis* which grows in most sub-alpine areas of western Oregon. This tree is distinguished from other junipers by its dark, lustrous green, keenly pointed leaves or needles as opposed to the scaly gray green leaves of *Juniperus occidentalis*. See Sudworth, *Forest Trees of the Pacific Slope*, p. 176, *et seq*.

Junkins Cemetery, MORROW. William E. Junkins homesteaded southeast of Valby in 1883. When he died in 1887, his family donated this plot of land for a cemetery which now has 15 or 16 graves.

Juntura, MALHEUR. *Juntura* is the Spanish word for juncture. It was applied to a community in Malheur County because it was near the junction of the North Fork with the main Malheur River. The name is said to have been selected by B. L. Milligan who settled in the locality in the early 1880s and was later county school superintendent. Juntura post office was established May 5, 1890 with Edw. Ashley first postmaster. After World War II development flagged and on Nov. 2, 1976, the town voted 29 to 1 to disincorporate.

Kah-Nee-Ta, JEFFERSON. Kah-Nee-Ta Vacation Resort is north of Warm Springs on Warm Springs River. Once privately owned, it was acquired in the early 1960s by the Warm Springs Tribal Council and developed as one of their self-governed activities. The compiler does not know the time or circumstances of the naming but Kah-Nee-Ta was in use prior to World War II. In 1966, Vern Jackson, Tribal Secretary, said the name meant "gift of the Gods" in Warm Springs dialect but the writer believes this is modern paraphrase.

Kaleetan Butte, DESCHUTES. This butte near Devils Lake is named with the Chinook jargon word for arrow.

Kamela, UNION. The compiler has been furnished with several explanations as to how this community got its name, and there is much discrepancy in the various stories that are told. Several early residents of northeastern Oregon say that the word was made up by combining the initials of civil engineers during railroad construction but this is not agreed to by other equally reliable pioneers who say that the word is Cayuse Indian for a tree. Kamela was, during the stagecoach period, known as Summit Station. This was unsatisfactory to the railroad company and J. C. Mayo of Stayton informed the compiler in 1927 that Dr. W. C. McKay was asked to furnish a number of names of Indian origin which could be used at various points on the line. From this list Kamela was selected. Mr. Mayo said it meant black pine, although as far as the compiler knows there are not many of these trees in the neighborhood. The official interpreter at Umatilla Agency said in 1927 that *kamela* was a Nez Perce word meaning tamarack, and this ought to settle the matter. Miss L. C. McKay, daughter of Dr. McKay, was certain that the word means summit. There was at one time a station on the railroad known as Mikecha, which was made up from the names of three civil engineers, Mink, Kennedy and Chalk, and the writer is of the opinion that this name has been confused with Kamela by those who think that Kamela was a compiled name. Mikecha was at or near the station now known as Gibbon.

Kane Creek, JACKSON. According to Walling, in *History of Southern Oregon*, p. 377, the stream near Gold Hill was named for a Doctor Kane who settled nearby in 1853. It was at one time known as T'Vault Creek for W. G. T'Vault, Oregon's pioneer editor, who lived at Dardanelles, near what is now Gold Hill.

Kane Springs, HOOD RIVER. Kane Springs just east of Bonney Meadows was named by USFS ranger Eric Gordon for his wife whose maiden name was Marion Kane.

Kansas City, WASHINGTON. Kansas City is the name of a crossroads community about six miles north-northwest of Forest Grove. It is said that the name was applied because some settlers from Kansas City, Missouri, established themselves there. The writer has not been able to find the name Kansas City on the Washington County post office list and apparently the locality never had a post office called Kansas City.

Kapka Butte, DESCHUTES. This butte near Tumalo Mountain was named with the Klamath Indian word for lodgepole pine.

Karl Lake, LANE. Karl Lake and nearby Ruth Lake are at the base of Lowder Mountain on the headwaters of East Fork McKenzie River. They were named to honor Karl W. Onthank and his wife, Ruth. Onthank was born in New Jersey but came to Oregon as a boy and entered the University of Oregon in 1909. After graduation, he joined the staff of the University where he spent his entire professional career. In additon to his university duties, he was active in many civic and outdoor organizations and, with his wife, a tireless worker for conservation and wilderness preservation. He died on Oct. 27, 1967 in Eugene and Ruth MacLaren Onthank died Apr. 14, 1978. The names of both lakes were approved by the USBGN in *Decision List 8902*.

Karlson Island, CLATSOP. Karlson Island is in the south part of Columbia

River near Knappa. It has been variously known as Carlson, Carlsen and Karlson. Arthur Dempsie of Astoria informed the compiler that the United States issued a patent on the land on the island in Dec. 1892, running to the name of Karl Karlson. The property was apparently a homestead. The transaction is filed in Clatsop County Transfer Records, v. 26, p. 84, Government certificate 2576. In 1941 Mrs. Karlson was still alive and vigorous. The USBGN has adopted the spelling Karlson, although some of the younger members of the family spell the name Carlson.

Kaser Butte, JEFFERSON. Kaser Butte, in the eastern part of the county on the upper reaches of Muddy Creek, is named for Jacob "Jake" Kaser. Kaser was born in Glarus, Switzerland in 1868, and emigrated to the United States in 1888. He came to eastern Oregon in 1893, and started in the sheep business. By the turn of the century he had aquired considerable acreage including the Grimes ranch at the base of the butte that now bears his name. Kaser died in Portland in 1948. The *OHQ*, v. 81, pp. 281, *et seq.*, has an interesting autobiography with many details of ranching in the area. Julius Kaser of The Dalles was a younger brother.

Kaser Ridge, WASCO. In 1913 Julius Kaser moved onto this high ground on the south bank of Columbia River about five miles east of The Dalles. The USC&GS established a triangulation station named Kaser on the ridge in 1930, but the name Kaser Ridge was first officially applied by the USGS in 1960 when they needed a designation for a water survey.

Kaskela, WASCO. This is a railway station on the east side of Deschutes River in the south part of the county. The name was suggested by Malcolm A. Moody. Kaskela was the first Warm Springs Indian chief after the establishment of the agency. He was a signatory of the Treaty of June 25, 1855 as chief of The Dalles Branch of the 'Wascoes' where his name is written Cush Kella.

Katsuk Butte, DESCHUTES. This butte, west of Sparks Lake in the Cascade Range, was named with the Chinook jargon word for middle, presumably because of its location. There is another Katsuk Butte in Lane County five miles southeast of Blue River.

Kawak Butte, DESCHUTES. This butte in Paulina Mountains was named with the Chinook jargon word meaning to fly. The name was selected arbitrarily by the USFS.

Keasey, COLUMBIA. Keasey was named for a local settler, Eden W. Keasey, who was instrumental in securing the post office. This office was established on Aug. 5, 1890, with Keasey the first postmaster. In 1924 the writer was informed that Keasey had moved from the community some years before.

Keating, BAKER. "Uncle Tom" Keating, a jovial British sailor, was one of the first settlers in this community, and owned much of the adjacent land, although he lost most of it in subsequent financial reverses. The office was established about 1880.

Keck Canyon, MORROW. Keck Canyon was apparently named for Edward Keck who, before World War I, settled near where it empties into Rhea Creek.

Keen, WASCO. A post office with the name Keen was established Apr. 14, 1911, with Owen Jones postmaster. The office was closed Mar. 31, 1912 but there is some question as to how long it was in actual operation. The compiler has tried unsuccessfully to get the significance of the name but there is an unconfirmed report that prospective patrons thought it "keen" that they would have postal service. Judge Fred W. Wilson informed the compiler that Owen Jones, who was later murdered, lived near the intersection of the Tygh Ridge road and the old road leading from The Dalles southeast to Sherars Bridge. For a short biography of Jones, *see Illustrated History of Central Oregon*, p. 367.

Keene Creek, JACKSON. This stream was named for Granville Keene, who was killed nearby by Rogue River Indians about Sept. 1, 1855. The spellings Keen, Kean and Keane are incorrect.

Keener Gulch, WALLOWA. This canyon running south into Imnaha River in T 4S, R 48E, takes its name from the G. W. Keener homestead near its mouth.

Keeps Mill, WASCO. Keeps Mill Camp of the USFS commemorates Joseph R. Keep who just after the turn of the century had a sawmill where Clear Creek flows into White River.

Keeton Creek, WHEELER. Keeton Creek is tributary to Mountain Creek south of Waterman. It was apparently named for James L. Keeton who took up a homestead in 1887 about two miles above its mouth. Keeton was mayor of Mitchell in 1898.

Keizer, MARION. Keizer is a city on the east bank of Willamette River north of Salem. For many years it was considered a suburb of Salem and Keizer post office, established in 1948, was a Salem Rural station. In 1982, the community incorporated and in 1989 had a population of 20,160. It was named for T. D. and J. B. Keizer, pioneers of Oregon, who took up donation land claims nearby in early days. Thomas D. Keizer (Kaizur) was born in Buncombe County, North Carolina, in 1793. In 1828 he moved to Giles County, Tennessee; in 1833 to Van Buren County, Arkansas. He died in 1871. He was an active leader of the 1843 emigration. He was a member of the legislative committee of 1844, of the provisional government.

Kelleher, DOUGLAS. Kelleher post office, a few miles west of Yoncalla, was named for William J. Kelleher, a native of County Cork, Ireland, who was an early settler in Douglas County, Oregon. He acquired a number of holdings, including a sawmill at a place he named for himself. The post office was established Apr. 5, 1904, with William H. Sykes first postmaster. Kelleher sold to an eastern lumbering concern, headed by one Skelley, and the name of the office was changed to Skelley, Dec. 21, 1904. The office was discontinued Oct. 31, 1910.

Kelley Point, MULTNOMAH. On Jan. 6, 1926, the USBGN, at the request of several citizens of Portland bestowed the name Kelley Point on the projection of land between the Columbia River and the Willamette River. This projection is the north point of Pearcy Island, and up to 1926 had no name. It once was the site of a small lighthouse. This action on the part of the Board was taken in honor of Hall

J. Kelley, a prominent character in the early exploration of Oregon. About 1817, Kelley, who was a Boston school teacher, began to work on behalf of the development of the Oregon country. He was an enthusiastic eccentric and as early as 1820 began to publish pamphlets on Oregon. He addressed memorials to Congress on Oregon, worked up schemes for colonizing the country, talked Oregon and wrote Oregon, in season and out, until he succeeded in drawing the attention of "many persons in public and private life." In 1830 he issued *A Geographical Sketch of Oregon*, which contained 80 pages and a map. Space does not permit a full discussion of Kelley and his difficulty in reaching Oregon, which he did in 1834. Five years before, in 1829, he drew up a plan for a city in Oregon on the peninsula between the Columbia and Willamette rivers. Real estate men note with interest the prescience of this gentleman 100 years ago. He even got out a "prospectus." He left Oregon in 1835 and died in Massachusetts in 1874, still writing about Oregon at the age of 85 years. It is appropriate to attach Hall J. Kelley's name to the point where he predicted there would be a great city. The development of Portland is ample vindication of Kelley's judgment and nationally known docks and shipyards are within a few miles of the spot he chose for his metropolis. In 1979 the City of Portland acquired 96 acres from the Port of Portland including frontage on both the Willamette and Columbia Rivers and Kelley Point. This has been developed as Kelley Point Park for picnic and day use. For information about Kelley's proposal to name mountain peaks in Oregon after various presidents, *see* Cascade Range. For information about Kelley and his influence on N. J. Wyeth, *see* Scott's *History of the Oregon Country*, v. 1, p. 199. Broughton visited the mouth of the Willamette River on Oct. 29, 1792, and named the southeastern point Belle Vue Point. However it seems apparent that at that time there was a different arrangement of channels and islands in this vicinity from that which exists today. Federal mapping agencies have applied the name Belle Vue Point to a locality on the east shore of Sauvie Island just northwest of the mouth of Willamette River. *See* Belle Vue Point for additional information.

Kellogg, DOUGLAS. S. D. Evans of Roseburg wrote the compiler in July 1927, as follows: "The above name was given to a place kept by two brothers, Lyman and Adna Barnes "Barney" Kellogg, on the Umpqua River, where freighters hauling from Scottsburg to the mines in southern Oregon found accommodations. A post office was established in early days and may be there yet, but I think it was discontinued a few years ago." This post office is no longer in operation. For additional information about Kellogg, *see* the *Oregonian*, June 21, 1927, editorial page.

Kellogg Creek, CLACKAMAS. This stream flows into Willamette River at Milwaukie. It was named for Joseph Kellogg, a pioneer of 1848. The widened part of the stream at Milwaukie is known as Kellogg Lake.

Kellow Creek, TILLAMOOK. This tributary of Little Nestucca River above Meda was named for Thomas Kellow who settled there in 1896. Clarence Dunn of

Meda told the compiler in 1967 that it was first called Norton Creek after Seba Norton who homesteaded there in 1891.

Kelly Butte, LANE. Kelly Butte, near Springfield, was named for John Kelly, a native of County Wexford, Ireland, who came to Oregon from Milwaukee, Wisconsin, about 1843, in the employ of the Hudson's Bay Company. He returned to the United States and took part in the Mexican War, and came to Oregon again with the U.S. Mounted Rifles in 1849 as wagonmaster. He traded in stock between Oregon and California, and finally took a donation land claim near Roseburg. Later he became engaged in milling and other enterprises near Springfield. He married Elizabeth Parker. He was one time collector of customs in Portland, and also receiver or registrar of the land office at Roseburg.

Kelly Butte, MULTNOMAH. Kelly Butte bears the name of Plympton Kelly, a son of pioneer Clinton Kelly. Clinton Kelly, a Methodist preacher, was born in Kentucky, June 15, 1808, and came to Oregon in 1848. He took up a donation land claim east of the Willamette River, in what is now the east part of Portland. He platted Kelly's Addition to Portland. *See the Oregonian,* Jan. 6, 1872, p. 3. He died at Portland June 19, 1875. *See* OPA *Transactions,* 1887. His biography appears in the *Oregonian,* June 21, 1875, p. 3. *See also* editorial in Portland *Telegram,* June 22, 1926. Kelly Butte is just north of Powell Valley Road and has an elevation of 577 feet.

Kelly Creek, MULTNOMAH. Kelly Creek, which rises southeast of Gresham and flows northward to join Beaver Creek, bears an old family name, sometimes incorrectly spelled Kelley. Kelly Creek was named for Gilmore Kelly, who had a donation land claim through which the stream flowed. Gilmore Kelly was the brother of Clinton Kelly, one of Oregon's well-known pioneers.

Kelly Gulch, WASCO. Kelly Gulch runs north towards Pine Grove west of Wapinitia. It was named well before the turn of the century for Hampton Kelly, the son of Portland pioneer Clinton Kelly, who settled near Pine Grove about 1880. Hampton's son, Lucern B. Kelly, was also a well-known resident of Juniper Flat.

Kelsay Valley, DOUGLAS. This valley is along North Umpqua River north of Diamond Lake. It was named for an early day stockman, "Ves" Kelsay, who ran sheep in that part of the Cascade Range, according to information furnished the compiler by George H. Kelly of Portland.

Kelso, CLACKAMAS. Kelso is a cross-roads community near the Mount Hood Loop Highway about three miles northwest of Sandy. According to information furnished by William H. Stanley of Gresham, in July 1947, the place was named for Kelso, Washington. Mr. Stanley got this information from Joel Jarl, the only postmaster the Clackamas County office ever had. In the 1890s Jarl built a little store on his mother's property at this location. The first name proposed for the place was Martinville, but this was rejected by postal officials. The next name to be selected was High Forest for the local High Forest School which had been named for the tall fir trees of the vicinity. This name was also rejected, probably because it was in two words. Jarlson was then suggested, with another veto. T. G. Jonsrud suggested Kelso in compliment to Kelso, Washington, and with the help of Captain Robert Smith of Orient, Kelso post office was established May 31, 1894. The office was closed May 26, 1904, due to the extension of rural delivery.

Kennedy, HARNEY. Kennedy post office was west of Harney Lake and in the westward half of the county, several miles northeast of the OO ranchhouse. It was in service from Mar. 10, 1906, to Sept. 15, 1908, with Julius E. Chandler postmaster. It was closed out to Narrows. The office bore the family name of Mrs. Chandler, *nee* Kennedy. Mrs. Chandler's mother, Mrs. Kennedy, was living with the Chandlers at the time the office was established, and the name was doubtless applied on that account.

Keno, KLAMATH. This place has had several names, and their history is confusing. Post office records are not as complete as they might be. A post office called Whittles Ferry was established at or near what is now Keno on Sept. 22, 1876, with Robert Marple first postmaster. Apparently the ferry was operated by Robert Whittle and the office was named for him. There was some objection to the name of the office, possibly because it was in two words. Captain O. C. Applegate told the writer that he suggested the name Klamath River, but postal officials also objected to this, for some undisclosed reason. Captain Applegate then suggested the name Plevna, a word then prominent in the news from the Russo-Turkish War. Accordingly the name Whittles Ferry was changed to Plevna on Jan. 9, 1878, but later the office was moved northeast a couple of miles to Juniper Ridge, along with the name. This incensed local patrons and they secured a new office in Aug. 1887, and named it Keno for Captain D. J. Ferree's dog. Nellie Doten, postmaster at Keno in Jan. 1926, informed the writer that her father surveyed and platted the townsite, and called it Doten. This name was objected to for a post office because of the similarity to Dayton. According to her version, the name Keno was then adopted for the office on account of Captain Ferree's bird-dog. Keno, the dog, was named after the popular card game of earlier days.

Kent, SHERMAN. J. E. Norton, postmaster at Kent in 1926, wrote the compiler that a petition was circulated in Jan. 1887, for a post office where the community of Kent is now situated. In order to select a name a number of persons wrote their preferences on slips of paper, which were subsequently stirred in a hat. The name, Kent, was drawn and was the one suggested by R. C. Bennett. M. H. Bennett was the first postmaster. The only reason R. C. Bennett gave for the selection of the word Kent was that it was "nice and short." However, Giles French of Moro told the writer in 1975 that R. C. Bennett was not involved and that Milton H. Bennett was alone in the Kent venture and named the post office on his own.

Kent Creek, DOUGLAS. Kent Creek flows into South Umpqua River at Dillard. It is named for Lewis D. Kent who was born at St. Charles, Missouri in 1814. Kent came to Oregon in the fall of 1852 and took a donation land claim including the creek. He died on his claim on Jan. 20, 1857.

Kent Station, DOUGLAS. Kent Station was a military establishment of sorts during the Indian disturbances of 1855–56. It was at the L. D. Kent place on Tenmile Prairie, and was for the protection of the settlers between Roseburg and Coos Bay. Captain W. W. Chapman stationed 30 men there. *See* Victor's *Early Indian Wars of Oregon*, pp. 368–69.

Kenton, MULTNOMAH. This post office is now a branch of the Portland main post office. Kenton community was established by Geo. F. Heusner. Heusner platted this addition to the city of Portland for an industrial section in 1905. He originally intended to name the addition Kenwood, but found he could not do this because there had been an addition to the city dedicated with that name. He then selected the name Kenton. He told the writer that the name had no particular significance.

Kentuck Slough, COOS. Kentuck Slough is fed by Kentuck Creek, and flows into Coos Bay from the east. It was named for George W. Thomas, a native of Kentucky, who settled on the slough in pioneer days. He was generally called Kentuck. About 1860 he had a contract to furnish elk meat to Charles Merchant for the North Bend mill. *See Pioneer History of Coos and Curry Counties*, p. 358.

Kerby, JOSEPHINE. Kerby is a very old community in Oregon, and was established in the days of gold mining in the southwest part of the state. It was named for James Kerby or Kerbey, who was not consistent in the way he spelled his last name. The name of the community has had even more variations. Josephine County was established by an act passed Jan. 22, 1856, and it was provided that the county seat was to be selected at the next county election. Among the polling places was listed Kirbey's Ranch. Kerby and Samuel Hicks were in the general mercantile and supply business, and according to James T. Chinnock of Grants Pass, in a letter in the Grants Pass *Courier*, Dec. 21, 1928, probably founded a town for the county seat race. The election was held in June 1857, and Kerbyville was selected. In 1857–58 Dr. D. S. Holton got a large interest in the town of Kerbyville. He was probably responsible for an act of the legislature Dec. 18, 1856, changing the name from Kirbeyville to Napoleon. This was either because of the association of the name of the county and the Empress Josephine, or because Holton was an admirer of Napoleon III. The new name was not popular, and an effort was made to get a bill through the next legislature to adopt the old name. In the fall of 1860 the house passed a bill to change the name from Napoleon to Kirbeyville, but on Oct. 10, Holton succeeded in getting the bill referred to the senate judiciary committee, where it is still embalmed. The county commissioners used the name Napoleon for a short time, but seem to have dropped it in favor of Kerbyville about Apr. 1860. A list of county seats in the Oregon *Statesman*, Feb. 11, 1861, includes Kerbyville, and that is the name that was used for a good many years, despite the fact that the legislature declined to restore it. Later still the name was changed to Kerby in the interest of simplicity, and Kerby it now is. The name of the first post office has had a much simpler history. Kerby office was established in

Sept. 1856, with James Kerbey postmaster. It is still operating with the original name. It is said that in the mining days one of the founders of the original town brought a pool table on his pack train from Crescent City. The table was intended for another mining camp, but on arrival near the site of the present town of Kerby, the mule packing the principal part of the table strayed away one night, loaded, and the weight of his load was so great that he died before morning. The packer concluded that the location was as good a place for a pool hall as any, and after burying the mule, set up shop on the spot. On Dec. 4, 1937, the Grants Pass *Courier* printed an interview with B. Kerbey Short of Auburn, Washington, in which Short said he was a grandson of the man for whom Kerby was named and that the family spelling was Kerbey. It seems improbable that the name of the community will be changed.

Kerby Creek, JACKSON. Mrs. Frances Pearson, a long time resident of the area, told the compiler in 1979 that this creek east of Prospect and nearby Kerby Hill in Klamath County were both named for USFS ranger Ed Kerby.

Kernan Point, WALLOWA. Kernan Point is in the northeast part of the county in T 2N, R 50E. It was named for John Kernan, due to the circumstance that he and one Nate Tryon killed a deer nearby. He ranged sheep in the vicinity of the point. Kernan and Wilkes Jennings were drowned in Snake River on Mar. 4, 1894, while attempting to cross in an Indian boat or canoe.

Kernville, LINCOLN. In Apr. 1943, Miss Grace Kern of Portland wrote the compiler about the beginnings of this community. Kernville was named by the late Daniel Kern of Portland, who with his brother, John H. Kern, operated a salmon cannery on Siletz River not far from its mouth. The business was known as Kern Brothers Packing Company and was started in 1896. The locality was isolated and could be reached only by water. The cannery was sold in 1898 to Mat P. Kiernan and J. W. Cook of Portland. Later it passed to the hands of Sam Elmore of Astoria. Kernville is now near US-101, the Oregon Coast Highway, a great change from 1896. The cannery was on the north bank of Siletz River about two miles up stream from the old Oregon Coast Highway bridge and the location of Kernville in 1945. The sawmill, post office and original community of Kernville were on the southwest bank about a mile up stream from the present site of Kernville which since the completion of the new Siletz River bridge and the rerouting of US-101 in the 1980s, is also no longer on the main highway. *See* also story by Ben Maxwell in *Sunday Oregon Journal*, magazine sect. Nov. 4, 1945. Kernville post office was established July 6, 1896, with John H. Kern first postmaster. Matthew P. Kiernan became postmaster Aug. 7, 1899. The office has been out of service at times.

Kerr Notch, KLAMATH. This is the lowest part of the rim above Crater Lake and is about 500 feet from the surface of the water. It was named for Mark B. Kerr, USGS engineer in charge of the party that surveyed the lake in 1886. He pronounced his name as "Kar." Kerr Valley is just southeast of Kerr Notch.

Kerry, COLUMBIA. Kerry is at the site of the junction of what was the Columbia and Nehalem River Railroad and the Spokane, Portland and Seattle Railway. It was named for A. S. Kerry, who started the community in 1912, when he was interested in the development of the first named railroad, extending it into his extensive timber holdings in the Nehalem Valley. Kerry was for many years a prominent business man of Portland and Seattle. He died at Seattle on Apr. 27, 1939. The Columbia and Nehalem River Railroad has been dismantled, and Kerry is no longer a railroad station, but it is a community on US-30, the Columbia River Highway.

Ketchketch Butte, DESCHUTES. This butte is southwest of Crane Prairie. The name comes from the Klamath Indian word *Ketchkitchli*, meaning rough. A derivative of the same word is *ketchkatch*, the rough-furred little gray fox. The USFS applied the name because of its distinctive sound and with the desire of perpetuating Indian words.

Ketchum Ranch, HOOD RIVER, WASCO. William K. Ketchum came to The Dalles as a boy in 1883 and homesteaded this ranch on Mosier Creek in 1900.

Kettle Creek, JACKSON. Kettle Creek is in the north part of the county and flows south to join Sugarpine Creek on the north line of T 32S, R 1E. In May 1946, Howard L. Ash of Trail, an oldtimer in that part of Oregon, wrote the compiler that the stream was named because Andy Pool and Sam Gray found a kettle on its banks in 1905. They were on a hunting trip. This old iron kettle held a few lumps of what appeared to be coal, and the hunters turned prospectors. They searched the stream and also the rock point just to the west, but found no coal. This rock point is now called Kettle Rock. Later what appeared to be coal was found a few miles to the northwest, but the compiler has been told that it is just a black rock. *See* Coalmine Creek.

Kettle Creek, WALLOWA. According to J. H. Horner of Enterprise this stream was named in 1883 because a broken camp kettle lay in the creek. A packhorse belonging to Enoch G. Vaughan and David M. Dennis bucked his pack off and jammed the kettle beyond use. The kettle lay in the water for many years. The creek flows into Imnaha River in S 10, T 2N, R 48E. When the area was remapped by the USGS in the late 1980s, The name was changed to Buck Creek. There are over forty Buck creeks in Oregon and the local inhabitants should be ashamed to give up a good, historic name for one of no distinction. *See* USBGN *Decision List 8903*.

Keyes Creek, WHEELER. Keyes Creek was named for James E. Keyes who settled near Mitchell, and nearby Keyes Mountain was probably named for his cousin Zachary Keyes. The two drove 600 Cotswold ewes from Philomath to the Bridge Creek area in 1873 to start the local sheep industry. Judge Henry D. Keyes, the well-known rancher and county judge, was the son of Zachary.

Kiechle Arm, LANE. This arm of Siltcoos Lake was named for Simon Kiechle who filed on his nearby homestead in 1895.

Kiger Creek, HARNEY. The name of this stream is frequently misspelled Kieger and Keiger. It was named for the Kiger family, who were well-known pioneers near Malheur Lake. For additional information about the Kiger family, *see* Kiger Island, also *OHQ*, v. 32, p. 125, and Lockley article on editorial page of the *Oregon Journal*, June 25, 1927.

Kiger Island, BENTON. Kiger Island is southeast of Corvallis between the main channel of the Willamette River and the Booneville Channel. It was named for Reuben C. Kiger, a pioneer resident of Benton County. He was born in 1828 and died in 1907. In 1874 the Kiger family moved to Harney County and settled near Steens Mountain, but Kiger moved back to western Oregon in 1878 because of Indian troubles. Kiger Creek in Harney County was named by his wife Minerva J. (Morgan) Kiger, better known as Dolly Kiger. She also named McCoy Creek and Cucamonga Creek in the Steens Mountain country. She was born July 28, 1850, and was married to Reuben C. Kiger on Nov. 18, 1866. She died at Corvallis on Jan. 8, 1928.

Kilbride, GRANT. Kilbride was a post office near Middle Fork John Day River about six or eight miles northwest of and down stream from Galena. The office was established Mar. 22, 1901, with Margaret Hamilton first of four postmasters. It was discontinued May 31, 1908, with mail to Susanville. Margaret Hamilton was Mrs. Robert Hamilton. Mrs. Hamilton named the office for Kilbride, Scotland, which was at or near the place of her birth.

Kilchis Point, TILLAMOOK. Kilchis Point is on the east shore of Tillamook Bay, and Kilchis River is close by. These features were named for Kilchis, a chief of the Indians of the Tillamook Bay region. He was friendly to the whites. Kilchis post office was established about 1872 with W. D. Stillwell first postmaster. The office was closed about 1890, because the community of Bay City had been established nearby, with a post office, and there was no longer a need for an office at Kilchis. The locality of Kilchis Point was called Jawbone in pioneer days, it is said, because a sawmill enterprise was built on "jawbone" when no cash was available.

Kilkenny Fork, MORROW. Kilkenny Fork is a tributary of Hinton Creek about eight miles east of Heppner. It was named for John S. Kilkenny, a native of Ireland, who came to Morrow county in 1890 and settled along the creek in 1914.

Killam Creek, TILLAMOOK. Killam Creek is a pleasing stream that finds its way into Tillamook River southeast of the town of Tillamook. It bears the name of Leonard Killam who took up a claim in 1879, his land bordering on the stream. Various other spellings such as Kilham, Killum and Killiam are wrong according to county authorities.

Killamacue Creek, BAKER. This stream drains Killamacue Lake and flows into Rock Creek. Old maps show a variety of spellings, but the USBGN has adopted this as best representing the pronunciation of the name. The compiler has been unable to learn the meaning of the name.

Killgaver, MULTNOMAH. Killgaver post office was in operation from Aug. 5,

1886, to Oct. 9, 1899, with John Howard the only postmaster. This office was in the Howard home on the Section Line road, now SE Division Street in the vicinity of what is now SE 112th Avenue. In July 1947, the compiler was informed that the Howards were either born in Ireland or were of Irish descent and named the Oregon post office for a place in the Emerald Isle. Modern atlases do not show such a place in Ireland, but Killgaver may have been used as an Irish place name in the early 1880s.

Kilts, JEFFERSON. Kilts post office was established Sept. 15, 1914, with Ruth A. Kilts first postmaster. It was named for Jesse Kilts, an early resident of the place. The office was discontinued June 29, 1940. While Kilts was the post office name, the local residents called the locality Donnybrook. An earlier name was Axehandle, but Donnybrook was adopted as the result of a gathering in Calf Gulch at which there was considerable disorder and some blood was shed. An editorial in the Bend *Bulletin*, Apr. 20, 1943, says that Kilts was a homesteader and relatively a newcomer. The editorial contains the following paragraph: "But old timers have long resented a community name which honors a newcomer, a member of the homesteading fraternity whom elderly stockmen referred to as 'scissorbills.' To Dan Crowley, one of the few old time survivors of the olden days, Kilts is still Donnybrook. And if you stop in Ashwood on your way east to the Horse Heaven mines to ask about the country beyond Ash Butte and the Red Jacket mine, folks of the Trout Creek village will tell you that the community up on the highlands is known as Donnybrook. Only postal inspectors are told that the region is known as Kilts." Another editorial in the Bend *Bulletin*, Sept. 18, 1937, says that Kilts post office was originally on the John Day side of the divide, but when Dan Crowley became postmaster he had the office moved to the locality of Donnybrook in the Deschutes drainage.

Kimball Hill, CURRY. Kimball Hill is near the south bank of Rogue River about seven miles east of the Pacific Ocean. It was named for Ira Kimball who, with his wife, Amanda, located on the small river bottom near the western base of the hill. Kimball Creek nearby received its name from the same source.

Kimberly, GRANT. The name of this post office was suggested by Elizabeth C. Murphy. She chose the name because the Kimberly family was well known thereabouts.

Kime, MALHEUR. Kime station was named for William Kime, a former resident of the vicinity. It was just west of Harper.

Kincaid Canyon, MORROW. This canyon is in the Eightmile drainage north of Utts Butte. John L. Kincaid patented the adjacent land in 1890.

Kincheloe Point, TILLAMOOK. This is the south point at the entrance of Tillamook Bay. It bears the name of Sub-Assistant Julius Kincheloe, of the USC&GS who was drowned at the mouth of the bay on May 20, 1867. An account of this tragedy appears on p. 11 of the *Report of the Superintendent* of the Coast Survey for 1867. Kincheloe joined the Coast Survey in 1854, and from the remarks of the superintendent, appears to have been an efficient and experienced officer, and was held in high esteem by his associates. At the time of his death Kincheloe was attempting to complete a line of soundings across the bar, and when his boat was capsized, five of his crew of six were drowned with him. Miss Lucy E. Doughty of Bay City, an early resident of the community, wrote the compiler that Mrs. Kincheloe was on the shore at the time of the accident and saw her husband swept into the sea. Later, she completed her husband's report, copied all the necessary notes and sent them to Washington with an account of the tragedy.

Kindred, CLATSOP. A post office named Kindred was established on the Clatsop County list May 19, 1894, with Mabel N. Ford postmaster. The National Archives says that the office was discontinued Aug. 14, 1894. It seems apparent that the establishment was never in actual operation as a post office. The office was doubtless named for Bartholomew C. Kindred who lived at what was known as New Astoria or Kindred Park on the Kindred donation land claim near what is at present known as Flavel. The office may have been intended to serve the community now known as Hammond, which is on the original Kindred property. Mr. and Mrs. Bartholomew C. Kindred came to Oregon in 1844.

King, MARION. King post office was in the west part of T 8S, R 1E, probably near Drift Creek. A map of 1911 shows it near the south line of section 17. This office was established Aug. 21, 1890, with William H. King first of four postmasters. With one intermission the office operated until Sept. 1903, when it was closed to Jefferson. This move seems strange to the compiler as there were other operating offices much nearer than Jefferson. It is apparent that the office was named for the first postmaster.

King Canyon, MORROW. Albert T. King was one of the earliest Morrow County settlers and he took a homestead near this canyon south of Ione in 1882. His daughter Dollie's marriage to Bert Haney in Mar. 1885, was the first recorded in Morrow County. King had three sons, Benjamin, John and William, who also took up land nearby.

King Canyon, WASCO. Cold Camp Creek flows through King Canyon just before it empties into Antelope Creek. It was named for Zachary T. King who homesteaded there in 1903.

King City, WASHINGTON. King City is a planned adult community organized by the Tualatin Development Company, Inc., and incorporated in Mar. 1966. The name was an arbitrary selection by R. B. Sorensen, the president of the development company, who also used the royalty theme in naming streets and certain other facilities.

King Creek, COOS. King Creek is a tributary of Middle Fork Coquille River. It was named for a Dr. King, who settled nearby in pioneer days.

King Creek, LINN. This creek flows south into Calapooia River at King Camp. It was named for Andy King who lived on its upper reaches after World War I. The compiler has been told that King found the solitude particularly suitable for the manufacture of a certain type of refreshment at that time not available through regular commercial channels.

King Creek, LANE. This King Creek is tributary to Horse Creek south of McKenzie Bridge. It is apparently named for William King who patented a homestead along it in 1891.

King Mountain, HARNEY. King Mountain is about 20 miles north of Harney. It was named for E. H. King, who established a mountain sawmill nearby about 1880. He came to Oregon from Red Bluff, California. The name Trout as applied to this mountain is an error, and is caused because the point is near the head of Trout Creek. The name King Mountain is now generally accepted by the public.

King Slough, LINCOLN. King Slough is a fairly large inlet on the south side of Yaquina Bay. In the 1880s one Jack King had a homestead near the head of this slough and the feature took his name. King also ran a small camp in the locality. In earlier days the inlet was called Hinton Slough, but that name did not persist.

King Well, DESCHUTES. This well was on the property of Orlea O. King who settled four miles west of Brothers before World War I.

Kingman, MALHEUR. Kingman was a station on the Union Pacific Railroad south of Nyssa. It was named for A. G. Kingman, a resident and founder of the small community. The only use of the name on maps of the 1970s is Kingman Road.

Kings Landing, COOS. Kings Landing was the name of a locality about nine miles south of Coos Bay, on the west side of Isthmus Slough, at or about the same place that in recent years has been called Delmar. It was named for one King, who lived there. Kings Landing was the transfer point where passengers and goods were set ashore at the head of navigation from Coos Bay. At Kings Landing a narrow gauge railroad took off and extended south to Coaledo, at which point there was a transfer back to boats again. There was no post office with the name Kings Landing.

Kings Valley, BENTON. Kings Valley was named for Nahum King, the first settler, who was an Oregon pioneer of 1845. The flour mill was built by Rowland Chambers in 1853. Kings Valley post office was established on Apr. 13, 1855, with Chambers first postmaster.

Kingsley, WASCO. Judge Fred W. Wilson informed the compiler in 1927 that Kingsley was named by his mother, Mrs. E. M. Wilson, about 1878 when she was postmaster at The Dalles. A delegation from Kingsley called on Mrs. Wilson at The Dalles post office with a petition for a new post office to serve a part of the county south of Dufur. The petition suggested a commonplace name. Mrs. Wilson had been reading Charles Kingsley's *Westward Ho!* and the book lay in her lap. She immediately suggested the name of the great English clergyman and writer for the new office and the suggestion was accepted on the spot. The town plat was filed on May 16, 1893. Kingsley was not a post office in Apr. 1927.

Kingsley Field, KLAMATH. Kingsley Field is a USAF Base and Klamath Falls

Municipal Airport. During World War II the field was a U.S. Naval Air Station. This was deactivated in 1946 and replaced in 1956 by the present USAF installation. It was named for Lieutenant David R. Kingsley of Portland, Oregon, who was killed in action over Ploesti, Rumania, on June 23, 1944. Kingsley was posthumously awarded the Medal of Honor for heroic action when he sacrificed his own life to save a wounded companion.

Kingsley Guard Station, HOOD RIVER. This USFS Guard Station and Forest Camp east of Mount Defiance are at the site of an early summer home of Edward D. Kingsley, president of the West Oregon Lumber Company. Kingsley was active in lumber circles in the Northwest. He died in Portland Sept. 4, 1940.

Kingston, LINN. This was a station near the North Santiam River, not far from Stayton. It is said to have been named for Samuel King, who lived there many years before the railroad was built.

Kingston Creek, TILLAMOOK. This tributary of Neskowin Creek was named for Paul Kingston, an early settler who lived near the site of the old Neskowin Forest Camp.

Kinton, WASHINGTON. Kinton is a place on the Scholls Ferry Road south of Cooper Mountain. It was named for Peter Kindt, who took up a donation land claim nearby in pioneer days. For information about Kindt and Kinton, *see* the Hillsboro *Argus*, Jan. 21, 1932.

Kinzel Creek, CLACKAMAS. This stream, which flows into Salmon River south of Rhododendron, is near a mining prospect owned by Tom Kinzel, and was named on that account. Kinzel was a prospector and packer in this part of the Cascade Range. The small lake or pond drained by Kinzel Creek is known as Kinzel Lake.

Kinzua, WHEELER. Kinzua lumber town and post office was established in 1928. The place was named by the Kinzua Pine Mills Company for Kinzua, Warren County, Pennsylvania, a community on the Allegheny River. At the time, it was said that Kinzua meant a place of many fishes. On Oct. 16, 1930, the postmaster at Kinzua, Pennsylvania, told the compiler that highway signs in that community said Kinzua was an Indian name meaning waters of many and big fish. However, an inquiry to an old Indian in the vicinity brought the information that he believed that the word actually meant that there were always fish for the spear rather than for other methods of catching.

Kirby Creek, BAKER. Kirby Creek, in Eagle Valley, was originally called Little Eagle Creek, because it was a separate channel of Eagle Creek. This caused confusion with another Little Eagle Creek, tributary to the main stream, about eight miles further north. Local residents recommended that the creek in Eagle Valley be called Kirby, for a local resident, which was done by the USBGN.

Kirk, KLAMATH. Kirk is the name of the family upon whose allotment the community is situated. Jesse Kirk was a prominent and respected Indian, an ordained Methodist minister. The name was first chosen by the Southern Pacific

Company for a station name at a point that was for several years the end of the line north of Klamath Falls. The post office was established in 1920, with the name Kirkford; why the additional syllable no one seems to know, although it is true there is a ford in Williamson River nearby. The scheme of different names for station and for post office has always been unsatisfactory and in 1925 the postal authorities changed the office name to Kirk to agree with the station name.

Kirkbride Canyon, JEFFERSON. J. A. Rooper of Antelope told the writer in 1969 that this canyon near upper Trout Creek was named for Al Kirkbride who ranched there with his brother about the time of World War I.

Kirkendall Branch, DOUGLAS. James A. Kirkendall homesteaded near this creek in Camas Valley in 1877.

Kirkland Spring, WALLOWA. This spring in S 13, T 4N, R 45E, was named for Wright Kirkland, a pioneer stockman of the locality.

Kishwalks, WASCO. Kishwalks is a locality on the Warm Springs Indian Reservation, north of the agency. It bears the name of an old Indian, very lame, who lived there. It is possible that the word in some way referred to his infirmity and that it was a mixture of the Wasco and English languages, but in Jan. 1944, Indians at the agency were not definite about the origin.

Kist, COLUMBIA. Kist post office was in the southwest part of the county near Nehalem River, several miles upstream from the mouth of Clear Creek. The office, which was established Jan. 21, 1899, is said to have been named for a local homesteader who had the misfortune of being frozen to death a short time before the office was established. Kist post office was discontinued May 31, 1912, and the business was turned over to Timber. Nearby Kist Creek retains the name.

Kitson Hot Springs, LANE. Dave Kitson of Springfield, a left-handed English carpenter, took up these springs many years ago and established a summer resort there. The springs and Kitson Ridge just to the north bear his name. Lawrence D. Hills of Oakridge said that Kitson built a bath house and a large pool out of hewn cedar logs. The timbers for the pool were grooved with a hand plane. The pool structure was destroyed by an avalanche in 1898.

Kittredge Lake, MULTNOMAH. This was the correct name of the small overflow lake on the west banks of the Willamette River east of Oilton, not Kittridge. It was named for George Kittredge, a pioneer settler who was born in Vermont in 1808. The lake was filled in in the 1940s, but since then the Kittredge Viaduct has been an important overpass over the Burlington Northern tracks.

Kiwa Butte, DESCHUTES. This butte southwest of Bend was named by the USFS with the Chinook jargon word for crooked or bent. The name is descriptive.

Kizer Creek, LANE. Kizer Creek is a tributary of Mosby Creek about five miles southeast of Cottage Grove. It was apparently named for Thomas C. Keizur who took up a donation land claim along its banks in 1863.

Klak Butte, DESCHUTES. This butte southwest of Bend, was named by the USFS with the Chinook jargon word for cut off, indicating its shape.

Klamath Agency, KLAMATH. Klamath Agency was established May 12, 1866, on the shore of what is known as Agency Lake, about three miles south of the last site of the agency. It is now on Crooked Creek. The Klamath Indian Reservation was abolished in 1961 but the community of Klamath Agency continues. For the origin of the name Klamath, *see* Klamath County.

Klamath County. Klamath County was created Oct. 17, 1882, by the state legislature. It was taken from Lake County as it existed at that time. It was named for the tribe of Indians called Klamath by the white travelers. The first appearance of the name as far as the compiler knows is in a letter from Peter Skene Ogden, dated Burnt River, July 1, 1826, which refers to the "Claminitt Country." *See* Merk's *Fur Trade and Empire*, p. 274. On Oct. 5, 1826, David Douglas wrote of looking into the country called "Clamite" by the natives who inhabited it. Ogden, who used the form "Clammitte" on Nov. 5, 1826, reached the headwaters of the Klamath drainage on Nov. 27 of that year, but indicates in his diary that McKay and McDonald, of his party had been there before. The theory has been advanced that the name originated with the French words *clair metis*, meaning light mist, which frequently lies above Upper Klamath Lake. The trouble with this notion is that the French style would be *metis clair*, and if these words mean anything, they mean a light colored halfbreed. However that may be, both Indians and white men used the name at an early day, the former for the lakes, and the latter for the Indians. The name may be a corruption of *Mak-laks*. *See* Maklaks Pass. Among the spellings used by early writers are: Clemmat, Clam-ath, Klamet, Clemet, Tlamath and many others. For references, *see* OGN, 1928 edition, p. 186. The Klamath Indians are classed as a Lutuamian tribe, living about Upper Klamath Lake, also on Williamson and Sprague rivers. They call themselves *Eukshikni*, or *Auksni*, "the people of the lake." For information about the lakes, *see* Lower Klamath Lake and Upper Klamath Lake. According to ODOT in 1990, Klamath County has an of 6113 square miles.

Klamath Falls, KLAMATH. The community of Klamath Falls is situated at the falls of Link River, where that stream flows into Lake Ewauna. The place was originally known as Linkville and was named for Link River. The Klamath Indian name for the place was *Yulalona*, or *Iuauna*, which referred to the peculiar blowing backward of the waters of Link River during strong south winds. For information about these Indian names, *see* Lake Ewauna and Link River. The Klamath name for the falls in Link River was *Tiwishkeni*, or rush of falling waters place. George Nurse founded the town of Linkville in 1867, and a bronze memorial tablet commemorating the event is installed in one of the concrete columns of the Link River bridge, in the west part of Klamath Falls. The name was changed to Klamath Falls in 1892–93.

Klamath Marsh, KLAMATH. This marsh is fed principally by Williamson River, of which it is an enlargement, and by small streams flowing from the Cascade Range. Its main outlet is Williamson River. Its elevation is just about 4500 feet. It was named for the Klamath Indians. These Indians called the marsh *Eukshi*, and used the same word to indicate the whole of the Klamath territory from Modoc Point up along the east shore of Upper Klamath Lake to the marsh. By slight differences in intonation, they indicated different localities with the same word, *Eukshi*. At the southern part of the marsh are Wocus Bay and Little Wocus Bay. For information about these features, *see* the respective headings. In the fall of 1826 Peter Skene Ogden took a trapping and exploring party into the Klamath country. Apparently on Nov. 30, 1826, the party reached the neighborhood of Klamath Marsh, although at just what point the compiler is not certain. On Dec. 6 of that same year Ogden mentions in his diary that Finnan McDonald, one of the Hudson's Bay Company men, had been that far the year before. At that date Ogden was further south than Klamath Marsh, so in all probability McDonald was the first white man to reach Klamath Marsh. For additional data, *see* Klamath County. John C. Fremont reached and very accurately described Klamath Marsh on Dec. 10, 1843, although at that time he thought he was at "Tlamath lake." Much of the marsh has been drained.

Klamath Mountains, CURRY, DOUGLAS, JACKSON, JOSEPHINE. This is the name used by Dr. J. S. Diller in USGS *Bulletin 196, Topographical Development of the Klamath Mountains*, to describe part of the Coast Range of Oregon and California between the 40th and 43rd parallels of latitude. The name is used by geologists rather than by geographers and map makers. The Klamath Mountains are made up of subordinate terranes, including the Siskiyous. Geologically they resemble the Sierra Nevada to a considerable extent. The bulletin mentioned gives a detailed account of the topographic development of these mountains, and explains why they are considered a separate group.

Klamath River, KLAMATH. Klamath River receives the drainage of Upper Klamath Lake through Link River and Lake Ewauna. *See* these two entries for information about their Indian names. The Klamath Indian name for Klamath River was *Koke*, the general name for river, and the hearer had to judge from the context which river was meant, Williamson, Lost, Sprague or Klamath. For information about the name Klamath, *see* Klamath County. Klamath River has a total drainage area of 11,850 square miles in Oregon and California, and has a total length of 180 miles between Lake Ewauna and the Pacific Ocean. About five miles above Keno the river is connected to Lower Klamath Lake by a stream, now under dike control, known as Klamath Strait. Water formerly flowed through Klamath Strait either way, depending on the relative stages of Klamath River and Lower Klamath Lake.

Klamath Strait, KLAMATH. Klamath Strait is the correct name of the outlet of Lower Klamath Lake, not Klamath River. Klamath River flows from Lake Ewauna, and the river is connected with Lower Klamath Lake by Klamath Strait. This strait formerly flowed either way, but its course has been interfered with by the Southern Pacific Company railroad grade.

Klaskanine River, CLATSOP. For information about this name, *see* Clatskanie. The Klaskanine River affords a route of travel from the mouth of the Columbia River to the place in the Nehalem Valley where part of the Tlatskani Indian tribe lived. The name of the stream in Clatsop County is spelled differently from the name of the Columbia County stream. In recent years, and as a result of more accurate mapping, the names of the branches of this stream have become established. South Fork Klaskanine River presents no problem. North Fork Klaskanine River heads south of Wickiup Ridge and joins the South Fork about two miles east of Youngs River, the two forks forming Klaskanine River. North Fork North Fork Klaskanine River flows into the North Fork at Klaskanine Hatchery. It heads west of Wickiup Ridge. Southeast of this branch is Middle Fork North Fork Klaskanine River which also heads west of Wickiup Ridge and flows into North Fork about five miles upstream from the hatchery.

Klawhop Butte, DESCHUTES. *Klawhop* is the Chinook jargon word for hole, and this butte southeast of Bend was named by the USFS, presumably because it had a crater in the top.

Klickitat Mountain, LANE. This is a prominent peak near the east end of Klickitat Ridge, in the Coast Range in the extreme north part of Lane County. It is unusual that the name of an Indian tribe, whose dwelling place was near The Dalles of the Columbia River, should be attached to a mountain so far away, and yet there is good evidence to verify the story that the Klickitat Indians traveled over a wide area. In pioneer days there was a trail near Rickreall Creek known as the Klickitat Trail, and there was a definite Klickitat camping place near the Boyle Lakes, northwest of the present community of Rickreall. J. W. Nesmith, in a letter in the *Oregonian*, Feb. 7, 1877, says that in Sept. 1849, he and General Joseph Lane went from the Willamette Valley to the Siletz River over a trail used by Klickitat Indians at that time living in Kings Valley. For description of the origin of the name Klickitat, *see* Meany's *Origin of Washington Geographic Names*. Early writers spelled the word in a variety of ways. General Hazard Stevens says that the word meant robber and tradition in the Willamette Valley in Oregon favors this meaning. The writer has been told by a number of Indians that the correct definition of the word was robber or marauder. General Stevens had first hand information, and the writer is inclined toward his opinion in the matter. David Douglas mentioned the tribe as *Clickitats* on June 20, 1825, which is as far as the writer knows the first use of the word by early explorers.

Klingers Camp, WASCO. Louis J. Klinger was born in Missouri in 1837 and came to Oregon ten years later. He settled in the Eightmile area in 1863 where he ranched and freighted on the Barlow and Canyon City roads. At one time he maintained a supply camp on the Barlow Road near the present USFS marker above White River. In 1889 he retired to Dufur and later served a term as mayor. He was an indefatigable supporter of the then proposed road from Dufur west to the Mount Hood area. Clinger Spring near Brooks Meadows above East Fork

Hood River was quite probably named for him because it was on the early road alignment.

Kloan, WASCO. This station on the Oregon Trunk Railway was named with the Chinook jargon word for three, since it was the third station from the north end of the line up Deschutes River.

Klondike, SHERMAN. The post office at Klondike was established Jan. 11, 1899 with A. B. Potter first postmaster. Due and French in *Rails to the Mid Columbia Wheatlands*, p. 49, says that when the Columbia Southern Railway was being built to Shaniko it reached Klondike in the summer of 1898. Most of the construction crew deserted the job and headed for the northern gold mines so it was decided to so name the station. For many years the railway used the form Klondyke but the compiler has been unable to find out why. Klondike post office was closed Nov. 30, 1951.

Klone Butte, DESCHUTES. Klone Butte, in the north part of the Paulina Mountains, was named with the Chinook jargon word for three, it being the third of a series of buttes named at one time by the USFS. This is a variation of the spelling Kloan.

Kloochman Creek, CROOK. Kloochman Creek flows south from the Maury Mountains into Bear Creek. *Kloochman* is the Chinook jargon word for woman, and Kloochman Creek is just another way of saying Squaw Creek.

Kloster Mountain, LANE. BLM records show that in 1898, Wilhelm Kloster patented a homestead near this high ground three miles south of Dexter.

Klovdahl Bay, LANE. This bay on Waldo Lake and Klovdahl Lake to the north were named for Simon Klovdahl, an engineer connected with the development of the Waldo Lake irrigation and power project. Klovdahl died at Eugene Nov. 26, 1932.

Klumb, MARION. A half century ago Klumb post office served a small area about three miles northwest of Mehama, not far from Fern Ridge School. It was named for Mrs. Jacob Siegmund, whose maiden name was Mary Margarethe Klumb. The Siegmunds were early day settlers in the locality. The writer has had an interesting letter from Mrs. Matilda S. Jones, *nee* Siegmund, of Amity, who was reared in the vicinity of Klumb post office. When Jacob Siegmund became interested in getting an office established, he submitted the name Klumb for his wife's family, and Cope, in compliment to Mrs. Lucy A. Pugsley, a neighbor and wife of Walter Pugsley. Mrs. Pugsley's maiden name was Cope. Mr. Siegmund was active in local civic and improvement matters, which may have influenced postal officials to select Mrs. Siegmund's maiden name, but it is also probable that the authorities thought that the name Cope was too much like that of Cove in Union County. The department was anxious to steer clear of names that might be confused. In any event Klumb post office was established Jan. 4, 1893, with Mrs. Pugsley first postmaster. Her husband, Walter Pugsley, was the first mail carrier, and he made the regular round trip to Mehama on horseback. The Pugsley family soon moved away, and on June 10, 1893, Jacob Siegmund was made postmaster and the office was moved to the Siegmund home where it remained until it was closed Feb. 15, 1910, because of the extension of rural free delivery from Stayton.

Knapp Creek, LANE. This upper tributary of Chickahominy Creek north of Walton was probably named for George W. Knapp who homesteaded there about 1900.

Knappa, CLATSOP. Knappa was named for Aaron Knapp, Jr. He was a pioneer settler who resided in the community many years. According to Silas B. Smith, the Indian name for the locality was *Tle-las-qua*. *See OHQ*, v. 1, p. 321. For information about the Indian village found by Lewis and Clark nearby, *see* Big Creek and Cathlamet Bay.

Knieriem Canyon, MULTNOMAH. Knieriem Canyon heads southwest of Crown Point and runs southwest to Big Creek and Sandy River. It bears the family name of George Knieriem who was born in Germany in 1844 and came to the United States as a boy. He came west in the 1890s and located in the Corbett area in 1896.

Knight, MARION. Knight post office was near Silver Creek at a point near the north line of T 8S, R 1E, about ten or twelve miles upstream from Silverton. The office was named for Daniel E. Knight, a local resident and the first postmaster. Knight post office was established Feb. 16, 1880, and was in service until July 27, 1895, when it was closed to Argenti.

Knight Creek, WALLOWA. Knight Creek flows into Snake River in T 4N, R 48E. It was named by the USFS for M. V. Knight who had some mining claims along the stream. In early days it was known as Bear Creek because R. M. Downey and Jerard Cohorn killed a bear there in 1881. The name was changed because there were too many Bear creeks in the county.

Knox Butte, LINN. This butte has an elevation of 634 feet, and is situated about six miles east of Albany. It was named for James Knox, a pioneer of 1845, and a cousin of James Knox Polk, president of the United States. James Knox was a native of Pennsylvania and lived in Ohio and Iowa before he came to Oregon.

Knox Ranch, WHEELER. This ranch on the headwaters of Cove Creek northeast of Clarno was homesteaded by Frank A. Knox in 1884.

Knutson Saddle, MARION. This saddle between Sardine Mountain and Dome Rock bears the name of Carl Knutson, an early day logger.

Koch Butte, CROOK. Koch Butte is east of Marks Creek just above its confluence with Ochoco Creek. It is named for Henry and Ella Koch who came from eastern Washington in 1907 and settled in the upper Ochoco.

Koch Mountain, LANE. This long mountain ridge is west of Waldo Lake. It is named for an early trapper, Louis Koch, who ran his trap line from the Waldo Lake Irrigation and Power Company cabin at the lake. Koch disappeared in 1916 while returning to the cabin after picking up the mail in Oakridge.

Kokostick Butte, DESCHUTES. This butte near Devils Lake is named with the Chinook jargon word for woodpecker.

Kolb Reservoir, BAKER. This reservoir on the southwest edge of Baker is named for the family of Franz H. Kolb who homesteaded the property prior to the turn of the century.

Koler, DOUGLAS. For many years there was a station on the Southern Pacific Company railroad four miles west of Glendale bearing the name Reuben, probably derived from Mount Reuben not far away. When residents at Reuben station wanted a post office after the beginning of the century they could not use the name Reuben because of duplication with the name Reuben post office in Columbia County. Accordingly, the name Koler was selected apparently in compliment to Richard Koehler, for many years manager of the Southern Pacific Company lines in Oregon. Mr. Koehler was a native of Germany and was brought to Oregon by Henry Villard. He had an outstanding career as a railroad administrator. He died in Portland in 1932. Along the line of the Southern Pacific he was always called by the Americanized form of his name which accounts for the style used by postal authorities. Koler post office was established Sept. 17, 1907, with Alonzo W. Moon first postmaster. The office was closed to Glendale Nov. 15, 1923.

Koosah Falls, LINN. These falls are immediately above Carmen Reservoir on McKenzie River. Before the development of the Clear Lake recreation area, they were known as Middle Falls but the USBGN confirmed the present name in *Decision List 6103. Koosah* is the Chinook jargon word for sky.

Koosah Mountain, DESCHUTES, LANE. This mountain at the summit of the Cascade Range has the Chinook jargon word for sky.

Kotan, KLAMATH. Kotan was a station on the Cascade line of the Southern Pacific. Railroad officials say the name is an Indian word for horse. It is probably an adaptation of the Chinook jargon word *cuitin*, from the Chinook *ikiuatan*, a horse. There does not appear to be a Klamath Indian word of this sound.

Kotzman Basin, DESCHUTES. This basin southeast of Pine Mountain was apparently named for Charles V. Kotzman who settled there about the time of World War I.

Kramer Canyon, UMATILLA. Jacob Kramer ranched near the head of this canyon east of Vinson in the 1890s.

Kroll, DOUGLAS. Kroll is a station on the Southern Pacific Company railroad on the east side of Tahkenitch Lake in the extreme west part of the county. The station was named for a member of the firm of Sparrow and Kroll who owned a large tract of timber nearby. There was a post office at Kroll from Nov. 2, 1920, to Sept. 30, 1921, with William L. Forsythe postmaster.

Kronenberg, MULTNOMAH. In July 1947, William H. Stanley of Gresham wrote the compiler in part as follows: "Kronenberg post office was named for Joseph Kronenberg, the only postmaster. It was at the present site of

Meadowland dairy at 162nd (Barker Road) and Powell Valley Road. The old Kronenberg house is still standing and occupied by the Andregg family which owns the premises and dairy. I did not know that the Kronenbergs had a post office, but I knew the entire family. One son is still living somewhere in California." Kronenberg post office was established Apr. 10, 1893, with Joseph Kronenberg first and only postmaster. The office was closed Feb. 8, 1897, with papers to Rockwood.

Krumbo Creek, HARNEY. Krumbo Creek flows off Krumbo Mountain, a foothill of Steens Mountain. It was named for a pioneer settler in the neighborhood. The spelling given here, Krumbo, is in accordance with official plats and with the best local use. Krumbe and Crumbo are incorrect.

Kuamaksi Butte, DESCHUTES. This butte, southwest of Bend, was named by the USFS with the Klamath Indian name of a locality near Sprague River, literally "at the cave." Gatschet gives the spelling *Kumakshi*. The word is derived from *kumme* or *kume*, meaning cave or cavern. The USFS used the word in order to perpetuate an Indian name, even though the butte is a long way from Sprague River.

Kubli, JACKSON. Kaspar Kubli came to Oregon from Switzerland in 1852, and his brother Jacob came some years later. Both settled in Jackson County, where they became prominent citizens. Jacob Kubli bought the Barnes claim near Applegate River in the extreme west part of the county in the locality called Missouri Flat. His son, Kaspar J. Kubli was born on this place, and in June 1891, was appointed postmaster at Kubli post office, which was but a few hundred feet east of the Jackson-Josephine county line. The office was closed Nov. 30, 1907, due to the establishment of rural delivery. Kaspar J. Kubli died July 2, 1942. He was postmaster at Kubli during the entire existence of the office.

Kuckup Park, JEFFERSON. This is a natural park just east of the summit of the Cascade Range and slightly south of Breitenbush Lake. Kuck-up and Kuck-ups were sub-chiefs among the signers of the 1865 Treaty with the Middle Oregon Tribes. The compiler has been unable to find why this name was applied to this specific area although it is on the extreme west side of the Warm Springs Indian Reservation.

Kuder Creek, WASHINGTON. Kuder Creek flows east into West Fork Dairy Creek near Manning. It bears the name of David E. Kuder, a pioneer sawmill operator. There have been numerous spellings of the name including Cueter but the present form was established in *Decision List 7801*.

Kuhn Ridge, WALLOWA. Kuhn Ridge is a well-known divide between Mud and Buck creeks in T 4N, R 43E. It was named for Henry and Dave Kuhn who ranged stock there in early days. Henry Kuhn took up the first homestead on this ridge.

Kweo Butte, DESCHUTES. This butte in Paulina Mountains was named by the USFS with the Chinook jargon word for ring or circle, which well describes it.

Kwinnum Butte, DESCHUTES. Kwinnum Butte, in the Paulina Mountains, is named with the Chinook jargon word for five, it being the fifth in a series of buttes all named at the same time by the USFS.

Kwolh Butte, DESCHUTES. Kwolh Butte, elevation 7349 feet, is about two miles south of Bachelor Butte. *Kwolh* or *kwalh* is the Chinook jargon word for aunt, and the name was applied to this butte arbitrarily as a means of identification in fire fighting. Tot Mountain, a point between Kwolh Butte and Bachelor Butte, is named with the Chinook jargon word for uncle. These two names of relationship appear to have been suggested because of the proximity of such features as the Three Sisters, Bachelor Butte, The Husband and The Wife, all prominent points in the Cascade Range. *See also* Wanoga Butte.

Kyser, COLUMBIA. Kyser was a locality on the Lost Creek drainage south of Delena, and near the center of the southwest quarter of T 7N, R 3W. It was named for a local resident. Kyser post office was established June 20, 1892, with William H. Kyser postmaster. Ella M. Kyser became postmaster May 8, 1908, and the office was closed to Rainier on May 30, 1918.

La Brie Lake, LAKE. There are two La Brie lakes in Oregon, both in the vicinity of Silver Lake. The northern one is about four miles south of Duncan reservoir and the other is some eight miles further south in S 2, T 31S, R 15E. Thomas J. La Brie filed on a homestead near the cummunity of Silver Lake in 1901. The lakes are obviously named for him or some member of his family.

La Butte, MARION. This hill, elevation 427 feet, is between Butteville and Champoeg. It was named in pioneer days by the French-Canadian settlers on French Prairie. Butteville was named for the hill.

Lachmund, MARION. This railroad station east of Salem was named for Louis Lachmund, a prominent resident of Salem, who owned a farm nearby.

Lacomb, LINN. J. E. Turnidge, a pioneer settler in this community, liked the name Tacoma and tried to have postal authorities adopt it, but they did not do so on account of duplication. W. J. Turnidge, a son, finally compromised the matter by suggesting the name Lacomb, which was chosen. This was in 1889.

Lacy, CLACKAMAS. In May 1948, Isaac V. Trullinger wrote from 217 NE Skidmore Street, Portland, that the old Lacy post office was named for a local family. Mr. Trullinger was a pioneer of Clackamas County and should have known the facts. Lacy post office was established in Mar. 1892, with John R. Lewis first and only postmaster. It ran four or five years but the compiler does not know the exact date it was discontinued. Mr. Trullinger said that the office was in the north part of the county on a mail route that served such places as Eagle Creek, Viola, Clarkes and other offices.

Ladd Canyon, UNION. This canyon was named for John R. Ladd who ran a hotel at the foot of the hill where the immigrant road came into the Grande Ronde Valley. For information about Mr. and Mrs. Ladd and their activities in the days of the eastern Oregon and the Idaho gold rush, *see* Lockley's article on editorial page of the *Sunday Journal*, Jan. 13, 1946. W. W. Curtis, who was familiar with eastern Oregon history, wrote the compiler in 1927 that in early days pioneer wagons were let down the slopes of Ladd Hill, near the canyon, with log drags attached to the wheels. In early days there were hundreds of pine logs at the bottom of the hill.

Ladd Glacier, HOOD RIVER. Ladd Glacier was named for William Mead Ladd of Portland who, with C. E. S. Wood, built Cloud Cap Inn. It is on the northwest slope of Mount Hood west of Pulpit Rock above Barrett Spur and is the source of Ladd Creek which flows into West Fork Hood River. Although the name Ladd Glacier has been in general use for many years, Captain Henry Coe in an article in the Hood River *News*, Mar. 6, 1918, says that in 1886 he named it Stranahan Glacier in honor of Oscar Stranahan, a close friend and associate.

Lady Creek, YAMHILL. This is the first tributary of South Yamhill River east of Gold Creek. Old maps show this as Sady Creek but this has been corrected on the USGS Grand Ronde quadrangle of 1979. Several nearby residents said the stream was named for an old time settler whose surname was Lady. This obviously was John T. Lady who settled near Willamina in the 1860s. However, James W. Sady in 1866, patented a claim on upper Rock Creek some seven or eight miles to the northeast. This may have been the cause of the confusion.

Lafayette, YAMHILL. Lafayette was founded in 1846 by Joel Perkins, and named after Lafayette, Indiana. It was the county seat of Yamhill County until 1889, when that designation was transferred to McMinnville. The post office was established Mar. 14, 1851, with Hardin D. Martin first postmaster.

LaFollette Butte, DESCHUTES. Jerome B. LaFollette made his camp at this butte in early days and let his horses run at large nearby. Later he was killed in central Oregon when he fell off a load of hay. The butte is near Lower Bridge.

La Grande, UNION. It is said that at one time an effort was made to call this place Brownsville for one Ben Brown, who settled there in 1861. A meeting was held for a discussion of the matter, and instead, the name La Grande was adopted, doubtless suggested by the name of Grande Ronde Valley and its impressive scenery. This may have taken some time for Nancy Glenn, who later settled at Summerville, states in a letter dated Oct. 8, 1862, referring to La Grande: "this little town" was known as "Grand Rond City." The Glenn letter was uncovered by John Evans of La Grande who in 1990 added to the mystery by sending a letter dated 1973 signed by Mrs. Violet La Grandeur of Edmonton, Alberta. Mrs. La Grandeur stated that the town was probably named by a Frenchman, Charles Dause to honor her late father-in-law, Mose La Grandeur, who came to the Grande Ronde Valley in the early 1860s. La Grande post office was established May 28, 1863, with Benjamin P. Patterson first postmaster.

Laidlaw Butte, DESCHUTES. Laidlaw Butte is about a mile west of Tumalo. It was named in compliment to W. A. Laidlaw, one of the promoters of the town now called Tumalo, but originally called Laidlaw. *See* Tumalo.

Lake, COOS. Lake post office was named for the Tenmile lakes. The office was established Feb. 8, 1892, with Jane E. Fox first postmaster, and was discontinued Oct. 12, 1903, with all mail to Templeton, which was about five miles eastward. Lake post office is shown on the post route map of 1900 as being on the peninsula between Tenmile Lake and North Tenmile Lake, but the scale of the map is small and this location may not be exact. In any event it was not far from the community later called Lakeside.

Lake, LAKE. Lake post office was formerly near Christmas Lake, about four miles from its later location. Christmas Lake as a name for the office was not acceptable to the authorities. A name of one word was wanted, so Christmas was dropped. The office was established in 1906 during the homestead surge and closed July 31, 1943. Mary Long, the mother of R. A. Long, well-known author and rancher of Fort Rock, was the first postmaster.

Lake Abert, LAKE. Lake Abert is one of the large lakes of Oregon with a normal area of about 60 square miles. It is fed principally by the outlets of Chewaucan Marsh and by Crooked Creek. The water has high levels of sodium carbonates and other salts. The elevation of high water is about 4250 feet, and the lowest part of the bed is about 4244 feet, according to surveys of the Oregon State Highway Commission. John Work and his brigade of 1832–33 reached the north end of this lake on Oct. 16, 1832, and called it Salt Lake. *See California Historical Society Quarterly*, Sept. 1943, p. 204. Work does not say so, but his diary implies that this was not a new discovery and that trappers had been there before. Arrowsmith's map of North America, corrected to 1832–33, shows this Salt Lake with reasonable accuracy. The lake was visited on Dec. 20, 1843, by then Captain John C. Fremont, and named for his chief, Colonel J. J. Abert of the U.S. Topographical Engineers. The lake was reported entirely dry in 1924, but has contained water since that year. Very complete descriptions of the lake and its surroundings including the Abert Rim, the imposing fault scarp on the eastern shore, are in USGS *Water-Supply Papers 220* and *363*.

Lake Ann, LINN. Lake Ann is immediately north of Marion Lake. It is named for Pamelia Ann Berry, cook for the Minto road viewing party. *See* Pamelia Lake.

Lake Billy Chinook, JEFFERSON. The water impounded by Round Butte Dam on Deschutes River was named Lake Billy Chinook in honor of a Wasco Indian born about 1827. Chinook joined Fremont in 1843 and accompanied him to California and thence to Washington, D.C., in 1844. He returned west with the emigration of 1845 and settled near The Dalles in 1851. In 1856 he moved to the Warm Springs Indian Reservation where he resided until his death. In 1866–67 during the Shoshone Indian War he served a year as acting first sergeant of Captain John Darragh's Indian Scouts. Billy Chinook was one of the nominal chiefs of The Dalles band of Wascos and as such was a signer of the "Treaty With the Tribes of Middle Oregon, 1855." He died Dec. 9, 1890 and was buried in the Warm Springs cemetery.

Lake Bonneville, HOOD RIVER, MULTNOMAH, WASCO. This is the impoundment of Bonneville Dam stretching east to The Dalles Dam. It has a normal pool elevation of 72 feet. *See* Bonneville.

Lake Charline, DOUGLAS. This lake four miles southwest of Cowhorn Mountain was named for Charline Thurston. She was the daughter of USFS ranger Charles Thurston.

Lake Chetlo, LANE. Lake Chetlo is northwest of Waldo Lake. *Chetlo* is a Chinook jargon word meaning oyster. It was applied to this lake because of its shape.

Lake County. Lake County was created Oct. 24, 1874, by the state legislature, and received its name because of the number of large lakes within or partly within its borders, including the Klamath lakes, Lake Abert, Summer Lake, Goose Lake, Silver Lake and the lakes of the Warner Valley. The territory comprising Lake County was taken from Wasco and Jackson counties. Lake County in 1989 had an area of 8275 square miles, according to ODOT. Klamath County was formed from the west part of Lake County in 1882, and the Klamath lakes are not now in Lake County. In 1876 there was a lively squabble about the selection of a county seat for Lake County. For details, *see* Bullard Creek.

Lake Creek, DESCHUTES. Lake Creek is the outfall of Suttle Lake. It flows toward the Metolius River, but about two miles from its source it splits and partly disappears later to form three forks which rejoin prior to entering the Metolius River south of Camp Sherman.

Lake Ewauna, KLAMATH. This is an enlargement or elbow in the outlet of Upper Klamath Lake. The connection to the north from Upper Klamath Lake is Link River. The outlet of Lake Ewauna is Klamath River. The name of the lake is from the Klamath Indian *Iuauna*, a condensed form of *Yulalona*, the name of a place below the falls of Link River.

Lake Harriet, CLACKAMAS. Lake Harriet was named for the daughter of Franklin P. Griffith, the first president of Portland General Electric Company. It was formed when a predecessor company dammed Oak Grove Fork Clackamas River for hydro-electric power.

Lake Harriette, KLAMATH. In 1988, Shannon Applegate provided the following information about this name with the comment that it came from Elizabeth Applegate Barry, granddaughter of O. C. Applegate. Lake Harriette is at the headwaters of Moss Creek west of Upper Klamath Lake between Mount Harriman and Aspen Butte. It was named by O. C. Applegate, probably about the same time he named nearby Lake of the Woods. Oliver Cromwell Applegate, the son of Lindsay Applegate, was a first cousin of Harriet Applegate, daughter of Lindsay's brother Charles. The young cousins had a warm relationship as both were of a literary and artistic bent. Harriet was a budding novelist and believed that Harriette had a grander look than plain Harriet. She died at age 16 and a short time later when her cousin named Lake of the Woods, he named nearby Lake Harriette, being careful to preserve the 'grander' spelling.

Lake Kiwa, LANE. Lake Kiwa is north of Waldo Lake. The name is from the Chinook jargon word meaning crooked, and was applied to this lake because it was elbow shaped. The word is said to have come originally from the Wasco Indian language.

Lake Labish, MARION. This is a marshy area east of Brooks and Chemawa, now almost completely drained and in cultivation. Lake Labish ditch, which flows into Little Pudding River, is practically all that is left of the original lake. The lake was named by early settlers on French Prairie for *la biche*, the female deer, although French-Canadians frequently used the word to mean elk. In the evening of Nov. 12, 1890, a Southern Pacific train, bound for California, plunged through the Lake Labish trestle. Five persons were killed and many injured.

Lake Lytle, TILLAMOOK. This is a seashore lake about five miles north of the entrance to Tillamook Bay. It has an intermittent outlet. There was once a post office nearby of the same name. These features were named for E. E. Lytle, a prominent Oregon railroad builder, who, among other things, constructed the Pacific Railway and Navigation Company line from Hillsboro to Tillamook, later owned by the Southern Pacific Company.

Lake Marr, LANE. This small pond is about a mile from the Pacific Ocean and five miles north of the Siuslaw River. It was named for Ezra E. Marr, who at one time owned a ranch adjoining the lake. In 1925 it was reported that he was a lighthouse keeper in the state of Washington.

Lake Merritt, COOS. Lake Merritt is the former Lower Pony Creek Reservoir constructed by the Coos Bay-North Bend Water Board. On Nov. 6, 1967 the board voted to name this body of water Lake Merritt to honor Byron W. "Barney" Merritt who went to work for them in 1929 and continued until his death in Mar. 1967.

Lake Miller, KLAMATH. Lake Miller is the large drained meadow that US-97 crosses just north of the California line. It was named for a very early ranching family in Klamath County. *History of Central Oregon*, p. 940, mentions a Mr. Miller and his three sons, John H., William and Warren, settling here in 1868. John H. and W. Y. Miller both took up government land in 1873 but the compiler can only assume the lake was named for the family in general.

Lake of the Woods, KLAMATH. This is a descriptive name, given because of the dense stand of timber nearby. The lake is about three and a half miles long on the east slope of the Cascade Range, partly fed by a stream rising southeast of Mount McLoughlin. Its elevation is about 4950 feet, and SH-140 between Medford and Klamath Falls skirts its northern end. In a letter to Will G. Steel, dated Oct. 28, 1925, Captain Oliver C. Applegate of Klamath Falls says that he named Lake of the Woods in 1870 when he was building a road by the lake. He built a cabin at the south end of the lake in that year. A post office called Lake of the Woods was established to serve the area on May 17, 1930, with Fred E. Wahl postmaster. This office was closed Aug. 15, 1931. It was near the north end of the lake. In the late

1930s an effort was made to establish the mongrel form Lake O' Woods and a post office using that style was established July 19, 1941. The USBGN in *Decision List 6103* adopted the original form, Lake of the Woods, for the lake and the community. The post office soon followed suit and in 1981 was operating as a community post office under Klamath Falls.

Lake Oswego, CLACKAMAS. The original community of Oswego was named for Oswego, New York, by A. A. Durham, a pioneer of Oregon of 1847. At one time he operated a sawmill in the Oregon community which he named for his former home in the East. For information about his activities in Oregon, *see* Durham. Oswego post office was established on Dec. 31, 1853, with Wesley C. Hull postmaster. On May 1, 1959, the residents of Oswego and those of Lake Grove at the west end of Oswego Lake voted to merge into a single city that was called Lake Oswego.

Lake Penland, MORROW. Lake Penland was formed in the 1970s when Mallory Creek was dammed at Penland Prairie about 20 miles southeast of Heppner. The lake is named for William Penland, the founder of Lexington, who came to what is now Morrow County in 1868. The prairie was named in the early 1900s when three of Penland's sons, William, Lanes and Henry Penland formed the Penland Stock Company to own the land along Mallory Creek.

Lake Simtustus, JEFFERSON. When Pelton Dam on Deschutes River was built in 1958 by Portland General Electric Company, the Warm Springs Indians chose this name for the impounded waters to honor Kyuslute Simtustus, a warrior of the tribe, who served as a scout for the U.S. Army in the 1867–68 campaign against the Paiutes. After his discharge, he returned to the the Warm Springs Reservation and lived there until his death in 1926. Simtustus was equally well known by his nickname, Pipsher.

Lake Umatilla, GILLIAM, MORROW, SHERMAN, UMATILLA. This lake was formed in 1968 when the Columbia River was impounded by John Day Dam. It is the final link providing slack water for navigation from Bonneville Dam, just above tidewater, to the Washington State line passing through Lake Wallula. The name comes from the town of Umatilla at the east end of the pool. For a discussion of the name, *see* Umatilla River.

Lake Wallula, UMATILLA. Lake Wallula is formed by the Columbia River impounded at McNary Dam near the town of Umatilla. The lake was named for the town of the same name at the confluence of Columbia and Snake rivers in Washington. *Walla* is an Indian word for "running water" in several languages and *Wallula* is a variant in a manner similar to Walla Walla meaning "fall after fall" or "small, rapid river." For additional information, *see* Scott's *History of the Oregon Country*, v. 2, p. 314.

Lakecreek, JACKSON. Lakecreek post office takes its name from Lake Creek, an important stream that flows into Little Butte Creek. Lake Creek post office was established Dec. 10, 1886, with Joseph T. Delk first of a long list of postmasters. In the 1890s the Post Office Department had an attack of efficiency, and consolidated the names of a great number of offices made up of two words, though for some reason names like New York, San Francisco, and Niagara Falls were overlooked. In any event, the name of the office in Jackson County was changed to Lakecreek on Apr. 24, 1894, and that was the official style until the office was closed after World War II.

Lakeport, CURRY. Lakeport was the name of a locality in the northwest part of the county, so called because it was established on Floras Lake about three miles southeast of Langlois. In 1894 it was planned to dig a canal to connect the lake to the Pacific Ocean so that timber products could be transported by ship. Floras Lake is several feet higher than the ocean so this scheme was abandoned. About 1908 a few summer residences were built along the lake front and a real estate promotion was put into high gear along with renewed talk of a channel. Lakeport post office was established June 22, 1910, with Emil Burg first postmaster and a number of buildings were constructed including a substantial hotel. The post office was closed June 30, 1915. In June 1946, Louis L. Knapp of Port Orford told the compiler that the project at Lakeport, including the plan to cut a channel from the lake to the ocean to accommodate ocean vessels, turned out to be impracticable. By the 1970s, trees and undergrowth had obliterated the townsite. The locality was first called Crittenden and later Pacific City, but that name could not be used for a post office because of duplication with an office in Tillamook County. *See Lakeport: Ghost Town of the South Oregon Coast*, by Bert and Margie Webber.

Lakeside, COOS. Lakeside is situated near the shores of Tenmile and North Tenmile lakes, and was named on that account.

Lakeview, LAKE. Lakeview is said to have been named at a citizens' meeting held in 1876. John A. Moon suggested the name. A post office was established late in 1876. Goose Lake was larger in those days and the water was nearer the town, hence the selection. Lakeview is one of the highest towns in Oregon. The bench mark in the county courthouse has an elevation of 4800 feet. M. W. Bullard was one of the first settlers arriving in 1869, and in the first county seat election, offered 20 acres of land should his place be chosen. This choice was made at an election in 1876, and Bullard gave land for the courthouse. He sold 300 acres to Moon, who filed the plat for the town on May 26, 1877. In May 1900, every business house in town but two was burned, and by October reconstruction was nearly complete. For story of the county seat fight of 1876, *see* Bullard Creek.

Lamberson Butte, HOOD RIVER. This is a well-known point east of Mount Hood, with an elevation of about 6600 feet. It was named for Lewis H. Lamberson of Portland, an early day member of Mazamas. He spent several summers at Cloud Cap Inn, and members of the Langille family named the butte for him because he made a trip to its top. This was about 1895.

Lambert Slough, YAMHILL. Lambert Slough empties into Willamette River south of Dayton and Lambert Bend is at its mouth. They bear the name of James

W. Lambert, who settled in the area in 1868. In the 1870s, he and William Lambert operated the Willamette Sawmill on Lambert Slough.

Lamonta, JEFFERSON. Harold Baldwin of Prineville informed the compiler in 1927 that this place was named by Miss Kate Helfrich, the name referring to Grizzly Mountain nearby. *History of Central Oregon*, p. 734, says the townsite was platted in Apr. 1905, by John C. Rush. While the intent of the name is obvious, the words "la monta" are not part of any language with which the compiler is familiar. Lamonta post office was established Sept. 7, 1898, with Miss Helfrich first postmaster. The office was closed in Apr. 1918.

La Mu, HARNEY. A post office with the odd name La Mu was established in Harney County Nov. 6, 1889, and discontinued Mar. 19, 1890. Elizabeth Newman operated the office for this short period, and when it was closed, what little business there was was turned over to Harney. It was in Crane Creek Gap, near what was later the site of Crane.

Lampa Creek, COOS. Lampa Creek is tributary to Coquille River a few miles east of Bandon. The name has been spelled several ways. It was originally called Lamper or Lampa Creek, for an old settler. The name of this settler is given as Seth Lampa in *Pioneer History of Coos and Curry Counties*, p. 395. The stream was later called Lampy Creek by a local property owner, and the style Lamprey was used on some government maps. Local usage finally crystallized on Lampa, and that style has been employed for a good many years. A post office called Lampa was established near this stream on May 9, 1905, with James L. Bean first and only postmaster. This office was closed to Bandon on Oct. 15, 1918. Highway signs use the style Lampa.

Lancaster, MALHEUR. This station was named for Lancaster, Pennsylvania, by D. M. Brogan, who was born there. Lancaster was between Vale and Brogan.

Lancaster Falls, HOOD RIVER. Lancaster Falls is a fine cascade on the first stream west of Warren Creek about a mile west of Starvation Creek State Park. In 1970 at the suggestion of Gertrude G. Jensen and Donald J. Sterling, Jr., the OGNB applied the name of Samuel C. Lancaster, the engineer who designed the Historic Columbia River Highway prior to World War I. Lancaster was born in Magnolia, Mississippi, Jan. 11, 1864. After attending college in Tennessee, he worked on the Tennessee highway program, one of the first hard-surfaced networks in the United States. He came to Oregon in 1908 and first designed the campus at Linfield College in McMinnville. He then proceeded to his best-known work, the Columbia River Highway, which was opened to traffic in 1915. Lancaster died on Mar. 4, 1941 and in 1963 a bronze plaque was dedicated to him at the Vista House on Crown Point. For editorial comment, *see Oregon Journal*, Nov. 11, 1970. An interesting letter from Mrs. Jensen is printed adjacent to the editorial.

Lancelot Lake, LANE. Ray Engels of the USFS named this lake along with nearby Camelot Lake because of a fancied resemblance to the terrain of an old time jousting field. *See also* Camelot Lake.

Landax, LANE. The name Landax was first used by the Southern Pacific Company for a siding but the compiler has been unable to determine why the selection was made. When the post office was established in Dec. 1914, the name was used for the office. Wilbur H. Hyland was the first postmaster. The name of the office was changed to Signal on June 16, 1927, and this office was discontinued in Nov. 1938. The writer does not know if Landax and Signal were in exactly the same place.

Landes Creek, LANE. Landes Creek flows into Hills Creek southeast of Oakridge. It was named for Joe Landess, an early USFS employee. The final "s" has been lost for many years.

Landrith Bridge, COOS. This bridge is over South Fork Coos River east of the town of Coos Bay. In May 1943, Mrs. S. B. Cathcart, formerly Dora Landrith, of Coos Bay, wrote the compiler that the correct spelling of this pioneer family name is Landrith and not Landreth. The bridge was named for a member of the family who owned land nearby.

Lane County. Lane County was created Jan. 28, 1851, by the territorial legislature. In 1989 it has an area of 4611 square miles. It was named for Joseph Lane, who came to Oregon in 1849, as first territorial governor. In 1851 and 1853 he led the campaigns against the Rogue River Indians. In 1859 he was elected United States Senator. He supported the contentions of the seceding states in 1860–61, and when his term as senator expired in 1861, he retired to private life. In 1860 he was nominee for vice-president with Breckenridge. His death occurred Apr. 19, 1881, at Roseburg. Joseph Lane was born in North Carolina, Dec. 14, 1801. Prior to coming to Oregon, he had distinguished himself in the Mexican War, and had been a member of the Indiana legislature. His attitude on secession wholly changed his political standing in Oregon. For references to Lane, *see* OGN, 1928 edition, pp. 193–194. For history of early boundaries of Lane County, by F. V. Holman, *see* *OHQ*, v. ii, p. 33.

Lane Creek, DOUGLAS. This Lane Creek flows into Booth Arm of Siltcoos Lake. BLM records show David Lane filed on land there in 1908.

Lane Creek, JACKSON. Lane Creek is a short stream that flows into Willow Creek from the west about three miles west of Central Point. Walling, in *History of Southern Oregon*, p. 377, says the stream was named for an old man named Lane, who was murdered on its banks in very early days. There was active gold mining along Lane Creek in the early 1850s. The community of Willow Springs, one of the first settlements in Jackson County, was situated near the junction of Lane and Willow creeks.

Lane Mountain, DOUGLAS. This mountain, about 12 miles east of Roseburg, was named in honor of General Joseph Lane, who was an early settler in the Umpqua Valley and the first territorial governor. For data concerning him, *see* Lane County.

Lane Ranch, KLAMATH. W. G. Lane founded this ranch in the northwest corner of Klamath Marsh in the early part of the 20th century. Lane Creek also bears his name.

Lane Ranch, LAKE. Lane Ranch northwest of Silver Lake was started in the 1870s by Andrew V. Lane. He was the first justice of the peace in Silver Lake.

Lang Canyon, GILLIAM. Lang Canyon drains into the Columbia River from the south at a point about five miles west of Arlington. The canyon was named for Thomas Stackpole Lang, 1826–1896, a native of Maine, who came to Oregon in 1875 and for a time engaged in the sheep business in the vicinity of Heppner. He loaded wool on the Columbia River boats by means of a chute or tram in the canyon that now bears his name. Thomas Lang held a number of prominent positions in Maine, both in business and in politics. The latter years of his life were spent at The Dalles and for four years he was receiver of the U.S. Land Office at that place. For biography, *see Illustrated History of Central Oregon*, p. 261. *See also* Rockville.

Langdon Lake, UMATILLA. This lake is near the summit of the Blue Mountains and is skirted by the highway between Weston and Elgin. It is an artificial lake made by damming one of the sources of Lookingglass Creek. The elevation of the lake is about 4875 feet. It was named for John W. Langdon of Walla Walla, who furnished a substantial part of the money necessary for surveying the ground and building the dam. Langdon did this from public spirit, to provide a camp ground.

Langell Valley, KLAMATH. Langell Valley is a natural geographic feature, and a post office bears the same name. Both were named for Arthur Langell, an early settler, who took part in the Modoc War. He was afterward killed in an altercation with a neighbor named Swingle. The post office was established about 1871 and has been moved about to several locations. It is now near the Oregon-California boundary line.

Langille Crags, HOOD RIVER. These crags north of Eliot Glacier were named for the Langille family, early settlers in the Hood River Valley and for many years associated with the development of transportation and hotel facilities on Mount Hood. William Langille was a pioneer guide on the mountain.

Langlois, CURRY. This post office is near Floras Creek. It was named for the Langlois family which has for many years been prominent in Curry County. William V. Langlois was born on the Island of Guernsey, English Channel, and came to Curry County in 1854. His wife was Mary A. King. A number of their children have been prominent in Curry County affairs. For additional information about the Langlois family, *see* editorial page, *Oregon Journal*, June 28, July 1, 1927.

Langrell Gulch, BAKER, UNION. This gulch runs northwest and empties into Big Creek valley at the Union County line southwest of Medical Springs. It was named for Richard T. Langrell, an early Baker County settler, who operated a local sawmill.

La Pine, DESCHUTES. La Pine was named by Alfred A. Aya. The name was suggested by the abundance of pine trees in the neighborhood. When the post office was established the postal authorities consolidated the two parts of the name into Lapine. The original form continued in some popularity and on Apr. 1, 1951 the Post Office Department changed to La Pine. This temporarily compounded the confusion as certain progressive elements had previously conformed with the Post Office. At this writing, La Pine prevails uncontested, but if this form is supposed to indicate a French origin, it is of course incorrect, as the French word would be *Le Pin*. Lapine post office was established in Sept. 1910, by change of name from Rosland.

Lapover Lake, WALLOWA. Lapover Lake, which is in S 27, T 3S, R 43E, is named for Lapover Cabin on Lostine River. The cabin was named because an addition to the original structure lapped over the main part of the building.

Laraut, DOUGLAS. Postal records show that Laraut post office was established June 16, 1890, with Narcisse LaRaut postmaster, and was closed Mar. 19, 1891, with all papers to Wilbur. The LaRaut home was about eight or ten miles west of Wilbur and near the Umpqua River. In Feb. 1946, Kenneth F. Barneburg of Wilbur dug up some history of the office, which was apparently never in actual operation. Mr. Barneburg located Narcisse LaRaut, Jr., then living in Salem, who reported that the elder LaRaut received a supply of stamps and other equipment but for some reason the office was not operated.

Larch, YAMHILL. This office named for the forest tree was established at the Summit House station on the Trask toll road 17 miles west of Yamhill. Miss Clara Rhude was the only postmaster the place ever had. She was the daughter of Mr. and Mrs. Oliver Rhude, who operated the Summit House. In addition to post office duties Miss Rhude helped in cooking, in general housekeeping and in making a dozen beds for travelers and residents. It is reported that the post office was established to provide a legal but fictitious and temporary address for persons proving up their homesteads. The Summit House was built in 1889 by Martin T. Record and was in use for many years after the post office was closed. *See* McMinnville *Telephone-Register*, Sept. 5, 1946, p. 1, for news story and picture. Postal records show that Larch post office was established Sept. 9, 1891, and was closed Feb. 10, 1894, with papers to Byersville. It is more than probable that the name Larch was used because of the presence of the noble fir rather than of any of the true larches.

Larch Mountain, MULTNOMAH. Larch trees probably do not grow on Larch Mountain. Forest experts assert that the tree grows only in that part of the state east of the Cascade Range. The tree on Larch Mountain known by lumbermen as the larch is really the noble fir, *Abies nobilis*, and is not related to the larch in any way. The name Larch Mountain is, however, well established for an important and beautiful geographic feature, and there it will doubtless remain. Larch Mountain has an elevation of 4058 feet.

Larison Rock, LANE. This rock and Larison Creek nearby were named for

George Larison, a resident of the valley of Middle Fork Willamette River. He was a son-in-law of B. J. Pengra, a pioneer of Oregon. The spelling Lairson is wrong. In the 1880s Larison logged at the mouth of the creek and floated the logs down the Middle Fork to Springfield.

Larson Creek, JACKSON. Larson Creek flows into Rogue River about three miles north of Prospect. Mrs. Frances Pearson, who was born in the area, told the compiler in 1979 that this creek was named for an early homesteader and BLM records show that John A. Larson filed for a homestead nearby in 1902.

Larwood, LINN. Larwood post office was in operation from July 25, 1893, until Aug. 12, 1903, and was named in honor of the postmaster, William T. Larwood. This office was approximately ten miles east of Crabtree in the foothills of the Cascade Range.

Last Chance Creek, WALLOWA. This stream flows into Minam River in T 4S, R 42E. It was named by George Miller in the fall of 1890. Miller was a sheep man and the last chance he had to make camp before getting out of the mountains was on this creek.

Latham, LANE. Latham was a station on the Southern Pacific Company railroad a little more than a mile south of Cottage Grove. It was established when the railroad was built through towards Roseburg in 1872. Milton S. Latham was governor and then United States senator from California. He was interested in Ben Holladay's financial activity and was one of the trustees of the Oregon & California Rail Road Company's bond issue of Apr. 1870. This is the issue that was widely sold in Germany and eventually led to the activity of Henry Villard. Latham post office was established Sept. 16, 1878, with James J. Comstock first postmaster. The office was closed Feb. 14, 1888.

Lathrop Creek, JOSEPHINE. This creek rises in Grants Pass and flows west about four miles to join Vannoy Creek. It was originally called Dutcher Creek, but there is another Dutcher Creek emptying into Rogue River at Finley Bend about nine miles west of Grants Pass. The Josephine County Planning Commission voted in 1965 to change the name to Lathrop Creek to honor the late Judge Raymond Lathrop who resided near the creek for many years and was county judge of Josephine County when he died in 1961. This was duly approved by the USBGN in *Decision List 6602*.

Lathrop Glacier, DOUGLAS. In 1966 Dr. Theodore G. Lathrop discovered a small glacier on the north side of Mount Thielsen, apparently the southernmost glacier in Oregon. Studies were made of the glacier and these were reported in *Mazama*, 1968, 1971 and 1976. Dr. Lathrop, who was also an authority on hypothermia, died in 1979 and, at the instigation of the mountaineering community, the OGNB named this glacier in his honor.

Latigo Creek, GRANT, HARNEY. This creek rises on the south slopes of Snow Mountain and flows southeast into Whiskey Creek about 30 miles northwest of Burns. *Latigo* is the Spanish word for whip that in western America has come to mean saddle strap. There is also a Latigo Lake appropriately near Cincha Lake near the headwaters of North Santiam River in Linn County.

Latourell Falls, MULTNOMAH. Latourell Falls is the name of a beautiful feature adjacent to the Historic Columbia River Highway, and also the post office name of the early community. The railroad station name was Latourell. Joseph Latourell was a prominent settler in the locality and it was named for him. The name Latourell frequently appears in print with a final "e," which is wrong. The falls are on property formerly owned by Guy W. Talbot of Portland, who had them accurately measured and found their height to be 249 feet. Latourell Prairie, on the bluffs above the Columbia River east of Latourell Falls received its name from the same source. For information about Joseph Latourell and the dedication of the falls to the state, *see OHQ*, v. 19, p. 78. Early in 1929, Mr. and Mrs. Talbot gave the state of Oregon about 220 acres of land adjoining the Historic Columbia River Highway and Latourell Falls. This property is known as Guy W. Talbot State Park. In 1934 the heirs of George W. Joseph also gave property for a park on the upper part of the stream and this is known as the George W. Joseph State Park. Rooster Rock was the name of the first post office in this vicinity. It was established in May 1876, with John Gilstrap postmaster, and was named for the natural feature nearby. Joseph Latourell became postmaster in Aug. 1876, and the name was changed to Latourell Falls in Aug. 1887. The compiler does not know if the office was moved when the name was changed.

Latta Crater, DESCHUTES. This crater is on the northwest slope of Black Crater. Professor Edwin T. Hodge in *Mount Multnomah*, p. 112, names it Lotta Crater for the discoverer of Lost Creek Canyon, but he misspells the name. John Latta was an early settler in Lane County and went to the Prineville area in the 1860s. At one time he was interested in the McKenzie toll road and was an associate of John T. Craig. *See OHQ*, v. 31, p. 261.

Laughlin Hills, WASCO. These hills lie south of SH-216 between Bear Springs and Wapinitia. They are named for Robert A. Laughlin who settled on Juniper Flat in 1872.

Laughlin Hollow, WASCO. Laughlin Hollow north of Antelope was named for Benjamin Franklin Laughlin who homesteaded near Antelope in the 1870s. Laughlin was the son of William O. Laughlin, one of the founding settlers of The Dalles.

Laurance, MARION. On July 7, 1898, Ellsworth Benjamin Fletcher was appointed postmaster at Laurance by Charles Emory Smith, then postmaster general. The post office was established in Mr. Fletcher's home at the North Howell crossroads. M. Louetta Carwood was appointed postmaster Nov. 23, 1900, and the office was discontinued Dec. 22, 1902, with papers to Gervais.

Laurance Lake, HOOD RIVER. Laurance Lake was formed in 1969 when the Middle Fork Irrigation District completed their dam on Clear Fork southwest of Parkdale. It is named in honor of Sheldon Laurance who served as the chairman of the district during the dam's planning and construction period. Laurance died in Hood River on Dec. 23, 1968 just before the completion of the project.

Laurel, WASHINGTON. Laurel was named early in 1879 at a meeting held at a school about a quarter of a mile east of the present site of the community. C. W. (Cooney) Williams suggested the name because there were so many laurel trees in the vicinity. The post office was established Mar. 14, 1879, with Alfred Mulloy postmaster. The office was first at his home, approximately a mile south of the present site of Laurel but was moved to the present location about 1890. For additional information about the community, see Hillsboro *Argus*, Nov. 26, 1931. Laurel community should not be confused with Laurelwood, about five miles due west. This is the site of Laurelwood Academy, a Seventh Day Adventist school founded in 1904 and named for a fine stand of what were supposed to be laurel trees. The compiler was told in 1981 that one of the original trees was still standing but that it was a madrone or *Arbutus menziesii*, a pleasing and common tree in western Oregon.

Laurel Hill, CLACKAMAS. Laurel Hill lies between Zigzag River and Camp Creek and is traversed by US-26, the Mount Hood Highway, over a fine grade. It was one of the terrors of the emigrants who traveled the Barlow Road. Wagons had to be let down the slopes of this hill with ropes. The name Laurel Hill was applied in the earliest pioneer days. For comments on this name and Zigzag River, see Barlow Creek and Zigzag River. It is probable that the pioneers named Laurel Hill for the rhododendrons that grew thereon rather than true laurels.

Lava, DESCHUTES. Lava was the name once applied to a post office near the Deschutes River south of Bend in what was then Crook County. The name was derived from Lava Butte and its remarkable lava flows, which were a little to the northeast. The locality was from time to time served by offices with other names. Crater post office was established Feb. 18, 1888, with David A. Findley first postmaster. This office, which was discontinued May 21, 1890, is shown on a map of 1889 as being just a little north of the Vandevert ranch. It was obviously named for Lava Butte and the nearby lava flows. A post office named Carlisle was established at the Vandevert ranch on May 10, 1893, with William P. Vandevert postmaster. Vandevert family tradition says that Mrs. Vandevert, who was from Kentucky, was an admirer of John G. Carlisle of that state who became secretary of the treasury in 1893. She named the office in compliment to Carlisle. This office was closed Apr. 6, 1895. It was planned to reestablish the office with a new name Lava, and this was done on June 11, 1895, with Sarah J. Potter postmaster. However, this order was rescinded and Lava post office was not actively established until Apr. 8, 1896, when David W. Aldridge was appointed postmaster. Lava office was on the Aldridge ranch a few miles north of the Vandevert place. On Dec. 29, 1899, Mrs. Sadie Vandevert was appointed postmaster of Lava and the office was moved to the W. P. Vandevert ranch. The office operated until Nov. 1908.

Lava Butte, DESCHUTES. Lava Butte is a conspicuous lapilli cone with a deep crater in its summit. From the south base of this butte a stream of basaltic lava poured out, which flowed to the northwest and dammed Deschutes River which resulted in Benham Falls. For detailed information about Lava Butte and its flow, *see* USGS *Bulletin 252*, by I. C. Russell, p. 110. The butte is composed of cinders and scoriaceous fragments and volcanic bombs. The name Lava described the flow at the base of the butte rather than the butte itself. Russell gives the opinion that in 1903 the flow was more than 150 years old. There was once a post office called Lava not far from the butte, but it has been discontinued.

Lava Cast Forest, DESCHUTES. In 1970 Phil Brogan of Bend provided the following information regarding this region: "This interesting feature, recently set aside by the USFS as a place of special geologic interest, is midway up the north slope of Newberry Crater. Here some 5000 years ago a massive flood of lava spilled through a forest of pines, congealing around bases of trees and enveloping toppled conifers." The USFS has designated Lava Cast Forest a Special Interest Area and built a special trail with interpretive signs.

Lava Lake, DESCHUTES. This is the apparent source of Deschutes River and it takes its name from the surrounding lava flows. Lava Lake ordinarily has no surface outlet, but during high water flows through an open channel to Little Lava Lake nearby, from which flows Deschutes River. Phil Brogan in the *Sunday Oregonian*, Apr. 4, 1976, p. B-8, has an interesting article on Deschutes River in which he states that geologists now consider Elk Lake the true source as water from that lake moves through underground lava channels to Lava Lake. The name Big Lava Lake is wrong.

Lava River Cave, DESCHUTES. Lava River Cave is really a lava tunnel about two miles long, caused by the outflow of the molten lava after the top had hardened. It is near Lava Butte. It is open at one place for a distance of about 400 feet, and is 30 to 40 feet deep and 50 feet wide. In this section the roof has fallen in. The floor of the cave is covered with fine sand, apparently deposited by a stream. Land along the course of the Lava River was given by The Shevlin-Hixon Company to the state for a park adjacent to US-97, The Dalles-California Highway. The lava flow forming the river came at an earlier date than the outflow from the base of Lava Butte. For additional information, *see* editorial page of the *Oregonian*, Dec. 9, 1925, and USGS *Bulletin 252*.

Lavacicle Cave, DESCHUTES. This cave is located 35 miles southeast of Bend and two miles northwest of Antelope Butte. It was discovered in 1959 by Dan Beougher, Max Stenkamp and Lester Martin and contains remarkable lava drip formations. The name Lavacicle was coined by Phil Brogan of Bend.

Lavadoure Creek, DOUGLAS. Lavadoure Creek flows into South Umpqua River about five miles above Days Creek and nearby is Lavadoure Community Hall. Lavola Bakken of the Douglas County Museum informed the compiler in 1976 that Joseph Lavadoure was a fur trader who may have been in western Oregon as early as 1825. He spent many years as a resident of the South Umpqua River region although he is buried near Pendleton. She added that the dates on his tombstone are 1791–1892.

Laverty Lake, WALLOWA. Laverty Lake is in the Wallowa Mountains in T 3S, R 43E. It was named for Frank Laverty by J. H. Jackson who stocked the lake with fish in 1914. This information came from J. H. Horner and R. L. Forsythe of Enterprise. Laverty lived at Lostine for a number of years.

Lawen, HARNEY. This place, according to one writer, was named after Henry Lauen, who settled in the neighborhood about 1887. No explanation is given as to the difference in spelling. Another correspondent has informed the compiler that the place was named because of the green lawn-like appearance of the neighboring shore of Malheur Lake. This version of the story maintains that the local applicant for the post office misspelled Lawn into Lawen. It seems likely to the writer that the first version is the more probable. Lawen post office was established in 1891.

Lawhead Creek, LINN. Lawhead Creek empties into North Santiam River a mile downstream from Detroit Dam. It was named for Loren W. Laughead who patented a homestead nearby in the 1890s. Laughead was the son of William M. and Elizabeth Laughead who were very early settlers in Marion County. The family used both spellings of the name and at one time Loren W. also went by the name William.

Lawler Canyon, UMATILLA. Milton P. Lawler settled along this canyon near McKay Creek shortly after the turn of the century.

Lawrentz, KLAMATH. Lawrentz post office was established Jan. 31, 1894, and was discontinued Apr. 17, 1895. It was named for Martha A. Lawrentz, the first and only postmaster. In Jan. 1947, Mrs. Fred G. Brown wrote that Lawrentz post office was situated where Pelican Bay Lodge resort was later established. It was at the site of Rocky Point post office, which was later called Harriman. Mrs. Brown adds an interesting paragraph to the effect that Lawrentz post office may have been discontinued because of a letter sent by Mrs. Lawrentz, the postmaster, to officials in Washington in reply to an inquiry about an alleged irregularity. She told her superiors: "If you will attend to your affairs in Washington, we shall run the post office here." Mrs. Brown adds that the mail was carried on horseback from Klamath Falls to Lawrentz.

Lawson Creek, CURRY. This stream, which heads near Fairview Mountain, was named for a pioneer prospector.

Lawson Creek, LANE. Lawson Creek is tributary to Siuslaw River east of Cushman. In Dec. 1942, Earl H. Hill wrote the compiler that the stream was named for John Lawson, a homesteader who lived near its mouth. He had a large family and has been dead many years.

Lawson Mountain, WHEELER. Gilbert Lawson settled near West Branch after the turn of the century and applied for a homestead on the slopes of this mountain in 1911.

Lawton, GRANT. Lawton was a mining camp in the northeast part of the county in the Blue Mountains. This camp was a couple of miles down stream from

Granite. The place was named for Major-General Henry Ware Lawton, who was born in Ohio in 1843. General Lawton had a distinguished career in the United States Army. He was killed in the battle of San Mateo, Philippine Islands, on Dec. 19, 1899. Lawton post office was established on the Grant County list on May 14, 1900, with Frank G. Hull first of three postmasters. The office was discontinued to Granite, June 15, 1905. The country was ringing with the praises of General Lawton at the time the post office was petitioned.

Laycock Creek, GRANT. This creek is tributary to John Day River from the south between Mount Vernon and John Day. It is named for John A. Laycock who took up land at its mouth in 1872. Laycock was born in Illinois in 1847 and came to Canyon City in 1865. He was a well-known rancher who also had substantial holdings in Bear Valley. In 1898 he was elected county judge of Grant County. *See History of Baker, Grant, Malheur and Harney Counties*, p. 473.

Layne Creek, LANE. Layne Creek empties into Siuslaw River in S 22, T 19S, R 7W. It is named for George W. Layne who homesteaded by it in the 1890s. On maps made shortly after World War II, it is incorrectly shown as Luyne Creek.

Layng Creek, LANE. Layng Creek is southeast of Cottage Grove. It was named for George Layng, a nearby resident. He filed a Homestead Entry in 1892 spelled George Laying.

Layton Point, HARNEY. This is the correct name of the point on the east side of Harney Valley, not Laton. It was named for a pioneer resident.

Lazarus Island, TILLAMOOK. Lazarus Island, in the Nehalem River opposite Wheeler, was named for one Lazarus, a homesteader who tried to develop the land but had little success.

Leaburg, LANE. Leaburgh post office was established Jan. 29, 1877, with Leander Cruzan as first postmaster. The name of the office was adapted from Cruzan's first name. Later the spelling was changed to Leaburg, but the compiler cannot tell when. The name was changed to Deerhorn on May 25, 1907, and that style was used until the office was closed in Sept. 1913. The change to Deerhorn also included a change of location about two miles west and a new Leaburg office was established Sept. 20, 1907. As of 1981 it is a CPO out of Eugene.

Leader, MULTNOMAH. Leader post office in the east part of the county did not last long but the name is of historic interest. The office was established on July 15, 1881, and was given the name of Joseph H. Leader, the first postmaster. The name of the office was changed to Taylor on May 25, 1882, at which time Ervine J. Taylor was postmaster. In Apr. 1949, William H. Stanley wrote from Gresham that he recalled that the old Joseph Leader home was on Corbett Heights at what is now the junction of the Historic Columbia River Highway and the Corbett Hill Road. Corbett Heights, of course, is now the rural community of Corbett. After Taylor became postmaster, he moved the office down on the river front to his home about .5 mile west of what is now Corbett Station. This was about the time the railroad was being built east up the Columbia River.

Leander, LINN. This station was just east of Albany on the Oregon Electric Railway. C. H. Stewart of Albany told the compiler in 1927 that it was on the donation land claim of Leander C. Burkhart, a pioneer of 1846, and was named for him. The facilities were incorporated into the railway's Albany Yard in the early 1940s.

Leap, WALLOWA. Leap is a place north of Enterprise in s 8, T IN, R 44E. According-ing to J. H. Horner of Enterprise it was first planned to call this community Fairview, but postal authorities would not accept that name because of duplica-tion. Mrs. F. W. Heskett suggested that the office be named Leap because it was leap year. That name was accepted, and the office was established at the Heskett house in Apr. 1892. Ben Weathers carried the mail in from Wallowa to Leap on horseback. Leap had not been a post office for some years prior to 1944.

Leaver Creek, LANE. Leaver Creek is a small tributary of Nelson Creek south of Greenleaf. It is named for James H. Leaver who settled along the creek in 1896. He lived on the property off and on until his death in 1918.

Lebanon, LINN. Lebanon was first called Kees Precinct for Morgan and Jacob Kees, who came there in 1848. Jeremiah Ralston had the site surveyed and record-ed in 1851 and adopted the name Lebanon after his birthplace, Lebanon, Tennes-see. The first post office in the vicinity, Santyam, was established Mar. 14, 1851, with Russel T. Hill postmaster. The name was changed to Washington Butte July 30, 1852, with John W. Bell as the new postmaster. At the time the change was made, the old name was put down as Santiam and not Santyam. Leland H. Wake-field became postmaster on Mar. 29, 1855. Later the post office name was changed to Lebanon to agree with the townsite. Early post office lists show that a Lebanon post office was established on June 5, 1851, with Jno. S. Hunt postmaster. The place was about 12 miles east of Salem, in Marion County, and had nothing to do with Lebanon in Linn County. The Marion County office Lebanon was discontinued in June 1858.

Le Conte Crater, DESCHUTES, LANE. This crater is on the summit of the Cascade Range south of the South Sister. Dr. E. T. Hodge of the University of Oregon named it for Professor Joseph Le Conte, famous Pacific Coast scientist of the University of California. Le Conte Crater is just southwest of Rock Mesa and has an elevation of 6574 feet.

Lee, COOS. Lee post office was established in 1888. William P. Mast was the first postmaster and was a native of North Carolina. He named the office for the great Confederate leader General Robert E. Lee. Lee was not a post office in 1929.

Lee Wood Spring, JEFFERSON. This spring was on the property of Lee Wood, the son of Whitfield Wood of Ashwood.

Leeds, JACKSON. Leeds post office, about ten miles up Rogue River from Trail, was named for W. H. Leeds, a newspaper publisher of Ashland and onetime state printer for Oregon, by A. J. Florey, for many years postmaster at Eagle Point. Florey was postmaster at Eagle Point in Apr. 1890, when Leeds post office was established with Frank M. Manning first postmaster. For information about W. H. Leeds, *see* Turnbull's *History of Oregon Newspapers*, p. 260. The post office apparently did not operate continuously and was finally closed Feb. 28, 1913. *See also* Peyton.

Leeds Island, DOUGLAS. Leeds Island is in the Umpqua River northwest of Reedsport, and was named for Captain Josiah B. Leeds, a pioneer of Gardiner. Captain Leeds was born in New Jersey, Dec. 1, 1829, and went to sea with his father when he was eight years old. He sailed into San Francisco Bay in June 1851, as mate of the schooner *Frances Helen*. He was made master of the schooner and sailed her in the coastwise trade. He crossed the bar into the Umpqua River May 10, 1853. He gave up seafaring and settled in Gardiner in 1865. He operated a boat on the Umpqua River and went into the sawmill business with G. S. Hinsdale and Edward Breen. This enterprise later became the Gardiner Mill Company. He sold his interest in 1882 and after four years in the stock business, sold out in 1886 and moved to San Francisco with his family. He died there in 1889. For additional data, *see* Walling's *History of Southern Oregon*, p. 532.

Lees Camp, TILLAMOOK. About 1939 Rex Lee bought approximately 16 acres of the Reeher property on Wilson River near the mouth of North Fork and the place was later developed into a tourist and sportsmen's camp with the name Lee's Wilson River Camp. In 1947 it was reported that H. M. Slauson was associated in the establishment, which is about 25 miles upstream from Tillamook on the Wilson River Highway and not far from the summit of the Coast Range. The post office, established in 1947 with the name Lee's Camp and with Mrs. Slauson postmaster, is very nearly in the same location as the much earlier office called Wilson. It now operates as a CPO out of Tillamook.

Leggins Spring, WHEELER. Grover Blake, an early USFS ranger, told the writer that this spring north of Spanish Peak was named for Frank Leggins, a miner in the early days.

Lehman, UMATILLA. Lehman, which is the site of Lehman Springs, was named for a pioneer settler, James Lehman, probably about 1873. The springs were discovered by Dr. John Teel, an old time physician. Lehman post office operated from Sept. 8, 1899, to Feb. 29, 1928.

Lehman Meadow, HARNEY. This meadow at the headwaters of Burnt Cabin Creek northeast of Delintment Lake was named for Mike A. Lehman (1935–1986), USFS Fire Management Officer for the Ochoco National Forest.

Leland, JOSEPHINE. Leland is an historic name in southern Oregon, used for a railroad station and for a post office about four miles west of the original location, which was known in early days as Twogood's, Leland, Fort Leland and the Grave Creek House. The old location is just north of where the old Pacific Highway crosses Grave Creek north of Grants Pass. Miss Martha Leland Crowley, a member of the emigration of 1846, died on what is called Grave Creek, and was buried there under a prominent oak tree. For the history of this event, *see* Grave Creek.

See also Grants Pass *Courier*, Jan. 23, 24, 26, 1934. In Jan. 1854, the legislature passed an act to change the name of Grave Creek to Leland Creek in honor of Miss Crowley, but the public never accepted the name. About 1852 Bates and Twogood operated a ranch on Grave Creek and packed into the mines. Preston's map of 1856 shows Twogood's place approximately in the southeast corner of S 3, T 34S, R 6W, although the real point may have been in section 2 or 11. About 1853, McDonough Harkness bought out Bates, and continued with James H. Twogood, operating the packing business and keeping the travel. The place was called the Grave Creek House, and also Leland Creek House. Leland post office was established Mar. 28, 1855, with Harkness postmaster. He was killed by Indians near lower Rogue River Apr. 27, 1856, and apparently Twogood took his place as postmaster at Leland. About 1860 Twogood sold out to the Harkness family. During the Rogue River Indian War of 1855–56 a military post called Fort Leland was established at this point, where Twogood and Harkness had already built a stockade for the protection of local settlers. In the early 1880s the railroad was built about four miles west of the old locality of Leland. A station named Leland was established on the railroad and it has been in service for over a century. Leland post office was closed Apr. 30, 1943.

Lemish Butte, DESCHUTES. This butte, west of Crane Prairie, is named with the Klamath Indian word for thunder, or the mythical genii of the Thunder, five in number, and their parents, Old Thunders.

Lemiti Meadow, CLACKAMAS. Lemiti Meadow is near the summit of the Cascade Range north of Olallie Butte. It drains into Clackamas River through Lemiti Creek. This name presents the curious but not infrequent application of a descriptive geographic name that does not describe the feature to which it is attached, but something entirely different. *Lemiti* is the Chinook jargon word for mountain, and is a corruption of the French *la montagne*. The compiler has been told that Ephraim Henness, pioneer resident in the valley of North Santiam River and one of the first forest rangers in the north Cascade Range, established and named Lemiti Ranger Station. The word *lemiti*, or mountain, was later applied to a nearby point, Lemiti Butte, and also to Lemiti Meadow and Lemiti Creek by someone who did not understand its exact significance.

Lemolo Falls, DOUGLAS. These falls are on North Umpqua River below Kelsay Valley. They were named by the USFS. *Lemolo* is a Chinook jargon word meaning wild or untamed. It is from the French-Canadian *le moron*, a corruption of *marron*, a runaway negro. The spelling Lemolo has been approved by the USBGN.

Lemolo Lake, DOUGLAS. This reservoir was formed by damming North Umpqua River at the lower end of Kelsay Valley approximately two miles upstream from Lemolo Falls from whence came the name. The lake is primarily for hydroelectric power but is also a popular recreation area with a nearby campsite. Normal elevation is 4148 ft.

Lemon Island, MULTNOMAH. Lemon Island is a low body of land west of Government Island in the Columbia River. It is occasionally spelled Lemmon Island. Investigations by George S. Shepherd, attorney at law, Portland, Oregon, indicated that this island once belonged to Peter Lemon who was unable to sign his name and used a cross on legal documents. His name was variously spelled Lemmons and Lemons, but later use is invariably Lemon, and deeds given by Lemon to correct title to the island were apparently made for the purpose of eliminating the uncertainty caused by the spelling Lemmons, Lemons, etc. As a result of Shepherd's investigation it may be assumed that Lemon spelled his name as indicated herein.

Lena, MORROW. The postmaster at Lena in 1926 wrote the compiler that this post office was named by J. S. Vinson and C. E. Hinton, local residents. It was understood that the name was selected because it had a pleasing sound. This is all the information the writer has been able to get. Lena post office was established June 11, 1873, with Hinton postmaster and closed Aug. 31, 1942.

Leneve, COOS. Leneve post office was established about 1917. The name Conlogue was suggested to postal authorities but it was considered too difficult. Leneve is the name of a pioneer family of Coos County. Leneve was not a post office in 1935.

Lenhart Butte, CLACKAMAS. Lenhart Butte, south of Cherryville, was named for Joe Linhart who homesteaded there in 1888. His son, Frank, was still living on the old homestead in 1970 and he told the compiler that the family name had been misspelled on an early map. The form Lenhart is firmly established.

Lenox, WASHINGTON. David T. Lenox, a pioneer of 1843, was one of the most prominent early settlers in Washington County. His land claim was about three miles east of the present community of North Plains. Lenox post office, named in compliment to this pioneer, was established in Mar. 1895, with Peter Jossy postmaster. This office was about a mile south of what is now Helvetia and about a half a mile north of Germantown road. It was a little south of the center of s 10, T 1 N, R 2W.The office operated until Aug. 4, 1903.

Lent Canyon, WALLOWA. Lent Canyon empties into Cottonwood Creek in the northeast part of the county in T 5 N, R 46E. It bears the name of one Joe Lent, who squatted on a claim in the canyon and built a cabin near the canyon mouth.

Lents, MULTNOMAH. Oliver P. Lent settled where the town of Lents stands in 1866, on a tract of 190 acres. He was born near Marietta, Ohio, Aug. 31, 1830; died at Mount Tabor, Portland, Apr. 22, 1899. His wife, Martha A. Buckley, was born at Parkersburg, Virginia, Mar. 19, 1833; died Apr. 5, 1905. Soon after arriving in Oregon, about 1852, Lent settled on the site of Sycamore, east of Lents. During many years he engaged in the sawmill business. He was a prominent and resourceful man, and served as school director, road supervisor and justice of the peace.

Lenz, KLAMATH. Lenz, a station on the Cascade Line of the Southern Pacific Company, was named for Charles A. Lenz who settled nearby before the turn of the century. His wife, Anna Corbell Lenz, lived in Klamath County for over 100 years.

Lenz Butte, HOOD RIVER. This butte near Odell was named for John Lenz, an early settler.

Leona, DOUGLAS. The town of Leona was named for a young girl, Leona Perkins. This was about 1900. In earlier years the place was called Hudson, and a post office with that name was in operation from June 1889, until Oct. 1890. Leonard M. Perkins was the first postmaster. When it was planned to revive this office, it was found that the old name, Hudson, could not be used because of duplication. Leona post office was established Feb. 14, 1901, with Thomas E. Bledsoe first postmaster. Miss Leona Perkins was the granddaughter of Newt Mulvaney, a prominent local resident.

Leonard Creek, DOUGLAS. Leonard Creek flows into Umpqua River near Tyee in S 33, T 24S, R 7W. It was named in 1973 at the request of the local residents to honor Bessie Leonard who was born in New York in 1878 and moved to Tyee in 1914. Mrs. Leonard served many years as postmaster as well as clerk of the Tyee School. She died in Apr. 1968.

Lepage Park, SHERMAN. This park at the mouth of John Day River was one of several constructed along the borders of Lake Umatilla after John Day Dam was placed in service in 1968. Lewis and Clark passed the mouth of John Day River on Oct. 21, 1805, and named it LePage's River for Baptiste LePage, one of their boatmen. It is most fitting that the park should recall the original name.

Leslie Gulch, MALHEUR. The Rev. Melville T. Wire, in the *Oregonian*, Dec. 5, 1926, sect. 5, p. 5, gives the story of the name of this feature. The gulch originally drained into Owyhee River from the east not far from the old post office called Watson, but now drains into Owyhee Reservoir. It bears the name of a cattleman, one Leslie, who was killed there by lightning about 1880. For an illustrated story about a Mazama expedition to Leslie Gulch, *see* magazine sect. *Sunday Oregonian*, Aug. 17, 1947.

Leuthold Couloir, CLACKAMAS. Joseph R. Leuthold was born in Switzerland in 1906 and came to this country as a small boy. He was an ardent skier and one of the founders of the Mount Hood Ski Patrol as well as an accomplished mountain climber with numerous first ascents of northwest peaks. Leuthold died on Dec. 12, 1965, and in 1970 at the instigation of representatives of the American Alpine Club, Mazamas, Wy'East Climbers and Crag Rats, the "Hourglass" gully climbing route above Reid Glacier on Mount Hood was named Leuthold Couloir in his honor. For his obituary, *see Mazama*, 1965.

Levage Creek, LANE. Levage Creek flows into Munsel Lake from the north. Jerry A. Levage patented a homestead along it in the early 1890s.

Lewis, WALLOWA. Postal authorities informed the compiler that this post office was established Sept. 11, 1913, with Alta E. Lewis first postmaster. She was the wife of Frank Lewis, and the post office was apparently named for the family. J. H.

Horner of Enterprise told the compiler that the name was suggested by a neighbor, Herbert L. Dunbar.

Lewis and Clark River, CLATSOP. Lewis and Clark mentioned this stream as Netul River. This was on Dec. 7, 1805. Their winter quarters for 1805–06 were on this river, and were called by them Fort Clatsop. Since that time the Indian name has been abandoned, and the form Lewis and Clark River is universally accepted. It was named in honor of the explorers. The earliest use of the modern name that has come to the compiler's attention is in Lee and Frost, *Ten Years in Oregon*, 1844, p. 15. Silas B. Smith, the authority on Clatsop County history, says that the name *Netul* referred to a point on the bank of the river rather than to the stream itself. It seems not to have been the custom of many Oregon tribes to name streams, but places along streams. The Klamath Indians were an exception to this rule. The site of Fort Clatsop was acquired by the Oregon Historical Society in 1901 but is now part of the Fort Clatsop National Monument. It comprises three acres of land, two miles from Youngs Bay, on Lewis and Clark River. For description of the place, *see* the *Oregonian*, June 27, 1885, p. 3. For details of Fort Clatsop and its restoration, *see* that heading.

Lewis Rock, WHEELER. This high point south of Mitchell was named for Charles G. Lewis who settled there in 1887. Lewis later moved to West Branch where nearby Lewis Butte also carries his name.

Lewis Glacier, DESCHUTES. This small glacier is on the southeast slope of South Sister and was named in 1924 for Meriwether Lewis by Professor Edwin T. Hodge of the University of Oregon. The most comprehensive information about Meriwether Lewis is to be found in Elliott Coues *History of the Expedition of Lewis and Clark*, v. 1. Lewis was born Aug. 18, 1774, near Charlottesville, Virginia, of distinguished family. At the age of 20 he enlisted in the militia to suppress the Whisky Insurrection, and three years later had reached the rank of captain. In 1801 he became private secretary to President Thomas Jefferson. Jefferson accepted, in 1803, Lewis' offer to become a member of the expedition to explore the West. On Apr. 30, 1803, the treaty concluding the Louisiana purchase was signed at Paris, and in the summer of that year the party under the joint command of Meriwether Lewis and William Clark set out for the Pacific Ocean. The expedition was successful, and the leaders were in Washington again in Feb. 1807. Lewis was rewarded by being made governor of Louisiana. His death occurred Oct. 11, 1809, in the exact center of what is now Lewis County, Tennessee, this county having been created in his honor. The manner of his end is a mystery. There is some belief that he committed suicide during a fit of mental derangement, but the weight of evidence seems to indicate that he was murdered for his money. Coues discusses this at some length in the above-mentioned volume. For other information about Lewis and the expedition, *see* Thwaites, *Original Journals of the Lewis and Clark Expedition*.

Lewisburg, BENTON. Haman C. Lewis, a pioneer of 1845, settled near this place on a donation land claim, and the station bears his name. Lewis was a member of the Oregon constitutional convention.

Lewisburg, MARION. Lewisburg post office was named for a family of pioneer settlers, information about which will be found in Down's *History of the Silverton Country*, p. 92. Daniel P. Lewis came to Oregon in 1851 and settled near Drift Creek in the Waldo Hills. Lewisburg post office was established in Apr. 1889, with Samuel Lewis first of seven postmasters. The office was closed in Apr. 1904. The office was probably moved around, but was generally about eight miles south-southeast of Silverton. In later years the locality was called Victor Point but the writer has not been able to learn why.

Lewisville, POLK. John T. Ford of Dallas wrote the compiler on Oct. 3, 1927, that Lewisville was named for David R. Lewis, a pioneer of 1845. The community was on the Lewis donation land claim. David R. Lewis' certificate was no. 2995. By the 1980s, nothing remained to mark its location.

Lexington, MORROW. The town of Lexington was named by William Penland, a prominent and successful pioneer resident of that part of Morrow County. He was a native of Lexington, Kentucky, and when he founded the new town he called it for his birthplace. Lexington post office was established Nov. 11, 1885, with Nathaniel A. Yeats first postmaster.

Libby, COOS. Libby is a place on Coalbank Slough a little south of Coos Bay, named for a well-known Indian woman, Libby, who was kind to white settlers. The locality was once called Eastport and was the location of coal mining activity. Libby post office was established June 11, 1890, with Enoch Gore postmaster. This office was closed July 5, 1892, but the locality still goes by the name Libby. The historic name Eastport could not be used for the post office in 1890 because of possible confusion with East Portland, then an incorporated community with its own post office. For additional information about Libby Tinilon and the mines at Libby, *see* Beckham, *Coos Bay, The Pioneer Period*, pp. 18 through 26.

Liberal, CLACKAMAS. Liberal is a community about four miles north of Molalla. It is said to be named for Liberal, Missouri. The late Dee Wright told the compiler that Liberal, Missouri, was named because of liberal credit terms by a pioneer storekeeper in the community. However, reference works say that the Missouri town was named because of the liberal views of its citizens. Harrison Wright, a pioneer of 1844, settled near the present site of Liberal, Oregon, and was instrumental in securing a pioneer post office with the name Molalla, established Apr. 9, 1850, with Wright first postmaster. This office was not at the present site of Molalla, but was moved to that place in the 1870s. Liberal post office was established Mar. 25, 1893, with Katie Willett postmaster. The office was discontinued Apr. 30, 1918.

Liberty, BENTON. Gill's map of Oregon, 1874, shows a place called Liberty to the northeast of Corvallis and about a mile south of what is now Wells. The post office was established in Apr. 1856, with James Gingles first postmaster. The office was finally discontinued in May 1867. The compiler does not know the reason for the name unless it was a patriotic one.

Liberty, MARION. Liberty is a well-known community situated about four miles south of Salem on the old highway south to Albany. It is about a mile west of the Pacific Highway East. It is the center of a very productive fruit section. Liberty post office was established Jan. 24, 1895, with J. R. Willard postmaster. The office was closed Mar. 19, 1901, and the community is now served through the Salem office. The community took its name from Liberty School, which was probably established prior to 1875. H. R. Crawford of Salem wrote the compiler in Nov. 1945, that Liberty School apparently was named because it was on the Liberty road running south from Salem, and the road got its name because it was an extension from Liberty Street in Salem itself.

Liberty, WHEELER. Liberty post office was on West Branch Bridge Creek about 12 miles southwest of Mitchell on the old road to Prineville, now the Ochoco Highway. It was near the foot of the hill where the road started upgrade over the Ochoco Mountains. Liberty post office was established Jan. 2, 1889 with James M. Mansfield postmaster. The office was closed July 24, 1894. G. C. Blake of Roseburg wrote the compiler in Jan. 1966 that Mrs. Mansfield's mother was Sarah Ann Ross, not Liberty Ann Ross, and that the post office and church were named for Liberty, Missouri, the former home of Caleb and Coanza Woodward, early settlers in Wheeler County.

Lick Creek, JACKSON. Lick Creek empties into Little Butte Creek near Brownsboro. Margaret Pool, whose family settled in Browsboro in the early days, told the compiler this creek was named for the salt licks along its banks.

Lick Creek, WALLOWA. Lick Creek was named in early days by hunters and stockmen because of the alkali and salt licks which attracted elk and deer. Lick Creek flows into Little Sheep Creek in T 4S, R 46E.

Lightning, WALLOWA. In Apr. 1907, Lightning post office was established with Eva P. Johnston postmaster. The office operated until July 1909. Lightning post office was near the mouth of Lightning Creek where that stream flows into the Imnaha River about 20 miles north of and downstream from Imnaha, and was named for the creek.

Lightning Creek, WALLOWA. Lightning Creek was so named because of the frequent storms in the neighborhood. The stream flows into Little Sheep Creek east of Enterprise.

Lightning Creek, WALLOWA. This is an important tributary to Imnaha River, into which it flows in T 3N, R 49E. According to J. H. Horner of Enterprise, it was named because of an incident connected with Abe Tharp who later homesteaded on the creek. Tharp and James Wilson once had great difficulty working their way down the creek and when they met Jack Johnson on the Imnaha, they told him they had had a "lightning" time making the trip because it was so rough. Johnson told Horner this was the origin of the name.

Lillard Ditch, BAKER. Several members of the Lillard family homesteaded east of Haines in the first decade of the present century. Shortly thereafter they banded together and formed the Lillard Ditch Company to handle irrigation water.

Lillian Falls, LANE. Lillian Falls are on Nettie Creek below and west of Waldo Lake. They are named for Lillian Ryker McGillvrey, the daughter of Augustus V. Ryker, the USFS man in charge of building the original trail through the area. Through error sometime in the 1930s a sign was erected using the form Lithan. This persisted on some maps and it was not until 1986 that the OGNB, after a field inspection by Chairman Tom McAllister, was able to correct the spelling. Lillian McGillvrey died in 1985 at age 78.

Lilly Lake, WALLOWA. This lake in T 4S, R 43E, was named for Samuel W. Lilly, a resident of Wallowa Valley. The name was applied by J. H. Jackson, who stocked the lake with fish about 1914.

Lilyglen, JACKSON. Lilyglen is a locality on the Dead Indian Road northeast of Ashland, at the Lindsay ranch, owned by William and Charles Lindsay. The name was suggested by Mrs. Lindsay, mother of the two ranchers, on account of the wild mountain lilies that grew in the surrounding meadows. Lilyglen post office was established Aug. 13, 1904, with William Lindsay postmaster. The office was closed May 31, 1909, but the locality is still called Lilyglen. It is in the east part of T 38S, R 3E.

Lime, BAKER. The post office at Lime was established on Sept. 4, 1899 to serve the community that grew around the lime processing business. The large deposits of limestone provided lime for a considerable area of eastern Oregon and western Idaho. In 1925 the Sun Portland Cement Company built a plant at Lime to provide cement for the Owyhee Dam. After the dam was completed in 1928, the operation was sold to the Oregon Portland Cement Company who ran the plant for many years. They were absorbed by Ash Grove Cement West and when the nearby high grade limestone deposits were depleted in the mid 1970s, raw material was brought in from the vicinity of Nelson, some 15 miles northwest on Burnt River. A new plant was built at Nelson which opened in 1979 and the Lime operation was closed in 1980. In 1990 the plant was still standing but vacant. Lime post office was closed in 1964.

Limpy Prairie, DOUGLAS. There are several features that include the name Limpy in T 27S, R 1E. G. C. Blake of Roseburg informed the compiler in 1966 that they were all named for an aged Indian who made his home on Little River or East Fork as it was then known. He took his nickname from an injured leg and a halting gait.

Lincoln, JACKSON. Lincoln is a community on the Green Springs Highway a little west of Pinehurst. A story about this lumbering town in the Medford *Mail-Tribune*, Sept. 29, 1929, says that it was named for Lincoln, New Hampshire, by the Henry family, which owned the Oregon mill and formerly operated in New England.

Lincoln, POLK. This community, which is on the west bank of Willamette River north of Salem, is said to have been named for Abraham Lincoln. The post office was established May 31, 1867, with Daniel J. Cooper postmaster. There had previously been an office at or near this location, called Valfontis. *See* Valfontis. For story about Lincoln community, *see* Salem *Capital Journal*, June 17, 1941. Lincoln post office was discontinued about 1901 and patrons have been served by a rural route from Salem.

Lincoln Beach, LINCOLN. Lincoln Beach is a summer resort area about three miles north of Depoe Bay on the Oregon Coast Highway. It was so named because it was in Lincoln County. The post office was established May 22, 1933, with George W. Betts postmaster.

Lincoln City, LINCOLN. On Dec. 8, 1964 the cities of Oceanlake, Delake and Taft and the unincorporated communities of Cutler City and Nelscott voted to combine to form a new single community. The name Lincoln City was, of course, derived from the county and was a non-controversial solution to the often thorny surviving name problem. For information on the components, *see* the individual headings.

Lincoln County. Lincoln County was created Feb. 20, 1893, by the state legislature and was named for Abraham Lincoln, the sixteenth president of the United States. The county has an area of 983 square miles in 1989 according to ODOT.

Lincton Mountain, UMATILLA. In 1862 a group headed by Samuel Linkton and Dorsey Baker of Walla Walla formed a company to build a road across the Blue Mountains to the Grande Ronde Valley to compete with the road from Umatilla Landing on the Columbia River. The route ran generally south from Walla Walla and crossed this high ground between Walla Walla River and Couse Creek where Linkton had previously built a steam powered saw mill. Advertisements and news accounts in the *Washington Statesman* in the 1860s show that Linkton probably spelled his name with a "k" but the form Lincton has been in general use for many years.

Lindros Arm, COOS. Lindros Arm runs east from North Tenmile Lake. It is named for Adolph Lindros who was born in Finland and came to Coos County in 1907. He worked on the Coos Bay jetty and then settled on a homestead and dairy farm near Lakeside. Saima Lindros Caughell, Adolph's eldest daughter, stated in 1985 that her father told her the name was orginally spelled Lindross but he dropped the final "s." The 1956 USGS Reedsport quadrangle uses the form Lindross but this was corrected in USBGN *Decision List 8602*.

Lindsey Creek, HOOD RIVER. This stream is reported to have been named for one John Lindsey, who took up a claim near the creek afterwards known as Lindsey Creek. Lindsey is said to have taken part in the battle at the Cascades in 1856 and was wounded therein. He was at one time a fireman on one of the river steamers. The stream is now well known by the name of Lindsey Creek.

Lindsley Creek, LANE. Lindsley Creek empties into North Fork Siuslaw River east of Munsel Lake. It is named for Samuel G. Lindsley who homesteaded near its mouth in 1880.

Line Creek, UMATILLA. Charles Kopp of Ukiah stated in 1969 that this tributary of Hidaway Creek was so named because it was at one time the dividing line between two sheep grazing allotments.

Link River, KLAMATH. This short stream connects Upper Klamath Lake with Lake Ewauna, and is named on that account. It is within the limits of the city of Klamath Falls, formerly known as Linkville. The Klamath Indian name for this stream was *Yulalona*, which meant to move back and forth, referring to the fact that during strong south winds the waters of Link River were blown back above the falls, leaving the bed of the stream, including the falls, partly dry. The name *Yulalona* was also used to refer to the settlement of Linkville near the falls. A condensed form of the name was *Iuauna*, which white people have adopted in the name Lake Ewauna. The Indian name for the falls in Link River was *Tiwishkeni*, literally rush of falling waters place. *See* Duwee Canyon, and *also* Lake Ewauna. The name Link River has been adopted by the USBGN.

Linn County. Linn County was created Dec. 28, 1847, by the provisional legislature. It was named for Senator Lewis F. Linn of Missouri, who nearly a decade before had been urging the American occupation of Oregon. Linn County was the first county to be taken from the original Champooick District, and comprised all of Oregon between the Willamette River and the Rocky Mountains, and between Santiam River and North Santiam River and the northern boundary of California. It was subsequently much reduced in size, but is still a large county, with an area of 2300 square miles. Lewis Fields Linn was born near the site of the city of Louisville, Kentucky, Nov. 5, 1795. He was the author of the donation land law, which gave free land to settlers in the West, and which was the forerunner of the homestead law. He was appointed United States senator for Missouri in 1833, elected in 1836 and re-elected in 1842, and served until his death. His work in the Senate was highly important to western settlement and acquisition of Oregon. His activity in the Senate, in support of his bill to occupy Oregon and granting land to actual settlers, was his last work of importance, for he died Oct. 3, 1843. Calhoun, McDuffie and Dayton led the fight against the Linn bill. They contended the bill would make a breach of faith with Great Britain, and cause international complications. The donation land act, based on Linn's idea, passed Congress Sept. 27, 1850. For history of his work for Oregon, *see* the *Oregonian*, Apr. 8, 1901, p. 6; May 8, 1887; *OHQ*, v. 19, pp. 283–305, by Lester Burrell Shippee. Senator Linn was a surgeon and lived at Ste. Genevieve, Missouri. His nephew, Lt.-Commanding William Pope McArthur, U.S. Navy, made the first survey of the Pacific Coast for the U.S. Coast Survey, 1849–50. His grand-nephew, Lewis Linn McArthur (1843–97) came to Oregon in 1864 to practice law, and was at one time a member of the supreme court of the state. His great grand-nephew, Lewis A. McArthur, was the original author of this book.

Linnemann, MULTNOMAH. This station on the Portland Traction Company line was two miles west of Gresham. It was named for Mr. and Mrs. John G. D. Linnemann, pioneers of 1852, who owned land nearby. Linnemann died in 1892, and Mrs. Linnemann Nov. 15, 1926, at the age of 98. For information about the family, *see* the *Oregonian*, Nov. 17, 1926, p. 4. The name is persistently misspelled. A. C. Giese, in a letter in the *Oregonian*, Sept. 22, 1927, calls attention to the fact that the platted name of the community is Cedarville, part of the Giese donation land claim. Apparently the railroad company and the Giese family were unable to agree on a name for the station.

Linney Creek, CLACKAMAS. This stream flows into Salmon River from the south, east of Linney Butte. The two features were named for an engineer connected with the Mount Hood Railway and Power Company project.

Linnton, MULTNOMAH. Peter H. Burnett and M. M. McCarver, pioneers of 1843, laid out the town of Linnton soon after their arrival in Oregon. They named it for Senator Lewis Fields Linn of Missouri. *See* Linn County. Burnett said of his town: "I have no doubt that this place will be the great commercial town of the territory." Burnett was afterwards first governor of the state of California. Linnton is now within the city of Portland.

Linslaw, LANE. In 1917 a petition was sent to Washington for a post office, and on Aug. 7, 1917 it was established with the name Linslaw. Ada Sutherland was first postmaster. Local residents are at a loss to explain the name, and say that they had nothing to do with its selection. The writer has a theory that the postal authorities had the name Siuslaw on file and the handwriting was not clear, with the result that the name Linslaw was applied to the office. This confusion could occur very easily. The office was discontinued Mar. 31, 1957. Linslaw is near the Siuslaw River.

Lint Slough, LINCOLN. Lint Creek flows into Lint Slough and Lint Slough empties into Alsea Bay at Waldport. These streams were named for one Lint Starr, reported to have been the first white man to claim land in the vicinity of the creek. The name Indian Slough is no longer applicable by decision of USBGN.

Linville, LINCOLN. Linville post office was named for the first postmaster, Robert W. Linville. The office was near Drift Creek a few miles east of Bayview. It was established May 26, 1896, and continued in operation until Apr. 15, 1915. Recent government maps do not show the place.

Little Applegate River, JACKSON. This is the correct name of an important tributary of Applegate River, not North Fork Applegate River. *See* decision of the USBGN, which agrees with local use. For origin of the name, *see* Applegate River.

Little Brother, LANE. Little Brother is a small butte northwest of the North Sister. It was so named because of its position in respect to the Three Sisters.

Little Crater Lake, CLACKAMAS. For many years this lake, some four miles north of Clackamas Lake, was called Crater Lake because of a peculiar crater or sink hole in the grassy marsh surrounding it. There was a notion that the name was not particularly apposite, especially on account of the much more important Crater Lake in Oregon and after World War II, the name was altered by the addition of the diminutive. The name Turquoise Lake had been suggested and when the matter was brought to the OGNB in 1967 others were also brought forward. However, past usage prevailed and the USBGN approved the present form in *Decision List 6802*.

Little Deschutes River, KLAMATH, DESCHUTES. This stream heads on the east slopes of the Cascade Range north of Mount Thielsen. It joins Deschutes River between La Pine and Bend. For several years federal authorities called the stream East Fork, but it was locally known as Little River. In 1926, at the suggestion of the writer, the USBGN officially named the stream Little Deschutes River, and this name has come into general use.

Little Eagle Creek, BAKER. This stream joins Eagle Creek on the range line between ranges 44 and 45 east. The name Little Fork is incorrect. *See* decision of USBGN.

Little Luckiamute River, POLK. This stream rises in the Coast Range southwest of Dallas. It joins Luckiamute River south of Independence. In the interest of simplicity government mapping agencies have dropped the word "Big" from the main branch. *Luckiamute* is an Indian word the meaning of which is unknown. Stories to the effect that it is based on an incident having to do with a deaf mute may be dismissed as fiction.

Little Nestucca River, POLK, TILLAMOOK, YAMHILL. As far as the writer knows, there is no translation into English of this Indian name. S. H. Rock, postmaster at Oretown, was authority for the statement that the real name of Little Nestucca River as given by the Indians was *Nestachee*. This probably referred to the lower part of the stream or to a point on its banks. *See* Nestucca River. Little Nestucca River flows into Nestucca Bay.

Little Niagara Falls, CLACKAMAS. This 15-foot-high falls on Salmon River is about six miles downstream from the mouth of Linney Creek. It is the third of six falls between Linney Creek and Welches and was named because it resembles its eastern namesake. For details of this group, *see* Stein Falls.

Little North Santiam River, MARION. This is the correct name of the main tributary of North Santiam River, which it joins at Mehama. Little North Fork is incorrect, and has been ruled against by the USBGN.

Little Santiam River, MARION. This stream is a by-pass from the main Santiam River into Willamette River, and is about two miles long.

Little Summit Prairie, CROOK. Little Summit Prairie is similar to and named in contradistinction to Big Summit Prairie some 12 miles to the west. USFS ranger Ralph Elder's notes at the Ochoco National Forest say this was once known as Camas Prarie as it was a favorite place for the Indians to gather camas root. A large ranger station was started in 1908 but never completed. The Connelly brothers had homesteaded the lower part and it was then known as Connellys Little Summit. By 1938, drought, erosion and over-grazing had seriously reduced its carrying capacity.

Little Wocus Bay, KLAMATH. This bay is at the south end of Klamath Marsh. Wocus is the English form of the name given by the Klamath Indians for the seed of the yellow pond lily, *Nuphar advena*. This plant grows in immense numbers in the marshes of Klamath County. The seeds were roasted by the Indians and ground for food.

Littlefield Spring, BAKER. This spring in Blue Canyon near the site of Auburn was on the ranch of David Littlefield, one of Henry Griffin's three companions when he discovered gold nearby in 1861.

Live Oak Mountain, DOUGLAS. Live Oak Mountain is a prominent geographic feature, elevation 3429 feet, near the head of Olalla Creek, and in the extreme northwest corner of S 26, T 30S, R 8W. The history of the name is unknown to the writer, but it was obviously applied because of a patch of canyon live oak trees on its slopes. Live oaks are not numerous in Oregon, although they constitute a prominent part of scattered forests in California. This live oak is known botanically as *Quercus chrysolepis* Liebman. Live oaks are sufficiently scarce in Oregon that a good sized grove is immediately conspicuous. Information about this patch of live oaks was secured from the supervisor of the Siskiyou National Forest and from District Assistant Edwin Frye. Mr. Frye visited this grove many years ago.

Liverpool, LINN. Liverpool post office was in operation in Linn County from Aug. 6, 1877, to Feb. 19, 1879, with Frank Sutter postmaster. The only reference to the place that the compiler can find is in the *Historical Atlas Map of Marion & Linn Counties*, 1878, p. 55, in the biography of Thomas Alford, where it is stated that the village of Liverpool was on his property about four miles northeast of Harrisburg. *See* Muddy Station. The locality is now known as Alford.

Llano, MALHEUR. *Llano* is a Spanish word meaning flat or plain. A post office was established with this name on June 5, 1888. It was closed to Vale on Sept. 18, 1894. Francis O'Neill was the only postmaster. The compiler has not been able to get the exact location of Llano post office, but it was probably at or near the location of a later post office Fangollano in the central part of the county. *Fangollano* is a Spanish name meaning mud flat.

Llao Rock, KLAMATH. This is a great bluff on the northwest rim of Crater Lake. Its top is 8046 feet above sea level, and 1869 feet above lake level. A bay at its foot is called Llao Bay. These two features were named by Will G. Steel on Aug. 15, 1885, for a Klamath Indian deity supposed to be associated with the lake. The rock was once called Mount Jackson for Colonel James Jackson, U.S. Army, veteran of Indian wars and a well-known resident of Portland for many years. He was at one time in command at Fort Klamath.

Llewellyn, LANE. Llewellyn was about 11 miles west of Eugene on the old Crow stage road, where it crossed Coyote Creek. The post office was established Feb. 18, 1886, with Mrs. Lilias Llewellyn Perkins first of three postmasters. The office was discontinued Sept. 17, 1904, due to the extension of rural free delivery. The name was, of course, taken from Mrs. Perkins' middle name. Henry Clay Perkins, her husband, was a prominent pioneer farmer and nurseryman, who had a place on Coyote Creek.

Loafer Creek, DOUGLAS. This creek forms the south border of Thorn Prairie on the upper reaches of North Umpqua River. It was named by the USFS for the intermittent sections of running water and dry creek bed. The creek just "loafs" along.

Lobert Draw, KLAMATH. Lobert Draw south of Chiloquin was named for a well-known early family. There were several Loberts in the general area but the draw was probably named for Hager Lobert who took up an Indian Allotment near its mouth.

Lobster Creek, CURRY. This stream is tributary to Rogue River a few miles above Wedderburn. It was doubtless named for the native crawfish or crayfish, as there are no real lobsters in Oregon waters, although there are many on land. The name was applied in very early days. Glisan, in *Journal of Army Life*, mentions the name several times when he was stationed at Fort Orford in 1855–56 and indicates that the expression Lobster Creek was already established and well known. There is another Lobster Creek in Lincoln, Benton and Lane counties, apparently named for the crawfish, but the compiler does not know the circumstances. A post office called Lobster was established on the Benton County list in Mar. 1883. It was in operation until July 1896. Old maps show the place in Lobster Creek valley about a mile east of the west boundary of Benton County.

Lockhart Creek, COOS. This tributary of South Fork Coquille River east of Eden Ridge was apparently named for Herbert Lockhart who took up property at its mouth in 1907. Lockhart was the son of Freeman G. Lockhart the early, well-known Coos County pioneer.

Lockit, WASCO. Lockit is a station on the Burlington Northern named with the Chinook jargon word for four, since it was the fourth station from the north end of the line up Deschutes River.

Lockit Butte, DESCHUTES. Lockit Butte, in the north part of Paulina Mountains, is named with the Chinook jargon word for four, it being the fourth butte of a series named all at the same time by the USFS.

Locoda, COLUMBIA. Locoda was a station on Spokane, Portland and Seattle Railway northeast of Clatskanie. It was once called Bradbury. The name Locoda was made by taking letters from the corporate title of the Lower Columbia Cooperative Dairy Ass'n and telescoping them into one word.

Locust Grove, DOUGLAS. A pioneer post office with the name Locust Grove was established on the Umpqua County list on Feb. 9, 1858, with Richard Smith first and only postmaster. The office was discontinued Sept. 10, 1863. Locust Grove, which was obviously given a descriptive name, was in one of the parts of Umpqua County that was annexed to Douglas County. Locust Grove was on the route of travel about six miles south of Yoncalla on the road to Oakland, but the compiler does not know its exact location. Old maps show it near what is now known as Rice Hill.

Log Cabin, KLAMATH. Log Cabin post office was short lived. It was situated at the Log Cabin service station and lunch rooms on US-97, The Dalles-California Highway, about five and a half miles south of the north boundary of Klamath County. The post office operated from June 13, 1930, until Dec. 31, 1930, when it was closed and the business transferred to Crescent. George H. Davis was postmaster. The main structure was of rustic construction, hence the name. The last time the compiler saw this establishment, the name had been changed to The Timbers.

Log Creek, WALLOWA. Log Creek was named for a pile of old logs lying across the trail along the stream. Log Creek flows into Imnaha River in T 2N, R 48E.

Log House Spring, JEFFERSON. Log House Spring is on Cherry Creek just above Wyman Creek. This is the site of the log house built by Andrew Jackson Schrum about 1870. Schrum was the first settler on upper Cherry Creek. For a picture and other details, *see* "Autobiography of Jacob Kaser," *OHQ*, v. 81, p. 281.

Logan, CLACKAMAS. Logan community and post office were named for Major-General John A. Logan of Civil War and political fame. The post office was established June 13, 1884, with Lafayette Hunniston, first postmaster. This office was on the flat or table land west of Clackamas River and east of Clear Creek. The locality is well known although the post office was closed Oct. 12, 1903, doubtless as the result of the extension of rural delivery. General John A. Logan was Republican candidate for vice-president in 1884 when the post office was established. His name had been frequently in the news which may have been the reason that the post office was named for him.

Logan Butte, CROOK. Logan Butte is a well-known landmark in the south part of T 18S, R 20E. Some of the butte may overlap into the township adjoining on the south. In Feb. 1948, Fisher C. Logan of Bend wrote that the butte was named for his uncle, Thomas Logan, who acquired nearby property in the early 1870s. An interesting feature of this area is the extensive deposit of bones of extinct animals.

Logan Creek, LANE. Logan Creek is tributary to Portland Creek near Sinker Mountain. A. J. Briem states in his *Recollections* that the creek was named for Burt Logan, a long time USFS employee during the first part of the twentieth century.

Logdell, GRANT. Logdell post office was established Aug. 7, 1916, with Ella Sproul first postmaster. The locality is southwest of Canyon City, and was once served by an office called Homer. The history of the name Logdell is not as clear as it might be, but it is said that the word Logdale was included on a list submitted to postal authorities. The spelling Logdell was officially adopted, but whether due to poor writing on the original list the compiler does not know. In any event it was intended to be a name descriptive of logging activity in the vicinity and either Logdell or Logdale is apposite.

Logie Trail Road, MULTNOMAH. James Logie was one of the earliest settlers on Sauvie Island. He was a Hudson's Bay Company employee, and was sent to the island about 1840 to take charge of butter making in one of the company's dairies. He worked on the old Indian trail over the hills into the Tualatin Valley, and made a better route out of it. It was named for him on that account. James Logie was born in the Orkney Islands. He died Mar. 24, 1854, and his widow, Isabella, also from the Orkneys, married Jonathan Moar. *See* letter by George B. Roberts in Oregon Historical Society files. Much of the original trail is now the route of Johnson Road.

Logsden, LINCOLN. Mrs. Hazel Schaffer, postmaster at Logsden in Apr. 1927, informed the writer that this place was named for an old Indian of the community, a Mr. Logsden. This is an unusual Indian name and may be a corruption of some other form. Logsden was a very old resident on the Siletz Indian Reservation. The post office was established in June 1914, with the name Orton, in compliment to a local family. The name of the office was changed to Logsden in June 1921.

Lolah Butte, DESCHUTES. This butte is northeast of Crane Prairie. The compiler is told the name is from the Chinook jargon. If that is true, the name is probably a form of *lo-lo*, meaning round, whole or complete. The accent is on the second syllable. This word is not the same as *lolo*, meaning to pack, or carry, which has the accent on the first syllable. There is a Lolo Butte not far from Lolah Butte.

Lolo Butte, DESCHUTES. This butte southwest of Bend was named by the USFS with the Chinook jargon word for pack or carry, apparently because supplies had to be carried to it.

Lolo Pass, CLACKAMAS, HOOD RIVER. Lolo Pass lies at the summit of the Cascade Range about two miles south of Bull Run Lake. From the west it is reached by way of Clear Fork Sandy River. Its elevation is about 3400 feet. It was named by Thomas H. Sherrard of the USFS for Lolo Pass in the Bitterroot Range in Idaho-Montana. John E. Rees, in his pamphlet *Idaho*, says that Lolo Pass in the Bitterroot Range received its name from a hunter and trapper named Lawrence who was buried on the banks of a stream on the Montana side. The Indians called the creek Lolo Creek because that was the best they could do with the name. They pronounced the name Loulou Creek. This stream heads northeast of the pass. It was called Travelers Rest Creek by Lewis and Clark. The attention of the compiler has been called to the fact that the Chinook jargon word for carrying and backpacking is *lolo*, and it is said that the pass in the Bitterroot Range was named from this source. Pioneers familiar with the Lolo Pass do not seem to have considered this to be the origin of the name. Gannett has yet another theory about *lolo*, and says that it is Nez Perce for muddy water.

Loma, HARNEY. *Loma* is a Spanish word meaning rising ground, or slope, frequently used for a locality from which there is a good view. Loma post office in Harney County was about eight miles north of the place called Narrows, in what was known as Sunset Valley. At one time there were 35 or 40 homesteaders in Sunset Valley, who later moved from the area. Loma post office was established Jan. 20, 1911, with Nathaniel Henney postmaster. The office was closed to Burns Jan. 15, 1912. Henney had made a previous effort to get postal service. An office named Henney, with Henney as the postmaster, was established June 4, 1908, but was never put in active service. The order was rescinded as of Jan. 31, 1909. The Loma post office was in the Henney home, just about south of the east end of Wright Point, near the center of the Henney homestead. This homestead claim was at the southeast corner of the intersection of the road east to Lawen and the road south to Narrows.

Loma Vista, LAKE. The name Loma Vista was made up of Spanish words meaning rising ground where a view was to be had. It is the same sort of a name as Viewpoint. Loma Vista post office was established in the Fort Rock Valley on Sept. 6, 1913, and was closed May 31, 1918. The office was in the home of Charles Mittge and his wife, Elsie Mittge, was first postmaster.

London Peak, JOSEPHINE. Up to recent times this peak had no name, but in 1939 Mrs. Helen Paul of Wolf Creek requested that it be named London Peak in honor of Jack London, the writer. Mrs. Paul was authority for the statement that Jack London spent several months in the vicinity when he was writing *Valley of the Moon*, and the peak was one of his favorites. London Peak is a mile and a half southwest of the town of Wolf Creek and a mile west of I-5 and has an elevation of about 3000 feet. The USBGN adopted Mrs. Paul's suggestion.

Lone Grave Butte, LAKE. Lone Grave Butte is in the southeast corner of Lake County and has an elevation of 6582 feet. It takes its name from a solitary grave near its east base. The eroded inscription on the headstone apparently reads "W. Kilbey NOV 28129," but the date could also be "NOV 28 29." The grave is on BLM property and they report that the marker was stolen in the fall of 1980. *See Oregon Journal*, Dec. 1, 1980.

Lone Ranch Creek, CURRY. Lone Ranch Creek flows into the Pacific Ocean south of Cape Ferrelo. The name comes from Lone Ranch, the 1860 homestead of John Cresswell. In 1872 Cresswell discovered borate of lime, now known as priceite, and in 1890 one Fleming took an option on the property with the intent to open the deposit. He allowed the option to lapse and Walter Gray purchased the land for the Pacific Coast Borax Company. After two years of desultory mining, operations ceased and the area returned to obscurity until 1961 when the new route of US-101 was opened for traffic. Part of the original ranch lying between the highway and the ocean was donated to the state in 1950 by Borax Consolidated Limited, parent company of Pacific Coast Borax Company. A second parcel was donated in 1960 by United States Borax & Chemical Corporation, successor to Pacific Coast Borax Company. Both parcels are now part of Samuel H. Boardman State Park.

Lonely, LAKE. Lonely post office with a descriptive name was established in the Warner Valley June 11, 1891, with Coelia Lemberger first and only postmaster. The office was closed June 10, 1895. The best available information is to the effect that Lonely was at or near the place later called Adel. Adel office was established in Apr. 1896, with Erastus C. Sessions first postmaster. Mrs. Lemberger was postmaster at Adel from Dec. 1896, to Aug. 1901. In July 1947, Mrs. Orvilla Stein, daughter of Mrs. Lemberger, wrote from Lakeview that she had never heard of Lonely post office, and there was a doubt in her mind that the office ever was in actual operation. In any event little is known about the place called Lonely with its appropriate name.

Lonerock, GILLIAM. Lonerock has been so called for many years. The place gets its name from a rock about 100 feet high and some 60 feet in diameter. It is a prominent landmark not far from the central part of the community. The post office was established in Nov. 1875. Lone Rock Creek takes its name from the same source. The town of Lonerock was founded by R. G. Robinson and Albert Henshaw in 1881 and was platted in 1882 by Robinson. The name used by the platters was Lone Rock, but the post office is Lonerock.

Lonesomehurst, HARNEY. Lonesomehurst post office was established Jan. 16, 1917, and discontinued Feb. 28, 1918. Henry K. Hardisty was the only postmaster. In the summer of 1946 Archie McGowan of Burns interviewed Mrs. Hardisty, widow of the postmaster, and among other things she reported as follows: "This post office was in our ranch home on Trout Creek about twenty miles south of Silvies post office, on the main road at that time. The mail was picked up at Silvies. I sent in several suggested names and they were rejected. In reading the 'funny' pages in the paper I found the name Lonesomehurst, which I submitted." Mrs. Hardisty appears to have had a keen sense of humor, and her selection of a name was certainly appropriate.

Long, MALHEUR. This station was named because of the length of the siding. It is on the Union Pacific Railroad between Riverside and Juntura.

Long Creek, GRANT. Long Creek is an important stream in Grant County and is said to have been so called because it is the longest creek in that part of the state. An inspection of the map indicates that this is probably not founded on fact although it may be the longest in the John Day River drainage. The name of the community Long Creek was suggested to postal authorities because it was near the stream.

Long Tom, LANE. Long Tom post office was established Sept. 3, 1853, with Augustus L. Humphrey first postmaster. It was out of service for about six months in 1884, but was reestablished. The name was changed to Madison on Sept. 19, 1904. The office was west of Eugene in the general vicinity of Elmira or Veneta, but it was doubtless moved around to suit the convenience of the various postmasters. It was never very far from Long Tom River. The change to Madison was doubtless in compliment to Madison Canaday, a local resident, and for many years postmaster at Long Tom office. For information about the history of the name, *see* Long Tom River.

Long Tom River, BENTON, LANE. George H. Himes stated this stream bears an imitation of an Indian tribal name, *Lung-tum-ler*. While on his way to the Umpqua River in 1834, John Work called it Sam Tomeleaf River. On his return trip, Work used the name Lamitambuff on July 1, 1834. David Douglas used the form Longtabuff River. Wilkes spelled it Lumtumbuff in 1841. *See OHQ*, v. 24, p. 264.

Long Walk Island, UMATILLA. When Lake Umatilla was formed behind John Day Dam in 1968, a number of islands were created. This one west of Irrigon is over a mile and a half long and only a few hundred yards wide. The name is descriptive but the circumstances of application are unknown.

Lookingglass, DOUGLAS. Lookingglass Valley was visited in 1846, according to local stories, by Hoy Flournoy, and he is said to have named the valley because of the beautiful appearance of the green grass in the valley, which reflected the light almost as well as a mirror.

Lookingglass Creek, UMATILLA, UNION. This stream flows into Grande Ronde River from the west. It bears the name of Lookingglass, a chief of the Nez Perce, who was so called by the whites because he carried with him a small looking-glass. His Indian name was *Apash-wa-hay-ikt*. For information about him *see The Life of Isaac Ingalls Stevens*, by Hazard Stevens. There is also a Lookingglass Lake, presumably named for the same man, in townships 5 and 6S, R 44E, on the boundary between Baker and Union counties.

Lookout Creek, BAKER. This stream is in T 14S, ranges 35 and 36E. It was at one time known as Sheep Creek, but the USBGN was prevailed upon to rename it Lookout Creek because there were already too many Sheep creeks in that part of the state.

Lookout Creek, WALLOWA. Lookout Creek flows into Snake River in the southeast part of T 3N, R 50E. The stream was named because of the difficulty in operating pack trains on the ridge above. Packers had to be on the lookout to see that their horses did not roll off the trail. It is said that the name was given by James and Nate Tryon.

Lookout Rock, CURRY. This is a well-known and peculiar landmark on the Oregon coast about four miles south of Humbug Mountain. It is just west of US-101, the Oregon Coast Highway, and rises almost vertically several hundred feet above the ocean. This descriptive name was given in the 1850s, probably during the mining excitement. George Davidson in the *Coast Pilot*, 1889, p. 373, says the Indian name for the rock was *Nog-gi-sa*, but gives no explanation.

Loon Lake, DOUGLAS. Walling, in *History of Southern Oregon*, p. 439, says that in 1852 L. L. Williams, Joseph Peters and Job Hatfield, while on an exploring expedition from Scottsburg, found this lake. In the center was a floating log with a loon's nest containing two eggs. Two loons were observed at some distance in the water. The eggs were packed in moss and taken to Wilbur Academy. In view of these facts the lake was named Loon Lake. Gabrielson and Jewett in *Birds of Oregon*, p. 64, *et seq.*, describe three loons that are found in Oregon.

Looney Butte, MARION. Looney Butte is a few miles north of Jefferson and is skirted on its east slope by the old Pacific Highway East. It has an elevation of 630 feet. It was named for Jesse Looney, who came to Oregon in 1843. He was one of the leaders of the migration that year. He died Mar. 25, 1869, aged 88 years. His home was near Looney Butte, where his descendants still reside. His wife, Ruby Crawford Bond, died there May 7, 1900, aged 92 years. For biography of Jesse Looney, *see* the *Oregonian*, Mar. 27, 1869, p. 2. For information about the Looney family, *see* the *Oregonian*, Aug. 1, 1926, sect. 1, p. 11.

Looney Creek, CROOK. Looney Creek empties into Porter Creek in S 22, T 14S, R 22E. USFS ranger J. O. F. Anderson said the creek was named for Gene Looney, an early settler on Summit Prairie. Looney Reservoir is at the headwaters of the creek. Eugene Looney also had timber filings in the area and later was a well-known citizen of Mitchell. The second stream to the east of Looney Creek is Crazy Creek, named for a mentally disturbed sheep herder. The proximity of Looney and Crazy creeks probably gave rise to the name of the stream between them, Stupid Creek. *See* Crazy Creek.

Looney Spring, WHEELER. This spring near US-26 above Keyes Creek was named for Eugene Looney. Looney was an early day rancher and businessman of Mitchell.

Lorane, LANE. This post office was established May 27, 1887, with William N. Crow postmaster. In Feb. 1947, Mrs. L. H. Johnson of Eugene, a niece of Crow, wrote that postal authorities asked Crow to submit several names for the proposed office. The name Loraine was suggested by Mrs. Crow because it was the name of a favorite niece. Officials accepted this suggestion but changed the spelling to Lorane as a matter of simplicity and also because there were already several Loraines in the country.

Lord Flat, WALLOWA. This flat is near Snake River. It is sometimes known as Buckaroo Flat. It was named for James Lord, who hunted and ranged stock there.

Lorella, KLAMATH. Lorella was first known as Haynesville, and the post office was established Aug. 3, 1887, with Joseph K. Haynes postmaster. It is said that the place was confused with Haines, Baker County, and as a result the name was changed to Lorella on Dec. 13, 1894. Captain O. C. Applegate of Klamath Falls told the compiler that this was in honor of Mrs. Lorella Wisner, a local resident.

Lost Cabin Creek, BAKER. This is a tributary of Paddy Creek in T 7S, R 44E. In early days a miner had a cabin on this creek and after the diggings were abandoned the brush grew so profusely that it was passed unnoticed by travellers on the trail a few feet away.

Lost Creek, LANE. This stream flows north into Middle Fork Willamette River near Dexter and it drains a north-south valley several miles long. In earlier days the vale was generally called Lost Valley, and the valley may have been named before the creek. Walling in *Illustrated History of Lane County* says that Elijah Bristow named the valley, but the exact reason is uncertain. It is probable that the name was applied because the valley was quite secluded.

Lost Forest, LAKE. The Lost Forest is a curious 9000 acre oasis of juniper and ponderosa pine about 50 miles northeast of Christmas Lake. Ponderosa pine normally will not survive in an area as arid as this but unusual sub-surface soil conditions maintain this stand of trees. *See* an article by Leverett Richards in the *Sunday Oregonian*, June 24, 1973, p. F-5.

Lost Lake, HOOD RIVER. This lake is said to have been originally known as Blue Lake, and it is stated that the Walk Up Trail from The Dalles to Sandy River passed by it. This does not agree with information printed in *Mazama* for Dec. 1920, which is to the effect that the lake was discovered by Joe and John Divers. Acting on information gathered from these two men by E. L. Smith of Hood River, a party of 12 was organized in 1880 for the purpose of locating the lake. It is of course possible that the Divers brothers called it Blue Lake. The searching party started to look for the lake on Aug. 18, 1880. Dr. T. L. Eliot wrote an account of this search which appeared in the *Oregonian* on Aug. 27, 1880. The party found the lake and christened it Lost Lake. Owing to the smoke and some misunderstanding of routes the party did not find the search any too easy, and the old story: "Indian not lost, wigwam lost," furnished the basis for the name. Dr. Eliot made several efforts to learn the Indian name of this lake, but was unsuccessful.

Lost Prairie, LINN. This prairie is along Hackleman Creek between Fish Lake and Tombstone Prairie. Roy A. Elliott in *Profiles of Progress*, p. 97, tells how Andrew Wiley came to name this place in 1859. After enduring a bad spring snow storm while camped on Browder Ridge, he saw the meadow below when the weather broke. He knew they were out of the Santiam drainage and facetiously said they were lost.

Lost Prairie, WALLOWA. Lost Prairie is an area not well defined, lying southeast of Grande Ronde River, north of Courtney Creek and west of East Bear Creek. It is not exactly a prairie, but a series of benches separated by canyons. The locality was named by A. C. Smith in the late 1870s. He and a party of settlers were following a band of renegade Indians who had run off with some stock. Smith and his party got to a place where the trail ran out on them, and they named the locality Lost Prairie. There was a post office called Lost Prairie, established about 1887. R. H. Bacon was postmaster. The postal map of 1900 shows this office a little south of the Oregon-Washington state line and close to Grande Ronde River. It was in the south part of S 19, T 6N, R 44E.

Lost River, KLAMATH. This stream rises in California and flows into Oregon. It formerly debouched into Tule Lake, but it is now controlled for irrigation, and as a result Tule Lake is being dried up and reclaimed for farm land. During its course through Langell Valley Lost River disappears for several miles, hence its name.

The famous natural stone bridge, by which the Applegate party crossed Lost River on July 6, 1846, was near Merrill. The rocks were submerged when seen by the compiler, and seemed more like a series of stepping stones than a natural bridge. *See* Bancroft's *History of Oregon*, v. 1, p. 548, and *OHQ*, v. 22, p. 24. A dam of the u.s. Bureau of Reclamation has been built at the natural bridge and the stones are covered. Lost River was discovered by Fremont early in May 1846, and named McCrady River for a boyhood friend, but that name did not prevail. There was a pioneer post office called Lost River on or near this stream, probably at the Horton ranch above Olene. It was in service from Feb. 1875, to Apr. 1876, with W. H. Horton postmaster.

Lost Spring, CROOK. This spring on the slopes of Black Mountain in S 9, T 14S, R 22E, was dug out and named by William Meyer and Dillard Lowery in the early 1890s. It was used for livestock for many years and had numerous improvements.

Lost Valley, WHEELER. The compiler has not been able to get definite information about the origin of the name Lost Valley other than it is supposed that the valley was named because some soldiers lost their way in it during the early Indian wars in eastern Oregon. Many years ago the *Oregonian* contained the following news item: "Lost Valley, Gilliam County, is looking forward with unmitigated delight to a grand ball next Friday night at which time William D. Johnson, of Lost Valley, will be united in marriage to Miss Edith Waddle, of Thirty-mile. Tickets to the ball, including the wedding supper and horse feed, are going freely at $1.50 per couple." This social affair apparently took place before Wheeler County was established in 1899. The community was always located in what is now Wheeler County but Vere A. McCarty of Salem in 1981 called attention to the fact that the Lost Valley School was always a little to the north in Gilliam County.

Lostine, WALLOWA. Lostine is a town on Lostine River in the Wallowa Valley. Local authorities wrote the compiler in 1927 that the place was named by a pioneer settler for Lostine, Kansas. The meaning of the name Lostine is unknown to the compiler. Lostine was a place in Lowell township, Cherokee County, Kansas. The census of 1870 gives it as a post office for farmers. The post office was discontinued before 1880 and the name does not appear in modern gazetteers. Lostine, Oregon, is an important trading center and does not seem to be headed for the fate that met Lostine, Kansas. The post office at Lostine, Oregon, was established Aug. 6, 1878, with W. R. Laughlin first postmaster.

Lostine River, WALLOWA. This stream has been called South Fork, and also Middle Fork Wallowa River, but local use is in favor of Lostine River, and the USBGN has adopted that name. *See* Lostine.

Loughs Mine, DOUGLAS. Loughs Mine is on North Umpqua River about two miles northwest of Horseshoe Bend. Ed Lough was a packer for the USFS in early days and worked this claim when not employed elsewhere.

Louse Canyon, MALHEUR. Louse Canyon heads just north of the Nevada line a few miles east of McDermitt. It runs east and north into the Owyhee River south of Three Forks. The story is that in the early 1900s a cow camp in the canyon became infested with the ubiquitous vermin. During the 1960s the OGNB received a plausible and earnest plea to change the name to La Rosa Canyon, supposedly given by Basque sheepherders for the profusion of wild roses therein. In due course this change was effected in *Decision List 6402*. The canyon is in an out of the way area and little more was heard of the matter until the late 1970s when the USGS started a major mapping project and the change of name received some attention. The locals took umbrage, declaring vehemently that the graybacks had been there in force while roses were conspicuous by their absence. After due progression through channels, Louse Canyon was restored in *Decision List 8004*.

Louse Creek, JOSEPHINE. This creek north of Grants Pass was originally so called because of an Indian camp on its banks that was infested with vermin. Sporadic efforts have been made to change the name to something more romantic, such as Grouse Creek, but there does not appear to be much steam behind such movements.

Lousignont Lake, WASHINGTON. Lousignont Lake, now almost entirely drained, is about five miles northwest of Forest Grove. It bears the name of a pioneer family of the county. Lousignont Creek northwest of Timber was named for the same family.

Love Lake, LANE. This small body of water east of Junction City was named for Hugh Love who took up a donation land claim there in 1852. In the early days this body of water drained north to Long Tom River but by the 1950s it had become intermittent.

Love Reservoir, BAKER. Love Reservoir in Ritter Creek drainage south of Keating was named for Walter S. Love. Love was the son of early Baker County settlers and was one of the first proponents of irrigation and water diversion. His brother, Avon Love, was equally well known.

Lovely, WALLOWA. Lovely post office was established May 10, 1902, with Sarah A. Lovely postmaster. It was situated about three miles northeast of Minam and operated until June 1907. The place was named for Walter Lovely who homesteaded there.

Low Gap Creek, JOSEPHINE. This stream is in the extreme southeast corner of the county. It was named because it heads in a low pass between Lake and Whisky peaks. The name Whisky Creek is incorrect.

Lowell, LANE. Amos D. Hyland, who came from Lowell, Maine, in the 1850s, established the community and helped secure a post office, of which he was once postmaster. He named the place for his former home. He was a successful stockraiser, and, the writer is informed, was an energetic and hard-working man. He brought up a family of 14 children! The first post office in this locality was called Cannon. It was established Aug. 9, 1880, with C. E. Byers postmaster and named for A. D. Cannon, a local resident. The name was changed to Lowell on Feb. 19, 1883.

Lowell Creek, LANE. This stream is tributary to Christy Creek northeast of Oakridge. According to Mrs. Lina A. Flock of Oakridge, the creek was named for E. D. Lowell. Lowell at one time pastured his stock in the surrounding area. Nearby Lowell Mountain takes its name from the creek.

Lower Bridge, DESCHUTES. This name is purely descriptive and originated at the time when the bridge was downstream from Tetherow bridge, which was the other important bridge in the upper Deschutes country. There was a post office of the same name not far from the bridge. This bridge is six miles west of Terrebonne, and near its western end is the well-known diatomite deposit.

Lower Klamath Lake, KLAMATH. This is the correct name of the smaller of the two Klamath lakes, not Little Klamath Lake. Lower Klamath Lake is on the boundary between Oregon and California, and part of it is in California. Its outlet is Klamath Strait, which connects it with Klamath River. Klamath Strait formerly flowed either way, depending on the stage of water in Lower Klamath Lake, but this characteristic has apparently been interfered with by the construction of a railroad embankment. For information about the origin of the name, *see* Klamath County. The Klamath Indian name for Lower Klamath Lake is *Aka-ushkni E-ush*, the latter word meaning lake. Attempts at reclamation have caused much variation in the size of Lower Klamath Lake in recent years.

Lower Land Creek, COOS. This creek, together with Upper Land Creek nearby, was named for T. C. Land, a pioneer settler on South Fork Coquille River.

Lowersoda, LINN. A post office with the name Lower Soda was established in the vicinity of what is now Cascadia on Aug. 27, 1892, with John Atkinson postmaster. The office was discontinued May 21, 1894, but was reestablished in about two weeks with the name Lowersoda and with Atkinson continuing as postmaster. The office was finally closed Apr. 21, 1899, and the business transferred to Cascadia office which had been established on May 12, 1898. Lowersoda, which was very close to Cascadia, was at the old roadhouse of William R. Finley. According to William R. Mealey, of Foster, who wrote in Sept. 1946, this old roadhouse was built in the late 1860s or early 1870s. The soda springs at Cascadia were at one time known as Lower Soda springs in contradistinction to the Upper Soda springs about ten or twelve miles further east.

Lowullo Butte, DESCHUTES. *Lowullo* is the Chinook jargon word for round. The name was applied to this butte three miles north of East Lake by USFS officials when they gave Indian names to a number of features.

Lubbing Flat, WASCO. W. D. Ketchum of The Dalles told the writer in 1967 that this flat between Mosier Creek and Mill Creek was named for an early settler. A check of BLM records in Portland showed that Heinrich Lubbing filed for a homestead in S 17, T 1N, R 12E, on Aug. 24, 1893. For a number of years this feature was shown on maps as Lugan Flat but this error was corrected by the USBGN in *Decision List 7701*.

Lucas Creek, POLK. Lucas Creek flows into Big Rock Creek southwest of

Valsetz Lake. John Lucas filed a homestead nearby in 1896. He was later a principal in the Bryan and Lucas Lumber Company who owned timber in the area.

Luce Creek, GRANT. Luce Creek is tributary to John Day River three miles west of John Day. The *History of Baker, Grant, Malheur and Harney Counties*, p. 488, says that John Luce was born in Iowa in 1843 and came to Oregon in 1859. He was one of the party that discovered gold at Canyon City in 1862. He settled on his farm that included the stream west of John Day.

Luckiamute, POLK. The Luckiamute River has given its name to two places in the Willamette Valley, a post office and a railroad station, neither of which survived the march of time. The meaning of the name, which is of Indian origin, is unknown. A post office with the name Lackemute was established Mar. 14, 1851, and was therefore one of the earliest in the county. Harrison Linville was the first postmaster. The compiler has been unable to find this place on a map, but it appears from the list of postmasters that the office was close to the Luckiamute River, probably a little west of the present Pacific Highway West, and in the extreme south part of the county. It also appears that the office was moved to suit the postmasters. It was finally closed on Nov. 23, 1874. In later years there was a railroad station Luckiamute on the Oregonian Railway narrow gauge line a little north of the Luckiamute River and about four miles northeast of Pedee. This place never had a post office. Time has done much to obliterate the community.

Luckiamute River, BENTON, POLK. This is an Indian tribal name, the meaning of which is unknown. Bancroft says the Lakmiut tribe was of the Kalapooian nation. The name Luckiamute is an old one, and has nothing to do with a deaf mute who is said to have operated a ferry on the stream. This derivation is purely fanciful. The southern stream is the main fork and is officially known as Luckiamute River, not Big Luckiamute River. The northern branch is officially called Little Luckiamute River.

Luckman Canyon, MORROW. Luckman Canyon south of Lena was named for Joseph Luckman, an early settler, who took up land there in 1896.

Lucky Creek, CROOK. Lucky Creek flows through Conant Basin into Conant Creek. It was not named for some fortuitous circumstance but for John L. Luckey who filed on a homestead along the creek in 1871. Luckey was deputy sheriff in Prineville when Lucius Langdon and W. H. Harrison were lynched in 1882.

Lucky Creek, CURRY. Lucky Creek is in the Siskiyou Mountains, at the extreme east edge of the county and southeast of Mount Billingslea. It flows into Tincup Creek. Along it was started the backfire used to stop the 1938 Chetco 30,000-acre fire. The fire was held at this creek, which became known as Lucky Creek by the firefighters.

Lucky Queen, JOSEPHINE. The Lucky Queen mine is one of the best known in southwest Oregon and bears a name redolent of high hopes. The property is in the north part of Josephine County, just southeast of Sexton Mountain. This mine is described briefly in Walling's *History of Southern Oregon*, p. 463. Little or no work has been done at this mine for many years. Lucky Queen post office was established Dec. 13, 1876, with David H. Sexton postmaster. The office was closed July 24, 1896, and local commercial activity is at a standstill.

Luckyboy, LANE. Luckyboy post office was established Feb. 16, 1901, with George A. Dyson first postmaster, to serve the Lucky Boy mine four or five miles north of Blue River community. The mine was of course named in a spirit of optimism. The office was closed Nov. 26, 1906, with papers to Blue River.

Luda, COOS. Luda post office was named for Luda Krantz, the daughter of the postmaster, David C. Krantz. The office was on East Fork Coquille River a few miles upstream from Gravelford. The locality was on the main road between Myrtle Point and Brewster Valley. Luda post office was established June 3, 1901, with Krantz first and only postmaster. The office was closed Aug. 28, 1902.

Ludwick Cabin, WHEELER. Ludwick Cabin northeast of Stephenson Mountain was the location of the homesteads of Walter and Elmer Ludwick just prior to World War I.

Lumrum Butte, DESCHUTES. *Lumrum* is a Chinook jargon word meaning whisky or rum, although the form *lum* is more generally used. The name has been applied to a butte northeast of Crane Prairie by the USFS, possibly because of some incident connected with the making or using of whisky in the vicinity.

Lund Park, LANE. Loren W. Hunt of Cove told the compiler that this spot was a stopping place for travellers to the Bohemia mines. The name is a combination of the original residents Alec Lundberg and Tom Parker.

Lundell Canyon, MORROW. Frank Lundell came to Morrow County in 1887 and took up a homestead at the mouth of this canyon near Gooseberry. Lundell was born in Sweden in 1848 and died at Ione, Apr. 4, 1932.

Luper, LANE. Luper was a station on the Southern Pacific line north of Eugene. Rhea Luper, state engineer, wrote the compiler on July 1, 1927, as follows: "This station was located on property owned by my father, James N. Luper, and his brother Lewis (Bud) Luper. My father when 19, and his brother about 21, bought this property about 1869 or 1870. When the railroad came through, my father had a spur constructed and built a warehouse, and this was at one time quite a wheat shipping point. The warehouse burned and was never rebuilt. The spur track was taken up, but it is still a whistling post. Incidentally, this is the place on which I was born."

Lurley, DOUGLAS. In Feb. 1947, Charles V. Stanton of the Roseburg *News-Review* started a systematic program to harvest information about old Douglas County post offices, with some very commendable results. The following paragraph from the issue for Feb. 14, 1947, slightly condensed, refers to Lurley post office: Lurley post office was on the Buckhorn road about 12 miles east of Roseburg. It was established by the late James J. Webb, father of Percy Webb, Roseburg, the latter having served for a number of years as sheriff of Douglas County. The office was named for Blanche Lurley Webb, a granddaughter of the postmaster and daughter of Percy Webb. She died at Lurley when she was but seven years of age. The site was later occupied by the Justin Eifert home. According to official records the post office was established Dec. 18, 1897, with James J. Webb first and only postmaster. It was discontinued Feb. 28, 1901, with mail to Roseburg.

Luse, MALHEUR. This place was named for F. N. Luse, formerly a dispatcher on the Oregon Short Line Railroad. The station is between Ontario and Vale.

Lutsey Point, CROOK. Lutsey Point overlooks Gray Creek and Gray Prairie seven miles south of Big Summit Prairie. It is named for Clarence J. Lutsey who took a homestead on Lytle Prairie in 1904.

Lyle Gap, JEFFERSON. The Dalles-California Highway, US-97, traverses Lyle Gap at a point about 13 miles northeast of Madras, where it goes through the ridge just west of Hay Creek. The gap was named for Alfred R. Lyle, a prominent settler on Hay Creek, in Wasco County as it was in 1877. Lyle went to central Oregon from Polk County to take charge of the cattle ranch of his brother-in-law, Edmund F. Veazie, who died in mysterious circumstances in John Day River in 1877. Lyle prospered in the business, added to the holdings, and became a prominent citizen of Crook County, which was established in 1882. He represented the county in the state legislature and died in 1906.

Lyman, WALLOWA. According to J. H. Horner of Enterprise the post office at Lyman in the north part of Wallowa County was named for Harry Lyman Murdock, the first postmaster. The office was established in May 1910, and operated until the following May. Lyman was in S 21, T 5N, R 43E, about three miles northeast of Powwatka. Local settlers who wrote the petition for the office selected Murdock's middle name.

Lyman Mountain, JACKSON. Lyman Mountain has an elevation of 2730 feet and overlooks Rogue River near the mouth of Sams Creek about three miles northeast of Gold Hill. It was named for George S. Lyman, a pioneer apple grower, who discovered gold on its slopes in 1894.

Lyons, LINN. Lyons was named for the family that established the community. They were early settlers. Lyons is in the valley of North Santiam River.

Lyons Ridge, JEFFERSON. James Lyons homesteaded near this ridge south of Currant Creek in 1923.

Lytle Creek, CROOK. Lytle Creek is in the northwest corner of the county near Prineville. It is named for Andrew Lytle, a pioneer settler. Lytle was born in Ohio in 1833 and came to Oregon in 1860 via California. In 1870 he and his wife, Sarah Ramp Lytle, settled on a ranch along Lytle Creek. Andrew Lytle was a prominent citizen of Crook County. He died in 1895 and was buried in the Pioneer Cemetery near Prineville.

Mabel, LANE. This post office was named for Miss Maud Mabel Drury, second daughter of the first postmaster, Alfred Drury. The post office has not always been in its present location. It was established about 1878.

Macduff Peak, LANE. This peak lies in the Cascade Range about four miles airline south of McKenzie Bridge. It bears the name of the late Nelson F. Macduff, for many years supervisor of the Cascade National Forest. The suggestion which led to the naming of the peak was made by Smith Taylor, formerly USFS ranger at McKenzie Bridge. The name has been officially adopted by the USBGN.

Mace Mountain, DOUGLAS. Mace Mountain is on North Umpqua River about six miles west of Steamboat. G. C. Blake of Roseburg told the writer the mountain was named for Mace, an Indian born about 1860, who was raised by the Meshach Tipton family near Lone Rock. Mace, known as Indian Mace or Mace Tipton, hearded sheep on the mountain for Tipton in the summers.

Macey Cove, DOUGLAS. Mrs. R. W. Williams of Reedsport wrote the compiler about 1925 that the name of the little cove on the east side of Umpqua River about two miles northeast of Winchester Bay is Macey Cove and not Macy Cove. She said the cove was named for a Colonel Charles Macey who was at one time at Fort Umpqua, Umpqua City. In 1925, Macey's descendants were still living in the neighborhood. Heitman's *Historical Register* lists no officer with the name Charles Macey. Possibly Macey was a civilian attached to the post or resident of Umpqua City.

Mack Arch, CURRY. The name Mack is applied to the prominent natural rock arch about one mile offshore as well as a reef, point and cove nearby, all 13 miles south of Gold Beach on US-101. The name is very old as the USCS chart of 1854 not only uses the name Mack's but also has a fine pictorial engraving of the landfall. The form Max's in honor of Maxime Langevin who later homesteaded nearby, while logical, is incorrect, and the story that the name comes from Mack Anderson, a transient of indifferent reputation, also completely fails the chronological test. The first survey of this part of the coast was made in 1850 by a USCS party commanded by Lt.-Commanding William P. McArthur. The 1854 chart was the first revision and it was made only three years after William P. McArthur's death. The compiler believes it was probably named in his memory by some of his old co-workers.

Mack Hall Creek, CLACKAMAS. This is a small tributary of South Fork Salmon River above Welches. It was named to honor Mack Henry Hall, a part time USFS employee. Hall attended school in Eugene and graduated from the University of Oregon in 1931 where he had been active in college journalism. He was killed in an automobile accident near Eugene in 1933.

Macklyn Cove, CURRY. This cove near the mouth of Mill Creek in Brookings was the best protected anchorage in the area. Elza J. Macklin homesteaded on the shore in 1864. In 1901, a wharf was built and borax brought by scows from Lone Ranch was transferred to ocean going vessels. Following current usage the USBGN decided on the present spelling in 1960 but the early records indicate that Macklin used this form.

Macksburg, CLACKAMAS. Macksburg is about five miles east of Canby. The little community was named for the Mack family, well known in the locality.

Macksburg post office was established Mar. 6, 1884, with Geo. H. McPherson first postmaster and was discontinued in Sept. 1903.

Macleay, MARION. Donald Macleay, a prominent merchant of Portland, was interested with William Reid in the Oregonian Railway Company, Limited. This company built the narrow gauge railroad in the east part of the Willamette Valley, subsequently a branch of the Southern Pacific Company. Mr. Macleay gave several hundred dollars to build a school house at a station in Marion County which was forthwith given his name. For a short history of the community, *see* Salem *Statesman*, Dec. 20, 1931.

Mad Creek, LINN. This stream just east of Gates, was named by Thomas J. Henness in 1863 because of the turbulent waters. *See* Salem *Capital Journal*, June 18, 1927, p. 1. There is no truth in the story that the creek was named for an insane woman. Some maps show the stream as Mud Creek, which is wrong.

Madden Butte, CURRY. Cyrus Madden came to Curry County in 1865 from Ohio and settled north of Sixes near the butte which bears his name. He was of contentious nature and always acted as his own attorney. There is a story to the effect that once, when incarcerated, he prepared his own *habeas corpus* and procured his release by serving it himself on the dumbfounded sheriff. He obviously was an early advocate of the rights of the accused.

Madras, JEFFERSON. Madras is in a more or less circular valley, and in earlier days the place was known as The Basin. When the community became established, and the post office was applied for, the name Palmain was suggested to postal authorities in Washington, in honor of John Palmehn, a well-known resident. Palmehn platted part of the town now called Madras with the name Palmain, which he thought would be easier spelled than Palmehn. However, the authorities objected, fearing confusion with a post office called Palmer. On Feb. 10, 1944, the Madras *Pioneer* published a letter from Bert Doze, a newspaperman in Wichita, Kansas, saying that he was sent to the new community about 1903 by his uncle, Joshua Hahn, to open a store. The name of the place was still undetermined. Willow Creek was suggested but was thought to be too cumbersome. Finally Hahn or Doze suggested the name Madras, which was taken from a bolt of cloth in the store. Madras is a well-known cotton fabric named for the city in India. Howard W. Turner, a long-time resident of Madras, did not accept the Doze story and thought that the Post Office Department named the place. The compiler queried postal authorities some years ago and was told the department had no record of suggesting the name Madras. The name of the Oregon town is generally pronounced with the accent on the first syllable, but the name of the place in India is pronounced with the accent on the second syllable.

Magic Lantern Creek, GRANT. This creek empties into South Fork John Day River in S 30, T 15S, R 27E. Wayne Stewart, a long time resident of Grant County, gives the following account in the Malheur National Forest records: "the light in a small cabin on the head of this creek, gleamed through a small window about eight inches by ten inches on the west side of this cabin. The light was visible for several miles and the natives were thus led to use the name of Magic Lantern Creek." A magic lantern was a device whereby a picture on a glass slide was focused and projected on a screen. They were popular in the nineteenth century long before our modern color positive slides and slide projectors.

Magone Lake, GRANT. Patsy Daly of Prairie City informed the compiler in 1927 that this lake was named for Major Joseph W. Magone, a resident of Canyon City. Magone stocked the lake with fish, and it was named for him on that account. The spelling Magoon is wrong. Magone was born in New York in 1821 and came to Oregon in 1847. He was a miller by occupation. He served in the Cayuse War with the rank of major. He lived in the Willamette Valley until 1872, when he went to eastern Oregon. He served in the Bannock War under General O. O. Howard as a guide and express messenger. When he was over 70 years old, Major Magone walked all the way from Canyon City to Chicago to see the World's Columbian Exposition and won a wager for the feat. He died at Ogdensburg, New York, Feb. 15, 1902. For additional information, *see OHQ*, v. 3, p. 276, *et seq.*, and v. 9, p. 309. *See also* several references in Down's *History of the Silverton Country*.

Magpie Peak, BAKER. This butte is near Haines. J. Neilson Barry told the writer that during early days in Baker County this was a convenient place for cattle round-ups. As a result of stock being driven to the peak for sorting, a great many magpies flew in with the cattle, and the country around the place became covered with them.

Mahogany Creek, WALLOWA. This stream, in T 4S, RANGES 47 and 48E, as well as several other geographic features in eastern Oregon, is named for the curlleaf mountain mahogany, *Cercocarpus ledifolius*.

Mahon Creek, HARNEY. Mahon Creek flows west from the Stinkingwater Mountains into Harney Valley. It is named for James F. Mahon, who settled nearby in the 1870s. *See* Mule and *History of Baker, Grant, Malheur and Harney Counties*, p. 672.

Maiden Gulch, BAKER. This gulch is near Sparta. For the history of this locality during the mining days, *see* editorial page, the *Oregonian*, Oct. 7, 1927, and the Baker *Morning Democrat* of Oct. 19, 1927. Dunham Wright, of Medical Springs, told the compiler that the prospects in Maiden Gulch were discovered by a bachelor who was of a romantic turn of mind and decided to compliment the opposite sex.

Maiden Peak, DESCHUTES, LANE. Explanations of this name are not satisfactory. One is to the effect that the mountain, which is at the summit of the Cascade Range, was named in contradistinction to the Three Sisters and Bachelor Butte to the north. Another is that the shape of the mountain resembles a reclining female figure, while a third is that the shape is like a woman's breast. The compiler thinks the first named reason is most likely the correct one. Maiden Peak has an elevation of 7818 feet. The Pacific Crest National Scenic Trail crosses the Cascade Range at a

6150 foot saddle about halfway between Willamette Pass and Maiden Peak. In 1986 the usfs proposed to designate this Maiden Peak Saddle, a name used in their trail log as early as 1936. This was confirmed by the usbgn in *Decision List 8701*.

Maidu Lake, DOUGLAS. Maidu Lake is the source of North Umpqua River. The name is that of an Indian family or tribe of the Sierra Nevada region of California. The writer does not know how it got transferred to Oregon.

Maiers Butte, JEFFERSON. This butte near the headwaters of Muddy Creek, is named for Ludwig Maier, an early settler. *See OHQ*, v. 81, p. 306.

Majors Prairie, LANE. Dee Wright told the compiler that Majors Prairie and Majors Creek nearby, both in the valley of North Fork northeast of Oakridge, were named for one Majors, a stockman. The form Major is wrong.

Makin Creek, WALLOWA. Makin Creek drains into Cherry Creek in T 4N, R 48E. It bears the name of Elzie O. Makin who bought a squatter's right from George Cusker, built a cabin near the stream and moved his family into it. He was a sheep man.

Maklaks Pass, KLAMATH. This pass is in a spur running southeast from the rim of Crater Lake. It divides Dutton Ridge to the north from Grayback Ridge to the south. *Maklaks* is a Klamath Indian word meaning literally the encamped, hence a body of Indians encamped, or a community, or tribe. It is also a generic term for Indian. The usfs has named a mountain in northwestern Klamath County between Davis and Odell lakes Maklaks Mountain.

Malheur, MALHEUR. This post office is in the valley of Willow Creek in the extreme north part of the county. There seems no doubt in the mind of the writer that the post office name came from the same source as the name of Malheur River. *See* Malheur River. The community of Malheur was a center in the gold excitement in the late 1860s, and there is a story to the effect that the place was named Malheur (French for evil hour or misfortune) because a tunnel caved in and killed a French miner. The compiler has no evidence that this event did not happen, but thinks it highly improbable that the name of the town originated in such a manner, and places no credence in the story.

Malheur County. Malheur County was created Feb. 17, 1887, and was taken from Baker County as that county was then constituted. Subsequently there were several readjustments in the Malheur County boundary. The county was named Malheur because Malheur River flowed through it. For the origin of the name Malheur, *see* Malheur River. The county has an area of 9868 square miles, according to ODOT and is the second largest county in Oregon. In Feb. 1931, a bill was introduced in the Oregon legislature to change the name of Malheur County to Sinnott County, in honor of Nicholas J. Sinnott, representative in Congress from the second Oregon district, 1913–28, who died July 20, 1929. The bill passed the house, but died in the senate. Despite the high esteem in which Mr. Sinnott was held, it appeared to be the sentiment of the citizens of the county to leave the name alone.

Malheur Lake, HARNEY. Peter Skene Ogden's party discovered this lake in Oct. 1826. Details of the discovery are given under the heading Harney Lake. Ogden did not name the lake, and referred to it simply as a freshwater lake. He described the ridge or dike that separated the fresh lake from the salt water, to the west, now known as Harney Lake. On July 7, 1859, Captain H. D. Wallen of the Fourth Infantry, while on an expedition from The Dalles to Great Salt Lake, reached the salt water and named it Lake Harney. He found and described the dike between the two lakes. His stock would not drink the alkaline water and stampeded over the dike eastward to what is now Malheur Lake. Wallen thereupon named the fresh water Lake Stampede. That name has not prevailed. Later Malheur Lake was named for Malheur River. For the origin of the name, *see* Malheur River. The compiler does not know who gave the lake its present name, which has been used for many years. Wallen's name Lake Stampede may actually have been applied to a part of Malheur Lake frequently called Mud Lake, which is west of the Narrows. At high stages Malheur Lake flowed over the dike and into Harney Lake, with the result that the latter lake tended to become more alkaline. In 1882 water was so high in Malheur Lake that it cut a wide passage through the dike. *See OHQ*, v. 32, p. 129. Malheur Lake is always relatively shallow and substantial changes in precipitation have produced wide variations in the size of the lake. Each one foot change in water level inundates or uncovers about 8500 acres. In the 1980s the inflow was large enough to combine Malheur, Mud and Harney lakes into one body of water with a surface elevation of 4102 feet, temporarily quite the largest lake in the state. By the end of the decade, the level had receded sufficiently to again separate the three. For details, *see* USGS *Water Resources Investigation Report 89–4111*, by Larry R. Hubbard.

There has been a good deal of litigation about the ownership of the lake bed. The Malheur Lake region has been one of the most productive waterfowl breeding places in western North America. It was formerly a mecca for plume hunters, market hunters and fur trappers. In 1908 President Theodore Roosevelt dedicated the area as a bird refuge. In 1935 the federal government purchased a large part of the old P Ranch in the Blitzen Valley and thus assured the lake of a permanent water supply. The Malheur Migratory Bird Refuge now comprises nearly 160,000 acres of open water, vast tule swamps, wild meadows and wooded areas. Stanley G. Jewett of the Fish and Wildlife Service said: "It ranks first in the number of breeding waterfowl, upland gamebirds, big game and fur bearers. During the fall and spring migrations hundreds of thousands of ducks and geese stop to feed and rest within the refuge. Among the abundant nesting waterfowl to be found are mallards, pintails, redheads, gadwalls, shovelers, cinnamon teal, bluewinged teal and canvasbacks. Canada geese nest abundantly in the meadows and even lay eggs and rear their young on the basaltic rimrocks along the edge of the Blitzen Valley. Here, too, are found nesting each year numbers of sandhill cranes, great colonies of ring-billed and California gulls, Foster's and black terns and white-faced glossy ibis. Malheur Lake marks the northern limit for breeding colonies of American egrets and the black-necked stilts. Long-billed curlews, western willets, avocets and Wilson's snipes are found nesting abundantly in the meadow lands. The heron family is also well represented." Jewett said that about 220 species of birds have been found on and adjacent to the Malheur Refuge. The compiler is prepared to believe the statement, and without reservation can say that the bird colonies of this area are among the most remarkable things he has ever seen.

Malheur River, BAKER, GRANT, HARNEY, MALHEUR. This stream rises on the southern slopes of the Blue Mountains. The name Malheur River is attached to the main stream which has in the past been known as Middle Fork but which the USBGN recognizes as Malheur River. There is also a North Fork Malheur River which joins the main stream at Juntura and a South Fork which joins the main stream at Riverside. The South Fork and its tributaries undoubtedly at one time drained the Harney Valley, but at the present time there is a low divide between the head waters of South Fork and Malheur Lake. The name Malheur was used by Peter Skene Ogden, a Hudson's Bay Company trader, who made an expedition into the Snake River country in 1825–26. In Ogden's journal, in Hudson's Bay House, appears the following entry: "Tuesday, Feb. 14, 1826 We encamped on *River au Malheur* (unfortunate river) so called on account of property and furs having been hid here formerly, discovered and stolen by the natives." Ogden was accompanied by French-Canadian hunters. *See Ogden's Snake Country Journal*, Hudson's Bay Record Society, v. 13, also article of T. C. Elliott, *OHQ*, v. 10, p. 353; v. 11, p. 364. The literal translation of the French *mal heur* is "bad hour," an idiom for misfortune used by the French-Canadian hunters after they discovered their cache had been rifled.

Malin, KLAMATH. Malin is a community on land that was formerly at the bottom of Tule or Rhett Lake. Tule Lake bed has been almost entirely reclaimed. On Sept. 30, 1909, some 50 families of the Czech Colonization Club began to arrive and settle at the site of Malin. The club was formed in Nebraska early in 1909 to locate suitable property for a group of Czechs who were anxious to relocate. A suitable name was needed for the new community and when Mrs. Frank Zumpfe found a large horseradish root growing nearby, all agreed to name the town Malin for the famous Bohemian horseradish of Malin, Kutna Hora, Czechoslovakia. For an account of the settlement, *see* "Czech Colonization Club," *Journal of the Shaw Historical Library*, v. 1, no. 1, 1986, Klamath Falls, Oregon. For information about fossil remains near Malin, *see Oregonian*, Dec. 3, 1925, editorial page. Malin postoffice was established Aug. 11, 1910, with W. W. Adams postmaster.

Mallett, MALHEUR. Mallett was named for C. W. Mallett, a pioneer rancher and nearby landowner. The station was just east of Vale.

Mangriff Lake, JEFFERSON. This lake directly south of Olallie Lake was named for Mangold Griffith, a fish biologist and one time purchasing agent for the Oregon Fish and Game Commission.

Manhattan Beach, TILLAMOOK. This is a summer resort in Tillamook County. The name strongly savors of real estate activity. In 1926 the postmaster wrote that the town was named Manhattan Beach by its promoters because it was a watering place. There seems to be something peculiarly inappropriate about the name being used for a watering place because Gannett in USGS *Bulletin 258* says the name *Manhattan*, as applied to the island in New York, was an Indian word, probably meaning place of drunkenness. The Indian name may well describe the locality of New York City, but it is generally understood that no one gets drunk in Oregon, certainly not at watering places. No indeed.

Manila, YAMHILL. Manila was a post office with a very short life. It was about five miles airline west of McMinnville or about eight miles by road, on the headwaters of Muddy Creek. It was named because the name Manila was so prominent in the news of the Spanish-American War in the Philippines in the summer of 1898. Manila post office was established June 27, 1898, with Moses Morgan first of two postmasters. The office was closed to McMinnville on Nov. 30, 1898.

Mann Lake, HARNEY. This small lake is in the north end of Alvord Valley. It is fed by small streams from Steens Mountain. It was named for a nearby rancher, Phillip Mann.

Mann Ridge, UNION. This ridge about four miles north of Wolf Creek Reservoir near North Powder is named for Minerva Mann who took up land near its southern end in 1907.

Manning, WASHINGTON. This community has been known as Manning for many years. It was named for Martin Manning, a local landholder.

Manzanita, TILLAMOOK. Manzanita is a beach resort and was surveyed and platted in 1912. The post office was established in 1914, with Emil G. Kardell first postmaster. *Manzanita* is Spanish for little apple, and the name is used on the Pacific Coast to designate shrubs of the *Arctostaphylos* group. They bear little fruits like miniature apples. Sweetser states that the shrub growing in Oregon is *Arctostaphylos tomentosa*. It grows at various places along the coast.

Maple Grove, POLK. Maple Grove is a prominent highway intersection about four miles northeast of Pedee and two miles north of Airlie, characterized by some fine Oregon maple trees. There was a post office called Maple Grove in operation in this locality from July 27, 1903, to Jan. 19, 1904, with William S. Bristow postmaster. In the 1980s, there was no evidence of human habitation.

Mapleton, LANE. The consensus of western Lane County is that Mapleton was named by "Grandma" Bean because of the presence of so many maple trees. These are the *Acer macrophyllum*, or bigleaf maple, also called the Oregon maple. "Grandma" Bean was born at Cadiz, Ohio, Feb. 25, 1838, and her maiden name was Julia Ann Sharp. She was married to Obediah Roberts Bean on Oct. 24, 1853, at the Nelson ranch north of Newberg, and the couple lived in the Chehalem Mountains until 1855, when they moved to Lane County. They were outstanding citizens and were the parents of 11 children, the eldest of whom was Oregon's famous judge, Robert Sharp Bean. The Beans moved to Mapleton about 1886 and the place was named shortly thereafter. Obediah R. Bean died in 1890, but Mrs. Bean continued to live in Mapleton until about 1906, when she moved to Eugene, where she died on Feb. 19, 1908. The Beans were both pioneers of 1852. A post office called Seaton was established near this locality in Nov. 1885, with William W. Neely postmaster. Mrs. Bean became postmaster in Apr. 1889, and the name of the office was changed to Mapleton Mar. 26, 1896.

Maplewood, MULTNOMAH. When the Oregon Electric Railway was built this station was called Kusa for the Kusan family of Indians. Some objection arose to the name Kusa and the name was changed to Maplewood because of the trees in the vicinity.

Marble Creek, BAKER. Marble Creek rises on Elkhorn Ridge of the Blue Mountains west of Baker and flows northward toward the ghost town Pocahontas. The stream drains Marble Gulch, which received its name in the 1860s because of the large marble deposits near its headwaters. *See* Hiatt's *Thirty-one Years in Baker County*, p. 33. Marble Point on Elkhorn Ridge has been a controversial feature. The USGS Sumpter quadrangle of 1939 showed a Marble Point but the small scale made the exact spot difficult to pinpoint. When the new 1/24,000 Elkhorn Peak quadrangle was made in 1972, both the OGNB and the USBGN agreed on a subsidiary peak with an elevation of 7791 feet in S 15, T 9S, R 38E. This was approved in *Decision List 7504* and so appears on the map. However, the USFS objected on the grounds that peak 7931 in adjoining section 22, while originally named in error, was now the accepted summit. This alteration was made in *Decision List 7603* and now all reigns serene. According to Norman Wagner of Baker, a geologist well informed on such matters, this area does have limestone deposits and is also in line above both the original east side quarry of the Chemical Lime Company on Marble Creek and the newer west side quarry on Baboon Creek above Sumpter.

Marcola, LANE. The post office of this community was once known as Isabel. About 1885 the railroad was built through the Mohawk Valley and a station known as Marcola was established near the post office. As a result of this the post office name was changed to agree with the station name. The wife of the founder of the town was Mary Cole and the name Marcola was made up in her honor.

Margaret, GRANT. Margaret post office was established May 23, 1898, with Walton H. Wilcox first and only postmaster. The office was discontinued Dec. 31, 1900, with papers to Prairie City. The post route map of 1900 shows the office about 11 miles southeast of Prairie City. In a letter printed in the John Day *Ranger*, Mar. 7, 1947, R. R. McHaley, long a resident of Grant County, says that Margaret post office was situated at Blue Mountain Hot Springs, and was probably named for the foster mother of Postmaster Wilcox.

Marial, CURRY. Marial was named for Marial Billings, daughter of the first postmaster, Thomas W. Billings. The office was established Jan. 29, 1903, and closed Aug. 31, 1954.

Marion, MARION. This station was named because it was situated in Marion County. A. N. Bush of Salem was authority for the statement that when the railroad was built the officials decided to build a station near Mill Creek, at the present site of Turner. This proposed station was to be called Marion. Material for a station and warehouse was sent out from Portland, but the man in charge of the shipment made a mistake and threw it off at the present site of Marion. When the officials found this had been done they concluded to finish the building and retain the name of Marion for the present community of that name. They subsequently had an additional shipment sent to the place they first had in mind and built a station there and called it Turner, for a prominent pioneer resident of the neighborhood, Henry L. Turner.

Marion County. Champooick District, as originally created and named, comprised all that part of Oregon south and east of the mouth of Pudding River. The eastern boundary was the Rocky Mountains, and the southern boundary was the 42nd parallel. The district was created July 5, 1843. In 1847 Linn County was created, and the new boundary between the two counties was put on Santiam River and North Santiam River, thence to the Rocky Mountains. This was the situation when on Sept. 3, 1849, the territorial legislature changed the name of Champoeg County, as it was then called, to Marion County. The name was in honor of General Francis Marion of Revolutionary War fame. The Weems-Hory *Life of General Francis Marion* was then largely read in Oregon and other frontier settlements, and the praise of Marion in this book greatly appealed to the settlers. Marion County had an area of 1201 square miles in 1989, according to ODOT.

Marion Creek, WASCO. This small creek is tributary to Fifteenmile Creek just east of the Hood River County line. It and nearby Marion Point were both named for Marion Gordon, wife of USFS ranger Eric Gordon.

Marion Lake, LINN. This lake was named in 1874 by the Marion County road viewing party under the leadership of John Minto. *See OHQ*, v. 4, p. 249. The outlet of this lake is now known as Marion Creek, and not Marion Fork Santiam River.

Markham Creek, DOUGLAS. Markham Creek is tributary to Calapooya Creek near Nonpareil. Both Nathaniel and David Markham had donation land claims including the stream but it is probably named for Nathaniel Markham.

Marks Creek, CROOK. Marks Creek is northeast of Prineville and US-26 follows it eastbound into the Ochoco Mountains. It was named for William H. Marks who was born in Indiana in 1826 and came to Oregon in 1853. He settled in Linn County with Bluford and William Marks, apparently a brother and a cousin. In 1868 he went to Crook County along with Bluford Marks and settled along Marks Creek. There is no evidence that the other William Marks ever lived in Crook County but two of his daughters and one son did settle there presumably at the instigation of their uncles or cousins. William H. Marks' donation land claim in Linn County was two miles north of Sweet Home on Marks Ridge which is also named for him.

Marks Prairie, CLACKAMAS. Marks Prairie is three miles south of Canby. Marks Memorial Park is the family cemetery and there is a lengthy bronze plaque affixed to a large grave monument. It states that John Mark was born in Virginia, served in the War of 1812 and brought his family to Oregon in 1847. He had a number of children who settled in the area and took donation land claims. These included Alexander K. Mark and his second wife, Mary Hill Mark, who gave the land for the cemetery. It is interesting to note that John's youngest son, Samuel Marks added a terminal "s" to his name.

Marley Creek, UNION. Leonard Marley came to the Starkey area about 1885 and took up government land in 1890 where Marley Creek flows into Meadow Creek. The creek bears his name.

Marmot, CLACKAMAS. Adolf Aschoff, for many years a forester and guide about Mount Hood, settled at the present site of Marmot on Mar. 16, 1883. He found an abundance of peculiar burrowings, especially in the fern growth near the borders of the timber. Local residents told him that these holes were dug by marmots, but Aschoff determined otherwise, and found that they were made by the so-called mountain beaver, or *Aplodontia rufa*. When the post office was established Aschoff and two cronies decided to call the place Marmot on account of this error. One of these friends of Aschoff's was an old miner, Fauntleroy S. Peake, who became first postmaster about 1886. Aschoff became postmaster in 1891. For information about him, *see* Aschoff Buttes.

Marquam, CLACKAMAS. Marquam post office was established in 1889, by change of name from Butte Creek, and named for early settler Alfred Marquam.

Marquam Hill, MULTNOMAH. Marquam Hill in southwest Portland bears the name of Philip A. Marquam, who was born near Baltimore, Feb. 28, 1823, and came to Portland in 1851. In 1862–70 he was county judge of Multnomah County. He was elected to the legislature in 1882. In the late 1880s Judge Marquam financed and built the Marquam Grand Opera House, one of Portland's historic landmarks. The opening performance, *Faust*, was given Feb. 10, 1890. The building was on the north side of Morrison Street, between what were then Sixth and Seventh. Marquam died in Portland, May 8, 1912. For additional biographical data, *see* Scott's *History of the Oregon Country*, v. 2, p. 273.

Marquam Lake, MULTNOMAH. Marquam Lake is on the east part of Sauvie Island. W. H. H. Morgan, one of the pioneer settlers on the island, told the compiler that in pioneer days, a French-Canadian employee of the Hudson's Bay Company operated a dairy near this lake. He was called Marquam, and the Morgan family named the lake for him. Marquam Lake drains into Columbia River through Dairy Creek. This stream was also named by the Morgan family, because of the dairy mentioned above.

Marr Creek, WALLOWA. This stream is in the southeast part of the county and flows into Sheep Creek. It heads near Marr Flat. These features were named for William Marr, who settled near the head of the stream in the early 1880s.

Marshall Butte, WHEELER. Marshall Butte is two miles northeast of Mitchell and has an elevation of 4538 feet. It was named for Alfred Marshall who settled in Mitchell in 1874.

Marshfield, COOS. G. A. Bennett, a pioneer of Coos County, is authority for the statement that the land upon which the city of Marshfield was built was once a part of a claim taken up by Wilkins Warwick in 1855, and that it was the general understanding of Oregon pioneers that Warwick named part of his claim for Marshfield, Massachusetts. The records of Coos County show that Warwick sold part of his claim on Mar. 11, 1856, to Andrew J. Davis for $3000, and the description of this property states that the land is particularly "known and designated as the Marshfield claim at the mouth of Wapello Slough." Wapello Slough is now known as Isthmus Slough as it leads to the isthmus over which there was a trail to Beaver Slough on the Coquille River side of the county. There is another version of the history of the name, according to S. B. Cathcart, also a pioneer resident of Coos County. Cathcart wrote that the name was applied by J. C. Tolman, who settled on the claim prior to Warwick, and inasmuch as he was a great admirer of Daniel Webster, Tolman named the Marshfield claim after Webster's home in Massachusetts. While the details of these two stories differ somewhat, it is apparent that Marshfield, Oregon, was named about 1854 for the Massachusetts community. Tolman later was surveyor-general of Oregon. Marshfield did not make progress until John Pershbaker started lumber and shipbuilding industries there in 1867. In that year there were but two buildings at the place. (Dodge's *Pioneer History of Coos and Curry Counties*, p. 154.) For description of the town in 1902, *see* the *Oregonian*, Dec. 25, 1902; description in 1903, Sept. 3, 1903, p. 14; description in 1890, Jan. 1, 1891. On Nov. 16, 1943, an election was held on a proposal to consolidate Marshfield, North Bend and an unincorporated area between the two places with the name Coos Bay for the new municipality. The proposal carried in Marshfield but lost elsewhere, hence did not go into effect. However, at the general election a year later, Nov. 7, 1944, the people of Marshfield adopted a new charter and a new name, City of Coos Bay. The change in name was confirmed at a special election held Dec. 28, 1944, and the name Marshfield, in use nearly a century, became a thing of the past. This change did not affect the community of North Bend. In subsequent years both Empire and Eastside have been consolidated with Coos Bay.

Marshland, COLUMBIA. When Z. B. Bryant settled on the marshy prairie west of Clatskanie about 1862, the place was known as Skunk Cabbage Flat. The post office of Marshland was established about 1873, and it is understood that Bryant selected the name as being more suitable than Skunk Cabbage Flat. It is quite descriptive.

Mart Davis Creek, COOS. Mart Davis Creek is a small tributary of Millicoma River. It was named for an early settler on its banks, J. M. Davis, better known as Mart. The name Mark Davis Creek is wrong.

Marten Buttes, MARION. These buttes, north of Detroit, were so named because trappers caught a number of martens there. Charles C. Giebeler of Detroit furnished the compiler with this information, adding that the name is not an old one. Marten Creek rises east of the buttes and takes its name from them. The marten is an important member of the *Mustellidae* family.

Martin Creek, LANE. Martin Creek rises southeast of Divide and flows northeast along the Southern Pacific tracks into Coast Fork Willamette River. It bears the name of Nathan Martin, an early settler. Martin was postmaster at Cottage Grove in the late 1860s when the office was moved to the extreme southwest part of the town. *See* Cottage Grove.

Martin Creek, LANE. This creek flows into Big River north of Black Butte. It is named for Van Buren Martin who took a homestead nearby in 1871.

Marx, TILLAMOOK. Marx post office was established Apr. 9, 1904, with Franklin C. Varner first of two postmasters. The office was about two miles southeast on Neskowin Creek from the place called Neskowin, on the Varner ranch. Varner was a great admirer of Karl Marx, the German socialist, and named the office for him. Maps showing the name Mary and Marks are incorrect. The Marx office was later moved northwest toward Neskowin, and finally to a point near the mouth of Neskowin Creek. The Neskowin post office had been discontinued in Oct. 1905, and that locality was without an office. The name of Marx office was changed to Neskowin on Mar. 30, 1910, and thus the fine old name of Neskowin was revived.

Marylhurst, CLACKAMAS. The compiler remembers when this locality was called Villa Maria. That was about 1910. In Apr. 1943, Father Leo J. Linahen was kind enough to look into the history of the name Marylhurst, and he reported as follows: "Since a modest count showed that there were altogether too many Villa Marias in the country, a more distinctive name was sought. A Sister Mary Claudia (MacIntosh) is credited with the choice of Marylhurst, or at least with the suggestion of the insertion of the "l," for euphony. This was in 1913. The Mary part is easily explained. The Sisters of the Holy Names of Jesus and Mary try always to put some reference to the Virgin in the names of their schools witness their many St. Mary's Academies. The hurst part is not too mysterious, either. When the property was acquired, the Sisters thought, as did everyone else, that the proposed highway would be below their holdings, along the river. This would have put their buildings among the trees on the heights above the river, on the hurst. The front of the College faces upward toward the new highway, but the older buildings, Christie Home and the Provincial House, face downward toward the river and toward the place where the Sisters thought the highway was going to be built. From the new road, they seem to be not on a height but in a hollow; they thought they were going to be precisely on a hurst."

Marys Creek, CLATSOP. This stream is about ten miles east of Astoria. It was named for Mary Burnside, whose husband was a settler at the place known as Burnside station.

Marys Peak, BENTON. Marys Peak, elevation 4097 feet, is one of the best-known points in western Oregon. It is just southwest of Corvallis. It is the highest peak in the Oregon Coast Range north of Coquille River, but there are a number of mountains in the Coast Range south of Coquille River that are higher. The Indian name is said to have been *Chintimini*, with the accent on the second syllable, but the compiler does not know the meaning of the word. An editorial in the Corvallis *Gazette-Times*, Sept. 20, 1935, says that the Indian name *Chintimini* was not used in earliest pioneer days, but the peak was called Mouse Mountain, a translation of an Indian name. This statement is attributed to Cal Thrasher, a well-known pioneer resident. Some color is given to this story by the fact that in the days of the fur traders, Marys River was called Mouse River or Mice River. *See* Marys River. The compiler has not found the name *Chintimini* in early records nor is there any contemporary evidence that the fur traders used the style Saint Marys Peak. It is probable that the name Marys Peak came as the result of the naming of Marys River, a stream which heads north of the mountain. The name Marys River was in use in 1846 and possibly earlier.

Marys River, BENTON. In the early days of the fur traders Marys River, which heads north of Marys Peak, was known as Mouse River. In his journal for Oct. 17, 1833, John Work refers to this stream as River *de Souris*, or Mouse River, and the context seems to show that the name Souris was already established. Duflot de Mofras used the name *Riviere des Souris*, Mice River, in 1841, and Joel Palmer called the stream Mouse River in 1845–46. Cal Thrasher, a Benton County pioneer, is authority for the statement that Marys Peak in early days was called Mouse Mountain, a translation of an Indian name. *See* editorial page of the Corvallis *Gazette-Times*, Sept. 20, 1935. The name Marys River appears in an act passed by the Oregon legislature Dec. 12, 1846, and it was apparently in public use at that time. There are at least two stories about the origin of the name Marys River. One is to the effect that it was applied by Adam E. Wimple, an early settler from Oneida County, New York, for his sister, who had never been in Oregon. Wimple murdered his young wife, Mary, Aug. 1, 1852, whom he had married the year before, and he was hanged at Dallas on Oct. 8, 1852. She had attacked him with a pistol. For narrative of the murder, *see* the *Oregonian*, Aug. 8, Sept. 11, 25, 1852. The other story is that the stream was named by Wayman St. Clair for Mary Lloyd, daughter of John Lloyd, who came to Oregon from Clay County, Missouri, in 1845, and in 1846 settled near the present town of Monroe in Benton County. She was said to be the first white woman to cross Marys River, in 1846 (George H. Himes). She married John Foster in Benton County, June 20, 1846; died in Aug. 1854. Lloyd was born in Buncombe County, North Carolina; died in Benton County, Oregon, Jan. 6, 1880. His house is said to have been the farthest south in

the Willamette Valley at one time. Wayman St. Clair was a member of the territorial legislature in 1850–51, representing Benton County in the lower house; also in
1854. He was an immigrant of 1845. He and John Lloyd were alternate captains of
the last party that followed the Meek Cutoff. In the winter of 1847 Joseph C.
Avery began to lay out a town at the mouth of Marys River, and the place was
called Marysville. In 1853 the name was changed to Corvallis. *See* Corvallis. Marysville was probably named for the stream, although there may have been additional
reasons. Mrs. John (Mary) Stewart, one of the first settlers, said that Avery told
her he would apply the name Marysville in her honor. *See* Corvallis *Gazette-Times*,
June 7, 1935. It has been suggested that French-Canadian employees of the Hudson's Bay Company may have named the stream Saint Marys River, but there
seems to be no contemporary record of the event.

Mascall Ranch, GRANT. Richard Mascall, a native of England, came to Canyon
City in 1864, and settled on his ranch five miles below Dayville in 1872. His son,
William R. Mascall, later ran sheep from the ranch and Mascall Corrals in Wheeler
County was on one of his ranges. The Mascall Ranch is best known for being the
headquarters of J. C. Merriam and other fossil hunters in the early 1900s. They
described the Mascall formation as middle and late Miocene containing fauna
fossils typical of that time.

Mast Creek, COOS. Mast Creek is tributary to Middle Creek about two miles
north of McKinley. William P. Mast was born in Watauga County, North Carolina in 1834. He came to Oregon in 1872 with a group of about 60 people from that
state including several other members of his family. Mast settled in Lee Valley
where he named the post office and was first postmaster. The creek was named for
him or some other member of his family.

Masten Butte, DESCHUTES. This butte, elevation 4881 feet, is about eight miles
southwest of La Pine. It bears the name of John N. Masten who at one time ran a
sawmill on Little Deschutes River about two miles east of the butte.

Matheny Creek, COOS. Matheny Creek is just west of Myrtle Point. It was
named for James H. Matheny, who took up a land claim on its banks in pioneer
days.

Matlock Canyon, MORROW. Matlock Canyon drains into Butter Creek in T 1N,
R 28E, on the extreme east edge of the county. The canyon was named for three
Matlock brothers who settled and lived in the canyon. The spelling Mattlock is
wrong.

Matney, WASCO. Matney post office was on South Fork Mill Creek some ten
miles southwest of The Dalles. It was in the extreme northeast corner of S 12, T 1N,
R 11E. Isaac Matney was the only postmaster and the office operated from June
1895 to Apr. 1896. At that time there was considerable sawmill activity in the area.

Matney Flat, GILLIAM. Matney Flat southeast of Condon takes its name from
H. C. Matney who settled there in 1872. Matney post office was established on
Dec. 4, 1886 with Godfrey Schilling postmaster and was closed on Apr. 20, 1892.

Matney School was located at the extreme northeast corner of s 20, t 4s, r 22e, and the post office was probably nearby.

Matoles, JEFFERSON. Matoles, an early spelling for Metolius, was the style used for a post office established Mar. 17, 1888, with Isaac Blanton first postmaster. According to O. D. Allingham of Bend, this office was in the southwest corner of what is now Jefferson County, north of Black Butte. It was on Lake Creek, west of what was later called the Hansen Resort and in more recent years Lake Creek Lodge. Blanton sold his holdings to E. R. Carey of Prineville, who did not care to operate the post office. Benjamin Hoover was then appointed, May 27, 1889, and moved the office half to three quarters of a mile east. The office was closed Sept. 12, 1890. Matoles post office was reestablished June 2, 1893, with Mrs. Margaret J. Allingham postmaster on the Allingham ranch, about two miles north of and downstream from its original location. The office was discontinued Aug. 29, 1896. All this information was gathered from Allingham by Robert W. Sawyer of Bend in Sept. 1946. For information about the name Metolius, *see* Metolius. The later post office Metolius, is a good many miles northeast of the place once called Matoles.

Matson Creek, COOS. Matson Creek flows into Catching Slough from the east. BLM records show that Matt Mattson took a homestead at the mouth of the creek in 1881. Mattson was born in Finland in 1851 and came to Coos County in 1879. However, Peterson and Powers in *A Century of Coos and Curry* list Alfred Mattson and John Mattson, both born in Finland in 1852 and 1855 respectively and, in the 1880s, involved in farming in the same neighborhood. The compiler suspects that the three were related and they are jointly responsible for the name. Matt Mattson apparently decided to spell his family name with one "t" and this is the form of the creek name

Matterhorn, WALLOWA. The Matterhorn, named because of a fancied likeness to the great mountain of Switzerland and Italy, is one of the highest peaks in the Wallowa Mountains, and is situated southwest of Wallowa Lake. *Matterhorn* means a peak or horn with green meadows at its base. The village of Zermatt in Switzerland, at the foot of the Matterhorn, is so named because it is on a meadow.

Matthieu Lakes, DESCHUTES. The name Matthieu Lakes was bestowed in 1924 by Professor Edwin T. Hodge of the University of Oregon on two small lakes on the southern part of Black Crater, near the summit of the Cascade Range. Professor Hodge thus honored Francis Xavier Matthieu, a pioneer of the Oregon country, who was born near Montreal, Apr. 2, 1818, and died near Butteville, Oregon, Feb. 4, 1919. He came to Oregon in 1842 with the Hastings company. He settled in the Willamette Valley not far from Butteville and was present at the meeting held at Champoeg on May 2, 1843, to consider a provisional government. He was one of those who favored a provisional government and his name is one of the most honored in pioneer history. *See* memorial address of Charles B. Moores, published in *OHQ*, v. 15, p. 73 *et seq*.

Maud, JEFFERSON. Maud post office was situated at the Samuel A. Sandvig homestead about ten miles west of Ashwood. The office was established May 9, 1912, with Sandvig postmaster, and was in operation until Mar. 31, 1914. The office was named for Maud Sandvig, wife of the postmaster. It was near Pony Butte.

Maupin, WASCO. Maupin bears the name of one of the most celebrated of Oregon pioneers. Beside being applied to the post office, the name is also used for several geographic features in the central part of the state including two Maupin Buttes. Howard Maupin was born in Kentucky in 1815, and when he was about 15 years old moved to Missouri. He came to Oregon in 1863 and after spending a short time in the Willamette Valley, went to central Oregon. He first settled in Antelope Valley. The famous central Oregon Chief Paulina and his renegade Indians stole all of Maupin's stock shortly after he settled in Antelope Valley. Maupin established a stopping place for travelers and in 1871 was the first postmaster of the town of Antelope. Maupin also lived and operated at other points in central Oregon. He had a farm at the forks of Trout Creek and it was near that location that Paulina stole more of his stock. Maupin pursued the Indians and surprised them near Paulina Basin, where he killed the old chief, who had been the terror of settlers for several years. Maupin was a veteran of the Mexican War and was said to be a crack shot. Later he had a ferry on Deschutes River near the mouth of Bakeoven Creek, which was subsequently owned by W. E. Hunt. The place was then called Hunts Ferry. W. H. Staats bought the townsite when the railroads were built up Deschutes Canyon and named the place Maupin Ferry, but the postal authorities cut off the last word and since about 1909 the place has been called Maupin.

Maury Mountains, CROOK. Maury Mountains are south of Crooked River, near the central part of Crook County. They form an isolated group of dissected hills drained by various tributaries of Crooked River. They were named for Colonel R. F. Maury, who was prominent during the various Indian wars fought in central Oregon in the 1860s. For information about Colonel Maury and his participation in these Indian wars, *see* Bancroft's *History of Oregon*, v. 2, p. 488, *et seq*. In 1887 a post office was established near Maury Mountains and it was intended that it should be named in Colonel Maury's honor, but in the petition the name was incorrectly spelled Mowry. This post office was discontinued about 1899. *See also* Camp Maury.

Maxville, WALLOWA. Maxville was a logging camp owned by the Bowman-Hicks Lumber Company. At the time the town was started the lumber company superintendent's name was J. D. McMillan, and the first part of his name was used to form the name of the community Maxville. The name was suggested by H. N. Ashby, of La Grande, general manager of the lumber company. The post office was discontinued about 1933, but the community was still in existence in Apr. 1943.

Maxwell, COOS. Maxwell community and post office were situated six or seven miles south of what is now the city of Coos Bay, on the right or east of Isthmus Slough. William A. Maxwell came to the place about the turn of the century and started to develop a coal property. Bunkers and housing were built, but the mines failed to become a paying proposition. Maxwell post office was established Jan. 29, 1902, with Fred Ward first postmaster. The office was closed May 15, 1907, and the place is now quite deserted.

Maxwell Point, TILLAMOOK. John W. Maxwell was one of the early Tillamook County settlers. He homesteaded at Oceanside in 1883.

Maxwell Pond, BAKER. This is a small impoundment on Favorite Slough. E. W. Coles of Haines told the compiler in 1973 that James O. Maxwell was an early settler in the area and the pond bears his name. He added that Maxwell did his bit to populate the West by fathering ten children.

Maxwell Spring, WHEELER. This spring near the Wheeler Monument east of Mitchell was named for William T. Maxwell who homesteaded there in 1882. Maxwell married the sister of the well-known Nelson brothers.

May, COOS. May post office, which was near the shore of Haynes Inlet north of Coos Bay, was named for May Peterson, daughter of the first postmaster. The office was established June 21, 1898, with Peter Peterson first postmaster in a series of two. The office was closed Nov. 15, 1904.

Mayflower Creek, MARION. This stream flows into North Santiam River west of Detroit. It was sometimes known as Watertank Creek, because of a railroad water tank nearby. C. C. Giebeler of Detroit told the compiler in 1920 that Mayflower was the older name and in his opinion the one in general use. He was not able to explain the origin of the name.

Mayger, COLUMBIA. C. W. Mayger, a native of France, came to Oak Point, Washington, about 1865, and later settled at what is now Mayger. The post office, established in 1889, was named for him, and he was first postmaster.

Mays Canyon Creek, WASCO. This creek east of Dufur commemorates one of the earliest stockmen in central Oregon. Robert Mays came to Oregon with the emigration of 1852 and settled near Dufur in 1858. In 1862 he moved to the Tygh area and also bought an interest in Sherars Bridge. He subsequently enlarged his operation to several ranches in Wasco and Wheeler counties. Mays Rock near the headwaters of Muddy Creek and May Basin near Amine Peak were both named for his ranges.

Mayville, GILLIAM. Mayville is said to have been named for an incident connected with the establishment of the post office in 1884, possibly for the month in which the petition was sent in. The office was put in operation in Oct. 1884, with Sam Thornton postmaster. William McConnell platted the townsite with the name Clyde, but the place is commonly called Mayville.

Maywood Park, MULTNOMAH. The city of Maywood Park was incorporated by vote of the residents Aug. 1, 1967. The triangular area northeast of Rocky Butte was opened as a subdivision in 1926 and by 1940 was a fully developed suburb. In the 1960s the OSHD located I-205 through the edge of Maywood Park and this sparked a movement to incorporate as some opponents of freeway construction felt city status could prevent the highway encroachment or minimize its effect. Arthur M. Taylor, son of F. E. Taylor, the developer, wrote the compiler in 1968 to say that the name was selected by his mother one wintry evening when they were remembering what a lovely spot the woods were in May.

Mazama Creek, DOUGLAS. Mazama Creek is a small stream in the extreme southeast part of the county. It flows into the Rogue River. It was named because of its proximity to Mount Mazama in Crater Lake National Park. *See* Mount Mazama for origin of the name. Several other features in Oregon are named Mazama.

McAlister Creek, WALLOWA. This creek was named for James W. McAlister, a stockman. It is in T 3N, R 43E. McAlister Ridge and McAlister Spring in the same locality are named for the same man.

McBee Island, BENTON. J. W. McBee, a pioneer of Oregon, took up a donation land claim in early days northeast of Peoria, and this island in the Willamette River was named for him. *See* land office certificate 3958. McBee Slough nearby was named for the same man.

McBride, COLUMBIA. This was a station named for Judge Thomas A. McBride, for many years a distinguished member of the judiciary of Oregon, and chief justice of the state supreme court. He had a farm near the station that bore his name.

McBroom Spring, LAKE. This spring is on property that was part of the ranch started by Frank McBroom about 1914.

McCaffery Slough, LINCOLN. McCaffery was the name of a pioneer settler who lived near this slough and tonged for oysters in the waters of Yaquina Bay. The slough flows into the bay on the south side, about a mile west of the locality called Oysterville. It is shown as Johnson Slough on some maps but the best authorities favor the name McCaffery Slough. Andrew L. Porter, who settled in Lincoln County in the 1860s, was one of those who said that McCaffery is the correct name.

McCall Creek, LAKE. McCall Creek is a small tributary of Duncan Creek southwest of Silver Lake. William H. McCall came to the Silver Lake country in 1873 where he was one of the earliest settlers. *See Illustrated History of Central Oregon*, p. 921. However, the creek was probably named for his son, Claud McCall, who bought government land along the creek in 1906.

McCall Point, WASCO. McCall Point is the 1722-foot-high nose a mile southwest of and above Rowena Crest on the Historic Columbia River Highway. It is named to commemorate Tom McCall, 30th governor of the State of Oregon. Thomas Lawson McCall was born Mar. 22, 1913, in Massachusetts but spent his youth on the family ranch near Prineville. He graduated from the University of Oregon and spent a number of years working in radio and television. In 1964 he was elected secretary of state and in 1966, governor. His eight years in that office were marked by a number of environmental actions including the Oregon land use legislation. After he left office, he spent much time espousing conservation activities including the wildflower habitat at Rowena Crest. In due course, the area there outside Mayer State Park was acquired by the Nature Conservancy. McCall died on Jan. 8, 1983, and in the following March it was dedicated as the Tom McCall Preserve. After his death many suggestions were made to name or rename some feature for McCall and in June 1987, the OGNB approved a proposal to name McCall Point. The USBGN concurred in *Decision List 8801. See* the *Oregonian*, Jan. 13, 1983, p. 1, and Mar. 24, 1983, p. F-12.

McCallister Soda Spring Forest Camp, JACKSON. BLM records show Simon McCallister filed on government land here in 1884. The camp is on North Fork Little Butte Creek about five miles west of Fish Lake.

McCarty Spring, UNION. McCarty Spring, two miles southwest of Starkey, was on the property of John McCarty who settled in the area at the turn of the century.

McCauley Creek, LANE. Gordon McCauley took a donation land claim along Row River near where Smith Creek empties into Dorena Lake. McCauley Creek flows into Smith Creek.

McClellan Creek, GRANT. McClellan Creek rises on McClellan Mountain and flows north to John Day River three miles west of Mount Vernon. According to USFS files, both were named for Theodore McClellan who ran sheep along the creek in the old days.

McClellan Meadow, UNION. This meadow and spring near the headwaters of McCoy Creek in the extreme west part of the county were named for an old couple who settled in the meadow and were later killed by Indians.

McComb Butte, LAKE. McComb Butte is about ten miles southwest of Paisley and has an elevation of 6468 feet. It was named to honor Scott McComb, the second USFS ranger at Paisley. McComb, who came to Oregon shortly after the turn of the century, died in 1917 at the age of 41.

McConville Peak, JACKSON. This peak east of Wimer and nearby McConville Gulch are apparently named for Arthur McConville who filed for a homestead in the gulch in 1889. BLM records indicate that he died before proving up, for this was done by his heirs.

McCord Creek, MULTNOMAH. This creek has had several names, including Pierce Creek and Kelly Creek. A committee representing various historical organizations recommended that it be named McCord Creek, and that name was adopted by the USBGN. This was in honor of W. R. McCord, a pioneer of Oregon, who built the first fish wheels near the mouth of the stream. The falls near the highway are named Elowah, and the creek runs through John B. Yeon State Park.

McCorkle Spring, JEFFERSON. This spring was named for Chester L. McCorkle who had a homestead south of Ashwood in the 1880s.

McCornack Point, KLAMATH. This point on the southwest corner of Upper Klamath Lake was near the site of the McCornack Brothers Ranch operated by Frank H. and Eugene P. McCornack.

McCoy, POLK. E. T. Hatch of Vancouver, Washington, informed the compiler in Dec. 1926, that McCoy was named for Isaac McCoy, who owned the land on which the town was built. He gave right-of-way for the railroad and requested that the station be named McCoyville, however, the railroad officials clipped off the last syllable.

McCoy Creek, HARNEY. The writer is informed that this stream, which drains the northwest slope of Steens Mountain, was named by Mrs. Dolly Kiger for a local resident, Mace McCoy.

McCoy Creek, UMATILLA, UNION. McCoy Creek rises in the Blue Mountains and runs southeast to Meadow Creek and Grande Ronde River. It was named for James G. McCoy, an early settler who came to Umatilla County prior to 1870. He filed on government land near the mouth of the creek in 1883 but he had probably lived in the area for some years previously. His son, Olney P. McCoy, was one of the four freighters killed at Deadman Pass in July 1878. In earlier days some maps showed this stream as Ensign Creek but this name has not prevailed.

McCredie Springs, LANE. McCredie Springs on Salt Creek were named for Judge William Wallace McCredie, well-known Portland baseball enthusiast. They are on the Southern Pacific Cascade line and on the Willamette Highway about ten miles southeast of Oakridge. Mrs. Paul Sims of McCredie Springs wrote the compiler that Judge McCredie bought an interest in the springs about 1916. They were then known as Winino Springs. For additional information, *see* Winino Springs. There was once a post office on Salt Creek called Winino. There are several hot springs of varying temperatures, and a resort development. McCredie Springs post office was established Sept. 14, 1926, with Mrs. Vivian Cartwright postmaster. This office was out of service for a time, reestablished and finally closed Oct. 2, 1953. Judge McCredie used the resort as a training quarters for the Portland baseball players. His nephew, Walter McCredie, was also interested in the activities of the Portland team.

McCubbin Basin, WALLOWA. This basin, in T 2S, R 43E, was named for Leander McCubbin, who ranged sheep thereabouts.

McCubbins Gulch, WASCO. This gulch starts two miles east of Bear Springs and runs towards Wapinitia. William H. McNeal in *History of Wasco County*, p. 255, says it was named for an early day sheep man who had been gone so long that even old timers had forgotten his given name. It obviously was named for the same family as McCubbin Basin since *History of Union and Wallowa Counties*, p. 537, states that Abraham McCubbin settled in Wasco County in the 1880s and his son, Leander, was raised there before he moved to Wallowa County in 1889. The USBGN *Decision List 6604* adopted the form McCubbins.

McCully Creek, WALLOWA. McCully Creek was named for Frank D. McCully, who ranged sheep there with Charles Christy. He was the second merchant in Joseph, Oregon.

McCurdy, KLAMATH. A post office named McCurdy was established on the Klamath County list in Feb. 1882, and ran for a little over a year when it was closed to Linkville. Martin V. McCurdy was the first postmaster. The following quotation from the editorial column of the Klamath Falls *Herald and News*, June 4, 1948, contains useful information: "Yesterday, Jesse Drew was in from Hildebrand with the story of McCurdy post office. He said this post office, located about three miles from the present Lakeview-Hildebrand intersection at the Bliss store, was run for just about one year." Drew went on to say that he was living in the former McCurdy house, which he had remodeled. This house is situated about a quarter of a mile south of the northeast corner of s 10, T 38S, R 11E. It is about four miles north and a half mile east of Dairy.

McDaid Springs, MORROW. These springs on the upper reaches of Juniper Canyon were named for Ed McDaid, an early homesteader. The spelling McDade is incorrect. When they mapped the area in 1968, the USGS reported the springs had filled up and little evidence remained.

McDermitt, MALHEUR. A post office with the name McDermitt was in service in the extreme south end of Malheur County from May 20, 1904, to May 26, 1908, when it was changed to the list for Humboldt County, Nevada. As far as the compiler can determine, the office has been in operation in Nevada ever since it was moved from the Oregon list. What there is of the community is very close to the state line. The writer has been unable to get the early history of this office, which was apparently established in Nevada. It was named for Fort Dermit, and the fort was named for Lieutenant-Colonel Charles McDermit of the Second Cavalry, California Volunteers, who was killed by Indians Aug. 7, 1865, while scouting along a creek westward of what was later the post office. The name McDermitt is used for a voting precinct in southern Malheur County. The compiler does not know what brought about the discrepancy in the spelling of the name. McDermitt for the post office is well established, and it is the official name of the voting precinct. Maps show the stream with the name spelled either way.

McDevitt Springs, MORROW. McDevitt Springs in Juniper Canyon near Strawberry were named for Bernard McDevitt who took up land nearby in 1896.

McDonald, SHERMAN. McDonald post office was established near the John Day River on the east border of the county on Mar. 15, 1904, with William G. McDonald postmaster, and remained in service until Oct. 14, 1922, when it was closed to Klondike. It was of course named with the family name of the postmaster. This office was at the McDonald Ferry on John Day River at the mouth of Grass Valley Canyon. The Oregon Trail crossed the river at this point. For the history of earlier post offices in this locality, especially on the Gilliam County side, *see* Rockville.

McDonald Canyon, UMATILLA. McDonald Canyon enters McKay Creek south of Table Rock. Angus McDonald was born in Canada in 1855 and came to Umatilla County in 1881. In 1891 he purchased land along McKay Creek where he was one of the first to farm and raise sheep. The family was numerous, and it is possible that the canyon may have been named for Charles McDonald who took up land near its mouth in 1910.

McDowell Creek, LINN. This stream flows into South Santiam River not far southeast of Waterloo. It was named for James McDowell, an early settler of the vicinity.

McDowell Peak, LAKE. McDowell Peak and McDowell Creek which rises on its east slope were named for Major-General Irvin McDowell. McDowell Peak is between Drake and Crook peaks about two and one half miles south of the site of New Camp Warner. McDowell was commanding the Military Department of the Pacific in 1866 when troops were using the military road along Honey Creek but the features probably were not named until Camp Warner was relocated to the west side of Warner Valley in 1867. Irvin McDowell was born in Ohio and graduated from West Point in 1838. He served in the Mexican War and as a brigadier-general was in command at the first battle of Bull Run at the start of the Civil War. After involvement in the disastrous Union operations of 1862, he was relieved of command in the field and sent to the Pacific Coast in 1864. During a second tour as commander of the Military Department of the Pacific, he was General Howard's superior during the Nez Perce War.

McElligott Canyon, MORROW. In the 1890s Richard McElligott homesteaded near the head of this canyon and Jeremiah, his brother, settled near its mouth. In 1969, Richard's family was still living in the area and stated that while Jeremiah McElligott left Morrow County in 1903, the canyon was probably named for him.

McEwen, BAKER. This community was named for Thomas McEwen, a pioneer settler.

McFarland Butte, LANE. This butte is just northwest of Cottage Grove and lies between Bennett Creek and Silk Creek. It was named for James McFarland, who came to Oregon in 1850 and settled near what is now Cottage Grove in 1853. His brother, John W. McFarland, was also an early settler in the vicinity. Several descendants have been prominent in the community.

McGlynn, LANE. McGlynn was the post office name for the railroad station of Penn. Postal authorities were unwilling to accept the name Penn as a post office name because of possible confusion. McGlynn was suggested because Thomas McGlynn owned the land on which the post office was established. This was in 1923. McGlynn post office was closed Nov. 21, 1938.

McGraw Creek, WALLOWA. McGraw Creek was named for an early day hunter and trapper. It flows into Snake River in T 5S, R 49E, in the extreme southeast corner of the county.

McGribble Guard Station, CURRY. This guard cabin three miles northeast of Humbug Mountain was built in 1906 by two USFS employees who combined their names, Macduff and Gribble. In 1975 Mrs. Ivan F. Duff of Ann Arbor, Michigan, wrote to say that she was certain the Macduff was her father, Nelson F. Macduff, for whom Macduff Peak was named. He had just graduated in the first class of the new Forestry School at the University of Michigan and had moved to Oregon to start a long career with the USFS.

McIntyre Ridge, CLACKAMAS. McIntyre Ridge is the high ground that runs to Wildcat Mountain east of Brightwood and south of US-26. John T. McIntyre came to the Salmon River area in the early 1880s. He built a hotel and kept the travel and trading post near the mouth of Salmon River. He was a prominent citizen and was with Roark when Perry Vickers was murdered near Government Camp in 1893. He also gave the property for the first school in Brightwood. His wife, Winifred McIntyre, was postmaster of the Salmon post office.

McKay, UMATILLA. This post office was named McKay because of its proximity to McKay Creek and because of a desire to honor Dr. William C. McKay. *See* McKay Creek, Umatilla County.

McKay Creek, CROOK. This stream is in the northwest part of the county. It was named for Donald McKay, a well-known scout in the Indian troubles in central Oregon, who took a conspicuous part in the Modoc War. He was a son of Thomas McKay and a grandson of Alexander McKay, who was blown up with the Astor ship *Tonquin* at Clayoquot Sound in June 1811. Thomas McKay came to Oregon with his father in 1811. Alexander McKay's widow, Marguerite Wadin McKay, married Dr. John McLoughlin and came to Oregon. Thomas McKay was married twice. Dr. William C. McKay was a child of the first marriage, and Donald McKay of the second.

McKay Creek, UMATILLA. This stream rises on the west slopes of the Blue Mountains and flows into the Umatilla River just west of Pendleton. It was named for Dr. William C. McKay, who was born at Astoria in 1824 and died in Pendleton in 1893. He settled near the mouth of McKay Creek in 1851-52, and called the place Houtama. Dr. McKay was the son of Thomas McKay. For a biography of Dr. McKay, *see* Pendleton *East Oregonian*, Jan. 2, 1889.

McKay Creek, WASHINGTON. This stream drains a considerable area north of Hillsboro. It was named for Charles McKay, a pioneer settler, who took up a donation land claim nearby. The stream has also been known as Johnson Creek and Davis Creek, because it passes through land once owned by early settlers with these names. The USGS, however, used the form McKay Creek when it mapped the Hillsboro quadrangle, and C. G. Reiter, city manager of Hillsboro, informed the compiler in Oct. 1927, that McKay Creek was the name generally used in the county.

McKay Dam, UMATILLA. McKay Dam is so called because it dams McKay Creek. For the origin of the name McKay Creek, *see* McKay Creek. McKay Dam is part of the Umatilla reclamation project and is situated about seven miles south of Pendleton. The dam was built for the purpose of storing water in McKay Creek and the reservoir created by the dam has a capacity of about 73,000 acre feet. This water is used to supplement the natural flow of Umatilla River for irrigating 38,000 acres of land near Echo, Stanfield and Hermiston. The post office of Mc-Kay Dam was established about 1923, and was discontinued in the summer of 1925. For additional details about this dam, *see New Reclamation Era* for Sept. 1925.

McKee, MARION. McKee station north of Mount Angel was named for a pioneer family of the neighborhood.

McKenzie Bridge, LANE. McKenzie Bridge has long been an important crossing of McKenzie River, and was named for the stream. For many years the post office was called McKinzie Bridge, and after much protesting, postal authorities agreed to correct the spelling, which was done in Nov. 1918. One of the enthusiastic supporters of the McKenzie road project was John Templeton Craig who is buried in McKenzie Pass. In the 1860s Craig lived like a hermit near what is now McKenzie Bridge, and the location was called Craigs or Craigs Pasture. *See* Craig Lake, and *also OHQ*, v. 31, p. 261. It is said that the location of McKenzie Bridge was once called Strawberry Prairie.

McKenzie Canyon, DESCHUTES. This canyon lies between Sisters and Lower Bridge. It is said to have received its name, not because of any local settler named McKenzie, but because the cattle trail from Lower Bridge up this canyon led to McKenzie Pass.

McKenzie Pass, DESCHUTES, LANE, LINN. Authorities who are presumed to know about such matters have informed the writer that nowhere are there such remarkable evidences of comparatively recent volcanism as in central Oregon. The writer is prepared to believe this, and is of the opinion that the lava fields and flows of McKenzie Pass present the most unusual aspect of nature that he has ever seen. Fortunately the development of an excellent highway over McKenzie Pass brought these lava flows within view of many people who knew little of them. McKenzie Pass is named for McKenzie River, and besides being well known for its unusual lavas, is also historically interesting by reason of the construction by pioneer citizens of Oregon of a toll road over the Cascade Range at this point. After toll collecting was abandoned, the road over the summit languished until active reconstruction was taken up about 1920. The road was relocated and widened, and on Sept. 21, 1925, the highway project was completed between Blue River and Sisters, a distance of about 50 miles. *See* Bend *Bulletin* of that date. The highest point on the highway through the pass is 5325 feet, according to computations made by the writer.

McKenzie River, LANE. As a fine mountain river the McKenzie may be equalled in Oregon, but it is surely not surpassed. It was named for Donald McKenzie, a member of Astor's Pacific Fur Company. In 1812 he explored the Willamette Valley, and it was doubtless this expedition that caused his name to be attached to what is now McKenzie River. It was called McKenzie's Fork by John Work in 1834, and during pioneer days the name was shortened to McKenzie

Fork. This term was used in contradistinction to Middle Fork and Coast Fork Willamette River. The name is now universally McKenzie River. A South Fork heads southwest of the Three Sisters. Donald McKenzie, a kinsman of Alexander Mackenzie, was an old "North Wester," before he joined the Astor enterprise. He came west with the overland party and arrived at Astoria Jan. 18, 1812. He went east to Fort William in 1814. He returned to the Columbia River with the North West Company in 1816, and thereafter made notable expeditions in the Snake River country. He accumulated a fortune in the fur trade and retired to New York, where he died at Mayville, Chautauqua County, in 1851. McKenzie was a remarkable rifle shot, skilled in woodcraft and Indian warfare, and was an able trader with the Indians. Ross Cox describes him favorably; "To the most cautious prudence he united the most dauntless intrepidity; in fact, no hardships could fatigue, no dangers intimidate him." Franchere calls him "a very selfish man, who cared for no one but himself." However, Alexander Ross, in *Fur Hunters of the Far West*, v. 1, pp. 281–83, presents a much more agreeable picture of McKenzie, credits him with some excellent qualities and winds up by calling him "Perpetual Motion." For data about McKenzie's activities in the Pacific Northwest, *see* article "Snake River Fur Trade," by W. T. Atkin, *OHQ*, v. 35, p. 295. For a short biography, *see* *Colin Robertson's Correspondence Book*, Hudson's Bay Record Society, 1939, p. 233.

McKinley, COOS. McKinley post office was established in July 1897, and was named in honor of William McKinley, president of the United States, by Homer Shepherd, who took the necessary steps to have the office established. Shepherd was the first postmaster.

McKinley Ranch, KLAMATH. Hartley B. McKinley settled on this ranch west of Antelope Flat prior to World War I.

McKinney Bottom, MARION. McKinney Bottom, east of Jefferson, was named for a pioneer landowner, William McKinney.

McKinney Butte, DESCHUTES. McKinney Butte is about a mile northeast of Sisters. In Nov. 1943, George E. Aitken of Sisters told the compiler that it was named for Jesse O. McKinney, who at one time owned a ranch near the base of the butte. McKinney died about 1942 at Stevenson, Washington.

McKinney Creek, LINN. This stream is a tributary of North Santiam River and was named by Thomas J. Henness because William McKinney, a pioneer settler of the Santiam Valley, in 1861 found a gold nugget worth $5 at the mouth of the stream. *See* the Salem *Capital Journal*, June 18, 1927, p. 1.

McKinney Creek, MORROW. Willis E. McKinney settled on this creek near Ruggs in the 1870s.

McLean Point, LINCOLN. McLean Point is a well-known place on the north shore of Yaquina Bay about a mile and a half east of Newport. It was named for Rufus McLean, who settled there in the late 1860s and had a house on a small bench above the bay. He used to haul freight to the Siletz Agency.

McMahan Branch, POLK. This stream rises on the west slopes of the Eola Hills and flows into Mud Slough, a tributary of Rickreall Creek. It was named for Richard McMahan, who was born in Kentucky in 1812 and who settled on a donation land claim nearby in Mar. 1851.

McMillan Canyon, MORROW. John F. and George L. McMillan were brothers who settled along this canyon just east of Ione. The family came from Tennessee to Morrow County in 1886.

McMinnville, YAMHILL. McMinnville was named by William T. Newby, who was born in McMinnville, Warren County, Tennessee, in 1820, and came to Oregon in 1843. He settled near the present site of McMinnville early in 1844, and in 1853 built a grist mill and founded the town. In 1854 he started a store. He was county assessor in 1848 and state senator in 1870. McMinville post office was established on May 29, 1855, with Elbridge G. Edson postmaster. The name was later changed to the present spelling.

McMullin Creek, JOSEPHINE. This is a tributary of Deer Creek near Selma. It bears the name of William McMullin, a pioneer of the Illinois Valley. *See* Walling's *History of Southern Oregon*, p. 452.

McNab, MORROW. This station west of Ione was named for Wesley T. McNab, who came to Pendleton from Iowa, and subsequently settled in Morrow County. He was a stockman and later a grain buyer.

McNary, POLK. McNary was a station on the Southern Pacific railroad about one and one-half miles west of Eola. It was named for the McNary family, pioneer settlers in Polk County.

McNary Dam, UMATILLA. This dam on the Columbia River near Umatilla was built by the USCE for flood control and hydroelectric power. It was named for Charles Linza McNary, United States senator from Oregon from 1917 to 1944. McNary was born of a pioneer family near Salem on June 12, 1874. He practiced law and from 1913 to 1915 was a member of the Oregon Supreme Court. He died in Miami, Florida, on Feb. 25, 1944. For additional information, *see* the *Oregon Journal* for Feb. 25, 1944. McNary post office was established Sept. 1, 1949.

McNeece Flat, WHEELER. This flat near West Branch was the site of the 1910 homestead of Flora McNeece.

McNeil Point, CLACKAMAS, HOOD RIVER. This prominent point is at timberline on Bald Mountain ridge of Mount Hood. It lies on the Cascade divide at an approximate elevation of 6000 feet between McGee Creek and Muddy Fork Sandy River. The nearly level promontory is about a quarter mile above the "Round the Mountain" trail and is marked by one of the stone shelters constructed during the 1930s. The point and the forest camp on Sandy River were named for Fred H. McNeil, a long time mountain and outdoor enthusiast. McNeil was born in Illinois in 1893 and moved to Oregon in 1912. His newspaper career, principally with the *Oregon Journal*, lasted more than 45 years until a few months before his death on Dec. 28, 1958. He was an active Mazama and was instrumental in organizing the Pacific Northwest Ski Association. During World War II he trained and directed the volunteer fire lookout and guard station personnel that formed the USFS Reserves. For additional information, *see* the *Oregon Journal*, Dec. 29, 1958, and July 13, 1959.

McNulty Creek, COLUMBIA. This stream and a railroad station were named for John McNulty, a pioneer of Oregon, who took up a claim not far from the present site of Saint Helens.

McSherry Creek, POLK. This stream flows into South Fork Siletz River above Valsetz Lake. Gordon Clarke says it was named for Charles L. McSherry but BLM records show that Samuel A. McSheery filed a homestead in 1901 that was subsequently patented. Clarke notes that the name was spelled both ways.

McTimmonds Valley, POLK. This valley, about three miles west of Lewisville and draining into Luckiamute River, was named for Lambert McTimmonds, who received a patent for land in the vicinity in 1875.

McVay Rock, CURRY. William R. McVay came to Curry County in 1861 and settled near this rock south of Brookings.

McVey Spring, WASCO. This spring west of Mosier Creek was named for the McVey family who homesteaded nearby just after the turn of the century.

Meacham, UMATILLA. Meacham is a station on the Union Pacific Railroad near the summit of the Blue Mountains. It is where H. A. G. Lee established Lees Encampment in the 1840s. Meacham was named for Harvey J. and Alfred B. Meacham, brothers, who operated Meacham Station in the 1860s and early 1870s. *See* interview with Mrs. Nellie Frances Meacham Reddington, editorial page of the *Oregon Journal*, Nov. 9, 1935. She was the daughter of A. B. Meacham. Harvey J. Meacham, already in Oregon, urged his brother to come here from California, which he did between February and March 1863, and the two started a small stage station at Lees Encampment. A larger station was built in the spring of 1865 and called Meacham Station. The following notice appears in the La Grande *Mountain Sentinel* of Oct. 17, 1868: "Meacham Bros. are closing out business and earnestly request those indebted to us to 'settle up' immediately. We have made arrangments to consolidate the Meacham Road and Lee's Encampment with the Ruckel & Thomas Road and Warm Springs. Until further notice A. B. Meacham will conduct the business at Warm Springs and H. J. Meacham at Lee's Encampment, henceforth doing only a cash business." The notice is dated July 25, 1867, some 15 months earlier. The brothers apparently had been a little generous in their credit policy. The Warm Springs location of A. B. Meacham was what is now Bingham Springs. *See* Bingham Springs. Harvey Meacham was killed at the original station May 29, 1872, when a tree fell on him. Alfred B. Meacham was born in Orange County, Indiana, Apr. 29, 1826. He joined the gold rush to California in 1850, and came to Oregon in 1863. On May 1, 1869, he was appointed Superintendent of Indian Affairs by President U. S. Grant. For his activities in trying to bring about peace with the Modocs, *see* his book, *Wigwam and Warpath*, and *The Indian History of the Modoc War*, by Jeff C. Riddle. In the Modoc Lava Beds attack on Apr. 11, 1873, General E. R. S. Canby and the Reverend Eleazar Thomas, D.D., were killed, and Meacham was severely wounded and left for dead. *See* Canby in this book. After the Modoc War Meacham interested himself in Indian affairs in various parts of the United States. He died Feb. 16, 1882, at Washington, D.C. After the railroad began operating over the Blue Mountains it built an eating house at Meacham, which later became famous under the management of "Grandma" Munra. Encampment post office was established May 8, 1882, with Mary M. Strickland first postmaster. The name of the office was changed to Meacham on Mar. 26, 1890.

Meadow, CROOK. Meadow was the name of a post office established on the Crook County list on Dec. 21, 1910, with Emma J. Merritt first postmaster. This office was operated until July 9, 1919, when the name was changed to Ochoco. The office is said to have been moved to a new location at that time. The compiler has not been able to learn the location of Ochoco post office of which Claud W. Martin was the only postmaster. Meadow post office was given a descriptive name because of its proximity to Big Summit Prairie. Many parts of this big prairie simulate a meadow. The prairie covers a large part of T 14S, R 21E, and Meadow post office was in section 13 of this township. At least that is where it is shown on a map of Ochoco National Forest dated 1915.

Meadow, LANE. Meadow was a place in the west part of the county on Siuslaw River about a mile south of the north line of T 18S, R 8W. Meadow Creek flows into the river nearby. In Jan. 1947, Elwin A. McCornack of Eugene wrote the compiler as follows: "After a road had been cut through over Badger Mountain, down Wildcat Creek to the Siuslaw and to Swisshome, the mail and stage coaches from Eugene followed this new route. Stage stations were established every 20 or 30 miles where horses were changed and passengers fed or put up for the night. One of these stations on the Siuslaw was known as Meadow and was owned and operated by a Mr. Tallman. I always assumed this place was called Meadow because of the fact that in a very restricted valley the Tallman ranch had a good expanse of hay meadow." Meadow post office was established Aug. 30, 1887, with Levi P. Tallman first postmaster. The office was closed Aug. 31, 1908, with papers to Walton.

Meadow Creek, UMATILLA, UNION. Meadow Creek is a good size stream flowing eastward in the Blue Mountains and draining into Grande Ronde River near Starkey. Some old maps show this as Starkey Creek, but letters from the postmaster at Starkey in 1933 and from the USFS say that Meadow Creek is the correct name and the one in general use.

Meadowbrook, CLACKAMAS. The name Meadowbrook, as applied to a locality a few miles northeast of Molalla, is mildly sentimental and certainly not very original. The place may have been named for Milk Creek which flows nearby, but that stream hardly merits the name "brook." Meadow Brook post office was established May 13, 1889, with Charles Holman postmaster. The name was changed to Meadowbrook Sept. 5, 1895, and the office was closed May 20, 1905.

Meadows, UMATILLA. In pioneer days that part of the county in the vicinity of what is now Hermiston was called the Meadows because of its characteristic appearance and in contradistinction to the canyon of Umatilla River west of Pendleton. There was an early post office on or near the Meadows called Meadowville. It was closed in 1874 and on May 10, 1880, a new office was established called Meadows. The office was closed to Echo on Dec. 19, 1882.

Meadowville, UMATILLA. One of the pioneer post offices of Umatilla County was called Meadowville. It was situated near what is now Stanfield, but it passed from the picture many years ago. Meadowville post office was established Feb. 2, 1867, with Hawkins Shelton first postmaster. The office was closed Oct. 26, 1874.

Mealey, LINN. The place called Mealey was near the foot of Moss Butte about seven miles southeast of Foster on the military road. It was named in compliment to Charles Mealey and his wife Mary Jane, *nee* Settlemier, who came to Oregon in separate wagon trains in 1852. After marriage, the Mealeys lived in Brownsville and also in Albany, before homesteading near the South Santiam River in 1874. This homestead was near the middle of s 4, T 14S, R 2E. Mealey post office was established Aug. 19, 1892, with Orange J. Mealey first and only postmaster. The office was discontinued Mar. 1, 1898, with papers to Foster. Information about the Mealey family was sent the compiler in Sept. 1946, by William R. Mealey of Foster, son of Mr. and Mrs. Charles Mealey and brother of Orange J. Mealey. William Mealey was born in Albany in Sept. 1870, and was brought up on the Mealey place described above.

Mecca, JEFFERSON. Mecca was a place on the east bank of Deschutes River a few miles east of Warm Springs Agency and in days gone by it sported not only a post office but it was a station on the Oregon Trunk railway line. The old wagon road from Madras to Warm Springs Agency came down from Agency Plains on a hair-raising grade, and crossed the Deschutes at Mecca. There is some uncertainty about the origin of the name Mecca as applied to the railroad station, but it is generally believed that the name was used because when the railroad was built to this point it was out of the worst part of Deschutes Canyon and one of its main objectives had been reached. Mecca post office was established Sept. 18, 1911, with Edward Chaoupka first postmaster. The office was discontinued May 31, 1924. When US-26 was built from Madras to Warm Springs, a new bridge was installed more than a mile upstream from Mecca. The railroad has been torn out. Mecca, Oregon, is not now a focal point for tourists and pilgrims.

Meda, TILLAMOOK. Meda post office was on Little Nestucca River about midway of Oretown and Dolph. This post office was established May 11, 1887, with Wallace Yates first postmaster. In May 1948, Mrs. Affolter of Hebo told the compiler that Meda was the name of Yates' sweetheart in England. The sentimental side of this story is tinctured with melancholy because Meda is reported to have died just before or just after Yates left England. In any event it was in her memory that he named the post office. This office was out of service from 1892 to 1915. It was discontinued again in Sept. 1920. The Meda schoolhouse is still in service. Meda post office had seven different postmasters and it seems probable that it moved around a little as time went on.

Medford, JACKSON. Richard Koehler, a resident of Oregon for more than half a century and for many years operating head of Southern Pacific Company lines in this state, told the compiler that the town of Medford was named by David Loring who was at the time of construction a civil engineer connected with the right-of-way operations for the Oregon & California Rail Road Company. The railroad was opened to traffic from Grants Pass to Phoenix in 1884. The name was apparently applied shortly before that date. In Aug. 1927, David Loring was living in Portland, and in conversation with the compiler confirmed Mr. Koehler's statement. Mr. Loring said that while the form of the name was suggested by Medford, Massachusetts, he really named the new community in Oregon because it was situated at the middle ford on Bear Creek. Mr. Loring was a native of Massachusetts. People in Jacksonville were not enthusiastic about the new rival community of Medford and referred to it as Chaparral City. The best authorities seem to agree that the name of Medford, Massachusetts, comes from the old English words *mead* and *ford*, meaning a ford at a meadow. Mr. Loring may have had in mind a combination of mede and ford, in which mede is an obsolete abbreviation for medium, hence middle.

Medical Springs, UNION. Medical Springs is a descriptive name applied to the hot sulphur springs at that place.

Medicine Creek, WALLOWA. Jake Sheets got sick on this stream, and his companions, Charles and James Rice, mixed up all the medicine they had and forced him to take it. The mixture nearly killed him. The stream was named to commemorate the dose.

Medicine Rock, LINCOLN. Medicine Rock is a well-known point on the north or left bank of Siletz River about five miles upstream from the mouth. In this locality the river flows eastward. The geography of the location is shown on the USGS map of the Devils Lake quadrangle. The rock was named because of an Indian custom of leaving offerings at its base. The rock was supposed to be the abode of a skookum, or bad medicine man, whom the Indians propitiated by giving articles of food, pieces of cloth and sometimes native tools and fishhooks.

Medley, CLATSOP. Medley post office was established early in 1890 with William Medley first and only postmaster. It was named in his compliment. The office was nearly three miles west of and up Fishhawk Creek from Jewell, and was therefore not far from an earlier post office called Denver, which had been closed in 1888. Medley post office was closed Jan. 2, 1904, with papers to Jewell.

Meek Lake, KLAMATH. This small lake is west of Crescent Lake and near the summit of the Cascade Range. It is said to have been named because of some incident connected with a party of immigrants traveling over the Meek Cutoff through central Oregon. However, the Meek Cutoff was not in the vicinity of the lake, although a party of immigrants may have left the cutoff and passed by the lake.

Meengs Canyon, GRANT, UMATILLA. This canyon and the springs by North Fork John Day River about three miles east of Dale were named for Dr. Peter C. Meengs who homesteaded there in 1905. The spelling Mings is incorrect.

Mehama, MARION. This town was named for Mehama Smith, wife of James X. Smith, who laid out the townsite and who operated a ferry on North Santiam River in pioneer days. A post office with the name of Mehamah was established Mar. 12, 1877, with John J. Blair first postmaster. The error was corrected and the name of the office changed to Mehama on Mar. 30, 1881. Lewis Stout ran a ferry at this place before Smith Ferry was put in operation. Mehama Smith died on Apr. 8, 1895.

Mehl Creek, DOUGLAS. Mehl Creek, near Elkton was named for Gottlieb Mehl, an early settler in Douglas County who took a donation land claim including the mouth of the creek. The military road built along the Umpqua River in the late 1850s went along Mehl Creek while cutting off one of the numerous oxbow bends in the river. After an unsuccessful venture with a combination grist mill and saw mill, Mehl sold out in 1864 and moved to Roseburg where he operated a brewery.

Mehlhorn Butte, BAKER. In 1906, Henry, Louis, Albert and Edward Mehlhorn all bought government land adjacent to this butte in sections 22 and 23, T 7S, R 46E.

Melrose, DOUGLAS. Melrose was named for Melrose Abbey in Scotland, by Henry Scott. Scott was a native of Scotland and came from near Melrose Abbey. A post office named Hogan was established at or near the place in Douglas County on May 18, 1887, with James McKinney first postmaster. Henry Scott became postmaster on Nov. 10, 1887. He was not satisfied with the name of the office and had it changed to Melrose on Oct. 10, 1890. Hogan was the name of a nearby resident.

Melville, CLATSOP. This place is said to have been named for the oldest son of D. J. Ingalls, who resided there. It is on Lewis and Clark River.

Melvin Butte, DESCHUTES. This butte is in the foothills of the Cascade Range about ten miles southeast of Sisters. It was named for J. L. Melvin, who took up a timber claim nearby about 1902. Melvin got into a controversy with S. H. Dorrance, which is said to have started because Dorrance put sawdust in Melvin's irrigation ditch. As a result of this altercation Melvin killed Dorrance on the side of the butte now known as Melvin Butte. Melvin was cleared by a jury which considered that he was not to blame for the difficulty.

Memaloose Island, WASCO. There are a number of geographic features in

Oregon bearing the Chinook jargon word for death or dead. They were so named because they were Indian burial places. Several islands in the Columbia River are named Memaloose. The most important is near the south bank of the river between The Dalles and Mosier directly opposite the rest area on I-84. On it is buried Vic Trevitt, a prominent pioneer citizen and for many years a resident of The Dalles. His monument is easily seen from the mainland. Memaloose is given by Gibbs as *memaloost*, who says it is from the Chinook Indian word *memalust*, meaning to die. Memaloose is the spelling adopted by the USBGN and is in general use.

Mendi Gorri, MALHEUR. This ridge east of US-95 and the community of Basque has a descriptive name. *Mendi* is the Basque word for hill and *gorri* means red. Mendi Gorri Posue, east of the ridge, is an area that at times may hold water and *posue* means puddle or pond. The USGS 1982 Basque quadrangle uses the forms Gori and Gore but Taquita Garatea, a student of the local language, informed the compiler that these forms are incorrect.

Meno, HOOD RIVER. This station, west of Hood River, was originally named Menominee, for the place in Michigan. The naming was at the request of J. E. Cameron, who had formerly lived in the Michigan town, and when he established a sawmill in Oregon, he desired to perpetuate the name of his old home. After the mill was abandoned, the railroad company shortened the name of the station because the long form of the name was awkward in telegraphing. For obituary of J. E. Cameron, *see Oregon Journal*, Sunday, May 22, 1927, sect. I, p. 2. A post office with the name Nicolai was established in this locality on Nov. 13, 1900, with George H. Nicolai first postmaster. The name was changed to Menominee on Oct. 13, 1903. The office was discontinued Mar. 31, 1909.

Mercer, LANE. This post office was named Mercer because of its proximity to Mercer Lake. It was established in June 1904. For the origin of the name, *see* Mercer Lake.

Mercer Lake, LANE. This lake is about five miles north of Florence and was named for a government surveyor, George Mercer. Mercer surveyed the line between T 17 S and ranges 11 and 12W in 1879, and his name became applied to the lake on that account. The line passed through the lake. The name Mercer Lake is shown on maps prepared in 1883. The compiler is informed that the Indian name for Mercer Lake was *Kow-y-ich*, meaning the place of the lake.

Merganser, KLAMATH. Merganser was the name of a town that lived for a decade then passed into limbo. The place was established about 1870 by J. P. Roberts and Albert Handy to compete with the nearby village of Linkville, now Klamath Falls. It was situated about two miles below Klamath Falls, on the west bank of Klamath River not far from the bridge for US-97, The Dalles-California Highway. The first post office was called Klamath. It was in service from June 1872, to Apr. 1873, with Albert Handy postmaster. On Apr. 9, 1873, the name of the office was changed to Lakeport, and Handy continued in office. On May 19, 1875, the name of the office was changed to Merganser. John P. Roberts was postmaster at the time. Merganser office was closed May 12, 1879. The name Merganser was selected because of some incident connected with the shooting of a merganser duck in the vicinity. The town petered out about 1880. For short history of this place, *see Illustrated History of Central Oregon*, p. 983.

Meridian, MARION. Meridian is a crossroads locality about two miles south of Monitor, named because of its position on the Willamette Meridian. Meridian post office was established in Oct. 1900, with B. W. Otto first postmaster. The office was discontinued in Oct. 1903.

Meriwether, CLATSOP. Meriwether was a station east of Warrenton, and was platted with that title in 1890 by S. D. and Mary R. Adair. It was named for Captain Meriwether Lewis, because it was near the bay called Meriwether Bay by Lewis and Clark but now known as Youngs Bay. For additional information, *see* Youngs Bay and Lewis and Clark River.

Merlin, JOSEPHINE. David Loring, of Portland, for many years engaged in civil engineering in Oregon, and at one time in the employ of the railroad company building from Roseburg to Grants Pass, informed the compiler in Aug. 1927, that he named the community of Merlin for the merlins that he saw in the neighborhood about 1882. These birds were probably what are locally known as pigeon hawks. John G. Lanterman was the first postmaster.

Merrill, KLAMATH. Merrill was named for Nathan S. Merrill, who was born in New Hampshire in 1836, and moved to California in 1869. He moved to Chehalis County, Washington, in 1881, and in 1890 settled at the present site of Merrill. He bought a ranch in the spring of 1894 and laid out part of the town of Merrill, which was named for him.

Merrill Creek, COLUMBIA. George Merrill, for whom this stream was named, was born in Ohio on Sept. 11, 1826, and came to Oregon with his parents in 1847. His father died on the overland journey. Merrill went to the California mines but returned to Oregon in 1850. In 1851 he married Ann Martin and settled on a donation land claim on Deer Island where he lived the rest of his life. Merrill was once assessor of Columbia County and served three terms as county clerk. He was an amateur geologist, naturalist, and botanist. He died at his home on Deer Island Nov. 8, 1912, aged 86. His obituary is in the *Oregonian*, Nov. 24, 1912. Merrill Creek rises in the hills west of Deer Island and drains eastward to the Columbia River.

Merritt Spring, KLAMATH. This spring southwest of Kirk was named for an Indian family who took up land nearby.

Mesa Creek, LANE. So named because it heads near Rock Mesa, south of the Three Sisters. *Mesa* is Spanish for table.

Metlako Falls, HOOD RIVER. These falls are on Eagle Creek. They were named for an Indian legendary goddess of the salmon.

Metolius River, DESCHUTES, JEFFERSON. Three of the western tributaries of the Deschutes have their sources in giant springs, Metolius, Spring and Fall rivers, and of these three the Metolius is the largest and longest. It flows from the north base of Black Butte, full bodied and icy cold, and after winding northward through beautiful pine forests, swings around the north end of Green Ridge through a canyon of great depth and majestic grandeur, joining the Deschutes just north of the mouth of Crooked River. The gorge of the Metolius is more than 1500 feet deep in places, with sides sufficiently precipitous to make a descent a real problem. The source of the water from Metolius Springs was a matter of conjecture for many years. In the spring of 1972, N. V. Peterson and E. A. Groh published "Geology and Origin of the Metolius Springs" in the *Ore Bin*, v. 34, no. 3, pp. 41–51. Their investigation shows that the water comes from the south and west sides of Black Butte. Dry Creek and Cache Creek lose most of their water to underground seepage west of Black Butte and other streams to the south drain into Black Butte Swamp. These waters follow the prehistoric course of Metolius River under the geologically more recent Black Butte to emerge at the springs at a relatively constant rate of 50,000 gallons per minute. As far as the writer knows, the first mention of Metolius is in the Pacific Railroad Surveys *Reports*, v. 6, where the name is given Mpto-ly-as. The army officers who compiled these reports visited the valley of the Deschutes in the latter part of 1855, and apparently heard the name from Indians at that time. Other early forms were Metoluis and Matoles, but modern use has standardized on Metolius. Around Bend there is a story to the effect that *metolius* is a Warm Springs Indian word meaning spawning salmon, but Warm Springs Indians informed the writer that *metolius* means white fish, indicating by that expression that they meant a light colored salmon rather than a whitefish. The two translations may both be correct. There was a post office in Jefferson County named Metolius, for the river. Fremont forded what we now call the Metolius River on Dec. 1, 1843, but gave it no name. His Indian guides told him it was a salmon-water.

Metteer Canyon, WHEELER. This canyon east of Porcupine Butte in the Pine Creek area was named for a well-known family of early settlers. There were several homesteads and George Metteer is mentioned in *Illustrated History of Central Oregon*, p. 693.

Metzger, WASHINGTON. Metzger townsite was laid out by Herman Metzger, a prominent pioneer merchant of Portland, who was born in Bavaria, and was in business in Portland for many years. The property was actively marketed in 1908–09. The post office was established in 1912, with C. C. Taylor first postmaster, and closed Feb. 28, 1954.

Metzler Creek, UNION. This is a small tributary of Wolf Creek four miles above Wolf Creek Reservoir. It is apparently named for Eugene Metzler who, in 1908, bought land to the south of the creek's mouth.

Meyer Draw, CROOK. The *History of Crook County*, by the Crook County Historical Society, gives a short biography of George M. Meyer. Meyer was born in

Pennsylvania and in 1897 followed his older brother, Isadore, to the Rabbit Valley area where Isadore and Michael Brown had started a ranch some years before. George Meyer only worked on the ranch for a year or so and then moved to Prineville. Thus it may be assumed that both Meyer Draw and Isadore Butte are named for the older brother, Isadore Meyer.

Meyer Hill, JACKSON. In 1875, August Meyer homesteaded near the hill just north of Lakecreek that now bears his name.

Meyers Canyon, WHEELER. In 1863 Christian W. Meyer settled beside The Dalles-Canyon City Road where this canyon joins Bridge Creek. Phil Brogan in *East of the Cascades*, p. 85, describes his activities as an inn keeper and early irrigationist. F. A. Shaver in *History of Central Oregon*, p. 638, describes the Indian attack on H. H. Wheeler and states that this occurred three miles east of Mitchell. He adds that the survivors fled two miles further east to Meyer's establishment which he later notes as five miles east of Mitchell. The compiler has checked BLM records and talked to people who knew Meyer's son and had visited the original acreage. The location was five miles west of Mitchell and as no one has ever questioned the place of the attack, one must assume that Shaver was incorrect in his directions.

Miami River, TILLAMOOK. Miami River empties into Tillamook Bay at the lower end, that is, toward the ocean. In pioneer days the stream was referred to as *Mi-me Chuck*, a Chinook jargon expression meaning a tributary creek or river coming in downstream. George Gibbs in *Dictionary of the Chinook Jargon*, 1863, gives *mi-mie*, meaning downstream, with accent on the first syllable. In 1927, T. B. Handley of the Portland bar wrote the compiler that Tillamook Indians and others used the expression Mime Chuck for the locality of the river down the bay, but the name has been corrupted into the style used in Ohio, Florida and elsewhere.

Michael Creek, TILLAMOOK. This small tributary of North Fork Trask River is named for Michael J. McMullen, a 14-year-old Aloha boy who was killed in Washington by a falling tree. Eugene McMullen and his young son joined the Beaverton Chapter of the Northwest Steelheaders. They were active in the STEP, Salmon Trout Enhancement Program, of the Oregon Department of Fish and Wildlife where the Beaverton Chapter worked on the Trask River and its tributaries. Michael Creek was the site of a major restoration effort in which both father and son participated. The stream was unnamed and after Michael's death, the Beaverton Steelheaders proposed the name in Michael's memory. The USBGN approved in *Decision List 8901. See also* Step Creek.

Middle Fork Willamette River, DOUGLAS, LANE. This is the main tributary of Willamette River, and it has been known as Middle Fork since early pioneer days. It heads in Timpanogas Lake. The name is well established. It was named in contradistinction to Coast Fork and to McKenzie Fork, now McKenzie River. From time to time there have been efforts to change the name of Middle Fork

Willamette River to that of the main stream, Willamette River. Popular sentiment has always been against the proposal.

Middle Mountain, HOOD RIVER. This mountain is the high ground east of Hood River and west of Neal Creek that marks the north end of the Upper Hood River Valley. Its name comes from its position in the center of the Hood River drainage. In early days it was called Gilhouly or Gilhooley and today old timers protest the prosaic modern term. The compiler has been told that Gilhouly is of Indian origin. This appears fanciful but the name does have a firm base in local slang and legend.

Middle Santiam River, LINN. This is the name given this stream by the USBGN, not Middle Fork. The largest tributary is Quartzville Creek, from the north. *See* Santiam River.

Middleton, WASHINGTON. Will G. Steel is authority for the statement that this place was once known as Stringtown. When the railroad was built the name was changed to Middleton because the station was about half way between Portland and Lafayette.

Midland, KLAMATH. Messrs. Campbell and Reams platted this townsite about 1908, and named it Midland. It is said that the name was chosen because the place was about half way between Portland and San Francisco on the new Cascade line of the Southern Pacific. However, the station is not half way between the two cities, and could not have been named on that account. Midland was on land partly surrounded by marshes, and was probably named for that reason.

Midnight Spring, DOUGLAS. Midnight Spring is about a mile east of Steamboat Creek and just south of the Lane County line. It was named because USFS ranger Fred Asam and packer Jack Illeg were benighted on the trail and it was very late before they found this suitable camping spot.

Midway, MORROW. The pioneer post office Midway was approximately 12 miles south-southwest of Heppner. It was obviously named because it was approximately midway between Heppner and some other place. Early maps indicate that this other place may have been Adamsville, Dairyville or Hardman. These three places were all in the same general locality. Dairyville is not on the county post office list and it is believed the name referred to the place now known as Hardman. Midway post office was established Oct. 27, 1874, with Henry C. Myers first postmaster. Except for one lapse the office operated continuously until Feb. 1, 1881.

Mikkalo, GILLIAM. Mikkalo was named in 1905, for John Mikkalo, an early settler in the community. This was at the time the railroad was built from Arlington to Condon. The post office was established a few years later.

Milbury Mountain, CURRY. Milbury Mountain was named for William Milbury who was a USFS ranger in the Siskiyou Mountains for many years. The mountain is about ten miles southeast of Port Orford in T 33S, R 13W, south of Elk River. It has an elevation of about 2600 feet.

Miles, BAKER. Miles was a locality name for a place near the upper or northwest end of Lower Powder Valley northeast of Baker. The post office, which was established May 22, 1901, was named for the first postmaster, William Miles, and it was in service a little over 11 years. It was near Powder River in the south part of T 7S, R 41E.

Miles Lake, TILLAMOOK. This lake and nearby Miles Mountain northeast of Cape Kiwanda were named for Heman A. Miles who settled on the lake about 1890. His daughter, Mrs. Clarence Dunn, told the compiler in 1967 that when she was a little girl, the lake was known as Kiwanda Lake.

Milk Canyon, MORROW. Rachel Harnett of Heppner wrote the compiler in 1970 to say that John A. Williams had a dairy farm in this canyon south of Sand Hollow in the 1880s and he delivered milk and butter to Heppner. Williams later purchased land near Williams Canyon by Utts Butte.

Milk Creek, CLACKAMAS. This stream, a tributary of Molalla River, flows over a deposit of rock resembling soapstone, and receives a milky color therefrom. This deposit is near Colton.

Milk Creek, JEFFERSON. This stream drains one of the glaciers on the east slope of Mount Jefferson, and flows into Whitewater River. It carries a considerable quantity of glacial silt of a light color, and received its name on that account. There is another Milk Creek on the west part of Mount Jefferson, in Linn County, that is so called for the same reason.

Mill City, MARION. Mill City is on North Santiam River. The post office is in Marion County. Part of the community is on the south side of the river in Linn County. John Shaw and others moved the sawmill from Stayton to this place in 1887 and in the following year had a post office established with the name Mill City. Shaw was a son of Angus Shaw, who established the town of Shaw in Marion County. For story about Mill City by Fred Lockley, *see* the *Oregon Journal*, editorial page, July 9, 1932. Just west of the highway bridge across North Santiam River is the old railroad bridge. This interesting structure is largely made of wrought iron although some steel reinforcement was added in 1919 when it was relocated to its present position. It was made by Phoenix Bridge Company in 1888 for the crossing of Cienega Creek south of San Jose, California on the Southern Pacific Company Coast Line. The compression members are segmented wrought iron sections rivetted together to form tubes. These sections are similar to the iron framework of the Washington Monument and the columns used to support the first elevated railways in New York City. When the Southern Pacific Company abandoned the Mill City branch, they gave the bridge to the city. It is now decked over for a foot path.

Mill Creek, CROOK. Old residents of Prineville say that the first sawmill of the county was built on this stream, hence the name. The creek flows into Ochoco Creek east of Prineville.

Mill Creek, MARION. This stream joins the Willamette River in the north part of Salem. It was named for the pioneer sawmill established on its banks as part of the operations of Jason Lee's Methodist mission, which was begun on Mission Bottom in 1834. The sawmill was probably built in 1840–41. The canal from North Santiam River, augmenting the flow of Mill Creek, was finished in 1857. The stream in the south part of town, sometimes called South Mill Creek, is largely artificial and is not the original Mill Creek.

Mill Creek, UMATILLA. Mill Creek is for the most part a stream of the state of Washington, but not far from its source in the Blue Mountains it flows through Oregon for several miles. The Rev. Myron Eells is authority for the statement that Dr. Marcus Whitman rebuilt his flour mill in the Walla Walla Valley in 1844, and the next year went up the stream about 20 miles into the Blue Mountains and built a sawmill, which caused the stream to be called Mill Creek. Eells' *Marcus Whitman*, p. 135.

Mill Creek, UNION. Mill Creek, near Cove, is so called because one of the pioneer sawmills of Grande Ronde Valley was built on the stream by James M. De Moss. *See* De Moss and North Powder.

Mill Creek, WASCO. The neighborhood of Mill Creek, which flows into the Columbia River at The Dalles, was called *Quenett* by the local Indians, which was a name for salmon trout. When the government decided to establish Fort Dalles, an officer was sent to build a sawmill to be operated by mule power. Upon his arrival he found a small waterpower site and built a mill on this stream, now known as Mill Creek, just north of the present site of the bridge on Ninth Street. The writer is informed that the officer was court-martialed and discharged from the service for disobeying orders and not using mule power. Dr. William C. McKay is authority for the statement that the mouth of Mill Creek was called *Will-look-it* by the Indians. This meant looking through an opening or gap.

Mill Slough, LANE. This slough through the outskirts of Coburg originally carried water for the old Booth-Kelly sawmill. It emptied into Canterbury Creek, a tributary of McKenzie River. Both Mill Slough and Canterbury Creek are now dry and barely discernible after years of farming.

Miller, MALHEUR. Miller was a mining community about 18 miles north of Brogan. Miller post office was established July 18, 1913, with William Miller first and only postmaster, and the office was given his name. The office was closed Mar. 31, 1917, with papers to Rye Valley. Miller was in the extreme north end of the county, and a change of county lines between Baker and Malheur counties may have put the locality in what is now Baker County.

Miller, SHERMAN. Miller is the railroad station and community on the south bank of the Columbia River just east of Deschutes River. It is named for C. S. Miller, an early settler who built and operated the Miller Bridge across Deschutes River. There is a Miller Island in the Columbia River but it is in Klickitat County, Washington. The early emigrants forded Deschutes River near its mouth where it was shallow but as traffic increased other facilities were needed. Nathan Olney started the first ferry in 1853. In 1854 he sold the ferry to William Nix who built the first bridge in 1858 or 1859. This bridge was washed out in the big flood of 1861 and the following year Nix relocated upstream 2 miles where he again operated a ferry. Stephen Coffin also had a ferry site further upstream and Nix then built a second bridge near this location. In 1864, James Fulton and others built a bridge at the mouth of the river near Nix's original site but this lasted only two years. Miller built his bridge in 1867 and it carried traffic until 1920 when the highway bridge on the new US-30 was opened. Prior to 1920, tolls were charged at all these crossings. This fact was the impetus for the construction in 1880 of the "Free Bridge" some eight or ten miles upstream on the Deschutes River. *See* Freebridge. The locality of Miller has had several names at various times. It was once called Deschutesville and later Fultonville in compliment to Colonel James Fulton of Sherman County. For a time the railroad station now known as Miller was called Deschutes. For the history of the name Deschutes as applied to places in Oregon, *see* Deschutes and Ainsworth.

Miller Arm, LANE. This arm of Siltcoos Lake was apparently named for Elisha B. Miller whose homestead bordered it.

Miller Butte, MARION. This butte, elevation 556 feet, is about two miles west of Marion. It was named for a family of pioneer settlers. The head of the family was Charles Miller. At the exposition at Philadelphia in 1876, a sample of flax sent by "Uncle Charley," beat the whole world.

Miller Creek, MARION. Miller Creek drains the hills east of Ankeny Bottom, in the southwest part of the county. It was named for W. F. Miller, a pioneer settler on its banks.

Miller Hill, KLAMATH. Miller Hill and Miller Island on the southern outskirts of Klamath Falls were named for Colonel J. N. T. Miller, Commissary General of Oregon Volunteers during the Modoc War. His ranch was near the base of the hill. Colonel Miller should not be confused with the Miller family of Lake Miller.

Miller Lake, CROOK. Miller Lake is east of Shotgun Creek southeast of Post. It is named for Richard and Celestine Miller who settled nearby about 1885. Jeff Apperson filed the original homestead but sold it to a man named Grizzle who proved up. Grizzle, who was blind, sold in turn to the Millers who lived there until Richard Miller's death from spotted fever in 1913.

Millers, LINN. Millers post office was established a few miles northeast of Albany on Feb. 7, 1873, with Henry Newman first postmaster. The office was in operation for more than 20 years with several different postmasters. The office was named in compliment to Isaac Miller, a prominent pioneer resident of the vicinity. Millersburg is the name of the railroad station that still serves this locality. It seems possible that the post office may have moved with the various postmasters and in that event the railroad company used a different form of name for the station so as to avoid confusion.

Millersburg, LINN. This is a station on the Southern Pacific a few miles north of Albany, now distinguished by the aroma from a large kraft paper mill. Isaac Miller took up a donation land claim in pioneer days and members of the family have lived in the area for over a century. The family came from Millersburg, Mercer County, Illinois.

Millican, DESCHUTES. George Millican was a prominent stockman of central Oregon. He was born near Otsego, New York, Nov. 22, 1834, and came to the Pacific Coast when he was a young man. He visited mining camps from California to Idaho, and finally settled on the McKenzie River east of Eugene in 1862. He made a trip into the Ochoco country as early as 1863, and subsequently became interested in developing the toll road over McKenzie Pass. He took a band of cattle into the Crooked River country in 1868 and settled there. A few years later he located a ranch near the present site of Millican in Millican Valley, about 27 miles southeast of Bend. He carried on the business of raising high grade stock, and finally sold out in 1916. He died on Nov. 25, 1919. *See* Carey's *History of Oregon*, v. 3, p. 714. Millican was at one time postmaster at Walterville, Lane County, which he named for his son, Walter Millican. Walter Millican was born in 1870, and is said to have been the first male white child born in central Oregon. Millican Crater, just south of Black Crater, in northwest Deschutes County, was named for George Millican. The old Millican store was on the P. B. Johnson homestead on the Bend-Burns road a little over a half a mile south of the 1942 location and the post office was established in 1913, with Johnson postmaster. Johnson proposed the name Mount Pine, and Mrs. George Millican suggested her husband's name, which was adopted. There was some objection to Mount Pine because of possible confusion with La Pine. Johnson later sold out to J. A. Smith and a man named Moore became postmaster. William A. Rahn was made postmaster about 1920 and the community became a one-man affair. In Oct. 1930, the Central Oregon Highway, now US-20, was opened on a new location to the north and Rahn found it necessary to move his one-man town, which was done to the accompaniment of suitable publicity. Nearly everything was shifted but the well. In 1941 and 1942 Millican and "Billy" Rahn received nation-wide publicity as a one-man town and its sole citizen. In the fall of 1942 Rahn reached the age of retirement for postmasters, and it was necessary to close the office as no one was available to take it. For illustrated story about Millican and Billy Rahn by Phil Brogan, *see* magazine sect. of the *Sunday Oregonian*, Sept. 1, 1940. On Apr. 7, 1946, Bill Mellin bought the 80-acre community and operated the store, gas station and post office. The post office was finally closed in Oct. 1953, but Mellin continued the remainder of the business for over 30 years. In the spring of 1985, he put the town up for sale and the *Oregonian*, Apr. 22, 1985, p. A10, has a full page story with pictures. In 1988 Mellin was murdered and his estate sold the community to Eric Cooper. This latest development is covered in the *Oregonian*, Feb. 6, 1990, p. B4.

Millican Creek, YAMHILL. Millican Creek rises in the Red Hills of Dundee and flows south to Yamhill River at Lafayette. It was named for Elijah and Lucinda

Millican whose donation land claim was along the creek near the present town of Lafayette.

Millicoma River, COOS. Millicoma River is the main north branch of Coos River and is sometimes called North Fork Coos River, although the USBGN has adopted the style Millicoma. In 1929 S. B. Cathcart, pioneer surveyor of Coos County, told the compiler that Millicoma was the original Coos Indian name for the stream and not North Fork. The meaning of the word is not known.

Mills Butte, CROOK. Ike Mills was born in Massachusetts in 1862 and came to Oregon in 1877. In the 1920s he owned the ranch in S 18, T 16S, R 24E, where Wolf Creek breaks out into Beaver Creek valley. Mills Butte is about a half mile north of the ranch house called in 1981 the Sartain Ranch. A short distance up Wolf Creek was the famous Sheep Shooter Tree under which the Paulina Sheep Shooters were organized in 1898.

Mills Creek, LANE. In 1894 George R. Mills filed on a homestead where this creek empties into Maple Creek just above Siltcoos Lake.

Millwood, DOUGLAS. Will G. Steel told the writer that this place was named by W. B. Clarke, who built a sawmill nearby. Millwood post office was established on the Umpqua River just west of Coles Valley on June 7, 1886 with Clarke as first postmaster. It was closed on July 31, 1931 with papers to Oakland.

Milo, DOUGLAS. Milo was established as a post office on Mar. 13, 1923, with Cora E. Buker first postmaster. Amos O. Buker, the husband of the postmaster, was born in Milo, Maine, and suggested the name. Milo post office is at the site of a former post office called Perdue. The Perdue office was closed in 1920, because no one could be found to accept the position of postmaster after Amos O. Buker had been removed from office for acting as a census enumerator when he was postmaster at Perdue, contrary to the rules of the postal authorities. Milo, Maine, was named for the Grecian island of Milo.

Milton-Freewater, UMATILLA. There are several stories about the naming of this community including one that it was first called Freeport and another that it was Milltown because a mill was projected for the locality. However, an article in the Walla Walla *Union-Bulletin*, Apr. 5, 1959, p. 10, appears definitive. Mrs. Katherine Steffenson states that her grandfather, W. A. Cowl, was the first postmaster and he named the town for his birthplace, Milton, Ulster County, New York. Cowl came west in 1867 and bought the "Inn at the Stage Crossing" on the Walla Walla River near what is now Milton. In 1873 he applied for a post office with the name Milton which was duly established on Feb. 3, 1873, with Cowl first postmaster. The long time rivalry between Milton and neighboring Freewater was terminated in 1951 by the merger of the two communities. Milton-Freewater post office was established Sept. 1, 1951. For additional information, *see* Freewater.

Milton Creek, COLUMBIA. The town of Milton in Columbia County was one of the early rivals of Portland. It was laid out as a town in 1851 and was founded by Captain Nathaniel Crosby and Thomas H. Smith. It was once swept away by a flood. Crosby and Smith ran advertisements in the *Oregonian* in 1851 offering to give two lots to each married man and one lot to each single man who would make his home there and build a house. A district school advertisement for the town is in the *Oregonian*, Sept. 13, 1851. About 1890 efforts were made to secure a post office, and it was necessary to change the name of the community because there was already a post office named Milton in Umatilla County. Milton in Columbia County was accordingly renamed Houlton. *See* Houlton. Houlton post office was near Saint Helens railroad station. The name of Milton is still attached to a creek that flows near the post office and railway station. The name Milton was adopted for the town because of the location nearby of a pioneer sawmill. The original townsite of Milton was near the mouth of Milton Creek, and not where Houlton was situated.

Milwaukie, CLACKAMAS. Lot Whitcomb founded Milwaukie in 1847, as a rival to Oregon City. It was named probably for the Wisconsin city, the spelling of which, in its early days, was varied. Milwaukie had a population of 500 in 1850 (Bancroft's *History of Oregon*, v. 2, p. 251). For narrative of pioneer episodes, *see* the *Oregonian*, June 7, 1903, p. 15; Apr. 3, 1884, p. 3. For information about various spellings of Milwaukee, Wisconsin, *see Steel Points*, by Will G. Steel, issue for Mar. 1917. The derivation of the name is Indian, but its meaning is in dispute. It is said to mean council place, and also good land. Postal authorities inform the compiler that Milwaukie post office was established Feb. 1, 1850, with Lot Whitcomb first postmaster.

Minam, WALLOWA. Minam is the name of a community which is situated at the junction of the Wallowa and Minam rivers. The name of the town was taken from the Minam River. For the origin of the name Minam, *see* Minam River. Minam post office was established June 25, 1890, with Elizabeth Richard first postmaster. The office was closed Feb. 4, 1891, and was not reestablished until June 1910. The opening of the railroad branch through to Joseph in 1908 was doubtless the reason for the revival of the Minam post office.

Minam River, UNION, WALLOWA. J. H. Horner of Enterprise told the compiler that the Indian name for the locality of this stream was *E-mi-ne-mah*, with the accent on the second syllable. This name described a valley or canyon where a certain sort of plant was abundant. This plant, which the compiler has been unable to identify, is said to have resembled a small sunflower, and the root, growing in loose rocks, was used for food. The suffix *mah* was the Indian word for valley or canyon. The form Minam River was used as early as 1864. There is a town named Minam on Wallowa River at the mouth of Minam River. Minam Lake, in southwestern Wallowa County, is remarkable for the fact that it has an outlet at each end. Minam River flows from the south end, and Lostine River from the north.

Mine Creek, MALHEUR. Mine Creek flows into McDermitt Creek just north of the Nevada border. It takes its name from the Opalite Mine which began operations during the 1930s and produced quicksilver until after World War II.

Mineral, BAKER. So named because prospectors struck ore on the opposite side of Snake River, and named their prospect Mineral. Mineral, Oregon was only the site of the ferry landing for the access to what has long been an Idaho ghost town.

Mineral, LANE. Mineral post office was in a mining area in the west part of T 23S, R 1E, a few miles west of Bohemia. It was named for the mineral prospects of the region. The office was established July 31, 1903, and was discontinued July 31, 1908. Ulysses C. LeRoy was the first postmaster.

Minerva, LANE. When the post office at Minerva was petitioned for in the early 1890s the name of Bays Landing was suggested to the department out of respect to James E. Bay, a local resident. The authorities suggested that a name of one word would be more convenient, and L. C. Akerly, who had framed the petition, decided to name the office Minerva, which was Mrs. Bay's first name.

Mink Lake, LANE. Mink Lake is the largest lake in Mink Lake Basin at the headwaters of South Fork McKenzie River. In the early days the basin was a favorite area for mink and marten trappers but most of the smaller lakes in the basin were named by fish planting crews after World War II. They are now popular for anglers and campers.

Minney Creek, LANE. Minney Creek flows into Gate Creek northeast of Vida. It is named for Benjamin F. Minney who homesteaded along it in the 1890s.

Minnie Scott Spring, LANE. In 1971 Ray Engels, the retired USFS ranger at McKenzie Bridge, told the compiler that he named this spring four miles south of McKenzie Pass at the suggestion of Dee Wright. Engels understood Wright to say that Minnie was the wife of Felix Scott, Jr., but this is incorrect as she was his niece, the daughter of his brother Rodney. Felix Scott the younger died in Nevada in 1876 unmarried. For additional information about him, *see* Scott Mountain.

Minniece Point, LINN. This 4432 high point nine miles south of Detroit Dam was named for John Minniece, an early USFS employee in the Detroit District.

Minnow, LANE. Minnow is a station on the Southern Pacific Cascade Line southeast of Lookout Point Dam. It is named for Minnow Creek which in turn is named for an early settler and not for its piscatorial denizens.

Minor Gulch, WALLOWA. This gulch drains into Tope Creek in T 3N, R 43E. It was named for William Minor, who came into the Wallowa Valley in 1878 and ranged his stock near the gulch.

Minthorn, UMATILLA. This station east of Pendleton bears the name of a prominent Indian, Gilbert Minthorn. Minthorn's Cayuse Indian name roughly translates as "Blackhawk." His grandson, Antone Minthorn, was chairman of the Umatilla Tribal Council in the 1980s. There is a picture of Gilbert Minthorn and his family in the *Oregonian*, Feb. 3, 1985, p. C4.

Minto, MARION. Minto, a locality on North Santiam River two miles east of Gates, was named for Douglas Minto, a son of John Minto. He was interested in lumbering in the North Santiam Valley. Minto post office was in service near this station from Jan. 29, 1892, to Apr. 1904. Thomas S. Ball was the first postmaster.

Minto Mountain, LINN. John Minto was for many years champion of the plan to develop transportation facilities up the North Santiam River and over the Cascade Range by what he considered an especially favorable route. For a description of the investigations of this route made by Marion County, *see OHQ*, v. 4, p. 241. As a result of Minto's interest in this matter a number of geographic features in that section of the state were named for him about 1879. These include Minto Mountain. John Minto is a leading authority, among early pioneers, on subjects of Oregon history and his contributions are of high value. He was born Oct. 10, 1822, at Wylam, Northumberland, England; came to the United States in 1840, with his father's family and came to Oregon in 1844. In 1867 he purchased a 250 acre island in the Willamette River just south of Salem. The land soon took the name of Minto Island and today, though no longer a true island, is part of Minto-Brown Island Park. John Minto died at Salem Feb. 25, 1915. For a biography and portrait, *see* the *Oregonian*, Apr. 27, 1901, p. 10. Minto wrote frequently for the *Oregon Historical Quarterly*. His narration of the migration of 1844 appears in OPA *Transactions*, 1876, pp. 35–50. For references to other writings, *see* Scott's *History of the Oregon Country*, v. 1, p. 307.

Miranda Creek, HARNEY. Miranda Creek flows into Wildhorse Creek below Kueny Ranch. Manda Miranda, a Mexican from California, first settled near Diamond. He later bought Peter Andrews' holdings and established a cattle and horse ranch. In the 1920s, Frank Kueny aquired the property.

Mishawaka, CLATSOP. Mishawaka post office was established Mar. 26, 1878, with James F. Kimberlin first postmaster. It was near Nehalem River a little eastward of the location now called Elsie. The office is said to have been named for Mishawaka, the well-known manufacturing town of Indiana, but the compiler has been unable to learn the circumstances. The place in Indiana is said to have been named for an Indian chief. The Clatsop County office was closed May 15, 1901, with papers to Vinemaple. The list of county precincts of 1940 contains Mishawaka precinct.

Mission Bottom, MARION. Mission Bottom is on the east side of Willamette River south of Wheatland. It was here that Jason Lee established his Methodist Mission in the fall of 1834, and the bottom was named on that account.

Mission Creek, MARION. Mission Creek flows through Saint Paul, and was named for the pioneer Catholic mission of that place. Mission Landing on Willamette River, about a mile and a half northwest of Saint Paul, is named for the same reason.

Mission Creek, UMATILLA. Mission Creek is about six miles east of Pendleton and slightly east of the Umatilla Indian Agency Headquarters. Professor Theodore Stern of the University of Oregon spent considerable time investigating the history and location of the Catholic mission church of Saint Anne. The original building was destroyed during the Cayuse War but was replaced by a new structure with the same name. There has been controversy as to its exact site with

Clifford Drury even placing it as far east as Thorn Hollow. However, Professor Stern's studies show the church was near the present agency headquarters about a mile and a half west of the mouth of Mission Creek. The name was in use at the turn of the century for the 1892 Oregon Railroad & Navigation Company timetable shows the station, Mission, where it is today, near the agency.

Mississippi Head, CLACKAMAS. Mississippi Head is the prominent rock buttress on the southwest side of Mount Hood at the bottom of Zigzag Glacier and the head of Zigzag Canyon. It was named in 1905 by Will G. Steel for the Mississippi delegation to the National Editorial Association meeting in Portland that year. The delegation had asked Steel to illuminate the mountain with red fire on the top of the bluff which he, along with E. G. Jones and A. J. Capron, did. *See Steel Points*, v. 2, no. 1.

Missouri Bottom, DOUGLAS. This bottom, along South Umpqua River south of Myrtle Creek, took its name from the fact that a number of Missourians were pioneer settlers thereon. *See* Walling's *History of Southern Oregon*, p. 423.

Missouri Flat, BAKER. A substantial number of early Oregon emigrants literally were from Missouri. E. W. Coles of Haines told the compiler that this section of Baker Valley was settled by a number of Missourians including his future wife, Ollie Ann Taylor who was born in Monroe County.

Mist, COLUMBIA. There was a post office called Riverside not far from this community, established about 1874. This caused confusion with another place in Oregon with the same name, and in Apr. 1888, the office was moved and the name changed to Mist, describing the atmospheric condition prevailing in the Nehalem Valley. The townsite of Mist was surveyed and platted with the name of Esto. It has never been so called.

Mistletoe, JACKSON. Mistletoe was a station on the Southern Pacific Railroad south of Ashland named for the Mistletoe Lumber Company which was established there prior to World War I. At the turn of the century, the station was called Clawson. In 1983 a fine example of the old wigwam burner was still standing at the mill.

Mitchell, WHEELER. Mitchell was named for John Hipple Mitchell, former U.S. senator from Oregon, and for many years prominent in the political history of the state. The name was suggested by W. W. "Brawdie" Johnson, the first postmaster, and the post office was established in Apr. 1873. J. H. Mitchell was senator from Oregon in 1873–79, 1885–97 and 1901–05. He was born in Pennsylvania in 1835, came to Oregon in 1860, and died in Portland Dec. 8, 1905. In 1884 the town of Mitchell experienced its first catastrophe. Water rushed over the bluff above the community, carrying boulders and mud. In Mar. 1885, I. N. Sargent platted the townsite of Mitchell. It was incorporated in 1893. About half the town was consumed by fire in Aug. 1899. It was rebuilt. On July 11, 1904, it was almost destroyed by a cloudburst; two lives were lost. On Sept. 25, 1904, it was visited by another flood, but the damage was slight.

Mitchell Point, HOOD RIVER. Beyond the fact that a man named Mitchell lived and died near this point, there is little information available. He is reported to have been a trapper. Although there have been efforts made to change the name to Storm Crest, the public has not looked with favor on the suggestion, and prefers the old name.

Mixup Spring, KLAMATH. This spring is in the northeast corner of T 38S, R 15E, very close to the Lake County line. In Apr. 1944, Ida M. Odell of Klamath Falls told the compiler that it was named because two bands of sheep once got mixed up nearby.

M & M Creek, LINN. This creek was named for the M & M Woodworking Company of Portland. After World War II they logged its watershed above the southwest finger of Detroit Reservoir.

Moccasin Lake, WALLOWA. Moccasin Lake is in the Lake Basin north of Eagle Cap. The lake, when seen from the north side of Eagle Cap, looks like a moccasin, hence the name.

Mocks Crest, MULTNOMAH. Mocks Crest is named for John Mock who came to Portland with his family in 1852. He located in north Portland on the bluff overlooking Swan Island where he was active in real estate development. He gave the land for what is now the University of Portland. His third house, built in 1894, is now a City of Portland Landmark and listed on the National Register of Historic Places. The low land northeast of Swan Island is Mocks Bottom, named for John's father, Henry Mock, who settled his family there in 1852. In the 1980s the Port of Portland developed much of the bottom for an industrial park. They felt "bottom" was not dignified so they chose the name Mocks Landing for their improvement. For a short article and pictures of Mocks Bottom, *see* the *Oregonian*, Nov. 1, 1990, sect. MW, p. 4.

Modoc Point, KLAMATH. This is a prominent point on the east shore of Upper Klamath Lake, about 15 miles north of Klamath Falls. It bears this name because the Modoc Indians, under Captain Jack, lived there from Dec. 31, 1869, to Apr. 26, 1870, and then escaped and went to their old habitat further south. Modoc Point is a well-known locality in Klamath Indian folklore, where it is spoken of as *Kiuti* and also *Muyant*. Will G. Steel is authority for the statement that the mountain is also known as *Nilakla*, which is the Klamath Indian name for dawn or sunrise. The Indian name *Modoc* is derived from the Klamath words *moa*, meaning south, and *takni*, meaning a native of that place or country, hence from the point of view of the Klamath Indians, natives of the country just to the south. The term Modoc Lake was formerly used in the Klamath country to refer to Tule Lake, because Modoc Indians lived nearby.

Moffat, WASHINGTON. This station on the Oregon Electric Railway was near the east city limit of Hillsboro. It was named for George Barclay Moffat, a prominent New York banker and president of the railway company. While on a visit, George B. Moffat died in Portland Dec. 4, 1911.

Moffett Creek, MULTNOMAH. Investigation by H. H. Riddell of Portland indicated that the family for which this stream is named spelled its name Moffett and not Moffatt. The Historic Columbia River Highway crossed Moffett Creek on a remarkable concrete arch. At the time it was built it was said to have been the longest three-hinged, flat arch bridge in America. *See* S. C. Lancaster's *The Columbia, America's Great Highway*. This bridge, now unused, is still standing just north of I-84.

Moffitt Butte, KLAMATH. This 4900 foot butte is just east of SH-31 about ten miles south of the junction with US-97. It was named for James A. Moffitt who took up government land nearby in 1888. After World War II this name appeared on maps as Moffit but the proper spelling was restored in USBGN *Decision List 7101*.

Mohawk River, LANE. According to Gustavus Hines, Mohawk River was named for the stream in the state of New York. The Oregon stream was probably named by Jacob C. Spores, a pioneer of 1847 and a native of Montgomery County, New York, a county drained in part by the original Mohawk River. For a short biography of Spores, *see Illustrated History of Lane County* by Walling, p. 481. Darrel Spores, great-grandson of Jacob Spores, and a resident of the Mohawk Valley in Oregon, said that Jacob Spores and a few other whites chased a band of Indians into the valley in 1849 and that Spores, viewing the locality from a high bluff, said that it reminded him of the valley of his birthplace in New York state. The name Mohawk River came into use as a result of this incident. Jacob Spores was one of the earliest settlers in Lane County and operated a pioneer ferry on McKenzie River not far from the present site of Coburg. A post office named Mohawk was established on the banks of the Oregon stream on Dec. 20, 1862, with Robert M. Robertson first postmaster. This office did not operate continuously and was converted to a Rural Station on Jan. 1, 1958. This, in turn, was terminated Dec. 31, 1961. Gannett in *The Origin of Certain Place Names*, says that the name of the eastern Mohawk tribe signifies an eater of live meat.

Mohler, TILLAMOOK. Mohler post office was originally established as Balm in May 1897, with Everett R. Bales postmaster. The office was on Foley Creek, a little above the mouth, and about two miles southeast of the present site of Mohler. In Dec. 1911, the name of the office was changed to Mohler and it was moved to the new location. The change is said to have been made at the request of E. E. Lytle, who built the Pacific Railway and Navigation Company line into that part of Tillamook County. The station and post office were named in compliment to A. L. Mohler, a prominent railroad official and one-time president of the Union Pacific.

Mokst Butte, DESCHUTES. This butte in the Paulina Mountains was named by the USFS with the Chinook jargon word for two, as it was the second of a series all named at the same time.

Molalla, CLACKAMAS. This is an important community that takes its name from Molalla River nearby. *See* Molalla River. Molalla post office was established Apr.

9, 1850. It was at or near the present site of Liberal and was discontinued Aug. 25, 1851. Harrison Wright was the postmaster. The office was reestablished Dec. 2, 1868, with Wright postmaster, but available records do not give its location. It operated until Mar. 1874. It was reestablished again in Jan. 1875, and it seems probable that this was the date it was placed at the present community of Molalla.

Molalla River, CLACKAMAS. Molalla was the name of the tribe of Indians that inhabited much of the territory now in Marion and Clackamas counties. The Molallas were a Waiilatpuan tribe akin to the Cayuses, forming the western division of the family. The Cayuses have a tradition that the Molallas were detached and driven west in wars with hostile tribes. The Molalla dialect shows that the separation from the Cayuses took place in remote times. Whether the Indians took their name from what is called Molalla River, or *vice versa*, is not known. For a short account of the Molalla Indians *see Handbook of American Indians*, v. 1, p. 930. Many methods of spelling the name by a variety of authors are listed. By decision of the USBGN, the name Molalla River extends to the headwaters of the main south branch of the stream. The style South Fork is wrong. The middle branch is Table Rock Fork. Pudding River empties into Molalla River which extends another mile to the Willamette. In the past there has been confusion regarding the correct name of this last stretch. Alexander Henry in his diary quoted in *OHQ*, v. 25, p. 308, says: "called by our people Pudding River." However, the name Molalla is now firmly established for the final mile.

Monitor, MARION. Robert H. Down says that local residents have a story to the effect that this place was named for a certain type of flour mill known as a Monitor mill, which was in use at Monitor in early days. This sounds reasonable, and may be the origin of the name. However, in 1990, Kenneth W. Battleson of Eugene informed the compiler that his father, Ben W. Battleson, bought the three story mill in 1923 and operated it for many years. His father was told by the previous owner that the mill was named after the Civil War for the *U.S.S. Monitor*. Down's *A History of the Silverton Country*, p. 202, says the town of Monitor did not exist in 1869. The flour mill was built much earlier. Monitor post office was established Nov. 16, 1869, apparently the first use of the name, so Battleson's origin appears more probable.

Monkland, SHERMAN. N. W. Thompson of Moro told the compiler that his father named the community of Monkland, presumably for Monkland, Ontario, because several nearby residents had formerly lived in the Canadian town.

Monmouth, POLK. The town of Monmouth was named for Monmouth, Illinois. In 1852 a group of citizens of the Illinois community crossed the plains to Oregon, and after spending the first winter at Crowley, five miles north of Rickreall, settled in 1853 near the present site of Monmouth. Members of the party gave 640 acres of land on which to establish the town and a college under the auspices of the Christian Church. The place was surveyed in 1855 by T. H. Hutchinson. The money secured from the sale of lots was devoted to the building of the Christian college, which was known as Monmouth University. At a mass meeting the people selected Monmouth as the name of the new community, in honor of their old home. In 1856 mercantile buildings were erected. The first house was built in 1857. The post office was established Feb. 25, 1859, with Joseph B. V. Butler first postmaster. In 1871, due to the influence of the church, the name of Monmouth University was changed to Christian College. The college underwent vicissitudes due to lack of funds, and was once offered to the state for a state university. In 1882 the Oregon legislature passed a bill creating the Oregon State Normal School at Monmouth, which absorbed the Christian College. The name of the school was later changed to the Oregon College of Education and more recently renamed Western Oregon State College. For information about the names of Monmouth pioneers, *see* the *Oregonian*, Aug. 13, 1916.

Monon Lake, JEFFERSON. This lake south of Olallie Butte was named by forest ranger Joe Graham. The name was selected because it had a pleasing sound.

Monroe, BENTON. The town Monroe was started in 1853 on the land of Joseph White, who had built a small sawmill in the neighborhood about 1850. The first post office in the vicinity was Starrs Point. Starrs Point was established Apr. 22, 1852, and was a little north of the present site of Monroe. Starrs Point was named for George Starr who had a store nearby. The name Starrs Point was changed to Monroe on Feb. 2, 1874, for James Monroe, fifth president of the United States. The first postmaster of Starrs Point was Samuel F. Starr.

Monroe Roughs, WHEELER. Monroe Roughs is a piece of mountainous terrain cut by steep canyons filled with mountain mahogany and other brush. The roughs lie between Girds Creek and Flock Mountain and form the headwaters of Monroe Creek. Thomas J. Monroe, one of the earliest settlers in the Mitchell area, was born in Ohio in 1837 and came to Oregon in 1865. He moved to Wheeler County in the early 1870s and settled where Monroe Creek joins Girds Creek.

Montague, GILLIAM. Montague, the name of a locality in Eightmile Canyon about eight miles southeast of Arlington, came from a local family. Montague was at the place where the Oregon Trail crossed this canyon three miles east of Shutler. Montague post office was established Apr. 1, 1911, and was discontinued Jan. 15, 1915. L. C. Montague was the postmaster.

Montavilla, MULTNOMAH. Montavilla post office was established Sept. 21, 1891 but for many years operated as a station of the Portland office. The name Montavilla is a contraction of Mount Tabor Villa. Mount Tabor Villa addition to the city of Portland was platted June 11, 1889. The name was cumbersome and the place was immediately known as Montavilla, and has been ever since. Besides being cumbersome the original name was more or less meaningless. Mount Tabor was taken from the nearby geographic feature. *Villa* is a Latin word, meaning a county-seat, or sometimes farm buildings. It is also used to refer to a detached suburban residence. The addition of Montavilla, platted July 13, 1904, was named long after the name Montavilla was applied to that part of Portland.

Monte Rico Ridge, LANE. This ridge is in the southeast part of the Bohemia mining district. *Monte Rico* is Spanish for rich mountain, and in this case the name probably refers to the ore prospects.

Montgomery Ranch, DESCHUTES. This ranch on Little Deschutes River south of Vandevert Ranch was the headquarters of James and Charles Montgomery who homesteaded land to the west in 1899.

Monument, GRANT. This post office was established Oct. 27, 1874, with Prior S. Wilson postmaster. It was named for a peculiar rock or mountain nearby which resembles a pulpit or rostrum. This peak is called Monument Mountain.

Moody, WASCO. Moody is a station on the Oregon Trunk Line near the mouth of Deschutes River. It was named for Malcolm A. Moody of The Dalles, who was a member of a prominent pioneer family, and at one time U.S. representative in Congress from eastern Oregon. He owned a power site near the mouth of the Deschutes River. When the Oregon Trunk Railway was built there was a large material yard at Moody, and a post office was established to take care of mail for construction camps along the line in Deschutes Canyon. When the work was completed the town of Moody faded to only a station. Moody post office was established Dec. 7, 1911, with Ida Carlisle postmaster. On May 4, 1922, the post office of Moody was moved across the river about a mile northeast in Sherman County and the name was changed to Miller. The office was finally closed on June 30, 1953. The move and the name change of the post office did not affect the name of Moody station in Wasco County, which remains as originally established.

Moolack Creek, LINCOLN. Moolack Creek, named with the Chinook jargon word for elk, is a couple of miles north of Agate Beach. The style Moloch Creek, commemorating the bull-headed idol of the Canaanites, is wrong, and is due to a mishearing of the real name.

Moolack Mountain, LANE. This mountain was formerly known as Elk Mountain because of the local abundance of that animal. Of late years it has been called Moolack Mountain, which is the Chinook jargon word for elk. The name was changed because there were a number of other Elk mountains in the state. Moolack Mountain has an elevation of 5500 feet, and is north of Waldo Lake.

Moon Creek, LINN. Moon Creek heads north of Marion Lake and runs into Marion Creek. It is named for Hal Moon who drowned in Marion Lake many years ago.

Moon Creek, TILLAMOOK. There were several members of the Moon family who settled along this creek which flows into Nestucca River at Blaine. Mr. Frank Kumm of Blaine stated in 1968 that he believed the creek was named for John Moon as the others left at an early date.

Mooney Mountain, JOSEPHINE. Walling, in *History of Southern Oregon*, p. 452, says that one Mooney was the first settler in the Illinois Valley to avail himself of the privilege of the donation land law. Samuel Mooney's claim was in the valley just south of Mooney Mountain. His certificate was no. 57.

Moore Park, KLAMATH. This City Park in Klamath Falls was donated by members of the Moore family as a memorial to early pioneers Charles S. and Rufus Moore.

Mooreville, MALHEUR. The locality called Mooreville is in the high country about 25 miles south-southeast of Riverside, airline. It bears the name of a local family. Mooreville post office was established Sept. 23, 1912, and was closed June 30, 1919, with mail to Crowley. Esther M. Moore was the only postmaster.

Moorhouse, UMATILLA. Moorhouse post office was established with the name Morehouse on Jan. 5, 1880, and with Thomas L. Moorhouse postmaster. The name should have been spelled Moorhouse, and accordingly the Post Office Department changed the record to Moorhouse, with Moorhouse postmaster, on Mar. 25, 1880, and it remained that way until it was discontinued June 6, 1883. Thomas L. Moorhouse was the same man as Thomas Leander Moorhouse, but far better known as Major Lee Moorhouse. Major Moorhouse was one of eastern Oregon's most prominent characters and in later years became famous for the remarkable Indian pictures that came from his camera. Moorhouse post office was at the Prospect Ranch of the John R. Foster Company, on the old stage road northwest of Pendleton five or six miles northeast of what is now the town of Stanfield. It was on what were called the Meadows, a large, inexactly defined area near the Umatilla River in the northern part of the county.

Moosmoos Creek, CLATSOP. This stream flows into Youngs River about a mile north of Youngs River Falls. *Moosmoos* is the Chinook jargon word for cattle, which have been plentiful in the locality for many years.

Morgan, MORROW. The original name of this post office was Saddle for Saddle Butte about three miles to the south. Saddle post office was established Nov. 20, 1882, with Ozwell T. Douglas postmaster. The name of the post office was changed to Douglas on Dec. 31, 1890. About 1906 the name was changed to Morgan, apparently in compliment to Alfred C. Morgan, a local resident who had been postmaster. For a time there was a discrepancy between the names of the post office and the railroad station, but it is probable that one of the changes listed above composed the difficulty.

Morgan Butte, WALLOWA. This butte is in the southeast part of the county. It was named for Albert Morgan, a sheepman.

Mormon Basin, BAKER, MALHEUR. Mormon Basin was named in 1862 at the time of the eastern Oregon gold rush. A party of prospectors from Salt Lake City found pay dirt and the basin was named either by or for these miners. About the same time a group of miners from the Humboldt River region found gold in another part of the basin, and the name Humboldt Basin was at once applied in compliment to this group. The Nevada miners had been working at Auburn with poor results and were on their way back home when they made a strike in Humboldt Basin. *See* Fred Lockley's article in *Oregon Journal*, Apr. 29, 1932. The two names, Mormon Basin and Humboldt Basin were used concurrently for a time, but the style Humboldt gradually gave way to Mormon Basin and modern usage is well crystallized in favor of the latter name. The stream draining the area is generally called Mormon Basin Creek. For postal history of the locality, *see* Humboldt Basin.

Mormon Flat, WALLOWA. This flat is in the east part of the county. It was named for W. H. Winters, an early settler, who was of the Mormon faith. He was drowned in Snake River.

Moro, SHERMAN. Moro is the county seat of Sherman County, and has an elevation of 1807 feet. It is generally believed that Henry Barnum was the first resident of the place, settling there in 1868, and establishing a trading post some 11 years later. There are several stories as to how the town got its name. One version is that it was named for Moro, Illinois, by Judge O. M. Scott, who formerly lived in that place. Another version is that it was named for Moore Brothers, who were interested in the townsite. Still another story is that it was named Moro for the Moors, which seems unlikely to the compiler. The reader may choose.

Morris Canyon, MORROW. In 1876 Frederick M. Morris settled where this canyon empties into Butter Creek.

Morris Creek, LANE. The *Siuslaw Pioneer*, 1982, p. 103, says this creek flowing into North Fork Siuslaw River at The Portage was named for James Morris who took a pre-emption claim at its mouth in 1880. BLM records show a number of claims by A. J. Morris as well as Joseph E. Morris. The compiler suspects that A. J. and James were the same man.

Morrison, CLATSOP. This station was named for Robert W. Morrison, an early settler. It was on Clatsop Plains. Robert W. Morrison was born in Kentucky in 1811, came to Oregon in 1844 and died in May 1894.

Morrow County. Morrow County was created Feb. 16, 1885, by the state legislature and was taken from the western part of Umatilla County. For data about the boundaries of Morrow and Umatilla counties at the time Morrow County was created, *see OHQ*, v. 11, p. 1, which contains an article, "Oregon Counties," by Frederick V. Holman. The following editorial from the *Oregonian* for Nov. 5, 1909, gives details concerning the naming of this county: "A letter to the *Oregonian* asserts that Morrow County, Oregon, was named for Colonel H. A. Morrow, a soldier of the Civil War, stationed later at Vancouver; and the writer desires to correct the *Oregonian*'s statement that it was named for an early pioneer. But the *Oregonian*'s statement was correct. The county was named for Jackson L. Morrow, one of the very earliest settlers there. He first settled on Puget Sound, and Shelton Bay, in 1853; a few years later, he went to eastern Oregon, and was a member of the legislature from Umatilla when Morrow was formed out of a part of that county. In the debate about what the name of the new county should be, some one said: "Let's call it for Jack Morrow; he is entitled to the honor." For

Morrow's biography, *see* the *Oregonian*, Apr. 18, 1898. Morrow County has an area of 2055 square miles.

Morrow Well, JEFFERSON. This well northwest of Grizzly bears the name of Andrew Morrow who homesteaded along Willow Creek in 1880.

Morton Butte, CURRY. William Morton homesteaded on the north edge of this butte in 1903. It is located about six miles north of Brookings.

Mosby Creek, LANE. This stream has its source on the western slopes of the Cascade Range, and has a length of approximately 20 miles. It flows into Row River, about two miles southwest of Cottage Grove, at an elevation of about 665 feet. It was named for David Mosby, who settled on its banks near its mouth in pioneer days. The creek was once known as Brumbaugh Creek, but that name did not prevail.

Mosier, WASCO. Mosier is a pioneer settlement on the Columbia River. J. H. Mosier started the community about 1853–54 by settling on a claim near the mouth of Mosier Creek. Mr. and Mrs. Mosier ran an impromptu stage station, a stopping place for travelers. Jonah H. Mosier was born Mar. 10, 1821, in Maryland, and moved to Missouri in 1839, and learned cabinet making. He went to California in 1849, but returned to the eastern states. He came to Oregon in 1853, and soon settled on his homestead. He served in the Oregon legislature and died in 1894. Pierce Mays, prominent Wasco County resident, told the writer that Mosier's large collection of artificial books in a handsome cabinet was one of the best of its kind in Oregon. He once tried to read one of the wooden books.

Mosquite, MALHEUR. Mosquite was a locality in the northeast corner of the county, on the west bank of Snake River ten or a dozen miles north of Ontario. Mosquite post office was established Apr. 18, 1893, with Laura Shepherd first postmaster. The office was finally closed May 31, 1911. The name was perhaps intended to be that of a shrub, the mesquite, but as far as the compiler can determine no variety of the mesquite grows in Oregon. However, in Nov. 1979, Beth Magrini of Ontario wrote to say that the place may have been named for the familiar pesky insect. She added that there were many Italian emigrants brought in to work on the railroad when it was built in the 1880s and that a common Italian pronunciation was "mosquit" without the "o." The compiler has also heard older Italians use the same pronunciation and must agree that this is an equally probable origin.

Moss Butte, LINN. Moss Butte, elevation about 2600 feet, is a prominent cone standing near the middle of s 3, T 14S, R 2E, just south of South Santiam River at a point about ten miles eastward of Sweet Home. In Sept. 1946, W. R. Mealey of Foster wrote the compiler that the butte was named for Mack Moss, a very early settler of the Sweet Home area, who roamed the South Santiam hunting and exploring. Moss came from Illinois and settled near Sweet Home in 1852.

Moss Lakes, CLACKAMAS. These two small lakes are between Oregon City and Park Place. They were originally one lake, but have been much reduced in size by draining. They were named for Sidney Walter Moss, who was born in Benton County, Kentucky, Mar. 17, 1810, and who came to Oregon in 1842. He organized the Falls Debating Society at Oregon City in 1843, and built the first hotel in Oregon City in 1844. He also engaged in the merchandise business. He died Sept. 24, 1901, and his biography is in the *Oregonian* for Sept. 25, 1901, and Mar. 6, 1898, p. 19. Moss claimed to have written the original tale of the *Prairie Flower*, which he gave to William Johnson for publication and which was expanded by Emerson Bennett of Cincinnati. This became a popular sketch of border life. Moss wrote many articles about pioneer life in Oregon. He carried an advertisement in the *Oregonian* in 1852, of his "Main Street House" at Oregon City, signed by himself and "The Widow," announcing that, "owing to pressing necessities and our cheap rate of fare, we are compelled to say:

To *all*, high or low,
Please down with your dust,
For he's no friend of ours,
That would ask us to trust."

"The Widow" was Mrs. Richardson, before she married Moss. For reminiscences of Sidney W. Moss, *see* the *Oregonian*, Sept. 29, 1901, p. 22.

Motanic, UNION. Motanic is a station on the Union Pacific Railroad about halfway from the Grand Ronde River to Kamela. It was established in the 1920s and named for Parsons Motanic, a prominent Indian on the Umatilla Indian Reservation. Motanic was a renowned athlete and amateur wrestler. His son, Art Motanic, was also active in Indian affairs.

Mother Lode Mountain, MARION. This mountain was named for the Mother Lode mine nearby. It is about 12 miles north of Detroit.

Mound, LANE. For nearly two decades a post office with the name Mound served an area close to Siuslaw River in western Lane County. The place was about a mile and a half east of Alma, in s 30, T 19S, R 6w. Postal records indicate the office was established June 1, 1892, with Joseph B. Beebe first of three postmasters. The office was closed Sept. 30, 1910, and the business turned over to Alma post office, but the name Mound was not changed to Alma as is sometimes reported. Alma post office was already in service in 1910. As a matter of fact Alma post office was established in 1888. In the summer of 1946 P. M. Morse, Lane County engineer, gathered some data about Mound post office from Hazen Johnson, who reported that his grandfather, Bowker Beebe, moved to the Siuslaw Valley from Mound, Nebraska in 1890, and when the new post office was established, Beebe asked to have it named for his former home. Mound, Nebraska was an office in Howard County, about 20 miles from Saint Paul. Mr. Johnson reported that Bowker Beebe had formerly been postmaster at Mound, Nebraska. It is probable that Joseph B. Beebe and Bowker Beebe were the same person.

Mount Angel, MARION. The community of Mount Angel was named in 1883 by the Reverend Father Adelhelm Odermatt, O.S.B., in compliment to Engelberg,

Switzerland. Mount Angel is the anglicized version of the German name Engelberg. Benjamin Cleaver came to Oregon in 1848 and in 1850 settled at the present site of Mount Angel. Some years later he planned a townsite to be named Roy, and his adjoining neighbor, George Settlemier, actually platted a place in 1881 with the name Frankfort. Cleaver bought the Settlemier townsite in 1882 and changed the name to Roy. A post office was established in 1882 with the name Roy. The compiler does not know the reason for selecting either of the names Frankfort or Roy. In 1880 a narrow gauge railroad was built through the locality and in the following year a station was established with the name Fillmore, in compliment to James M. Fillmore, an official of the railroad company. Father Adelhelm Odermatt had received his theological training at Engelberg in Switzerland, came to Oregon in 1881, and was soon in charge of the parishes at Gervais, Fillmore and Sublimity. After overcoming many difficulties, Father Odermatt succeeded in establishing a Benedictine community in Gervais in 1882–83. In 1883 a pilgrimage chapel was built on the summit of Lone Butte or *Tapalamaho*, and in the same year Father Odermatt applied the name Mount Angel to the butte and the community. He had the name Mount Angel adopted both for the railroad station and for the post office and the old designations Fillmore and Roy were discarded. The City of Mt. Angel was incorporated Apr. 3, 1893 and the railroad station also uses the abbreviation although the post office is Mount Angel. In 1884 the Benedictine establishment was moved from Gervais to Mount Angel. *See* Saint Benedict. For history of Mount Angel and its Benedictine institutions, *see Mt. Angel, Oregon, 1848–1912*, by Sister Ursula Hodes, University of Oregon Thesis Series, No. 20. T. W. Davenport, in *OHQ*, v. 5, p. 36, says the Indian name for the butte southeast of Mount Angel was *Tap-a-lam-a-ho*, indicating a mountain used by the Indians for communion with the Great Spirit. Early settlers called it Lone Butte, Lone Tree Butte, and also Graves Butte for John P. Graves, a nearby resident. The new name Mount Angel quickly superseded the old forms.

Mount Ashland, JACKSON. This mountain lies about eight miles due south of Ashland and was named for that community. In the past it has been known as Ashland Peak and sometimes Siskiyou Peak. It is now universally known as Mount Ashland and that form is shown on the USGS map of the Ashland quadrangle, published in 1983. The elevation is now accepted as 7532 feet. Accurate mapping indicates that Siskiyou Peak, elevation 7149 feet, is about three miles to the southwest. The two points were formerly confused one for the other. Mount Ashland is now better known for the downhill ski facilities installed in the 1980s.

Mount Avery, CURRY. This mountain is near the headwaters of Sixes River. It was named for Frederick S. Avery, who owned a small ranch just west of the mountain and lived there for many years. Mount Avery has an elevation of 2613 feet.

Mount Bachelor, DESCHUTES. Mount Bachelor has an elevation of 9065 feet and is one of the imposing isolated peaks of the middle Cascade Range. It is just southeast of the Three Sisters and received its original name, Bachelor Butte, because it stands apart from them. John C. Todd of Bend told the compiler in 1928 that in early days Bachelor Butte was frequently called Brother Jonathan, in contradistinction to the Three Sisters. After World War II, a major ski area was started on its slopes. The developers felt that skiing on a butte would be considered small-time, so they named their operation Mount Bachelor Ski Area. Over the years, the combination of excellent skiing and effective advertising brought the form Mount Bachelor into general use. While some people deplored this change, the OGNB, in a divided decision, voted to accept this *fait accompli* and the USBGN confirmed in *Decision List 8304*. Commercial interests succeeded in replacing a fine, old, euphonious name with a commonplace form.

Mount Bailey, DOUGLAS. This is an important peak in the Cascade Range and has an elevation of 8368 feet. It lies west of Diamond Lake. The writer has been unable to get much information as to the origin of the name. Older maps show the mountain as Old Baldy and Old Bailey. It is possible that Old Bailey is the result of a draftsman's error. The summit of the mountain has a bald, burnt-over appearance. The compiler has found no record of any person named Bailey connected with the peak, but it has been known as Mount Bailey for many years. Will G. Steel wrote in 1927 that the Klamath Indian name for the mountain was *Youxlokes*, which meant Medicine Mountain. According to Indian tradition, the medicine men and priests often feasted on the summit of this mountain and communed with the upper world.

Mount Billingslea, CURRY, JOSEPHINE. This peak, elevation 4181 feet, is approximately 20 miles northwest of Kerby on the high divide south of Illinois River. It was named for James H. Billingslea, who served in the USFS for more than 15 years, including six years as supervisor of Siskiyou National Forest. He died Nov. 7, 1939.

Mount Bolivar, COOS, CURRY. Mount Bolivar, elevation 4319 feet, is at the extreme southeast corner of Coos County, and as far as the writer knows, is the highest peak in the Oregon Coast Range north of Rogue River, although there are higher peaks to the south. The elevation given above was determined by the USC&GS in 1907 and may be superseded. Mount Bolivar was named by a well-known Coos County surveyor, Simon Bolivar Cathcart, during a township survey carried on about 1900. While the name was his own, it was applied to the mountain in honor of the South American patriot, Simon Bolivar, 1783–1830, who was born in Caracas, Venezuela, and who spent his mature years and a large part of his fortune in securing the independence of Colombia, Peru and Ecuador. The name is frequently misspelled Boliver and generally mispronounced. The correct accent is on the second syllable of each word. For information about Simon Bolivar Cathcart, *see* Mount Cathcart.

In Sept. 1984, a delegation including Venezuelan Consul Oscar Hernandez, Peruvian Consul Fernando Casafranca and representatives of Panama, Colombia and Bolivia met with USFS District Ranger John Berry. The group hiked to the summit of Mount Bolivar where a bronze plaque was set commemorating bonds of friendship. The plaque is inscribed: "The United States was the first to teach us the path to independence—Simon Bolivar, Jamaica, 1815. From Venezuela to the people of Oregon—Mount Bolivar, 1984." A contemporary account states that though the weather was cold and wet, a feeling of warmth and friendship permeated the troop.

Mount Bonneville, WALLOWA. This mountain was formerly known as Middle Mountain, but in 1925 the USBGN, at the suggestion of J. Neilson Barry of Portland, changed the name to Mount Bonneville, in honor of Captain Benjamin L. E. Bonneville, U.S. Army, who was possibly the first white man to visit the Wallowa Valley. For additional information, *see* Bonneville. Mount Bonneville is just south of Wallowa Lake.

Mount Cathcart, COOS. This point is in the Coast Range east of Coos Bay, and bears the name of Simon Bolivar Cathcart, prominent civil engineer and surveyor of Coos County. S. B. Cathcart was born in Indiana in 1842, came to Oregon in 1853, and in the 1860s served in the First Oregon Cavalry. He engaged in the stock business at various places, and studied surveying. In 1872 he settled at the head of tide on Millicoma River. In 1929 he informed the compiler that Mount Cathcart was named for him by R. U. Goode and W. T. Griswold of the USGS. This was apparently about the time the Survey was mapping the Coos Bay area in 1895–96. Mr. Cathcart served as mineral surveyor and also as Coos County surveyor, and was a prominent citizen of southwest Oregon. He died on May 13, 1932.

Mount David Douglas, LANE. The USBGN, at the suggestion of the writer, adopted on Nov. 2, 1927, the name Mount David Douglas for a conspicuous, angular peak on the north side of Salt Creek Valley, opposite the Cascade line of the Southern Pacific Company. This peak has an elevation of 6253 feet. David Douglas was the great pioneer botanist of Oregon, and his discoveries in this state were of the first order. Douglas was born in Scotland in 1798. He served his apprenticeship as gardener to the Earl of Mansfield, and later received an appointment in the Glasgow botanical gardens. The Royal Horticultural Society became interested in the country of the Hudson's Bay Company, and asked to have an exploring botanist recommended for American research. Douglas received the appointment and sailed for America the first time in 1823. He worked along the Alantic Coast and returned to England in the fall of the same year. Douglas came to the Columbia River on Apr. 8, 1825. In the Oregon country he made extensive explorations. An interesting account of his activities appears in *The Scientific Monthly*, July 1926, p. 81, by Major John D. Guthrie of Portland. *See also OHQ*, v. 5 and 6. The Royal Horticultural Society published a *Journal Kept by David Douglas*, in London in 1914. After two years' activities in the Oregon territory and Canada, Douglas returned to England in Sept. 1827. Douglas later made some additional explorations in the Oregon country, and then went to the Hawaiian

Islands, where he met a tragic death in Aug. 1834. He fell into a cattle pit and was gored to death by a wild bull. For editorial comment on David Douglas and peak in Oregon named for him, *see* the *Oregonian*, Dec. 11, 1927. Douglas may have been the first white man to climb Mount Hood. *See OHQ*, v. 6, bottom of p. 309. The Douglas fir, Oregon's most important forest tree, was noted by David Douglas and he bestowed its early botanical name, *Pseudotsuga taxifolia*. It is most fitting that Douglas is remembered by the common name of this great tree although it is not a true fir but a false hemlock. For further information on the Douglas fir, *see* Firwood.

Mount Defiance, HOOD RIVER. This is a well-known landmark west of Hood River Valley and has an elevation of 4960 feet. It was named by Dr. P. G. Barrett, an early settler in the Hood River Valley, because the mountain was the last to hold its snow in spring, thus defying the elements.

Mount Elijah, JOSEPHINE. Mount Elijah, elevation approximately 6400 feet, is in T 40S, R 6W, and is about a half a mile southwest of Lake Peak. The Oregon Caves are under its northwestern slopes. The name Mount Elijah was adopted by the USBGN in 1930–31 in honor of Elijah J. Davidson, a prominent pioneer of southern Oregon, who discovered the caves in 1874. Previously the mountain was known as Cave Mountain and Sand Mountain, but these names were not well established.

Mount Emily, CURRY. F. S. Moore, a pioneer of the county, said this name is the white man's version of the Indian name *Emney. See Curry County Reporter*, Dec. 16, 1926. The meaning of the Indian name is not known. Maps show this mountain with various names including Mount Emery and Chetco Peak, but the real Chetco Peak is farther east. The government has officially adopted the form Mount Emily, even though it does not exactly conform to the reported Indian pronunciation. Mount Emily became famous in 1942 as the result of an attack, apparently by a small airplane based on a Japanese submarine. In September incendiary bombs were dropped on Wheeler Ridge southeast of the lookout, with negligible damage. Bert Webber treats this in detail in *Silent Siege: Japanese Attacks Against North America in World War II*.

Mount Emily, UNION. There is a story to the effect that a family named Leasy lived at the foot of this mountain in pioneer days. Leasy weighed about 100 pounds and his wife nearly 300, and it is said that he named the mountain for his wife, Emily, because of her great size. There is another history of the name to the effect that a very popular young lady named Emily lived on the slopes of the mountain in early times, and she was often visited by the young men of La Grande, who christened the mountain because they so frequently went up to Mount Emily.

Mount Fanny, UNION. "The beautiful peak on the summit of the mountain range east of the Cove is called 'Mt Fanny' in honor of Mrs. Fanny McDaniels, one of the first women to settle in the Cove in 1862 and the first white woman to reach its summit, which she did in June, 1863." This quotation is from Geer's *Fifty Years in Oregon*. The statement is incorrect, for the name should be Mrs. Fannie McDaniel. Her sons were well-known physicians in Portland. However the form Mount Fanny is too well established to change. Mount Fanny is a prominent peak to the east of Grande Ronde Valley and has an elevation of 7132 feet.

Mount Gauldy, TILLAMOOK. Mount Gauldy is a point south of Hebo and east of the Oregon Coast Highway. It is said to have been named for the Gauldy Trail and the Gauldy trail was named because it was so steep and hard on men and horses. Packers and animals sustained pack-strap and saddle galls so frequently that the trace became known as the Galldy trail which was transformed into Gauldy trail.

Mount Gurney, DOUGLAS. Mount Gurney is west of Reston. It was named for Robert M. Gurney who took up a donation land claim near its base in 1853.

Mount Harriman, KLAMATH. This prominent peak is west of Upper Klamath Lake. It was named to compliment Edward H. Harriman, financier and railroad magnate, who for a time had a summer camp on Pelican Bay nearby.

Mount Harris, UNION. Mount Harris, northeast of La Grande, was named for Joseph Harris, a pioneer resident nearby.

Mount Hebo, TILLAMOOK, YAMHILL. The compiler of these notes spent six years as a small boy on a farm in Polk County, and the most important landmark visible from his home was Mount Hebo. He speculated about Mount Hebo considerably, both then and later, and always had a notion that its name was corrupted from Mount Nebo. This does not seem to be a fact. On Jan. 7, 1919, Miss Lucy E. Doughty of Bay City wrote the compiler sending information about Mount Hebo that came from Warren N. Vaughn, a Tillamook County pioneer. Vaughn relates that the mountain was named by a viewing party to find a new route to the Willamette Valley. The party climbed the mountain to get a better understanding of the country. One of the party, Cadiler, was impressed by the fine view and said, "We are very high up, so I will call this mountain Hevo." Miss Doughty explains this peculiar name by saying that Isaac Alderman, a member of the party, told her parents that the name was intended to be Heave Ho, because from their position the mountain seemed to have been heaved up above the surroundings. However that may be, it is apparent that the name became distorted somewhere along the line, and the present form is Mount Hebo. In 1926 the postmaster at Hebo wrote the compiler that the name Hebo was a misunderstanding of the name Heave Ho, and attributed the original form to the Indians. This seems improbable to the compiler. Vaughn was a reliable citizen and his story plus Alderman's explanation is probably nearer the truth. A determination made some years ago by the USC&GS gives the elevation of Mount Hebo as 3154 feet.

Mount Hood, HOOD RIVER. This post office was in the upper Hood River Valley about three miles northeast of Parkdale. It is reported that the community developed on land owned by a man named Tieman, and when the post office was applied for, it was named Mount Hood for the reason that the mountain was the most important object in the landscape. In 1976 the Post Office Department consolidated the offices of Parkdale and Mount Hood. The former was the much larger community but the latter had the name preferred by the local residents so on Oct. 9, 1976, the Mount Hood office was relocated to the community of Parkdale and the Parkdale office closed.

Mount Hood, CLACKAMAS, HOOD RIVER. On Oct. 29, 1792, Lieutenant William Robert Broughton, of Vancouver's command, discovered Mount Hood and in his *Voyage of Discovery*, Vancouver makes the following comment: "A very distant high snowy mountain now appeared rising beautifully conspicuous in the midst of an extensive tract of low, or moderately elevated, land, lying S. 67 E., and seemed to announce a termination of the river." Broughton was somewhere near the mouth of the Willamette River when he had this view of Mount Hood, and the description which he gave Vancouver would be difficult to improve upon. The next day, while near Point Vancouver, Broughton saw the mountain again, and Vancouver wrote as follows: "The same remarkable mountain that had been seen from Belle Vue point, again presented itself, bearing at this station S. 67 E., and though the party were now nearer to it by 7 leagues, yet its lofty summit was scarcely more distinct across the intervening land which was more than moderately elevated. Mr. Broughton honored it with Lord Hood's name; its appearance was magnificent; and it was clothed with snow from its summit, as low down as the high land, by which it was intercepted, rendered it visible." Here Broughton's report shows him to be a keen observer and a judge of natural beauty. Professor Edmond S. Meany, in his *Vancouver's Discovery of Puget Sound*, has taken pains to present a suitable picture of Lord Hood, and the compiler hereof cannot do better than to paraphrase from Professor Meany's notes. The Lord Hood, to whom Vancouver referred, was Samuel Hood, born Dec. 12, 1724, and entered the Royal Navy as a captain's servant in 1741. As the result of his own efforts coupled with the fact that he served under splendid officers he rose to the rank of lieutenant in 1746, and after experiencing considerable service in America and elsewhere, reached post rank on the *Lively* on July 22, 1756, but just at his promotion, he was returned to England and paid off. He was forced to resort to temporary commands for a time, but was so successful in these that he was reinstated in regular line, and served in a number of places with no remarkable distinction, but always satisfactorily, until he was practically retired in 1778 as Commissioner at Portsmouth and Governor of the Naval Academy. The king visited Portsmouth and made him a baronet. Hood lived quietly enough when to the surprise of everybody in 1780, he was promoted to the rank of rear-admiral of the blue, and was sent with a squadron to reinforce Rodney in the West Indies. Hood remained second in command in American waters until the peace of 1783, and took part in nearly all the stirring engagements that marked the close of the War for Independence. As a reward for his services he was on Sept. 12, 1782, raised to the Irish peerage as Baron Hood of Catherington, Hampshire. This was before his return to England. On his return he was given other honors, and made vice-admiral of the blue. In 1788 he was made a member of the Board of Admiralty under the Earl of Chatham, and while in this position signed the original instructions for Vancouver's voyage. But Hood's career did not end here. He served in the Mediterranean during the French Revolution. Nelson was a captain under him, and praised his vigor of mind and judgment. Sir William Hotham wrote that he never saw an officer of more intrepid courage or warmer zeal. Before his recall he was elected an Elder Brother of Trinity House in Mar. 1795, and a little later was made an admiral. In 1796 he was appointed governor of Greenwich Hospital and created Viscount Hood in the peerage of Great Britain. His remarkable mind and body made him a noted man, and shortly before he died, on Jan. 27, 1816, at the great age of 92, he received the Grand Cross of the Bath. Mount Hood is an unusual mountain, and none can say but that it was named for an unusual man. Occasional statements to the effect that Mount Hood was named for other members of the Hood family, cannot be substantiated. It is certain that the mountain was named for Samuel Hood. He was Lord Hood, a baron, when he signed the original instructions for Vancouver's voyage. The mountain could not possibly have been named in honor of Alexander Hood, Lord Bridport, younger brother of Lord Hood and also an admiral. Alexander Hood was not raised to the peerage until after 1793, and never had the title Lord Hood, but instead that of Lord Bridport. He was a viscount when he died in 1814, after a long and distinguished life. Lord Hood and Lord Bridport had two famous cousins, also named Samuel and Alexander Hood, but in reverse order. Alexander was the elder of this pair and died in action at sea in 1798, but never received a title. His younger brother, Sir Samuel Hood, had a remarkably successful naval career, but was not a peer. It will be seen from the above that there was but one Lord Hood in 1792, when the mountain was named, and that was the first Samuel. It will also be seen that the statement that Mount Hood and the famous British warship *Hood* were named for the same man is difficult to prove. There have been several ships named *Hood*. In 1935 the compiler secured a copy of the picture hanging in the wardroom of H.M.S. *Hood*, and it turned out to be of Vice-Admiral Sir Samuel Hood and not that of Lord Hood. Alexander Hood, Lord Bridport, seems, from his biography, to have done more sea fighting than the other three, and was raised to the peerage even though his brother was already a peer. The *Oregonian* had an editorial on the name Hood on June 1, 1941, which says that the ships and the mountain are named for the same man, but offers no definite evidence and in fact fails to mention Admiral Alexander Hood, Viscount Bridport, who is obviously one of the most important men of the family group.

Lewis and Clark saw Mount Hood for the first time on Friday, Oct. 18, 1805, and wrote: "saw a mountain s. w. conical form Covered with Snow." On Oct. 25 Clark wrote at a point near The Dalles, "The Pinical of the round toped mountain which we Saw a Short distance below the forks of this river is s. 43 w. of us and abt 37 miles, it is at this time toped with Snow we called this the *falls mountain* or *Timm* mountain. [this the Mount Hood or Vancouver.]" Timm was a name given to a point at The Dalles of the Columbia, said to have been applied because the word sounded like the noise of falling water. It is obvious that Clark meant to write *this the Mount Hood of Vancouver*, and it is also obvious that he and Lewis must have had a reasonably accurate knowledge of Vancouver's discoveries, though it seems they did not have Vancouver's engraved charts. *See* Coues' *History of the Expedition of Lewis and Clark*, v. 1, p. xxiv. The fur traders had many other things to occupy their attention, and did not go in for mountaineering, and for the most part, neither did the pioneers. There are many references to Mount Hood in early day journals and diaries, but nothing of importance, except Hall J. Kelley's plan to change the name to Mount Adams (See under Cascade Range), until Joel Palmer made one of the earliest attempts by a white man to climb the mountain, on Oct. 12, 1845. *See* the volume containing Palmer's journals in *Thwaites' Early Western Travels*, p. 132, and *see also* Camp Creek and Palmer Peak in this book. David Douglas, the botanist, is said to have attempted to climb the mountain in 1833. *See OHQ*, v. 6, p. 309. Possibly the first ascent of Mount Hood was in Aug. 1854. *See* the *Oregonian*, Aug. 19, 1854. Joel Palmer is said to have been a member of the first party to make the complete ascent. For information about early ascents and references to interesting articles about the mountain, *see* Scott's *History of the Oregon Country*, v. 2, p. 302. The first reasonably accurate determination of the height of Mount Hood, 11,225 feet, was made on Aug. 23, 1867, by a party under direction of Lieutenant-Colonel Robert S. Williamson. *See* the *Oregonian*, Sept. 24, 1867, and Scott's *History of the Oregon Country*, v. 5, p. 119. For information about Williamson, *see* Williamson River. The Mazamas were organized on the summit of Mount Hood July 19, 1894. *See Mazama*, v. 1, no. 1. For additional information about Mount Hood, *see* the booklet *Mount Hood*, issued by Mazamas. It will be noted in this booklet that doubts are cast on the reliability of the reports on the ascent of Aug. 1854. For information on the movement of glaciers on Mount Hood, *see* Eliot Glacier. The best general books about Mount Hood are Fred H. McNeil's *Wy'east "THE Mountain,"* and *Mount Hood, A Complete History*, by Jack Grauer. For many years there was a mild controversy about the elevation of Mount Hood, the USGS and the USC&GS using different values in their publications. These differences were composed in 1939 when a USC&GS party under Lieutenant William M. Scaife established a triangulation station on the summit and fixed its elevation by means of vertical angles measured with great accuracy. The measurement was based on the elevation of a first-order bench mark near Warrendale, and produced an elevation of 11,245 feet. In 1958, the USGS field survey crew working on the Mount Hood remapping project made a revised determination of 11,235 feet. This reduction of ten feet is explained by the fact that vertical angles were taken from six control spots of known elevation instead of the two used in 1938. Improvements in instruments and techniques also contributed to more accurate results. The development of orbital measuring and surveying during the 1970s could possibly result in further revisions in the height of Mount Hood and other peaks of the Cascade Range but with minor exceptions, these would be computation differences and not physical change of the summits themselves. The official height of Mount Hood in 1990 was 11,239 feet.

Mount Hood, WASCO. A post office with this name was established May 27, 1872, with William Hollandsworth first postmaster. Other postmasters were named McAtee, Shannon, Paquet, Hinkle and Steers. The office was discontinued Jan. 11, 1878. The writer has not been able to associate this office with the place called Mount Hood in Hood River County. Old maps show a community called Mount Hood in the general vicinity of Tygh Valley, Wasco County, but not always in the same place. It is obvious that such a place was named because of the fine view of Mount Hood that is obtained in that part of the country.

Mount Hood, YAMHILL. John Richardson was a pioneer settler in Yamhill County and his claim was at the east foot of the Amity Hills about two miles north of the present site of Hopewell. A post office named Mount Hood was established Oct. 14, 1854, with Richardson postmaster and it may be assumed that it was on or near this claim. Richardson probably named the office because of the view of the top of Mount Hood, although the mountain was a long way from the locality. This office was closed in Jan. 1862. Other postmasters included James M. Belcher and Daniel C. Doherty.

Mount Horeb, MARION. This butte, with an elevation of nearly 4500 feet, lies about eight miles northeast of Mill City. An article published in the Salem *Capital Journal*, June 18, 1927, p. 1, says that it was named in 1873 by David Smith, a local Bible enthusiast.

Mount Howard, WALLOWA. This was formerly Signal Peak, and lies southeast of Wallowa Lake. The name was changed in 1925 by the USBGN at the suggestion of J. Neilson Barry, of Portland, to honor Major-General Oliver Otis Howard (1830–1909), who graduated from West Point in 1850 and served with great distinction in the Civil War and throughout the Indian uprisings. He was not only brevetted for gallantry at the battle of Ezra Church, but received a vote of thanks of the Congress for heroic valor at the battle of Gettysburg, and the coveted Congressional Medal of Honor for distinguished bravery at the battle of Fair Oaks, where he lost his right arm. He was in command of the Department of the Columbia at the time of Chief Joseph's uprising in the Wallowa Valley, and took the field in person against that famous Indian, driving him into Montana. He was accused of dilatory tactics, but time has had the effect of establishing General Howard's reputation as a soldier. *See* Howard's *My Life and Experiences*, and Scott's *History of the Oregon Country*, v. 2, p. 332.

Mount Ireland, BAKER, GRANT. This peak, which is on the summit of the Blue

Mountains, has an elevation of 8330 feet. It was known for some years as Bald Mountain, but the name was changed to Ireland Mountain by the USBGN at the request of the USFS and eastern Oregon citizens. This was in honor of Henry Ireland who was for many years supervisor of the Whitman National Forest, and who died May 31, 1916. Before being connected with the USFS he was with the Department of the Interior. The form Mount Ireland was set in *Decision List 7502*.

Mount Isaac, DOUGLAS. Mount Isaac is about a mile west of Riddle. George W. Riddle of Roseburg informed the compiler that the mountain was named for Isaac Flint, a nearby pioneer settler of 1852.

Mount Isabelle, JACKSON. Mount Isabelle, elevation about 4500 feet, is ten miles south-southwest of Gold Hill. The peak was named for Isabelle Smith, daughter of a pioneer settler, Jakey Smith. He and his Indian wife squatted on a little ground on the east side of the mountain. In 1946 there were remains of the old Smith cabin and possibly a few apple trees in the clearing.

Mount Jefferson, JEFFERSON, LINN, MARION. This is the second highest peak in Oregon and has an elevation of 10,497 feet, according to the USGS. Gatschet in his 1877 manuscript says the Molalla Indian name for the mountain was *Kuassal Teminbi*. It was seen by Lewis and Clark on Sunday, Mar. 30, 1806, from a point near the mouth of the Willamette, and it was named by them in honor of Thomas Jefferson, president of the United States. Since it was already named for a president, Hall J. Kelley did not attach a new name to it when he rechristened the Cascade Range Presidents Range and tried to change the names of the individual peaks. Kelley's geographic position of Mount Jefferson was in error, and so was Farnham's in his *Travels in the Great Western Prairies*, but the latter mistake in text is possibly due to a typographical error in notes, "44 1/2" being misprinted "41 1/2." *See* Cascade Range for details of Kelley's scheme. Mount Jefferson is really in north latitude 44° 40′ 28″. While the mountain has rarely been referred to by any other name, Thornton in *Oregon and California* mentions the fact that the British used the name Mount Vancouver but gives no reference. He may have seen either Arrowsmith's map of *British North America*, 1834, or the *Territory of Oregon* map drawn by Washington Hood for the Bureau of Topographical Engineers under Colonel J. J. Abert, dated 1838. On both maps Mount Jefferson is clearly shown as Mount Vancouver. However, Wheat in *Mapping the American West*, pp. 87–88 states that Captain Hood apparently disregarded then recent North American sources and relied heavily on the 1834 Arrowsmith. It is important to note that David Douglas uses the name Mount Jefferson in his *Journal Kept by David Douglas* under date of Apr. 19, 1825, and again on Oct. 5, 1826, thus indicating that he, at least, did not know the mountain by the name Mount Vancouver. Douglas does, however, use the name Mount Vancouver in his journal on Oct. 13, 1826, referring to a snowy peak south of Mount Hood, but it seems obvious from his text that he never saw such a mountain and mentions it only by hearsay. It is not clear just what mountain he refers to.

Mount Jefferson by any route is considered by mountaineers to be the most difficult of the major Oregon peaks. While there are some questions, the first ascent is generally credited to E. C. Cross and Ray L. Farmer via the south ridge on Aug. 12, 1888. There were a limited number of other successful climbers until after the turn of the century when, in Aug. 1903, S. S. Mohler climbed the true north ridge from Jefferson Park, alone, a truly remarkable achievment. The best available information about Mount Jefferson is contained in the following publications: USGS *Bulletin 252, Geology and Water Resources of Central Oregon*, by Israel C. Russell; *Mineral Resources of Oregon*, v. 2, no. 1, and *Mazama*, v. 2, no. 3, for July 1903; v. 3, no. 1, for Mar. 1907; v. 4, no. 3, for Dec. 1914; v. 5, no. 2, for Dec. 1917, and v. 7, no. 2, for Dec. 1925. More recently, Don A. Hall in *On Top of Oregon*, 1975, gives an excellent layman's account of the geology along with considerable climbing history.

Mount June, LANE. Mount June is about 15 miles due east of Cottage Grove and has an elevation of 4616 feet, according to the USGS. Mount June was named by Elijah Bristow because he saw snow on its summit in that month when he was making an early exploring trip.

Mount Mazama, KLAMATH. Mount Mazama is the name of a prehistoric mountain, the caldera of which is now occupied by Crater Lake. For information about the discovery and naming of Crater Lake, *see* Crater Lake. The rim enclosing the lake formed part of the base of Mount Mazama. It was named for the Mazamas, the mountaineering organization of the Pacific Northwest, at the annual outing Aug. 21, 1896. *Mazama* is the Spanish name of the mountain goat. *See Mazama*, v. 1, nos. 1 and 2. For information about Mount Mazama, *ibid.*, v. 1, no. 2, and the booklet on Crater Lake issued in 1922 by Mazamas. For geography of Crater Lake and picture of Mount Mazama restored, *see* USGS 1/62,500 map of Crater Lake National Park. The entire area was remapped by the USGS in 1985 at 1/24,000. The highest points on the rim of Crater Lake are Hillman Peak, 8156 feet; Applegate Peak, 8135 feet; Garfield Peak, 8060 feet; Llao Rock, 8046 feet, and The Watchman, 8025 feet.

Mount McLoughlin, JACKSON. This mountain is called Mount McLoughlin on a map issued in 1838, accompanying the *Journal of an Exploring Tour Beyond the Rocky Mountains, in 1835, '36 and '37*, by the Reverend Samuel Parker. It was later called Mount Pit, for Pit or Pitt River, which was named for the pits dug by Indians to trap game. Peter Skene Ogden mentions the name Pit River in his journal for May 21, 1829, and spells it Pitts River. *See OHQ*, v. 11, p. 394. Sir George Simpson in *Narrative of a Journey Round the World*, London, 1847, v. 1, p. 351, refers to Pit Mountain in this locality, "so called from the number of pitfalls dug by the neighbouring savages for the wild animals." T. J. Farnham in *Travels in the Great Western Prairies*, New York, 1843, p. 96, refers to Mount McLaughlin, but is inaccurate as to location. Mount McLaughlin is shown on Wilkes' map in the *U. S. Exploring Expedition*, 1841. The name Mount Pitt appears for the first time on a map made by Charles Preuss, Fremont's cartographer, in 1843, but no mention is made of it by Fremont in his report. The compiler has never found any evidence that associates this name with that of William Pitt, British statesman. Lieutenant R. S. Williamson of the corps of topographical engineers explored the region of Pit River in 1855, and the report of this expedition, prepared by Lieutenant Henry L. Abbot, was published by the government in v. 6, of the Pacific Railroad Surveys *Reports*. Under date of Aug. 8, 1855, the journal says: "We passed many pits six feet deep and lightly covered with twigs and grass. The river derives its name from these pits, which are dug by the Indians to entrap game." On this account Williamson always spelled the name with a single "t," although on most maps it is written with two. Early settlers in the Rogue River Valley called the mountain Snowy Butte and Big Butte. As early as 1839 Hall J. Kelley tried to have the name John Quincy Adams applied to this mountain, but his plan for a Presidents Range fizzled out. *See* Cascade Range. The name Mount Pitt came into common use about 1864, supposedly due to George H. Belden, a civil engineer in the employ of the United States surveyor general of Oregon. Klamath Indians called the mountain *M'laiksini Yaina*, or mountain with steep sides.

The name Mount McLoughlin was restored by the legislature in 1905, to honor Dr. John McLoughlin, and was recognized by the USBGN in 1912 through the efforts of Will G. Steel and George H. Himes. The spelling McLaughlin is wrong. Dr. John McLoughlin, as chief factor of the Hudson's Bay Company, at Fort Vancouver, in 1824–46, possessed almost autocratic power in affairs in the Oregon country up to the time of the provisional government, and has therefore been called the first governor of Oregon. He was a man of broad views and ideas, generous and kind instincts and of large physical proportions. He was born in parish La Riviere du Loup, Canada, about 120 miles below Quebec, on the Saint Lawrence River, Oct. 19, 1784. Young McLoughlin was educated in Canada and became a physician. He joined the North West Company, and became a partner and was one of the factors in charge of Fort William, the chief depot and factory of the North West Company, at the time of the consolidation with the Hudson's Bay Company. His wife, Marguerite Wadin McLoughlin, was the widow of Alexander McKay, who had been killed in the *Tonquin* disaster at Clayoquot Sound, Vancouver Island, in June 1811. Dr. McLoughlin built Fort Vancouver in 1824–25, and there he created a farm of 3000 acres and established a sawmill and a flour mill. His district of the Hudson's Bay Company (the Columbia) grew to be profitable. There were numerous forts and posts tributary to Fort Vancouver, there being, in 1839, about 20 of these besides Fort Vancouver. In the development of the fur business, of agriculture and commerce, and in the government of the country, Dr. McLoughlin displayed rare powers of organization. He met the American traders with kindness, but with severe competition, and the American missionaries and settlers, with benevolence. He left the service of the Hudson's Bay Company in 1846, and became an American citizen at Oregon City May 30, 1849. After his resignation he carried on a milling and merchandise business at Oregon City, where he died on Sept. 3, 1857. Dr. McLoughlin's house at Oregon City, built in 1845–46, and occupied by him until his death, was moved, by the McLoughlin Memorial Association, to the bluff overlooking Willamette River, and restored to its first condition. It was dedicated as a permanent memorial Sept. 5, 1909. For narrative, *Dr. John McLoughlin and His Guests*, by T. C. Elliott, *see Washington Historical Quarterly*, v. 2, pp. 63–77; for biography, *see* F. V. Holman's *Dr. John McLoughlin*; *John McLoughlin: Patriarch of the Northwest*, by Robert C. Johnson, and Richard G. Montgomery's *The White-Headed Eagle*. For a long list of references to published material about Dr. McLoughlin, *see* Scott's *History of the Oregon Country*, v. 1, pp. 295–96. McLoughlin's *Fort Vancouver Letters* have been published by the Hudson's Bay Record Society in three volumes. *See also Letters of Dr. John McLoughlin*, edited by Dr. Burt Brown Barker, 1948.

Mount Mitchell, CLACKAMAS. This mountain, elevation 5110 feet, was named for Roy Mitchell, a veteran of World War I, who was killed while fighting a forest fire Aug. 20, 1919. The mountain was formerly called Oak Grove Mountain, an unsatisfactory name because there were no oak trees on the mountain, and also the name caused confusion with Oak Grove Butte, seven miles to the south. Oak Grove Mountain had been applied because the feature was near Oak Grove Fork Clackamas River.

Mount Moriah, UNION. This mountain is in T 1S, R 41E, and has an elevation of about 5500 feet. It is flat on top. In early days it was called Stubblefield Mountain in compliment to Jasper Stubblefield who had a homestead west of the mountain in about 1878. Later some Bible enthusiast named it for the place in Palestine, about which a great deal seems to be unknown.

Mount Nebo, DOUGLAS. Moses viewed the Promised Land from the summit of biblical Mount Nebo. The name was applied by pioneers to the high ground in the bend of South Umpqua River that has a commanding view of the entire Roseburg area but affords an especial overlook of fertile Garden Valley to the northwest.

Mount Pisgah, LANE. Mount Pisgah is the prominent high nose just southeast of the confluence of Coast and Middle forks Willamette River. The Paul Bristow notes in the Lane County Pioneer Museum state that Elijah Bristow bestowed this name because of the overview of the fertile upper Willamette Valley. Moses' view of the Promised Land was from Mount Nebo, a summit of Biblical Mount Pisgah.

Mount Pisgah, POLK. J. L. Ford, many years a resident of Dallas, wrote the compiler in Aug. 1927, as follows: "I find that Colonel Cornelius Gilliam named the little butte southeast of Dallas 'Mt. Pisgah' for a butte so named near his old home in Missouri, and probably also because of his veneration for biblical names." Pisgah was a mountain of Abarim, Moab, northeast of the Dead Sea. Mount Nebo was one of its summits.

Mount Pleasant, LINN. Mount Pleasant is a descriptive name for a nice viewpoint mostly in s 30, T 9S, R 1E. This hill rises about 200 feet above the surrounding land but it pleased the early settlers to call it a mount. The compiler does not know who was responsible for this but probably members of the Irvine family who took up property there in the early fifties. The locality was once known as the Irvine District and it was called The Hill. There is a cemetery on the top of Mount Pleasant and there are also nearby school grounds probably set aside by Robert Irvine. The church property was set aside by Washington Crabtree and it is reported that Ben Irvine raised the money for the various necessary buildings. A post office called Mount Pleasant was established in Aug. 1874, with Elijah Richardson first of several postmasters. This office was discontinued Oct. 10, 1887. Mount Pleasant is about seven miles northeast of Scio.

Mount Popocatepetl, LANE. This mountain, elevation 1020 feet, is a well-known point in the Oregon Coast Range, but not one of the highest. The peak was named about 1888 by R. O. Collier, a government surveyor, because it was so hard to climb. The crew was smoking hot when it reached the top. The original Mount Popocatepetl is the second highest mountain in Mexico and is named with the Aztec word for smoking mountain. This information was furnished by E. A. Collier of Salem.

Mount Ray, LANE. Mount Ray is just south of Waldo Lake. It is named for Frederick and Nellie Ray who, along with Amos Black of Black Creek, promoted the Waldo Lake Irrigation and Power Company prior to World War 1.

Mount Reuben, DOUGLAS, JOSEPHINE. Mount Reuben is a prominent peak about ten miles west of Glendale on the divide between the waters of Cow Creek and those of Rogue River. It was named for Reuben Field of Linn County, who was a member of Captain Jonathan Keeney's company who fought Indians in this part of Oregon in 1855. While the company was trying to cross Rogue River not far from this mountain Field made a jocular prediction that the Indians would make an attack. The prediction was soon fulfilled and Mount Reuben and Reuben Creek nearby have since borne his name.

Mount Scott, CLACKAMAS. This well-known butte is in the southeast outskirts of Portland and is 1083 feet above sea level. It was named in 1889 for Harvey Scott, editor of the *Oregonian*, by W. P. Keady. In that year, and in 1890, Mr. Scott bought 335 acres of land on the north and west slopes of the hill. From that time until Nov. 1909, when he sold the land to Mount Scott Park Cemetery Corporation, the editor continually kept men working the soil and clearing away the forest and stumps. In this effort Mr. Scott expended considerable money, but he was determined to "tame that wild land," as he frequently expressed it. For a detailed description of Mr. Scott's life, *see* Scott's *History of the Oregon Country*. For W. P. Keady's part in the development and naming of Mount Scott, *see* editorial page of the *Oregon Journal*, Sept. 24, 1928. There it is said that the butte was once called Mount Zion.

Mount Scott, DOUGLAS. Mount Scott post office was established Oct. 14, 1854, and discontinued Oct. 5, 1857. Andrew J. Chapman was postmaster. It was reestablished May 8, 1879, with Matilda Blakely postmaster and finally closed Sept. 14, 1886. An army map of Dec. 1887, shows the place at a point on North Umpqua River a few miles west of what is now Glide. The office was of course named for Scott Mountain, a prominent point a little to the northeast, which was in turn named for Captain Levi Scott.

Mount Scott, KLAMATH. This mountain lies east of Crater Lake and is one of the important peaks of the Cascade Range. It was named for Levi Scott, a pioneer of 1844, and the founder of Scottsburg, in Douglas County. For additional information, *see* Scottsburg. Mount Scott has an elevation of 8929 feet. The Klamath Indian name for Mount Scott was *Tum-sum-ne*, according to the treaty of 1864. Barker in his *Klamath Dictionary*, Berkeley, 1963, gives *Walmsini*.

Mount Sylvania, MULTNOMAH. Mount Sylvania is in the extreme southwest part of the county. It has an elevation of about 950 feet. I-5 skirts its northwest shoulder. The name is derived from *Silvanus*, the deity or spirit of the Italian woodlands. Silvanus is not wholly associated with the wild woodlands, but those near civilization, and partly cleared, so to speak, or the bordering and fringing woodlands. Silvanus' name came from *silva*, the Latin name for wood. His name is generally misspelled, Sylvanus, and from this we have the name Sylvan and Sylvania. The post office list of 1853 shows Mountsylvania, an office not far from the present site of Metzger, and a short distance from the mountain now known by the same name. The writer has been unable to learn who established the name, either for the post office or for the mountain, but he was told by the late Colonel Henry E. Dosch of Hillsdale that the mountain had been so called since pioneer days. Information furnished the compiler by postal authorities in Washington in 1927 does not agree with that printed in the list of post offices in the *Oregonian*, Mar. 26, 1853. The records in Washington indicate that the name of the office was in two words, Mount Sylvania. This office was established Aug. 6, 1852, and was discontinued Nov. 14, 1854. It operated again for a short time in 1856. Israel Mitchell was the only postmaster. John B. Preston's *Map of Oregon and Washington* of 1856 shows the name in still another style, Montsylvania. The compiler has been unable to reconcile these discrepancies.

Mount Tabor, MULTNOMAH. Mount Tabor was named by Plympton Kelly, son of Clinton Kelly, pioneer resident of Portland. He had been reading *Napoleon and His Marshals*, by Joel T. Headley, and was impressed among other things by the battle fought by the French against the Moslems on the Plain of Esdraelon not far from the base of Mount Tabor in Palestine. He therefore named the hill near his home Mount Tabor for the mount in the Holy Land. It was first planned to call Mount Tabor in Oregon Mount Zion. *See* OPA *Transactions*, 1887, p. 60. Mount Tabor post office was in operation many years.

Mount Talapus, MULTNOMAH. This peak is between the headwaters of Tanner

Creek and north branches of Bull Run River. It bears an Indian name for coyote, or barking wolf of the plains. The coyote was a sort of deity or supernatural being in Indian mythology. Chinook jargon, *Talapus*; Chinook Indian, *Italipas*; Yakima Indian, *Telipa*. This peak was once called Shellrock Mountain, but the USBGN was prevailed upon to change the name because there were more than enough Shellrocks already. *See* Coyote Creek.

Mount Thielsen, DOUGLAS, KLAMATH. This mountain is one of the most remarkable in the state because of a great pinnacle or spire that forms its summit. Its elevation is 9182 feet. In early days it was known as the Big Cowhorn in contradistinction to Little Cowhorn farther north, now called Cowhorn. It is also said to have been called Diamond Peak, but the compiler has seen no written evidence of this. About 1872 it was named Mount Thielsen by John A. Hurlburt of Portland, in honor of Hans Thielsen, prominent pioneer railroad engineer and builder. For references to Thielsen, *see* Scott's *History of the Oregon Country*. For information about the mountain, *see* article by Ira A. Williams in *Mazama*, Dec. 1921. The Indian name of the mountain was *His-chok-wol-as*. *See also* Cascade Range.

Mount Vernon, GRANT. Herman Oliver of John Day stated that David W. Jenkins, an early settler, owned a prize black stallion named Mt. Vernon. Both the town and the rocky eminence just to the north were named for the horse and the animal was stabled in a small stone building constructed especially for him as protection against Indians and thieves. During the Indian War of 1878 neighbors crowded into the stout little fortress along with the horse. In 1990 the building was still standing, unfazed by over 100 years, just north of US-26 about one and one half miles east of Mount Vernon. The post office was established May 14, 1877 with Wm. J. Gray postmaster.

Mount Washington, DESCHUTES, LINN. In elevation, Mount Washington may be counted as one of the lesser peaks of the Cascade Range, but its unusual appearance and the fact that it is difficult to climb make it an important mountain. It has an elevation of 7794 feet. It doubtless received its name because of the proximity of Mount Jefferson, but who applied the name, and when, is apparently unknown. It was of course named for George Washington. It was not mentioned by any early explorers, or shown on early maps but it does appear on the survey for the Willamette Valley and Cascade Mountain Military Road compiled by James A. Warner dated July 19, 1867. The survey, in the Oregon State Archives, uses the form Washingtons Peak. The top part of Mount Washington is a rocky spire that defied all attempts at climbing until Aug. 26, 1923, when six men from Bend managed to reach the summit. In recent years it has become one of the popular ascents as varying routes on all three main ridges and faces range from moderate to extremely difficult. The first attempts to climb the peak are covered in *Mazama* for 1922 and 1923. Don A. Hall in *On Top of Oregon*, 1975, has an excellent summary of the geology and climbing history.

Mount Wilson, CLACKAMAS, WASCO. This mountain, with an elevation of 5595 feet, is an important lookout station on the summit of the Cascade Range. It was named for Bruce Wilson of Portland, when he was supervisor of forest areas in the northern part of the Cascade Range in Oregon. Older maps show the mountain as Tamarack Mountain. This name was unsatisfactory because of duplication, and USFS map makers changed it to Mount Wilson. At that time there was no rule against naming geographic features for living members of the Forest Service. However, Wilson protested against the change, but without result. Dee Wright of Eugene, long a USFS employee, informed the compiler that there was no doubt that the mountain was named for Bruce Wilson, because Wilson told him of the circumstances. Robert Bruce Wilson, son of Dr. and Mrs. R. B. Wilson, was born in Portland on June 2, 1877. He graduated from Yale in 1901, and received a degree from the Yale Forest School in 1904. Shortly thereafter he entered the USFS and before he resigned, in 1908, he was supervisor of the forests of the Cascade Range between Columbia and McKenzie rivers. He died near Medford on June 19, 1919. He was not married.

Mount Yoran, LANE. The top of Mount Yoran, elevation 7100 feet, is just west of the summit of the Cascade Range north of Diamond Lake. It was named for Louise C. Yoran of Eugene, who was at the time employed by the USFS. She married C. A. E. Whitton of Eugene.

Mount Zion, LANE. According to the Paul Bristow notes in the Lane County Pioneer Museum collection, Mount Zion was named by his grandfather, Elijah Bristow, at the same time that he named Lost Creek just to the west.

Mountain, JOSEPHINE. The place called Mountain, obviously for the surroundings, was a few miles north of Grants Pass in the southwest part of T 34S, R 5W. It was at or near the location of the Lucky Queen mine. The *Oregon Almanac*, 1915, says it was a lumbering community. Mountain post office was established Nov. 30, 1908, with Allison Burnham first postmaster. The office was closed to Threepines on Mar. 31, 1913, apparently having served its usefulness. Mountain was just southeast of Sexton Mountain.

Mountain Home, WASHINGTON. Mountain Home is a locality or neighborhood about three miles south of Scholls. There is a Mountain Home School. The place was named for the Mountain Home farm of the Schmeltzer family, well known in that part of the country. Mountain Home School is on the northwest slopes of the Chehalem Mountains. It was formerly called Schmeltzer School and the place where it stands was known as Fir Clearing. For a history of these matters, *see* Hillsboro *Argus*, Dec. 24, 1931.

Mountain House, YAMHILL. Mountain House appears to have been an institution that moved westward as better transportation became available. According to available information it was first the home of Wilson Carl, two miles west of Carlton, but later there was another locality called Mountain House about seven miles northwest of Carlton and the same distance southwest of Yamhill. The compiler has not been able to learn the exact relationship, if any, between these various establishments. According to post office records Mountain House post office was established Oct. 19, 1866, with Charles W. Cogle first postmaster. Wilson Carl became postmaster Nov. 9, 1868, and Lewis C. Thompson took over the office in Jan. 1874. Mountain House post office was closed in Nov. 1874, but the use of the place name continued a good many years after that. It is assumed that the Mountain House was named because it was where travelers stopped before climbing westward over the Coast Range toward Tillamook.

Mountain Sheep Creek, WALLOWA. This creek flows into Snake River in T 4N, R 48E. It was named by Charles Holmes and R. F. Stubblefield who were looking for winter range and saw mountain sheep on the range above the stream.

Mountaindale, WASHINGTON. Mountaindale is a descriptive name applied to a locality where East Fork Dairy Creek emerges from the hills at the north border of the Tualatin Valley. Mountain Dale post office was established June 11, 1873, with David O. Quick postmaster. The name was changed to Mountaindale probably in 1895, as the *Postal Guide* issued at the end of that year is the first to contain the name in one word. The office was discontinued in July 1935.

Mouse Island Lake, COLUMBIA, MULTNOMAH. This lake is on Sauvie Island. It received its peculiar name because there was an island in the lake infested with field mice.

Mouth of the Willamette, MULTNOMAH. This pioneer post office was established on Sauvie Island, close to the south end, June 30, 1851, with Ellis Walker postmaster. It was first put on the list for Clark County, Washington, but it never was actually in that county. The name of the office was changed to Sauvies Island on Mar. 5, 1852, and on May 19, 1853, it was moved to the Washington County, Oregon, list with Benjamin Howell postmaster. The locality is now in Multnomah County. *See* Post Office Bar.

Mowich, KLAMATH. *Mowich* is a Chinook jargon word meaning deer and it has been applied to a number of geographic features in Oregon. The word is used for a station name on the Southern Pacific Cascade line about twelve miles north of Chemult, and while there are doubtless deer in the locality many of these station names are Indian words selected because of their pleasing sound. Mowich post office was established Jan. 3, 1936, with R. J. Watt postmaster. It was closed Mar. 15, 1948.

Moyina Hill, KLAMATH. Moyina Hill is a prominent landmark about midway between Klamath Falls and Dairy and north of Olene. Many years ago Will G. Steel told the compiler that the name was a Klamath Indian word meaning big mountain. The spelling Moyina is that used on maps of the USFS. Apparently it comes from the Indian word *yaini*, meaning mountain, with the prefix *muni* for big or bulky.

Mud Creek, WALLOWA. Mud Creek flows into Grande Ronde River in T 5N, R 43E. It was named for the mud springs and mud flats at its head. It has been known as Mud Creek for a long time.

Muddy Creek, JEFFERSON, WASCO. This stream rises in Jefferson County east of Ashwood and flows into Currant Creek, a tributary of John Day River. Its occasional turbidity caused its name. H. H. Bancroft in his *History of Oregon*, v. 1, p. 787, says that when in 1862 Joseph H. Sherar and his party were packing into the John Day mines, they named this as well as a number of other features.

Muddy Creek, LANE, LINN. This stream drains the eastern floor of the Willamette Valley. It rises in the hills east of Coburg and flows generally to the Willamette River, finally joining it east of Corvallis. It is a sluggish stream, and it is no surprise that the pioneers named it as they did. The name Muddy Creek appears in the *Oregonian* as early as Nov. 7, 1857. Muddy Creek has two main tributaries, Dry Muddy Creek and Little Muddy Creek. There was a railroad station called Muddy, where the stream crossed the main line of the Southern Pacific, but that station is now Alford. There is another Muddy Creek, of similar characteristics, draining the western part of the Willamette Valley and flowing into Marys River south of Corvallis.

Muddy Station, LINN. A post office with the name Muddy Station was established Feb. 24, 1874, with William Landreth postmaster. Thomas Alford, Sr., became postmaster on Nov. 5, 1874, and the office was closed Feb. 19, 1875. Muddy Station was a place on the Oregon & California Rail Road about four miles northeast of Harrisburg at the place where the railroad crossed Muddy Creek. Most old maps show the place as Muddy, but the official post office name was Muddy Station. Some time after the turn of the century the name of the station was changed to Alford in compliment to Thomas Alford mentioned above. Alford was a pioneer of 1850 and a well-known resident of Linn County. For a biography of Alford, *see Historical Atlas Map of Marion & Linn Counties*, 1878, p. 55, wherein it is stated that the village of Liverpool was situated on Alford property. *See* Liverpool.

Mudjekeewis Mountain, KLAMATH. Mudjekeewis Mountain, maximum elevation 6616 feet, is in the Cascade Range, on the west border of Klamath County, about four miles south of the southwest corner of Crater Lake National Park. It was named for an Indian deity, *Mudjekeewis*, spirit of the four winds, made famous by Henry W. Longfellow as the father of Hiawatha. As applied to the feature in Klamath County, the name is relatively modern. It may have been used because the mountain is in an unusually windy situation or because some forest ranger landed in the clutches of poetical romance.

Mugwump Lake, LAKE. One of the Warner Lakes. Will G. Steel told the compiler it was named Mugwump because it was so changeable from wet to dry and back again.

Muir Creek, WALLOWA. Muir Creek is a small stream in a canyon draining into Snake River in T 1N, R 51E. It was named for a Scottish prospector, one Muir, who worked in the canyon with a fellow countryman.

Mule, HARNEY. Mule post office was established Feb. 11, 1895, with James F.

Mahon postmaster. It was in operation until Feb. 14, 1901. It was reestablished May 13, 1903, with Lucy R. Mahon postmaster, and continued until Jan. 14, 1906. In Dec. 1945, Archie McGowan wrote the compiler in substance as follows: "Mule post office was at the ranch home of James F. Mahon, early pioneer and noted mule breeder at his famous Anderson Valley ranch 55 miles southeast of Burns. The office was likely discontinued in 1901 because of lack of patrons. Its reinstatement in 1903 with Lucy R. Mahon, wife of James F. Mahon, was justified by the last wave of homesteaders that spread over the West. Mahon was a prominent Democrat and the appointment of his wife as postmaster by Theodore Roosevelt in 1903 was likely political. During the last years of the post office, Mahon had one John Hoss working on the ranch, who of course was a patron of the office. It was quite common to note letters and other mail addressed to John Hoss, Mule, Oregon. I think Ripley has used this item in his pictures."

Mule Creek, CROOK. John Beoletto, who was raised in the Conant Basin, stated in 1969 that this tributary of Wickiup Creek near Pollard Butte was named for a homesteader named Yule. The name was mistakenly altered to Mule. The compiler has been unable to find the later history of Mr. Yule.

Mule Creek, CURRY. Mule Creek is in the extreme northeast corner of the county and flows into Rogue River. Many years ago William H. Packwood told the compiler that the stream was named in the summer of 1852 when a company of soldiers from Fort Orford was trying to open a trail along Rogue River. Packwood was a soldier in the party. Lieutenant R. S. Williamson rode a mule named John, and when it was turned loose to graze near this stream, it wandered off and despite a search, the animal was not recovered. The stream was named John Mule Creek because of this incident. Old maps show the name in full, but in recent years the name has been reduced to Mule Creek. There is a Mule Mountain nearby. Packwood also said that a few years later he found the mule at Siletz in the possesion of an Indian, who had apparently salvaged it. Stories to the effect that the stream was named for a prospector, John Mule, cannot be substantiated.

Muleshoe Ridge, WHEELER. Muleshoe Ridge is east of Service Creek, and Muleshoe Creek is just east of the ridge. J. H. Tilley of Service Creek told the compiler that there was a story in the neighborhood to the effect that someone found a muleshoe near the head of this creek, which accounts for the name. On the other hand it is also said that the ridge itself is shaped something like a muleshoe with the toe to the north. The reader is free to choose one of the above explanations.

Mulino, CLACKAMAS. Mulino was named by C. F. Howard in 1882, and the name was a corruption of the Spanish word, *molino*, which means mill. Postal authorities would not accept the name Molino because it was too much like the nearby Molalla. Richard R. Howard, father of C. F. Howard, erected a flour mill at Mulino in 1851, and the place was known as Howards Mill. The mill building, still standing in 1989, although enlarged and altered, is probably the oldest surviving industrial building in Oregon. Mulino post office was established Mar. 21, 1882, with James G. Foster first postmaster.

Multnomah, MULTNOMAH. The community of Multnomah took its name from Multnomah County. The Oregon Electric Railway was built from Portland south to Salem in 1907 and began operation in 1908 and it was the policy of the officials to apply Indian names, wherever possible, to the stations as they were established. For the origin of Multnomah, *see* Multnomah County. The post office at Multnomah was established Feb. 7, 1912, with Nelson Thomas first postmaster. It was closed Apr. 15, 1940 but has operated since as a Portland station.

Multnomah Channel, COLUMBIA, MULTNOMAH. For many years the channel between Sauvie Island and the mainland to the west was known as Willamette Slough, probably because its southern entrance was close to the mouth of Willamette River. Commercial interests and citizens interested in historical matters prevailed upon the USBGN to adopt the name Multnomah Channel for this stream. Multnomah Channel was discovered on Oct. 28, 1792, by W. R. Broughton, and named Calls River, apparently for Sir John Call. *See* Meany's *Vancouver's Discovery of Puget Sound*, p. 261. Lewis and Clark called this channel Wappato Inlet because it lay to the west of what they called Wappato Island, now Sauvie Island. Wilkes used the name Warrior Branch because the stream joined the Columbia at Warrior Point. Sauvie Island was referred to as Multnomah Island by Wilkes.

Multnomah County. Multnomah County was created Dec. 22, 1854, and was taken from Washington and Clackamas counties as they then existed. Multnomah County has an area, according to ODOT, of 474 square miles and is the smallest county in the state. Multnomah is an Indian name. The word is first used by Lewis and Clark in their journals for Nov. 3, 1805, with the style Mulknomah, referring to the stream now known as the Willamette. On the following day the explorers record a village of *Mulknomans* on the east side of what is now known as Sauvie Island. On Apr. 2, 1806, the stream is mentioned again in the spelling Multnomah, and this form is used on the maps prepared by the party, not only for the stream but also for the village on the east side of Sauvie Island. Coues thinks that the name as applied to the stream meant only that part of the Willamette below the falls, and says the word is a corruption of *nematlnomaq*, meaning down river. The Multnomah Indians were of the Chinookan tribe. The map of Lewis and Clark indicated that Multnomah River headed about where Great Salt Lake is now known to be. The map is said to have established the 42nd parallel as the boundary with Spain.

Multnomah Falls, MULTNOMAH. The compiler has been unable to learn who named these falls on Multnomah Creek, but Geo. H. Himes said that they were called Multnomah Falls in the 1860s, and he was of the opinion that S. G. Reed may have named them with the idea of trying to popularize points along the river for steamboat excursions. Lewis and Clark, Wilkes, and many others mentioned the falls on the south bank of the Columbia between the mouth of the Sandy and the Cascades, but no individual names seem to have been applied. Pioneer estimates of the height of Multnomah Falls, amounting to as much as 1000 feet, were grossly in error. In 1916 the USGS made detailed computations of the height of the falls and found the following elevations above standard sea level: Top of upper falls, 659.8 feet. Base of upper falls, 117.5 feet. Top of lower falls, 103.1 feet. Base of lower falls, 39.8 feet. Total drop of two falls, 620.0 feet. Floor of concrete bridge, above lower falls, 134.7 feet. The lodge adjacent to the Historic Columbia River Highway was designed by Portland architect A. E. Doyle and has been listed on the National Register of Historic Places. Multnomah Falls is the most visited outdoor scenic location in the state, attracting some two million visitors a year.

Multorpor Butte, CLACKAMAS. This prominent butte, elevation 4657 feet, lies just south of Government Camp, and is easily seen from the Mount Hood Loop Highway. It was named for the Multorpor Republican Club of Portland. The name Multorpor was made by combining the first parts of Multnomah, Oregon and Portland. The name Multiple for this mountain is wrong.

Muncey Creek, BAKER. This creek is a small tributary of Pine Creek about a mile upstream from the mouth of North Pine Creek. It bears the name of Edwin F. Muncey who took up land along it about the time of World War I. Muncey was postmaster at Halfway for many years. The stream shows on the 1957 USGS Copperfield quadrangle as Mitchell Creek but this was corrected by the USBGN in *Decision List 8701*.

Munkers, LINN. This station west of Scio was named for the Munkers family, prominent early-day settlers of Linn County. One of the family owned the land where the station was established.

Munra Point, MULTNOMAH. Munra Point was named in 1915 in honor of "Grandma" Munra, who for many years kept a railroad eating house at Bonneville, and later at Meacham. She was a widely known pioneer woman, and her name was attached to the point in question by a committee representing various Oregon historical organizations. Munra Point is just south of Bonneville, between Tanner Creek and Moffett Creek. The name has been approved by the USBGN. In 1928 the Union Pacific Railroad named a station (siding) east of Pendleton for "Grandma" Munra.

Munsel Lake, LANE. This lake is about two miles north of Florence. It was named for David L. Munsel, who operated a small furniture factory and repair shop on Munsel Creek. Munsel, who was a French cabinet maker, also spelled his name Munselle, but Munsel is now the well established style for the name of the lake and creek.

Munson Creek, TILLAMOOK. Munson Creek and Munson Falls about six miles south of Tillamook were both named for Goran Munson who came from Michigan and settled along the creek in 1889. This information was provided by Mr. Munson's daughter, Mrs. D. H. Near of Tillamook.

Munson Point, KLAMATH. This point and the valley just to the east were named by Captain Oliver C. Applegate for a Doctor Munson, physician at Klamath Indian Agency, who died in 1871 from overexertion while climbing near the point. *See* article in Klamath *Record*, Mar. 22, 1918.

Murder Creek, LINN. This stream is just northeast of Albany. It owes its name to the fact that on Feb. 8, 1862, Andrew J. Pate killed George Lamb near its banks, and Pate was hanged at Albany on May 17, 1862. Pate was the first man to be hanged in Linn County. Additional details about this murder are contained in a very rare pamphlet in the files of the Oregon Historical Society, which gives Pate's confession. The stream has been called Fisher Creek and also Powell Creek for nearby settlers, but Murder Creek seems well established and is used on government maps.

Murderers Creek, GRANT. Colonel William Thompson, in *Reminiscences of a Pioneer*, p. 62, says this stream was named in the 1860s because Indians killed a party of eight prospectors who were exploring its banks. For additional information about the naming of this stream, *see* news article by Martha Stewart in Canyon City *Blue Mountain Eagle*, Oct. 21, 1927.

Murphy, JOSEPHINE. B. O. R. Murphy settled on Applegate River May 7, 1854, and took up a donation land claim. The stream running through the claim became known as Murphy Creek. On Jan. 7, 1875, Jacob O. C. Wimer had a post office established called Murphy in honor of the early settler.

Murphy Bar, POLK. Murphy Bar is on the south bank of the Willamette River about three miles southeast of Independence. It was named for William Murphy who lived nearby many years ago.

Murphy Creek, WALLOWA. This creek was named for one Murphy, a pioneer trapper and hunter, who built a cabin on the creek. In 1926 part of this cabin was still standing. The stream flows into Minam River.

Murphys Camp, TILLAMOOK. Murphys Camp is on Murphys Camp Creek on the upper reaches of East Fork Trask River. Both are named for the activities of the Murphy Timber Company prior to World War II. Ed M. Murphy, born 1870, died July 22, 1949, was a prominent Oregon timber man who, with his four sons, was active in logging the then recently burned Trask River drainage. Murphys Camp was where Murphy's logging railroad connected to the Flora Mainline operated by the Joe Flora Logging Company.

Mussel Creek, CURRY. This stream empties into the Pacific about two miles north of Sisters Rocks. Reinhart, in *The Golden Frontier*, p. 80, says it was named after a small band of Indians. They apparently were part of the Tututni tribe.

Mutton Mountains, WASCO. These mountains are in the northeast part of the Warm Springs Indian Reservation and have an extreme elevation of about 4500 feet. The eastern slopes are excessively steep down to the Deschutes River, and the group is so cut off from the routes of travel that it is little visited. Pierce Mays, a well-known resident of Wasco County, said that the Mutton Mountains were named for the large number of mountain sheep that formerly lived thereon. That eastern Oregon had at one time plenty of mountain sheep is attested by J. E. Snow, whose statement to that effect appears on the editorial page of the *Oregonian* for Dec. 10, 1925. The use of the name Mutton Mountains began before 1855. There is a good deal of information about the mountain sheep in Vernon Bailey's *Mammals and Life Zones of Oregon*, beginning on p. 63. The principal variety in Oregon is known as the rimrock or lava bed sheep, credited to David Douglas as of 1829, but mentioned by Ogden as early as 1825.

Muttonchop Butte, KLAMATH. Muttonchop Butte, elevation 5489 feet, is about ten miles north of Chemult and west of the Southern Pacific Cascade line. The first explanation of the name that the compiler can find is that when the area was mapped by the USFS about 1930, the contour lines of this butte made a very fair representation of a mutton chop. This may be seen by inspecting the USGS map of the Muttonchop Butte quadrangle. In June 1944, R. W. Crawford, supervisor of the Deschutes National Forest at Bend, wrote the compiler that he had been told that about 1913 a German took up a timber claim on Spruce Creek near this butte. This man grew some rather natty side whiskers and was generally called Old Muttonchops because of the hirsute adornment. Muttonchop Butte is said to have been named for this local settler. This story sounds reasonable.

Myer Creek, JACKSON. This creek empties into Bear Creek at Talent. It is named for Nathaniel Myer who settled in Jackson County in the 1850s. The form Meyer is incorrect

Myers Creek, CURRY. Myers Creek is just south of Cape Sebastian and is a well-known stream flowing into Pacific Ocean. The name is variously spelled, but the form Myers has been adopted by USBGN. This was done on the recommendation of F. S. Moore, formerly county assessor of Curry County. In a letter to the compiler, dated Mar. 29, 1932, Mr. Moore says that the stream bears the name of one Myers who settled nearby in the late 1850s and mined the beach sands. Myers abandoned his cabin. When F. S. Moore was about seven years old his father moved the family into the Myers cabin, and used the building while he built a new house on the Moore property about a mile to the north.

Myrick, UMATILLA. Myrick is a station on the Burlington Northern northeast of Pendleton. The place was originally known as Warren, but was changed to Myrick because of confusion with Warren in Columbia County. Samuel Jackson Myrick came to Oregon from Missouri in the spring of 1884 and settled near the station now known as Myrick. When it was found necessary to abandon the name of Warren it was decided to name the place for Myrick.

Myrtle Creek, DOUGLAS. Myrtle Creek was named for the groves of Oregon myrtle in the vicinity. The site was first settled upon by James B. Weaver, in 1851, who sold it to J. Bailey for a yoke of oxen. Bailey sold to Lazarus Wright in 1852, who sold it to John Hall in 1862. Hall laid out the town in 1865. Myrtle Creek post office was established on Feb. 18, 1854, with Lazarus Wright first postmaster. In the late 1860s a movement was on foot to divide Douglas County, and Myrtle Creek had hopes of becoming the county seat for the south part. This county division was not made. For information about Oregon myrtle, *see* Myrtle Point.

Myrtle Park, GRANT, HARNEY. In 1942, Archie McGowan of Burns became interested in the problem of the origin of this name for the natural park southwest of Canyon City. There were no myrtle trees in that part of Oregon and a botanical significance seemed improbable. Mr. McGowan concluded that the locality might have been named for Minnie Myrtle Miller, wife of Joaquin Miller. He wrote an interesting letter on the subject in Canyon City *Eagle* for Apr. 10, 1942. As to whether or not Mrs. Minnie Myrtle Miller ever lived in Grant County, the evidence seems positive that she did. Wagner's *Joaquin Miller* indicates that Mrs. Miller lived with the poet in Canyon City and the two youngest children were born there. In 1943 Mr. McGowan verified his theory. He found living near the park one Andy Pierce, aged 90, sound of mind and body, who joined the Canyon City gold rush in 1864. Pierce had lived in that vicinity ever since and was well acquainted with the Miller family. He made the positive statement that the Millers spent some time in an old cabin in the park and that Joaquin Miller named the place in honor of his wife.

Myrtle Point, COOS. The early history of this place is given by Dodge in his *History of Coos and Curry Counties*, chapter 14. It was a natural rendezvous of the Indians. Henry Meyers laid out the town about 1861 and named it Meyersville. It remained a paper community until 1866 when Chris Lehnherr bought the property and built a small flour mill. He named the place Ott in compliment to an old friend and his son. Lehnherr became the first postmaster in Aug. 1872. Binger Hermann and Edward Bender became interested in the townsite and suggested that the name be changed to Myrtle Point. Postal records show that the name of the post office Ott was changed to Myrtle Point in Dec. 1876. The name was due to the geographical location and also to the fact that the community was started where there was an abundance of myrtle. This Oregon or Coos Bay myrtle is the same as California laurel, *Umbellularia californica*. It is an evergreen tree, distinguished by a strong camphor odor. In favorable conditions it grows 80 feet high and four feet in diameter. In the dense forest it grows with a clean straight trunk, but elsewhere and more commonly it has a thick trunk and large low limbs. Its range in Oregon is in the Coast Range and Siskiyou Mountains. It has a beautiful grain and excels as a cabinet and finishing wood. It grows extensively in southwest Oregon.

Namorf, MALHEUR. Namorf station west of Harper was named for George Froman, a local resident, by spelling his name backward.

Nansene, WASCO. The name Nansene seems to have been derived from an Indian word used to describe Fifteenmile Creek. Fremont gives the style Tinanens Creek, but it is doubtless the same as Nansene. Nansene post office was established May 17, 1880, with William C. Adams postmaster. It was on the ridge southeast of Dufur and the name has been perpetuated by Nansene School. Nansene post office was closed in Feb. 1894.

Nan-Scott Lake, LINN. This lake near Marion Forks was named for Nan and Scott Young, long time residents of Marion Forks.

Napton, MALHEUR. This station was named for J. S. Napton, a local resident. The place is on the Union Pacific Railroad 17 miles south of Nyssa.

Narrows, HARNEY. Narrows is a descriptive name suggested by the narrow channel connecting Harney and Mud lakes to Malheur Lake. It is commonly referred to as The Narrows. A community was started by Charles A. Haines about 1892. A post office named Springer was established nearby in Aug. 1889, with Lewis B. Springer postmaster, and the name was changed to Narrows in Apr. 1892. The office operated with one intermission until closed in 1936. In dry years both Harney and Mud lakes have little or no water. However, the Harney Basin is exceptionally flat and one or two wet years can increase the area of all three lakes substantially. For many years the Burns-Frenchglen highway has crossed The Narrows on a bridge. In the early 1980s the water level came up several feet and it was necessary to raise the highway. At that time little remained of the community. By 1984 Malheur, Mud and Harney lakes had combined to become quite the largest lake in Oregon with an area of 280 square miles. The Union Pacific Railroad branch line from Ontario to Burns was flooded out as were numerous ranches. The level remained relatively constant in 1985 as plans were discussed to dig a drainage canal through Virginia Valley to Malheur River. The *Oregonian*, Apr. 15, 1966, p. 33, has an article describing the situation as of that date. Pauline Braymen describes the 1985 situation in the *Sunday Oregonian*, Apr. 28, 1985, p. 3M. By 1989, the water level had receded enough so there were again three distinct bodies of water. Undoubtedly, this will not be the last change in the size and shape of these lakes. *See also* Malheur Lake.

Nash Crater, LINN. This crater in the Cascade Range was named for Wallis Nash. *See* Nashville. The railroad enterprise in which Nash was interested, projected a line into eastern Oregon, and several geographic features near the survey were named for the promoters. Nash Crater is just south of the junction of the North and South Santiam highways and has an elevation of 4770 feet. Little Nash Crater, elevation 4401 feet, is just west of the junction.

Nashville, LINCOLN. Nashville was named for Wallis Nash, a native of England, who visited Oregon in 1877, and came to this state to settle in 1879. He was prominently identified with various enterprises in Benton and Lincoln counties, including the construction of the railroad between Corvallis and Yaquina Bay. He lived at Nashville for many years. For interesting notes on his career, *see* his *A Lawyer's Life on Two Continents*. Nash was born near London on Aug. 16, 1837, and died at Nashville in 1926.

Nasoma, WASHINGTON. Nasoma was a station on the Oregon Electric Railway southwest of Tualatin. When the railroad was built many Indian names were applied to the stations. The word *Nasoma* was apparently derived from one of the bands of Indians that originally lived near Port Orford in Curry County. The name was used by the railway company because it had a pleasing sound and not for any local reason.

Nasty Pond, LAKE. Nasty Pond is a small, intermittent lake two miles southwest of Alkali Lake. It was named in 1984 by Sandra Harrison and Sarah Metcalfe of Oxford University and Patricia McDowell and Jane Benjamin of the University of Oregon. The four were on a field expedition where they sampled water chemistry, soils, salt-tolerant algae and micro-organisms. A name was needed for use in scientific reports and Nasty Pond was appropriate because of the appearance and odor.

Natal, COLUMBIA. The name Natal was once applied to a post office situated on Nehalem River between Pittsburg and Mist. This post office was established Oct. 2, 1889, with Roderick D. Cole first and only postmaster. The office was discontinued to Mist on Jan. 26, 1891. Omar C. Spencer had a chance to dig up some evidence about the name Natal and on Mar. 2, 1949, reported, among other things, that it was Mr. Cole's notion that the name of the office should honor N. C. Dale, who had owned land in the locality in the early 1870s and had accommodated his neighbors by fetching their mail from Mist to his own home. He served as county clerk for Columbia County from July 1884, until July 1888. Dale's first name was Nathaniel and the best available information is that the name Natal was an arbitrary contraction of his first name. The locality is still called Natal and the name is used by Natal Grange.

Natron, LANE. Natron is a station on the Southern Pacific Cascade line just east of Springfield. In the 1920s, the new railroad through Klamath Falls was often referred to as the Natron Cut-off. The name was suggested by Thomas Condon to Richard Koehler, then manager of the Southern Pacific Company lines in Oregon for a proposed station on the East Side Branch. This was long before the railroad was completed to Oakridge in 1910. The following quotation is part of a letter from Condon to Koehler dated July 30, 1891, printed in full in Ellen Condon McCornack's *Thomas Condon, Pioneer Geologist of Oregon*, p. 220. "First, Natron. If your proposed station is, as I suppose it is, in sight of Mt. Pisgah, east of Springfield. The trap rock of this mountain has in it an abundance of fine specimens of the mineral Natrolite; the principal root of the Natrolite is Natron-Soda. Natron is a short pleasant name, and as far as I know, new."

Naylox, KLAMATH. Naylox was the name of a pioneer stage station or roadhouse on the east shore of Upper Klamath Lake about midway of Klamath Falls and Modoc Point. It was not far from the well-known Barkley Spring. For a story by Mary W. Case about this old stopping place, *see* magazine sect. of the *Oregon Journal*, Mar. 17, 1946. Naylox took its name from Naylox Ridge, a prominent geographic feature that stands just east of the highway. The Klamath Indian word *Nilaksh* or *Nilaks* was the basis of the name Naylox, meaning Daylight Mountain, or mountain over which the sun rose. White settlers also used the style Nailix, but the form Naylox has been in general use for the locality for many decades. For additional information, *see* Gatschet's *Dictionary of the Klamath Language*, p. 243. Naylox post office was established Feb. 7, 1882, with Leroy S. Dyar first postmaster. The office was finally closed June 30, 1896.

Neacoxie Creek, CLATSOP. This is a stream on Clatsop Plains. Its course has undergone several changes since pioneer days, largely because of drifting sands. Part of the stream flows north from Cullaby Lake, then around a hairpin bend near Camp Rilea. During recent years the south part of the stream has drained Neacoxie Lake southward into the estuary of Necanicum River. If the long sand ridges shift positions, the course of the stream may be interfered with still further. The name is derived from *Neahcoxie*, the Clatsop Indian name of the village at the mouth of the creek. The form *Neacoxie* has been adopted by the USBGN, and is in general use. George Gibbs, in *Alphabetical Vocabulary of the Chinook Language*, New York, 1863, says this name, which he spells *Ni-a-kok-si*, is said to refer to the small pine trees near the mouth of the stream. Neacoxie Lake is sometimes called Sunset Lake, but that is not the historic name. Sunset Lake is a style that has resulted from real estate activity.

Neahkahnie Mountain, TILLAMOOK. There has at times been some controversy about the meaning of the Indian name of this bold headland north of Nehalem River. Neahkahnie is a place of romance and mystery. Tales of buried treasure, marooned Spaniards, galleons laden with beeswax candles and suchlike, have drawn the attention of the white man for three-quarters of a century. Chunks of engraved wax and curious letters on half-buried stones have been all the more mysterious. Joseph H. Frost's diary of 1841 in *OHQ*, v. 35, p. 242, says: "This mountain is called Ne-a-karny—after one of the deities of these natives, who, it is said by them, a long time since, while sitting on this mountain, turned into a stone, which stone, it is said, presents a colossal figure of Ne-akarny to this day. And in our passage over the mountain, which is a prairie on the side next the ocean, we discovered a stone which presented a figure of this kind." Silas B. Smith says in *OHQ*, v. 1, p. 321, that *Ne-kah-ni* meant the precipice overlooking the ocean, the abode of *Ekahni*, the supreme god. Lee and Frost in *Ten Years in Oregon*, 1844, p. 343, give the Clatsop word *Acarna*, meaning chief deity. Mrs. Ed Gervais, a Nehalem Indian, is authority for the statement that the name *Neahkahnie* had its origin in the word used by the supposed Spanish wreck survivors when they saw elk on the side of the mountain, and exclaimed: "Carne," meaning meat. This is probably fanciful. *Neahkahnie* is one of a number of coast Indian names beginning with the prefix *Ne-*, which had to do with villages or places where certain tribes lived. These names include also Necanicum, Nehalem, Neskowin, Netarts, Nestucca and Neacoxie. John Gill informed the writer that a Clatsop Indian told him *ne* meant a place. Neahkahnie Mountain presents a bold front to the Pacific, and stands 1621 feet above the water, an imposing sight. The best collection of romances and facts about the place is in the book by S. J. Cotton, *Stories of Nehalem*. Thomas H. Rogers' *Nehalem* should be read by all interested in Neahkahnie. It contains an excellent picture of the glyphic rock. For additional references, *see* Nehalem.

Neal Camp Burn, JACKSON. This spot in the northeast part of the county was named for Carl B. Neal, an early USFS supervisor of the Umpqua National Forest.

Neal Creek, HOOD RIVER. Peter Neal ran a sawmill on what is now known as Neal Creek in the early 1880s, and the stream was named for him. He built a dam near what was later the Wilson Fike farm and the mill pond was a favorite fishing place.

Neathammer Gulch, JACKSON. This draw empties into Evans Creek from the north some five miles east of Wimer. Daniel E. Neathammer came to Oregon in 1853 and to Jackson County with his family in 1857. In 1874 he bought a farm along the creek and later added more property. His brother, Jesse Neathammer, also owned land closer to Wimer.

Neawanna Creek, CLATSOP. This stream flows into the estuary of Necanicum River just north of Seaside. In earlier days it was generally called Wahanna Creek, although some people called it Ohannah or Wahannah in the belief that it was named for a member of the R. W. Morrison family whose name was Hannah. This etymology always seemed dubious to the compiler, and was without substantial confirmation. The result of this variety of names was confusion. In 1930 Miss Clara C. Munson of Warrenton interested herself in the business of getting a better form of name for this little stream, and proposed Neawanna Creek, in the belief that the spelling more nearly expressed the original name. This style closely approximates the word *Newanah* which came to the compiler on the authority of the late John Gill of Portland, who was a reliable student of Chinook place names. Various official and civic organizations sponsored the change, and as a result, the USBGN on Feb. 4, 1931, adopted the style Neawanna Creek and apparently everyone in the vicinity is happy. The meaning of this Indian word is unknown, although it is probable that it referred to a location along the bank of this stream near a rapid, or a waterfall. A large number of Indian place names in northwestern Oregon began with the syllable *Ne*. See Neahkahnie Mountain.

Necanicum, CLATSOP. This community no longer has a post office. It was originally called Ahlers, for Herman Ahlers, a local resident. The name was changed to Push on Apr. 13, 1899. The post office was subsequently known as Necanicum on account of Necanicum River which flowed nearby. For the origin of that name, *see* Necanicum River. Necanicum post office was at the Sly place about twelve miles southeast of Seaside on US-26, the Wolf Creek Highway. Ahlers selected the name Push because he expected the place to turn into an enterprising community. The name was changed from Push to Necanicum on May 27, 1907. Ahlers was postmaster at all three offices mentioned.

Necanicum River, CLATSOP. Necanicum is one of the many Indian names in northwest Oregon beginning with *Ne*, which was apparently a prefix indicating place. This stream flows into the Pacific Ocean at Seaside. William Clark named it Clatsop River on Jan. 7, 1806, but that name did not prevail. *Necanicum* is derived from *Ne-hay-ne-hum*, the name of an Indian lodge up the stream, according to H. S. Lyman, *OHQ*, v. 1, p. 321. The name is given as *Nekonikon* in OPA *Transactions*, 1887, p. 86. In 1929 Herman Ahlers, for some years postmaster at Necanicum post office, wrote that the name meant a gap in the mountains, apparently referring to the valley. In pioneer days the stream was known as Latty Creek, for William Latty, who took up a land claim in what is now the south part of Seaside. Necanicum is the form of spelling in general use and has been adopted by the USBGN.

Neece Canyon, SHERMAN. Neece Canyon is the west fork of Frank Fulton Canyon starting near Locust Grove. It was named for the Neece family several of whom took up government land there in the 1880s. Giles French in the *Golden Land* refers to T. Clay Neece as a part-time preacher and music teacher.

Needy, CLACKAMAS. Geo. H. Himes told the compiler that this place was named, not because of the character of the soil, which was excellent, but because of the unfortunate condition of some pioneer settlers who lived there. Leslie M. Scott in *History of the Oregon Country*, says that the place was also known as Hardscrabble. Inquiries made by the compiler in 1943 failed to confirm stories of poor soil in the locality. Needy post office was established Feb. 16, 1855, with John M. Bacon postmaster. John S. Vinson in an article on the *Oregonian* editorial page, Mar. 17, 1928, says that James H. Brents originated the names Needy and Hardscrabble, and gives additional history of the place.

Neely Mountain, LANE. Neely Mountain is one of the minor points of the Coast Range lying a couple of miles northwest of Mapleton, within one of the bends of the Siuslaw River. It has an elevation of 1677 feet. The name was applied in 1948 at the request of the USFS to commemorate William Wallace Neely, a Lane County homesteader. There is an interesting editorial about W. W. Neely and the mountain in the *Oregonian*, Aug. 26, 1948. Thomas J. Neely took a Timber claim on its slopes in 1903. The compiler does not know how these two may have been related.

Neer City, COLUMBIA. Neer City is a ghost town on the Columbia River Highway at a county road junction about a half a mile north of Goble. This place was laid out by Abe Neer and the plat filed for record on Aug. 31, 1883. It was a point on the Columbia River where boats found it convenient to get cordwood for their boilers and a little settlement of woodcutters developed at Neer City. An account of the activity, by Mrs. Abe Neer, is in the Saint Helens *Sentinel-Mist*, Mar. 24, 1942. The *Postal Guide* for Jan. 1888, lists Neer post office, with that style.

Neet, DOUGLAS. Neet post office was near the middle of T 31S, R 2W, about five miles south of the place now called Tiller. The office was established Oct. 11, 1899, with Charles W. Neet first and only postmaster. The office was closed Feb. 28,

1901. The office was named in compliment to the postmaster. Charles Neet was a homesteader. In Mar. 1947, Mrs. Bertha B. Pennell of Tiller wrote the compiler that the office was in the log home of Neet, standing on the side hill west of Drew Creek, a little over a mile from the place now called Drew. This old building, apparently still standing in 1947, was a couple of miles upstream from the mouth of Drew Creek. Drew post office was not established until about a year after Neet was discontinued.

Negro Ben Mountain, JACKSON. For many years this 4500-foot peak in the Siskiyou Mountains, a little to the southwest of Ruch and Applegate River, was called Nigger Ben Mountain. The name was very old, and appears to have been derived from a Negro named Ben who operated a small blacksmith shop near the river and accommodated miners by sharpening picks and other tools. In his spare time Ben worked a tunnel on a small prospect he had developed. There are a number of stories about Ben, most of them probably apocryphal. Ben's last name appears to have been lost to posterity. In 1964, when integration was the watchword, the USBGN in *Decision List 6402* changed the name to its present form. There is no evidence the original name was derogatory, and if every name that might offend some ethnic group must be altered to suit the changing times, the authorities might just as well resort to a simple numerical designation.

Nehalem, TILLAMOOK. The Nehalem Indians were a Salish tribe, formerly living on Nehalem River. Duflot de Mofras gives the name as *Nahelem* in *Exploration*, 1844, v. 2, p. 104. The name is *Naalem* in Senate Executive Document 39, Thirty-second Congress, first session, p. 2, 1852; *Ne-ay-lem* in *OHQ*, v. 1, p. 320, by Silas B. Smith. The name is used for the town of Nehalem and Nehalem River. The latter flows in all four of the northwest counties of the state and cuts completely through the Coast Range. The first bold point extending to the sea north of Nehalem Bay is Neahkahnie Mountain. There is no little romance about Nehalem and Neahkahnie, having to do with treasure and marooned Spanish sailors. *See* Neahkahnie. In addition to references given thereunder, *see* Scott's *History of the Oregon Country*, v. 3, p. 125, for data on the Nehalem beeswax controversy. USGS Bulletin 590, *Geology of Northwestern Oregon*, goes into the geology of the Nehalem region and strongly supports the beeswax theory of the Nehalem wax as against the natural mineral theory. John Gill told the compiler in 1927 that many years ago he had discussed the origin of Clatsop County names with a Clatsop Indian, Mrs. Jenny Williams, the widow of Bill Williams, who lived near Seaside. Mrs. Williams informed Mr. Gill that the Indian word *Nehalem* meant "place where people live" and indicated that the prefix *Ne* used frequently in the Indian names of northwestern Oregon, meant a place or locality. Nehalem post office was established in Aug. 1870 or 1871, with Samuel Corwin first postmaster. This office was probably about two miles north of the present community at the locality sometimes called Upper Nehalem, which is not now organized. The post office was moved to suit the convenience of the available postmasters and was from time to time at the Hunt, Scovell and Alley places. When John M. Alley was postmaster the name of the office was changed on Feb. 6, 1884, to Onion Peak. By this time the office was some miles north up the valley of North Fork Nehalem River and it was of course named for the nearby mountain, Onion Peak, a conspicuous landmark. This office was closed Apr. 7, 1893. While all this was going on a new post office with the name Nehalem was established May 12, 1884, with Henry Ober postmaster. This office was at or near the present community and has been in continuous operation since it was established.

Neil Creek, JACKSON. Neil Creek is tributary to Bear Creek south of Ashland. It was named for Claiborne Neil, a pioneer settler who was born in Tennessee in 1821 and came to Oregon in 1853. He settled in Jackson County the following year and took a donation land claim that included the stream. Neil installed one of the earliest irrigation projects in the area when he diverted the creek through his large orchard.

Nekbobets Lake, MARION. This lake west of Olallie Lake was named after World War II by a fish planting crew. The name is a reversed combination of Ken, Bob and Steve Koski, sons of Reino Koski, crew chief. *See* Alice Lake. The form Neknoberts is incorrect.

Nellies Cove, CURRY. Nellies Cove is the middle of three coves just west of the bay at Port Orford and just southwest of the town of Port Orford. Nellies Point is the promontory on the east of Nellies Cove. These features were named for Sarah Ellen Tichenor, youngest daughter of Captain William Tichenor, the famous pioneer of the locality. She was known as Nellie and the cove and point were her favorite spots on the old Tichenor property. The cove to the east of Nellies Cove is Tichenor Cove. Sarah Ellen Tichenor was born in Illinois in 1848. She was brought to Port Orford probably in May 1852, and spent her girlhood there. Later she married E. W. McGraw and lived in San Francisco. In early days the town of Gold Beach was called Ellensburg, in compliment to Ellen Tichenor.

Nelscott, LINCOLN. This has become an important summer resort on the Oregon Coast Highway. A letter by Mrs. Alma Anderson, published in North Lincoln *Coast Guard* for May 4, 1939, indicates that the name was formed by combining parts of the names of Charles P. Nelson and Dr. W. G. Scott, who opened the townsite in Apr. 1926. Nelson died in Dec. 1946. For editorial comment about his activities, *see Sunday Oregonian*, Dec. 25, 1946. On Dec. 8, 1964, Nelscott voted to become part of a new community to be called Lincoln City.

Nelson Canyon, MORROW, UMATILLA. James Nelson settled along Butter Creek south of Vinson in the 1880s and later took up several parcels of land near the head of this canyon.

Nelson Creek, LANE. Nelson Creek is a small tributary of Champion Creek just north of Fairview Peak. Ray Nelson in *Facts and Yarns of the Bohemia, Oregon Gold*

Mines says it was named for Andy Nelson, his father, who mined in the area around the end of the 19th century.

Nelson Creek, WHEELER. Rufus K. Nelson was a native of Kentucky who settled near Mitchell in 1877 along the creek which bears his name. His large family included three sons who later ranched nearby, and Nelson Reservoir was built by a grandson, George W. Nelson. R. K. Nelson was killed in a horse drive accident in 1889.

Nena Creek, WASCO. Nena Creek rises in Mutton Mountains in the northeast corner of the Warm Springs Indian Reservation. It flows into Deschutes River. Indians inform the writer that the word means tall white cottonwood trees that grow near the stream. The style *Nee-nee* was used in the Pacific Railroad Surveys *Reports* in 1855. The form Nena Creek does not reflect the real Indian pronunciation, but it appears on government maps. It is also the name of a railroad station, and appears to be here to stay.

Nenamusa, TILLAMOOK. Nenamusa Falls are on the east border of the county in the west part of T 4S, R 7W, in the Nestucca River drainage. Nenamusa post office was established nearby Jan. 16, 1912, with Peter N. Forsyth first and only postmaster. The office was closed Aug. 31, 1917. It was about eight miles east of Blaine. Information about the origin of the name of the falls is unsatisfactory. The word is said to be Indian, meaning sweetheart, or love, but the writer has not been able to trace any such word or meaning in available Indian dictionaries. It is reported that the word may have been brought to Oregon from an eastern state. Indians known by the writer had no knowledge of the sentiment of love as known to white people, or of the word sweetheart, either. The prefix *ne* in the northwest Oregon area was used by Indians as a locative, and may be translated, roughly, as a place. The nearest approach to Nenamusa offered by the Chinook jargon is the expression *ne moosum*, which may be translated as place to sleep. It might refer to a place for a temporary camp. It has been suggested that Nenamusa means a place for a honeymoon, but all this is conjectural.

Neotsu, LINCOLN. Neotsu is a post office on US-101, the Oregon Coast Highway, near the north end of Devils Lake. The name is said to be an Indian word referring to the lake. The compiler has been unable to get a satisfactory translation. There are a number of Indian legends about Devils Lake. Apparently it was a place where evil skookums flourished. Davidson, in the *Coast Pilot*, 1889, uses the spelling *Na-ah-so*, but does not explain the word. The compiler has heard Devils Lake referred to as a *me-sah'-chie chuck*, which is Chinook jargon for evil water.

Neskowin, TILLAMOOK. Mrs. Sarah H. Page in a letter to the *Oregonian* published June 30, 1925, says that the name Neskowin is an Indian word, meaning plenty fish. Mrs. Page was appointed postmaster of this office in 1887 and the locality was then known as Slab Creek. Years before a ship had been wrecked on the coast and a quantity of slabwood washed up on the beach. One day she heard an Indian say as he pointed to the nearby stream, "Neskowin, Neskowin." She asked him what Neskowin meant and he said "plenty fish, plenty fish." In 1925 the USBGN was asked to change the name of the stream from Slab Creek to Neskowin Creek, and this was done, on Oct. 7 of that year. Neskowin post office was established Dec. 4, 1886, with Weston Burdick first postmaster. The office has not been in continuous service, and not always in the same place. When a small boy, the compiler always heard this locality referred to as Neskowin, with the accent on the second syllable, rhyming with how. Tillamook County pioneers have confirmed this pronunciation.

Nesmith Point, MULTNOMAH. Nesmith Point, elevation 3878 feet, is the highest point on the cliffs overlooking the Columbia River in the gorge through the Cascade Range. It is just south of Warrendale and east of Yeon Mountain. The point was named as the result of a suggestion made in 1915 by a committee of the Mazamas who selected a number of place names for unnamed geographic features adjacent to the new Columbia River Highway. James Willis Nesmith was born in New Brunswick July 23, 1820, while his parents, residents of Maine, were on a short visit. The Nesmith family was of Scottish ancestry, and came to New England from the north of Ireland in 1718. James W. Nesmith, as the result of his father's financial reverses, had no early advantages, and was forced to lead a more or less roving life eventually reaching the state of Ohio. He attempted to emigrate to Oregon in 1842, but was too late to join Dr. White's party that year. He was a member of the emigration of 1843, and was elected orderly sergeant. For his diary of events during the emigration *see OHQ*, v. 7, p. 329. For his reminiscences of the emigration *see* OPA *Transactions* for 1875. The diary describes a severe windstorm on the Columbia River below the Cascades, which compelled him to put ashore and finish the day reading *The Merry Wives of Windsor*. It was this incident that suggested his name to the committee for Nesmith Point. Nesmith was a judge under the provisional government, representative from Polk County, captain in the Cayuse and other Indian wars, colonel of volunteers in the Yakima War, United States marshal, and superintendent of Indian affairs. He served in the United States Senate from 1861 to 1867, and although a Democrat, served on the military committee, and upheld the cause of the Union in every possible way. He served as representative in Congress from 1873 to 1875, and spent the rest of his life on his farm at Rickreall, where he died June 17, 1885. For Harvey W. Scott's estimate of Colonel Nesmith, *see* the *Oregonian*, June 18, 1885, and also Scott's *History of the Oregon Country*, v. 5, p. 172, *et seq.* For description of Nesmith's grave and epitaph, *see* the *Oregonian*, May 8, 1895, p. 3; for tribute from U. S. Grant, Mar. 13, 1901, p. 8; for episodes of Nesmith's life, July 18, 1897, p. 6. For other references *see* Scott's *History of the Oregon Country*, v. 1, p. 308. There was a railroad station Nesmith, in Polk County, south of Rickreall, but a short distance from the Nesmith farm. There was also a railroad station Nesmith on the Oregon Electric in Washington County.

Nestocton, TILLAMOOK. The Nestocton post office was one of the oldest in

Tillamook County. It was established Feb. 7, 1867, with Leonard Killam first postmaster. This post office remained in service until June 13, 1904, when it was discontinued, probably because of the extension of rural delivery which brought about the closing of so many post offices about that time. The locality of Nestocton was settled in the sixties. It is about eight or nine miles south along US-101, the Oregon Coast Highway, from Tillamook. It is obvious from the names of its ten postmasters that the office was moved to fit their availability. Nestocton was the second post office in Tillamook County. The first post office was Tillamook, established Mar. 12, 1866. The name is obviously an Indian word, but the compiler has been unable to learn its meaning.

Nestucca River, TILLAMOOK, YAMHILL. Nestucca is an Indian name for a part of this stream or a point on its banks, or for a tribe living nearby. As far as the writer knows there is no English translation of the word *Nestucca*. This stream is frequently called Big Nestucca River in contradistinction to Little Nestucca River nearby, but federal map makers leave off the word Big from such names, and it is apparent that the Indian name of the stream was not Big Nestucca. As a matter of fact, the stream called Little Nestucca River was known to the Indians as *Nestachee*, so there would be no occasion for them to call the other river Big Nestucca. Little Nestucca River does not flow into Nestucca River but into Nestucca Bay. The spelling Nestugga is wrong. The *Handbook of American Indians* says the Nestucca Indians took their name from the country in which they lived, but that their real tribe name was *Staga-ush*. J. H. Frost in his journal of 1841, published in *OHQ*, v. 35, pp. 253 and 254, used the name *Nea-Stocka* in referring to a place on Nestucca River.

Netarts, TILLAMOOK. Netarts community is on Netarts Bay south of Tillamook Bay. Netarts post office was established Aug. 25, 1870, and operated with one interruption in the 1870s until May 31, 1957. William H. Hardman was the first postmaster. *Netarts* is one of the number of Indian names beginning with *Ne* which were probably used to indicate localities or the homes of certain tribes. See Neahkahnie Mountain and *OHQ*, v. 1, p. 321. George Davidson, in the *Coast Pilot* of 1889, p. 433, refers to this bay as *Na-ta-at* or Oyster Bay. He does not explain the meaning of the Indian name and does not imply that it is the same as oyster. Mrs. Mildred Phelps Edner, a long time resident, said the original name was Oyster Bay but it was changed to Netarts Bay after the post office was opened. She also said the best rendering of the Indian name would be *Ne ta ats*. This all agrees with George Davidson. Mrs. Edner added that in 1868, Claus Christensen began to harvest oysters from the bay for market in San Francisco and Portland.

Neubert Spring, KLAMATH. Neubert Spring on the east slope of Naylox Mountain was named for the family of Will Neubert, an early settler in Swan Lake Valley.

Neverstil, COLUMBIA. On Feb. 3, 1946, the *Oregonian* printed an editorial about Neverstil, inviting information. The place was described with some fidelity, and while it was referred to as a logging community, it was in fact the location of the repair shops for A. S. Kerry's logging railroad. A lively correspondence resulted from this editorial and letters were printed on Feb. 5, 6, 10, 12 and 13. A number of stories were furnished about the origin of the word Neverstil, some based apparently on high-geared imagination. An impartial review of the evidence indicates to the compiler that the name was coined by Mr. Kerry of the Kerry Timber Company to describe the bustle and noise attendant upon the timber company railroad shops. The place was at the old Harvey ranch about two miles south of Birkenfeld where Deep Creek flows into Nehalem River. Neverstil post office was established June 10, 1916, with Florence M. Bennett first postmaster. The office was closed Dec. 31, 1919. The logging railroad was in operation as early as about 1913 and it is said that the place was first called Evergreen, but that name could not be used for a post office because of duplication with another Evergreen, Oregon. There must have been some other reason for not continuing the name Evergreen, as there was no other post office with that name in Oregon during the period in question.

New Bridge, BAKER. New Bridge was originally on the banks of Eagle Creek near where an important pioneer bridge was built across the stream. The post office was established on July 22, 1878, and closed Sept. 8, 1967. Joseph Gale was the first postmaster. For information about him, *see* Gales Creek. When this office was established it was in Union County. In 1901 the county boundaries were altered and this long panhandle was eliminated.

New Era, CLACKAMAS. There are two stories about how this community got its name. Several persons have told the writer that the naming came about as the result of the construction of the railroad as far as the mouth of Parrott Creek, which made it possible for Willamette River boats to stop there and deliver produce. This was hailed as a new era in river transportation as boats then would not have to go to the falls below at Oregon City. This story has the earmarks of truth, but on the other hand it should be said that one correspondent has informed the compiler that a local family were spiritualists and devoted to a publication called the *New Era*, and named the place on that account.

New Pine Creek, LAKE. This is said to be the oldest town in Lake County. It was originally intended to name the place Pine Creek because of a nearby stream, but postal authorities objected to this because of duplication, so the name New Pine Creek was adopted. The post office was established Dec. 8, 1876, with S. A. Hamersley first postmaster.

Newberg, YAMHILL. C. B. Wilson, postmaster at Newberg, Oregon, in 1926, informed the writer that Newberg was named Nov. 5, 1869, by Sebastian Brutscher who was the first postmaster. Brutscher formerly lived in Germany at a place called Neuberg and adopted for the new office the English translation of the name of his former home. Neuberg is in Bavaria on the Danube River southwest of Ingolstadt.

Newbern, LINN. Newbern was the name of a short-lived post office established June 18, 1874, and closed Sept. 1 of the same year. The General Land Office map of Oregon of 1876 shows the place near the west edge of T 11S, R 2W, on the old road from Albany southeast toward Lebanon. The office was about six miles southeast of Albany and a mile or so north-northwest of what was later known as Tallman. The compiler has not been able to get the significance of the name Newbern, which is spelled Newburn on the map mentioned above. Benjamin N. Hardman was postmaster at the place. Newbern sounds like a family name and it may be represented by the postmaster's middle initial, though this is no more than a surmise.

Newberry Crater, DESCHUTES. Nature narrowly missed giving Oregon two crater lakes almost equal in size and beauty, but like many other attempts to improve upon a masterpiece, this one failed. Twenty-five miles south of Bend lies Newberry Crater, a result of volcanism much more recent than the caldera occupied by Crater Lake. Newberry Crater is situated in the summit of the isolated Paulina Mountains and in this crater are two lakes, Paulina Lake and East Lake, at an elevation of about 6350 feet or several hundred feet higher than Crater Lake. It is apparent that the caldera was at one time occupied by one lake, but subsequent volcanic action has built up a series of small craters running north and south across the middle which divides the depression and leaves East Lake with neither inlet nor outlet. Paulina Lake overflows to the west down Paulina Creek, a tributary of Little Deschutes River. Paulina Creek is blessed with several pretty waterfalls. Newberry Crater broke down its western side and if it had not been for this break it is apparent that the water level would be much higher in the crater, and the surroundings would have more nearly resembled Crater Lake itself. At some points around the two lakes the walls are precipitous and high and Paulina Peak, which is just south of Paulina Lake, affords one of the finest views in Oregon. It stands 7985 feet high, or 1600 feet above the lake, and its sides to the north are rough and jagged. From the USFS lookout on top the writer has seen the great snow peaks of the Cascade Range spread out like a fan in magnificent panorama, extending from Mount Adams on the north to Mount McLoughlin on the south. In 1903 Dr. I. C. Russell examined this part of Oregon for the USGS and attempted to name the Paulina Mountains and Paulina Peak Mount Newberry, for Dr. John Strong Newberry, who explored central Oregon for the Pacific Railroad Surveys in 1855. Dr. Russell's proposal has never been adopted in local practice, but instead the great caldera is now generally known as Newberry Crater, and Dr. Newberry is well honored, though not in the manner intended by Dr. Russell. Additional information may be found under Paulina Peak.

Newbill Creek, CROOK, JEFFERSON. Newbill Creek rises northeast of Grizzly Mountain and flows into Willow Creek. It was named for Jesse Newbill who homesteaded along its banks in 1873. The form Newhill is incorrect.

Newell Creek, CLACKAMAS. Newell Creek is a small stream east of Oregon

City, flowing north into Abernethy Creek. This little creek was named for one of the most prominent and picturesque pioneer citizens of the Oregon country. "Doctor" Robert Newell rated his title by affectionate courtesy rather than by professional training. He was a mountain man when he was scarcely out of his teens, and it was in the mountains that he learned to plug bullet wounds, set broken bones and prepare natural remedies for sick dogs, horses, Indians and fellow trappers. His companions held him in esteem for his timely help and doubtless the dogs licked his hands. Robert Newell was born in Ohio, probably in 1807. He started trapping out of St. Louis when he was 22. T. C. Elliott has written entertainingly of his career in *OHQ*, v. 9, p. 103. Not much is known of his life in the Rocky Mountains, but in Dec. 1840, he was in Oregon City. He played a conspicuous part in the formation of the provisional government; he was a member of the Legislative Committee and twice speaker of the House of Representatives. He took an active part in Indian problems. He moved to Lapwai, Idaho, in the 1860s and died at Lewiston in Nov. 1869.

Newell Spring, JEFFERSON. Newell Spring is on the old Madras-Ashwood road near Hay Creek. It was named for Roy Newell who took up a homestead there in 1906.

Newman Canyon, MORROW. Newman Canyon northwest of Lena was named for William R. Newman who settled near Heppner about 1890.

Newport, LINCOLN. This post office was established July 2, 1868, with Samuel Case postmaster. The compiler has not succeeded in learning who christened the community, although the name is obviously intended to be descriptive, and was doubtless suggested by Newport, Rhode Island.

Newsome Creek, CROOK. Newsome Creek east of Post was named for Samuel J. Newsom who was born in Springfield, Illinois on Mar. 13, 1834 and came to Oregon with his parents, David and Mary Newsom, in 1851. Newsom lived in Marion County then moved to eastern Oregon in the 1870s. He was a prominent rancher in the vicinity of Post and later developed Newsom's Addition to the City of Prineville. The superfluous terminal "e" is fixed by current usage. For a short biography, *see Illustrated History of Central Oregon*, p. 786.

Newton Clark Glacier, HOOD RIVER. This glacier is on the southeast part of Mount Hood. Newton Clark was a native of Illinois, and after living for a time in Wisconsin, he served in the Civil War, and then settled in what is now South Dakota. It is said that Clark County in that state was named for him. Clark came to Hood River Valley in Sept. 1877 and was both a teacher and land surveyor. He was interested in nature and spent considerable time around Mount Hood. Captain Henry Coe and Oscar Stranahan reportedly named Newton Clark Glacier for him in 1886. Clark died on June 21, 1918.

Newton Creek, HOOD RIVER. This stream, together with Clark Creek to the south, drains Newton Clark Glacier. The two creeks were named by splitting the name of the glacier. *See* Newton Clark Glacier.

Niagara, MARION. Niagara, a place on North Santiam River about eight miles east of Mill City, was named for the adjacent constriction in the river. After the railroad was built through here in 1889, it was believed that the narrow gorge, only five feet wide in one spot, would be an excellent waterpower site. A masonry dam was constructed and a paper mill planned but not completed. Electric power was generated but variations in stream flow coupled with maintenance problems on the dam caused the operation to be abandoned in 1912. Niagara post office was established as Niagora on Oct. 3, 1890 with William H. Burns first postmaster. The spelling was corrected to Niagara in July 1893 and the office operated intermittently until June 14, 1934. As of 1990, there is a pleasant Marion County Park there with a good flight of steps down to the narrow gorge and the remains of the original masonry. Maynard Drawson has an interesting history of the dam in *OHQ*, v. 71, pp 349 *et seq*.

Nibley, UNION. This place was named for C. W. Nibley, a well-known member of the Mormon Church and prominent in various industrial enterprises in the Pacific Northwest. It was near Conley Lake, northeast of La Grande, on property purchased from Frank Conley in 1900 by the Oregon Land Company. Nibley, David Eccles and George Stoddard organized the Oregon Sugar Company in 1898 and promptly constructed a factory in La Grande to process sugar beets, the first in the Pacific Northwest. Local beet production was less than expected and the land company was organized to attract experienced beet farmers from Utah. By 1902 there was a flourishing village of 20 families but unfavorable weather and lack of water kept beet production low. A typhoid epidemic and bad weather in 1905 precipitated the end. On Dec. 29, 1906, all community functions stopped and the town ceased to exist. The compiler is indebted to John Evans of La Grande for searching out this information.

Nice, LINCOLN. Nice was a community on the north side of Alsea Bay. J. H. Middleton, who lived there, informed the compiler in 1927 that the place was named for Harry Nice, who was born in New Brunswick about 1828 and came to California about 1867 and to Oregon about 1869. He fished for salmon and built boats on the Columbia River, and after having spent a short time in British Columbia, returned to the United States and was employed by the government in the construction of jetties near Newport. He later became interested in salmon packing on Alsea Bay. He died about 1922. The post office situated near the present site of Nice was established with the name Drift Creek on Aug. 6, 1874, with Matthew Brand first postmaster. The name was changed to Collins on Jan. 31, 1876, with Brand postmaster. On June 17, 1881, the name was changed to Waldport with David Ruble postmaster. The name was changed back to Collins on Feb. 23, 1882. Collins was the name of a local family. The name of the office was changed to Lutgens on May 17, 1890, and Albert H. Lutgens was appointed postmaster on the same day. On July 29, 1893, the name of the office was changed to Stanford and W. C. Shepard was appointed postmaster. The name was changed again to Lutgens on June 21, 1897, and Albert H. Lutgens was appointed postmaster. The name was changed to Nice on Apr. 24, 1917, with Nona L. Strake postmaster. The office was discontinued on Nov. 15, 1919.

Nichols, DOUGLAS. For many years Nichols was a railroad station in Cow Creek Canyon. It was southwest of Riddle, and was named for a well-known Douglas County family. Nichols post office was established Dec. 31, 1914, with Mrs. Viola B. Nichols postmaster. It was discontinued Dec. 31, 1929. The railroad station Nichols was established when the railroad was built in the early 1880s.

Nichols Canyon, UMATILLA. Nichols Canyon is just south of Milton-Freewater. It was named for William Nichols who settled near its mouth in 1871 and later platted Nichols' 1st and 2nd additions to what was then Milton City. The Oregon Historical Society in *Scrapbook #270*, p. 163, has an unidentified newspaper clipping giving an interesting interview with Nichols and his comments on the early days. The form Nicolis used on the USGS Milton-Freewater quadrangle dated 1964 is a typographical error.

Nichols Creek, BENTON. This creek is a mile southwest of Alpine. It is named for H. B. Nichols who came to Bellfountain in 1853 and taught the local school. The schoolhouse, finished in 1850, was about half a mile southeast of Alpine. *see OHQ*, v. 38, p. 289.

Nichols Creek, DOUGLAS. This creek is a tributary of Jackson Creek about eight miles east of Tiller. Benjamin F. Nichols, who had a ranch along its banks, was the son of I. B. Nichols and grandson of William H. Riddle.

Nicholson Spring, WHEELER. This spring in S 12, T 9S, R 20E, was named for a family of early settlers.

Nick Eaton Ridge, HOOD RIVER. This ridge runs south from the Columbia River just east of Herman Creek. Mrs. Clifford L. Gorton of Cascade Locks stated that the ridge was named for Nick Eaton who had a farm between Wyeth and Cascade Locks about 1905.

Nickel Mountain, DOUGLAS. This mountain is four miles west of Riddle and has the only known major deposit of green silicate of nickel (garnierite) in the United States. Commercial production was started in 1954 by a subsidiary of the M. A. Hanna Company.

Nish, SHERMAN. Nish was a railroad station near Moro. It was named for Alexander Nish who was born in Scotland on Feb. 15, 1847, and came to the United States in 1852. He served during the Civil War and later settled in Sherman County. It is said that his name was originally McNish or MacNish, but he changed his name at the time he entered the army.

Nixon, LINN. This was a station on the Oregon Electric Railway southwest of Halsey. C. H. Stewart of Albany told the compiler that it was named for a pioneer resident, Samuel Nixon.

No Name Creek, HOOD RIVER. Stanley Walters, USFS ranger, named this tributary of Lake Branch when the area was logged about 1950. He said that everything else was named so "No Name" would have to suffice.

Noah Butte, COOS. Noah Butte is east across Coos Bay from the town of Coos

Bay and north of Coos River. Members of the Noah family were early settlers in the county and the butte was named for one, but the compiler does not know which.

Noble Creek, COOS. Noble Creek was named for William H. Noble who was born in Arkansas in 1844. He came to Coos County as a small boy in 1853 and grew up in Empire. He and his brother Lyman Noble were early loggers and renowned for their "Bull Team" operations. In 1902, Noble homesteaded near the mouth of Noble Creek east of Lakeside. Peterson and Powers in *A Century of Coos and Curry* say that at the time of Noble's death in 1910 he had a large dairy farm on Hopkins Creek east of Lakeside. Modern maps show no such stream and the compiler is of the opinion that Hopkins and Noble creeks are the same. Noble's sister, Emily Oregon Noble, the first white child born in Coos County, married William H. Saunders of Saunders Lake.

Noble School, MARION. Noble School and the Noble district, about three miles southeast of Scotts Mills, were named for William Noble, who settled on the Abiqua some time prior to 1848. He sold out to Samuel Allen in the spring of that year, and went to Oregon City, where he soon died. *See* Down's *History of the Silverton Country*, p. 41. Noble post office served this section from Feb. 1893, to May 1908. Charles W. Roberts was the first postmaster of a series of six.

Noel Creek, DOUGLAS. Noel Creek flows into Smith River from the north a few miles northeast of Gardiner. It bears the name of Stephenson C. Noel who came to Oregon from Missouri. In pioneer days, he and some companions left Eugene on a prospecting expedition and finally reached lower Smith River. Noel settled on the stream that now bears his name. *See* Reedsport *Courier*, Apr. 10, 1936.

Nofog, DOUGLAS. Nofog post office bore a strictly descriptive name. It was on the upper reaches of Cavitt Creek about due east of Roseburg. Nofog post office was established June 7, 1915, and Hezekiah J. Robinett, the first and only postmaster, named the place because of the clear atmosphere. The office was discontinued Feb. 28, 1918. The compiler has an interesting letter by Victor Boyd of Roseburg, written in Feb. 1948, about his experiences teaching school in 1903–04 in a log building on the Cavitt place. Except for the window sash, floor, desks and seats, the whole school building was hand split from cedar logs. Mr. Boyd writes that at one time eight of the seventeen pupils were from the family of S. W. Turnell. Robinett later bought the Turnell home. In 1984, Winona A. Sellard, a granddaughter of Robinett, sent the writer a letter telling of her visits to Nofog where her family used the abandoned schoolhouse as a hunting cabin. She enclosed a snapshot of the old building.

Nohorn Creek, CLACKAMAS. This stream is in the southern part of the county and flows into the Hot Springs Fork of Clackamas River. Nohorn is the popularized version of the name Nachand. John Nachand was a pioneer prospector of eastern Clackamas County, with James Russell and Joe Davis. It is said that Nachand had formerly mined in the Cariboo district in British Columbia. Little is known of his history except that during the later years of his life he lived at Park Place, north of Oregon City. He died about 1905. He was universally called Nohorn, and the name Nohorn is well established for the stream.

Nonpareil, DOUGLAS. A locality on Calapooya Creek six or seven miles airline east of Oakland is called Nonpareil, a word meaning unrivaled or unique. Whoever named the place thought well of it. Nonpareil post office was established in Dec. 19, 1882, with Elizabeth C. Sacry postmaster. The office was discontinued July 10, 1884. The name was derived from the nearby Nonpareil quicksilver mine, which at one time produced a considerable quantity of the mineral. The Nonpareil mine has not been worked in recent years.

Norfolk, DOUGLAS. Norfolk was a pioneer post office on Smith River in the west part of the county. It was near the mouth of North Fork Smith River. A report from Reedsport says that the post office was to have been called Norfork for the stream. However that may be, the spelling Norfolk was adopted by postal authorities and that is the way it appears on all records available to the compiler.

Norris, CLACKAMAS. This station near Barton was named for G. Norris who took up a homestead nearby. His land office certificate was no. 3012.

North Bend, COOS. The original settlement of North Bend was on the peninsula around which Coos Bay bends between the town of Coos Bay and the ocean. It is said that the name North Bend was originally applied in 1856 by Captain A. M. Simpson, the founder of the city. The post office was established Feb. 27, 1872, with C. H. Merchant first postmaster.

North Fork Smith River, CURRY. This is the principal Oregon tributary of a river in California, which is named for Jedediah Strong Smith, explorer and fur trader. Smith discovered the river in California on Thursday, June 19, 1828. *See The Ashley-Smith Exploration* by Professor Harrison C. Dale. For information about Smith's exploration along the Oregon coast, *see* Smith River, in this volume. Smith River in Oregon and Smith River in California are so far apart that they are not confused. The California stream is shown as Smiths River on a map accompanying Senator Lewis F. Linn's report dated June 6, 1838. The Reverend Samuel Parker uses the same name on his map of Oregon Territory published the same year. North Fork Smith River heads just west of Chetco Peak. The important tributary that heads southeast of Chetco Peak is Chrome Creek.

North Fork Smith River, DOUGLAS, LANE. This is the largest tributary of the main stream. The name West Fork is wrong. West Branch is a small stream tributary to North Fork Smith River. For origin of the name, *see* Smith River. This refers to the Oregon river.

North Junction, WASCO. North Junction station was established on the east bank of Deschutes River when the two railroads were built upstream from the mouth. From North Junction to South Junction, a distance of about 12 miles, but one track was provided. Later the Union Pacific track was torn up north of North

Junction, so that the station name is no longer descriptive. The post office was established in June 1927, some years after the railroads were built in the canyon. J. C. McCarty was the first postmaster. The place was not listed in the *Postal Guide* in the fall of 1933.

North Minam River, UNION, WALLOWA. This important tributary of Minam River heads in Steamboat Lake. The name North Fork River is incorrect.

North Plains, WASHINGTON. The name North Plains is used for a post office in the northern part of Tualatin Valley. This locality was known in pioneer times as North Plains, and the office gets its name from that source. Stories to the effect that a farmer named Nord lived hereabouts and gave his name to the plains do not appear to be founded on fact, for the plains were known as North Plains long before any settler of that name lived thereon.

North Pole Ridge, WASCO. Dolph Kimsey, who was raised near Antelope, told the writer that a Scot named Finlayson had a sheep spread near Black Rock and he claimed that in the winter this cold, desolate ridge compared favorably with its namesake. Since Finlayson presumably had had experience with the rigours of winter in Scotland, the compiler feels his opinion must be given considerable weight.

North Portland, MULTNOMAH. This post office was established Mar. 24, 1910, and was named because of its position in respect to Portland. The first postmaster was Vaughn D. Crosby. It is said that the name was suggested by a representative of Swift & Company, which concern operated a large meat packing plant in the community. The area is now served by Kenton Station out of Portland.

North Portland Harbor, MULTNOMAH. North Portland Harbor lies between Hayden Island and the flats north of St. Johns. The harbor is really a branch of the Columbia River. For many years it was known as Oregon Slough but at the request of Portland commercial interests the name was changed to North Portland Harbor because of rapidly developing activity in that part of Portland. The USBGN approved the change.

North Powder, UNION. North Powder took its name from North Powder River, a tributary of Powder River. For the origin of that name, *see* Powder River. North Powder was a pioneer station. James M. De Moss is said to have been the founder of the stage station. *See* De Moss. Maps of Lewis and Clark show North Powder River as *Ta-kin-par*. North Powder post office was established Dec. 2, 1866, with Joseph Austin first postmaster.

North Santiam River, LINN, MARION. This is the correct name of the main tributary of Santiam River, and not North Fork. South Santiam River is the correct name of the other important branch that combines with North Santiam River near Jefferson to form the main stream. *See* Santiam River. The principal tributary of North Santiam River is Little North Santiam River, not Little North Fork.

North Scappoose Creek, COLUMBIA. This is the correct name of the main north tributary of Scappoose Creek, not North Fork. *See* Scappoose Creek.

North Sister, DESCHUTES, LANE. This is the fourth highest mountain in Oregon, and has an elevation of 10,085 feet. The Three Sisters have been so known since pioneer days, but the compiler has been unable to find out who first used the name. There is an old story to the effect that in early days the three peaks were known as Faith, Hope and Charity, the North Sister being Mount Faith. These names have not prevailed. *See* Three Sisters.

North Tenmile Lake, COOS, DOUGLAS. This lake is known by the name given, and also by the name North Lake. The USBGN has officially declared in favor of North Tenmile Lake. Its outlet is into Tenmile Lake, which in turn drains into the ocean through Tenmile Creek. The two lakes and other nearby features doubtless received their names from Tenmile Creek, which flows into the Pacific Ocean about ten miles south of Winchester Bay. *See* Tenmile Creek and Tenmile Lake.

North Umpqua River, DOUGLAS. This is the correct name of the north branch of Umpqua River, not North Fork. It rises on the west slopes of the Cascade Range, north of Diamond Lake, and joins South Umpqua River near Winchester, forming Umpqua River. For origin of the name Umpqua, *see* Umpqua River.

North Yamhill River, YAMHILL. This is the correct name of the main north tributary of Yamhill River, not North Fork. *See* Yamhill River.

Norton, CLACKAMAS. A pioneer post office, named Norton for a local family, was established Dec. 1, 1871, with Benjamin C. Lewis first postmaster. Zach C. Norton was the second postmaster. The office was closed June 9, 1881. The place is shown on old maps at a point about four or five miles northwest of Springwater, close to or actually on the Clackamas River, probably not far from the place known as Feldheimer Ferry. In response to an inquiry, the Oregon City *Banner-Courier* on Jan. 1, 1946, published a statement by R. B. Holcomb, a pioneer resident of the county who was in the late 1880s a mail carrier. Mr. Holcomb avers that he recalled a building known as Norton's Hall at a point about four miles north of Springwater, although it does not appear from his statement that the building was on the river. Norton's Hall was apparently a meeting place of sorts, and bore insignia, possibly of the Masonic fraternity.

Nortons, LINCOLN. This railroad station was in the extreme east part of the county. It was named for the Norton family, who owned a ranch nearby. The place was originally called Norton but postal authorities did not accept this name as there was another post office in Oregon of the same name, so the "s" was added. The post office was established in 1895.

Norway, COOS. Norway station and post office got its name from the fact that in early days the community was settled by Norwegians. The post office has been moved a few miles since it was first established in May 1876.

Norwegian Creek, LANE. Ray Engels of McKenzie Bridge told the writer in

1971 that this creek north of Belknap Springs was named about the turn of the century after a Norwegian committed suicide nearby.

Nostoc Creek, LANE. Nostoc Creek empties into Lookout Creek four miles north of McKenzie Bridge. It was named by personnel of the USFS H. J. Andrews Experimental Forest. Nostoc, a blue-green nitrogen fixing algae, was found in abundance in the creek. This is an interesting name in contrast to nearby Saddle Creek and Colder Creek also given descriptive names at the same time.

Noti, LANE. Postmaster H. G. Suttle told the writer in Feb. 1926, of the unusual origin of this name in the following words: "In the early days an Indian and a white man were traveling together from a point on the coast into the Willamette Valley with one horse between them. In order to make as rapid progress as possible they were doing what was known as 'riding and tying.' One would take the horse and ride ahead a distance, tie the horse and proceed on foot. When his companion reached the point where the horse was tied, he in turn mounted and rode a given distance beyond his partner and tied the horse again. It is said that the white man had agreed to tie the horse at about the point where the Noti Creek joins Long Tom River, where the present town of Noti is now located, but instead double-crossed the Indian and rode on to Eugene and left the Indian to walk. When the Indian discovered that he had been jobbed, he is said to have exclaimed, 'Him no tie,' and therefrom the place received its name."

Noyer Creek, CLACKAMAS. This creek north of Barton was named for Peter Noyer, who took up a donation land claim nearby in pioneer days. His land office certificate was no. 3876.

Nugget, DOUGLAS. This post office was named Nugget because of gold mines in the vicinity.

Numbers Creek, LANE. Numbers Creek flows into Coast Fork Willamette River south of Cottage Grove Reservoir. It bears the name of Phillip Numbers who in 1872 purchased the sawmill built nearby by William Payne in 1867.

Nute Slough, LINCOLN. Nute Slough forms the eastern border of Boone Island west of Toledo. It is named for Hezekiah C. Nute who homesteaded near there in 1876.

Nye, UMATILLA. Nye post office was about eight miles southwest of Pilot Rock near the present three-way highway junction. This junction is still referred to as Nye and the general impression is that the locality was named for A. W. Nye, a well-known early resident of Umatilla County. The post office was established Mar. 9, 1887, with Henry C. Wright first postmaster. The office was discontinued June 30, 1917.

Nye Beach, LINCOLN. Nye Beach on the ocean at Newport was once a separate community. John T. Nye was one of the earliest settlers at Yaquina Bay. He took a homestead along the beach and was instrumental in the development of the area. His property is now occupied by motels and houses facing the beach in front of Newport.

Nyssa, MALHEUR. This post office was established June 15, 1889. The name was first applied to a station when the railroad was built, but the town was not incorporated until about 1903. Accurate information about the application of the name is not available. It is said that a Greek section hand named the place for a town in Greece, but the compiler has been unable to find such a place in any modern atlas. However, in 1973 Professor William G. Loy of the University of Oregon provided the interesting information that the town Messene in Messenia was once known as Nissi. The geographical situation is remarkably similar. Both are situated on slight rises of land with a substantial river to the east and a ditch or small stream to the west. He adds that the word *nissi* meant island. As Loy has done extensive work on Greek geography, the the compiler feels this explanation should be given considerable weight. There are numerous other versions including an acronym for New York Sheep Shippers Association and that it is an Indian name for sagebrush. In botany, Nyssa is the name of the tupelo tree commemorating one of the so-called water nymphs. In Greek mythology Jove charged the Nysaean nymphs with rearing the infant Bacchus. The locale was not specified but Alexander the Great discovered the ancient city of Nysa at the foot of Mount Koh-i-nor west of Peshawar, Pakistan. Tradition says Nysa was founded by Bacchus.

Oak, COOS. On Feb. 28, 1901, a post office named Oak was established about eight miles by road southeast of Myrtle Point near the banks of Middle Fork Coquille River, probably very close to Endicott Creek which flows in from the north. Solomon S. Endicott was the first and only postmaster. The office was closed Aug. 22, 1902. It was named for the forest growth of the locality.

Oak Creek, BENTON. Oak Creek is near Corvallis. There are many geographic features in Oregon named for oak trees. Sudworth, in *Check List of Forest Trees of the United States*, p. 105, lists but one oak in northern Oregon, *Quercus garryanna*, Oregon white oak, and most of the features named for the oak are named because of the nearby existence of this species. *Quercus kelloggii*, California black oak, is listed as growing as far north as McKenzie River, and *Quercus chrysolepis*, canyon live oak, is listed as far north as Cow Creek.

Oak Creek, DOUGLAS. Oak Creek, a locality about ten miles northeast of Roseburg, took its name from the stream on which it is situated. The stream name is very old and came of course from the oak trees which are so prominent in that part of the county. Oak Creek post office was established Oct. 18, 1878, with Jeptha Thornton first postmaster. In 1896, when postal officials were in the throes of efficiency, the name was consolidated to Oakcreek, but the general public continued to use the style Oak Creek. The writer does not know when the post office was closed, but apparently it was some time between 1910 and 1912.

Oak Grove, CLACKAMAS. Harvey G. Starkweather, a resident of this neighborhood, was authority for the statement that the name of Oak Grove was suggested by Edward W. Cornell, a member of the surveying party that platted the townsite in the early 1890s. The company developing the property had not been able to secure a satisfactory name and Cornell's suggestion came as a result of a crew eating lunch in a fine grove of oak trees in the northwest part of the tract. The townsite was originally served from Milwaukie post office. About 1904 Creighton post office was established to serve the community. This name was adopted in honor of Susan Creighton who took up a donation land claim where the post office then stood. Postal authorities did not use the name Oak Grove because of duplication. The first postmaster was Thomas Howell, Oregon's great botanist. What was known as Oak Grove station was originally called Center station and what was St. Theresa was originally known as Oak Grove station. In order to prevent the confusion created by this state of affairs, postal authorities were prevailed upon in 1907 to change the post office name to Oak Grove and the name of Center station was changed to Oak Grove station, so that peace and happiness reigned insofar as the name was concerned. As of 1980 the tracks were gone and the station only a dim memory. The post office is a branch of Portland.

Oak Grove, HOOD RIVER. This was originally part of the Barrett district on the west side of Hood River Valley. The first school was called Crapper School, but when the church was constructed it was called Oak Grove Church. About 1904 when the present school was constructed, residents changed the name of Crapper district to Oak Grove district.

Oak Grove Butte, CLACKAMAS. This butte, elevation 4626 feet, was named for Oak Grove Fork Clackamas River to the north and not because of any grove of oaks on its slopes.

Oak Grove Fork Clackamas River, CLACKAMAS. This is a principal tributary of the Clackamas. In early days Wapinitia, on the east side of the Cascade Range, was known as Oak Grove, and because this fork headed in that general direction it was known as Oak Grove Fork. For other information, *see* Wapinitia.

Oak Hill, LANE. This hill west of Eugene was named by John Bailey for a fine grove of oak trees that grew thereon. Bailey, who took a donation land claim there in 1850, later moved five miles southeast to the hill which now bears his name. The record is filed under Roseburg Land Office #1770 with the spelling Baily. Edward F. Bailey, a grandson, told the compiler in 1968 that other family records used both spellings.

Oak Point, COLUMBIA. On June 1, 1810, Nathan Winship, William Smith and others of the Winship expedition on the ship *Albatross* came upon a grove of oak trees on the south bank of the Columbia River. These were the first oaks the party had found since entering the river on May 26 and the locality was named Oak Point. This point is west of and across Bradbury Slough from the west end of Crims Island where the Beaver ammunition shipping depot was located during World War II and the Portland General Electric Company auxiliary generating plant was built in the 1970s. Bancroft, in *History of the Northwest Coast*, v. 2, pp. 129 *et seq.*, gives an account of the settlement and the difficulties experienced. Later the name Oak Point emigrated across the Columbia River to the Washington side where it is now the name of a community. Lewis and Clark passed this locality on Mar. 26, 1806, and named what is now Crims Island Fannys Island in compliment to Frances Clark, sister of William Clark. The extensive flat or prairie on the south bank of the river was named Fannys Bottom. It is perhaps just as well that Miss Clark was unable to foresee modern English usage. The explorers mention the prominent grove of oak trees at the point at the north corner of Fannys Bottom. Oak Point and vicinity are described in Coues' *Henry-Thompson Journals*, v. 2, pp. 794–95, under date of Jan. 11, 1814, and the name seems to have been well established. Wilkes charted Oak Point on his maps and charts as of 1841. A few years later the Abernathy mill drew the name across the river to the Washington shore and there it has remained. In 1792 Broughton applied the name Oak Point to a place on the Washington side of the Columbia River a little below the present community of St. Helens. This Oak Point seems to have been in the same locality as Caples Landing.

Oakerman Ranch, HARNEY. The name of this ranch is frequently misspelled. It bears the name of J. Fred Oakerman, who received his land patent from the United States. The ranch was a little north of US-20 and is well known in central Oregon.

Oakland, DOUGLAS. Oakland post office was established Feb. 21, 1852. In 1856 the office was on a prairie surrounded by oak trees, about three miles north of the present town. At that time the office, which was in charge of a preacher named Hull Tower, was the terminus of four mail routes, one to Jacksonville, one to Scottsburg, one via the pass to the Coast Fork and Eugene, and the other through Yoncalla to Corvallis. All mail was carried on saddle and pack horses. The office received its name on account of the oak trees that are so plentiful in the vicinity. *See* University of Oregon Extension *Monitor* for Sept. 1924. The first postmaster at Oakland was David C. Underwood.

Oakley, HARNEY. Oakley was a post office in the east part of the county, in Crane Creek Gap, a little more than a mile east of the town now known as Crane. The significance of the name Oakley has not been determined. Oakley post office was established Nov. 4, 1889, with Philander H. Gray postmaster, who served until the office was discontinued July 29, 1895. When the office was established in 1889, Mrs. Gray suggested the name Fairview, which was well suited to the locality, but this turned out to be a duplicate of another Fairview, in Coos County, and postal officials would not approve it. Mrs. Gray then suggested Oakley, a name apparently selected at random.

Oakridge, LANE. This name was suggested by Major R. L. Edwards, a right-of-way agent of the Southern Pacific Company. It accurately describes the topography and surrounding timber cover. Oakridge post office was established in 1912. In earlier days the community was known as Hazeldell.

Oakville, LINN. Oakville is a locality about six miles airline southwest of Albany, but it is not now classed as a commercial community. The prominent

Oakville church has long been a landmark. The name was of course derived from the Oregon white oak trees native to the land. Oakville post office was established May 16, 1878, with James B. Coney first postmaster. This office served the area for nearly a quarter of a century and was not closed until Aug. 15, 1902. Its demise was doubtless due to the extension of rural free delivery.

Oar Creek, DOUGLAS. Oar Creek flows into Scholfield Creek southeast of Reedsport. Despite the adjacent marine activity, the name has no nautical significance as it was named for Alfred R. Oar who took up land there in 1896.

Oard Flat, HARNEY. A. G. Oard, supervisor of the Wallowa-Whitman National Forest, wrote in 1976 giving the origin of this name. Six Oard brothers came to the Harney Valley in the late 1860s and two remained. His grandfather, John A. Oard, settled south of Lawen and his great-uncle, James H. Oard, homesteaded on Oard Flat some seven miles north of Buchanan. He later ranched on nearby Rock Creek. Oard Flat was a stopover for the Oard brothers when trailing sheep from the Harney Valley to summer range near Calamity Butte. Rock Creek was so called because the passage through the rocky area was difficult for the sheep. Oard Spring, named for the brothers, is on the slopes of Calamity Butte.

Oasis, GILLIAM. Oasis post office was given a descriptive name. It was established May 5, 1884, with Thomas Fairhurst first and only postmaster. The office was closed to Arlington Nov. 3, 1886. On Aug. 6, 1948, J. D. Weed, an early settler in Gilliam County, wrote the compiler from Condon as follows: "Oasis post office was in what is known as Eightmile Canyon, about four miles south of and up the canyon from the site of a later post office called Montague, which was established in 1911. I was well acquainted with the son of Thomas Fairhurst and visited at the old Fairhurst home where the Oasis post office was situated. There was a large spring that broke out in this canyon and when I was a boy, there were about twenty-five acres of irrigated alfalfa land. On all sides of this place there was dry, arid bunchgrass land." It seems apparent that Oasis post office was well named.

Oatfield Road, CLACKAMAS. This road extends southeast from Milwaukie. It bears the name of a well-known pioneer family. For additional information, *see* obituary of Mrs. Minerva Thessing Oatfield, *Oregon Journal*, Apr. 9, 1943.

Oatman Flat, LAKE. Burton R. Oatman settled on this flat west of Silver Lake just after the turn of the century.

Obenchain Mountain, JACKSON. Obenchain Mountain is five miles west of Butte Falls. It is named for John Obenchain who came to Oregon in 1861 and took a homestead near the mountain in 1864. A son, John A. Obenchain, was postmaster at the nearby Big Butte office in 1888.

O'Brien, JOSEPHINE. O'Brien is a community and post office on the Redwood Highway about ten miles south of Kerby, at the junction with the old stage road to the southwest up West Fork Illinois River. The place bears the name of John O'Brien, one of the first settlers of the locality. The spelling O'Bryan is wrong.

Obsidian Cliff, LANE. Dr. E. T. Hodge, in his *Mount Multnomah*, p. 103, *et seq.*, describes Obsidian Cliff quite fully. Obsidian is black volcanic glass composed of acid lava which cooled so rapidly that it did not have time to crystallize. Obsidian Cliff is a prominent point west of the Three Sisters. *See* Glass Buttes.

Oceanside, TILLAMOOK. Nothing could be simpler than this.

Oceola, WASHINGTON. Oceola was a post office of pioneer days and was established June 24, 1854, with Laurence Hall postmaster. Preston's *Map of Oregon*, 1856, shows the place near the present site of Beaverton, but spelled Oseola. It passed from the picture many years ago. There are many places in the United States named for the famous Seminole Indian chief, and the spelling generally used is Osceola.

Ochoco Creek, CROOK, WHEELER. Ochoco Creek and other geographic features in central Oregon are said to have been named for Ochoco or Ocheco, a Snake or Paiute chief, and a contemporary of Paulina and Howlock. However, this is disputed by old-timers in Crook County, who say the chief was named for the stream because he lived nearby. It is also said that the word *ochoco* was a local Indian word for willows and the stream was named on that account. The compiler knows no way to compose these differences in legend.

O'Conner Meadow, KLAMATH. O'Conner Meadow is south of Tea Table Mountain. Denis O'Conner settled there at the time of World War I.

Odell, HOOD RIVER. This is a well-known community in the middle Hood River Valley. It was named for William Odell, who settled nearby as early as 1861, and whose son, Milton D. Odell, was the first white child born in the valley. Roswell Shelley started a store at Odell and applied the present name. William Odell was a native of Tennessee. Milton Odell was born in 1863. A news item in the Hood River *Glacier*, Oct. 14, 1932, cites Mrs. Troy Shelley as authority for the statement that the name of the town was originally suggested by S. F. Blythe, the pioneer editor of the *Glacier*. Post office records show that when the post office was established in June 1910, it was first called Newtown. The name was changed to Odell in Mar. 1911. The name Newtown did not refer to Hood River's famous apple, but to the new settlement that sprang up at the railroad station about three-quarters of a mile southeast of the old Crossroads.

Odell Creek, KLAMATH. Odell Creek is the name applied to the outlet of Odell Lake. The stream flows into Davis Lake. For many years there was considerable confusion about the names of the streams in the upper Deschutes River drainage basin. A committee of USFS officials codified the names, and the term Odell Creek was chosen to indicate the stream described above. It has come into universal use.

Odell Lake, KLAMATH. William Holman Odell was born in Indiana in 1830. He came to Oregon in 1852, and engaged in farming and teaching, and later in surveying and was connected with the construction of the military wagon road up the Middle Fork Willamette River. He was appointed surveyor general for Oregon in 1871, and was a presidential elector in 1876, and later engaged in the newspaper business. He died in Portland, Apr. 27, 1922. Odell Lake, one of the finest mountain bodies of water in the state, was named for him. The name was applied in 1865, by B. J. Pengra. In July 1865, Pengra and Odell made a reconnaissance in the vicinity of Diamond Peak for the Oregon Central Military Road, and part of Pengra's report is on file at the Oregon Historical Society. The report says that Pengra and Odell visited what is now known as Odell Butte, apparently on July 22, 1865. On July 26, Odell climbed to the top of the butte and discovered a fine lake to the northwest. On July 27, the two explorers visited the lake and Pengra named it for Odell. The report contains a very good description of Odell Lake. Odell Lake has an elevation of 4792 feet, and the Cascade line of the Southern Pacific Company skirts its southern shore. The Willamette Highway, SH-58, is on the north bank of the lake. Other features in the neighborhood named for W. H. Odell include Odell Butte and Odell Creek, the outlet of Odell Lake. Odell Lake is fed from melting snows on Diamond Peak and Maiden Peak, and is about six miles long. Its western end is but a few minutes walk from the summit of the Cascade Range over the tunnel of the Southern Pacific. This lake occupies a depression cut by a glacier, and the terminal moraine on the southeast end makes the dam that impounds the water. Odell Creek connects this lake with Davis Lake to the northeast.

Odell Spring, CROOK. This spring on the south edge of the county near West Butte was on the early day ranch of Clint Odell.

Odessa, KLAMATH. Odessa post office was established northwest of Klamath Falls and near Upper Klamath Lake on May 16, 1902. Mrs. Blanche Griffith was one of a long string of postmasters. The office operated with one intermission, until July 31, 1919, when it was closed to Recreation. The compiler is not satisfied with the available information about the origin of the name of this office. In 1948 Mrs. Griffith, then living in San Diego, wrote the compiler that the place was named by the wife of her husband's brother. This Mrs. Griffith had lived in France and it is said that the name Odessa came to her attention in that country, but the compiler knows of no Odessa in France. It seems more probable that the name came from the important city in the southwest part of Russia.

Odin Falls, DESCHUTES. These falls are said to have been named by Joe Houston, a nearby resident. Odin was the name, in Norse mythology, of the chief god corresponding to the Germanic Woden. He was considered to be the supreme being.

Offatt Spring, JEFFERSON. Offatt Spring is on Blizzard Ridge south of Ashwood. It was named for Z. B. Offatt who settled in the area in 1869.

Officer Creek, GRANT. Officer Creek flows west into Lewis Creek in S 18, T 17S, R 29E. It is named for R. V. Officer who homesteaded along it in the 1890s. Officer was later mayor of John Day. There were several members of the Officer family in Grant County in the early days.

Ogle Creek, CLACKAMAS, MARION. Ogle Creek was named for Bob Ogle, of

Molalla, who prospected on this stream and located some claims thereon. The stream flows into Molalla River in the south part of the county.

O'Hara Creek, TILLAMOOK. This creek was named for William C. O'Hara who settled at Netarts in 1876.

Ojalla Creek, LINCOLN. Ojalla Creek is tributary to Siletz River near Ojalla Bridge. Ojalla is a Finnish name, apparently that of a local settler. It should not be confused with the Indian word *olalla* or *olallie*, meaning berries.

O K Butte, DOUGLAS. Shortly after World War I, Theo and Leroy Bond, USFS employees, cut a way trail near this butte on Calf Creek south of North Umpqua River. Upon completion they asked approval of ranger Fred Asam. He replied: "It's O K," and the name was fixed from then on.

O K Gulch, WALLOWA. This is a dry gulch about a mile and a half long. Its mouth is in S 1, T 2S, R 45E. J. H. Horner of Enterprise told the compiler that the gulch was named for John Creighton, who built a corral in the gulch and rounded up his cattle there and branded them with the letters OK, connected. Creighton served with John W. Cullen in the Bannock War.

Olalla, DOUGLAS. This was formerly a post office on Lookingglass Creek, but the community is now served through other offices. For origin of the name, *see* Olallie Butte.

Olalla Slough, LINCOLN. This is the tidal reach of Olalla Creek where it enters Yaquina River east of Toledo. The original spelling of both slough and creek was Olallie but the USBGN adopted the present form in *Decision List 6202*. For origin of the name, *see* Olallie Butte.

Olallie Butte, JEFFERSON, MARION. The most important geographic feature in Oregon bearing the name Olallie is Olallie Butte at the summit of the Cascade Range between Mount Hood and Mount Jefferson. The USGS gives it an elevation of 7215 feet. The name is used in a number of other places, particularly along the Cascade Range. The word is from the Chinook jargon and means berries in general, or salmon berries. Gibbs gives it as a derivative of the Chinook word *klalelli*, meaning berries. Its use along the Cascade Range generally meant huckleberries. The USBGN has adopted this form of spelling.

Old Maids Canyon, JEFFERSON. This canyon runs to Mud Springs Creek north of Gateway. Cecily Beasley homesteaded there in 1911 and Turner in *Reminiscences of Jefferson County*, p. 193, tells how this canyon was named for Miss Beasley, a maiden lady of strong religious bent.

Oldenburg Lake, KLAMATH. This lake is about four miles south of Crescent Lake on the Pacific Crest Trail. It is named for Emil Oldenburg, one of the early day packers who was stocking the high lakes with fish. Family tradition has it that Oldenburg was stocking lakes out of Crescent Lake and came upon this body of water when he strayed from the primitive trail. The spelling Oldenberg, found on some maps, is incorrect.

Olene, KLAMATH. Steel says this name is an Indian word meaning eddy place, or place of drift, and that it was applied by Captain O. C. Applegate in 1884. The original location of the post office was up Lost River from the present site.

Oler Spring, WHEELER. Oler Spring is on the upper reaches of Cherry Creek. It takes its name from Andrew A. Oller who homesteaded there after World War I. The compiler cannot reconcile the two spellings.

Olete, KLAMATH. About 1890 Mr. and Mrs. William T. Wilson of Sacramento moved into eastern Klamath County for the purpose of developing a stock ranch. They settled in or near what was known as the Horsefly Valley. The locality was so named because of the prevalence of the insect pests. Wilson was conspicuous because of his fine red beard and to distinguish him from other Wilsons in Klamath County he was familiarly known as "Horsefly" Wilson. In due season there came to be a demand for a post office which is said to have been based to some extent on Mrs. Wilson's desire to get the home papers from Sacramento. In any event a petition was sent in and also a list of suggested post office names. Accordingly Olete post office was established Mar. 25, 1892, with Wilson first postmaster. Wilson suggested the name Olete by coining the word from the names of his daughter, Ora Letetia Wilson. That the name Olete was approved by postal authorities when there was an office not far away in the same county with the name Olene is remarkable. The post office was about 12 miles northeast of Lorella, on the road to Vistillas. Olete post office was closed to Lorella in Jan. 1904.

Olex, GILLIAM. When this post office was established it was intended to honor one Alex Smith, a local resident, but the enthusiasm of the petition writer was better than his handwriting, and the authorities at Washington misread Alex into Olex, and so it has been for many decades. The office was established Oct. 27, 1874, with James H. Butler first postmaster.

Olney, CLATSOP. Cyrus Olney was a native of Ohio. He was appointed supreme court justice of Oregon Territory in 1853, and resigned in 1857. He was a member of the constitutional convention of 1857. He died at Astoria Dec. 21, 1870, aged 55 years. The town of Olney bears his name. *See* Scott's *History of the Oregon Country*, v. 5, pp. 220–21.

Olson Creek, LINCOLN. This creek flows south through Newport into Yaquina Bay. Early maps show both Olsen's Addition and Olssonville near its mouth but the entire area is now part of Newport.

Ona, LINCOLN. Ona is a place on Beaver Creek about three miles east of Seal Rock. It is shown as a post office in 1890, and did not have an office in 1944 nor for some years prior. Ona may have been named with a Chinook jargon word. The jargon word *ona* generally refers to the razor clam. The community is not on the seashore and not near the clam beds, but someone may have imported the name. However, the compiler has a notion that the jargon word *ee-na* is the basis for the name. *Ee-na* means beaver and is appropriate to the location of the place on Beaver Creek.

Oneatta, LINCOLN. Oneatta is a ghost town on the northeast side of Yaquina

River and about a mile and a half upstream from Yaquina. The place was first settled and named by Ben Simpson in 1871. *See History of Benton County*, p. 490. A sawmill was operated there for a time and a post office was established in May 1876. The community appears to have been named for an Indian princess, who was, as usual, beautiful, accomplished and virtuous. A. B. Meacham, in *Wigwam and War-path*, chapter 5, gives a lugubrious story about her, but it is hard to tell whether it is fiction or fact.

O'Neals Mills, POLK. Apparently the first post office in Polk County was O'Neals Mills, established Jan. 8, 1850, with James A. O'Neal postmaster. The name was changed to Nesmiths on Aug. 21, 1850, with James W. Nesmith postmaster, and the office was discontinued Oct. 22, 1852. It was about two miles west of the present site of Dallas. For the history of the locality, *see* Ellendale.

O'Neil, CROOK. William G. O'Neil and family immigrated from Illinois to a place near the present site of Bend about 1881. Members of the family lived at various places in central Oregon and three of the sons at one time owned a store at the place now called O'Neil, which is west of Prineville. Philip Grinder Carmical settled in this general locality and built a cabin in the spring of 1872. He brought his family in July 1873, and the place became known as Carmical Station, as it was on a main route of travel. Carmical was born in Illinois on Aug. 27, 1821, and died at London, near Cottage Grove, Oregon, on Feb. 18, 1909. Carmical Station was apparently a little north of O'Neil. Francis Forest established himself in the vicinity in 1876. His first place was near Carmical Station but he later moved his store to the present site of O'Neil. Forest Crossing on Crooked River nearby bears his name.

O'Neil Creek, CROOK. This creek is tributary to Eagle Creek just south of Eagle Rock. George W. O'Neil took up government land there in 1888.

Oneonta Gorge, MULTNOMAH. The origin of this name is obviously the place in New York. The compiler has not been able to find out why the name was applied to the gorge in Oregon. Oneonta is said by Gannett to mean "place of peace." A handsome steamboat of the Mississippi-River-side-wheel type was built at the Cascades in 1863 and named the *Oneonta*. She was operated by the Oregon Steam Navigation Company on the Columbia River until 1877, both above and below the Cascades. While the evidence is by no means conclusive, it seems probable that Oneonta Creek and Gorge were named after the steamboat was built, and it is possible that the geographic features were named because of some incident connected with the boat.

Onion Peak, CLATSOP. Onion Peak, elevation 3057 feet, is one of the highest points in Clatsop County, and its rugged summit makes it an outstanding landmark. The peak is east-northeast of Arch Cape and about two miles north of the south line of the county. In Dec. 1945, Mrs. H. V. Alley of Nehalem informed the compiler that the peak was named for the wild onions growing near the summit. Mrs. Alley came to the Nehalem settlements as a girl in 1879 and said the name was used in the early days. There are a number of varieties of wild onion growing in Oregon and the compiler does not know what sort grows on Onion Peak.

Onion Springs Mountain, JACKSON, JOSEPHINE. Onion Springs Mountain is an important geographic feature at the north joint corner of the two counties. It is a main triangulation point of the USC&GS, and has an elevation of 5240 feet, according to that survey. The name comes from the presence of the wild onion, *Allium acuminatum*, which grows near the springs. This mountain is sometimes called King Mountain, but that is not its official name. There are a number of geographic features in western Oregon named for the wild onion.

Ontario, MALHEUR. The following quotation is from the *History of Baker, Grant, Malheur and Harney Counties*, p. 545: "Ontario was so named at the request of James W. Virtue, one of the founders, who wished thus to honor the place of his nativity Ontario, Canada. In 1883, William Morfitt, Daniel Smith, James W. Virtue and Mrs. Mary Richardson, all of Baker City, exercised desert land rights under United States laws and took up four adjoining sections of desert land." In 1927 Robert E. Strahorn told the compiler that he laid out the town in the early 1880s, presumably in connection with the construction of the Oregon Short Line Railroad, and that the name Ontario had been selected by a landowner before he got there. James W. Virtue was a prominent citizen of Baker and one-time sheriff. Inquiries made at Baker in Apr. 1943, to members of his family, elicited the fact that he was born in Ontario, Canada, and came to Oregon in the 1860s. Family tradition is to the effect that he spent some time at what is now Ontario, Oregon, and named the townsite.

Ooskan Butte, LAKE. This butte southeast of the Paulina Mountains was named by the USFS with the Chinook jargon word for cup or bowl, indicative of the crater in the top.

Opal City, JEFFERSON. Opal City was named for Opal Springs in the Crooked River Canyon not far away.

Opal Lake, MARION. This lake and Opal Creek north of Detroit Dam were named for Opal Elliot, the wife of early USFS ranger Roy Elliot.

Opal Springs, JEFFERSON. Opal Springs are the largest of the remarkable springs on the lower reaches of Crooked River. They issue in a sand-lined basin that contains small opal-like pebbles, and from this they have received their name. They discharge over 80 million gallons of water a day.

Ophir, CURRY. The name Ophir occurs in the Bible, and refers to a region celebrated for its proverbially fine gold. Efforts to localize the place have not been successful. The compiler has been unable to learn who named the place on Euchre Creek in Curry County, or when the name was applied, but the word is said to have been chosen because of fine gold in the black beach sands nearby. Ophir post office was established on the Curry County list on June 5, 1891, with Elizabeth J. Burrow first postmaster. It has not been in continuous service, but was operating in 1980.

Opie Dilldock Pass, LANE. This spot on the Skyline Trail about five miles south of McKenzie Pass is where the route leaves the lava fields and begins the descent to White Branch and the Sunshine Shelter. It was named in 1932 by Dee Wright and Ralph Engels, then USFS district ranger at McKenzie Bridge. They had had difficulty finding a good way down into White Branch canyon but finally found one small, practical passage. They were both reminded of a comic strip character of the early 1900s named Opie Dilldock who always found some way out of impossible situations so they decided to honor the pass with his name. The compiler spent many hours trying to locate a copy of this comic strip to give credit to the cartoonist and verify the spelling. Donald J. Sterling, Jr., of the *Oregon Journal* and Robert Frazier of the Eugene *Register-Guard* also gave generously of their time and in the fall of 1974, the former of these two came upon the true facts of the matter. *The Comics* by Jerry Robinson, New York, 1974, lists the strip *Old Opie Dilldock* by Frank M. Howarth. In Dec. 1974, the OGNB, backed by such an authority, voted unanimously to correct the spelling from the earlier form, Oppie Dildock. Only one other small nugget can be added to this gold mine of historical information. The name is a variant spelling of Knight's Opedildock, a well-known camphor and soap linament of bygone days.

Orcal, JACKSON. Orcal was a station on the Southern Pacific, near the Oregon-California line. The name was coined by railway officials who took the first parts of the names of the two states. The station was not in service in 1945.

Ord, LANE. Ord post office was named in compliment to Ord, Nebraska. Horace N. Fiske was first postmaster of Ord in Oregon, and he had formerly lived in Ord, Nebraska. When it came to naming the place in the Coast Range in Lane County, he selected the name of his old home. Ord post office in Oregon was established May 18, 1898, with Fiske postmaster. The office was in service, with one intermission, until Oct. 31, 1912, when it was closed to Earl. It was six or seven miles northeast of Earl, on the extreme south edge of Lane County, and on the very headwaters of North Fork Smith River. Ord, Nebraska, was named for Major-General Edward O. C. Ord, U.S. Army, who made a distinguished military record in the Civil War.

Ordnance, UMATILLA. In the fall of 1941 the War Department put into commission an establishment in the north part of Umatilla County, with the name Umatilla Ordnance Depot. On Dec. 6, 1943, Ordnance post office was established to serve this depot with Lorena Lane Bounds first postmaster.

Oregon. But one important contribution to our knowledge of the origin of the word Oregon has been made in the last hundred years. That was the discovery, not unexpected, that Jonathan Carver may have appropriated the name, but not the spelling, from a Major Robert Rogers, an English army officer who was commandant at the frontier military post at Mackinac during the time of Carver's journey into the upper valley of the Mississippi. Elliott has written on this point in *OHQ*, v. 22, p. 91. Major Rogers used the form Ouragon or Ourigan in a petition or proposal for an exploring expedition into the country west of the Great Lakes. This was in London in 1765. His petition was not granted, but he was sent to Mackinac as commandant. Carver is the first person to have used the form Oregon in referring to the River of the West. For a short account of Carver, *see* Carver Glacier. His *Travels Through the Interior Parts of North America* was first published in 1778 and in the introduction occurs the following passage purporting to list the names of the four great rivers of the continent: "The River Bourbon, which empties itself into Hudson's Bay; the Waters of Saint Lawrence, the Mississippi and the River Oregon, or the River of the West, that falls into the Pacific Ocean at the Straits of Annian." It is important to get clearly in mind the chronological sequence of Carver's book and the petition prepared by Major Rogers. Carver's *Travels* was first published in London in 1778 from a manuscript finally prepared just previous to its publication, but to use Carver's own words, was based upon "journals and charts" claimed to have been made during his journey to the west in 1766–67, and while at Mackinac in the fall of 1767. Kenneth Roberts' historical novel *Northwest Passage*, 1937, has a good deal to say about Carver and his relations with Rogers. Rogers' petition containing the name Ouragon was dated Aug. 1765, and his second petition containing the spelling Ourigan was dated Feb. 1772. A petition by Carver to the King's Privy Council showing the original association of Carver with Rogers for the purpose of the western exploration was acted on in May 1769, and another petition by Carver showing that the journals and charts previously mentioned had been and were still deposited with the Board of Trade in London is dated Nov. 1773. Not only did Major Rogers put into writing the name Ouragon during the year before he engaged Carver, but also none of Carver's petitions, so far examined, contains the name Oregon as we spell it, although he mentions other localities. Malcolm H. Clark, Jr., in *OHQ*, v. 61, p. 211 discusses the foregoing chronology in considerable depth and gives details of the respective travels of Rogers and Carver and the relationship of the two men. The subsequent history of the word Oregon, and some of the theories of its origin were favorite themes of Harvey W. Scott, the famous early editor of the *Oregonian*. The compiler cannot do better than to reprint some of Mr. Scott's editorial comments on the subject, but it must be borne in mind that these comments were not originally printed together as they are here reproduced. "But the name Oregon came very slowly into notice. It was long after the publication of Carver's book when it again made its appearance. The name seems not to have been known either to Vancouver or to Gray, since neither uses it. The latter, entering the river as a discoverer, called the river, not the Oregon, but the Columbia, for his ship a fact which shows that the name Oregon was quite unknown. The name was not used by Lewis and Clark in the report of their travels; in Astor's petition to Congress, presented in 1812, setting forth his claim to national assistance for his undertaking, on the ground that his efforts to establish trade here, under the sovereignty of the United States, would redound to the public security and advantage, the name

Oregon is not used to designate or describe the country; nor is it used in the act of Congress passed in response to his petition, by which the American Fur Company was permitted to introduce here goods for the Indian trade. At this time, indeed, the name appears to have been quite unknown, and perhaps would have perished but for the poet Bryant, who evidently had happened, in his reading, upon the volume of Carver's travels. The word suited the sonorous movement and solemn majesty of his verse, and he embalmed it in 'Thanatopsis' published in 1817. The journal of Lewis and Clark had been published in 1814–17, and the description therein of the distant solitudes and 'continuous woods' touched Bryant's poetic spirit and recalled the name he had seen in Carver's book. There are men whose susceptibility to literary excellence, whose skill and power in producing literary effects, give us results of this kind.

"The textbooks in the hands of our children in the public schools continue to furnish them with erroneous information that the name of the state of Oregon was derived from the word *oregano*, the Spanish name for the plant we call 'marjoram.' This is a mere conjecture absolutely without support. More than this, it is completely disproved by all that is known of the history of the name. There is nothing in the records of the Spanish navigators, nothing in the history of Spanish exploration or discovery, that indicates, even in the faintest way, that this was the origin of the name, or that the Spaniards called this country, or any part of it, by that name. There is marjoram here, indeed; and at a long time after the Spaniards had discontinued their northern coast voyages, it was suggested that the presence of marjoram (*oregano*) here had led the Spaniards to call the country Oregon. From the year 1535 the Spaniards, from Mexico, made frequent voyages of exploration along the Pacific Coast toward the north. The main object was the discovery of a passage connecting the Pacific and Atlantic oceans. Consequently, the explorers paid little attention to the country itself. After a time, finding the effort to discover a passage fruitless, they desisted for a long period. But, after the lapse of two centuries, they began settlements on the coast of California; and then voyages toward the north were resumed by some of their navigators. In 1775 the mouth of the Columbia River was seen by Heceta, but, owing to the force of the current, he was unable to enter. The fact here to be noted is that the Spaniards of that day did not call the country Oregon, or, if they did, they have left no record of it. Others have professed or proposed to derive the name Oregon from the Spanish word *oreja* (the ear), supposing that the Spaniards noted the big ears of the native Indians and named the country from the circumstance. But the Spaniards themselves have left no record of the kind; nor has it been noted, so far as we are aware, that the ears of our Indians were remarkably large. The word *orejon* is nearer our form; it signifies 'slice of dried apple,' we may suppose, from its resemblance to the form of the ear. Many years ago Archbishop F. N. Blanchet, of Oregon, while in Peru, noted a peculiar use of the word *orejon* in that country, which he ingeniously conjectured might throw some light on the origin of the name Oregon. We believe it probable that the name Oregon arose out of some circumstances connected with western explorations of the French. Earlier than the English the French had pressed on westward from the Great Lakes to the Red River, to the Saskatchewan and to the foot of the Rocky Mountains. They were ranging the country of the upper Mississippi in search of furs and for trade with the natives; they were full of curiosity and active in inquiry about the great distant West and the unknown western sea. Of this sea they possessed Spanish charts and perhaps used among the natives the word *Aragon* as a homonym of Spain. When Jonathan Carver, of Connecticut, was on his expedition to the upper Mississippi country, in 1767–68, he made all possible inquiries, he tells us, about the country toward the west, the western river, and the sea and the word Oregon. Recent writers have shown that much of Carver's book is made up of unacknowledged extracts from French explorers before him, particularly from Hennepin, Lahontan and Charlevoix; and, as Carver had no scholarship, it is believed the book was compiled in London, partly from Carver's own story and partly from the records of French and English exploration." Scott's quoted comment that the name appears to have been quite unknown at the time of Astor's expedition cannot be accepted as correct. Arrowsmith's 1798 map of the river made from Broughton's sketch is plainly titled *Plan of the River Oregan, made from an Actual Survey*.

The most plausible present explanation of the name Oregon is given by George R. Stewart. In an article in *American Speech*, Apr. 1944, and *Names on the Land*, 1967, he propounds that the origin was an engraver's error naming the Ouisconsink (Wisconsin) River on certain French editions of Lahontan's map published in the early 1700s. In early editions the name was not only misspelled Ouariconsint but also hyphenated after Ouaricon—with the final syllable oddly offset. Stewart feels that Rogers heard secondhand of the River Ouaricon that flowed west somewhere beyond the Great Lakes and that he mistakenly or carelessly transformed the word first to Ouragon and then to Ourigan. The odd nomenclature did not occur in the English editions of the map so if Rogers had seen one, he would have had no reason to suspect the Ouaricon was merely the Wisconsin by another name. Previously for more than 50 years, the best opinion has been that the name originated from one of three sources, French, Indian or Spanish. T. C. Elliott, in the *OHQ*, mentioned in the first paragraph under this heading, associated the names used by Major Rogers with the French word for storm, *ouragan*. William H. Galvani wrote of the possible Spanish origin of Oregon in *OHQ*, v. 21, p. 332. Joaquin Miller suggested the Spanish *oye agua*, hear the water, as a source of Oregon in the *Oregonian*, Oct. 21, 1907, but this seems fanciful to the compiler. Thus the matter rests.

Oregon Caves, JOSEPHINE. This is the name of a summer post office established to serve visitors to Oregon Caves. Oregon Caves post office was established July 10, 1924. The caves were formerly known as Josephine Caves.

Oregon Caves, JOSEPHINE. For information about the discovery of Oregon Caves, *see OHQ*, v. 23, 1922, pp. 271 and 274. The caves were discovered about 1874 by Elijah J. Davidson, a well-known pioneer citizen of southern Oregon. The caves were first known as Elijah Caves and later as the Marble Halls and Josephine Caves. President Taft by proclamation dated July 12, 1909, set the caves aside as a national monument with the name Oregon Caves. *See OHQ*, v. 20, p. 400. For obituary of Elijah Davidson, *see* the *Oregonian*, Sept. 11, 1927, sect. 1, p. 21.

Oregon City, CLACKAMAS. Oregon City was laid out and named in 1842, by Dr. John McLoughlin, chief factor of the Hudson's Bay Company, who located his land claim there in 1829. A Methodist church was built there in 1843. For narrative of the early settlement, *see* the *Oregonian*, Jan. 1, 1895, p. 15; description and location of pioneer buildings, June 16, 1893, p. 9; history of Oregon City, Mar. 11, 1900, p. 13; description in 1872, July 8, 1872, p. 3. The paper mill at Oregon City was first operated in 1867, *OHQ*, v. 31, p. 276. The first name of the locality was Willamette, or Willamette Falls. It is referred to by that name in correspondence of the Methodist mission, established there in 1840 on the arrival of the "great reinforcement" in the *Lausanne*. After 1840 the place grew as a political and trade center. According to Mrs. Mary Waller Hall, daughter of the Reverend Alvin F. Waller, who was one of the missionary party which came to Oregon on the *Lausanne* and settled at Oregon City in June 1840, the first apple tree in that place grew in the lot where the Methodist church was first built, from seed that her mother threw outdoors after preparing dried apples for cooking. Oregon City post office was established Mar. 29, 1847, with David Hill first postmaster.

Oregon Coast Highway, CLATSOP, COOS, CURRY, DOUGLAS, LANE, LIN-COLN, TILLAMOOK. A short sketch of early highway projects along the Oregon coast, by Leslie M. Scott, appears in *OHQ*, v. 33, p. 268. On June 3, 1919, partly as a result of feeling aroused by World War I, a measure was passed at a special election approving a bond issue of $2,500,000 to be used in cooperation with the federal government to build the Roosevelt Coast Military Highway. The name was in honor of Theodore Roosevelt. Later it became apparent that this name was not strictly suitable. In the fall of 1928 the compiler of these notes suggested to Robert W. Sawyer, then state highway commissioner, that the name Oregon Coast Highway be adopted. This change was made by the legislature in 1931. It is now known as US-101.

Oregon Trail. More than 100 years ago Francis Parkman coined a geographic name of ideal simplicity, the Oregon Trail. These two words captured the interest of millions of Americans and visitors from abroad. For almost a century the name Oregon Trail stood every test. However, in recent years efforts have been made to call this great route the Old Oregon Trail, which is just a touch of overripe sentimentality. It is unfortunate that the name Oregon lends itself to alliteration with the adjective Old. The possibilities of this sort of thing are very great. We may have the Pure Pacific Ocean, the Cute Cascade Range, Perpetual Portland. Perhaps the worst feature of the business is the official use of the name Old Oregon Trail for a modern high-speed highway, many parts of which are not close to the routes used by the great immigrations to the Pacific Northwest.

Orejana Canyon, HARNEY. Orejana is a name applied to a canyon in the southwest part of Harney County near the outside corner of Lake County. Orejana is a word used in the cattle country to indicate a young, unbranded calf and sometimes a colt. These animals are also referred to as "slick-ears" and are liable to be branded by the first finder. The canyon was named because the young animals were frequently found therein. The spelling Oreana originally used in Harney County for this and some other geographic features followed that used for a post office in Idaho, named in the 1880s. However, the present form was adopted in *Decision List 7304*. There is no doubt that the word is derived from the Spanish or from the Basque, but its exact origin is a little uncertain. In some places it is spelled *Orijana* and even *orina*. *Orijana* does not appear in any Spanish dictionary available to the compiler and *orina* is a little impolite. It seems probable that there is some connection between the word orejana meaning a "slick-ear" and the Spanish word *oreja* meaning ear.

Orenco, WASHINGTON. Orenco is a community about four miles east of Hillsboro. Oregon Electric Railway officials made up the name in 1908 by taking parts of the title of the Oregon Nursery Company, which operated several large plantations in the locality.

Oretown, TILLAMOOK. James B. Upton and S. H. Rock settled in this part of the state in 1875–76 and in 1877 sent a petition to Senator John H. Mitchell asking for a mail route to Grand Ronde and a post office. Upton had a seal with Oregon City cut in the die, and he suggested that the proposed post office be named Ore City, for he had an idea that he could alter the seal in such a way that it could be used for the new community. Senator Mitchell knew that confusion would result with Oregon City and suggested to the postal authorities that Oretown would be a better name, which was adopted. C. C. Christensen was the first postmaster. The subsequent history of the seal has not transpired.

Orient, MULTNOMAH. There are two stories about the origin of the name of this well-known place southeast of Gresham. While they do give conflicting sources for the name, together they tell the early history of Orient community and Orient School, names in use long before the post office was established. In Aug. 1946, Mrs. Louise M. Nelson wrote to say that her father moved into the community in 1872. A new school building was built in 1875 and the ground was dedicated by her father to school purposes. She added that she was a pioneer in that part of the country and the name Orient was given to the school because it was the most eastward in Multnomah and Clackamas counties. This explanation appears unlikely to the compiler because here, due to our location on the shore of the Pacific Ocean, we tend to look west to the Orient rather than east. A more reasonable explanation is given by Barbara Yasui in *OHQ*, v. 76, p. 228, where she tells how Andrew McKinnon brought Miyo Iwakoshi to Oregon as his bride in 1880. Miyo along with her younger brother, Rikichi, and her five-year old adopted daughter were the first Japanese to settle permanently in Oregon. After their arrival in Portland, McKinnon with his new family and an old friend, Captain Robert Smith, established a sawmill near Gresham which was named Orient Mill in honor of the bride. The community which grew around the mill thus received its name. Orient post office was established in Mar. 1896, with James N. Campbell first postmaster. The office was discontinued Nov. 30, 1908, and the business was turned over to Gresham. It is probable that the post office had previously operated with the name Pleasant Home. The Pleasant Home office was moved several times and while it was located at Orient, the name was changed.

Orleans, LINN. The compiler has been unable to get much information about this pioneer community, in fact none at all about the origin of the name. The place was established a little before 1850 on the Moore donation land claim, just east of and across the river from what is now Corvallis. Floods in the 1860s eliminated the settlement but not the name, which is now used for an important voting precinct in Linn County. There is also an Orleans school. The name Orleans does not appear on any of the Oregon post office lists.

Orodell, UNION. Orodell is a locality, a ghost town, on Grande Ronde River just northwest of La Grande. It is where the river leaves the canyon and enters the valley. Paul Van Scoy of La Grande wrote the compiler in Jan. 1944, that a man named Fox started a sawmill at this point in the early 1860s, the first mill in Grande Ronde Valley. A store and a post office followed in due time. The post office was named Orodell, and the name was apparently originated by a Captain Harlow, who worked for W. J. Snodgrass, storekeeper and for a time the postmaster. The name was coined by taking part of the Greek word *oros*, meaning a mountain, and adding the English word dell as a suffix. The place is still known as Orodell, but there has been no community there for many years.

Oroville, HARNEY. Oroville is a synthetic name derived from the Spanish word *oro* meaning gold. The word has been applied in many places by miners and prospectors. In Mar. 1947, Archie McGowan of Burns wrote the compiler as follows: "Oroville post office was situated at the Melvin Doan ranch near the base of Pueblo Mountain, in the south part of the county, about five miles south of the place now known as Fields. The locality was long known for its various minerals and float quartz. Messrs. Catlow and Doan were always interested in this mineral showing and gathered more or less quartz for exhibition. Presumably they named the post office for this rock." Oroville post office was established July 19, 1911, with Byron T. Tiscal first postmaster. Edwin J. Catlow was appointed postmaster Jan. 8, 1914, and the office was closed to Fields on June 30, 1915.

Orphan Butte, DESCHUTES. Orphan Butte, which is northeast of Paulina Mountains, received its name because it stands alone.

Orseco, LANE. Orseco was a post office established Nov. 23, 1903, at the site of the Champion Mine. Its name was made up from parts of the Oregon Securities Company who had just aquired the property. The name of the office was changed to Champion on Sept. 15, 1909.

Ortley, WASCO. Ortley was named for the Ortley apple, a variety that was planted there in considerable numbers. About 1911 it was planned to develop Ortley as a model orchard or fruit growing community and the growers were to live in the town and operate their orchards from there. The place is on the heights above Rowena and is about seven miles southeast of Mosier. The post office was established about 1911, with L. D. Firebaugh first postmaster. It was discontinued Nov. 30, 1922, and many of the apple trees have been taken out.

Orville, CLACKAMAS. Orville post office was established Apr. 29, 1892, with Lawrence J. Perdue first postmaster. It was discontinued June 15, 1896 with mail to Needy. Orville post office was about eight miles south of Barlow where the road from Barlow to Monitor crosses the road east to Yoder. The Perdue family were among the early settlers in this part of Clackamas County and a close friend was Orville Byland who taught the Oak Lawn school. Mr. Byland later moved to Oregon City and became county school superintendent. There is an interesting editorial about this part of the county in the Canby *Herald*, June 17, 1948. The compiler is indebted to Mr. Alvin Perdue, Route 1, Hubbard, for much of this history. He lived on part of the old Perdue farm where the post office was situated. It is a little to the north of Oak Lawn school.

Orville, MARION. Orville is a station on the Oregon Electric Railway about two miles east of Independence. It was named for Orville Butler who owned land nearby.

Oswego Creek, CLACKAMAS. This is the outlet of Lake Oswego. The stream was once known as Sucker Creek, and Lake Oswego was called Sucker Lake. Many years ago the USBGN changed the name of the lake, but the name of the creek was not disturbed. In 1927 local residents asked to have the name Sucker Creek changed to Oswego Creek to agree with the lake, and the board took the necessary action on Feb. 2, 1927.

Oswego Lake, CLACKAMAS. Oswego Lake was known as Sucker Lake during pioneer times because of the fish of that name. Local residents objected to the name and it was subsequently changed to Oswego Lake for the town of Oswego nearby, and it is now universally so known. It is said that the Indian name was *Waluga* which meant wild swan.

Othello, LANE. This post office was in service from Mar. 28, 1855, to July 8, 1859, with Jerome B. Zumwalt the only postmaster. Early maps do not show the place but in 1968 Jax Zumwalt told the compiler that the office was on the Andrew Zumwalt donation land claim along US-99W just south of the Benton County line.

Otis, LINCOLN. This post office was established Apr. 24, 1900, with Archibald

S. Thompson, postmaster. It was named for Otis Thompson, nephew of the postmaster. For more information about Thompson and the Salmon River country, *see Pioneer History of North Lincoln County*, p. 128.

Otter Rock, LINCOLN. Otter Rock was a post office near the ocean. The name originated from a rock situated about a half mile offshore and three and a quarter miles north of Yaquina Head. The rock is 36 feet above low water. About a mile to the north is a larger rock. Sea otter formerly inhabited these rocks. The writer has been unable to learn who suggested the name either for the rock or for the post office.

Ottertail Lake, HOOD RIVER. This lake about one mile east of Wahtum Lake was named in 1955 by the Oregon State Game Commission. The name was arbitrary and selected to avoid duplication.

Outerson Mountain, MARION. Outerson Mountain, near Detroit, was formerly called Bald Mountain, but because of much duplication the USFS changed the name to Outerson Mountain in honor of the late John Outerson, a pioneer of the North Santiam Valley.

Ouxy, KLAMATH. Ouxy, once a railroad station north of Klamath Falls, bore a name derived from the Klamath Indian word *E-ukshi*, meaning Klamath Lake. Ouxy Spring remains nearby.

Overholt Creek, GRANT. Overholt Creek comes into Canyon Creek from the west three miles above Canyon City. David Overholt was an early Canyon City merchant who was born in Bucks County, Pennsylvania in 1830, and came to Canyon City in 1863. For a short biography, *see History of Baker, Grant, Malheur and Harney Counties*, p. 480.

Overstreet, MALHEUR. This station was named for Robert R. Overstreet, a resident of the vicinity. It is on the Union Pacific south of Nyssa.

Overtime Spring, UMATILLA. Overtime Spring near where Texas Bar Creek enters North Fork John Day River was named in the 1960s by the USFS. Lloyd Waid of Ukiah said that truck drivers for Georgia Pacific Company stopped nearby for their coffee breaks and thus were often forced to exceed the eight hour straight time limitations of the Federal Wage and Hour Act.

Owens, TILLAMOOK. Owens post office was situated in Gods Valley and was named for a nearby landowner. The office was established Jan. 16, 1912, with William Schultz first postmaster. The office was closed Jan. 15, 1917.

Owings Creek, UMATILLA. In 1885, John A. Owings took up property near the mouth of this creek about five miles south of Nye. At one time Owens Creek southeast of Battle Mountain was erroneously shown on some maps as Owing Creek.

Owyhee, MALHEUR. A post office called Owyhee Ferry was established on the Baker County list as of Mar. 19, 1867, with William Hill postmaster. This office, which was in what is now Malheur County, was closed Sept. 16, 1868. The writer is informed that the ferry was on Snake River near the mouth of the Owyhee, and was not on Owyhee River itself. It was not far from the site of Fort Boise, Idaho. A post office with the name Owyhee was established on Jan. 4, 1886, with William Grimes postmaster. This office was closed Sept. 8, 1887, with papers to Jordan Valley. This seems to indicate that the office was farther south than the mouth of Owyhee River. An office with the same name was established July 11, 1890, with Belle Dryden postmaster. This office was on the lower reaches of Owyhee River, not far from Owyhee Ferry, and was closed in 1932. An Army map of 1887 gives the name Kinney's Ferry for the establishment on Snake River near Fort Boise.

Owyhee Rapids, GILLIAM. Judge Fred W. Wilson of The Dalles informs the compiler that these rapids in the Columbia River just west of Arlington were named for some event in the history of the steamer *Owyhee*. It is said that the boat grounded in the rapids. For the history of the *Owyhee*, see Lewis & Dryden's *Marine History of the Pacific Northwest*. The *Owyhee* was built at Celilo about 1864, and operated for about 12 years. These rapids were inundated in 1968 when John Day Dam was completed.

Owyhee River, MALHEUR. On Saturday, Feb. 18, 1826, Peter Skene Ogden, then on his second expedition into the Snake River country, "reached Sandwich Island River, so called, owing to 2 of them murdered by Snake Indians in 1819." There seems to be no doubt that the Owyhee River was named for these Hawaiians, for on June 15 of the same year Ogden uses the word *Owyhee*. The name *Owyhee* was used before 1800 for Hawaii. Owyhee River drains a large area in Oregon and western Idaho, and there are other geographic features bearing the name, derived from the name of the river. There is a community of Owyhee near the mouth of Owyhee River and also an Owyhee Ridge in Malheur County.

Oxbow, BAKER. Western pioneers were so familiar with ox bows that the descriptive name was often used for geographic features. The best-known ox bow in Oregon was that of Snake River near Ox Bow station on the now inundated railroad down the river. Oxbow is the form now used for the community established in the 1960s when the Idaho Power Company built the Oxbow Dam on Snake River. It is near the site of the old town of Copperfield, see Copperfield. Oxbow post office was established May 1, 1965, by move from Homestead.

Oxman, BAKER. This station on the Union Pacific Railroad between Pleasant Valley and Durkee was originally called Unity. Because of confusion with the more important Unity west of Bridgeport, a movement was started by the Durkee Grange to change the name to Oxman in honor of Frank C. Oxman, a local rancher. This was accomplished in 1935. Oxman was an important prosecution witness at the trial of Thomas J. Mooney for bombing the San Francisco preparedness day parade in 1916.

P Ranch, HARNEY. The P Ranch is one of the historic and romantic landmarks of eastern Oregon. It is in the valley of the Donner und Blitzen River south of Burns and west of Steens Mountain. For many years it was the headquarters of Peter French, one of the West's great cattle kings. For information about him, *see*

Frenchglen. It is frequently said that the P Ranch was named for a brand based on Pete French's first name, but in Sept. 1943, Archie McGowan of Burns, wrote the compiler that this is not a fact. French came to Oregon in the early 1870s as a scout for Dr. Hugh James Glenn, the great landowner of the Sacramento Valley. Among others, French bought out an old prospector and trapper named Porter who had a small ranch in the place that French wanted for headquarters. This man was already using a **P** iron, according to McGowan. French bought him out, iron and all, and made the brand famous throughout the west. It was a coincidence that it was the initial of Pete French's first name. For more information, *see* the *Oregonian*, Nov. 11, 1983

Pacific City, TILLAMOOK. Pacific City was named because of its proximity to the Pacific Ocean. The post office was established July 31, 1909, with Peter Murray postmaster.

Pacific Ocean, Western boundary of Oregon. After crossing the Isthmus of Panama in Sept. 1513, Vasco Nunez de Balboa discovered the ocean which he called *Mar del Sur* or Sea of the South. In Nov. 1520, Fernando Magellan, also under the Spanish flag, sailed through the straits which have since borne his name. On sailing into the great sea, he found it calm and bestowed the name of Pacific Ocean. Both names were used for many years. The Lewis and Clark expedition, 1803–1806, used these names: "Entrance of the Columbia River into the Great South Sea or Pacific Ocean" and again, "The Great Western Ocian, I can't say Pacific, as since I have seen it, it has been the reverse." (Thwaites *Original Journals of the Lewis and Clark Expedition*, v. 3, pp. 235 and 162.)

Packard Creek, LANE. This stream is six miles south of Oakridge. It was named for a logger who took a contract for getting out some sugarpine logs. He used ox carts for hauling logs from the woods to the river. This took place in the early 1870s.

Packsaddle Creek, BAKER. This short tributary of Gold Creek in S 3, T 7S, R 44E, was named because in early days a burro packsaddle was abandoned on a deer skinning pole near the creek. It was a familiar sight for many years and a reminder that trailside litter started before the twentieth century.

Packsaddle Mountain, WHEELER. This high ground west of Girds Creek near John Day River has two rock walls that simulate a packsaddle.

Paddys Valley, DOUGLAS, LANE. This is the valley of Middle Fork Willamette River where that stream crosses the county line west of Emigrant Butte. George H. Kelly of Portland told the compiler that the name was very old, and that he had been unable to learn its origin. When he was a young man the place was called Paddys Marsh.

Padgett Canyon, MORROW. This tributary of Butter Creek south of Vinson was named for Elisha H. Padgett who took up government land there in 1886.

Paisley, LAKE. There is conflicting information about the reason for the name Paisley. The compiler has been informed that the place was named by Charles

Mitchell Innes, a Scot, for Paisley in his native land. This was about 1873. The writer was told that Innes bestowed the name because the Oregon townsite reminded him of Paisley in Scotland. Whatever the reason may have been, it certainly could not have been this. A letter from E. J. McDonald printed on the editorial page of the *Oregonian* July 21, 1927, says that the place was named by a Mr. Steele, also a native of Scotland. The reader is free to choose either origin. The post office was established May 12, 1879, with Samuel G. Steele first postmaster. Presumably he is the man referred to by McDonald.

Palanush Butte, DESCHUTES. This butte, southeast of Crane Prairie, is named with the Klamath Indian word indicating a place that is dried up.

Palatine Hill, MULTNOMAH. Since the 1880s the hill or ridge just west of the west bank of the Willamette River and east of Tryon Creek has been called Palatine Hill. The Palatine Hill road traverses the summit of this hill, which has a maximum elevation of 506 feet. The Romans used the word palatine in referring to something pertaining to the emperor or king. The only clue that suggests itself about the name in Multnomah County is the fact that the plat of Palatine Hill was filed by A. N. and Melinda King Feb. 24, 1886. It may be possible that the Kings selected the name Palatine Hill because of the historic significance.

Palestine, MULTNOMAH. Palestine post office was established June 30, 1891, with James Howe first postmaster. Later postmasters were Henry S. Lewis and Albert Vail. The office was closed Feb. 16, 1903, with all papers to Lents. Palestine post office was situated in a store operated by Henry S. Lewis at SE 39th and Division streets. The name Palestine was given by James Howe, an Englishman, who is said to have visited the Holy Land and liked the name. The store and post office were later moved to the vicinity of the South Mount Tabor school, near the old cemetery.

Palmateer Meadows, WASCO. These meadows are along Barlow Creek just south of the Hood River County line and east of Bird Butte. They and Palmateer Creek, just north in Hood River County, are named for an early Wasco County sheepman, Jack Palmateer.

Palmer, MULTNOMAH. Palmer post office was in service near Bridal Veil Creek in the hills about three miles east of Bridal Veil, from Feb. 21, 1898, to Dec. 15, 1919. Idona A. Pulley was the first postmaster. The office was near the mill and logging railroad of the Bridal Veil Lumber Company and was named for the president, Loren C. Palmer.

Palmer Butte, CURRY. This butte five miles northeast of Brookings was named for D. H. Palmer who homesteaded on its slopes before the turn of the century.

Palmer Creek, JACKSON. Palmer Creek is tributary to Applegate River in the southwest part of the county. It rises on the southeast slopes of Palmer Peak, elevation about 4700 feet. The creek was named for one Palmer, an early-day miner who was the first to discover gold on the stream. The peak was named for the creek.

Palmer Glacier, CLACKAMAS. There was an unusually light snowfall in the winter of 1923–24 and as a result of this a new glacier was discovered on Mount Hood in the summer of 1924. This glacier is west of White River Glacier. Because it drained into Salmon River it was decided to name it Salmon River Glacier. The name was not satisfactory but was eventually adopted by the USBGN. At the suggestion of the compiler of these notes and with the approval of the Mazamas and other interested organizations the USBGN changed the name on Feb. 3, 1926, to Palmer Glacier, in honor of General Joel Palmer, who may have been the first white man to attempt to climb Mount Hood. That was in 1845. For information about General Palmer and his activities in Oregon, *see* Palmer Peak. In a letter printed in *OHQ*, v. 6, p. 309, Archibald McDonald says that David Douglas attempted to climb Mount Hood in 1833. The compiler has been unable to get any facts about this attempt.

Palmer Junction, UNION. Palmer Junction, at the confluence of Lookingglass Creek and Grande Ronde River, was the name given the junction of the Palmer Lumber Company's railroad and the line into the Wallowa Valley now operated by the Union Pacific Railroad Company. The lumber company railroad is abandoned and the present railroad station, now named Looking Glass, is about a quarter of a mile northeast of the former community. A post office named Palmer Junction was established Apr. 17, 1909, with F. Eldrich postmaster. The office was closed July 16, 1937.

Palmer Peak, MULTNOMAH. Palmer Peak is a high point in the northeastern part of Multnomah County not far from the cliffs above the Columbia River. It has an elevation of 4010 feet and was named for General Joel Palmer, a pioneer of 1845, and a noted character in Oregon history. He was born of American parents in Canada in 1810. He came to Oregon from Indiana, and helped Samuel K. Barlow locate the Barlow Road. He made an attempt to climb Mount Hood on Oct. 12, 1845, and while he did not reach the top, his diary indicates that he climbed well up on the mountain, and assured himself that the summit could be reached. The next day he named Camp Creek. Palmer settled in the Willamette Valley and was one of the founders of Dayton, Yamhill County. He became superintendent of Indian affairs for Oregon in 1853, and later was president of the Columbia River Road Company that opened a toll road from Sandy River to the Cascades in 1863. It operated ferries at Sandy River and at Dog (Hood) River. He occupied important political positions, and was once a candidate for governor. He died at Dayton June 9, 1881. Palmer Peak was at one time called Cub Peak, a name without significance. Palmer Creek in Yamhill County, was also named for Joel Palmer.

Palos, LINN. Palos post office was established Mar. 4, 1856, and was closed Oct. 30, 1857. Samuel G. Thompson was the first postmaster. The compiler does not know why this pioneer post office was named with the Spanish word meaning sticks or stones and sometimes timbers, but he has come to the conclusion that Thompson was a student of history and was familiar with the name of the port near the southwest corner of Spain from which Columbus sailed on Friday, Aug. 3, 1492, on his eventful first voyage of discovery. The Spanish place-name Palos was doubtless the origin of the name of the Linn County post office.

Palouse Creek, COOS. How this stream tributary to Haynes Inlet on the north part of Coos Bay got the name of Palouse River in eastern Washington is a problem that the writer has been unable to solve. Lewis and Clark called the stream in Washington Drewyers River after a member of the expedition, and referred to the Indians as *Palloat-pallah*. Canadian members of the Astor party in 1812 used the name Pavion for the river and *Pallatapalla* for the tribe. David Douglas called the tribe *Pelushpa*. For other forms of the name, *see Handbook of American Indians*, v. 2, p. 195. Palouse is the style now used in referring to a large area of rolling country and to other geographic features in eastern Washington. The French word *pelouse* is used to describe terrain covered with fine grasses, a characteristic of the Palouse country before it was cultivated. Whether the name Palouse came from the French-Canadian trappers or from the Indians, or both, is a matter of conjecture.

Pamelia Creek, LINN. Pamelia Creek, at the southwestern base of Mount Jefferson, was named for Pamelia Ann Berry, a girl cook in the Marion County road locating party described by John Minto in *OHQ*, v. 4, p. 249. Minto named the stream in 1879, and gave as his reason, the unfailing cheerfulness of Miss Berry. It may be added that the wording of the article is ambiguous, and Miss Berry may have been with the party that opened the trail to Black Butte in 1879. Pamelia Lake was named for the creek, probably by Judge John B. Waldo.

Panky Spring, KLAMATH. Panky Spring and Panky Lake are west of Gerber Reservoir and east of Bonanza. They were named for the family of Lewis Panky, ranchers in the vicinity.

Pansy Mountain, MARION. This mountain is in the extreme north part of the county, north of Detroit. It was named for the Pansy Blossom copper mine, which was operated by Joe Davis and Robert Bagby. The ore at this mine was peacock colored, and the mine was named on that account.

Panther, LANE. More than 50 Oregon streams have been named for the cougar or the panther, not because of the popularity of these animals but because early settlers disliked them so. Ordinarily panthers did not attack human beings, but they killed such an abundance of deer and livestock that they were held in great aversion. Most of the Panther creeks in the state were named because they were the scenes of the visits of the giant cats, or the scenes of their exterminations. An important Panther Creek in western Oregon is that in Lane County, southwest of Eugene. This stream rises southwest of Crow and flows southwest to join Wolf Creek. Panther Creek was named in very early days. Panther post office was established near the mouth of this creek on Feb. 5, 1894, with Demetrius D. Hooker first postmaster. The office was closed May 15, 1909, but the locality retained the name Panther, despite the fact that what local business there was for the place eventually evaporated. There are two varieties of panthers or mountain lions in

Oregon, the one in the west part of the state called the Oregon cougar and the Rocky Mountain cougar in the east part of Oregon. Vernon Bailey in *Mammals and Life Zones of Oregon* has a good account of these animals.

Paquet Gulch, WASCO. Francis Xavier Paquet came to the Wapinitia area in 1876 and opened the first store. He settled southwest of the community near the gulch which bears his name. The spelling Pacquet is wrong.

Paradise, WALLOWA. This place was named by Sam Wade, Pres Halley and William Masterson, who went from Wallowa Valley about Oct. 1878, to look for winter range. On returning to the valley, they informed the settlers that they had found a regular paradise, with fine grass. Settlers with about a thousand cattle went to the new range in Nov. 1878. Notwithstanding the appearance of the country the winter was severe and many cattle were lost.

Paris, LANE. Paris, Oregon, is justly famous for two things. It was not named for Paris, France, or "Pah-is," Kentucky. George E. Parris asked to have the place made a post office, and was the first postmaster. The office was named for him with one "r" eliminated.

Park Place, CLACKAMAS. The plat for Park Place, written as two words, was filed for record Aug. 10, 1889, and the post office was established the following year. Postal authorities soon consolidated the name into one word. Park Place was originally called Clackamas, but that name was subsequently moved to a station about three miles to the north and the former station of Clackamas was called Paper Mill. Remains of the old paper mills were in evidence about 1910. The name Park Place was chosen for the townsite because of the park in a nearby oak grove, and Paper Mill was no longer appropriate. The post office name was later changed from Parkplace to Park Place.

Parkdale, HOOD RIVER. Parkdale is a descriptive name rather accurately describing the community and its surroundings. The name is said to have been selected by Ralph Davies about 1910, when the post office was established. In 1976, after much public discussion, the name of the post office was changed to Mount Hood. Simultaneously, the Mount Hood office, three miles to the northeast, was closed. The community retains the name Parkdale.

Parker, POLK. This place was named for one "Lon" Parker, a pioneer landowner. Bloomington post office was established on May 25, 1852, near the site of Parker, with Eli W. Foster first postmaster. The office was closed in 1863. The railroad was built through this area in the late 1870s and Parker's station was then established. Many years later the name of the station was changed to Parker. Parker post office was established in Sept. 1880, and was closed in Mar. 1882. From 1884 to 1907 it was operated with the name Parkers. In 1914 it was reestablished as Parker and was closed in 1927. The community of Parker passed from the scene after World War II.

Parkers Mill, MORROW. Benjamin H. Parker was born in Canada in 1827. He came to Oregon in 1862 and to Morrow County in 1876. "Uncle Ben" Parker, as he was usually called, established the Parker and Gleason sawmill on Rock Creek at the mouth of Board Creek, this latter name probably due to the activity at the mill. The mill had a daily capacity of 10,000 board feet of cut stock. Parker later bought out Gleason and the place became known as Parkers Mill. "Uncle Ben" was also a stockman, and well known in central Oregon. *See History of Umatilla and Morrow Counties*, p. 496.

Parkersburg, COOS. This place got its name from Captain Judah Parker, who built a sawmill in the community about 1876. For history of Captain Parker by Fred Lockley, *see Sunday Journal*, Mar. 3, 1946.

Parkersville, BAKER. In Mar. 1917, R. R. McHaley of Prairie City, Oregon, wrote as follows: "Parkersville was on the old mail stage road leading from Austin to McEwen and Auburn near the headwaters of Burnt River and about three miles west of Whitney. Mr. and Mrs. Parker kept a stage station for years until the railroad bypassed the station, and the town of Whitney was established. Parkersville is in Baker County about four miles from the Grant County line." Parkersville post office was established Aug. 1, 1874 and was discontinued June 29, 1876, on the Grant County list. By all reports, it was never in Grant County, always in Baker. This is a set of puzzles the reader will have to solve.

Parkersville, MARION. This place was about three miles west of the present site of Mount Angel. Parkersville post office was established Sept. 29, 1852, with Freeman E. Eldriedge first postmaster. The office was discontinued on Dec. 2, 1861. The community was named for William Parker, a pioneer of 1846. *See* Down's *A History of the Silverton Country*, pp. 31, 36, 224 and 226. The name is now used for Parkersville school.

Parkrose, MULTNOMAH. Parkrose is a branch post office of Portland serving an area northeast of the city. Prior to the incorporation of Maywood Park in 1967, the whole area was considered Parkrose and the name in 1990 is still in general use although a sizeable part is within the corporate limits of the new community. The plat of Parkrose was filed on Oct. 5, 1911, and the name was doubtless suggested because of the proximity of Rose City Park, the plat of which was filed in Mar. 1907. It is said that a Portland business man, Frank E. Beach, was the originator of the name Rose City as applied to Portland.

Parkwood, MULTNOMAH. Parkwood post office was established about 1913 with J. W. Spencer first postmaster. The name has a pleasant rustic suggestion which seems to be about the only reason it was selected. The post office was closed in 1928.

Parrett Mountain, YAMHILL. This well-known landmark lies about four miles east of Newberg. Its lower slopes extend into Clackamas and Washington counties. It is crescent shaped and the highest point is in its central section, with an elevation of 1247 feet. It is easily seen from the hills southwest of Portland and has become a point of interest since it serves to locate Newberg and the Pacific Highway West. Parrett Mountain is a spur of the Chehalem Mountains from which it is separated by Chehalem Gap. It was named for the Parrott brothers, who were born in England and who settled in this vicinity in 1853. The three brothers spelled their name as indicated, but members of later generations who have investigated the matter in England, use the form Parrett, which they say is correct.

Parrish Gap, MARION. This gap is in the hills about a mile northeast of Marion. It was named for E. E. Parrish on whose donation land claim the gap is situated.

Parrott Creek, CLACKAMAS. The stream flowing through New Era was named for Joseph Parrott, a pioneer of 1844.

Parrott Creek, DOUGLAS. This creek in the south part of Roseburg was named for Moses Parrott, a pioneer settler from Tennessee who owned a large acreage in the area. His large, Queen Anne house built in 1891, was still standing in 1990 and was entered on the National Register of Historic Places.

Pass Creek, DOUGLAS. This creek bears a descriptive name because of the fact that it heads in a comparatively low divide between the waters flowing into Willamette River and those flowing into the Umpqua River. In early days William Ward built a corduroy road through the canyon of Pass Creek and operated a toll gate. *See* Wards Butte. J. J. Comstock built a sawmill on Pass Creek about the time the railroad was built and was given the privilege of using cut timber along the right of way. He had previously been in business with Ben Holladay, and Holladay favored him on that account. The name of the creek was used for an early day post office, Pass Creek, established May 31, 1867, with William A. Mulvaney first and only postmaster. The office was closed to Yoncalla on Jan. 7, 1869. Drain post office had not yet been established. The compiler has been unable to get the location of Pass Creek post office, except that it was near the stream Pass Creek somewhere between Divide and Drain.

Pataha Creek, LANE. Pataha Creek, which flows into Wildcat Creek east of Austa, is one of several features in the Oregon Coast Range that have Indian names imported from the state of Washington. The compiler does not know the reason for the application of the name Pataha to the stream in Lane County unless it was by someone who had once lived in southeastern Washington or who liked the name because he saw it on a map. Pataha is the name of a village near Pomeroy, Washington, on a creek bearing the same name. *Pataha* is said to be a Nez Perce word meaning brush. *See* Meany's *Origin of Washington Geographic Names*, p. 208.

Patawa Creek, UMATILLA. Patawa Creek and its tributary, South Patawa Creek, rise on the west slopes of Emigrant Hill and flow northwestward to join Tutuilla Creek near Pendleton. Patawa is the name of a large and well-known Indian family of Umatilla County, members of which have lived on the banks of Patawa Creek for many years. The spelling Parawa is wrong.

Patjens Lakes, LINN. These lakes west of Santiam Pass are one and one-half miles southwest of Big Lake. The 45-minute walk on a pleasant forest trail is a popular summer hike for young and old. They were named for Henry Patjens, a member of a Sherman County sheep family, who had summer range near Mount Washington at the turn of the century.

Patrick Creek, CURRY. According to John Quiner of the OSHD, this creek west of Carpenterville was named for Mrs. Patrick, an adjacent property owner, by the survey party who relocated US-101 in the 1950s.

Patterson Mountain, LANE. This mountain about six miles west of Westfir was named for A. W. Patterson. Patterson was an original incorporator of the Oregon Central Military Road Company and also made a number of the early land surveys during the 1850s.

Pattersons Mills, DOUGLAS. Pattersons Mills were a very well-known Douglas County commercial enterprise that began operations in pioneer days. The mills were near North Umpqua River not far from the place called Glide. The post office Pattersons Mills was established in Aug. 1878, with William Patterson postmaster. The office was closed in June 1886, and the business turned over to Mount Scott post office a few miles to the west.

Patton Valley, WASHINGTON, YAMHILL. Patton Valley was named for a family of early settlers. William and Mary Patton came from Missouri in 1850 and later settled in the valley. Their son, Robert Patton, owned land therein and lived nearby for many years. The valley lies along Tualatin River from a point near Gaston westward to Cherry Grove.

Paulina, CROOK. In the opinion of the writer there are more than enough geographic features in Oregon named for this belligerent Snake Indian. We have Paulina town, Paulina Mountains, Paulina Peak, Paulina Marsh, Paulina Creek, Paulina Prairie and Paulina Lake. The Southern Pacific Company also had Paunina station in the early days of the Cascade line. There may be honest sentimental differences of opinion about naming these features for the Oregon chief, but practically, confusion is the sure result of such a process, especially when the various features are not in the same locality, but yet are not widely separated. For an account of Paulina and his activities, *see* Bancroft's *History of Oregon*, v. 2, pp. 504 *et seq*. The name is spelled in a variety of ways, but Paulina is generally accepted. Paulina was a skillful antagonist and his activities covered a large territory. Bancroft's pages are full of Indian atrocities in central and eastern Oregon during the years 1866–68 and scores of miners, trappers and settlers were exterminated. It is generally believed that Paulina was to a large extent responsible, though of course we have only the white man's side of the story. In the summer of 1867 Paulina raided several ranches in the John Day country. He was pursued by J. N. Clark, Howard Maupin and William Ragan, and was shot down while he was feasting on a roasted ox. Bancroft says that Clark killed him, but in central Oregon it is generally believed that Maupin fired the shot. For additional information, *see* Maupin. Col. William Thompson of Alturas, California, published a book entitled *Reminiscences of a Pioneer*. He gives a graphic description of the activities of Paulina, and confirms the generally accepted belief that Maupin killed him in

Paulina Basin. Paulina Basin is near the junction of Trout Creek and Little Trout Creek north of Ashwood in the northeast part of Jefferson County. Paulina post office was established on May 23, 1882 on Beaver Creek in the east part of Crook County. John F. Bowen was the first postmaster.

Paulina Creek, DESCHUTES. According to Captain O. C. Applegate, the Paiute Indian name for this stream and the vicinity of Paulina Prairie was *Mil-ka-ke*. Captain Applegate told the compiler in Nov. 1927, that he did not know the translation of the name.

Paulina Peak, DESCHUTES. Paulina Peak, elevation 7985 feet, is a high point on the south edge of Paulina Lake in the Paulina Mountains. For information about this part of Oregon, *see* Newberry Crater. Paulina Peak, shown on older maps as Pauline Peak, is one of a number of central Oregon geographic features named for Paulina, the famous Snake Indian chief. There are several spellings, including Paunina, Panina, Panaina and Palihi. He was of the Walpapi tribe of Snakes. For information about his activities, *see* Paulina. For a description of the neighborhood of Paulina Peak, *see* the *Oregonian*, Jan. 16, 1916.

Paunina, KLAMATH. Paunina was a station on the Southern Pacific Cascade line named for the famous central Oregon Indian chief. *See* Paulina. During the construction period. Paunina was called Skookum.

Pawn, LANE. The name of Pawn post office was composed by taking the first letter in the names of four local residents who were instrumental in getting the post office established. These four men were named Poole, Ackerley, Worthington and Nolen. Willis Nolen suggested manufacturing the name in this manner. Monroe Poole was the first postmaster and the office operated from Dec. 13, 1915, to Oct. 17, 1930.

Pawnee Lake, MARION. Pawnee Lake is in the basin west of Olallie Lake. It was named after World War II by a fish planting crew that was supplied by a Piper Pawnee airplane. *See* Alice Lake.

Paxton, JEFFERSON. Paxton is a station on the Burlington Northern north of Madras named for G. L. Paxton, a nearby landowner.

Payn, CLACKAMAS. Payn post office was on the extreme north edge of Clackamas County just about south of Lents and close to the west base of Mount Scott. It was named for the postmaster, William S. Payn. This office was established Apr. 6, 1898, and was closed Jan. 12, 1904. As with so many other small offices, its death was caused by the advent of rural free delivery.

Payne Creek, WHEELER. Payne Creek is tributary to Girds Creek. George Nelson of Mitchell told the compiler that James Payne was a well-known early homesteader with a family of ten daughters.

Paynesville, CLACKAMAS. Paynesville was about three miles north of Sandy and a little to the west of the Bluff Road. The post office was established Dec. 31, 1885, with John G. P. Lawlor first and only postmaster. The office was closed June 6, 1888. Paynesville was named for a local landowner who owned property adjacent to Lawlor. Later Lewis Hoaglum acquired some or all of this property. The site of the post office was said to be owned by a man named Pratt in 1947.

Peach, MALHEUR. This Union Pacific Railroad station was named for a peach orchard nearby. The place was about nine miles east of Juntura, and in 1943 it was reported that the station was no longer in service.

Peach Canyon, UNION. Peach Canyon between Hilgard and Perry was apparently named for John Peach who bought government land along it in 1882. Peach was a cousin of William G. Peach of Island City.

Peach Creek, UNION. Peach Creek is northwest of North Powder. William G. Peach first came to the Grande Ronde Valley in 1873. He later moved to the Willamette Valley but returned permanently in 1883. Peach and his two sons, James S. and George W. Peach, then established what grew to be a large dairy farm near Island City. In the 1890s all three men bought government land along Peach Creek, probably for its timber.

Peak, BENTON. Peak post office was a few miles northwest of Marys Peak and was named for the mountain. It was on the extreme west edge of Benton County in the Coast Range and was relatively isolated. The office was established Oct. 11, 1899, with Virgie Davidson postmaster. Peak post office was discontinued Oct. 15, 1917.

Peak, WASHINGTON. A post office with the name Peak was established in Washington County on Mar. 13, 1874, with Bentley George postmaster. It was discontinued June 9, 1876. Peak post office was two or three miles northwest of Forest Grove and near Gales Creek. It was named for Gales Peak, a prominent feature a little to the northwest.

Pearcy Island, MULTNOMAH. This island is in the angle formed by the junction of the Columbia and Willamette rivers. South of the island is Pearcy Slough. These features bear the name of Nathan Pearcy, a pioneer of Oregon, who took up a donation land claim on the island in 1850. Drainage and reclamation projects have changed the character of islands and sloughs in this locality.

Pearse Peak, CURRY. Pearse Peak is four miles east of Humbug Mountain. Charles H. Pearse took up a homestead on its west slope in 1906 but probably did not personally prove it up as he was born in 1826 in Boston. He came to Oregon in 1871 and a short time later was lighthouse keeper at Cape Blanco. His son, Stoner P. Pearse, was at one time in the state legislature and reportedly had mining claims on the mountain so the homestead could have been a family enterprise.

Pebble Creek, COLUMBIA, WASHINGTON. Pebble Creek, which bears a descriptive name, rises in the extreme north part of Washington County, and after crossing the Columbia County line flows northward to join the Nehalem River in the east part of Vernonia. It has been called Pebble Creek since pioneer times. Pebble post office was established Jan. 31, 1891, with Richard J. Tyacke postmaster. It was on the Pebble Creek road about three miles south of Vernonia, on the Tyacke property. The office was in operation until Dec. 1895, when its affairs were turned over to the Vernonia office. The Pebble Creek road or trail was one of the first routes of travel into the upper Nehalem Valley, and many pioneer settlers went in that way from the Willamette Valley. *See* Fred Lockley's interview with Mrs. Sarah Spencer on editorial page of the *Oregon Journal*, Aug. 18, 1928.

Pebble Springs, GILLIAM. Pebble Springs, three miles southeast of Arlington, was the site of the proposed controversial nuclear generating station planned by Portland General Electric Company in the late 1970s. The name comes from Pebble Springs Camp and not because nature provided a constant and bountiful supply of cold, crystal clear water at this location. Rather, according to information provided by long-time Arlington resident Alfred "Buzz" Clough, Pebble Springs Camp was part of Krebs Brothers Sheep Ranch. When they put in a cistern and other facilities, they needed a name. An observant worker noticed an abandoned (and empty) bottle of Pebble Springs whiskey and all agreed that that name would serve admirably.

Peck, DOUGLAS. When the Oregon & California Rail Road was built south of Roseburg in the early 1880s a station called Nichols was established 13 miles southwest of Riddle. This station was named for a well-known family of the vicinity. It did not have a post office however until Dec. 31, 1914, when Nichols post office was established with Viola B. Nichols first and only postmaster. This office operated until Dec. 31, 1929. The railroad company had difficulty with the station named Nichols due to the fact that there were other places on the line with the same name. Shipments went astray. As a result, the company changed the name of Nichols station to Peck. The origin of the name Peck is a mystery to the compiler and it is not certain just when the railroad made the change. In any event, a post office was named Peck and established Dec. 29, 1931, with Homer V. Cook postmaster. This was just two years after the Nichols office had been closed. For some reason Mr. Cook never got the Peck office into operation and his appointment was rescinded June 2, 1932. As far as the compiler knows, there has been no post office at this point since that date. The railroad station Peck has also succumbed to the paucity of travelers and shippers in the Cow Creek Canyon.

Peck Gulch, JACKSON. Peck Gulch, just west of Lakecreek, is on the 1876 homestead of Henry Peck.

Pedee, POLK. Pedee owes its name to Colonel Cornelius Gilliam who was born in North Carolina in 1798 and came to Oregon in 1844. *See* Gilliam County. He was killed in 1848. Either he, or members of his family, named Pedee Creek, a tributary to Luckiamute River. Pedee community is near the mouth of this creek. The name is, of course, from the famous river of North and South Carolina which was doubtless frequently in the minds of the Gilliams. The stream in the South is officially Peedee, but the place in Oregon is spelled Pedee.

Pedro Mountain, BAKER. Pedro Mountain is west of Rye Valley in the southeast part of the county. In Dec. 1945, LeRoy Grettum of Baker wrote the compiler that old mining men of that area reported that the mountain was named by a group of Portuguese miners who operated there during the eastern Oregon gold rush of the 1860s. There was a Pedro Mine on the mountain, and it seems probable that the mountain took its name from the mine. Pedro post office was in operation for a few months in the early summer of 1879 with Lyman S. Brown postmaster. Doubtless it was connected with some work at the mining claim.

Peel, DOUGLAS. Peel post office was on Little River, a branch of North Umpqua River, about 25 miles east of Roseburg, and a few miles up Little River from Glide. The office was established Jan. 18, 1888, with Robert McKure first postmaster. According to a story in the Roseburg *News-Review*, Feb. 21, 1947, the office was named for Samuel West Peel, of Bentonville, Arkansas, by Hiram L. Engels, who became second postmaster at Peel on Feb. 15, 1888. Peel and A. A. Engels, father of H. L. Engels, had been schoolmates many years before. Peel post office was closed Dec. 15, 1921. S. W. Peel, 1831–1924, was a well-known citizen of Arkansas, of which state he was a native. He served in the Confederate army in the Civil War and reached the rank of colonel. He studied law, and held several political offices, including that of prosecuting attorney on one of the circuits. He was elected representative in Congress and served from 1883 to 1893.

Peepover Saddle, WALLOWA. This saddle, in the southeast part of the county, is very narrow, and its summit is sharp. It is called Peepover on that account, and the name is usually written P. O. Saddle. The initials conveniently suggest other forms of the name.

Peg Gulch, JEFFERSON. This tributary of Little Muddy Creek east of Axehandle bears the name of a local homesteader, Daniel W. "Peg Leg" Morissey. Time has obliterated the details concerning the loss of Mr. Morissey's leg.

Peggy Butte, WHEELER. Peggy Butte northeast of Mitchell was named for Margaret Reynolds whose family came from Tennessee and raised stock in the area.

Pelican, KLAMATH. For the history of the post offices called Pelican and Pelican Bay, *see* Rocky Point.

Pelican Bay, KLAMATH. Pelicans are much in evidence about the Klamath lakes, and this name was appropriately applied to an arm of Upper Klamath Lake. A few other geographic features in the state are also named for the pelican. The Oregon bird is *Pelecanus erythrorhynchos*, the American white pelican. The habits of this pelican, particularly in Oregon, are well described in Bulletin 121 of the United States National Museum, *Life Histories of North American Petrels and Pelicans*, p. 285. The Klamath Indian name for these birds was *kumal* or *yamal*. Pelican Bay was named by Captain O. C. Applegate in 1866. There was at one time a post office called Pelican near the west shore of Pelican Bay and later another office named Recreation. For the most part these offices served summer patrons.

Pelican Butte, KLAMATH. This butte was named for Pelican Bay nearby. One of the Indian names for the butte was *Mongina*. The USC&GS formerly listed it under the name Lost Peak, elevation 8026 feet.

Pelican City, KLAMATH. Pelican City is the suburb of Klamath Falls north of Link River along the shore of Upper Klamath Lake. It is so called because it was the site of the mill that belonged to the Pelican Bay Lumber Company. Pelican Bay itself is in the extreme northwest corner of the lake.

Pelican Creek, UMATILLA, UNION. Pelican Creek, prominent in the history of northeastern Oregon, rises in the Blue Mountains east of Kamela and flows southeast to join Dry Creek just northwest of Hilgard. In Nov. 1945, C. C. Fisher of the U.S. Bureau of Reclamation, then stationed at Salem, wrote the compiler as follows: "When I was a small boy my parents ran the old Pelican stage station on Pelican Creek a few miles above Hilgard. A short distance above the stage station is Pelican Prairie on the old stage road. It was reported that Pelican Creek and Pelican Prairie were named because someone saw a flock of pelicans flying over that area. This was quite an unusual event, as I never saw any pelicans during my young life in the Blue Mountains." Some very early maps show the stream as Tilliacum Creek or Tillicum, but if this was the origin of the name, it has not persisted. *Tillicum* is an Indian word meaning friendly people or associates.

Pelton Dam, JEFFERSON. Pelton Dam is a 203-foot-high structure on Deschutes River five miles south of Warm Springs built by Portland General Electric Company for hydroelectric power. It takes its name from the one time Oregon Trunk Railway station of this name on Willow Creek just east of Deschutes River. When this line was built, James J. Hill, president of the railway, had several stations named for local residents. John Sisemore, the first postmaster at Bend, married the widow of Enoch C. Pelton of Jackson County. She had three sons by her first marriage and two of them, John and James Pelton, settled in central Oregon where they were well-known citizens at the turn of the century. *Pelton* is also the Chinook jargon word for crazy, but it is only coincidence that it described the emotions of some ardent anglers. Feeling ran high and old friends faced off on this issue of the first high dam on Deschutes River.

Pemberton Canyon, GILLIAM. This canyon is southwest of Condon. It was named for Pemberton Cason, a nearby resident. Pemberton F. Cason was born in Missouri in 1843 and came to Oregon in 1864. After experiences in the mines and elsewhere, he settled in what was later Gilliam County in 1881. Cason Canyon, west of Pemberton Canyon, was named for the same man.

Pendleton, UMATILLA. George Hunt Pendleton, of Ohio (1825–89), was Democratic candidate for vice-president in 1864. Pendleton was named in his honor, in 1868, by the commissioners of Umatilla County, J. S. Vinson, James Thompson and Samuel Johnson, on suggestion of G. W. Bailey, then county judge. In that year the Oregon Democratic state convention instructed its delegates to vote for Pendleton for president. The town of Pendleton was designated the county seat against the rivalry of Umatilla Landing, which was just east of the mouth of Umatilla River. The Pendleton townsite was owned chiefly by M. E. Goodwin and G. W. Bailey. For progress of the town until 1890, *see* the *Oregonian*, Jan. 1,

1890. Efforts to establish a trading center in what is now the locality of Pendleton began as early as 1851, when Dr. William C. McKay started a post at the mouth of McKay Creek and called it Houtama. Later, one Marshall established Marshall Station about a half mile to the east, on the north bank of Umatilla River. This was also known as Swift Station. Marshall is said to have been a "White Collared Man," a euphemism for gentleman gambler. Marshall Station was about two miles west of the present business district of Pendleton. About 1863 Marshall Station was known as Middleton because it was believed to be about half way between Umatilla Landing and the Grande Ronde Valley. When Umatilla County was created in 1862, the temporary seat of government was put at Marshall Station. *See* Umatilla County, and Fred Lockley's article in the *Sunday Journal*, June 3, 1945. Marshall post office was established on Apr. 21, 1865, with Jonathan Swift postmaster. The name of the office was changed to Pendleton on Oct. 8, 1869.

Pengra, DESCHUTES. Pengra post office was established on the Crook County list Jan. 18, 1886, with Walter O'Neil postmaster. The office was closed Dec. 22, 1888, but reopened Apr. 10, 1893 with B. J. Pengra postmaster and finally closed Apr. 6, 1895 with papers to Crater. Crater was an office a little southwest of Lava Butte and just north of the Vandevert Ranch, close to Deschutes River. According to the Polk Gazetteer of 1889–90, Pengra was ten miles south of Crater, at or close to the present site of La Pine where B. J. Pengra had some interests.

Pengra, LANE. Pengra was a station on the Cascade line of the Southern Pacific Company. It was named for B. J. Pengra, a pioneer of 1853, who was for a time a newspaper publisher, and in 1862 surveyor general for Oregon. He was an advocate of the Humboldt or Winnemucca railroad route from the Willamette Valley. Pengra had charge of the construction of the military road up Middle Fork Willamette River. He died at Coburg Sept. 18, 1903. For many references to his activities, *see* Scott's *History of the Oregon Country*.

Pengra Pass, KLAMATH, LANE. The USBGN, at the suggestion of the compiler of this book, adopted on Nov. 2, 1927, the name Pengra Pass for the pass in the Cascade Range just west of Odell Lake used by the Cascade line of the Southern Pacific Company. This action was taken in honor of B. J. Pengra, one of Oregon's pioneer railroad enthusiasts and an early advocate of a railroad from the Willamette Valley across the Cascade Range to Nevada. It was therefore thought proper that an important strategic point in the Cascade Range should be named in his honor. The proposal made by the compiler was approved by the government bureau concerned. At the time the compiler suggested the name Pengra Pass for this feature, he did not know that B. J. Pengra was its actual discoverer. The Oregon Historical Society has been provided with part of a report by Pengra, who, with W. H. Odell, made a reconnaissance of the Diamond Peak region for the Oregon Central Military Road in July 1865. Writing as of July 21, 1865, Pengra mentions the probability of a good pass to the north of Diamond Peak. On July 27

Pengra and Odell visited Odell Lake and Pengra confirmed his belief that there was a good pass through the Cascade Range at this point. He gives the elevation of the pass as 5000 feet, or 600 feet lower than Willamette Pass, now Emigrant Pass, west of Summit Lake. Both of these observations are remarkably correct. For editorial comment on B. J. Pengra and pass in Oregon named for him, *see* the *Oregonian*, Dec. 11, 1927. For the crossing of SH-58 just north of Odell Lake, *see* Willamette Pass.

Peninsular, MULTNOMAH. Peninsular post office was established Apr. 25, 1890, with Anna B. Lyman first postmaster, to serve a growing suburban area that was later taken into Portland. The name was descriptive and had its origin in the Peninsular Addition and some additions to that addition. The writer does not know when Peninsular post office was closed, but it is shown as active on the post route map of 1900. The addition was named because it was on the peninsula between Columbia and Willamette rivers. The plat was filed in March 1889.

Penn, LANE. Penn was a railroad station for McGlynn post office. The name Penn was used for the railroad station because of the Penn Timber Company, which was operating nearby. *See* McGlynn.

Penola, GRANT. A post route map dated 1880 shows a post office with the name Penola at a point 16 miles northeast of Prairie City on the road to Sumpter. Other postal records show that the Penola post office was established Jan. 27, 1876, and was discontinued Apr. 19, 1878. John R. Roy was the only postmaster. The compiler has been quite unable to get information about the origin of the name or word Penola. It does not appear in any available reference works except that it is used for a post office in Virginia. Correspondence with the postmaster in Virginia has failed to produce any explanations of the name.

Peoria, LINN. This name came from Peoria, Illinois. The village of Peoria is below the mouth of Lake Creek, on Willamette River, 15 miles southwest of Albany and eight miles northwest of Halsey. The first settlement was by H. A. McCartney, in 1851. In 1875 the place contained four grain warehouses on the river bank, having a capacity of 60,000 bushels of wheat. There were 30,000 bushels in the warehouses. The school contained 60 pupils. The village was a shipping point for considerable business until the Oregon & California Rail Road drew the business to Halsey and Shedd. *See Material Resources of Linn County*, A. S. Mercer, 1875, p. 53. A post office called Burlington was established in this locality on Nov. 17, 1855, with William M. McCorkle postmaster. The name of the office was changed to Peoria on Nov. 7, 1857.

Pepper Canyon, WHEELER. This small canyon in the northwest part of the county about eight miles northeast of Clarno was apparently named for Marion Pepper who patented a homestead on its upper reaches in 1915.

Perdue, DOUGLAS. Perdue post office was named for John Perdue, Sr., its first postmaster. The office was first situated on South Umpqua River at the mouth of Elk Creek, and was called Elk Creek. John Perdue, Sr., became postmaster of the Elk Creek office on June 11, 1884, and on the following Aug. 22, the name of the office was changed to Perdue. About this time the office was moved down South Umpqua River about six miles, but the writer cannot determine just when this move was made. For nearly 40 years Perdue post office continued to serve the territory, until it was closed rather abruptly on Aug. 31, 1920, because Amos O. Buker, then postmaster, ran afoul of postal regulations prohibiting dual government employment. Buker took on the job of local census enumerator and the government quickly put a stop to his postal activities. The locality was without a post office for three years, until Milo post office was established with Mrs. Cora E. Buker first postmaster. *See* Milo. Perdue was about half way between Days Creek and Tiller.

Perdue Creek, LANE. Perdue Creek is tributary to Christy Creek. It is named for Raymond Perdue, an early settler on High Prairie north of Oakridge.

Perham, CROOK. On Aug. 9, 1946, Remey M. Cox, editor of the Prineville *Central Oregonian*, wrote the compiler: "Gardner Perry, for many years stage driver on the Prineville-Paulina run, reports he lived near Bear Creek buttes while Perham post office was open. The place was named for Ad Perham, who ran sheep on Bear Creek buttes. The post office was operated by Sadie E. Moore, wife of one of Perham's hands. Moore was carrying the mails from Prineville to Silver Lake at the time while his wife ran the post office in their home. There wasn't much of a settlement there, Perry reports. The Perrys lived about two miles north of the Perham post office. When the Moores moved to Prineville, the post office was closed. Moore ran a harness shop in Prineville." According to postal records, Perham post office was established Dec. 26, 1888, with Sadie E. Moore postmaster. The office was closed Nov. 1, 1890.

Perham Creek, HOOD RIVER. This stream flows under the Columbia River Highway and into the Columbia River about seven miles west of Hood River. It was named to commemorate Eugene L. Perham who emigrated from Indiana to Oregon in 1850. After living at various places in Oregon he married the daughter of the Reverend Edward R. Geary, who came to Oregon in 1851. The newly married couple settled at The Dalles about 1857 or 1858, where Perham was connected with river navigation interests that became part of the Oregon Steam Navigation Company in 1860. The family remained in The Dalles for about 25 years and Perham took an interest in public affairs. He then moved to the vicinity of what is now Perham Creek, but later disposed of his holdings. He died in 1891 and Mrs. Perham died in 1926. The Perhams were a much respected family.

Peris, COLUMBIA. Peris was the strange name of an early day post office on the road from Saint Helens west to Mist. Omar C. Spencer, a native of Columbia County, informed the compiler that Peris was named by Christoph Sauervein, a homesteader, native of Switzerland. It was Sauervein's idea to name his post office for the great French metropolis but there was defective handwriting. Officials in Washington could not believe that there would be a Paris in the wilds of Oregon and they misinterpreted the spelling as Peris. The office was established Nov. 19, 1891, and discontinued May 9, 1901. Sauervein was the first of two postmasters.

Periwinkle Creek, LINN. Periwinkle Creek heads near Midway School southeast of Albany and flows northwest through the east part of town and into the Willamette River. In earlier days this stream was known as Periwinkle Creek on account of the presence of a small mollusc, well known to fishermen. The name of this little mollusc has many forms, including the popular variation pennywinkle. About 1911 USGS map makers used the name First Periwinkle Creek for the stream in contradistinction to Second Periwinkle Creek to the northeast, but applied the title to the wrong fork. In 1942 the USBGN changed the name of Second Periwinkle Creek to its pioneer style, Cox Creek, and adopted the name Periwinkle for the creek that flows through Albany. The name should be used for the longer branch and not for the shorter fork to the northeast. The business now seems to be adjusted to the satisfaction of local citizens.

Perkins Creek, LANE. This tributary of Mosby Creek was named for Joseph Perkins who settled on its banks in 1883.

Perkins Ditch, BAKER. This ditch in the Lower Powder River Valley was named for Edmond P. Perkins whose ranch at Keating was a stop on the stage line from Baker to Sparta. This information was supplied by Catherine Tyler of Baker, a descendant.

Perkins Flat, MALHEUR. Perkins Flat is an area on the west shore of Lake Owyhee about ten miles south of Owyhee Dam where the BLM has leased sites for recreation cabins. It is named for Fred Perkins who farmed the land before it was inundated by the lake.

Pernot Mountain, LANE. This mountain was named for John F. Pernot, who was in charge of forest insect studies in the Pacific Northwest, for the USFS. He was killed by a runaway horse in the Ochoco National Forest, and this peak in the Cascade Range was named for him. It is in the northwest part of T 18S, R 3E.

Perrin Canyon, WHEELER. Perrin Canyon opens into Pine Creek six miles south of Fossil. It was named for John P. Perrin who homesteaded there in 1887.

Perrin Island, MALHEUR. Perrin Island is in Snake River about two miles downstream from Nyssa and just east of Arcadia. It is named for Thomas L. Perrin who had a claim on it about the time of World War I. BLM records indicate Perrin came and went several times between 1918 and 1922 and the claim was apparentlty relinquished and settled by file Serial #06126. The compiler has been unable to get additional information about Mr. Perrin. ODOT maps have shown this as Crow Island and some local citizens have occasionally used the form Sullivans Island. The USBGN decided in favor of Perrin in *Decision List 8304*.

Perry, UNION. Perry was a community and railroad station on the Grande Ronde River northwest of La Grande. It was a company town for the Grande Ronde Lumber Company mill, and the post office was established Aug. 26, 1890, with Robert Smith first postmaster. G. Earl Stoddard, postmaster in 1926, informed the compiler that the town was first called Stumptown and then Stanley, but post office officials would not accept these names and selected Perry arbitrarily. George W. Perry was postmaster during World War I but this may have been just coincidence. The Grande Ronde Lumber Company mill burned Sept. 8, 1924 and was not rebuilt, but Perry survives as a small residential community. The post office was closed Mar. 14, 1931.

Perry Butte, DOUGLAS. Perry Butte is north of North Umpqua River and four miles north of Toketee Falls. USFS ranger Fred Asam named it for Perry Wright of Cap's Illahee who grazed cattle nearby.

Perrydale, POLK. Perrydale was named by William Perry, a pioneer landowner. The post office was established in 1870.

Persist, JACKSON. William W. Willits came to Oregon from Iowa in 1875, and his wife was born in 1858 at Talent, Oregon, of pioneer parents. They settled on a homestead at the present site of Persist post office in 1884, and after 18 years of persistent effort, secured an office to serve their immediate neighborhood in 1902 with Willits first postmaster. The name Persist means all it implies to those who, for many years, pioneered in this part of Oregon with road work, school development and other problems. Mail was first had at Trail post office, 22 miles away by trail, or ten miles by trail to Prospect. The Willits suggested the name Persist on account of their pioneering.

Peter Paul Prairie, DOUGLAS. This prairie is near Red Butte south of Little River. In the early 1920s USFS supervisor Carl Neal and ranger Fred Asam were on a pack trip in the area. They camped one night in this nearly alpine meadow and since it was covered with fine grass for the animals, named it in honor of Neal's saddle and pack horses, Peter and Paul.

Peter Skene Ogden Park, JEFFERSON. Peter Skene Ogden was the explorer of central Oregon during the period of the fur traders. He was born in Quebec in 1794 and entered the service of North West Company in 1811. He entered the Oregon country in 1818 at the head of a trapping party with headquarters at Fort George, now Astoria. He discovered and named Mount Shasta, California, Feb. 14, 1827. He was one of the first to describe and name geographic features in eastern Oregon. He discovered the Humboldt River in Nevada in 1828, and the city of Ogden, Utah, is named in his honor. He was a chief factor of the Hudson's Bay Company at Fort Vancouver; he rescued the survivors of the Whitman Massacre in Dec. 1847; and died in Oregon City on Sept. 27, 1854. He is buried in Mountain View cemetery in Oregon City, where a monument was erected by pioneer and historical organizations, and dedicated to his memory on Oct. 27, 1923. Summaries of Peter Skene Ogden's Journals, edited by T. C. Elliott, appear in the *OHQ*, v. 10, p. 331; v. 11, pp. 201, 229 and 355. The complete Ogden journals of 1824–25 and 1825–26 were published in 1950 by the Hudson's Bay Record Society. The Oregon State Highway Commission gave the name Peter Skene Ogden Park to land adjacent to the Crooked River bridge on US-97, The Dalles-California highway in the south part of Jefferson County, to commemorate Ogden's explorations into central Oregon. For article by John W. Kelly about Peter Skene Ogden, *see* the *Oregonian*, magazine sect. June 26, 1927, and for information about the dedication of Peter Skene Ogden Park, July 16, 1927. The name Peter Skene Ogden Park was suggested by Robert W. Sawyer of Bend.

Petersburg, WASCO. Petersburg was established in 1905 as a station on the Great Southern Railroad. W. H. McNeal in *History of Wasco County*, p. 275, states it was named for Peter Strohler who homesteaded along Fifteenmile Creek about 1900. The *Illustrated History of Central Oregon* has a short biography of this man using the spelling Stoller and the reader is free to make his own choice. After the railroad was taken up in the 1930s, the population diminished but the name is retained by Petersburg School.

Peterson Butte, LINN. Peterson Butte is southwest of Lebanon and has an elevation of 1430 feet. It was originally called Washington Butte, but in the course of time local custom changed the name to Peterson. It was named in honor of Asa H. Peterson, who crossed the plains in 1845, and settled in that locality. He was one of the party that was piloted from Fort Hall westward by Stephen Meek.

Peterson Ridge, UMATILLA. This ridge north of Blalock Mountain was named for Nels Peterson who had extensive land holdings north of North Fork Walla Walla River.

Petes Mountain, CLACKAMAS. Petes Mountain, maximum elevation 830 feet, is a well-known ridge south of Tualatin River and west of the town of Willamette. In July 1945, Raymond P. Caufield of Oregon City informed the compiler that Peter A. Weiss received a patent for land on the slopes of this mountain in June 1868, and that as far as could be learned the ridge was named for him. Weiss had a donation land claim, certificate no. 3034, on the eastern slope above the mouth of Tualatin River.

Petes Point, WALLOWA. Petes Point is south of Wallowa Lake. This point was named for Peter Beaudoin, a Frenchman who was at one time one of the largest sheep owners in eastern Oregon. He started in the sheep business in the Wallowa Valley about 1884.

Petteys, MORROW. A post office with the name Pettysville was closed in 1887. Postal records show that a new office with the name Petteys was opened Nov. 9, 1900, with S. Pearl Jones postmaster. This office was in service until May 15, 1901. It was named for Amanuel C. Petteys, who came to Oregon about 1854 and for a time lived near Salem. He was interested in livestock and moved to the Willow Creek country in 1868 where he settled near the mouth of Rhea Creek. The name of the old post office Pettysville represented a misspelling of the family name and produced some irritation. Petteys operated the stage station until the railroad came about 1888. *See also* Pettysville.

Pettysville, MORROW. Pettysville was an important stopping point for early day travel. It was near the present site of Ione, perhaps a little to the east at the point where Rhea Creek flows into Willow Creek. A post office with the name Willow Forks was established in this locality on June 3, 1872, with Amanuel C. Petty postmaster. The name of the office seems to be descriptive of the juncture of the two streams at this point. The name Willow Forks was changed to Pettysville on Dec. 24, 1878. The office was closed May 19, 1887, and the business turned over to Ione. The family says the name of the man was Amanuel C. Petteys. For a short biography of Petteys *See History of Umatilla and Morrow Counties*, p. 568. *See also* the entry Petteys.

Peyton, JACKSON. Peyton is a locality on upper Rogue River about midway between Trail and Prospect, named for a local family. The post office was established Aug. 30, 1900, with Anna B. Jones first of four postmasters. The name of the office was changed to Leeds Jan. 16, 1912, and the office may have been moved a couple of miles west and downstream at that time. Leeds had already been a post office, operating from 1890 to 1906. Available records do not give a clear history of the movements of some of these old post offices.

Phantom Ship, KLAMATH. This peculiar, spired island in Crater Lake bears an appropriately descriptive name.

Pharmacy Hill, MALHEUR. Pharmacy Hill is the high ground northwest of the community of Jordan Valley. In the early days it was known as Skinner Butte for Silas Skinner, one of the original settlers and also apparently called Holler Hill, possibly a translation of the Paiute *wa a geet do ya be*. During the depression two unemployed painters came to Jordan Valley and solicited work from Dr. Walter W. Jones who also owned the local drug store. He engaged them to paint "PHARMACY" on the hill in large letters. The paint faded with the years but the name remains. Jones was the town's second doctor, having arrived in 1910. He practiced medicine until his death in 1963. Hanley and Lucia have an interesting account of Doctor Jones and his activities in *OWYHEE TRAILS, The West's Forgotten Corner*.

Phelps Creek, HOOD RIVER. This stream is named for A. C. Phelps who conducted a small cooperage business near Frankton. On May 14, 1864, Phelps, James Laughlin of The Dalles and William Jenkins with his young son Walter were ferrying a load of oak kegs out to the freight steamer. Young Walter Jenkins fell into the Columbia and his father and Laughlin were both drowned in a vain rescue effort.

Philippi Canyon, GILLIAM. This canyon debouches into the Columbia River east of John Day Dam. Roy Philippi wrote the compiler in 1970 that his father, Albert, homesteaded this land in the 1880s and that four generations of the family have lived on the ranch. In 1970 the USCE developed Albert Philippi Park at slack water on John Day River on land that was part of the Philippi Ranch.

Phillips, WASHINGTON. Phillips post office was established June 20, 1895, with Charles Hanson first postmaster. The office was in operation until Dec. 23, 1904, when it was closed because of the advance of rural free delivery. Phillips was on the west side of the Cornelius Pass road a few hundred feet north of the 1945 location of Rock Creek School. The office was named in compliment to Phillip Pezoldt, a prominent local resident.

Phillips Lake, BAKER. This artificial lake on Powder River about 17 miles west of Baker was formed when Mason Dam was built by the USBR in 1965. It was named for Fred Phillips, a prominent Baker resident and long time advocate of the project. For an editorial comment on Phillips, *see* the Baker *Record-Courier*, May 21, 1964.

Philomath, BENTON. *Philomath* is a Greek word meaning a lover of learning, an astrologer or prognosticator. Philomath College was opened in 1867, founded by the United Brethren Church. About the time the college was started, a post office was applied for, and named for the college.

Phoca Rock, MULTNOMAH. This rock, sometimes known as Lone Rock, is in the middle of the Columbia River north of Bridal Veil. It is conspicuous from Crown Point. It was named for the harbor seal, *Phoca vitulina*. Lewis and Clark passed this rock on Nov. 2, 1805, and described it accurately but did not refer to it by name. However, it may be definitely attributed to Captain Clark as it appears in "Clarks Summary Statement of Rivers, Creeks, and Most Remarkable Places," Thwaites, *Original Journals of the Lewis and Clark Expedition*, v. 6, p. 67. Wilkes, in *U. S. Exploring Expedition*, v. 23, Hydrography, refers to the rock as Hermit Islet.

Phoenix, JACKSON. Phoenix was settled in the early 1850s. Samuel Colver took a land claim there in 1851. In 1852 his brother, Hiram, settled adjoining him. In 1854 Samuel Colver laid out the town. Phoenix reached the height of its prosperity in 1864. Ten years later the town had greatly dwindled. For several months, in 1884, it was the terminus of the Oregon & California Rail Road. During the Indian troubles in the fall of 1855, Milton Lindley's sawmill was running wide open providing timbers for a blockhouse as well as for a new flouring mill belonging to Sylvester M. Wait. A young lady named Kate Clayton was employed by Mrs. Wait to help with the cooking for the mill hands and for many years the place was known as Gasburg because of the loquacity of this fluent and attractive woman. The town was named by Wait (*Oregonian*, Jan. 3, 1892), after whom later was named Waitsburg, Washington. Wait not only owned the flouring mill but was also the agent for the Phoenix Insurance Company of Hartford, Connecticut and he took that name for the post office which opened Jan. 3, 1857. The Phoenix was a fabulous sacred bird of the Egyptians. There are many legends about the phoenix, which was described as a bird of the size and shape of an eagle, but with red and gold plumage. There was but one phoenix at a time, and it came to Egypt every 500 years from Arabia. The bird played a part in the mystic religion of Egypt, and popular legend says it flew to Heliopolis every 500 years, and was burned on the altar of the temple. The next day there was a new phoenix on the altar.

Phys Point, UNION. This was named for John Phy, whose farm was nearby. It is about two miles west of Cove.

Pickett Butte, DOUGLAS. This prominent peak five miles east of Tiller is the site of a USFS lookout. It was named for William T. Pickett who homesteaded nearby in 1898.

Picnic Spring, UNION. Bernal D. Hug in *History of Elgin, Oregon* states that when the Woodward Road was finished from Spout Springs to Summerville in 1879, a celebration picnic was held at this spring in S 25, T 2N, R 38E.

Picture Gorge, GRANT. This is an imposing canyon, through which flows John Day River, a few miles northwest of Dayville. On its western walls are several Indian pictographs, hence the name. The USGS has issued a splendid map of this gorge and its surroundings. *See* editorial page the *Oregonian*, Dec. 10, 1925.

Picture Rock Pass, LAKE. Between Silver Lake and Summer Lake the Fremont Highway, SH-31, goes through a pass at an elevation of about 4830 feet, and the gap is known as Picture Rock Pass. The name comes from some strange designs or pictures on the rocks about a hundred feet south of the highway. These peculiar marks, made by Indians, are strongly suggestive of a WPA style painting project operated by the aborigines.

Pierce Creek, LINN. This stream flows into Little Muddy Creek east of Harrisburg. It was named for James A. Pierce, a pioneer settler.

Piety Knob, MARION. Piety Knob is now an island in Detroit Reservoir but before the dam was built it was the prominent high ground north of North Santiam River. Earl Stahlman of Detroit told the compiler in 1968 that this was originally known as Mayborn Hill after an early homesteader but that it was renamed by Roy Elliot, a USFS ranger. He was unable to explain the religious significance.

Pika Lake, LINN. Pika Lake is at the headwaters of North Santiam River. It was named after World War II by a fish planting crew because there was a rock slide with pika burrows near the lake. The pika is a small rodent similar to a guinea pig. *See* Alice Lake.

Pike, YAMHILL. Considering the large number of persons who emigrated to Oregon from Pike County, Missouri, it is not suprising that the name was used here, but it is remarkable that some effort was not made to name a county for the famous middle western soldier and explorer. Zebulon Montgomery Pike was born in 1779 in New Jersey. He entered the army before he was of age, and was a lieutenant when he was 20. He explored the Mississippi River, and later went to the Rocky Mountains in what is now Colorado. Pikes Peak bears his name. He was killed at York, Upper Canada, Apr. 27, 1813, in an engagement with the British. He was then a brigadier-general. Pike, in Oregon, is a small community northwest of Yamhill.

Pike Creek, TILLAMOOK. Pike Creek heads in the hills east of Bay City and flows south and west into Hathaway Slough, which joins Tillamook Bay. The stream flows through the homestead of Dan Pike, a pioneer settler, and was named on that account. It is the next stream east of Doughty Creek.

Pikes Camp, LINCOLN. Pikes Camp is on the northeast or right bank of Siletz River about a mile upstream from the mouth of the river and the location of Kernville in 1945. It is near the old ferry landing and about opposite the former Kernville post office, which was on the southwest bank. The camp was named for a fisherman who camped there while he fished for the Kern cannery.

Pilcher Creek, UNION. Pilcher Creek drains Tucker Flat and empties into North Powder River near the mouth of Anthony Creek. In 1882, James A. Pilcher took government land about a mile above its mouth so it is assumed the stream is named for him.

Pilot Butte, DESCHUTES. Pilot Butte, which is at the east city limits of Bend, has been a prominent landmark for travelers for many years. Farewell Bend on Deschutes River was the objective of emigrant trains because it afforded a suitable place to cross the river and was a convenient camp ground. Pilot Butte was an excellent signal to this stopping place. Some early maps refer to it as Red Butte because of its characteristic color, but the name has not prevailed. For information about the importance of this locality to pioneer travelers, *see* Bend. There is an automobile road to the top of the butte from which an impressive panorama may be seen. Pilot Butte has an elevation of 4139 feet according to the USGS. On Sept. 30, 1928, Pilot Butte and Pilot Butte Park on its summit were given to the state of Oregon by F. R. Welles, Kempster B. Miller and Charles A.Brown, as a memorial to their former business associate, Terrence Hardington Foley. T. H. Foley was a prominent resident of Bend who died in 1925 as a result of an automobile accident.

Pilot Knob, CURRY. Preston's *Map of Oregon and Washington*, 1856, shows a prominent peak about ten miles southeast of Port Orford which is lettered Pilot Knob. This was a well-known landmark for mariners, and while the name may have been used to some extent on land, people on shore generally called this point Bald Mountain. For additional information, *see* Bald Mountain.

Pilot Rock, JACKSON. Pilot Rock is an outstanding landmark in the Siskiyou Mountains south of Ashland, and some five miles southeast of Siskiyou Summit on I-5. It has been so known since pioneer days because it served as a guide for travelers crossing the pass between Oregon and California. It has an elevation according to the USGS of 5914 feet. This rock is mentioned in Wilkes' *Narrative*, v. 5, p. 236. Wilkes named it Emmons Peak after Lieutenant George F. Emmons, U.S. Navy, of his expedition. Emmons saw the rock on Sept. 28, 1841. The name Emmons Peak did not come into use.

Pilot Rock, UMATILLA. Pilot Rock was named for a large bluff of basalt near the community. The post office was established in Dec. 1868, but the town was not platted until about 1876. Andrew Sturtevant was the first postmaster.

Pilpil Butte, DESCHUTES. Pilpil Butte is in the northern part of Paulina Mountains. It is composed of red cinders, characteristic of the area, and bears the Chinook jargon word for red.

Pinchot Lake, GRANT. Pinchot Lake is on the north slope of Aldrich Mountain near Stewart and Roosevelt lakes. They were named, apparently by USFS personnel, for President Theodore Roosevelt and his chief forester, Gifford Pinchot.

Pine, BAKER. Pine post office was first established on June 27, 1878, with the name Pine Valley and with Reese W. Pindell postmaster. The office was on the Union County list and the compiler does not know its exact location. Andrew P. Greener became postmaster on Apr. 3, 1879, and the office was then at the Greener farm about two and a half miles from where Pine is now situated. The name was changed to Pine on June 1, 1892. The office was so named because it was in the Pine Creek Valley. There are many geographic features in Oregon named for pine trees. The timbered area of Oregon east of the Cascade Range is largely covered with species of pine. The pines have needle-like leaves and are distinguished from larches, spruces, hemlocks and firs by the length of the needles and the arrangement of the bundles. The only other tree which has its needles in bundles is the larch, but larch needles are short and have as many as thirty needles in a bundle. Pines do not shed all of their needles, and larches do, in the winter. Western white pine, sugar pine and white-bark pine all have five needles in a bundle. Western yellow pine has three needles in a bundle. Lodgepole pine has two needles in a bundle. The three pines of Oregon which have five needles in a bundle can be distinguished from each other by the cones and by the locality in which they occur. Western white pine, *Pinus monticola*, has a slender cone usually five or six inches in length and is made up of very thin scales. It is scattered through the Cascade Range. It is not considered a common tree and is found generally at altitudes above 2000 feet. Sugar pine, *Pinus lambertiana*, is the largest and most magnificent of the Pacific Coast members of the white pine family. It attains a diameter of from four to seven feet. It has a slender cone generally more than a foot in length made up of thin scales. Sugar pine does not occur in Oregon much further north than Mount Jefferson. The white-bark pine, *Pinus albicaulis*, has a short cone about three inches in length and made up of thick scales. It occurs on both sides of the Cascade Range at high altitudes generally near the timber line. Western yellow pine, *Pinus ponderosa*, is the only three-needle pine in Oregon. It has dark bark in its youth and yellow bark when it becomes older. Its needles are long. It is the most common of all forest trees east of the Cascade Range and even west of the range it occurs occasionally in small groups scattered through the Willamette Valley. It is of great commercial importance. Lodgepole pine, *Pinus contorta*, is a two-needle pine and is very common east of the Cascade Range. West of the Cascade Range it is found mostly along the seacoast. Owing to the dark color of its bark it is frequently called black pine and is also known as bull pine and jack pine. The cones are small and have a tendency to remain attached to the tree, sometimes for many years. These cones may break open during a forest fire and scatter the seeds in all directions. In central Oregon and on the east slopes of the

Cascade Range there are in many places dense thickets of small lodgepole pine. This tree is not yet of great commercial importance but experiments are being made to develop new uses for its wood.

Pine, LINN. Pine post office was situated about ten miles east-southeast of Harrisburg near the Lane County line. It was named for the yellowpine trees growing in the foothills. The office was established Aug. 19, 1853, with the name Lat Shaw's Mill, and with William H. Latshaw postmaster. The name of the office was changed to Pine on Jan. 3, 1855, with Thomas M. Weger postmaster. When the name was changed it was noted that the old name was Latshaw's Mill and not with the peculiar arrangement shown above. Pine office continued in operation until Oct. 7, 1887, when the business was turned over to Coburg. It was doubtless moved from time to time but was always in the same general neighborhood.

Pine Creek, BAKER. Pine Creek heads on the northeast slopes of Elkhorn Ridge of the Blue Mountains and flows generally eastward and northeastward to join Powder River near Haines. This stream was named in the gold excitement of the 1860s because of the prominent yellowpine trees near its banks. In 1862 John McLain laid out a town called Pine City on or near this stream with the intention of providing facilities for traveling miners. Before it was well established, Pine City was moved to and consolidated with Pocahontas. *See* Pocahontas. *See also* Hiatt's *Thirty-one Years in Baker County*, pp. 34 and 35.

Pine Creek, UMATILLA. This stream rises in the western slopes of the Blue Mountains and flows northward through Weston and thence into Walla Walla County, Washington. N. W. Durham says it is probably the *Te-hoto-nim-me* of Steptoe. (*Spokane and the Inland Empire*, p. 222.)

Pine Grove, UMATILLA. It is not surprising that many geographic names in Oregon include references to the pine tree, generally by implication to the western yellow pine, *Pinus ponderosa*, or to use its trade name, Pondosa pine. Pine Grove in Umatilla County was a post office ten or a dozen miles south of Pilot Rock on one of the branches of Birch Creek. Pine Grove post office was established Jan. 20, 1911, with Maud Warner first postmaster. The office was discontinued Aug. 9, 1934.

Pine Mountain, DESCHUTES. Named in pioneer days because its high slopes are covered with conifers. Pine Mountain is a prominent landmark at the edge of the High Desert six miles south of US-20 and 35 miles southeast of Bend. From its 6405-foot top there is a sweeping view of much of Oregon's interior plateau and the USFS established a permanent lookout there in 1921. Phil Brogan of Bend supplied this description to the compiler in 1967 when Pine Mountain was in the news spotlight as a site for a proposed University of Oregon astronomical observatory. The observatory was placed in service in the 1970s.

Pine Ridge, KLAMATH. A descriptive name. The place was first known as Aspgrove, presumably for a grove of quaking aspen trees nearby.

Pinehurst, JACKSON. Pinehurst is a place on the Green Springs Highway in the east part of the county between Ashland and Klamath Falls. The name is a combination of the word pine with the old English word hurst, referring to a wooded eminence or just woods. The name is appropriate to the locality. Old maps show an early post office in this vicinity with the name Pioneer. This office was established Mar. 26, 1878, with James Purvis postmaster. John Van Horn became postmaster Dec. 29, 1880, and the office was closed Dec. 19, 1882. The compiler does not know its exact location. The next post office to serve this area was called Shake. It was established in Aug. 1886, with George W. Bailey first postmaster. This office operated until Nov. 1911, when the name was changed to Pinehurst. Pinehurst office is said to be about a mile southwest of the old locality Shake. The name Shake was applied to this locality in early days because it was a place where shakes were riven from sugarpine bolts. These shakes were used extensively by early settlers in the Rogue River Valley for various types of buildings.

Pinewan Lake, KLAMATH. This lake about one mile south of Crescent Lake was named by the Campfire Girls about 1953 when they began using it in connection with their summer camp. Pinewan is Campfire Girl jargon for "among the pines."

Piney, LANE. Piney post office was established July 6, 1852, with Benjamin Richardson postmaster. The office was discontinued Nov. 18, 1852. The place was a little northeast of Elmira and was apparently named by someone interested in trees.

Pinto Mountain, LANE. Pinto Mountain, elevation 6355 feet, is in the Cascade Range near the headwaters of South Fork Salt Creek. Dee Wright of Eugene told the compiler that the mountain was named for a pinto pony that strayed away from his owner and ranged near the mountain.

Pioneer, LINCOLN. Pioneer was a post office near Yaquina River. The post office was for some years known as Morrison, but the name was changed in 1900 because of confusion with Morrison Street in Portland. Barney Morrison was the first postmaster. The name Pioneer was selected because of the operations in that section of the Pioneer Sandstone Company. Barney Morrison continued to act as postmaster at Pioneer after the name was changed.

Pioneer City, LINCOLN. The post office at Pioneer City, which was established July 2, 1868, with George Kellogg first postmaster, was one of the first in what is now Lincoln County. Newport office was established the same day, Newton was established July 12, 1868, and Little Elk, Toledo and Yaquina were established on July 14 of the same year. These six offices took care of the postal needs of that part of Oregon for several years. Pioneer City was named in honor of the steamer *Pioneer*, owned by Kellogg and engaged in general transportation from the mouth of Yaquina Bay to the new community at tidewater. It was about two and one quarter miles up Yaquina River from the place later known as Elk City and about three quarters of a mile downstream from the place later known as Morrison and still later Pioneer. Pioneer City and Pioneer were not in the same place, though they were not more than a mile apart. Pioneer Mountain and Pioneer Summit are west of these old post office locations, and the compiler has been told that the mountain was so named before the Pioneer City post office was established in 1868. Pioneer City post office was closed Aug. 10, 1868, so it was in operation but little more than a month. It was in the southeast quarter of s 2, т 11s, R 10W.

Pioneer Gulch, LANE. This gulch northwest of Emigrant Pass was named because the ill-fated wagon train of 1853 followed it down to Middle Fork Willamette River. According to C. B. McFarland of the USFS the wagon tracks were clearly visible for many years.

Piper Canyon, MORROW. This canyon is named for John and Ernest Piper who settled near its upper end at Swaggart Buttes in the 1890s. The form Pieper used in the fifth edition of this book is incorrect.

Pirtle, LINN. Pirtle was a station on the Oregon Electric Railway south of Albany. It was named for Grant Pirtle, at one time proprietor of a hotel in Albany, and owner of land in the vicinity of the station.

Pistol River, CURRY. James Mace lost a pistol in this stream in 1853 and it has been known as Pistol River since that time.

Pitcher Creek, LANE. The Pitcher Creek which flows into Row River near Dorena was named for Miles Pitcher who homesteaded near its mouth in 1888. Loren Hunt told the compiler in 1967 that the Pitcher Creek which flows into Layng Creek near Disston was named for Miles Pitcher's son, Ben Pitcher.

Pitcher Point, TILLAMOOK. Pitcher Point is the northernmost point on the road around the southwest side of Tillamook Bay to Cape Meares. John A. Biggs of Portland told the compiler in 1971 that his grandfather, Webley Hauxhurst, named the place because of a prominent rock that resembled a milk jug. The Biggs family at that time lived at nearby Biggs Cove. The rock was covered or destroyed when the present road was built in the 1930s.

Pitner, TILLAMOOK. Pitner post office in the extreme southeast corner of the county was named in honor of the postmaster, Mrs. Sarah Paul, *nee* Pitner. The office was established in Aug. 1901, and was discontinued Apr. 30, 1910. This office was on or very close to what is now the Salmon River Highway, SH-18, at a point two or three miles southwest of the locality now known as Boyer. However, in those days Boyer post office was a mile or so southwest of Pitner, in what is now Lincoln County.

Pitsua Butte, DESCHUTES. This butte, southwest of Bend, is named with the word used by Klamath Indians to describe an eminence about two miles southwest of the old site of Klamath Agency. Its use near Bend is to perpetuate a pleasant Indian name. The compiler has been unable to learn the meaning of the name of the butte near the old Klamath Agency. In 1939 Fred M. White of Portland called attention to the fact that the Paiute Indian name for the Columbia five-toed kangaroo rat is *wapota pitsua*. Inquiries to authorities about the name of the butte on the Klamath Indian Reservation have not been wholly successful. In

1944, Indians professed to know very little about the word *pitsua*, although a few of them said they thought it referred to a rodent of some sort.

Pittsburg, COLUMBIA. Pittsburg is on Nehalem River at the mouth of East Fork and at the junction of the Nehalem Highway and the highway east to Saint Helens. The place was named by Peter Brous, who made settlement there in 1879 and built a sawmill and a gristmill operated by waterpower. Brous had formerly lived in Pennsylvania and named the new settlement for the city in that state. The post office at Pittsburgh, Oregon, was established Apr. 17, 1879, and Peter Brous was the first postmaster. The name was changed to Pittsburg Apr. 26, 1892, and the office was discontinued Nov. 30, 1908. There is now not much left at Pittsburg except a substantial highway bridge and a popular cafe. Omar C. Spencer was kind enough to dredge up the facts given above. The place was within his field of activities when he was a small boy in the 1880s.

Pivot, COLUMBIA. Pivot post office was in service from Apr. 1894 to May 1895, when it was discontinued to Keasey. Omar C. Spencer said this office was situated up Rock Creek from Vernonia, in the general vicinity of an important road junction. While in that locality the traveller could take his pick and go in any one of several directions. Most of the time he would be adjacent to good fishing. Mr. Spencer said that some bright mind decided to call the post office Pivot because of its pivotal situation.

Pix, BAKER. Pix post office was apparently established to serve the Pyx Mine. The word can be spelled either way but probably Pyx is the more modern form. Pix office was established Aug. 27, 1890, with William Parker postmaster. It was discontinued June 11, 1895. There is no doubt as to the spelling of the post office name Pix, and the office is said to have been in the extreme west part of Baker County. It may actually have been over the line in Grant County but officials in Washington did not know it. The Pyx mine was close to the divide but all the records say it was in Grant County. It was in s 2, T 10S, R 35E. Whether the post office was actually at the mine or over the hill in Baker County the compiler does not know. The Pyx mine was in what was called the Greenhorn District. The word pyx has several meanings. One, of course, is ecclesiastical; the other important meaning is associated with metallurgy. It refers to the box used at the Royal Mint in London, in which are deposited sample coins struck off in the mint. These are examined annually in the "trial of the pyx" by a committee of the Goldsmiths' Company under direction of the King's Remembrancer. This trial is well known to metallurgists and may have been the reason for naming the Pyx Mine.

Placedor Gulch, GRANT. Placedor Gulch drains into South Fork John Day River just south of the mouth of Murderers Creek. It is about a dozen miles south of Dayville and drains a small area east of the river. It is said to bear the name of a Mexican, Placedor Bravo, well known in that part of the state. Bravo came into central Oregon probably about 1890 and was much interested in horses and horse-races. He died at Mount Vernon Hot Springs about 1940.

Placer, JOSEPHINE. Placer was named for the placer mining in the vicinity. The place was on Grave Creek a few miles east of I-5. Placer post office was established Aug. 10, 1894, with Newell F. Inman first postmaster. The office was closed May 31, 1924 with mail to Leland.

Placer Lake, LINCOLN. Placer Lake is on Reynolds Creek about four miles south of Waldport. It was named by the USFS in 1966 as this part of the Siuslaw National Forest was developed for recreation. Sometime in the 1870s a promoter staked mining claims in the area and constructed an elaborate system of ditches and flumes to fool prospective purchasers. The scheme fell through but later Chinese miners moved in and reportedly recovered a sizeable quantity of gold by placer mining with water from the creek and lake. Evidence of the old ditches could still be seen in 1966.

Placidia Butte, HARNEY. Placidia Butte, elevation 5513 feet, is at the west edge of the county, about ten miles west of Riley and a little to the south of US-20. The name has long been a puzzle and its origin uncertain, but in the summer of 1946 Alphene Venator, pioneer resident of the Harney Valley, told the compiler the butte was named for a Mexican horse trader many years ago. This man is said to have moved north from the Harney Valley into Grant County. For a good many years there lived in the John Day Valley a Mexican named Placedor Bravo, an experienced character with horses. He died at Mount Vernon Hot Springs about 1940. For additional information, *see* Placedor Gulch. While the evidence is certainly not conclusive, it seems probable that Placidia Butte was named for Placedor Bravo. The difference in spelling would be of little consequence to Senor Bravo.

Plainview, LINN. This was a station on the eastside branch of the Southern Pacific Company north of Brownsville. Plainview Church, erected about 1857, was about three miles northeast on a low ridge extending westward from Peterson Butte. The area around the railroad station was flat but the overview from the church site and cemetery on the ridge made the name emminently suitable.

Plank Hill, MARION. Plank Hill is a point on Croisan Ridge about five miles southwest of Salem. It has an elevation of about 850 feet. It was named for E. C. Plank who owned a farm nearby.

Plano, BAKER. A post office with the name Plano was established on the Baker County list July 28, 1897, with Frances Smith first postmaster. The office was discontinued Oct. 12, 1899. Plano was in Burnt River Valley between Durkee and Weatherby. The reason for the name is not on record, but the compiler is of the opinion that the word Plano was intended to be in compliment to some local farm equipment. The Plano line of farm vehicles and harvesting machinery was well known in the 1890s and for some years thereafter.

Plaza Guard Station, CLACKAMAS. This station is near South Fork Salmon River. It was named by T. H. Sherrard of the USFS because of a natural plaza or clearing, which afforded a fine view of Mount Hood.

Pleasant Hill, LANE. Pleasant Hill is east of Goshen. In earlier days there was a nearby post office of the same name. The origin of the name is given in *OHQ*, v. 5, p. 135. Elijah Bristow and several companions made a trip into the valley of the Middle Fork Willamette River in 1846. Bristow was struck with the beauties of the locality now known as Pleasant Hill, and said: "What a pleasant hill. This is my claim." He finished his house in the fall of that year, and it is said to have been one of the first built in Lane County. The name Pleasant Hill was given to his claim by an act of the legislature passed Dec. 27, 1847. Pleasant Hill post office was established on Apr. 9, 1850, with Elijah Bristow postmaster.

Pleasant Home, MULTNOMAH. Pleasant Home, a locality on the headwaters of Johnson Creek about a mile east of Orient, had a post office in pioneer days. Pleasant Home office was established on the Clackamas County list on July 10, 1876, and was given a descriptive name. Orlando S. Murray was the first postmaster. The office was soon changed to the Multnomah County list, but the record does not show just when. This office operated until Dec. 14, 1918, when it was closed out to Gresham. Wm. H. Stanley of Gresham said that Pleasant Home post office never was in Clackamas County, but the fact that it was less than a quarter of a mile from the county line may be the reason that postal officials placed the office on the Clackamas County list in error. *See also* Orient.

Pleasant Valley, BAKER. Pleasant Valley post office was established Sept. 28, 1868, with Jared Lockwood first and only postmaster. The office was in service for two months. A later office with the name Pleasant Valley was established Mar. 21, 1890, with Thomas B. Moore postmaster. This office was closed in 1962 and recent reports state development has constricted to a motel and the Union Pacific Railroad station.

Pleasant Valley, JACKSON. Pleasant Valley, which is on the extreme west edge of the county north of Rogue River, is drained by Evans Creek and by a tributary, Pleasant Creek. The valley and creek got their names in pioneer days as a result of the battle of Evans Creek in the Rogue River Indian War, fought on Aug. 24, 1853, on which day Pleasant Armstrong of Yamhill County was killed. Armstrong was a prominent citizen and was acting as an aid to General Joseph Lane, in command of the white troops. *See* Walling's *History of Southern Oregon*, p. 219 and also p. 380. The valley has always lived up to its name, although the title was not applied descriptively.

Pleasant Valley, TILLAMOOK. Homer Simmons of Tillamook, who was born and raised nearby, sent the compiler the following interesting comment on this community: "Pleasant Valley on US-101 about seven miles south of Tillamook was probably named because of the pleasant surroundings. My father jokingly said it should have been called Wrangletown because of the disputes and feuds among the residents."

Plum Hills, KLAMATH. These hills are north of Klamath Falls. They have been so called since pioneer days on account of wild plums that grew there. Stock have grazed on these hills for so long that the plum trees have practically disappeared. *See* editorial in the *Oregonian*, July 1, 1927, about the wild Pacific plum, *Prunus subcordata*.

Plum Valley, POLK. Plum Valley is a little vale in the west part of Eola Hills. It is just south of Bethel and east of McCoy, and it drains westward into Ash Swale. Its name came from the wild plums that grew in the vicinity, and according to John E. Smith in his booklet, *Bethel*, the name was probably selected by Amos Harvey. Plum Valley post office was established Nov. 30, 1854, on the Absalom H. Frier claim, a little to the south of the valley and about on the south line of section 20. Frier was the first postmaster. In 1856 Plum Valley post office was moved into Plum Valley proper. It was moved several times later but never far from Bethel. It was discontinued Aug. 13, 1863.

Plush, LAKE. The town of Plush was named for a local Indian celebrity who was a member of the Paiute tribe. The name was suggested by Dr. H. Wright who was for a time postmaster at Lakeview. A letter of C. A. Moore, published in the *Oregonian*, Feb. 16, 1926, tells how the Indian received the name Plush. This was the result of a poker game that he got into. The game was a frame-up. The Indian was dealt a flush by another member of the party, who held a better one. He could not pronounce the word "flush" and called it "plush," and that was the name he subsequently went by.

Plympton Creek, CLATSOP. Plympton Creek is at Westport. It was named for Silas B. Plympton who took up a land claim nearby in 1861. Plympton was the first postmaster at Westport, 1863.

Pocahontas, BAKER. Pocahontas is a ghost town at the base of the Blue Mountains a few miles northwest of Baker. It was established in the mining days of the 1860s, but so far the compiler has not had any success in getting the origin of the name or even much of value about the history of the place. Beyond the fact that it was named for the famous Indian princess of Virginia, little has transpired. Hiatt in his *Thirty-one Years in Baker County*, pp. 34 and 35, says that a number of persons went up into the timber near the foot of the Blue Mountains and laid out a town called Pine City. It may be assumed from the text that this took place in 1862 and the place was on Pine Creek west of what was later Pocahontas. The community was laid out for the purpose of accommodating travel, which was forced to go close to the mountains to avoid spring waters. One John McLain had taken up a ranch at or near what was later Pocahontas and he persuaded the Pine City people to move to Pocahontas, which soon boasted a hotel, express office and blacksmith shop. Pocahontas was not primarily a mining town, but for the accommodation of travel through Baker Valley. One Morrison had a rival place a couple of miles to the south and Hiatt has some amusing comments about this rivalry. Pocahontas post office was established Aug. 4, 1863, with Thomas McMurran postmaster. Available records about the closing date are inconclusive. In one place the date is given as June 24, 1864, and in another place the year is 1872.

Poe Valley, KLAMATH. This valley which is southeast of Olene, was named for James M. Poe, who lived there a few years at the time of the Modoc War. Later he moved to Chehalis, Washington, where he spent the rest of his life. In 1945 his Poe Valley homestead was owned by members of the Liskey family. The Poes were the parents of Mrs. William H. Horton, wife of a prominent and long-time stockman of the Poe Valley-Bonanza area.

Pogue Gulch, COOS. Pogue Gulch opens into Isthmus Slough about a half mile north of Delmar. BLM records show that William R. Pouge patented a land claim along the gulch on Aug. 3, 1874. There is no further history of the family and the compiler does not know if the form Pouge was correct or a misspelling.

Point Adams, CLATSOP. This is on the Oregon side at the mouth of the Columbia River. The name was given by Captain Robert Gray on May 18, 1792, in honor of John Adams. *See* "Boit's log of the Columbia" in *Washington Historical Quarterly*, v. 12, Jan. 1921, p. 35. Later in the same year Vancouver recognized the name, saying: "Point Adams is a low, narrow, sandy, spit of land, projecting northerly into the ocean, and lies from cape Disappointment, S 44 E about four miles distant." (*Voyage of Discovery*, 1798 edition, v. 2, p. 53.) Point Adams was first described by Captain Bruno Heceta on Aug. 17, 1775, and was named by him *Cabo Frondoso*, or Leafy Cape, "from the great number of trees which covered it." *See California Historical Society Quarterly*, v. 9, p. 235. Heceta was at the mouth of the Columbia River but he did not know it. *See* Greenhow's *History of Oregon and California*, p. 430, *et seq*.

Point Meriwether, CLATSOP. Point Meriwether is the middle of the three small points south of Hug Point and north of Arch Cape. It was named in the 1890s by Samuel Adair to honor Meriwether Lewis. Adair's homestead was just to the north of Point Meriwether. *See* Adair Point.

Point Terrace, LANE. Point Terrace was named by Mrs. Josephine R. Styles, the first postmaster. This was about 1890. The name is descriptive and refers to the three steps or beaches nearby. This was a popular Indian hunting ground in early days and a great deal of game was dried and smoked in this neighborhood.

Poison Creek, HARNEY. This stream is on the northwest slopes of Steens Mountain and is tributary to Kiger Creek. It was so called in early days because a number of cattle were poisoned nearby by eating wild parsnips.

Poison Creek, HARNEY. This stream is east of Burns. Like many others in eastern Oregon it was named because cattle were poisoned nearby when they ate wild parsnips.

Pokegama, KLAMATH. In the early part of the century there was excitement in Klamath County because of prospects of a railroad. This line was surveyed from Thrall, a station on the Southern Pacific near Klamath River, in California, northeastward to the southwest corner of Klamath County, Oregon. Construction started in Nov. 1901, and in May 1903, the line was completed to Pokegama, the Oregon terminus. The Pokegama Lumber Company was responsible for the project, and the name of the line was the Klamath Lake Railroad. It was about 24 miles long. Pokegama post office was established by change of name from Snow on Sept. 2, 1899. The office was in operation until Oct. 31, 1911. Snow post office was established in June 1894, with Adelbert B. Smith postmaster. The writer does not know its location in respect of Pokegama. The lumber company got its name from the place in Pine County, Minnesota. Pokegama, Oregon, ceased to exist many years ago.

Poker Jim Ridge, LAKE. This ridge is the high ground east of Warner Valley above Campbell and Bluejoint lakes. The local tradition is that it was named for Poker Jim, an Indian Scout during the Bannock War of 1878. The compiler has been unable to find any mention of such a man in the available campaign accounts but the *Sunday Oregonian*, Dec. 7, 1952 has a long article telling of Poker Jim, a well-known Pendleton Indian who was born about 1854 near Wallula and died in 1936 at Cayuse. His Indian name was *Sap-At-Kloni* and he is reported to have been a scout under Collier in the Bannock War. Collier is not identifiable and may be Captain Patrick Collins, 21st Infantry. There is nothing to connect any of this with the east side of Warner Valley but some activity could have occured during or after 1878 to fix the name. In view of Poker Jim's well documented affinity for the card game, he may also be responsible for the naming of nearby Plush.

Polallie Creek, HOOD RIVER. This tributary of East Fork Hood River rises southwest of Cooper Spur. Over the centuries it has cut a deep canyon in the powdery soil. In the early days it was called Sand Creek and Sand Canyon but in the 1920s the USFS started a program to replace repetitious or mundane names. Sand Creek fits both these qualifications as "sand" carries far more than its share of the place-name burden. *Polallie* is a Chinook jargon word meaning sandy or powdery. George Gibbs says that *polallie* was undoubtedly from the French *poudre*, and was not originally a Chehalis or Chinook word.

Pole Bridge Creek, KLAMATH. Soldiers from Fort Klamath built a bridge over this stream in the 1860s, using small lodgepole pine trees, and the name arose on that account.

Pole Creek, WASCO. J. A. Rooper of Antelope told the compiler that this tributary of Ward Creek was named because of the excellent supply of juniper fence posts available in the canyon.

Pole Gulch, BAKER. Pole Gulch is the correct name of a drain in townships 12 and 13S, R 36E, not Sawmill Creek. *See* USBGN decision.

Polk, POLK. The name Polk has been used for two different post offices in Polk County, both named in compliment to the county. An office called Polk was established Mar. 9, 1885, with Lycurgus Hill first and only postmaster. This office was closed Dec. 7, 1885. Lycurgus Hill lived in the locality called Bridgeport, and since Bridgeport post office had been abandoned in 1874, it is possible that Polk office was organized to fill the local need. However, the record of this Polk post office is far from clear. Members of the Hill family are of the opinion that the office never functioned, and some color is lent to the statement by the fact that the compiler has not been able to find the office on any contemporary maps. There have been a number of cases in Oregon postal history where post offices have been established, only to have local sponsors lose interest in the prospects. The other Polk office was about three miles northeast of Dallas. The name Polk for this locality was in use in the 1880s as a station on the Oregonian Railway narrow gauge line, and confusion between the two places may have been the reason that Hill's post office did not actively furnish service. Polk railroad station northeast of Dallas did not get a post office until Apr. 12, 1899, when Peter R. Graber was appointed postmaster. This office was closed Feb. 15, 1902. The locality is still called Polk Station, though both post office and railroad service are things of the past as far as the locality is concerned.

Polk County. Polk District, or County was created by the provisional legislature, Dec. 22, 1845. It was named for James Knox Polk, then president of the United States. It comprised all that part of the original Yamhill District south of the south line of that district, which had been reestablished by an act of Dec. 19, 1845, and the California line. Information about the establishment of Polk County will be found in the article on Oregon counties by Frederick V. Holman, in *OHQ*, v. 11, p. 28. In his notes on Polk County Mr. Holman calls attention to the fact that he was unable to find the act of the legislature establishing the south boundary of the county immediately prior to the creation of Benton County. However, the act was printed in the *Oregon Spectator*, Feb. 10, 1848. This act was passed on Dec. 9, 1847, and was approved Dec. 23, 1847. In 1990, Polk County had an area of 744 square miles.

Pollard, JOSEPHINE. Pollard was a station on the Southern Pacific Railroad four miles southwest of Wolf Creek near the mouth of Water Tank Gulch. In the days of steam locomotives it was an important water stop for apparently Wolf Creek had no such facility. The station was named for Joseph P. Pollard who in 1882 filed a homestead including the mouth of Water Tank Gulch. He sold some of this claim to the Oregon & California Rail Road for right of way and relinquished the balance in favor of a new location about one mile east. In 1912, Pollard died at age 82 and was buried in the Wolf Creek Cemetery. In 1983 nothing remained at the station site.

Pollard Creek, TILLAMOOK. This creek flows into Three Rivers about five miles above Hebo. It was named for an early homesteader near Sears Lake, Aaron B. Pollard, who was postman at Woods around 1900.

Pollman Dam, BAKER. This dam on Baldock Slough was named for William Pollman.

Poly Top Butte, DESCHUTES, LAKE. This butte southeast of Paulina Mountains has several tops, hence the name.

Pompadour Bluff, JACKSON. This bluff is a peculiar, basaltic rock formation in the valley east of Ashland. It resembles, in a general way, the style of haircut made famous by the Marquise de Pompadour and by Jim Corbett. The bluff was probably named during the 1890s when Corbett was the world's heavyweight boxing champion.

Pompeii, CLACKAMAS. Pompeii post office came as the result of the activities of Oliver C. Yocum, for many years a guide at Mount Hood. He started a community near the present site of Government Camp and chose the name Pompeii because of the volcanic soil in the vicinity. The office was established Oct. 15, 1902, but available records do not give the closing date. It probably was never in service.

Pondosa, UNION. Pondosa is a lumber town not far from Medical Springs. It was named with the word Pondosa, the trade name for lumber from the western yellowpine tree, *Pinus ponderosa*. The post office was established Sept. 28, 1927, with Holger M. Larsen first postmaster, to serve the Grande Ronde Pine Company, millers of western yellowpine. The office was not in service in 1973.

Pony Butte, JEFFERSON. Pony Butte is a landmark in the eastern part of the county. Mrs. Chester Kennedy, the daughter of early settler Bidwell Cram, told the writer in 1971 that the butte was named because of an Indian drawing or petroglyph resembling a pony. She recalls as a small girl riding with her mother to view this rock near the top of the butte but said she had not been able to find the spot in later years. Pony Creek rises on the north slopes of the butte.

Pony Slough, COOS. Pony Creek runs directly through North Bend into Pony Slough. The name is very old and supposedly was applied in the early days when a pony belonging to an Indian boy mired and drowned in the tidal marsh.

Poole Hill, JACKSON. Poole Hill is south of South Fork Little Butte Creek in s 17, T 37S, R 3E. Margaret Pool of Portland told the compiler in 1971 that the hill was named for her great-grandfather, Arthur Pool, who was born in Ohio and came west about 1860. He owned a store in Brownsboro and kept the hotel in Eagle Point. The terminal "e" for the hill was added in error.

Poole Lake, DOUGLAS. Poole Lake is in s 29, T 29S, R 3E, on the upper reaches of Jackson Creek. It was named for Andrew T. Poole who was a forest ranger in the area for many years. The name Toad Lake is incorrect as this is about a mile north.

Poole Slough, LINCOLN. According to information received in 1945 from Andrew L. Porter of Newport, Poole Slough was named for an oysterman and homesteader who settled on the west bank, near the mouth. Government records show Newton Pool filed a homestead there in 1874. The different spellings cannot be reconciled. The USGS Toledo quadrangle of 1957 used the form Pooles but local usage dropped the "s" as did the USGS on the 1984 Toledo South quadrangle.

Poore Creek, DOUGLAS. Fred Asam of Canyonville told the compiler that this tributary of Little River west of Taft Mountain was named by logger Harold Church. Church had so much difficulty logging in the rugged terrain that he called the job a "poor set-up" and subsequently Poor Creek. The terminal "e" is an affectation reflecting an attempt to change a poor situation.

Popcorn School, POLK. Popcorn School in the Eola Hills about five miles northwest of Salem started as a one room schoolhouse built in 1876. The first teacher was Napoleon Franklin Nelson, nicknamed "Poley." Nelson was small in stature, smaller than some of his pupils. At the end of the first term, several youngsters demanded that Poley treat the school. When no treat was forthcoming, the boys took their teacher to the ravine behind the school and held him upside down over the creek. The unfortunate pedagogue capitulated and was set back on dry ground. He returned to the school and produced a bag of popping corn which was duly popped and eaten, giving the school its name from then on.

Pope Creek, LANE. Pope Creek flows into Lake Creek near Blachly. It was apparently named for either Thomas C. or John Pope, the sons of Thomas Pope who had the first farm on Deadwood Creek. Pope, Sr., settled at the site of Deadwood in 1882 and was the first postmaster. The two sons moved to the Blachly area in the early 1900s.

Poplar, WHEELER. Poplar post office was established Apr. 10, 1894, with Zachariah J. Martin first postmaster, and was discontinued Sept. 22, 1899. A map of 1897 shows the office on Haystack Creek about a mile north of and upstream from John Day River. The office is said to have been named for some poplar trees on a nearby ranch.

Port Orford, CURRY. Cape Blanco is about seven miles north of Port Orford. On Apr. 24, 1792, Captain George Vancouver sighted what we now know as Cape Blanco, and named it Cape Orford in honor of George, Earl of Orford, his "much respected friend." *See* Cape Blanco for history of that name. McArthur's chart of the Pacific Coast, issued by the USC&GS in 1851, shows the name Ewing Harbor attached to what is now called Port Orford. He apparently named the harbor for his ship, the *Ewing*, which was used in the survey in 1850. The name Ewing did not prevail, and the place has been known since the early 1850s as Port Orford because of its proximity to the cape named by Vancouver. Tebenkoff's chart shows the name Indian Bay. George, third Earl of Orford (1720–1791) was the grandson of Sir Robert Walpole, first Earl of Orford and was the nephew of the fourth Earl of Orford, the famous Horace Walpole. Port Orford has given its name to a valuable lumber, Port Orford cedar, botanically known as Lawson cypress, *Chamaecyparis lawsoniana*. It is considered one of the most beautiful cedars in cultivation. Port Orford post office was established Mar. 27, 1855, with Reginald H. Smith first postmaster.

Porter Hill, UMATILLA. Porter Hill is a spur of Rocky Ridge north of East Birch Creek. It was named for a prominent early settler, William T. Porter, who took up property along its slopes in 1895.

Porter Spring, UNION. Porter Spring is three miles north of the confluence of Meadow Creek and Grande Ronde River. It was named for William Porter who took a land claim there in 1900.

Porterville, LAKE. Porterville was a homesteaders' post office situated a few miles southwest of Silver Lake town, in the north part of S 7, T 29S, R 13E. This is on the Buck Creek drainage. The post office was established Feb. 3, 1898, with James C. Porter first and only postmaster, and was discontinued June 15, 1899, with papers to Silver Lake. The office was named for the Porter family, several members of which had homesteads in the vicinity.

Portland, MULTNOMAH. Portland was named for Portland, Maine, in 1845, by Francis W. Pettygrove. Whether the name should be Portland or Boston was decided by Pettygrove and A. L. Lovejoy by the toss of a copper coin. Pettygrove was born at Calais, Maine, in 1812, and came to Oregon by sea in 1843 with a stock of merchandise. He built a warehouse at Champoeg, had a store in a log house at the southwest corner of Front and Washington streets, Portland, and a store called the Red House in Oregon City. There is uncertainty about the exact date that Portland was established. William Johnson and his Indian wife had a cabin as early as 1842 near what is now Southwest Macadam Avenue and Curry Street, but Johnson apparently had no notion of starting a town and his house was some distance south of the locality that became Portland in 1845. Etienne Lucier may have settled in what was later East Portland as early as 1829, but this was not in the original Portland townsite. A. L. Lovejoy and William Overton landed at the site of Portland in Nov. 1843, on the way from Fort Vancouver to Oregon City. That winter they returned and took a land claim of 640 acres. Lovejoy was the first proprietor, and Overton, his hired man. Overton took a share of land for his services, and in 1844 sold it to Pettygrove for $50. The subsequent history of Overton is unknown. In the winter of 1844, the first building was erected at the foot of Washington Street. In 1845, Lovejoy and Pettygrove laid off 16 blocks of the townsite and named the place Portland by the process mentioned above.

Captain John Couch of Newburyport, Massachusetts, had been in the Columbia River trade and soon recognized the strategic importance of the locality of Portland. He made settlement in the place in 1845–46, and became an important addition to the community. In the fall of 1845, Lovejoy sold his interest to Benjamin Stark and moved to Oregon City. Daniel H. Lownsdale located on what later was called the King claim, and built a tannery. In Sept. 1848, Lownsdale bought out Pettygrove, then in sole possession of the 640 acres, for $5000 in tanned leather. The sale included a wharf at the foot of Washington Street, which was built in 1846. In 1851 Pettygrove became one of the founders of Port Townsend, Washington, where he died on Oct. 5, 1887. Lovejoy was born in Massachusetts in 1808 and came to Oregon first in 1842, went to Bents Fort on the Arkansas River with Dr. Marcus Whitman and came to Oregon again in 1843. He died in Portland Sept. 10, 1882. For references to Pettygrove and Lovejoy, *see* Scott's *History of the Oregon Country*, v. 2, pp. 266 and 319. For references to Captain Couch, v. 1, p. 301. For synopsis of first hundred years of Portland history by the compiler, *see* the *Oregon Sunday Journal*, Aug. 15, 1943. Portland post office was established Nov. 8, 1849 with Thomas Smith first postmaster. At that time Astoria and Oregon City already had post offices and the Salem office was established the same day. For an interesting account of Portland's first years, *see Early Portland: Stump-town Triumphant* by Eugene E. Snyder.

Portland Creek, LANE. According to A. J. Briem, long time USFS district ranger, a group of miners from Portland staked a claim and built a cabin at the forks of Portland Creek northwest of Sinker Mountain. They were known as the "Portland Outfit" and thus gave their name to the creek.

Portola, LANE. The plat for Portola townsite was filed in Jan. 1912, to provide for a community at the mouth of Noti Creek, where that stream flows into Long Tom River. The name Portola had been much in the news during the preceding few years of the Portola Festival held at San Francisco in Oct. 1909. This was in honor of Don Gaspar de Portola, commander of the expedition sent from Mexico to found the first European settlement in what is now the state of California. Portola reached San Diego about July 1, 1769, and continued northward to search for the famous Monterey Bay, which theretofore had been reached only by sea. Portola did not recognize Monterey, went far beyond it and on Nov. 1, 1769, discovered San Francisco Bay. It is believed that the celebration of 1909 inspired the selection of the name Portola for the Lane County townsite. Portola post office was established Mar. 19, 1912, with Herbert G. Suttle, postmaster. The name Portola for the new community did not prove satisfactory. Mail, freight and express were missent to Portland, in error. In addition, there was a Portola station in California on the recently completed Western Pacific Railroad, and this caused confusion. Residents of Portola, Oregon, petitioned to have a new name, and Noti was selected because of Noti Creek nearby. The name of the post office was changed to Noti on Mar. 29, 1913. For information about that name, *see* Noti.

Post, CROOK. Post, southeast of Prineville, was named for the postmaster, Walter H. Post. The office was established June 6, 1889.

Post Canyon, HOOD RIVER. David Cooper told the compiler in 1967 that this canyon southeast of Mitchell Point was named because it was an abundant source of fence post stock in the early days.

Post Office Bar, MULTNOMAH. This is a bar in the Willamette River, about a mile above the mouth. W. H. H. Morgan of Sauvie Island told the compiler that it was named because the former Sauvie Island post office was once on the island, opposite the bar. This office was established with the name Mouth of Willamette, June 30, 1851, with Ellis Walker postmaster. It was listed in Clark County, Washington, in error, and never actually was in that county. The name was changed to Sauvies Island Mar. 5, 1852, and was moved to the Washington County, Oregon, list May 19, 1853, with Benjamin Howell postmaster.

Postage Stamp Butte, WASCO. Postage Stamp Butte is at the extreme west end of Tygh Ridge, about two miles west of The Dalles-California Highway, and has an elevation of 2902 feet. There once was a USFS lookout on the summit. The name was applied in 1925 by James Frankland, during observations for USFS triangulation. When seen from a distance, an arrangement of ground colors on the slopes of the butte simulated a letter with a postage stamp stuck in one corner.

Potamus Creek, GRANT, MORROW. Potamus Creek flows into North Fork John Day River about nine miles northwest of Ritter. The name is a redundancy for *potamus* is the Greek word for river. The stream apparently was named by a classical scholar.

Potato Hill, LINN. This hill, elevation about 2000 feet, is five miles east of Mill City. It was named in 1863 by Thomas J. Henness on account of its shape. *See* Salem *Capital Journal*, June 18, 1927, p. 1. This hill is locally known as Tater Hill.

Potterf Creek, LANE. Potterf Creek is a small tributary of Elk Creek above Noti. It is named for William F. Potterf who was born in Ohio in 1861 and moved to Lane County in 1890. He took a homestead along this creek and for a short while in the 1890s operated a shingle mill on the property. He died in Eugene in Feb. 1935.

Pounder Creek, MULTNOMAH. James Pounder was born in 1870 and came to Corbett in 1891. For many years he farmed about a mile south of Corbett along Pounder Creek. He died in Aug. 1951.

Powder River, BAKER. The name Powder River is probably first recorded by Peter Skene Ogden, in his journals, but he does not give any circumstances or history of its origin. *See* his journals in the *OHQ*, v. 11, pp. 361 and 362. The river was probably named by Donald McKenzie. Dr. William C. McKay, born at Astoria in 1824, grandson of Alexander McKay, a partner of John Jacob Astor, says that the name Powder River came from the Chinook jargon words *polallie illahe*, meaning a sandy or powdery ground used to describe the soil along the stream. The first white people to visit the vicinity of Powder River were the Astorians in 1811. Lewis and Clark show Powder River on their map as *Port-pel-lah* River.

Powder Springs, HOOD RIVER. David Cooper told the writer in 1967 that these springs on the Brooks Meadows road were named because the powder house was located nearby when the road was built in the 1920s.

Powell Butte, CROOK. Powell Butte is the name of the post office near the northwest foot of Powell Buttes. It was named, of course, on account of the buttes, but the writer has not been able to ascertain why the singular form was used rather than the plural. Powell Butte post office was established Mar. 12, 1909, with Moses Niswonger first postmaster.

Powell Buttes, CROOK. Powell Buttes form a well-known landmark between Bend and Prineville. These buttes are much dissected and there are a number of summits, the highest of which has an elevation of about 5100 feet. They were named for some member of the family of Jacob Powell of Linn County, probably for Daniel or John Powell. Several of the Powells crossed the Cascade Range into central Oregon in the early days to range stock.

Powell Creek, CROOK, WHEELER. Powell Creek rises on the west end of Wolf Mountain and flows south to North Fork Beaver Creek. Near its mouth was the Thomas J. Powell ranch. Powell was born in Missouri in 1845 and came to Crook County in the 1870s. In later years his son, Fred A. Powell, ran the ranch and was active in cattlemen's affairs. *See Illustrated History of Central Oregon*, p. 776. Powell Mountain is two miles south of the ranch house.

Powell Creek, DOUGLAS. Powell Creek empties into Umpqua River in s 32, T 24S, R 7W. It was named in 1973 to honor William Powell, one of the first mail carriers to operate out of Tyee. The proponents of the name informed the OGNB that the mail was first carried on horseback and that 27 gates had to be opened and closed twice during each round trip. They also added the curious fact that it was a "backward" route where all mail was carried to the end of the line and delivered on the return trip. No explanation was given but one cannot help but imagine that even then officials were experimenting with new ways to prolong the arrival and heighten the suspense of the waiting patrons. William Powell died in Roseburg on May 15, 1970, just a few days short of his 101st birthday.

Powell Creek, JOSEPHINE. Powell Creek was named for John L. Powell who settled on a donation land claim near the stream in 1855.

Powell Hills, LINN. Powell Hills are northwest of Brownsville and have a maximum elevation of 516 feet. They were named for Silas Powell, a nearby resident and member of the family of Linn County's famous preacher, Joab Powell.

Powell Valley, MULTNOMAH. Powell Valley was named for three pioneer settlers, James Powell and Jackson Powell, of 1852, and Dr. J. P. Powell, of 1853. They were not related. *See* the *Oregonian*, July 19, 1899, p. 9; Nov. 5, 7, 1909. Powell Valley is east of Gresham. A post office with the name Powell's Valley was established Feb. 13, 1873, with William H. Bond first postmaster. Theodore K. Williams was appointed postmaster Dec. 16, 1874, and ran the office for nearly 20 years. On Apr. 5, 1894, Albion B. Elliott was appointed postmaster and the name of the office was changed to Powell Valley. It was closed to Gresham on Feb. 28, 1903. For most of its life the office was near Powell Valley School No. 26.

Powers, COOS. Powers was named in 1914 for A. H. Powers. Powers was then vice-president and general manager of the Smith-Powers Logging Company. Powers post office was established July 24, 1915, with Gustaveous A. Brown first postmaster. Albert H. Powers was born of American parents in Ontario, Canada, Nov. 6, 1862, and followed the logging and lumber business all his life, in several places. He was with the Smith-Powers Logging Company in Coos County from 1907 to 1922, and later with other organizations. He died at Indio, California, Jan. 2, 1930, as the result of an automobile accident. Powers was an ardent sports enthusiast. For obituary, *see* the *Oregonian*, Jan. 5, 1930.

Powwatka Ridge, WALLOWA. J. H. Horner of Enterprise told the compiler that the name Powwatka is the modern spelling of the Indian name *Paw-wa-ka*, meaning high, cleared ground, from where a view could be had. The form Powatka has been discarded by the USBGN. Powwatka post office was near the north end of Powwatka Ridge. It was established Aug. 15, 1900, with Amanda F. Harris first of four postmasters. The office was discontinued Nov. 30, 1920.

Prahl, CLACKAMAS. This was a station on the Oregon Electric Railway at the south end of the bridge over the Willamette River at Wilsonville. It was named for Fred Prahl, roadmaster for the railway, who had charge of the construction of the bridge. He died in 1908.

Prairie Channel, CLATSOP. This is the south channel of the Columbia River east of Tongue Point. It has been called Prairie Channel since pioneer days because of the prairie-like islands on either side. Wilkes, in *U. S. Exploring Expedition*, v. 23, Hydrography and accompanying atlas, refers to this channel as Dicks Run, but gives no explanation of the origin of that name. The name Dicks Run has not persisted.

Prairie City, GRANT. Prairie City is purely a descriptive name and quite accurately describes the community. *The History of Baker, Grant, Malheur and Harney Counties*, p. 447, says that the first community was Dixie, started in 1862 about three miles up the stream of the same name. By 1870 much of the area had been destroyed by placer operations but a new townsite had already been selected at the mouth of the creek near John Day River. The name Prairie City is reported to have been chosen by J. W. King. Prairie City post office was established Aug. 8, 1870, with Jules Le Bret first postmaster.

Prairie Creek, WALLOWA. Prairie Creek and Prairie Basin are east and southeast of Joseph. These features were named in early days by Robert M. Downey, a pioneer settler of the Wallowa Valley who came from Missouri. He applied the names because of the fine stands of bunchgrass on the nearby prairies. Prairie Creek post office was established in Jan. 1876, with Downey the first postmaster. The office was closed in July 1893. Prairie Creek was the second post office in what is now Wallowa County. Wallowa, established Apr. 10, 1873, was the first. When first established the Prairie Creek office was in S 11, T 3S, R 45E, about two miles east of Wallowa Lake.

Prater Creek, HARNEY. Prater Creek is about six miles east of Burns. It was named for Thomas Prather who was born in Clermont, Ohio on Dec. 21, 1843 and came to Douglas County, Oregon in 1859. In 1872 he settled in the Burns area, then part of Grant County, where he stayed until 1882 when he moved to Montana. The name Prather is pronounced to rhyme with crater. In 1980, the OGNB attempted to have the spelling corrected to Prather but the USBGN decided in *Decision List 8104* that the form Prater should be retained.

Prattville, WASCO. Prattville post office is listed on the Wasco County list with Mrs. Mary J. Mackie postmaster. It operated from Nov. 1879 to Sept. 1880, near the locality later called Wamic. Jason C. D. Pratt came to Oregon in 1859 and was one of the first settlers in the area in 1862. Even after Wamic post office was established in 1884, the name Prattville was continued for some years. *See*

McNeal's *History of Wasco County*, p. 244 where he quotes Gladys McAllister, a member of an early family.

Pratum, MARION. *Pratum* is a Latin word meaning meadow. The name is said to have been applied to the place by a group of the Mennonite Church established in the community. The railroad was built through this locality about 1880, and it is said a Mr. Larson opened the first store and called the place Enger, for a friend. This name was confused with Eugene, hence the change to Pratum. Postal authorities inform the compiler that Pratum post office was established with the name Switzerland on Feb. 28, 1887, and with John Green first postmaster. The name of the office was changed to Enger on Aug. 21, 1897, and to Pratum Oct. 1, 1898. There is a community named Switzerland nearby, and the office may have been moved in addition to having its name changed.

Preachers Peak, HOOD RIVER, MULTNOMAH. This name, sometimes misprinted Preachers Rock, refers to a point on the Hood River-Multnomah county line at the extreme southeast corner of Multnomah County. R. S. Shelley of the USFS named the peak for his father, Troy Shelley, a well-known minister of upper Hood River Valley. Shelley senior had a crippled foot. About the turn of the century he rode a horse to the summit and his son named it in his honor. According to Ralph Lewis of Parkdale, who supplied this information, Devils Pulpit nearby was named because the remark was made that if the preacher was there, the devil wouldn't be far away.

Prescott, COLUMBIA. Prescott was named about 1905 for owners of the sawmill. Prescott post office was established May 21, 1907, with Anna Barker first postmaster.

Preston, LANE. Government records show that Preston post office was established Oct. 11, 1853, and discontinued Mar. 30, 1855. Henry Small was postmaster. The compiler has been unable to get the location of the place, but it was probably on Small's donation land claim now in the southwest part of Cottage Grove.

Preuss, COOS. Preuss post office was established Apr. 17, 1917, and was at the Beaver Hill coal mines of the Southern Pacific Company. The mines are now closed and the post office has been discontinued. It was named for Rosa Preuss, a school teacher, who helped to have the post office established.

Prevost, BAKER. This station on the railroad along Snake River was named for Jean Baptiste Prevost, a member of the Astoria overland party under Wilson Price Hunt. Prevost was drowned in Snake River in Dec. 1811. *See* Irving's *Astoria*, first edition, v. 2, p. 52. The railroad was inundated when Brownlee Dam was completed in 1959 and Prevost is now history.

Price, CROOK. Price post office was established Nov. 16, 1886, with Mrs. Elmira Logan first postmaster. With one short intermission the office was in operation until July 11, 1902. The office was named for T. B. Price, one of the signers of the petition. It was in Camp Creek area, in S 15, T 19S, R 20E, about 47 miles southeast of Prineville. Although the office was established on Nov. 16, Mrs. Logan's commission was not actually dated until Dec. 9, 1886. The office was first in the living room of the log home of the Samuel Allen Logan family. Later the office was moved to other homesteads, but never very far from Camp Creek.

Prichard, BAKER. Prichard post office was named for a local resident. It was situated about 15 miles airline east-northeast of Baker, in the Lower Powder Valley, about four miles north of Prichard Flat. Modern maps are lettered Middle Bridge at this point. Prichard post office was established May 24, 1872, with Royal A. Pierce first postmaster. The office was later on the Union County list, but it was when Union County included that part of what is now Baker County. Prichard post office was closed Feb. 23, 1876. Postal records use the spelling Prichard for this office, but the name appears as Pritchard in other places. The writer does not know which style was used by the family in question.

Priday Agate Beds, JEFFERSON. East of Hay Creek is the site of the old Priday Ranch. This was part of the Teal & Coleman holdings purchased by Albert James Priday who came to this country in 1880 from Westbury, England. Phil Brogan was kind enough to provide the following facts about the rock deposits: "These beds, world known for the fine material, especially plume agates, which they produce, have been known since early days, and were among the first agate localities to bring fame to Oregon for its fine quality gem stones. The beds are in ancient formations near Trout Creek which slashes through a land of tilted mountains. The bedrock, dipping to the John Day formations and Clarno rocks, are mostly in rhyolite. Nearby on Pony Creek are the well-known Polka Dot Agate beds." Priday Reservoir in Warner Valley is on property that belonged to a son, Ernest Priday.

Prill Lake, LINN. This is a small mountain lake near the summit of the Cascade Range, about eight miles south of Mount Jefferson. The lake was discovered by Dr. A. G. Prill of Scio, and about 1912 was named by representatives of the State Board of Fish and Game Commissioners, who stocked the lake with fish that year. Dr. Prill, long an enthusiastic amateur naturalist, conveyed his extensive bird and egg collection to the University of Oregon in 1945. *See* news story in *Sunday Journal*, Sept. 23, 1945.

Prince Lake, LANE. This lake southwest of Scott Mountain was named for Prince Glaze who was USFS guard at Frog Camp during the 1920s. Nearby Glaze Lake was named for the same man.

Princeton, HARNEY. Archie McGowan wrote the compiler in Aug. 1927, as follows: "Princeton originated as a small rural post office in about 1912. C. B. Smith, a Bostonian and professional musician, settled on a homestead there about three years prior to the birth of the post office, and named the place for Princeton, Massachusetts, which was a town of his childhood." Postal authorities inform the compiler that Princeton post office was established Oct. 15, 1910, with David Williams first postmaster. The compiler has been unable to reconcile the discrepancy in dates. When SH-78 was improved from Burns to Burns Junction, the original site was bypassed and the present community, a short distance away, is called New Princeton.

Prineville, CROOK. Prineville was named after the first merchant of the place, Barney Prine. His stock consisted of a barrel of first rate whisky in the front room of his establishment and some blacksmithing equipment in the back room. The prevailing opinion around Prineville is to the effect that most of the business was done in the front room. For article about Barney Prine by Fred Lockley, *see* the *Oregon Journal*, Mar. 31, 1927, editorial page. Prineville post office was established with the name Prine on Apr. 13, 1871, and with William Heisler first postmaster. The name of the office was changed to Prineville on Dec. 23, 1872.

Pringle Creek, MARION. This stream rises in the hills south of Salem, and flows through the southern part of the town. Virgil K. Pringle, who arrived at Salem on Dec. 25, 1846, took up a donation land claim near the stream, which was accordingly named for him. The Pringles left Missouri on Apr. 15, 1846, and Octavius M. Pringle, son of Virgil K. Pringle, wrote an account of the trip under the heading *Experiences of an Emigrant Boy of 1846*. Octavius M. Pringle subsequently moved to central Oregon. *See* Pringle Falls.

Pringle Falls, DESCHUTES. Pringle Falls on Deschutes River were named for O. M. Pringle who, in 1902, made a Timber and Stone Act purchase of 160 acres of government land near the site of the falls. Pringle came into central Oregon about 1874, from Salem, and for some years lived near Prineville. The locality of Pringle Falls is also known as the Fish Trap. Indians guddled salmon at this point, lying on the bank and grasping the fish in the gills as they swam up through the shallow channels.

Progress, WASHINGTON. When Progress was named, optimism was fairly singing in the air. Progress post office was established Aug. 28, 1889, with Joseph Hingley postmaster. The office was closed July 11, 1904, but Progress continued as a county crossroads, about three miles southeast of Beaverton. It is at the crossing of the Scholls Ferry Road and Hall Boulevard. In the 1970s, a large shopping mall, Washington Square, was erected in Progress and by 1989 the community had become part of a heavily built suburbia stretching from Beaverton to Tigard.

Promise, WALLOWA. John C. Phillips and W. Mann settled near the present site of Promise about 1891 and took up homesteads. Mann called the place "Promised Land" and "Land of Promise." The post office was established Dec. 22, 1896 and was called Promise on that account. Thomas C. Miller was first postmaster.

Proposal Rock, TILLAMOOK. Proposal Rock is a well-known feature at the mouth of Neskowin Creek. The various trails through sallal to the top are popular scrambles for both young and old. Alexandria L. Rock, who came to the Little Nestucca in the 1880s, in her recollections on file at the Oregon Historical Society says the name was applied by Mrs. Henry Page when Charley Gage proposed to her daughter about the turn of the century. She added the Indian name was *Schlock*.

Prospect, JACKSON. In 1979 Mrs. Frances Aiken Pearson of Medford gave the compiler some interesting history of this small community on the Rogue River north of Medford. It was first established as Deskins and a post office with this name was opened on July 5, 1882 with Harvey P. Deskins postmaster. In the fall of 1883 Deskins, after a misguided business venture, fell on hard times and sold all his holdings to Squire Stanford Aiken, Mrs. Pearson's father. Eventually Aiken became postmaster and on Nov. 9, 1889, had the name changed to Prospect because some preliminary plans had been run for a railroad up the Rogue River.

Prospect Creek, TILLAMOOK. Prospect Creek flows into Neskowin Creek. Ralph Sutton, a long time resident, said that the name was given many years ago by a cowboy who claimed to have discovered gold along its banks, and in due course a company was organized, stock sold, furnace built and company bankrupted in that sequence. At least the promoters picked an original area for their operation.

Prosper, COOS. Prosper post office was established Aug. 8, 1893, with Adam Pershbaker postmaster. The name was apparently selected because of hopes that the locality would be prosperous. The office was discontinued in June 1928.

Prouty Glacier, DESCHUTES. Prouty Glacier is on the northeast side of the South Sister. It was named for Harley H. Prouty who was born in Vermont June 26, 1857, of a distinguished New England family. He was engaged for a time in the lumbering business after he came to Oregon. Later he retired from active business and devoted much time to mountaineering, and was president of the Mazamas. He died Sept. 11, 1916, and it was his wish that his remains be buried in the Cascade Range. As a result of this a party of Mazamas took his ashes to Obsidian Cliff, near the Three Sisters, and placed them in a cairn. Nearby is placed a bronze tablet bearing a suitable inscription. Prouty may have been the first man to climb the North Sister and the higher of the two summits or pinnacles at the top of the mountain is known as Prouty Pinnacle. A short biography appears in *Mazama*, 1916, and information about the bronze plate is in *Mazama* for 1917.

Providence Creek, DOUGLAS. Providence Creek flows into Umpqua River west of Reedsport. The name perpetuates a settlement called Providence, established in the early 1850s, but gone long ago. The compiler has been unable to get the history of the place, by whom it was settled and why it was named. In June 1944, Mrs. Alice B. Maloney told the compiler that she had found an interview with C. C. Mann in The Bancroft Library at the University of California, Berkeley. Mann was a member of the *Samuel Roberts* party visiting Umpqua River in July 1850. He stressed the fact that he was a graduate of Brown University, Providence, Rhode Island. It is possible this is the genesis of the name, but the evidence is of course rather tenuous.

Provolt, JACKSON. This post office was named for a pioneer family of the community. The office was established Apr. 29, 1895, with Mary E. Provolt postmaster. It was then in Josephine County.

Proxy Point, LANE. Proxy Point is just west of the Three Sisters. It was named by USGS surveyors during the time when the triangulation net was being extended along the Cascade Range. This point and Substitute Point were both selected for possible stations, where but one was to be occupied.

Pryor, LANE. Pryor, a station on the Cascade line of the Southern Pacific Company, was named for a member of the Lewis and Clark expedition, Nathaniel Pryor.

Pucci Glade, CLACKAMAS. In 1936 Emilio Paola Pucci dei Marchese di Barsento came from Italy to pursue graduate studies at Reed College. He also undertook to coach the then fledgling Reed College ski team. Pucci picked for a practice slope this open glade immediately south and west of the present site of Timberline Lodge. Reed College was one of the early local entrants in Alpine downhill skiing competition and by the time the lodge was opened in 1937, the name was firmly entrenched. Emilio Pucci completed his studies and returned to Italy where he achieved considerable fame as a fashion designer and was also active in politics. He maintained his friendships with members of the Mount Hood skiing community and on Mar. 10, 1978 the Friends of Timberline arranged a reunion of the ski team and a testimonial dinner at Timberline Lodge. The name of the glade was formally recognized and Pucci was able to demonstrate that he still retained his skiing dexterity. At the evening banquet he was presented with a handsome engraved replica of the present wood descriptive marker.

Puckett Glade, KLAMATH. This small meadow is in sections 20 and 21, T 39S, R 5E, near Surveyor Mountain. The USFS says it was named for an early settler and BLM records show that Prentiss S. Puckett homesteaded there in 1887.

Pudding River, CLACKAMAS, MARION. This stream rises in the Waldo Hills, east of Salem, and joins Molalla River just before that stream flows into the Willamette. Little Pudding River drains an area to the west of Pudding River, and joins that stream just west of Mount Angel. Pudding River is a name that originated in the days of the fur trade. W. H. Rees, in an address in OPA *Transactions*, 1879, p. 23, gives the story of the name. The substance is that about 1821–22 Joseph Gervais and Etienne Lucier and their families were camped on the stream, which was called *Hons-u-cha-chac*, and in a period of severe weather had the good fortune to shoot some elk. Their Indian wives immediately made a favorite French dish, known as a blood pudding, which went a long way toward overcoming the discomfort of rain and snow. While this feast was being enjoyed, Gervais and Lucier christened the stream *Riviere au Boudin*, or Pudding River. *See also Ten Years in Oregon*, by Dr. Elijah White, edited by Miss A. J. Allen, p. 70. Rees is doubtless right in his account of the origin of the name, but wrong about the date, for Alexander Henry mentions Pudding River in his diary on Jan. 23, 1814. The river was probably named in 1812–13. *See* Gervais. Pudding River appears on the Wilkes map of 1841. Another form of the Indian name was Anchiyoke River, which was used in the act of July 5, 1843, creating Champooick District. Early writings show different spellings. *See Handbook of American Indians* under the heading "Ahantchuyuk."

Pueblo Mountain, HARNEY. Pueblo Mountain is in the extreme south end of the county, south of Steens Mountain. It is named with the Spanish word for city or village. The name was applied in the early 1860s by prospectors and miners from Nevada, and a news item in the *Humboldt Register*, Unionville, Nevada, Dec. 5, 1863, copied from the Virginia City *Union*, attributes the discovery of the "Puebla" district to Major M. D. Harmon of Carson City. The form *Puebla* is the wrong gender for the Spanish word, and has been supplanted by Pueblo. In May 1946, James F. Abel, then at The Bancroft Library in Berkeley, sent the compiler a transcript of the item about Harmon, which will be found in *OHQ*, v. 47, p. 210. Mr. Abel concludes: "Puebla Mining District was in existence as early, at least, as the summer of 1863. It may have been established in 1862 but that is not probable. The district was believed to be in Nevada and is shown on Milleson's Map of the Reese River and Humboldt Silver Mines dated 1864. In reality the Territorial line ran south of or through it and all or most of it was in Oregon. Mentions of Puebla Mining District are numerous in 1864. Pueblo Mountain, Butte, Valley and City are shown with considerable accuracy on Lieutenant Colonel R. S. Williamson's map published in 1866."

Puget Bar, CLATSOP. Puget Bar lies in the Columbia River east of Tenasillahe Island and west of Puget Island. Broughton discovered Puget Island on Oct. 26, 1792, and named it for Lieutenant Peter Puget, and the name Puget has by custom become attached to the bar. Puget Island is in Washington. Tenasillahe Island is in Oregon. Lieutenant Peter Puget was a member of the Vancouver expedition and it was for him that Puget Sound in Washington was named. Not a great deal is known about Peter Puget, though diligent search has been made, particularly by Professor Edmond S. Meany of the University of Washington. He was lieutenant on Vancouver's sloop *Discovery* at the time Vancouver visited the Pacific Northwest. What is known about Puget is printed in Meany's *Vancouver's Discovery of Puget Sound. See also British Columbia Coast Names*, by John T. Walbran.

Pulpit Rock, HOOD RIVER. Pulpit Rock is the prominent buttress on Mount Hood dividing Coe and Ladd glaciers at the 9000-foot level. The earliest reference to this rock is in a letter from Dr. T. L. Eliot written in the summer of 1887 describing what must be assumed to be the first ascent of Cathedral Ridge. Dr. Eliot calls it "The Cockscomb" but this form has not prevailed. The present descriptive name, Pulpit Rock, is now in general use.

Pulpit Rock, KLAMATH. This rock outcrop is west of and overlooks Rosary Lakes. It was so called by the USFS as early as 1936 in their Trail Log, but it was not until 1986 that the name was made official in USBGN *Decision List 8701*. The rock is visible from a number of places in the Willamette Pass-Odell Lake area and is used as a reference point by hikers and cross-country skiers. The name is, of course, descriptive.

Pulpit Rock, WASCO. Pulpit Rock is a peculiar formation of stone within the city limits of The Dalles. It is a pillar about 20 feet high, cleft at the top in such a way as to make it a natural pulpit, with a seat attached. Missionaries of the Methodist mission in The Dalles used this pulpit when they preached to the Indians. On the seventieth anniversary of the founding of the mission, a bronze tablet was unveiled and Pulpit Rock was dedicated in the presence of about 500 persons. For information about the mission and Pulpit Rock, *see* Lulu D. Crandall's article in the *Oregonian*, Oct. 24, 1927, editorial page.

Puma Creek, LANE. A. J. Briem, in his notes on file at the Oregon Historical Society, says that this creek was named because the small daughter of a road camp cook saw a cougar on its banks.

Pumpkin Creek, WALLOWA. This stream is east of Imnaha and was named because Ike Bare camped on its banks while hunting, and cooked some pumpkins, of which he was fond.

Pursel, JACKSON. Pursel post office and community were named in compliment to the postmaster, C. C. Pursel. The office, which was in the Applegate Valley about ten miles north of Watkins, operated from Feb. 1898, until Jan. 1904, and was then closed out to Buncom.

Pyburn Hollow, SHERMAN. Jacob Pyburn homesteaded in this canyon west of John Day River in the 1890s.

Pyle Canyon, UNION. This canyon, south of Union, was named for James M. Pyle, a pioneer settler of that part of Oregon, and one of the first members of the legislature from Baker County as it then existed.

Pyle Creek, LANE. This creek is a small tributary of West Fork Indian Creek west of Reed. According to Dale Steinhauer in the *Siuslaw Pioneer*, 1980, p. 25, it was named for John Pyle who came to California just before the Gold Rush and moved to the Lake Creek area in 1882. Some years later he left Blachly and worked a small farm near the mouth of Pyle Creek.

Pyramid, COLUMBIA. This station on the south bank of the Columbia River west of Rainier was named for a peculiar pyramidal rock standing above the railroad track.

Quail Creek, CURRY. This stream, a tributary of Rogue River, was named for Peter Quail, a pioneer prospector.

Quaking Aspen Swamp, LANE. This is a feature of the Quaking Aspen Swamp Botanical Area between French Mountain and South Fork McKenzie River in T 17S, R 6E. The swamp itself is a prime example of mountain sphagnum bog and is named because a small grove of aspen or *Populus tremuloides* grows at the upper end. The name Quaking Asp Swamp is incorrect. For further information on aspen, *see* Aspen Lake.

Quartz Creek, WASCO. Quartz is not a rare mineral in the Cascade Range, nevertheless it is not plentiful as compared with other rocks. As a result, when it occurs, it attracts attention. Quartz Creek in the north part of the Warm Springs

Indian Reservation was named for the mineral in very early days. Captain H. D. Wallen of the Fourth Infantry conducted a military expedition from Fort Dalles to Great Salt Lake in 1859, and on the night of June 10 of that year camped at a place about 50 miles south of The Dalles which he named Quartz Spring because of the first quartz seen on the march. This was after passing Tygh Valley and Oak Grove (Wapinitia). However, in the table of distances given for the trip Wallen uses the name Quartz Creek. *See* 36th Congress, 1st Session, Senate Executive Document 34, pp. 7 and 46.

Quartz Mountain, LAKE. Quartz Mountain is a ridge about 30 miles northwest of Lakeview, crossed by SH-140, the Klamath Falls-Lakeview Highway. The mountain got its name from a narrow but rather prominent ledge of quartz, something out of the ordinary for the locality. The name of the mountain has spread to other nearby geographic features. Quartz Pass is the highest point on SH-140, and Quartz Creek heads just east of the pass and flows southeast into Quartz Valley. On Nov. 24, 1930, a post office with the name Quartz Mountain was established on the highway a little to the southeast of the pass. Mrs. Vera A. Real was the only postmaster. The office was closed to Lakeview Aug. 31, 1943.

Quartzville, LINN. Quartzville was once an important locality, due to gold discoveries in Dry Gulch in the early 1860s. The place was laid off as a town in 1864, and a stamp-mill was erected in the same year. For information about routes to the Santiam mines, *see* the *Oregonian*, July 9, 1864. For other information, June 9, 16, 30; Sept. 1 and 8, 1860; Oct. 14 and 22, 1863; June 30 and Nov. 12, 1864, and Oct. 29, 1869, p. 3. *See also* Down's *History of the Silverton Country*, p. 85. The excitement of the times is well expressed by the following text of a broadside described in detail as item 739 of *Oregon Imprints 1845–1870*, by George N. Belknap: "Ho! For Quartzville. All persons who want to go to Quartzville, will meet at the court-house, armed and equipped, at 3 o'clock this (Thursday) evening. Every man must furnish his own rations (say for 4 days) horse, and other necessaries gratis. Salem August 25, 1864." For further information, *see Sunday Oregonian*, Aug. 14, 1960, sect. 1, p. 22. When mining activity was resumed in the 1890s, the place was called Anidem, *see* Anidem. One of the largest tributaries of Middle Santiam River is Quartzville Creek, named for the town.

Quinaby, MARION. Quinaby was a station on the Oregon Electric Railway named for a self-appointed chief of a small group of Calapooia Indians who lived north of Salem in the early days of statehood. Os West in an article in the magazine section, *Sunday Oregonian*, Oct. 22, 1950, tells of old Quinaby and how he wintered in a camp about one half mile north of the Capitol and just west of Capitol Street in what were then the environs of Salem. Quinaby died in 1883.

Quincy, COLUMBIA. Quincy was settled about 1882, and named for Quincy, Illinois, by J. W. Barnes, who came from that place. The post office was established Oct. 8, 1892.

Quines Creek, DOUGLAS. Quines Creek flows north into Cow Creek near where 1-5 leaves Upper Cow Creek Valley to ascend to Canyon Creek Pass. There is a small roadside community which takes its name from the stream. Henry and Elizabeth Quine came to Oregon from Missouri in 1853. They first located in Benton County but in 1854 took a donation land claim including the mouth of the creek.

Quinn, COLUMBIA. The locality and post office called Quinn was near the south bank of the Columbia River on the low land northwest of Quincy. The post office was named for James Quinn, the first postmaster. He was appointed May 4, 1876, and served until June 30, 1909, at least that is the date the office was discontinued. There was never any other postmaster there.

Quinn Lakes, LANE. These lakes north of Waldo Lake were named for a pioneer sheep man, William E. Quinn of Grizzly. In 1894, at age 25, he was fatally injured while hunting in the Cascade Range near Waldo Lake. Quinn died near Crane Prairie while being packed out to the Deschutes River. He was buried on the banks of the stream now known as Quinn River, which is in Deschutes County. William E. Quinn's sister was married to Samuel A. Lytle, the son of Andrew Lytle, well-known Crook County pioneer.

Quinton, GILLIAM. Quinton is a railroad station that derives its name from an early settler named Quinn. The place was formerly called Quinn. For a few years there was a post office called Quinook, and this name was made up by taking part of the name Quinton and part of the name Squally Hook, which was the name of a railroad station to the west. For information about Squally Hook, *see* Hook. Quinook post office was discontinued in the fall of 1925.

Quitters Point, MARION. Quitters Point is south of Firecamp Lakes above South Fork Breitenbush River. It is a long, steep trail from the river at the 3000-foot level up to this 5000-foot-high nose near the lakes. It was named by USFS personnel who found their enthusiasm for the outdoors temporarily dimmed by the climb.

Quosatana Creek, CURRY. This name is said to come from an Indian word *Quosaten*. F. S. Moore of Gold Beach wrote the compiler that George W. Meservey, a half-blood Indian, told him that the Indian word meant a beautiful or fine creek. Quosatana Butte near the headwaters of the creek got its name from the stream. J. Neilson Barry calls attention to the entry under Tututni, *Handbook of American Indians*, v. 2, p. 857, which lists among the bands of that tribe the Cosuttheutun, and other similar forms. The name is translated as "people who eat mussels," in v. 1, p. 749. Possibly Quosatana is derived from it.

Rabbit Ears, DOUGLAS. These two peculiar rocks are in the mountains west of Rogue River opposite Crater Lake. The higher has an elevation of 6031 feet. The Indian name was *Kalistopox*, according to Will G. Steel. Two forest rangers, William E. White and Melvin E. Layton climbed one of them in 1912 and built a cairn on its summit. A stream nearby is Rabbitear Creek.

Rachel, LINN. Rachel post office was situated on what is known as Middle

Ridge at a point about five miles southeast of Sodaville. It was at the home of James W. Pierpoint, the first and only postmaster, and was named for his mother, Rachel Pierpoint. Rachel post office was established Feb. 16, 1915, and discontinued June 15, 1916, with papers to Sodaville.

Rackheap Creek, TILLAMOOK. This stream is in the extreme north part of the county and flows into North Fork Nehalem River from the east. Little Rackheap Creek is just to the north and flows into Rackheap Creek. In Jan. 1944, J. H. Scott of Nehalem wrote the compiler that the term "rackheap" was used by loggers to indicate a heap or pile of logs to be driven down stream by splash dam operations. It also means an accumulation of waste and scrap logs and debris. An eddy in the North Fork Nehalem River piles up a collection of debris and brush at the mouth of Rackheap Creek, which is the reason for the odd name of the stream.

Rader Creek, DOUGLAS. William Rader came to Douglas County in the 1880s with a large family. He eventually settled northwest of Tyee near the headwaters of this creek that bears his name.

Rager Creek, CROOK, WHEELER. Rager Creek flows into Powell Creek in the northeast corner of Crook County. The USFS Rager Ranger Station is located near the mouth of the creek which was named for James Rageor, a German rancher who settled there in 1885. The Northwest Electric Cooperatives house publication, *Ruralite*, Oct. 1984, has a fine account of this isolated ranger station.

Ragged Ridge, DOUGLAS. Ragged Ridge is the high ground forming the divide between North Umpqua River and Steamboat Creek. The descriptive name was applied by USFS ranger Fred Asam in the 1920s.

Ragic, CURRY. Ragic is Cigar spelled backward. G. W. Meservey wrote from Illahe saying that a distinctive name was wanted, and Ragic was the result! Ragic post office was established Sept. 10, 1898, with John H. McElhaney first postmaster. The office was closed Oct. 5, 1900, and mail sent to Wedderburn. Ragic was about nine miles up Rogue River from Wedderburn, apparently on the McElhaney place about a mile west of the mouth of Lobster Creek.

Railroad Creek, DOUGLAS. This stream is in the west part of the county and is tributary from the east to North Fork Smith River at a point about a mile and a half up stream from the mouth of North Fork. In May 1948, William Wroe, a local resident, wrote that the name Railroad was applied because there was once a logging railroad near the creek. Wroe added: "That was way over fifty years ago and there is no trace of the railroad left."

Railroad Gap, JACKSON. The name Railroad Gap has been used in the upper Evans Creek area for many years. It is applied to a natural pass and also to a USFS shelter, both of which are situated in the southwest corner of T 32S, R 2W. When the Oregon & California Rail Road was being projected south from Roseburg in the 1870s, a survey was run through this section in hope of finding a practicable route from the drainage of Cow Creek into the Rogue River. This location was not used but the fact of the survey gave rise to the name Railroad Gap. Railroad

Gap Creek takes it name from the gap. For the geography of the locality, *see* USGS map of the Cleveland Ridge quadrangle, issued in 1983.

Rainbow, LANE. The name of this post office was suggested by Mrs. L. Quimby, whose husband bought the property where the office is situated in May 1922. The office was established July 1, 1924, and closed Aug. 31, 1937 with mail to Blue River. Mrs. Quimby selected the name because McKenzie River nearby is the home of the popular rainbow trout, *Salmo gairdneri*.

Rainbow Point, KLAMATH. This point is on the south shore of Crescent Lake. It was named by F. W. Cleator of the USFS in 1925 because of the presence of many rainbow trout in the water nearby.

Rainier, COLUMBIA. The town of Rainier was founded by Charles E. Fox, who settled there in 1851, and was the first postmaster. The name of the town was taken from Mount Rainier. The earlier name was Eminence. Mount Rainier, in Washington, has been the center of one of the most acute geographic name controversies in the history of the country. It was named by George Vancouver on May 8, 1792, for Rear-Admiral Peter Rainier, of the Royal Navy. For facts about the discovery and Admiral Rainier, *see* Meany's *Vancouver's Discovery of Puget Sound*, p. 99. For additional information about the mountain and the name Tacoma as applied thereto, *see Mount Rainier*, by the same author. Eminence post office was established June 5, 1851, with Charles E. Fox first postmaster. The name of the office was changed to Rainier on Jan. 6, 1852.

Rainrock, LANE. This railroad station was west of Eugene. The name was applied by H. L. Walter of the operating department of the Southern Pacific Company. Walter told the compiler he selected this name arbitrarily and it had no particular significance.

Rajneeshpuram, WASCO. Rajneeshpuram was the city and commune developed by Bhagwan Shree Rajneesh in the 1980s. The Bhagwan, as he was popularly known, was born Mohan Chandra Rajneesh on Dec. 11, 1931, in Kuchwada, India. After a career of study and teaching, he founded a cult in India and in 1981 moved, with a number of followers to Montclair, New Jersey. The facilities were not to his liking so later that year he purchased the 64,000 acre Big Muddy Ranch near the John Day River for $5,750,000. His followers immediately began constructing a large commune which in 1982 was incorporated as Rajneeshpuram. Friction developed at once between the red-clad disciples and Wasco County residents. In 1983, Oregon Attorney General David Frohnmeyer filed suit to invalidate the city. Meanwhile, the commune had grown to over 4000 people and expanded to take over the old communtiy of Antelope which they renamed Rajneesh. *See* Antelope. In 1984, members of the commune introduced *Salmonella* organisms into salad bars at restaurants in The Dalles and 750 people were taken sick. In October of that year, busloads of homeless people were brought to the commune from various parts of the United States and registered to vote, apparently in an attempt to take over the county government. This was thwarted and subsequent investigation brought matters to a head in 1985. On Sept. 13, 1985, Anand Sheela, the Bhagwan's general factotum, resigned and fled to Germany where she was later arrested on a variety of charges ranging from theft to attempted murder. The Bhagwan was being pursued by the U.S. Immigration authorities and on Oct. 27, 1985, he attempted flight but was intercepted at Charlotte, North Carolina on his way to Bermuda. In due course, he was deported to India where he settled on his original commune at Pune. He died in Pune on Jan. 19, 1990. In 1988, the Connecticut General Life Insurance Company, the mortgage holder, filed to repossess the ranch property and title passed to them in 1989. For much information on this bizarre bit of Oregon history, *see* an *Oregonian* series of articles in July 1985 and the *Oregonian*, Jan. 20, 1990, pp. A1, 16 and 17.

Raker Point, HOOD RIVER. This point on the west end of Sawtooth Mountain was named for its similarity to a raker tooth in a cross cut saw. Raker teeth clean out chips cut by the other teeth.

Raleigh, WASHINGTON. The name Raleigh was derived from an old-time resident of the neighborhood, Raleigh Robinson. The place was on Scholls Ferry Road at a point about a mile southwest of the Hillsdale-Beaverton Highway crossing, and just northeast of the Portland Golf Club. Raleigh post office was established Apr. 26, 1892, with Frank T. Berry first postmaster, and closed Apr. 29, 1904, with papers to Beaverton. In recent years the locality has been called Raleigh Hills, which sounds like a name coined by real estate operators.

Rambo Creek, BENTON. Rambo Creek is two miles west of Alpine and flows through the donation land claim of Isaac Rambo in T 14S, R 6W. The form Rainbow, used on some maps, is incorrect.

Ramo Flat, UNION. This flat is southeast of Union. Dunham Wright of Medical Springs informed the compiler in 1927 that it was named for a Frenchman, one Raymou, who lived thereon.

Ramona Falls, CLACKAMAS. Ramona Falls is a heavily visited spot where the Pacific Crest National Scenic Trail crosses the upper reaches of Sandy River. The *Sunday Oregonian*, Sept. 16, 1973, p. 4M, has an interesting article by Leverett Richards on the Civilian Conservation Corps or the CCCs. He recounts an interview with John E. Mills, a USFS employee who supervised a great deal of trail and bridge building by the enrollees. Mills stated that he discovered and named the falls on Aug. 8, 1933, while locating trail. He further said he was courting his wife-to-be and his head was full of the romantic song "Ramona." The compiler remembers as a young man a popular movie and song of that time based upon the novel by Helen Hunt Jackson.

Ramsey Lake, MULTNOMAH. This lake south of the mouth of the Willamette River was filled in by the Rivergate development during the 1970s. It was named for F. H. Ramsey, who was a pioneer settler of the neighborhood.

Ran Creek, GRANT. Ran Creek empties into John Day River five miles west of Mount Vernon. BLM records show that Caleb Ran took a homestead near its mouth in 1872. In 1889, Charles W. Rann filed on land about a mile upstream. The compiler does not know which spelling is correct.

Rancheria Creek, JACKSON. Rancheria Creek rises on the west slopes of the Cascade Range south of Rustler Peak and flows southwestward to join South Fork Big Butte Creek east of Butte Falls. This name has been shown on maps since pioneer days. *Rancheria* is a Spanish word used to refer to an Indian village or frequently for creeks flowing by such villages. The compiler has been told that Rancheria Creek was named because of the Indian village not far from its mouth and also not far from the old military freight road from Jacksonville to Fort Klamath.

Rand, JOSEPHINE. Rand is a community on Rogue River three miles north of Galice. Edith A. Keyte in *Josephine County Historic Highlights* states that it was the housing for the workers at the Almeda Mine a mile further downstream, and that it was named for the Rand, or more accurately the Witwatersrand, a ridge in the Transvaal of South Africa famous for its gold bearing soil. At one time there was a USFS ranger station at this site.

Randall Butte, JEFFERSON. Zenery P. Randall took a homestead on the slopes of this Axehandle Country butte in 1916.

Randleman Creek, COOS. Randleman Creek, which flows into Bear Creek east of Bandon, was named for Michel Randleman, who settled near the stream in 1874. The Randleman family has been prominent in Coos County affairs for several generations.

Randolph, COOS. Randolph is a community on the north side of Coquille River about three miles from the Pacific Ocean. Walling's *History of Southern Oregon*, p. 492, says the place was established in the days of the Coos County mining excitement, by Dr. Foster and Captain Harris and was named for John Randolph of Roanoke, Virginia. Randolph was first situated several miles northwest of the present location, near the mouth of Whisky Run, a small stream flowing into the ocean. Nearby sands were mined with feverish activity between 1853 and 1855. A dreary picture of Randolph in Oct. 1855, after the fever, is given in an article by William V. Wells, in *Harper's Magazine*, Oct. 1856, p. 595.

Range, GRANT. This post office was established June 4, 1908, and was named by its patrons because of the good stock range in the vicinity. Craig Thom was the first postmaster.

Rankins Horse Pasture, LANE. SH-58 passes through Rankins Horse Pasture about two miles west of Willamette Pass. Earl Walker of Oakridge said Rankin was a locating engineer for the railroad who pastured his stock in this meadow. This was C. R. Rankin who worked in the area around 1906 when the Harriman interests were planning to run a railroad through central Oregon from Eugene to Ontario.

Rann, GRANT. Rann post office was established Apr. 8, 1886, with William D. Baker first of two postmasters. The office was closed to Canyon City, Feb. 29,

1888. Rann and Ryan were in the livestock business in the central part of the Silvies Valley, and Rann post office was at or near the Rann ranch. It may be assumed that the office was named for this stockman.

Ransom Creek, CURRY. This Ransom Creek is tributary to Bravo Creek near Palmer Butte. Hiram C. Ransom who homesteaded at its mouth was the father of Edwin Ransom who later lived on the Ransom Creek at Brookings.

Ransom Creek, CURRY. This creek entering the Pacific Ocean on the north edge of Brookings was originally named Iler Creek. Edwin Ransom, son of Hiram Ransom, bought the Iler homestead prior to World War I and the creek name changed with the land title.

Rath Creek, LANE. Rath Creek flows into Sutton Lake from the north. Francis M. Rath homesteaded along it in the early 1890s.

Rattlesnake Creek, LANE. Rattlesnake Creek flows into Middle Fork Willamette River east of Pleasant Hill and west of Trent. Rattlesnake Butte, elevation 1374 feet, is just east of the south end of the stream. The creek was named by Elijah Bristow in pioneer days because of the prevalence of rattlesnakes in the vicinity. *See* Walling's *Illustrated History of Lane County*, p. 447. The place now called Trent was once called Rattlesnake because it was on the banks of Rattlesnake Creek.

Rattlesnake Grade, MORROW. Don McElligott wrote the compiler in 1969 regarding the name of this stretch of county road up McElligott Canyon. He stated that when the present road was built in 1923, his father and several other local ranchers contracted the grading which they did with horse drawn fresnoes, a type of scoop grader. There were a lot of rattlesnakes in the canyon and after the crews uncovered one exceptionally big den, the road was known as Rattlesnake Grade.

Ray Gold, JACKSON. This was the railroad name for Gold Ray. Colonel Frank Ray built a power plant on Rogue River nearby and named the place for himself with Gold added because it was hoped the enterprise would be a gold mine. The power plant is still known by its original name, but the railroad reversed the order of things because of confusion with Gold Hill nearby.

Rebel Hill, GRANT. This small eminence in the southeastern part of Canyon City was named during the Civil War because some southern sympathizers lived on the hill and made their presence in the community very much noticed.

Rebel Rock, LANE. Rebel Rock is on the west slope of the Cascade Range near South Fork McKenzie River. It is said to have been named for a pioneer sheep herder who boasted that he was the only rebel who had never been whipped, captured or surrendered.

Rector, TILLAMOOK. When the Wheeler Lumber Company established a logging camp at this place about 1909, it was named after Edward Rector, the manager of the company. The post office was established Aug. 1, 1913, with Mrs. Elizabeth M. McClure first postmaster.

Red Blanket Creek, JACKSON, KLAMATH. Red Blanket Creek flows into Middle Fork Rogue River south of Prospect. Mrs. Frances Aiken Pearson, who was born in Prospect in 1885, told the compiler in 1979 that she understood it received its name when early settlers gave the Indians red trade blankets for the fertile land east of Prospect. This became the site of the Red Blanket Ranch which in turn gave the name to the creek and Red Blanket Mountain.

Red Creek, HOOD RIVER, WASCO. This creek rises on Bonney Butte and flows southwest to White River. Lewis D. Reavis who worked for the USFS in the 1920s told the compiler that this is a descriptive name.

Redboy, GRANT. Redboy post office was established to serve the Redboy Mine in the Blue Mountains a few miles southwest of Granite. The office was put in service Dec. 5, 1907, with Percy W. Brick first of two postmasters. It was closed out to Granite on Dec. 15, 1910.

Redess, HARNEY. Redess was named for the "Red s" brand of the Pacific Live Stock Company's nearby ranch. It is between Burns and Crane on the Union Pacific Railroad. The stock company had acquired large acreage through the Swamp Act implementation of 1870 when overflow federal lands were marked with a capital "s" in red ink on land maps and deeded to the state. The administration of this law was marked by large scale abuse and some cases of outright fraud. The lands were generally known as Red s and it is probable that this was the origin of the brand.

Redland, CLACKAMAS. Redland is a locality six or seven miles east of Oregon City, so called because of the color of the soil. Redland post office was established Mar. 21, 1892, with William J. Johnson first of five postmasters. The office was closed Oct. 12, 1903, apparently because of the extension of rural free delivery.

Redmans Tooth, DOUGLAS. This is a prominent tooth-shaped rock on the end of Ragged Ridge above the junction of Steamboat Creek and North Umpqua River. According to Fred Asam, an early USFS ranger, nearby Redman Creek was originally known as Buck Tooth Creek for the rock, but for some unknown reason it was changed to Dead Indian Creek. Asam combined the two elements and gave the present names to both creek and rock.

Redmond, DESCHUTES. Redmond was named for Frank T. Redmond, who settled near the present site of the town in 1905. His house was a stopping place for transients. The town was laid out in 1906. For history of Redmond, *see* University of Oregon *Commonwealth Review*, April–July 1924. Redmond post office was established on Aug. 29, 1905, with Carl N. Ehret first postmaster.

Redne, MARION. Redne post office was established Jan. 10, 1918, with Gladys Grafe first postmaster. The office was discontinued Aug. 31, 1921. The writer was told in Jan. 1947, that the office was at a logging camp or headquarters on North Santiam River between Niagara and Detroit. It is said that the name was coined by spelling the proper name Ender backward. Ender was also a logging station, previously in service just east of Niagara, but it was not a post office.

Reed, LANE. Reed post office was established Feb. 8, 1900 on Indian Creek.

John L. Taylor, the first postmaster, drew up the petition and suggested the name in honor of Thomas Brackett Reed, for many years speaker of the United States House of Representatives. Originally the office was on the Taylor Ranch at the mouth of Taylor Creek but in later years it shifted around and its final location was about two thirds of a mile upstream near the mouth of Herman Creek.

Reed Creek, DOUGLAS. This creek in Camas Valley was named for Alexander Reed who took up a donation land claim along its banks in 1854.

Reeder Point, MULTNOMAH. Reeder Point is on the west bank of Columbia River and on the east shore of Sauvie Island in the extreme northwest corner of Multnomah County. It is about a mile south of the north boundary of the county. It is not a sharply defined point, in fact no more than a simple bend in the river. It bears the name of pioneer settlers in the locality, Simon M. and Catherine Reeder. The Reeders established themselves on their donation land claim in the 1850s. *See* Sauvies.

Reeds Creek, BAKER. Reeds Creek empties into Burnt River southwest of Dooley Mountain. It was named for Tabor M. Reed, a well-known early settler and prospector.

Reedsport, DOUGLAS. This town was named in honor of Alfred W. Reed, a pioneer resident of the western part of the county. The name was first applied about 1900 when the townsite was platted. The post office was established July 17, 1912.

Reedville, WASHINGTON. This town was named for Simeon G. Reed, who was a prominent figure in Columbia River transportation during the years 1859–79. He was a leading member of the Oregon Steam Navigation Company, and a large part of his fortune came from the sale of that company to the Villard syndicate in July 1879. Reed was born at East Abington, Massachusetts, Apr. 23, 1830, and came to Oregon in 1852. In 1859 he became a partner in the mercantile firm of Ladd Reed & Company. He engaged in various activities after the sale of the Oregon Steam Navigation Company. He died at Pasadena, California, on Nov. 7, 1895. For his biography, *see* the *Oregonian*, Nov. 8, 1895, p. 10; June 26, 1904, p. 33. Reed operated a blooded stock farm at what is now Reedville. For description of the farm and the livestock, the *Oregonian*, Oct. 12, 1875. His property became the endowment of Reed College after the death of his wife, Amanda Wood Reed. Mrs. Reed was born at Quincy, Massachusetts, Aug. 26, 1832; was married to S. G. Reed in Oct. 1850, and came to Oregon in 1852. She died at Pasadena on May 16, 1904. Reedville post office was established Jan. 2, 1877, with George Thing postmaster. The office was closed Jan. 31, 1954.

Reese Lake, LANE. This small lake southwest of the South Sister was named for Professor Hamit Darwin Reese of Oregon State University. Reese was born in Colorado in 1917 and graduated from Brigham Young University. He was a member of the OSU faculty from 1947 to 1980 and received numerous awards for teaching excellence. Reese was very active with the Boy Scouts and led many trips to the Three Sisters Wilderness. The lake was one of his favorite spots and after his death in 1987 the USFS proposed his name.

Reid Glacier, CLACKAMAS. This glacier is on the west slope of Mount Hood. It was named in 1901 for Professor Harry Fielding Reid, of Johns Hopkins University, an authority on glaciers. For his articles on glaciers, *see Mazama*, July 1903, and "Glaciers of Mount Hood and Mount Adams," *Mazama*, Dec. 1905. Professor Reid was born in Baltimore, May 18, 1859; died June 18, 1944.

Reids Mill, MORROW. Reids Mill was on Thorn Creek in S 18, T 5S, R 27E. James Reid was born in Oxford, Wisconsin in Nov. 1854. He married Mary Jane Roberts in 1874 and they brought their family to Oregon in 1901. The elder Reids settled on the Thorn Creek claim first but their sons, Arthur and Martin Reid, were the long-time operators of the sawmill.

Reinhart Creek, CURRY. In the spring of 1854 Herman and Charles Reinhart homesteaded on this creek about three miles north of Sisters Rocks. Herman Reinhart was born in Prussia in 1832 and emigrated with his family to the United States. In 1851 he and his brother came west and for the next 18 years followed most of the important mining discoveries from the Siskiyou country to Fraser River in Canada and the Rocky Mountains in Montana. His recollections published in *The Golden Frontier*, University of Texas Press, 1962, are a classic description of day to day life on the frontier and contain innumerable references to people and events in southwest Oregon. Reinhart died in Chanute, Kansas, Jan. 14, 1889. At the instigation of the OGNB the spelling Reinhart was approved by USBGN in *Decision List 6801*.

Remote, COOS. Remote was named in pioneer days because of the location which was well removed from other settlements. The post office was established June 1, 1887, with Herman S. Davis first postmaster. A century has wrought little change in Remote for while it once straddled SH-42, between Roseburg and Coquille, a recent highway relocation left it several hundred yards removed from the present highway. The *Oregonian*, Sept. 7, 1982, p. B4, has a short account with a picture of the gas station that houses the post office.

Renfrew Glacier, LANE. This glacier, on the northwest slope of the Middle Sister, bears the name of P. C. Renfrew, one of the incorporators of the McKenzie toll road project.

Reserve, LANE. This station on the Cascade line of the Southern Pacific was named many years ago when national forests were called reserves. It was at the boundary of the Cascade Forest Reserve. When the railroad was relocated around Lookout Point Lake after World War II, the station and name were abandoned.

Rest, HARNEY. A post office with the agreeable name Rest was established on the Harney County list on Apr. 3, 1890, with Samuel F. Hutton first and only postmaster. This office was closed to Riley on Apr. 29, 1891. In Mar. 1947, Archie McGowan wrote the compiler as follows: "Samuel F. Hutton was a pioneer settler in the vicinity of Wagontire Mountain. This area became quite famous during the last homestead era because of the feuds between the pioneer stockmen and the later settlers over the famous Wagontire waterholes. Mrs. America Sutherland, daughter of S. F. Hutton, reports that there were very few patrons for this early post office. It was situated in her father's home, and since patrons had to come so far for their mail, they had to rest before starting on their return journey. The name Rest was applied on that account."

Reston, DOUGLAS. This place is said to have been named by a traveler who sat on the front porch of Edmond E. Weekly's stage station. Weekly was considering a name for the post office, which was established Aug. 25, 1890, and the stranger suggested Rest because of the conveniences furnished to tired travelers. Weekly found there was another post office named Rest and he added an additional syllable. The place has been called Reston ever since, but it was not a post office in 1941.

Retlaw, WASHINGTON. This station was on the line of the Southern Pacific Company and was named by spelling the word Walter backward. The place was named for H. L. Walter, a member of the operating department of the company in Portland.

Retz Creek, CURRY. M. S. Brainard wrote the compiler in 1967 that this creek south of Port Orford was named for William Rhetz who lived near its banks. Rhetz was a long-time local resident and a county commissioner in 1873. Posterity decided that his memory be preserved in four letters instead of the original five.

Reuben, COLUMBIA. On Feb. 29, 1940, the Rainier *Review* published a short article about Goble and Reuben. Reuben is a place about a mile south of Goble and apparently it was named for Reuben R. Foster who was the second postmaster. The post office was established Sept. 5, 1890, with Eli G. Foster the first postmaster. The office ran with one interruption until it was discontinued to Goble on Oct. 25, 1923. Members of the Foster family were prominent in the history of Goble and vicinity. The place called Reuben is at or near a locality once known as Enterprise. It was planned to name the post office Enterprise in 1890, but that proposal fell by the wayside because there was already an Enterprise in Wallowa County, where the post office was established in 1887.

Reuben Creek, JOSEPHINE. Reuben Creek is a tributary of Grave Creek west of Leland. It was named for Reuben Field, who fought in the Rogue River War. *See* Mount Reuben.

Rex, YAMHILL. Rex is a community in Chehalem Gap a few miles east of Newberg, very near the Washington-Yamhill county line. The writer has not been able to learn why the name was selected. Some time in the 1890s Charles F. Moore, a local landowner, platted some property in the place and named it Charleston, presumably for his own given name. A railroad station was installed with the name Charleston and on Mar. 27, 1900, Charleston post office was established with Harry L. Ward postmaster. Very soon confusion developed with the town of Carlton in the same county. Mail and railroad shipments went astray. The railroad changed the station name from Charleston to Rex and on May 14, 1901, the name of the post office was changed to Rex. Local residents say the railroad selected the name Rex, but no one seems to know why.

Rhea Creek, MORROW. The name Ray Creek is incorrect. The stream was named for Columbus Rhea, son of Elijah Rhea, pioneer of Lane County. Columbus Rhea settled in eastern Oregon about 1870, near the junction of Willow and Rhea creeks. Other brothers settled in the neighborhood. Columbus Rhea was engaged in a number of enterprises beside farming and was living in Heppner in 1928. He died on July 11, 1934.

Rhine Hollow, WHEELER. Rhine Hollow is north of Mountain Creek about 12 miles east of Mitchell. It was shown on old maps as Wren Hollow but in 1986, Jim Collins, a local rancher, said it was named for an old homesteader named Rhine. He added that remnants of an old cabin and shed were still visibile at the site.

Rhinehart, UNION. Rhinehart is a small community and formerly a flag stop on the Union Pacific Railroad a few miles south of Elgin, but the name is misspelled. Henry Rinehart and other members of the family were early and prominent settlers in the locality, and the place is supposed to bear the family name, but has too many of the letter "h." For information about members of the Rinehart family, *see Illustrated History of Union and Wallowa Counties*, pp. 337, 344, and 411.

Rhoda Creek, COOS. This stream flows into South Fork Coquille River south of Myrtle Point. It was named for William Rhoda, one of the so-called Baltimore party that settled nearby in pioneer days. Rhoda is said to have been a skilled cabinet maker.

Rhodes Creek, LANE. Rhodes Creek empties into Lookout Point Lake near the site of the one-time community of Blakelyville. It was named for Willaim Rhodes, an early settler.

Rhodes Creek, WALLOWA. This stream flows into Lightning Creek in the northeast part of the county. It was named for one Doc Rhodes, a local resident.

Rhododendron, CLACKAMAS. Rhododendron is on the Mount Hood Loop Highway. It was once a popular summer colony but with the increased popularity of skiing it has become a year-round community. The place was originally called Rowe for Henry S. Rowe, who was one time mayor of Portland and interested in the development of Oregon's scenic attractions. Later the post office was known as Zigzag. Still later the name was changed to Rhododendron because of the large number of rhododendron shrubs growing in the neighborhood.

Ribbon Ridge, YAMHILL. Ribbon Ridge is a spur in the southwest part of the Chehalem Mountains, about east of Yamhill. The top of the ridge twists like a ribbon, hence the name. A story in the Newberg *Graphic*, Apr. 25, 1940, says that Ribbon Ridge was named by Colby Carter, who came to Oregon from Missouri in 1865, and was an early settler in the Chehalem Mountains.

Rice, WASCO. Horace Rice settled on upper Fifteenmile Creek in the 1860s. He planted the first crop of wheat in upland Wasco County and through subsequent years increased his land holdings to 1000 acres. When the Great Southern Railroad was built up Fifteenmile Creek in 1905, Rice's name was given to the station near the mouth of Dry Creek. In 1980 there was little evidence of urban activity.

Rice Creek, DOUGLAS. Rice Creek is east of Dillard. It was named for Harrison Rice, who settled near this creek in 1852.

Rice Hill, DOUGLAS. Rice Hill was named for I. F. Rice, who settled there in 1850. It is a summit on the Southern Pacific Siskiyou line on the watershed between Elk Creek and Umpqua River. For many years Rice Hill was the bugaboo of pioneer travelers and it even presented a problem in railroad construction. The elevation of the government bench mark near the top of Rice Hill is 710 feet.

Rich Gulch, MALHEUR. This gulch is in the very north part of the county, and drains south into Willow Creek a few miles west of Malheur. It was named during the gold fever in the 1860s when rich placers were found in the vicinity.

Richard G. Baker Park, DOUGLAS. This is a county park on North Umpqua River ten miles east of Glide. It was named for R. G. Baker, a long time Douglas County employee and county commissioner at the time of his death.

Richards Butte, DOUGLAS. This butte is about four miles north of Wilbur, and west of I-5. It was named for James Richards, one of the earliest settlers in the lower Calapooya Creek section of the county.

Richardson Butte, LANE. This butte is northeast of Elmira. It was named for a pioneer family. *See OHQ*, v. 5, p. 136. Richardson Butte has an elevation of 812 feet.

Richardson Gap, LINN. Richardson Gap is east of Franklin Butte and southeast of Scio. It was named for a family of early settlers who resided nearby. Plats dated 1878 show several members of the family owning land in the vicinity of the gap. The principal man in the clan was W. W. Richardson. This gap connects the valleys of Thomas and Crabtree creeks.

Richland, BAKER. W. R. Usher platted this community and named it Richland on account of the character of the soil. The post office was established in 1897 with James Calhoun postmaster.

Richmond, WHEELER. Richmond was named by R. N. Donnelly. He gave the site and was the prime mover in establishing the community. The writer is informed that Donnelly selected the name as a result of a controversy he got into with William Walters, another pioneer resident, who objected to Donnelly's selection of the site for a school building. Donnelly called Walters "Jeff Davis" because of Walters' rebellious tendencies about the school, and applied the name Richmond because it was the name of the capital of the confederacy.

Rickard, BENTON. Rickard post office was named for John Rickard, a well-known Benton County pioneer. The office was established Apr. 28, 1879, and was closed Oct. 5, 1880. Robert S. Brown was the only postmaster. The office was situated on the Rickard claim about two miles east of Bruce.

Rickey, MARION. The community of Rickey was southeast of Salem and about a mile south of Penitentiary Road. The locality, which was not incorporated, was named for James Rickey, a very early settler. Rickey School was the principal landmark. For a short account of the place, *see* Salem *Statesman*, Oct. 10, 1931. After World War II, Rickey was absorbed into growing southeast Salem.

Rickreall Creek, POLK. Few geographic names in Oregon have caused such a dispute as the name of this stream, which rises in the Coast Range and flows eastward through Dallas and Rickreall to the Willamette River west of Salem. Members of pioneer families living along its banks have written fully on both sides of the subject, without converting those of opposite belief. The controversy deals with two problems, one concerning the original, pioneer name of the stream, and the other about the meaning of the word Rickreall. One group of early settlers is of the opinion that the pioneer name of the creek was La Creole, and that this name had its origin in the fact that an Indian was drowned at the ford near the present site of Dallas. The French-Canadians referring to the event used the word *la creole*, meaning "the native." Another group insists that the first name of the stream was *rickreall*, an Indian word. The matter is complicated by the belief by some that Rickreall is a perversion of *la creole*, and not an original name, while others insist that Rickreall comes from *hyak chuck*, Chinook jargon for "swift water." It has also been suggested that the word Rickreall was an Indian name for a locality near the stream. As far as the compiler knows, the first use of the name is in Wilkes *Narrative*, 1841, v. 5, p. 222, Creole Creek. Joel Palmer uses the name Rickreall in 1845–46 in his *Journal of Travels*, published in 1847. A school at Dallas (La Creole Academy) retains the early name. This school was founded by Horace Lyman. *See* letter of J. T. Ford in the *Oregonian*, Aug. 4, 1916, p. 8, on Indian origin of the name Rickreall. The school was chartered with the name Rickreall, by the territorial legislature in Dec. 1853. The name is given Ricrall in an advertisement in the *Oregonian*, Feb. 7, 1852. The references given above indicate that there was a difference of opinion about the name of the stream in the early days of pioneer settlement. It seems to the writer that different localities near the stream might have had different names, and while La Creole was used to refer to the creek near Dallas, Rickreall might have been an Indian name for another place on its banks. This would explain some of the discrepancies. The USBGN has adopted the name Rickreall Creek, and Rickreall is the name of the post office. Rickreal post office was established June 30, 1851, with Nathaniel Ford postmaster, but was discontinued Apr. 11, 1857. The office was reestablished June 19, 1866, with the spelling Rickreall and with Colonel Ford again postmaster. It has been in continuous operation since it was reestablished. The controversy over the name Rickreall was particularly acute during the summer of 1916. Letters on the subject were printed in the *Oregonian* July 23, 26, 30, Aug. 4, 5, 11, 13, 14, 18, 19, 20, 21, 24, Sept. 10, Oct. 2 and 8, 1916. During the Civil War and for some time thereafter Rickreall village was frequently referred to as Dixie because of Southern sentiment in the community. The name Dixie was used colloquially for several decades, but it was never the name of the post office.

Riddle, DOUGLAS. Riddle is a town on the Siskiyou line of the Southern Pacific, south of Roseburg. It was named for William H. Riddle, who came to Oregon from Springfield, Illinois, in 1851, and settled near the present site of the town. The old form Riddles is wrong. For information about the Riddle family, *see* the *Oregonian*, Mar. 29, 1925.

Riddle Creek, HARNEY. This creek and Riddle Mountain, just to the north, were named for Stilley Riddle, an early settler. The mountain is about ten miles southeast of Malheur Lake and has an elevation of 6351 or 6352 feet, according to the USGS Anderson Mountain 15' or 7 1/2' quadrangles, both dated 1974. The compiler assumes that government map makers will reconcile this difference in due course. The highest point is near the east end. T. S. Riddle was a member of a pioneer family of Oregon. For his biography, *see* Walling's *History of Southern Oregon*, p. 539.

Ridge, UMATILLA. Ridge post office was given a name descriptive of its situation which was about a dozen miles southwest of Pilot Rock. The ridge was the watershed between the Birch Creek and Butter Creek drainages, and there was sufficient local timber to provide business for a sawmill and for an output of poles and posts. Ridge post office was established Oct. 5, 1882, and was in service until May 15, 1906. William R. Stansell was the first postmaster.

Ridgeway, WASCO. Ridgeway post office was established Mar. 3, 1892, with Mary S. Cooke first postmaster. The office was finally closed Oct. 31, 1905, with papers to Shaniko. The locality called Ridgeway was west of Antelope in the southeast part of the county. In May 1946, Judge Fred W. Wilson of The Dalles wrote the compiler in part as follows: "Mrs. D. V. Bolton, wife of our county clerk, was the daughter of H. C. Rooper and raised right in the Ridgeway country. She remembers all about it. When she was a girl, the stagecoaches going to Canyon City on the one hand and to Prineville on the other used one road from The Dalles to Bakeoven. Then at Bakeoven the roads branched and the road for the Canyon City coaches went by way of Antelope, Cold Camp, Burnt Ranch and Mitchell, while the other road to Prineville went from Bakeoven to the head of Cow Canyon and then through Cross Keys and Hay Creek. Mrs. Bolton says that when she was a little girl there was a post office at Ridgeway and that she used to ride a horse to get the mail. The reason for the name is easily explained. The road, after it left Bakeoven, went along a rather high ridge until it reached the head of Cow Canyon, and it was by reason of this ridge that the office got the name Ridgeway, and the area out there is still called the Ridgeway country, though the post office has long since been abandoned."

Ridgeway Butte, LINN. This butte, east of Lebanon, was named for a pioneer settler, James Ridgeway. The name Chamberlain Butte is incorrect.

Rieth, UMATILLA. When the railroad company constructed new shops and terminals west of Pendleton, the station was named Rieth after a family of pioneer settlers who owned land nearby. The postal authorities named the post office

Reith. This discrepancy in spelling prevailed for some time until the writer made an investigation of the matter, and found that local opinion was in favor of Rieth, and the post office name was accordingly changed. For an obituary of Louis Rieth, one of the two brothers who owned the land where the town now stands, *see* the *Oregonian*, Sept. 23, 1926. Rieth post office was closed in June 1971. The principal Union Pacific yard in eastern Oregon is now located at Hinkle.

Rietmann Canyon, MORROW. Ernst and Paul Rietmann homesteaded in the late 1880s in this canyon tributary to Willow Creek at Ione.

Rigdon Meadows, LANE. This was the site of the Rigdon Guard Station of the USFS on the Middle Fork Willamette River. Steve Rigdon of Pleasant Hill maintained a post here from 1871 to 1896. The post was on the Oregon Central Military Wagon Road, an important link between the Willamette Valley and central Oregon. Rigdon kept careful records both of the westbound emigrants and eastbound travellers and cattle drives. He was married to Zilphia Bristow, daughter of Elijah Bristow of Pleasant Hill. Rigdon Point to the south and Rigdon Lakes and Rigdon Butte north of Waldo Lake were named for the same man.

Riggs Lake, LINN. Riggs Lake is on Scar Creek a mile and a half southeast of Scar Mountain. It was named for Albert Riggs who was born in Missouri in 1857 and came to Oregon in 1862. Riggs trapped in the Scar Mountain area in the 1880s and later worked as a lookout for the USFS prior to World War I.

Riggs Meadow, LANE. This meadow is just northwest of Odell Lake. Dee Wright of Eugene informed the compiler that it was named for Dave Riggs, a sheepman of central Oregon, who pastured his flocks nearby.

Riley, HARNEY. William Hanley of Burns told the compiler that this place was named for Amos Riley, an early stockman. Archie McGowan, also of Burns, wrote the compiler as follows: "This rural post office was named about 1885 for Riley of Riley and Hardin. Prior to the birth of Riley post office there was an office located about 75 miles north and west named Hardin, which was named for Mr. Hardin of this firm, so it was suggested by residents of Silver Creek that the new office be named Riley." The office was closed Nov. 15, 1919 but was reestablished Jan. 1, 1949, after the closing of the Suntex office.

Riley Camp, UNION. This spot in S 36, T 3S, R 33E, was the site of a cabin built by one Riley, the railroad station agent at Pilot Rock. There are several stories about the facilities which were in the heart of good elk country but the most intriguing says that one of Riley's associates, Ed Smith of Pilot Rock, put the torch to the building to stop its continued use by a superior force of intruders.

Riley Creek, CURRY. Riley Creek flows under US-101, the Oregon Coast Highway, at Gold Beach. It was named for Judge Michael Riley, who was born in New York state in 1827 and came to Curry County in 1853. He was a well-known pioneer citizen. He served as sheriff and also in the state legislature. For many years he was county judge of Curry County. Additional biographical information will be found in Dodge's *Pioneer History of Coos and Curry Counties*. Riley Creek is about a quarter of a mile south of the main part of Gold Beach. The stream should not be confused with Dean Creek which flows through the main part of town.

Riley Creek, GRANT. Riley Creek rises in Riley Creek Meadow at the base of Riley Creek Butte and flows north past Riley Mountain to John Day River west of Mount Vernon. All these names come from Augustus Riley who in 1871 filed on land at the mouth of the creek.

Ringo Point, CLACKAMAS. In pioneer days a locality about 15 miles southeast of Oregon City was called the Ringo settlement, named for the Ringo family. It was near the place that was later called Clarke. Ringo Point post office was established May 16, 1876, with William J. Allison first postmaster. The office was closed Apr. 3, 1878. The compiler has not been able to identify the exact geographic feature called Ringo Point and it does not appear on available maps.

Ritner Creek, POLK. Ritner Creek north of Kings Valley is named for Sebastian Ritner who came to Oregon with the emigration of 1845 and whose donation land claim included the stream. At one time there was a station named Ritner on the Valley and Siletz Railroad about two miles north of Kings Valley.

Ritter, GRANT. The post office at Ritter was named for the Reverend Joseph Ritter at whose ranch it was first established. The office has not always been in its present location. It is now near hot mineral springs, formerly known as McDuffee Hot Springs, but now known as Ritter Hot Springs. Joseph Ritter was a pioneer Baptist minister of the John Day Valley. The springs were discovered by William Neal McDuffee, an early day packer between Umatilla and the John Day mines.

Ritter Creek, BAKER. Ritter Creek is tributary to Powder River five miles southeast of Keating. It was named for Andrew J. Ritter who settled in Lower Powder River Valley at the turn of the century.

River Mill, CLACKAMAS. This station and power plant north of Estacada were so named because they were established near a sawmill on the banks of Clackamas River.

Riverdale, TILLAMOOK. Shortly after the turn of the century a post office with the descriptive name Riverdale was in service for a little over a year at a point about three miles north of Tillamook. This office was close to Kilchis River and was named on that account. The office was not far from the locality later called Cloverleaf. Riverdale post office was established in June 1901 and was closed in Aug. 1902. Theodore P. Bowlby was the postmaster.

Rivergrove, CLACKAMAS. This community is south of Lake Oswego just east of I-5. On Jan. 27, 1971, 105 voters of a population of 319 voted 57 to 48 to incorporate. The name is taken from Tualatin River on the south and the old Lake Grove area on the north. Rivergrove is another example of a small area and population group incorporating to avoid ultimate annexation into a larger community.

Rivers, DESCHUTES. Rivers post office was in the extreme north part of T 20S, R 19E, a little to the northeast of Brothers. Post route and other maps show this place as on the north border of Deschutes County, just over the line from Crook County. An office with the descriptive name Highland was established on the Crook County list Sept. 6, 1913, with Mrs. Mary T. Rivers postmaster. This was before Deschutes County was established. On Mar. 9, 1914, the name of the office was changed to Rivers in compliment to the family of the postmaster. The office was discontinued Dec. 21, 1918. The later record of this office was put on the Deschutes County list by postal authorities and it is assumed that the Highland-Rivers office was always in what is now Deschutes County, but by a narrow margin.

Riverside, MALHEUR. Riverside was given a descriptive name because the place was on the banks of Malheur River near the junction of the South Fork. Riverside post office was established Nov. 21, 1889, with Teresa E. McRae first postmaster.

Riverton, COOS. Riverton is a community on the Oregon Coast Highway about 12 miles east of Bandon. It is on the east bank of Coquille River and got its name on that account. Riverton post office was established June 30, 1890, with Orlando A. Kelly first postmaster. Riverton was laid out by E. Weston, a civil engineer, in 1889. The townsite was originally part of the Nathaniel Thrush property. Kelly, a teacher, is said to have been the first settler in the place. For more information about Riverton, *see* Dodge's *Pioneer History of Coos and Curry Counties*, p. 249.

Roache Creek, LANE. Roache Creek flows into Maple Creek two miles above Siltcoos Lake. BLM records show that Jon Roche filed on a homestead along the creek in 1891. The compiler cannot account for the variation in spelling.

Roaring Springs, HARNEY. These springs are at the western foot of Steens Mountain at the Roaring Springs Ranch. They are so called because of the peculiar noise they make. For details of the ranch, *see* the *Oregonian*, Nov. 16, 1983.

Robert W. Sawyer State Park, DESCHUTES. This 41-acre park along Deschutes River just north of Bend was named to honor one of central Oregon's most distinguished citizens. Robert William Sawyer was born May 12, 1880 in Bangor, Maine. He was a graduate of Harvard University and practiced law in Boston until 1912 when he moved west to Bend. Shortly after his arrival he took a job writing for the Bend *Bulletin* then owned and edited by George Palmer Putnam. In 1914 Sawyer took over the management and continued as editor and publisher until 1953. His position on the paper provided him with a base for many other activities. He was county judge of Deschutes County from 1920 to 1927 and then a member of the State Highway Commission. During his tenure on the Highway Commission he showed particular attention to the parks program and was instrumental in the establishment of the Parks Engineer and the initial appointment of Samuel H. Boardman to this post in 1929. Sawyer was active in irrigation affairs and served as president of both the Oregon Reclamation Congress and the National Reclamation Association. He was a member of the Capitol Reconstruction Commission in 1935 and later served on the Capitol Planning Commission.

Robert W. Sawyer was an active outdoorsman with a great interest in nature.

He was a tireless worker for both conservation and the proper and orderly development of central Oregon, his adopted home. He died in Bend on Oct. 13, 1959 after a long and useful life.

Roberts, CROOK. Roberts, on Alkali Flat between Crooked River and Bear Creek, was named for an early settler in Crook County, J. E. Roberts, who was for a time postmaster, but not the first. The post office was established May 6, 1910, and closed Feb. 29, 1940.

Roberts, LINN. Roberts is a place on Quartzville Creek not far above the mouth. It seems to have been named for John Roberts, a miner and prospector, who lived beside the stream for many years, mining at various localities. For an account of his activities, *see* Sweet Home *New Era*, July 3, 1941.

Roberts, MARION. Roberts was a station on the Oregon Electric Railway four miles southwest of Salem. When the railway was built south of Salem about 1911, the station was named Livesley in compliment to T. A. Livesley, a prominent hop grower of the locality. Livesley was associated with John J. Roberts and the style of the firm was T. A. Livesley & Company. In 1925 Roberts bought the Livesley interest and the firm became John J. Roberts & Company. The name of the station was changed to Roberts at that time.

Roberts, YAMHILL. Roberts post office was in service in the north part of the county from Apr. 5, 1892, to Aug. 28, 1895. It was about east of Wapato and near the south end of Wapato Lake. James H. Robertson was the first postmaster of Roberts post office and the name of the office is said to have been derived by abbreviation from the postmaster's family name.

Roberts Butte, JEFFERSON. Roberts Butte, west of Cherry Creek, is named for Willis D. Roberts who patented a homestead nearby in 1893. He sold to Jacob Kaser in 1900.

Roberts Butte, WALLOWA. This butte is about 14 miles north of Enterprise and was named for Mrs. Nellie (Stillwell) Roberts Averill, who ranged stock nearby about 1885.

Roberts Creek, COOS. Roberts Creek is tributary to Johnson Creek east of Templeton. It is named for Benjamin Roberts, an early homesteader.

Roberts Mountain, DOUGLAS. This mountain, and Roberts Creek, just to the north, were named for Jesse Roberts, a pioneer landowner. The mountain is important because the early stage road passed through a gap on its summit and the steep grade and narrow road resulted in many accidents and not a few deaths. In modern times, I-5 also traverses the same gap to avoid the circuitous route along South Umpqua River through Dillard. The *Sketch Map of Military Road from Myrtle Creek to Scottsburg*, prepared by 1st Lieutenant Jonathan Withers, 4th Infantry, shows the feature as Burnett Hill, apparently for John S. and James E. Burnett, father and son, who arrived in the area in 1853 and 1852 respectively and who both took donation land claims.

Robideau Landing, DESCHUTES. In 1972, Lloyd E. Robideaux wrote to give the origin of the name of this spot on the southwest edge of Crane Prairie Reservoir. He stated that his nephew, Fay Robideau, built the South Twin Lakes Resort in the early 1920s and was a fishing guide for many celebrities including Herbert Hoover. Robideau built a small summer cabin at South Twin Lake for Mr. Hoover who in turn named Robideau's Landing for his guide. Lloyd Robideaux added that members of his family used both forms of the last name.

Robinette, BAKER. James E. Robinette, born in Maryland in 1852, emigrated to Nevada about 1870 and came to Union County, Oregon, in 1884. He was associated with various mining enterprises, and in Oct. 1887, settled at what was Robinette on the west bank of Snake River near the mouth of Powder River. When the railroad was built from Huntington down Snake River about 1909, a station and a townsite were named for Robinette. A post office was established about the time the railroad was built. For a biography of James E. Robinette, *see* Gaston's *Centennial History of Oregon*, v. 3, p. 715. The spelling Robinett is wrong. The townsite was inundated when Brownlee Dam was built.

Robins Nest, CLACKAMAS. Robert Moore, who came to Oregon from Illinois with the Peoria party in 1840, used the name Robins Nest for his little settlement on the west bank of the Willamette River across from Oregon City. The place was later called Linn City and now is known as West Linn. On Dec. 20, 1945, Ernest E. East of the Illinois Historical Society wrote the Oregon Historical Society as follows: "It is not impossible that Robert Moore got the poetic inspiration for 'Robin's Nest' from the name of the log house in which lived Philander Chase, first bishop of the diocese of Illinois, Protestant Episcopal Church. Chase bought land in the valley of Kickapoo Creek about 12 miles west of Peoria and established Jubilee College. His first house was called 'Robin's Nest,' because, as he said, it was 'built of mud and sticks, and filled with young ones.' Robin's Nest was a United States post office. Philander Chase was the first postmaster. Robin's Nest farm today occupies part of the original Jubilee College farm. The chapel and dormitory, erected in or about 1839, with 90 acres, is maintained by the state and Jubilee College Park."

Robinson, WASHINGTON. Robinson was a station where the Scholls Ferry Road crosses the Southern Pacific line south of Beaverton. It was named for William J. Robinson, whose donation land claim was situated nearby.

Robinson Canyon, WHEELER. Granville C. Robinson homesteaded in this canyon off Pine Creek in 1881.

Robinson Ridge, JEFFERSON. Robinson Ridge near the headwaters of Currant Creek was the scene of a strange murder. In 1923, Alvin Robinson left his ranch home near Coyote Mountain for a day's work on the range. His horse returned riderless and no trace was found of the missing man until his wife told of a dream which showed in unbelievable detail her husband dead on the trail. Deputies found Robinson in the exact spot, shot through the back, but as of 1971 his murderer had not been discovered nor has there been any explanation of Mrs.

Robinson's remarkable extrasensory powers. Phil Brogan describes this incident in *East of the Cascades*, p. 226.

Robisonville, GRANT. Robisonville was one of the early post offices in the Blue Mountain mining region, in the extreme east part of Grant County. The post office was established June 27, 1878, and was discontinued July 23, 1884. Charles W. Daggett was the only postmaster. The name of the office has been spelled in several different ways on government maps, but Miles F. Potter in *Oregon's Golden Years*, p. 78, says that the place was named for William Robinson and that the form Robisonville is incorrect. The post office records all use Robisonville but the USGS Greenhorn quadrangle of 1972 shows the site as Robinsonville. William Robinson is long gone and the compiler must leave it to others to determine whether the Post Office Department erred originally or if later history altered William's name from Robison to Robinson.

Roby Hill, MARION. Roby Hill lies in the bend between Willamette River and Santiam River and is just south of Ankeny Bottom. It has an elevation of 345 feet. It was named for R. Roby, who took up a donation land claim nearby in pioneer days.

Rocca, POLK. Rocca post office was on Rock Creek in the extreme southwest corner of the county, and during its entire existence it was in the Hampton home. The office was established Apr. 30, 1895, with Miss Maggie Hampton first of four postmasters. The office was closed on Aug. 31, 1918. When the office was first proposed it was planned to have Sam Center act as postmaster, but as he was moving from the neighborhood, other arrangements were necessary. Center asked to have the office named for his daughter, Mary Rocca Center. This girl had been named for a friend of her mother who had married an Italian.

Rock Creek, BAKER. The 1988 GNIS lists 89 streams in Oregon called Rock Creek, a name applied by early-day residents with the greatest of ease and not without reason. One of the best known of these creeks is that which flows eastward out of the Blue Mountains to join Powder River near Haines. This Rock Creek was named during the days of the mining excitement of the 1860s. There is a community area about six miles west of Haines that goes by the name Rock Creek. A post office was established in this locality shortly after the turn of the century, with Edward P. Castor postmaster, but available information about its life history is meager. The compiler finds it listed as Rockcreek in the *Postal Guide* as of Dec. 1, 1903, but elsewhere the style Rock Creek is used. The office doubtless gave way to rural free delivery.

Rock Creek, GILLIAM. Rock Creek post office was on Rock Creek very near present Olex. It was established June 3, 1872, with Alexander Smith postmaster. The second postmaster was James R. Alfrey. The office was discontinued Mar. 11, 1874. Olex office was established Oct. 27, 1874 and named for Smith, albeit a misspelling of his first name.

Rock Creek, HOOD RIVER, WASCO. This stream is west and south of Wamic.

Joel Palmer crossed a stream in this vicinity on Oct. 4, 1845, and named it Rock Creek. *See* his *Journal of Travels*. While exact identification is impossible, it may be assumed that the stream now called Rock Creek is the one Palmer named.

Rock Creek, JACKSON. This stream is north of Lower Table Rock and flows westward into Sams Creek. It has been known in the past as Table Rock Creek, but in 1937 Paul B. Rynning recommended that the name Rock Creek was more suitable and that is the form used on the USGS Sams Valley quadrangle. *See also* Snider Creek.

Rock Creek, WASHINGTON. Early maps show the stream as Stony Creek, but for many years Rock Creek has been the universally accepted name. The name Dawson Creek, applied to the lower part of the stream, is incorrect, and was ruled against by the USBGN on Oct. 6, 1926.

Rock Mesa, LANE. The word *mesa* is Spanish for table, and is used in geographic nomenclature to describe hills and peaks with more or less flat tops. Rock Mesa is south of the Three Sisters.

Rock Point, JACKSON. Rock Point is now principally famous because of a fine concrete arch over Rogue River carrying the old Pacific Highway. It is two miles west of Gold Hill, and is named because of the geologic formation. In pioneer days this general locality was known as Dardanelles, and there was a post office by that name established Oct. 19, 1852, with William G. T'Vault first postmaster. It was also an important travelers' station and the tavern building built in the 1870s, and similar to the Wolf Creek Tavern, is still standing. The T'Vault place was on the south bank of the river about two miles east of the Rock Point Bridge. Dardanelles post office operated intermittently until Dec. 1878. There was also a post office named Rock Point, established in Nov. 1859, with John B. White first postmaster. This office operated until Oct. 1912. Early writers sometimes referred to this locality as Point of Rocks.

Rockaway Beach, TILLAMOOK. Rockaway Beach is north of Tillamook Bay. The Rockaway Beach Company projected this summer resort and named the townsite. The place is obviously named for Rockaway, Long Island, New York, a famous eastern seashore resort. For many years the simple form "Rockaway" sufficed but about 1987 it was changed to the more stylish Rockaway Beach.

Rockcreek, GILLIAM. Rock Creek takes the name of the longest creek in the county. The name of the creek is accurately descriptive. The community name is generally used in two words, but the post office used the form Rockcreek. Rockcreek post office was established Dec. 10, 1906 with Philip J. Mulkey postmaster and was discontinued Mar. 31, 1942. It should not be confused with the early Rock Creek post office near Olex.

Rockford, HOOD RIVER. This is a community on the west side of Hood River Valley and is said to have been named because of the rocky character of the surroundings.

Rockland, DOUGLAS. Rockland post office was given a name descriptive of the surroundings. It was a few miles southeast of Dixonville, and in the southeast quarter of T 27S, R 4E. The office was established June 28, 1910, with Alfred Mathews first and only postmaster. The office was discontinued in Oct. 1913.

Rockville, GILLIAM. Rockville was a place on Rock Creek not far above the mouth, probably not more than two or three miles and not as far as the railroad station now known as Rock Creek. The writer cannot determine the exact location. The first post office in this locality was called Scotts, and it was established Feb. 4, 1867, with Daniel G. Leonard first postmaster. This office was at or close to the mouth of Rock Creek near the place known as Leonards Bridge. Leonards Bridge was over John Day River and was a toll enterprise. The name Scotts seems to have been derived from a local settler or landowner. There is a Scott Canyon making into John Day River a few miles south of Rock Creek. The name of the post office called Scotts was changed to Rockville on Nov. 26, 1878, and Thomas S. Lang became postmaster. It was in operation until Aug. 2, 1889. It is apparent from a War Department map of 1887 that when the name was changed to Rockville, the office was moved eastward two or three miles. Thomas Lang was an early-day sheep raiser in the Heppner area and he carried on part of his activities near lower Rock Creek in what is now Gilliam County. Later he was a well-known citizen at The Dalles. He used a canyon to the northeast of Rockville to get his wool down to the Columbia River boats, and this canyon is still known as Lang Canyon. Scotts post office referred to above was apparently the first post office in what is now Gilliam County.

Rockville, MALHEUR. Rockville is on the east border of the county in the Succor Creek drainage and about 15 miles north of Sheaville. There is plenty of rock in the area and the name is descriptive. Rockville post office was established Jan. 27, 1912, with Etta E. Mullinax first postmaster. The office was discontinued June 30, 1948.

Rockwood, MULTNOMAH. Rockwood community at the intersection of SE Stark Street and Burnside extension was named for the rocks and trees that characterized the locality in earlier days. The post office was established Mar. 14, 1882, with Cyrus C. Lewis first postmaster. The office was closed Feb. 28, 1903, with the advent of rural delivery. Lewis, the first storekeeper, wanted a post office to help his mercantile establishment. Francis Tegart, frequently called Lord Tegart, local landowner, is said to have applied the name Rockwood in the hope of impressing members of his family in Ireland with his "estate." When the post office was established, he insisted on the selection of the name Rockwood.

Rocky Butte, MULTNOMAH. This butte has been known in the past as Wiberg Butte, but that name has fallen into disuse. The present name is appropriate because of the quarry on the east face. In the 1940s a large quantity of rock was removed from the quarry and incorporated into a new Multnomah County Jail. After the jail was razed in the 1980s to make way for I-205, much of the stone was reused along the Historic Columbia River Highway and other suitable spots.

Rocky Point, KLAMATH. Rocky Point bears a descriptive name for a place on the shore of Pelican Bay of Upper Klamath Lake. It is an area that has been used for some years by summer residents. A post office called Pelican was established in this vicinity on July 5, 1888, with Charles Stidham first of five postmasters. This office ran along until Oct. 29, 1907, when it was closed to Ashland. The next office for the Pelican Bay area was named Recreation, established Oct. 15, 1913, with May D. Willson first postmaster. This office operated on and off until Feb. 11, 1924, when the name was changed to Pelican Bay. The name Pelican Bay was changed to Rocky Point on June 30, 1924, and this persisted until Oct. 1, 1947, when it was changed to Harriman. *See* Harriman. It may be noted that there was at one time a railroad station on the east side of Upper Klamath Lake opposite Pelican Bay with the name Pelican.

Rocky Ridge, UMATILLA. The old Indian Treaty boundary ran along this ridge just north of East Birch Creek. The ridge was a natural stock driveway for this part of the route from Pilot Rock to Starkey and Tom Gibson and others constructed a series of drift fences with the rails blocked by rock cribs. In many spots the continuous trample of hooves removed the soil to bedrock and the naming of the ridge logically followed both these circumstances.

Rocky Top, MARION. This conspicuous mountain is near Niagara. It was named in 1863 by Thomas J. Henness, a pioneer of the North Santiam Valley, because of its formation at the summit. *See* the Salem *Capital Journal*, June 18, 1927, p. 1.

Rodeo, HARNEY. This railroad station was named with the Spanish word for roundup. It was a cattle shipping point. The correct pronunciation is with accent on the "e." Rodeo was on the Union Pacific Railroad just southeast of Burns.

Rodgers Creek, MARION. Rodgers Creek rises in the hills south of Salem and flows eastward to join Battle Creek near Turner. The Pacific Highway East crosses this stream a little to the east of Jackson Hill. Rodgers Creek has been known as Taylor Creek, but on Apr. 12, 1940, the USBGN adopted the name Rodgers Creek. The name of the stream commemorates Clark and Sarah Adams Rodgers, pioneers of 1852, who were married in Marion County in 1856 and settled near the banks of the stream in 1857. In 1939 residents of the vicinity petitioned to have the name Rodgers Creek officially adopted, and this petition was approved by the county commissioners and by various state agencies.

Rodley Butte, DOUGLAS. Rodley Butte, elevation 6838 feet, is about two miles west of the north end of Diamond Lake and bears the name of Oscar Rodley, a fire guard of the USFS who was drowned while swimming in Diamond Lake on July 14, 1928. He was brought up near Lookingglass, was a graduate of Lookingglass High School and had worked for the USFS several seasons. The name Rodley Butte was adopted by the USBGN on Jan. 8, 1930, in place of Bald Butte on the theory that there were more than enough Bald buttes in Oregon to meet existing needs.

Rodman Rim, CROOK. William Rodman and his son Seth homesteaded near the east end of this rim north of Brothers in the 1880s.

Roger Creek, BAKER. Roger Creek empties into Anthony Creek just north of North Powder Valley. It is named for Benjamin F. Rogers who, in 1887, bought land near its mouth.

Roger Lake, WALLOWA. This small lake just east of Aneroid Lake bears the name of George Roger, long-time state game warden for Wallowa County. He worked for the Oregon State Game Commission from 1921 to 1931 and then was commissioned by the State Police when they took over enforcement of game laws. He continued as enforcement officer until his retirement in 1947. Roger was a friend of naturalist Stanley G. Jewett and accompanied him on numerous collecting trips. *See* Jewett Lake.

Rogers Creek, LANE. Rogers Creek flows into West Fork Indian Creek. Its name probably comes from Walton Rogers who, in 1900, filed a homestead claim along the creek. His claim was not patented.

Rogers Peak, TILLAMOOK. This 3700-foot peak south of Blue Lake Guard Station in T 2N, R 7W, is one of the two highest points in the Coast Range north of Marys Peak. It was named for Nelson S. Rogers, Oregon state forester from 1940 to 1949, who played a prominent part in the rehabilitation of the Tillamook Burn. Rogers Forest Camp on SH-6 was also named for him. For further information on Rogers, *see* the *Oregon Journal*, Sept. 19, 1949.

Rognes, WALLOWA. Rognes post office was short lived. It was established in Aug. 1909, with Louis O. Roggs postmaster and was discontinued in Nov. 1910. It was situated in the north part of S 10, T 2N, R 44E, about 18 miles airline north of Enterprise. The office was named for Rognes Sever, a Norwegian Lutheran minister, who lived in the locality.

Rogue River, CURRY, DOUGLAS, JACKSON, JOSEPHINE, KLAMATH. Rogue River rises in the extreme northwest corner of Klamath County at Boundary Springs near the northern boundary of Crater Lake National Park. On Dec. 20, 1904, Max Pracht wrote a letter to the *Oregonian* giving a well-known but incorrect version of the origin of the name Rogue River, ascribing it to the French word *Rouge* on account of the alleged red color of the water during flood seasons. This letter was printed in the *Oregonian* for Dec. 22, 1904, p. 11. Harvey W. Scott wrote a spirited reply to the Pracht letter, giving the real source of the name and printing it on the same page with the communication. The reply is as follows: "This is fanciful, purely so, though the 'Rouge' story is old. There would have been reason for calling the Klamath River Rouge River, or Red River; for its waters are much discolored by the marshes of the lake basin which it drains. But Rogue River is one of the clearest of streams, and even in flood its waters are not red. An old French map has been mentioned though no such map is known to be in existence whereon the Klamath and Rogue rivers are united and called Rouge-Clamet, or Red Klamath. But Rogue River, as an individual stream, has been known by its present name ever since white men first visited the country. Bishop Blanchet's account of the Catholic Church in Oregon says the French were first to call it by this name. The Indians there were a peculiarly troublesome lot; 'hence,' says Blanchet, 'the name "Les Coquins" (the Rogues) and "La Riviere aux Coquins" (The Rogue River) was given to the country by the men of the brigade.' So far then is it from the fact, that Rogue River is a corruption or change from the alleged 'Rouge' River of the French. The actual truth is that the French called it Rogue River themselves. Everything is against the assumption that it once was 'Rouge River' changed by Missourians to Rogue River, on the theory that 'them French couldn't spell'." In his journal for Monday, Sept. 16, 1833, John Work of the Hudson's Bay Company uses the name River Coquin, referring to what is now known as Rogue River, and the text indicates that the name Coquin was already in use by the fur brigades. In Sept. 1841, Henry Eld of the Wilkes Expedition used the names Rogue River and Rascally River in his journal. Wm. P. McArthur charted this stream as Rogue River for the USC&GS in 1850. Rogue River was called by the Indians *Trashit*, and by act of the territorial legislature, Jan. 12, 1854, Gold River. *See Session Laws*, p. 29; and the *Oregonian*, Nov. 15, 1883; letter by "Pioneer." The old name was restored in 1855. For history of the name, *see* the *Oregonian*, Nov. 15, 1883. For entertaining editorial about name Rogue River, larded with poetry, May 23, 1935.

Rogue River, JACKSON. Rogue River is the name of a town on Rogue River at the mouth of Evans Creek. It was for many years known as Woodville, but about 1912 the name was changed to Rogue River, presumably on account of the better advertising the community would get with that name. In the early 1850s the settlers near the mouth of Evans Creek and west to Evans Ferry were served through Gold River post office, which was at the ferry about three miles from the present site of Rogue River office. *See* Evans Creek. Woodville post office was established Feb. 8, 1876, with John Woods first postmaster. Presumably the place was named for Woods. The post office was changed to Rogue River on Mar. 11, 1912.

Rogue River, POLK. This stream flows into South Yamhill River. It was named because Rogue River Indians lived along its banks after they came from southern Oregon to Grand Ronde Agency.

Roland, COOS. Roland post office was established Feb. 12, 1880, with William N. Warner first and only postmaster. The office was closed Nov. 20, 1882, and what business there was turned over to Myrtle Point. The name of the office was intended to compliment William Rowland, a noted pioneer settler in the south end of the county, but there was a slip in the spelling. Information about William Rowland will be found under Rowland Prairie and Fort Rowland.

Rolling Grounds, DOUGLAS. These are about 15 miles west of Diamond Lake. They are so called because stock comes from some distance to roll in the light volcanic soil that abounds thereabout.

Rolyat, DESCHUTES. Rolyat is Taylor spelled backward. The post office was established in what was then Crook County on Sept. 15, 1910, and closed July 1, 1929. It is said that Taylor was the name of a postal official in Washington who had something to do with establishing the office. Victor Schreder was first postmaster and the office was near Hampton in T 22S, R 21E.

Roman Nose Mountain, DOUGLAS. This name is said to have been applied by government surveyors of the USGS, who determined its elevation, 2859 feet. The pioneer name was Saddle Mountain, which was considered unsatisfactory because of frequent duplication.

Rome, MALHEUR. This post office was established July 26, 1909. The first postmaster was Leonard R. Duncan. The writer is informed that the place was named by Wm. F. Stine because the peculiar geologic formations nearby suggested the ruined temples of Rome, Italy.

Rome, MARION. Rome post office was established June 30, 1851, with Christopher C. Cooley postmaster. It was discontinued Mar. 19, 1852. It is not shown on early maps available to the writer but the Cooley claim was a little east of the present site of Woodburn and it may be assumed that the office was in that locality. There seems to be no record of the reason for the name.

Rondeau Butte, DOUGLAS. This butte four miles north of Tiller was named for John Rondeau, an early USFS employee and member of a pioneer Douglas County family who homesteaded nearby.

Rondowa, WALLOWA. Rondowa is a made-up name. The station and eating house were at the junction of the Wallowa and Grande Ronde rivers. The name was given by John Anthony, a native of Switzerland, who operated the hotel and restaurant. He also applied the name "Switzerland of North America," a subtitle still borne by the Wallowa Mountains. Anthony was christened Johann Anton Koelbener and was not related to William Anthony of Anthony Lakes. For an interesting article on John Anthony, *see* La Grande *Observer*, Nov. 10, 1955.

Roney Creek, LANE. Roney Creek was named for Peter Runey, one-time owner of Foley Springs. It flows into Horse Creek.

Rooper Ranch, WASCO. Herbert C. Rooper was an early settler on Ward Creek southwest of Shaniko where his family is still well known. Rooper was born in England in 1852 and died at Antelope in 1935.

Roosevelt Beach, LANE. For some years this community was known as Heceta, in honor of the Spanish explorer who is mentioned under the heading Heceta Head. Heceta post office was near the lighthouse, but a few years ago the office was moved several miles north to a ranch near the mouth of Big Creek. The name was changed to Roosevelt Beach in 1922, at the suggestion of Mrs. Gladys Murrow of Portland. This was because the Roosevelt Coast Military Highway was projected through the ranch, and the name Heceta seemed no longer appropriate because the office had been moved from the cape. The name comes, of course, from Theodore Roosevelt. The place was not on the post office list in 1939. The 1900 post route map shows a post office named Samaria near the mouth of Big

Creek. Richard Helbock in *Oregon Post Offices, 1847–1982*, says the office was named for the ship *Samaria* which was wrecked nearby. It operated from 1897 to 1905 with Dollie Lanham first postmaster.

Rooster Rock, CLACKAMAS. This conspicuous peak, elevation 4663 feet, is in the south part of the county near Molalla River. It was named by Bob Ogle of Molalla, a prospector of the early 1860s, because of its resemblance to a rooster's comb. This information was furnished by Dee Wright of Eugene.

Rooster Rock, CROOK. USFS ranger J. O. F. Anderson, in his 1948 notes on file at the Ochoco National Forest, says this prominent rock in S 13, T 12S, R 18E, was named by an old-time sheepherder who claimed he could always hear a rooster crowing up on the rock. It is said "solitude makes strange company." Rooster Rock Spring is nearby.

Rooster Rock, MULTNOMAH. This is probably the rock mentioned by Lewis and Clark as their camping place on the night of Saturday, Nov. 2, 1805. Wilkes, in *U. S. Exploring Expedition*, v. 23, Hydrography, refers to it as the Obelisk, a name that has not persisted. The modern name is of phallic significance. A post office called Rooster Rock was established in May 1876, with John Gilstrap first postmaster. The name was changed to Latourell Falls in Aug. 1887. There is nothing in the records to show that the office was always in the same place. In 1938 the OSHD acquired the immediate area as part of the right-of-way for the water level highway, and after World War II developed the beach and adjoining low ground. Rooster Rock State Park is now one of the popular bathing and boating spots near Portland.

Roots Creek, LINCOLN. This stream flows into Siletz River from the east about a mile north of Mowrey Landing. It was named for a local settler. Roots post office was established in this locality on May 24, 1897, with Thomas A. Roots first postmaster. The office was closed on Oct. 15, 1906. The post office seems to have been moved from time to time if maps of that period are to be relied on.

Ropers Bunion, JACKSON. This eminence at Ashland bears an unusual name derived from a local resident. It is just south of the business center of the city and east of Lithia Park.

Rosa, LINN. Rosa post office was established Apr. 4, 1892, with Joseph D. Cosgrove first postmaster. The office was closed Oct. 17, 1895. The compiler has been informed by Rex Peery of Bay City that the office was named for his sister, Rosa Peery. The office was a few miles southwest of Scio, in an area previously served by Dotyville office.

Rosary Lakes, KLAMATH. These lakes are in the extreme northwest corner of the county and are very close to the summit of the Cascade Range. They are in a series, simulating to some extent a string of beads and are named on that account. The lakes are very popular among summer residents around Odell Lake. A stream heading at the lakes was formerly known as Maiden Creek because it headed near Maiden Peak, but about 1939 the USBGN changed the name to Rosary Creek to fit popular use.

Rose Lodge, LINCOLN. Rose Lodge post office was established Feb. 8, 1908, at the home of Julia E. Dodson, the first postmaster. Mrs. Dodson had a rose bower or "gazebo" over her front gate, and named the office on that account. The office was closed in Dec. 1964.

Roseburg, DOUGLAS. Roseburg was named for Aaron Rose who settled at the site of the community on Sept. 23, 1851. Rose was born June 20, 1813, and came to Oregon from Michigan in 1851. During many years his house at Roseburg was a public tavern. He was a well-known character in southern Oregon. He died Mar. 11, 1899. The locality, Roseburg, was first known as Deer Creek, being at the junction of Deer Creek and South Umpqua River. Roseburg's rival was the town of Winchester. In 1854 Roseburg won the county seat by popular vote, aided by settlers of Lookingglass Valley. Rose gave three acres of land and $1000 for the courthouse. The important buildings of Winchester were moved to Roseburg prior to 1860. For references to Roseburg, *see* Scott's *History of the Oregon Country*, v. 2, p. 299. Deer Creek post office was established Sept. 28, 1852, with William T. Perry postmaster. Lewis L. Bradbury became postmaster Mar. 31, 1854. The name of the office was changed to Roseburgh on July 16, 1857. It operated with that name until Mar. 1894, when the spelling was changed to Roseburg. During that time people of the community generally used the form Roseburg and not Roseburgh.

Rosedale, MARION. Rosedale, which is about six miles south of Salem, has borne its descriptive name for many years. It is at the point where the old highway from Salem to Albany crosses Battle Creek and its pleasing little dale. There are plenty of wild roses in the vicinity. Rosedale post office was established Apr. 20, 1892, by change of name from Dencer, with James M. Lawrence first postmaster. The Dencer office had been in operation since Feb. 12, 1889, at the home of Jacob Dencer about two miles northwest of Rosedale.

Rosland, DESCHUTES. The origin of the post office name Rosland is one of the mysteries of central Oregon nomenclature. This office was just a little north of the present location of La Pine, on the old stage road, west of The Dalles-California Highway. Rosland post office was established Apr. 13, 1897, with B. J. Pengra first of seven postmasters. It is probable that Pengra named the office, but so far the compiler has failed to discover the reason. The name of the office was changed to Lapine on Sept. 21, 1910.

Ross Flat, WHEELER. Howard Ross was an early settler near West Branch and his homestead was near this flat.

Ross Island, MULTNOMAH. This island was named for Sherry Ross, who owned and lived on it in pioneer days. *See* the *Oregonian*, Dec. 23, 1926, and *Oregon Journal*, editorial page, July 12, 1927. The name Ross Island is correctly applied to the northwestward of two islands that lie near each other. The southeast island is known as Hardtack Island by decision of the USBGN. There is a third small island, not more than a gravel bar, lying westward of the south end of Ross Island. These islands are shown as Oak Islands in the atlas accompanying Wilkes'

U. S. Exploring Expedition, v. 23, Hydrography. Early in 1943 Henry E. Reed of Portland sent the compiler additional information about the small gravel bar island. A special plat of this island, approved by Surveyor-General E. L. Applegate on Jan. 23, 1869, shows it as Toe Island, obviously because of its shape. Another survey was made in 1883 and the gravel bar was shown as Island No. 3. For additional information, *see* Hardtack Island. A good deal has been written about the famous Blue Ruin whiskey of pioneer days and some narratives say it was made on Ross Island. It was a fluid of high voltage. Some early settlers drank it neat, or barefoot, as the saying goes. Others reduced its ferocity by making it into long toddy. Blue Ruin was probably made from a mash of wheat, shorts or middlings and molasses. The topers played bean poker for Blue Ruin. Every now and again temperance enthusiasts swooped down on the stills and dumped the stuff in the river. It may be coincidence that the steelwork of the Ross Island Bridge is painted blue.

Ross Mountain, MULTNOMAH. Nelson Ross brought his family to Oregon from Michigan in the 1870s. About 1877 he moved to the Crown Point area and cleared a homestead on what is now known as Ross Mountain.

Ross Slough, COOS. This is a tributary of Catching Slough, southeast of Coos Bay. It was named for Frank Ross, a respected pioneer resident of Coos County.

Rouen Gulch, BAKER. Rouen Gulch drains northward from a spur of the Blue Mountains at a point about six miles west of Baker and whatever water it carries finds its way into Salmon Creek. According to Isaac Hiatt in *Thirty-one Years in Baker County*, p. 33, the creek was named in the summer of 1862 by a prospector who found paying gold in the gulch. Hiatt does not give this man's name, but says that he named the stream Ru Ann Creek for his eldest daughter. This is an unusual name for a girl, but of course not impossible. There is nothing to explain how the spelling got changed by later users, but Rouen has been the style for many years and is doubtless here to stay.

Rough and Ready Creek, JOSEPHINE. Rough and Ready Creek rises in the Siskiyou Mountains and flows eastward to join West Fork Illinois River. It flows under the Redwood Highway about two miles north of O'Brien. Rough and Ready Creek was named in the mining excitement of the fifties when Waldo was a boom area in the Illinois Valley. Rough and Ready was the affectionate nickname given to General, later President, Zachary Taylor. The stream was probably named by a veteran of the Mexican War who admired General Taylor, or perhaps for some miner named Taylor who appropriated the nickname. The former is more likely. General Taylor died in 1850 and the Josephine County goldrush began but a few years after that.

Round Butte Dam, JEFFERSON. This dam on Deschutes River west of Madras was completed in 1964 by Portland General Electric Company for hydroelectric power generation. It is an earth and rock fill structure 440 feet high which holds a reservoir of 535,000 acre-feet of water and can generate 300,000 kilowatts of electric energy. The dam is named for Round Butte, a prominent cone rising from the high ground directly to the east.

Round Prairie, DOUGLAS. Round Prairie is a well-known place on South Umpqua River between Roseburg and Myrtle Creek. It bears a descriptive name. Round Prairie post office was established Nov. 22, 1853, with James D. Burnett postmaster. This office has operated intermittently.

Rover Creek, TILLAMOOK. This creek empties into the Pacific Ocean about one mile south of Cape Lookout. It is on Camp Meriwether, Boy Scout property, and was named because the mounted troop of "Rover Scouts" had their campsite on its banks.

Row River, LANE. This stream rises on the western slopes of the Cascade Range and flows into the Coast Fork Willamette River at Cottage Grove. In the early days it was known as East Fork Coast Fork, but its present name came after a dispute between George Clark and Joseph Southwell over a stock trespass. The two men were brothers-in-law as well as neighbors but the disagreement ran so deep that Clark lost his life as a result. The present name, of course, rhymes with *cow* not *slow*.

Rowe Creek, WHEELER. In 1868 J. W. Rowe moved into what is now Wheeler County and engaged in the stock business on the banks of a stream flowing into John Day River. The stream is south of Fossil and its name commemorates this early settler.

Rowena, WASCO. Pierce Mays, for many years a resident of Wasco County, told the compiler that this place was named for H. S. Rowe in the early 1880s. Rowe was an official of the railroad company that was building along the south bank of the Columbia River. Mrs. Lulu D. Crandall of The Dalles confirmed this statement, but Miss A. M. Lang, also of The Dalles, thinks Rowena was the name of a girl who lived in the vicinity. Rowena is near the center of Rowena Gap where the Columbia River has cut four miles through the Columbia Hills anticlinal ridge. This geologic formation is easily discernible from the highway.

Rowena Dell, WASCO. This is a peculiar canyon in the basaltic rock on the Columbia River Highway between Rowena and Mosier. In early days it was known as Hog Canyon, but after the highway was built, a more elegant name was desired, and residents of The Dalles selected Rowena Dell.

Rowland, LINN. Rowland was a station on the Southern Pacific Company Springfield line five miles east-northeast of Harrisburg. It was named for a local resident. Rowland post office was established Dec. 29, 1886, with Jere T. Rowland postmaster. The office continued in operation with various postmasters until Feb. 15, 1905, when it was closed out to Harrisburg. Rural free delivery brought an end to the establishment.

Rowland Prairie, COOS. In 1853 William Rowland and his wife, who was a dusky maiden of the forest, settled in the valley of South Fork Coquille River on what has become known as Rowland Prairie. Rowland was a well-known pioneer, and a fragment of his history is found in Dodge's *Pioneer History of Coos and Curry Counties*, pp. 187–88. During the Indian troubles of 1855–56 the Rowland place was provided with some defense works and was called Fort Rowland. Rowland Creek, a tributary of South Fork Coquille River, is named for the same family.

Roxy Ann Peak, JACKSON. Will G. Steel was the authority for the statement that this well-known feature in the Rogue River Valley near Medford was at one time kmown as Skinner Butte. This was probably for A. A. Skinner, an early resident who was Indian Agent in 1851–53. He said that the present name was bestowed in 1854 in honor of Roxana Baker but this is not correct. Research by Jeff LaLande for the City of Medford indicates that the name is in compliment to Roxy Ann Bowen, wife of John Bowen. The Bowens settled near the base of the peak in the 1850s, long before the advent of Roxana Baker.

Roy, WASHINGTON. Railroad officials applied this name to a station about 1906, which became a post office in 1907. It came from the Roy family, pioneer settlers of the vicinity.

Roy Creek, TILLAMOOK. Roy Creek flows into Nehalem River a mile or so east of Mohler. It was named for Felix Roy, a local landowner.

Royal, LANE. The USGS map of the Cottage Grove quadrangle shows a place named Royal about five miles northwest of and up Silk Creek from Cottage Grove. There is not much left of this little community except the school. Royal post office was established Apr. 6, 1887, with Royal H. Hazleton postmaster. The office operated until Sept. 19, 1899, and it was doubtless named for the first post-master. Incidentally Silk Creek was at one time known as Hazleton Creek. Royal H. Hazleton received two patents for government land in this vicinity in 1867.

Royce Mountain, KLAMATH. This mountain is northeast of Crescent Lake. It was named for George Royce, an early-day stockman of the Deschutes Valley.

Royston, KLAMATH. Royston was a post office in the east part of the county about 18 miles northeast of Bonanza. The name Royston is still preserved at Royston Spring which is a little to the east of Yainax Butte on the old road from Bonanza to Bly. Royston post office was established Dec. 14, 1892, and operated continuously until Aug. 6, 1908, with Mrs. Lura E. White the only postmaster. Mr. and Mrs. Sanders White moved to a ranch in that part of Klamath County in the early nineties and soon felt the need of a post office. Erle R. White, a son, wrote the compiler from California in June 1948, saying that his mother wanted the name Agnes for the office but this name in the form Agness was already in use in Curry County. Mrs. White selected the name Agnes in compliment to a sister living in Illinois. The name Royston was then suggested and accepted. Mr. White is of the opinion that his mother selected the name because she found it in a book she was reading. There are at least two places in England named Royston and it is possible that one of them may have been the source of the name of the Klamath County post office.

Ruby, DOUGLAS. Ruby post office, which was in operation from June 1895 to Aug. 1901, was just east of Tahkenitch Lake in the extreme west part of the county. It was on the old Coast wagon road. The office was named at the request of Myrtle E. Wilson, daughter of Joseph E. Wilson, the first postmaster. This young lady liked the name Ruby because it had a pretty sound. Mrs. Mary Slonecker was postmaster at Ruby from 1898 to 1901. Ruby was ten or twelve miles north of Gardiner, and when Mr. Wilson had the office it was on Perkins Creek. When Mrs. Slonecker was postmaster the office was on Fivemile Creek.

Ruch, JACKSON. Ruch was named for C. M. Ruch who bought a small tract of land in 1896 where the community is now situated and built a blacksmith shop, a store and a house. In 1897 he was appointed postmaster and was given the privilege of naming the post office, which he did, for himself.

Ruckel Creek, HOOD RIVER. This was formerly Deadman Creek, a melancholy designation. At the request of the OGNB, federal authorities adopted the name Ruckel in honor of J. S. Ruckel, who built the portage tramway on the south side of the Columbia River at the Cascades, completing the project in May 1861. He was an original incorporator of the Oregon Steam Navigation Company. Ruckel signed his name as here written and not Ruckle nor Ruckles. *See also* Thomas Creek, Umatilla County.

Ruckles, DOUGLAS. This place was named for M. C. Ruckles, who owned land where the Southern Pacific Company now has its station. The community was formerly known as Oak Grove, but when the post office was established this name could not be used on account of duplication so Ruckles was selected. The railroad station is Dole. It is understood that the railroad objected to the use of the word Ruckles because it sounded so much like Riddles and this presented the possibility of confusion in train orders. Riddles was the former name of the station now known as Riddle. Ruckles post office was established on Feb. 10, 1898 and operated until Jan. 15, 1934.

Ruckles Creek, BAKER. Ruckles Creek rises near the Virtue Mine northeast of Baker and flows northeast to Powder River at Keating. It takes its name from Colonel J. S. Ruckel who, after he sold his interest in the Oregon Portage Railway at Cascade Locks, moved to Baker County and operated a mine and stamp mill. Ruckel shares with Binger Hermann the distinction of bestowing two spellings of the same name on two different features.

Ruddock, UMATILLA. Ruddock post office was established July 25, 1888, with Isaac Ruddock postmaster. The office was closed Oct. 12, 1895, and the business turned over to Gibbon. The office was at or near the railroad station North Fork, at the junction of that stream and Meacham Creek. The writer has been told that Ruddock, which was obviously named for the postmaster, was a post office established to serve people engaged in wood cutting operations in the Blue Mountains.

Rudio Mountain, GRANT. Rudio Mountain is in the west part of the county and Rudio Meadow and Rudio Creek are in the same general locality. Rudio

Creek flows into North Fork John Day River. About 1930 J. E. Snow of Dayville wrote the compiler that these features were named for one Rudio, a cattleman, who settled near the mouth of the creek in the early 1870s. His first name was probably Peter.

Rufus, SHERMAN. Rufus was named for Rufus C. Wallis, the original settler in the community. Wallis later moved across the Columbia River and settled in Klickitat County, Washington. He received a U.S. patent for the Klickitat County land on Dec. 13, 1876, for 163.75 acres.

Rugg Canyon, UMATILLA. Alfred H. Rugg was born in Franklin County, Massachusetts in 1831. He moved gradually west coming to Oregon in 1882 and Umatilla County in 1885. Two of his sons, Alby and Emery took up property near Nye in the 1890s and members of the family are still active in the area.

Ruggs, MORROW. This community on Rhea Creek was named for Ed Rugg who ranched nearby after World War I and at one time operated the local store and service station. It has now fallen victim to the urban migration.

Rujada, LANE. Rujada was a lumber camp at the eastern terminus of the Oregon & Southeastern Railroad, east of Cottage Grove. It is said the name was taken from a telegraph code book, and means "a considerable body of standing timber is available." Another theory is that it was made up from the first letters of Reserve and United States followed by those of several involved individuals. Rujada does not appear on recent maps, but the name is preserved in Rujada Point Lookout on Rose Hill nearby.

Rural, COOS. The community called Rural was named for its surroundings, which were well described by the name. The place is in the south part of the county on South Fork Coquille River near the mouth of Salmon Creek. Rural post office was established Aug. 21, 1890, with James D. Hayes first postmaster of a series of ten. The post office was discontinued Sept. 30, 1915.

Rush Creek, WALLOWA. This stream is near Paradise. It received its name because of bulrushes growing on its banks.

Russ Creek, CLACKAMAS. This creek is a tributary of Collawash River. It was named for Hiram R. Wilcox of Estacada, formerly of the USFS, and universally known as Russ.

Russell Creek, CLACKAMAS, MARION. This stream which flows into Molalla River, was named for Henry Russell of Molalla who, with several friends, prospected in this part of the state for a number of years.

Russell Lake, MARION. North of Mount Jefferson, wedged in between living glaciers on the south and a rough precipitous mountain wall 1000 feet high on the north, lies Jefferson Park, a natural playground, invitingly level, directly athwart the Cascade Range. There is snow in this park even as late as the first of September, but generally during August the park is a mass of flowers. There are several lakes in the park, and the largest is but a few hundred feet in diameter, but looking down into it from the north, one gets a fine reflection of Mount Jefferson. This lake was named in honor of Dr. Israel C. Russell, one of the early geologists of the USGS, who was an investigator in Oregon beginning in the early 1880s. His principal contribution to the knowledge of Oregon geology is USGS Bulletin 252, *Geology and Water Resources of Central Oregon*. Russell Lake forms South Fork Breitenbush River until late in the season, when evaporation reduces its level to a point below the outlet. Its elevation is about 5900 feet.

Russellville, MULTNOMAH. Russellville is an area on SE Stark Street about a mile east of Montavilla. The best information available to the writer is to the effect that the locality was named in compliment to Russellville, Illinois. In July 1947, Mrs. H. A. Lewis, a resident of the Russellville community, wrote the compiler that in 1888 Leander Lewis circulated a petition for a post office, and it was planned to use the name Lewisville. Officials at Washington would not approve this name because it duplicated the name Lewisville in Polk County. Mr. Lewis then suggested Russellville in compliment to a place in Illinois where he had relatives. The Multnomah County office was established Feb. 11, 1889, with George W. Stafford first of a long list of postmasters. Russellville post office was closed as of July 15, 1904, probably as the result of rural delivery. According to Mrs. Lewis the Russellville post office was for most of its life in a store on the north side of SE Stark Street near the present SE Ninety-seventh Avenue.

Rustler Peak, JACKSON. This peak in the Cascade Range is said to owe its name to an incident connected with stock rustlers in early days.

Ruthton Point, HOOD RIVER. Ruthton Point is on the Columbia River just west of Hood River. Joseph W. Morton bought a farm including this point in 1886 and applied the elided name of his daughter, Ruth Morton. This information was uncovered by Ruth M. Guppy of Hood River.

Rutledge, SHERMAN. Rutledge post office was established June 6, 1884, with Joseph H. Rutledge first postmaster. This office continued in service until Mar. 23, 1908. It served a territory a few miles east-southeast of Grass Valley. For information about the Rutledge family, *see Illustrated History of Central Oregon*, p. 520. "Uncle Joe" Rutledge and his family came to central Oregon from California in the fall of 1882 and took up land south of Moro. However, actual residence on the land did not begin until the spring of 1883.

R. W. Spring, MALHEUR. This spring three miles west of Harper owes its name to a change in government policy. When the Bureau of Land Management became responsible for the administration of federal lands outside the national forests, all lands with water resources formerly administered by the Bureau of Reclamation were among those turned over to the BLM. This typical perennial spring was properly coded R.W. for "reclamation withdrawal."

Ryan Ranch Meadow, DESCHUTES. This meadow along Deschutes River near Benham Falls was named for John Ryan, an early-day lumberman.

Rye Valley, BAKER. When the immigrants and miners came to Oregon, natural forage was more suitable than gasoline to the motive power then available. A good many geographic features in the state have been named for the native grains and grasses that have grown so abundantly in favorable places. Rye Valley is a name that had its start in the mining boom in northeastern Oregon in the 1860s. This valley is in the Dixie Creek drainage about 30 miles southeast of Baker. Rye Valley post office was established Sept. 27, 1869, with Nayson S. Whitcomb first postmaster. This office operated on and off for many years, but was not in service in 1945. A prominent mesa in eastern Crook County just southeast of Paulina bears the descriptive name Ryegrass Table. The writer does not know just what types of ryegrass grow in the locations mentioned. William Andrews, a retired range management consultant, advised the compiler in 1990, that the most likely species was *Elymus cinereus*. Peck, in his *Manual of Higher Plants of Oregon*, lists no fewer than 13 varieties of ryegrass native to Oregon, but a number of them do not grow east of the Cascade Range. The various species of the genus *Elymus* should not be confused with the species of the genus *Lolium*, the valuable commercial seed crop of the Willamette Valley. While contemplating the fascinating subject of rye it should be noted that there is a locality in Sherman County known as Bourbon. Geographic nomenclature plays no favorites.

Sacajawea Peak, WALLOWA. This mountain is one of the highest points in the Wallowa Mountains south of Enterprise. It bears the name of the famous Shoshone Indian woman who was with the Lewis and Clark party. It was once called Legion Mountain in compliment to the American Legion. There has been ample controversy about Sacajawea, about the value of her services, the place of her death and even about the spelling of her name, a matter which doubtless bothered her but little. Grace Raymond Hebard's *Sacajawea* gives a general account of her story. An editorial by Albert Hawkins in the *Oregonian*, Oct. 13, 1929, ably discusses some of her problems. *See also* C. S. Kingston's article in *Pacific Northwest Quarterly*, Jan. 1944.

Saddle Bag Mountain, LINCOLN. In 1980, William Erdmann of the State Forestry Department wrote to give the origin of the name of this high ground south of Salmon River between Otis and Grand Ronde. About 1900 the mail was delivered out of the Butler store in Grand Ronde. The mail route ran along Salmon River near the base of the mountain but as local residents were widely scattered, the letters were left in an old saddle bag which hung on a prominent snag. Mail service improved over the years and the saddle bag is long gone. However, after World War II the name mysteriously changed to Saddleback Mountain. Mr. Erdmann brought the matter to the attention of the OGNB in 1980 and the USBGN corrected the matter in *Decision List 8104*.

Saddle Creek, WALLOWA. Saddle Creek is so named because it heads near Freezeout Saddle, on the divide between the waters of Snake River and Imnaha River.

Saddle Mountain, CLATSOP. Gustavus Hines, in *Oregon and Its Institutions*, says the Indian name of this prominent landmark was *Swallalah-oost*. There was an

Indian tradition that one of the great chiefs, after being killed by enemies, assumed the form of an eagle and became the creator of thunder and lightning at the top of this peak. Hines further says that the name Saddle Mountain was applied by Wilkes in 1841. The name is unusually descriptive. Saddle Mountain is one of the highest peaks in the north part of the Coast Range in Oregon and has an elevation, according to the USGS, of 3283 feet. Lewis and Clark mention the mountain but give it no name.

Saddlebutte, HARNEY. Saddlebutte post office was established Sept. 26, 1916, with T. C. Albritton first postmaster, to serve the area near the physical feature Saddle Butte not far from the northeast shore of Malheur Lake. Saddle Butte is a prominent point a few miles west-southwest of Crane. Saddlebutte post office was closed May 15, 1920, and the business turned over to Crane. The butte was named for its shape.

Sage Hen Creek, HARNEY. The sagehen or sage grouse, *Centrocerus urophasianus*, was formerly plentiful throughout the West, and its name has been applied to a number of geographic features, but as far as the compiler knows, the only place the name has been used in Oregon is in Grant, Harney and Lake counties. We have a good description of the sagehen as it is found near the Oregon creek that bears its name in U.S. National Museum Special Bulletin No. 1, *Life Histories of North American Birds*, by Captain Charles Bendire, p. 106. This bird is, next to the wild turkey, the largest game bird found in the United States. During the winter the sagehen feeds largely on the leaves of the sagebrush, but that is not its exclusive diet, and some authorities assert that sage leaves are only eaten when other food is not available. Captain Bendire spent several years studying the birds of Oregon, particularly in the Harney Valley. The USBGN adopted the two-word form for this stream in *Decision List 6202* although several other features use one word.

Sageview, HARNEY. Sageview post office served an area in the sage plains west of Catlow from Feb. 1916, until Nov. 1918. It would be difficult to suggest a better name for an office in such surroundings.

Saginaw, LANE. R. A. Booth, vice president of the Booth-Kelly Lumber Co., informed the compiler that this place was named by J. I. Jones for Saginaw, Michigan. The community was established about a year before the lumber company began to operate there. Gannett says that *Saginaw* is an Ojibwa Indian word meaning Sauk place, referring to the Sauk or Sac Indians. Saginaw post office, with Laura Weaver first postmaster, operated from Mar. 1898 to July 1957.

Sahale Falls, HOOD RIVER. These falls of East Fork Hood River are on the original Mount Hood Loop Highway just east of Bennett Pass. They bear the Chinook jargon word for high. The name was bestowed on the falls by George Holman of Portland, as a result of a prize competition conducted by the Portland *Telegram*, in which it was judged that Mr. Holman had suggested the best name. The word *sahale* is composed of three syllables with the accent on the first.

Sahalie Falls, LINN. This 140-foot waterfall on McKenzie River is between Carmen Reservoir and Clear Lake. At one time they were called Upper Falls but the present name came into general use about 1950 with the development of the Clear Lake recreation area. The USBGN confirmed this in *Decision List 6202*. *Sahalie* is a variant spelling of the Chinook jargon word for high.

Sain Creek, WASHINGTON. This creek rises in s 33, T 1N, R 5W, and flows generally southeast into Scoggins Creek. It was named for Thomas W. Sain who settled there in 1875 and owned much of the land along the creek. The forms Sein and Seine are both incorrect and the USBGN adopted the present spelling in *Decision List 6402*.

Saint Benedict, MARION. In 1881 a Benedictine monk, the Rev. Adelhelm Odermatt, came to Oregon and soon established a Benedictine community, which is now known as St. Benedicts Abbey. This community was first started at Gervais, but in 1884 it was moved to the town of Mt. Angel. Since it was less than a mile from the Mount Angel post office, the authorities would not establish a new post office for the abbey. In 1903 a new abbey was completed on the butte southeast of Mt. Angel town and in 1914 the post office of Saint Benedict was established at the abbey. The first postmaster was Wendel Neiderprum. Father Odermatt came from Engelberg, Switzerland. He translated this name into Mount Angel, thus naming the town and the butte although the town was incorporated with the form Mt. Angel. Saint Benedict was named for the founder of the Benedictine Order, who was born in Nursia, Italy, in the year 480, and died at Monte Cassino, Italy, in 543. For additional information, *see* Mount Angel. The butte on which St. Benedicts Abbey is built has an elevation of 485 feet.

Saint Helens, COLUMBIA. The community of Saint Helens was founded by Captain H. M. Knighton, a pioneer of 1845. Available records seem to indicate that Knighton, who was a mariner, was born in New England, which may have been the reason he first applied the name Plymouth to the new townsite. There is a tradition that this name was suggested by a prominent rock which Knighton found on the river bank. It made a natural wharf. The name Plymouth appears in an advertisement in the *Oregon Spectator*, July 22, 1847. The Rev. George H. Atkinson mentions the little Plymouth community on June 18, 1848, and says there were but two people there. See *OHQ*, v. 40, p. 180. Theodore Talbot calls the place New Plymouth in his *Journals*, p. 88, on May 13, 1849, and mentions two houses. On Aug. 25, 1849, Knighton signed a deed in which he refers to "Plymouth and now called Kasenau." This new name was in compliment to Chief Cassino, a prominent Indian who lived nearby. This name is spelled in many ways. For Omar C. Spencer's article about Chief Cassino, *see OHQ*, v. 34, p. 19. It is hard to determine the exact status of the name Kasenau mentioned by Knighton, because within a year he was using the name Plymouth for the post office. *See* below. Also on May 6, 1850, Knighton refers to "Casenau now called St.

Helens" at the very time he was using the name Plymouth for his post office. In any event, the name of the place was changed to Saint Helens in the latter part of 1850, apparently because of the proximity of Mount Saint Helens, Washington. Saint Helens is advertised in the *Oregon Spectator*, Nov. 28, 1850, as a terminus of a proposed railroad from Lafayette because of its deep water for ships. Vancouver named the mountain in honor of Baron Saint Helens (Alleyne Fitzherbert, 1753–1839), British ambassador to Spain in 1790–94, who negotiated the Nootka treaty in Madrid. For information about Baron Saint Helens, *see* article by Professor Edmond S. Meany, *Washington Historical Quarterly*, v. 15, p. 124. Saint Helens post office was established with the name Plymouth, Apr. 9, 1850, with Henry M. Knighton postmaster. The name was changed to Saint Helen Nov. 4, 1850, with William H. Tappan postmaster. Saint Helen was an error in spelling at Washington, D.C. The name was later changed to Saint Helens. Tappan, a native of Massachusetts, came to Oregon in 1849 with the Mounted Rifles. He may have had a hand in naming Saint Helens, as he became interested in the townsite, but he was not in Oregon when Plymouth was named.

Saint Johns, MULTNOMAH. James John crossed the plains to California in 1841, with General John Bidwell, and came to Oregon in 1843. He settled first at Linnton, and several years later moved to the area that bears his name. He operated a ferry there in 1852. He died May 28, 1886. For history of the town and of James John, *see* the *Oregonian*, Aug. 29, 1907, p. 11; Mar. 29, 1903, p. 40; May 29, 1886, p. 5. The plat for Saint Johns was filed on July 20, 1865. Efforts to change the name to Saint John have been unavailing, and the style Saint Johns has been approved by USBGN. The town was annexed to Portland in 1915.

Saint Joseph, YAMHILL. This place was named by Ben Holladay, probably for Saint Joseph, Missouri, but Mrs. Harriet McArthur informed the compiler in 1926 that she was once told that Holladay selected the name on account of his brother, Joseph Holladay. Holladay founded Saint Joseph as the terminus of his west-side Oregon Central Railroad, apparently to encourage competition between McMinnville and Lafayette. The McMinnville *West Side*, May 17, 1872 gives more information.

Saint Louis, MARION. Saint Louis is a very old settlement in the Willamette Valley about three miles northwest of Gervais. In 1844 a Jesuit missionary, the Reverend Aloysius Verecuysee, visited the early settlers and in 1845 he built a log church at Saint Louis. In Nov. 1847, the parish was first organized with a resident priest, the Reverend B. Delorme. The parish was named for Saint Louis, King of France, and not for the metropolis of Missouri. The compiler has been to Saint Louis, Oregon, many times and has always been impressed by the quiet simplicity of the place. Saint Louis post office was established Oct. 26, 1860, with S. C. Matthieu first postmaster. With a couple of intermissions this office remained in service until the summer of 1901 when it was closed to Gervais. The remains of

Madame Marie Dorion, famous member of the Astor overland party, are buried at Saint Louis Church.

Saint Marys, WASHINGTON. Saint Marys, once a separate community but now part of Beaverton, is close to the Tualatin Valley Highway and sw 148th Avenue or Murray Road. The locality is well known because of the girls school, Saint Marys of the Valley, and a little to the west of the girls school is Saint Marys Home for Boys. These institutions are in charge of the Sisters of Saint Mary, an order founded in 1886 at Sublimity. In 1891 the Sisters assumed charge of the Saint Marys Home near Beaverton. That institution is no longer in its original location but has been moved westward toward Huber. On May 31, 1902, Saint Marys post office was established on the Washington County list with Dominic Faber first postmaster. However, this office was never completely organized and the appointment was rescinded in June 1903.

Saint Paul, MARION. Saint Paul was named by Archbishop Francis Norbert Blanchet, who came to Oregon in 1838, and established Saint Paul Mission in 1839 at the Catholic church on French Prairie. The mission was named for the Apostle Paul. The writer has been told that the first postmaster was John F. Theo. Brentano. The post office was established June 24, 1874.

Saint Peters Dome, MULTNOMAH. This basalt monolith in the Columbia Gorge near Dodson was a conspicuous challenge to the mountain-climbing fraternity for many years. In 1940 it was first climbed by Joe Leuthold and five others including a woman, Ida Darr. For details, *see* the *Mazama*, 1940. In early days this was called Cathedral Rock and the name Saint Peters Dome described the higher summit to the south now called Yeon Mountain. The name is most descriptive but the compiler has not been able to learn when it was first applied to the present peak.

Salado, LINCOLN. The post office Salado was established in Apr. 1891. The compiler has been told that George Hodges named the place for Salado, Texas, where he had formerly lived. *Salado* is a Spanish word meaning salty or saline, or a plain encrusted with salt.

Salem, MARION. The Indian name for the locality of Salem was *Chemeketa*, which is said to have meant meeting place or resting place or possibly both. Chemeketa also may have been the name of one of the bands of the Calapooya Indians. In 1840–41 the Jason Lee Mission was moved from its old location near the Willamette River upstream about ten miles to the Chemeketa plain and extensive improvements were started. While the new establishment was called Chemeketa, it was probably better known as the Mill, on account of the installation on Mill Creek. In 1842 the missionaries established the Oregon Institute and a building was started. From that time the place was often spoken of as the Institute. There is argument as to who selected the name Salem. Bancroft, in *History of Oregon*, v. 1, p. 222, says that after the mission was dissolved in 1844, it was decided to lay out a townsite on the Institute lands. This was done and David Leslie, president of the trustees, named the place Salem. Leslie came to Oregon from

Salem, Massachusetts. Leslie M. Scott, in *History of the Oregon Country*, v. 2, p. 298, says the place was named by W. H. Willson. The late R. J. Hendricks of Salem, a diligent student of the community, was strongly of the opinion that Leslie named the place. *See* articles in the Salem *Statesman*, Mar. 8, 1931, and Mar. 28, 1940. Salem post office was established Nov. 8, 1849, with J. B. McClane postmaster. Three plats forming what is now the main part of Salem were filed in 1850–51. Salem is the anglicized form of the Hebrew word *shalom*, meaning peace. In Dec. 1853 efforts were made in the territorial legislature to change the name from Salem to Thurston or Valena. Chester N. Terry petitioned to have the name changed to Corvallis, but after spirited debate the name Corvallis was given to the Benton County community then known as Marysville. The names Chemawa, Willamette and Bronson were also suggested. Pike and Victoria were mentioned, but by this time the members concluded that they had wasted enough time over the matter and the various bills were postponed. The final vote was in Jan. 1854. The name Valena is said to have been suggested because it was the name of Velina Pauline Nesmith, later Mrs. Wm. Markland Molson, but she was not born until 1855. In 1907 a station on the Oregon Electric Railway north of Salem was named Chemeketa to perpetuate that name, but it was later changed to Hopmere because of local sentiment. The location of the Oregon capital caused a spirited contest that lasted for nearly 15 years. The first legislative assembly of the provisional government met at Oregon City (Willamette Falls) in 1844. By an act of 1851 the capital was moved to Salem, and in 1855 it was moved to Corvallis, only to be moved back to Salem in the same year. Destruction of the capitol at Salem, Dec. 29, 1855, was considered as an incendiary part of this controversy. For history of this squabble, *see* article by Walter C. Winslow, *OHQ*, v. 9, p. 173. For many references to the history of Salem and the capital controversy, *see* Scott's *History of the Oregon Country*, v. 2, pp. 298 and 312.

Salem Hills, MARION. These hills form the high ground south of Salem bordered generally on the east by the Southern Pacific Company main line, on the south by Santiam River and on the west by Willamette River. They have been variously known as the Salem Hills, Red Hills and Illahee Hills. In 1963 the OGNB voted to recommend the name Chemeketa Hills, an Indian name of historic significance now applied only to a Salem street and Chemeketa Community College. This action provoked a spirited dissent from a large group who claimed that the area had been known as the Salem Hills for many years. In Dec. 1964 the matter was given a full hearing and the proponents of Salem Hills led by ex-Governor Charles A. Sprague and state geologist Hollis Dole carried the field as the board rescinded their action of 1963 and voted to approve the present form. In this case, as in many others, long usage prevailed over an excellent historic name.

Salene Lake, COLUMBIA. This lake is near the west bank of Multnomah Channel north of Scappoose. It was named for the Salene family, pioneer residents of the neighborhood.

Saleratus Creek, LANE. Saleratus Creek is in the west part of the county. It drains south into Wolf Creek, a well-known tributary to Siuslaw River southwest of Austa. The compiler has been told that the stream was named to commemorate the baking of a batch of biscuits by some accomplished surveyor. Saleratus is the common name originally for bicarbonate of potash but now also used for bicarbonate of soda, both when used as an ingredient in baking powder. In bygone days *saleratus* was used frequently and interchangeably with *baking powder* when describing biscuits.

Salineville, MORROW. Salineville was 13 miles northwest of Heppner and was undoubtedly named for the alkaline soil in the valley of Willow Creek. If early maps are to be relied on, the place was a little to the northwest of the community now known as Lexington. Salineville post office was established Jan. 9, 1884, with Mrs. Mary L. Benefiel postmaster. The office was discontinued Apr. 2, 1886, and the records were turned over to Heppner. Lexington post office was established in Nov. 1885, and doubtless supplied the post office needs of the area.

Saling Creek, TILLAMOOK. Saling Creek was named for William Saling who homesteaded along it in 1892. It flows into Nestucca River about a mile below Beaver.

Salisbury, BAKER. Salisbury was a place on the Sumpter Valley Highway near Powder River about ten miles southwest of Baker. The locality was once known as Bennett, probably for a local resident. A post office called Salisbury was established Mar. 23, 1906, with Charles R. Foster postmaster. This office was closed May 31, 1907, but the locality still retains the name Salisbury, which came from Hiram H. Salisbury, superintendent of logging operations for the W. H. Eccles Lumber Company. In 1980 there was little evidence of commercial activity.

Salisbury, UMATILLA. Salisbury post office was established Aug. 18, 1894, with Francis M. Salisbury postmaster. The office was closed Jan. 24, 1896. It was named for the postmaster. A railroad map dated July 1903 shows Salisbury on McKay Creek near the western boundary of the Umatilla Indian Reservation. It was about midway between Pendleton and Pilot Rock.

Salishan, LINCOLN. In 1964 John Gray of Portland began the development of a planned community and resort motel at the south end of Siletz Bay. The careful planning of architect John Storrs and landscape architect Barbara Fealy integrated the public facilities east of US-101 into the rolling terrain and typical coast vegetation. The name was taken from the *Salish* Indian, the linguistic group that included the Tillamook and Siletz languages. Salishan is an excellent example of a well-chosen name for a commercial development.

Sallal Springs, CURRY. These springs are about five miles east of Humbug Mountain. *Sallal* is an Indian name for the fruit of the *Gaultheria shallon,* called by white people the sallal bush or sallal berry. This shrub grows in dense thickets in the Coast Range, and in other parts of the state as well. The berry is a purplish black, and not particularly palatable. The name has been used in a number of places in Oregon and Washington to describe geographic features. Sallal is spelled in several ways but the style here given is that used by government map makers.

Sallee Creek, LANE. This creek flows into Row River from the east a mile north of Dorena. In 1986, the OGNB voted to name this stream Sallee Creek for John T. and Mary Sallee who patented the first timber claim along it and lived nearby with their family for many years. John Sallee was at one time postmaster at Star when that office was a few hundred yards downstream from the mouth. The creek was formerly known as Cedar Creek but as there are more than 50 Cedar creeks in Oregon including four tributaries of Row Rover, the change will do little to diminish the importance of the western red cedar or *Thuja plicata*.

Salmon, CLACKAMAS. Salmon post office was established to serve the area at the mouth of Salmon River, where that stream flows into Sandy River on the Mount Hood Loop Highway. The office was named for the river, but the naming of Salmon River is a matter probably lost to history. Salmon post office was established Apr. 2, 1891, with Winnie McIntyre first postmaster. The office was discontinued May 6, 1910. Salmon post office was moved and the name changed to Brightwood when it was discontinued. The two places are very close together.

Salmon Harbor, DOUGLAS. Salmon Harbor is the name of the Douglas County Park system boat basin development at the community of Winchester Bay. Prior to the 1950s a hydrographic feature, Winchester Bay, existed in the estuary of Umpqua River and it was here that Heman Winchester established his settlement in 1850. The embayment was a popular docking site for small fishing and pleasure craft but it was also subject to damage by winter storms. In 1951 a comprehensive plan was developed and given the name Salmon Harbor. This plan was implemented over the years by dredging and landfill. By 1987 there were two large docking areas, East Basin and West Basin, and Winchester Point, a substantial breakwater on the west. Natural and man-made actions have eliminated the bay but the community flourishes with the original name. *See* Winchester Bay and Winchester.

Salmon River, LINCOLN, POLK, TILLAMOOK. Considering the importance of the salmon in the history of Oregon, it is not surprising that a number of geographic features should be named for the fish. Salmon River mentioned in the heading rises in the Coast Range and flows into Pacific Ocean just south of Cascade Head. The Salmon River Highway, SH-18, follows the stream for many miles. George Davidson, in *Coast Pilot*, 1889, says the Indian name for this Salmon River was *Nechesne*. Another well-known Salmon River rises on the south slope of Mount Hood and flows into Sandy River. It is in Clackamas County. There are streams named for the salmon in other counties. A good deal has been written about the various varieties of salmon frequenting Pacific Coast waters. The opinions of some of the experts are highly controversial, and the compiler does not feel that he has the energy to join the battle. He knows but four sorts of salmon—

fresh, salt, tinned and kippered, and if the reader requires further information, he will have to look elsewhere.

Salmonberry, TILLAMOOK. There are several geographic features in Oregon named Salmonberry, the most important being Salmonberry River, in Tillamook and Washington counties, and the railroad station near its mouth. They are named for the *Rubus spectabilis*. The form Salmon Berry is wrong when used as a geographic name. Preston's *Map of Oregon*, 1856, gives Salmonberry Creek for the stream mentioned above. Salmonberry post office was established Mar. 15, 1923, with Ernest B. Graham postmaster, and closed Feb. 28, 1924.

Salt Butte, CROOK. *A History of the Ochoco National Forest*, says that this butte north of McKay Creek was named for nearby Salt Spring. The spring was not named because the water was brackish but by a party of hunters camped there who found they had forgotten this essential commodity.

Salt Caves, KLAMATH. Salt Caves were much in the news in the late 1980s when the City of Klamath Falls proposed a scheme to divert the Klamath River for a hydroelectric plant. The city planned to sell the electric power and use the money for economic development. The proposal met intense opposition from the fishing and rafting communties and the issue was still unresolved in the fall of 1990. Francis Landrum of Klamath Falls informed the compiler that the name came from salt deposits on the banks of the river just north of the California border.

Salt Creek, LANE. This large tributary of Middle Fork Willamette River has been called Salt Creek since pioneer days because of the salt springs along the stream used as licks by deer.

Salt Creek, POLK, YAMHILL. Salt Creek rises in the foothills north of Dallas and flows northeast into South Yamhill River. John Ford of Dallas told the compiler that it was named in pioneer days because of the salt licks found on its banks. The advance of civilization has apparently obliterated the licks. Preston's *Map of Oregon*, 1856, shows Salt Creek post office six miles northwest of Dallas. This office was established July 6, 1852, with James B. Riggs first postmaster.

Salt Creek Falls, LANE. These falls are among the finest in the state. They are estimated to be 300 feet high, and were discovered by Frank S. Warner and Charles Tufti in Mar. 1887. *See* the *Oregonian*, July 3, 1927, sect. 4, p. 5. The rock at the top of the falls is so shaped as to make the water form a letter "s" as it plunges over. Warner was a member of a pioneer family of the valley of the Middle Fork Willamette River, and Tufti was his Indian friend. Tufti Mountain was named for the Indian.

Sam Creek, LANE. Sam Creek is named for Samuel Woolsey who filed on government land near the site of Pawn where this creek forms the head of North Fork Siuslaw River. Woolsey filed in early 1915. Pawn post office was established in December of the same year. *See* Pawn.

Sam Creek, LINCOLN. Sam Creek is tributary to Siletz River from the south about three miles east of Siletz. In 1856 the Siletz Indian Reservation was established in this area and about 600 Indians from southern and southeastern Oregon were moved to the new reservation. *See OHQ*, v. 30, p. 348. Sam Creek was undoubtedly named for Chief Sam of the Rogue River Indians. *See* Sams Valley. Nearby Klamath Creek was named for the same reason.

Sam Davis Spring, WHEELER. This spring in the southwest corner of T 13S, R 24E, was named for Sam Davis who ranged sheep nearby from his ranch on John Day River.

Sampson, DOUGLAS. Sampson post office was named for Rear-Admiral William Thomas Sampson, famous American naval officer who made a remarkable record in the war with Spain. Sampson post office was established Aug. 27, 1898, and was in service until Sept. 15, 1912. George B. Balderree was the first postmaster. Admiral Sampson was at the height of his fame in the summer of 1898. Sampson post office was six or seven miles south of Gardiner. The town of Reedsport had not yet been founded.

Sampson Mountain, JEFFERSON. Sampson Mountain forms the south end of Blizzard Ridge south of Ashwood. It was named for Frank F. Sampson who homesteaded there in 1886.

Sams Valley, JACKSON. Chief Sam of the Rogue River Indians formerly lived in this valley and it was named for him. There is also a small community with the same name and Sams Creek flows through the valley. The Rogue River Indians were relocated to the Grand Ronde Indian Reservation and a number of geographic names such as Sams Creek and Rogue River were duplicated in Polk County. *See* Rogue River, Polk County.

San Antonio Creek, LANE. This stream is tributary to Siuslaw River near Beecher. The form San Antone is not considered correct.

Sand Creek, KLAMATH. This stream heads in Crater Lake National Park and flows east toward Klamath Marsh. Captain O. C. Applegate wrote on July 21, 1911, as follows: "The old Indian trail and later the wagon road crossed Sand Creek in the valley of the Klamath Marsh. The pumice and sand was a menace to travel and teams and saddle horses were mired there. Even until a bridge was constructed over the stream a couple of months ago, the crossing was treacherous on account of the quicksands. The danger from these uncertain sands gave the name to the stream and was a reminder of the need of vigilance."

Sand Hollow Battleground, MORROW. In 1964 Judge John F. Kilkenny proposed this name to commemorate the battle between the Cayuse Indians and troops under the command of Colonel Cornelius Gilliam in Feb. 1848. The site is east of Finley Buttes and about a mile north of the OSHD marker indicating where the Oregon Trail crossed Sand Hollow.

Sand Mountain, LINN. Sand Mountain is a double summit about three miles south of the junction of US-20 and SH-22 west of Lost Lake. Each summit has a distinct crater and the whole is considered a textbook example of a cinder cone occuring above a deep fissure. In the 1980s an effort was made to save the early

USFS lookout. This culminated in the complete restoration of the building which now doubles as a lookout during fire season and as an interpretive center for the regrowth of the area of the Big Lake Fire of 1967.

Sand Ranch Well, MORROW. This well is at the site of John S. Kilkenny's 1911 Sand Hollow ranch house. John F. Kilkenny tells of the housewarming party and other details of this establishment in "Shamrocks and Shepherds," *OHQ*, v. 69, p. 101, *et seq*. It appears congenial combat was not confined to Donnybrook.

Sand Ridge, UNION. On Apr. 6, 1875 a post office with the name Sand Ridge was established in the Grande Ronde Valley with Cyrus G. Enloe first postmaster. This office was in service only until July 9, 1877, and even at that there was a period of several months when it did not function. It was named for a local topographic feature. The post office was in the northeast part of s 16, T 2S, R 39E, at a station on the old stage route from Union to Summerville. *See also* Slater.

Sanders Creek, TILLAMOOK. This creek flows towards Nestucca River north of Cloverdale but turns abruptly west and parallels the river nearly to Woods. It is named for Americus Sanders who homesteaded near Cloverdale in 1882 and raised goats nearby. At one time this stream was confused with Smith Creek just to the east but this was clarified in *Decision List 8701*.

Sandlake, TILLAMOOK. Sandlake post office was not far from Sand Lake, which is near the shore of the Pacific Ocean. As is customary, many names of this type were telescoped into one word by postal authorities. The post office was established with the name Hembree on July 10, 1890, with A. J. Hembree first postmaster. The name was changed to Sandlake on Jan. 18, 1898.

Sandy, CLACKAMAS. Sandy is near Sandy River and received its name on that account. *See* Sandy River for the origin of the name of the stream. J. H. Revenue, of Boring, sent the compiler information about the history of the town. His father settled near the present site of Sandy in 1853, and in those days of pioneer influx over the Barlow Road, all that territory lying north and east of Eagle Creek was known as Sandy, and the particular place where the community now stands was called Revenue. About 1870 Richard Gerdes, who had been operating a store at Eagle Creek with Henry Wilbern, bought property near the Revenue farm and opened a store. He soon applied for a post office, which was established Feb. 13, 1873, and it is generally believed Gerdes suggested the name Sandy, as he was more familiar with that name than with Revenue. On June 1, 1854 a post office named Sandy was established, apparently near the present site of Troutdale, with Emsley R. Scott postmaster. This post office was discontinued Feb. 26, 1868.

Sandy, MULTNOMAH. In 1977 the Union Pacific Railroad, as part of their track modernization program, replaced the limited siding facilities at Troutdale with a new long siding east of the Sandy River. The new station, Sandy, takes its name from the nearby river.

Sandy Creek, COOS. This stream is a tributary of Middle Fork Coquille River just west of Remote. It was named for a pioneer settler, "Sandy" Brown.

Sandy River, CLACKAMAS, MULTNOMAH. Sandy River was discovered by Lieutenant W. R. Broughton of Vancouver's expedition and was named Barings River on Oct. 30, 1792. This was probably for the great English family of bankers and financiers. Francis Baring (1740–1810) was for many years a director of the East India Company, and his second son Alexander (1774–1848) was better known as Lord Ashburton. Lewis and Clark passed the mouth of Sandy River on Sunday, Nov. 3, 1805, and made the following notation in their journals: "we coasted and halted at the mouth of a large river on the Lard. Side, this river throws out emence quantitys of sand and is very shallow, the narrowest part 200 yards wide bold current, much resembling the river Plat." The presence of the two mouths of the river was noted, and the stream was called Quicksand River. This name continued nearly 50 years, in American and British maps and writings. The name seems to have shortened to Sandy River on the tongues of Americans, between 1845 and 1850. Joel Palmer's *Journals of Travel*, written as of 1845, mentions Quicksand, Big Sandy, and Alexander Ross gives Quicksand River.

Sanford Canyon, MORROW. This canyon in Rhea Creek drainage south of Heppner was named for an early settler, one Sanford, who married a member of the Ayers family.

Sanger, BAKER. This place bears the name of one of the owners of the mining property nearby. The early name for this place was Hogum. *See* editorial page the *Oregonian*, Oct. 7, 1927, and the Baker *Morning Democrat*, Oct. 19, 1927. Dunham Wright of Medical Springs told the compiler that the place was named Hogum because of the greediness of some prospectors. The name was changed to Augusta in honor of Miss Augusta Parkwood. This change in name came about as the result of an agreement on the part of some of the miners to name the place for the first unmarried woman resident. The name Sanger has been established for many years, having displaced Augusta. Augusta post office was in operation for about a year in 1871–72. Sanger post office was established Aug. 17, 1887, with William R. Aldersley first postmaster. Augusta and Sanger may not have been in exactly the same place. *See also* Augusta.

Santiam, LINN, MARION. The name Santiam, with varied spellings, has been used for several Oregon post offices. For the derivation of the word, *see* Santiam River. An office called Santyam Forks was established in Linn County, Apr. 9, 1850, with Jacob Conser postmaster. John Crabtree became postmaster Oct. 4, 1850, and the office was discontinued July 27, 1852. It is known that Jacob Conser was living near the present site of Scio early in 1850, and John Crabtree lived in the same general locality. It may be assumed that the office was in the neighborhood. Santyam post office was established in Linn County Mar. 14, 1851, with Russel T. Hill postmaster. For the history of this office, *see* Lebanon. An office named Syracuse was established in Marion County Oct. 4, 1850. The place was about two miles downstream from the present site of Jefferson, but all available records show that it was really in Linn County and not Marion. *See* Jefferson for details.

On July 27, 1852 the name of the office was changed to Santiam City, and in the official records is a note that on Oct. 16, 1852, the office was in Linn County, but here again, the record at Washington, D.C. does not fit early maps and records in Oregon, which show Santiam on the Miller claim and in Marion County. These discrepancies may have been due to shifts in the Santiam River channel, here the boundary between Linn and Marion counties. The office was later moved to Jefferson, with a change in name. The post route map for 1900 shows an office called Santiam near South Santiam River between Lebanon and Sweet Home. This office has been discontinued and the community has almost evaporated.

Santiam Pass, JEFFERSON, LINN. In earlier days Santiam Pass was considered to be that used by the old South Santiam road which crossed the summit of the Cascade Range just east of Big Lake. Hogg Pass was about three miles to the north and was the point selected by Col. T. Egenton Hogg for his railroad location. As a result of the topographic mapping of this area by the USGS in 1928–29 and also of the building of the Santiam Highway through the Cascade Range, the USBGN on Apr. 3, 1929 adopted the name Santiam Pass for both of these routes of travel. This was done on the theory there was one wide pass and not two narrow ones, which is generally substantiated by the USGS Three Fingered Jack quadrangle. The name Hogg Pass, as applied to the location of Santiam Highway, is now obsolete. For editorial on this change, *see* the Salem *Capital Journal*, June 13, 1929. The name Santiam Pass appears to have been accepted very rapidly by the traveling public. The name of Colonel Hogg is perpetuated at Hogg Rock, a prominent point west of the pass and just north of Santiam Highway, which skirts its base. Andrew Wiley went through Santiam Pass as early as 1859. *See* Wiley Creek and Hogg Rock.

Santiam River, LINN, MARION. Santiam River and North Santiam River form in part the boundary between Linn and Marion counties. In addition to the two streams named, other important tributaries to the Santiam drainage are the South Santiam, Little North Santiam and Breitenbush rivers, and Crabtree, Thomas and Quartzville creeks, all heading on the western slope of the Cascade Range. The main stream was named for the Santiam Indians, a Kalapooian tribe, living near the Santiam River. The remnants were moved to Grand Ronde Agency in 1906. Variant forms of the name are *Ahalapam, Sandeam, Santiams, Santainas, Santian, Santians, Sandeham*. A detailed map of the North Santiam River and some of its tributaries may be found in USGS *Water-Supply Paper 349*.

Sardine Creek, JACKSON. Sardine Creek flows into Rogue River west of Gold Hill. In a letter signed "Pioneer," published in the *Oregonian* for Nov. 15, 1883, it is said that this stream was named by J. W. Hayes of Rock Point. Hayes was a gold seeker, and his pack mule one morning kicked him into the creek. Hayes jumped up with the remark that he was no sardine. Some of the information contained in "Pioneer's" letter mentioned above is erroneous, and the data on Sardine Creek may be incorrect. Walling, in *History of Southern Oregon*, p. 380, has another story of the origin of the name, to the effect that prospectors used sardines for food near the stream in the 1850s. Possibly the name had its start in both events.

Sardine Creek, MARION. This tributary of North Santiam River was named in 1867 by Thomas J. Henness because he found an empty sardine can in the stream while he was on a prospecting expedition from his home near the present site of Gates. Sardine tins were unusual in the Oregon mountains in those days. The name spread from the creek to Sardine Mountain nearby. For information about the Henness family, *see* the Salem *Capital Journal*, June 18, 1927, p. 1.

Sargent Butte, WHEELER. This 3300 foot butte is just north of the mouth of West Branch. It was named for Allie E. Sargent who homesteaded nearby in 1893. Grover Blake, who knew Sargent well, told the compiler in 1968 that he was unable to find any relationship between A. E. and I. N. Sargent, the man who made the original plat of Mitchell.

Saunders Creek, CURRY. This stream, which flows into Rogue River about four miles from the Pacific Ocean, was named for John Saunders who, with a man named Hastings, settled there about 1860 and built a saw and grist mill on the creek. This information was furnished by F. S. Moore of Gold Beach, Oregon.

Saunders Creek, LANE. Saunders Creek is a small tributary of Siuslaw River from the north about two miles east of Beck Station. BLM records show George Saunders filing on a homestead along this creek in 1888.

Saunders Lake, COOS. Saunders Lake is four miles southwest of Lakeside. It is drained by Saunders Creek which flows into Tenmile Creek. There is also a small adjacent community named Saunders Lake. These were all named for William Saunders who took up land there in 1884. Saunders was born in Pennsylvania in 1844 and came to Oregon as a boy. He married Emily Oregon Noble, the first white child born in Coos County and a sister of William H. Noble. Saunders died in 1914 and his wife in 1929.

Sauvie Island, COLUMBIA, MULTNOMAH. This is the largest island in the Columbia River, and is for the most part low land and lakes. The highest point on the island is only about 50 feet above sea level. Lewis and Clark called it *Wap-pa-to* and *Wap-pa-too* in 1805–06, the Indian name for the arrowhead or sagittaria. This was the wild potato, a valuable article of Indian food. There have been several forms of this native word, now generally spelled *wapato*. N. J. Wyeth built Fort William on this island in 1834–35 and some early maps have the name Wyeth Island. Wilkes used the name Multnomah Island. The name Sauvie Island comes from a French-Canadian employee of the Hudson's Bay Company who worked at the dairy farm on the west side of the island. The lettering Sauvies Island appears on Preston's *Map of Oregon*, 1856. Bancroft's *History of the Northwest Coast*, v. 2, p. 599, is authority for the statement that the island was named for one Jean Baptiste Sauve, but information has transpired that indicates this statement is wrong. In the files of the Oregon Historical Society is a letter from George B. Roberts to Mrs. F. F. Victor, dated Nov. 7, 1879, in which he says that Sauve Island bears the name of a

Canadian, Laurent Sauve, also called LaPlante. Many of the French-Canadians were known by two names. Mrs. Victor was one of the authors of Bancroft's history. The parish register of Saint James Catholic Church, Vancouver, has the marriage of Laurent Sauve to Josephte (Indian) on Feb. 11, 1839, and records that Sauve was from the district of Montreal. The burial of Laurent Sauve is entered in the parish register of Saint Paul Catholic Church on Aug. 3, 1858. In these registers the name of Laurent Sauve occurs a number of times, as godfather or burial witness. The name of Jean Baptiste Sauve does not occur at all. George B. Roberts came to Fort Vancouver in the service of the Hudson's Bay Company in 1831 and knew well the employees of the company. It may be inferred that Mrs. Victor erred in transcribing Roberts' letter. The USBGN has adopted the style Sauvie Island rather than the possessive Sauvies Island. It is interesting to note the following in a letter from Roberts to Mrs. Victor on July 5, 1882: "We say Sauvie (an old Canadian), not Sauvies—Puget, not Pugets, as we say Washington and not Washington's Territory."

Sauvies, MULTNOMAH. A post office named Sauvies was established in the extreme northwest corner of Multnomah County on Apr. 3, 1882, with J. L. Reeder postmaster. This office was on the west bank of Columbia River and on the east shore of Sauvie Island, at Reeder Point, and it was of course named for the island. Reeder ran the office until it was closed Apr. 6, 1906. Omar C. Spencer has informed the compiler that mail was brought to this and other Columbia River post offices by boat.

Savage Creek, JACKSON, JOSEPHINE. This creek, together with Little Savage Creek in Jackson County, and Savage Rapids in Rogue River in Josephine County, were named for a pioneer settler, and not for Indians. James Savage came to Oregon from Illinois in 1853, and took up a donation land claim near the geographic features that now bear his name.

Savage School, BENTON. This school, north of Corvallis near Soap Creek, was named for Morgan R. Savage who once owned a donation land claim nearby. *See* land office certificate 2326.

Sawmill Canyon, MORROW. When Heppner was being built in the 1870s, the closest lumber came from Van Armen's mill located where this canyon opens into Little Butter Creek east of Freezeout Ridge. In common with most Mill creeks, all that now remains is the name.

Sawyer Bar, LANE. The Pacific Crest Trail crosses the outfall of Collier Glacier two miles northwest of the North Sister. Ray Engels of the USFS named this crossing Sawyer Bar in honor of Robert W. Sawyer of Bend. Sawyer had a great love for the outdoors and a tremendous knowledge of the geography and history of the Cascade Range. For additional information, *see* Robert W. Sawyer State Park.

Scappoose, COLUMBIA. Scappoose post office was established Apr. 25, 1872. The name is of Indian origin and is said to mean gravelly plain. In addition to being used for the post office the name is also used for a well-known stream nearby, which drains the southern part of Columbia County. This stream is composed of two main branches, the correct names of which are North Scappoose Creek and South Scappoose Creek. "The History of Scappoose" is the title of an article in the Rainier *Review*, Oct. 23, 1931, which says among other things that the Scappoose post office of 1872 was at what is now known as Johnson Landing. It was moved to the present community about 1886. Samuel T. Gosa was the first postmaster of the Scappoose post office. Records of this office are confusing. It may have been in operation previously for a short time with the name Columbia. Gosa was also postmaster of the Columbia office.

Scaredman Creek, DOUGLAS. Scaredman Creek flows into Canton Creek about three miles north of North Umpqua River. USFS ranger Fred Asam stated that the name came from Scaredman Camp near the headwaters. A group of hunters had camped at this spot in the days when wolves were still plentiful in the mountains. The nocturnal howlings so disturbed the nimrods that at daybreak they hastily packed and departed to more civilized surroundings.

Schaff, MARION. This was a railroad station two miles south of Aumsville. It was named for Walter Schaff who owned the land on which the station was built.

Schieffelin Gulch, JACKSON. This draw is about a mile and a half southeast of the town of Rogue River and south of the river. It is named for Clinton Schieffelin who, with his wife Jane, took a donation land claim nearby. The spelling Shefflein is incorrect. Edward L. Schieffelin, Clinton and Jane's son, discovered the Lucky Cuss Mine in Arizona and founded the famous town of Tombstone. Ed Schieffelin returned to Oregon in 1895 and took up prospecting in the Northwest. The following year he was found dead of a heart attack in a lonely cabin on upper Days Creek. There were several tins of high grade ore and a cryptic note: "Struck her rich again, by God." The lode, dubbed the Red Blanket Mine, has never been found. *See* the article by Carl Gohs in the *Sunday Oregonian*, Dec. 26, 1971, *Northwest Magazine*, p. 9. The lost Red Blanket Mine has nothing to do with Red Blanket Creek in the Prospect area.

Scholfield Creek, DOUGLAS. This is an important tributary of the Umpqua River at Reedsport. It was named for Socrates Scholfield, a member of the party that came to the Umpqua River in 1850 in the schooner *Samuel Roberts*, and founded Umpqua City. He was the son of Nathan Scholfield of Norwich, Conn. There is a discrepancy in the way the name is spelled by Bancroft in his *History of Oregon*, v. 2, p. 176, and in *OHQ*, v. 17, p. 341. Bancroft uses the form Schofield, but Scholfield himself uses the style with a second "l." Scholfield family papers and letters at the Oregon State Library all confirm the spelling here used. Nathan Scholfield was one of the leaders of the party, and it is not clear why the stream was named for the son rather than the father, although Bancroft says such was the case. Possibly some incident of the exploration connected the name of the younger man with the stream. Attention is called to the fact that there is a discrepancy in the name of the schooner, the form *William Roberts* sometimes being used. However, the contemporaneous newspaper accounts, marine records, and George Davidson of the USC&GS all use the form *Samuel Roberts*, and it may be assumed that that style is correct.

Scholls, WASHINGTON. Scholls, Scholls Ferry and Scholls Ferry Road are all well-known geographic names in the Tualatin Valley. These features were named for Peter Scholl, a pioneer of 1847, who took up a donation claim nearby. In early days Scholls Ferry was one of the important crossings of the Tualatin River. Peter Scholl was born in Kentucky on Oct. 20, 1809. He was related to the family of Daniel Boone. He died in Portland in Nov. 1872. For information about Peter Scholl, *see OPA Transactions*, 1887, p. 80. Scholls Ferry post office was established Sept. 12, 1871, with J. R. Bennett first postmaster. The name was changed to Scholls on Feb. 2, 1895, and the office was discontinued in Nov. 1905.

School Creek, LANE. A. J. Briem, in his notes on file at the OHS, says that when the railroad was built up the Middle Fork Willamette River in 1909, the old Eula School was torn down to clear the right of way. The USFS then gave a permit to build a new school on government land alongside what at once became known as School Creek.

School Section Cabin, WHEELER. School Section Cabin is appropriately located in S 16, T 10S, R 22E, some ten miles north of Mitchell. This application of "School Section" applies to a number of features and originated with one of the earliest grants of public lands by the federal government to the state. The Oregon Territorial Act of 1848 provided that sections 16 and 36 of each township were to be reserved to the territory for the support of common schools. Where these sections were already occupied by donation land claim or other valid possession, an equivalent area of "lieu land" could be selected from other federal lands. This grant totaled 3,457,340 acres, the bulk of which were sold prior to 1910. For an excellent and concise report on this and other land laws, *see The Disposition of the Public Domain in Oregon*, Jerry A. O'Callaghan, a doctoral dissertation printed for the U.S. Senate Committee on Interior and Insular Affairs, Government Printing Office, 1960.

Schoolmarm Spring, WASCO. Schoolmarm Spring is on Mill Creek Ridge southwest of The Dalles. It was not named for a popular pedagogue but for a forked tree or *schoolmarm* in logger's parlance. There is also a Schoolmaam Creek in Jackson County west of Prospect.

Schooner Creek, LINCOLN. Schooner Creek is a well-known stream that flows into Siletz Bay just south of Taft. In 1945 Andrew L. Porter of Newport told the compiler that the stream was named for a schooner that came in over Siletz Bar about 1890 and ran aground on the rocks on the east side of the bay just south of the creek. Mr. Porter reported that some of the ship's ribs were still showing above the sand at low tide. Mr. Porter also said that he understood that about 1894 the ship's bell was taken to Grand Ronde and used at the Indian school.

Schooner Creek, LINCOLN. This paragraph refers to a stream called Schooner Creek that flows into the Pacific Ocean about a mile north of Yaquina Head. The stream was named for a small schooner that came ashore on the beach near the creek about 1890. The writer has not been able to identify this vessel and little is known of her except that she was about 50 feet long. The schooner was hauled above high tide by means of oxen and tackle and in 1944 it was reported that some of her remains were on the ground. A small point of rocks about a quarter of a mile north of the mouth of the creek is called Schooner Point.

Schott Canyon, GILLIAM. Schott Canyon is southwest of Condon. It was named for Conrad Schott, a pioneer settler.

Schreiner Peak, CLACKAMAS. Schreiner Peak, elevation 5678 feet, is a point in the Cascade Range near the headwaters of Collawash River. It was formerly called Pikes Peak, a name without local significance, but in 1935 the USFS recommended that the name be changed to Schreiner Peak in honor of the late Professor Fred J. Schreiner, a member of the faculty at Oregon State University. Beside being held in public esteem, Professor Schreiner had spent much time in the Mount Hood National Forest in the vicinity of the peak carrying on surveys for fire control. The USBGN adopted the name Schreiner Peak on Mar. 29, 1935.

Schrum Creek, LANE. In the 1890s Stephen J. Schrum homesteaded at the mouth of this creek a mile from Siltcoos Lake.

Schweitzer Creek, LANE. This creek flows northeast from Hardesty Mountain. It is named for homesteader Jacob Schweitzer who settled near its mouth in the early 1900s.

Scio, LINN. Scio was named for Scio, Ohio, which was in turn named for Scio, or as it is also known, Chios, an island off the west coast of Turkey in Asia. Mrs. C. A. Davis of Turner told the writer that Henry L. Turner and William McKinney built the flour mill at Scio, and when the work was completed, Turner suggested that McKinney give the new community a name. McKinney chose the name of his former home in Ohio. Another version of the story is to the effect that Mrs. McKinney really chose the name. Having been married, the compiler inclines toward the latter tradition. Scio post office was established Oct. 3, 1860, with Euphronius E. Wheeler first postmaster. *See also* Santiam.

Scissors Creek, CROOK. The writer has had several requests for information about the origin of the name Scissors Creek for a stream east of Prineville, flowing into Ochoco Creek. So far no data about this odd name have come to light. A map of 1889 shows a place called Scissorsville near this stream, with the probability that it was a mining locality.

Scofield, WASHINGTON. Scofield was a small community and station on the Southern Pacific Company Tillamook branch. Robert Benson of Washington County reported that it was named for Alva Scofield, an early settler. Scofield post office was established June 25, 1926 with Elmer H. Stewart postmaster and operated until Jan. 13, 1934. Logging and lumber, the principal industries in the area, ceased after the disastrous 1933 Tillamook Burn and the community faded into obscurity.

Scoggins Creek, WASHINGTON. Scoggins Creek was named for Gustavus Scoggin, a pioneer settler. The original form was Scoggin Creek but the use of the terminal "s" without the possessive was so prevalent that the USBGN adopted the present form in *Decision List 6402*.

Scorpion Mountain, MARION. According to Dee Wright of Eugene, this mountain received its name at the time the nearby USFS trail was built because there were so many small wood scorpions in the rotting logs that were moved.

Scotch Creek, WALLOWA. Scotch Creek is west of Joseph. It was named by Mat Inglehorn, who was a Scotsman, in the 1870s. He and his brother had a homestead on the stream.

Scott Butte, WHEELER. Scott Butte is east of Girds Creek and is 4304 feet high. It bears the name of Raleigh E. Scott who came from Tennessee and settled here before the turn of the century. Scott called his ranch "Fairview."

Scott Canyon, SHERMAN. Owen, Elihu and John Scott were the sons of Polly Scott, a widow who homesteaded the upper reaches of this canyon near Rufus. The Scott brothers were among the earliest wheat farmers in what is now Sherman County.

Scott Creek, CURRY. Raleigh Scott settled on this creek east of Carpenterville in 1882. Although there was no established community, he operated a store and trading post for residents of the area.

Scott Mountain, DOUGLAS. This peak was originally known as Scotts Point, but nearby settlers changed the name to Scott Mountain. It is about 4300 feet in elevation and is clearly seen from the neighborhood of Sutherlin. It was named for Captain Levi Scott, the founder of Scottsburg. *See* Scottsburg.

Scott Mountain, LANE. This peak is in the Cascade Range west of McKenzie Pass. Scott Lake is nearby. These two geographic features were named for Felix Scott, the younger, who was one of the promoters of the McKenzie toll road project. *See* Hodge's *Mount Multnomah* for information on the subject. Felix Scott was the brother of Mrs. John E. Lyle, a pioneer resident of Dallas. This Scott family was not related to that of Captain Levi Scott of Scottsburg. About a mile east of the summit of the Cascade Range is Scott Pass, in Deschutes County. It is a gap in the ridge between Black Crater and North Sister. Scott Trail goes through Scott Pass. These two features were also named for Felix Scott.

Scott Spring, UMATILLA. In 1895 William Scott took up land near this spring in T 5S, R 33E.

Scotts Campground, CROOK. Scotts Campground is on the divide just north of Big Summit Prairie. It was probably named for James H. Scott who was born in Scotland in 1866. He came to this country in 1903 and worked for the Hahn interests on Big Summit Prairie until just before his death in 1939.

Scotts Mills, MARION. Robert Hall Scott and Thomas Scott had a sawmill and a flour mill at this place in early days, and the settlement was named Scotts Mills about 1866. The post office was established Nov. 1, 1887, with Thomas Scott first postmaster.

Scotts Valley, DOUGLAS. Scotts Valley is a broad opening where I-5 crosses Elk Creek south of Curtin. John Scott and J. J. Scott both took donation land claims in the valley.

Scottsburg, DOUGLAS. Scottsburg was founded in 1850 by Levi Scott, a pioneer of Oregon of 1844, from Iowa. Scott led the party that went into southern Oregon and thence to Fort Hall in 1846, locating the southern or Applegate route. Scottsburg became the metropolis of southern Oregon, but the establishment of Crescent City in California in 1852, and other diversions of transportation, caused the decline of the community. Scott was a member of the territorial council from 1852 to 1854, and of the constitutional convention in 1857. He died in Malheur County in 1890, aged 93 years. Mount Scott in Crater Lake National Park was named in his honor. For detailed information about the Scott family, *see* editorial page, *Oregon Journal*, Nov. 25, 26, 27, 1926. Copies of Scott family records in the possession of the compiler do not substantiate the statement that Levi Scott died in Lane County in 1878. Historical information about Scottsburg is contained in an article in the *Oregon Journal*, Portland, for May 21, 1939, compiled by Ben Maxwell. There appear to have been two parts to the community, separated by about a mile of river, and Lower Scottsburg was the port of entry. The big flood of 1861 is the important event in the history of the place, and is said to have obliterated Lower Scottsburg. The names Myrtle City and Scottsburg seem to have been applied to this locality at first, but whether they were for the separate places the compiler cannot determine. The early history of the post offices is confusing. Myrtle City post office was established June 30, 1851, with Levi Scott postmaster. It was discontinued July 27, 1852. In the meantime Scottsburg post office was established Oct. 8, 1851, with Stephen F. Chadwick postmaster. Eugene R. Fisk became postmaster Oct. 12, 1852. Preston's map of 1851 shows Myrtle City just east of and very close to Scottsburg. A place called Gagniersville is shown just east of Myrtle City, but Scottsburg is the only one of the three shown on Preston's map of 1856. The other two places did not persist. Postal records are not consistent about the name Scottsburg, and in a number of instances the spelling is Scottsburgh, but the public generally has used the style Scottsburg and that is the official spelling at present.

Scotty Creek, GRANT. This creek, south of Mount Vernon, was named for a pioneer sheep man, Scotty Hay, who had a camp and cabin on the stream. Scotti is incorrect.

Scout Lake, HOOD RIVER. After the Boy Scout camp was built at Wahtum Lake about 1918, many of the campers would hike to this small lake about a half mile south for undisturbed fishing or swimming. The name Scout Lake became fixed by association although the Boy Scout camp was always at Wahtum Lake.

Scout Lake, MARION. This is one of the larger lakes in Jefferson Park. It was named in Aug. 1931 by a group of Boy Scouts from Troop #20, Albany, who camped by it for several days. Before they left they marked "Scout Lake" with a heavy pencil on a split limb pointer and wedged it into a tree alongside the Skyline Trail. On a subsequent trip they found the pencil markings unreadable so the words were carved into the limb. This troop was redesignated Troop #21 in Dec. 1931.

Seaforth, CURRY. Seaforth post office was established Nov. 12, 1890, with Robert McKenzie postmaster. The office was closed Mar. 8, 1892, and mail sent to Port Orford. According to Dodge in his *Pioneer History of Coos and Curry Counties*, appendix p. 66, McKenzie lived on a large farm near the mouth of Elk River and it may be assumed that was the site of the post office Seaforth. Dodge gives a short biography of McKenzie on the page indicated. Members of the Mackenzie family have at various times been the earls of Seaforth in Scotland and the Mackenzies and McKenzies have a strong sentimental interest in the Scottish name.

Seal Rocks, LINCOLN. These form a ledge of partly submerged rocks extending parallel to the coast for about two and a half miles and a distance of half a mile from the beach. The highest rock rises about 20 feet above water. The *Coast Pilot* uses the name Seal Rocks, and that was the style used in pioneer days for the locality along the shore about ten miles south of Newport. There is one large rock at the shoreline and several smaller ones. The place was called Seal Illahe, Chinook jargon for seal place or seal home. The post office, now a CPO out of Waldport, is on US-101, the Oregon Coast Highway. It is named for the rocks, but is called Seal Rock. This form of name is not completely descriptive and seems to refer only to the large rock at the shoreline. The post office was established Apr. 25, 1890, with J. W. Brasfield postmaster. In those days the rocks were well covered with seals and sea lions.

Sears Creek, CROOK. Sears Creek empties into Marks Creek in s 36, T 13S, R 18E. USFS records state it was named for a family who once had a substantial ranch along Marks Creek. Census records show the David A. Sears family ranching in the Ochoco area at the turn of the century and Sears filed on a homestead near the mouth of Marks Creek in 1914.

Seaside, CLATSOP. Silas B. Smith, in *OHQ*, v. 1, p. 321, says that the Clatsop Indian village at the site of what is now Seaside was called *Ne-co-tat*. The name Seaside came from Ben Holladay's famous hostelry and resort, the Seaside House. The first post office in the locality seems to have been Summer House, established Dec. 1, 1871, with A. J. Clontire first postmaster. The name was changed to Seaside House on July 23, 1873, with Charles H. Dexter postmaster. The name was changed to Seaside on Mar. 29, 1882. The old Seaside House was about a mile south of the present business section of Seaside. Seaside was at one time divided into two municipalities, east and west of the Necanicum River, but they are now consolidated. The Spokane, Portland and Seattle Railway was completed in 1907 to Seaside and the end of the line was a mile further south at Holladay. Until World War II, it did a thriving passenger business to the north coast beach resorts but the line has been removed south of the Columbia River. For an interesting article about the railroad, *see* the *Oregon Journal*, Sept. 3, 1979, p. 1. Lewis and Clark sent a detail of men who established a salt-making cairn at the present site of Seaside about Jan. 1, 1806. This site is now a detached section of Fort Clatsop National Monument. For a description of the cairn in 1899, *see* the *Oregonian*, Aug. 19, 1899, p. 8. For narrative of Lewis and Clark expedition to the salt cairn, by L. B. Cox, June 17, 1900, p. 8.

Seaton, LANE. Seaton was an early-day post office in western Lane County, a little to the north of what was later Mapleton. Seaton office was established Nov. 13, 1885, with William W. Neely first postmaster. The name Seaton was suggested by a Mr. Anthony, in compliment to a place in England called Seaton. There are several places in England called Seaton and the compiler has no means of knowing which one Mr. Anthony had in mind in 1885. Mrs. Julia A. Bean was appointed postmaster at Seaton Apr. 1, 1889, and the name of the office was changed to Mapleton on Mar. 26, 1896. It is believed that the office was moved to the present site of Mapleton in 1889, seven years before the name was changed.

Second Lake, LINN. Second Lake is the name applied to the second of a series of four lakes on the east bank of Willamette River northeast of Albany, and it is so named because of the position it occupies.

Seekseequa Creek, JEFFERSON. Seekseequa Creek is a tributary of Deschutes River and drains the south part of the Warm Springs Indian Reservation. Indians have informed the compiler that the word is from the Paiute language and means a variety of coarse rye grass that grows near the stream. The spelling *Psuc-see-que* is used in Pacific Railroad Surveys *Reports*, v. 6, and there are several other forms. The USBGN originally adopted the form Seekseekwa but this was altered to the present spelling in *Decision List 6302*.

Seeley Creek, DOUGLAS. Seeley Creek is a small stream flowing eastward under the Territorial Road and into Pheasant Creek in S 19, T 21S, R 4W. This creek or brook flows through the ranch of Mr. and Mrs. Ernest J. Martin a few miles north of Anlauf and south of Lorane. Seeley Creek was named to commemorate Seeley Douglas Martin, son of Mr. and Mrs. Martin. Seeley was a seaman in the U.S. Navy, reported missing in action May 23, 1942, during the Midway campaign. He was a graduate of the Navy Communications School at San Diego. The application of the name Seeley Creek was approved Apr. 12, 1947, by the Douglas County court and shortly thereafter the USBGN approved the selection.

Seghers, WASHINGTON. Seghers is a station on the Southern Pacific line north of Gaston. It was named for the Most Rev. Charles Seghers, Catholic archbishop of Oregon in the early 1880s, who was murdered in Alaska in 1886. *See Catholic*

History of Oregon, p. 152 *et seq*. Seghers post office was established June 21, 1898, with Augustine A. Roth postmaster. The office was closed June 14, 1924.

Seits Ridge, LINCOLN. This two-mile long ridge lies south of Five Rivers just north of the Lane County line. It bears the name of Henry Seits who settled there in the first decade of the twentieth century.

Selah, MARION. This station was on the Southern Pacific Company Springfield branch west of Silverton. *Selah* is a Hebrew term meaning to pause, and is used as a place name to indicate a place of rest.

Sellers Butte, LANE. Sellers Butte is about a mile south of Pleasant Hill. Its name comes from James R. Sellers who was born in Illinois in 1827. He came to California in 1863 and to Oregon in 1871. The following year he bought 450 acres near Sellers Butte where he, and later his son, John R. Sellers, farmed for many years. Another son, William Sellers, taught at Pleasant Hill School in the late 1880s. James R. Sellers died Feb. 3, 1911.

Sellwood, MULTNOMAH. This part of the city of Portland was named for the Rev. John Sellwood. The name was first applied about 1882, and the post office was established in Oct. 1883. Sellwood was taken into the city of Portland in 1893.

Selma, JOSEPHINE. Selma post office was established by change of name from Anderson on July 10, 1897. When the name of the Anderson office was changed to Selma the office was moved south a few miles. The first postmaster at the new office was Robert C. Churchill. Mrs. Churchill selected the name Selma in honor of the little town Selma, in Van Buren County, Iowa, near where she was raised.

Seneca, GRANT. This post office was named for Judge Seneca Smith of Portland. The name was given by Minnie Southworth, the first postmaster. The office was established Sept. 17, 1895. Postal authorities wanted a short name, and the word Seneca suggested itself to Mrs. Southworth because her sister-in-law was Mrs. Seneca Smith.

Senecal Spring, HOOD RIVER. This spring near Lookout Mountain was named for John Batiste Senecal who was USFS ranger in Dufur from 1895 to 1913. He was commonly called Batt and at one time ran horses in the meadow near Red Hill that now bears his nickname. Senecal's father, Gideon Senecal, came to Oregon in 1840 with the Hudson's Bay Company and subsequently took a donation land claim near Champoeg. He later moved to eastern Oregon and left a substantial family in Wasco and Crook counties.

Senoj Lake, DESCHUTES. Senoj Lake is near the summit of the Cascade Range and about four miles west of Lava Lake. The name is in compliment to some person called Jones, with the spelling reversed.

Sentinel Peak, CLACKAMAS, HOOD RIVER. R. S. Shelley of the USFS named this peak for its commanding position overlooking West Fork Hood River. According to Ralph Lewis, who was with him, this took place in July 1906.

Sepanek, MORROW. Sepanek post office was established Aug. 2, 1917, with Bertha Sepanek first and only postmaster. The office, which was obviously named with the postmaster's family name, was closed Sept. 14, 1918. It was about six miles northeast of Lexington, in the southwest part of T IN, R 26E.

Separation Creek, LANE. Separation Creek heads west of the South Sister, and flows westward, its waters eventually reaching McKenzie River. The creek was so named because it flows between The Husband and The Wife, two lesser peaks west of the summit of the Cascade Range and members of the Three Sisters group.

Serrano Point, HARNEY. Serrano Point is between Alvord Desert and Alvord Lake, on the west side of Alvord Valley. *Serrano* is Spanish for mountaineer or highlander.

Service Buttes, UMATILLA. Service Buttes, which lie about eight miles southwest of Echo, have an extreme elevation of 1685 feet. Service Canyon is southwest of the buttes, and Service Springs to the north. These features are named for the serviceberry, otherwise called shadbush or Juneberry. The bush is of the *Amelanchier* family. The name is probably the most mispronounced botanical word in the west, the uneducated invariably making it sarvis berry.

Service Creek, WHEELER. This was the name of a post office near the mouth of Service Creek, a tributary of John Day River. The creek was formerly called Sarvis Creek, spelled as pronounced colloquially. The post office was established on May 23, 1918, with the name Sarvicecreek and with May Tilley first postmaster. At the request of the compiler of these notes the name was changed to Servicecreek on Dec. 4, 1918. The 1941 *Postal Guide* lists the office as Service Creek, the change to two words having taken place early in 1929. The post office was not operating in 1980.

Serviceberry Camp, DOUGLAS. This out-of-the-way spot in T 30S, R IE was named by Durk Van Dike, a USFS employee and part-time trapper in the early days, apparently for the abundance of serviceberries or *Amelanchier florida*.

Seufert, WASCO. Seufert station is east of The Dalles. It bears the name of two brothers, Theodore J. and Frank A. Seufert. They were natives of New York, and came to Oregon in the early 1880s. They were engaged in various branches of the packing business, principally of salmon and fruit. For biography of Theodore J. Seufert, *see Illustrated History of Central Oregon*, p. 327.

Seven Devils, COOS. In describing the coast south of Cape Arago, George Davidson in the *Coast Pilot* of 1889 says: "The hills are covered with dense forests and underbrush, and are cut by deep ravines running at right angles to the shoreline. From the number of these ravines the coast is locally known as 'the *Seven Devils*.'" R. R. Monbeck of the USGS furnished the compiler with information about this name in 1943 and it seems apparent that the name Seven Devils was originally applied because of the difficulty in cutting the coast trail across these ravines. The earliest mention of these ravines that the compiler has seen is in the Harrison G. Rogers journal in *The Ashley-Smith Exploration* on July 4, 1828: "The travelling pretty bad, as we were obliged to cross the low hills, as they came in close to the beach, and the beach being so bad that we could not get along, thicketty and timbered, and some very bad ravines to cross."

Seven Sixty Spring, GRANT. This spring in S 8, T 14S, R 26E is so called because in the early days a sheep herder was asked the elevation. He replied: "Seven sixty feet by blankety-blank-blank." Government accounts did not contain *verbatim* records of profanity in those days.

Sevenmile Creek, COOS. Sevenmile Creek flows into Coquille River about seven miles upstream from the river's mouth and is so named on that account.

Sexton Mountain, JOSEPHINE. This mountain is a prominent peak north of Grants Pass and I-5 crosses its western flank at an elevation of 1960 feet. It takes its name from a family of early settlers. William M. Colvig of Medford wrote the compiler on July 1, 1927, as follows: "In about the year 1853 a widow by the name of Niday settled on a location at the foot of the mountain. She kept a wayside tavern on the road and travelers were delighted to enjoy the restful hospitality of the place. In the 1850s she married David Sexton and the stopping place became known as Sextons. Their son Charles Sexton now lives there." Later investigation shows that Hiram and Caroline Niday took a donation land claim in what is now S 40, T 34S, R 6W. Hiram Niday died in Mar. 1856, and David Sexton came to this spot in Pleasant Valley, presumably, shortly thereafter.

Sexton Mountain, WASHINGTON. Edward S. Sexton was born in Ohio in 1822, and settled on land southwest of what is now Beaverton in the spring of 1853. Sexton Mountain was named for him. The spelling Saxton is incorrect.

Shady Cove, JACKSON. Shady Cove is on Rogue River between two and three miles south of Trail. The post office is on SH-62, the Crater Lake Highway, near the concrete bridge which carries the highway over the river, but the cove itself is upriver a few hundred yards and on the southeast side of the stream. The name is descriptive of a little nook on the river bank, but is not particularly applicable to the locality of the post office and the highway bridge. Shady Cove post office was established in Sept. 1939, with Mrs. Lillian F. Hukill postmaster. The compiler has been informed that the name Shady Cove was applied to the place upstream from the post office some years before the office was established, by one J. Powell of Medford.

Shamrock Creek, WALLOWA. Shamrock Creek and Shamrock Flat are near Flora. These features are said to have been named by some soldiers from Walla Walla who crossed the Grande Ronde River at Hanson Ferry about 1885 or 1886. These soldiers had difficulty in fording the river and lost part of their equipment. After traveling near Bear Creek and Buford Creek they camped on a small flat at the head of what is now known as Shamrock Creek. When they left they painted a sign on a tree with a shamrock on it, and the flat has been known by that name ever since.

Shanahan Place, LAKE. Shanahan Place on the west edge of Antelope Flat was the homestead of Tom Shanahan. He settled there after World War I.

Shaniko, WASCO. Shaniko was named for pioneer settler August Scherneckau. Scherneckau came to Oregon after the Civil War and bought a farm near the present site of Shaniko. Indians pronounced the name Shaniko, and that is how the locality got its name. The Scherneckau ranch was on the stage route from The Dalles to central Oregon and August Scherneckau opened a stage station and kept the travel. Scherneckau some years later moved to Astoria, and after residing there several years moved to California, where he died. This locality was first called Cross Hollows, and a post office with that name was established May 23, 1879, with Scherneckau first postmaster. The office was closed May 27, 1887. The name Cross Hollows was descriptive of the local topography. Shaniko post office was established Mar. 31, 1900, with John D. Wilcox first postmaster. For additional information about Shaniko, *see* Bend *Bulletin*, Sept. 24, 1930, and for a story about early days in Shaniko by Giles L. French, *see* news section of the *Oregonian*, Dec. 12, 1943.

Shark Creek, CLATSOP. Shark Creek flows into Asbury Creek east of the community of Arch Cape. The section of the deck and the cannon of the wrecked *Shark* drifted ashore just north of the mouth of Asbury creek. The compiler has no positive information but assumes Shark Creek takes its name from the ship of the unfortunate Lieutenant Howison. *See* Cannon Beach.

Sharps Creek, LANE. This stream was named for a well-known pioneer character, James H. "Bohemia" Sharp. He was an early prospector and road builder. For an interesting account of some of his activities, *see* the Cottage Grove *Sentinel*, July 13, 1967.

Shasta Costa Creek, CURRY. Shasta Costa Creek is a tributary of Rogue River. It bears the name of the *Shas-te-koos-tee* Indians. Orvil Dodge spells the name of the Indian tribe in this manner and says that it numbered about 145 in 1854. The name of the creek does not seem to have anything to do with either Mount Shasta or the Spanish word *costa* meaning coast, but is merely the white man's convenient method of writing the Indian name. The *Handbook of American Indians*, v. 2, p. 857, lists the tribe or band as the *Chastocosta*, part of the Tututni Indians.

Shasta Gulch, MALHEUR. Shasta Gulch is in the extreme north end of Malheur County, and drains south into Willow Creek. This gulch was named in the gold rush of the 1860s by miners from the Shasta region of northern California.

Shattuck, MULTNOMAH. Erasmus D. Shattuck was one of the foremost jurists of Oregon. He came to Oregon in 1853 from New York, and conducted the Oregon City College and the Clackamas County Female Seminary in 1853–55. He served at Pacific University as professor of ancient languages, beginning in 1855, and was elected superintendent of schools for Washington County in 1855, and probate judge for the same county in 1856. In 1857 he was a member of the constitutional convention, and, in 1858, a member of the territorial legislature; in 1862–67 he was supreme and circuit judge; in 1874–78 he was judge of the supreme court; in 1886 he was elected to the circuit court, and served until 1898. He also served in the Portland city council and on the school board of Portland. Judge Shattuck was born at Bakersfield, Vermont, Dec. 31, 1824; died at Portland on July 26, 1900. *See* various estimates of his work and character in the *Oregonian*, July 6, 1898. For tributes to him in 1896, Jan. 1, 1896. Judge Shattuck owned a farm near the Southern Pacific line about two miles west of Hillsboro. The station at the crossing with the Shattuck Road was named for him.

Shaw, MARION. This is a station east of Salem. It was named for Angus Shaw. Shaw came to Oregon from Ontario, Canada, and bought a farm near the present site of Shaw in 1876.

Shaw Mountain, UNION. Shaw Mountain, elevation 5493 feet, is northwest of North Powder. John, Louellen and Alex Shaw all settled on government land nearby during the first decade of the twentieth century. The compiler does not know how the three were related.

Shaw Stewart Ditch, BAKER. Daniel Shaw filed on government land in Bowen Valley on Jan. 11, 1875.

Sheaville, MALHEUR. Sheaville is in the cattle country on the extreme east edge of the county and just about midway north and south. It was named for Con Shea, a pioneer stockman. Sheaville post office was first established Nov. 3, 1887, with Morris Oberdorfer first postmaster. The office was not in continuous operation and was closed permanently prior to 1980.

Shedd, LINN. A post office near the place now known as Shedd was established with the name Boston Mills, on Sept. 22, 1869, with William Simmons first postmaster. The name of the office was changed to Shedd on Aug. 28, 1871, at the time when the railroad was being built south from Albany. The new name came from Captain Frank Shedd, upon whose land the community was started. For a time the place was called Shedds, but that form has passed into oblivion. For information about the Shedd family, *see* editorial page of the *Oregon Journal*, Oct. 18, 1930.

Sheep Rock, GRANT. Sheep Rock is in the south part of Butler Basin, north of Picture Gorge. J. E. Snow of Dayville told the writer that this rock was not named because of any fancied resemblance to a ram's head, but because of the prevalence of mountain sheep nearby in pioneer days. The rock has an elevation of 3360 feet. *See* editorial page the *Oregonian*, Dec. 10, 1925. There is another Sheep Rock in Grant County about seven miles south of John Day. It is between US-395 and Strawberry Mountain and has an elevation of 6400 feet.

Sheep Rock, JEFFERSON. This Sheep Rock is west of Trout Creek near the Maupin Cemetery. It is so called because from certain angles it resembles the head of a sheep.

Sheep Shooter Tree, GRANT. This tree was located in the narrow bottom of Wolf Creek a short distance upstream from what is now (1981) the Sartain Ranch in the center of s 18, T 16s, R 24E. The Paulina Sheep Shooters were organized under this tree in July 1898. USFS ranger C. S. Congleton has an interesting account of "Sheep Shooters" and a photograph of the tree in his *Report* to Forest Supervisor Harpham dated Feb. 8, 1927. This and other information are in *History of the Ochoco* in the Ochoco National Forest files.

Sheepshead Mountains, MALHEUR. These mountains separate Wildhorse Valley east of Steens Mountains from the Owyhee River. In the early days they were the haunts of large bands of rimrock sheep, *Ovis canadensis californiana*, that ranged most of eastern Oregon. In the 1880s domestic sheep entered this range and infected the wild animals with "sheep scab." This quickly exterminated the bighorns and the mountains were named because for many years thereafter large numbers of horned skulls were scattered throughout the area. Vernon Bailey in *Mammals and Life Zones of Oregon* describes this fine animal and its unfortunate demise. The form Sheepshead Mountains is in general use but Mary Kueny who was raised in the area claimed the correct form was Sheephead Mountain.

Sheet Iron Jack Creek, WHEELER. The compiler was told by Mrs. Lily Collins of the Fopiano Ranch that an early settler named Jack built a cabin covered with sheet iron in the meadow where this creek heads northwest of Waterman.

Shelburn, LINN. In Apr. 1927 the postmaster at Shelburn wrote the compiler that the name Shelburn was supposed to be a combination of parts of the names of two pioneer residents, Shelton and Washburn. Riley Shelton of Scio, in 1927, confirmed the statement and told the compiler that the name was made up by Rosa and Mary Miller.

Sheldon Ridge, WASCO. Joseph L. Sheldon settled on this ridge east of Mosier Creek in 1910.

Shell Rock, HOOD RIVER. A post office with the name Shell Rock was established on the Wasco County list Apr. 14, 1873, with David Graham postmaster. This office was in what is now Hood River County and was in the vicinity of Shellrock Mountain on the south bank of the Columbia River between Cascade Locks and Hood River. The office was of course named for the mountain. Shell Rock post office later was moved north across the Columbia River into Washington Territory and the name changed to Collins Landing, but the compiler cannot tell when. Shell Rock post office was in operation again on the Oregon side between May 20 and Aug. 19, 1878, with John Cates postmaster. John Cates, of a well-known Wasco County family, operated a sawmill at a point a couple of miles west of the present site of Wyeth. The post office was apparently reestablished to serve people connected with the Cates mill. It was about three miles west of Shellrock Mountain, but named for that feature nevertheless.

Shellrock Creek, CLACKAMAS. Shellrock Creek, which takes its rise in Shellrock Lake, is in the east part of the county. It flows into Oak Grove Fork Clackamas River. The lake and stream were so named because they were near Shellrock Mountain, which had shale slides on its slopes. Several years ago the name of this mountain was changed by the government to Frazier Mountain because there were too many other Shellrock mountains in the state, but the name of the lake and creek remained as before because there was no duplication.

Shellrock Mountain, HOOD RIVER. Mountains of this name are so called because the rock of which they are composed breaks off in platy chunks and piles up in long slopes, like shelled corn. There are several Shellrock mountains in Oregon, the best known being on the Columbia River Highway east of Cascade Locks.

Shepperds Dell, MULTNOMAH. This dell on the Historic Columbia River Highway just west of Bridal Veil was presented to the public in May 1915, by George Shepperd, as a memorial to his wife. The tract consists of 11 acres. The creek is spanned by a fine concrete arch about 100 feet long.

Sherar Burn, CLACKAMAS. This clear area north of Salmon River about five miles west of Salmon River Meadows was burned by one of the big fires of the mid-nineteenth century. It went to grass and Joseph Sherar grazed sheep there before it became national forest. For a biography of Sherar, *see* Sherars Bridge.

Sherars Bridge, WASCO. Peter Skene Ogden took an exploring party into central Oregon in 1826–27, and on Thursday, Sept. 22, 1826, he noted in his journal: "Proceeded down River of the Falls (Deschutes) to the Falls where we found an Indian camp of 20 families. Finding a canoe also a bridge made of slender wood, we began crossing, 5 horses were lost thro' the bridge." *See OHQ*, v. 11, p. 205. Apparently in pioneer times there was no bridge at the present site of Sherars Bridge, for Bancroft, in his *History of Oregon*, v. 1, p. 787, says that it had to be forded or crossed in Indian canoes. John Y. Todd built a bridge in 1860, but it was carried away and had to be rebuilt in 1862. For Todd's reminiscences, *see OHQ*, v. 30, p. 70. Todd later took in Ezra L. Hemingway and Robert Mays as partners. Hemingway bought out the other two, and then sold to O'Brien, who sold out to Joseph Sherar in 1871. Sherar was a prominent character in central Oregon. He was born in Vermont on Nov. 16, 1833, of Irish parentage, and was reared in St. Lawrence County, New York. He came by sea to California in 1855. He mined in northern California, and in 1862 he started with passengers and freight by pack train to the John Day mines, and on this trip his party named Antelope Valley, Muddy Creek, Cherry Creek and Burnt Ranch, and laid the foundation for Bakeoven. Sherar married Jane A. Herbert in 1863 and settled in Wasco County. He paid $7,040 for Sherars Bridge and spent $75,000 improving roads leading to it. He was interested in various milling enterprises on White River and kept a stage station at the bridge which bears his name. He died at The Dalles on Feb. 11, 1908. Apparently there was a post office at this locality as early as 1868 with the name Deschutes. *See* Deschutes.

Sheridan, YAMHILL. Sheridan is on the South Yamhill River and was named for Philip Henry Sheridan, who as a lieutenant, did efficient and courageous work against the Indians at the Cascades in 1856. He arrived at Fort Vancouver in Oct. 1855, from California, and remained in Oregon and Washington until the outbreak of the Civil War. In Apr. 1856, he was ordered to Grand Ronde Agency, and was stationed not far from the town that now bears his name. He was stationed at Fort Hoskins in 1857, 14 miles from Corvallis, as quartermaster and commissary. He went east in Sept. 1861, and as a result of his great work in the Civil War was made lieutenant-general in 1869, and general before he died, Aug. 5, 1888. He visited Portland, Salem and Yamhill County in 1875; arrived at Portland Aug. 31; left for California Sept. 8. *See* his *Memoirs* for narrative of the Yakima War; also the *Oregonian*, Dec. 9, 1888, Dec. 23, 1888. Sheridan post office was established Apr. 4, 1866, by change of name from Willamina, with Thomas N. Faulconer postmaster. The office had been serving an area a few miles west of Sheridan, and was moved eastward to the new location. Another office was established for Willamina in Aug. 1878.

Sheridan Mountain, DESCHUTES. Sheridan Mountain, elevation 6948 feet, is a prominent point in a string of craters that extends south from Mount Bachelor. It is about five miles from Mount Bachelor and the same distance from Lava Lake. It was formerly called Tent Mountain, because of its shape when seen from the west, but on Mar. 4, 1931, the USBGN adopted the name Sheridan Mountain, in honor of General Philip H. Sheridan, who, in 1855, as a second lieutenant with the Pacific Railroad Surveys, explored central Oregon. It seems probable that Sheridan ascended this peak on Aug. 30, 1855. *See also* Williamson Mountain.

Sherman, SHERMAN. This station west of Biggs was once known as Deschutes Junction, because it was at one end of the railroad branch line up Deschutes River. Fred S. Stanley later asked to have the name Deschutes given to a point between Redmond and Bend, and it then became necessary to change the name at the north end of the line. The name Sherman was selected because it was in Sherman County. This was in 1912. In 1930 the name Sherman was changed to Ainsworth, because Sherman duplicated the name of other stations. *See* Ainsworth for additional information. The north end of the Deschutes Canyon line was abandoned in 1936 and as a result the junction at Ainsworth was eliminated. There was no station there in 1940.

Sherman County. Sherman County was created Feb. 25, 1889, by the state legislature. It was taken from the northeast part of Wasco County, as that county was then organized, and in 1990 had an area of 835 square miles. Sherman County was named for General William Tecumseh Sherman, the great northern leader in the Civil War. W. T. Sherman was born at Lancaster, Ohio, Feb. 8, 1820, and graduated from West Point in 1840. He resigned from the army in 1853. He accepted a colonelcy in the Union Army in 1861, and gained rapid promotion on account of his recognized ability. He was made a lieutenant-general in 1866 and general in command of the army in 1869. He died Feb. 14, 1891, at New York City. It was first planned to name this county Fulton County for Colonel James Fulton, a pioneer resident, and the bill providing this name went through two readings in the house of representatives, but before it was passed, the name Fulton was changed to Sherman, at the instigation of J. W. Maxwell of Tillamook and Yamhill counties. It is said that this was done because Colonel Fulton objected to extending an invitation to General Sherman to visit the house of representatives some years previously when General Sherman was a visitor in Oregon. For an editorial about naming Sherman County, *see* the *Oregonian*, Nov. 27, 1942.

Sherod Meadow, WALLOWA. Sherod Meadow is in the northwest corner of T 2N, R 43E, and bears the name of William Sherod, who ranged his sheep there in 1887–88.

Sherrard Point, MULTNOMAH. Sherrard Point was named in honor of Thomas H. Sherrard who was associated with the USFS for more than 40 years. It comprises the viewpoint on the northeast extremity of the summit ridge of Larch Mountain and is marked with a bronze plaque. During his tenure with the USFS, Sherrard served as supervisor of the Mount Hood National Forest from 1907 to 1934 and took a keen interest in the development of recreation facilities as well as assisting in the establishment of the Bull Run water preserve. He was born in Brooklyn, Michigan and studied forestry at Yale. After graduate study, he went to Washington, D.C. to be Gifford Pinchot's first assistant. Sherrard died in Portland on Jan. 22, 1941. *See* the *Oregon Journal*, Jan. 22, 1941 and editorial comment the following day in the same paper.

Sherrill, LAKE. Elmer Sherrill was the first postmaster at Sherrill and the office bore his family name. Sherrill post office was established Sept. 17, 1914, and operated until June 29, 1918. It was situated about 15 miles southwest of Wagontire Mountain.

Sherwood, WASHINGTON. Sherwood was founded and laid out as Smockville by James C. Smock in 1889. The post office was established in that year with George B. Seely first postmaster. The name of the place was changed to Sherwood in the summer of 1891. The new name was adopted at a meeting of the citizens and was suggested by Robert Alexander. It is supposed he did so because he had formerly lived near Sherwood, Michigan, although there is a local tradition that the name was chosen in compliment to Sherwood Forest, England.

Shevlin, DESCHUTES, KLAMATH. From time to time Shevlin post office was in the news because of its mobility. It served loggers for The Shevlin-Hixon Company, and when logging was completed for a local area, the camp buildings were put on cars and moved to a new location. Most of the buildings were glorified trailers. When the compiler first knew the camp, it was about ten miles south of Lava Butte and two or three miles east of The Dalles-California Highway. It was later moved to a point about three miles southeast of La Pine. Both of these sites were in Deschutes County. The next move was to Summit Stage Station on the Fremont Highway in the very extreme east border of Klamath County. Shevlin post office was established in Deschutes County June 27, 1931, with William J. Baer first postmaster. It first appears on the Klamath County list in Sept. 1936. The office was discontinued Apr. 1, 1951, with business transferred to Chemult. For illustrated story about Shevlin, *see* the *Sunday Oregonian*, June 15, 1947, sect. 2.

Shevlin Park, DESCHUTES. This natural park along Tumalo Creek is west of Bend. The land comprising the park was given to the city of Bend by a deed dated Dec. 22, 1920, by The Shevlin-Hixon Company. The idea of setting this land aside for a park originated with T. A. McCann, then general manager of the company at Bend, who had witnessed the cutting over of an entire lumber district in the Midwest, and did not want to see the operation repeated. The park was dedicated to the memory of Thomas H. Shevlin, famous football player and former president of the lumber company.

Shiloh Basin, COLUMBIA. Shiloh Basin and Shiloh School are six miles north of Trenholm. The Columbia County Historical Society in *Columbia County History*, v. 2, 1963, p. 53, says the area was settled in the early 1880s by a number of Civil War veterans, some of whom had been present at the battle of Shiloh. It is said that J. P. Archibald was the first to use the name.

Shirk, HARNEY, LAKE. Members of the Shirk family were among the early settlers in Catlow Valley and for a time lived at the famous Home Creek Ranch. Shirk post office was established at or near this ranch Sept. 22, 1890, with Leonore Mott first postmaster. Frances M. Shirk, the wife of Dave Shirk, was appointed postmaster Aug. 31, 1892. The office was closed to Diamond May 31, 1902. Later some members of the family transferred their ranching operations to eastern Lake County, and Shirk post office was reestablished in that area Sept. 10, 1903, with Olive G. Shirk, a daughter of Dave and Frances, postmaster. The office was closed to Cedarville, California, May 5, 1905.

Shirttail Gulch, BAKER. Shirttail Gulch is north of Rye Valley. J. Tracy Barton, in *OHQ*, v. 43, p. 228, gives a glowing account of the origin of the name. In 1869, John Richardson, a rancher in Rye Valley, went foraging about five miles for a load of wood. He unhitched his team in a likely spot and began to assemble the load, when suddenly he was surprised by the singing of bullets from the guns of a band of rambling Snake Indians. Richardson abandoned his equipment and ran for home. His speed was so great that his shirttail fanned out behind him and even the jackrabbits were amazed. The place has since been called Shirttail Gulch.

Shitike Creek, JEFFERSON. This stream is in the south part of the Warm Springs Indian Reservation. It heads in a magnificent gorge cutting into the Cascade Range north of Jefferson Park. The stream is mentioned in the Pacific Railroad Surveys *Reports*, under date of 1855, as Chit-tike Creek, but the meaning of the name is not given. The Klamath Indians used the name *Sidaikti* to indicate the general locality of the Warm Springs Indian Reservation, and also the stream mentioned above. The compiler has been unable to get a satisfactory translation of the name. Indians indicate that it is a very old locality name.

Shivigny Mountain, DOUGLAS. Shivigny Mountain is a prominent summit with an elevation of 3782 feet in T 26S, R 2W. It is near the confluence of Emile Creek and Little River. Both the mountain and the creek were named for Emile Shivigny, a native of France, who settled nearby about 1875.

Shobe Creek, MORROW. Shobe Creek is south of Heppner. Allen J. Shobe was educated as a druggist in New Mexico and came to Heppner about 1873. He eventually bought the local drugstore and was universally known as "Doctor" Shobe while he prescribed IXL and other popular remedies of the times. Shobe died in Heppner in 1901 at the age of 81. Shobe Creek watercourse is called Shobe Canyon until just south of Heppner. Here it enters Donaldson Canyon but the name of the creek continues.

Shonquest Ranch, DESCHUTES. The name of this pioneer ranch on the old road south of Bend is frequently misspelled.

Shorter Creek, LANE. This is the shortest of four creeks in the H. J. Andrews Experimental Forest given descriptive names by the USFS. It is just north of Lookout Mountain north of McKenzie Bridge. *See also* Nostoc Creek.

Shortridge Butte, LANE. James Shortridge came to Oregon in 1851 and in 1853 with his wife, Amelia, settled on Coast Fork Willamette River near the present Cottage Grove Dam. The butte just to the east bears their name as does a park with an historical marker. Shortridge Creek near London School was named for James' brother, William Wallace Shortridge, who built a sawmill nearby about 1883 and took up a homestead. He was postmaster at the community which was then called Wallace. The form Short Ridge Creek for the creek is incorrect.

Shotgun Creek, CROOK. This creek rises on Drake Butte and flows north to Crooked River. Its name comes from Shotgun Spring in S 4, T 17S, R 20E, just west of the mouth of Drake Creek and north of the old county road. The mineral water from the spring is supposed to taste and smell like the residue of discharged black powder used in old shotguns. There are also East and West Shotgun springs but they are several miles south near the creek's headwaters.

Shotpouch Creek, BENTON, LINCOLN. According to Jerry E. Henkle, Benton County pioneer, Shotpouch Creek was named in 1856 when a party of Benton County settlers was exploring the Coast Range looking for grazing land. George Knowlton, a member of the party, lost a shotpouch near the stream, which was named on that account. This story was reported to the compiler in 1937 by Mark Phinny of Philomath, who interviewed Henkle about Benton County history. Shotpouch Creek flows northwest from Marys Peak.

Showalter Creek, LANE. This stream is in the Mohawk Valley west of Mabel. The creek bears the name of W. B. Showalter, who built a cabin on its banks in early days and operated as a hunter in the locality.

Shroyer Ridge, BENTON. This high ground between Marys and Tumtum rivers was named in 1969 in honor of Oliver J. Shroyer, local teacher and landowner. Shroyer lived there from 1910 until shortly before his death in 1961.

Shuck Mountain, COOS. Shuck Mountain, a ridge with a maximum elevation of nearly a thousand feet, lies southeast of Coquille in the big bend between Coquille River and North Fork Coquille River. The mountain was named for

Samuel Shuck, who came to Oregon in 1863 and settled in Coos County in 1872. *See* Dodge's *Pioneer History of Coos and Curry Counties*, supplement p. 90.

Shultz Creek, LANE. This tributary of Maple Creek west of Goodwin Peak is named for John Shultz who filed a homestead along it in 1891.

Shutler, GILLIAM. Shutler is a place in Alkali Canyon about eight miles south of Arlington. Shutler Flat is in the same locality. In Apr. 1947, Mark V. Weatherford of Albany wrote as follows: "Schuttler Flat was named for the Schuttler wagon. The first plowing was done on the flat by W. W. Weatherford and A. H. Weatherford in 1880, and the first crop was raised in 1881.... Most of the early settlers moved from Willow Creek to Schuttler Flat and this movement was coincident with the building of the railroad along the Columbia River. Most of them had been cattle men." Peter Schuttler, 1812–1865, a native of Germany, came to the United States in 1834. He learned wagonmaking, and tried several ventures in the business. Finally he established himself in Chicago and supplied many of his wagons to emigrants and gold seekers en route to Oregon and California. His wagon was lighter than the old prairie schooners and easier running. It commanded a premium over other makes, and was widely used in many parts of the west. The compiler does not know the reason for the discrepancy in spelling for the name used in Oregon, except that it was simpler. A post office called Shutlers was established June 5, 1914, with May Piper postmaster. It was apparently named for the nearby railroad station, also called Shutlers. In Nov. 1915, the name of the post office was changed to Shutler, and the office was discontinued Dec. 14, 1918. The name of the railroad station was changed to Shutler about the same time as the change in the post office name.

Shutter Arm, COOS. Shutter Arm, Shutter Landing and Shutter Creek are all on the south side of Tenmile Lake. They bear the name of John Shutter who filed for homestead near the mouth of the creek in 1901. Shutter failed to prove up but his name has prevailed.

Shy Creek, CURRY. Early road surveys show a crossing of this creek on the property of Henry Shigh just north of Brookings. Curry County probate records refer to him as "Henry Schaich, also known as Shy or Shigh."

Siah Butte, DESCHUTES. This butte southwest of Bend was named by the USFS with the Chinook jargon word for far or far off, indicating its more or less inaccessible position. The name should be pronounced as though spelled Si-ya with accent on the last syllable.

Siboco, LANE. Siboco was a station on the Southern Pacific Company railroad at the mouth of South Inlet on the south side of Siuslaw River about two miles south of Cushman. The name was made synthetically by taking parts of the name of Siuslaw Boom Company which operated in those parts.

Sickfoot Creek, WALLOWA. This stream is about 20 miles north of Wallowa. It was named for David Rochester, a clubfoot, who homesteaded along the creek.

The Indians named him Sickfoot. Sickfoot Creek drains into the Grande Ronde River in T 5N, R 42E.

Sidney, MARION. Sidney is a station on the Burlington Northern in Ankeny Bottom. J. M. Wallace started a flour mill at Sidney in pioneer days and is said to have named the place because of his wife's family name.

Sidwalter Buttes, WASCO. The Sidwalter Buttes lie on a northwest-southeast axis between Badger and Mill creeks in the south part of the county and near the west edge of the Warm Springs Indian Reservation. The maximum elevation of about 3600 feet is near the northwest end of the series. The buttes are named for an old Wasco Indian family of the vicinity. There are several spellings, including Sid Walter, Sidwalter, Sidwallo, Sidewalder and other styles. Sidwalter is the spelling used on the USGS map of the Sidwalter Butte quadrangle and reflects the general modern usage.

Signal Buttes, CLACKAMAS. Signal Buttes are near the head of Roaring River. T. H. Sherrard of the USFS told the compiler that the name was intended to be descriptive, because as far as he knew there never were any signals of any kind on these buttes. The pointed summits gave rise to the name.

Signal Buttes, CURRY. M. S. Brainard told the compiler that this descriptive name was applied because of early Indian activity and that remnants of fire pits were still visible.

Signal Hill, WASCO. Signal Hill is the rounded bluff one mile east of and overlooking the east abutment of The Dalles Dam. It was first named in 1956 in the USCE *Foundation Report on The Dalles Dam*. Since that time it has been the site of numerous radio and other electronic installations which make the name even more significant.

Silcox Hut, CLACKAMAS. Silcox Hut was the upper terminus of the "Magic Mile" ski lift on Mount Hood above Timberline Lodge. It was built in 1939 and named for Ferdinand A. Silcox, then chief of the USFS. Silcox was born in Georgia in 1882 and died in office on Dec. 20, 1939. Timberline Lodge was designed to attract skiers and other winter sport enthusiasts and the mile-long chairlift rising 1000 vertical feet attracted skiers from all over the west. Its exposed position caused operating difficulties and in 1962 it was replaced by a newer and faster lift. Silcox Hut was abandoned and partly vandalized. In 1985 it was placed on the National Register of Historic Places and a movement was started to rehabilitate the building for use as a hostel. By 1991 much work had been accomplished and it was expected to be open to the public in 1992.

Silent Creek, KLAMATH. This creek rises in the northeast corner of Crater Lake National Park and flows east to Beaver Marsh. R. A. Long of Fort Rock told the writer in 1969 that despite a fairly rapid current the stream was so quiet as to be a curiosity.

Siletz River, LINCOLN, POLK. The Siletz Indians were the southernmost Salishan tribe on the coast. The name now designates all the tribes on the former

Siletz Reservation: Athapascan, Yakonan, Kusan, Takilman, Shastan and Shahaptian linguistic families. The name had been called *Celeste, Neselitch, Sailetc*. Leo Frachtenberg, the philologist, in a letter to Professor Franz Boas from Siletz, Oregon dated Sept. 5, 1915, states that Rogue River Indians first applied the name *Silis* meaning black bear to what is now known as Siletz Lake. The Indians and the river took their name from the lake. There was for many years a Siletz Indian Agency in Oregon. For an editorial on the closing of this agency, *see* the *Oregonian*, Nov. 18, 1925. It is estimated there were 2000 Indians at Siletz Agency in 1867. The Siletz Reservation is described in the *Oregonian*, May 22, 1862, by Philip Ritz. For description of the Siletz Indians in 1869, see the *Oregonian*, Sept. 24, 1869, p. 3. A writer in the *Oregonian*, Feb. 2, 1877, p. 3, identifies the word with the French *celeste*. This theory is controverted by James W. Nesmith, Feb. 7, 1877, p. 2. The town of Valsetz was named for the Valley & Siletz Railroad.

Silica, GILLIAM. This station east of Arlington was named by the railroad company because of the presence of so much sand.

Silica Mountain, DOUGLAS. Silica Mountain is just south of the Lane County line on the headwaters of Mosby Creek. It was originally named Quartz Mountain but USFS ranger Fred Asam changed it to Silica about 1920 to avoid duplication with the more prominent Quartz Mountain near Little River. Much of the surface of western Oregon is covered with volcanic material and in some areas, usually associated with mining activity, the centers or sources of the volcanism are exposed. Because of the importance of early-day mining in local history, the author asked Hollis M. Dole, state geologist, for a few comments on this type of formation. He replied as follows: "Silica Mountain probably represents a center of volcanism to the early Tertiary volcanics of the Western Cascades. Due to uplift and erosion, these former sources of volcanism have been exposed and are represented by coarsely crystalline rocks. Silica Mountain is complex but its core is dacite porphyry. Altered rocks and highly siliceous rocks occur close by. The dacite may be related to the implacement of the larger nearby Bohemia Mountain intrusives and therefore also to the mineralization of that area."

Silk Creek, LANE. This stream flows into Coast Fork Willamette River at Cottage Grove, and according to Elbert Bede, was once known as Hazleton Creek. A letter by Frances E. Morss Baker in the Eugene *Register*, Apr. 17, 1929, says that a miner named Turpin returned from California, where he had been forced to take part of his wages in merchandise, which included enough handsome silk to make a dress. A woman living on the stream liked the silk so much that she traded a cow for it and the name Silk Creek had its origin in this swap. *Golden Was The Past*, the story of Cottage Grove, adds some additional information on p. 223. The woman was Mrs. Lewis Martin and her husband sold the cow to purchase the silk. They had to ford the creek on the way home. The creek was in flood, the wagon was jostled and the package of silk fell out and was lost.

Siltcoos Lake, DOUGLAS, LANE. Not much is known about the origin of this name, except, of course, that it is Indian. It is said to be the name of a local chief and also that it is an Indian family name. This version seems to be substantiated by an entry under Kuitsh, a small Yakonan tribe on the lower Umpqua River, in *Handbook of American Indians*, v. 1, p. 732, where the village *Tsiakhaus* is listed. The proximity of Coos Bay could easily produce a distortion in the name of the lake, although the Indians of the two regions were not related. The name was formerly spelled Tsiltcoos, but the USBGN adopted the shorter form. The lake is a fine body of water covering several square miles, and has an elevation of eight feet. Siltcoos River connects it with the Pacific Ocean.

Silver Butte, CURRY. Silver Butte is a small point close to the Oregon Coast Highway about two miles north of Port Orford. On June 1, 1946, Louis L. Knapp, of Port Orford, told the compiler an amusing story about the origin of the name, a story that was told him when he was a small boy. The butte was named in the very early days at a time when there was plenty of panning for gold on the black beach sands. Some enthusiast got the notion of starting a silver stampede to property that he owned or controlled. He melted up some small silver coins and poured the metal so that it would resemble silver grains. He used these to salt the property and then announced a discovery of silver-bearing ground. Wise prospectors soon exposed the scheme, but the name Silver Butte has remained attached to the feature to this day.

Silver Creek, HARNEY. Silver Creek heads in the northwest part of the county and flows southeast to Harney Lake. A little to the northwest of Harney Lake is Silver Lake, which at times receives water from Silver Creek. The compiler has not been able to get definite information about the origins of the names of these features, but is of the opinion that they are the result of mixed identity with Silvies River, an important stream just to the east. Early in July 1859, Captain H. D. Wallen, of the 4th Infantry, in charge of a military expedition, passed Silver Lake and called it Whatumpa Lake, but gave no explanation of the name. *See* 36th Congress, 1st Session, Senate Executive Document 34, which gives an account of this expedition. For early history of this area by Robert C. Clark, *see OHQ*, v. 33, p. 101. On June 23, 1878, the 12th Cavalry, commanded by Colonel Reuben Bernard and augmented by a force of local residents, including Pete French, surprised and drove off the large band of Paiute and Bannock Indians camped along Silver Creek. These were the Indians who had just raided the Harney Valley and killed George Smyth and his son. *See* Smyth Creek and Chickahominy Creek.

Silver Creek, JOSEPHINE. This stream is in the western part of the county. Walling, in *History of Southern Oregon*, p. 452, says the stream was named because of a pretended discovery of silver ore on its banks in 1879.

Silver Creek, MARION. Silver Creek was named in pioneer days, and the town of Silverton was named for the stream. There are two stories about the origin of the name. The first is to the effect that a traveler on horseback had some silver in his saddle bags and tried to ford the stream near where the town of Silverton now stands. His horse got into deep water and in the struggle that ensued the saddle pockets were lost, silver and all. The loss was not recovered, and as a result the stream was named Silver Creek. The second and more probable story is that the stream was named for James Smith, who was called "Silver" Smith because he brought a quantity of silver dollars into the locality, possibly a bushel of them. Smith and John Barger built a sawmill at Milford, two miles above Silverton, about 1846. Old-timers generally favor this version. A post office with the name Silver Creek was established in Marion County Nov. 16, 1854, with E. M. Waite postmaster. The compiler has not been able to get its location, but it was doubtless not far from the present site of Silverton.

Silver Creek Falls, MARION. These falls are about 15 miles southeast of Silverton, in Silver Creek Falls State Park. They constitute one of the important scenic attractions of Oregon and in ordinary times are visited by large numbers of sightseers. North and South Silver creeks join to form Silver Creek in the park, and the larger falls are on the two streams above the forks. In Apr. 1943, S. H. Boardman, state parks superintendent, had the heights of the falls accurately measured with the following results: North Falls, 136 feet; Winter Falls, 134 feet; Middle North Falls, 106 feet; Drake Falls, 27 feet; Double Falls, 178 feet; Lower North Falls, 30 feet; Lower South Falls, 93 feet; Twin Falls, 31 feet; South Falls, 177 feet. Below the junction of North and South Silver creeks are five small falls within the park, with the following heights; Crag Falls, 12 feet; Elbow Falls, 20 feet; Canyon Falls, 10 feet; Lisp Falls, 5 feet; Sunlight Falls, 5 feet. A community called Silver Falls City sprang up near these falls many years ago. The town was platted in 1888, with ambitious dimensions, but the enterprise folded up. *See* story by R. J. Hendricks, Salem *Statesman*, May 16, 1937.

Silver Falls, COOS. These falls are on Silver Creek, northeast of Allegany. They were named in contradistinction to Golden Falls nearby, in the belief that Golden Falls were named for the metal. According to information from S. B. Cathcart in 1929, Golden Falls were actually named for Dr. C. B. Golden, first Grand Chancellor of the Knights of Pythias of Oregon.

Silver King Mountain, MARION. This mountain, elevation 5238 feet, is in the north part of the county, north of Detroit. It was named for a mining claim nearby which was located by some Portland men.

Silver Lake, LAKE. Silver Lake is about six miles east of Silver Lake town. It formerly had an area of about 20 square miles, but is now quite dry. The lake apparently bears a descriptive name, but it is not known who first applied it. Residents of central Oregon attribute the name to John C. Fremont, but the compiler cannot find that Fremont had anything to do with it, and certainly did not see or name Silver Lake on his first trip into Oregon in 1843. The Klamath Indian name for Silver Lake was *Kalpshi*. This appears to have been derived from the word *kalapsh*, meaning a decayed log, and was used because of the presence of petrified wood near the lake.

Silver Lake, LAKE. Silver Lake post office was established on Dec. 9, 1875. It was first in the home of G. C. Duncan at a point considerably east of the present site of the town of Silver Lake. Duncan was the first postmaster. The office was discontinued in Mar. 1880, and reestablished in July 1882, at the ranch of C. P. Marshall one and one-half miles west of where the town now stands. The most important happening in the history of the community was a fire which occurred on Dec. 24, 1894, in which 43 people lost their lives in the burning of one building. *The Oregon Desert* by Jackman and Long, pp. 126–127 has an account of the tragedy and Ed O'Farrell's 100-mile ride to Lakeview for medical help. Silver Lake town was named for Silver Lake, six miles to the east. *See* that heading. Silver Lake town has an elevation of 4345 feet. For history of the community, *see Illustrated History of Central Oregon*, pp. 853–57.

Silver Point, CLATSOP. Silver Point is sometimes erroneously referred to as Sylvan Point. This small promontory on Cannon Beach was called Silver Point because of the characteristic color of the weathered spruce trees on its face. The land adjacent to the point was platted and recorded as Silver Point Cliff on Apr. 21, 1894. On Feb. 16, 1898, Sylvan Park was platted and recorded a half a mile north of Silver Point. In 1929 Rodney L. Glisan, long familiar with the geography of this part of Oregon, recommended that the name Silver Point be adopted, and this style was also favored by the compiler of these notes. On Dec. 4, 1929, the USBGN adopted the name Silver Point rather than Sylvan Point.

Silver Wells, CROOK. The compiler has had an inquiry for the history of the place called Silver Wells. A post office with this name was established on the Wasco County list Aug. 16, 1878, with Joseph J. Brown postmaster. The office was finally closed in 1881. It was on Camp Creek south of the east end of Maury Mountains. The name is intended to be descriptive, probably of the white sand near the wells.

Silverton, MARION. Silverton took its name from the fact that it is situated on Silver Creek. The early history of the community is given in Down's *A History of the Silverton Country*, p. 223. The first settlement was at a locality called Milford, where James Smith and John Barger established a sawmill about 1846. This was about two miles upstream from the present site of Silverton. Down says that the town of Silverton itself dates from 1854, but that the name did not come into use until the following year. Various milling and mercantile establishments along Silver Creek as far south as Milford were finally concentrated in Silverton, the other locations being abandoned. The name Bargerville was suggested for the new community in honor of John Barger, a nearby landowner. This was rejected because of confusion with Parkersville nearby. Mrs. T. R. Coon, a member of a pioneer Silverton family, wrote the compiler that Polly Crandall Coon Price actually selected the name of Silverton. She came to Oregon in 1852, following her husband, T. L. Coon, who had arrived shortly before. Her husband died on Jan. 10, 1854, before securing title to his donation land claim. Mrs. Coon remained on the land and secured the title and sold town lots, naming the place Silverton. This was probably in the fall of 1854 or early in 1855, as the Silverton post office was established July 16, 1855, with Charles Miller postmaster. Mrs. Coon married Stephen Price in Sept. 1855.

Silvies River, GRANT, HARNEY. Silvies River was named for Antoine Sylvaille, who, with a party of trappers, was sent into central Oregon by Peter Skene Ogden in 1826. *See OHQ*, v. 10, p. 354, and v. 11, p. 202. Sylvaille, on his return from central Oregon, reported finding a stream very rich with beaver, to which the name Sylvailles River was at once given. The Arrowsmith maps published between 1830 and 1850 showed the stream as Sylvailles River. In the Ogden journals, under date of Oct. 8, 1826, mention is made of the fact that Sylvaille discovered this river. On Nov. 1, Ogden mentions the river as flowing into a lake, now known as Malheur Lake. Dr. Robert C. Clark, in *OHQ*, v. 33, p. 113, says that the party under Major Enoch Steen, 1860, named this stream Cricket River, because of the swarms of insects. That name did not supplant the older name, Sylvailles River, or its anglicized form, Silvies River, which had been in general use for many years. Silvies post office was established near this stream in the extreme north part of Harney County in Feb. 1892, with Adelaide Cross first postmaster. The office was closed in July 1906, but was reestablished in 1915 in the south part of Grant County. It was not in operation in 1980.

Simax Bay, KLAMATH. This bay is at the northern end of Crescent Lake. It is reported that the word *simax* is an Indian expression meaning landing place. The compiler has been unable to find the word in the Klamath Indian language, or any other language for that matter.

Simmons Creek, TILLAMOOK. Homer Simmons of Tillamook informed the writer in 1968 that this creek five miles south of Tillamook was named for his grandfather, Leonard Simmons, who came to Oregon from Indiana in 1865 and settled along its banks in the 1870s.

Simmons Draw, WALLOWA. Simmons Draw is east of Maxville. It was formerly known as Deadhorse Draw because a horse was drowned therein.

Simnasho, WASCO. This was a post office on the Warm Springs Indian Reservation. Pierce Mays is authority for the information that the original Indian word was pronounced as though spelled *Sini-massa*. Warm Springs Indians have corroborated this and inform the compiler that the word means thorn bush.

Sinamox, WASCO. A station on the Burlington Northern named with the Chinook jargon word for seven, since originally it was the seventh station from the north end of the line up Deschutes River. Sinamox post office was established Jan. 2, 1914. The office was closed Dec. 31, 1914, with papers to Moody.

Sink, LAKE. Sink post office, in the extreme north part of the county, took its name because it was near the sink of Peters Creek. It was established in Apr. 1911, and operated until Aug. 1920. Anna M. Long was the first postmaster.

Sink, SHERMAN. Sink railroad station was named for George P. Sink who was born in Illinois June 2, 1847, and came west in 1876. He took up a homestead in Spanish Hollow in 1882.

Sinker Mountain, LANE. Sinker Mountain, elevation 4752 feet, is the highest point on Alpine Ridge between Christy Creek and Fall Creek. George H. Kelly of Portland told the compiler that the peak received its name as the result of a camping experience of some hunters who were forced to eat biscuits made with soda, popularly known as sinkers. A. J. Briem in his notes on file at the Oregon Historical Society, p. 37, says the men were Jack and John Hills.

Sinnott, MORROW. Sinnott post office was established in the southwest corner of the county, on one of the headwaters of Rock Creek, and about six miles south of Hardman, on Apr. 29, 1916. Scott H. Osborn was the first postmaster. Sinnott post office was discontinued effective Feb. 28, 1918. Sinnott was named in compliment to Nicholas Sinnott of The Dalles, a representative in Congress from Oregon from 1913 to 1928, who doubtless assisted in getting the post office established. N. J. Sinnott was one of Oregon's most esteemed citizens. He was born at The Dalles Dec. 6, 1870, and was graduated from the University of Notre Dame in 1892. He was admitted to the bar and practiced law at The Dalles. He was a member of the Oregon State Senate in 1909 and 1911. His service in Congress at Washington was brought to a close by an appointment to the United States Court of Claims. However, his term on the court was cut short by his death on July 20, 1929.

Sisi Butte, CLACKAMAS. Sisi Butte, elevation 5614 feet, is a prominent point in the Cascade Range in the southern part of the county, just west of Lemiti Butte. *Sisi* is the Chinook jargon word for blanket or cloth. Gibbs gives the form *pa' seesie,* but it is the same word. In 1927, Dee Wright, who was a walking encyclopedia about Cascade Range place names, told the compiler that he had never been able to get a good explanation as to why the name was applied to Sisi Butte, although Indians told him that it was correct.

Siskiyou, JACKSON. The name Siskiyou as applied to a post office did not appear until Apr. 1895, well over a half a century after Hudson's Bay Company trappers had named the pass through the Siskiyou Mountains. The compiler does not know the exact location of the first Siskiyou post office, which was in charge of Alice E. Ager, but for many years this office was near the Southern Pacific Company station Siskiyou at the northeast end of the Siskiyou tunnel and very close to I-5. This post office was closed Oct. 31, 1932. The compiler has been asked about where the golden spike was driven on completion of the Siskiyou line of the Southern Pacific Company. In Mar. 1947, G. H. Kilborn, superintendent of the Southern Pacific Company's Shasta Division at Dunsmuir had a search made of the old records and reported that the golden spike was driven on Dec. 17, 1887, at about 5:04 P.M. on the east side of the track at the south end of the Ashland yard at mileage 428:8. The spike was driven at survey station 1154 + 05. The driving of this spike completed the Siskiyou line of the Southern Pacific.

Siskiyou Mountains, JACKSON, JOSEPHINE. George Gibbs, in his *Dictionary of the Chinook Jargon*, 1863, gives the following version of the origin of this name: "Siskiyou. Cree. *A bobtailed horse.* This name, ludicrously enough, has been bestowed on the range of mountains separating Oregon and California, and also on a county in the latter state. The origin of this designation, as related to me by Mr. Anderson, was as follows: Mr. Archibald R. McLeod, a chief factor of the Hudson's Bay Company, in the year 1828, while crossing the mountains with a pack train, was overtaken by a snow storm, in which he lost most of his animals, including a noted bob-tailed race horse. His Canadian followers, in compliment to their chief, or 'bourgeois,' named the place the Pass of the Siskiyou, an appellation subsequently adopted as the veritable Indian name of the locality, and which thence extended to the whole range, and the adjoining district." Alexander C. Anderson was connected with the Hudson's Bay Company. On p. 598 of Lacombe's Cree dictionary, Montreal, 1874, published in French, is the Cree word *sisikiyawatim*, which refers to a spotted horse or possibly a packhorse. The obvious similarity between the first part of this word and the word *Siskiyou* is too great to need comment. The compiler feels that when Gibbs attributed Siskiyou to the Cree, he was on firm ground. The story that the name Siskiyou comes from the French *six cailloux*, meaning six stones, has always seemed fanciful to the compiler. It is alleged that the six stones were used in fording various streams, but there are several versions of the story, and none is well authenticated. They cover too much territory and are very indefinite. Professor A. L. Kroeber of the University of California said of this etymology: "(it) looks too much like a typical case of folk-etymology to engender much confidence. The usual assumption of an Indian origin, though not necessarily from a tribal name, is more credible." The Siskiyou Mountains are part of what geologists call the Klamath Mountains, which lie as a connecting uplift between the Coast Range and the Cascade Range. Joseph S. Diller, in his *Topographic Development of the Klamath Mountains*, USGS Bulletin 196, gives an interesting description of the geography and geology of this part of Oregon. Attention is called to the fact that there is some confusion about the given name of the McLeod, referred to by Gibbs. Presumably this is the same person generally mentioned as Alexander R. McCleod, for whom McCloud River in northern California is said to have been named.

Sisters, DESCHUTES. Sisters is just east of the summit of the Cascade Range, and is named for the imposing nearby peaks, the Three Sisters. There was previously a post office at Camp Polk, about three miles away, and in 1888 it was found advisable to move the office. As a result of the move, the name was changed, as Camp Polk was no longer significant. It is said that Jacob N. Quilberg selected the new name, and John J. Smith was the first postmaster in the new office. The townsite plat was filed for the record July 15, 1901, by Alex and Robert Smith. For a news story about the fortieth anniversary of the town of Sisters, *see* Bend *Bulletin*, Sept. 24, 1941.

Sitkum, COOS. About 1873, J. A. Harry established a tavern or roadhouse about half way between Roseburg and what was known as Coos City. As a result of a competitor putting up another halfway house nearby, a new name was selected, Sitkum, which is the Chinook jargon word for half. The post office got its name from the name of the tavern. It was established on May 9, 1873, with Wm. H. Flook first postmaster.

Sitkum Creek, LANE. Sitkum Creek flows into Salmon Creek from the north about 11 miles east of Oakridge. *Sitkum* is the Chinook jargon word for half, and in this case means that the stream is rather piddling.

Siuslaw River, LANE. Siuslaw was the Indian name of a locality, tribe or chief, and has become the name of a river in western Oregon. The Siuslaws are classed as a Yakonan tribe. The first mention of the name that the compiler has seen is by Lewis and Clark, in *History of the Expedition*, Biddle edition, v. 2, p. 118, where it is given as *Shiastuckle*. Alexander R. McCleod in his journal of 1828 gives *Saoustla*; Samuel Parker in his *Journal of an Exploring Tour* gives *Saliutla*; Hale gives *Saiustla* in Wilkes' *U. S. Exploring Expedition*, v. 6, p. 221. The name has many other variations. *See Handbook of American Indians*, v. 2, p. 584. The forms Linslaw and Linslow are probably due to misreading of poor handwriting, mistaking S and u for L and n. A post office with the name Siuselaw was established Apr. 23, 1852, with James Heatherby postmaster. Henry Coleman became postmaster June 1, 1854. Preston's *Map of Oregon*, 1856, shows this office at a point five miles north of the present site of Lorane, but with the spelling Siuslaw. Postal records of later dates show an office called Siuslaw, but the compiler does not know when the spelling of the name was changed. *See also* Linslaw and Lorane.

Sixes River, CURRY. Sixes River is an important stream flowing into the Pacific Ocean just north of Cape Blanco, and draining a considerable part of northern Curry County. L. B. Spurgeon, postmaster at Sixes office in 1926, wrote that it was named for a local Indian chief. George Davidson, in the *Coast Pilot* for 1869, has a different history of the name, and says that in 1851 it was usually called Sikhs River, the Chinook jargon word for friend. On some maps he found the name of a stream in that locality shown as Sequalchin River. The Indian village on Sikhs River was known as *Te-cheh-kutt*. Captain Wm. Tichenor, in *Pioneer History of Coos and Curry Counties*, p. 26, says the Indian name of Sixes River was *Sa-qua-mi*. *Handbook of American Indians*, v. 1, p. 746, under the heading Kwatami, a subdivision of the Tututni, lists a number of alternative forms of the tribe name. One of these forms, *Sik-ses-tene*, is said to mean "people by the far north country." This is probably the real origin of the name, but the form of spelling, Sixes, was doubtless applied during the southern Oregon gold rush by miners who were familiar with the Chinook jargon word for friend. The spelling Sixes was used as early as Oct. 1855. *See Harper's Magazine*, Oct. 1856, p. 591.

Sixmile Canyon, MORROW. This canyon, opening onto Columbia River, was named on the assumption it was six miles east of the mouth of Willow Creek.

Sixmile Creek, GILLIAM. This stream flows into Rock Creek east of Condon. The headwaters average about six miles from Condon and the stream is said to have been named on that account.

Sixteen Butte, LAKE. Sixteen Butte was named by W. O. Harriman of the USFS, because the butte was largely in s 16, T 23S, R 15E.

Skeeters Flat, JACKSON. Skeeters Flat is southeast of Butte Falls some eight or ten miles and Skeeters Creek is nearby. These two geographic features were named for Isaac Skeeters, who was one of the first white settlers in the vicinity and operated a rived shingle camp. Skeeters was one of the party that discovered Crater Lake on June 12, 1853. The name Skeeter Flat is wrong, as the etymology has nothing to do with the unpopular insect. The USFS maintained a guard station at this point called Mosquito Guard Station which seems to carry dignity a little too far.

Skeleton Cave, DESCHUTES. Skeleton Cave, three miles north of Arnold Ice Cave on the Deschutes Plateau, was named for the accumulation of fossil and modern bones that were found in a natural sink near its mouth. Phil Brogan has an interesting article about this cave in the *Oregonian*, Jan. 1, 1956.

Skell Head, KLAMATH. A point on the east shore of Crater Lake named by Will G. Steel in 1908 for a Klamath Indian deity of the plains, represented by the marten.

Skelley, DOUGLAS. *See* Kelleher.

Skinner Butte, LANE. This butte is between the main business section of Eugene and the Willamette River and has an elevation of 681 feet. It was named for Eugene F. Skinner, who settled at its foot in 1846. For references to Eugene F. Skinner and his family, *see* Eugene. The University of Oregon at one time maintained an observatory near the east end of the top of this butte. The Indian name was reported to be *Yapoah*.

Skinner Dam, MALHEUR. Skinner Dam near Danner is named for Silas Skinner who was one of the original settlers at Jordan Valley in 1864. He operated the road from the mines to Boise and was a prominent citizen.

Skipanon River, CLATSOP. Lewis and Clark called this stream Skipanarwin Creek on their charts, and for a century most maps used that form and Skeppernawin Creek. These spellings did not lend themselves to easy use, and for many years the stream has been locally known as Skipanon, a fact that the USBGN finally took notice of, and included in a decision: Skipanon Creek. Subsequently (Apr. 1, 1925) the decision was changed to Skipanon River, which fits the universal Oregon use. Preston's map of 1856 uses the form Skippenon Cr. There was a station named Skipanon on the railroad south of Warrenton. Skipanon was originally known as Lexington. Lexington was surveyed in 1848 by W. Hall and the plat recorded Apr. 19, 1854. It was part of the Jeremiah G. Fuller donation land claim. The place was also known as Upper Landing. Silas B. Smith is authority for the statement that the Clatsop Indian name *Skippernawin* referred to a point at the mouth of the stream rather than to the stream itself, *OHQ*, v. 1, p. 321. *See* Warrenton. Lexington post office was established Nov. 28, 1850, with David E. Pease first postmaster. It was discontinued Feb. 24, 1853. It was in operation again with other postmasters from Apr. 1856, to Sept. 1857. Skipanon post office was in service from Aug. 1871, to Apr. 1903.

Skiphorton Creek, UMATILLA. Kirk Casper of Walla Walla wrote the compiler in 1975 regarding this tributary of South Fork Walla Walla River. He said that supposedly well before 1900, a man named Horton came to Milton and built a cabin near the mouth of this creek. Word came to the sheriff that Horton was wanted for murder but before the law caught up with him, he fled the country. The sheriff returned empty handed to report that Horton had skipped so the creek became known as Skiphorton.

Skookum Lake, CLACKAMAS. This small lake on the north slope of Thunder Mountain drains into Fish Creek, a tributary of Clackamas River. It is named with the Chinook jargon word which originally meant a strong or powerful malign deity, and later came to mean simply strong or stout. When used in connection with localities, the word *skookum* generally indicated a place inhabited by a *skookum*, or evil god of the woods. It sometimes meant a place used as a burial ground. There are several geographic features in Oregon described with this name. Indians avoided skookum places and considered them haunted. A *skookum chuck* did not mean a strong, swift stream, but a place to stay away from. The modern meaning of the word *skookum* is quite different from the earlier connotation. In contradistinction to a skookum, a *hehe* was a good spirit and a *hehe chuck* was a fine place for games, races and other sports and festivities.

Skookum Rock, CROOK. This is a large rock rising vertically from Trout Creek near its headwaters east of Bull Mountain. For the meaning of *skookum*, *see* Skookum Lake. In this instance, the name was introduced by whites and refers not to the original Indian meaning but to the "big" or "strong" corruption.

Skookumhouse Butte, CURRY. Indians near the mouth of Rogue River built a fort or stockade on the south bank of the stream about 15 miles from the ocean. It was named with the Chinook jargon word *skookum* for stout or strong, and the name has been applied to various geographic features nearby. White settlers drove the Indians out and took the fort. *See* Port Orford *News*, Dec. 14, 1926. Skookumhouse was also a word used by early settlers to describe a jail.

Skull Spring, MALHEUR. Skull Spring was so called long before the post office was established. The compiler was told many years ago that the name was applied because the bleached skull of a melancholy steer lay near a useful spring. Skullspring post office was established June 13, 1902, with Anna G. Riley first postmaster. The office was finally closed in Oct. 1927. It was in the high country about 20 miles east-southeast of Riverside, possibly not always in the same location. The name of the post office was in one word.

Skunk Creek, JOSEPHINE. It is surprising how many people have the notion that a geographic feature may be made more attractive by changing its name. Every now and again someone wants to change the name of Skunk Creek, which is an agreeable brook flowing through the city of Grants Pass. Up till now champions of the old name seem to have had the best of the argument. If the compiler lived on Skunk Creek he would be glad of the publicity and would print a picture of the little black and white animal on his letterpaper. The skunk is independent, brave and capable. It produces, among other things, a fine fur that can be made into coats for women who don't object to the name skunk. There are several varieties of skunk in Oregon, all of which are ably described in Vernon Bailey's *Mammals and Life Zones of Oregon*, beginning on p. 308. The skunk is an animal of distinction.

Slagle Creek, JACKSON, JOSEPHINE. Slagle Creek is a tributary of Applegate River about ten miles southeast of Grants Pass. It was named for Conrad Slagle, a pioneer settler. A letter by Logan Wooldridge, of Murphy, Oregon, printed in the Grants Pass *Bulletin*, June 4, 1937, says that Slagle was born in Tennessee and came across the plains to Oregon in 1852. He first settled in Lane County, but sold out and went to Jackson County in 1858, where he took up a claim on the creek which now bears his name. He died many years ago and was buried in the Sparlin cemetery on Williams Creek.

Slater, UNION. Slater was a post office with an unusually short life. It was situated in the Grande Ronde Valley, probably near the middle of T 2S, R 39E, on the old stage road from Union to Summerville. The post office was established June 9, 1881, with Stowell L. Payne first and only postmaster. The office was discontinued Jan. 31, 1882, and the business turned over to Summerville. The office was at or near the site of an older office, Sand Ridge. *See* that heading. At the time the post office was established James H. Slater of Union County was United States senator from Oregon and it was doubtless named in his honor.

Sled Springs, WALLOWA. These springs in T 3N, R 44E were named in the 1880s for a broken sled that lay nearby for many years. The sled belonged to Ed Renfrew who, with James Alford and Alford's family, tried to cross the Blue Mountains in the middle of winter. The trip was completed safely but the snow was so deep the party was compelled to abandon the sled. For an interesting history of the people involved, *see* the Wallowa County *Chieftan*, Thursday, Oct. 29, 1959.

Sleepy Creek, WALLOWA. This is a tributary of Lightning Creek. It was named by James and Charles Rice, Fred Gaylord and Len Snell, who had a camp there, and since the sun did not fall on the camp until late in the morning they lay abed and snoozed.

Slick Creek, DOUGLAS. This creek flows into Boulder Creek in S 1, T 29S, R 1W. Grover Blake, who tried unsuccessfully to ride a horse down the creek in the 1930s, told the writer in 1968 that it was named for its slippery bed.

Slick Rock Creek, LINCOLN. Elmer Calkins of Otis told the compiler that in the early days there were seven important fords on the trail down Salmon River. The last of these was at Slick Rock Creek and was so named because the smooth, mossy rock of the streambed was a bad spot for horses.

Slide Mountain, CLACKAMAS. Slide Mountain is in the northeast part of the county and was named because of a large landslide on the southwest shoulder.

Sloan Creek, TILLAMOOK. This tributary of Neskowin Creek was named for John S. Sloan who patented land nearby in 1901.

Slough, MULTNOMAH. Slough post office was one of the earliest in what is now Multnomah County, and was put in service just about a year after the Portland office was established. Slough post office was established Nov. 25, 1850, with John Switzler first postmaster, and was in operation until Jan. 6, 1852. It was near what was then called Oregon Slough on the south bank of the Columbia River. Oregon Slough is now North Portland Harbor. John Switzler was an early settler in that area.

Sluice Creek, WALLOWA. This stream heads near Hat Point and flows into Snake River. It was named by Alex Warnock because a miner named Corby sluiced for gold there in the early days.

Slusher Canyon, UMATILLA. This canyon empties into Butter Creek south of Echo. It was named for William M. Slusher who settled north of Vinson in the 1890s. Slusher was one of the early members of the Umatilla Wool Growers.

Sly, DESCHUTES. A post office with the name Sly was established on the Crook County list as of Jan. 17, 1900, with G. Sly first postmaster. The order was rescinded May 12, 1900, and the office was never put in operation. George Sly had a place in the extreme south part of what is now Deschutes County, and the Sly office would have been about four miles south of La Pine, on Long Prairie within a few hundred feet of the Klamath County line.

Smith, HARNEY. Smith post office in Harney County was near the stream known as Smyth Creek. Smith was the correct spelling of the post office, which was established Mar. 2, 1895 with Ida C. Smith first postmaster. The creek was named for D. H. Smyth, but the post office was named for another family. The office was closed Oct. 31, 1913, with mail to Diamond.

Smith Canyon, DESCHUTES. This canyon five miles north of Millican was named for several members of the Smith family who settled there in 1919. The father, John A. Smith, built a fine home that was a local showplace but it was a dry homestead and hauling water during the arid years after World War I was too great a problem. Vandals have since largely destroyed another early landmark.

Smith Creek, DOUGLAS. This stream is tributary to Cow Creek north of the old Southern Pacific railroad station called Peck. In the 1880s, William O. Smith patented government land at its mouth.

Smith Creek, MULTNOMAH. Smith Creek flows into Sandy River south of Springdale. It was named for Fred Smith, a native of London, England. Smith came to Oregon in the 1860s and settled along Smith Creek in 1879 where he later developed one of the early prune orchards. He died on Feb. 28. 1927.

Smith Creek, TILLAMOOK. This stream flows into Nestucca River from the north at Cloverdale. It is named for Lester P. Smith who settled there in the 1890s. On early maps it was called Sanders Creek but this is incorrect. *See* Sanders Creek.

Smith Falls, LANE. These falls are on Champion Creek about two miles north of Fairview Peak. There is a story that one "Bohemia" Smith, the discoverer of the Twin Rocks Mine, was on his way home from Lund Park one evening with a substantial internal load of liquid refreshment. He stepped off the trail, fell over a cliff and landed in a small tree, unharmed. When found, he was singing merrily and holding his empty jug, undamaged.

Smith Hill, BENTON. Smith Hill is southeast of Airlie. It was named for Green Berry Smith, a prominent pioneer settler of the county. Smith, who was frequently called Greenberry Smith, was born in Grayson County, Virginia, in 1820 and came to Oregon in 1845 with the Meek party. He settled in Benton County in 1846 on a claim near the butte that now bears his name. *See* land certificate 2322. He later moved to a farm south of Corvallis and then to Corvallis. For biography, *see History of Benton County*, p. 526. *See also* Greenberry.

Smith Hill Summit, JOSEPHINE. Smith Hill Summit, elevation 1730 feet, is the pass on I-5 between Wolf Creek and Sunny Valley. It takes its name from Henry Smith who came to Josephine County in 1858 and took up land at Wolf Creek in 1872. Smith was a prominent local citizen. Smith Hill is not identified on current maps so the name may have been applied either to the high ground east of the highway or to the grade on the old stage road where it ascended 500 feet from Wolf Creek to the pass. The historic Wolf Creek Tavern, restored in 1979 by the Oregon State Parks Department and now operated under their supervision, is built on land originally owned by Henry Smith.

Smith Hollow, WHEELER. Smith Hollow five miles east of Waterman was named for Leander R. Smith who bought government land there in 1885.

Smith Lake, CLATSOP. Smith Lake is at the north end of Clatsop Plains, west of the Oregon Coast Highway and a short distance south of Skipanon. It was named for Solomon Howard Smith, one of the early American settlers in Oregon. Solomon H. Smith was employed by Dr. McLoughlin to teach school at Fort Vancouver in 1832, a few weeks after John Ball had quit schoolteaching there. He settled near the mouth of Chehalem Creek, and afterwards at Clatsop Plains. Ball was a member of Wyeth's first party and returned to the East in 1834. Smith taught school, also, at French Prairie, near the home of Joseph Gervais. Smith was one of the organizers of the provisional government in 1843. He died at Skipanon June 19, 1891. For biographical narrative, *see* OPA *Transactions*, 1887, pp. 81–89. The name of Smith Lake was *O-mo-pah*. *See OHQ*, v. 1, p. 322.

Smith Point, CLATSOP. Smith Point is at the western extremity of Astoria, and was named for Samuel C. Smith, who took up a donation land claim that included the point. The Indian name for this point was *O-wa-pun-pun*. See *OHQ*, v. 1, p. 321. Vancouver's expedition named it Point George, for George III of England. Wilkes charted this with the name Youngs Point. *See* the atlas for *U. S. Exploring Expedition*, v. 23, Hydrography.

Smith Ridge, DOUGLAS. This ridge south of Red Butte was named for William C. Smith, an early USFS employee and native of the area.

Smith River, DOUGLAS. Smith River is a large tributary of Umpqua River, into which it flows at a point opposite Reedsport. It was named for Jedediah Strong Smith, a western fur trader and explorer, who was born in the Mohawk Valley, New York, June 24, 1798, and was killed by Comanche Indians in the summer of 1831 while on the way from St. Louis to Sante Fe. When he was 13 years old Smith obtained a position on a freight boat on the Great Lakes, and when he was about 18 he was in St. Louis, attracted by the fur trade. In 1826 Smith started from St. Louis with William Henry Ashley on the first stage of what was to be the first journey of a white man from the Mississippi to the Pacific Ocean over the midland route. He traveled to southern California by way of Great Salt Lake, then returned to Utah and in 1828 started for northern California and southern Oregon. His party made its way up the Pacific Coast, and reached the Umpqua River, which was crossed very close to the mouth early on July 12, 1828. The party then made its way up the west and the north side of the river until the evening of July 13, where camp was pitched on the north bank just west of the mouth of what is now Smith River. Gordon's land office survey of 1857 gives the location as about a quarter of a mile west of the east line of S 26, T 21S, R 12W, or about the same distance southwest of what is now East Gardiner or Gardiner Junction on the Southern Pacific railroad. On the morning of Monday, July 14, Indians attacked the party, while Smith and two companions were away from camp. Arthur Black was the only man who escaped from the camp. He made his way north to Tillamook, thence to Fort Vancouver. Smith and his two companions escaped toward Willamette Valley. Fifteen men were killed. These figures are from the account by R. C. Clark, *OHQ*, v. 38, p. 115. Through the aid of Dr. John McLoughlin, Smith's furs were recovered and the dead were buried. Smith eventually returned to St. Louis and continued in the fur trade until his death. He was a devout Christian, and a reliable geographer, and entitled to great credit for his explorations. For details of his life, *see The Ashley-Smith Explorations* by Harrison C. Dale; *The Travels of Jedediah Smith* by Maurice S. Sullivan and *Jedediah Smith, Trader and Trail Breaker*, also by Sullivan. The main tributary of Smith River is North Fork Smith River, not West Fork. A tributary of North Fork is known as West Branch. There is another Pacific Coast stream named Smith River, for Jedediah Smith. It is in northern California. The north fork of this stream rises in southern Oregon, so that there are two North Forks Smith River in this state, but not two Smith rivers, named for Jedediah Smith.

Smith Rock, DESCHUTES. This interesting formation is in the extreme north-

east corner of the county. Here Crooked River is forced by geologically recent lavas on the west bank to undercut Clarno ash and tuff formations on the east. Ellen Morris Bishop has an interesting column on the geology of the area in the Oregonian, June 22, 1989, p. F3. The name Smith Rock is strictly applied to the 3200-foot ridge in the southwest end of the large bend in the river. However, Smith Rock State Park, acquired in 1960, now includes most of the land west of North Unit Main Canal. A small day park site has been established south and west of Crooked River but the more inaccessible rock formations on the opposite bank are frequented by mountaineers who find rock climbs of every degree of difficulty. There is a popular story that the name comes from one Smith, a soldier who in the 1860s fell to his death while his company was camped nearby. However, a letter in the Albany *States Rights Democrat,* Aug. 10, 1867, signed "Ochoco" describes a trip made in July 1867 over Santiam Pass to what is now the Prineville area. The five travelers, Captain J. A. White, Jackey Settle, W. S. Elkins, John Smelser and W. Usher, described Smith's Rocks and state specifically that they were named for their discoverer, John Smith, then sheriff of Linn County. "Ochoco" describes the 4200-foot-high point east of the present irrigation canal rather than the lower ridge but it is this high ground along with Gray Butte that is visible from the north and west. John Smith was born in Kentucky and came to Oregon in 1852. He settled in Linn County where he was sheriff from 1855 to 1859 and then representative in the 1862 legislature. He was appointed Indian agent at Warm Springs Indian Agency and occupied that position with one short exception from 1866 until just before his death in 1886.

Smith Springs, DOUGLAS. In 1889 Owen E. Smith took up a homestead on North Umpqua River east of Glide at the springs that now bear his name.

Smith Well, DESCHUTES. Smith Well is on the south edge of Millican Valley. It was named for Levi Smith who homesteaded the land in 1913.

Smithfield, LANE. Daniel Smith came to Oregon in 1852 and shortly thereafter settled in Lane County on the Territorial Road southwest of what is now Junction City. In 1857 R. V. Howard built a store in the vicinity and began to call the place Smithfield. In the meantime Franklin post office had been established in the same general locality. This has resulted in a controversy about the names Franklin and Smithfield that has at times been acute. For a history of the business, *see* Franklin-Smithfield.

Smithfield, POLK. Smithfield, formerly a railroad station about five miles northeast of Dallas, bears the name of Absalom Smith, a pioneer settler. Smithfield post office was established July 28, 1893, with Ira Kimball postmaster, but the railroad station was in service before that date. The compiler cannot tell when the post office was closed, but it was before Mar. 1900. The railroad through this place was originally the narrow gauge line of the Oregonian Railway Company, later standardized by the Southern Pacific Company. The track has been removed and the site is now mostly farmland.

Smock Prairie, WASCO. Smock Prairie is southwest of Wamic. McNeal in *History of Wasco County*, p. 247, says Smock was named for the Smock family and was a much older community than nearby Wamic. Smock post office was established Oct. 28, 1899 with Elizabeth Ledford first postmaster. The office was closed May 31, 1909, and the name is remembered only by the prairie.

Smoky Creek, GRANT. J. E. Snow of Dayville told the writer that this stream probably received its name because of mist and fog that collects against the mountain where it heads.

Smuggler Cove, TILLAMOOK. This snug little harbor is between Cape Falcon and Neahkahnie Mountain, and its shore has been called Short Sand Beach for many years. It is not a landing place, but fish boats sometimes anchor there in rough weather. The name Smuggler Cove is purely romantic as there is nothing to indicate that smugglers ever used the place. *See also* Treasure Cove.

Smyth Creek, HARNEY. Smyth Creek was named for George C. Smyth and his family. Smyth came to the Harney Valley in 1873 with his four sons. He and his son, John Smyth, were killed by Indians at Happy Valley in June 1878. His second son, Darius Hynson Smyth, nicknamed "Rye," was born in Lincoln County, Missouri, Oct. 29, 1844, and came to Oregon in 1853. He spent nearly 20 years in Lane County, but also roamed in Nevada and California. He settled in Harney County in 1872 and established himself in Happy Valley in the winter of 1873–74. He was a prominent resident for many years. For reminiscences of D. H. Smyth, *see OHQ*, v. 33, p. 125. He died at his home in Happy Valley, May 13, 1942.

Snake River, BAKER, MALHEUR, WALLOWA. Snake River forms the north part of the eastern boundary of Oregon. Its name comes from the Snake Indians (Shoshones and Paiutes). The Lewis and Clark journals called the Indians *Choshonnes* and *Sosonees*. The name Snake came out of the fur trade period. Alexander Ross, in *Fur Hunters of the Far West*, v. 1, p. 275, comments on the facility of these Indians in concealing themselves, and adds: "They are very appropriately named Snakes." De Smet said the Indians were called Snakes because of their poverty, and necessity of digging in the ground for food. *See* Chittenden and Richardson's *Life, Letters and Travels of Father De Smet*, p. 217; also *OHQ*, v. 20, p. 3, "The Snake River in History," by Miles Cannon. The habitat of these Indians was extremely barren, and their eating habits were repulsive to the early writers. Snake River has had various names: Lewis, for the explorer; *Shoshone, Nez Perce, Sahaptin, Kimeonim*. Captain William Clark named the river Louis, or Lewis, when a few miles below the confluence of the Salmon and Lemhi rivers. *See* Thwaites' *Original Journals of the Lewis and Clark Expedition*, v. 3, p. 10. For editorial by Harvey W. Scott on the name of Snake River, *see* Scott's *History of the Oregon Country*, v. 2, p. 209. For notes by Leslie M. Scott and comments by T. C. Elliott of Walla Walla about the application of the name Lewis River and other references, *ibid.*, p. 324, *et seq.*

Sneddon Creek, COOS. Charles Sneddon came to Coos County in 1861 and patented land east of Libby where his claim included this creek. The form Snedden is incorrect.

Snell Creek, WALLOWA. Snell Creek was named for George Snell, a nearby rancher. This stream is in T 1S, R 48E.

Snell Lake, KLAMATH. This lake three miles west of Crescent Lake was named in 1948 by a fish planting crew of the Oregon State Game Commission for Earl W. Snell, the twenty-third governor of Oregon, who was killed in a plane crash on Oct. 28, 1947.

Snider Creek, JACKSON. For some years there has been a difference in the names applied to the stream that flows southward between Upper and Lower Table rocks, and it has been shown on maps as Snider Creek, Table Creek, and Table Rock Creek. In 1937 the USGS adopted the name Snider Creek for this stream, apparently for an early settler. This was the recommendation of Paul B. Rynning, county engineer. The name Rock Creek is now given to the stream north of Lower Table Rock which flows into Sams Creek to the west. The geography of the area is shown on the map of the Sams Valley quadrangle.

Snow, KLAMATH. The post office called Snow was in the extreme southwest corner of Klamath County. It was established June 22, 1894, with Adelbert B. Smith first of four postmasters. The office ran along with its original name until Nov. 22, 1898, when it was changed to Pokegama. This change doubtless came about because the Pokegama Lumber Company projected a railroad north into Oregon from Thrall, a station on the Southern Pacific near Klamath River, California. For a time this railroad was an important factor in the development of Klamath County. Snow post office was probably named for Snow Peak, a point about 12 miles to the northeast. There are two distinct peaks here, Chase Mountain and Hamaker Mountain. In the old days one of these was called Snow Peak but the compiler does not know which one or when the change was made. Emphasis must be called again to the fact that when the names of post offices were changed the offices themselves were frequently moved, sometimes a considerable distance. The compiler does not know if the Snow post office was in the same building as the Pokegama office or not. The situation is further complicated by the fact that the Pokegama office had more than one location before it was closed in 1911.

Snow Creek, COOS. Snow Creek rises on Eden ridge and flows northwest to Myrtle Creek and Coquille River. In 1923, Ura F. Snow applied for a timber allottment on its upper reaches. He was not able to patent it.

Snow Shoe Rock, CROOK. Charles Hutchinson in the Prineville *Central Oregonian*, Sept. 11, 1969, says this name originated in a pair of snow shoes cached in a crevice in the rock. Remains of the snow shoes were there for a long time and many local people wrote their names on them.

Soap Creek, BENTON, POLK. This stream rises in the eastern foothills of the Coast Range and flows into Luckiamute River about two miles from the junction of that stream with the Willamette. There is a belief that Soap Creek was so called because of its white, soapy appearance, but David L. Stearns of San Francisco, in a letter in 1963, recalled hearing both from his grandparents and at Oregon Pioneer Association gatherings how the early travelers stopped at Soap Creek ford to do the laundry as it was well known that the waters contained some detergent mineral which eliminated or reduced the need for soap. In view of relative impurity of 1972 surface water in the Willamette Valley, chemical analysis would probably add little to the pioneer's empirical knowledge. Soap Creek post office was established in Benton County Nov. 4, 1854, with David D. Davis postmaster. The compiler does not know its location, but it was doubtless near the stream. The name of this office was changed to Tampico on Dec. 3, 1854, and it was closed Nov. 3, 1860. The compiler has not learned the significance of the name Tampico as applied to this office.

Soap Creek, DESCHUTES. This stream flows east from North Sister. Hodge, in *Mount Multnomah*, says it was named because of the white, glacial silt carried by the water.

Soap Flat, WALLOWA. This flat is in s 18, T 5N, R 45E, and was named because of the soapweed that grew there. William Ralls took up the first homestead there about 1890.

Social Ridge, MORROW. This high ground lies north and east of Rhea Creek. Rachel Harnett of Heppner told the compiler in 1969 that it was named in the 1880s by Mrs. William L. T. Benge, the widow of a pioneer Walla Walla doctor, who homesteaded there with a large family. The few neighbors of that time were so helpful that the widowed mother chose to call it Social Ridge. A son, Ralph L. Benge, was later county judge.

Soda Creek, DESCHUTES. This stream is tributary, from the north, to Sparks Lake. It was named for a well-known soda spring about three miles from its mouth.

Soda Springs, JACKSON. There are several places in Jackson County with the name Soda Springs, but only one had a post office of the same name. Soda Springs office was on Emigrant Creek ten or twelve miles southeast of Ashland, in the extreme north part of T 40S, R 2E. The locality is often called Wagner Springs because of the ownership. Soda Springs post office was established in Sept. 1886, with John Marshall Wagner postmaster. The office continued under Wagner's direction until May 1911, when it was closed to Ashland. The Wagner family was among the early settlers of the valley.

Soda Springs, LINN. The valley of South Santiam River has been well endowed with mineral springs and it is not surprising that the localities of these springs have had communities and some post offices, such as Soda Springs, Soda Stone, Sodaville, Lower Soda, Upper Soda, and others. Soda Springs is shown on old maps in the east part of T 13S, R 1E, northeast of the present community of Foster. This was the first of the springs to have an office. Soda Springs post office was established Sept. 24, 1869, with Daniel D. Gibson first and only postmaster. The office was discontinued Dec. 7, 1873.

Sodaville, LINN. Sodaville was named for a cold mineral spring situated nearby. Jo Dana has a short article in the *Oregonian*, Sept. 1, 1969, editorial page, in which she says the springs were discovered in 1848 by Reuben Coyle. She also describes improvements going back to the late 1880s.

Sodhouse, HARNEY. This historic spot, sometimes written Sod House, is immediately west of the Malheur National Wildlife Refuge Headquarters at Malheur Lake. Sodhouse was, literally, constructed of blocks of sod. It was probably built by John Chapman, James Weaver and Pete Stenger about 1872. A marker erected in 1937 by the Sod House CCC Camp says the cabin was built in 1862 by the Stenger and Chapman brothers who wintered there in 1862. The marker may be correct as to the party but the compiler feels the date is in error. At one time there was a small community called Sodhouse nearby.

Soldier Camp Mountain, CURRY. This is a well-known point on the north side of Rogue River about ten miles airline east of the Pacific Ocean. It was named during the local Indian disturbances of the 1850s. The north end of the ridge is known as Sawtooth Rock Mountain, which is a little higher than Soldier Camp Mountain, a mile to the south. Troops under the command of Captain C. C. Augur, U.S. Army, camped at the point on Mar. 17, 1856, and an account of the event is given in Glisan's *Journal of Army Life*, p. 295, *et seq*. On Mar. 20 the detachment returned to the place and Glisan mentions it specifically as "Soldiers' Camp." The name also appears in other contemporaneous records. The compiler believes that the name probably was in use before Glisan's visit, although that may be debatable.

Soldier Creek, HARNEY. This stream is just west of Harney. It was named because soldiers camped there in the Indian wars in the 1860s.

Soldier Creek, MALHEUR. This creek is so named because Camp Winthrop, a military post after the Civil War, was located on its upper reaches across the border in Idaho.

Soloman Butte, KLAMATH. Soloman Butte, 5763 feet high, is located just east of Williamson River near Kirk. It and the nearby flat were named for Sam Soloman Lalakes who had an Indian land allotment nearby. Soloman was the son of the well-known and powerful regional chief, Lalakes.

Somerange, HARNEY. When the petition was sent in for the establishment of this post office local residents suggested the name Steens because of Steens Mountain nearby. The name was not acceptable to the postal authorities so another name, Somerange, was suggested. This name had its origin in the words "summer range," the stockmen's term for summer feeding grounds. Somerange post office was established Dec. 19, 1923, with Robert W. Bradeen first postmaster. Bradeen was a member of the firm of Bradeen Brothers, merchants in the Catlow Valley, who kept a supply camp in Steens Mountain during summer months for the accommodation of their customers. In 1926 the Bradeens abandoned this project, and Somerange post office was moved off the mountain to a point a little west of the P Ranch and the name was changed to Frenchglen on Dec. 1, 1926. On the death of Robert Bradeen, Jesse L. Bradeen became postmaster June 30, 1930, and the office was closed on Decmber 31, 1943 only to be re-opened in Mar. 1947. *See* Frenchglen.

Somers Creek, WALLOWA. This is a tributary of Snake River in the east part of the county. It was named for Frank P. Somers, who ran stock near this creek for many years.

Songer Butte, JACKSON. Songer Butte is the high ground between the arms of Emigrant Reservoir. It takes its name from William F. Songer, early Jackson County resident, whose donation land claim was in ss 18 and 19, T 39S, R 2E.

Sonny, HOOD RIVER. This station, west of Hood River, bore an unusual name. It was formerly called Mitchell, but owing to confusion with another place in the state of the same name, it was decided by railroad officials to make a change. Mr. and Mrs. Charles Parker, owners of the Little Boy Ranch, just west of Mitchell Point, tried to have the station named Little Boy, but this was not acceptable to the railroad because it was awkward in telegraphy. Mrs. Parker's nickname Sonny was finally selected as the next best thing.

Soocup Canyon, MORROW. This tributary of Balm Fork south of Heppner was named for William Soucup who settled there before World War 1. The form Soocup has been in general use for many years.

Soosap Peak, CLACKAMAS. This peak, elevation 4693 feet, lies east of North Fork Molalla River. Dee Wright, for many years a packer in the Cascade Range, told the compiler that it was named for Soosap, a well-known Indian of Oregon City, who occasionally hunted in the neighborhood of the mountain. This Indian was also known as Joe Suisap and Joseph Andrews, and was part Klickitat and part Molalla, according to Wright. Soosap died Jan. 18, 1916, and his obituary is printed in the Oregon City *Enterprise*, Jan. 21, 1916. He was 61 years old at the time of his death. Soosap Peak was at one time known as Arquette Point, for a settler who lived nearby, but the name has not persisted.

Southbeach, LINCOLN. This is a descriptive name for a community near the south side of Yaquina Bay. It has been so known since the turn of the century, although the post office was not established until May 18, 1916. Harborton is the name of the place on the official plat, but that name is not in general use. Margaret F. Conrad was the first postmaster. An 1893 map uses the form South Beach.

South Canyonville, DOUGLAS. Under the heading Canyonville mention is made of a place called South Canyonville. South Canyonville was the name used for a locality, but not for a community, about ten miles south of Canyonville, in the Cow Creek Valley where the road from Canyonville first reaches that valley. It was at the Hardy Elliff place, later called Johns. It was at this locality that pioneer settlers "forted up" at Camp Elliff at the time of the Indian wars of the 1850s.

South Canyonville was not a post office, but the use of the words as a locality name made it necessary to use the name North Canyonville for the post office at Canyonville, ten miles to the north. The post office name North Canyonville was changed to Canyonville in 1892, as by that time South Canyonville was no longer used as a place name.

South Dickey Peak, CLACKAMAS. This peak, elevation about 5300 feet, lies in the Clackamas drainage basin in the extreme south part of the county. North Dickey Peak and Dickey Creek are nearby. These geographic features were named for J. K. Dickey, a native of Pennsylvania, who came to Oregon from Missouri in 1845 and settled in a small valley near the present site of Molalla, in the spring of 1846. He hunted a great deal near Collawash River, and it is thought that government surveyors named the features for him because of this fact. This information was furnished the compiler of these notes in Oct. 1927, by J. O. Dickey, a son of J. K. Dickey.

South Inlet, COOS. South Inlet post office was established Apr. 18, 1912, with Lillian Saunders first and only postmaster. The office was closed Dec. 15, 1914. It was situated near the head of South Slough, about 12 miles by road south of Empire. The name was supposed to be descriptive.

South Junction, WASCO. When the two railroads were built up Deschutes Canyon, an arrangement was made for the use of joint track for a distance of about 12 miles in the south part of Wasco County. The station at the north end of this joint track was named North Junction and the station at the south end was named South Junction. Subsequently one of the duplicate tracks between South Junction and Metolius was abandoned, so that South Junction is no longer a junction point, although the original name has been retained.

South Saddle Mountain, WASHINGTON. Oregon has ten Saddle Buttes and seven Saddle Mountains, an adequate supply. This peak is five miles south of the summit crossing of the Wilson River Highway and about 33 miles south and east of the well-known Saddle Mountain near Seaside. Its official name was also Saddle Mountain but to avoid confusion, local usage for years had been South Saddle Mountain. In 1983 at the instigation of Robert Benson and others, the OGNB voted to change the name to the current form. The USBGN concurred in *Decision List 8301*. The southwestern hump is the higher at 3507 feet.

South Santiam River, LINN. This is the correct name of the southern large tributary of Santiam River. The name South Fork is wrong.

South Scappoose Creek, COLUMBIA. This seems to be the form of name in general use, not South Fork.

South Umpqua River, DOUGLAS. This is the correct name of the southern branch of Umpqua River, not South Fork.

South Yamhill, POLK. This was a pioneer post office situated near the present site of Broadmead. It was named for South Yamhill River nearby. This office was established July 6, 1852, with Marshall B. Burke first postmaster. The name was changed to Lawn Arbor on Apr. 12, 1855, and the office was discontinued Feb. 22, 1865.

South Yamhill River, POLK, YAMHILL. This is the correct name of the southern branch of Yamhill River. It was so named in pioneer days.

Souvies Island, MULTNOMAH. This was the name of a pioneer post office near the mouth of Willamette River. The office was established under the name Mouth of Willamette on June 30, 1851, with Ellis Walker first postmaster. The name of the office was changed to Souvies Island on Mar. 5, 1852. The office was discontinued Aug. 1, 1860. The island is now officially known as Sauvie Island. For information about the island, *see* that heading and Post Office Bar.

Spanish Charlie Basin, MALHEUR. This spot is near the headwaters of Succor Creek just west of the Idaho border. In 1978 Jeffrey Ford of Ontario was kind enough to turn up some information on this name during an interview with Alfred McConnell. McConnell spent most of his early years in the area and he said that in the old days the land was owned by two Charlies, Spanish and Scarface. Spanish Charlie was shot to death on his own doorstep by a neighboor and he was commemorated by having the basin named for him.

Spanish Gulch, JACKSON. This gulch is on the extreme west edge of the county and drains into Wooldridge Creek, a tributary of Slagle Creek. In a letter published in the Grants Pass *Bulletin* on June 4, 1937, Logan Wooldridge says that the gulch was named for a company of Spaniards who mined there during the Rogue River Indian War. The Spaniards deserted their camp in 1855 and never returned.

Spanish Hollow, SHERMAN. This is the hollow that opens upon the Columbia River at Biggs. It is said to have received its name because a Spanish ox died in the canyon during the days of the immigrations. The name Spanish Gulch for this hollow is incorrect.

Sparks Lake, DESCHUTES. This is a long, kidney-shaped lake just east of the summit of the Cascade Range. Its weedy banks originally provided a rendezvous for many varieties of water fowl, some of which have unfortunately been driven away by automobile travel. The lake was named for "Lige" Sparks, a pioneer stockman of central Oregon.

Sparta, BAKER. Sparta was named for Sparta, Illinois, by William H. Packwood, a prominent Oregon pioneer. Packwood and others visited the diggings near lower Powder River in 1871 and the name of Sparta was selected at that time. Sparta post office was established Oct. 29, 1872, with William W. Ross postmaster. This office was first established with the name Gem on Aug. 7, 1871, with William Lynn White postmaster, and the Sparta office was provided by changing the name. The office may have been moved, possibly some little distance, when the name was changed. Facts about these changes in early post offices are not always clear from the records. Gem was the name of a mine. The compiler has a copy of a statement made by Packwood on June 26, 1916, the substance of which is that Packwood, I. B. Bowen, Ed Cranston and C. M. Foster left Baker on Jan. 8, 1871, to visit the locality where Packwood was preparing to build what is now the Sparta Ditch. They laid out a townsite and decided to name the place by spinning a four-sided wooden top with a proposed name on each face. Packwood wrote Sparta for his home in Illinois, and that side of the top turned up. H. S. Daly, in a letter on the editorial page of the *Oregonian*, Oct. 7, 1927, says that Packwood did not name Sparta, but Dunham Wright, of Medical Springs, takes issue with him in a letter in the Baker *Morning Democrat*, Oct. 19, 1927. Wright says he got his information first hand from Packwood. Irving Rand, of Portland, a grandson of Packwood, confirmed the Packwood story. In view of all this the compiler thinks that Packwood was responsible for the name. Both Daly and Wright say that the locality was first called Koster, for Tom Koster, who discovered gold nearby. Daly also says the place was called Eagle City before it was named Sparta.

Speaker, JOSEPHINE. Josephine Speaker was the only postmaster this office ever had and it was named in her honor. The office was on Wolf Creek about six miles east of and upstream from Wolf Creek community. It was in the northeast part of the county and depended on farming, lumbering and mining. The office was established Sept. 20, 1905, and was discontinued Mar. 31, 1925.

Specht Rim, WHEELER. Specht Rim east of West Branch was named for the Henry Specht family. Specht was an early settler and his son, Henry Jr., homesteaded near the rim in 1907.

Speece, GILLIAM. Speece was a railroad station north of Condon. It was named for William Speece, a local resident.

Speelyais Columns, MULTNOMAH. These rock columns are on the south bank of the Columbia River near Shepperds Dell. They are the cores of old basalt volcanic vents, the softer coverings of which have been eroded away. They are named with the Indian word *Speelyai*, the name of the coyote god of the mid-Columbia region. *See* Lyman's *Columbia River*, p. 8, *et seq*.

Spencer Butte, LANE. Spencer Butte, elevation 2065 feet, is just south of Eugene and is a well-known landmark in the south part of the Willamette Valley. Spencer Butte was named in July 1845, by Dr. Elijah White, while making an exploration along the foothills of the Cascade Range for the purpose of locating an emigrant road to the eastern states. Dr. White and a companion, Batteus Du Guerre, climbed the mountain, and the following passage quoted from his book, *Ten Years in Oregon*, (compiled by Miss A. J. Allen and published in 1848), describes their experiences on the summit: "They now took a delightful survey of the general features of the landscape before them. On one hand was the vast chain of the Cascade mountains, Mt. Hood looming in solitary grandeur far above its fellows; on the other hand was the Umpqua Mountains, and a little farther on, the coast ridge. Between these lay the whole magnificent panorama of the Willamette valley, with its ribbon streams, and carpet-like verdure. The day was fine, and such was the clearness of the atmosphere that the scene was very distinct, grand and imposing. In enthusiastic admiration of the noble site, the doctor named the elevation Mt. Spencer, in compliment to John C. Spencer, the then secretary of war...." For additional information about the discovery of Spencer Butte and Baptiste (Batteus) Du Guerre, *see* article by Fred Lockley on editorial page *Oregon Journal*, June 7, 1927. This article indicates that Du Guerre's nephew used the spelling DeGuire. Walling, in *History of Lane County*, p. 327, has quite a different story about the naming of Spencer Butte, based on tradition, to the effect that the butte was named for a young Englishman, Spencer, who had wandered away from a Hudson's Bay Company party and was killed on the mountain by Indians. He says the Indian name was *Champ-a-te* meaning rattlesnake, a reptile still present in the late 1900s. The compiler inclines to Miss Allen's version, which was written nearly 40 years before Walling's and was not based on a legend although a careful examination of her text gives no good clues to the party's exact route of travel or the exact summit they ascended. It should be noted that Mount Hood viewed from Spencer Butte does not loom far above its fellows for Mount Jefferson is much closer. Spencer's Butte post office was established July 14, 1853, with Milton S. Riggs postmaster and was discontinued Apr. 2, 1855. It was near the west base of the butte.

Spencer Creek, KLAMATH. Captain O. C. Applegate in 1926 informed the compiler that Spencer Creek was named for an early settler who lived on a ranch on the creek.

Spencer Creek, LINCOLN. Spencer Creek flows into Pacific Ocean at Ocean Park about a mile south of Otter Rock. The creek was named for Doke Spencer, an Indian who lived near its mouth. Spencer and his family were allotted land in this locality.

Spencer Well, DESCHUTES. This well northwest of Pine Mountain was on the homestead of Frank S. Spenser. The compiler has been unable to determine if the form Spenser was an error in the early records or if it changed through continued use of the more usual spelling.

Spicer, LINN. Spicer, about five miles northwest of Lebanon, was first called Leng, apparently for a local landowner. The Oregonian Railway narrow gauge line was built south through the area in 1880, but the compiler does not know if the station Leng was established at that time or not. In any event, Leng appears as the station name in Polk's *Directory of 1886–87*, but Spicer post office was established Aug. 17, 1886, with Adam A. Bashor first of a long series of postmasters. The post office was named for a local resident, W. E. Spicer, and the railroad adopted the post office name for its station. The post office was closed Nov. 30, 1904, as the result of the extension of rural delivery. The railroad through this part of the county was abandoned in 1910.

Spikenard, JACKSON. The reason for the application of the name Spikenard to a Jackson County post office is another puzzle in Oregon geographic nomenclature. On Nov. 21, 1879, a post office called Thomas Mill was established in the north part of the county with Thurston T. Thomas postmaster. The name of the office was changed to Spikenard on Mar. 22, 1883, with Joseph Satterfield post-master, and the office was finally closed in Oct. 1903. Old maps show Spikenard on the upper reaches of Evans Creek in T 34S, R 2W, but the exact location is a little indefinite. Dictionaries give several definitions of the word spikenard, including an ancient aromatic ointment, an essential oil or one of a number of plants allied to the lily. The compiler does not know which of these was in mind when the post office was named, although the place was probably christened for the *Smilacina racemosa* or false Solomon's seal, often called spikenard.

Spikes Gulch, UMATILLA. Spikes Gulch runs north to Echo Meadows. Elting J. Spike took up land near its upper end in 1909 but it is possible the name was applied for his nephews, Robert and Steve Spike, who farmed the property for many years.

Spinning Lake, WASCO. This small lake east of Bonney Meadows is named for early USFS employee Bill Spinning.

Spino Spring, UMATILLA. This spring on Little Johnson Creek in the southeast corner of the county was named for an early Indian family.

Spirit Falls, LANE. Spirit Falls are on Alex Creek, a tributary of the upper reaches of Layng Creek. They are a 30- to 40-foot falls in a beautiful, grotto-like setting. When a local Boy Scout troop built the trail to the falls, they asked to have the name applied to honor the spirit of Scouting. This was in the 1980s.

Spirit Mountain, YAMHILL. This mountain, about a mile north of Grand Ronde, was so named because the Indians thought spirits or skookums lived on it. It was at one time called Cosper Butte for a family of early settlers. Dr. Rodney Glisan and other officers stationed at Fort Yamhill climbed this mountain on Oct. 30, 1856, but Glisan does not mention a name in *Journal of Army Life*, pp. 374–75.

Splintercat Creek, CLACKAMAS. This stream is a tributary from the south to Roaring River in range 7E. It received the fantastic name of the legendary flying cat of the woods which was supposed to splinter branches from trees and tear out dead stumps. *See* editorial page of the *Oregonian*, Apr. 17 and 24, 1944.

Split Falls, CLACKAMAS. This double falls on Salmon River is about one mile downstream from the mouth of Linney Creek. It is the second of six falls between Linney Creek and Welches and was named because it is divided into 35- and 55-foot drops. For details of this group, *see* Stein Falls.

Spores Point, LANE. When I-5 was built it crossed McKenzie River at the site of the old Spores Ferry. In 1967 at the suggestion of the OSHD the OGNB recommended the name Spores Point for the high ground just east of the highway. Jacob C. Spores, a native of Montgomery County, New York, came to Oregon in 1847 and was one of the earliest settlers in Lane County. He operated a pioneer ferry on McKenzie River south of what is now Coburg, a few hundred feet upstream from the old Southern Pacific Company railroad bridge. This enterprise was of course named Spores Ferry in compliment to the owner. For information about Spores, *see Illustrated History of Lane County*, p. 481 and also under Mohawk

River. Travelers on the highway should note the Southern Pacific Company railroad bridge, an historic structure. It is a 400-foot single span double intersection, pin connected, Pratt through truss constructed of wrought iron and as of this writing in 1990, one of probably only four wrought iron bridges of any size in the state. The bridge was originally erected about 1887 at the Oregon Railroad & Navigation Company crossing of John Day River. In 1907, when the Columbia River line was rebuilt, it was sold to the Southern Pacific Company and relocated on the Springfield branch. This accounts for the incongruity of the date, 1887, cut into the headplates at each end.

Sprague River, KLAMATH. There have been two different post offices in Oregon with the name Sprague River, established at different times and places. They were both named for the stream. The first Sprague River office was established Nov. 12, 1873, with John W. Gearhart postmaster. The office was at first on the Jackson County list, but since it was east of the Cascade Range, it was not in what is now Jackson County. Later the office was moved to the Lake County list. John A. Smith became postmaster on Mar. 24, 1876, and the office operated with other postmasters and with some intermissions until Jan. 31, 1883, when the name was changed to Bly. The record does not show if the office was moved when the name was changed. The Gearharts were stock raisers on the upper reaches of Sprague River and the compiler is of the opinion that this office was in what is now Klamath County and never far from Bly. The second Sprague River office was established Sept. 14, 1923, with Benjamin E. Wolford first postmaster, to serve a well-known lumber community. The office is much further west of and downstream from the old office and is about 15 miles westward of Beatty.

Sprague River, KLAMATH, LAKE. Sprague River was named for Captain F. B. Sprague, who was a participant in various phases of the Snake and Paiute Indian wars, and who was in command at Fort Klamath in 1866. His name was applied to the stream at least as early as 1864. The Klamath Indian name for Sprague River was *Plai*, or *Plaikni Koke*. *Koke* was the general word for river, and *plai* indicated that the stream came from the upper or higher country. *See* Bly.

Spray, WHEELER. Spray was named for its founder, John Fremont Spray, and his wife, Mary E. Spray. Spray was born in Iowa in 1859, and came to the Willamette Valley in 1864. He moved to the site of Spray in 1900, and the town plat was filed for record May 19, 1900, by Mrs. Spray. Spray post office was established May 31, 1900, with John F. Spray first postmaster. For information of the Spray family, *see* editorial page of the *Oregon Journal*, Dec. 13, 1934. John F. Spray died at Fossil Jan. 11, 1930. *See* the *Oregonian*, Jan. 18, 1930, for obituary.

Spring Hill, BENTON. Spring Hill is a prominent landmark west of the old wagon road between Albany and Independence. It has several tops, the highest 519 feet in elevation. A fine spring fed a water trough by the roadside, and for many years travelers pulled up their tired horses for a drink.

Spring Valley, POLK. Spring Valley is in the northeast corner of the county, between the Eola Hills and Willamette River, and has been so called since pioneer days. The name is descriptive. Spring Valley post office was established Mar. 5, 1852, with Sanford Watson postmaster. Solomon Allen became postmaster Nov. 30, 1854. When Watson was postmaster, the office was at his home on the extreme west edge of the valley in the north part of s 26, T 6s, R 4W. When Allen became postmaster, he moved the office to his home near the middle of s 33, T 5S, R 4W, about two miles southeast of Amity and a considerable distance from Spring Valley. The office was closed on Sept. 1, 1855. *See* Valfontis.

Spring Valley, WHEELER. A post office with the descriptive name Spring Valley was established on the Wasco County list Feb. 28, 1876, with Henry H. Wheeler first and only postmaster. The office was discontinued Apr. 14, 1880. Old maps show the place in the extreme northeast corner of what is now Wheeler County, on the south bank of John Day River between Spray and Kimberly. H. H. Wheeler, for whom Wheeler County was named, was a prominent pioneer character of the John Day country. His biography appears in *Illustrated History of Central Oregon*, p. 688. In 1864 he started the stagecoach service between The Dalles and the newly discovered mining area near Canyon City. In the early 1870s he located in the John Day Valley where he was associated with French Brothers in the stock business at the place called Spring Valley. About 1880 he bought property at a point six miles northwest of Mitchell where he lived until he sold out in 1904 and retired to Mitchell, where he died in 1915.

Springbrook, YAMHILL. Springbrook was for several years called Hoskins, for Cyrus E. Hoskins, a pioneer settler. When the post office was established June 30, 1893, it was impossible to use the name Hoskins because of confusion with a place of the same name in Benton County. Hoskins' farm was known as Springbrook and the name of the community was therefore changed to Springbrook. Hoskins was one of the pioneer horticulturists of the state.

Springdale, MULTNOMAH. Springdale is a community between Troutdale and Corbett on the Historic Columbia River Highway. In the 1890s the east end was called Springdale and the west end Gage. When the post office was established in 1900, it was named Gage to avoid confusion with a number of other places in Oregon whose names began with Spring. William M. Northway was the first and only postmaster and the office was closed Oct. 31, 1903. Subsequently the name Springdale was used for the entire settlement. Mrs. Grant Bell picked the name because of the many springs in the area.

Springfield, LANE. Springfield appears to have been named for a natural spring, which sent up its water in a prairie or open field. In the early 1850s the spring and the land near it were fenced off, and the place came to be known by its present name. Elias Briggs was the first settler there in 1849. During many years he ran a ferry on the Willamette River. The town is described in the *Oregonian*, Apr. 23, 1903; also, Sept. 4, 1867, by Preston W. Gillette. Springfield post office was established May 15, 1868, with Albert G. Hovey first postmaster.

792 OREGON GEOGRAPHIC NAMES

Springville, MULTNOMAH. The following note by Leslie M. Scott in Scott's *History of the Oregon Country*, v. 2, p. 328, is a good summary of the history of Springville: "Springville was south of Linnton, one mile, and north of Portland, six miles, at the place known (1922) as 'Claremont.' At that place C. B. Comstock and Lafayette Scoggin established a warehouse, which served as a shipping point for farmers of Tualatin Valley, and which, about 1860, was regarded with jealousy by Portland and Saint Helens. It was the nearest shipping point to North Plains of Washington County, and Comstock and the farmers opened a road across the hills to Springville. The Springville road, from Tualatin, was a favorite route to the Willamette River before the Canyon Road to Portland was improved. When the west side railroad was opened, the Springville road fell into disuse, and, in 1872, the buildings there burned." Springville was named for a well-known spring on the slope of the hills to the west. The place was near the old Saint Johns ferry landing and just north of the modern Saint Johns Bridge. Springville post office was established Feb. 27, 1860, with C. B. Comstock first postmaster. The office was discontinued Apr. 18, 1873.

Springwater, CLACKAMAS. The locality known as Springwater, about three miles south of Estacada, has borne the descriptive name since early days. Springwater was one of the first places on the upper Clackamas River to have a post office, which was established June 24, 1874, with George A. Crawford first postmaster. The office called Zion, later Currinsville, was established the same day. Springwater office was discontinued May 31, 1914.

Sproats Meadow, KLAMATH. This meadow in s 28, T 26S, R 10E, apparently bears the name of William L. Sproat who in 1916 filed for a homestead nearby. Sproats application was later cancelled.

Spruce, TILLAMOOK. Spruce post office, named for the Sitka spruce trees in the vicinity, was established at a point about 12 miles south of Tillamook in Nov. 1894, with Henry Peters first postmaster. The office was not far from the place later called Hemlock. Spruce office was moved around to suit the postmasters and was finally moved a few miles to the north to Pleasant Valley. It was discontinued in May 1907. In the meantime the locality now called Hemlock was left without an office, so Hemlock office was established in Apr. 1906, with James W. Beaty first postmaster. Hemlock post office was closed in Nov. 1921.

Squaw Back Ridge, JEFFERSON. This name is supposed to be descriptive, but the compiler has been unable to see the similarity between the ridge and what the name describes.

Squaw Creek, DESCHUTES, JEFFERSON. Fremont camped on this stream on Dec. 2, 1843, but gave it no name. Lieutenant R. S. Williamson camped on Squaw Creek on Sept. 1, 1855, and wrote that the Indian name was *Why-chus*. *See* Pacific Railroad Surveys *Reports*, v. 6, p. 78. The compiler has been unable to learn who gave Squaw Creek its modern name.

Squaw Gulch, WALLOWA. This gulch drains into Sheep Creek in T 1N, R 48E. It was named in the early 1880s by Elisha Chase for an old Cayuse mare called Squaw, generally found ranging in the gulch.

Squaw Island, COOS. One of the islands at the mouth of Sunset Bay southwest of the mouth of Coos Bay is called Squaw Island. There is a fairly well authenticated account of an Indian battle near Sunset Bay. The Indian women were put on the island so that when the tide came up they could not be captured. This encounter was between a roving band of Chetco Indians in war canoes and some Indians living near what is now Sunset Bay.

Staats Creek, BENTON, POLK. This creek and Staats Hollow nearby were named for Isaac Staats, who was born in Albany County, New York, in 1814, and settled on his donation land claim near the creek in Sept. 1849. He married Orlena M. Williams May 10, 1846. *See* land certificate 4710.

Stacey, DOUGLAS. Stacey post office was established Jan. 19, 1901, with T. B. Fagan first postmaster. This office, named for a local family, was situated on Elk Creek a few miles northeast of Yoncalla. The office was closed Oct. 31, 1906.

Stafford, CLACKAMAS. This place was named by George A. Steel, a prominent pioneer of Portland, for his native town, Stafford, Ohio.

Stahlbusch Island, BENTON. This island is the upper part of a land area in the Willamette River above Corvallis. The lower part is Fischer Island, and the two are separated by water at high river stages. About 210 acres of the land were deeded to John and Herman Stahlbusch in Dec. 1888, and Robert Johnson of Corvallis informed the compiler that this is the correct spelling, not Stallbush.

Stahlman Point, LINN. This point overlooking the east end of Detroit Reservoir was named for Fred Stahlman, the first USFS ranger at Detroit.

Staley Ridge, DOUGLAS. This ridge is in the Calapooya Mountains, and just to the east is Staley Creek. Staley Creek flows into the Middle Fork Willamette River in Lane County. These features were named for W. F. Staley of the USFS. Staley Creek was known in early days as South Fork Middle Fork.

Staleys Junction, WASHINGTON. In 1948 Charles G. Staley built a service station at the intersection of the then new US-26 and SH-47 running north to Buxton. Staley was a relative newcomer to the area.

Stalter Canyon, MORROW. Stalter Canyon four miles southeast of Heppner was named for Daniel B. Stalter who took up government land near its mouth in 1891. Stalter's wife and six of his seven children were drowned in the Heppner flood of 1903.

Standcliff Creek, HARNEY. In the 1880s George M. Stanclift homesteaded along this creek on the south edge of Anderson Valley. Stanclift was born in New York and settled in Harney County in 1877. A son, Lewis L. Stanclift, also located nearby. *See History of Baker, Grant, Malheur and Harney Counties*, p. 669. The spelling has been corrupted for a good many years.

Stanfield, UMATILLA. Stanfield was first known as Foster. Mrs. J. M. Cornelison of Pendleton wrote in 1959 that John R. Foster was a Portland associate of Allen & Lewis who had commercial interests at Umatilla. They bought 4000 acres northeast of Echo where they established a large farm followed by a small community and branch store all named for one of the proprietors. Foster post office was established May 14, 1883, with Frank B. Clopton first postmaster. The name of the place was later changed to Stanfield, for Robert N. Stanfield, subsequently U.S. senator from Oregon. Senator Stanfield owned land nearby, hence the application of his name to the community. Stanfield post office was established in 1907.

Stanley, CLACKAMAS. The locality called Stanley is in the extreme north edge of Clackamas County about two miles northeast of Milwaukie. When the interurban line was built along Johnson Creek the company asked John H. Gibson, a local resident, to name the place. This he did in compliment to his son, George Stanley Gibson. Stanley post office was established Nov. 16, 1904, and was discontinued Apr. 29, 1905. Mary A. Morris was the only postmaster. The office was about a third of a mile west of Wichita.

Stanley Lake, CLATSOP. Stanley Lake is a short distance northeast of Seaside. It was named for S. K. Stanley, an early settler on Clatsop Plains.

Stanley Rock, HOOD RIVER. This is a prominent rocky bluff on the south bank of the Columbia River just east of the mouth of Hood River. It is surmounted by a steel transmission tower of the Pacific Power & Light Company. The top of the rock is about 140 feet above the river level. It was named for John Stanley, who operated a farm at this point, and also a ferry to the Washington side.

Stapleton, POLK. This station, near Independence, was named for John Stapleton, who came west from Canada in 1863, and after spending a few years in Idaho, settled in the Willamette Valley, near the place that now bears his name. His sons, George Stapleton and James P. Stapleton, were prominent members of the Oregon Bar for many years.

Star, LANE. Star was a post office that operated from Apr. 1891 to Dec. 1923. It was on Row River about two miles downstream from the present site of Dorena. When Dorena Dam was built in 1949, Dorena was moved about five miles upstream. Star was so named because it was located at the Star Ranch but the compiler does not know if this was a family name or merely the name of the ranch. James B. Stewart was the first postmaster.

Starkey, UNION. Starkey was a post office in the west part of the county near, but not on, Starkey Creek. Both were named for the first postmaster, John Starkey, who settled there in the 1870s. The post office was established Dec. 10, 1879 and closed in the early part of 1935.

Starr Creek, BENTON. Starr Creek is southwest of Corvallis. It bears the name of a pioneer family. *See* Monroe.

Starr Creek, LANE. Starr Creek is tributary to South Fork McKenzie River from the west at a point just about due south from McKenzie Bridge. It flows into South Fork about a half mile north or downstream from the mouth of Augusta Creek. It bears the family name of a former forest assistant who was stationed at McKenzie Bridge. The compiler has been informed by competent authorities that young Starr began to pay his respects to (was a settin' of) Miss Augusta Young, daughter of Carl Young, an early day USFS ranger in the neighborhood, and by the time their engagement was announced, their names had been joined in a sort of nomenclative couple. The two streams were named Starr Creek and Augusta Creek and thus sylvan romance has been preserved for posterity.

Starr Spring, WHEELER. This spring above Stone Cabin Creek southwest of Fossil was named for early homesteader Felix Starr.

Starvation Creek, HOOD RIVER. This creek was originally called Starveout in Dec. 1884 when two trains of the recently completed railroad were snowbound nearby. There is a story that men were paid $25.00 per day to pack food on skis from Hood River and that the railroad offered the stranded passengers who were willing and able $3.00 per day to shovel snow. For more information on this intense, early storm, *see* The Dalles *Times Mountaineer*, Dec. 20 and 27, 1884.

Starvout, DOUGLAS. The locality called Starvout is on Starvout Creek which flows into Cow Creek a few miles east of Galesville. The place has been so called since early days. Early in 1946 Miss Bess A. Clough of Canyonville was able to get the history of this name from her uncle, George Elliff, then mining gold in northern California. The Elliff family were well-known Douglas County pioneers. Some time in the 1850s Hardy Elliff grubstaked one George Walton and sent him up on the creek to prospect. Gold was scarce and when Walton came out in the spring, neighbors said he had starved out, hence the name of the stream. Some good diggings were found later on, farther up the creek. Starvout post office was established on the banks of Starvout Creek on Feb. 18, 1888, with H. L. Miser postmaster. For the subsequent history of this office, *see* Azalea.

Stauffer, LAKE. Stauffer was in Lost Creek Valley, and local residents wanted the post office called Lost Creek. Postal authorities objected to the name because of duplication, and instead selected the name Stauffer, for C. J. Stauffer, the first postmaster. The post office was established Sept. 13, 1913, and closed to Hampton on June 30, 1950.

Stavebolt Landing, CLATSOP. This landing was named because it was the place where bolts or logs were dumped into Lewis and Clark River and towed away to the mills. Stavebolt Landing is about eight miles airline south of Astoria. Stavebolt Creek flows into Lewis and Clark River about a half mile above the landing. These names have been in use for many years.

Stayton, MARION. Stayton was named for Drury S. Stayton, who founded the community. The following news item printed in the *Oregonian* for Nov. 18, 1875, tells of early days in Stayton: "The new town of Stayton in Marion County has grown rapidly during the past season. A new flour mill and a sawmill have been built. It now contains 20 families." Stayton was platted in 1872, and the post office established on May 7 of that year. Samuel D. McCauley was first postmaster.

Steamboat, JACKSON. Many old mining camps have this name applied to one or more geographic features, and it does not mean that a steamboat has ever been in the neighborhood. When mines have been worked out, or where prospects do not come up to expectations, either naturally or through fraud, they are said by miners to have been "steamboated." In addition to a place and a mountain in the southwest part of Jackson County bearing this name, there is also a stream named Steamboat Creek which rises in the Calapooya Mountains in Lane County and flows through Douglas County into North Umpqua River. It is said to have received its name in this manner.

Steamboat Creek, WALLOWA. Steamboat Creek flows into Snake River in T 4S, R 49E. This is near the site of the Copper Ledge Falls where the steamer *Shoshone* temporarily came to grief in 1870 and the *Norma* also had difficulty in 1895. These two steamers were the only boats to successfully make the trip from the upper Snake River down to Lewiston.

Steamboat Lake, WALLOWA. So called because of a rock in the lake resembling a steamboat. The lake is about 18 miles airline south of Lostine.

Stearns, DESCHUTES. Harry Stearns of Prineville wrote the compiler in 1969 to say that this station on the Burlington Northern north of La Pine was named for his brother Cecil. Their father, Sidney Stearns, had large land and cattle holdings near both La Pine and Prineville.

Stearns Butte, CROOK. This butte, four miles south of Prineville, is at the S. S. Stearns ranch, and got its name on that account. A prominent tree on the summit was for many years a surveyor's bearing mark.

Steel Bay, KLAMATH. This bay is in the north shore of Crater Lake, and was named in honor of Will G. Steel, for a half a century a prominent explorer, mountaineer and nature lover of Oregon. William Gladstone Steel was born in Stafford, Ohio, Sept. 7, 1854, the son of William and Elizabeth Steel. His father's mother, Jean Gladstone, was a sister of Thomas Gladstone, Jr., and was therefore the great aunt of William Ewart Gladstone who became premier of England. Steel moved to Pittsburgh with his parents in 1865 and in 1868 to Kansas. Here the boy read an account of the discovery of a mysterious lake in Oregon. This fired his imagination and filled him with a desire to come to this state and see the natural wonder. He reached Oregon in 1872, and it was nine years before he could get authoritative data about the lake he was looking for. He finally visited Crater Lake in 1885, and immediately started a movement to have the locality made into a national park. He was successful in this after 17 years of effort. Steel devoted a large part of his life to matters pertaining to the natural history and attractions of the Pacific Northwest and was the authority on Crater Lake. He died at Medford Oct. 21, 1934.

Steel Cliff, HOOD RIVER. This cliff is on the south face of Mount Hood, and was named for Will G. Steel by E. L. Coldwell, better known as Jerry Coldwell, for many years a reporter on the *Oregonian*.

Steens Mountain, HARNEY. The first reference to this mountain that the writer has seen is in the journal of John Work, for Friday, June 29, 1831. *See OHQ*, v. 14, p. 308. Work describes the mountain as covered with snow. Pioneer maps use the name of Snow Mountains for the range. In 1860 a joint expedition was sent into southeastern Oregon under the command of Major Enoch Steen, U.S. Army. Steen reached the mountain that now bears his name early in August, and drove a band of Snake Indians over its summit. *See* Bancroft's *History of Oregon*, v. 2, p. 467. The name Steens Mountain has been in general use ever since, although it is frequently misspelled Steins Mountain. The USBGN has adopted the form Steens Mountain. The mountain is the highest in southeastern Oregon, and is much longer north and south than east and west. Its east face is a notable escarpment that extends for 5000 feet above Alvord Valley. Enoch Steen was born in Kentucky, and was commissioned second lieutenant in the mounted rangers in 1832. He reached the rank of lieutenant-colonel on Sept. 28, 1861, retired from the army on Sept. 23, 1863, and died Jan. 22, 1880. He was brevetted major in 1847 for gallant conduct in the battle of Buena Vista, Mexico.

Stein Falls, CLACKAMAS. These are a double falls on Salmon River just below the mouth of Linney Creek. They were named in honor of Bobby and Johnny Stein of Welches who were killed in World War II. In 1963 W. Kirk Braun proposed this name along with six others on Salmon River and Tumbling Creek. In order downstream from Linney Creek they are Stein Falls, Split Falls, Hideaway Falls on Tumbling Creek, Little Niagara Falls, Vanishing Falls, Frustration Falls and Final Falls. There is a trail from the end of the road above Welches to the upper reaches of Salmon River, but it traverses some of the roughest country in Clackamas County. A subcommittee of the OGNB consisting of Herbert Stone, Thomas Vaughan and Donald Sterling made a field inspection of this area in the summer of 1963. They reported that names such as Frustration and Vanishing were most appropriate as much of the river bank is almost inaccessible from the trail. For further information, *see* the separate headings.

Stein Gulch, JACKSON. Julius Stein must have been an early resident here for BLM records show that in 1896 he filed a protest of record against an Oregon & California Rail Road allotment in T 35S, R 4W.

Steinhauer Creek, LANE. This creek empties into Lake Creek a mile above Greenleaf. It is named for Herman Steinhauer who, along with his brother Gerhard, emigrated from Germany in 1884 and settled along Lake Creek in the late 1880s.

Steinman, JACKSON. Steinman station south of Ashland was established in 1887 when the Central Pacific completed the railroad north into Ashland. It was named for Ben Steinman, a jeweler, pawnbroker and money lender of Sacramento. He was well known to railroad officials and employees, who wished to perpetuate his memory in a kindly way by naming a station for him.

Steinnon Creek, COOS. This stream, which is southeast of Coos Bay town, flows south from Blue Ridge. In 1929 S. B. Cathcart of Coos Bay told the compiler that it was named for a Belgian farmer who settled nearby about 1900.

Steins Pillar, CROOK. Steins Pillar is a 350-foot-high monolith south of Mill Creek and northeast of Mahogany Butte. Tradition has it that it bears the name of Major Enoch Steen, U.S. Army. In 1860 Steen commanded an expedition from Fort Dalles against the Snake Indians in the Harney Basin. On June 3, 1860 camp was made on Mill Creek not far from the pillar which is plainly visible from the valley. In the report by Lieutenant Joseph Dixon of the U.S. Topographical Engineers who accompanied the expedition Mill Creek is called Cottonwood Creek. On June 6, 1860 Dixon writes: "Road good with the exception of a few narrow and rocky places in the canon of Tooth Rock." However, this was along Crooked River well east of Post. Steins Pillar is 120 feet in diameter and 350 feet high with a slight overhanging cap. It obviously offered a major rock climbing challenge but it was not until 1950 that it was first climbed by a party of five men, Floyd and Glenn Richardson, Don Baars, Leonard Rice and Rodney Shay. The surface has been hardened by weathering but the rock immediately beneath is soft and friable. This makes the use of pitons and other direct aids difficult and dangerous.

Steiwer Hill, MARION. Steiwer Hill is south of Salem just east of the I-5 north Jefferson exit. It is named for one of Oregon's pioneer families. Frederick Steiwer was born in Frankfort, Germany in 1828, and came to the United States as a boy in 1836. He came to Oregon in 1850 and took a donation land claim south of Salem including this hill. He married Susan Looney, daughter of Jesse Looney who settled at nearby Looney Butte. One son, John Steiwer, was a resident of the Willamette Valley and the father of Frederick Steiwer, a United States senator in the 1930s. Another son, W. W. Steiwer, settled in Gilliam County where his branch of the family is still prominent. Frederick Steiwer died at Salem in 1903.

STEP Creek, DOUGLAS. STEP Creek is a small stream flowing into Umpqua River north of Bolon Island. It is the site of a volunteer Salmon Trout Enhancement Program project and its name is the acronym. The mile long creek is dammed for what was once the Gardiner water supply but that community now receives its water from the City of Reedsport. After it was no longer needed for water source, volunteers initiated a fish enhancement program that included stream improvement to create small pools and spawning areas as well as an egg collection and rearing facility. While this is one of a number of private volunteer efforts, public agencies have also been active. The USFS improvement on Axtell Creek near Yachats is an excellent example. The *Oregonian*, Nov. 10, 1986, p. D10, has an article on the STEP program including pictures.

Stephens, DOUGLAS. Stephens is a place on Calapooya Creek about four miles west of Sutherlin. It was named for the family of Ebenezer Stephens who took a donation land claim nearby. Stephens post office was established Jan. 6, 1890, with Mrs. Eliza Ottinger postmaster. The office operated until Oct. 31, 1912, when it was closed out to Oakland. Stephens was never a large community. The post office list for Umpqua County contains the name of an office called Stephensville, which operated in the late 1850s with Winslow P. Powers postmaster. This list appears to be for that part of Umpqua County which was added to Douglas County in 1862. It may be that Stephensville was an early name for what was later Stephens.

Stephenson Mountain, JEFFERSON. This mountain and adjoining lake were named for Thomas J. Stephenson who homesteaded the old Stephenson Ranch in 1870. The mountain is in the extreme southeast corner of Jefferson County while the ranch was in Wheeler County. Stephenson was the first settler in the area. He died in 1898 but his family retained the property until 1967.

Sterling Creek, JACKSON. There have been a number of geographic features in southwest Jackson County with Sterling as part of the name, including Sterling Peak, Sterling Creek, Sterling Mine and Sterlingville. Many years ago the writer was told by Will G. Steel that these names all came from one James Sterling, presumably a miner, who operated in the area in the 1850s. Sterling Peak was named in 1853, according to Steel, but the name Dutchman Peak has supplanted the older name. Sterling Creek flows into Little Applegate River near Buncom, and Sterling Mine was well known because of its hydraulic works, shown on popular picture post cards. Sterlingville post office, a short distance upstream from the mine, was established Apr. 21, 1879, with George Yandes first and only postmaster. This office was closed to Jacksonville on July 31, 1883.

Steve Fork, JACKSON, JOSEPHINE. Steve Fork is a tributary of Carberry Creek. Jeff LaLande in *From Abbott Butte To Zimmerman*, says the creek and nearby Steve Peak were both named for Stephen Oster who was prospecting in the area in the 1870s. The name Steamboat Creek is incorrect.

Stevens Gulch, BAKER. Stevens Gulch empties into Ruckles Creek south of Keating. Azor L. Stevens settled near its mouth during World War I.

Stewart Cabin, GRANT. This cabin on Murderers Creek in the southeast corner of S 10, T 15S, R 28E, was the early home of Eminger "Billy" Stewart. Stewart was born in Ohio in 1843, came to Oregon in 1849 and settled in the Dayville area in 1862. He built the cabin and corrals and brought in shorthorn cattle. In 1878 marauding Paiute Indians killed his cattle and ran off his horses. Five years later he settled on a ranch near Dayville where he was a well-known citizen. Stewart died on Aug. 2, 1916. Stewart Lake, on the north slope of Aldrich Mountain, is named for Billy Stewart.

Stewart Creek, CROOK. Stewart Creek empties into Crooked River just above its confluence with North Fork Crooked River. It bears the name of T. J. Stewart who lived most of his life along the stream not far from the site of Camp Maury.

Stewart Lake, BENTON. This lake, northeast of Corvallis, was named for Archimedes and John Stewart, who took up donation land claims around it. *See* land office certificates 175 and 176.

Still Creek, CLACKAMAS. This stream flows into Zigzag River at Rhododendron. It was named in pioneer days because emigrants coming down the Zigzag, which is turbulent, noted the difference in the character of the flow of the two streams.

Stillwell Creek, TILLAMOOK. This creek which flows into Little Nestucca River one mile above Dolph was named for Fred Stillwell, an early USFS ranger.

Stinger Gulch, DOUGLAS. This draw a mile west of Days Creek was named for Leonard Stinger, an early day prospector and settler. Stinger took up donation land claim #354 near Canyonville in 1854.

Stinkingwater Creek, HARNEY. William Hanley of Burns told the compiler that this stream has been so known since the 1870s, because of the disagreeable fumes that are prevalent near some of the mineral springs along the creek. These disagreeable fumes are said to contain arsenical gases. The late George E. Davis, corporation commissioner of Oregon, who died in Nov. 1927, informed the compiler that, according to his understanding, the name of the stream was a corruption of the name of a pioneer German settler who lived on its banks. Hanley denied this, however, and said he never heard of such a settler and was positive this version was incorrect. However, US-20 east of Drewsey crosses Drinkwater Pass on the north edge of Stinkingwater Mountains west of the creek. The pass was named for a family who settled in Drewsey about 1900.

Stipp, MARION. Among the pioneer settlers in Marion County was John L. Stipp, who took up a claim just west of the community now known as Macleay. Stipp was pastor of the local Baptist Church, and was referred to as Elder Stipp. He gave land for what is called the J. L. Stipp Memorial Cemetery, just west of the community. Stipp post office, named for Elder Stipp, was established May 4, 1880, with William Taylor postmaster. The name of the office was changed to Macleay Feb. 3, 1882. *See also* Macleay.

Stone Bridge, LAKE. Stone Bridge is a well-known place near the south end of Hart Lake in the Warner Valley. The bridge was built in the summer of 1867 under the direction of Major-General George Crook, then a lieutenant-colonel in the regular army. In the previous year Old Camp Warner had been established on the east side of the Warner Valley and not in the place specified in the orders. When Crook arrived in the valley in 1867 he wanted to know why the camp had been built on the wrong side of the valley and was told that the troops were on the east side and could not get across the lakes. Crook immediately ordered the army wagons and carts to haul chunks of lava out to the narrowest crossing, and, using rock for a foundation, built a causeway to the west side. A new Camp Warner was then established. *See Illustrated History of Central Oregon*, p. 812. Stone Bridge is listed in the National Register of Historic Places. It is difficult to locate as in the 1980s the roadway was inundated but still passable at low water stages.

Stonehouse Creek, HARNEY. Stonehouse Creek and nearby Little Stonehouse Creek both rise on the east slopes of Steens Mountain. In the 1870s James Rankin Crow and his wife, Ann Elizabeth, homesteaded in s 3, T 31S, R 35E, a little north of Mann Lake. They built a stone house, this being the material readily at hand, and the creek takes its name from their home.

Stookey Flat, DESCHUTES. This flat west of Horse Ridge was named for Seth Stookey who settled there in 1917.

Stotts Landing, MULTNOMAH. This landing, just west of the mouth of Little Sandy River, was named for J. M. Stott, who took up a donation land claim nearby.

Stout Creek, MARION. Stout Creek was named for Ephraim Stout and his son Lewis, who emigrated from Iowa in 1852 and operated pioneer sawmills near this stream. Lewis Stout was born in 1829 and died in 1922. His donation land claim was at the mouth of Stout Creek, and his sawmill was operated by water from the creek.

Stouts Creek, DOUGLAS. Stouts Creek is an important tributary of South Umpqua River from the south at Milo. Benjamin Stout took a donation land claim just east of the creek and probably gave his name to the stream. However, his brother, Milton Stout, is mentioned in the 1860 census and Reinhart in *The Golden Frontier*, p. 158, mentions seeing Ben and George Stout in 1858. He later adds that George Stout was killed by George Green in 1860 so all three brothers may have contributed.

Straightsburg, HOOD RIVER. Straightsburg was the name given to a post office established on the Wasco County list Oct. 19, 1888, with Henry D. Straight postmaster. The office was in the Hood River Valley and within the limits of what is now Hood River County. Straightsburg post office operated only until Nov. 18, 1891. Old gazetteers say the office was on Neal Creek about seven miles south of Hood River town.

Strait Spring, MORROW. This spring in s 22, T 2N, R 25E, was on the property of Alpheus L. Strait who settled there about the time of World War I.

Stranahan Ridge, HOOD RIVER. Stranahan Ridge is on the northeast side of Mount Hood and divides the drainages of Eliot and Coe branches. It was named for Oscar L. Stranahan. Stranahan was one of the organizers of the Mount Hood Trail and Wagon Road Company along with Captain Henry C. Coe and David R. Cooper.

Strassel, WASHINGTON. Strassel and Strassel Creek were both named for Mary Strassel. She was an early settler, who took up a homestead, and with pioneer spirit made a home in what had been a wilderness. When the railroad was built near her place, E. E. Lytle, president of the Pacific Railway and Navigation Company, named a station for her. A post office was established on June 18, 1913 and operated until June 22, 1934. It closed after the disastrous Tillamook Burn of 1933 ended logging and lumbering in the area.

Straw Fork, WHEELER. This stream flows into Butte Creek southeast of Fossil. It was named for Al Straw who settled there about 1869. *See Illustrated History of Central Oregon*, p. 640. Stories to the effect that the stream was named for straw-stacks are wrong.

Strawberry, MORROW. Strawberry is a locality about nine miles north of Lexington, supposedly named for the wild strawberries that grow there. The place has not grown into a community. Strawberry post office was established Mar. 7, 1904, with Jesse C. White first and only postmaster. The office was discontinued Dec. 31, 1908. Expected development did not become a fact.

Strawberry Mountain, GRANT. Patsy Daly of Prairie City, for many years a resident of the John Day country, told the compiler in 1927 that white settlers and miners first called this mountain Logan Butte for Camp Logan, nearby. This was in the 1860s. To the north of the butte was Strawberry Creek. "Grandfather's Story" by William R. Fisk, in *The History of Grant County, Oregon, 1862–1983*, pp. 156 and 157, tells how Fisk's father, Nathan Wills Fisk, located a homestead and "because there were wild strawberries in abundance there, he called it Strawberry Creek, and the mountain Strawberry Butte, and the names remain to this day." Fisk's 1870 homestead was in S 24, T 13S, R 33E. Gradually the name Strawberry spread to the valley so that the forms Strawberry Valley and Strawberry Butte came into universal use. The name Logan Butte became obsolete. During the past three decades the name Strawberry Mountain has supplanted Strawberry Butte, and the form with the word "Mountain" now appears on official maps. It seems to be in general use. It is the highest point in the southwest part of the Blue Mountains. The elevation determined by the USGS is 9025 feet.

String Creek, CLACKAMAS. This stream is in the Salmon River drainage basin. It was so named because of its small, stringy appearance.

Stringtown, CLACKAMAS. There are several localities in Oregon called Stringtown, generally because they are or were strung out along a road or highway. One of the best known with this name is about a mile southwest of Canemah. It was called Stringtown long ago, long before there was a through highway. There were a number of houses built on the narrow strip between the railroad and the steep bluff to the southeast, and these houses were called Stringtown, especially by people living in more thickly settled areas such as Oregon City and Canemah. The place is now well known because it is on SH-99E, the Pacific Highway East.

Stubblefield Mountain, UNION. Stubblefield Mountain in S 24, T 1N, R 40E, is east of Elgin and just south of Minam Summit on SH-82. It was named for James Jasper Stubblefield, who ranched on its west slope in 1874. The main wagon road from La Grande over Minam Summit to Wallowa Valley ran north past the foot of the mountain about a quarter mile west of Jasper's place and parts are still visible today. In 1879 one of his brothers, Thomas J. Stubblefield, took up property two miles away on the mountain's north slope near the old Pine Grove Church. From

1878 to 1883, Thomas J.'s son and founder of Enterprise, Robert F. Stubblefield, lived just west of Jasper's farm. A third brother, William K. Stubblefield, settled in Imnaha. About 1881, Jasper moved to La Grande, and in 1885 he moved on to Wallowa County to join his nephew, Robert. The mountain was named for J. J. Stubblefield who was the first of the family in the area. This information was provide by Barbara Brice of Portland, Stubblefield's great-granddaughter.

Stukel Mountain, KLAMATH. Stukel Mountain was named for Stephen Stukel, a pioneer settler. It is about ten miles southeast of Klamath Falls, and is shown on some maps as Laki Peak, but it is not known by that name locally. Laki is probably derived from the Klamath Indian word *laki* meaning chief.

Stulls Falls, COOS. Stulls Falls are on West Fork Millicoma River 13 miles southwest of Scottsburg. They bear the name of Walter Stull who settled nearby in the early 1900s. For a number of years they were incorrectly shown on various maps as Stalls Falls but this was corrected in USBGN *Decision List 7302*.

Sturgeon Lake, COLUMBIA, MULTNOMAH. Omar C. Spencer of Sauvie Island in a letter of Jan. 18, 1946, says *inter alia*: "Before the hand of man despoiled its natural characteristics through the medium of the public levee built at government expense, Sturgeon Lake was a large body of water consisting of approximately 2500 acres, through which Gilbert River found its way to an outlet in Multnomah Channel of the Willamette River. Now the upper part of Gilbert River has been cut off from flowing through Sturgeon Lake, but the lake still has its Gilbert River outlet to Multnomah Channel. Originally Sturgeon Lake was of sufficient importance that it had its Little Sturgeon Lake, which has been taken from it by the levee above mentioned." Sturgeon Lake was named in very early days, but the exact circumstances of the event are not known to the compiler. The white sturgeon, *Acipenser transmontanus*, is the largest fish found in fresh water in North America. The biggest specimen on record was taken from the Columbia River near Vancouver in 1929. It was over 12 feet long and weighed 1285 pounds. These big sturgeon in the Columbia River are largely a thing of the past, and the fish now caught seldom exceed five feet in length. Sturgeon is much appreciated locally as a food fish, but is relatively scarce. Squire Spencer's letter contains a lively tradition that Sauvie Island sturgeon came ashore from the lake and stripped the fruit from the nearby apple trees. A fish weighing 1285 pounds might be able to do anything, even reach up into an apple tree.

Sturgill, BAKER. In 1925 railroad company officials wrote that this station was named for an early settler and prospector. This was probably Francis H. Sturgill who came to Baker County in the early days and claimed land on the lower Powder River in 1877. One of his sons, George B. Sturgill, came to the same area in 1893. The railroad has been taken up and what community there was is long gone. The site is inundated by the reservoir behind Brownlee Dam.

Sturgill Peak, WALLOWA. Sturgill Peak in the Wallowa Mountains was named for Jacob Sturgill. *See* Corral Basin.

Sturgis Fork, JACKSON, JOSEPHINE. This stream is a tributary of Carberry Creek. It is named for Alonzo J. Sturgis, a local miner who developed several hydraulic operations nearby shortly after 1900. Sturges is wrong.

Sturtevant Creek, LANE. This stream flows into Coyote Creek not far from Crow. It was named for Joseph K. Sturtevant, an early settler.

Sublimity, MARION. According to information furnished the writer, Sublimity was named by James M. Denny who established the town and said he called it Sublimity "for the sublime scenery in the hills around the town." Sublimity post office was established Sept. 29, 1852. Denny was the first postmaster.

Substitute Point, LANE. Substitute Point, elevation 6340 feet, is just west of the Three Sisters. It was named in 1916 by a USGS party in charge of J. G. Staack, which was extending triangulation in that part of the Cascade Range. Two unnamed peaks were selected for possible stations, where but one was to be used. The other peak was called Proxy Point. *See* that heading. The station was installed on Substitute Point and later a lookout was established there.

Succor Creek, MALHEUR. There has been a good deal of controversy over this name and it is to be hoped that the OGBN decision of Dec. 1965 and the USBGN decision of June 8, 1966 will finally lay the matter to rest. The stream rises north of Sheaville and flows northward near the east border of the county, then northeast into Idaho, where it empties into Snake River near Homedale. The decision in favor of Sucker Creek was made by USBGN on June 6, 1906. Postal history shows that there was a post office called Sucker established on the lower reaches of the stream on Oct. 4, 1895, with Sara McConnell postmaster. This office was close to the Idaho line. It was closed Oct. 13, 1899. Apparently the name was changed and the office moved to DeLamar, Idaho. The existence of a post office with the spelling Sucker seems to indicate that that style was acceptable to local residents about the turn of the century. In the summer of 1929 the problem was presented again and after another study, the USBGN decided to stand by the earlier decision. The style Sucker Creek appeared to be based either on the prevalence of sucker fish or a story to the effect that some miners were played for suckers during early day mining excitement, and the spelling adopted by the Post Office Department in 1895. In 1965 the Oregon State Highway Department announced plans to establish a recreation area in the Succor Creek canyon between SH-201 south of Adrian and US-95 north of Sheaville. The canyon contains spectacular rock formations, fossil plants and petrified wood, and is a favorite hunting ground for thunder eggs, the Oregon state rock. The resultant publicity stirred up the old controversy as most of the local civic organizations and elder citizens protested that because of the intermittent nature of the stream there were few piscatorial suckers and there was no evidence of the gullibility of the early inhabitants. Horace L. Arment of Ontario and L. E. George of Salem took up the cudgel in behalf of Succor and unearthed references spelled in this manner as early as the John Tucker Scott diary entry for Aug. 19, 1852, and the diary of Major G. G. Kimball in 1865.

The account of the 1860 Vanorman massacre in *OHQ*, v. 20, p. 16, and the reminiscences of Wm. Schnable printed in the Malheur *Enterprise* on Mar. 8, 1930 also use this spelling. As Scott uses the name eight years before the Vanorman incident, it was not applied because the survivors of the massacre were saved by hiding in the willows along the bank. The origin of the name is obscure but there is a legend that travelers south of the Snake were saved by the fresh water found in the creek and applied the name as a corruption of the Spanish word *socorro*, meaning aid or help.

Sucker Creek, JOSEPHINE. Sucker Creek flows into East Fork Illinois River. Walling, in his *History of Southern Oregon*, p. 454, says the stream was named on account of some Illinois miners who prospected nearby. Illinois is known as the Sucker State.

Sugarbowl Creek, UMATILLA. This stream rises on the Butter Creek divide five miles south of Gurdane and flows north ultimately to North Fork John Day River. It was named because the meadow at its source is bowl shaped.

Sugarloaf, POLK. Sugarloaf post office served the Siletz Basin in the locality of what is now Valsetz. The office was named for a conical point just north of South Fork Siletz River, called Sugarloaf Mountain. Sugarloaf post office was established on Apr. 16, 1895, with John S. Wright first postmaster. It continued in operation until Apr. 30, 1904, when it was closed out to Rocca.

Sugarpine Mountain, KLAMATH. There are few geographic features in Oregon named for the sugar pine, *Pinus lambertiana*, and of these features Sugarpine Mountain north of Klamath Indian Reservation is probably the most important. The sugar pine is the largest of the Pacific pines, from 160-180 feet tall with a diameter as great as six feet. The long, chestnut brown cones are characteristic, reaching a length of 16 inches. The range of the tree does not generally extend north of the latitude of Mount Jefferson.

Sullivan Creek, BAKER. This stream is in T 6S, R 44E. It was named for a pioneer prospector who is buried on its banks.

Sullivan Gulch, MULTNOMAH. Timothy Sullivan, for whom this gulch in east Portland was named, settled on a donation land claim in the eastern part of S 35, T IN, R IE, on Jan. 27, 1851. The record of this claim, certificate 1478, shows that Sullivan was born in Ireland in 1805. He appears to have traveled extensively, for he was married to Margaret, last name unstated, in Van Dieman's Land (Tasmania), Jan. 8, 1841. He was made a citizen of the United States by Judge Cyrus Olney on Apr. 16, 1855, and appears to have received title to the claim about 1863. His house was on the south edge of the gulch, in the north part of his claim. For additional information about the Sullivan family, *see* editorial in the Portland *Telegram*, May 3, 1927, and article in *Oregon Journal*, May 15, 1927, sect. 1, p. 10.

Sullivan Gulch, UNION. Sullivan Gulch is west of Starkey. it was named for Andrew Sullivan who came to the Starkey area in 1888 with 2500 horses. He also had a large horse ranch on Juniper Creek in Umatilla County where a band of cowboys broke the animals raised near Starkey. This information came from John Evans and Jon Skovlin of La Grande.

Sulphur Springs, DOUGLAS. Sulphur Springs are close to the north bank of Smith River a couple of miles east of North Fork. These springs, which flow cold mineral water, have been known from pioneer days. Sulphur Springs post office was one of the earliest offices in the west part of the county. It was established Feb. 6, 1878, with John Cowan first postmaster. That was the same day that Norfolk post office was established not very far away. Sulphur Springs post office was closed to Reedsport on Mar. 31, 1920.

Sumac Creek, WALLOWA. Sumac Creek is near Chico, in T 3N, R 45E. The stream was named for the sumac, *Rhus glabra occidentalis*.

Summer Lake, LAKE. Summer Lake is one of the larger lakes of the arid part of the state and has an area of about 60 square miles. Its main source of supply is Ana River which is a spring-fed stream attaining great volume within a short distance from its source. Summer Lake has no outlet and as a result its water is strongly impregnated with salts, particularly of sodium. The lake was discovered and named by then Captain John C. Fremont, of the U.S. Topographical Engineers, on Dec. 16, 1843. As he looked down from the ridge which his party had climbed from the west he saw the sun shining on the lake, bordered with the green grass and the contrast was so great that he named the mountain Winter Ridge and the lake Summer Lake.

Summerville, UNION. William Patten, one of the founders of this community, named it for his friend and one time neighbor, Alexander Sommerville. The two had lived about six miles from Harrisburg in the Willamette Valley. Edgar J. Sommerville, a son of Alexander reported that his father and Patten had settled near Summerville in 1857. This is incorrect as the earliest permanent settlement in the Grande Ronde Valley was in 1861 although the two may have made a previous trip to the area. Patten probably arrived about 1864 as he was station agent for the Thomas and Ruckel Road which was completed late that year. Summerville post office was established May 30, 1865, with Patten first postmaster. The compiler does not know why the spelling was changed from Sommerville to Summerville. It may have been a mistake or postal authorities may have preferred the more common spelling. Edgar J. Sommerville moved from the Willamette Valley to Pendleton in 1879 where he became a well-known citizen.

Summit, BENTON. Summit is on the watershed between Willamette Valley and Yaquina River and the name is descriptive. At one time the place was called Summitville.

Summit Lake, KLAMATH. Summit Lake, elevation 5554 feet, is in the extreme northwest part of the county and drains eastward into Crescent Lake. It is very close to the summit of the Cascade Range, hence its name. Summit Lake must have been known in the days of the immigrations, but the first use of the name that has come to the compiler's attention is in a report on the Oregon Central

Military Road, by B. J. Pengra, dated Nov. 29, 1865. Part of this report is on file at the Oregon Historical Society. The report seems to indicate that the name Summit Lake was applied in July 1865, by Pengra and W. H. Odell while making a reconnaissance of that part of Oregon.

Sumner, COOS. Steel says this community was founded in 1888 by John B. Dalley and named for Charles Sumner, (1811–1876), Massachusetts statesman. The date must be wrong, for the post office was established on Sept. 18, 1874, with Dalley first postmaster.

Sumpter, BAKER. C A. Moore of Baker informed the compiler in 1927 that Sumpter was settled during the early days of the Civil War, and was named for Fort Sumter, South Carolina, because of the prominent position occupied by the name in the news dispatches. Post Office records show that an office with the name Sumter was established on the Grant County, Oregon, list June 24, 1874, with Joseph D. Young first postmaster. The office was soon changed to the Baker County list and was discontinued Oct. 1, 1878. It was reestablished Dec. 13, 1883, with the spelling Sumpter and F. Beagle postmaster. However, the records are obviously in error for the compiler has a photocopy of Joseph D. Young's commission as postmaster of Sumpter dated Dec. 13, 1883. His grandson, Frederick Young of Cove, supplied this in 1981 along with the information that his grandfather was told he could not use the form Sumter. As all supplies were packed in by mule train, he stayed as close as possible to the original form by changing to Sumpter as in sumpter mule. A news item in the Baker *Democrat-Herald*, May 3, 1929, says that the immediate reason for selecting the name for the Oregon town was that a local resident found a rock, as perfectly spherical as a cannon ball, and this, along with the name of Fort Sumter in the news, suggested the use of the name. This rock was on display in Baker in 1929.

Sundial Lake, MULTNOMAH. This lake is on the south side of the Columbia River near Fairview. It was named for the Sundial Ranch nearby. Charles F. Swigert of Portland told the compiler that the ranch was named by his business associate, the late Homer C. Campbell, also of Portland. Swigert said he did not know why Campbell chose the name Sundial Ranch, because as far as he knew, there never was a sundial on the place.

Sunny Valley, JOSEPHINE. Sunny Valley post office was established in the summer of 1945 at the point where I-5 now crosses Grave Creek, about 18 miles north of Grants Pass. The name takes the place of several that have had great historic significance in Oregon. The first establishment in this vicinity was the Grave Creek House of Harkness and Twogood, also called Fort Leland in the Indian wars of the 1850s. The first post office here was Leland, on Mar. 28, 1855, with McDonough Harkness first postmaster. For the history of the name Leland, *see* Leland. Some time after the railroad was extended from Roseburg south in the 1880s, Leland post office was moved about four miles west to the railroad location. There had already been a railroad station at Altamont at or near the station later called Leland. The compiler cannot learn when the name Leland was moved to the railroad, but it must have been in the early 1890s. On July 24, 1894, a post office named Grave, with Samuel B. Pettengill postmaster, was established to serve the locality on Grave Creek from which Leland post office had been moved. Grave office was operated until Oct. 1913. It was opened again in Mar. 1928, with the name Grave Creek, and with Mrs. Nora Dunham postmaster. This office continued to serve the locality until the office Sunny Valley was established by change of name from Grave Creek. Local residents were apparently a little morbid about the old name and selected Sunny Valley because the locality is often free of the low fogs that frequent the general area. For the origin of the early name, *see* Grave Creek.

Sunnyside, CLACKAMAS. The area called Sunnyside lies south of Mount Scott and is rather loosely defined. There is a Sunnyside Road, well known and also a Sunnyside School about two miles west of Damascus. These features are all near the north border of the county. Sunnyside post office was established Dec. 17, 1888, with John R. Welch first postmaster. The office was closed Aug. 12, 1903, probably because of the extension of rural free delivery. The compiler does not know the exact location. The fact that this office was in operation in the early 1890s made it impossible to have a Sunnyside post office to serve Sunnyside, now a part of Portland. Accordingly the Sunnyside addition in Multnomah County was served by an office called Sunnyview.

Sunnyview, MULTNOMAH. That part of Portland known as Sunnyside in the vicinity of SE Belmont Street between SE Twenty-ninth and SE Thirty-seventh avenues was once served by a post office with the name Sunnyview. The name Sunnyside could not be used because there was already a Sunnyside office in neighboring Clackamas County. Sunnyview office was established Aug. 21, 1890, with Queen M. Bower first of three postmasters. The office was closed Dec. 4, 1894, with all papers to Portland. The name was optimistically descriptive.

Sunriver, DESCHUTES. This is a planned resort and residential community 15 miles southwest of Bend on the site of World War II Camp Abbot. Sunriver post office was established with Lawrence J. Doherty first postmaster on July 18, 1969, at the same time that the first public facilities were opened. Sunriver is a coined name selected by John Gray and Donald V. McCallum, developers of the project. For information on Camp Abbot, *see* that heading.

Sunset, COOS. Sunset post office was named for Sunset Bay, where it was situated, about three miles west of Charleston. The office was established Jan. 24, 1910, with William S. Denning postmaster. It was closed Mar. 31, 1911. Sunset Bay is a little cove on the north part of Cape Arago and is said to have been named by Thomas Hirst.

Sunset Bay, COOS. Sunset Bay is a snug little cove on the north part of Cape Arago, at the mouth of Big Creek. According to an article in the Marshfield *Coast Mail*, Aug. 14, 1892, the name was first suggested by Thomas Hirst.

Sunset Highway, CLATSOP, COLUMBIA, MULTNOMAH, TILLAMOOK, WASH-INGTON. Sunset Highway is the official name of the state road, which was built largely with the name Wolf Creek Highway. The name Wolf Creek was derived from a small stream flowing eastward into Nehalem River near Sunset Camp. For many months during the construction period the name Wolf Creek Highway was used for this important link in the state road system but it became apparent that the name caused confusion because of other Wolf creeks in Oregon. Accordingly on Jan. 17, 1946, the Oregon State Highway Commission adopted a resolution changing the name to Sunset Highway. This was in compliment to the 41st or Sunset Division of the United States Army which played a conspicuous part in both World Wars I and II. The late M. R. Chessman of Astoria suggested the name Sunset Highway because the Sunset Division had such a large proportion of men from the Pacific Northwest. Chessman was a member of the Highway Commission. Sunset Camp in Washington County was named long before the name Sunset was applied to the highway. Sunset Camp was named for a logging enterprise that had nothing to do with the Sunset Division. Sunset Tunnel to the southeast was named for the camp. All this presents an interesting coincidence.

Sunset Shelter, DOUGLAS. This trail shelter on the west slope of Big Squaw Mountain was built in 1930. Fred Asam named the camp because of its exposure to the evening sun.

Suntex, HARNEY. W. F. Sturges, of Scio, Oregon, was the first postmaster of Suntex. Sturges informed the compiler in Jan. 1927, that postal authorities selected the name of this post office and he did not know why they chose the word Suntex. It has no local significance. The office was established on Feb. 7, 1916 and closed Jan. 1, 1949, with mail to Riley.

Suplee, CROOK. Annie Senecal, postmaster at Suplee, informed the compiler that Charles Dorling suggested his mother's maiden name, Suplee. The office was established Oct. 31, 1894, with Joel C. Abbott first postmaster.

Surveyor Ridge, HOOD RIVER. This ridge is the high ground between East Fork Hood River and West Fork Neal Creek three miles east of Parkdale. Tradition says it was named by Newton Clark, the early Hood River surveyor, because of the difficulty running the 2-3 section line of T 1S, R 10E on top of the ridge. BLM records show that Clark did both the township and section line surveys in the spring of 1884.

Susanville, GRANT. Was settled in 1865 as a mining community on Middle Fork John Day River near the mouth of Elk Creek. A Canyon City correspondent signing himself "Bruney" wrote in the *Oregonian*, May 9, 1865, that John N. Reid had discovered the Elk Creek lode and that the new town was named Susanville in compliment to Mrs. Susan Ward, one of the earliest inhabitants. Susanville post office was established Sept. 12, 1888, but in 1901 was relocated some two miles up Elk Creek while Galena post office was established at the original location. Susanville office was closed Dec. 31, 1952 with papers to Bates.

Sutherlin, DOUGLAS. Sutherlin was named for Fendel Sutherlin, who was born in Greencastle, Indiana, in 1822, and after graduating from Greencastle College in 1846 came to Oregon in the following year. In 1849 Sutherlin joined the gold rush for California, but soon returned to Oregon. Fendel Sutherlin's parents came to Oregon, arriving in the fall of 1850, and in 1851 moved into the valley that now bears his family name. Sutherlin spent much time and energy in developing the valley and irrigating fruit land. Fendel Sutherlin died in 1901. *See* University of Oregon *Extension Monitor* for Sept. 1924.

Suttle Lake, JEFFERSON. C. H. Stewart of Albany wrote the compiler in Aug. 1927, as follows: "This lake was named for John Settle, or Uncle Jackie, as he was familiarly known. He was one of the pioneers of the Lebanon district, where he took up a donation land claim about two miles north of that town. He was one of the organizers and directors of the Willamette Valley and Cascade Mountain Military Wagon Road project in 1866. He was one of the men who had actual supervision of the building of the road. It is said that while out on this expedition he went hunting one day and found the lake which was named for him and also Blue Lake in the same vicinity." This lake has been known for many years as Suttle Lake, a corruption of the correct name, but the compiler is of the opinion that it would be useless to attempt to revert to the spelling Settle. The form Suttle has been used in many legal documents, including irrigation district records, and is firmly established.

Sutton Lake, LANE. This lake is about five miles north of Florence. It was named for Orrin W. Sutton, a pioneer homesteader who settled on its banks in early days.

Sutton Mountain, WHEELER. Sutton Mountain, which has an extreme elevation of 4680 feet, lies north of Mitchell. It was named for Al Sutton, a pioneer stockman who settled in The Dalles in 1858 and moved to what is now Wheeler County in 1865. He was a native of England and well known throughout central Oregon.

Suver, POLK. Joseph W. Suver, who was born in Virginia in 1819, was a pioneer of Oregon, and settled on a donation land claim at the present site of Suver in 1845. The community bears his name. His wife was, according to land office records, Deliley Suver. For history of the community, *see* Independence *Enterprise*, Jan. 27, 1939.

Svensen, CLATSOP. This is the correct spelling and not Svenson. The USBGN has adopted the form Svensen for the community and also for a nearby island along the south bank of Columbia River. These features were named for Peter Svensen, a seafaring man, who settled near the Columbia River in early days.

Swaggart Buttes, MORROW. This high ground east of Lexington was named for Benjamin F. Swaggart who was born in Creswell in 1854 and homesteaded on the buttes which bear his name in 1879.

Swallow Lake, LINN. There are conflicting stories concerning the origin of the name of this body of water east of Marion Lake. A story in the Eugene *Register Guard*, Oct. 11, 1959, says that one John Cooper found a body in Swallow Lake and buried it marking the grave with a combination of his given name and the lake as a patronym. Why he buried the man a mile and a half from the lake and why the lake was named Swallow to begin with are both unexplained. Another tale claims that John Swallow was an early sheepherder who drowned in the lake. His friends attempted to pack out his body but the delay in discovering the corpse coupled with summer heat caused them to abandon the project and perform a hasty burial. Swallow's grave alongside the Skyline Trail has apparently made him better known in modern times than at his death near the turn of the century.

Swan, KLAMATH. Swan post office was about 12 miles northeast of Klamath Falls in the Swan Lake Valley. Swan Lake was once much larger than it is now and was much frequented by wild swan. It was named on that account. Arthur Cleveland Bent, in his splendid series of bulletins of the U.S. National Museum, *Life Histories of North American Wild Fowl*, and similar titles, has painted a graphic picture of the tragedy of some of the most picturesque of our birds. Bulletin 130, pp. 281–301, contains a fine account of *Cygnus columbianus*, the whistling swan, and *Cygnus buccinator*, the trumpeter swan, both of which use the western United States for winter range. The ruthless destruction of these birds has been without the slightest excuse. As Bent says, no opportunity has been neglected to kill these magnificent swans, by fair means or foul, until they have been sadly reduced in numbers and are now confined to certain favored localities. For letter about swans along Columbia River, *see* editorial page the *Oregonian*, May 4, 1927.

Swan Island, MULTNOMAH. The origin of this name is obvious, but the compiler has been unable to find out by whom the name was applied. The island was charted by Wilkes in the atlas accompanying *U. S. Exploring Expedition*, v. 23, Hydrography, as Willow Island, but the name has not persisted. For editorial protest against changing the name of Swan Island, *see* the *Oregonian*, Sept. 27, 1927. For similar editorial, Nov. 2, 1939. Despite the fact that the land is no longer an island, the name Swan Island is firmly and affectionately fixed in the public mind.

Swart, UMATILLA. Swart post office was established Sept. 15, 1897, and was closed to Duncan on May 31, 1902. John H. Swart was postmaster all this time, and the office was named for his family. It was about seven miles south of Gibbon. The Swarts were well known in the Blue Mountain area, and several of the family were in the railroad service. Swart post office was established to serve people in the vicinity of the railroad spur which was installed on Meacham Creek to allow for the shipment of cordwood. At the time two of the Swart family were loading and shipping wood from this area.

Swartz Creek, LANE. This Swartz Creek is near Deadwood. It is named for

John Swartz, an early settler who was killed in a hunting accident in 1888. The spelling Schwartz is incorrect. Information about both Swartz creeks was supplied in 1984 by Mrs. Elma Rust of Blachly.

Swartz Creek, LANE. Swartz Creek near Horton was named for George Swartz who settled along its banks about 1900. Swartz and his three sons, Harry, William and Raymond, all worked on the family homestead. They were not related to the Swartz family near Deadwood.

Swastika, JACKSON. Swastika post office was in the extreme east part of the county, in the northeast part of T 38S, R 4E, at or near Deadwood. The office was established Dec. 11, 1909, with Clayton E. Burton first of two postmasters. The office was discontinued Sept. 15, 1912. The name of the office was derived from the stock brand of C. E. Burton, who branded his livestock with a swastika. It is apparent that the name Deadwood could not be used for this office because that name was already in use in Lane County. Hitler had not yet been heard of and there was no objection to the use of Swastika as a place name.

Swede Cabin, JACKSON. Swede Cabin is just south of Willow Creek Reservoir. BLM records show that Carl and William Erickson both filed on land at the site in the early 1900s.

Sweet Creek, LANE. Sweet Creek rises in the Coast Range in the west part of the county and flows generally northward to join Siuslaw River near the locality called Point Terrace, a few miles down stream from Mapleton. BLM records show both Cecil C. Sweet and Zara T. Sweet with homesteads near its mouth taken up in the early 1880s. The name of the stream came from these people and was not applied because of any excellence of the water.

Sweet Home, LINN. At the approach of spring in 1930 Oswald West applied his talents to the early history of Sweet Home. His kindly letter on the subject and an equally sympathetic editorial appear in the *Oregonian* for Mar. 5 of that year. Both are well worth reading. Governor West says, and it has not been disputed, that an early name for the locality of Sweet Home was Buckhead. This name, savoring of pioneering days, finally gave way to Sweet Home. There is nothing to indicate the date of this transition, but the post office of Sweet Home was established on Mar. 13, 1874, with John B. Hughes first postmaster. It is apparent that Governor West could not have had much to do with the boisterous behavior of the young men of Buckhead which he so well describes. The calendar proves otherwise. In Dec. 1926, B. H. Watkinds told the writer that the place was called Sweet Home in the 1840s by Lowell Ames, Sr., but in Oct. 1927, C. H. Stewart of Albany wrote that this could not be true, because Ames did not arrive in the vicinity of Sweet Home until about 1860. Ames may have applied the name to his homestead. A letter in the Sweet Home *New Era*, Mar. 28, 1930, by Mrs. O. Feigum, a well-known local resident, says that the name Sweet Home was first applied in the form Sweet Home Valley. The first community to be called Sweet Home was in the east part of what is now the town. Buckland was the name of a saloon on Ames Creek west of the community. It was decorated with a large pair of antlers over the front door. Mrs. Feigum says that about 1880 the community buildings were moved west to Ames Creek and the name Sweet Home supplanted the name Buckhead.

Sweetbrier, MULTNOMAH. Sweetbrier post office was established Jan. 10, 1900, and was in service until Aug. 31, 1901, with Robert G. Combs postmaster. This office was a little to the west of the center of s 1, T 1S, R 3E, about a half a mile south of Base Line Road at the 15-mile post on the old road down to Sandy River. This was before the Base Line extension was cut through. The office was named for the well-known Sweet Briar Farm then owned by Emmet B. Williams, Portland attorney, and in 1947 owned by Mr. Williams' daughter, Mrs. Lenore W. Althaus. Variations in the form of this name for one of the most popular bushes in Oregon are familiar to most people. Sweet Briar Farm is the style in the registration certificate held by Mrs. Althaus. Frequently one meets the forms Sweetbriar, Sweet Brier and Sweetbrier. The last spelling was the one used by postal officials at Washington, but Mrs. Althaus says that a signboard nailed to a maple tree in front of her house uses the form Sweet Brier for the old post office. This gives a four-way choice. In addition, there is the romantic name *eglantine* also used for this wild rose. For editorial comment about the sweetbrier, *see* the *Oregonian*, June 27, 1947, and for letters on the subject, June 25, July 3 and July 4, 1947.

Sweetser, HARNEY. A map of 1889 shows a place called Switzer a few miles southeast of Crane, but whether it was a real community or a proposed station for the projected Oregon Pacific Railroad the compiler does not know. In any event the name appears to be misspelled. Alphene Venator, J. W. Biggs and Phil Metschan said the place was intended to be named for Frank Sweetser, who, with Stauffer, operated horse ranches in the Harney Valley, and elsewhere in eastern Oregon. Sweetser died in 1895, and his widow, maiden name Meriah Sutherlin, married Phil Metschan, Sr., in 1896.

Swim, CLACKAMAS. The name Swim was given to this post office early in 1925. Boyd Summers was the first postmaster and the originator of the name. There was a large, outdoor, warm mineral-water swimming pool nearby and this suggested a title for the post office. Swim was on US-26 just east of Government Camp.

Swiss Spring, KLAMATH. Swiss Spring is in s 29, T 27S, R 7E. It was at one time called Coyote Spring, but due to duplication with another Coyote Spring in the neighborhood, the USFS asked to have the name changed to Swiss Spring in compliment to a Swiss who was associated with the locality. The style Swiss Spring was adopted by the USBGN in 1940.

Swisshome, LANE. The name Swisshome originated because a Swiss family, Mr. and Mrs. Heinrich Zweidler, lived about a mile west of the present site of the post office. The locality where they lived was called Swisshome and when the post office was established on Mar. 5, 1902 with Mrs. Zweidler postmaster, the name followed naturally.

Switchback Falls, HOOD RIVER. These falls were named May 6, 1925, by the

USBGN because the title suggested was unusually descriptive. They are near where the Mount Hood Loop Highway crosses Iron Creek, southeast of Mount Hood.

Switzler Lake, MULTNOMAH. This was a slough lake on the south shore of the Columbia River near Portland. It has long since been reclaimed for industrial land but it was centered about the present intersection of Vancouver and Union avenues. The lake was named for John Switzler, who brought his family to Oregon, from Missouri, in 1845, and on Sept. 30, 1846, settled on the south side of the Columbia, opposite Vancouver, and north of Woodlawn, which is a part of the city of Portland. This was the old landing of the Vancouver ferry. *See* map of W. W. Chapman, surveyor-general of Oregon, dated Sept. 20, 1860, Eugene, Oregon, in the surveyor-general's office at Portland, Oregon. Switzler was born in Virginia and served in the War of 1812. He died in 1856. *See* Scott's *History of the Oregon Country*, v. 2, p. 289, and land office certificate 137. Slough post office was established in the vicinity of Switzler Lake Nov. 25, 1850, with John Switzler postmaster. The office was discontinued Jan. 6, 1852.

Sycamore, MULTNOMAH. Sycamore is a locality on Johnson Creek about three miles east of Lents, near the south border of the county. A story about George Flinn, in Fred Lockley's column of the *Oregon Journal*, July 16, 1927, tells of the origin of the name. Sycamore State is a name used in referring to West Virginia. The Flinn family came to Oregon about 1844 from West Virginia and settled at the present site of Sycamore. Nelson A. Flinn, the head of the family, named the locality Sycamore. A post office with that name was established May 29, 1889, with Flinn first postmaster. This office was closed Mar. 23, 1901. Some of the family later moved to the vicinity of Cherryville east of Sandy.

Sycan Marsh, KLAMATH, LAKE. Sycan Marsh gets its name from the Klamath Indian words *saiga* and *keni*, literally, the level, grassy place. The marsh covers a considerable area west of Summer Lake, and its outlet is Sycan River, a tributary of Sprague River. Most of it was aquired in 1980 by the Nature Conservancy to be preserved as a natural area. The best information about Sycan Marsh may be found in the cooperative report issued by the state engineer entitled *Silver Lake Project*. There are many spellings of the name, but the USBGN has officially adopted Sycan. It seems probable that the name Thompson Valley was at one time applied by white people to Sycan Marsh as well as to what is now known as Thompson Valley, to the north. The name Sycan has become applied to Sycan River as a result of the association of the stream with the marsh, and also rather inappropriately, considering its literal Indian meaning, to Sycan Butte, near the northeast corner of Sycan Marsh. There are many other examples of this misapplication of names by association and proximity. *See* Lemiti.

Sylvan, MULTNOMAH. Nathan B. Jones, a pioneer of 1847, settled at the pass at the head of Tanner Creek in 1850 and lived there until he was murdered early in 1894. He called the locality Zion Town and platted lots with that name in 1892–93. Whether he chose the Bible name for religious reasons or because of the place called Mount Zion about a mile to the southeast the writer cannot tell. There was no community at Mount Zion, which was named about 1860–61. Jones may have adopted the unusual form Zion Town to show that it was the community or trading center for Mount Zion. When a post office was desired in the late 1880s postal authorities would not use the name Zion, on the grounds of confusion that might result from duplication. There had already been at least two Zions in Oregon and the names had been changed because of difficulties with the mails. T. H. Prince, resident of Zion Town, suggested the name Sylvan and an office with that name was established June 6, 1890, with Charles C. Prince first postmaster. This office was closed Oct. 11, 1906. The locality is now generally called Sylvan. The name is derived from *Silvanus*, the Roman deity of the woods. For additional information, *see* Mount Sylvania. Nathan B. Jones was born in Salem, New Hampshire, in 1819. Four years after he settled at the place now called Sylvan he built a dwelling called the Hermitage, which was destroyed by fire in 1893. Jones was considered to be an eccentric hermit. It is said that one of his schemes was to develop a town that would become Oregon's seat of government. The outside of his home was decorated with weird paintings that anticipated the modern fad for fantastic murals. In Jan. 1894, Jones disposed of some property to Henry E. Reed of Portland and took a check for the balance due, which he promptly deposited in a Portland bank. He was supposed to have retained the cash in his house, and was clubbed on January 17, apparently with the idea of robbery. He died Jan. 25, 1894, and was buried at the little cemetery at Sylvan.

Symbol Rock, LANE. Symbol Rock is on the divide between McKenzie River and Fall Creek south of Nimrod. USFS ranger A. J. Briem said that it was named because of the distinctive, almost geometric, formations of rock on the west face. It was used by Indians for ceremonial vigils prior to the coming of the white man.

Syracuse, POLK. Syracuse post office was established in the valley of Luckiamute River on Feb. 8, 1885, with Frank K. Hubbard first of two postmasters. James P. Starr became postmaster on Jan. 9, 1889. On Oct. 28 of the same year the office was moved westward about two miles to Falls City. When this move was made Starr was appointed postmaster of Falls City and retained the position until the summer of 1890. The origin of the name Syracuse is not based on water-tight evidence, but it is generally thought that the word was applied by some of the first settlers, who are said to have come from Syracuse, New York. However, there is another theory that should be mentioned. The Oregon post office may have been named by someone interested in classical history. There were several such students in the area.

Table Creek, DOUGLAS. Table Creek flows into Cow Creek from the north at a point about a mile due west of Peck. The stream got its name because it drained the south slopes of Table Mountain. Table Mountain is a conspicuous landmark north and west of Cow Creek Canyon. It has an elevation of 3335 feet. The name is of course descriptive.

Table Mountain, LINCOLN. This mountain, elevation 2820 feet, has a characteristic flat top and has been known as Table Mountain since pioneer days. Except for the fact that it is much too far south it might be La Mesa of Heceta. *See* Cape Falcon.

Table Rock, CLACKAMAS. This Table Rock is in the south part of the county between the upper reaches of Molalla River and Table Rock Creek. Don Onthank of Portland wrote the compiler in 1979 describing a climb to the top via a recently completed trail around from the north. He was much impressed by the north face: "a perpendicular wall of black lava made up of four distinct layers of lava such as I have never seen before." The name Table Rock is, of course, descriptive.

Table Rock, JACKSON. For nearly a century Upper Table Rock and Lower Table Rock have been well-known landmarks north of Central Point in the Rogue River Valley. They are real mesas, standing nearly a thousand feet above nearby Rogue River. The historic meeting between Rogue River Indians and white soldiers and settlers took place on the southwest slope under Upper Table Rock on Sept. 10, 1853. Table Rock post office was in service near these two landmarks from Apr. 25, 1872, until Sept. 14, 1895, when in a fit of efficiency postal authorities changed the name to Tablerock, and that was the style until the office was discontinued Nov. 15, 1906. Thomas Gianini was the first postmaster in 1872. After inspecting the list of postmasters of this office, Judge J. B. Coleman of Medford, long familiar with Jackson County history, gave it as his opinion that the office did a good bit of moving about to suit the convenience of the postmasters, but it was never far from the valley between the two mesas.

Taft, LINCOLN. The community of Taft was named for William Howard Taft, twenty-seventh president of the United States. The post office was established Jan. 22, 1906, and was named when Mr. Taft was secretary of war. John W. Bones was first postmaster, and is said to have suggested the name. On Dec. 8, 1964, Taft voted to become part of a new community to be called Lincoln City.

Taft Mountain, DOUGLAS. Former USFS ranger Fred Asam supplied the following information about the mountain north of Little River. He said that a huge Douglas fir stood about a half mile from the summit. It was known far and wide as the Taft tree and apparently had been named by then district ranger Oscar Houser before World War I for President William Howard Taft. The mountain and Taft Creek to the south took their names from the tree.

Taghum Butte, DESCHUTES. This butte in the Paulina Mountains is named with the Chinook jargon word for six, it being the sixth of a series all named at the same time by the USFS.

Tahkenitch Lake, DOUGLAS. Tahkenitch Lake is in the western part of the county. It is of very irregular shape, and the Indian name is said to mean many arms.

Takilma, JOSEPHINE. Takilma is on East Fork Illinois River about a mile southeast of Waldo. It was formerly called Taklamah, and is said to have been named by Colonel T. W. Draper of the Waldo Copper Company, for an Indian chief. Since 1902 the place has been called Takilma, a modification of the name Takelma, applied to an Indian tribe that lived on the middle course of Rogue River. *See Handbook of American Indians*, v. 1, p. 673. Takilma post office was established Aug. 2, 1902, with George F. Morgan first postmaster. The writer was told in 1926 that the style Taklamah could not be used for a post office in Oregon because it duplicated the name of a place in Oklahoma. However, available post office records do not substantiate this statement.

Talapus Butte, DESCHUTES. This butte, west of Sparks Lake, is named with the Chinook jargon word for coyote. *See* Mount Talapus.

Talbot, MARION. Guy W. Talbot was the first vice-president and general manager of the Oregon Electric Railway Company, and after he resigned and entered the public utility business, the new owners of the railway extended it south from Salem and this station near the Santiam River was named for him. Talbot station was at first known as Roby, for a pioneer family of the vicinity, but this name was confused with Ruby, a station in Multnomah County, so the change was made.

Talent, JACKSON. This place was named in the early 1880s by A. P. Talent, who platted the town. Talent suggested the name of Wagner, but postal authorities gave the place his own name. He came to Oregon about 1876 from Tennessee. In pioneer days the place was known as the Eden District and also Wagner Creek for a family of early settlers.

Tallman, LINN. This station northwest of Lebanon was named for a nearby settler, James Tallman.

Tallow Butte, DOUGLAS. Tallow Butte is on the divide between South Umpqua River and Jackson Creek in T 29S, R 1E. Grover Blake of Roseburg told the compiler this was so named because in early days some very fat deer were found nearby.

Tallowbox Mountain, JACKSON. Tallowbox Mountain, elevation 5021 feet, is a prominent point in the Siskiyou Mountains a little south of Applegate. Thomas V. Williams of Medford submitted a story about the name, which he said may be fact or fiction, but in either event it is the best available. About 1880 some hunters in the locality shot more deer than they were able to get home with facilities available. They wished to save the tallow for future use, so they packed it in a box to keep it from birds and animals and fastened the box up in a tree. The story is to the effect that the tallow was never salvaged and the box gave the name to the mountain.

Tam McArthur Rim, DESCHUTES. This prominent ridge runs east from Broken Top and is clearly visible from Lava Butte on the south to Madras on the north. It was named by the USBGN in *Decision List 5401* to honor Lewis A. "Tam" McArthur, the author of the first three editions of this book. After McArthur's death in 1951 many people felt that some geographic feature in Oregon should have his name and one of his oldest friends, Robert W. Sawyer of Bend, was instrumental in selecting this particular ridge. In retrospect it is interesting to note two curious facts: the Broken Top alpine uplands was one of the few spots in central Oregon that McArthur had not visited, and he probably would have expressed some dissatisfaction at the inclusion of a nickname in otherwise serious nomenclature. The preface to this edition of *Oregon Geographic Names* contains a biography of Lewis A. McArthur and the background of this book.

Tamanawas Falls, HOOD RIVER. These falls on Cold Spring Creek a mile west of Mount Hood Loop Highway were named by the USFS. *Tamanawaas* or *Tahmahnawis* is the Chinook jargon word for friendly or guardian spirit. The name was first applied with the curious spelling Tamanawaus, but in Dec. 1971, the OGNB decided upon the present form. *See* USBGN *Decision List 7301.*

Tamarack, UMATILLA. Tamarack was the name given a post office in the Blue Mountains, about 15 miles east of Weston on the road to Elgin. This office was established June 2, 1896, with Lewis A. Rambo first postmaster. It was finally closed after the turn of the century, but the writer does not know the exact date. In the Blue Mountains the name tamarack is generally given to the western larch, *Larix occidentalis.* Not all authorities agree and in the Pacific Northwest the terms larch and tamarack are often used interchangeably. There are many of these western larch trees near the locality of the Tamarack post office and that is how it got its name.

Tamarack Creek, WALLOWA. This creek is in T 5N, R 45E. Other geographic features in Oregon are also named for the tamarack, which is, correctly, the western larch, *Larix occidentalis.* This tree has a variety of common names. It grows in many places in Oregon, particularly in the Blue and Wallowa mountains. *See* Tamarack.

Tamolitch Falls, LINN. This 60-foot waterfall on McKenzie River is about two miles downstream from Carmen Reservoir. Before the development of the Clear Lake Recreation Area, they were known as Lower Falls but the USBGN confirmed the present name in *Decision List 6103. Tamolitsh* is the Chinook jargon word for tub or bucket.

Tanasbourne, WASHINGTON. Tanasbourne is a substantial real estate development on the Sunset Highway, US-26, in the vicinity of NW 181st Avenue. It was developed by the Standard Insurance Company and named for a combination of Chinook and Anglo Saxon words meaning small, pretty creeks. The Chinook jargon word is *Tenas* meaning small or little. *Bourn* is a Middle English variant of *burn*, a small brook.

Tandy Bay, KLAMATH. This bay is at the southwest end of Crescent Lake. In 1925 the USFS made a detailed map of Crescent Lake, and at the suggestion of Lewis A. McArthur, this bay was named for William Tandy, who was a member of the pioneer road exploration party sent out by the state in 1852. For information about this exploration, *see* Scott's *History of the Oregon Country*, v. 4, p. 8.

Tandy Creek, LAKE. Tandy Creek is south of Lakeview and flows westward into Goose Lake. It is about four miles north of the Oregon-California state line. William and Robert Tandy, pioneer settlers in the Willamette Valley, moved into the Goose Lake Valley about 1869, and Tandy Creek was named for some member of the family. The style Tansy Creek is wrong.

Tangent, LINN. This station on the Southern Pacific line south of Albany was named because of the long stretch of straight track to the north and south. This tangent is more than 20 miles long.

Tangerman Creek, LINCOLN. This creek is tributary to Siletz River near Siletz. Apparently it is named for Otto Tangerman who homesteaded along it prior to World War I.

Tanks, UMATILLA. This was a summer settlement near the summit of the Blue Mountains on the road between Walla Walla and Elgin. It was named for water tanks used by freight haulers, and not by a railroad, as there is no railroad near the place. Tanks post office was established June 2, 1896, with DeWitt C. French first postmaster. It was discontinued May 14, 1906.

Tanner Creek, MULTNOMAH. Daniel H. Lownsdale settled on what was later the King Claim, now in the city of Portland, in 1845 and built a tannery. Tanner Creek got its name from this enterprise. The creek drained the canyon at the head of Jefferson Street, and flowed under the present location of the Civic Stadium, and through a ravine where upper Alder Street is situated. Canyon Road, an important factor in the development of Portland, was named because it was built up the canyon of Tanner Creek.

Tanner Creek, MULTNOMAH. J. T. Tanner took up a donation land claim near the mouth of this stream in pioneer days, and his name became attached to the creek. It is just west of Bonneville. Tanner Butte near the headwaters of the creek was once known as Tanner Creek Butte, but the government has eliminated the unnecessary part of the name.

Tanners Pass, DOUGLAS. In 1948 the U.S. Plywood Company was building a private road north of Sampson Butte heading toward Evarts Creek. The powderman, one Tanner, encountered so much difficulty because of bad rock and limited equipment that crew members referred to the place where the work was delayed as Tanners Pass.

Tansy Point, CLATSOP. The name Tansy Point is applied to a place on the south bank of Columbia River just north of Warrenton, and has been in use for many years. The tansy plant, *Tanactum huronense*, grows there in abundance and the name of the point is appropriate. Tansy ragwort is extremely harmful to cattle and in some areas much time and effort has been spent in attempted eradication. Sir Edward Belcher's chart of 1839 uses the name Racoon Point, presumably in commemoration of the visit of HMS *Racoon* in 1813.

Target Meadows, UNION. Caroline Davis of the Umatilla National Forest wrote to give the origin of this name. Target Meadows is about a mile and a half north of Tollgate. It was used by the soldiers from old Fort Walla Walla for target practice when they were in the area. Jay Hughes, an old time USFS employee, said the target mounts and impact areas behind were still visible in the 1960s.

Target Spring, WALLOWA. Target Spring, southeast of Wallowa Lake, was named because of the fact that the ground nearby was used as a hunting camp and hunters practiced there, shooting at marks on trees.

Tartar Gulch, JOSEPHINE. Tartar Gulch drains into Althouse Creek southeast of Holland. It is shown on various maps as Carter Gulch and Tarter Gulch, but in May 1943 USFS officials wrote the compiler that these forms were wrong and that Tartar Gulch was correct. An old-time resident of Selma is authority for the statement that the gulch bears a name applied in mining days indicating that gold in this gulch was in very spotted pockets and the term "tartar" was used to describe that condition. A tartar gulch was considered not good for mining. The compiler has not been able to verify this meaning for the word, but assumes it to be correct.

Tarter Gulch, BAKER. Tarter Gulch runs into Snake River near the site of Robinette. On some maps it has been shown as Robinette Gulch but this is incorrect. It is named for Daniel Tarter, Jr., who ran horses along Snake River. His father and mother, Daniel and Nancy Tarter, came to Union County in the 1860s. This information was supplied by Walter Tarter in 1987 when the USGS was remapping the area.

Tate Spring, WHEELER. Grover Blake, the first USFS ranger in the area, told the compiler that this spring north of Spanish Peak was named for one or more of the several Tate brothers who ranched nearby.

Taylor, MULTNOMAH. Taylor was a siding west of Corbett on the south bank of the Columbia River. Land office records indicate that E. J. Taylor took up a homestead nearby, entry 76, in pioneer days, and the place was named for him. A post office named Leader was established in this locality July 15, 1881, with Joseph H. Leader first postmaster. The name was changed to Taylor on May 25, 1882, at which time Ervine J. Taylor was postmaster. The office was discontinued in June 1895. Mrs. Lydia Taylor Ostrand, daughter of E. J. Taylor, has an interesting account of the early days in *History of East Multnomah County Pioneers*, v. 1.

Taylor Butte, LANE. Taylor Butte has an elevation of 5835 feet. It is west of the summit of the Cascade Range, three miles north of Waldo Lake. It and other nearby geographic features were named about 1898 for one Joe Taylor, a stockman of the Deschutes country, who ranged sheep in the neighborhood. This information was furnished the compiler by Geo. H. Kelly of Portland and W. P. Vandevert of Bend, both of whom were familiar with central Cascade Range history.

Taylor Creek, CURRY. This creek enters the Pacific Ocean two miles north of Brookings. It was named for William Taylor who settled near its mouth about 1870.

Taylor Creek, LANE. Most of Taylor Creek is in the extreme west part of T 16S, R 9W. It flows west over the township line into Indian Creek. The stream was named in compliment to John L. Taylor, who settled on its banks in 1888 and lived for nearly 20 years. John L. Taylor named Reed post office that operated for 40 years on Taylor Creek. This was to honor Thomas B. Reed of Maine. Mr. Taylor was the father of ten children, several of whom, including Smith L. Taylor of McKenzie Bridge, were well known in Lane County.

Taylor Lake, LINN. This is an enlargement of Courtney Creek and is northeast of Halsey. Land plats of 1878 show that S. Z. Taylor owned land nearby, and the lake was probably named for him.

Taylor Sands, CLATSOP. These sands in the Columbia River are just northeast of Astoria. They were named for Tom Taylor of Mayger, who owned the grounds and seined them for salmon. Taylor was a son of E. J. Taylor of Taylor, Multnomah County. At one time the sands may have been known as Taylors Island for in the *Clatskanie Chief*, Jan. 23, 1975, p. 8, there is an article about Mayger with a picture of Tom Taylor "of Taylor's Island."

Taylors Ferry Road, MULTNOMAH, WASHINGTON. John A. Taylor was born in New York state on Sept. 12, 1825. He crossed the plains with an ox team in 1852, and, upon arrival in October of that year, took up a donation land claim ten miles from Portland on the Tualatin River, and installed a ferry there. Afterwards he built a toll bridge to take the place of the ferry. He was at one time the county judge of Washington County. He died in Walla Walla, Washington, Feb. 12, 1919. Taylors Ferry Road led from the south part of Portland over the north end of Palatine Hill to the ferry. Most of the road southwest of West Portland is now incorporated in Capitol Highway and Barbur Boulevard leaving the name to be applied only to a short section of the old road between Fulton and West Portland. The long tangent west of the intersection of Capitol Highway and Barbur Boulevard is of recent construction and has nothing to do with the original Taylors Ferry Road. Taylors Ferry post office was in service from Oct. 8, 1869, to Dec. 13, 1869, with John A. Taylor postmaster.

Taylorville, CLATSOP. Taylorville is in the east part of the county on US-30 a mile west of Westport. It is named for Lawrence and Olive Taylor who platted the community in the 1920s. The Taylors managed the Westport Hotel for many years. Both Olive and Lawrence Taylor died in Portland in the spring of 1940. *See* the Astoria *Evening-Astorian Budget*, Mar. 8, 1940, p. 12.

Taylorville, WASCO. Taylorville is a locality on Fifteenmile Creek about eight miles southwest of Dufur. For the geography of the place, *see* USGS map of the Wolf Run quadrangle. At late reports there was not much stirring in Taylorville and it no longer is shown on the map. It was in the northwest corner of S 13, T 2S, R 12E. Taylor post office was established on Aug. 20, 1909, and discontinued Sept. 30, 1910, with Albert Taylor postmaster. The community was apparently named for the postmaster. According to Judge Fred W. Wilson of The Dalles, who wrote the compiler in 1946, a sawmill was established near this locality, and to accommodate the employees, Taylor opened a store and had the post office established. When the mill stopped operating, the post office was closed.

Teal Creek, POLK. Teal Creek rises in the Coast Range south of Black Rock and flows eastward to join Little Luckiamute River near Bridgeport. In pioneer times the stream was called Brown Creek in compliment to Adam Brown, an early settler, through whose farm it ran. Later John B. Teal moved into the mountains south of Falls City and gradually the name Teal Creek supplanted the name Brown Creek. The change in name took place during the 1890s. Teal was a carpenter, wagonmaker and also a sawmiller. He was at times county commissioner and also county judge. He was a much-respected resident of Polk County. The spelling Teel is wrong.

Teardrop Pool, LANE. Teardrop Pool is a small melt pond usually in the northwest corner of the crater of the South Sister. It is only a few feet below the actual summit so it is easily the highest lake in Oregon. It was named in 1969 by Elizabeth, Patricia and Peggy Falconer, daughters of David Falconer, a well-known photographer. The Falconer family had completed a successful ascent of the mountain when the young girls asked the name of the lake. When they learned it had none, they suggested Teardrop Pool. This was duly submitted to the OGNB and approved by the USBGN in *Decision List 7003*.

Teaser Creek, WALLOWA. This creek, which was named for a stallion that ranged thereabouts, flows into Deep Creek in T 3N, R 50E.

Techumtas Island, UMATILLA. This was the Indian name for an island in the Columbia River east of Umatilla. It was also known as Switzler or McComas Island, for men who had owned land on it. In the fall of 1940 the compiler mentioned this name to William Switzler of Umatilla, and was told that Techumtas was the name given by the Cayuse Indians to J. B. Switzler, father of William Switzler, and one time owner of the island. J. B. Switzler always referred to the island as Techumtas Island, not Switzler Island, and that was the family custom. In 1941, the USBGN adopted the name Techumtas for this island and applied Switzler to another island slightly upstream. Both Techumtas Island and Switzler Island were inundated when Lake Wallula was impounded behind McNary Dam.

Tecumseh Creek, KLAMATH. Tecumseh Creek is a stream about one and one-half miles north of Klamath Agency. It is sometimes erroneously known as Spring Creek, which is unsatisfactory because this duplicates the name of a stream not far to the east. Klamath County pioneers used the expression Tecumseh Creek because a well-known Klamath Indian, Tecumseh, was found dead near the stream many years ago in circumstances that indicated that he had been murdered. He was of course named for the famous chief in Ohio.

Teeter Creek, LANE. Teeter Creek runs into Dorena Lake from the east near the lakehead. It is named for James H. Teeters who homesteaded along it in the 1870s. Census records use the form Teeter while the BLM original entry records use Teeters with the terminal "s." Readers must search elsewhere to determine which form was used by the family.

Tegart Bluff, MULTNOMAH. Tegart Bluff is on the south bank of the Columbia River immediately north of Blue Lake and is named for an early landowner. Francis Tegart was born in County Cavan, Ireland, in 1819. In 1863 he emigrated to the United States with his four children and settled in Pennsylvania. Here he became a friend of Benjamin Wister Morris, later to be Episcopal Bishop of Oregon. Tegart came to Portland in 1870, apparently after some discussion with Morris, and settled in the present Rockwood area, the name which he selected for his farm. He died in Portland on Nov. 14, 1907. For other information, *see* Rockwood.

Telephone Flat, KLAMATH. Telephone Flat, in S 2, T 36S, R 7E, is named because an important long distance telephone line crosses this ground. The many wires on multiple crossarms are a distinctive feature.

Tellurium Peak, DOUGLAS. Tellurium is a rare metallic element, generally found associated with other elements such as silver and gold. Tellurium Peak, just southwest of Canyonville, was named because the metal has been found there.

Telocaset, UNION. This place was once called Antelope Stage Station. When the railroad was built through the Blue Mountains, Dr. William C. McKay was asked to suggest new names for stations that had names duplicating others in Oregon. Among those he suggested was Telocaset. This word is from the Nez Perce language and means a thing at the top, or put on top, such as a tree growing on a hill, summit or plateau, overlooking a valley. The Indians pronounced the word *Taule-karset*, according to O. H. Lipps, of Fort Lapwai Indian Agency, Idaho, in a letter dated Mar. 2, 1927. Telocaset post office was established Feb. 25, 1885, with William A. Cates first postmaster.

Temperance Creek, WALLOWA. This stream flows into Snake River in T 1N, R 50E. It was named by Ben Johnson and others with him as a result of the coffee giving out. The party had nothing but water to drink and named the stream on that account.

Templeton, COOS. Templeton post office was established June 21, 1898, and was discontinued Feb. 28, 1917. Albina Coleman was the first of five postmasters. When a petition was circulated asking for a post office Robert Templeton, a local resident, sponsored the document and the office was thereupon named in his honor. Templeton was in the extreme north end of the county, east of Tenmile Lake. It was in several locations, at least twice on Benson Creek and twice on Johnson Creek, but as far as the compiler knows it was always in T 23S, R 12W. The Templeton name is preserved in Templeton Arm of Tenmile Lake.

Ten O'Clock Church, CLACKAMAS. This is not the name of a community although it is so indicated on road signs and maps. It is a church two miles southeast of Beavercreek founded by a German reform congregation in 1880 and more recently used by the United Church of Christ Congregational. When the original building was erected a clock tower was included but the congregation could not afford the machinery, so a dummy face was installed with hands fixed at ten o'clock, the time of Sunday service.

Tenasillahe Island, CLATSOP. The name Tenasillahe is composed of two Chinook jargon words, *tenas* meaning small or little, and *illahe*, meaning land, hence, "little land." There are many ways of spelling Chinook words, but the USBGN as a matter of standardization has adopted the form shown at the head of this paragraph. This island is low, and marshy in places, which doubtless accounts for the Indian name. Maps prepared by Lewis and Clark show this and other islands nearby in the Columbia River marked *marshy islands*, but the expression was apparently not used as a geographic name. Lieutenant W. R. Broughton passed Tenasillahe Island on Oct. 25, 1792, and describes it as a "long, sandy, shallow spit." His report on this part of the Columbia River is not entirely clear, but it may be that he camped on the island that night as he mentions "the dampness of the situation." Wilkes used the name *Kathlamet* for this island, a form of Cathlamet. *See* Cathlamet.

Tencent Lake, HARNEY. This is a small lake at the extreme north end of the Alvord Valley. It is fed largely by ditches, which are also its outlet. Tencent Lake has an elevation of about 4400 feet, and it was so named because it was small and round like a dime.

Tenino Creek, JEFFERSON. This stream on Warm Springs Indian Reservation bears the name of the Tenino Indians, a Shahaptian tribe of the Columbia and Deschutes valleys. They are now classed with the Warm Springs Indians. *See Handbook of American Indians*, v. 2, p. 729. In Dec. 1942, J. W. Elliott, superintendent at Warm Springs Indian Agency, wrote the compiler that he had discussed with several older Indians the origin of the name. At the time of the treaty of 1855 the Teninos had as their habitat a locality on the Columbia River a few miles down stream from Celilo. This locality was known as the Tenino Fishery, and as nearly as Mr. Elliott could understand the translation, the name meant a river channel where the water was confined by steep rock walls. When the Teninos were moved to the Warm Springs Indian Reservation they took the name with them to the new location. Many of them return to the Tenino Fishery during the fishing season.

Tenmile, DOUGLAS. The name of the post office of Tenmile is derived from the fact that a man who lived in Happy Valley drove cattle from the valley and grazed them at the place now known as Tenmile. The distance was about ten miles, hence the name. This incident happened in pioneer days. The office was established June 13, 1870, and was still in operation in 1980 about halfway between Winston and Camas Valley.

Tenmile Creek, COOS. This creek was undoubtedly named because it emptied into the Pacific Ocean about ten miles south of Winchester Bay, at the mouth of Umpqua River. It is also about ten miles north of the northern bend of Coos Bay, but Winchester Bay was settled earlier than any settlement on the northern part of

Coos Bay, and the compiler thinks that the first explanation is the correct one. Tenmile Creek has given its name to Tenmile Lake, to Tenmile Butte, southeast of Tenmile Lake, and to North Tenmile Lake.

Tenmile Creek, LANE. This stream, which flows into Pacific Ocean south of Cape Perpetua, was named by surveyors because it was about ten miles long. Tenmile Ridge to the north was named for the stream.

Tenmile Lake, COOS. This lake was once known as Johnson Lake. The USBGN has officially named it Tenmile Lake. North Tenmile Lake is nearby. Both lakes probably received their names from Tenmile Creek, which connects Tenmile Lake with the ocean. Tenmile Creek was named because it was supposed to be about ten miles south of the pioneer settlement at Winchester Bay. The name South Tenmile for this lake is incorrect. It was approved by the USBGN, but subsequently the decision was revised.

Tenmile Rapids, WASCO. These rapids of the Columbia River were named by USCE because of their distance east from the boat landing at The Dalles. They formed part of The Dalles of the Columbia, and were formerly known as the Little Narrows, Short Narrows, and *Les Petites Dalles. See* The Dalles in this book, and *OHQ*, v. 27, p. 115. Part of Tenmile Rapids was in the state of Washington. They were inundated after The Dalles Dam was completed.

Tepee Camp, WALLOWA. This is an old Indian campground in T 5N, R 46E. It was used generally during hunting seasons.

Tepee Draw, DESCHUTES. This is a draw on the northeast slopes of Paulina Mountains. It was so called because remains of Indian tepees were found therein.

Tepee Springs, WALLOWA. These springs are about six miles north of Enterprise and about a mile west of the Lewiston Highway. They were named for a group of tepees, the poles of which were left standing by Indians. They were on a piece of land reported filed on by Chancy Akin, but Akin did not prove up for title. A post office named Teepy Springs was established Aug. 3, 1886, with Akin postmaster. This spelling is from Post Office Department records and does not agree with local style. The office operated until the summer of 1890.

Terrebonne, DESCHUTES. The community of Terrebonne was first known as Hillman, a word made by taking parts of the names of two prominent railroad men, James J. Hill and E. H. Harriman, whose lines ran a race to see which could reach central Oregon first. Shortly after the town was founded a man named Hillman, a prominent real estate operator in the Deschutes Valley, got into trouble with the government, amidst unpleasant notoriety. This was disquieting to the good people of Hillman, who changed the name of the place to Terrebonne, a French expression meaning good earth. It is said that a Mr. Stevens suggested the new name. The name of the post office was changed in Sept. 1911.

Terry, MULTNOMAH. On Oct. 13, 1899, a post office named Bement was established at or near the road intersection at Twelvemile Corner on SE Stark Street north of Gresham. Francois M. Graham moved a store building from Fairview and set it up at the Twelvemile Corner. He was appointed first postmaster at Bement. Shortly thereafter the name of the office was changed to Terry, and it was closed Oct. 31, 1903. The patrons were then served by rural delivery. It has been reported that Terry was named for some postal official, but the compiler has not been able to identify any such official.

Testament Creek, TILLAMOOK. This creek flows into Nestucca River in the south part of the county. It was named by association with Bible Creek just to the south. *See* Bible Creek.

Tetherow Butte, DESCHUTES. Tetherow Butte is about three miles north of Redmond, and Tetherow Bridge across Deschutes River is three miles west of the butte. These geographic features were named for a local settler, A. J. Tetherow, a pioneer stockman and a member of a prominent early pioneer family of the Willamette Valley. He had a farm on Crooked River and a ferry on Deschutes River, near the present site of the bridge. This information was furnished by J. N. Williamson of Prineville.

Texas Bar Creek, UMATILLA. This creek flows into North Fork John Day River east of Dale. In the days of the mining excitement, a man named Tex kept a saloon and roadhouse at the mouth of the creek and the place was known as Tex's Bar. The change to present form occurred sometime during the intervening years.

Tharp, DOUGLAS. Tharp was a station on the Southern Pacific Coos Bay branch on the upper reaches of Wind Creek south of Reedsport. It was probably named for Jack Tharp who came to Oregon in 1851 and to the Alsea area in 1883. He later lived at Tidewater. During this time there was considerable railroad activity along the coast.

Thatcher, WASHINGTON. Thatcher is a cross-roads community about three miles northwest of Forest Grove and close to the northeast slope of David Hill. The place was named for Harmon and Jemima Thatcher who took up a homestead in the locality in early pioneer days. The Thatchers were married in Indiana in 1847 and came to Oregon soon afterward. Thatcher post office was established Aug. 3, 1895, with Thomas J. Clark first postmaster. The office was closed Aug. 21, 1902.

Thayer Glacier, DESCHUTES. This glacier is on the eastern part of the North Sister. It was named by Professor E. T. Hodge of the University of Oregon for Eli Thayer, representative in Congress from Massachusetts, who assisted in securing the passage of the bill admitting Oregon to the Union. *See Mount Multnomah*, p. 75. For information about Oregon's debt to Thayer, *see* Scott's *History of the Oregon Country*, v. 5, p. 3.

The Dalles, WASCO. The name The Dalles is derived from the French word *dalle*, meaning flagstone, and was applied to the narrows of the Columbia River, above the present city of The Dalles, by French-Canadian employees of the fur companies. Among other things, *dalle* meant a stone used to flag gutters, and the peculiar basalt formation along the narrows doubtless suggested gutters. The word *dalles* signified, to the voyageurs, the river rapids flowing swifty through a narrow channel over flat, basaltic rocks. The name is common in America. Well-known *dalles* are those of the Saint Louis, Saint Croix, Wisconsin, and Columbia rivers. The best-known *dalles* were those of the Columbia. The name is not derived from the French *dale* meaning trough. As far as the compiler knows the first use of the name Dalles in Oregon is in Franchere's *Narrative*, on Apr. 12, 1814, where it is used to describe the Long Narrows. John Work, in his journal of 1825, speaks of *Dalls*. The name *La Grande Dalle de la Columbia* became established. The original name of the community was Dalles City, but for many years the style in universal use has been The Dalles, this style being adopted not only for historical and sentimental reasons but also to avoid duplication with Dallas, Polk County. On June 7, 1966, the name was changed by ordinance to the City of The Dalles to conform to current usage. The post office was established with the name Dalles on Nov. 5, 1851, with William R. Gibson first postmaster. On Sept. 3, 1853, the name was changed to Wascopum, and on Mar. 22, 1860, it was changed to The Dalles. The narrows of the river were generally known as The Dalles of the Columbia, and this collective term described the geographic features from the Big Eddy on the west to Celilo Falls on the east. All these rapids were inundated in Mar. 1957 when The Dalles Dam was completed, forming Lake Celilo. Just east of Big Eddy was Fivemile Rapids, formerly known as the Long Narrows, The Dalles or The Great Dalles. Further east was Tenmile Rapids, formerly known as the Short Narrows, Little Narrows or *Les Petites Dalles*. For information about The Dalles of the Columbia, *see OHQ*, v. 27, in the article by Henry J. Biddle entitled "Wishram." The neighborhood of Mill Creek at The Dalles was called *Quenett* by the Indians, which was a word for salmon trout. Lewis and Clark camped at the mouth of this stream on Oct. 25, 26 and 27, 1805, and recorded the form *Que-nett* in their journals and maps. In Apr. 1806 they named this place "Rockfort camp." Dr. William C. McKay, in an article in The Dalles *Mountaineer*, May 28, 1869, gives the Indian names of a great many places in the vicinity of The Dalles. Dr. McKay says that long before the white men came, the Indians called the locality of what is now the city of The Dalles *Win-quatt*, signifying a place encircled by rock cliffs.

The Dungeon, CLACKAMAS. This locality is on the east side of Molalla River about three miles southwest of Table Rock. The place was named by Andy Wyland and Joe Davis of Molalla, who built a rough shelter of cedar shakes there in the early 1880s. Most of the structure has since disappeared, but the place is still known by its original name. The building was low and without windows and this name was quite descriptive. Joe Davis, a well-known character of Molalla, was a prospector and trapper. He died on Molalla River and was buried about 150 feet south of the original site of The Dungeon. Dee Wright of Eugene furnished this information.

The Flatirons, JEFFERSON. These flat-top rocks three miles east of Willowdale are named for their resemblance to the sad irons of pioneer days.

The Meadows, DOUGLAS. This place on upper Cow Creek at the mouth of Meadow Creek was the site of James W. Thomas' Meadow Ranch at the end of the nineteenth century. Thomas was the first postmaster at Anchor and the post office was probably at or near the ranch.

The Watchman, KLAMATH. The Watchman, elevation 8025 feet, is one of the highest points on the western rim of Crater Lake. It was named because a party of topographic engineers was placed on its summit in 1886 to take observations while the lake was being sounded. It had previously been christened Bentley Peak by Captain O. C. Applegate in honor of A. Bentley of Toledo, Ohio, who visited Crater Lake in 1871 with Sir (then Mr.) William F. Maxwell, of Edinburgh, Scotland, and a Dr. Munson of Klamath Agency. Munson died of over-exertion and Maxwell faithfully watched his body all night while Bentley went for assistance. For an account of this event, *see* Klamath *Record*, Mar. 22, 1918. *See also* Glacier Peak and Munson Valley.

Thelake, HARNEY. Thelake post office was in service from Nov. 3, 1914, to Mar. 1, 1919, with Rose G. Balcomb the only postmaster. It was at the east border of the Mann Lake Ranch, about ten miles south of the old Alberson post office. The name was intended as an allusion to Mann Lake, an intermittent feature named long ago. Mann Lake was named for a local settler, Phillip Mann.

Theora, LAKE. Theora post office, situated near the middle of S 7, T 40S, R 19E, was established Dec. 4, 1916, with Hubert E. Koons first and only postmaster. The office was discontinued to Lakeview on Mar. 15, 1918. Theora office was named for Theora Swift, sister of Alvin J. Swift. Swift was secretary of the local irrigation district.

Thief Valley, UNION. This little valley east of North Powder is now partly inundated by the reservoir behind Thief Valley Dam. Previously the place was an isolated valley with good pasture hemmed in by steep hills. An article in the Baker City *Democrat-Herald*, Sept. 27, 1989, tells how a group of citizens organized by William Huffman ambushed three thieves who were stealing horses and holding them in the valley before moving them to Nevada. The thieves were promptly terminated with the aid of a large willow tree nearby, giving the valley its name. This event occured during the 1870s. Another story says the valley is where John Wetherly was hanged in Dec. 1864, for stealing mules from an emigrant at Boise. The Huffman account is more probable although both may be correct.

Thielsen, POLK. This is a station on the Southern Pacific line between Salem and Dallas, and is near the farm of the late Henry B. Thielsen, who was for a number of years engaged in railroad surveying and construction work in Oregon and in Washington, and subsequently operated a farm near the site of Thielsen station. For several years before his death Mr. Thielsen resided in Salem. He was a son of Hans Thielsen, a prominent Oregon pioneer railroad builder for whom Mount Thielsen in the Cascade Range was named.

Thimble Mountain, CLACKAMAS. This point in the northeast corner of the county was named by T. H. Sherrard of the USFS because of its resemblance to a thimble.

Third Lake, LINN. Third Lake is the third of a series of four lakes extending along the east bank of Willamette River north of Albany. These lakes are named in accordance with their position, First Lake being the one nearest Albany.

Thirsty Creek, DOUGLAS. This creek rises southeast of Lemolo Lake. It is intermittent and finally goes underground, later to form Spring River. In 1919 a fire crew found the stream dry when they needed it the most, thus naming it. The compiler believes "thirsty" is temperate language for men in this situation.

Thirty-two Point Creek, WALLOWA. This creek is in the extreme southeast part of the county. There are two theories about the name, one to the effect that a pair of antlers with 32 points was found nearby, and the other to the effect that there are 32 points of land fronting on the creek between its mouth and its source. The reader may choose.

Thomas, LINN. Thomas was a railroad station on the Oregon Pacific Railroad, later the Corvallis & Eastern, near the mouth of Thomas Creek. Edwin D. Culp in *Stations West* has a picture of the building on p. 89. Thomas post office operated from May 4, 1898 until Jan. 31, 1921 in the same vicinity. Both were named for the Frederick Thomas of Thomas Creek.

Thomas Creek, LINN. Thomas Creek is one of the important streams of the county. It was named for Frederick Thomas who in 1846 settled on the banks of the stream, where he took up a donation land claim. Other nearby settlers named the stream.

Thomas Creek, UMATILLA. George F. Thomas and J. S. Ruckel established the stage line from Walla Walla to the Grande Ronde Valley in 1865. South of Bingham Springs on Umatilla River the Ruckel Road, as it is still called, follows Thomas Creek to the summit of the Blue Mountains at an elevation of about 4500 feet. The compiler believes this Thomas Creek bears the name of the first partner as the second is also commemorated by Ruckel Ridge and Ruckel Spring immediately adjacent to the pass.

Thompson Creek, LANE. Thompson Creek empties into Siuslaw River from the north at Rainrock. It is named for Manly Thompson who filed on government land nearby in 1884. The spelling Thomson is incorrect.

Thomson, LANE. Thomson was an early-day post office on McKenzie River, but should not be classed as a pioneer establishment. Mary C. Thomson was appointed postmaster Apr. 15, 1891. She ran the office until June 24, 1893, when it was closed to McKenzie Bridge. An effort was made to revive the office in May 1895, when Cynthia J. Isham was appointed postmaster, but the order for some reason or other was rescinded in July 1895. The C. W. Thomson homestead was in S 17, T 16S, R 5E, just across the McKenzie Highway from Belknap Bridge, but bridge and highway were not there when the Thomsons settled. Thomson post office was between Blue River and McKenzie Bridge.

Thorn Hollow, WALLOWA. Thorn Hollow drains into Cougar Creek in T 4N, R 45E. In 1885 J. Pern Averill and James Alford killed two bears there that were found feasting off the thornberries, and the name Thorn Hollow resulted.

Thorn Prairie, DOUGLAS. Thorn Prairie is on North Umpqua River just above Toketee Lake. It is a comparatively level bench covered with thorn brush which sprang up after the area was burned over many years ago. G. C. Blake of Roseburg informed the compiler that the name was applied in 1917 by Perry and Jessie Wright of nearby Caps Illahee.

Thornberry, SHERMAN. This station, formerly known as Grebe, was named for a local resident and stockman. It is south of Biggs. Grebe post office was established in Feb. 1916, with Henry Grebe postmaster. Harvey B. Thornberry became postmaster in Jan. 1919, and the name of the office was changed to Thornberry in Oct. 1920. The office was discontinued in Nov. 1923.

Thornhollow, UMATILLA. Thornhollow was the name of a post office situated in the natural geographic feature Thorn Hollow about 18 miles east of Pendleton. The name Thorn Hollow was applied in the 1870s, but the post office was not established until 1923. Marietta Jones was the first postmaster. At that time postal authorities made the name one word. Thorn Hollow was originally named by a stage driver because of an abundance of thorns along the road. Thornhollow post office was closed Nov. 30, 1926, but Thorn Hollow railroad station lasted until the 1970s.

Thornton Lake, BENTON. This is a narrow lake about a mile northwest of Albany. It is on what was the donation land claim of J. Quinn Thornton, one of Oregon's prominent pioneers, and was named for him. Thornton was born in Mason County, West Virginia, Aug. 24, 1810. He came to Oregon in 1846. He rendered important service toward creation of Oregon Territory. He wrote *Oregon and California in 1848*, in two volumes, Harper & Brothers, New York, 1849. He died at Salem on Feb. 5, 1888. His address on the migration of 1846 to Oregon appears in OPA *Transactions*, 1878, pp. 29–71; history of the provisional government, 1874, pp. 43–95. Thornton was a member of the emigration that came by the Applegate Route in 1846, and for many years was especially bitter against Jesse Applegate and other members of the party who went from the Willamette Valley to prepare a road for the emigration. Particulars of this difficulty may be found in Bancroft's *History of Oregon*, v. 1, p. 542, *et seq.* Thornton challenged the integrity of David Goff, a member of the Applegate party, and James W. Nesmith, Goff's son-in-law, challenged Thornton to a duel. As a result of Thornton's failure to accept Nesmith's challenge, the latter prepared a poster and tacked it up on trees about Oregon City in June 1847, calling Thornton a variety of names. Judge Deady describes the poster as "a wealth of adjectives." C. H. Stewart, of Albany, calls attention to the fact that Thornton called this lake Fairmount Lake, presumably for a small hill to the north. The name Fairmount has not persisted for the lake, although it is applied to a school nearby. When Thornton settled on his homestead in Nov. 1846, he called the place Forest Grove. The name seems to have been unusually attractive to him, for on Jan. 10, 1851, he suggested it for the locality which is now a town in Washington County. *See* Forest Grove for details.

Thorp Creek, WALLOWA. Thorp Creek is just southwest of Wallowa Lake. It was named for C. H. Thorp by Fred McClain.

Three Creek Lake, DESCHUTES. This lake is about 17 miles south of Sisters and three miles east of Broken Top. It is directly below and to the north of Tam McArthur Rim and is a favorite fishing lake as well as the site of a USFS Forest Camp. About a mile north of the lake is a meadow where three streams, the outfall of Three Creek Lake, that of Little Three Creek Lake and Snow Creek Ditch come together to form Three Creek. This flows north past Three Creek Butte into Squaw Creek but the bulk of the water is diverted south of Three Creek Butte into the continuation of Snow Creek Ditch and thus eventually into Tumalo Canal.

Three Fingered Jack, JEFFERSON, LINN. While this peak is one of the lesser ones of the Cascade Range, as far as altitude is concerned, its unusual appearance has given it much prominence. Its elevation is 7841 feet, or practically the same as that of its neighbor, Mount Washington. Its name is in a way descriptive, but the writer has been unable to learn who named it, or when. It has three main rock spires. It is not mentioned by any writer of the exploratory period. Some time in the 1870s it was called Mount Marion because of the activities of a Marion County road locating party under the leadership of John Minto, who investigated passes over the Cascade Range nearby. The writer was told about 1900 that the present name had been applied because of a three-fingered trapper who lived nearby, whose name was Jack. Judge John B. Waldo in one of his letters dated July 27, 1895, says: "Left Big Meadows, crossed summit just north of the peak heretofore called Three Fingered Jack, we called Trident Peak." This name has not prevailed. As far as known the first ascent of Three Fingered Jack was on Labor Day, Sept. 3, 1923, when six men from Bend, some of whom had made the first ascent of Mount Washington on Aug. 26, reached the summit. This party found a series of lava chimneys to ascend in mounting the almost perpendicular walls of the highest finger. For particulars about Three Fingered Jack, *see Mazama*, for Dec. 1917.

Three Lynx Creek, CLACKAMAS. This stream, a tributary of Clackamas River below Oak Grove Fork, bears a name that has provoked much controversy. Old maps show the name Three Links, and there is a legend in eastern Clackamas County to the effect that this name was the result of loss, by a surveyor, of three links out of a surveying chain. Ernest P. Rands and William C. Elliott of Portland, for many years civil engineers in Oregon, both informed the compiler that there was no truth in the three links story. They were in the neighborhood of the stream at the time it was named. They are authority for the statement that one of the Austen family, early settlers nearby, named the stream Three Lynx Creek because he saw three bobcats on its banks. The USBGN has adopted the name Three Lynx.

Three Rocks, TILLAMOOK. This community on the north bank of Salmon

River takes its name from three prominent rocks just offshore. The form 3 Rox was, fortunately, only a temporary affectation.

Three Sisters, DESCHUTES, LANE. These peaks are among the most interesting in Oregon. There are but two higher mountains in the state, and the Three Sisters, together with Broken Top, comprise the most majestic alpine group in the Cascade Range in Oregon. The writer has been unable to learn who named the Three Sisters, and they are not frequently mentioned either by explorers or pioneers. The earliest mention of these mountains, as far as known, is by David Douglas, as follows: "Thursday 5th Oct. 1826. After a scanty breakfast proceeded at nine o'clock in a south course. Country more hilly. At one o'clock passed on the left, about twenty-five or thirty miles distant, Mount Jefferson, of Lewis and Clarke, covered with snow as low as the summit of the lower mountains by which it is surrounded. About twenty miles to the east of it, two mountains of greater altitude are to be seen, also covered with snow, in an unknown tract of country called by the natives who inhabit it 'Clamite'." (*Journal Kept by David Douglas*, London, 1914, p. 216.) From certain positions the Three Sisters appear as two mountains, and Douglas' mistake was natural. The mountains appear as the Three Sisters on Preston's *Map of Oregon*, 1856. There is a story to the effect that at one time the three mountains were known as Mount Faith, Mount Hope and Mount Charity, beginning at the north. In 1927 William P. Vandevert of Bend, a native son of Oregon, confirmed this, and informed the compiler that when a youth, he was often told that the name Three Sisters was originally applied by members of the Methodist mission at Salem in the early 1840s, and that the individual peaks were given the names mentioned above. In 1928 John C. Todd of Bend told the compiler that in early days he heard the Three Sisters called Faith, Hope and Charity many times. The best information about the Three Sisters is that contained in USGS Bulletin 252, by Dr. I. C. Russell; in *Mineral Resources of Oregon*, v. 1, No. 1; in *Mazama* for Oct. 1912 and Dec. 1916 and 1922; in *Mount Multnomah* by Professor E. T. Hodge and in *National Geographic Magazine*, June 1912. In the summer of 1944 the University of California Press issued Howel Williams' *Volcanoes of the Three Sisters Region*, a valuable contribution to the knowledge of the area. It contains some very fine plates. Williams controverts the notion that there was a Mount Multnomah.

Three Trappers, DESCHUTES. The Three Trappers are three adjoining buttes about six miles east of Crane Prairie Reservoir. They were named in the 1920s to commemorate Roy Wilson, Dewey Morris and Ed Nichols who were murdered in the early spring of 1924 while tending a fox farm at Little Lava Lake. Circumstantial evidence pointed strong suspicion at an escaped convict who had been seen near Bend, but no direct link was established and the crime remains unsolved today. Phil Brogan, who covered the story as a young reporter for the Bend *Bulletin*, gives more details in *East of the Cascades*, p. 224.

Threebuck Creek, WALLOWA. This stream flows into Little Sheep Creek in T

2S, R 46E, and was named by J. J. Blevans and his son Murat Blevans, in 1878, because the two had good luck there hunting. They were getting food for the white settlers who were in the Prairie Creek stockade.

Threemile Canyon, MORROW. Threemile Canyon is about three miles east of the mouth of Willow Creek, and is so called on that account.

Threemile Creek, COOS. The Coos County gold rush of 1853–55 was largely centered at Randolph, a mining town near the mouth of Whisky Run north of Coquille River. Threemile Creek was named because it was about three miles north along the beach from Randolph.

Threemile Creek, DOUGLAS. This is a small creek flowing into the Pacific Ocean north of the mouth of Umpqua River. It was named on the assumption that its mouth was three miles from the river. As a matter of fact it is about four miles.

Threemile Creek, HARNEY. Threemile Creek flows westward from Steens Mountain into Catlow Valley at a point about three miles south of Home Creek and the Home Creek Ranch. It got its name on that account.

Threemile Creek, WASCO. This stream was so named because the pioneer road from The Dalles into central Oregon crossed it about three miles from town. The mouth of the stream is also about three miles east of The Dalles, but the compiler is of the opinion that this fact was not the original reason for the name.

Threepines, JOSEPHINE. Threepines was the name of a post office on the Southern Pacific line a few miles south of Hugo that operated from Nov. 1910, until Nov. 1921. W. E. Daniel was the first postmaster. The railroad station was Three Pines. The place was named by Jefferson D. Cook and George A. Steele, founders of the townsite. It was not named for three prominent pine trees but for the three main types of pine cut and milled nearby. These were sugar pine, western yellow pine and Oregon pine, which was an early commercial name for Douglas fir.

Thunder Rock, CLACKAMAS. This rock, in the northeast corner of the county, was named by R. S. Shelley of the USFS in the fall of 1906 because he was caught there in a violent thunder storm.

Thurston, LANE. Geo. H. Kelly of Portland told the compiler in 1926 that this town was named for George H. Thurston, a pioneer settler of Lane County. Among other things, he was one of the early-day land surveyors of the county. He was born in Burlington, Iowa, Dec. 2, 1846, and was the son of Samuel R. Thurston, who was later Oregon's first territorial delegate in Congress. George H. Thurston was brought to Oregon before he was a year old. For biographical information, *see* Hines' *Illustrated History of the State of Oregon*, pp. 475 and 1272. Thurston post office was established Mar. 16, 1877 and operated until July 1, 1973. An earlier post office named Thurston was established Dec. 31, 1853, with Gamaliel Parrish postmaster. It was near the present site of Harrisburg, Linn County, and had nothing to do with the place in Lane County. It was discontinued Dec. 3, 1856.

Tiara, HARNEY. Tiara was a word originally used to refer to an ancient royal Persian headdress, but the meaning has been extended to include several forms of head ornament, including a style of coronet. On May 18, 1916 Tiara post office was established in Harney County with Mrs. Minerva Benson first and only postmaster. The office was closed Jan. 15, 1917. It was in T 32S, R 31E, near the north end of Catlow Valley. In June, 1947 Mrs. Benson, then living in Albany, wrote the compiler that the name Tiara was selected for the post office by her son, Hill M. Benson, because it was at the head of the valley.

Tichenor Rock, CURRY. Tichenor Rock is south of The Heads and southwest of Port Orford, and is a well-known landmark. It was named for Captain William Tichenor, who was born at Newark, New Jersey, in 1813. In 1843 he settled in Illinois and in 1848 was elected state senator from Edgar County. In 1849 he started for California and engaged in the sea trade. In 1851 he commanded the steamer *Sea Gull*, one of the first in the San Francisco-Columbia River trade. He lost the steamer at Humboldt Bay on Jan. 22, 1852, but saved the lives of all on board and was given a gold watch for heroism. Captain Tichenor founded the town of Port Orford, Oregon, in 1851, and brought his family there in May 1852. For history of the first attempts at settlement, *see* Battle Rock. He gave up sea life in 1868 and settled down at his home in Port Orford. He died in San Francisco July 28, 1887, and was buried in the family cemetery at Port Orford. He was a public spirited and highly respected citizen of southwest Oregon.

Tidbits Mountain, LINN. This mountain is an important triangulation station and lookout north of Blue River. It received its name because the top is shattered into fingers or tidbits.

Tide Creek, COLUMBIA. The name Tide Creek as applied to a stream in the east part of Columbia County is very old and doubtless resulted from the fact that there were manifestations of small tides in the creek. Tidecreek post office was established near the lower reaches of this stream on Nov. 29, 1902, with Fred A. Bucher first and only postmaster. Mr. Bucher was apparently not able to develop a heavy postal business as the office was closed to Goble on June 24, 1903.

Tidewater, LINCOLN. Tidewater lies east of Waldport, and received its name because it is near the head of tide on Alsea River.

Tiernan, LANE. The post office at Tiernan was established about 1919. It was named for R. Tiernan of San Francisco who, at the time, was leasing a sawmill in the neighborhood. Some maps use the name Beck Station, so called because of an early railroad station master, but this was never the name of the community.

Tierra Del Mar, TILLAMOOK. This community north of Cape Kiwanda was named by Marie F. Pollock who started the real estate development. *Tierra Del Mar* is Spanish for land by the sea.

Tigard, WASHINGTON. Tigard was named for Wilson M. Tigard, who came from Arkansas to Oregon in 1852 and took up a donation land claim near the present site of the town. The community first bore the name of Tigardville and was situated about a half a mile west of the railroad station at Tigard. The village of Tigardville existed many years before the development at the railroad station.

Tiger Creek, UMATILLA. Tiger Creek flows northwest into Mill Creek about three miles east of where that stream passes into Washington. Kirk Casper of Walla Walla wrote in 1975 to say that in the early days a Swede went up the creek looking for timber to cut ties. On his return he reported seeing a tiger though the locals assumed it was actually a cougar.

Tillamook, TILLAMOOK. For the origin of this name, *see* Tillamook County. The locality of the town of Tillamook was, in early days, called Lincoln, Hoquarton, The Landing and Tillamook Landing. The word Tillamook by itself generally meant the county. *Hoquarton* was an Indian word the meaning of which is unknown to the compiler. This word, now spelled Hoquarten, is applied to a slough at Tillamook. Even though the place was called by other names, a post office named Tillamook was established Mar. 12, 1866, with George W. Miller first postmaster. Stories to the effect that the office could not be named Lincoln because of another Oregon office with that name are wrong, because the Lincoln office in Polk County was not established until more than a year later, on May 31, 1867. It is possible that at some later date an effort was made to change the name of Tillamook to Lincoln but the existence of the Polk County office may have put a stop to the proposal. The Tillamook airbase for blimps was put in commission Dec. 1, 1942, with the name U.S. Naval Air Station, Tillamook, Oregon. It was closed after World War II, but the two immense wood-framed hangars are prominent landmarks.

Tillamook County. *Tillamook* was the name of a large tribe of Salish Indians whose habitat was near and south of Tillamook Head. In the journals of Lewis and Clark, this name is spelled *Kilamox* and *Killamuck*. Gass' journal gives it *Callemeux* and *Cal-a-mex*; the journals of Henry and Thompson, by Coues, give it *Callemex*. For references to various spellings used by early writers, *see OHQ*, v. 28, p. 183. Tillamook County was created by the territorial legislature Dec. 15, 1853, and has an area of 1105 square miles according to ODOT. For further information about its name and establishment, *see* Holman's "Oregon Counties," *OHQ*, v. 11, pp. 1–81. Apparently the spelling Killamook was changed to Tillamook about the time the county was created. In addition to the county, the name is used for Tillamook (city), Tillamook Bay, Tillamook Head and Tillamook River. Dean Collins' book *Cheese Cheddar*, Portland, 1933, contains information about the early history of Tillamook County and a popular account of the Tillamook cheese industry, a business of great importance.

Tillamook Head, CLATSOP. For the origin of the name Tillamook, *see* Tillamook County. The first white man of record to visit Tillamook Head was William Clark, who spent the night of Jan. 7–8, 1806, near the top of the head, and in his journals comments on the fine view to be had, which gave the place the name of Clarks Point of View. Clark was on his way to what is now called Cannon Beach on a short exploring expedition to inspect a reported whale beaching. The wording of his diary has caused several authorities, notably Greenhow and Thwaites, to confuse Tillamook Head with other features further south along the coast. Clark crossed over but one head though his journal seems to indicate two. For additional information, *see* Capes, Cannon Beach and Ecola Creek. Tillamook Head triangulation station, on the highest point, has an elevation of 1136 feet. Steel says the Clatsop Indian name for Tillamook Head was *Nah-se-u'-su*.

Tillamook Rock, CLATSOP. Tillamook Rock takes its name from Tillamook Head. It is famous because upon it is built Tillamook Rock Lighthouse. An act approved June 20, 1878, made an appropriation of $50,000 for a first-class light on Tillamook Head. Subsequent appropriations of 1880–81 added $75,000 to this sum. The heavy cost of a road, and the fact that the light would be 1000 feet above the sea led Major G. L. Gillespie, U.S. Army, then light-house engineer for the 13th District, to recommend a light on Tillamook Rock. An inspection was made of the rock, and H. S. Wheeler, superintendent of construction, was landed on the rock from the revenue-cutter *Corwin* on June 26, 1879. This was probably the first time a white man ever stood on the rock. An attempt by Wheeler to land on June 22 was a failure. John R. Trewavas, of Portland, a mason who had had experience in England working on lights, tried to land on Sept. 18, 1879, to make a preliminary survey, but was drowned in the attempt. Construction was started in October. A little over 29 feet of rock was blasted off the pinnacle to provide a platform for the station. The rock was originally 80 feet high and a mile from shore, and had a sharp overhang to the west. All materials and supplies were landed by derricks. After World War II, improved navigation systems and high maintenance costs combined against the installation and the light was finally extinguished at 12:10 AM on Sept. 1, 1957. It was replaced by a radar buoy. The lighthouse and rock were designated surplus property and in 1959 sold to a pair of Las Vegas businessmen. They did not use it and after several changes of ownership, it was purchased in early 1980 by a Portland real estate consortium headed by Mimi Morisette. Work began at once to restore the exterior and convert the interior to a columbarium or repository for the ashes of cremated persons. The proprietors deliver the permanent residents about twice a year by helicopter, a modern device which disturbs no one except the hordes of seabirds. The compiler can only quote Gray's *Elegy*, composed upon a similar theme: "of such as wandering near her secret bower, molest her ancient, solitary reign."

Tiller, DOUGLAS. Tiller was named for a pioneer settler, Aaron Tiller. The post office was established Oct. 15, 1902, with Alfred B. Marquam postmaster.

Tilley Canyon, WHEELER. Tilley Canyon is in Horse Mountain east of Girds Creek. Albert N. Tilley homesteaded there in 1893.

Tillicum Creek, LANE. *Tillicum* is a Chinook jargon word that has been in popular use in the Pacific Northwest for well over a century, but not always with exactly the same meaning. The early Chinook use referred to people, or tribe or even relatives. With the passage of time the word came to mean also friendly people or even a friend. It also means friendly, or agreeable, as in the case of Tillicum Creek. The older Chinook jargon word for friend, applied to persons rather than things, is *siks* or *six*. Tillicum Creek flows into Salmon Creek northeast of Oakridge.

Tilly Jane Creek, HOOD RIVER. This stream on the northeast flank of Mount Hood, was named for Mrs. William M. Ladd of Portland. *See* Ladd Glacier and Cloud Cap Inn. The Ladd family spent many summers at Cloud Cap Inn, and the stream heading near the inn was given Mrs. Ladd's nickname.

Timber, WASHINGTON. When this post office was established a number of local residents suggested names and a list was sent to the government. Postal officials chose the word Timber. The name was suggested on account of the heavy forests in the neighborhood.

Timber Culture Gulch, JEFFERSON. Columbus Friend, a well-known early settler, filed a timber culture claim in 1886 near the mouth of this canyon in Trout Creek drainage north of Ashwood. Timber culture filings were authorized in 1873 when Congress passed "An act to encourage the growth of timber on western prairies." The act provided that a man could file on a quarter section of 160 acres and put 40 acres into a tree farm of prescribed standards. At the end of ten years if the trees had shown adequate growth and care, the claim could be patented at no additional cost. It also provided that certain homesteads under the 1862 law could be patented in like manner. Proper administration and supervision were difficult and the results were not too satisfactory. The bill was amended at various intervals and finally repealed in 1891 but isolated stands of poplar, locust and other trees still mark the locations of these claimants.

Timberline, CLACKAMAS. Timberline and Timberline Lodge are names that have developed naturally and spontaneously because such names fit the physical conditions. The writer had some correspondence from Francis E. Williamson, Jr., of the USFS, which gives some interesting history about the origin of this name. The following quotations are from Mr. Williamson's letter of Jan. 31, 1947: "The popularity of Timberline Lodge, combined with the public's idea that the area was new and possibly unexplored until recent years, causes me to assume that many people claim the distinction of naming it. Historically, I believe that you will find the following steps in the development of the lodge are correct and have some bearing on the actual naming. Plans and drawings for the formal compilation of a recreation plan for the south slope of Mount Hood were started by me in 1927. My ideas were the result of several trips over the area with Fred Cleator and a reconnaissance with Cecil Lord in which we ran a p-line for a road. The plan, as developed, authorized a *lodge at the timberline* along with ski club and mountain climbing club chalets." E. J. Griffith became interested in the project and soon thereafter became head of the WPA in Oregon. Timberline Lodge as it now stands was a cooperative project and had the name Timberline Lodge from the very first.

The name was natural and undoubtedly came about as the result of conferences between the USFS and the WPA. The post office was first called Timberline Lodge and established Aug. 19, 1939, with Arthur V. Allen first postmaster. This office was closed as of Dec. 19, 1942, when due to war conditions the lodge was shut up. The office was reopened in 1946 with the name Timberline and finally closed July 31, 1951. Richard L. Kohnstamm took over operation of the facilities in the middle 1950s and instigated renovations to the building and ski lifts. Aided by both public and private financial support, it has become a unique resort known throughout the country. The lodge is now a National Historic Landmark and receives large numbers of visitors throughout the entire year. Timberline Lodge post office was re-established Sept. 28, 1982.

Timon, COOS. In the spring of 1894 J. H. Timon opened a vein of coal on the east side of Coquille River about four miles south of the community called Riverton. The Timon Mine was diligently operated for a number of years and coal was shipped to California. For an account of this enterprise, *see* Dodge, *Pioneer History of Coos and Curry Counties*, p. 250. The place was near what is now known as Lampa Creek. On Jan. 22, 1902, Timon post office was established in this locality, with James L. Bean postmaster. The office was closed Oct. 9, 1902. The compiler does not know if the mine was in operation at the time the post office was established or not. Bean also ran a store. Three years later Bean had a new office established with the name Lampa, at or close to the site of the Timon office.

Timothy Lake, CLACKAMAS. This artificial lake was formed when Portland General Electric Company dammed Oak Grove Fork Clackamas River for hydroelectric power and the impoundment flooded Timothy Meadows. In 1967 Lige Coalman told the compiler that before the National Forest the meadows were a favorite summer sheep graze and sheepherders sowed timothy seed to augment the natural grass.

Timpanogas Lake, DOUGLAS. This lake, so named on the map of the Cowhorn Mountain quadrangle, is the principal source of Middle Fork Willamette River. The compiler has been informed that the name was applied to the lake in the Cascade Range by J. G. Staack, formerly topographic engineer for the USGS and later chief topographic engineer. The name was used in 1913–14 when Mr. Staack was mapping the area. It is reported that he found the name while reading in the Library of Congress, Washington, D.C., apparently in one of the Hall J. Kelley publications. Kelley published a *Geographical Sketch of Oregon* in Boston in 1830, and in this book it is stated that the Multnomah River, now known as the Willamette, had one of its sources in Lake Timpanogos. This is the name used by Mr. Staack, with slightly different spelling. Timpanogos was an early name for Great Salt Lake, derived from the name of a stream. Fremont says the word means rock river. *See* his *Report*, Washington, 1845, p. 273.

Tioga, DOUGLAS. The name Tioga is probably taken from an Iroquois Indian word meaning "where it forks," referring to a place in Bradford County, Pennsylvania, which was the southern gateway to the Iroquois country. Several important trails met there. For a discussion of the word, *see Handbook of American Indians*, v. 2, p. 755. Tioga, as a post office name, has been popular throughout the country. Tioga was once a post office on North Umpqua River about six miles northeast of Glide. The office was established Apr. 3, 1890, with J. S. Williams postmaster, and was discontinued Nov. 28, 1892. The name may have been selected because it was near this point that a trail forked away from the river and followed up Rock Creek. A later post office, Idleyld Park, has been established at this place. Tioga Creek is the name given a stream in the east part of Coos County, tributary to South Fork Coos River. It is probable that the name was used in this case because of its pleasing sound. There is a locality on this stream called Tioga, but it was not a post office in 1945.

Tipsoo Peak, DOUGLAS, KLAMATH. This peak is on the summit of the Cascade Range north of Mount Thielsen. It is named with the Chinook jargon word for grass. *Tipsoo* also meant hair.

Tipton, BAKER. Tipton post office was established at the summit of the Blue Mountains near the Baker-Grant county line west of Whitney at a high point on the Sumpter Valley Railway, and was named on this account. The office was put in service Feb. 13, 1904, with Robert W. Cecil first of two postmasters, and was closed Jan. 17, 1906. The locality has an elevation of a little over 5100 feet.

Tiptop, LANE. Tiptop post office was named with the nickname of the first postmaster, Isaac Hamner, who was frequently called Tiptop because of some hunting incident that suggested the name. The post office, which was established May 16, 1895, was in s 36, T 21S, R 3E, on or near Hills Creek. Isaac Hamner was the first and only postmaster. The office was discontinued Apr. 5, 1901. The locality of Tiptop post office is frequently called The Boulders and in 1948 the place was owned by Cliff Morgan.

Tire Creek, LANE. In May 1943, USFS ranger C. B. McFarland of Oakridge wrote the compiler as follows: "Tire Creek was named during the early days soon after the old military wagon road was constructed. A traveler broke his wagon wheel. The wagon tire rolled to the lower side of the road and was abandoned in the small creek bed. It lay there for many years and the creek was referred to as Tire Creek." The stream rises on Tire Mountain and joins Middle Fork Willamette River about two miles east of the head of Lookout Point Reservoir.

TNT Creek, LANE. This is a tributary of Hills Creek. It is named because, when the trail was being built, a USFS pack mule bucked off a box of TNT at this creek.

Tobin Cabin, KLAMATH. Tobin Cabin and Tobin Spring near Antelope Mountain bear the name of William Tobin who took up the surrounding land in 1902.

Todd Lake, DESCHUTES. Formerly called Lost Lake because of the difficulty in finding it. Citizens of Bend asked to have the name changed because of confusion with other Lost lakes, and the name Todd Lake was selected in commemoration of Uncle John Y. Todd, an early settler of central Oregon. John Young Todd was born in Carroll County, Missouri, Nov. 30, 1830, and died at Salem, Nov. 8, 1919. He fought in the Mexican War and arrived in Oregon in 1852, by way of California. He packed goods to the mines and engaged in other business, and settled on a homestead in Tygh Valley. He built Sherars Bridge in 1860 and rebuilt it later. Todd later moved to the Farewell Bend ranch at the present site of Bend and lived in that vicinity for many years. For additional data, see *OHQ*, v. 30, p. 70.

Toketee Falls, DOUGLAS. These falls are on the North Umpqua at the mouth of the Clearwater. *Toketee* is the Chinook jargon word for pretty, or graceful. The word is pronounced Tuck-et-tee, with the accent on the first syllable.

Toketee Lake, DOUGLAS. This is a reservoir with a normal elevation of 2430 feet formed by damming North Umpqua River above Toketee Falls but below the mouth of the Clearwater. It holds water for hydroelectric power and is named for the nearby falls.

Tokyo Slough, LINCOLN. Tokyo Slough lies between the Southern Pacific Company tracks and the Georgia Pacific mill in Toledo. In 1925, the C. D. Johnson Lumber Company, the predecessor of Georgia Pacific Corporation, imported 35 Japanese workers. They ran the green chain at the sawmill and were housed at a camp alongside the slough. As they were willing to work at a lower wage, they were the cause of much local unrest.

Toledo, LINCOLN. Toledo is on the homestead of John Graham, a pioneer resident, who emigrated from Ohio. It is said that when the post office was established in 1868, Joseph D. Graham, a son, was told that he could name the place. He said: "I am homesick for Ohio. We will call the place Toledo." Toledo post office was established on July 14, 1868, with William Mackey first postmaster.

Tolke Canyon, WASHINGTON. Whitcher Creek west of Manning flows through Tolke Canyon. Hubert E. Davies of Boring, who lived in the Manning area for many years, told the compiler in 1990 that this canyon was named for Chris, Gus and Hans Tolke, brothers, who owned a threshing machine and did custom threshing for all the local farmers.

Tollgate, UMATILLA. Sometime in the 1870s the proprietor of the toll road over the Blue Mountains in the northeast part of the county established a toll gate and for many years the locality of this barrier was called Tollgate. With the development of Langdon Lake close by, the name Langdon Lake came into general use as the locality name. However, when a post office was established in Sept. 1941, the old name Tollgate was revived and used for the post office. Mrs. Harry (Gertie) Hunter was the first postmaster. The toll road was generally referred to as the Woodward road. Its west end was at the junction of the Lincton and Weston mountain roads and the southeast terminus was at Summerville. The gate was at Woodward Meadow in S 32, T 4N, R 38E. The meadow is the site of the Tollgate Ranger Station of the USFS. The locality is now on the main Weston-Elgin highway. The post office was discontinued in Mar. 1954.

Tolman Creek, JACKSON. James C. Tolman took a donation land claim where this creek empties into Neil Creek south of Ashland. He was leader of the emigration of 1852, the first to take the direct route into southern Oregon from the east. In later years he was county judge of Jackson County and surveyor general of Oregon. For further information about Tolman, *see History of Jackson County*, pp. 352 and 541.

Tolo, JACKSON. Will G. Steel is authority for the statement that this place was named in error by postal authorities. Cleophas C. Ragsdale, formerly a resident of Yolo, California, was living in Willow Springs, Oregon, in 1885, and as he disliked the commonplace name of his adopted home, he petitioned to have it changed to Yolo. The Y was misread as a T in Washington, and on Mar. 30, 1886, postal authorities changed the name of the office from Willow Springs to Tolo, and so it has been ever since. *Yolo* or *Yolay* was the name of an Indian tribe in California. The word is said to mean a place abounding in rushes. Willow Springs post office was established Aug. 12, 1864, with Samuel P. Dean first postmaster.

Tolovana Park, CLATSOP. Tolovana Park is a place on Cannon Beach, named for Tolovana, Alaska. The town in Alaska is on Tanana River, about 100 miles above Fort Gibbon, established in 1905 as a telegraph station and post office. This Indian name was selected by the Signal Corps, but the compiler has been unable to get the exact meaning. Some say it is an Indian tribal name, others that it means a wooded country and another version is that it means a pile of driftwood or log jam. Mark Warren and his brother, William E. Warren, spent some time in central Alaska, and, after their return, they platted property on Cannon Beach. Mark Warren chose the name Tolovana Park for his tract, because he fancied the sound of the word as used in Alaska.

Tom Dick & Harry Mountain, CLACKAMAS. This is the half-mile-long ridge about one mile southwest of Government Camp that forms the cirque now called the Ski Bowl. Lige Coalman told the writer that the name was in use when he first came to Government Camp in 1897 and that he thought it was so called because it has three distinct summits. The form Tom Dick Mountain on some maps is an incorrect abbreviation.

Tom East Creek, CURRY, JOSEPHINE. While Tom East probably was no more peripatetic than many other early-day miners in southwest Oregon, he accomplished wonders in leaving his mark on the land. There are at least three Tom East Creeks, one in Curry County tributary to Rogue River near Potato Illahe Mountain and two in Josephine County tributary to Grave Creek, near Galice and further upstream near Placer. East was born in England and came to the United States as a young man. He was mining in Josephine County in 1855 and lived in southwest Oregon until his death on July 14, 1897.

Tom Taylor Canyon, DOUGLAS. This canyon east of Camas Valley was named for a homesteader of 1895.

Tomahawk Island, MULTNOMAH. This name was originally given by Lewis and Clark to a small island between what is now known as Hayden Island and the north shore of the Columbia River. The name was the result of an incident that took place on Nov. 4, 1805, when William Clark's tomahawk pipe was stolen. The incident is mentioned several times in Thwaites' *Original Journals of the Lewis and Clark Expedition*. While the theft took place on the mainland, a small island was a silent witness and received its name on that account. *See* atlas volume, plate 34. Eventually the island disappeared. After the construction of the interstate bridge between Portland and Vancouver another island gradually emerged from the river not far from the original Tomahawk Island. In 1927 a group of students from the Catlin school in Portland petitioned the USBGN to attach the name Tomahawk Island to the new island in the Columbia River, which occupies a position between Ryan Point and Hayden Island. The USBGN made the requested decision on Apr. 6, 1927, and thus perpetuated the old name.

Tombstone Gap, JACKSON. Tombstone Gap is at the north edge of the county, about a mile south of Richter Mountain. It is a pass through the watershed between the Umpqua and Rogue river drainages. It was named for an outcrop of gray rock nearby, which in a small degree simulates a gravestone.

Tombstone Lake, UNION. Tombstone Lake, in T 5S, R 43E, was not named because of a tombstone. In Jan. 1944, J. F. Irwin, for many years connected with the USFS, wrote the compiler that the lake was named because a prominent mountain peak stands immediately at one end, like a gravestone.

Tombstone Prairie, LINN. This is a pleasant place on the South Santiam Highway, despite its melancholy name. Hackleman Creek flows eastward from the prairie into Fish Lake, and just west of the prairie the highway crosses Tombstone Summit, the watershed between the South Santiam and the McKenzie River drainage. On the south edge of the prairie is a tombstone with the inscription: "JAMES A., son of J. W. & C. M. McKnight. From an Accidental Shot. Oct. 17, 1871. AGED 18 Y's 9 M's 9 D's." Below this inscription there are eight stanzas of poetry, apparently composed by Mrs. McKnight.

Tomlike Mountain, HOOD RIVER. This mountain is south of Wyeth. According to H. D. Langille of Portland, it bears the name of Tomlike, or Indian George, a familiar character in the Hood River Valley. He was the son of Chinidere, the last Indian chief in that part of Oregon.

Tomlinson Slough, TILLAMOOK. This waterway near the mouth of Tillamook River was named for Samuel Tomlinson who settled nearby about 1883.

Toney Butte, WHEELER. Toney Butte near the headwaters of Girds Creek was named for Jonathan Toney who took up a homestead near its base in 1882. The form Tony is incorrect.

Tongue Point, CLATSOP. As far as the writer knows Tongue Point was the first geographic feature in Oregon not fronting on the Pacific Ocean to be named by white men. Captain George Vancouver, at the head of his expedition, attempted to sail into the mouth of the Columbia River in his sloop *Discovery* on Oct. 19 and 20, 1792, but was forced to abandon the attempt on Oct. 21, and sailed southward, leaving Lieutenant William Robert Broughton on the armed tender *Chatham* safely inside the bar. On the day that Vancouver sailed south, Broughton noted "a remarkable projecting point, that obtained the name of Tongue Point, on the southern shore, appearing like an island." No one has ever suggested a better name. It speaks for itself. Lewis and Clark tried to attach the name Point William, for William Clark, but the name has not prevailed. *See* Youngs Bay. Silas B. Smith says that the Indian name for Tongue Point was *Secomeetsiuc. See OHQ*, v. 1, p. 321. About 1920 a submarine and destroyer base was authorized for Tongue Point but it was not finished. Prior to World War II, the name of the installation was changed to U.S. Naval Air Station, Tongue Point, Oregon. The station was developed rapidly and was commissioned Dec. 15, 1940. After World War II, the station was decommissioned and the Navy declared the property surplus in 1961. After several alternate proposals, a federal Job Corps center was established in 1965. Tongue Point again figured in the news in 1980 with a discussion of the transfer of part of the area to the state or county for industrial use.

Tonquin, WASHINGTON. When the Oregon Electric Railway was built in 1907 – 08, it was the policy of the company to establish stations with names of historic interest to Oregonians and the station Tonquin was named for the ship that brought the Astor party to Astoria. The *Tonquin* entered the Columbia River, with the Astor sea party from New York, Mar. 24, 1811; was destroyed at Clayoquot Sound, Vancouver Island, in June 1811, and all the crew were killed by Indians. Its fate makes one of the most terrible and heroic tales of the Pacific Coast. For description of the place where the vessel was destroyed, *see* the *Oregonian*, Apr. 17, 1887. For narrative of the tragedy, Apr. 23, 1887, p. 3.

Tony Creek, HOOD RIVER. Tony Creek, north of Mount Hood, was named by members of the Langille family for their Cayuse pony, Tony. The stream was named about 1885. This information was furnished by H. D. Langille of Portland, who told the compiler that stories to the effect that the stream was named for Thornton Ladd of Portland, better known as Tony, were wrong.

Tony Creek, TILLAMOOK. Homer Simmons of Tillamook told the writer in 1970 that this tributary of Nestucca River upstream from Beaver was named for an early resident, Antone "Tony" Dotesauer. He added that the spelling of the family name was questionable.

Too Much Bear Lake, LANE. This lake is about a mile south of SH-58 above Salt Creek Falls. In 1983 Dan Sellard of the Eugene *Register-Guard* was kind enough to request information in his column. A number of replies were received and, while Earl Clark's statement that it was named in the 1880s by Charlie Tufti seems possible, Carl Isom of Sheridan informed the writer that he was present when the name was applied in the 1920s. His story is corroborated by Mrs. Moses Evans whose husband, now deceased, was working nearby. A USFS crew was building a trail from Salt Creek Falls to the newly completed Cascade Line of the Southern Pacific. Delbert Brown, the USFS packer, stopped to spend the night at their camp and in the evening walked up to the lake to try the fishing. He came unexpectedly and unwantingly close to a large bear and promptly retreated. Later around the campfire the days events were rehashed and the name was proposed by Charlie Stone, one of the crew. The next day Stone whittled a cedar sign which was duly installed.

Toomey Gulch, WALLOWA. Toomey Gulch drains into Imnaha River from the west in T 4N, R 49E, and bears the name of Michael Toomey, who with Hamilton Vance, had some mining claims there.

Top, GRANT. Top is in the extreme northwest corner of the county. The post office was established Oct. 22, 1915, with James Porter postmaster. Porter resigned, however, without actually having served and S. V. Cochran was the first postmaster who really conducted the office. Local residents who signed the petition for the post office sent in six names and Top was selected. It was suggested by one of the prospective patrons of the office because it was the first name of a prominent local resident, Top Reasner.

Tope Creek, WALLOWA. This stream is north of Wallowa and flows into Mud Creek. It bears the name of William A. Tope and was named for him in 1883 when he had a homestead near the head of the stream.

Topsy, KLAMATH. Topsy post office got its name from the Topsy grade on the old road from Ager in northern California northeast to Linkville, now Klamath Falls. The name Topsy was descriptive and was supposedly applied by freight haulers. However, Francis Landrum of Klamath Falls informed the compiler that Harold Ashley, a local authority, said the name was a corruption of that of an old Siskiyou Indian *Thipsi*. The post office, which was established Jan. 9, 1884, was at the Overton ranch at the top of the grade leading up from Klamath River, not far north of the California-Oregon state line and east of the river. This establishment was about 15 miles southwest by road from what was later Keno. Major Overton was listed as the only postmaster and the office was closed Feb. 2, 1885. Dr. Eugene W. Rockey of Portland informed the compiler in 1948 that Overton's full name was Major Watson Overton. He had been a messenger boy during the Modoc War of 1872 but Major was his given name and had no military significance.

Torrey Lake, LANE. Torrey Lake, about two miles north of Waldo Lake, is named for Dr. Henry Beal Torrey. Dr. Torrey was a native of Boston and took his graduate work at Columbia University. He was professor of biology at the University of California when, in 1912, he was asked to head the department as an original professor at the newly started Reed College in Portland. He was an expert on the growth and diseases of salmon and trout. The lake was named for him in the summer of 1913 by two of his students, Carl G. and Glen R. Johnson, who had the first contract with the Oregon Fish and Game Commission to stock mountain lakes with trout.

Tot Mountain, DESCHUTES. Tot Mountain is not a mountain at all, but a butte or point on the south slope of Bachelor Butte. It is named with the Chinook jargon word for uncle. The word was applied by the USFS because it was necessary to have a name for the butte for convenience in fire fighting. A little to the south is Kwolh Butte, and *kwolh* is the Chinook jargon word for aunt. These two names were doubtless selected because of Bachelor Butte, Three Sisters, The Husband and The Wife in the same general locality.

Tower Mountain, UMATILLA. Tower Mountain is in S 13, T 6S, R 34E, and was formerly known as Lookout Mountain. There is another Lookout Mountain 66 miles northeast, and on June 2, 1925, the USBGN changed the name of the mountain here considered to Tower Mountain because that was the name used by the USC&GS for a triangulation station on the summit. This was done to avoid confusion with the other Lookout Mountain. The triangulation station is about a quarter of a mile east of the USFS lookout site.

Townsend, MARION. This railroad station north of Mt. Angel was named for a pioneer family of the vicinity.

Trail, JACKSON. Trail is a post office on Rogue River at the mouth of Trail Creek. Trail Creek is so known because an Indian trail from Rogue River to Umpqua River traversed its banks, forming a short-cut between the military road and Roseburg in pioneer days. Will G. Steel is authority for the statement that the earlier name of Trail Creek was Stewart Creek, but it does not now go by that name.

Trail Creek, WALLOWA. Trail Creek flows into Camp Creek west of Imnaha. J. H. Horner told the compiler that it was named for an important Indian trail extending west from Imnaha River to camps on Camp Creek. The Indian name for the creek and trail was *Wa-lim-isk-kit*, with the accent on the second syllable.

Trailfork, GILLIAM. Trailfork is a descriptive name for a locality situated about ten or twelve miles southeast of Condon. The name came into use in pioneer days, but the post office was not established until July 1, 1902, with Nancy M. Mattingly first postmaster. This office was discontinued Jan. 31, 1916. Government maps use the style Trail Fork, and there is a Trail Fork Canyon and Trail Fork School shown on the map of the Salmon Fork quadrangle.

Trapp Creek, LINCOLN. Trapp Creek in the Coast Range flows into Yaquina River from the south in the extreme southwest corner of T 10S, R 9W, at a point a little over a mile west of Chitwood. The stream was named for a well-known family of pioneer settlers of the vicinity. The spelling Trap is wrong.

Trapper Creek, KLAMATH. Trapper Creek empties into West Bay of Odell Lake. Judge John B. Waldo, in many notes of his Cascade Mountain trips, tells of camping at Odell Lake. His names have not survived but his camp was at the west end of the lake and he frequently mentions Trappers Bay nearby with the remnants of an old trapper's shack. The compiler does not know when the name was changed to West Bay but old timers still refer to Trappers Bay.

Trask River, TILLAMOOK. Elbridge Trask, a native of Massachusetts, first came to Oregon in Wyeth's brig *May Dacre* in 1834, and in the fall of 1835 he went to the

Rocky Mountains to trap and hunt. He returned to Oregon in 1842 and settled on Clatsop Plains, probably in 1843. Silas B. Smith says Trask worked on Hunt's Mill, pioneer sawmill of Clatsop County, built at Hunts Mill Point in the winter of 1843 –44. He moved from Clatsop Plains to Tillamook County in Aug. 1852. Trask River bears his name. Trask's land title certificate was no. 3926. He died June 22, 1863, aged 49 years.

Traverse Ridge, WALLOWA. This ridge is south of Lostine and east of Lostine River. It was named by R. L. Hensel about 1915 during some mapping operations, and on account of a survey traverse.

Treasure Cove, TILLAMOOK. This is an almost inaccessible cove in the northern base of Neahkahnie Mountain. It is said to have a cave in its face not far above the waters of the Pacific Ocean. The name was bestowed because of the many legends of pirate treasure in the neighborhood of Nehalem. *See* Cotton's *Stories of Nehalem*. Just north of Treasure Cove is a similar indentation called Devils Cauldron, and the much larger Smugglers Cove is still further north.

Tremont, MULTNOMAH. The plat for the addition called Tremont was filed June 4, 1892, covering an area in what is now southeast Portland, and about a mile westward of Lents. There are other additions with Tremont as part of the name, including Tremont Park and Tremont Place. The name Tremont is familiar to Bostonians and refers to three hills or mounts. It is possible that someone from Massachusetts named the Tremont additions. In the summer of 1892 a post office was petitioned for, and it was established Aug. 18, 1892, with J. A. Forbes postmaster, but to the surprise of the local enthusiasts the name turned out to be Fremont. Whoever wrote the petition did not have the benefit of the Spencerian method of handwriting. The mistake was soon corrected and the name of the office was changed to Tremont on Oct. 15, 1892. The office was closed to Lents on Feb. 18, 1903.

Trent, LANE. Rattlesnake post office was established near Rattlesnake Creek in 1868. The office name was changed to Trent on Oct. 8, 1875, but the compiler has been unable to learn why. The office was closed June 7, 1963.

Trester, GRANT. Trester was at one time a post office in Grant County at a point about six miles west of Fox, named for a local resident. The office was established Aug. 6, 1913, with Gertrude Trester first postmaster. The office was discontinued June 29, 1918, and the business turned over to Fox.

Trestle Creek, LANE. Trestle Creek is tributary to Brice Creek a mile upstream from Lundpark. When the Oregon Securities Company built the Bonita Placer in the early 1900s, they constructed a powerhouse at Lundpark. The flume supplying water for the turbine crossed Trestle Creek on an imposing wood structure.

Tri City, DOUGLAS. This is a community in Missouri Bottom centered among Myrtle Creek, Canyonville and Riddle. The name apparently originated with the Tri City School District and was taken up later by the sewer district and Tri City State Airport.

Tri-Club Island, MULTNOMAH. This island was formerly called Sand Island, one of many. It lies in the Columbia River northeast of Lemon Island and north of the west tip of Government Island. Larry Barber has an interesting account of its history in "River Ramblings," a column written for the June 1984, Jantzen Beach Center *Freshwater News*. The pertinent facts are as follows. Originally it was north of the main channel and consequently in the state of Washington. About 1929 Spencer Biddle and Mrs. Erskine Wood bought the island from Clark County and made it available to the public for recreation. Subsequently the channel was moved north and the island found itself in Oregon. In 1953 the Biddles and Woods sold it to a consortium of the Portland, Columbia River and Rose City yacht clubs. The clubs tried to maintain minimum sanitary facilities for boaters but after property taxes were increased 500 percent in two years, they capitulated and deeded the island to Oregon's Division of State Lands. In 1985 when new charts of the Columbia were being prepared, the OGNB voted to adopt the current common usage, Tri-Club Island. It was published in *Decision List 8602*.

Triangle, CURRY. Triangle post office was in the extreme north end of the county on the old mail road between Myrtle Point and Langlois. It was in service from Sept. 29, 1914, to Dec. 15, 1916. Mrs. Elinor Lehnherr was the only postmaster. The office was named for the Triangle Ranch, operated by the Lehnherr family, where a triangular stock brand was used.

Triangle Hill, DESCHUTES. A descriptive name, applied on viewing the hill from the east. The point is in the foothills of the Cascade Range east of the Three Sisters.

Triangle Lake, LANE. This prominent lake west of Blachly is named because of its shape. Before the completion of Fern Ridge Reservoir, it was the most popular local spot for water sports and it still has a large following. Mrs. Elma Rust of Blachly wrote in 1971 to give some of the early history which is paraphrased as follows. It seems to have had various names as an 1878 map shows it as Loon Lake while Walling's 1884 *History of Lane County* also has a map with Loon Lake but a text reference to Lake of the Woods. An early Eugene newspaper, *Oregon State Journal*, Sept. 23, 1882, mentions Echo Lake, formerly called Loon Lake and this is reiterated in an 1887 road petition that uses the form Echo Lake. This interesting variety appears to have ended with the advent of the motor car and the geometric forms of the age mechanical.

Triangle Moraine, CLACKAMAS. This glacial moraine on Mount Hood is at the 9000-foot level between Zigzag and White River glaciers and above Palmer Glacier. It is a conspicuous spot on the upper slopes and was the terminus of the snow cat run for spring skiers before the construction of the Palmer Lift. Fred H. McNeil says in *Wy-east "THE Mountain"*, p. 142 that it was named not because of its shape but by the Triangle Club, a YMCA organization of climbers who went that way in 1896.

Trolan Grade, JEFFERSON. This grade on the old Teller Creek road was named because it ran by the property of Daniel Trolan who settled in the area just after the turn of the century.

Trout Creek, JEFFERSON. Trout Creek post office was one of several established in the stock pioneering days northeast of what is now Madras. Cross Keys was another and also Hay Creek and Heisler. They were well-known places and have left a legacy of pioneer lore. Trout Creek post office was established July 3, 1878, with Jasper A. Friend postmaster. William Heisler became postmaster Oct. 17, 1878. It seems probable from an inspection of postal records that the name of this office was changed to Cross Keys on Feb. 13, 1879, but the record is not clear and the two offices may not have been in the same place, but they were both near the stream Trout Creek.

Troutdale, MULTNOMAH. The community of Troutdale was once known as Sandy. Sandy post office was established June 1, 1854, with Emsley R. Scott postmaster. The office was discontinued Feb. 26, 1868. It was apparently near the present site of the town Troutdale. Captain John Harlow, an Oregon pioneer from Maine, originated the name Troutdale, because of the fact there was a small dale near his house where he had a fish pond, which he stocked with trout. This occurred about 1880. Shortly thereafter he secured the establishment of Troutdale post office. This office was for a time discontinued. When the railroad built through this section of the country the station was named Troutdale, at the request of Captain Harlow, and so it has been known ever since.

Troy, WALLOWA. The postmaster at Troy informed the compiler in Dec. 1926, that at the time the post office was established, which was in 1902, several names were suggested, but the Post Office Department rejected them all. Finally the department suggested a list which included the name Troy. This was adopted. However, in 1931 J. H. Horner of Enterprise told the compiler that the place was probably named for Troy Grinstead, son of A. L. Grinstead. Mormons settled in the locality about 1898 and the place was generally called Nauvoo.

Truax Island, LINN. Truax Island is northeast of Corvallis, on the south side of Willamette River and north of Dead River. It was named for Wallace and Maud Truax, landowners. The spelling Traux is wrong.

Tryon, COLUMBIA. Tryon, the name of a locality in Columbia County, came from the family name of Socrates Hotchkiss Tryon, son of an Oregon pioneer of 1850. Dr. Socrates H. Tryon, Sr., settled near Oswego and Tryon Creek just west of Palatine Hill in Clackamas and Multnomah counties bears his name. The younger Tryon was left fatherless in 1855 and had to shift for himself most of his life. In 1869 he became a fisherman on the Columbia River and later engaged in logging and farming. Tryon post office was established near the Columbia River at a point between Rainier and Mayger on Dec. 1, 1884, with S. H. Tryon postmaster. The place was about a mile and a half south of Walker Island. The office was discontinued in Sept. 1894. There is an account of the activities of S. H. Tryon in Fred Lockley's column in the *Oregon Journal*, Aug. 25, 1928, editorial page. Records at the Oregon Historical Society do not substantiate the statement that Dr. Tryon was an Oregon pioneer of 1849. That was probably the year he arrived in California. He reached Oregon in 1850.

Tryon Creek, CLACKAMAS, MULTNOMAH. Dr. Socrates Hotchkiss Tryon was born in Vermont about 1815 and came to Oregon by way of Panama about 1850. He settled near Oswego, and Tryon Creek is named in his memory. He died in 1855. Tryon Creek drains the west slope of Palatine Hill and flows into Willamette River just north of Oswego. For information about the Tryon family, *see* article by Fred Lockley, *Oregon Journal*, Aug. 25, 1928.

Tryon Creek, WALLOWA. Tryon Creek flows into Snake River in T 3N, R 50E. It bears the name of Nate and James Tryon, who ranged sheep there and built a two-story cabin.

Tualatin, WASHINGTON. The town of Tualatin is near Tualatin River and was named on that account. There was formerly a discrepancy in spelling between the post office name and the railroad station name. The USBGN finally decided on Tualatin, which is now in universal use. The post office with the spelling Tualitin was established Nov. 5, 1869, with Marcellus S. Dailey first postmaster. The name was changed to Tualatin on Sept. 25, 1915. In the 1880s the place was sometimes called Bridgeport probably because of the construction of one of the first bridges over the nearby Tualatin River.

Tualatin River, CLACKAMAS, WASHINGTON. Tualatin is probably an Indian word meaning "lazy or sluggish," this being the character of the river's flow; other meanings are "land without trees," signifying the plains of Tualatin and "forks" or "forked" for the numerous upper tributaries including Gales and Dairy creeks. The "treeless plain" was vouched for by Tolbert Carter, pioneer of 1846, whose home was near Wells, Benton County to Geo. H. Himes. *Tualatin* was *Twha-la-ti*, according to Silas B. Smith in the *OHQ*, v. 1, p. 323. John Work gave *Faladin* in 1834. The name has had many variations, among them *Twality, Quality, Falatine* and *Nefalatine*. There is a town named Tualatin in Washington County. The settlements near what are now known as Hillsboro and Forest Grove were in pioneer days called East and West Tualatin precincts. One of the original districts or counties of Oregon was called Twality. *See OHQ*, v. 11, p. 11, v. 16, p. 278 and v. 28, p. 56. The spelling Tuality was also used officially.

Tub Spring, WALLOWA. Tub Spring is in T 2N, R 41E, and is so called because it was lined with a tub to keep the water clean. This was done about 1890 when the McDonald brothers had a cattle camp nearby.

Tub Springs, JACKSON. Tub Springs Wayside, a state park, is located at these springs 18 miles east of Ashland and two miles west of Lincoln on SH-66. The name is old and obviously refers to some improvement of the spring. Some maps, including the USGS Soda Mountain quadrangle, show this as Tubb Springs but this is incorrect.

Tub Springs, JEFFERSON. This spring and canyon of the same name are tributary to Trout Creek just south of the Wasco County line. In 1969 John Silvertooth of Antelope told the compiler there was a fine spring near the head of the canyon that was lined with an old wood tub to clarify the water.

Tub Springs, MORROW. This spring in Juniper Canyon five miles north of McDaid Springs was named in early days because the hole resembled a round tub. It was on an alternate trace of the Oregon Trail some two miles north of the main route and for 50 years was the home of James Carty, a pioneer sheepman.

Tucker Bridge, HOOD RIVER. B. R. Tucker built a bridge and a sawmill at this place about 1881, and the locality was named Tucker Bridge for him. Tucker post office was established Jan. 15, 1892, with B. R. Tucker postmaster. The office was discontinued June 2, 1900.

Tucker Creek, BAKER. Tucker Creek empties into Powder River at Keating. It was named for John A. Tucker, an early settler.

Tucker Creek, CLATSOP. J. B. Kilmore of Astoria wrote the compiler in 1927 that this stream, southeast of Astoria, was named for a wood scow operator who cut wood near the stream and brought it to Astoria for sale.

Tuffy Creek, TILLAMOOK. Tuffy Creek flows into South Fork Wilson River at South Fork Camp, a Department of Corrections minimum-security facility. A young salmon made its way through a supply pipe drawing water from the creek to a pond. Here it was hand fed by the inmates and named Tuffy for its resilience in surviving the unusual journey. The creek was named for the fish, to the compiler's knowledge the only individual fish ever so honored in Oregon. The Oregon Wildlife Heritage Foundation was instrumental in proposing official naming action. In 1987 they were doing preliminary engineering studies prior to constructing a substantial fish-rearing facility at the South Fork Camp site.

Tufti Mountain, LANE. Tufti Mountain is about six miles southeast of Oakridge. It was named for a local Indian celebrity, Charlie Tufti.

Tule Lake, KLAMATH, Oregon, and MODOC, SISKIYOU, California. Tule Lake was discovered May 1, 1846, by then Captain John C. Fremont, and was later named Lake Rhett for his friend, Barnwell Rhett of South Carolina. *See* Fremont's *Memoirs of My Life*, Chicago, 1887, p. 480. On July 6, 1846, the Applegate exploring party first saw this lake. *See OHQ*, v. 22, p. 1. It is possible that members of the exploring party named the lake Tule Lake at that time, because of its surroundings, although the article does not specifically say so. The article was not written at the time of the exploration. In any event, the name Tule Lake has come into general use and has been adopted by the USBGN in preference to Lake Rhett. Tule is the name of a certain kind of rush. Due to the fact that the waters of Lost River have been diverted, the lake is being gradually reclaimed and at the time of this writing does not exist in Oregon. *See* the *Oregonian*, Sept. 16, 1923, p. 2. There has been a post office called Tule Lake at various locations in Klamath County, but it was not in service in 1945. In 1944 there was a Tulelake post office just over the line in California, serving among others, a Japanese relocation center frequently in the news. Gatschet, in *Dictionary of the Klamath Language*, gives a number of Klamath and other Indian names for this lake. One was *Mayaltko E-ush*, meaning the lake overgrown with rushes or tule-grass. *Moatak* and *Moatokni E-ush* were words used by the Klamaths in referring to this lake, indicating that it was in the neighborhood of the Modoc Indians. The Pit River Indians, according to Gatschet, used the word *Lutuami* when speaking of this lake.

Tulley Creek, WALLOWA. Tulley Creek drains into Imnaha River in T 3N, R 48E. It was named for James Tulley, who, with Aaron Wade, drove cattle to the mouth of the stream in 1880 or 1881 for winter range.

Tumalo, DESCHUTES. The original name of the community of Tumalo was Laidlaw. It was named for W. A. Laidlaw, one of the promoters of the place, and Laidlaw post office was established Dec. 17, 1904 with William G. Stiles first postmaster. At that time the state was active in the development of the Tumalo irrigation project and a post office with the name Tumalo had been established near the construction camps on Oct. 15, 1904 with George W. Wimer postmaster. In 1913 after the work was terminated and the camps abandoned, Tumalo post office was closed with mail to Laidlaw. Meanwhile, the name Tumalo was coming into general use for the locality and on Jan. 20, 1915, the name of the Laidlaw post office was changed to Tumalo. The compiler is indebted to Mrs. May D. Fryrear of Salem for the preceding facts. Mrs. Fryrear's mother was acting postmaster at the first Tumalo post office when it was closed.

Tumalo Creek, DESCHUTES. Satisfactory information about the origin of Tumalo has not been forthcoming, but the compiler is inclined to the belief that it is from the Klamath Indian word *temolo*, meaning wild plum. This shrub was once quite plentiful in south central Oregon. The Klamaths had another word *temola* meaning ground fog, which may have been used to describe the vicinity of Tumalo Creek, but this is conjectural. Robert B. Gould of Bend informed the compiler that an old settler told him the original name was *Tumallowa*, and meant icy water. Any one of the above explanations might fit the facts, so there you are.

Tumalt Creek, MULTNOMAH. This stream in the eastern part of the county was formerly called Devil Creek and Devil Slide Creek, but at the instigation of the Mazamas in 1915 the name Tumalt was adopted by the government to commemorate an Indian who was killed by Sheridan's command during the Cascade engagement in 1856.

Tumia, UMATILLA. In 1928 the Union Pacific Railroad established a new station just west of Gibbon and called it Tumia. The word is an abbreviation of the Indian name *Toom-hi-ya*. The accent is on the middle syllable. Toom-hi-ya was an Indian woman living near the siding, the wife of Charles Shaplish. The station was closed before 1970.

Tumtum River, BENTON, LINCOLN. *Tumtum* is a Chinook jargon word meaning heart, and Tumtum River was so named because it was considered to be the heart of the valley through which it flowed. Mrs. H. G. Downing, of Burnt

Woods, wrote the compiler in 1927 that, when a post office was proposed, an effort was made to have the place called Tumtum, but the post office department selected the name Burnt Woods because of the forest fires that had swept over that part of the country many years ago.

Tunnel Canyon, UMATILLA. Tunnel Canyon is just west of Battle Mountain Summit and empties into East Fork Butter Creek. Prior to World War 1, O. D. Teel started the Teel Irrigation Project to bring water from Camas Creek to Butter Creek drainage. This included a tunnel under the pass south of Battle Mountain Summit with the north portal in what is now known as Tunnel Canyon. In the 1920s after about a quarter of the tunnel was completed, the company went bankrupt so we must conclude that in oil drilling parlance they ended with a "dry hole." Teel was the son of Dr. John Teel, the first physician on the Umatilla Indian Reservation.

Tunnel Creek, MARION. Tunnel Creek flows into North Santiam River just downstream from Whitewater Creek. The name is descriptive for the stream, despite a substantial watershed, flows underground in the vicinity of SH-22.

Tunnel Point, COOS. Tunnel Point is a natural rock formation on Bastendorff Beach at the south side of the entrance to Coos Bay. It has a hole in it, hence the name.

Tupper Rock, COOS. This was a well-known landmark near Bandon, and just south of Coquille River. It was named for John P. Tupper, who kept a hotel at Bandon for many years. Most of the rock has been removed and used to build the Coquille River jetty. There is a snappy picture of J. P. Tupper's Ocean House and Tupper Rock in Walling's *History of Southern Oregon*, p. 268.

Turnbull Creek, BAKER. In 1910 Milton S. Turnbull filed on land at the mouth of this tributary of North Pine Creek.

Turnbull Peak, MALHEUR. Turnbull Peak is at the north end of the Sheepshead Mountains. It and nearby Turnbull Lakebed bear the name of Tom Turnbull who came from Scotland in 1883, age 26. Turnbull first came to Shaniko where he was a succesful sheep rancher. He later expanded into Barren Valley and the Folly Farm area. He was a life-long bachelor and a well-known philanthropist. Turnbull died in 1942. Turnbull Mountain, well to the northeast in T 25S, R 40E, is named for the same man.

Turner, MARION. When the railroad was built through this part of the state the officials shipped a load of construction material to the present site of Turner, with instructions to build a station and warehouse to be known as Marion. A man in charge of the shipment unloaded it at the wrong place and built a station some six miles farther south which was called Marion and is in the present location of the station of that name. When the railroad officials discovered the material had been sent to the wrong place they sent a new consignment to the place originally intended to be called Marion, and after building a station named it Turner, for Henry L. Turner, a well-known pioneer resident of this vicinity.

Turner Creek, YAMHILL. The stream heading near the Yamhill-Washington county line and flowing south into North Yamhill River near Pike is generally known as Turner Creek. The name came from a family of pioneer settlers who at one time operated a small water-driven sawmill on the upper reaches of the stream. This creek has also been called Hay Creek and Hayes Creek, but local sentiment at Pike seems to be in favor of Turner Creek. That is the name used by the USGS on the Turner Creek quadrangle while Hay Creek is a small tributary north of Pike.

Turner Mountain, GRANT. Turner Mountain is in the extreme northwest corner of Grant County, in the southwest part of T 7S, R 27E. It was named for Joseph A. Turner, a pioneer homesteader on the Howell Ranch nearby.

Turtle Cove, GRANT. Turtle Cove is east of John Day River in the John Day Fossil Beds National Monument. It was named in 1864 by Professor Thomas Condon for the abundance of fossil remains of Miocene turtles. The area has also been known as Blue Basin because of the distinctive coloration. This latter name was first applied by the John C. Merriam party of 1899.

Tuskan, WASCO. This is a railway station on the Burlington Northern near Sherars Bridge. The Indian name of the locality near Sherars Bridge was *Tush-kan-ee*, and the modern form is a derivative. The form Tuscan is incorrect.

Tustin Lake, YAMHILL. This intermittent pond was named for Charles S. Tustin, a pioneer settler. The lake is near the North Yamhill River west of St. Joseph.

Tuttle Creek, DOUGLAS. This tributary of Cavitt Creek was named for Walter Tuttle who homesteaded near its source in 1912.

Tutuilla Creek, UMATILLA. Information about the origin of this name is conflicting. Judge Fred W. Wilson of The Dalles told the compiler in 1927 that there was a family tradition that this stream was named about 1870 by his father, the late Judge Joseph G. Wilson, because of some childish remark made by his sister, Lucy Wilson, later Mrs. Joseph T. Peters of Portland. Lucy Wilson's nickname was Toots and the story is that Judge and Mrs. Wilson and their little girl were camped near the mouth of this stream and the child referred to it as Toots Creek. Judge Wilson then made up the name Tutuilla Creek. Mrs. Wilson, in her reminiscences on file at the Fort Dalles Museum, gives a slight variation. She says her nickname was Tootie and she called the stream "Tuta-illa." The incident occured when she was two and a half years old so the exact wording may be obscure. Residents of the Umatilla Indian Reservation do not agree with this version. One old Indian says that the stream has been known as Tutuilla Creek by the Indians for several generations and that the word *tutuilla* means a thorn bush which grows along its banks. There is another story in circulation in Umatilla County to the effect the stream was named for a place in the South Seas, by an old resident. It is of course possible that the Indians originally named the stream and Miss Wilson or the old resident or both of them applied their own versions. Such coincidences are not unknown in geographic nomenclature.

Tututni Pass, KLAMATH. This pass is in Vidae Ridge, south of Crater Lake. It bears the name of a tribe of Indians that lived near the mouth of Rogue River. The name has no especial significance near Crater Lake, and was probably chosen for sentimental reasons.

Twelvemile Creek, LAKE. This stream flows generally eastward back and forth across the California-Oregon state line southeast of Lakeview. Its waters eventually find their way into the Warner Valley. Twelvemile Creek was so called because the old wagon road north from Fort Bidwell, California, crossed the stream about 12 miles north of Fort Bidwell. Fifteenmile Creek flows into Twelvemile Creek.

Twentymile Creek, LAKE. Twentymile Creek flows into the Warner Valley south of Adel. The stream received its name because the old road from Fort Bidwell, California, crossed it about 20 miles from the fort.

Twentythree Creek, LINCOLN. For most of its course Twentythree Creek flows through s 23, T 10S, R 10W, and for that reason was named for the section number. The stream is about six miles northeast of Toledo and is tributary to Simpson Creek.

Twickenham, WHEELER. Twickenham is a place on John Day River about 20 miles south of Fossil. In Aug. 1943, W. H. Steiwer of Fossil wrote the compiler that the locality was formerly called Contention, and that there was once a post office of that name, apparently commemorating a quarrel between Anthony "Pike" Helms and Jerome H. Parsons, local celebrities. Contention post office was established July 8, 1886, with Edward F. Horn first postmaster. Miss Frankie Parsons, daughter of Jerome H. Parsons, is said to have been responsible for changing the name of the office to Twickenham. While away at school she appears to have become familiar with Theophile Marzials' poem, *Twickenham Ferry*, the scene of which is laid at Twickenham, a western suburb of London on the River Thames. Upon her return from school, Miss Parsons is said to have objected to the name Contention as being undignified and she determined to get rid of it. Whatever the reason, the facts are that Twickenham post office was established on June 6, 1896, with Anthony Helms as postmaster. It is not clear whether this was a new office or a change of names, and the available records are not conclusive. Twickenham post office was discontinued on Feb. 28, 1917, and mail is now sent through Fossil.

Twilight Creek, CLATSOP. This stream is east of Astoria. It was named for W. H. Twilight who took up land on its banks in pioneer days. He was at one time sheriff of Clatsop County.

Twin Cities. The compiler has had several requests for information about a locality in Oregon known as Twin Cities. It may have been a mining camp.

Twin Lakes, DESCHUTES. The correct names for these two lakes are North Twin Lake and South Twin Lake. They straddle the center north-south section line in T 21S, R 8E. Thornton T. Munger, who started with the USFS in 1908, told the writer in 1972 that about 1911 he was surveying certain boundaries for the proposed experimental forest near Crane Prairie. This section line had been previously surveyed but no mention was made of its crossing any lakes so he was not only surprised to find these two bodies of water but also surmised that the previous surveyor had made generous use of the "armchair transit." Munger stated that he applied the name Twin Lakes at that time.

Twin Pillars, CROOK. This is a descriptive name for a tall stone formation whose top is separated into two distinct parts. It stands between Brogan Creek and East Fork Mill Creek.

Twin Rocks, TILLAMOOK. Twin Rocks post office served a summer resort, and was named for two large rocks more than 100 feet high in the Pacific Ocean just beyond low tide line. The office was established in the summer of 1914, with William E. Dunsmoor first postmaster.

Twin Sisters Creeks, DOUGLAS. These streams are in the northwest part of the county, in the Coast Range. They converge into one stream just before they flow into Smith River in s 18, T 20S, R 8W. The two creeks are very much alike, and of about the same size. They are known as North Sister Creek and South Sister Creek, and Twin Sister Guard Station is situated at the junction of the two streams. According to H. R. Oglesby, district fire warden, the names are very old and were applied in natural consequence of the similarity of the two creeks.

Two Corral Creek, WALLOWA. This stream flows into Snake River in T 1N, R 50E, and was named because W. H. Winters had two stock corrals there in the early days.

Twobuck Creek, WALLOWA. This stream is called Twobuck Creek because the Warnock brothers once killed two deer nearby at a time when they badly needed meat. It is in T 2S, R 49E.

Twocolor Creek, BAKER. This stream is in T 6S, R 43E. It was named because of the contrast in color of the two main forks.

Twomile Creek, COOS. This stream is about ten miles north of Bandon. It was named during the Coos County gold rush of 1853–55 because it was about two miles north along the beach from Randolph and Whisky Run, one of the important points of the excitement.

Twomile Creek, COOS. Twomile Creek south of Bandon is said to have been named because it was that distance south of the town and of the mouth of Coquille River. However, maps do not support this theory. The stream is more than five miles south of Bandon. *See* Fourmile Creek.

Tycer Creek, JOSEPHINE. Tycer Creek is about five miles southeast of Kerby. It was named for James E. Tycer who settled in Brownsville in 1853 and moved to Josephine County in 1866. He owned a ranch near the stream.

Tyee Mountain, DOUGLAS. *Tyee* is the Chinook jargon word for chief, and this mountain was so named because of its important position in its surroundings. The word comes from the Nootka language. Until 1939 there was a post office near the mountain called Tyee.

Tygh Valley, WASCO. Tygh Valley is a post office in the valley of the same name on the banks of Tygh Creek. To the north is an imposing range of hills more than 3000 feet high, known as Tygh Ridge. The name comes from the Tygh Indian tribe, now part of the Warm Springs Indians. The Pacific Railroad Surveys *Reports*, 1855, use the form Tysch Prairie. Fremont in his *Report* of 1845 gives Taih Prairie. *Handbook of American Indians*, v. 1, p. 860, gives other forms.

Tyler Creek, JACKSON. This is a tributary of Emigrant Creek south of Emigrant Reservoir. It apparently was named for James M. Tyler who homesteaded near its mouth in the 1870s.

Ukiah, UMATILLA. This post office was established Sept. 22, 1890, with DeWitt C. Whiting first postmaster. E. B. Gambee, of Portland, informed the writer in 1926 that he suggested the name of the Oregon community which had been platted Aug. 6, 1890, by the Camas Land Company. Gambee had previously lived in Ukiah, California, and offered the name on that account. The place in California was named for the Yokaia Indians, a division of the Pomo. The word is said to mean south valley. Gambee was born in Michigan about 1852 and came to Oregon from California about 1881. He died in Portland on Oct. 8, 1939. For obituary, *see* Pendleton *East Oregonian*, Oct. 10, 1939.

Ulvstad, JACKSON. Ulvstad post office was on or near Sugarpine Creek, which flows into Elk Creek 12 or 14 miles northeast of Trail. Martin Ulvstad served as the postmaster from July 16, 1904, to Oct. 4, 1905, and the office was given his name. There was no community, just a very few small mountain ranches.

Umapine, UMATILLA. This place in the north part of the county was formerly named Vincent, but when a post office was applied for, it was found that there was another Vincent in the state. This was doubtless Vincent in Wallowa County. Citizens of Vincent in Umatilla County then changed the name of their community to Umapine, for a Cayuse or Umatilla Indian chief of some prominence. Umapine post office was established in June 1916, with Edgar Holm first postmaster. The office was closed Dec. 30, 1966.

Umatilla, UMATILLA. The town now known as Umatilla was surveyed by Timothy K. Davenport in 1863. It was first known as Umatilla Landing, and later Umatilla City. Eight miles west was the locality known for a time as Grande Ronde Landing, near the site of what is now Irrigon. Umatilla and Grande Ronde landings sprang up as stopping places for traffic with the Boise and Owyhee mines, but Umatilla Landing soon controlled the business and Grande Ronde Landing ceased to be of importance. Umatilla was known as Columbia about 1863, but soon resumed the old name. For information about the laying out of the town, *see* the *Oregonian*, May 16, 1863. Umatilla is at the mouth of Umatilla River and was named on that account. Postal records at Washington D.C. show that Umatilla post office was established Sept. 26, 1851, with A. Francis Rogers postmaster. The office was discontinued Jan. 6, 1852. *See OHQ*, v. 41, p. 69. This was the first post office in eastern Oregon. The *Oregonian*, Aug. 2, 1851, says this office was at the Umatilla Indian Agency, about 150 miles east of The Dalles, on the route to Salt Lake. The news item gives the name of the postmaster as A. Francis Royer. Records at the Oregon Historical Society substantiate the name Royer and not Rogers. This pioneer post office was of course not near the present town of Umatilla, but probably near Echo. The post office for Umatilla town was established May 28, 1863, with Z. F. Moody postmaster.

Umatilla County. This county was created Sept. 27, 1862, and was carved out of Wasco County as it existed at that time. It was named for Umatilla River, which see. It now has an area of 3263 square miles. The temporary seat of government for the new county was put at what was then known as Marshall Station, on the north bank of Umatilla River near Houtama, William C. McKay's place at the mouth of McKay Creek. About 1863 Umatilla County citizens changed the name of Marshall Station to Middleton. This name was selected because it was thought that the place was about half way between Umatilla Landing and the Grande Ronde Valley. In 1865 Umatilla City was selected as the county seat and was continued so until 1868 when the legislature passed an act directing the citizens of the county to declare their choice between "the present location . . . and Upper Umatilla, somewhere between the mouths of Wild Horse and Birch Creeks." The election favored the new location, and it was accordingly made county seat and named Pendleton, for George H. Pendleton, Democratic nominee for vice president. Umatilla tried to rescue the seat by legal means, on the grounds of vagueness of the act of the legislature, but was not successful. For additional information, *see* Pendleton. *See also* Fred Lockley's article in *Sunday Journal*, June 3, 1945.

Umatilla River, UMATILLA. *Umatilla* is the Indian name for a river, given as *Youmalolam*, in Lewis and Clark journals; variously spelled in early books of Oregon. Alexander Ross gives *You-matella* and *Umatallow*; Townsend gives *Utalla* and *Ewmitilly*; Irving gives *Eu-o-tal-la*; Fremont gives *Umatilah*; Parker gives *Umatella*; Wilkes and Nesmith give *Umatilla*. The compiler knows of no reliable interpretation of the Indian name. For references to the name and to the locality, *see Oregon Geographic Names*, 1928 edition, pp. 363–64. The Umatilla Indians are a group of tribes formerly living on the Umatilla River and on adjacent banks of the Columbia River. Umatilla, as a tribe name, is of late application. These Indians were not originally Umatillas. The name came to be applied after the extermination of many of the Cayuses and Walla Wallas.

Umbrella Falls, HOOD RIVER. This descriptive name was suggested to the USBGN by Oregon residents, and adopted May 6, 1925. The falls are on one of the sources of East Fork Hood River about a mile and a half above the Mount Hood Loop Highway, near Mount Hood Meadows Ski Area.

Umpqua, DOUGLAS. Umpqua is an historic name in the state. It was used by the Indians to refer to the locality of the Umpqua River and came to be applied to

Umpqua River. For a discussion of the name, *see* Umpqua River. There have been several places known as Fort Umpqua. John Work visited the Umpqua River in 1834 and Fort Umpqua, which was later established by the Hudson's Bay Company near the present site of Elkton, did not then exist. Work mentions "umpqua old fort" which appears to have been established in 1832 near Calapooya Creek. *See* Elkton for additional information. In the summer of 1850 a party of prospectors, originally planning to visit the Klamath River, explored the Umpqua River and established Umpqua City on Aug. 5, 1850. It was on the east side of the river, near its mouth. West Umpqua was the name selected for the community planned for the other side. *See OHQ*, v. 17, p. 355. There was some development at both places, but the towns had petered out by 1867. *See* Scott's *History of the Oregon Country*, v. 3, pp. 42 and 46. Umpqua City post office was established on Sept. 26, 1851, with Amos E. Rogers postmaster. Samuel S. Mann became postmaster on Feb. 24, 1852. This office may have been on the east side of the river when first established but in 1860 the post office and community of Umpqua City were on the west side of the river about two miles north of the mouth. A military post was then at the same place. *See* Fort Umpqua. The present Umpqua post office is on Umpqua River near the mouth of Calapooya Creek and a long way from the places mentioned above. The post office now known as Umpqua was originally called Umpqua Ferry and was first established Mar. 16, 1877, with John C. Shambrook postmaster. About 1905 the word Ferry was eliminated from the name.

Umpqua River, DOUGLAS. *Umpqua* was the Indian name of the locality of Umpqua River, and the name came to be applied both to the river and to an Indian tribe; given as *Umptqua*, or *Arguilas* River, by David Douglas, in 1825, *OHQ*, v. 6, pp. 82, 84, 95. Peter Skene Ogden refers to *Umqua Mts.* on Nov. 25, 1826, writing of the Cascade Range, which he was viewing from the Deschutes River, *OHQ*, v. 11, p. 210. John Work used the style *Umquah Mountain* in his journal for Oct. 3, 1833, referring to the divide between the Umpqua and Rogue rivers. Alexander Ross gives *Imp-qua* in his *First Settlers on the Oregon*, p. 237, and *Umpqua* in his *Fur Hunters of the Far West*, v. 1, p. 108. Wilkes's map (1841) shows *Umpqua*. William P. McArthur uses the form *Umpqua* in his survey of the Pacific Coast in 1850. Hale gives *Umpquas* in *Ethnography and Philology*, 1846, p. 198, and *Umpqua* and *Umkwa*, p. 204. The Umpquas are classed as an Athapascan tribe of the upper Umpqua River. The territorial legislature created an Umpqua County Jan. 24, 1851. It ceased to exist Oct. 16, 1862, its area having been added to other counties. The Hudson's Bay Company had an establishment in the Umpqua Valley as early as 1832, probably on Calapooya Creek. It was generally called Old Fort Umpqua. The company later had another Fort Umpqua near the present site of Elkton. During the Indian wars there was a federal establishment called Fort Umpqua just north of the mouth of Umpqua River. For many references to Umpqua River and to Umpqua Valley, *see OHQ*, v. 44, p. 357.

Uncle Dan Mine, BAKER. This mine in the Encina district was located in the early 1900s by Dan Cochrane, universally known as "Uncle Dan." This information was provided by Cochrane's daughter, Mrs. J. P. Jackson of Baker.

Union, UNION. Dunham Wright, aged 84 in 1926, of Medical Springs, informed the compiler that the town of Union was founded in 1862 by E. H. Lewis, Fred Nodine and Samuel Hannah, and was named for patriotic reasons during the Civil War. The town was named before the county was formed. Homemade flags from dresses and sheets were in the celebration on July 4, 1863. Union post office was established on May 8, 1863, with John A. J. Chapman first postmaster.

Union County. Union County was created Oct. 14, 1864, and was taken from the north part of Baker County as that county then existed. Its name was taken from the town of Union, which had been established about two years. Union County has an area of 2053 square miles.

Union Creek, JACKSON. The locality known as Union Creek is on the upper reaches of Rogue River, about twelve miles north of Prospect and about ten miles west of the entrance to Crater Lake National Park. It took its name from the stream, which was in turn named for Union Peak in the park. Union Creek post office was established Apr. 22, 1924, with Mrs. Helen C. Herriott first postmaster. It was closed Apr. 30, 1945 although it had actually ceased operation in Oct. 1942.

Union Mills, CLACKAMAS. Union Mills is a well-known locality about three miles southeast by road from Mulino. It is adjacent to Milk Creek. The name of the place has had an interesting history. The Cutting family operated a post office in this vicinity as early as Sept. 1867. Charles Cutting, Sr., was the first postmaster and the office was named in his honor. It was called Cuttingsville. The office did not operate continuously. On Dec. 28, 1875, the name Cuttingsville was changed to Union Mills and Gabriel J. Trullinger became postmaster. With one short interval he ran this office until Aug. 1904. In Mar. 1948, Isaac V. Trullinger, then living in Portland, and a son of Gabriel J. Trullinger, sent some information to the compiler. Gabriel J. Trullinger came to Oregon in 1847 and took up a donation land claim on Milk Creek in 1852. He built a sawmill and later added wool-carding machinery. Still later he added a planing mill and as a result of these various activities he called his establishment Union Mills. A flour mill was built in 1877. In 1875 the post office had been moved from Cuttingsville. The post offices of Cuttingsville and Union Mills were not in exactly the same place. Isaac V. Trullinger adds an interesting note that the planer was bought from Dr. John McLoughlin, who imported it from England. It is said to have been the first power-driven planer to operate on the Pacific Coast. This piece of machinery is now in the museum of the Oregon Historical Society at Portland.

Union Peak, KLAMATH. This peak was named for patriotic reasons by a party of prospectors who climbed it on Oct. 21, 1862. Will G. Steel gives their names as follows: Chauncey Nye, H. Abbott, S. Smith, J. Brandlin, James Leyman and J. W. Sessions. The elevation of Union Peak is 7709 feet.

Union Point, LINN. Union Point post office was established Feb. 18, 1854, with

William B. Blain postmaster. Hugh Dinwiddie became postmaster Mar. 2, 1855. In 1989, Glenn Harrison of the Linn County Historical Society wrote the compiler as follows: "The town of Union Point was named for the church union that occurred there on Oct. 20, 1852 forming the United Presbyterian Church. Associate Reformed Presbyterian minister Wilson Blain settled on the Territorial Wagon Road three miles south of Brownsville in June 1849 and laid out plans for a town. He wrote to the Associate Presbyterian ministers working in the area and proposed a merger. After a series of meetings that began at the Mealey School House (Oakville) on Dec. 25, 1851 and ended in Rev. Blain's house on Oct. 20, 1852, the union took place. (Following this example the national merger of these Presbyterian branches occured in May 1858.)" There is no longer a community with the name, but there is a Union Point School. Union Point post office was discontinued in Aug. 1859. Blain died Feb. 22, 1861 and the town died also. The reader should note the given names of the postmaster and the minister. Wilson Blain is listed in the 1850 Oregon census but William Blain is not. Both are listed in the 1860 census in Brownsville precinct, Linn County. There is no evidence the two were related, so the reader must decide if both Blains were really involved in Union Point or if there was some clerical error.

Uniontown, CLATSOP. Uniontown is in the west part of Astoria and got its name from the Union Packing Company, which began operations in the early 1880s, in the vicinity of Bond and Washington streets. The company was not successful and its real estate was platted into lots and deeded to the stockholders. The locality was called Uniontown and the name eventually spread until it included the entire west end of Astoria. For details, *see* the *Astorian-Budget*, Mar. 4, 1938.

Uniontown, JACKSON. Uniontown was an early post office on Applegate River near the mouth of Little Applegate River. Theodoric Cameron, a native of Madison County, New York, and a pioneer of 1852, was the only postmaster the place ever had. Cameron was a staunch Republican and during the Civil War had pronounced views on upholding the Union. The place was named on that account. Uniontown post office was in operation at the Cameron store from Apr. 1879 to Sept. 1891.

Unit Lake, WALLOWA. This lake in T 4S, R 44E, in the Wallowa Mountains is separated from other lakes in the vicinity. It is named because it is a unit by itself.

Unity, BAKER. Robert Murray, whose grandfather settled in the valley east of Unity in 1861, told the author in 1968 that the first post office in the area was at Tucker Swamp on Job Creek on the freight road to Baker, about one and one half miles from the present site. This was apparently not a convenient place for the settlers who were all ranchers throughout the valley, so they had a meeting to decide where to move it and what to name it. They all agreed on the location and were so pleased with their agreement that they decided to call it Unity. Unity post office was established in Sept. 1891 but the compiler has been unable to identify any previous post office in the immediate area.

University Park, MULTNOMAH. Portland has had a liberal supply of platted additions with fancy names, although many of them actually came into being before the city became a metropolis. In fact some of them antedated the Portland-East Portland-Albina consolidation of 1891. A number of them, then suburbs, had post offices. An office called Portsmouth was established Apr. 17, 1891, with Chapman S. Pennock postmaster. This was to serve the area of Portsmouth addition, southeast of Saint Johns. It seems apparent that Pennock or the postal authorities were not satisfied with the name or location, for on Aug. 25, 1891, the name of the office was changed to University Park to agree with that of an addition with that title. The plat for University Park had been filed in Apr. 1891. The post office may have been moved when the name was changed. University Park office was in operation until Nov. 14, 1903, when it was closed out to Portland. In 1980 University Park was a station under the Portland office. The name of Portsmouth addition was doubtless suggested by the sight of waterborne commerce passing close at hand. University Park was named for Portland University, a Methodist institution established on the river bluff in 1890. This institution later became Columbia University, and is now University of Portland, both establishments of the Catholic church.

Unnecessary Mountain, KLAMATH. Francis Landrum of Klamath Falls told the compiler in 1969 that Scott Warren named this small hill east of Algoma. A favorite fairy tale of his children related a long list of "unnecessary" items and the hill was a humorous addition.

Upper Astoria, CLATSOP. Upper Astoria post office was established Mar. 19, 1877, with Christian Leinenweber first of five postmasters. The office was discontinued Sept. 11, 1886, but was not in continuous service between the two dates given. Leinenweber was a prominent early-day citizen of Clatsop County, and probably named the office himself. It was about a mile and a half east of what is now the main business part of Astoria, but probably not always in the same place. The name was of course descriptive, as it was upriver from the older post office at Astoria. The general locality of what was Upper Astoria is now frequently called Alderbrook.

Upper Klamath Lake, KLAMATH. The official and correct name of the largest lake in Oregon is Upper Klamath Lake and not Klamath Lake. There is a Lower Klamath Lake and a contradistinction is necessary. Beyond that, however, the name Upper Klamath Lake has a broad and deep historic background. In passing, it should be mentioned that John C. Fremont did not reach the shores of Upper Klamath Lake in the winter of 1843–44. In fact Fremont did not see the lake until his second visit to Oregon, in 1846. On Dec. 10, 1843, Fremont reached and very accurately described Klamath Marsh, although at the time he supposed he was at "Tlamath lake." It can hardly be contended that Klamath Marsh is part of Upper Klamath Lake. The north end of the marsh is about 30 miles from the lake and approximately 400 feet greater in elevation. For the history of the name Klamath, *see* Klamath County. Upper Klamath Lake has an area of about 142 square miles at high stages, and is the largest in the state except in the rare periods of extreme high water in the Malheur-Harney lakes basin when these bodies of water join.

Upper Land Creek, COOS. This creek, together with Lower Land Creek nearby, was named for T. C. Land, a pioneer settler on South Fork Coquille River.

Upper Ochoco, CROOK. The early-day post office Upper Ochoco was not on the upper reaches of Ochoco Creek at all. It was not more than about ten miles east of Prineville near the mouth of Mill Creek and near where the Claypool place was in 1946. Upper Ochoco post office was established Apr. 13, 1871, with James H. Miller first of seven postmasters. The office was discontinued Aug. 2, 1880.

Upper Table Rock, JACKSON. There are two table rocks north of Central Point. They are prominent landmarks, and well named. Upper Table Rock is the eastern one of the two. It is famous because of the council between the white soldiers and Rogue River Indians held on its southwestern slope, at the foot of the vertical cliff, on Sept. 10, 1853. For an account of this meeting by Colonel James W. Nesmith, *see OHQ*, v. 7, p. 211.

Upton Slough, TILLAMOOK. Upton Creek empties into Upton Slough and in turn into Nestucca River. The name comes from James B. Upton who homesteaded there in the 1870s.

Utopia, WALLOWA. The post office at Utopia was on the homestead of Charles N. Walker in S 24, T 4N, R 42E. Walker was not only a homesteader but also a schoolteacher and was so impressed with the surrounding country that he named the office for Sir Thomas More's imaginary paradise on earth. Utopia post office was established May 4, 1905 with Aurelia M. Walker postmaster, and it operated until May 1911. The place was on Middle Point between Wallupa and Wildcat creeks about two miles southeast of Promise, and the name of the office at Promise may have suggested the name Utopia.

Utter City, COOS. In Jan. 1946 Mrs. Mary M. Randleman of Coquille, who had an extensive knowledge of Coos County history, wrote the compiler as follows: "There were two brothers, Fred and William Utter, residents of San Francisco, who opened the Dale and Utter coal mine about a mile south of Coaledo. They had large holdings in Contra Costa County, but resided in Utter City while operating the mine here. Utter City was about a mile south of the Coos City bridge. The town was never recorded so it is hard to locate it geographically. Mr. Utter built the Isthmus Transit railroad from Coaledo to Utter City where the coal was put in bunkers and eventually shipped to San Francisco. Henry Sengstacken came from San Francisco to serve as bookkeeper and store manager. There was a store, post office, hotel, brewery and a number of houses." Utter City was on Isthmus Slough south of the town of Coos Bay. A post office with the name Isthmus was established Dec. 11, 1871, with Gilbert Hall postmaster. The name of the office was changed to Utter City on Feb. 11, 1875, and the office was discontinued

June 22, 1880. The compiler is told that the ravages of time have obliterated the community.

Utts Butte, MORROW. George W. Utt was born in Missouri and came to Morrow County in 1885. In 1887 he applied for a timber culture claim on this 2185-foot butte north of Eightmile Canyon and ranched there until 1924. He died in Los Angeles in 1944 at the age of 85.

Valby, MORROW. Valby, five miles north of Eightmile, is the site of the Swedish Lutheran Church built in 1897 by the large number of early Swedish settlers. Oscar Peterson, the son of one of the founders, offered the following information in 1970. *Valby* or *Vallby* was the Swedish term for a community or group of sheepherders and since many of the early members ran sheep, the name seemed humorously appropriate. After World War II, a group of the younger members endeavored to change the name to one more dignified but fortunately the old tradition prevailed. For an interesting account of Valby in recent years, *see* the *Sunday Oregonian*, May 8, 1983, p. F14.

Vale, MALHEUR. The compiler has never been able to learn who named this place or for what reason. Vale is on the Malheur River but its surroundings do not suggest a vale in the concise meaning of that word. Vale post office was established Feb. 20, 1883, with Henry C. Murray first postmaster.

Valfontis, POLK. This was a pioneer post office which eventually passed from the picture. Valfontis office was established Sept. 29, 1854, with Andrew J. Doak postmaster. C. C. Walker became postmaster June 12, 1855. The origin of its name has not transpired, though its meaning may be surmised. It was just another term for Spring Valley. Doak and Walker had claims close to the present site of Lincoln, a community at the east edge of Spring Valley, and Valfontis office was in that neighborhood. The office was discontinued in Aug. 1865.

Valley, COLUMBIA. Valley was the name given to a locality and post office about eight miles by road east of Pittsburg, where the road crossed Clatskanie River. There was a vale of sorts and Omar C. Spencer said that was the reason for the name. Valley post office was established Apr. 23, 1895, with Catherine Dupont postmaster. The office was discontinued Mar. 20, 1905. The office was a little to the west of the place later called Trenholm.

Valley Falls, LAKE. C. W. E. Jennings named this community about 1908 because of a small fall in Chewaucan River a mile or so to the north. Valley Falls post office was established on June 25, 1909, with Ernest L. H. Meyer postmaster, but Jennings later took over the position. The office was first situated near the base of Abert Rim, about a mile east of its location in 1942, but was moved westward so as to be on SH-31, the Fremont Highway, at the junction with US-395, the highway northeast to Burns. The office was closed in the summer of 1943.

Valsetz, POLK. Valsetz was a company town. After the bad forest fire of 1910, the William W. Mitchell Company built a railroad up the Luckiamute River to the summit of the Coast Range and began logging in western Polk County. In 1919 construction was started on a sawmill and a company town at the terminus of the railroad just over the divide into the Siletz River drainage. The town was named Valsetz, made-up from parts of the name of the Valley & Siletz Railroad. Valsetz post office was established Nov. 6, 1920. The mill and timber stands passed through various ownerships until 1959 when they became part of the Boise Cascade Corporation. After the old timber was depleted in the 1970s, the railroad was torn up. In Dec. 1983 the company announced that all operations would cease early the next year. The town was removed and the property added to the Valsetz Tree Farm. This was possible as all structures and property including streets were owned by the Boise Cascade Corporation. The post office was closed on June 30, 1984, and the community ceased to exist. The *Oregonian*, July 1, 1984, printed a special illustrated section in which Tom Hallman, Jr., gives an excellent history of the town and its demise.

Van, HARNEY. The postmaster at Van wrote the compiler in Dec. 1926, that the office was named for Van Middlesworth, a local settler. The office operated from Mar. 3, 1891 to Aug. 31, 1953.

Van Horn Butte, HOOD RIVER. This hill was originally called Julia Butte for Mrs. Peter Neal, but in 1906 the Van Horn brothers purchased the surrounding property and it has been called Van Horn Butte ever since. Willes and Bert Van Horn were residents of Buffalo, and in the cold storage business there. Willes Van Horn moved to Hood River Valley and built a home on top of Van Horn Butte. There was a nearby railroad station named Van Horn.

Vanderhoof Canyon, WASCO. This canyon empties into Currant Creek in the extreme south part of the county. Gilbert Vanderhoof homesteaded near its upper end before World War I. J. A. Rooper of Antelope told the compiler in 1969 that after Oregon went dry in 1916, it was understood that Gilbert and his brother John enlarged the scope of their livestock operation to include liquid grain by-products then not readily available.

Vandevert Ranch, DESCHUTES. Vandevert Ranch is on the old stage road south of Bend. It was for many years the home of William P. Vandevert. He was born near Saginaw, Lane County, on Apr. 22, 1854. His father, J. J. Vandevert, was a native of Ohio and came to Oregon in 1848. W. P. Vandevert was a forest ranger, rancher and stockman and an early settler in Deschutes Valley. He died Feb. 24, 1944. For biography, *see* the Bend *Bulletin*, Feb. 24, 1944.

Vanishing Falls, CLACKAMAS. This thirty-foot-high falls on Salmon River is about six miles downstream from the mouth of Linney Creek. It is the fourth of six falls between Linney Creek and Welches and was named because it vanishes into a narrow box canyon. For details of this group, *see* Stein Falls.

Vannoy Creek, JOSEPHINE. James N. Vannoy took up a donation land claim near this stream, five miles west of what is now Grants Pass, about 1851. He operated Vannoy Ferry across Rogue River. Bancroft, in *History of Oregon*, v. 2, p.

184, says that Perkins and Long operated ferries near this point before Vannoy. The spelling Vanoy is wrong. *See also* Fort Vannoy. Vannoy post office was established Sept. 4, 1856, with James N. Vannoy postmaster. The office was discontinued Oct. 11, 1859.

Vanora, JEFFERSON. The name Vanora was coined from the first two names of Ora Van Tassel. Vanora is a place on the east bank of Deschutes River about eight miles airline northwest of Madras. When the Oregon Trunk line was built through the area, there was a Vanora station in service, but the track in that locality has been torn out. Vanora post office was established Mar. 22, 1911, with John T. Dizney first of four postmasters. The office was closed Dec. 15, 1920, with mail to Madras. Ora Van Tassel was a real estate man and a farmer of the lands where Vanora railroad station and post office were situated. Later he was a grain buyer, active in civic affairs. He installed an elaborate water system, which was abandoned after he moved to Madras.

Vanport City, MULTNOMAH. Vanport City was the official name of the community built between Portland and Vancouver to house World War II workers. The name was made up in compliment to the two nearby cities. A full-page advertisement in the *Oregonian*, Aug. 12, 1943, gives a history of the project. On that date the place had 9942 dwelling units, prepared for 40,000 inhabitants, and was the nation's largest single war-housing town. Construction officially started Sept. 14, 1942, and from point of time, the development was remarkable. The place was frequently referred to as Kaiserville, an informal honor to the shipbuilder, Henry J. Kaiser. For an interesting account of the maintenance problems on a project of this sort, *see* the *Oregonian*, Aug. 16, 1943. Vanport was destroyed on May 30, 1948, by a disastrous flood.

Vansycle Canyon, UMATILLA. This canyon opens into the Walla Walla Valley east of Wallula. The name is universally spelled Vansycle, and most historical records indicate that it was given for J. M. Vansycle, a local resident. However, T. C. Elliott of Walla Walla investigated the matter for the compiler and found the name signed to a deed in the form J. M. Vansyckle. An advertisement of Wallula Hotel, in the *Washington Statesman*, 1864, is printed over the name J. M. Vansyckle. Vansyckle may have used different forms of his name at different periods of his life. In any event it would probably be impossible to get the spelling of the name changed at this late date. Vansycle post office operated from 1882 to 1900.

Varco Well, DESCHUTES. This well three miles east of Brothers was on the 1912 homestead of Elva and Joseph Varco. Elva E. Varco was later Deschutes County commissioner.

Vaughn Creek, LANE. Vaughn Creek flows into the upper reaches of Dorena Reservoir. Sidner H. Vaughn homesteaded near its mouth in 1891.

Veatch, LANE. This was a station on the Southern Pacific Company line about three miles southwest of Cottage Grove at an elevation of about 700 feet. It was named for Frank Veatch, a nearby resident.

Veazie Creek, CROOK. Edmund F. Veazie came to Oregon from Maine about 1858, and in 1868 settled in the Ochoco Valley, near what is now known as Veazie Creek. A short time later he moved to Hay Creek where he lived until he was drowned in John Day River in 1877, in mysterious circumstances. His home on Hay Creek was approximately the same location as what was later known as Heisler. He married Harriet Lyle, a member of a pioneer Polk County family, and their four children were prominent citizens of the Pacific Northwest. *See* editorial page *Oregon Journal*, Dec. 17, 1926.

Veda Lake, CLACKAMAS. This small lake lies on the western slope of the Cascade Range, about five miles south of Government Camp. It has an elevation of approximately 4300 feet. It was named in 1917 when Vern Rogers and Dave Donaldson packed into the lake with a load of trout fry. George Ledford, local forest ranger, named the lake for these two men by appropriating the first two letters of the first name of each.

Venator, HARNEY. Venator was named for Alphene Venator, (pronounced Venatta), a native of Linn County, who settled in the Harney Valley as a youth in 1872. He established himself on a stock ranch in the east part of the county in 1884, and the locality was soon known as Venator. The post office was established Feb. 18, 1895, with Mrs. Louella Venator first postmaster. This office was later moved about two and a half miles north to a station on the Union Pacific Railroad. The post office operated, with one intermission, until 1959.

Venator Canyon, HARNEY, LAKE. Venator Canyon heads in Harney County and drains west into the Alkali Valley. It was named for Jezreal Venator, a pioneer settler in the vicinity of Albany, who crossed the plains in 1852. He took part in the Rogue River Indian War and was wounded. He moved to the Goose Lake Valley, in the fall of 1870, buying the Crane property on Crane Creek south of what is now Lakeview. In Aug. 1881 he started on a business trip to Harney County to pick up some horses. His saddle horse got away from him, and he died of thirst about a half mile west of the canyon which bears his name.

Veneta, LANE. Veneta post office was established Nov. 3, 1914, to serve a community which was started in 1912 by E. E. Hunter. At the suggestion of Rev. Charles Dunham, Hunter named the townsite for his five-year-old daughter, Veneta. The Eugene *Register-Guard*, June 26, 1982, has an account of the seventieth anniversary party of the city which was attended by Mrs. Veneta Hunter Vincent.

Vera Creek, CLATSOP. Vera Creek flows into Adair Slough near US-101. It is named for Vera Owens Hill, the granddaughter of Dr. Bethenia Owens-Adair whose home was nearby. *See* also Adair Slough.

Verboort, WASHINGTON. This place was named for William Verboort, who owned part of the Henry Black donation land claim. The place is about two miles north-northeast of Forest Grove.

Verdure, LINN. This was a station on the Oregon Electric Railway. When the line was originally built the station was called Oakville, for the community of Oakville, a pioneer settlement about one mile to the west. Due to confusion with other places in the Pacific Northwest, the name of the station was changed to Verdure in Dec. 1916. The form Verdue is incorrect.

Vernie, MALHEUR. Vernie post office, about five or six miles northwest of Ontario, was established Mar. 29, 1909, with Cornelia Belknap first and only postmaster. The office was discontinued May 31, 1913, with mail to Payette, Idaho. In Apr. 1947, C. D. Warren of Chiloquin wrote that he was the son of the postmaster, and that the office was named for a boy named Vernie who was resident in North Carolina. A Mrs. Buchanan was to be served by the new Oregon office, and she wanted the place named Vernie for her grandson, who was the youth in North Carolina. Mrs. Buchanan's son Bert also put in a plea for the name Vernie, which was adopted, apparently to the annoyance of the postmaster elect.

Vernon, MARION. Gill's Oregon map of 1874 shows Vernon post office a few miles northeast of Salem, near the west line of s 2, T 7S, R 2W. This office was established Feb. 2, 1869, with Benjamin B. Wilson first postmaster. The office was closed Apr. 6, 1874. The place was named for a local family.

Vernonia, COLUMBIA. The community of Vernonia was first settled by Judson Weed and Ozias Cherrington, of Ohio, in 1876. Sometime thereafter when the question of getting a post office came up for consideration the matter of choosing a name had to be settled. At a meeting held in the schoolhouse the name of Auburn was suggested for Auburn, Minn., and Cherrington suggested the name of Vernonia for his daughter in Ohio. The community was named Vernonia and the precinct was named Auburn. This arrangement continued for some years but as a result of the confusion that followed the county court changed the name of the precinct to Vernonia. Some interesting facts have come to light about Miss Cherrington, the most important of which is that her name was not Vernonia at all, but Vernona, so the place does not bear her exact name. Vernona Cherrington became Mrs. W. H. Dawson, and on Mar. 15, 1942, she was living in Saxe, Virginia. On that day she wrote to Omar C. Spencer of the Oregon Bar and provided some biographic data. She was born Mar. 30, 1868, apparently in Ohio. Her mother died when she was a small child, and her father emigrated to Missouri and on to Oregon about 1873, leaving Vernona with his stepmother. She never saw him again, as he never went back to Ohio and she never visited Oregon. Miss Cherrington was married to William H. Dawson in 1890 and moved from Jackson, Ohio, to North Carolina in 1902, and later to Virginia. Her father was thrown from a hay tedder about 1894, while working on Sauvie Island and died a few months later at the home of Judson Weed, apparently near St. Helens. Vernonia post office was established Jan. 11, 1878, with David F. Baker, first postmaster.

Vesper, CLATSOP. Vesper is not now a post office, although it has been in the past. It is in the Nehalem Valley. It is said to have been named by William Johnston for the evening star. The name Vesper is generally applied to the planet

Venus when it is east of the sun, and therefore shines brightly after sunset. Vesper post office was established Jan. 30, 1879, with Johnston first postmaster. It was then on the Clatsop County list, but near the east boundary of the county. At times the office was in Columbia County, depending upon who was postmaster. It was finally closed on Nov. 30, 1919.

Vey Ranch, MORROW. This ranch on Butter Creek south of Service Buttes was the headquarters for one of the largest and best-known early day sheep operations in Morrow County. John, Joe and Antone Vey came from the Isle of Graciosa, Azore Islands. After sundry travels, the first two settled along Butter Creek in the early 1870s where Antone soon joined them. In 1878, friendly Indians warned them of the impending uprising but John Vey disregarded the advice and was murdered and scalped while tending the flock at Camas Prairie. Antone and Joe Vey continued together for a number of years but broke up after a serious fraternal argument. Legend has it that the disagreement was so deep that they literally severed their ranch house into distinct halves.

Vey Spring, UMATILLA. Vey Spring just east of Service Buttes was apparently named for Joseph Vey, a son of one of the early Vey brothers, who took up government land nearby in 1928.

Victor, WASCO. Victor was a post office serving an area on Juniper Flat about midway between Tygh Valley and Wapinitia. The office was established Nov. 14, 1893, with Viola Jones first postmaster. Victor apparently was a family name for Viola Jones had a son, Victor Jones, who was born in Apr. 1895 and died less than a year later. This, of course, was after the post office was named. The compiler has heard that Mrs. Jones's maiden name was Viola Victor but this is not confirmed. The post office was closed in Nov. 1912, and the business turned over to Maupin. The old USGS map of the Dufur quadrangle shows Victor School in s 32, T 4S, R 13E, as of 1930. By 1980 the school and all other buildings had disappeared.

Victor View, KLAMATH. Victor View is a natural viewpoint on the east wall of Crater Lake, north of Kerr Notch and above Sentinel Rock. It was named on Jan. 4, 1933, by the USBGN in honor of Mrs. Frances Fuller Victor, Oregon poet and historian, who visited Crater Lake in 1872. For information about Mrs. Victor, *see* Scott's *History of the Oregon Country*, v. 1, p. 142, and *OHQ* article by Hazel Mills, v. 62, p. 309 *et seq*. Mrs. Victor was born at Rome, New York, May 23, 1826, and died in Portland, Nov. 14, 1902. For many years a natural feature on the southwest rim of Crater Lake was called Victor Rock, but in 1930–31 the Sinnott Memorial was built on this rock, making it necessary to name another point for Mrs. Victor.

Vida, LANE. The original name of this place was Gate Creek. This name resulted in confusion with Gales Creek in Washington County. The name Vida was selected because it was the name of the daughter of the postmaster, Francis A. Pepiot. Vida post office was established Apr. 12, 1898. The community is where SH-126, the McKenzie Highway, crosses Gate Creek.

Vidae Ridge, KLAMATH. Vidae Ridge is a very prominent, rugged backbone extending south from the rim of Crater Lake. Applegate Peak is the highest point at its north end. The compiler has been unable to learn about the origin of the name.

Viento, HOOD RIVER. Dr. T. L. Eliot of Portland, who was familiar with the history of Hood River and vicinity, told the writer that this railroad station on the Union Pacific west of Hood River was named by taking the first two letters of the names, Villard, Endicott and Tolman. William Endicott of Boston was a capitalist who was heavily interested in Henry Villard's railroad enterprise. Tolman was a railroad contractor. *Viento* is also a Spanish word meaning wind and this word is peculiarly fitting when applied to this station, but Dr. Eliot said the Spanish origin had nothing to do with the matter. Viento State Park on the banks of Viento Creek has both picnicking and overnight facilities.

Viewpoint, LAKE. Viewpoint was the descriptive name of a post office established during the homesteading wave just after the turn of the century. This office, which was in the south part of the Christmas Lake Valley, was established Apr. 9, 1910, with Bertha C. Hach first postmaster. The office was discontinued Sept. 30, 1918. In 1946 Mrs. Delbert Cloud, New Pine Creek, Oregon, wrote about the homesteaders' post offices in Lake County. Mrs. Cloud said she visited the vicinity of Viewpoint office about the time it was discontinued. She said that the people had all left. The newspaper mail had not been distributed and was still scattered around. The office door had blown away, but the post office books were still there. *Sic transit gloria* Viewpoint.

Villard Glacier, DESCHUTES. This small glacier is on the north slope of the North Sister. It was named by Professor E. T. Hodge of the University of Oregon. *See Mount Multnomah.* Henry Villard was a great factor in the material development of Oregon, and did his share from a civic point of view as well. He should have had something more than a small glacier named for him. Villard was born Apr. 10, 1835, in Bavaria. His family name was Hilgard. He came to the United States when he was 18 years old, and here entered upon a career as teacher, editor, war correspondent and finally railroad builder that lasted nearly half a century, and made him an outstanding figure in the history of transportation in America. For detailed accounts of his railroad construction work in Oregon, *see* many references in Scott's *History of the Oregon Country*, and also Villard's *Memoirs*. He died Nov. 12, 1900. He was a firm supporter of the University of Oregon, where Villard Hall is named in his honor. *See also* under Hilgard.

Vincent, WALLOWA. J. H. Horner of Enterprise informed the compiler that this place was named for Vincent Palmer of the Palmer Lumber Company.

Vincent Creek, GRANT. This creek is west of Austin. Patsy Daly of Prairie City told the compiler that it was named for a nearby resident who was engaged in mining.

Vinemaple, CLATSOP. The vine maple or shrub, *Acer circinatum*, grows so abundantly and so persistently throughout western Oregon that it is surprising so few geographic features have been named for it, but such seems to be the case. About the turn of the century there was a post office in the Nehalem Valley called Vinemaple. This office was about six miles downstream, or southwest, from Jewell. Available records are not clear as to the opening and closing dates, but they were probably May 6, 1891, and May 12, 1902. The office was apparently closed out to Grand Rapids. Today the old name is retained by Vinemaple School and Vinemaple Log Church, both of which are a little south of the river on the road to Elsie.

Vineyard Mountain, BENTON. Vineyard Mountain, elevation 1755 feet, is north of Corvallis, in the east part of s 3, T 11S, R 5W, on the boundary of the McDonald Forest of Oregon State University. It bears the name of an early settler who had a land claim nearby. It is the southern and larger of two hills of about the same height and about a half mile apart. For many years it was known as Vineyard Hill but it was elevated to mountain status by the USBGN in *Decision List 8501*, apparently at the instigation of real estate interests.

Vingie Creek, LINCOLN. This stream flows into the Pacific Ocean about two miles north of Yachats. It bears the name of an early settler who owned land near the head of the creek. The name Divinity Creek is wrong and is due to a mishearing of the correct name.

Vinson, UMATILLA. Vinson was named for John S. Vinson, a pioneer settler, who once ran a store in the community. Vinson began operating as a merchant at Needy, Clackamas County, about 1854. In the early 1870s he preempted land at what was later Vinson and secured a post office. With Frank Newman he engaged in the livestock and farming business. Later they added a mercantile establishment and the place became an important stage station on the line between The Dalles and Pendleton by way of Heppner. Railroad development put a stop to the community. *See* editorial page of the *Oregonian*, Mar. 17, 1928. A post office named Butter Creek was established at this place on July 28, 1873, with J. S. Vinson postmaster. The name of the office was changed to Vinson on Sept. 15, 1881, and finally closed Nov. 30, 1907.

Viola, CLACKAMAS. Viola is a place a few miles west of Estacada. It is said to have been named for Mrs. Violet O. Harding, the wife of an early settler in the locality. Clear Creek post office was established in this vicinity on Oct. 30, 1867, with Oliver P. Mattoon first postmaster. The name was changed to Viola on Jan. 25, 1876.

Virginia Valley, HARNEY. Mrs. Thomas (Delta) Maupin told the compiler in 1990 that Virginia Valley was named by her two great-aunts, Augusta Kenneke and Nena Stevens who were born in Germany and came to Virginia in the United States. Later they homesteaded in Harney County and named the valley for their first location in this country. Augusta Haarstrich and Nena Haarstrich both filed homesteads south of Hat Butte on Oct. 18, 1907, under their maiden names.

Virtue Flat, BAKER. This flat was named for James W. Virtue, for many years a resident of the county, and one-time sheriff. For additional information about Virtue, *see* Ontario.

Vista Ridge, HOOD RIVER. Vista Ridge is a long slope north of Mount Hood and northwest of Wy'east Basin. Its west face forms the east wall of the Ladd Creek Canyon. It was named in 1922 by an exploring party from Hood River because of the extensive views from its summit. This information is in a letter from C. Edward Graves, Arcata, California, dated July 5, 1943. The name has been approved by the USBGN.

Vistillas, LAKE. In Feb. 1944, Ida M. Odell of Klamath Falls kindly dug up some information about the history of this post office. In the late 1880s there was an office with the name Loraton serving an area in the Barnes Valley near the Klamath-Lake county line. This office was discontinued after a short life, and later, about 1890, local settlers tried to get it reestablished. The old name Loraton was objected to because it was so much like Lorella, also in Klamath County. The name Fairview was suggested to postal authorities, but it was not acceptable because there was another Fairview in Oregon. The Post Office Department is said to have suggested the name Vistillas, and that is what it has been for more than half a century. The office has been moved several times, depending on who would assume its responsibilities. It has been in both Klamath and Lake counties. Edward Tull was probably first postmaster. One of the Batchelders later took the office. It has been at the Lapham Ranch and also at the Adams' and other places. *Vistillas* is a Spanish word meaning an eminence affording an extended view, or a viewpoint. This is very much the same as a fair view. The compiler thinks that somewhere along the line, after the name Fairview was rejected for this office, somebody selected the Spanish word that is nearly equivalent.

Voltage, HARNEY. Voltage was a post office just south of Malheur Lake. It was close to the site of Sodhouse which was for many years an important landmark in the Harney Valley. The post office at Voltage was established on Aug. 28, 1908, with Walter C. Botsford first postmaster. He suggested the name because he was interested in electricity and had the idea that sufficient "voltage" could be generated on Donner und Blitzen River to serve the entire Harney Valley. Botsford was not the first man to go astray and confuse force with power. The post office was closed in 1933 and hydroelectric power is still unavailable.

Voorhies, JACKSON. This station was named for Colonel Gordon Voorhies, who for many years operated an orchard nearby. Colonel Voorhies was a native of Kentucky and a graduate of West Point. He served in the Spanish-American War with rank of captain, and about 1899 retired from the army because of impaired health. He volunteered his services for World War 1 and reached the rank of lieutenant-colonel, serving with distinction. He died in Sept. 1940.

Vosburg, TILLAMOOK. Vosburg post office was established June 28, 1901, with J. L. Vosburg postmaster. The office was closed Dec. 15, 1903. Vosburg was named for the postmaster, who was an early-day lumberman and was later connected with the Wheeler sawmill. The office was at or near the site of the Wheeler mill and about a half mile west of what later became the community of Wheeler. Wheeler post office was established in Aug. 1910, and served the locality previously served by Vosburg office. Some years later the Wheeler office was moved eastward to the community of Wheeler and a third office, Hoevet, was established to serve the locality of the mill. Hoevet post office was closed Jan. 31, 1944.

Waconda, MARION. Waconda was a station on the Oregon Electric Railway north of Salem. It was named when the railroad was built about 1907, and the post office was established in 1912. Waconda is an old name in that part of the Willamette Valley, and was originally applied to a community about a mile south of Gervais, at the point where SH-99E, the present Pacific Highway East, is crossed by the old road from Parkersville to Saint Louis. The old community has disappeared. The name Waconda was probably brought to Oregon from the Plains. *Wakonda* is used by tribes of the Siouan family to mean something consecrated, and as a verb, it means to worship. It is hard to give an exact definition of *wakonda*. *See Handbook of American Indians*, v. 2, p. 897.

Wade Creek, LINCOLN. Wade Creek flows into the Pacific Ocean near Beverly Beach State Park. It bears the name of Lee Wade who homesteaded there at the turn of the century.

Wades Flat, DOUGLAS. Wades Flat is southwest of Reedsport. Captain Henry Wade and his brother settled on a ranch on this flat in early days, and the locality is named for them. For information about Henry Wade, *see Marine History of the Pacific Northwest*, p. 185.

Waespe Point, MULTNOMAH. This point is on Trails Club of Oregon property south of the Historic Columbia River Highway and just west of Oneonta Gorge. It was named in 1983 to honor Henry Waespe who was born in Minnesota in 1891 and died in Portland Nov. 19, 1981. Waespe came to Oregon as a child and as a young man worked for the USFS. He was active in the Trails Club of Oregon, was president of the club in the 1950s and was one of three members who selected the site for the club's Nesika Lodge near Waespe Point.

Wagner, WHEELER. Wagner post office was established Mar. 21, 1882, and was given the family name of the first postmaster, Carl N. Wagner. The office was then in Grant County, as Wheeler County had not yet been created. It was on or near the upper reaches of Kahler Creek and a few miles north of John Day River. The office was closed Apr. 27, 1901.

Wagner Creek, JACKSON. This stream is northwest of Ashland. It was named for Jacob Wagner, who was born in Ohio in 1820 and came to Oregon in 1850. He settled on Wagner Creek two years later, and in 1862 moved to Ashland, where he ran the Ashland flour mills. For additional biographical information, *see* Walling's *History of Southern Oregon*, p. 542. The community of Talent was once known as Wagner or Wagner Creek.

Wagner Mountain, JEFFERSON. Wagner Mountain is the high ground at the south end of Melendy Ridge between Muddy and Cherry creeks. It is named for Joe Wagner, a well-known local rancher at the end of the nineteenth century.

Wagontire Mountain, HARNEY, LAKE. Wagontire Mountain is one of the important landmarks in central Oregon. It has an elevation of 6504 feet, according to the USC&GS. It received its name in pioneer days because for many years a wagontire lay beside the road on its northern slopes. This tire is said to have come from an emigrant wagon which was burned by Indians. However, in *The History of Grant County, Oregon, 1862–1983*, pp. 156 and 157, there is an article titled "Grandfather's Story" written in 1929 by William Ralph Fisk, then age 78. Fisk relates his family's moving from the Yreka area to Canyon City in the spring of 1864 when he was a boy. There were several families in the party and they had the usual equipment failures. One wagon broke a wheel as they neared Wagontire Mountain and Fisk's father, Nathan Wills Fisk, who was a skillful mechanic, cut the wagon in two and fashioned a two-wheel cart. The broken wheel was abandoned at the site. Fisk says the place was known as Mountain Springs until some years later when the abandoned tire was found and the present name given to the mountain. North Mountain Spring is on the north slope of Wagontire Mountain in S 31, T 20S, R 24E. There was a post office named Wagontire southeast of the mountain. This post office was formerly known as Egli, for a prominent local stockman. The name was changed to Wagontire in the fall of 1919 at the suggestion of Loretta M. Addington, who thought the new name more appropriate. The office was closed Nov. 15, 1943 with papers to Burns.

Wahanna Lake, LANE. Wahanna Lake, north of Waldo Lake, bears an Indian name imported from Clatsop County. Wahanna was the name used for many years for the stream flowing into Necanicum River north of Seaside, now officially known as Neawanna Creek. For the history of these names, *see* Neawanna Creek. The lake in Lane County was named at a time when several other nearby features were given Indian names for better identification. The name Wahanna Lake was probably used because it had a pleasing sound and not for any local reason.

Wahclella Falls, MULTNOMAH. These falls are on Tanner Creek, and were named in 1915 by a committee representing the Mazamas and other organizations. *Wahclella* was the name of an Indian locality near Beacon Rock on the Washington side of the Columbia River, and was selected because of its pleasing sound.

Wahgwingwin Falls, HOOD RIVER. Wahgwingwin or Wah Gwin Gwin Falls are produced by Phelps Creek when it plunges over the cliff west of Hood River town into Columbia River. The falls, which are about 207 feet high, are near the east end of the Columbia Gorge Hotel and are a well-known scenic feature of the vicinity. The name is said to be of some Indian tongue and means tumbling or rushing waters. There are a number of geographic names in the Pacific Northwest with the initial syllable *Wah*, and they generally refer to water features. The repeated syllables are used for emphasis. Walla Walla is a name of this type.

Wahkeena Falls, MULTNOMAH. These falls were once known as Gordon Falls, for F. E. Gordon, a pioneer landowner. On account of confusion with Gordon Creek near Sandy River, and Gorton Creek at Cascade Locks, a committee appointed by the Mazamas in 1915 to name points on the Columbia River Highway changed the name to Wahkeena Falls and Wahkeena Creek. This name is said to be a Yakima Indian word meaning most beautiful. *See Wah-Kee-Nah, and her People*, by James C. Strong.

Wahtum Lake, HOOD RIVER. H. H. Riddle told the compiler in 1922 that Wahtum Lake was named by H. D. Langille in 1901 while making a map for the USGS. *Wahtum* is a Sahaptin language word meaning pond or body of water.

Wake Butte, DESCHUTES. This butte southwest of Bend was named by the USFS with the Chinook jargon word for no or none, indicating its unimportant character.

Wake Up Rilea Creek, CURRY. Peterson and Powers in *A Century of Coos and Curry*, p. 201, say that this tributary of Rogue River near Agness was named indirectly for Michael Riley, an early settler. Riley grubstaked a miner only to be routed out at midnight by his enthusiastic partner with the words, "Wake up Riley. We're rich." Unfortunately the bonanza proved to be iron pyrites so Riley lost both grubstake and sleep. While the foregoing may easily be correct, M. S. Brainard of Brookings told the compiler in 1968 that George Washington Rilea was a long-time postmaster and school teacher at Agness in the early part of the century. Then in 1981 John Scharf of Burns added that he had been a forest ranger in Agness in the 1920s and knew Rilea. He said the postmaster would stay up listening to the news on his primitive radio, which worked best at night. Rilea compensated by sleeping late in the mornings and early customers were forced to bang on the door to wake up Rilea.

Wakonda Beach, LINCOLN. This is the name of a small, unincorporated community south of Waldport. *Wakonda* is a Siouan word relating to worship. *See* Waconda.

Waldo, JOSEPHINE. According to James T. Chinnock of Grants Pass, Waldo was a specific place in the general locality known as Sailor Diggings, so named because a party of seafaring men found gold there. However the legislative act of Jan. 22, 1856, that created Josephine County, provided that Sailor Diggings was to be the county seat until the next county election. Waldo was not mentioned. This may mean that Sailor Diggings was also a specific place, or it may mean that the two names referred to the same locality. It is too late in the day to determine the situation exactly. The name Sailor Diggings passed out of use; Waldo survived. Reports that Waldo was named for Daniel Waldo, prominent Oregon pioneer of 1843, do not seem to be true. Daniel W. Bass, a grandson of Daniel Waldo and a prominent citizen of Seattle, wrote the compiler in 1928 that the Josephine County town was named for William Waldo, brother of Daniel Waldo. William Waldo was nominated for governor of California by the Whig party in 1853. He had been of service to settlers and miners in northern California and the residents of what was later Waldo, Oregon, close to the state line, all voted for William Waldo with the notion that they were actually living in California. This origin of the name is confirmed by Walling in his *History of Southern Oregon*. There is nothing to indicate that Daniel Waldo ever held court in this part of Oregon. Waldo post office was established on Sept. 4, 1856, with Lyman H. Guthrie first postmaster and closed Dec. 15, 1928.

Waldo Gulch, BAKER. This gulch is southeast of Bowen Valley. In 1899, Charles A. Waldo filed on government land near Waldo Spring at the head of the gulch.

Waldo Hills, MARION. The Waldo Hills are western foothills of the Cascade Range and lie east of Salem. Their geography is well shown on the USGS maps of the Stayton NE and adjoining quadrangles. They were named for Daniel Waldo who was born in Virginia in 1800; died at Salem Sept. 6, 1880. For his funeral eulogy, by J. W. Nesmith, *see* the *Oregonian*, Sept. 11, 1880; biography, by T. T. Geer, May 7, 1905, p. 19. He was a companion of the Applegates in the migration to Oregon in 1843. He was a member of the legislative committee of the provisional government in 1844, and a district judge for Champooick district in that government. He was a highly respected pioneer. "His name will be remembered as a synonym for independence and integrity" (Matthew P. Deady, Pioneer Address, 1875). Two of his sons, William and John B., were prominent in Oregon affairs. His daughters married James Brown, Samuel Bass and David Logan. In earliest pioneer days the name Waldo Hills was not generally used; the locality was referred to as the Waldo Settlement. The area was also called Lebanon, and Lebanon post office was in operation at a point about 12 miles east of Salem from 1851 to 1858. The name Lebanon was absorbed by the place in Linn County.

Waldo Lake, LANE. This is one of the largest mountain lakes in the state, and lies in the Cascade Range at an elevation of 5410 feet. The geography of the lake and its surroundings is shown on the USGS map of the Waldo Lake quadrangle. The lake was named for Judge John B. Waldo, son of Daniel Waldo for whom the Waldo Hills were named. Judge Waldo sought his recreation in the Cascade Range, and Waldo Glacier on the southeast slope of Mount Jefferson was also named for him. Judge Waldo died Sept. 2, 1907. This lake and others nearby were shown as the Virgin Lakes on a map dated Aug. 24, 1863, by the surveyor general of Oregon. Frank S. Warner, a pioneer resident of Lane County, in a letter printed in the *Oregonian*, Sept. 6, 1927, says that Waldo Lake was discovered by Charlie Tufti, and that its early name was Pengra Lake, for B. J. Pengra. Pengra was a pioneer railroad enthusiast, and championed the construction of a line approximately in the present location of the Cascade line of the Southern Pacific. Tom McAllister has an interesting article about Waldo Lake in the *Oregonian*, June 18, 1987, p. D6.

Waldport, LINCOLN. This community is said to have received its name in the early 1880s at the suggestion of P. V. Wustrow, then postmaster at Alsea. Waldport is a combination of the German word *wald*, meaning forest, and the English word port, referring to Alsea Bay. The name is descriptive, for the bay is closely surrounded by hills, once wooded. Waldport was founded by David Ruble, already in business in Alsea, and he is said to have asked Colonel Wustrow to suggest a name for the new community. Waldport post office was established June 17, 1881, by change of name from Collins. This office may have been on the north side of Alsea Bay. It was changed back to Collins on Feb. 23, 1882. *See* Nice. On Aug. 15, 1882 another Waldport office was established with Thomas Russell postmaster. He was succeeded on Sept. 27, 1883 by David Ruble who also had been postmaster of the earlier Waldport. Obviously there was some rivalry between the north and south side.

Waldron, WHEELER. The compiler has not been able to get an explanation of the origin of the name of this early-day post office except that it was named for a person. The office was established on the Wasco County list on Mar. 28, 1879, with William A. Helms postmaster. The place was on Shoofly Creek about ten or twelve miles northeast of Mitchell. On the USGS Toney Butte quadrangle Waldron School shows near Shoofly Creek while Waldron is about a mile and a half northeast on Tamarack Creek. It is doubtful much remains to establish this latter position. Several members of the Waldron family have been prominent in central Oregon affairs and Henry J. Waldron was once postmaster at The Dalles. Waldron post office was closed out to Richmond in July 1902.

Walker, LANE. Walker post office was established in 1891. Francis Smith, first postmaster, had come from Crawford County, Iowa, to seek a western home and a place to open a small mercantile business. He secured some property from Mrs. J. F. Walker, a pioneer resident of the neighborhood north of Cottage Grove. Mr. Smith was instrumental in securing the post office and named it for Mrs. Walker. The post office at Walker was discontinued about 1925.

Walker Creek, DOUGLAS. Walker Creek heads in Shoestring Valley and flows into Elk Creek. It runs through the donation land claim of Eli Walker in Shoestring Valley.

Walker Creek, JACKSON. Walker Creek is one of three streams that join east of Ashland to form Bear Creek. Three Walker brothers, John, Enoch and Minus, all had donation land claims along or near the stream, but John Walker and his wife, Mary Ann, were the best known.

Walker Island, COLUMBIA. This island in the Columbia River below Rainier was discovered by Lieutenant Broughton on Oct. 27, 1792, and was named Walkers Island for the surgeon of the ship *Chatham*. Modern usage, Walker Island, has been approved by the USBGN.

Walker Mountain, JOSEPHINE. Walker Mountain is east of I-5 and south of Jumpoff Joe Creek. It was named for Wesley R. and Augustus Walker who took adjoining donation land claims in Pleasant Valley.

Walker Mountain, KLAMATH. This is an important mountain a few miles south of Crescent. It is shown on maps as Walker Range, Walker Rim and Walker Mountain, but the last named is considered to be the best designation and the one in general use. In the opinion of the writer it was named for W. T. Walker, of the Middle Fork Willamette River road viewing party, who explored this part of the state in 1852. *See* Diamond Peak. It appears that two peaks were named for Walker, one the mountain described herein, and the other a point on the summit of the Cascade Range north of Mount Thielsen. The name of the latter peak has been changed from Walker Mountain to Howlock Mountain for an Indian chief. This was done to avoid the confusion that would result from two mountains of the same name so near together.

Walker Prairie, MULTNOMAH. Walker Prairie and Walker Peak are near Bull Run Reservoir. Ralph Lewis who was in the area in the early 1900s told the writer that an old trapper named Walker had lived on the prairie by one of the trails from Hood River to the Sandy drainage. The BLM plat book dated 1874 shows "Walkers Trail" in T 1S, R 5E.

Walker Road, WASHINGTON. For many years the name Walker Road has been applied to a thoroughfare which extends westward from Canyon Road through the area south of the Sunset Highway toward Hillsboro. Walker Road was named for Mr. and Mrs. William E. Walker who took up a farm a little southwest of Cedar Mill in 1852. For an account of Walker family history, *see* Fred Lockley's article in the *Oregon Journal* for Sept. 10, 1929, editorial page. In 1946 there was a painted sign over a gate on the north side of Walker Road near the crossing of Cedar Mill Creek, reading: "Mr. and Mrs. William E. Walker, 1852. The Old Meadow Farm."

Wall Creek, GRANT. Wall Creek is a tributary of North Fork John Day River. Little Wall Creek rises in Morrow County and flows into Wall Creek. J. L. Cochran, an early resident in the John Day country, informed the compiler that the stream was named because of the rimrocks or walls along its banks.

Wall Creek, GRANT. This Wall Creek is south of Canyon City and flows into Canyon Creek. Patsy Daly of Prairie City informed the compiler that it was named for a local resident.

Wall Creek, JACKSON. Wall Creek is tributary to Hill Creek south of Ashland. Andrew J. Walls homesteaded near its mouth in the 1870s. The Southern Pacific Shasta Line track crosses the creek three times in ascending the Siskiyou Mountains and the uppermost crossing is a high steel trestle set on footings of cut stone.

Walla Walla River, UMATILLA. The sources of Walla Walla River lie in Oregon. South Fork Walla Walla River is the main tributary, and this stream rises in the extreme northwest corner of Wallowa County. The north and south forks join about seven miles southeast of Milton, and the stream flows into Washington north of Milton, after having been divided into several channels and ditches, one branch being known as Little Walla Walla River. "In several languages *walla* means running water, and reduplication of a word diminutizes it; so *Wallawalla* is the small rapid river." (Coues in *History of the Expedition of Lewis and Clark*, p. 969.) According to Myron Eells, in *The American Anthropologist*, Jan. 1892, p. 34, the word is Nez Perce and Cayuse, the root of which is *walatse*, which means running, hence running water. Wallula is probably an anglicized corruption of Walla Walla. Lewis and Clark use the name *Wallow Wallow*, with several variations, and other early travelers use different spellings. The pronunciation, however, is more or less the same. *See Oregon Geographic Names*, 1928 edition, p. 373. Old Fort Walla Walla (Fort Nez Perce), at the mouth of Walla Walla River, in Washington, was established in 1818 by the North West Company, and was abandoned in 1855. The city of Walla Walla, 33 miles east, came into importance in 1860–61, amid placer gold mining activities on Clearwater, Salmon, upper Columbia, Owyhee and Boise rivers. It was first settled upon in 1855. Whitman's mission, at Wai-il-at-pu, was six miles west of the city of Walla Walla.

Wallace, CLACKAMAS. Wallace was a station on the Oregon Electric Railway about two miles south of Wilsonville, named for Mrs. Guy W. Talbot, of Portland, whose maiden name was Wallace.

Wallace, LANE. Wallace post office and what there was of a community were named for William Wallace Shortridge. The place was on Coast Fork Willamette River about ten or a dozen miles south of Cottage Grove, in T 22S, R 3W. The post office was established Dec. 8, 1885, with Shortridge postmaster, and it continued in service until Mar. 1, 1898. Shortridge had previously been postmaster at Ida, named for Ida Shortridge, at or near the same place as Wallace. Shortridge was born in Iowa. He came to Oregon in 1852 and to Lane County in 1853.

Wallace Canyon, WASCO. Nathan Wallace was born in Miami, Ohio, in 1832 and came to Oregon with the immigration of 1852. He settled near Currant Creek and was the second inhabitant of Antelope where he started a blacksmith shop at the old townsite in 1870. Wallace died in Antelope on Sept. 10, 1904.

Wallace Hill, POLK. Wallace Hill is a prominent landmark in the eastern part of the Eola Hills about three miles northwest of Salem. It has an elevation of about 400 feet and the highway between Salem and Dayton skirts its eastern shoulder. It was named for R. S. Wallace who planted nearby one of the largest orchards in Polk County.

Wallace Island, COLUMBIA. This is an island in the Columbia River north of Clatskanie. It is said to bear the name of an early settler who either lived thereon, or owned part of it. The compiler has been unable to get reliable information about the matter. Wilkes in *U.S. Exploring Expedition*, v. 23, Hydrography atlas, calls the western part of the island "Yapats I" and the eastern part "Kotse I," and the channel to the south, now known as Wallace Slough, is called by him "Natsox Run." Wilkes does not explain these names, though they are apparently of Indian origin.

Wallace Slough, COLUMBIA. This is probably the small river described by

Broughton, which he named Swaine's River on Oct. 26, 1792. Its appearance emerging from behind Wallace Island doubtless led Broughton to believe it was a real river.

Wallalute Falls, HOOD RIVER. These falls of Eliot Branch are on the northeast slope of Mount Hood. They were named in 1893 by Miss A. M. Lang of The Dalles. The word is the Wasco Indian term for strong water. Miss Lang and Will Langille explored the falls on Sept. 26, 1892. Langille and Will Graham had been there about a year before, but Miss Lang was the first white woman, as far as known, to visit the place. She asked Wasco Sally for a list of names from which to select, and Wallalute was the result. Sally told Miss Lang the word meant strong water, and her statement was confirmed by Sampson, a prominent Indian at the Warm Springs Agency. It should be noted that many old-time Hood River residents familiar with the mountain claimed that Wallalute Falls were on Compass Creek, the next creek north of Eliot Branch.

Wallooskee River, CLATSOP. Wallooskee River is a tributary of Youngs River, southeast of Astoria. It bears in modern form the name of a small band of Indians that lived nearby. They were of the Chinook tribe. In 1851 Wallooska was the sole surviving member of this band. *See OHQ*, v. 22, p. 61. The stream is known as a river and not a creek. For many years the name was spelled Walluski but this was changed in *Decision List 7504*.

Wallowa, WALLOWA. Wallowa was the first post office in that part of Oregon that now comprises Wallowa County. The office was established Apr. 10, 1873, with John Snodgrass first postmaster. It was on the Union County list at the time.

Wallowa County. Wallowa County is the extreme northeast county of Oregon. It has an area of 3188 square miles. *Wallowa* is a Nez Perce Indian word used to describe a structure of stakes set in a triangle, used to support a network of sticks called *lacallas*, for catching fish. These traps were put in Wallowa River below the outlet of Wallowa Lake. This information was furnished the compiler by Levi Ankeny of Walla Walla, who was thoroughly familiar with the early history and tradition of the Wallowa Valley and on intimate terms with many Indians, who knew the facts of the matter. This origin of the name has been disputed, but the compiler is disposed to place great weight on Levi Ankeny's opinion, which was confirmed by J. H. Horner of Enterprise. Wallowa County was created Feb. 11, 1887. *See* F. V. Holman's "History of Counties of Oregon," *OHQ*, v. 11, p. 60. Wallowa River is a tributary of Grande Ronde River, which Lewis and Clark named *Wil-le-wah*. The explorers also gave the name to a tribe of Indians.

Wallowa Mountains, BAKER, UNION, WALLOWA. The Wallowa Mountains are an important geographical feature in Oregon and represent a structure quite distinct from most of the other mountain ranges of the state. They are granitic and are not of volcanic origin, or the result of lava flows. They are rugged in character and alpine in appearance. They take their name from the Wallowa River. These mountains were formerly known by a number of names, most of which were applied by prospectors. These names included Granite Mountains, Powder Mountains and Eagle Mountains. J. Neilson Barry, at the time living in Baker, recommended to the USBGN that these local names be eliminated and the name Wallowa Mountains be used to describe the features in question. This was done and the new name is now in universal use. Wallowa Mountains are separate from and are not part of the Blue Mountains.

Wallowa River, UNION, WALLOWA. Wallowa River is one of the important rivers of the northeastern part of the state. It is formed by the confluence of the east and west forks about a mile south of Wallowa Lake. The river flows into Wallowa Lake at the south end and out of the north end and joins Grande Ronde River at Rondowa. For the origin of the name, *see* Wallowa County. There is a post office in Wallowa Valley named Wallowa.

Walls Lake, HARNEY. This is a small lake south of Harney Lake serving as a collecting place for spring runoff. It has an elevation of about 5000 feet. It was named for a pioneer stockman, Tom Walls.

Wallupa Creek, WALLOWA. J. H. Horner of Enterprise told the writer that *wallupa* was an Indian word and probably meant wildcat.

Walterville, LANE. Walterville was named by George Millican, a pioneer resident, for his son Walter Millican. For further information, *see* Millican.

Walton, LANE. The road from Eugene to Florence was started in 1881. It crossed the Coast Range near Noti and then followed a large tributary of Siuslaw River which was named Walton Creek to honor Judge Joshua J. Walton, a pioneer lawyer of Lane County and for some years county judge and secretary of the Board of Regents of the University of Oregon. Walton post office was established in 1884 to serve settlers along the new route and James L. Atkinson, the first postmaster, named the office for the stream. However, sometime after the turn of the century the name of the stream was changed to the mundane Wildcat Creek, the form now in universal use.

Walton Lake, CROOK. This artificial lake about 27 miles northeast of Prineville was formed by a dam near the headwaters of Camp Creek. The Prineville Chapter of the Izaak Walton League of America was instrumental in this work and the lake is named in honor of their well-known patron.

Waluga, CLACKAMAS. Indian tradition says that the lake now known as Oswego Lake by the town of Lake Oswego, was originally called Waluga Lake, *waluga* being an Indian term for wild swan. This name was used because of the peculiar sound made by these birds. When Waluga post office was established in Mar. 1916, near Oswego Lake, it was thought appropriate to use the old Indian name, but in June 1923, the name of the office was changed to Lake Grove, a move of no improvement in the opinion of the compiler. Lake Grove was incorporated into Lake Oswego in 1959.

Wamic, WASCO. Wamic was named for a family of early settlers named Womack. This family consisted of Asa and Levi, brothers, and a nephew Crawford. Pierce Mays, prominent resident of Wasco County, is authority for the statement that these three men had a remarkable plan of allowing each of the three in turn to determine what all should do during his day of leadership. Thus on Monday all worked in the blacksmith shop under the leadership of Asa. Levi was more socially inclined and on Tuesday all three sat in front of the shop and "chewed the rag and whittled." Crawford was the Nimrod of the family and on Wednesday the three went hunting or fishing. Thursday began the cycle anew. Wamic post office was established Nov. 25, 1884, with James W. Sanford postmaster. It replaced the early office of Prattville. Wamic post office was closed June 1, 1958.

Wampus, KLAMATH. Wampus is a word used by timbermen to refer to a legendary monster of the forests. No one has ever seen a wampus but plenty of woodsmen will undertake to describe one. Wampus post office was established June 27, 1908, with Eugene Spencer first and only postmaster. It was put in service just a few months after nearby Forest post office was discontinued. According to a letter from Devere Helfrich of Klamath Falls, written in Apr. 1948, Wampus post office was probably at the old Spencer stage and freight station at the east foot of Hayden Mountain. This would make it about three miles southwest of Forest. Wampus post office was discontinued Sept. 15, 1911.

Wampus Butte, DESCHUTES. The wampus is a legendary monster of the forest, about which there are many stories. Wampus Butte, named for this creature, is about eight miles west-northwest of La Pine, near the Deschutes River.

Wanderers Peak, CLACKAMAS. Dee Wright of Eugene, a native of the Molalla Valley, told the compiler that this peak was named because a party of hunters got lost nearby and wandered around several days before it found camp.

Wanoga Butte, DESCHUTES. Wanoga Butte, elevation 5740 feet, is about eight miles southeast of Bachelor Butte. It was named by the USFS with one form of the Klamath Indian word meaning son or male child. Other forms are *vunak, vunaga,* and *unak*. This butte was named about the same time as other nearby features were named with Indian words expressing family relationship. *See* Tot Mountain and Kwolh Butte.

Wapato Lake, WASHINGTON, YAMHILL. This intermittent lake, which covers considerable area in wet years, bears the Indian name for the arrowhead or sagittaria, commonly known as the wild potato. It grows in wet situations. For information about the wapato, *see* Chewaucan Marsh and Sauvie Island. The form Lake Wapato was frequently used in earlier days, but Wapato Lake is now in general use. A post office with the name Wapatoo was established July 14, 1853, with William E. Molthrop postmaster, on the Washington County list. It was a little southeast of the present town of Gaston. The office was discontinued in Aug. 1865. On Aug. 13, 1871, another post office, Wapatoe, was established in this vicinity. The name of the office was changed to Gaston on June 5, 1873. The office may have been moved at the time the name was changed. Both of the above offices were on the Washington County list. Wapato post office was established on the Yamhill County list on Sept. 26, 1883, with Frederic Florey postmaster. This office was discontinued Nov. 3, 1886. The railroad station at or near this place is shown on old time-cards with the spelling Wapato, but it was abolished prior to 1980.

Wapinitia, WASCO. *Wapinitia* is a Warm Springs Indian word. The correct spelling is said to be *Wapinita*. The compiler of these notes discussed the name with several Warm Springs Indians and finds that the word *Wapinitia* is difficult to translate but it suggests a location near the edge of something. One Indian says that it means the edge of the desert or cultivated land. Another version is that it means a point at the end of the brush, or coming out of the brush. These two meanings are not necessarily contradictory. In Wapinitia it is said the name means running water but this translation does not seem to be substantiated by Indians. Wapinitia was once known as Oak Grove because of the trees in the vicinity. One of the principal tributaries of Clackamas River is Oak Grove Fork, so called because it headed in the general direction of Oak Grove.

Wapiti Camp, UMATILLA. This forest camp on the Tower Mountain road was named by the USFS with a plains Indian word for elk or *Cervus canadensis*. *Wapiti* is used elsewhere as a placename and is a welcome relief from the surfeit of "Elk."

Ward Butte, LINN. Ward Butte is east of Shedd and south of Plainview. Here there are two buttes, one on each side of the Southern Pacific Company tracks, and the name Ward is always applied to the western one, which has an elevation of 858 feet. The eastern butte has no name, and an elevation of 442 feet. The compiler is informed that the hill known as Ward Butte is really on the Isom donation land claim, and should have been called Isom Butte, while the small hill is on the Ward claim and should be Ward Butte. Regardless of these facts, however, the larger hill to the west is always known as Ward Butte, and will probably continue to be so called. It was named for Thomas M. Ward.

Ward Butte, UMATILLA. This butte is west of Butter Creek south of Hermiston. It was named for Charles J. Ward who homesteaded near its base.

Ward Creek, JACKSON. Ward Creek is a tributary of Rogue River at Rogue River town, named for Oliver P. Ward, a pioneer settler.

Ward Creek, WASCO. This creek rises southwest of Shaniko and flows into Antelope Creek. It was named for John H. Ward who was born in New York and came to California with the gold rush. About 1864 he moved to Oregon and located near Cross Hollows where he farmed and later kept the hotel and drove stage. Ward moved to The Dalles about 1874 and died there some three years later. His son, Thomas A. Ward, was a well-known citizen and later sheriff of Wasco County.

Ward Lake, LAKE. Ward Lake is four miles northwest of the community of Silver Lake. It is named for Royal E. Ward who, with his wife, Minnie Lee Ward, homesteaded by it in the 1890s. The Ward's baby son Russell was one of those burned to death in the disastrous Silver Lake Christmas Eve fire of 1894. For a description of this tragedy and Ed O'Farrell's 100-mile ride to Lakeview for the nearest doctor, *see The Oregon Desert* by Jackman and Long, pp. 126–7.

Wards Butte, DOUGLAS. William Ward came to Oregon from Ohio in 1852. He was an early settler where Ward Creek empties into Pass Creek near Comstock and was the operator of the toll road which passed near Wards Butte. He died in 1871 and was the first person buried in the Anlauf Cemetery near Comstock.

Wardton, DOUGLAS. Wardton, a place near Champagne Creek about six miles west of Roseburg, was named for a local resident, Frazier Ward. Wardton post office was established Jan. 7, 1890, with Ward postmaster. An office named Wardville was established on Feb. 15, 1890, also with Frazier Ward postmaster but the order was rescinded on Mar. 20, 1890. Apparently both names were submitted in the application and through error, both were established. Wardton post office was closed on Feb. 28, 1907.

Warfield Creek, LANE. This tributary of Hills Creek southeast of Oakridge was named for Mrs. B. B. Warfield, the owner of Kitson Hot Springs.

Warm Springs, JEFFERSON. This place, the agency for the Warm Springs Indian Reservation, was named for natural features nearby. The name of the reservation was apparently taken from the much more important springs on Warm Springs River. Warm Springs post office was established Feb. 7, 1873, with Michael Flinn postmaster. The name of the office was telescoped into Warmsprings in 1894, and later to Warmspring. All this was confusing, for people found it difficult to adhere to two styles, one for the agency and one for the reservation. About 1929 postal authorities changed the name again to Warm Springs, and at length all was brought into agreement.

Warner Lake, LAKE. Warner Lake post office was in the south part of Warner Valley. There never was a geographic feature in Oregon called Warner Lake. Instead the name Warner Lakes was used collectively for a string of lakes, ponds, and playas in the Warner Valley. However, there was a Warner Lake post office which was established Aug. 28, 1889, with Alvin N. Bennett, first postmaster. This post office was about eight miles southwest of Adel. It remained in service until July 31, 1924.

Warner Mountain, LANE. This mountain is in the big bend of Middle Fork Willamette River south of Oakridge. It was named for Fred Warner, an early settler on the stream. Warner was a hunter and came to Oregon in 1853, according to information furnished in 1927 by his granddaughter, Mrs. Lina A. Flock of Oakridge.

Warner Valley, HARNEY, LAKE. There are several geographic features in Oregon named for Brevet Captain William Horace Warner who was killed by Indians in Sept. 1849, just over the line in northern California. These features include, besides the valley, the Warner Lakes, former Warner Lake post office, and Warner Canyon just north of Lakeview. There is no Warner Lake in Oregon, the term Warner Lakes being a collective name. The peak east of Warner Valley, once known as Warner Mountain, is now universally known as Hart Mountain. Arrowsmith's map of North America, corrected to 1832–33, shows a string of lakes connected by Plants River in the locality of what is now called Warner Valley. Plants River and the lakes are also shown on the map *Territory of Oregon*, prepared by direction of Colonel J. J. Abert of the u.s. Topographical Engineers, 1838. The compiler is of the opinion that John Work of the Hudson's Bay Company visited the Warner Valley on Oct. 12–15, 1832. *See California Historical Society Quarterly*, Sept. 1943, p. 203. Work left the main party to explore what "might with propriety be called the valley of the lakes," and there is an implication that the old hands had been there before. When Work made his little exploration, he took along C. Plante and J. Favel, two of his good men. Charles Plante was also known as Plant and it seems obvious that Plants River bears his name. Work gives a good description of Warner Valley and its string of lakes. Fremont explored what is now known as Warner Valley in Dec. 1843, and named one of the Warner Lakes Christmas Lake. This was probably Hart Lake of the present day. For many years the Warner Valley was known as Christmas Lake Valley, but the name of Christmas Lake was transferred to another and much less important body of water by a curious transfer that the writer is unable to explain. *See* Christmas Lake. Captain Warner, together with Lieutenant R. S. Williamson, left Sacramento in Aug. 1849, for the purpose of exploring the upper reaches of Pit River. Unfortunate delays hindered the work. Finally the leaders separated, Williamson remained at Goose Lake, while Warner went north to Lake Abert, and then to Warner Valley. He worked south along the west edge of the valley until his party was ambushed and massacred. Williamson gives Sept. 26, 1849, as the date of the massacre, and his map shows the place just south of the 42nd parallel. Williamson's map in Pacific Railroad Surveys *Reports* is on a large scale and shows the site of the massacre about four miles south of the state line. In 1864, Lieutenant-Colonel C. S. Drew of the First Oregon Cavalry, during the Owyhee Reconnoissance, visited and named Warner Valley for the murdered officer, in the belief that Warner had been killed in the valley itself. Drew says in his report that John S. Drum of Jacksonville told him later that Warner was killed in Surprise Valley, and not in Oregon. Drum was a member of the party that went to find Warner's remains in 1850. While it seems apparent that Warner was killed south of the state line, and not in Warner Valley, it also seems clear that he was not killed as far south as Surprise Valley. The massacre was possibly near Eightmile Creek. For additional information about Warner's death, *see Gold Rush*, Columbia University, New York, 1944, p. 624, *et seq.* The principal lakes and playas of Warner Valley, beginning on the north, are as follows:

Bluejoint Lake
Stone Corral Lake
Lower Campbell Lake

Campbell Lake
Flagstaff Lake
Mugwump Lake
Swamp Lake
Anderson Lake
Hart Lake
Crump Lake
Pelican Lake

The best information about Warner Valley may be obtained from the cooperative irrigation report issued by the state engineer entitled *Warner Valley and White
River Projects.*

Warren, COLUMBIA. Warren post office was established on Feb. 19, 1885. James
Gill, later a resident of Newberg, named the place for his old home, Warren,
Massachusetts. In 1888 the post office was discontinued and when it was reestablished two years later it was named Gillton, for Gill. This was due to the fact that
there was another post office called Warren in Umatilla County. Some years later
the post office in Umatilla County was discontinued and Gillton, Columbia
County, was changed to Warren again. The place formerly called Warren in Umatilla County is now known as Myrick.

Warren, UMATILLA. Warren was a station on the Northern Pacific Railway
about five miles southwest of Helix, named for a local family. The post office was
in service from Dec. 18, 1888, to Mar. 26, 1895, with William O. Warren postmaster.
From time to time there was confusion between this place and Warren in Columbia County. The name of the station in Umatilla County was changed to Myrick
in compliment to another local family. Myrick post office was established Aug. 1,
1902, with John W. Myrick first of several postmasters. The office operated, but
not continuously, until Mar. 31, 1908.

Warren Creek, HOOD RIVER. Warren Creek and Warren Lake were named for
Warren Cooper, an early USFS ranger and son of David R. Cooper. The curious
diversion tunnel west of the creek was constructed by the OSHD in 1938 to control
runoff water.

Warren Creek, LINN. Warren Creek flows into Calapooia River east of
Brownsville. It was named for Andrew J. Warren, a pioneer resident. He married
Eliza Spalding, daughter of pioneer missionaries of the Oregon country, the Rev-
erend Henry H. Spalding and Eliza Hart Spalding.

Warrendale, MULTNOMAH. Warrendale was a post office in eastern Multno-
mah County serving the territory west of Bonneville. Warrendale was named for
Frank M. Warren, Sr., a pioneer fish packer of Oregon, and a prominent citizen of
Portland. He was drowned in the wreck of the *Titanic* in Apr. 1912.

Warrenton, CLATSOP. Warrenton gets its name from D. K. Warren, an early
settler. The community of Lexington, which was laid out in 1848, was the forerun-

ner of Warrenton and was the first county seat of Clatsop County. Lexington was a post office in the early history of the state. The site of Lexington was near the south limits of Warrenton and about where Skipanon station was situated. The name Lexington fell into disuse and for many years the territory where Warrenton is now was known as Skipanon. Small boats went up Skipanon River to the place called Skipanon, or Upper Landing, and there unloaded passengers and goods for Clatsop Plains. Warrenton near the mouth of the river was platted by its proprietor in 1889 and the development of the community immediately began around Warrenton, with the result that Skipanon ceased to be of equal importance. For additional information, *see* Skipanon. Most of Skipanon is now within the city limits of Warrenton, although it is about a mile away from the business part of Warrenton. For reminiscences of D. K. Warren, *see OHQ*, v. 3, p. 296.

Warrior Point, COLUMBIA. Warrior Point is the north end of Sauvie Island, and Warrior Rock is on the Columbia River side of the island a little to the south. The following quotation from Vancouver's *Voyage of Discovery* for Oct. 28, 1792, indicates the reason for naming this point: "About three and a half miles from Oak Point Mr. Broughton arrived at another, which he called Point Warrior, in consequence of being there surrounded by 23 canoes, carrying from three to twelve persons each, all attired in their war garments, and in every other respect prepared for combat." Lieutenant Broughton made peace with these Indians, and no bloodshed ensued. The modern use Warrior Point has been approved by the USBGN. It is not possible to tell at this time if Broughton had his adventure at the point or at the rock not far away, but the latter is more likely.

Wasco, SHERMAN. Wasco owes its inception to the fact that the old Oregon emigrant trail and the road south from the Columbia River, intersected at this point. Despite its early establishment, it was not incorporated until 1898. It was named for Wasco County, in which it was formerly situated, before Sherman County was formed. The first post office in the locality was called Spanish Hollow. It was established Mar. 2, 1870, with Jesse Eaton postmaster. The name of the office was changed to Wasco on Mar. 17, 1882.

Wasco, WASCO. The postal history of Wasco County is complicated by the fact that when the county was established, it was of magnificent proportions. It is difficult to localize some of these early offices, as they may have been anywhere in eastern Oregon. Many are not shown on available maps. Some of the names are in duplicate. A post office called Wasco was in operation in Wasco County from Aug. 26, 1868, until June 3, 1872, with William D. Gilliam postmaster. This office was not for the locality, now named Wasco, in Sherman County. According to Anita Drake of The Dalles, it was at the old 12 Mile House two miles down Fifteenmile Creek from Dufur near the mouth of Long Hollow. The 12 Mile House was an important stage stop in the 1870s and 1880s. The original building burned in 1930. Wasco post office was of course named for the county.

Wasco County. When Wasco County was created, Jan. 11, 1854, it comprised all the area of the Oregon Territory between the Cascade Range and the Rocky

Mountains, an empire in itself. By successive takings for other states and counties, the area of Wasco County has been reduced to 2408 square miles. Wasco is the modern name for a tribe of Indians. Early writers used the name in many forms. Ross in *Fur Hunters of the Far West*, v. 1, p. 186, speaks of the *Wiss-co-pam* tribe. Lee and Frost in *Ten Years in Oregon*, p. 176, give *Was-co-pam*. For references to various spellings, *see Handbook of American Indians*, v. 2, p. 918. About the time of the immigrations white people shortened the name to *Wasco*. The Wasco Indians were a Chinook tribe, formerly living on the south side of the Columbia River, in the vicinity of The Dalles. The name *Wasco* is said to be derived from the Wasco word *wacq-o*, meaning a cup or small bowl made of horn. The *Handbook of American Indians*, v. 2, p. 917, says this referred to a cup-shaped rock near the main village of the tribe, but Dr. William C. McKay, in an article in The Dalles *Mountaineer*, May 28, 1869, said that the name *Wasco* meant makers of basins, and that the literal meaning of the word was horn basin. Some of these basins were fantastically carved. Both of the explanations may be correct. Dr. McKay said that the locality of the city of The Dalles was called *Winquatt*, signifying a place surrounded by bold cliffs.

Washboard Ridge, LANE. This ridge is near the summit of the Calapooya Mountains just north of the Douglas County line. The descriptive name was given by USFS ranger Fred Asam.

Washburn Butte, LINN. This butte is in the southwest part of s 18, T 13S, R 2W. It was named for James A. Washburn, a pioneer landowner nearby. It is about three miles north of Brownsville.

Washington, YAMHILL. There have been but two post offices in Oregon using the name of the first president. The first of these offices was known as Washington Butte. Its short history will be found under the name Lebanon. This post office, strictly speaking, was named for George Washington indirectly, because it was named for a nearby geographic feature. A post office called Washington was in service in southern Yamhill County from Sept. 30, 1858, to Oct. 13, 1860. Edward Dupuis was the only postmaster. While it is probable that Dupuis selected the name of this office the compiler has no written record to that effect. The name of the Dupuis family has been applied to a Yamhill County stream which flows into Deer Creek a little to the northeast of Sheridan. The name of this stream is generally given as Dupee Creek due to the inability of later settlers to struggle successfully with the French spelling. The compiler has not been able to determine the exact location of the Washington post office in Yamhill County.

Washington County. When the Oregon country was divided into counties by an act approved July 5, 1843, four districts were created. That part of the country between the Willamette River and the Pacific Ocean, north of Yamhill River, was called Twality. This is an Indian name and it is spelled in many different ways. For information about the origin of the name, *see* Tualatin River. That part of Oregon originally lying in Twality District was subsequently divided into several counties. The first of these districts, or counties, to be cut off of Twality District was Clat-

OREGON GEOGRAPHIC NAMES

sop District, which was created June 22, 1844. On Sept. 3, 1849, the territorial legislature passed an act changing the name of Twality County to Washington County, in honor of the first president of the United States, the act providing: "That the name of the county commonly called 'Twality' or 'Falatine' be and the same is hereby changed to Washington." The name Twality is so spelled in the written bills introduced in the legislature in 1849, but in the endorsements on the backs of the bills the word is Tuality. The law as printed in *Local Laws*, 1850 session, p. 54, uses the spelling Tualitz. The "z" is probably a typographical error for a written "y." Washington County had an area of 726 square miles in 1990.

Wasson Creek, COOS. Wasson Creek was named for George Wasson, a pioneer settler. The creek flows into Winchester Creek southeast of Cape Arago. *See* Dodge's *Pioneer History of Coos and Curry Counties*, p. 16.

Wastina, LAKE. The postmaster at Wastina in 1925 wrote the compiler that Wastina was a name of Indian origin and that it meant beautiful valley. He gave no indication as to what tribe used the word. *Wastina* is not found in the dictionary of the Klamath language. The office operated from 1915 to 1925.

Water Tower Mountain, MARION. When the Oregon Pacific Railroad was built to Detroit in 1889, a water tank was built at the mouth of Mayflower Creek just west of Detroit Dam. For a time the creek was known as Watertank Creek but the original name prevailed and the only memento is Water Tower Mountain at the top of the watershed.

Water Trough Canyon, CROOK. This canyon emptying into McKay Creek takes its name from an old watering trough on the Gail Demaris Ranch.

Waterloo, LINN. W. H. Klum of Lebanon informed the writer in Dec. 1926 that he was born and reared on the Klum donation land claim, and one of his first recollections was the saw and grist mill built by Elmore Kees at the falls of South Santiam River. The place was known as Kees Mill. After Kees died his widow leased the property to John F. Backensto. There was litigation among the Kees heirs and other persons. John Ambler, a local wit, suggested the name Waterloo after a court decision was handed down giving a substantial victory to one party to the contest. *See* a story in the Lebanon *Express*, Sept. 16, 1937. Waterloo post office was established by change of name from Harris Ranch on Jan. 5, 1875, with S. D. Gager postmaster. Harris Ranch office was established June 18, 1874, with W. S. Harris postmaster. The writer does not know if it was at the same location as Waterloo or not.

Waterman, WHEELER. Waterman is in the south central part of Wheeler County. It was named for John W. Waterman, better known as "Doc." He settled on the land where the post office was subsequently established. The place was known as Waterman Flat. Waterman belonged to the cattle firm of Smith & Waterman. There was at one time a post office not far from this place known as Caleb, for Caleb N. Thornburg. Thornburg at one time had stock at Spanish Gulch in John Day Valley and was receiver of the land office in The Dalles.

Waterman Mine, WHEELER. This mine and a homestead both near Antone were another center of operations for early settler John W. Waterman, the founder of Waterman.

Waters Creek, CURRY. M. S. Brainard of Brookings told the compiler in 1967 that this creek entering Rogue River just north of Illinois River was named for George M. Waters who lived nearby at the turn of the century.

Waterspout Creek, WALLOWA. This stream occupies a canyon that drains into Snake River in T 2S, R 50E. It was named by the Warnock brothers because of the heavy floods that washed so much material down to Snake River.

Waterspout Gulch, GRANT. Waterspout Gulch drains into John Day River just north of Picture Gorge. It is common practice in certain sections of Oregon, Washington and Idaho to name streams and gulches Waterspout, not because of the frequency of waterspouts, but because of the excessive flood discharge after cloudbursts. The terrific effect of these floods is nowhere more noticeable than along the canyon of Snake River between Riparia and Huntington. Great masses of boulders and earth are swept down narrow defiles and into the main stream in quantities sufficient to form serious obstructions in the river.

Watkins, JACKSON. For nearly 30 years Watkins was a post office in the upper Applegate River Valley near the mouth of Squaw Creek. The office was established in Mar. 1893, with the name of the first postmaster, Mark Watkins. The office operated in this locality until Nov. 30, 1920, when it was closed out to Jacksonville.

Watson, MALHEUR. The post office at Watson was established in July 1898. It was named for Harry Watson, a local stockman. Robert J. Ivers was the first postmaster.

Watson Cabin, DOUGLAS. Alma Watson wrote the compiler in 1967 that this cabin a mile and a half northwest of Red Butte was built in 1903 by Clair Watson, her husband's cousin, to prove up a timber claim. She said: "It was a nice one room cabin with a separate screened cooler over the creek, a nice place to keep a deer so the flies couldn't get it." She added that the hunters always stayed there the first night out from Wolf Creek. The author imagines the venison was more often poached than fried.

Watson Mountain, DOUGLAS. This 2288-foot peak is three miles southeast of Glide. It bears the name of James Watson who was born in South Carolina in 1801. In 1854 he settled on a donation land claim along nearby Fall Creek.

Waucoma Ridge, HOOD RIVER. Waucoma Ridge is a spur off the main divide of the Cascade Range. It is in the northwest part of the county and separates the drainage of Hood River on the east from that of Eagle and Herman creeks to the west. Around the city of Hood River *waucoma* is said to be an Indian word meaning cottonwood tree, and it was used sometimes to refer to the locality because of the trees near the Columbia and Hood rivers. The compiler has not been able to learn what tribe used the expression. There are probably no cottonwood trees on Waucoma Ridge and the name seems to have been applied to that feature by white people because it has a pleasing sound.

Waud Bluff, MULTNOMAH. Old maps show this as Waid Bluff, but an investigation by government authorities disclosed the fact that Waud Bluff is correct, the name coming from an old settler, John Waud. Waud Bluff is on the east bank of the Willamette River north of Swan Island. Waud's donation land claim was north of the bluff.

Wauna, CLATSOP. For the origin of the name Wauna, *see* Wauna Point. The name was applied to the Clatsop County community by Alfred W. Clark. Wauna post office was established Jan. 21, 1911, with James Pollock first postmaster, and closed prior to 1980.

Wauna Point, MULTNOMAH. *Wauna* is an Indian name, probably Klickitat. It describes a mythological being supposed to represent the Columbia River. *See The Bridge of the Gods*, by F. H. Balch. Wauna Point is on the Columbia River Highway between Tanner Creek and Eagle Creek. The highest point of the bluff near the river is about 2500 feet in elevation.

Wauneka Point, MULTNOMAH. This point is just south of I-84 between McCord Creek and Moffett Creek. It bears the Indian name of a locality on the south bank of the Columbia River west of Bonneville.

Waverly, HARNEY. Waverly was about seven miles southeast of Crane. It was a freight stop on the wagon road to the then railhead at Riverside some 30 miles east. David A. Brakeman operated a store and when the post office was established in June 1908, Brakeman was first postmaster. The railroad reached Crane in 1916 and that community became the important commercial center. Waverly post office was closed to Harriman on Nov. 15, 1916.

Waverly Lake, LINN. This lake is not large, but it has a pleasing aspect. It is just east of Albany, and came into being largely because of the construction of the grades of the old and new locations of the Pacific Highway East. It lies between the two alignments and is an attractive feature of the locality. It was named Waverly Lake at the suggestion of Charles Childs, well-known Linn County resident.

Wawa Creek, CLATSOP. Wawa Creek is a small tributary to Youngs River about a mile south of Youngs River Falls. *Wawa* is the Chinook jargon word for talk and may have been applied to the stream because the water makes a noise flowing over the gravel.

Weaver, DOUGLAS. This small community about two miles south of Myrtle Creek on South Umpqua River was named for William and Anna Weaver who settled nearby in 1851. Weaver Creek, a tributary of South Myrtle Creek, was named for the same family.

Weaver Creek, LANE. This tributary of Brice Creek north of Elephant Mountain was named for one Weaver who got lost and died nearby in the early days. This information was supplied by Loren W. Hunt of Cove who spent his boyhood near Disston.

Weaver Gulch, MARION. Weaver Gulch lies just east of the old Pacific Highway East, a mile north of Looney Butte. It was named for David Weaver, who took up a donation land claim nearby.

Web, YAMHILL. This station, northeast of Newberg, was named by consolidating the initials of W. E. Burke, a well-known politician of Portland, who owned land nearby. The station was not in service in 1940.

Webfoot Creek, BAKER. Webfoot Creek is near the old mining community of Auburn and lies just east of California Gulch. It was the favored area of the Oregon miners while the California Tarheads stayed on the other side of the ridge. *See also* California Gulch.

Wecoma, LINCOLN. John Gill in his *Dictionary of the Chinook Jargon*, 1909, says that *wecoma* is the jargon word for sea. The community of Wecoma is in the north part of Lincoln County, overlooking the ocean.

Wedderburn, CURRY. Wedderburn was established by R. D. Hume, a prominent Pacific Coast business man, who had fishing interests at the mouth of Rogue River. He named the community for an ancestral home in Scotland. Literally, Wedderburn means Sheep Creek. *Wedder* is an old form of wether, and *burn* is, of course, a stream or brook.

Weekly, DOUGLAS. A post office named Weekly was established on the Coos County list on Sept. 24, 1883, but about the same time it was moved to the Douglas County list and there it remained until it was discontinued Feb. 25, 1884. Smith Baily was the only postmaster. All the evidence available is to the effect that the office was at the west edge of Douglas County, probably about 20 miles west of Roseburg on the Roseburg-Coos Bay stage road. The Weekly family was well known, especially in Coos County and some members were interested in the construction of the road. It is probable that Weekly post office was at or near the place called Reston, a stage station on the road and a post office from 1890 to 1934. Edmond E. Weekly was the first postmaster at Reston and was the proprietor of the station.

Weekly Creek, COOS. The correct spelling of this name is Weekly and not Weakly, as sometimes written. The stream is a tributary of East Fork Coquille River about one mile east of Gravelford. It was named for a pioneer family of the Coquille Valley.

Wegner Creek, UMATILLA. Julius F. Wegner was born in Wallin, Germany in 1845 and came to this country as a young man. After living in Pilot Rock for a number of years, in 1885 he homesteaded on the upper reaches of the creek near Wegner Spring.

Wehrli Canyon, GILLIAM. William Wehrli came to Gilliam County from California in 1884 and filed on a homestead northwest of Mayville. For a brief biography, *see Illustrated History of Central Oregon*, p. 587.

Welch Butte, KLAMATH. Welch Butte is just northeast of Crater Lake National Park. In 1911, Samuel S. Welch filed on government land at its base.

Welches, CLACKAMAS. Welches was named for Samuel Welch, who took up a homestead nearby in 1882. The post office was established in 1905.

Wellen, JACKSON. Wellen is the neighborhood of the home of H. von der Hellen. He named it for the estate of his ancestors in Germany.

Well Spring, MORROW. Well Spring has been well known since the days of the immigrations. It is south of Boardman and close to Juniper Canyon. The exact location may be found on the USGS map of the Well Spring quadrangle. Well Spring is mentioned in several early journals written on the Oregon Trail, and was probably named because it was enlarged into a well. The compiler has been unable to associate the name of anybody called Wells with the spring.

Wells, BENTON. Wells was named for a man locally known as "Red" Wells, who owned a donation land claim nearby in pioneer days. Wells post office was established Feb. 24, 1880, with James Gingles first postmaster. The railroad station was put in service about the same time, but some years later the name of the station was changed to Wellsdale to avoid confusion with another Wells on the Southern Pacific railroad. Wells post office was continued with that name until Feb. 1936, when it was closed to Corvallis. The station name was still Wellsdale as of 1982.

Wells Island, HOOD RIVER. This island is in the Columbia River just west of Hood River town. Before Bonneville Dam was built it was part of the mainland. It later was called Morrison Island for its owner, George Morrison. In Mar. 1940 it was purchased by Dr. Stanley E. Wells of Hood River and it has been known as Wells Island ever since. This was confirmed in *Decision List 8602*.

Wemme, CLACKAMAS. Wemme is a place on the Mount Hood Loop Highway about four miles west of Rhododendron. It is named for a public-spirited citizen of Portland, E. Henry Wemme, who was instrumental in getting the Barlow Road into the possession of the state of Oregon. This road was for many years a toll road, but in 1912 Wemme bought it for $5400. After making a number of desirable improvements, Wemme died, but not before making arrangements to bequeath the road to the public. It is now incorporated in part in the US-26 section of the Mount Hood Loop Highway. Wemme post office was established June 21, 1916, with Leonard A. Wrenn first postmaster and discontinued Dec. 9, 1977.

Wenaha River, WALLOWA. This stream is also called Salmon River, but that name is unsatisfactory because of the more important Salmon River nearby in Idaho. J. H. Horner of Enterprise informed the compiler that the name *Wenaha* is derived from the Indian family or sub-tribe name *Wenak*, with a *ha* added to indicate the land governed by the sub-chief Wenak. *See* Imnaha.

Wenaka, WALLOWA. This place was to have been called Wenaha, but postal authorities at Washington mistook the spelling and changed the "h" to "k."

Wendling, LANE. Wendling was named for Geo. X. Wendling, a prominent Pacific Coast lumberman and at one time a director of the Booth-Kelly Lumber Company. The post office was established in 1899 and the first postmaster was Geo. H. Kelly.

Wendson, LANE. Wendson is a railroad station northeast of Cushman. The name was condensed from that of the Wendling-Johnson Lumber Company.

Wendt Ditch, BAKER. Henry Wendt came to Baker County in the 1860s and eventually filed on land near Bridgeport in 1885.

Wenner Creek, LINCOLN. This is a small tributary of Yachats River from the south about five miles upstream from Yachats. It is named for Richard Wenner, an early homesteader.

Wesley, BENTON. Wesley got its name from the given name of the first postmaster, Wesley C. Keeton. The office was established in Sept. 1900, and was discontinued in Oct. 1903. It was on the extreme west edge of the county and about five miles east of Harlan. Some maps show Wesley on the extreme east edge of Lincoln County, but the postal records in Washington put the office in Benton County.

West Branch, WHEELER. West Branch is a principal tributary of Bridge Creek some four miles west of Mitchell. It was originally called Taylor Creek for James M. Taylor, an early settler. It has also been known as West Branch Bridge Creek. Taylor was the first settler along the creek in a spread-out community that once boasted some 20 families.

West Buker Spring, WHEELER. This spring southwest of Antone near the Crook County line was named for Hal Buker, one of a number of brothers who ranched near the head of Pine Creek. The compiler has been unable to locate east Buker Spring.

West Chehalem, YAMHILL. West Chehalem is an area name, given in contradistinction to East Chehalem or Chehalem as it was more generally known. Chehalem meant the locality now usually called Newberg and vicinity. West Chehalem was on the upper reaches of Chehalem Creek six or eight miles northwest of Newberg. West Chehalem post office was established as early as Nov. 20, 1865, with Isaac Rogers first postmaster. The office operated until July 31, 1900, when it was closed to Gaston. West Chehalem post office moved to fit the availability of postmasters, but it was generally in the northwest part of T 3S, R 3W. In recent years there has been no specific community called West Chehalem.

West Creek, CLATSOP. West Creek is near Westport and was named for John West, who settled in the vicinity in pioneer days. *See* Westport.

West Creek, TILLAMOOK. West Creek near Beaver was named for a local settler, Walter West.

West Fork, DOUGLAS. West Fork was a railroad station on the Southern Pacific line in Cow Creek Canyon at the mouth of West Fork Cow Creek. For the post office name, *see* Dothan. At one time West Fork was an important stop on the railroad including an early day "eating house." By the 1980s, nothing remained but the main line tracks.

West Lake, CLATSOP. This is a long, narrow lake on Clatsop Plains south of the site of Carnahan station. It was named for Josiah West, a pioneer landowner. The Oregon Coast Highway, US-101, crosses the north end of this lake north of the old

West homestead. For story about Josiah West and the building of the West house, *see* the *Sunday Oregonian*, Dec. 1, 1946, magazine section.

West Linn, CLACKAMAS. This is the successor to Linn City, which was established as Robins Nest by Robert Moore, a pioneer of 1840. Moore took a prominent part in organizing the provisional government, and bought the *Oregon Spectator* in 1850. In 1844 the legislature authorized him to operate a ferry between Oregon City and Robins Nest. On Dec. 22, 1845, the legislature named the locality of his home Linn City, for Lewis F. Linn of Missouri. *See* Linn County. A flood swept away the place in 1861. Linn community is now incorporated with the name of West Linn. Linn City post office was established Jan. 8, 1850, with James M. Moore postmaster. The name was changed to West Linn on Feb. 18, 1854.

West Portland, MULTNOMAH. The name West Portland is used to describe the area near the crossing of Barbur Boulevard and Capitol Highway. There was a West Portland School and the name is otherwise perpetuated in West Portland Addition that lies generally south and southwest of Multnomah. In the 1890s a steam motor carline extended into the territory by way of Fulton Park. West Portland post office was established July 21, 1890, with Henry J. Osfield first postmaster. This office continued in service until Mar. 15, 1907, when it was closed out to Hillsdale. In Aug. 1946, Werner Raz, superintendent of the Multnomah branch of the Portland post office, wrote that for a time the old West Portland office was housed in a building numbered 4623 SW Taylors Ferry Road, a short distance west of Capitol Highway. Mr. Raz added that the building was being demolished.

West Side, LAKE. This post office was named by Will C. Fleming, who was the first postmaster when the office was established in June 1923. It was named for the West Side Store, which was on the west side of Goose Lake. The office was closed July 31, 1942.

West Stayton, MARION. West Stayton railroad station was established on the Oregonian Railway narrow-gauge line in the 1880s to serve the locality about four miles west of Stayton. The railroad did not go through Stayton, and West Stayton was the nearest shipping point on the narrow gauge. The station was of course named in contradistinction to Stayton. For origin of name, *see* Stayton. In the latter 1880s a post office was petitioned for to serve the locality of West Stayton, but postal authorities refused to establish an office with the name West Stayton for fear of mail confusion and suggested that the local people interested should choose another name. A meeting was held and Hugh McNeil suggested the name Ale which was short, and duplicated no other post office in the country. Mrs. Maude Porter Boone of Aumsville informed the compiler that the name was suggested by the finding of an empty ale bottle beside the road near the station. Ale post office was established on Dec. 18, 1888, with Levi J. Hollister postmaster. The office was discontinued on July 26, 1890. It was opened again on Jan. 21, 1891, with Henry B. Condit postmaster. Mr. Condit ran the office, in conjunction with the railroad station West Stayton, until Sept. 3, 1902, when Ale post office was closed due to the extension of rural free delivery from Aumsville. The later development of the locality brought new demands for a post office, and West Stayton office was established Oct. 12, 1911, with D. M. McInnis first postmaster. This office was closed July 31, 1953.

West Union, WASHINGTON. The name West Union, applied to various places in Washington County, is of great historic interest and has been in use over a century. On May 25, 1844, a few members of the Baptist Church met in the cabin of David T. Lenox, a pioneer of 1843, who had taken up a claim on the north part of Tualatin Plains. A constitution and covenant was drawn up for the West Union Baptist Church, the first Baptist Church established west of the Rocky Mountains. The text of this document, as printed in *OHQ* v. 36, p. 247 *et seq.* contains the express statement that the churchmen "have been thrown together in these Wilds of the West, and . . . Agree that we Constitute and come into union." West Union Baptist Church was built in 1853 on a site given by Lenox on the east edge of his claim. The congregation met in the new church on Dec. 24 and 25, 1853. The church still stands on the Germantown Road about a mile northwest of the community of West Union. West Union post office was established Jan. 27, 1874, with Stephen A. Holcomb first postmaster. This office was in operation until Mar. 17, 1894. The writer does not know its exact location, but it was probably near the present community of West Union, which is close to the Holcomb claim. West Union community is at an intersection just south of the Germantown Road and about a mile and a half northwest of Bethany.

West Woodburn, MARION. West Woodburn originated when the Oregon Electric Railway was built in 1907. The line ran on a tangent that missed Woodburn by about two miles and a spur was built east to the downtown area by the Southern Pacific tracks. This spur has long since been torn up while a large, new, populated section of Woodburn has grown around the I-5 freeway exit which is about halfway between the two places. For information about origin of the name, *see* Woodburn. West Woodburn post office was established in May 1912, with M. J. McCormick first postmaster. The office was closed in Mar. 1934.

Westfall, MALHEUR. Westfall was named for Levi Westfall, a pioneer who settled in Bully Creek Valley. The post office was first established with the name Bully in Apr. 1882, but was changed to Westfall in Feb. 1889. It was at one time on the old Westfall Ranch about two miles east of the present site of the town of Westfall. By the 1980s little remained to mark this community.

Westfir, LANE. Westfir was named for the Western Lumber Company. The name was first used July 19, 1923, according to a letter written the compiler by W. J. Norris. The Western Lumber Company was a large producer of fir lumber. The post office was established in Nov. 1923. Subsequently the lumber operations were taken over by the Edward Hines Lumber Company and the community was operated as a company town. Hines closed its mill in 1977 and sold the town along with the public facilities including water, sewers and the like. The new owners wished these utilities in public ownership and in Jan. 1979 the residents voted to incorporate.

Westimber, WASHINGTON. Westimber, a post office and railroad station west of the town of Timber, was named on that account. The railroad station was formerly called West Timber but about 1918 the railroad company changed the name to one word to agree with the post office name. The post office was established in 1916 with L. R. Kern postmaster, and closed Jan. 25, 1935.

Westlake, LANE. Westlake post office derives its name from the fact that the town site it serves is on the west shore of Siltcoos Lake. This community was established by W. P. Reed in 1914 and the post office was installed in Sept. 1915. The community was incorporated in 1962 with the name Dunes City. *See* that heading.

Westland, UMATILLA. Westland was a railroad station near the west bank of Umatilla River, about eight miles west of Stanfield, named because of its westward position as compared with other communities in the lower Umatilla River area. Westland came into being as a result of the construction by the railroad of the Messner-Hinkle cutoff. Westland post office was established Aug. 17, 1917, with Henry T. Schroeder first postmaster. This post office was closed Jan. 14, 1922, and the railroad station was not in service as of Feb. 1972.

Weston, UMATILLA. Weston was named for Weston, Missouri, by T. T. Lieuallen. Lieuallen came from the Missouri town and named his home in Oregon after his old home in the Midwest. He was first postmaster at Weston, Oregon. The writer has been informed by those who say they knew that Lieuallen said on several occasions that he intended to name the place Western, but the postal authorities circumvented him. In Carey's *History of Oregon*, it is said that Western was the name Lieuallen picked on, but this does not agree with other reports that have been received by the compiler. A post office named Mitchell's Station was established in Feb. 1867, with W. H. Abell postmaster. The name of this office was changed to Weston in Sept. 1869, at which time Lieuallen became postmaster. The compiler has been unable to learn if Mitchell's Station was at the present location of Weston, or if it was moved in 1869 when the name was changed.

Weston Landing, YAMHILL. Mrs. Harvey Stoller of Dayton investigated this name and informed the compiler that Weston Landing was on the donation land claim of Gabriel Chrisman. In the early 1850s, Chrisman platted a town named Weston and in May 1855, he sold lots to four people including Joel Palmer. Chrisman moved to California about 1857 and his town never materialized. Mrs. Stoller added that the Chrismans spent several years in Missouri and may have selected the name for Weston in that state. However, the donation land claim of David Weston, who was present at the Champoeg division, was only a few miles to the east so that coincidence cannot be completely ruled out. Weston Landing is two miles southweast of Dayton on the Willamette River and Weston Bar and Weston Bend are in the river

Westport, CLATSOP. John West settled in this locality about 1850, and the place was named for him. West was born in Linlithgowshire, Scotland, in 1809, and came to Oregon by way of Quebec and California. He was known as Captain West and was a millwright and lumberman. He ran a sawmill at Westport and also a salmon cannery. He died in 1887 and his widow, Margaret West, also a native of Scotland, died in 1894. For information about John West, and his large family, *see* article by Fred Lockley in the *Oregon Journal*, Jan. 31, 1943. Westport post office was established in Dec. 1863.

Wests Butte, CLACKAMAS, WASCO. This butte is on the summit of the Cascade Range about five miles southeast of Timothy Lake. It was named for John I. West who settled near Wapinitia about 1880.

Wetmore, WHEELER. Wetmore community was established in 1942 about 11 miles northeast of Kinzua at a location used by the Kinzua Pine Mills Company in handling logs in northeast Wheeler County. It was named for the late E. D. Wetmore of Warren, Pennsylvania, a large stockholder in the logging and lumbering concern who had previously named Kinzua for Kinzua, Pennsylvania. The post office was established in the summer of 1945, and discontinued July 8, 1948.

Weygandt Canyon, HOOD RIVER. In 1899 Marcus W. Weygandt homesteaded near the mouth of this canyon between Evans Creek and East Fork Hood River. Weygandt, usually known as Mark, was one of the early guides on the north side of Mount Hood.

Whale Cove, LINCOLN. Whale Cove is a well-known place on the Oregon Coast Highway at the north base of Cape Foulweather. The compiler was told about 1930 that it was named many years before by a party of white people who found some Indians busy at work on the carcass of a dead whale. Despite the aroma, the Indians were enthusiastic over a whale steak.

Whaleshead Island, CURRY. This rocky islet is in the Pacific Ocean, close to the shore 20 miles south of Gold Beach. It is hollow to seaward and has a hole in the top so that at certain stages of the tide water rushes into the cavity and spouts out the hole, simulating a whale. Whaleshead Island has been so known since very early pioneer days. The style of the name has included such forms as Whalehead, Whale Head and other variations. In 1943 the USBGN adopted the name Whalehead Island as being the most desirable arrangement. This was changed to the present form on the USGS 1986 Carpenterville quadrangle. A nearby stream is called Whaleshead Creek. Orvil Dodge, in *Pioneer History of Coos and Curry Counties*, says that Frances Fuller Victor's statement that Gold Beach was once known as Whalehead is wrong.

Wharf Creek, KLAMATH. When the Cascade Line of the Southern Pacific was built in the 1920s by the Utah Construction Company, supplies were loaded on

barges at the southeast end of Odell Lake. A wharf and construction camp were
built by Carleton & Fetter, a sub-contractor, at the mouth of Wharf Creek, giving
it the name. Debbs Potts of Grants Pass supplied this information, Debbs was a
teenager working for his father's C. R. Potts Lumber Company who had a mill at
the mouth of Trapper Creek where they cut timber for the numerous tunnels.

Wheatland, YAMHILL. Wheatland is in the extreme southeast corner of the
county and was named in pioneer days because it was an important shipping point
for wheat grown on nearby lands. The place was also called Wheatland Landing
and sometimes Matheny Ferry. Wheatland post office was established Jan. 29,
1867, with Marion B. Hendrick first postmaster. The office was discontinued Jan.
31, 1903, doubtless due to the extension of rural free delivery from larger offices.
The area tributary to Wheatland has been extensively developed by intensified and
diversified field and fruit crops.

Wheeler, TILLAMOOK. This place was named for Coleman H. Wheeler, of
Portland, a prominent lumberman and sawmill operator, who operated a mill in
the community shortly after the railroad was built. Wheeler died about 1920. For
his biography, *see* Carey's *History of Oregon*, v. 2, p. 72.

Wheeler, WHEELER. Wheeler post office was established Aug. 15, 1890, with
Lafayette Frizzell postmaster, and continued in operation until Sept. 5, 1895, when
it was closed to Waldron. Lafe Frizzell lived at the Frizzell Ranch on Girds Creek
about six miles north of Mitchell. It is reported that the office was named for
Henry H. Wheeler, prominent pioneer resident of central Oregon, for whom
Wheeler county was named in 1899.

Wheeler County. Wheeler County was created Feb. 17, 1899, and according to
ODOT has an area of 1715 square miles. It was named for Henry H. Wheeler, who
was born in Erie County, Pennsylvania, Sept. 7, 1826, of English and German
ancestry; went to Wisconsin in 1855; drove an ox team from Wisconsin to Yreka,
California, by way of Salt Lake, in 1857, in company with a family named Wells;
came to Oregon in 1862 and located at The Dalles in 1867, but soon went to the
Salmon River mines in Idaho. Mining being unprofitable, he secured work driving a stage. He returned to The Dalles, and began farming and stock raising in the
vicinity of Mitchell, Oregon, where he remained until his death, Mar. 26, 1915. He
was married Dec. 19, 1875, to Dorcas L. Monroe, who died at Mitchell in Mar. 1911.

Wheeler Creek, CURRY. This creek rises on the south slopes of Mount Emily
and flows into East Fork Winchuck River. It was named for James P. Wheeler
who settled near its mouth before the turn of the century. Wheeler Ridge, the
high ground on the south side of the creek was the area where the Japanese
dropped incendiary bombs from a float plane in Sept. 1942. They experimented
with a program to start massive forest fires but, because of damp weather, the
small fires were easily controlled. The Japanese abandoned the submarine-based
float plane scheme after a second attack east of Port Orford produced no results.
See Japanese Attacks Against North America in World War II, by Bert Webber.

Wheeler Creek, KLAMATH. This stream was named for James H. Wheeler, of Fort Klamath, one-time deputy sheriff. Wheeler was a trapper and spent a great deal of time, often alone for long periods, in the mountains with his traps.

Wheeler Creek, LANE. Wheeler Creek flows into Lake Creek at Greenleaf. It is named for William H. Wheeler, an early settler.

Whelpley, JACKSON. Whelpley post office was established in July 1882, and ran along to the following April when it was discontinued and the business turned over to Deskins post office. Whelpley post office was named for the postmaster, Thomas H. Whelpley. The compiler has not been able to find this place on any map. It is apparent from the fact that the office was closed to Deskins that it must have been in the upper Rogue River country. The name Deskins post office was later changed to Prospect.

Whetstone Creek, CLACKAMAS, MARION. This stream is on the northeast slope of Whetstone Mountain and flows northward. The creek was named by John Paine and Preston Pendleton (familiarly known as Doc Pendleton) because of the prevalence of a rock that could be used to sharpen knives.

Whetstone Point, JACKSON. This point is a prominent place near the south end of Bald Mountain, west of Rogue River and a few miles southwest of Prospect. It was named because of the local occurrence of a slate rock which forms a good abrasive whetstone for sharpening blades. The rock splits into suitable shapes and sizes.

Whig Lake, LANE. Whig Lake is directly west of and almost connected to Torrey Lake north of Waldo Lake. It apparently was named by someone who confused Torrey with the British Tory political party, rivals of the Whig party. Torrey Lake was named for Henry Beal Torrey. For more information, *see* Torrey Lake.

Whiskey Creek, TILLAMOOK. Mrs. Mildred Edner of Netarts told the compiler the humorous incident concerning the naming of this creek. One Charles Wiley had a campground on Netarts Spit. This was an eight or nine mile trip with a team and wagon and late starters would often spend a night along the way. Two couples travelling together were benighted at this stream and while the wives made camp, the men took the whiskey keg to cool in the creek. The cooling apparently required continuous supervision and sampling. The wives were unable to get the men to perform the routine chores such as gathering firewood. The matter was resolved and the creek named when the ladies dumped the whiskey in the creek and broke up the keg for the campfire.

Whiskey Hill, CLACKAMAS. Whiskey Hill is a locality about four miles south of Aurora, on the Meridian Road just east of Pudding River. On Mar. 9, 1945, the Oregon City *Banner-Courier* printed a letter from Mrs. Wilda Elliott Fish of Woodburn to the effect that when she was a small girl she drove through this neighborhood with her father and asked about a strange-looking building with steam coming out. Her father explained it was a distillery where whiskey was being made from apples. This sounds more like applejack than whiskey, but either fluid carries a stout kick. In the late 1940s a school was constructed nearby and the more conservative residents feared youth would stray from the path of temperance if the school were named indirectly for John Barleycorn's elixir. Ninety-One crossroads is a mile to the east so the school at Whiskey Hill was named Ninety-One School.

Whisky Creek, JACKSON. This stream is a tributary to Rogue River, not a great way from Crater Lake. Will G. Steel says that it was named as a result of an enterprising pioneer bootlegger, who planned to take a load of whiskey from Jacksonville over the mountains to Fort Klamath. Snow impeded his progress and he buried his load for the winter. Someone discovered his cache and the soldiers of Fort Klamath gradually cleaned out his stock so that when he returned in the spring there was nothing left. All this is said to have occurred about 1883. Times have not changed much.

Whisky Creek, WALLOWA. Whisky Creek drains an area northeast of Wallowa. The *Illustrated History of Union and Wallowa Counties*, p. 674, gives the origin of the name. Raz Tulley, a resident of Wallowa, is authority for the statement that in the summer of 1872 traders brought a supply of whiskey by pack train from Walla Walla and began to barter the firewater to the Indians for Indian goods. Local residents, including Tulley, Masterson, White, Cox, and several others, became much alarmed and went to the camp to put a stop to the business. A three-cornered fight ensued, which was won by the settlers. The kegs were broken and the whiskey ran into the stream, which has been known as Whisky Creek ever since. In 1931 J. H. Horner confirmed this story, and said he got his information from W. W. White.

Whisky Run, COOS. Whisky Run, just north of Coquille River, was named at the time of the Coos County gold rush of 1853–55. Excitement in the locality was at a high pitch, and it hardly seems possible that liquid stimulants were needed, but the name of the stream indicates otherwise. Remarkable stories are told of the results of panning the beach sands. The community of Randolph was established near the mouth of Whisky Run but was moved to Coquille River after the gold fever subsided.

Whistlers Bend, DOUGLAS. This oxbow bend in North Umpqua River is on the donation land claim of D. L. Whistler. It was once known as prosaic Horseshoe Bend but is now the site of Whistler Bend County Park.

Whitaker, DESCHUTES. Whitaker post office was a short-lived establishment on the High Desert about ten miles east of Millican. The office was named for John O. Whitaker, a property owner in eastern Deschutes County. The office was established Mar. 28, 1911, with Mary E. Gray first and only postmaster. It was discontinued Aug. 15, 1912, with mail to Bend. Mary E. Gray later became Mrs. John O. Whitaker.

Whitcomb, LINN. Whitcomb was a locality on Quartzville Creek about 15 miles northeast of Sweet Home, now inundated by Green Peter Lake. The name has been preserved in Whitcomb Island. The town was named for George B. Whitcomb, who had some interests there. A stream flowing into the lake from the northwest is called Whitcomb Creek. Whitcomb post office was established Dec. 26, 1889, and was closed May 15, 1899. George B. Whitcomb was the postmaster. The office was out of service from Apr. 13, 1893, until Aug. 12, 1896.

White Bull Mountain, LINN. White Bull Mountain, east of the site of Quartzville, was the location of one of the big gold strikes of 1864, the White Bull Ledge. A stock certificate of the Santiam Gold and Silver Mining Company dated 1864 and now in the possession of the University of Oregon Library lists the White Bull Ledge along with Dry Gulch and Driggs ledges. Quartzville community was located in Dry Gulch and Jeremiah Driggs made the first gold discovery in the area in Aug. 1863.

White Butte, WHEELER. George Nelson of Mitchell told the compiler that this 5664-foot-high butte was named because it was colored white by the thick cover of dead bunchgrass. It held this cover because it was too steep for easy grazing.

White City, JACKSON. When Camp White, north of Medford, was deactivated after World War II, the lumber industry was expanding rapidly. A group of local sawmill owners purchased 390 acres of the former camp and established White City Industrial Park. Although unincorporated, it is known today as White City and is comprised of lumber mills, light industrial and manufacturing plants, a residential neighborhood and the usual community amenities. White City post office was established Apr. 1, 1960, and was changed to a branch of the Medford office in June 1963. For the origin of the name, *see* Camp White.

White Creek, LINN. This stream flows into Little Muddy Creek east of Harrisburg. It was named for Luther White, through whose donation land claim the creek runs. White was a pioneer surveyor for that part of Oregon.

White Horse, HARNEY. The name White Horse as applied to a post office in then Baker County was long a puzzle in Oregon nomenclature. The office was established Feb. 13, 1867, with W. A. Mix postmaster and was closed on Aug. 6 of the same year. In 1980 information from Keith and Donna Clark of Redmond and Priscilla Knuth of Portland, the meticulous investigators of early matters military, indicates beyond a doubt that the office was at or near Camp C. F. Smith on Whitehorse Creek within the confines of what later became the Whitehorse Ranch. The *Owyhee Avalanche*, Ruby City, Idaho Territory, under date of Mar. 10, 1866 tells of Captain Walker, Mr. William Mix and others on their way through the area along with Walker's efforts to relocate Camp Alvord. This was accomplished shortly thereafter and Captain J. H. Walker, 23rd U.S. Infantry, assumed command at Camp C. F. Smith. The same paper on Apr. 21, 1866 tells of 40 men moving onto ranches along White Horse [sic] Creek and again, on Apr. 13, 1867 says "Documents for the postmaster at White Horse, Baker County, Oregon, are in the Ruby City Office, which makes it probable that an office has been established at that place." At that time Baker County included all this area as Harney County was not created until 1889.

White Lake, KLAMATH. This lake was so named because of the color of the lake bottom, which apparently consisted of some white diatomaceous material. The lake was an extension of the original Lower Klamath Lake, and much of its area was south of the Oregon state line and therefore in California. It was two or three miles southwest of Merrill. Irrigation and drainage projects have eliminated White Lake. White Lake City was named for the lake. One of the original promoters of the city, Mr. Bert C. Hall, was a resident of Klamath Falls in Apr. 1947, and kindly submitted some interesting information about the project. The Oklahoma and Oregon Townsite Company was organized to market a large number of lots which were to be made available by the passage of a bill in Congress to dispose of some Indian lands near Klamath Falls. The bill failed to pass and the company acquired the White Lake City area as a substitute townsite. The nucleus of the town was in S 16, T 41S, R 10E. White Lake City boasted a bank, built by Mr. Hall, a restaurant, a newspaper and small piers for waterborne traffic. Lots in the project were sold for $15 each, assignment made by lottery. When the Southern Pacific Company extended its line from Weed northeast to Klamath Falls and Kirk, White Lake City was left off the main route of travel, and the town expired. Most of the buildings have been salvaged for nearby farm structures. Whitelake post office was established Sept. 20, 1905, with Lillian H. Stilts first postmaster. The office was closed to Merrill Dec. 15, 1913.

White Pine, GRANT. White Pine post office was about five miles northeast of Austin, on the Sumpter Valley railroad, near the summit of the Blue Mountains. It was established Apr. 6, 1912, with Julius Gardinier first postmaster, and was discontinued Mar. 15, 1918, with mail to Austin. The post office was named for the Baker White Pine Lumber Company, then operating in those parts. The mill was doubtless cutting western yellowpine rather than western whitepine.

White Point, JACKSON. White Point was a post office on the old stage road from Ashland south over the Siskiyou Mountains to Yreka. It was about 16 miles south of Ashland. The post office was established Aug. 8, 1883, with Edward J. Farlow first postmaster. Byron Cole took office Oct. 17, 1883, and was apparently the cause for changing the name of the office to Colestin on Apr. 8, 1892. Colestin office was in service for many years. The name White Point came from a conspicuous outcrop or ledge of white rock, probably some form of granite, visible from many parts of the Cottonwood Creek Valley. The Southern Pacific Company had a railroad station in this locality called White Point, shown on the USGS map of the Siskiyou Pass quadrangle. This station was abandoned about 1938–40. The compiler does not know if this station was in the same location as the old White Point post office or not, but is of the opinion that the old White Point post office was in about the same location as the place called Colestin, also shown on the above map. White Point station and Colestin station were about a mile apart.

White River, HOOD RIVER, WASCO. This stream has a descriptive name, resulting from the color of the water when glacial silt and sand are present. William Clark's map accompanying the Biddle edition of the journals of the Lewis and Clark expedition published in 1814, shows the stream with the name Skimhoox River, but the compiler has been unable to find any mention of the name in the text. Peter Skene Ogden saw the stream on Monday, Dec. 5, 1825, and Fremont mentions it under date of Nov. 26, 1843, but neither of these explorers commented on its color. This is not remarkable, because in the winter the amount of silt carried by White River is small. Joel Palmer, in his *Journal of Travels*, as of 1845, mentions the river in a number of places, as a branch of the Deschutes, but does not use the name White River. He makes a note of the sand. White River, as a name, probably came into use in the late 1840s, but it is not known who was the first to apply it.

White Rock, DOUGLAS. This is purely descriptive. The mountain has an exposed white rock formation on the west side.

Whiteaker, MARION. Whiteaker post office was named for John Whiteaker, first governor of Oregon, but probably not because he held that position. Governor Whiteaker was Oregon's representative in Congress when the post office was established and was probably of some help in getting the new facility. Doubtless the office was named for some such reason. Whiteaker post office was established May 3, 1880, with George W. Hunt first of four postmasters. George W. Hunt was a well-known local resident who owned property in S 23, T 8S, R 1W. There was a store on the east-west road near the north part of his property and this is said to be the first location of the Whiteaker post office. The Hunt place was known as the Beaver Glen Farm because it was in the vale of Beaver Creek. Old maps show that this post office was moved around from time to time but it was generally a few miles north or northeast of Sublimity. The office was discontinued July 20, 1903. John Whiteaker was born in Indiana in 1820 and came to Oregon in 1852. He was first state governor of Oregon. He served one term as representative in Congress and also in several sessions of the Oregon legislature. He died in Eugene in 1902.

Whitehill, LAKE. Whitehill post office was about ten miles northwest of Paisley and just south of the south end of Summer Lake. It was named for a local topographic feature, apparently composed of some chalklike substance. The office, with one short intermission, operated from Dec. 9, 1875, to Apr. 28, 1879. The four postmasters were: William H. Miller, Mrs. Julia D. Hayes, William T. Hill, and Peter Withers.

Whitehorse Creek, KLAMATH. Will G. Steel informed the compiler in 1927 that when the government forces were constructing the road from Annie Spring west toward Rogue River in 1865, a white horse was used to carry supplies, and the stream and Whitehorse Bluff nearby were undoubtedly named for this animal.

Whitehorse Ranch, HARNEY. Whitehorse Ranch is one of the historic landmarks of southeast Oregon and much has been written about it. The ranch is on Whitehorse Creek, southeast of Steens Mountain. John S. Devine came to this part of Oregon about 1868 and soon was a member of the partnership of Todhunter and Devine. These two stockmen assembled a fine collection of blooded animals of one sort and another and the Whitehorse Ranch became famous throughout the West. A weather vane simulating a white horse was put on the cupola over the barn and there it has stood for many decades. This weather vane is kept carefully painted and is an object of considerable veneration. In May 1946 James F. Abel, then at Berkeley, California, wrote the compiler that the name Whitehorse Creek appears as early as 1866 on Colonel R. S. Williamson's map of the Steens Mountain country. Mr. Abel continues: "Some thirty years ago a vaquero from the ranch told me that it was named for a beautiful white horse ridden by an Indian chief who frequented that section in the early days." His statement is to some extent verified by the *Humboldt Register*. The issue of Sept. 23, 1865, in telling of an Indian fight in Quinn River Valley has the following: "One horse, which had often before attracted notice, was again conspicuous on this occasion a white animal that defied all efforts to approach its rider." There is another mention of this white horse in the issue of Dec. 30, 1865, where it is said that he was ridden by Black Rock Tom, a local sub-chief who was captured and killed at the Big Meadow on Humboldt River Dec. 26, 1865. The newspaper account says that Tom did not ride his "pale horse" in the last foray and as a result the animal remained with other Indians. It is Mr. Abel's belief that Whitehorse Creek and Whitehorse Ranch owe their names to Tom's pale horse, which appears to have ranged as far north as the Alvord Valley. For information about the post office, *see* White Horse.

Whiteman Bar, MARION. Whiteman Bar is on the east bank of Willamette River about one mile southwest of Sidney. It was named for S. J. Whiteman who owned land nearby in pioneer days.

Whiteson, YAMHILL. The postmaster in 1926 wrote the compiler that this place was named for Henry White, who gave the right-of-way to the railroad, and laid out the townsite. Will G. Steel says it was named for William White. The reader is free to guess which. Possibly there were two men of the same family. A post office called Whites was established here on Oct. 3, 1889, with Dennis A. Browne first postmaster. The name of the office was changed to Whiteson on Oct. 2, 1890. The writer recalls that when he was a very small boy, the railroad station was also called Whites. This was the place where the old narrow-gauge railroad from Portland to Airlie crossed the standard gauge line from Portland to Corvallis.

Whitewater Creek, LINN, MARION. This stream was named by the Marion County road surveying expedition in 1874. *See* an article by John Minto, *OHQ*, v. 4, p. 249. The name was applied because of the light-colored glacial silt held in suspension by the water.

Whitewater River, JEFFERSON. This stream rises on the northeast shoulder of Mount Jefferson and flows into Metolius River. It carries much silt from Whitewater Glacier and the name is descriptive. It was named many years ago, and for a time was known as Whitewater Creek, but this caused confusion with Whitewater Creek, a tributary of North Santiam River west of Mount Jefferson. As a result, the eastern stream is now generally known as Whitewater River.

Whitford, WASHINGTON. This station was named for W. A. White and A. C. Bedford, prominent capitalists of New York City, who were directors of the Oregon Electric Railway Company during the early history of the line.

Whitney, BAKER. This town was named for C. H. Whitney, a pioneer landowner of the county.

Whittaker Flats, UMATILLA. In 1969 Charles Kopp of Pilot Rock informed the compiler that these flats south of Nye were named for Harry Whittaker who settled there just before the turn of the century.

Whorehouse Meadow, HARNEY. In the early days "sin" was considered an unavoidable adjunct of life in the cattle and sheep country. During the summer one or more of the female entrepreneurs from Vale would set up facilities under canvas in this accessible but secluded meadow a mile east of Fish Lake. Houses of this category, wood and canvas, passed with the end of the open cattle range and all that remained was the name on the slopes of Steens Mountain. In the 1960s the BLM issued a recreation map and in deference to the moralists substituted a namby-pamby name, Naughty Girl Meadow. The USGS advance sheet of the Fish Lake quadrangle followed suit but in 1971 the OGNB took strong exception to the change. The compiler is happy to add that the old name was restored by *Decision List 8304. O tempora! O mores!*.

Wichita, CLACKAMAS. Wichita station was on the interurban line about two and a half miles northeast of Milwaukie at the extreme north edge of the county. The Wichita property was developed by George Parry, who had formerly lived in Wichita, Kansas. Mr. Parry applied the name of his old home in the Midwest.

Wickiups, DESCHUTES. This is an old stockman's name for a point on Deschutes River south of Crane Prairie. The place was a campground for Indians who gathered there to hunt and fish in the fall. They left their wickiup poles standing which gave the place its name. Wickiup Butte, elevation 4913 feet, is nearby and got its name from the locality. Wickiup Dam is also named for the locality. *Wickiup* is a plains Indian word for tepee or wigwam. In 1939 the USBGN adopted the spelling Wickiup rather than Wikiup.

Wicopee, LANE. Wicopee is a station on the Southern Pacific Company Cascade Line, situated in the Salt Creek Valley southeast of Oakridge. It was named at the time the railroad was built. *Wicopee* is an Indian word transplanted from New York state. It is said to mean "long hill," and it probably refers to a long grade or steep climb, rather than to an elongated hill or mountain standing by itself. The compiler has no idea how the name happened to be dug up in far away New York.

As far as the Indian meaning is concerned "long hill" is strictly accurate for the Lane County railroad station. It is about midway of the long climb from Oakridge up the summit of the Cascade Range. Wicopee in Lane County is not a community nor does it have a post office. It was just an operating point on the railroad with some company facilities. The name may be found in USGS Bulletin 258, *Origin of Certain Place Names in the United States*, by Henry Gannett.

Widby Loops, CLATSOP. Before World War II the lower Columbia River Highway ascended from the river level up to Clatsop Crest and part of the ascent was made by a series of hairpin bends called the Widby Loops. In 1914 J. L. Widby was resident engineer of the OSHD during the construction of these loops and an assistant, Earl Withycombe, prepared a sign reading "Widby Loops," which was nailed to a tree nearby. The name became permanently attached to this interesting example of engineering.

Widgeon Lake, LINN. Widgeon Lake is at the headwaters of North Santiam River. It was named after World War II by a fish planting crew who disturbed a flight of widgeons while stocking the lake. *See* Alice Lake.

Widows Creek, GRANT. This stream east of Dayville was named for a widow, Mrs. S. E. Heim, who lived on the creek, and was, according to reports, a typical frontierswoman.

Wilark, COLUMBIA. The name of Wilark post office was made by taking the first part of Wilson and the last part of Clark. These two names occur in the Clark & Wilson Lumber Company which operated a mill at Linnton and owned timber lands in Columbia County. The post office was established in 1924 and served the camp which was logging the company timber lands.

Wilbur, DOUGLAS. Wilbur was named for James H. Wilbur, D.D., who was born in Lowville, New York, on Sept. 11, 1811, and died at Walla Walla, Oct. 8, 1887. He was universally known as Father Wilbur and was one of Oregon's best-known pioneer Methodist ministers. He came to Oregon by way of Cape Horn in 1846–47. He was instrumental in founding several educational institutions, among others Umpqua Academy at Wilbur. The first building was a rough log structure on Father Wilbur's land claim upon which he settled Sept. 8, 1853. For short history of Father Wilbur and Umpqua Academy, *see OHQ*, v. 19, p. 1. A pioneer post office with the name Laurel was established near the present site of Wilbur on Oct. 14, 1854, with Willis Jenkins postmaster. It was discontinued in Nov. 1855.

Wilbur Mountain, UMATILLA. Wilbur Mountain is a prominent feature in the Blue Mountains about ten miles east of Meacham. It is almost on the southwest corner of S 6, T 1S, R 37E. It was named for Erastus J. Wilbur, who, as a member of the firm of Wilbur and Son, cut and milled a great deal of railroad timber from the vicinity of Wilbur Mountain.

Wild Cheat Meadow, MARION. This meadow is near the headwaters of Cheat Creek, a tributary of Whitewater Creek west of Mount Jefferson. It is named for the abundance of one of the grasses of the genus *Bromus*, commonly called "cheat grass." The form Wildcheat is incorrect. Cheat Creek takes its name from the meadow.

Wild Rose Point, DOUGLAS. This point north of Illahee Rock was named by USFS ranger Fred Asam for the thicket of wild roses around the nearby spring.

Wilderville, JOSEPHINE. Wilderville was named for Joseph L. Wilder, a local resident. Postal authorities informed the compiler that the first post office established at this place was called Slate Creek. It was established on Sept. 30, 1858, with Oliver J. Evans first postmaster. The name of the office was changed to Wilderville on Aug. 12, 1878. Joseph L. Wilder was then postmaster.

Wildhorse Creek, UMATILLA. This name is an old one. It occurs as Marron's Fork in Brouillet's *Account of the Murder of Dr. Whitman*, New York, 1853, p. 55. *Marron* is a French word, meaning, among other things, a domesticated animal gone wild. Brouillet uses the name as of 1847. Kip, in *Army Life on the Pacific*, 1859, p. 25, uses the form Wild Horse Creek. The origin of the name obviously had some connection with an early-day experience with stock, probably by fur traders. Government map makers use the form Wildhorse.

Wildwood, LANE. For a good many years Wildwood, with its descriptive rustic name, was an important locality in the Row River area. Wildwood post office was established Jan. 6, 1888, with Sarah E. Kerr first of a long series of postmasters. The office was closed Dec. 31, 1914, with papers to Disston. The office was a mile or so southeast of what was later Culp Creek post office.

Wilelada Creek, LANE. This creek west of Foley Springs has a composite name. Ray Engels, longtime USFS ranger at McKenzie Bridge, stated that the middle section, "ela" was for Mrs. Ella Haflenger of Foley Springs. He did not know the source of the first and last syllables. Mrs. Haflenger's first husband was Peter Runey and they had two children, a son, William, and a daughter who died at an early age. It is possible that son Will provided the first syllable.

Wiley Creek, GRANT. In 1877 William Wylie homesteaded at the mouth of this tributary of John Day River west of Mount Vernon.

Wiley Creek, LINN. This stream flows into South Santiam River near Foster. It bears the name of Andrew Wiley, a pioneer settler. It is also known as Rock Creek, but there are already too many creeks of that name in the state. C. H. Stewart of Albany wrote the compiler in 1927, as follows: "Andrew Wiley was a great hunter and was the pioneer explorer of the old Indian trail up the South Santiam River. Each year on his hunting expeditions he would penetrate farther into the recesses of the mountains, and in the year 1859, accompanied by two others, he made his way entirely across the Cascade Range and arrived in the locality of the present town of Sisters. He was thus the first man to discover the famous Hogg Pass. He was the chief pilot of the locators of the Willamette Valley and Cascade Mountain road project in 1866 and 1867, and the road followed the route of his memorable trip of 1859. Some surveyor has tried to change the name of Wiley Creek to Rock Creek, but the people of the vicinity still cling to the old name, and you never hear the other mentioned anywhere in the county." John Minto, in *OHQ*, v. 4, p. 241, mentions this pioneer trail, but misspells it Wyley. County records substantiate the spelling Wiley.

Wilhelm Creek, LANE. Wilhelm Creek is named for Frederick Wilhelm who homesteaded near its mouth in 1896. The creek flows into North Fork Siuslaw River from the north about six miles north of Beck Station.

Wilhoit, CLACKAMAS. John Wilhoit took up a land claim at the present location of Wilhoit post office about 1866. There were attractive mineral springs in the vicinity and Wilhoit took up the property on that account and operated a health and pleasure resort. The post office was established in 1882, and closed on Sept. 29, 1928.

Wilkesboro, WASHINGTON. The community of Wilkesboro was named about the time the United Railway was built through that part of Washington County. The post office was established in 1916, but the town was platted about four years before that. Wilkesboro was named for Peyton G. Wilkes, a pioneer of 1845, who settled at the present site of the community in pioneer days.

Wilkins, LANE. Wilkins was a station north of Coburg. It was named for Mitchell Wilkins, who settled near there in 1848. *See OHQ*, v. 5, p. 136.

Wilkins Creek, COOS, DOUGLAS. Peterson and Powers in *A Century of Coos and Curry*, p. 57, say that Harry Wilkins came to the Lakeside area in the 1880s. It is probable that this creek emptying into North Tenmile Lake is named for him.

Willamette, CLACKAMAS. This town is on the west bank of Willamette River at the mouth of the Tualatin. It takes its name from the Willamette River, which see. The locality of Oregon City was first known as Willamette Falls, and in pioneer days a community was projected on the west bank of Willamette River not far from the mouth of Clackamas River, to be called Willamette. These two places should not be confused with the town now known as Willamette, which is farther south. *See* Willamette River for information about the name. A post office named Willammette Forks was established on the Linn County list on Jan. 10, 1851, with William Spores postmaster. It was changed to the Lane County list on Mar. 4, 1852, with the style Willamette Forks, with Mitchell Wilkins postmaster. Preston's map of 1856 shows the place close to the foothills about three miles north of Coburg. The office was operated until about 1884. Willamette post office was established in Yamhill County Mar. 14, 1851, with John M. Forest postmaster. It was discontinued July 27, 1852. A pencil correction in the postal records changes the spelling to Willammette. John M. Forrest, who spelled his name thus, had a claim at the north bend of Lambert Slough about four miles southeast of Dayton and the office was probably in that locality. A post office named Wallamette was established Aug. 19, 1853, with Robert V. Short postmaster. It was on the Yamhill County list and was closed late in 1857. The Short claim was about a mile west of the present site of Wilsonville, in what is now Clackamas County.

Willamette Pass, KLAMATH, LANE. When SH-58 was completed in 1940, it was the most convenient route from the Willamette Valley to southeastern Oregon. It was also popular with California-bound travelers anxious to avoid the then curvacious Douglas and Josephine county sections of US-99. The initial stretch of the highway from Goshen to Oakridge follows Middle Fork Willamette River and the road was promptly and commonly called the Willamette Highway. It crosses the Cascade Range at elevation 5126 feet about one half mile north of Odell Lake and one mile northwest of the Southern Pacific summit tunnel under Pengra Pass. On Dec. 2, 1960 the OGNB moved to designate this Willamette Pass and the USBGN concurred in *Decision List 6103*. Historically Willamette Pass was the emigrant route crossing about one half mile west of Summit Lake and one and one half miles north of Emigrant Butte, several miles south of the present location. This original pass was renamed Emigrant Pass in simultaneous action.

Willamette River, BENTON, CLACKAMAS, LANE, LINN, MARION, MULTNOMAH, POLK, YAMHILL. This is the largest river entirely in the state of Oregon. Controversy over the spelling of the name continued many years. *Wal-lamt* was an Indian word, according to H. S. Lyman in *OHQ*, v. 1, p. 320, designating a place on the Willamette River near Oregon City on the west bank. Three ways of spelling the name have had their respective champions: *Willamette, Wallamette* and *Wallamet*. *Wilarmet* is the form used in David Thompson's *Narrative*, Toronto, 1916, p. 493, under date of July 9, 1811. Ross Cox, in his *Adventures on the Columbia River*, gives *Wallamat* (v. 2, p. 135), and *Wallamut* (v. 2, p. 164). Alexander Ross, in *Fur Hunters of the Far West* and *First Settlers on the Oregon*, gives *Wallamitte*; Franchere gives *Wallamat* and *Willamett*; Townsend's *Narrative* gives *Wallammet*; David Douglas, 1826, gives *Willamette*; Arrowsmith's map of North America, corrected to 1832–33, gives *Wallamatte*. A map of the Territory of Oregon, prepared by direction of Colonel J. J. Abert, U.S. Topographical Engineers, 1838, and attached to several government documents, shows the lower part of the stream as *Multnomah* or *Wilhamet*. The upper part is lettered *Walla Matte*. In 1841 Charles Wilkes used the spelling *Willamette* and this is the style throughout *U. S. Exploring Expedition* and atlas, 1845, as well as on the large charts prepared by Wilkes. Wilkes appears to have crystallized government use in favor of Willamette. For many references to the controversy over the spelling of the name, *see OHQ*, v. 44, p. 360. Harold Mackey in *The Kalapuyans*, p. 15 *et seq.*, also gives references generally supporting the various forms of *wal*. . . . The Willamette University *Willamette Scene*, Summer 1986, pp. 18 & 19 has a good account of the controversy between Judge Matthew Deady and Judge William Strong, the former supporting *Wallamet* and the later the conventional *Willamette*. The meaning of the word Willamette is not known, although there are several theories, including Mackey who says *Wallamet* means "spill water" and was applied to the river above the falls. Broughton discovered the river on Oct. 29, 1792, and named it the River Mannings, possibly for Boatswain's Mate Samuel Manning, a member of Vancouver's expedition. Lewis and Clark did not observe the stream on their westward trip, nor on their eastward trip either until their attention was called to it by Indians after they had gone as far as the Sandy River. Clark went back and entered the Willamette on Apr. 2, 1806, calling it the Multnomah.

Willamette Slough, MULTNOMAH. Willamette Slough post office was in service from Feb. 10, 1873, to Feb. 8, 1887, at a point on the mainland northwest of Linnton, and about opposite the south end of Sauvie Island. The office may have moved from time to time depending on who was postmaster. Thomas J. Howell, Oregon's famous botanist, was first to hold the office. The office was named for the channel on the west side of Sauvie Island, formerly Willamette Slough, now officially known as Multnomah Channel.

Willamette Stone, MULTNOMAH, WASHINGTON. The Willamette Stone is a surveyor's monument at the intersection of the Willamette base line and the Willamette meridian in the hills west of Portland. The mark was established on June 4, 1851, by John B. Preston, the first surveyor general of Oregon. The original mark was not a stone but a stake. This stake was officially replaced on July 25, 1885, by the present Willamette Stone. The replacement was carried on by another surveyor, W. B. Marye, and other officials, who made the replacement the occasion of a small ceremony. About 1985 vandals removed the stone, an obelisk about six inches square and three feet high. It was never recovered but has been replaced with a bronze plate. Preston selected the site of the Willamette Stone because it was thought at that time the meridian surveyed north from the stone would pass through the mouth of the Willamette River. The base line was established in its present location so that it would not cross the Columbia River and thus produce difficulties in surveying. In 1903 the USC&GS extended the triangulation net to include the Willamette Stone. The geographic position of the Willamette Stone, based on the 1927 datum, is 45° 31′ 10.831″ in north latitude and 122° 44′ 33.551″ in west longitude.

Willamina, YAMHILL. The community of Willamina was named for Willamina Creek, and the stream was named for Mrs. Willamina Williams, who is said to have been the first white woman to ride a horse across it. Some written reminiscences of Enos C. Williams are on file at the Oregon Historical Society. He says that Mrs. Williams was born in 1817 in Ohio and was married to James Maley in Mar. 1837, apparently in Illinois. Mrs. Maley came to Oregon in 1845 with her husband and her step-daughter and in the spring of 1846 the Maley family and a man named Burden went prospecting for land on which to settle. They found a stream flowing into South Yamhill River in the foothills of the Coast Range and named it in compliment to Mrs. Maley. Maley died in 1847 and on Feb. 24, 1848, Enos C. Williams and Willamina Maley were married, probably in Polk County. They settled on the land on which the town of Amity was built. They were much respected citizens of Amity and are buried at the old churchyard at that place. Willamina post office was established May 29, 1855, with James Brown first postmaster. The office was on the Brown claim about a mile east of the present town of

Willamina. On Jan. 1, 1863 Jeremiah Lamson became postmaster and the office was moved to his claim nearly two miles west of the Brown place. Brown had the office again on Mar. 24, 1865. On Apr. 4, 1866 the office was moved to and the name was changed to Sheridan, with Thomas N. Faulconer postmaster and there it has been ever since. This shift left Willamina Creek without a post office, and on Aug. 29, 1878 a new office was established with the name Willamina and with Jackson Monroe postmaster. From Dec. 1880 to Mar. 1891 Willamina post office was operated just over the line in Polk County.

Willard, MARION. The Willard area is about four miles east-southeast of Pratum and was named for Abner S. Willard, a pioneer of 1847. Willard was born in Ohio in 1827, and after reaching the Willamette Valley, settled near the middle of T 7S, R 1W. He died there in 1851. The Willard school district was organized as early as 1855 and in 1893 the Willard church was established. Willard post office was established in Apr. 1889, with Mary H. Starmer first postmaster. This office was finally closed in Apr. 1904.

Willbridge, MULTNOMAH. This station is the junction of the Astoria branch and the main line of the Burlington Northern Inc. It is southwest of the bridge over the Willamette River, and it has a composite name on that account.

Williams, JOSEPHINE. Williams is one of three post offices in southern Oregon named because of the proximity of Williams Creek. *See* Williamsburg and Williams Creek in this series of notes. In 1981 Williams post office was situated six miles southwest up Williams Creek from Provolt. Williams post office was established Oct. 11, 1881, with David John first of a long string of postmasters. The office is still in service as this note is being written. It is about two miles west of the Jackson-Josephine county line.

Williams Butte, LANE. Thomas Williams came to the Dexter area in 1854. He took a donation land claim near this butte which now bears his name.

Williams Canyon, MORROW. Williams Canyon is in the south part of T 1S, R 23E. It apparently was named for Nathaniel Williams who filed a timber culture claim in the canyon in 1883. However, John A. Williams who lived near Sand Hollow in the 1880s also bought land near the canyon in 1898.

Williams Canyon, YAMHILL. Williams Canyon runs south from Tualatin River three miles west of Gaston. It is named for Joseph Williams, who was born in England in 1850 and came to Oregon as a young man where he farmed in the canyon. In later years, his daughter and her husband, L. Wesley Walters, continued the operation. Hester Ann Walters died in Forest Grove in Mar. 1989, age 99 years.

Williams Crater, KLAMATH. Williams Crater is about one half mile west of Hillman peak near the west rim of Crater Lake. It was named in 1983 to honor Howel Williams, the renowned geologist and student of Crater Lake. Williams Crater, elevation 7747 feet, rises about 350 feet above the surrounding terrain and is of special geologic interest for its commingled andesite and dacite lavas. Williams calls this cone Forgotten Crater in *Geology of Crater Lake National Park, Oregon*, pp. 56–57 and pp. 142–143, but this name was never in general use. Howel Williams was born in Wales in 1899. For many years he was professor of geology, specializing in volcanology, at the University of California, Berkeley. He died at Berkeley, Jan. 12, 1980.

Williams Creek, DOUGLAS. Williams Creek rises north of North Umpqua River and flows into it about two miles west of Steamboat Creek. A USFS Forest Camp of the same name is located at the confluence of the two streams. The creek was named for Joe Williams who came from Ohio with several other families in the 1890s and settled near Lone Rock.

Williams Creek, JACKSON. Williams Creek post office was established Mar. 14, 1876. It was out of service for a time and the compiler does not know the dates of its later history. The first postmaster was John A. Lewman. This post office was very close to the center of the northwest quarter of s 7, T 38S, R 4W, and was therefore about a quarter of a mile east of the present Jackson-Josephine county line. It was also about the same distance southeast of the present Provolt post office. *See also* Williams and Williamsburg. The Williams Creek post office was not exactly on Williams Creek but not far from it.

Williams Creek, JOSEPHINE. This stream flows into Applegate River. Walling, in *History of Southern Oregon*, p. 458, says that it was named for Captain Robert Williams, an Indian fighter of local fame, who skirmished with the natives on the creek in 1853. Williams post office took its name from the stream.

Williamsburg, JOSEPHINE. Williamsburg was a pioneer post office on Williams Creek, named in compliment to Captain Robert Williams, a well-known Indian fighter in the Rogue River War. In June of 1948, the compiler had some interesting correspondence about early post offices in this area with R. F. Lewman, an old time resident of the vicinity. Mr. Lewman wrote that Williamsburg was in the north part of northeast quarter of s 26, T 38S, R 5W. Mr. Lewman says that at one time there were several hundred people in Williamsburg. The place was on a slight rise of ground at a point about three miles southwest of Provolt and about three miles northeast of the community presently called Williams. Williamsburg was a little to the east of the present highway from Grants Pass to Williams, but not much. Williamsburg post office was established Nov. 16, 1860, with P. C. Wood first and only postmaster. The office was discontinued July 5, 1861. The compiler was informed that there were a very few remains of the old post office structure, in fact just a little of the roof. The post offices called Williams Creek in Jackson County and Williams in Josephine County were also named for the stream and for Captain Williams, although they were not all in the same place.

Williamson Creek, CROOK. This stream rises in the Bear Creek Buttes and flows northwest to disappear into Dry River near the Deschutes County line. It was named for John N. Williamson who homesteaded near its headwaters in 1893.

Williamson, who was born in Lane County in 1855, served as sheriff of Crook County and later was both state representative and state senator.

Williamson Mountain, DESCHUTES. Williamson Mountain, elevation about 6300 feet, is just west of Lava Lake and near the summit of the Cascade Range. It was named for Lieutenant R. S. Williamson for whom Williamson River was named. *See* that heading. Williamson and Lieutenant P. H. Sheridan, attached to the Pacific Railroad Surveys, were in this part of central Oregon in the latter part of Aug. 1855, and Williamson Mountain was named to commemorate the event. The mountain was formerly known as Leloo Mountain. *Leloo* is the Chinook jargon word for wolf, derived from the French *le loup*. The name Williamson Mountain was adopted by the USBGN on Mar. 4, 1931.

Williamson River, KLAMATH. Williamson River drains a large part of northern Klamath County, and its enlargement forms Klamath Marsh. It empties into Upper Klamath Lake. The Klamath Indian name for the river was *koke*, and this word was generally used alone in referring to Williamson, Sprague, Lost and Klamath rivers, because of their importance. Sometimes the Williamson River was called *Ya-aga-Koke*, *ya-aga* being the word for willow trees not far from the mouth of the stream. This name was generally applied to that locality only. Lieutenant Robert Stockton Williamson explored parts of central Oregon for the Pacific Railroad Surveys in 1855, and Williamson River was named in his honor. He was the first man to determine with reasonable accuracy the height of Mount Hood, which he did in 1867. Fremont's party fought the Klamath Indians on this stream on May 12, 1846, and Fremont named it Torrey River for his friend Professor John Torrey, the botanist. *See* Fremont's *Memoirs of My Life*, pp. 493-5. The battleground was upstream from the former highway crossing, probably near the old Indian trail ford.

Willits Ridge, JACKSON. Willits Ridge is in the north part of the county a little southeast of Persist and about six miles airline west of Prospect. The ridge took its name from William W. Willits who in 1884 settled on a homestead at the place later called Persist. For a brief mention of Mr. and Mrs. Willits, *see* Persist.

Willoughby, JEFFERSON. Willoughby post office was established on the Wasco County list on May 20, 1872, with Robert Warren first of a series of five postmasters. The office was not in continuous operation, and was finally discontinued Mar. 7, 1879. It served a locality on Willow Creek not far from what is now known as Grizzly, Jefferson County. The compiler has not been able to learn the reason for the name of the office, though it has been suggested that it represents a play on the words willow by, that is, by Willow Creek. No other explanation has been suggested. There seems to be no record of any family with the name Willoughby ever having lived in the district.

Willow Creek, GILLIAM, MORROW. Lewis and Clark mention this stream as a "riverlit" in their journals for Sunday, Oct. 20, 1805. On the sketch map by Clark, in Thwaites' *Original Journals of the Lewis and Clark Expedition*, v. 4, p. 308, it is shown as *Choch*. It has been known as Willow Creek since pioneer days. Willow Creek Dam was constructed by the USCE in 1983, just upstream from Heppner and below the mouth of Balm Fork. It is designed to prevent another disastrous flood. *See* Heppner. The dam is of rolled compacted concrete construction and the normal storage of Willow Creek Lake is 2540 acre feet. The structure was much in the news in 1989 when it was suggested that leaching of the compacted concrete was weakening the dam. There are many Willow creeks in the state, which is not surprising, as Sudworth in *Check List of Forest Trees of the United States*, lists at least ten of this family that grow in Oregon.

Willow Creek, JACKSON. Willow Creek heads in the hills west of Central Point and flows northeast into Bear Creek. It received its name in the early 1850s and it was a prominent locality in the early Indian wars and also in the mining days. After it flows out of the hills, it receives Lane Creek from the west and it was at this point that the pioneer community of Willow Springs was established. *See* Walling's *History of Southern Oregon*, p. 377.

Willow Lake, JACKSON. Willow Lake was created in 1952 when Willow Creek, a tributary of Butte Creek, was dammed about eight miles east of Butte Falls by the Medford Water Commission as part of the municipal water system. The USBGN adopted the name Willow Lake in *Decision List 6303*. This drainage is in no way connected with the Willow Creek west of Central Point.

Willow Point, COLUMBIA. This point is on the northeast part of Sauvie Island. In the opinion of the writer, it is the place mentioned by Broughton in his report to Vancouver for the day of Oct. 28, 1792, when he stated that "he proceeded up what he considered the main branch of the river, until eight in the evening; when under the shelter of some willows, they took up their lodging for the night on a low sandy point." This was just after Broughton had passed the lower end of Sauvie Island. Older maps used the form Willow Bar Point.

Willowcreek, MALHEUR. Willowcreek post office took its name from the natural feature, Willow Creek, one of the prominent streams of the county. Willow Creek got its name in pioneer days, and it is doubtless too late to learn the circumstances. Willowcreek post office was established Aug. 19, 1937, at a point on Willow Creek about a dozen miles northwest of Vale. Mrs. Dorothy Sappe was the first postmaster. It was not in service in 1980.

Willowdale, JEFFERSON. Willowdale is in the north part of the county, a few hundred feet south of the bridge which carries The Dalles-California Highway over Trout Creek. The locality has been called Checkerboard because of the style of painting once used on the service station at that point. Willowdale post office was established May 23, 1928, with Mrs. Edna Chesnut first of five postmasters. The office was closed to Gateway on Mar. 11, 1937. Willowdale is in the same general locality as the pioneer post office Cross Keys. It was of course named for one of the many varieties of willow that grow in central Oregon.

Willows, GILLIAM. Willows post office, named for the many trees of that species that grow in Oregon, was established Dec. 17, 1878, on the Umatilla County list. Morrow and Gilliam counties had not then been created. The first Willows post office was very near what was later to be the Gilliam-Morrow county line, and the exact location is not clear from the available data, though it seems probable that the office was on the south bank of the Columbia River near the mouth of Willow Creek or just to the east. J. W. Smith was the first postmaster. This office was closed June 29, 1885, in the same year that Gilliam and Morrow counties were established. Willows office was reestablished on Jan. 29, 1895, with James A. Vawter postmaster. This time it was in Gilliam County, and it was at or near the mouth of Willow Creek, sometimes a little to the west. The railroad station at the mouth of Willow Creek is known as Heppner Junction.

Willsburg, CLACKAMAS. Willsburg is a junction point on the Southern Pacific line between Sellwood and Milwaukie. It was named for George W. Wills and his son, Jacob Wills, who emigrated to Oregon in 1848 from Iowa. They took up adjoining claims near Johnson Creek, the Jacob Wills claim being near the present site of Eastmoreland. Jacob Wills was a pioneer sawmill operator along Johnson Creek. His father was a "hardshell" Baptist preacher, and he did not allow his business of farming and building to interfere with his soul-saving activities. Willsburgh post office was established nearby in Multnomah County on Jan. 15, 1883, with Jacob F. Rhodes first postmaster. This office was in operation until Sept. 1900. The post route map for 1900 uses the spelling Willsburg for this office.

Wilson, TILLAMOOK. Wilson post office, named for Wilson River on which it was situated, was about 25 miles upstream from Tillamook and near the mouth of North Fork. The office was established in July 1896, with Walter J. Smith first postmaster. The office was discontinued officially in Dec. 1917, when it was closed out to Gales Creek. Wilson post office was apparently served over nearly 25 miles of mountain road from Gales Creek. Wilson post office actually went out of service in 1916 because no one would make a bid to carry in the mail from the outside. It was feared that there might be too much parcel post for a bidder to take chances. Wilson post office served Glenora station of the United States Weather Bureau. Postal officials would not accept the name Glenora for an office because of possible confusion with such places as Glenwood, Glendale and others with similar names. *See also* Glenora.

Wilson Creek, CLACKAMAS, MARION. Wilson Creek is in the Molalla River drainage basin and in the south part of Clackamas County. It was named for an early-day prospector who visited the vicinity of the stream and prospected there. His home was in the North Santiam Valley.

Wilson Creek, DOUGLAS. In 1918 Abraham Wilson homesteaded on this creek near where it flows into North Umpqua River just west of Copeland Creek. Wilson was an old time USFS packer and Abes Mountain near Red Butte was also named for him.

Wilson Lake, LINN. This lake is near the east bank of the Willamette River north of Albany. It was named for a nearby resident, John P. Wilson. Stories to the effect that it was named for Woodrow Wilson are not founded on fact, because the lake was called Wilson Lake before President Wilson came into political prominence.

Wilson Prairie, CURRY. In 1892 George Wilson homesteaded near Bravo Creek northwest of the prairie and Wilson Creek which now bear his name.

Wilson River, TILLAMOOK. Miss Lucy E. Doughty, one of the early residents of Tillamook County, wrote the compiler in June 1927 that much obscurity surrounded the origin of the name Wilson River. The stream was called Georgie or Georgia River in pioneer days. The name was later changed to Wilson River, in honor of an early settler who drove the first cows into the county from Seaside. Wilson was apparently the founder of the great Tillamook dairy industry. Warren N. Vaughn, a pioneer resident of the county, wrote a memoir in 1891–92, which was published in the Bay City *Tribune*, and in the series of articles mentions Wilson and tells about cattle being driven from Astoria about 1851. The story about Wilson is questioned in a letter on the editorial page of the *Oregonian*, Sept. 17, 1927, signed Mary Alderman Bird. Miss Doughty's reply, with quotation from Vaughn, is printed in the *Oregonian*, Sept. 26, 1927. Henry W. Wilson was an English printer. After leaving the Tillamook country, he moved to Salem, and was employed on the *Oregon Statesman*. There is a story to the effect that he secured the passage of the bill creating Tillamook County, but the compiler has been unable to secure confirmation. Wilson was not a member of the legislature in 1853, although his name is signed to the petition to establish the county. Miss Doughty calls the attention of the compiler to the fact that there was a Wilson River Road project as early as 1875. After the plan was organized, a party consisting of William T. Baxter, Jacob E. Elliott and William T. Doughty explored the Kilchis and Wilson rivers. They got lost, nearly starved to death, and the idea of a road was given up.

Wilsonia, CLACKAMAS. This station north of Lake Oswego was named for A. King Wilson, a well-known attorney of Portland, who made his home nearby.

Wilsonville, CLACKAMAS. The name of this community was derived from a local resident, Charles Wilson. R. V. Short suggested the name. This was in 1880. A post office named Boons Ferry was established in this locality on Dec. 7, 1876, with Charles Wilson postmaster. The name of the office was changed to Wilsonville on June 3, 1880. For information about the origin of the name Boones Ferry, *see* Boones Ferry in this volume. The writer does not know why the style used by postal authorities did not agree with the family name. A post office called Boon was in operation in Clackamas County from Apr. 1868 to Mar. 1869. The writer has been unable to learn its location. It seems probable it was at Boones Ferry, but that is just an assumption. Wilsonville was incorporated Oct. 10, 1968.

Wilts Creek, UNION. This small tributary of Grande Ronde River near the mouth of Meadow Creek was apparently named for George P. Wilt who filed on nearby government land in 1898.

Wimer, JACKSON. Wimer is a place on Evans Creek. On July 1, 1927, William M. Colvig of Medford wrote the compiler: "In 1886–7 William Wimer edited a paper at Grants Pass, 12 miles distant. He had something to do with getting a post office for the people there. He had a relative named Wimer who lived in the neighborhood. I do not know which one gave the name, but I think William Wimer did."

Win Ridge, LANE. This ridge four miles south of Monroe bears the name of John H. Winn who was born in Maury County, Tennessee and came to Oregon in 1852. His donation land claim included the ridge. Winn and his wife are buried in nearby Griffin Cemetery.

Winans, HOOD RIVER. Winans was a station on the Mount Hood Railroad near the forks of Hood River. It was named for Ross Winans who settled nearby about 1880, and operated a hotel for hunters.

Winant, LINCOLN. Winant post office was named for Captain James J. Winant who made his home nearby. Winant was the post office name for Oysterville station, and it operated from 1902 to 1946. For biography of Captain Winant, *see History of Benton County*, p. 530.

Winberry, LANE. Winberry post office was near the mouth of Winberry Creek. Winberry is simply another name for whortleberry, and is applied more or less indiscriminately to various species of *Vaccinium*. The form windberry is wrong. Winberry Creek is an important tributary of Fall Creek, but Winberry post office was discontinued in 1933.

Winchester, DOUGLAS. This place, which was founded by the Umpqua exploring expedition of San Francisco in 1850, was laid out by Addison R. Flint. *See* Bancroft's *History of Oregon*, v. 2, p. 183. For a number of years it was the largest settlement in the Umpqua Valley. It was the county seat until 1854, when Roseburg won that distinction. Winchester post office was established Nov. 3, 1851, with A. R. Flint first postmaster. There were two Winchesters in the expedition, Heman and John. The party sailed from San Francisco on July 5, 1850. Heman Winchester was captain. The expedition was headed for Klamath River, but actually first landed at Rogue River, and later established a settlement at the mouth of Umpqua River. Nathan Scholfield, a member of the party, kept a diary and used the form Heman Winchester, which is also the form used by Bancroft, and it may be assumed that the spelling Herman is wrong. The compiler has been unable to substantiate stories to the effect that Winchester was named for the younger brother John Winchester. Attention is called to the fact that there is also a discrepancy in the name of the schooner used by the party, various accounts giving *William Roberts* and *Samuel Roberts*. George Davidson of the USC&GS, authority on Pacific Coast marine history, used the name *Samuel Roberts*, Bancroft uses that form, and *Samuel Roberts* appears in Lewis & Dryden's *Marine History of the Pacific Northwest*, which seems conclusive. Nathan Scholfield's diary is in the State

Library at Salem. His son, Socrates Scholfield, wrote a summary of this diary, which was published in *OHQ*, v. 17, p. 341.

Winchester Bay, DOUGLAS. Winchester Bay is a town on the Umpqua River, near its mouth. Winchester Creek flows into Winchester Bay. These geographic features were all named for Heman Winchester, a member of the expedition that came to Oregon from San Francisco in 1850 and established itself on Umpqua River. *See* Winchester. Winchester Bay, the hydrographic feature, has been dredged and greatly altered. It is now called Salmon Harbor and for details, *see* that heading.

Winchester Creek, COOS. Winchester Creek, which flows into South Slough, drains a considerable area southeast of Cape Arago. Its geography may be found on the USGS topographic atlas sheets for the Charleston and Riverton quadrangles. It was named for T. D. Winchester, a pioneer who tried to develop a logging and milling project at the head of the slough. *See* Dodge's *Pioneer History of Coos and Curry Counties*, p. 16.

Winchester Lake, LANE. Winchester Lake is northwest of Waldo Lake. Lawrence D. Hills in *Tales From the Hills*, gives the origin of this name. Hills' father, Jasper, was employed as guide and packer for Dr. and Mrs. Lambert Wood of Portland on an excursion to Waldo Lake. The Woods were accompanied by their young son, Lambert, Jr., so Lawrence Hills, about the same age, also came along. They camped by this lake and the two boys ventured out on the water on a makeshift raft. Young Wood had a brand new Winchester rifle which he dropped overboard and only retrieved after some groping. On their return to shore, a board was duly carved with the name "Winchester Lake."

Winchuck River, CURRY. F. S. Moore, in *Curry County Reporter*, Dec. 16, 1926, says this stream was called by the Indians *Hasonta*, for the tribe living nearby. Moore had a theory that the modern name is derived from the Chinook jargon, *wind chuck*, or windy water. The compiler has been unable to identify the Hasonta Indians. Old maps show Windchuck, but modern use is generally Winchuck River, which seems to be the accepted local style. George Davidson in the *Coast Pilot*, 1889, p. 361, says that *winchuck* was the local Indian word for woman, and that the Indians called the stream *Neh'-saw*, but he does not explain that word. Davidson spent much time working on the Oregon coast and his observations are generally reliable. The compiler has been unable to reconcile the information under this heading.

Wind Cave, DESCHUTES. This cave is a mile north of Arnold Ice Cave on the Deschutes Plateau. It is named for the breeze that on warm summer days roars from its 5000-foot tube through the small surface opening.

Windigo Butte, DOUGLAS, KLAMATH. Windigo Butte, Windigo Pass and Windigo Lake are all on the crest of the Cascade Range south of Cowhorn Mountain. Virgil Vogel in *Indian Names in Michigan*, p. 102, describes the Ojibwa Indian tales of the *Windigo* or *Weendego*, a legendary tribe of giant and ferocious cannibals. He gives references as old as the 1823 *Narrative of an Expedition to the Source of* *the St. Peter's River*, by William H. Keating. The complier has no idea how the word came to be applied to the features in Oregon but the name Windigo Butte goes back to the early part of the twentieth century.

Windmill Canyon, UMATILLA. This canyon empties into Jack Canyon three miles east of Nye. Charles Kopp of Pilot Rock said in 1969 that the canyon was named for an old-fashioned windmill located near its mouth.

Windsor Island, POLK. Windsor Island is in the Willamette River in the extreme northeast corner of the county. It bears the name of a family of pioneer settlers that lived in the locality.

Windy, HARNEY. Windy Point is a projection westward onto the floor of Harney Valley, just east of Malheur Lake. It bears a descriptive name. On Aug. 3, 1908, a post office called Windy was established in this locality, with August Haarstuch postmaster. The name of the postmaster probably should be Augusta Haarstrich. For information about this early settler, *see* Virginia Valley. The order was rescinded Oct. 9, 1908, and the office accordingly never functioned. Waverly post office had just been established a very short distance south, which may account for the failure of Windy to get blowing.

Windy Brown Spring, JEFFERSON. This spring south of Priday Agate Beds was named for an early and apparently loquacious settler, William Brown, who took up his homestead nearby in 1913.

Windy Point, CROOK. John Beoletto, whose family has been in the area since the turn of the century, stated in 1969 that this spot north of Alkali Butte bears a descriptive name. It is an excellent spot to hold stock for branding as there is a good spring nearby.

Windy Spring, UNION. This spring is in the extreme west part of the county near the headwaters of McCoy Creek. Helen Stangier of Pendleton said in 1969 that it was named for William Porter, an early and well-known but extremely talkative settler.

Wineglass, KLAMATH. This peculiar rock slide on the northeast part of the inside rim of Crater Lake was named by J. S. Diller of the USGS. From across the lake the slide looks like a huge wineglass.

Winema, KLAMATH. The compiler does not know the exact location of Winema post office. It was some ten or twelve miles north of Kirk, but whether on the highway or on the railroad the compiler has not been able to learn, and there is nothing in the record to give a reason for its existence. Winema post office was established Jan. 27, 1928, with Mrs. Mae Allen postmaster. The office was closed to Kirk Nov. 30, 1929. Irrespective of its location there is no doubt that the office was named in compliment to Winema, otherwise Mrs. Frank Riddle, the Indian heroine of the Modoc Lava Beds massacre.

Winema Pinnacles, MULTNOMAH. These basalt spires high above the Columbia River Highway, are about half a mile east of Multnomah Falls. They were named for Winema, Mrs. Frank Riddle, the heroine of the Modoc Lava Beds massacre. For information about her, *see* Jeff C. Riddle's *Indian History of the*

Modoc War. She did not live near the Columbia River, but the pinnacles were named because it was thought her memory should be perpetuated somewhere in the state.

Wing, BAKER. This station is near the community of Wingville. *See* that heading. The railroad company shortened the name because of awkwardness in telegraphing.

Wing Ridge, WALLOWA. This ridge, southeast of Wallowa Lake, was named by surveyors because of its shape. It lies between Sheep Creek and Little Sheep Creek.

Wingville, BAKER. Major-General Sterling Price, of the Confederate Army, was active in Missouri and Arkansas in 1861–64. He was finally defeated by the Union forces in 1864. Many Southern Democrats thereafter migrated to Oregon. Numbers of them had been soldiers in Price's campaigns. The newcomers in Oregon were derisively termed by Republicans, "The left wing of Price's army." They contributed largely to the southern admixture in the pioneer population of Oregon. A community of these people near Baker was referred to as Wingville. Wingville post office was established June 23, 1871, with John R. McLain first postmaster. The office was closed in July 1879.

Winino, LANE. The name Winino appears to be of Indian origin, but the compiler cannot find it in any available Indian dictionary. The place is now known as McCredie Springs. The hot springs on Salt Creek have long been known. In 1914 John Harding of Portland obtained a lease on the springs property and applied the name Winino. Later, Judge William Wallace McCredie of Portland acquired an interest in the springs and used the resort as training quarters for his Portland baseball club. For additional information, *see* McCredie Springs. Winino post office was established July 8, 1924, with Vivian Cartwright postmaster. This office was discontinued Dec. 31, 1925, with mail to Railhead. This was at the time of construction of the Southern Pacific Cascade Line.

Winkle Bar, CURRY. This bar on Rogue River was named for William Winkle, a pioneer prospector. Winkle has long since passed into obscurity but his name is well preserved because his claim was later purchased by Zane Grey, the author, who built a summer cabin on the bar. Grey used his experiences there as background for some of his later novels. In 1962 the property was sold to Walter Haas of San Francisco who was still using the cabin during the 1970s.

Winkle Butte, BENTON. This butte is just east of the Pacific Highway West about nine miles south of Corvallis. It is on the donation land claim of Isaac W. Winkle, and was named for him. Winkle Lake, just to the east, is on the claims of Isaac W. Winkle and Wiley Winkle and may have been named for either or both of them. Winkle Butte has been known in the past as Irwin Butte for another pioneer family of the vicinity, but that name has not prevailed.

Winlock, WHEELER. Winlock post office was named for Winlock Steiwer, a pioneer settler in eastern Oregon. Steiwer was instrumental in having the office established about 1888, but not at its later site. *See* Steiwer Hill.

Winniford, DOUGLAS. This office was just east of the Umpqua River at a point about eight miles west of Wilbur. It was established in April or June 1890, with Thomas W. Winniford postmaster and was closed in Jan. 1891, with papers to Oakland. The office was situated in the Winniford home, which was still standing in Dec. 1945.

Winona, JOSEPHINE. A recent number of the *Postal Guide* shows more than a dozen post offices in the United States named Winona, a word of the Santee Indian dialect meaning first-born (if a girl). The name was well known for its use at Winona, Minnesota, and was apparently introduced to the reading public by Keating in his *Narrative* of Long's expedition, 1823. The musical sound of the word has made it popular as a name. The principal use of the name in Oregon has been for a place on Jumpoff Joe Creek, Josephine County, a few miles north of Grants Pass. A post office called Winona was established here in June 1897, with Herbert M. Gorham first postmaster. The office was closed on Jan. 31, 1905. The name Winona has also been applied to a place in Polk County between Salem and Eola.

Winopee Lake, DESCHUTES. This lake is just east of the summit of the Cascade Range and northwest of Cultus Lake. *Winopee* is a Chinook jargon word meaning by-and-by or wait. The name was applied to the lake by someone who was in no hurry to leave the place.

Winslow, WALLOWA. Winslow post office was situated in S 13, T 1N, R 45E, about ten miles northeast of Enterprise, airline. It was established in May 1890, with Fannie Root postmaster. The office was discontinued in Dec. 1900. The office was named directly for Edward Winslow Rumble, a teacher in the neighborhood, and indirectly for a General Winslow who fought in the Civil War. J. A. Rumble, father of E. W. Rumble, served under General Winslow and named his son for the officer. There were several generals named Winslow who served in the Civil War, but it may be presumed that the one complimented was Brigadier-General Edward Francis Winslow, who entered the forces from Iowa.

Winston, DOUGLAS. Winston is a locality a couple of miles north of Dillard and just west of South Umpqua River. A little further north is the old Pacific Highway bridge over the river, generally called Winston Bridge. Winston post office was established June 16, 1893, and bore the name of the first postmaster, Elijah Winston. The office was closed July 14, 1903. It was reestablished in 1948.

Winter Knight Camp, DOUGLAS. Winter Knight Camp is on Thorn Prairie near North Umpqua River. Jessie Wright of Caps Illahee said the spot was named for a man of this name who used it as a hunting camp prior to World War 1.

Winter Ridge, LAKE. Winter Ridge is the rimrock west of Summer Lake. It was discovered and named on Dec. 16, 1843, by then Captain John C. Fremont of the U.S. Topographical Engineers. Fremont applied this name because of the bad weather he encountered at the summit of the ridge, where he looked down to the sunshine on the green grass around Summer Lake. He named the lake at the same time. *See* Summer Lake.

Winters Spring, WALLOWA. This spring, sometimes called Mormon Spring, is in the northwest part of T 2N, R 50E. It was named for W. H. Winters, an early settler. Winters was of the Mormon faith and Mormon Flat in the same township was named on his account. The style Winter Spring is wrong.

Wise, CLATSOP. Wise post office, south of Astoria, was in what is known as the Tucker Creek district. The office was established in June 1895, with Hugh McCormick postmaster, and was discontinued in May 1903. Herman Wise was the postmaster at Astoria when the office was established and it is more than probable that it was named in compliment to him.

Witch Hazel, WASHINGTON. Witch Hazel was a place on the Tualatin Valley Highway and on the Southern Pacific railroad about a mile west of Reedville. Van B. DeLashmutt of Portland had a farm there in earlier days and is said to have named the place. In fact the writer once heard a statement to the effect that DeLashmutt named the farm for one of his racehorses. Oswald West was the authority on Oregon bang-tails and in Oct. 1945 told the writer that he never heard of an Oregon racehorse named Witch Hazel. That settles it as far as the writer is concerned. However, Governor West said that Mayor DeLashmutt once owned a building at SW Front and Madison streets in Portland, called the Witch Hazel Building. DeLashmutt seems to have had a fancy for the name. The witch hazel tree or shrub, *Hamamelis virginiana*, is not native to Oregon and has nothing to do with the hazelnut bush. Witch hazel wands are said to have the power of pointing to buried gold and silver and even to underground water. Oddly enough Jonathan Carver was one of the very first American authors to mention this belief, which he did in 1778. A post office was established at Witch Hazel in Aug. 1904, with Earl W. Anderson postmaster. It was closed in Nov. 1905.

Witches Cauldron, KLAMATH. The crater at the top of Wizard Island was named Witches Cauldron on Aug. 17, 1885, by Will G. Steel, because of its weird appearance.

Witt Butte, LANE. This butte three miles east of London Springs apparently was named for Henry Witte who homesteaded nearby in the 1880s.

Wizard Island, KLAMATH. This island in Crater Lake has a weird appearance, and was named on that account by Will G. Steel on Aug. 17, 1885. The top of the island is 763 feet above the surface of the lake.

Wocus Bay, KLAMATH. Wocus Bay, near the southeast part of Klamath Marsh, is named with the English form of the Klamath Indian word used to describe the seed of the yellow pond lily, *Nuphar advena*. This seed was roasted and ground for food. The Indians pronounced the word as though spelled *Wokash*.

Wolf Creek, JOSEPHINE. The post office for Wolf Creek community and railroad station was Wolfcreek but in 1951 it was changed to two words to conform. There were plenty of wolves in Oregon in early days, and a number of streams are known as Wolf Creek. This community was the locality of the famous Six Bit House, frequently mentioned in pioneer history. In 1936 James T. Chinnock of

Grants Pass wrote the compiler about this establishment, transmitting information from James Tuffs and George Riddle of Grants Pass, both familiar with the history of southern Oregon. The original Six Bit House was built during the Indian wars, probably about 1853, within the sharp hairpin curve of the Southern Pacific Company railroad about a mile east of town. It was at the mouth of a gulch on the old road location north of I-5 and the old Pacific Highway. There are several stories about the origin of the name. The most probable explanation is that 75 cents was charged for a night's lodging, compared with a dollar charged elsewhere along the road. Another story is that the proprietor interrupted some white men who were hanging an Indian nearby and declined to let them proceed with the business until the melancholy brave paid the inn-keeper six bits, then past due. This story seems fanciful to the compiler because of the improbability that a local Indian ever had six bits in currency. The building has long since disappeared, but Mr. Tuffs recalled seeing the remains during his youth. The second Six Bit House, built of logs, was in the north part of the town, close to the railroad. Mr. Tuffs lived in it several years. The present Wolf Creek Tavern, now on the National Register of Historic Places, was built later and had no connection with either of the Six Bit houses.

Wolverine Creek, DOUGLAS. Wolverine Creek is a small tributary of Canton Creek northeast of Mace Mountain. It is named for the wolverine, *Gulo luscus*, the largest member of the weasel family and an animal once fairly common in the Cascade Range. The last wolverine trapped of record in Oregon was taken in the Three Sisters area in 1912. Since then, one was shot by a deer hunter in 1965 and another was road-killed on I-84 at Starvation Creek in 1990. They had long been considered extinct in Oregon but this assumption was incorrect. The wolverine is a solitary animal that is truly omniverous, eating anything, live or dead, that it may come upon. Tom McAllister has a good article on the wolverine in the *Oregonian*, Jan. 22, 1990.

Womack Basin, WALLOWA. Womack Basin is on the northeast slope of Huckleberry Mountain in S 25, T 1S, R 42E. John William Womack was born in Missouri in 1849 and came to the Wallowa country in 1877 where he ranched and raised a large family. In 1990 several of his descendants asked the OGNB to place his name on this basin where he had grazed cattle. Womack died on Oct. 20, 1921 in Wallowa.

Wonder, JOSEPHINE. About 1902 a man by the name of John T. Robertson started a store at the present site of Wonder. He began to call this store Wonder Store because neighbors wondered where he would get his trade as the territory was sparsely settled. Later postal authorities used the name of the store for the name of the post office, which was established in Dec. 1903.

Wood Lake, WALLOWA. According to J. H. Horner of Enterprise, this lake in T 3S, R 43E, was named for John Wood, who helped J. H. Jackson stock it with young salmon in 1914.

Wood River, KLAMATH. Wood River is part of what was the west boundary of the Klamath Indian Reservation and flows into Agency Lake. During the early days of Fort Klamath, contractors cut wood for the fort in a lodgepole pine grove on the banks of the stream, hence the name. The Klamath Indians called it *Eukalksine Koke*.

Wood Village, MULTNOMAH. Wood Village was built during World War II as a housing project for the employees of the Troutdale plant of Reynolds Aluminum Company. Lester J. Wood of Commonwealth Inc., a Portland real estate firm, told the compiler in 1967 that while he arranged the financing, originally the Long-Bell Lumber Company was to have had charge of the actual construction. Supposedly the name was selected by them to go with a number of streets named for native trees, but in view of the major part played by Mr. Wood, the author suspects more than mere coincidence. The town was incorporated Feb. 9, 1951, with a mayor and commission form of government.

Woodburn, MARION. Woodburn was platted in 1871 by J. A. Settlemeier and the post office was established Dec. 28, 1871 with Adolphus Mathiot postmaster. It is said that when the railroad came through the place was first called Halsey, presumably for a railroad official. *See* Halsey. However, in 1981 Charles E. Nebergall of Portland told the writer that in the 1880s his grandfather had been a close friend of Settlemeier's and that a brochure in his possession, *Woodburn, Oregon*, Stewart & Doud, Printers, undated but apparently printed during the 1890s, gives the following origin of the name. Settlemeier platted the town and left a large grove of fir trees surrounded by cleared fields. When the railroad came through, their right of way went directly through the middle of the grove. The felled trees and brush were left alongside the track until winter when they were burned. The fire got out of hand and a substantial quantity of the standing timber was destroyed along with the brush. The name Woodburn commemorates this happening.

Woodcock Creek, JOSEPHINE. Woodcock Creek is about five miles south of Kerby and flows into the Illinois River. It was named for Horace Woodcock, a pioneer rancher.

Woodlawn, MULTNOMAH. Woodlawn was an outstanding separate community in the 1890s and rated a post office of its own. It was an important stop on the steam, later electric, railway from Portland to Vancouver. Woodlawn post office was established Dec. 24, 1890, with Hiram Parrish first postmaster. That was before the Portland-East Portland-Albina consolidation. The office was finally closed on Nov. 14, 1903. It was out of service for about a year in 1897–98. The name of the office followed Woodlawn addition, which was of course the product of real estate activity. The plat for Woodlawn was filed in Oct. 1889.

Woodley, UNION. Woodley post office was established Feb. 1, 1896, with Daniel M. Griffith first postmaster. The compiler does not know when the office was discontinued, but apparently it did not last long. Woodley is not shown on the post route map of 1900. The post office was named for the Woodley Mine, located by Frederick Woodley. The property was in the northwest part of T 6S, R 36E, near Grande Ronde River.

Woodrow, LAKE. A post office named Woodrow, apparently in compliment to Woodrow Wilson, was in operation during the last wave of homesteaders in northern Lake County. It was situated about ten miles east of Fort Rock and was established Apr. 24, 1914, with George W. Craig postmaster. The office was closed May 15, 1916.

Woodruff Creek, DOUGLAS, JACKSON. Woodruff Creek flows into Rogue River from the west eight miles north of Prospect. Anne and Newton Woodruff both patented homesteads in the area during the 1890s.

Woodruff Mountain, DOUGLAS. This mountain is on the west side of the Umpqua River, west of Wilbur. It was named for Jonathon W. Woodruff, a donation land claim owner nearby. His musical talents made him famous in pioneer days in Douglas County.

Woods, TILLAMOOK. Woods was named for Joseph Woods, who settled there about 1875. The post office was established in Apr. 1886, with William Booth first postmaster. Booth suggested the name in honor of Woods. The post office was closed on Aug. 29, 1935.

Woodson, COLUMBIA. Woodson got its name from Woods Landing on Westport Slough. Many years ago a man named Wood hauled logs to the locality and dumped them into the slough, where they were made up into rafts. Woodson post office was established Apr. 2, 1929, with Mrs. Alice Brooks first postmaster. It was in the northwest corner of the county, about a mile east of Kerry.

Woodstock, MULTNOMAH. Woodstock was a station of the Portland post office. It bears the name of a real estate tract platted in 1889. At that time there was a vogue for naming tracts after Sir Walter Scott's novels, and in the southeast part of Portland we have Woodstock, Ivanhoe, Kenilworth, Waverly, [sic], and even such flights of fancy as Waverleigh. The word *stoc* came from the Anglo-Saxon and means a stockaded place, and woodstock means a place fortified with wooden posts. Woodstock was an independent post office from 1891 to 1912.

Woodward Creek, COOS. This creek is a tributary to South Fork Coquille River. It was named for Henry H. Woodward, a pioneer settler nearby.

Woodward Creek, UMATILLA. Woodward Creek rises south of Langdon Lake and flows south into North Fork Umatilla River. It is named for David J. Woodward who was one of the organizers of the Sommerville and Walla Walla Road Company, named before the spelling of the town was changed to Summerville. It was later known as the Woodward Road and fees were collected at what is now Tollgate. Woodward later became sole owner and lived most of the time at Tollgate while his family retreated to Milton during the winter. In Jan. 1896 he came into Elgin for supplies and against the advice of friends, started the return journey in threatening weather. A bad storm ensued and Woodward disappeared without a trace. His son, Walter L. Woodward, succeeded his father as collector at Tollgate.

Wooldridge Butte, LANE. This low hill, elevation 380 feet, is about a mile east of Cheshire and bears the name of a well-known pioneer family of the vicinity. The spelling Waldridge is wrong. Wooldridge Creek, a stream in Jackson County flowing into Slagle Creek, is named for members of the same family. *See* a letter by Logan Wooldridge in the Grants Pass *Bulletin*, June 4, 1937.

Woolley, DOUGLAS. The Woolley family is very well known in northern Douglas County and when a post office was established Sept. 20, 1905, with Anna L. Woolley first postmaster it was natural that the office should be given the family name. Woolley was about 15 miles northwest of Drain on the Smith River Road. It was also about eight miles east of Gunter. The office was discontinued June 30, 1912. In Feb. 1948 Mrs. May Brown Woolley of Drain sent the compiler an interesting letter about early-day conditions in the upper Smith River area. Mrs. Woolley's letter with other useful information will be found in the Roseburg *News-Review*, Mar. 6, 1948.

Woolly Horn Ridge, HOOD RIVER. According to Ralph Lewis of Parkdale this ridge north of Tomlike Mountain was named by the Odell and Lenz brothers who once shot a buck in velvet on its slopes.

Worden, KLAMATH. William S. Worden was a member of a family of early settlers in Klamath County. During the time the Southern Pacific Company was building a railroad into Klamath Falls, Worden acted as right-of-way agent and while doing so purchased the land and laid out the present townsite of Worden. The post office was established in 1910. Worden was subsequently elected county judge of Klamath County.

Wren, BENTON. This place bears the name of George P. Wren, a pioneer settler.

Wrentham, WASCO. Wrentham was named by the Daniel Farrington family, who came to Oregon from Maine. It is said that the family had lived in New York near a point once known as Wrentham Hill and Wrentham, Oregon, was named on that account. Wrentham post office established in 1900 but was discontinued in June 1916.

Wright, JACKSON. Nicholas B. Wright was the only postmaster that Wright post office ever boasted and the place was named in his honor. It was about nine miles up Applegate River, or south, from the place called Uniontown, which was near the mouth of Little Applegate River. Wright post office was in service from Apr. 25, 1878, to Dec. 22, 1888, when it was closed out to Uniontown.

Wright Creek, CLACKAMAS. Wright Creek is a small stream just north of Liberal, flowing into Molalla River. It was named in compliment to Harrison Wright, a pioneer of 1844, who settled near the present site of Liberal. He was instrumental in getting a pioneer post office, which was named Molalla, and Wright was first postmaster. This office was established Apr. 9, 1850. The office was not at the present town of Molalla, but was moved to that place in the 1870s. The highway bridge over the Molalla River north of Liberal is also named for Harrison Wright.

Wright Point, HARNEY. This is a long neck of solid land extending into the flats north of Malheur Lake. It is an interesting example of an inverted river of lava. Some two million years ago a lava flow from the west filled an ancient valley. In time the land around the filled valley eroded leaving the point as a neck of land some 250 feet higher than the present plain. *See* an article by Alan R. Niem in *The Ore Bin*, v. 36, no. 3, Mar. 1974. The feature was named for Camp Wright, which was established in Oct. 1865, by Captain L. L. Williams, and named for Brigadier-General George Wright. For details concerning Captain Williams and his operations in the Shoshone War, *see* Bancroft's *History of Oregon*, v. 2, p. 514. George Wright was born in Vermont, and graduated from West Point in 1822. He served in various Indian campaigns and in the Mexican War, with distinguished gallantry, receiving three brevets. He came to the Pacific Coast in 1852, and was identified with operations in Oregon and Washington, finally reaching command of the Department of the Pacific in 1861, with the rank of brigadier-general. He and his wife were drowned in the wreck of the *Brother Jonathan*, which foundered off Crescent City, California, July 30, 1865, with a loss of about 300 lives. *See* Camp Wright.

Wroe, DOUGLAS. Wroe post office was on North Fork Smith River about four miles up stream from the mouth. The office was named for the family of the first postmaster. It was established Nov. 27, 1922, with Floyd A. Wroe first and only postmaster. The office was discontinued June 20, 1923. In Apr. 1948 William M. Wroe of Reedsport, brother of Floyd A. Wroe, wrote that by the time Wroe post office was set up for business many prospective customers had moved away from the valley of the North Fork. In these circumstances it was concluded not to operate the office, so it never actually functioned.

Wyatt Creek, LANE. Wyatt Creek is tributary to Brice Creek from the north upstream from Lund Park. It is named for M. F. Wyatt, an early miner.

Wy'east Basin, HOOD RIVER. Wy'east Basin is north of Mount Hood. *Wy'east* is said to be the legendary name for Mount Hood, but the word does not appear in available books on Chinookan dialects. H. H. Riddle of Portland, an authority on the names of the Columbia River Gorge, told the compiler that he was unable to get facts about the origin of the name, but that it was used in Indian myths. In 1943, C. Edward Graves, Arcata, California, wrote that the basin was named Wiyeast in 1922 by an exploring party from Hood River. Graves was the organizer of the party and was in 1922 living in Hood River. In June 1973 the OGNB voted to adopt the now current form, Wy'east, and this was duly approved by the USBGN in *Decision List 7402*.

Wyeth, HOOD RIVER. Oregon has seen fit to honor one of her notable explorers by attaching his name to a railroad station that achieved fame largely because it was for some years the site of a "tie pickling plant." Other than that, not much has been done to commemorate Nathaniel J. Wyeth. Wyeth, trader and patriot in one, had a definite plan to counteract the British fur-trading influence in the Pacific Northwest. Inspired by Hall J. Kelley, but compelled to dissolve a compact with him because of Kelley's procrastination, Wyeth crossed the plains in 1832 without the Boston school teacher. He was the first American after the Astor overlanders to make the journey to the Willamette. On a second expedition, in 1834, he convoyed the missionaries, Jason and Daniel Lee, built Fort Hall, near the present site of Pocatello, and named it for one of his financial backers. He established on Sauvie Island the trading post which he called Fort William. With him came Thomas Nuttall and J. K. Townsend, naturalists who share with David Douglas the honor of being pioneers in science in Oregon, and John Ball, first school teacher in the Pacific Northwest. Wyeth planned a more diversified program than that of the Hudson's Bay Company, studied salmon packing and envisioned an American trade with the Orient by way of the Pacific Coast, asking no exclusive privilege for his company. "Nothing on our part is desirable," he wrote, "excepting aid to get men out there and enacting some laws for their regulation when there, and leave us to ourselves." Wyeth's *Correspondence and Journals*, edited by Professor F. G. Young, have been published by the University of Oregon. For other information about Wyeth, *see* editorial in the *Oregonian*, Dec. 13, 1925. *See also* Kelley Point in this book.

Ya Whee Plateau, KLAMATH. This plateau is southwest of Saddle Mountain. The name is derived from a Klamath Indian word meaning eastern. Various forms have been in use, including *ye-wat*, *yah-wa*, etc. The name is properly written in two parts in order to indicate the proper pronunciation, as *Yawhee*, written as one word, is not satisfactory.

Yach, TILLAMOOK. Yach post office was in service from March to January 1908, when it was closed out to Dolph. Frank Yach was the postmaster. The Yach homestead was about four or five miles westward of Dolph, on the Little Nestucca River. The office was manifestly named for the postmaster.

Yachats, LINCOLN. This post office was established in 1887 about a mile north of its present location with the name of Ocean View. George M. Starr was the first postmaster. In 1916 the name of the post office was changed to Yachats for a tribe of Indians. These Indians had previously been moved to Siletz and they are now practically extinct. The name is pronounced Ya-hats. Indians say that the word means "at the foot of the mountain." This interpretation fits the facts. The name of the post office was changed to Yachats at the suggestion of J. K. Berry because it was at the mouth of Yachats River. *See Handbook of American Indians*, v. 2, p. 982.

Yager Creek, TILLAMOOK. Lon Yager was a cattle buyer who lived near Netarts after the turn of the century and this creek bears his name.

Yainax, KLAMATH. This place was for a number of years a sub-agency for the Klamath Indian Reservation. It took its name from the Klamath Indian word *Yainaga*, meaning little hill, which was the name the Indians used in referring to a little butte about two miles away, now known as Council Butte. The name Yainax Butte, originally applied to this feature, has become transferred to a mountain 12 miles southeast. *See* Yainax Butte.

Yainax Butte, KLAMATH. The government has officially adopted this name for a mountain, elevation 7226 feet, about 12 miles southeast of Yainax, and just south of what was the Klamath Indian Reservation. The butte has also been known as Modoc Mountain, Bald Mountain, and Yonna Butte. *Yainax* is a Klamath Indian word meaning little hill, and the name is not strictly suitable for a mountain, yet it has been used so long for the feature in question that the USBGN finally adopted it as official. *Yainax* was originally the name used for what is now Council Butte, near the settlement of Yainax.

Yakso Falls, DOUGLAS. This 70-foot fall is on Little River in S 16, T 27S, R 1E, near its source. *Yakso* is a Chinook jargon word meaning "hair of the head," and the falls resembles the long hair of a woman. The name was applied by USFS officials and approved by the OGNB on Dec. 2, 1966.

Yamada, LINCOLN. Yamada post office was in operation for a few months near South Beaver Creek, north of Alsea Bay. The office was established Mar. 26, 1898, with Newton L. Guilliams first and only postmaster, and was closed to Ona on Dec. 26, 1899. It is reported that Yamada post office was established as the result of some "feudin" between the people on South Beaver against the patrons of Ona post office, which was on the main Beaver Creek, or north branch. In any event, Yamada office had a short life. There are two places in Japan named Yamada, and this fact tends to substantiate the story that members of the Guilliams family ran across the name while sealing in Alaska and cruising off the coast of Japan. They liked the sound of the word and later applied it to the Oregon post office. The Japanese word *yamada* means a mountain field.

Yamhill, YAMHILL. The name Yamhill, in various forms, comes of course from the Yamhill River, but the exact meaning is a matter of doubt. A post office with the name Yam Hill Falls was established Jan. 8, 1850, with Jacob Hawn postmaster. This office, which was the first post office in Yamhill County, was closed Jan. 6, 1852. Yamhill Falls are directly south of the park square in Lafayette and not downstream near Yamhill Locks. Hawn's home was south of Hawn Creek on his donation land claim but old records show that Joel Perkins sold him "a certain mill seat at or near the town of Lafayette known as Falls of Yamhill River." He built a tavern or hotel on this property where on at least one occasion in 1850 Judge Matthew Deady held court so this was probably the site of the post office. Apparently it was replaced by the office of Lafayette established nearby on Mar. 14, 1851. Yam Hill post office was established Sept. 4, 1856, with Thomas Bailey postmaster. The office was closed Sept. 25, 1857. The writer has been unable to find this place on any old map, but Bailey's donation land claim was across the Willamette River from J. V. Boone in what was then Yamhill County near present-day Wilsonville. Bailey sold his property to Boone in 1857 and moved to McMinnville so it is possible this post office was actually on the Willamette River. North Yam Hill office was established Mar. 14, 1851, with Benjamin E. Stewart first postmaster. With one break, this office was in operation for more than a half a century at or near the North Yamhill River on the route of travel from McMinnville to Forest Grove. On May 9, 1908 the name of the office was changed to Yamhill and that has been its official title ever since.

Yamhill County. This county was created July 5, 1843, and now has an area of 728 square miles according to ODOT. It was one of the original four districts of Oregon and embraced the southwest part of the territory. Several counties have been taken from it. The origin and meaning of the name are uncertain, but the best evidence indicates that it is the white man's name for the Yamhill Indians. The Yamhill Indians were of the Kalapooian family, formerly living on Yamhill River, in Yamhill County. The remnants of the tribes were sent to Grand Ronde agency. The Henry-Thompson *Journals*, p. 812, under date of Jan. 23, 1814, refer to the *Yamhelas*, "who dwell in houses on Yellow river, a branch of the Willamette. They are great rogues, but not very numerous." John Work uses the name *Yamhill* in 1834. Lee and Frost, in *Ten Years in Oregon*, p. 90, give *Yam-hill*. The early pronunciation of the word was *Yam-il*. Nothing very definite is known about its meaning. In *All Over Oregon and Washington*, by Mrs. F. F. Victor, the origin is given as from *Che-am-il*, Indian word for bald hills, this being the character of the hills near the falls of Yamhill River, where there was a convenient ford. John Minto discusses the history of the word in the *Oregonian*, Oct. 7, 1890, p. 4. There is a town with the name Yamhill, formerly known as North Yamhill, presumably because it was near North Yamhill River.

Yamhill River, YAMHILL. For the origin of this name, *see* Yamhill County. The two main branches of Yamhill River are North Yamhill River and South Yamhill River, the latter being the larger. South Yamhill River has part of its course in Polk County.

Yampo School, YAMHILL. Yampo School is in the Eola Hills about a mile north of the Polk-Yamhill county line. The name is synthetic and is made up of parts of the two county names.

Yamsay, KLAMATH. Yamsay post office was established Feb. 28, 1930, with Claude Houghton postmaster. This office was about 40 miles by road northeast of Chiloquin and it was established to serve a lumbering activity. The office was near Yamsay Mountain and was named on that account. Yamsay post office should not be confused with Yamsay railroad station on the Southern Pacific Cascade Line about ten miles south of Chemult. The origin of the name of the railroad station is the same as that of the post office. Both are in Klamath County but some distance apart.

Yamsay Mountain, KLAMATH, LAKE. This is a well-known geographic feature with an elevation of more than 8000 feet. It is east of Klamath Marsh and just west of the Lake County line. The mountain and its extension to the south are drained to the west by Williamson River and its tributaries. The Klamath Indian name was *Yamsi*, a form of *Yamash*, the north wind, referring possibly to the abode of the north wind. The Weaslet was supposed to live at Yamsay Mountain. *See* Chaski Bay. Yamsay Mountain was also supposed to be the abode of *Kmukamtch*, the supreme being of Klamath mythology, who at times appeared as the Marten, elder brother of Weaslet.

Yankton, COLUMBIA. This community was settled about 1890 by several families from the state of Maine. It was known as Yankeetown. About 1894 a post office was petitioned for and local residents suggested the name Maineville. Postal authorities did not like this name, and when Yankeetown was suggested they shortened it to Yankton and Yankton it has been ever since.

Yapoah Crater, DESCHUTES, LANE. This crater has an elevation of 6737 feet and lies on the summit of the Cascade Range halfway between McKenzie Pass and the North Sister. *Yapoah*, signifying an isolated hill, was the Indian name for Skinner Butte near Eugene. Professor Edwin T. Hodge of the University of Oregon applied the name to this isolated crater in 1924 when he was studying the Three Sisters area.

Yaquina Bay, LINCOLN. Yaquina Bay, Yaquina station and Yaquina River which heads near the Benton-Lincoln county line, and flows into the bay, bear the name of the Yaquina Indians. In early days there was also a Yaquina City. The Yaquinas were a small tribe of the Yakonan family, formerly living about Yaquina Bay. Hale gives the name as *Iakon* and *Yakone*, in *Ethnography and Philology*, 1846, p. 218; Lewis and Clark give *Youikeones* and *Youkone*; Wilkes' *Western America*, 1849, gives *Yacone*. Another form of the word is *Acona*. (*OHQ*, v. 1, p. 320.)

Yaquina John Point, LINCOLN. Yaquina John Point is on the south side of the entrance to Alsea Bay just southwest of Waldport. It was named for Yaquina John, a chief or councillor of the Yaquina Indians, who lived in the vicinity of Alsea Bay.

Yarnell Canyon, MORROW. Yarnell Canyon, west of Utts Butte, is named for Henry Yarnell who came to Morrow County in the 1920s and bought the ranch at the head of the canyon.

Yellow Jacket Spring, UMATILLA. This spring east of Carney Butte was on the old road between Pilot Rock and Ukiah. Lester Hurst of Pendleton said that it had the first water on the way to Lehman Springs and was also a fine campsite with huckleberries in season. In the spring and fall it was also plagued with the well-known *Vespa vulgaris* or common yellow jacket which has given its name to so many similarly supplied features.

Yellowstone Creek, LINN. This stream flows into Quartzville Creek about 25 miles northeast of Sweet Home and bears a descriptive name. The creek was named in the early 1890s when there was a good deal of mining excitement along

Quartzville Creek. The miners became attracted by the abundance of a yellowish, quartz-like bedrock in the channel of a branch entering Quartzville Creek from the northwest and crossed by the old Quartzville trail near its mouth. This side stream became known as Yellowstone Creek, the name by which it is still called. Yellowstone Mountain was named in 1919 when it was first used as a forest lookout station. It was named for the creek. Yellowstone Mountain, elevation 4320 feet, is a little to the west of Yellowstone Creek.

Yeon Mountain, MULTNOMAH. Yeon Mountain is a prominent point on the south bank of the Columbia River east of Saint Peters Dome and west of Tumalt Creek. It is conspicuous from I-84. It was named for John Baptiste Yeon, who was born in Canada on Apr. 24, 1865. After working in various places, he came to Oregon in 1885, and began his career as a logger at $2.50 a day. He accumulated a large fortune, and for many years was interested in the good roads movement in Oregon. He was among those who developed the idea of the Columbia River Highway. He served, without pay, as roadmaster of Multnomah County during the early construction of the Historic Columbia River Highway, and later as state highway commissioner. John B. Yeon State Park to the east along the Columbia River was named in his honor. Yeon died on Oct. 15, 1928. For obituary, *see* the *Oregonian*, Oct. 16; for editorial, Oct. 17.

Yeoville, GRANT. All the available evidence shows that Yeoville was a post office in Bear Valley or vicinity, but old timers in the valley disclaim knowledge of the place. Yeoville post office was established Feb. 23, 1887, with Aaron Wickiser first and only postmaster. The establishment did not last long, for it was closed out to Canyon City May 18, 1887. The reason for the unusual name is not known.

Yoakam Point, COOS. For many decades this name has been applied to a small promontory about a mile west of Coos Head just south of the entrance to Coos Bay. It commemorates a family well known in the history of the county. John Yoakam settled in Coos County in the early 1850s. He was the father of seven children, five of whom were killed by a large tree which fell one night, Mar. 27, 1855, on the Yoakam cabin. This was the most unexpected and unusual tragedy in the early history of the county. It took place at a point sometimes called Yoakam Hill southwest of Coos Bay town and west of Libby. The family also lived for a time at Empire and also other places in the county. Dodge in *Pioneer History of Coos and Curry Counties* mentions John Yoakam in several places and spells the name in several ways. George Bennett in *OHQ*, v. 28, p. 334, mentions John Yoakum, in the late 1850s living near Coquille. In 1943 Mrs. Mary M. Randleman, authority on Coos County history, wrote the compiler that Yoakam was the correct spelling of the name.

Yoakum, UMATILLA. This spot on Umatilla River ten miles southeast of Echo was named for Hughy G. Yoakum who was born in Tennessee and came to Pendleton in 1867. Yoakum bought a stock ranch on Umatilla River and was elected county judge in 1872. He moved to Idaho in 1889 and the community, after a decent interval, passed into obscurity.

Yocum, LAKE. Yocum post office, in Yocum Valley, was in the extreme southwest corner of the county and was in service from Aug. 1917 to June 1937, when it was closed to West Side. An earlier office called Kriegh was established Mar. 8, 1915, with Margaret E. Kriegh postmaster. Belle Pardue became postmaster Aug. 4, 1917, on which date the name of the office was changed to Yocum. Yocum Valley bears an old name, the history of which has not been unravelled by the writer. The name has been in use for nearly 100 years, apparently to commemorate an early settler or squatter who departed long ago. There was once a cabin in the west end of Yocum Valley called Yocum Cabin, and the owner of the name apparently lived there many years ago.

Yocum Ridge, CLACKAMAS. This ridge is a western spur of Mount Hood. It bears the name of Oliver C. Yocum, who came to Oregon as a small boy with the emigration of 1847, and resided in Yamhill County and in Portland for many years. He developed the Government Camp hotel and resort in 1900, and lived there for 22 years. He guided many persons to the top of Mount Hood and was admired and respected because of his affection for the mountain. He returned to Yamhill County about 1922. Yocum Falls also bears his name. For additional information, *see* editorial page, *Oregon Journal*, July 3, 4, 1927.

Yoder, CLACKAMAS. This place was named for a pioneer family. It was formerly known as Yoderville, but that form has fallen into disuse. Daniel Yoder operated a shingle mill nearby in the early days and his brother, Levi Yoder, was a local farmer.

Yoncalla, DOUGLAS. Yoncalla is in a small valley called Yoncalla Valley. It was famous for many years as being the home of the Applegate brothers. The valley and the town were named for a prominent bald mountain to the northwest, which was known by the Indians as Yoncalla, or the home of the eagles. Eagles made their nests and reared their young on this butte. It is said that Jesse Applegate applied the name to the community. Bancroft, in *History of Oregon*, v. 2, p. 225, footnote, says the word is composed of *yonc*, eagle, and *calla* or *calla-calla* meaning bird or fowl in the Indian dialect. The compiler has been unable to identify the word *yonc* in any Indian dictionary available. The Chinook jargon borrowed the word *kal-lak'-a-la*, meaning bird, from the Chinook Indian language. The accent given by George Gibbs is on the second syllable, but the compiler heard the word frequently in the Willamette Valley in the 1880s and 1890s pronounced as though spelled *cully-cully*, with the accent on the first syllable of each part. This word was used by Indians in referring to birds generally but more especially to game birds such as grouse and quail. It seems to have been the same word used by Applegate in his name Yoncalla. Yoncalla post office was established on Mar. 14, 1851, with James B. Riggs postmaster. Jesse Applegate became postmaster on Sept. 15, 1851.

Yonna Valley, KLAMATH. Yonna Valley was at one time known as Alkali Valley, but that name was abandoned some time ago for the Klamath Indian name. *Yonna* may come from *yana*, meaning below, or low down, referring to the lower altitude of the valley, or it may be from *yaina*, meaning mountain. There are mountains nearby. There was at one time a post office at Yonna, in Yonna Valley northeast of Dairy.

Youngs Butte, GRANT. This butte, elevation 5330 feet, southwest of Dayville, was named for John M. Young, a Civil War veteran who lived on Youngs Creek, under the butte.

Youngs Canyon, MORROW. Youngs Canyon spills into Eightmile Canyon. Alex Young settled near a small spring two miles up this canyon in the 1880s. Members of his family owned the ranch until after World War II.

Youngs River, CLATSOP. Lieutenant William Robert Broughton, of Vancouver's expedition, discovered and explored Youngs Bay and Youngs River on Oct. 22, 1792. He named Youngs River for Sir George Young of the royal navy. The bay took its name from the river. Lewis and Clark named the bay Meriwether Bay for Meriwether Lewis, just as they named Tongue Point, Point William for William Clark, but neither of these new names was able to supplant the names attached to the features by Lieutenant Broughton in 1792. The Lewis and Clark maps indicate that Youngs River was called Kilhowanahkle River by the explorers, apparently from the Indian name, but Silas B. Smith is authority for the statement that this was the name of a place on the river and not of the river itself. Admiral Sir George Young was born in 1732 and became a midshipman in the royal navy in 1757. He served at various important stations and reached the position of flag captain to Sir Edward Vernon in the east Indies in 1777. He was knighted in 1781 and became an admiral in 1799. He was a fellow of the Royal Society and actively supported a proposal of Jean Maria Matra for establishing a colony in New South Wales in 1784. He was the promoter and one of the first proprietors of the Sierra Leone Company in 1791. He died in 1810.

Youtlkut Butte, LAKE. This butte is just south of the Paulina Mountains. It was named by the USFS with the Chinook jargon word for long.

Zena, POLK. Zena is a community in the southeastern part of Eola Hills. It was named for Arvazena Cooper, wife of Daniel Jackson Cooper. The Coopers moved to this place in 1863 and lived there until 1875, when they moved to Salem. Mrs. Cooper was living in The Dalles in 1927. This information was furnished by Norman Cooper of The Dalles, a son of D. J. Cooper. Subsequent history of Polk County schools adds the information that Cooper's brother, Jacob Cooper, was married to Melzena Stillman, Mrs. Cooper's sister. The Cooper brothers operated the local store and the post office, established in 1869, was named for both wives.

Zigzag River, CLACKAMAS. On Oct. 11, 1845, Joel Palmer crossed the deep ravine of Zigzag Canyon near timberline on Mount Hood. In his journal for that day he uses the following description: "The manner of descending is to turn directly to the right, go zigzag for about one hundred yards, then turn short round, and go zigzag until you come under the place where you started from; then to the right, and so on, until you reach the base." The members of the Barlow party, who crossed south of Mount Hood without wagons in Oct. 1845 used a trail that ascended White River nearly to timberline and then traversed west not far from the 1989 alignment of the Timberline Trail. After crossing Zigzag Canyon they descended one of the ridges of Zigzag Mountain. It is obvious that the principal stream was identified by the crossing. The river is no more crooked than adjoining streams and there is no reason to believe it was named for an especially irregular alignment. For a detailed account of the investigation of the south side of Mount Hood and the discovery of Barlow Pass, *see* the entries for Oct. 1845 in Joel Palmer's *Journal of Travels over the Rocky Mountains*, a photographic reproduction of which was made in 1966. The name Zigzag has also come to be applied to Zigzag Glacier on Mount Hood as well as to a community two miles west of Rhododendron. Zigzag post office was established in 1917 and operated intermittently until 1974. The form Zig Zag is wrong. *See* decision of USBGN. For discussion of the name Zigzag, *see OHQ*, v. 19, p. 75, where it is held that the use of the name for a stream east of Mount Hood is not likely.

Zinc Creek, DOUGLAS. Zinc Creek flows into South Umpqua River above Dumont Creek. It was named for a zinc mine development that has long since passed into obscurity.

Zion, LANE. Zion post office operated for more than a decade in the Lost Creek Valley south of Dexter. It was named because of the proximity of Mount Zion just to the east. Mount Zion was named in pioneer days by Elijah Bristow. It has an elevation of 2660 feet and is a prominent point. Zion post office was established Mar. 11, 1899, with Thomas H. Hunsaker postmaster. The office was finally closed Nov. 30, 1913, and the business turned over to Dexter. There is still a Zion School in the Lost Creek Valley.

Zollner Creek, MARION. Robert Zollner settled near this stream in pioneer days and it was named for him. Zollner Creek flows into Pudding River northwest of Mount Angel.

Zosel Hill, MARION. Zosel Hill is about five miles southwest of Salem. It has an elevation of about 600 feet. It was named for William Zosel, a landowner nearby.

Zuckerman Island, KLAMATH. Francis Landrum of Klamath Falls informed the writer in 1969 that this high ground in Lower Klamath Lake near Worden was named because nearby land was owned or farmed by Weyl-Zuckerman, a California agricultural corporation.

Zumwalt, WALLOWA. Zumwalt got its name from Henry Zumwalt, a local resident. The community was northeast of Enterprise. The post office was established Aug. 25, 1903, with Josie Zumwalt first postmaster.

Zwagg Island, CURRY. M. S. Brainard of Brookings provided the following curious information about the early days on this island just offshore from Brookings. Folker Von Der Zwaag was born in The Netherlands in 1835 and came to Curry County in 1889. He was obviously fond of solitude as he lived alone on the island with his dog Sniff. The island had no fresh water and the local mechanical marvel was the trolley with the self-filling attachment by which he drew water from the mainland.

INDEX

Bald Peak, p. 170, **Chehalem Mountains**
Bald Peter, p. 377, **Green Peter**
Bald Peter Butte, p. 40, **Bald Peter**
Bald Peter Creek, p. 40, **Bald Peter**
Bald Point, p. 438, **Indian Beach**
Ballsville, p. 41, **Ballston**
Banner Valley, p. 47, **Barren Valley**
Barings River, p. 741, **Sandy River**
Barlow, Camp, p. 122, **Camp Barlow**
Barlow Butte, p. 44, **Barlow Creek**
Barlow Pass, p. 44, **Barlow Creek**
Barnes Heights, p. 46, **Barnes Road**
Barrett Spur, p. 47, **Barrett**
Bashop Creek, p. 73, **Bishop Creek**
Basin, p. 113, **Butler Basin**
Basin, p. 429, **Humboldt Basin**
Bateman, p. 312, **Fir**
Bates, p. 36, **Bade**
Battery Russell, p. 330, **Fort Stevens**
Battle Mountain, p. 50, **Battle Creek**
Baxterville, p. 51, **Baxter Creek**
B. C. Basin, p. 53, **B. C. Creek**
Beal Lake, p. 53, **Beale Lake**
Beals Mountain, p. 53, **Beals Creek**
Bear Butte, p. 348, **Garwood Butte**
Bear Chute, p. 54, **Bear Island**
Bear Creek, p. 69, **Big Canyon**
Bear Creek, p. 480, **Knight Creek**
Beatys Springs, p. 55, **Beatys Butte**
Beaver, p. 56, **Beaver Creek**
Beaver, p. 628, **Oak Point**
Beavercreek, p. 56, **Beaver Creek**
Beck Station, p. 834, **Tiernan**
Belknap Creek, p. 308, **Ferguson Creek**
Belknap Settlement, p. 59, **Belknap Creek**
Belknap Settlement, p. 398, **Hawley Creek**
Belknap Spring, p. 59, **Belknap Creek**
Belknaps Settlement, p. 60, **Bellfountain**
Bellevue, p. 385, **Halfway**
Belpassi, p. 59, **Belle Passi**
Bement, p. 825, **Terry**
Ben Holladay, p. 417, **Holladay**
Bendire Mountain, p. 62, **Bendire Creek**
Bennett, p. 736, **Salisbury**
Bennett Prairie, p. 62, **Bennett Butte**
Berry Creek, p. 65, **Berry**
Berry Way Meadow, p. 55, **Bearway Meadow**
Bethel Hills, p. 294, **Eola Hills**
Bethesda Hot Springs, p. 320, **Foley Springs**
Bieberstedt Creek, p. 69, **Bieberstedt Butte**
Big Butte, p. 592, **Mount McLoughlin**
Big Canyon Creek, p. 69, **Big Canyon**
Big Cowhorn, p. 597, **Mount Thielsen**
Big Creek, p. 446, **Jamestown**
Big Fall Creek, p. 304, **Fall Creek**
Big Hole Butte, p. 69, **Big Hole**

Big Howard Spring, p. 427, **Howard Valley**
Big Luckiamute River, p. 525, **Luckiamute River**
Big Pine Opening, p. 134, **Campers Flat**
Big Sandy, p. 741, **Sandy River**
Big Summit Prairie, p. 512, **Little Summit Prairie**
Biggs Cove, p. 143, **Cape Meares Lake**
Biggs Junction, p. 70, **Biggs**
Billingslea, Mount, p. 583, **Mount Billingslea**
Bingham Basin, p. 71, **Bingham Lake**
Bingham Ridge, p. 71, **Bingham Lake**
Bingham Spring, p. 72, **Bingham Prairie**
Birdseye, Fort, p. 322, **Fort Birdseye**
Bitter lakes, p. 393, **Harney Lake**
Bitterlick Creek, p. 73, **Bitter Lick**
Black Butte, p. 113, **Butte Creek**
Black Butte, p. 262, **Donnelly Butte**
Blackbutte, p. 74, **Black Butte**
Blakelyville, p. 299, **Eula**
Blanco, Cape, p. 139, **Cape Blanco**
Bland Creek, p. 77, **Bland Mountain**
Blazed Alder Butte, p. 77, **Blazed Alder Creek**
Blevins Spring, p. 265, **Double Corral Creek**
Blitzen, p. 263, **Donner und Blitzen River**
Blossom, Camp, p. 122, **Camp Blossom**
Blue Basin, p. 853, **Turtle Cove**
Blue Lake, p. 521, **Lost Lake**
Board Creek, p. 651, **Parkers Mill**
Bolivar, Mount, p. 583, **Mount Bolivar**
Bolland Creek, p. 83, **Bolan Creek**
Bollon Creek, p. 83, **Bolan Creek**
Bolt Mountain, p. 84, **Bolt**
Bone Island, p. 84, **Bolon Island**
Boner Spring, p. 84, **Boner Flat**
Bonita Placer, p. 846, **Trestle Creek**
Bonneville, Lake, p. 486, **Lake Bonneville**
Bonneville, Mount, p. 584, **Mount Bonneville**
Bonneville Dam, p. 84, **Bonneville**
Bonney Meadow, p. 85, **Bonney Butte**
Boon, p. 916, **Wilsonville**
Boone Island, p. 85, **Boone Slough**
Booneville, p. 86, **Booneville Channel**
Boons Ferry, p. 916, **Wilsonville**
Boring Junction, p. 87, **Boring**
Bowdens, p. 89, **Bowden Crater**
Bowline Island, p. 84, **Bolon Island**
Bowling Creek, p. 83, **Bolan Creek**
Bradley Creek, p. 92, **Bradley Trail**
Brant Island, p. 91, **Bradford Island**
Brasfield Ferry, p. 278, **Echo**
Braun, p. 93, **Braunsport**
Breitenbush Hot Springs, p. 94, **Breitenbush**
Bridal Veil, p. 95, **Bridal Veil Falls**
Bridal Veil Creek, p. 95, **Bridal Veil Falls**
Bridgeport, p. 849, **Tualatin**

Mayborn Hill, p. 668, **Piety Knob**
Mays Rock, p. 544, **Mays Canyon Creek**
Maywood Park, p. 652, **Parkrose**
Mazama, Mount, p. 592, **Mount Mazama**
McAlister Ridge, p. 545, **McAlister Creek**
McAlister Spring, p. 545, **McAlister Creek**
McBee Slough, p. 545, **McBee Island**
McClellan Mountain, p. 546, **McClellan Creek**
McConville Gulch, p. 546, **McConville Peak**
McCrady River, p. 521, **Lost River**
McDermid Cone, p. 365, **Gordon**
McDowell, Camp, p. 129, **Camp McDowell**
McDuffee Hot Springs, p. 711, **Ritter**
McKenzie, p. 27, **Armitage**
McKibbin, p. 397, **Haskin Butte**
McKinley, Camp, p. 129, **Camp McKinley**
McKinzie Bridge, p. 551, **McKenzie Bridge**
McLoughlin, Mount, p. 592, **Mount McLoughlin**
McNary, p. 553, **McNary Dam**
McNary Dam, p. 488, **Lake Wallula**
Meadow Creek, p. 555, **Meadow**
Meadow View, p. 370, **Grand Prairie**
Meadows Ranch, p. 18, **Anchor**
Meares, Cape, p. 142, **Cape Meares**
Mendi Gorri Posue, p. 559, **Mendi Gorri**
Menominee, p. 559, **Meno**
Menzies Island, p. 399, **Hayden Island**
Mercer Reservoir, p. 1, **Aaron Mercer Reservoir**
Meriwether, Camp, p. 129, **Camp Meriwether**
Meriwether Bay, p. 934, **Youngs River**
Merritt, Lake, p. 487, **Lake Merritt**
Meva, p. 94, **Braymill**
Meyersville, p. 606, **Myrtle Point**
Middle Bridge, p. 689, **Prichard**
Middle Falls, p. 481, **Koosah Falls**
Middle Mountain, p. 584, **Mount Bonneville**
Middle North Falls, p. 767, **Silver Creek Falls**
Middleton, p. 659, **Pendleton**
Mikecha, p. 353, **Gibbon**
Mikecha, p. 460, **Kamela**
Miles Mountain, p. 564, **Miles Lake**
Milford, p. 768, **Silverton**
Mill Creek, p. 410, **Hess Creek**
Miller, Lake, p. 487, **Lake Miller**
Miller Island, p. 566, **Miller Hill**
Miller Stage station, p. 431, **Huntington**
Miller's Island, p. 367, **Government Island**
Millican Crater, p. 567, **Millican**
Millican Valley, p. 567, **Millican**
Millicoma Tract, p. 289, **Elliott State Forest**
Millra, p. 295, **Erskine**
Milton, p. 568, **Milton Creek**
Milton, p. 568, **Milton-Freewater**
Minam Lake, p. 569, **Minam River**

Miner, Fort, p. 328, **Fort Miner**
Miner's Fort, p. 328, **Fort Miner**
Miners Fork, p. 193, **Collawash River**
Mink, p. 56, **Beaver Creek**
Mink Lake Basin, p. 570, **Mink Lake**
Minnehaha, p. 20, **Anglersvale**
Minnow Creek, p. 570, **Minnow**
Minto Island, p. 571, **Minto Mountain**
Mission, p. 571, **Mission Creek**
Mission Landing, p. 571, **Mission Creek**
Mitchell, Mount, p. 594, **Mount Mitchell**
Mitchell Creek, p. 603, **Muncey Creek**
Mitchell's Station, p. 896, **Weston**
Mocks Bottom, p. 573, **Mocks Crest**
Mocks Landing, p. 573, **Mocks Crest**
Modoc Mountain, p. 929, **Yainax Butte**
Mohawk, p. 574, **Mohawk River**
Moloch Creek, p. 577, **Moolack Creek**
Monroe Creek, p. 576, **Monroe Roughs**
Monument Mountain, p. 577, **Monument**
Moriah, Mount, p. 594, **Mount Moriah**
Mormon Spring, p. 922, **Winters Spring**
Morrison, p. 672, **Pioneer**
Morrison Island, p. 892, **Wells Island**
Mount Charity, p. 832, **Three Sisters**
Mount Conley, p. 199, **Conley**
Mount Faith, p. 625, **North Sister**
Mount Faith, p. 832, **Three Sisters**
Mount Franklin, p. 429, **Humbug Mountain**
Mount Hope, p. 832, **Three Sisters**
Mount Jackson, p. 513, **Llao Rock**
Mount Marion, p. 831, **Three Fingered Jack**
Mount Multnomah, p. 832, **Three Sisters**
Mount Pit, p. 592, **Mount McLoughlin**
Mount Vancouver, p. 591, **Mount Jefferson**
Mount Zion, p. 376, **Green Hills**
Mountain House, p. 150, **Cartwright**
Mountain Springs, p. 873, **Wagontire Mountain**
Mountain View, p. 290, **Ely**
Mouse Mountain, p. 540, **Marys Peak**
Mouse River, p. 540, **Marys River**
Mouth of Willamette, p. 684, **Post Office Bar**
Mowry, p. 543, **Maury Mountains**
Mt. Angel, p. 581, **Mount Angel**
Mud Flat, p. 305, **Fangollano**
Mud Lake, p. 393, **Harney Lake**
Mud Lake, p. 425, **Hosmer Lake**
Mud Lake, p. 532, **Malheur Lake**
Muddy, p. 12, **Alford**
Muddy, p. 60, **Bellevue**
Muddy, p. 600, **Muddy Creek**
Muddy Station, p. 12, **Alford**
Mule Mountain, p. 601, **Mule Creek**
Muleshoe Creek, p. 601, **Muleshoe Ridge**
Multnomah Creek, p. 602, **Multnomah Falls**

Multnomah Island, p. 743, **Sauvie Island**
Multnomah River, p. 909, **Willamette River**
Munsel Creek, p. 603, **Munsel Lake**
Munson Falls, p. 603, **Munson Creek**
Murderers Harbour, p. 52, **Bays**
Murphy Creek, p. 604, **Murphy**
Murphys Camp Creek, p. 604, **Murphys Camp**
Muskrat Camp, p. 434, **Idanha**
Muslin Creek, p. 119, **Calico Creek**
Myrtle City, p. 749, **Scottsburg**
Mysterious Lake, p. 217, **Crater Lake**
Nailix, p. 608, **Naylox**
Namanu, Camp, p. 130, **Camp Namanu**
Nansene Creek, p. 310, **Fifteenmile Creek**
Napoleon, p. 467, **Kerby**
Natsox Run, p. 878, **Wallace Island**
Naughty Girl Meadow, p. 905, **Whorehouse Meadow**
Nauvoo, p. 848, **Troy**
Naylox Ridge, p. 608, **Naylox**
Neacoxie Lake, p. 609, **Neacoxie Creek**
Neal Creek, p. 71, **Bilyeu Creek**
Neal's Folly, p. 320, **Follyfarm**
Nebo, Mount, p. 594, **Mount Nebo**
Neknoberts, p. 613, **Nekbobets Lake**
Nellies Point, p. 613, **Nellies Cove**
Nelson, p. 508, **Lime**
Nelson Reservoir, p. 614, **Nelson Creek**
Nenamusa Falls, p. 614, **Nenamusa**
Nesmith, p. 615, **Nesmith Point**
Nesmiths, p. 288, **Ellendale**
Nesmiths, p. 635, **O'Neals Mills**
Nestucca Bay, p. 616, **Nestucca River**
Netarts Bay, p. 616, **Netarts**
Nettie Creek, p. 74, **Black Creek**
Netul River, p. 505, **Lewis and Clark River**
New Albany, p. 8, **Albany**
New Astoria, p. 472, **Kindred**
New Castle, p. 278, **Eckley**
New Plymouth, p. 732, **Saint Helens**
New Princeton, p. 689, **Princeton**
New Walla Walla, p. 338, **Freewater**
Newellsville, p. 165, **Champoeg**
Newton, p. 285, **Elk City**
Newton Creek, p. 180, **Clark Creek**
Newtown, p. 631, **Odell**
Niagora, p. 620, **Niagara**
Nichols, p. 657, **Peck**
Nicolai, p. 559, **Meno**
Nicolis Canyon, p. 621, **Nichols Canyon**
Nigger Ben Mountain, p. 612, **Negro Ben Mountain**
Ninety-One, p. 899, **Whiskey Hill**
Noonday Mine, p. 21, **Annie Creek**
North Beach, p. 272, **Dunes City**
North Canyonville, p. 137, **Canyonville**

North Dickey Peak, p. 785, **South Dickey Peak**
North Falls, p. 767, **Silver Creek Falls**
North Fork Applegate River, p. 511, **Little Applegate River**
North Fork Coos River, p. 568, **Millicoma River**
North Fork River, p. 624, **North Minam River**
North Lake, p. 625, **North Tenmile Lake**
North Mountain Spring, p. 873, **Wagontire Mountain**
North Sister Creek, p. 855, **Twin Sisters Creeks**
North Slough, p. 397, **Hauser**
North Twin Lake, p. 854, **Twin Lakes**
Norton Creek, p. 464, **Kellow Creek**
Oak Cut, p. 293, **Encina**
Oak Grove, p. 727, **Ruckles**
Oak Grove, p. 882, **Wapinitia**
Oak Grove Mountain, p. 594, **Mount Mitchell**
Oak Islands, p. 392, **Hardtack Island**
Oak Islands, p. 723, **Ross Island**
Oakville, p. 866, **Verdure**
Oard Spring, p. 630, **Oard Flat**
Obelisk, p. 722, **Rooster Rock**
Ocean View, p. 928, **Yachats**
Ochoco, p. 555, **Meadow**
Ochoco Mines, p. 426, **Howard**
Odell Butte, p. 631, **Odell Lake**
Odell Creek, p. 631, **Odell Lake**
Olalla Creek, p. 633, **Olalla Slough**
Old Bailey, p. 583, **Mount Bailey**
Old Baldy, p. 583, **Mount Bailey**
Olds Ferry, p. 306, **Farewell Bend**
Olney Creek, p. 171, **Chenoweth Creek**
Olssonville, p. 634, **Olson Creek**
O'Neals Mills, p. 288, **Ellendale**
Oneonta Creek, p. 635, **Oneonta Gorge**
Onion Peak, p. 612, **Nehalem**
Opal Creek, p. 636, **Opal Lake**
Oppie Dildock, p. 637, **Opie Dilldock Pass**
Oreana, p. 642, **Orejana Canyon**
Oregon Slough, p. 624, **North Portland Harbor**
Oregon Slough, p. 776, **Slough**
Orford, Fort, p. 329, **Fort Orford**
Orient Mill, p. 642, **Orient**
Orla Falls, p. 348, **Gatch Falls**
Orton, p. 516, **Logsden**
Osborn Grove, p. 381, **Grove City**
Oseola, p. 631, **Oceola**
Oswego, Lake, p. 488, **Lake Oswego**
Ott, p. 606, **Myrtle Point**
Ouxy Spring, p. 645, **Ouxy**
Owl Creek, p. 113, **Butte Creek**
Owyhee Ferry, p. 645, **Owyhee**
Owyhee Ridge, p. 646, **Owyhee River**
Ox Bow, p. 646, **Oxbow**

The Great Dalles, p. 316, **Fivemile Rapids**
The Hill, p. 595, **Mount Pleasant**
The Hogsback, p. 188, **Coalman Glacier**
The Hourglass, p. 504, **Leuthold Couloir**
The Institute, p. 734, **Salem**
The Landing, p. 835, **Tillamook**
The Mill, p. 734, **Salem**
The Narrows, p. 607, **Narrows**
The Point, p. 226, **Crown Point**
The Portage, p. 199, **Condon Creek**
The Table, p. 140, **Cape Falcon**
Thielsen, Mount, p. 597, **Mount Thielsen**
Thomas Mill, p. 788, **Spikenard**
Thompson Valley, p. 814, **Sycan Marsh**
Thorn Hollow, p. 830, **Thornhollow**
Three Brothers, p. 99, **Brothers**
Three Brothers, p. 142, **Cape Meares**
Three Creek, p. 831, **Three Creek Lake**
Three Creek Butte, p. 831, **Three Creek Lake**
Three Links, p. 831, **Three Lynx Creek**
Three Notches, p. 221, **Criterion**
Three Pines, p. 833, **Threepines**
3 Rox, p. 831, **Three Rocks**
Thurston, p. 396, **Harrisburg**
Tichenor Cove, p. 613, **Nellies Cove**
Tichenors Humbug, p. 429, **Humbug Mountain**
Tigardville, p. 834, **Tigard**
Tillamook Landing, p. 835, **Tillamook**
Tillamook River, p. 835, **Tillamook County**
Tillasana Creek, p. 69, **Big Creek**
Tilliacum Creek, p. 659, **Pelican Creek**
Tillicum, p. 659, **Pelican Creek**
Tilly Ann Creek, p. 69, **Big Creek**
Tilly Jane Creek, p. 69, **Big Creek**
Timberline Lodge, p. 837, **Timberline**
Timothy Meadows, p. 838, **Timothy Lake**
Tinanens Creek, p. 310, **Fifteenmile Creek**
Tioga Creek, p. 838, **Tioga**
Tire Mountain, p. 839, **Tire Creek**
Toad Lake, p. 681, **Poole Lake**
Tobin Spring, p. 839, **Tobin Cabin**
Toe Island, p. 392, **Hardtack Island**
Toe Island, p. 723, **Ross Island**
Tom Dick Mountain, p. 841, **Tom Dick & Harry Mountain**
Tom McCall Preserve, p. 545, **McCall Point**
Tombstone Summit, p. 842, **Tombstone Prairie**
Torrey River, p. 913, **Williamson River**
Trail Creek, p. 845, **Trail**
Trail Fork Canyon, p. 845, **Trailfork**
Trapper Creek, p. 103, **Buck Creek**
Trappers Bay, p. 845, **Trapper Creek**
Traux Island, p. 848, **Truax Island**
Trident Peak, p. 831, **Three Fingered Jack**

Trout Mountain, p. 473, **King Mountain**
Tsiltcoos Lake, p. 765, **Siltcoos Lake**
Tualatin, p. 321, **Forest Grove**
Tubb Springs, p. 849, **Tub Springs**
Tucker, p. 850, **Tucker Bridge**
Tunnel Mountain, p. 174, **Chief Joseph Mountain**
Turnbull Lakebed, p. 852, **Turnbull Peak**
Turnbull Mountain, p. 852, **Turnbull Peak**
T'Vault Creek, p. 461, **Kane Creek**
12 Mile House, p. 886, **Wasco**
Twelvemile, p. 390, **Hardin**
Twin Falls, p. 767, **Silver Creek Falls**
Twogood, p. 501, **Leland**
Tyee, p. 855, **Tyee Mountain**
Tygh Creek, p. 856, **Tygh Valley**
Tygh Ridge, p. 856, **Tygh Valley**
Tysch Prairie, p. 856, **Tygh Valley**
Ukah Creek, p. 298, **Euchre Creek**
Umatilla, Lake, p. 488, **Lake Umatilla**
Umatilla Landing, p. 856, **Umatilla**
Umpqua, Fort, p. 331, **Fort Umpqua**
Umpqua Canyon, p. 137, **Canyonville**
Umpqua City, p. 857, **Umpqua**
Umpqua County, p. 265, **Douglas County**
Umpqua Ferry, p. 857, **Umpqua**
Unavilla, p. 106, **Bull Run River**
Unity, p. 646, **Oxman**
Upper Basin, p. 113, **Butler Basin**
Upper Falls, p. 732, **Sahalie Falls**
Upper Landing, p. 773, **Skipanon River**
Upper Meadow, p. 339, **Fremont Meadow**
Upper Table Rock, p. 816, **Table Rock**
Upton Creek, p. 862, **Upton Slough**
Van Dusen, p. 239, **Day**
Van Dusen, p. 451, **John Day River**
Van Horn, p. 864, **Van Horn Butte**
Vancouver Island, p. 399, **Hayden Island**
Vannoy, Fort, p. 331, **Fort Vannoy**
Vansycle, p. 865, **Vansycle Canyon**
Varien, p. 172, **Chesher**
Vernon, Mount, p. 597, **Mount Vernon**
Victor Point, p. 506, **Lewisburg**
Victor Rock, p. 868, **Victor View**
Viento Creek, p. 869, **Viento**
Villa Maria, p. 539, **Marylhurst**
Villard, p. 373, **Grant**
Vincent, p. 856, **Umapine**
Vineyard Hill, p. 870, **Vineyard Mountain**
Virgin Lakes, p. 875, **Waldo Lake**
Wagner, p. 872, **Wagner Creek**
Wagner Springs, p. 782, **Soda Springs**
Wagontire, p. 873, **Wagontire Mountain**
Wahanna Creek, p. 610, **Neawanna Creek**
Wahkeena Creek, p. 874, **Wahkeena Falls**
Waid Bluff, p. 890, **Waud Bluff**

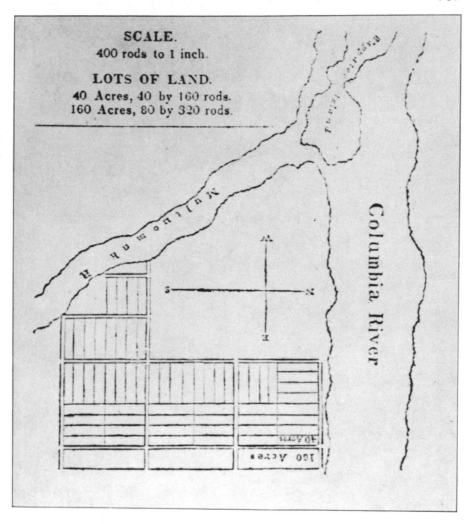

Hall J. Kelley's diagram of townsite at mouth of the Willamette River, published in his *Geographical Sketch of Oregon* in 1830. This diagram was published as the frontispiece in the first edition of *Oregon Geographic Names. See* Kelley Point entry (pp. 463-64).